Britannia: or, a chorographical description of Great Britain and Ireland, ... Written in Latin by William Camden, ... and translated into English, ... Revised, digested, and published, with large additions The third edition Volume 2 of 2

William Camden

Britannia: or, a chorographical description of Great Britain and Ireland, ... Written in Latin by William Camden, ... and translated into English, ... Revised, digested, and published, with large additions, by Edmund Gibson, ... The third edition. Illustrated with maps .. Volume 2 of 2
Camden, William
ESTCID: T145183
Reproduction from British Library
The pagination is erratic.
London : printed for R. Ware, J. and P. Knapton, T. Longman, C. Hitch, D. Browne, H. Lintot, C. Davis [and 6 others in London], 1753.
2v.([66]p.,cclxviii columns,[2]p.,1526 columns,[177]p.),plates : ill.,maps,port. ; 2°

Gale ECCO Print Editions

Relive history with *Eighteenth Century Collections Online*, now available in print for the independent historian and collector. This series includes the most significant English-language and foreign-language works printed in Great Britain during the eighteenth century, and is organized in seven different subject areas including literature and language; medicine, science, and technology; and religion and philosophy. The collection also includes thousands of important works from the Americas.

The eighteenth century has been called "The Age of Enlightenment." It was a period of rapid advance in print culture and publishing, in world exploration, and in the rapid growth of science and technology – all of which had a profound impact on the political and cultural landscape. At the end of the century the American Revolution, French Revolution and Industrial Revolution, perhaps three of the most significant events in modern history, set in motion developments that eventually dominated world political, economic, and social life.

In a groundbreaking effort, Gale initiated a revolution of its own: digitization of epic proportions to preserve these invaluable works in the largest online archive of its kind. Contributions from major world libraries constitute over 175,000 original printed works. Scanned images of the actual pages, rather than transcriptions, recreate the works ***as they first appeared.***

Now for the first time, these high-quality digital scans of original works are available via print-on-demand, making them readily accessible to libraries, students, independent scholars, and readers of all ages.

For our initial release we have created seven robust collections to form one the world's most comprehensive catalogs of 18th century works.

Initial Gale ECCO Print Editions collections include:

History and Geography
Rich in titles on English life and social history, this collection spans the world as it was known to eighteenth-century historians and explorers. Titles include a wealth of travel accounts and diaries, histories of nations from throughout the world, and maps and charts of a world that was still being discovered. Students of the War of American Independence will find fascinating accounts from the British side of conflict.

Social Science

Delve into what it was like to live during the eighteenth century by reading the first-hand accounts of everyday people, including city dwellers and farmers, businessmen and bankers, artisans and merchants, artists and their patrons, politicians and their constituents. Original texts make the American, French, and Industrial revolutions vividly contemporary.

Medicine, Science and Technology

Medical theory and practice of the 1700s developed rapidly, as is evidenced by the extensive collection, which includes descriptions of diseases, their conditions, and treatments. Books on science and technology, agriculture, military technology, natural philosophy, even cookbooks, are all contained here.

Literature and Language

Western literary study flows out of eighteenth-century works by Alexander Pope, Daniel Defoe, Henry Fielding, Frances Burney, Denis Diderot, Johann Gottfried Herder, Johann Wolfgang von Goethe, and others. Experience the birth of the modern novel, or compare the development of language using dictionaries and grammar discourses.

Religion and Philosophy

The Age of Enlightenment profoundly enriched religious and philosophical understanding and continues to influence present-day thinking. Works collected here include masterpieces by David Hume, Immanuel Kant, and Jean-Jacques Rousseau, as well as religious sermons and moral debates on the issues of the day, such as the slave trade. The Age of Reason saw conflict between Protestantism and Catholicism transformed into one between faith and logic -- a debate that continues in the twenty-first century.

Law and Reference

This collection reveals the history of English common law and Empire law in a vastly changing world of British expansion. Dominating the legal field is the *Commentaries of the Law of England* by Sir William Blackstone, which first appeared in 1765. Reference works such as almanacs and catalogues continue to educate us by revealing the day-to-day workings of society.

Fine Arts

The eighteenth-century fascination with Greek and Roman antiquity followed the systematic excavation of the ruins at Pompeii and Herculaneum in southern Italy; and after 1750 a neoclassical style dominated all artistic fields. The titles here trace developments in mostly English-language works on painting, sculpture, architecture, music, theater, and other disciplines. Instructional works on musical instruments, catalogs of art objects, comic operas, and more are also included.

BRITANNIA:

OR, A

Chorographical Defcription

OF

GREAT BRITAIN

AND

IRELAND,

Together with the Adjacent Islands.

Written in LATIN

By *WILLIAM CAMDEN*, Clarenceux, King at ARMS:

And Tranflated into ENGLISH, *with* ADDITIONS *and* IMPROVEMENTS.

Revifed, Digefted, and Publifhed, with large ADDITIONS,

By EDMUND GIBSON, D. D. Late Lord Bifhop of LONDON.

THE THIRD EDITION.

Illuftrated with MAPS of all the COUNTIES, and PRINTS of the BRITISH, ROMAN, and SAXON COINS

VOL. II.

LONDON:

Printed for R. WARE, J. and P. KNAPTON, T. LONGMAN, C. HITCH, D. BROWNE, H. LINTOT, C. DAVIS, J. HODGES, A. MILLAR, W. BOWYER, J. WHISTON, J. and J. RIVINGTON, and J. WARD.

MDCCLIII.

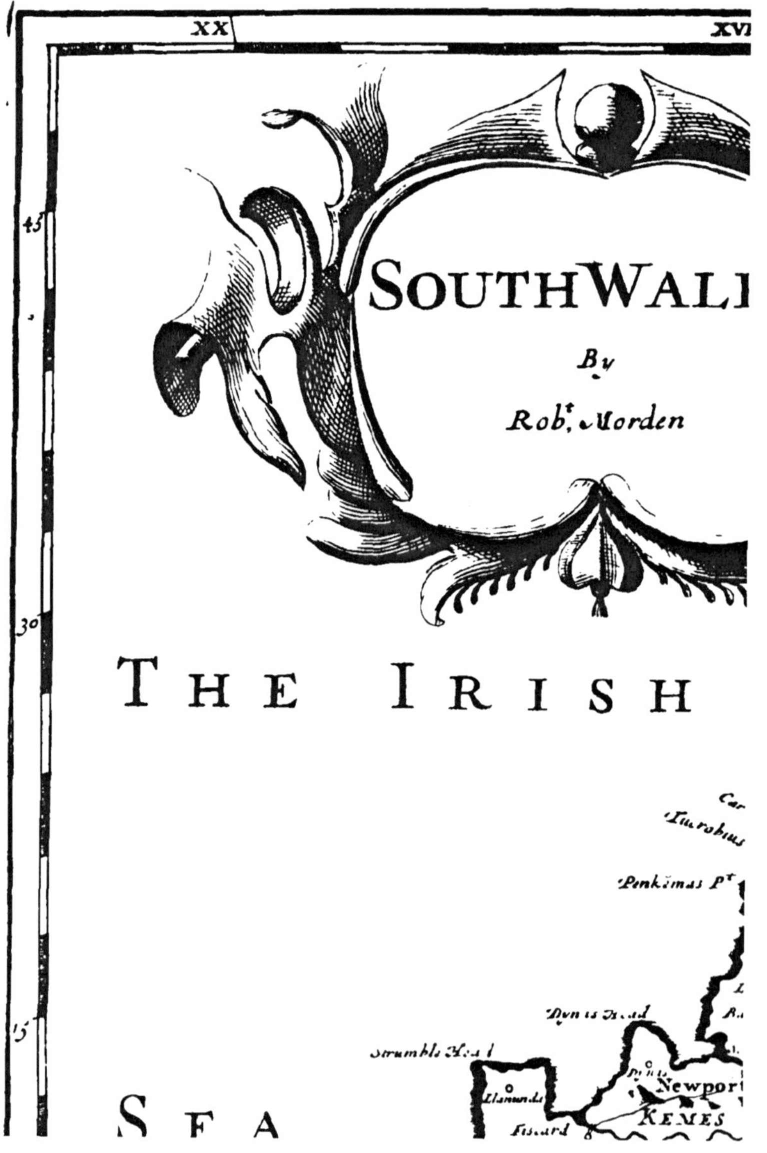
XX
SOUTH WALE
By
Robt. Morden
THE IRISH
SEA
Penkemas Pt
Newport
KEMES

XII
N of Time
WALES
P OF SHROP
SHIRE
30
Llanidlos
KNIGHTON HUN
SILVRES
Knighton
RHAYADERGOWY HUN
Rhyader Gowy
RADNOR SHIRE
Presteign
New Radnor
RADNOR HUN
Kyneton
15
COLLOWINI HUN
PAINS CASTLE HUN
Hay
SILVR
MERTHYR HUN
BRECKNOCK SHIRE
Brecknock
Part of Hereford Shire
52
CRICKHOEL HUN
DYVYNNOCK HUN
Aberge Venny

St Ketterus
Llanrian
S Davids Head
The Bishop and his Clarks
Ramsey I
DEWYSLAND
HUN
Llandeloy
Treuegare
St Davids
PEMBROKSHI
Lamiton
Haverford West
St Briedes Bay
RHOS
HUN
Johnston
Stanton
Rosemarket
or
Stokeholme I
Milford Haven
S^T GEO
52
30
5

CARMARDHEN SHIRE
Carmarthen
DERLLYS
NERBERTH HUN
Tenbye
Pembrok
KIDWELLYE
Kidwelly
Llanelly
SWANSEY HUN
WEST GOWRE
Cheriton
Ilston
Wormes head Pt
Oxunch Point
Uumbles Pt
Ludsop Pt
Templeton
Redhare
Llanon
Llangennech
GLAM

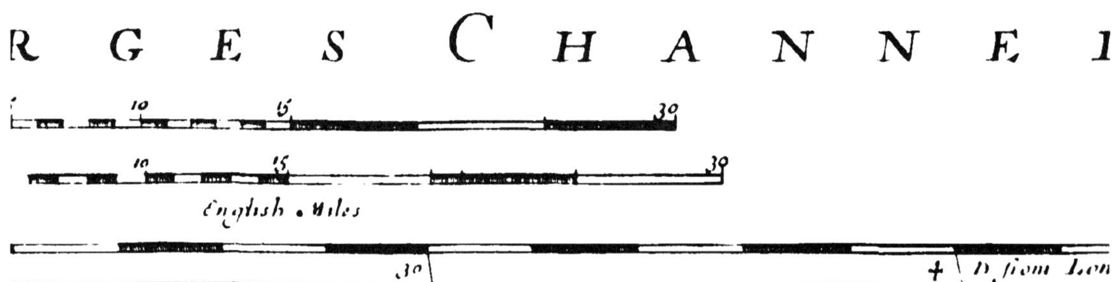
RGES CHANNE
10
15
30
10
15
30
English Miles
30

Cap Tarechan
PART OF MONMOUTH SHIRE
O-R-G-A-N SHIRE
Aberavon
CASTLE HUN
Bridgend
Cowbridg
Llandaf
Caerdiff
OGMOR HUN
Landogh
COWBRIDG HUN
DENISPOWYS HUN
St Fagans
Penmark
Barrye
Funmun
Funtgary
Sully
Sully I
Barri I
Flatholm I
Stepholmes I
Nashe Point
30
45

BRITANNIA:

OR, A

CHOROGRAPHICAL DESCRIPTION

OF

Great-Britain and Ireland.

RADNORSHIRE.

N the north-west of Herefordshire, lies *Radnorshire*, in British *Sir Vaesived*, of a triangular form, and gradually more narrow as it is extended further westward On the south, the River Wye divides it from Brecknock, and on the north part lies Montgomeryshire The eastern and southern parts are well cultivated; but elsewhere it is so uneven with mountains, that it is hardly capable of tillage, though well-stor'd with woods, and water'd with rivulets, and in some places with standing lakes

Towards the east it hath to adorn it (besides other castles of the Lords Marchers, now almost all Castelh Pain bury'd in their own ruins) *Castelbpain*, which was built by Pain a Norman, from whom it had the Colwen name and *Castel Colwen*, which (if I mistake Maud castle v Castelh Colwn not) was formerly call'd *Maud Castle in Colwent* For there was a Castle of that name, much noted, whereof Robert de Todncy, a very eminent person, was governour in the time of Edward the second It is thought to have belonged before, to the *Breoses*, Lords of Brecknock, and to have received that name from Maud of St *Vale-* † Procaciffima Matth Par *rie*, a † malpert woman, wife of *William Breos*, who rebell'd against King John This Castle being demolish'd by the Welsh, was rebuilt of stone by King Henry the third, in the year 1231 Radnor But of greatest note is *Radnor*, the chief town of the County; call'd in British *Maesived*, fair-built, but with thatch'd houses, as is the manner of that country Formerly it was well fenc'd with walls and a Castle, but being by that rebellious *Owen* Owen Glyndwr Old Radnor *Glyn Dowrdwy* laid in ashes, it decay'd daily, as well as old *Radnor* (call'd by the Britains *Maes rled hên*, and from its high situation *Pencraig*) which had been burnt by Rhys ap Gruffydh, in the reign of King John If I should say that Magi this Maesived is the city Magos, which Antoninus seems to call *Magnos*, where (as we read in the *Notitia Provinciarum*) the Commander of the *Pacensian* regiment lay in garrison, under the Lieutenant of Britain, in the reign of Theodosius the younger; in my own judgment (and perhaps others may be of the same mind) I should not be much mistaken For we find that the writers of the middle age call the inhabitants of this Country *Magasetæ*, and also mention *Comites* Magesetæ *Masegetenses* and *Magesetenses* and the distances from *Gobannium* or *Aber-Gavenni*, as also from *Brangonium* or *Worcester*, differ very little from Antoninus's computation Scarce three miles to the east of Radnor, lies *Prestean*, in British Presteän *Lhan Andras*, or St *Andrews*; which from a small village, in the memory of our † grandfathers, did, by the favour and encouragement of † So said, ann 1603 Martin Lord Bishop of St David's, become so eminent and beautiful a market town, as in some measure to eclipse Radnor Scarce four miles hence, lies *Knighton* which may vye with Pres- Knighton tean) call'd by the Britains, as I am informed, *Trebuclo* for *Trevyklawdh*, from the dike lying Offa Dike under it; which was cast up with great labour and industry, by *Offa* the Mercian, as a boundary between his Subjects and the Britains, from the mouth of Dee, to that of the River Wye, for the space of about ninety miles, whence the Britains have call'd it *Klawdh Offa* or Offa's Dyke Concerning which, *Joannes Sarisburiensis*, in his *Polycraticon* saith, that *Harald establish'd a law, that whatever Welshman should be found arm'd on this side the limit he had set them, to wit*, Offa's-Dike, *his right-hand should be cut off by the King's Officers* [The tracing of this Dike gives us the exact bounds of the Britains and Saxons It may be seen on *Bracky hill*, and near *Rhyd ar Helig*, and *Lanterden*, in Herefordshire and is continued northwards from *Knighton*, over a part of Shropshire into Montgomeryshire; and may be traced over the long mountain call'd in Welsh Kevn Digolh, to *Harden castle*, cross the Severn and Lhan Drinio Common, from whence it passes the *Vornwy* again into Shropshire, not far from Oswaldstry, where there is also a small village call'd Trevyrclawdh In Denbighshire, it is visible along the road between Rhywabon and Wrexham,

Wrexham; from whence being continu'd thro' Flintſhire, it ends a little below *Holywell*, where that water falls into Dee, at a place formerly the ſite of the Caſtle of *Baſingwerk* This limit ſeems not afterwards to have been well maintain'd by the Engliſh for although we find that the Britiſh tongue decreaſes daily on the borders of Wales yet not only that language, but alſo the ancient Britiſh cuſtoms and names of men and places remain ſtill for ſome ſpace on the Engliſh ſide, almoſt the whole length of it]

Melienydh

All the land beyond this, toward the weſt and north, call'd by the natives *Melienydh*, from the *yellowiſh* mountains, is for the moſt part a barren and hungry ſoil Which, notwithſtanding, ſhews the ruins of ſeveral Caſtles, but eſpecially of Kevn Lhys, and of *Tinbod* ſtanding * on the ſummit of a cop'd hill, which was deſtroy'd by Lhewelyn Prince of Wales in the year 1260 This Country of *Melienydh* reaches to the River *Wye*, (which word, though it be here the name of a River, ſeems to have been anciently an appellative, either for *River*, or *Water* For although it be not uſed at preſent in that ſenſe, nor preſerv'd in any Gloſſary, or other books, yet I find it in the termination of the names of many of our Rivers *ex gr* Lhugwy, Dowrdwy, y Vyrnwy, Edwy, Conwy, Elwy, Hondhwy, [illegible] Mowdhwy, Tawy, Towy, *&c* Now, that [illegible] final ſyllable [*wy*] in theſe names of Rivers, is the ſame with *gwy*, ſeems more than probable, in that we find the River Towy call'd in the Book of Landaff *Tiugui (ab hoſtio Taratir ſ per ripam Gui, uſque ad ripam Tiugui*, &c) and alſo the River *Elwy*, call'd *Elgui* And that *gwy* or *wy* ſignified *water*, ſeems further to be confirmed from the names of ſome aquatick animals, as *G[illegible]ch*, *Giach*, *eog*, alias *oog*, &c This being granted, we may be able to interpret the names of ſeveral Rivers, which have hitherto remained unintelligible as *Lhugwy*, *clear water*, from *lhug*, which ſignifies *light* or *brightneſs* *Dowrdwy*, *loud water*, from *Dwrdh*, *noiſe* *Edwy*, *a ſwift or rapid ſtream*, from *Ehed*, *to fly*, &c]

Kevn y Lhys,
* *Acuminato colle*

Gwy or Wy, what it ſignifies

The Wye croſſes the weſt angle of the County; and having its rapid courſe ſomewhat abated by the rocks it meets with, and its chanel diſcontinu'd, it ſuddenly falls headlong over a ſteep precipice Whence the place is called *Rhaiadr Gwy*, that is, the *Cataract* or *fall of the River Wye*. And I know not whether the Engliſh might not from that word *Rhaiadr* impoſe the name of *Radnor*, firſt on the county, and afterwards on the chief town therein [Several places in Wales are thus denominated, all which have cataracts near them and the word is ſtill uſed appellatively among the mountains of *Snowdon* in Caernarvonſhire, where ſuch falls of water are very frequent *Rhaiadar-caſtle* (whereof not the leaſt ruins are now remaining) was very advantageouſly ſituated in a nook of the River, cloſe by this Cataract But what ſeems very remarkable, is a deep trench on one ſide of the Caſtle-yard, cut out of an exceeding hard and ſolid rock About two furlongs below this place, where the caſtle ſtood, I obſerved a large *Tumulus* or Barrow, call'd from a Chapel adjoyning, *Tommen lhan St Ffrêd* and on the other ſide, at a farther diſtance, there are two more, much leſs than the former, called *Krigeu Kevn Keido*, viz the Barrows of Kevn Keido, a place ſo call'd, where, it is ſuppos'd, there ſtood heretofore a church, in regard a piece of ground adjoining is call'd *Klyttieu'r Eglwys*

Rhaiadr Gwy

Barrows or Lows call'd in Welſh *Krigeu*

Gwaſtedin

On the top of a hill, call'd *Gwaſtedin*, near Rhaiadr Gwy, there are three large heaps of ſtones, of that kind which are common upon mountains in moſt (if not all) the Counties of Wales; call'd in South Wales *Karneu*, and in North Wales *Karned-beu* They conſiſt of ſuch leſſer ſtones from a pound weight, to a hundred, *&c* as the neighbouring places afford, and are confuſedly pil'd up without any farther trouble, than the bringing them thither, and the throwing them in heaps On *Plin Lhimmon*, or, as otherwiſe call'd, *Pym Lumnon* mountain, and ſome other places, there are of theſe *Karnedbeu* ſo conſiderably big, that they may be ſuppos'd to conſiſt of no leſs than a hundred Cart-loads of ſtones, but, generally ſpeaking, they are much leſs They are alſo found in the North, and probably in other parts of England; and are frequent in Scotland and Ireland, being called there by the ſame Britiſh name of *Karn* whereof I can give no other account to the curious Reader, than that it is a primitive word, and appropriated to ſignify ſuch heaps of ſtones That moſt of theſe *Karnedbeu* (not to ſay all) were intended as memorials of the dead, I am induced to believe, for that I have myſelf obſerv'd near the ſummit of one of them, a rude ſtone monument (which I ſhall have occaſion to prove Sepulchral hereafter) ſomewhat of the form of a large *Coffer* or Cheſt, and have received unqueſtionable information of two more ſuch monuments, found of late years in the like places But what removes all ſcruple, and puts this queſtion beyond further debate, is that it is ſtill the cuſtom in ſeveral places, to caſt heaps of ſtones on the graves of malefactors and ſelf-murderers And hence perhaps it is, ſince we can aſſign no other reaſon, that the worſt of Traytors are call'd *Karn-bradwyr*, the moſt notorious thieves *Karn Lhadron*, &c That this was alſo the cuſtom amongſt the Romans, appears from that Epitaph aſcrib'd to Virgil, on the infamous Robber Baliſta:

Karn, what it ſignifies

Monte ſub hoc lapidum tegitur Baliſta *ſepultus,*
Nocte, die, tutum carpe, viator, iter

Under this ſtone *Baliſta* lies inter'd,
Now (night or day) no danger need be fear'd

But that this was nevertheleſs uſual among the Britains, before they were known to the Romans, ſeems evident, for that they are common alſo in the *Highlands* of Scotland, and in Ireland, where the Roman Conqueſts never reach'd

Now, if it be demanded whether Malefactors only were thus ſerv'd in ancient times, or whether other perſons indifferently had not ſuch heaps of ſtones erected to them, as Sepulchral monuments I anſwer, that before Chriſtianity, men of the beſt quality ſeem to have had ſuch Funeral Piles, conformable to a cuſtom among the Trojans, as we find by Homer's deſcription of *Hector*'s Funeral, at the end of the *Iliads* And ſuch I take to have been the largeſt of them, thoſe eſpecially that have the monuments abovemention'd within them But ſince the planting of Chriſtianity, they became ſo deteſtable and appropriated to Malefactors, that ſometimes the moſt paſſionate wiſhes a man can expreſs to his enemy is, *that a Karn be his monument* and (as we have already obſerved) the moſt notorious and profligate Criminals are diſtinguiſh'd by that word

Karn ardy Wyrth

By the aforeſaid *Cataract* there was a caſtle, which, as we find it recorded, was repaired by *Rhys*, Prince of South-Wales, in the Reign of King Richard the firſt Near this place is a vaſt Wilderneſs, render'd very diſmal by many crooked ways and high mountains into which, as a proper place of refuge, that bane of his native Country, King *Vortigern* (whoſe very memory the Britains curſe) withdrew himſelf, when he had at laſt repented of his abominable wickedneſs, in calling in the Engliſh Saxons, and inceſtuouſly marrying his own daughter But God's vengeance purſuing him, he was conſum'd by

Vortigern

Lightning together with his City *Kaer-Gwortigern*, which he had built for his refuge Nor was it far from hence (as if the place were fatal) that not only this *Vortigern*, the last British Monarch of the race of the Britains, but also *Lhewelyn*, the last Prince of Wales of the British line, being betray'd and intercepted in the year of our Lord 1282, ended his life From this Vortigern, Ninnius calls that small region *Gwortigern-mawr*, nor is the name yet lost; but of the city there is not any memorial remaining, but what we have from Authors Some are of opinion, that the Castle of *Gwethrénion* arose out of the ruins of it, which the Welsh, out of hatred to Roger *Mortimer*, laid even with the ground, An 1201 This part of the Country hath been also call'd *Gwarth Ennion*, as we are inform'd by Ninnius, who writes, that the forementioned Vortigern, when he was publickly and sharply reproved by St German, did not only persist in his obstinacy, and his wicked practices, but also cast false and malicious reproaches on that godly saint *Wherefore* (saith *Ninnius*) *Vortimer, the Son of Vortigern, to make amends for his father's fault, ordain'd that the Land where the Bishop had receiv'd so great an indignity, should be his own for ever Upon which, and in memory of St* German, *it has been call'd* Gwarth Enian, *which in English signifies a* slander justly requited

Lhewelyn.

Gwerthrynion

Gwarth in British *Calumny*, and *Ennian* Just

The * *Mortimers*, descended from the Niece of *Gonora*, wife of Richard, the first Duke of Normandy, were the first of the Normans, who having overcome *Edric* † *Sylvaticus* a Saxon, gain'd a considerable part of this small territory And having continu'd for a long time the principal part of the County, at length Roger *Mortimer*, Lord of *Wigmore*, was created * Earl of *March*, by Edward the third, about the year 1328, who soon after was sentenced to death, having been accus'd of insolence to the government, of favouring the Scots to the prejudice of England, of conversing over familiarly with the King's mother, and of contriving the death of his father, King Edward the second He had by his Wife, *Jane Jenevil* (who brought him large revenues, as well in Ireland as England) a Son call'd *Edmund*, who suffer'd for his father's crimes, and was depriv'd both of his inheritance, and the title of Earl But his Son *Roger* was receiv'd into favour, and had not only the title of Earl of *March* restor'd, but was also created Knight of the Garter, at the first institution of that noble Order This Roger marry'd *Philippa Mountague*, by whom he had *Edmund*, Earl of March, who marry'd *Philippa*, the only daughter of *Leonel*, Duke of Clarence, the third Son of King Edward the third, whereby he obtain'd the Earldom of Ulster in Ireland, and the Lordship of Clare After his decease in Ireland, where he had govern'd with great applause, his Son *Roger* succeeded, being both Earl of March and Ulster; whom King Richard the second design'd his successor to the Crown, as being in right of his mother the next heir but he dying before King Richard, left Issue *Edmund* and *Anne*. King Henry the fourth (who had usurp'd the government) suspecting Edmund's interest, and title to the Crown, expos'd him to many hazards, insomuch, that being taken by the Rebel *Owen Glyn Dwr*, he dy'd of grief and discontent, leaving his sister *Anne* to inherit She was marry'd to *Richard Plantagenet*, Earl of Cambridge, whose posterity in her right became afterwards Earls of March, and laid claim to the Crown, which in the end (as we shall shew elsewhere) they obtain'd, and Edward the fourth's eldest Son, who was Prince of Wales, Duke of Cornwall, &c had also confer'd on him by his Father, as an additional honour, the title of Earl of *March* [From which time, this title lay dead, till it was reviv'd by King James the first, and bestow'd upon *Esme Steward*, Lord Aubigny, and afterwards Duke of Lennox, who was succeeded by James his Son, and *Esme*, his Grandson Which Esme dying young, the Honour descended to Charles, the fourth Son of Esme, the first Duke of Lennox, who also dying without issue, in the year 1672, this honourable Title, among others, was confer'd by King *Charles* the Second, in the Year 1675, upon *Charles Lenos*, created at the same time Duke of Richmond] As for the title of Radnor, † [it was erected into an Earldom by King Charles the Second, in the person of *John Roberts*, Lord Roberts of Truro whose Son Robert, stil'd Lord Viscount *Bodmin*, dying in the life-time of his Father, the honour descended to *Charles* his Grandson, the present Earl]

* *Mortuoma ris sive de mortuo mari* Earls of March G Gemet l ult c 10

† *Weald* or *Wild*

* *Hujus limitis Wallici, vel (ut loquuntur) Marchiæ Comes*

Lib Monast *Lantlony* 19 Ed 3

See in *York shire*, towards the end of the County

† No Person that I know of hath enjoy'd it since rally, C

In this County are [illegible] *Parishes*

BRECK-

BRECKNOCKSHIRE.

IN the South of Radnor lies *Brecknockshire*, in British *Brychetnog*, so call'd, as the Welsh suppose, from
* Girald Camb. Prince * *Brechanius*, who is said to have had a numerous and holy off spring, to wit, twenty four daughters, all *Saints* This County is considerably larger than *Radnorshire*, but more mountainous, though in many places it has also fruitful Vales It is bounded on the East with *Herefordshire*, on the South with *Monmouthshire* and *Glamorganshire*, and on the West with *Caermardinshire* But since nothing can be added in the description of this small province, to what the industrious Giraldus Cambrensis hath al-
† Four, C ready written, (who was Arch-deacon hereof † five hundred years since,) I may do well for some time to be silent, and to call him to my assistance

Brechiniauc (saith he, in his Itinerary of Wales,) *is a Land sufficiently abounding with Corn, whereof if there be any defect, it is amply supply'd from the borders of England, and is well stored with Pastures, Woods, Wild Deer, and Herds of Cattle It hath also plenty of River-fish, on one side from* Usk, *and on the other from* Wy; *both abounding with Salmon and Trout, but the* Wy *with a better sort call'd* Umbræ. *It is inclosed on all parts except the North, with high mountains having on the West, the Mountains of* Cantre bychan, *and towards the South, the Southern hills, whereof the chief is call'd* Kader Arthur, *or* Arthur's Chair, *from two peaks on the top of it, somewhat resembling a Chair Which, in regard it is a lofty seat, and a place of strength, is ascribed in the vulgar appellation of it, to* Arthur, *the most puissant and absolute Monarch of the Britains A Fountain springs on the very top of this hill, which is as deep as a draw well, and four square, affording Trouts, tho' no water runs out of it Being thus guarded on the South with high mountains, it is defended from the heat of the Sun with cool breezes, which, with an innate wholsomeness of the air, renders the Country exceeding temperate On the East it hath the mountains of Talgarth and Ewias*

On the North (as he saith) it is a more open and champain Country, where it is divided from *Rhadnorshire* by the River *Wye* upon which there are two Towns of noted Antiquity, *Bualht*
Bualht and *Hay* *Bualht* is a Town pleasantly seated, with Woods about it, and fortified with a Castle, but of a later building, *viz* by the *Breoses* and *Mortimers*, when *Rhys ap Gryffydh* had demolished the old one At present it is noted for a good Market but formerly it seems to have been a place very eminent; for Ptolomy sets down the Longitude and Latitude of it, and calls it *Bullæum Silurum* [Of this Town, in the
Bullæum year 1690, a considerable part (being that side of the Street next the River *Wye*) was by a casual fire totally consumed Whether this *Bualht* be the ancient *Bullæum*, or whether that City or Fort, (allowing it to have been in this County) was not a place call'd *Kaereu*, some miles distant
Kaereu from it, may be question'd At least it is evident, that there hath been a Roman Fort at *Kaereu* for, besides that the name implies as much (signifying strictly the *Walls* or *Rampire*,) and that it was prefix'd by the Britains to the names of almost all the Roman Towns and Castles; they frequently dig-up Bricks there, and find other manifest signs of a Roman work It is now only the name of a Gentleman's House, and not far from it, there is also another House call'd *Castelban* If it be urg'd in Favour of *Buelht*, that it seems still to retain its ancient name, which Ptolomy might render Βουλλαῖον·
it may be answer'd, that *Buelht*, which I interpret *Colles Boum*, (*Ox-Cliff*, or else *Oxen-Holt*,) Buellt, what it signifies
was the name of a small Country here, from whence in all likelihood the ancient *Bullæum* (it it stood in this Tract) was denominated, but that being totally destroy'd, and this Town becoming afterwards the most noted place of the Country, it might also receive its name from it, as the former had done But (that I may dissemble nothing) since the congruity of the Names is the main argument for assigning this situation to the ancient *Bullæum Silurum*, we shall have occasion of hesitating, if hereafter we find the Ruins of a Roman Fort or City, in a † neighbouring Country of the *Silures*, the † See Caer...
name whereof may agree with *Bullæum*, no less than *Buelht*] From this Town, the neighbouring part (a mountainous and rocky Country) is also call'd *Bualht*, into which, upon the Incursion of the Saxons, King Vortigern retired And there also, by the permission of Aurelius Ambrosius, his Son *Pascentius* govern'd, as we are inform'd by Ninnius, who in his Chapter of *Wonders*, relates I know not what prodigious Story of a heap of Stones here, wherein might be seen the footsteps of King Arthur's Hound.
Hay *Hay*, in British *Tregelhi* (which in English we may render *Hasely*, or *Hasleton*) lies on the bank of the River *Wye*, upon the borders of Herefordshire, a place which seems to have been well known to the Romans, since we often find their coins there, and some Ruins of Walls are still remaining But now being almost totally decay'd, it complains of the outrages of that profligate Rebel, *Owen Glyn Dowrdwy*, who, in his March through these Countries, consum'd it with fire

[Of this *Oven Glyn dwr*, or *Glyn-Dowrdwy*, is Owen Glyndwr
found the following Account, in some notes of the learned and judicious Antiquary *Robert Vaughan*, of *Hengwrt*, Esq; "Sir *Davydh Gam* "was wholly devoted to the interest of the "Duke of Lancaster, upon which account it "was, that *Owen ap Gryffydh Vychan* (commonly call'd *Owen Glyn-Dwr*) was his mortal "enemy This *Owen* had his education at one "of the Inns of Court, and was preferred to "the service of King Richard the second, whose "*Scutifer* (as Walsingham saith) he was *Owen* "being assured that his King and Master *Richard* was deposed and murder'd, and being "withal provoked by several Affronts and "Wrongs done him by the Lord Grey of Ruthin his neighbour, whom King Henry very "much countenanced against him, took arms, "and looking upon Henry as an Usurper, "caus'd himself to be proclaim'd Prince of "*Wales* And though himself were descended "paternally but from a younger brother of the "house of *Powis*, yet (as ambition is ingeni- "ous) he finds out a way to lay claim to the "Principality, as descended by a daughter "from *Lhewelyn ap Gryffydh*, the last Prince of "the British race He invaded the lands, and "burnt and destroy'd the houses and estates of

" all those that favour'd and adher'd to King " Henry He call'd a Parliament to meet at " *Machynleth* in Montgomeryshire whither the " Nobility and Gentry of Wales came, in obe- " dience to his summons, and among them the " said *David Gam*, but with an intention to " murder *Owen* The Plot being discover'd, " and he taken before he could put it in execu- " tion, he was like to have suffer'd as a Traitor " but intercession was made for him by *Owen's* " best friends, and the greatest upholders of his " cause; whom he could not either honourably " or safely deny Yet notwithstanding this Par- " don, as soon as he return'd to his own Coun- " try, where he was a man of considerable in " terest, he exceedingly annoy'd *Owen's* friends " Not long after, *Owen* enter'd the Marches of " Wales, destroying all with fire and sword, " and having then burnt the House of Sir *David* " *Gam*, it is reported that he spake thus to one " of his tenants "

O gwels di wr côch cam,
Yn ymofyn y Gwrngwen,
Dywed y bôd hi tan y lan,
A nôd y glo ar ei phen

But to return]

Usk, whence denominated

As the river *Wy* watereth the Northern part of this County, so the *Usk*, a noble river, takes its course through the midst of it [The British name of this river is *Wysk*, which word seems a derivative from *Gwy* or *Wy*, whereof the Reader may see some account in *Radnorshire* At present it is not significative in the British, but is still pre serv'd in the Irish tongue, and is their common word for *water* There were formerly in Britain many rivers of this name, which may be now distinguish'd in England by these shadows of it, *Ex*, *Ox*, *Ux*, *Ouse*, *Usk*, &c But because such as are unacquainted with Etymological Observations, may take this for a groundless conjecture, that it is not such will appear, in regard that in Antonine's Itinerary we find *Exeter* call'd *Isca Danmoniorum* from its situation on the river *Ex*, and also a City upon this river *Usk*, for the same reason, call'd *Isca Leg II*]

Brecknock

Aberhodni, Giraldo Camb

The *Usk* falling headlong from the *Black-mountain* and forcing a deep Channel, passes by *Brecknock*, the chief Town of the County, and placed almost in the Center of it This Town the Britains call *Aber Hondhy*, from the conflu ence of the two rivers, *Hondhy* and *Usk* That it was inhabited in the time of the Romans, is evi dent from several Coyns of their Emperors, sometimes found there; [and from a Roman Brick lately discover'd with this Inscription, LEG II AUG as also from a square Camp near this place, commonly called *y Gaer*, that is, the Fortification, where Roman Bricks are fre quently turn'd up by the Plough, with the same Inscription] *Bernard Newmarch*, who conquer'd this small County, built here a stately Castle, which the *Breoses* and *Bohuns* afterward repaired; and in our † Fathers memory King Henry the eighth founded a Collegiate Church of fourteen Prebendaries (in the Priory of the Dominicans) which he translated thither from *Aber Gwily* in *Caermardhinshire*

† So said [illegible]

Lhyn Savadhan

Brecknockmere

Two miles to the East of Brecknock, is a large Lake, which the Britains call *Lhyn Savadhan*, and *Lhyn Savadhan*, i e a *Standing Lake* Giraldus calls it *Clamosum*, from the terrible *noise* it makes, like a clap of thunder, upon the break- ing of the Ice In English, it is called *Brecknock-mere* it is two miles long and near the same breadth; well stored with Otters, and also with Perch, Tench, and Eel, which the Fishermen take in their *Coracles* *Lhewenny*, a small river, having enter'd this Lake, still retains its own colour, and, as it were disdaining a mixture, is thought to carry out no more, nor other water, than what it brought in It hath been an ancient tradition in this neighbourhood, that where the Lake is now, there was formerly a City, which being swallow'd up by an Earthquake, resign'd its place to the waters And to confirm this, they alledge (besides other arguments) that all the high-ways of this County tend to this Lake If this be true, what other City may we suppose on the river *Lhewenny*, but *Loventium*, placed by Ptolemy in this tract, which I have diligently search- ed for, but there appear no where any † remains, either of the name, or the ruins, or the situation of it Marianus (which I had almost forgotten) seems to call this place *Bricenaumere*; who tells us that *Edelfleda, the Mercian Lady, enter'd the Land of the Britains* Anno 913, *in order to re- duce a Castle at* Bricenaumere, and that *she there took the Queen of the Britains prisoner* Whether that Castle was Brecknock itself, or *Castelh Dinas* on a steep tapering Rock above this Lake, remains uncertain, but it is manifest from the publick Records, that the neighbouring Castle of *Blaen Lhevenny*, was the chief place of that Ba rony, which was the possession of *Peter Fitz Herbert*, the son of *Herbert* Lord of *Dean forest*, by *Lucy* the daughter of *Miles* Earl of Hereford

See Caermarthenshire

Loventium

† Vid Cardiganshire

Bricenaumere

Brecknock Castle

Blaen Lhevenny Castle

The sinking of a Town at the *Savadhan*, an erroneous tradition

[As to the sinking of *Lhyn Savadhan* abovemen tioned, we find the tradition of Cities being drown'd, apply'd to many other lakes in Wales, as *Pwlh Kynffig* in Glamorganshire, *Lhyn Lhan Lhwch* in Kaermardhinshire, *Lhyngwyn* in Rad norshire, *Lhyn Dekwyn ucha* in Merionydshire, and *Lhyn Lhynklys* in Shropshire All which I suspect as fabulous, and not to be otherwise re- garded, than as one of those erroneous traditions of the Vulgar, from which few (if any) Nations are exempted It cannot be denied, but that in *Sicily* and the Kingdom of Naples, and in such o- ther Countries as are subject to violent earthquakes and subterraneous fires, such accidents have hap- pened, but since no Histories inform us, that any part of Britain was ever sensible of such Ca lamities, I see no reason we have to regard these oral traditions

Maen y Morynnion

At a place call'd *y Gaer* near Brecknock, there stands a remarkable Monument in the highway, commonly call'd *Maen y Morynnion*, or the *Maiden stone* It is a rude pillar, erected in the midst of the road, about six foot high and two broad, and six inches thick On the one side, where it inclines a little, it shews the portraitures of a man and woman in some ancient habit It seems to have been carv'd with no small labour, though with little art, for the Figures are con- siderably rais'd above the superficies of the stone, and all that part where they stand is depressed lower than that above their heads or under their feet That it is very ancient, is unquestionable; but whether a British Antiquity, or done by some unskilful Roman Artist, I shall not pretend to determine; but recommend it (together with the tradition of the neighbours concerning it) to the farther disquisition of the curious

Inscription at Pentre Ysky throg

And at *Pentre Ysky throg* in *Lhan St Fred* pa rish, there is a stone Pillar erected in the high way, about the same height with the former, but somewhat of a depress'd cylinder form, with this mutilated Inscription, to be read downwards

I suppose this Inscription (notwithstanding the name *Victorinus*) to have been of somewhat later date than the time of the Romans; and that it is only a Monument of some persons buried there, containing no more than his own name and his father's, *N* ——— *filius Victorini*

Inscription at Vaenor

But this upon a Cross in the Highway at *Vaenor*-parish, is yet much later, the Inscription whereof, though it be intirely preserv'd, is to me unintelligible, for I dare not rely on a slight conjecture that I made at first view of it, that it might be read, *In nomine Dei Summi*, *Iltus Tilaus* or *Teilaw* being an eminent Saint, to whom many Churches in South-Wales are consecrated

St Iltut's Cell

In *Lhan Hammwich* Parish, there is an ancient Monument commonly call'd *Ty Ilhtud* or St *Iltut*'s Hermitage It stands on the top of a hill, not far from the Church, and is composed of four large Stones somewhat of a flat form, altogether rude and unpolish'd Three of which are so pitch'd in the ground, and the fourth laid on the top for a cover, that they make an oblong square Hut, open at the one end, about eight foot long, four wide, and near the same height. Having enter'd it, I found the two side Stones thus inscrib'd with variety of Crosses

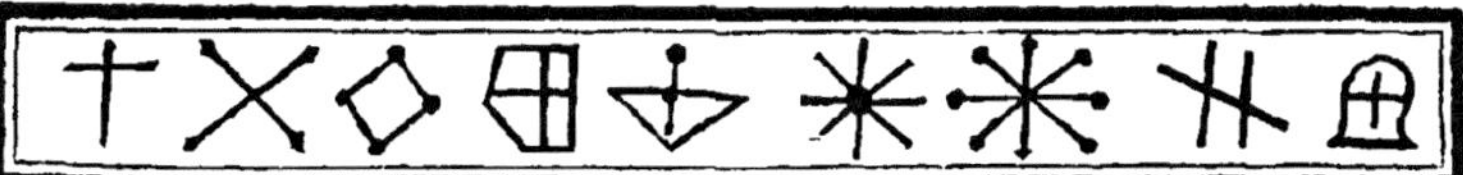

I suppose this Cell, notwithstanding the crosses and the name, to have been erected in the time of Paganism, for that I have elsewhere observ'd such Monuments (to be hereafter mention'd) plac'd in the center of circles of stones, somewhat like that at *Rolrich* in Oxfordshire And though there is not at present such a circle about this, yet I have grounds to suspect that they may have been carried off, and applied to some use For there has been one remov'd very lately, which stood within a few paces of this Cell, and was call'd *Maen Ilhtud*, and there are some Stones still remaining there]

* *De novo mercatu* Lords of Brecknock

In the reign of William Rufus, *Bernard* * *Newmarch* the Norman, a man of undaunted courage, and great policy, having levied a considerable Army both of English and Normans, was the first that attempted the reducing of this Country [Having discomfited and slain in the field *Bledhyn ap Maenyrch*, and seised on the Lordship of *Brecon*, and forced his son and heir *Gwgan* to be content with that share of it, which he was pleas'd, by way of composition, to appoint him, he gave him the Lordship and Manours of *Lhan Vihangel Tal y Lhyn*, part of *Lhan Lhyeni* and *Kantrev Selis*, with lodgings in the Castle of Brecknock; where, in regard he was the rightful Lord of the Country, there was such a strict eye kept over him, that he was not permitted at any time to go abroad without two or more Norman Knights in his company]

Bledhyn ap Maenyrch

R Vaughan

Which *Bernard Newmarch* having at length, after a tedious war, got this country out of the hands of the Welsh, he built Forts therein, and gave Possessions of Lands to his Fellow soldiers, amongst whom the chiefest were the *Aubreys*, *Gunters*, *Haverds*, *Waldebeofs*, and *Prichards*, [of these, *Roger Gunter*, a younger brother of that Family, intermarrying with the daughter and heir of *Thomas Stodey*, 8 Hen 4, settled at *Kintbury* or *Kentbury* in Barkshire] And the better to secure himself amongst his enemies the Welsh, he married Nest, the daughter of Prince Gruffydh, who being a woman of a licentious and revengeful temper, at once depriv'd herself of her reputation, and her son of his inheritance For *Mabel* the only son of this *Bernard*, having affronted a young Nobleman with whom she convers'd too familiarly, she, (as the Poet saith)

—— *Iram atque animos à crimine sumens*,

Spur'd on by Lust to anger and revenge;

depos'd upon Oath before King Henry the second, that her son *Mabel* was begotten in adultery, and was not the son of *Bernard* Upon which, *Mabel* being excluded, the estate devolved to his sister *Sibyl*, and in her right to her husband *Miles* Earl of Hereford, whose five sons dying without issue, this Country of Brecknock fell to the share of *Bertha* his daughter, who

The County of
MONMOUTH
By Robt. Morden
PART OF
BRECKNOCK
SHIRE

XII
XI minutis of Time
Clodock
Llangua
PART
SKENFRITH
Grosmont al Grysmond Cast
OF HE
SH
PART OF HEREFORD SHIRE
Hatterel Hills
Patrissun
Stanton Chap
Modny R
Llangattok Kelenyg
THE SILVRES
Skinfrith
Cast
Norton
Bettus Chap
Crycorne
White Cast
Llanvaner chap
HUN
Llanfyrren
Peny vale Hill
The Chappell
Llanwenarth
Aber Gavenny
Kebby R
Gowenni R
Trothy R
Llantelio Gryssenny
Llanvihangel
Blorenge Hill
Colbrok
Hardwick Chap
BERGAVENNI HUN
Llanarthe
Treagare
Penrose
Brynguin
Llanelen
Llanouer
Cleytha
Ragland Cast
Iska
Kylgeden
Bettus newith
Trostrey
Burrium or Uske
Llandenny
Pyll R
Coytre
Chap Newith
Kemeys Comaunder
Birthin R
Llanvihangel
Ponty moil
Lanbadock
Llangowan
Panteage
Wolfsnewton
Kelyoruck

REFORD
IRE
Whitchurch
Welshe towne
Gennirew
S Michael
Stanton
PART OF MONMOUTH SHIRE
Welshe Bycknor
PART OF
GLOCESTER
Pennallte
Chapel
Lindogan
Trylech
St Breuale
Trylech Grange
Brockweare
Little Tyntarn
Chapelhill
Llancant Chap
Penterye Chap
St Aruan
Tydnam
50
45
40

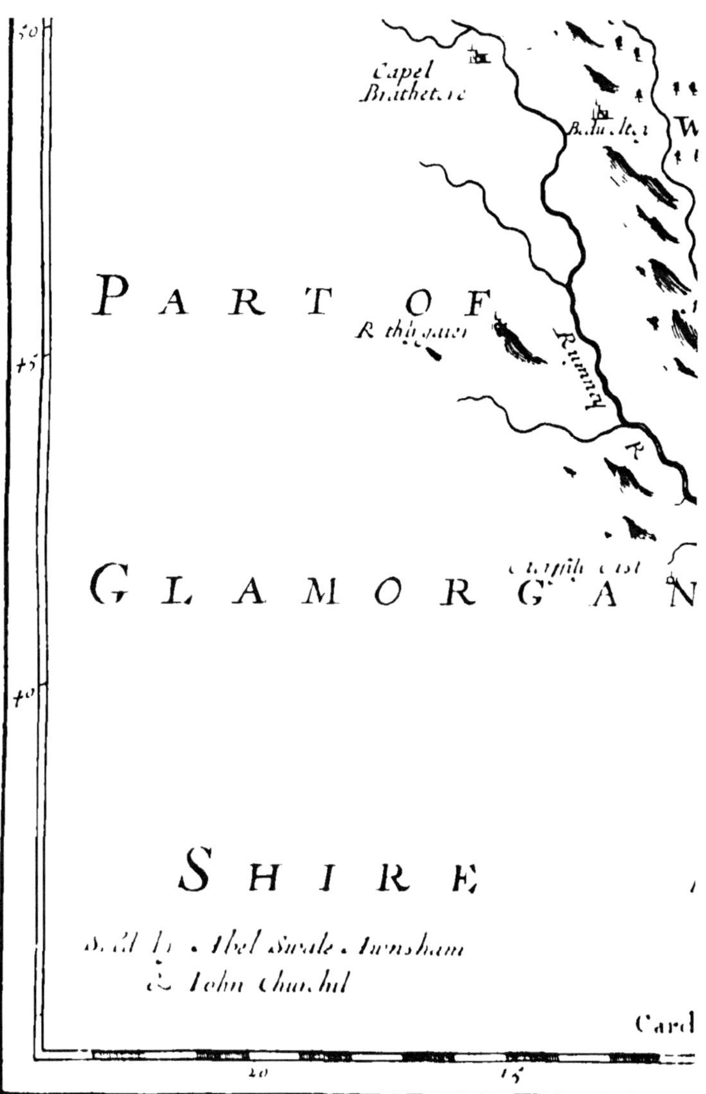
Capel
P A R T O F
G L A M O R G A N
S H I R E
50
45
40
20
15

Ponty pool
USKE
LOOGE HUN
HUN
Llantrissant
Tredunock
Lanthewe
Llanthewell Chap
Isca Legio
Kaer Lleon
Newport
The More
Bettus Chapell
Rishka
Christ Church
Langston
Lanmartin
Llanwern
Grenefeld cast
Wense Wood
Penhow
Pennycoyd
Erles Wood
Magor
Perthollie Chap
Kemis
Llanhenog
Penrose
Bassalig
Llanbeder
Marshfeld
Peterston
Ramny
St Melans
Colkhurst
Goldcliff Point
Bysshopston cast

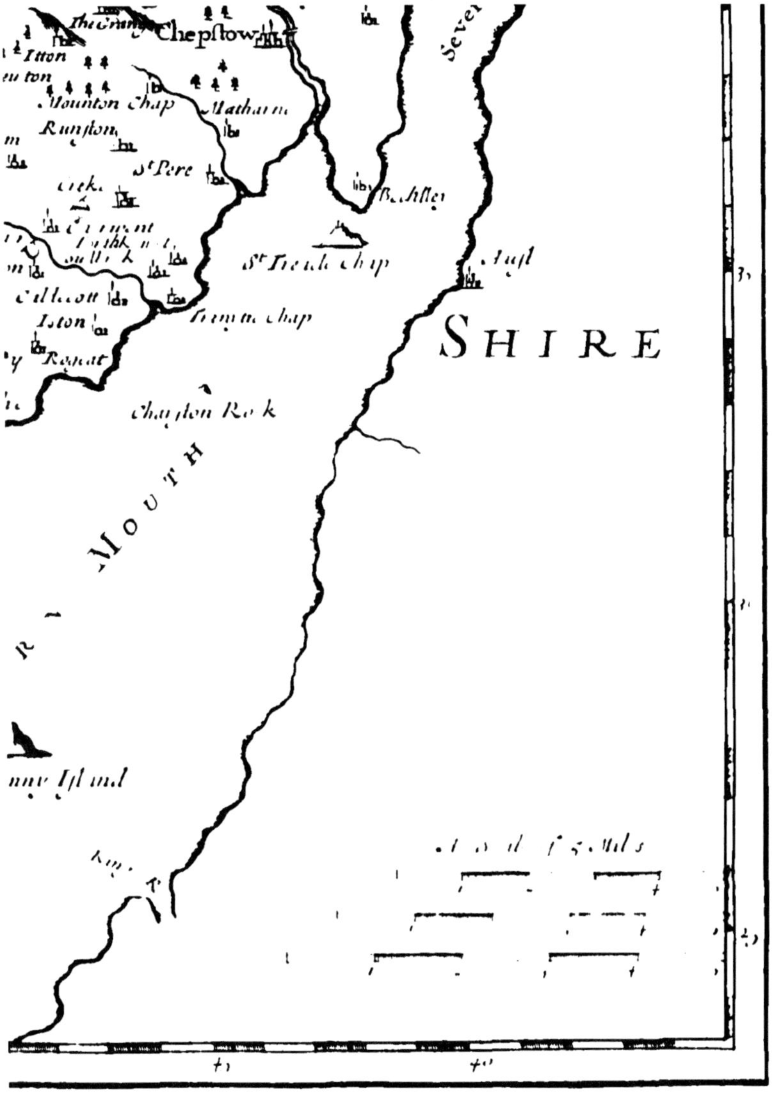
Chepstow
Itton
Mounton Chap
Runston
St Pere
St Treacle Chap
Aust
SHIRE
Chapston Rock
MOUTH
Iston
Rogiat
Sever

Call'd also Braus and Breus. * Procax. ‖ Matildis de Haia.

who had, by *Philip de Breos*, a Son, *William de Breos*, Lord of Brecknock; upon whom the seditious spirit and * shrewd tongue of his ‖ wife drew infinite calamities. For when she had utter'd reproachful language against King John, the King strictly commanded her Husband, who was deep in his debt, to discharge it immediately Who after frequent demurrings, at last mortgaged to the King his three castles of *Hay*, *Brecknock*, and *Radnor*; which soon after he surprized with a mixt multitude, that he had got together, and put the Garrisons to the Sword, he also burnt the Town of *Lemster*, and with Fire, Sword, and Depredations, continu'd to annoy the Country, omitting nothing of the usual practices of Rebels But upon the approach of the King's forces, he withdrew into Ireland, where he associated with the King's enemies yet, pretending a submission, he returned, and surrender'd himself to the King, who was about to follow him, but after many feigned promises, he again rais'd new commotions in Wales At last, being compell'd to quit his native country, he died an Exile in France But his wife being taken, suffer'd the worst of miseries; for she was starv'd in prison, and so, did severe penance for her scurrilous language His Son, *Giles*, Bishop of Hereford, having (without regard to his Nephew, who was the true heir) recover'd his father's estate by permission of King John, left it to his brother *Reginald*; whose Son *William* was hang'd by *Lhewelin*, Prince of Wales, who had caught him in adultery with his wife But by the daughters of that *William*, the *Mortimers*, *Cantelows*, and *Bohuns*, Earls of Hereford, enjoy'd plentiful fortunes This County of *Brecknock* fell to the *Bohuns*, and at length from them to the *Staffords*, and upon the attainder of Edward Stafford, Duke of Buckingham, considerable revenues were forfeited to the Crown in this County

[*James Butler*, afterwards Duke of *Ormond*, was created Earl of *Brecknock*, upon the Restoration of King Charles the Second, in the year 1660] Earl of Brecknock.

This County has 61 Parishes

MONMOUTHSHIRE.

THE County of *MONMOUTH*, call'd formerly *Wentset*, and *Wentsland*, and by the Britains *Gwent*, from an ancient City of that name) lies South of *Brecknockshire* and *Herefordshire* On the North it is divided from Herefordshire by the river *Mynwy*, on the East from Gloucestershire by the river *Wye*, on the West from Glamorganshire by *Rhymni*, and on the South it is bounded by the Severn Sea, into which those rivers, as also *Usk*, (that runs through the midst of this County) are discharged It affords not only a competent plenty for the use of the inhabitants, but also abundantly supplies the defects of the neighbouring Counties The East part abounds with pastures and woods, the West part is somewhat mountainous and rocky, but yet rewards to a good degree the pains of the husbandman The inhabitants (saith Giraldus, writing of the time when he liv'd) *are a valiant and courageous people, inur'd to frequent Skirmishes, and the most skilful archers of all the Welsh borderers*

Ewias. Lantoni.

In the utmost corner of the County, Southward, called *Ewias*, stands the ancient Abbey of *Lantoni*, not far from the river *Mynwy*, amongst *Hatterel hills*; which, because they bear some resemblance to a chair, are call'd *Mynydd-Kader* [For *Kader* is the name of many mountains in Wales, as *Kader* Arthur, *Kader* Verwin, *Kader* Idris, *Kader* Dihnmael, *Kader* yr Ychen, &c which the learned Dr *Davies* supposes to have been so called, not from their resemblance to a *Kadair* or Chair, but because they have been either fortified places, or were looked upon as naturally impregnable, by such as first impos'd those names on them For the British *Kader* (as well as the Irish word *Kathair*) signify'd anciently a *Fort* or *Bulwark*, whence probably the modern word *Kaer* of the same signification, might be corrupted] As for Lantoni, it was founded by *Walter Lacy*, to whom William Earl of Hereford gave large possessions here, and from whom those *Lacies*, so renown'd among the first Conquerers of Ireland, were descended Giraldus Cambrensis (to whom it was well known) can best describe the situation of this small Abbey *In the low vale of* Ewias (saith he) *which is about a Bow shot over, and enclos'd on all sides with high Mountains, stands the Church of St* John Baptist, *cover'd with Lead, and, considering the solitariness of the place, not unhandsomely built, with an arched Roof of stone in the same place, where formerly stood a small Chapel of St* David, *the Archbishop, recommended with no other Ornaments than green moss and ivy A place fit for the exercise of Religion, and the most conveniently seated for canonical discipline, of any Monastery in the Island of Britain built first (to the Honour of that solitary Life) by two Hermits in this Desert, remote from all the noise of the world, upon the River* Hodeni, *which glides through the midst of the vale Whence it was call'd* Lhan Hodeni, *the word* Lhan *signifying a Church or Religious place But to speak more accurately, the true name of that place in Welsh is* Nant Hodeni, *for the Inhabitants call it at this day* Lhan Dhewi, yn Nant Hodeni *i e St* David's *Church on the River Hodeni The Rains which mountainous places usually produce, are here very frequent, the Winds exceeding fierce, and the Winters almost continually cloudy Yet notwithstanding that gross air, it is so temper'd, that this place is very little subject to diseases The Monks sitting here in their cloisters, when they chance to look out for fresh air, have a pleasing prospect on all hands, of exceeding high mountains, with plentiful herds of wild Deer, feeding aloft at the farthest limits of their Horizon The * Body of the Sun surmounts not these hills, so as to be visible to them, till it is past One o'clock, even when the air is most clear* And a little after —— *The fame of this place drew hither* Roger *Bishop of Salisbury, prime Minister of State, who having for some time admired the situation and retired solitariness of it, and also the contented condition of the Monks, serving God with due reverence,* and

Hodnes al. Hondhi

* This is contradicted by such as know the place

and their most agreeable and brotherly conversation; and being return'd to the King, and having spent the best part of a day in the Praises of it, he at last thus concluded his discourse What shall I say more! all the Treasure of your Majesty and the Kingdom would not suffice to build such a Cloyster At which both the King and Courtiers being astonish'd, he at last explain'd that Paradox, by telling them he meant the mountains *wherewith it was on all Hands enclos'd*

But of this enough, if not too much

Lhan [It may be here observed, that *Lhan* or *Lan*, properly signifies a *Yard*, or some small *Inclosure*, as may be taken notice of in compound words For we find a *Vineyard* call'd *Gwyn-lan*, an Orchard, *Per-lan*, a Hay-yard, *Yd lan*, a Church-yard, *Korph-lan*, a Sheep fold, *Kor-lan*, &c However (as *Giraldus* observes) it denotes separately a Church or Chapel, and is of common use, in that sense, throughout all Wales probably because such Yards or Inclosures might be places of worship in the time of Heathenism, or upon the first planting of Christianity, when Churches were scarce]

Grossmont. Skinffrith. On the river *Mynway* are seen the Castles of *Grosmont* and *Skinffrith*, which formerly, by a Grant of King *John*, belonged to the *Breoses*, but afterwards to Hubert de Burgh, who (as we are informed by † Matthew Paris) *that he might calm a Court-tempest of Envy*, and be restor'd to favour, resign'd up these and two other Castles, to wit, *Blank* and *Hanfeld*, to King Hen the third

† Hist Min

In another corner North eastward, the river *Mynwy* and *Wy* meeting, do almost encompass the chief town of this County, which is thence denominated, for the Britains call it *Mynwy*, and we *Monmouth* On the North side, where it is not guarded with the rivers, it is fortify'd with a wall and a ditch In the midst of the town, near the market-place, stands the castle, which (as we find in the King's Records) flourish'd in the time of William the Conqueror, but is thought to have been rebuilt by John, Baron of Monmouth From him it came to the House of Lancaster, when King Henry the third had depriv'd him of his Inheritance, for espousing so violently the Barons Interest against him Or rather (as we read in the King's *Prerogative*) for that his Heirs had pass'd their Allegiance to the Earl of Britain in France Since that time, this town has flourish'd considerably, enjoying many privileges granted them by the house of Lancaster But for no one thing is it so eminent, as for the birth of King Henry the fifth, that triumphant Conqueror of France, and second ornament of the Lancastrian family, who, by direct force of Arms, subdu'd the Kingdom of France, and reduc'd their King, Charles the sixth, to that extremity, that he did little less than *resign* his Title Upon whose prosperous Success, *John Seward*, a Poet in those times, and none of the lowest rank, bespeaks the English Nation in this lofty stile

Monmouth

Ite per extremum Tanain, pigrosque Triones,
Ite per arentem Lybiam, superate calores
Solis, & arcanos Nili deprendite fontes
Herculeum finem, Bacchi transcurrite metas;
Angli juris erit quicquid complectitur orbis
Anglis rubra dabunt pretiosas æquora conchas
Indus ebur, ramos Panchaia, vellera Seres,
Dum viget Henricus, dum noster vivit Achilles
Est etenim laudes longe transgressus avitas

March on, brave Souls, to *Tanais* bend your arms,
And rouze the lazy North with just alarms
Beneath the torrid Zone your Armies spread,
Make trembling *Nile* disclose its secret head
Surprize the World's great Limits with your Haste,
Where not *Alcides* nor old *Bacchus* past.
Let daily triumphs raise your vast renown,
The World and all its Treasures are your own
Your's are the Pearls that grace the *Persian* Sea,
You rich *Panchæa*, *India*, and *Catav*,
With spicy, ivory barks, and silk supply,
While *Henry*, great *Achilles* of our land,
Blest with all joys, extends his wide command
Whose noble deeds and worthy fame surpass
The ancient glories of his heavenly race

Monmouth also glories in the birth of *Galfridus Arthurius*, Bishop of St *Asaph*, who compil'd the British History, an Author well skill'd in Antiquities, * but, as it seems, not of entire credit so many ridiculous Fables of his own invention hath he inserted in that work Insomuch that he is now rank'd amongst those writers that are *prohibited* by the Church of *Rome* [But altho' this, *Jeffrey of Monmouth* as (well as most other writers of the Monkish times) abounds with Fables, which is not deny'd by such as contend for some Authority to that History; yet that those Fables were of his own Invention, may seem too severe a censure, and scarce a just accusation since we find most or all of them in that British History he translated; of which an ancient copy may be seen in the Library of *Jesus-College* at Oxford, which concludes to this effect *Walter, Arch-deacon of Oxford, compos'd this book in Latin, out of British Records which he afterwards thus render'd into modern British* We find also many of the same Fables in *Ninnius*, who writ his *Eulogium Britanniæ* about three hundred years before this *Galfridus Arturius* compos'd the British history As to the regard due to that History in general, the judicious Reader may consult Doctor *Powel*'s Epistle *De Britannica Historia recte intelligenda*, and Dr *Davies*'s Preface to his British Lexicon, and ballance them with the arguments and authority of those who wholly reject it

Geofrey of Monmouth, or Ap-Arthur
* *Fide, (ut videtur) non antiqua*

Near *Monmouth* stands a noble House, built by *Henry* late Duke of *Beaufort*, call'd *Troy*, and heretofore the residence of his eldest Son *Charles*, Marquiss of Worcester, who was owner of it, and of the Castle and Manour of Monmouth, which were settled upon him, with other large possessions in this County, by the Duke his Father] Troy

The river *Wye* (wherein they take Salmon plentifully from September to April) is continued from hence Southward with many Windings and Turnings It is now the Limit between Gloucestershire and Monmouthshire; but was formerly the Boundary betwixt the Welsh and English, according to that verse of *Necham*

Inde vagos Vaga *Cambrenses, hinc respicit Anglos*
Hence *Wye* the *English* views, and thence the *Welsh*

Near

Near its fall into the *Severn Sea*, it passes Chepstow by *Chepstow*, which is a Saxon name, and signifies a *market* or *place of trading*. In British it is call'd [*Kasgwent* or] *Castelh Gwent*. It is a town of good note, built on a hill close by the river, and guarded with walls of a considerable circumference, which take in several Fields and Orchards. The castle is very fair, standing on the brink of the river: and on the opposite side there stood a Priory, whereof the better part being demolish'd, the remainder is converted into a Parish Church. The bridge here over the *Wye* is built upon piles, and is exceeding high, which was necessary, because the tide rises here to a great height. The Lords of this place were the *Clares* Earls of Pembroke; who from a neighbouring castle call'd *Strighul*, where they liv'd, were commonly call'd *Earls of* Strighul *and Pembroke*: Earls of Strighull of whom Richard the last Earl, a man of invincible courage and strength (sirnam'd *Strong bow* from his excellency in *Archery*,) was the first that made way for the English into Ireland. By his daughter it descended to the *Bigots*, &c. and now it belongs to the Earls of Worcester, [created since Dukes of Beaufort.] This place seems to be of no great antiquity, for several do affirm, and not without reason, that it had its rise not many ages past, from Venta the ancient city *Venta*, which flourish'd about four miles from hence in the time of Antoninus, who calls it *Venta Silurum*, as if it was their chief city. Which name neither arms nor time have been able to consume, for at this day it is call'd *Kaer went*, or Kaer went the city *Venta*. But the city it self is so much destroy'd by the one or the other, that it only appears to have once been, from the ruinous walls, the checquer'd pavements, and the Roman coins.

[In the year 1689 there were three checquer'd Pavements discover'd in a * Garden here, which being in frosty weather expos'd to the open air, upon the thaw the cement was dissolv'd, and this valuable antiquity utterly defac'd. So that at present there remains nothing for the entertainment of the Curious, but the small cubical stones whereof it was compos'd, which are of various sizes and colours, and may be found confusedly scatter'd in the earth, at the depth of half a yard. Checquer'd Pavements consist of oblong cubical stones, commonly about half an inch in length; whereof some are natural stones, wrought into that form, and others artificial, made like brick. These are of several colours; as white, black, blue, green, red, and yellow; and are close pitch'd together in a floor of fine plaster, and so dispos'd by the Artist, with respect to colour, as to exhibit any figures of men, beasts, birds, trees, &c. In one of these Pavements, as the owner relates, were delineated several flowers, which he compar'd to *Roses*, *Tulips*, and *Flowers de Luce*; and at each of the four corners, a Crown, and a Peacock holding a Snake in his Bill, and treading it under one foot. Another had the figure of a man in armour from the breast upward. There were also Imperial Heads, and some other variety of Figures, which, had they been preserv'd, might have been instructive, as well as diverting, to the Curious in the study of Antiquities. In their Gardens, and elsewhere in this village, they frequently meet with brass Coins: which have been diligently collected by an ingenious and worthy † Gentleman of that neighbourhood. In that Collection, there is an adulterated Coin of *Antoninus Pius*, which seems to have been counterfeited not of late, but anciently, when that Emperor's Coins were current money. It is a brass piece, of the bigness of a *denarius*, and cover'd with a very thin leaf of silver; which when rubb'd off, the letters disappear. Also *Julia Mæsa*, of embas'd metal, not unlike our tin farthings. Others were of *Valerianus*, *Gallienus*, *Probus*, *Dioclesianus*, *Constantius Chlorus*, *Constantinus Magnus*, *Julius Crispus*, *Constans*, and both *Valentinians*. Again, in the year 1693, one *Charles Kenton* shew'd me part of a Roman brick pavement in his yard: the bricks were somewhat above a foot long, nine inches broad, and an inch and a half thick, all mark'd thus

σ ⅂

* Fr. Ridley's

† George Kemeys of Than Vair, Esq;

The City took up about a mile in circumference on the south side, a considerable part of the wall is yet remaining, and more than the ruins of three Bastions. What repute it had heretofore, we may gather from hence, that before the name of Monmouth was heard of, this whole Country was call'd [from it] *Guent*, *Went-set* or *Wents-land*. Moreover (as we read in the life of *Tathaius* a British Saint) Lib. Landaff. it was formerly an Academy, or place dedicated to Literature, which the same *Tathaius* govern'd with great commendation, and also founded a Church there, in the reign of King *Kradok ap-Ynyr*, who invited him hither from an Hermitage.

[The foresaid English names of *Went-set* and Wentset &c. *Wents-land* have indeed their orginal from the British *Gwent*, by which almost all this Country, and part of Glocestershire and Herefordshire, were call'd, till Wales was divided into Counties. But it is made a question by some, whether that name *Gwent* be owing to the City *Venta*, or whether the Romans might not call this City, *Venta Silurum*, as well as that of the *Iceni*, and that other of the *Belgæ*, from the more ancient British names of part of their Countries. Had the Country been denominated since the Roman Conquest, from the chief City, it had been more properly call'd *Gwlâd Gaer Lheion*, than *Gwlâd Gwent*. But of this enough, if not too much.] Five miles to the west of *Kaer-went*, is seated *Strighul*-castle at the bottom of the hills, which now we call Strigle *Strugle*, but the Normans *Estrig-hill*; built (as we find in Domesday-book) by William *Fitz-Osbern* Earl of Hereford, and afterwards the seat of the *Clares*, Earls of Pembroke, whence they have been also commonly call'd *Earls of* Strighull. Beneath these places, upon the Severn Sea, not far from the mouth of the river Wy, lies *Port Skeweth*, call'd by Marianus *Port-* Port Skeweth *Skith*, who informs us, that Herald built a Fort there against the Welsh in the year 1066, which they immediately overthrew, under the conduct of *Karadok*. Near *Caldecot*, where the Caldecot river *Throgoy* enters the Severn Sea, I observ'd Inq. 3 E. 1. the wall of a castle, which formerly belong'd to the Constables of England, and was held by the service of the *Constableship* of England. Not far from hence are *Wondy* and *Pen how*, the Wondy and Pen how seats formerly of the illustrious family of St. St. Maur or Seimour *Maur*, now corruptly call'd *Seimour*. For we find that about the year 1240 (in order to wrest *Wondy* out of the hands of the Welsh) *G. Marescal* Earl of Pembroke was oblig'd to assist William of St. *Maur*. From whom was descended Roger of St. *Maur* Knight, who marry'd marry'd one of the coheirs of the illustrious *J. Beauchamp*, Baron of Hach, who was descended from Sibyl one of the coheirs of that most puissant *William Marshall* Earl of Pembroke, from *William Ferrars* Earl of Derby, *Hugh de Vivon*, and *William Mallet*, men of great Eminence in their times The Nobility of all which, as also of several others (as may be made very evident) center'd in the Right Honourable Edward de St *Maur* or *Seimour*, * Earl of Hereford, a singular encourager of virtue and learning, for which he is deservedly to be celebrated

* The present Earl, C

The Moor

The Fenny tract, extended below this for some miles, is call'd the *Moor*, which at my † present reviewing these notes, has suffer'd a most lamentable devastation For the Severn-Sea after a Spring tide, having before been driven back by a south-west wind (which continu'd for three days without intermission) and then again repuls'd by a very forcible Sea wind, rose to such a high and violent Tide, as to overflow all this lower tract, and also that of *Somersetshire* over against it, throwing down several Houses, and overwhelming a considerable number of cattle and men In the borders of this fenny tract, where the land rises, lies *Gold-cliff*, *so call'd* (saith Giraldus) *because when the Sun shines, the stones appear of a bright gold colour Nor can I be easily persuaded* (saith he) *that nature hath bestow'd this colour on the stones in vain, or that it would be found to rely a flower without fruit, should some skilful Artist search the veins and bowels of this rock* In this place there remain some ruins of an old Priory, founded by one of the family of *Chandois*

† Circ ann 1607 An Inundation 1607 Jan

Gold cliff

From hence we come through a Fenny Country to the mouth of the river *Isca*, call'd by the Britains *Wysk*, in English *Usk*, and by others *Osca* This river (as we have already observ'd) taking its course through the midst of the County, passes by three small cities of great antiquity The first, on the north west border of the County, call'd by Antoninus *Gobannium*, is situate at the confluence of the rivers *Wysk* and *Gevenni*, and thence denominated It is at this day (retaining its ancient appellation) call'd *Aber Gavenni*, and by contraction *Aber Gaenn*, which signifies the *Confluence of Gavenni* or *Gobannium* It is fortify'd with walls and a castle, which (as Giraldus observes) has been oftener stain'd with the infamy of treachery, than any other castle of Wales First, by *William* Son of Earl Miles, and afterwards by *William Breos*, both having upon publick assurance, and under pretence of friendship, invited thither some of the Welsh Nobility, and then basely murder'd them But they escaped not the just vengeance of God, for *Breos* having been depriv'd of all his effects (also, his wife and son starv'd with hunger) dy'd in exile The other having his brains dash'd out with a stone, while *Breulas castle* was on fire, receiv'd at length the due reward of his villany The first Lord of *Aber Gavenni*, that I know of, was one *Hamelin Balun*, who made *Brien Wallingford*, or *Brient de l'Isle* (call'd also *Fitz Count*) his Heir And he having built here an Hospital for his two sons, who were Lepers left the greatest part of his Inheritance to *Walter* the son of *Miles*, Earl of Hereford This *Walter* was succeeded by his brother *Henry*, whom the Welsh slew, when they invaded his Territories, which the King's Lieutenants defended, though not without great hazard and danger By the sister of Henry it descended to the *Breoses*, and from them, in right of marriage, by the *Cantelows* and *Hastings*, to Reginald Lord *Grey* of *Ruthin* But *William Beauchamp* obtain'd it of the Lord *Grey*, * by Conveyance and he again, in default of Issue-male, entail'd it on his brother *Thomas* Earl of Warwick, and on his heirs male *Richard* son of William Beauchamp, Lord of *Aber-Gavenni*, who, for his military valour, was created Earl of *Worcester*, and being slain in the wars of France, left one only daughter, who was marry'd to *Edward Nevil* From henceforth, the *Nevils* became eminent under the title of *Barons of Aber-Gavenni* But the castle was a long time detain'd from them, by reason of the conveyance before mention'd The fourth of these dying † in our memory, left one only daughter *Mary*, marry'd to Sir *Thomas Fane* Knight, between whom and Sir *Edward Nevil* the next heir male (to whom the castle and most of the estate had been left by Will, which was also confirm'd by authority of Parliament) there was a trial for the title of *Baron of Aber-Gavenni*, before the House of Lords, in the second year of King James [the first,] the Pleadings on both sides taking up seven days But in regard the question of right could not be fully adjusted, and that each of them seem'd to all (in respect of descent) very worthy of the title, and that moreover it was evident, that both the title of Baron of *Aber-Gavenni*, and that of *Le Despenser*, belong'd hereditarily to this family, the Peers requested of his Majesty, that both might be honour'd with the title of *Baron*, to which he agreed It was then propos'd to the Peers by the Lord Chancellor first, Whether the heir-male or female should enjoy the title of *Aber Gavenni*, upon which the majority of voices gave it for the heir male And when he had again propos'd, Whether the title of Baron *Le Despenser* should be confer'd on the female and her heirs, they unanimously agreed to it, to which his Majesty gave his Royal Assent And *Edward Nevil* was soon after summon'd to Parliament by the King's Writ, under the title of Baron of *Aber Gavenni* And being according to the usual ceremony introduc'd in his Parliament-Robes between two Barons, he was plac'd above the Baron *de Audely* At the same time also, the King's Letters Patents were read before the Peers, whereby his Majesty *restor'd, advanc'd, prefer'd*, &c Mary Fane, *to the state, degree, title, stile, name honour, and dignity of Baroness le Despenser, and that her heirs successively should be Barons le Despenser*, &c But the question of Precedency being propos'd, the Peers refer'd the decision thereof to the Commissioners for the office of Earl Marshal of England, who, upon mature deliberation, gave it under their hands and seals for the Barony of *le Despenser* This was read before the Peers, and by their order register'd in their Journal, out of which I have taken this account, in short [Edward was succeeded in the honour of Baron of *Aber Gavenny*, by his son and heir of the same name, to whom succeeded *Henry* his son, and likewise John, son of the said Henry, and George (brother and heir to the said John,) who was also succeeded by *George* his son Who dying without issue, the title of Lord Aber-Gavenny descended to *George* (son of *George Nevil* of Sheffeld in the County of Sussex, great grandson to Edward Lord Aber Gavenny,) who now enjoys it] What ought not to be here omitted, is, that *John Hastings* held this Castle *by homage, ward, and marriage When it happens* (as we read in the Inquisition) *and there shall chance to be war between the King* of

The river Usk

Gobannium

Aber Gavenni

Lords of Aber Gavenni

19 Rich 2

* *Virtute cujusdam Transcriptionis, & Conventione*

† So said ann 1607 Claus 19 & 21 Hen 6 &c

Baroness le Despenser

6 Edw 2

of England and Prince of Wales, he ought to defend the Country of Over *went at his own charge, to the utmoſt of his power, for the good of himſelf, the King, and Kingdom*

Burrium

The ſecond town, call'd by Antoninus *Burrium* (who places it twelve miles from *Gobannium*,) is ſeated where the river *Byrdhin* falls into *Uſk* It is call'd now in Britiſh, by a tranſpoſition of letters, *Brynbiga* for *Burenbegi*, and alſo *Kaer-wyſk*, by Giraldus *Caſtrum Oſkæ*, and in Engliſh *Uſk*

Uſk

At this day, it ſhews only the ruins of a large ſtrong Caſtle, pleaſantly ſeated between the river *Uſk*, and *Olwy* a ſmall brook, which takes its courſe from the eaſt, by *Ragland*, an elegant and caſtle like houſe of the Earl of Worceſter [now Duke of *Beaufort*,)] and paſſes under it

Iſca

The third City, call'd by Antoninus *Iſca* and *Legio ſecunda* (ſeated on the other ſide of the river Uſk, and diſtant, as he obſerves, exactly twelve Italian miles from *Burrium*) is call'd by the Britains *Kaer Lheion* and *Kaer Lheion ar wyſk* (which ſignifies *the city of the Legion on the river Uſk*) from the *Legio Secunda Auguſta*, which was call'd alſo *Britannica ſecunda*

Kaer Lheion ar Wyſk

This Legion, inſtituted by Auguſtus, and tranſlated out of Germany into Britain by Claudius under the conduct of Veſpaſian to whom, upon his aſpiring to the Empire, it proved very ſerviceable, and did alſo ſecure him the Britiſh Legions, was plac'd here at length by *Julius Frontinus* (as ſeems probable) in garriſon againſt the *Silures* How great a City this *Iſca* was at that time, our Giraldus informs us, in his Itinerary of Wales *A very ancient City this was* (ſaith he) *and enjoy'd honourable privileges, and was elegantly built by the Romans with* * *brick wall There are yet remaining many footſteps of its ancient ſplendour Stately Palaces, which formerly with their gilded Tiles emulated the Roman grandeur, for that it was firſt built by the Roman nobility, and adorn'd with ſumptuous edifices Alſo, an exceeding high tower, remarkable hot* † *Baths, ruins of ancient temples, theatrical places encompaſs'd with ſtately walls, which are, partly, yet ſtanding Subterraneous edifices are frequently met with, not only within the walls, but alſo in the ſuburbs, as, aqueducts, vaults, and (which is well worth our obſervation) Hypocauſts or ſtoves, contriv'd with admirable artifice, conveying heat inſenſibly through ſome very narrow vents on the ſides Two very eminent, and (next to St* Alban *and* Amphibalus) *the chief Protomartyrs of* Britannia major, *lye entombed here, where they were crown'd with martyrdom, viz* Julius *and* Aaron, *each of whom had a Church dedicated to him in this City For in ancient times there were three noble Churches here One of* Julius *the Martyr, grac'd with a Quire of Nuns, another dedicated to St* Aaron *his companion, ennobled with a famous order of Canons, and the third honour'd with the Metropolitan See of Wales* Amphibalus *alſo, teacher of St Alban, who ſincerely inſtructed him in the Faith, was born here This City is excellently ſeated on the navigable river Uſk and beautified with meadows and woods Here, the Roman Embaſſadors receiv'd their audience at the illuſtrious Court of the great King* Arthur *And here alſo Archbiſhop* Dubricius *reſign'd that honour to David of* Menevia, *by tranſlating the Archiepiſcopal See from this City thither*

* The circuit of the walls about three miles

† Ann 1654 Hot baths were diſcovered near St *Julians* the Bricks equilaterally ſquare about an inch thick, like thoſe at St Albans Mr *Aubrey*

Thus far Giraldus But in confirmation of the antiquity of this place, I have taken care to add ſome ancient Inſcriptions † lately dug-up there, and communicated to me by the right reverend Father in God *Francis Godwin*, Lord Biſhop of Landaff, a great Lover of Antiquity, and all other valuable parts of Learning In the year 1602, ſome labourers digging in a meadow adjoyning, found on a chequer'd pavement, a ſtatue of a perſon in a ſhort truſs'd habit, with a Quiver and Arrows, the head, hands, and feet broken off and alſo the fragment of an Altar with this Inſcription in fair large characters about three inches long erected by *Haterianus* Lieutenant General of Auguſtus, and Proprætor of the Province of *Cilicia*

† So ſaid, ann 1607

ISVS.C
ILIVS.Q.I
HATERIANVS
LEG.AVG.PR.PR.
PROVINC.CILIC.

These *Inſcriptions* are in the wall of the Garden at *Moinſcourt*, [formerly] the houſe of the Biſhop of *Landaff*

The next year, this Inſcription was alſo diſcover'd hard by, which ſhews the Statue before mentioned to have been of the Goddeſs Diana, and that *Titus Flavius Poſthumus Varus*, a Veteran perhaps of the fifth Cohort of the ſecond Legion, had repair'd her Temple

T FL POSTVMIVS VARUS
V C LEG TEMPL DIANÆ
RESTITVIT

Also this votive Altar, out of which the name of the Emperor * Geta seems to have been rased, when he was depos'd by his brother Antoninus Bassianus, and declar'd an enemy, yet so as there are some shadows of the Letters still remaining

* See Phil Trans numb. 145.

PRO SALVTE
AVGG N N
SEVERI ET ANTONI-
NI ET GETÆ CÆS
P SALTIENVS P F † MAE
CIA THALAMVS HADRI
PRÆF LEG II AVG
C VAMPEIANO ET
LVCILIAN

In printed Copies *Claudius Pompeianus*, and *Lollianus Avitus* Coss An Chr 210
† He was of this Family

And this fragment of a very fair Altar, the Inscription whereof may perhaps be thus supply'd

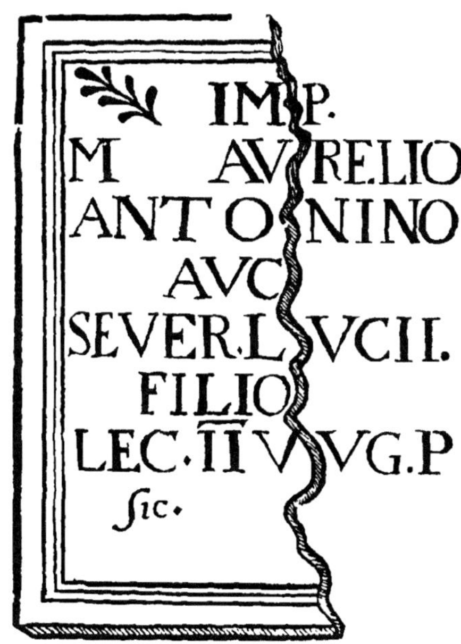

Together with these two fragments

* 7 VECILIANA

[which, not long since, was in the wall of the School at *Kaer Lheion*, but is now rased out]

* Centurio

VIII
7 VALER
MAXSIMI

[which is in the Garden wall at Moin's Court; but the first line [VIII] and the character [7] are not visible

Vid Reinef p. 977

In the year 1654 some workmen discover'd at St *Julian*'s near *Kaer Lheion*, a Roman Altar, the Inscription whereof was soon after copy'd by a learned and ingenious * person, a true lover and promoter of real knowledge, and of equal industry and curiosity The Altar, he says, was of Free-stone, four foot in length, and three in breadth; the Inscription he was pleas'd to communicate out of his excellent Collection of *British Monuments*, to be publish'd on this occasion

St. Julian's

* *J. Aubrey*

2

It

It seems worth the enquiry of the curious, upon what occasion *Jupiter*Jupiter Dolichenus. is here stil'd *Dolichenus*; for that I take to be the meaning of this word *Dolichv*. It seems probable, that this Altar was erected, to implore his Tuition of some Iron Mines, either in the Forest of Dean, or some other place of this Country. The grounds of which conjecture are taken from this Inscription in Reinesius;Rein. Syntagma Inscriptionum CL.I. n.XV. *Jovi optimo maximo Dolycheno, ubi ferrum nascitur, C. Sempronius Rectus, cent. Frumentarius* D.D. For unless Caius Sempronius, who dedicates this Altar *Jovi Dolicheno*, makes his request to *Jupiter* that he would either direct them to find out Iron Mines, or be propitious to some they had already discover'd, why should he add the words *ubi ferrum nascitur*? which were not only superfluous, but absurd, if they imply'd no more than barely that Iron-ore was found at *Doliche*, a Town of Macedonia, whence Jupiter was call'd *Dolichenus*. *Augustorum monitu* is a Phrase we find parallel instances of, in Reinesius, p.42. where he tells us, that the Pagans would be thought to do all things at the command of their Gods, *ex monitu Dei, imperio Deorum Dearumque, ex jussu Numinis*.

At *Tre-Dyno-Church*,Inscription at Tredonok. about three miles distant from *Kaer-leion*, is preserv'd this fair and entire Monument of a Roman Soldier of the Second Legion. The Stone is a kind of blue slate: the four oblique lines are so many Grooves or *Canaliculi*; and the small squares without the lines are holes bored through the stone; by which it was fasten'd with Iron-pins to the Ground-wall of the Church on the outside; and was discover'd by the Sexton about forty years since, at the digging of a Grave. Considering that this was the Monument of a Heathen, and must be about fourteen or fifteen hundred years standing; it seems strange it should be reposited in this place, and thus fasten'd to the Foundation of the Church; unless we suppose it laid there by some pious Christian in after-ages, out of a mistaken respect to the name *Julianus*, or rather that the Church was built on some old Roman burial-place. But however that happen'd, that it was there found is most certain, and testify'd by a worthy Gentleman of the neighbourhood, who was present at the discovery of it, and took care to preserve it.

Diis Manibus JVLius JVLIANVS MILes LEGionis IIdæ AVGustæ STIPendiorum octodecim, ANNORum quadraginta, HIC SITVS EST: CVRA AGENTE AMANDA

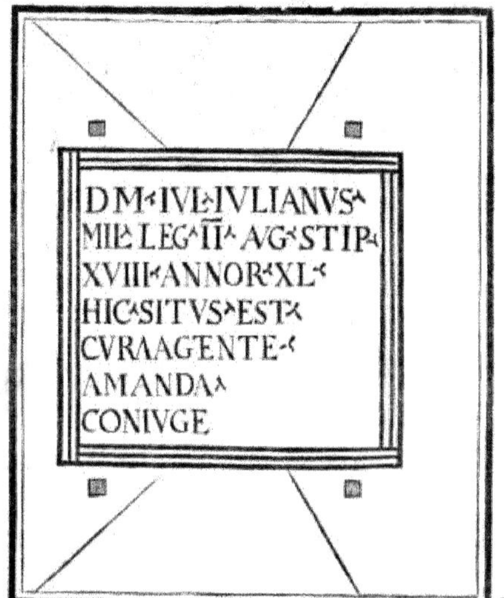
D M IVL IVLIANVS
MIL LEG II AVG STIP
XVIII ANNOR XL
HIC SITVS EST
CVRA AGENTE
AMANDA
CONIVGE

CONJVGE. Rein. Inscr. p.543.–
Cura agentibus, Semp. Pudente, Mil. frum. & Curio Eupla.
Ministro Spec.

Very lately also was discover'd, in plowing, near Kaer-Leion, on the bank of the river, a Stone with the following Inscription:

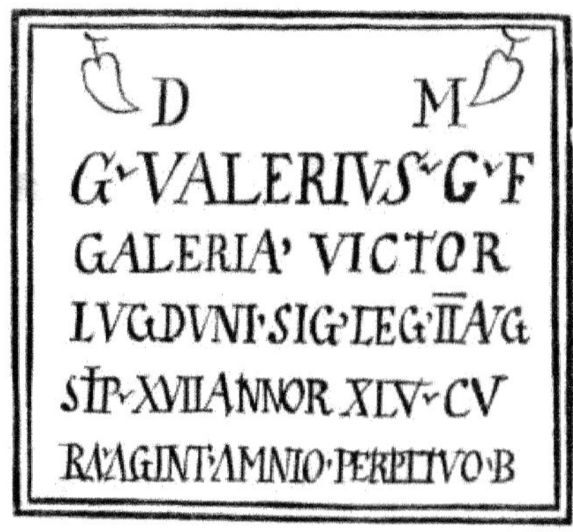
D M
G VALERIVS G F
GALERIA VICTOR
LVGDVNI SIG LEG II AVG
STIP XVII ANNOR XLV CV
RA AGINT AMNIO PERPETVO B

At the same *Kaer Leion,* they frequently dig-up Roman Bricks with this Inscription.

LEG. II. AVG.

The Letters on these Bricks are not *inscrib'd* (as on Stone) but *stamp'd* with some Instrument; there being a square cavity or impression in the midst of the Brick, at the bottom whereof the Letters are *rais'd*, and not *insculpt'd.* One of these Bricks may be seen (together

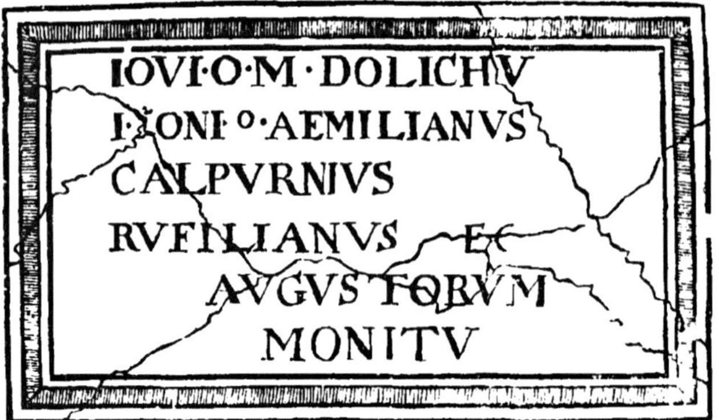

IOVI Optimo Maximo DOLIcHeno IunONI Optimae AEMILIANVS CALPVRNIVS RVFILIANVS [illegible] AVGVSTORVM MONITV

Jupiter Dolichenus.

It seems worth the enquiry of the curious, upon what occasion *Jupiter* is here stil'd *Dolichenus*, for that I take to be the meaning of this word *Dolich.* It seems probable, that this Altar was erected to implore his Protection of some Iron Mines, either in the Forest of Dean, or some other place of this County. The grounds of which conjecture are taken from this Inscription in Reinesius, *Jovi optimo maximo Dolycheno, ubi ferrum nascitur, C. Sempronius Rectus, cent. frumentarius* D. D. For

Reines. Syntag. Inscrip. Antiqu. Cl. I. n. XI.

that is Caius Sempronius, who dedicates this Altar *Jovi Dolicheno*, makes his request to *Jupiter* that he would either direct them to find out Iron Mines, or be propitious to some they had already discover'd, why should he add the words *ubi ferrum nascitur?* which were not only superfluous, but absurd, if they imply'd no more than barely that Iron-ore was found at *Doliche*, a Town of Macedonia whence Jupiter was call'd *Dolichenus*. *Augustorum monitu* is a Phrase we find parallel instances of in Reinesius, p. 4? where he tells us, that the Pagans would be thought to do all things at the command of their Gods, *ex monitu Dei*, *imperio Deorum Dearumque*, *ex jussu Numinis*.

At *Tr-Dino Church*, about three miles distant from *Kaer-leon*, is preserv'd this fair and entire Monument of a Roman Soldier of the Second Legion. The Stone is a kind of blue slate; the four oblique lines are so many Grooves or *Canaliculi*, and the small squares without the lines are holes bored through the stone, by which it was fasten'd with Iron pins to the Ground-wall of the Church on the outside, and was discover'd by the Sexton about forty years since, at the digging of a Grave. Considering that this was the Monument of a Heathen, and must be about fourteen or fifteen hundred years standing, it seems strange it should be reposited in that place, and thus fasten'd to the Foundation of the Church, unless we suppose it laid there by some pious Christian in after-ages, out of a mistaken respect to the name *[illegible]*, or rather that the Church was built on some old Roman burial place. B[illegible] however that happen'd, [illegible] it [illegible] most certain [illegible] testify'd [illegible] Gentl. [illegible] present at the discovery of it, and took care to pre[illegible]

Inscription at Tredonok.

It seems worth the enquiry of the curious, upon what occasion *Jupiter*Jupiter Dolichenus. is here stil'd *Dolichenus*; for that I take to be the meaning of this word *Dolichv*. It seems probable, that this Altar was erected, to implore his Tuition of some Iron Mines, either in the Forest of Dean, or some other place of this Country. The grounds of which conjecture are taken from this Inscription in Reinesius;Rein. Syntagma Inscriptionum CL.I. n.XV. *Jovi optimo maximo Dolycheno, ubi ferrum nascitur, C. Sempronius Rectus, cent. Frumentarius* D.D. For unless Caius Sempronius, who dedicates this Altar *Jovi Dolicheno*, makes his request to *Jupiter* that he would either direct them to find out Iron Mines, or be propitious to some they had already discover'd, why should he add the words *ubi ferrum nascitur*? which were not only superfluous, but absurd, if they imply'd no more than barely that Iron-ore was found at *Doliche*, a Town of Macedonia, whence Jupiter was call'd *Dolichenus*. *Augustorum monitu* is a Phrase we find parallel instances of, in Reinesius, p.42. where he tells us, that the Pagans would be thought to do all things at the command of their Gods, *ex monitu Dei, imperio Deorum Dearumque, ex jussu Numinis*.

At *Tre-Dyno-Church*,Inscription at Tredonok. about three miles distant from *Kaer-leion*, is preserv'd this fair and entire Monument of a Roman Soldier of the Second Legion. The Stone is a kind of blue slate: the four oblique lines are so many Grooves or *Canaliculi*; and the small squares without the lines are holes bored through the stone; by which it was fasten'd with Iron-pins to the Ground-wall of the Church on the outside; and was discover'd by the Sexton about forty years since, at the digging of a Grave. Considering that this was the Monument of a Heathen, and must be about fourteen or fifteen hundred years standing; it seems strange it should be reposited in this place, and thus fasten'd to the Foundation of the Church; unless we suppose it laid there by some pious Christian in after-ages, out of a mistaken respect to the name *Julianus*, or rather that the Church was built on some old Roman burial-place. But however that happen'd, that it was there found is most certain, and testify'd by a worthy Gentleman of the neighbourhood, who was present at the discovery of it, and took care to preserve it.

Diis Manibus JVLius JVLIANVS MILes LEGionis IIdæ AVGustæ STIPendiorum octodecim, ANNORum quadraginta, HIC SITVS EST: CVRA AGENTE AMANDA

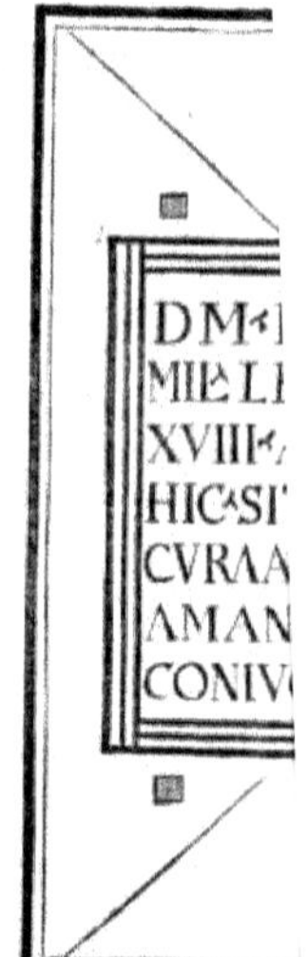

CONJVGE.
Cura agentibus, Semp. Pudent
Ministro Spec.

Very lately also was discover'
Stone with the following Inscri

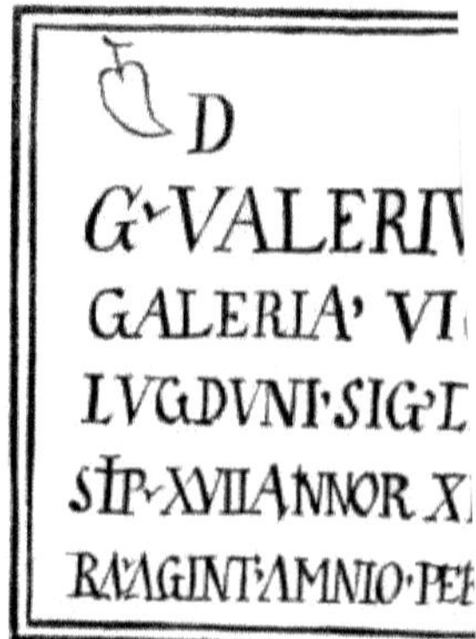

At the same *Kaer Leion*, they fre

LEG. II. AVG.

The Letters on these Bricks are n
Instrument; there being a square c
whereof the Letters are *rais'd*, an

Diis Manibus JVLius JVLIANVS MILes LEGionis IIdæ AVGuſtæ STIPendiorum octodecim, ANNORum quadraginta HIC SITVS EST CVRA AGENTE AMANDA CONJVGE

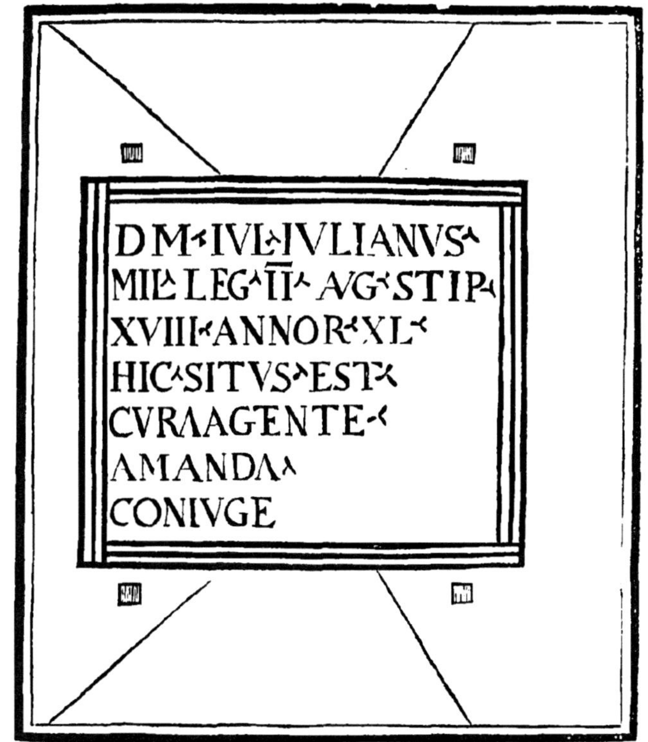
D M·IVL·IVLIANVS·
MIL·LEG·II·AVG·STIP·
XVIII·ANNOR·XL·
HIC·SITVS·EST·
CVRA AGENTE·
AMANDA·
CONIVGE

Rein Inſcr p. 543 ---- Cura agentibus, Semp Pudente Mil ſrum & Curio Lupli Miniſtro ſpec

¶ Very lately alſo was diſcovered, in ploughing, near Kaer-Leion, on the bank of the river, a Stone with the following Inſcription

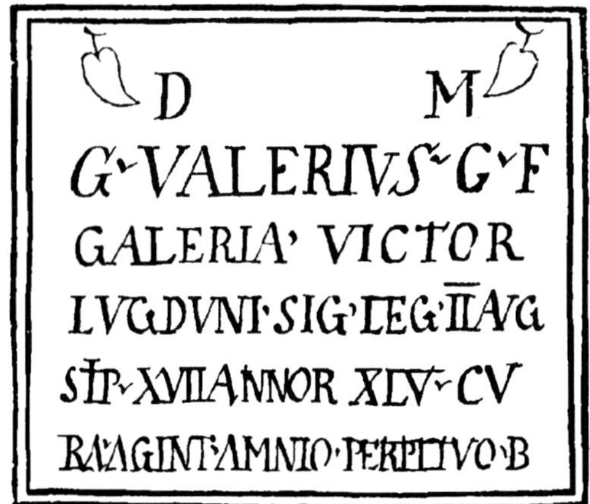
D M
G·VALERIVS·G·F
GALERIA·VICTOR
LVGDVNI·SIG·LEG·II·AVG
STIP·XVII·ANNOR XLV·CV
RA·AGINT·AMNIO·PERPETVO·B

At the ſame *Kaer Leion*, they frequently dig up Roman Bricks with this Inſcription

I I G II AVG

8

The Letters on theſe Bricks are not *inſcribed* (as on Stone) but *ſtamped* with ſome Inſtrument, there being a ſquare cavity or impreſſion in the midſt of the Brick, at the bottom whereof the Letters are *raiſed*, and not *inſculped* One

of

of these Bricks may be seen (together with the first of the foregoing Inscriptions) in the Garden-wall at *Moinscourt* (the seat of the worshipful *Thomas Lyster* Esq;) and some others at *Kaer Leion*.

In the year 1692 a chequered pavement was discovered in the grounds of *Henry Tomkins* of Kaer Leion, Esquire. It was found by workmen who were ploughing in a field close adjoining to his house. And here we may observe, that these ancient Pavements are not buried so deep in this County, as that in the Church-yard at *Woodchester* in Glocestershire. For whereas that lies at about three foot deep, this at *Kaer Leion* (as also some others formerly discovered,) lay no deeper than the plough-share; and that above mentioned at *Kaer-went*, not much lower. The said worthy person took all possible care, to preserve what the servants had not spoiled of this valuable Antiquity, by removing a considerable part of the floor in the same order it was found, into his garden; and was pleased to communicate a draught of the whole to be * published upon this occasion. The diameter of it is about fourteen foot. All the arches, and that part of the border they touch, were composed of white, red, and blue Stones, varied alternately. The bills, eyes, and feet of the birds were red, and they had also a red ring about the neck, and in their wings, one or two of the longest feathers red, and another blue. The inside of the cups were also red; and elsewhere, wherever we have not excepted it, the whole *area*, is variegated of umber or dark-coloured Stones and white.

* See it at the end of Wales.

About sixty years since, some Labourers digging in a Quarry betwixt *Kaer Leion* [illegible] and *Christ-church* (near a place called *Porth-sini-kran*) discovered a large Coffin of free-stone, which being opened, they found therein a leaden sheet, wrapped about an iron frame, curiously wrought; and in that frame a Skeleton. Near the Coffin they found also a gilded Alabaster Statue of a person in a coat of mail, holding in the right hand a short sword, and in the left a pair of scales. In the right scale appeared a young maiden's head and breasts; and in the left (which was out-weighed by the former) a globe. This account of the Coffin and Statue I received from the worshipful Captain *Matthias Bird*, who saw both himself; and, for the further satisfaction of the curious, was pleased to present the Statue to the Ashmolean Repository at Oxford. The feet and right arm have been broken some years since, as also the scales; but in all other respects, it is tolerably well preserved; and some of the gilding still remains in the *interstices* of the armour. We have given a figure of it, amongst some other Curiosities relating to Antiquity, at the end of these Counties of Wales; but must leave the explication to some more experienced and judicious Antiquary; for though at first view it might seem to be the Goddess *Astraea*, yet I cannot satisfy my self as to the device of the *Globe* and *Woman* in the scales; and am unwilling to trouble the Reader with too many conjectures.

Amongst other Roman Antiquities frequently dug-up here, we may take notice of the curious earthen Vessels, of which some are plain, and the same with those red *Patellae* or earthen Plates often discovered in several parts of England; but others are adorned with elegant figures, which, were they preserved, might be made use of for the illustration of Roman Authors, as well as their Coins, Statues, Altars, &c. That, of which I have given a figure, represents to us, first, an emblem of *Piety*, the celebrated History of the woman at Rome, who being denied the liberty of relieving her father in prison with any food, yet obtaining free access to him, fed him with the milk of her own breasts. I am sensible, that in * *Pliny*, and in most printed copies of such Authors as mention this History, we are informed she exercised this piety to her mother; but this figure (though it be somewhat obscure) seems to represent a bearded man: however, whether I mistake the figure, or whether we may read with *Festus*, *Patre* [illegible], or rather, do suppose the tradition to have been erroneous (in some Provinces at least) amongst the vulgar Romans; that the same History was hereby intended, is sufficiently evident. In the second place, we find an *Haruspex* or Soothsayer looking upwards to observe the motion of a bird, or rather perhaps a *Cupid* (according to the Potter's fancy) performing the office of a Soothsayer. And in the third, a woman sacrificing with *Vervain* and *Frankincense*: for I am satisfied, that the plant on the altar is no other than Vervain, and it seems very probable, that the Woman who reaches her hand towards the Altar, is casting Frankincense on the Vervain, since we find that Women, a little before their time of lying in, sacrificed to *Lucina* with Vervain and Frankincense. Thus the Harlot *Phronesium* in Plautus, pretending she was to lie in, bids her maids provide her *Sweet-meats*, *Oil of Cinnamon*, *Myrrhe*, and *Vervain*. (a)

* Hist. nat. l. 7. c. 36.

We may also collect out of Virgil (b), that Women sacrificed with *Vervain* and *Frankincense* upon other occasions.

(b) Eclog. 8.

Effer aquam, & molli cinge haec altaria vitta,
Verbenasque adole pingues, & mascula thura;
Conjugis ut magicis sanos avertere sacris
Experiar sensus ———

Bring running Water, bind those Altars round
With Fillets, and with Vervain strow the Ground,
Make fat with Frankincense the sacred Fires,
To reinflame my Daphnis with desires.

As for the naked person on the other side of the Altar, I shall not pretend to determine whether it be her husband, or who else is intended by it. In regard we find the other figures repeated alternately, I suppose there were no other delineations on the whole vessel, than what this piece, included within the crack (which is all I have of it) represents. By the figures on this vessel, we might conjecture that it was a bowl used in those Feasts which they called *Matronalia*, and observed on the Kalends of March, when the married women sacrificed

(a) *Date mihi huc stactam atque ignem in aram, ut venerem Lucinam meam.*
Hic apponite atque abscedite ab oculis,———
Eho, Astaphium, fer huc verbenam mihi, thus & strebulas. Plautus, Trucul. Act. II. Sc. 5.

to

to *Juno*, for their happy delivery in child-births, and for the preservation of their husbands, and the continuance of their mutual affections. And from its form, I should guess it was that sort of Vessel they call'd *Phiala*; because in Welsh the only name we have for such Vessels is *Phiol*, which is doubtless of the same origin with the Greek and Latin *Phiala*, and is very probably one of those many words left amongst us by the Romans, which we may presume to be still preserv'd in the sense they us'd them.

I shall only mention two other Curiosities found here, and detain the Reader no longer in this County: the first is, a *Ram's horn* of brass, much of the bigness and form of a lesser Ram's horn, broken off at the root, as if it had been formerly united to a brass head. One of these heads and horns (though somewhat different from ours) may be seen in * *Lodovico Moscardo's* Museum, who supposes such heads of Rams and Oxen to have serv'd at once both for ornaments in their Temples, and also for religious types of sacrifice.

* Pag. 8.

The other is a very elegant and an entire *Fibula vestiaria*, of which (because it would be difficult to give an intelligible description of it) † I have given two figures, one being not sufficient to express it. It is of brass, and is curiously chequer'd on the back part, with enamel of red and blue. It should seem that when they us'd it, the ring at the upper end was drawn down over the *acus* or pin, and that a thread or small string ty'd through the ring, and about the notches at bottom, secur'd the *acus* in its proper place. Such a *Fibula* in all respects, but that it is somewhat less, was found Anno 1691, near Kings-Cote in Glocestershire. They that would be farther satisfy'd of the various forms and matter of these Roman *Fibulæ*, and the several uses they were apply'd to, may consult, amongst other Authors, the learned and ingenious *Joannes Rhodius de Acia*, and *Smetius Antiquitates Neomagenses*.]

† See at the end of *Wales*.

Here also, at this *Kaer Lheion*, about the time of the Saxon Conquest, was *an Academy of two hundred Philosophers, who being skill'd in Astronomy and other Sciences, observ'd the courses of the Stars*, as we are inform'd by *Alexander Elsebiensis*, a very scarce Author, out of whom much has been transcrib'd for my use by the learned *Thomas James* of Oxford, who may deservedly be stil'd Φιλόβιβλος, as one who is wholly intent upon Books and Learning, and is † *at present* (God prosper his endeavours) out of desire of promoting the publick good, employ'd in searching the Libraries of England, on a design that is like to be of singular use to the Commonwealth of Learning.

Tho. James.
* Ann. 16—
† Ann. 160—

In the time of King Henry the second, when Giraldus wrote, the City seems to have been a place of considerable strength. For we find, that *Iruith* [(or rather, perhaps, *Iorwerth*)] of *Kaer Lheion*, a courageous Briton, defended it a long time against the English, till at last, being over-power'd by the King, he was dispossess'd of it. But (as a fair instance that Cities as well as Men have their chances and vicissitudes) that is become a small inconsiderable town, which once was of so great extent on each side the river, that they affirm St *Gilian's* (* the house of the honourable Sir *William Herbert*, a person no less eminent for wit and judgment, than noble extraction) to have been part of the city; and in that place the Church of *Julius* the Martyr is said to have stood, which is now about a mile out of the town.

* Ann. 160—

From the ruins also of this City, *Newport* had its beginning, which is seated a little lower, at the mouth of the river *Usk*. By Giraldus it is call'd *Novus Burgus*. It is a town of later date, but of considerable note for a Castle and a convenient harbour, where was formerly some Military way, mentioned by Necham in these verses:

Newport.

Intrat, & auget aquas Severni fluminis Osca
Præceps, testis erit Julia strata mihi.

Increas'd with *Usk* does *Severn* flow,
As *Julia Strata* testifies.

That this *Julia Strata* was a way, we have no reason to question; and if we may be free to conjecture, it seems not absurd to suppose it took its name from *Julius Frontinus* who conquer'd the *Silures*. *Not far from this Newburgh*, saith Giraldus, *there glides a small stream call'd* Nant Pencarn, *unpassable but at some certain fords, not so much for the depth of its water, as the hollowness of the chanel, and deepness of the mud. It had anciently a ford called* Rhyd Pencarn, *i.e. a ford under the head of the rock; which has been long since discontinu'd.* Henry the second King of England having by chance pass'd this ford, the Welsh (who rely too much upon old prophecies) were presently discourag'd, and reckon'd their Case desperate, because their Oracle *Merlin Sylvester* had foretold, that whenever a strong Prince with a freckled face (such King Henry was) should pass that ford, the British Forces should be vanquish'd.

During the Saxon Heptarchy, this County was subject to the Mountain Welsh, call'd by them Dunsetan, who, notwithstanding, were under the government of the West-Saxons, as appears by the ancient Laws. At the first coming in of the Normans, the Lords Marchers grievously plagu'd and annoy'd them; especially the above-mention'd *Hamelin Balun*, *Hugh Lacy*, *Walter* and *Gilbert de Clare* and *Brien* of *Wallingford*. To whom the Kings having granted all they could acquire in these parts, some of them reduc'd by degrees the upper part of this County, which they call'd *Over-Went*, and others the low lands, call'd *Nether-Went*.

Dunsetan.

[In the first year of King Charles the first, Robert Lord *Carey* was created Earl of *Monmouth*, and was succeeded by *Henry* of the same name; who dying without issue-male, James *Fitz-Roy*, among other honours, was created Duke of *Monmouth*, 15 Car. 2. And in the first year of King William and Queen Mary, Charles, son of John Earl of Peterborough, by Elizabeth, daughter of *Thomas Carey* second son to Robert Earl of *Monmouth*, was created Earl of *Monmouth*; who at present enjoys that title, together with his other of Earl of *Peterborough*.]

Earls and Duke of Monmouth.

Parish Churches in this County, 127.

GLAMORGANSHIRE.

Glamorgan, whence so called

HE farthest County of the *Silures* seems to be that which we call *Glamorganshire*, and the Britains *Morganwg Gwlâd Morgan*, and *Gwlâd Vorganwg*, which signifies the County of *Morganwg* It was so call'd (as most imagine) from *Morgan* a Prince, or (as others suppose) from an Abbey of that name But if I should deduce it from the British *Mor*, which signifies the *Sea*, I know not whether I should deviate from the Truth However, I have observ'd that Maritime Town of Armorica, which we now call *Morlais*, to have been call'd by Ptolemy and the ancient Gauls *Vorganium*, or *Morganium* (for the Consonants M and V are often counterchanged in this language) and whence shall we suppose it so denominated, but from the *Sea*? And this our *Morganwg* also is altogether Maritime, being a long narrow Country, wholly washed on the South-side by the Severn Sea As for the inner part of it, it is border'd on the East with *Monmouthshire*, on the North with *Brecknockshire*, and on the West with *Kaermardinshire*

On the North, it is very rugged with Mountains, which, as they come nearer the South, are by degrees more fit for Tillage, at the bottom whereof we have a spacious Vale or Plain open to the South Sun, a situation which *Cato* preferr'd to all others, and for which Pliny doth so much commend Italy For this part of the Country is exceeding pleasant, both in regard of the fertility of the Soil, and the Number of Towns and Villages

The Conquest of Glamorgan [illegible]

In the reign of William Rufus, *Jestin ap Gwrgant* Lord of this Country, having revolted from his natural Prince *Rhys ap Tewdwr*, and being too weak to maintain his Rebellion, did very unadvisedly, which he too late repented, call to his assistance (by the mediation of *Einon ap Kadivor* a Nobleman, who had married his daughter) *Robert Fitz Hamon* a Norman, son of *Hamon Dentatus* Earl of *Corboil* Who forth with levied an Army of choice Soldiers, and taking to his assistance twelve Knights as Adventurers in this Enterprize, first gave *Rhys* Battle, and slew him, and afterwards being allur'd with the fertility of the Country, which he had before conceiv'd sure hopes to be Lord of, turning his Forces against *Justin* himself, for that he had not kept his Articles with *Einon*, he soon deprived him of the Inheritance of his Ancestors, and divided the County amongst his Partners The barren Mountains he granted to *Einon*, but the fertile Plains he divided amongst the twelve Associates (whom he called *Peers*, and himself, on this condition,

Robert Fitz Hamon

12 Knights

that they should hold their Lands [illegible] in Vassalage [illegible], to assist each other [illegible], and [illegible] defend his [illegible] in his Castle of Cardiffe and attend him in his Court for the [illegible] Justice It may not perhaps be foreign to our purpose, if we add their names out of a Book written on this subject, either by Sir [illegible] Stradling, or Sir [illegible] Mansel (for it is ascribed to both of them) both being very well skill'd in Genealogy and Antiquities

Cardiffe

William of [illegible] or de Londres

R[illegible] Granv[illegible]

Pain Turbervil

Oliver St John

Robert de St Quintin

Roger Bekeroul

William Easterling (so called, for that he was descended from Germany) whose Posterity were call'd *Stradlings*

Gilbert Humfranvil

Richard Siward

John Flemming

Peter Score

Reginald Sully

The river *Rhymny*, coming down from the Mountains, makes the Eastern limit of this County, whereby it is divided from Monmouthshire, and in the British, * *Remny* signifies to divide In a Moorish bottom, not far from this river, where it runs through places scarce passable, among the hills, are seen the ruinous Walls of *Caer-phili* castle, which has been of that vast magnitude, and such an admirable structure, that most affirm it to have been a Roman Garrison, nor shall I deny it, though I cannot yet discover by what name they called it However, it should seem to have been re-edified, in regard it has a Chapel built after the Christian manner, as I was informed by the learned and judicious Mr *J Sanford*, who took an accurate survey of it It was once the possession of the *Clares* Earls of Glocester, but we find no mention of it in our Annals, till the reign of Edward the second For at that time, the *Spensers* having by under-hand practices set the King and Queen and the Barons at variance, we read that *Hugolin Spenser* was a long time besieged in this Castle, but without success [It is probably the noblest ruin of ancient Architecture now remaining in Britain For in the judgment of some curious persons, who have seen and compared it with the most noted Castles of *England*, it exceeds all in bigness, except that of Windsor That place which Mr *Sanford* call'd a Chapel, was probably the same with that which the neighbouring Inhabitants call the Hall It is a stately room about seventy foot in length, thirty four in breadth, and seventeen in height On the South side we ascend to it by a direct Stair case, about eight foot wide, the roof whereof is vaulted and supported with twenty arches, which are still gradually higher as you ascend The entry out of the Stair case, is not into the middle, but somewhat nearer to the West end of the room, and opposite to it on the North side, there is a Chimney about ten foot wide On the same side there are four stately windows (if so we may suppose them) two on each side the chimney, of the fashion of Church windows, but that they are continued down to the very floor, and reach up higher, than the height of this room is supposed to have been, so that the room above this Chapel, or Hall, had some part of the benefit of them The sides of these windows are adorned with certain three leav'd knobs or husks, having a fruit or small round ball in the midst On the walls, on each side the room, are seven triangular pillars, like the shafts of Candlesticks, placed at equal distance From the floor to the bottom of these pillars, may

* Rhamni

Caerphily castle

be

Taking it for granted that this place was of Roman foundation, I should be apt to conjecture (but that BVLLÆVM hath been hitherto placed in another County) that what we now call *Kaer-phyli*, was the *Bullæum Silurum* of the Romans. And if there was no other ground to place it at *Bualht* in Brecknockshire, but the affinity of the names, and the situation in the Country of the Silures; we also may urge, that the name of *Caer-phyli* comes as near *Castrum Bullæi*, as *Bualht*. For they who understand the British tongue, will readily allow, that *Bullæum* could not well be otherwise expressed in that language, than *Kaer Vwl, Kaer Vul* (which must be pronounced *Kaer-Vyl*) or, like some other names of places, from the genitive case, *Kaer-Vyli*. That this place was also in the Country of the *Silures*, is not controverted: and farther, that it has been a Roman garrison, is so likely, from the stately ruins still remaining, that most persons of Curiosity who have seen it, take it for granted. Whereas I cannot learn that any thing was ever discover'd at *Bualht*, that might argue it to have been inhabited by the Romans; much less a place of note in their time, as *Bullæum Silurum* must needs have been.

On a Mountain call'd *Kevn Gelhi Gaer*,Kevn Gelhi Gaer. not far from this *Kaer-Phyli*, in the way to *March-nad y wayn*; I observ'd (as it seem'd to me) a remarkable Monument, which may perhaps deserve the notice of the curious. It is well known by the name of *Y maen hîr*,Y maen hîr *near* Gelhi Gaer. and is a rude stone pillar of a kind of quadrangular form, about eight foot high; with this Inscription to be read downwards.

It stands not erect, but somewhat inclining; whether casually, or that it was so intended, is uncertain. Close at the bottom of it, on that side it inclines on, there is a small bank or intrenchment, inclosing a space of about six yards; and in the midst thereof a square *Area*, both which may be better delineated than describ'd.

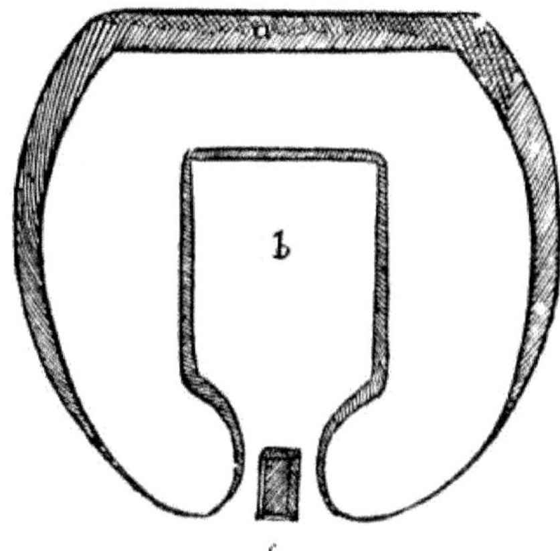

The Bank.*b* The Bed or *Area* in the midst of it.
c The place where the Stone is erected.

I suppose, that in the bed or Area in the midst, a person has been inter'd; and that the Inscription must be read *Tefroiti* or *Deffroiti*; which is doubtless the same with the British proper name *Dyvrod*, expressed otherwise in Latin *Dubrotus* and perhaps *Dubritius*.] Upon the river *Rhymny* also (tho' the place is uncertain) *Ninnius* informs us, that *Faustus* a pious godly son of *Vortigern* a most wicked father, erected a stately Edifice. Where, with other devout men, he daily pray'd to God, that he would not punish him for the sins of his father, who, committing most abominable Incest, had begotten him on his own daughter; and that his father might at last seriously repent, and the Country be freed from the Saxon War.

A little lower, Ptolemy places the mouth of *Rhatostabius*, or *Rhatostibius*,The mouth of Rhatostabius. a maim'd word for the British *Traeth Tâv*, which signifies *the sandy Frith of the river Taf*. For there the river *Taf* coming down from the Mountains, falls into the Sea at *Lan-daf*,Landaffe. that is, *the Church on the river Taf*, a small place seated in a bottom, but dignified with a Bishop's See (in the Diocese whereof are one hundred fifty four Parishes) and adorn'd with a Cathedral, consecrated to St. *Teiliau*, Bishop thereof. Hist. Landavensis. This Church was then erected by the two Gallick Bishops *Germanus* and *Lupus*, when they had suppres'd the Pelagian Heresie which prevail'd so much in Britain: and *Dubricius*, a most devout man, was by them first prefer'd to the Bishoprick, to whom *Meurick* a British Prince granted all the Lands between the rivers *Taf* and *Eli*. From hence *Taf* continues its course to *Caerdiffe*,Caerdiffe. in British *Kaer Dŷdh* ** Corruptly, I suppose, for *Caer Dyv*., a neat Town considering the Country, and a commodious Haven; fortified with Walls and a Castle by the Conqueror *Fitz-Haimon*, who made it both the Seat of War, and a Court of Justice. Where, besides a standing Army of choice Soldiers, the twelve Knights or Peers were oblig'd, each of them, to defend their several stations. Notwithstanding which, a few years after, one *Ivor Bâch*, a Britain who dwelt in the Mountains, a man of small stature, but of resolute courage, march'd hither with a band of Soldiers privately by night, and seiz'd the Castle, carrying away *William* Earl of *Glocester*, Fitz-Haimon's grandson by a daughter, together with his wife and son, whom he detain'd prisoners till he had receiv'd satisfaction for all injuries. But how *Robert Curthose*,Robert Curthose Duke of Normandy. eldest son of William the Conqueror (a man in Martial Prowess but too adventurous and foolhardy) was deprived by his younger brothers of all hopes of succession to the Crown, and, being bereft of

be about twelve foot and a half, and their height or length seemed above four foot Each of these pillars is supported with three Busts, or heads and breasts, which vary alternately For whereas the first (for instance) is supported with the head and breast of an ancient bearded man and two young faces on each side, all with dishevelled hair, the next shews the face and breasts of a woman with two lesser faces also on each side, the middlemost or biggest having a cloth tied under the chin and about the forehead, the lesser two having also forehead-cloths, but none under the chin, all with braided locks The use of these pillars seems to have been, for supporting the beams, but there are also on the south side six Grooves or chanels in the wall at equal distance, which are about nine inches wide, and eight or nine foot high four whereof are continued from the tops of the pillars, but the two middlemost are about the middle space between the pillars, and come down lower than the rest, having neat stones jutting out at the bottom, as if intended to support something placed in the hollow Grooves On the north-side, near the east end, there is a door about eight foot high, which leads into a spacious Green about seventy yards long and forty broad At the east end there are two low-arched doors, within a yard of each other, and there was a third near the south side, but much larger, and another opposite to that on the west end The reason why I have been thus particular, is, that such as have been curious in observing ancient buildings, might the better discern whether this room was once a Chapel or Hall, &c and also in some measure judge of the Antiquity of the place, which, as far as I could hitherto be informed, is beyond the reach of history

That this Castle was originally built by the Romans, seems, indeed highly probable, when we consider its largeness and magnificence Though at the same time we must acknowledge, that we have no other reason to conclude it Roman, but the stateliness of its structure For whereas most or all Roman Cities and Forts of note, afford (in the revolution at least of fifty or sixty years) either Roman Inscriptions, Statues, Bricks Coins, Arms, or other Utensils, I could not find, upon diligent enquiry, that any of these Monuments were ever discovered here I have indeed two Coins found at this Castle, one of silver, which I received, amongst many greater favours from the right worshipful Sir John [illegible] of [illegible] Trydhyd, Baronet, and the other of brass, which I purchased at Kaer-phyli of the person that found it in the Castle Neither of these are either Roman, Saxon, Danish, or Norman That of silver is as broad as a Sixpence, but thinner, and exhibits on one side the image of our Saviour with this Inscription, GLORIA× TIBI R... and on the Reverse, two Persons with these Letters, MVGNETI R..... ON ¦ X This being compared with an account of a fairer Coin in the celebrated Collection of Mr Thoresby of Leeds, appears to have been a Venetian piece In this Coin, before the M, on the reverse, is S for *Sanctus Marcus*, whose figure is there, with a glory about the head, then follows the particular Doge's name with DVX, besides the Banner, which is jointly supported by both Upon the Reverse of some, we GLORIA, and upon others, LAVS TIBI SOLI The brass Coin is like the French pieces of the middle age, and shews on the obverse, a Prince crowned, in a standing posture, holding a Scepter in his right hand, with this Inscription ×ΛVΓΦ× XRSΩI [illegible] *Maria*, &c and on the Reverse a Cross *flore* with these Letters, + + + + Λ + + V+ + Θ + *Ave*

Taking it for granted that this place was of Roman foundation, I should be apt to conjecture (but that BVLLÆVM hath been hitherto placed in another Country) that what we now call *Kaer-phyli*, was the *Bullæum Silurum* of the Romans And if there was no other ground to place it at *Bualht* in Brecknockshire, but the affinity of the names, and the situation in the Country of the Silures, we also may urge, that the name of *Caer-phyli* comes as near *Castrum Bullæi*, as *Bualht* For they who understand the British tongue, will readily allow, that *Bullæum* could not well be otherwise expressed in that language, than *Kaer Vwl*, *Kaer Ful* (which must be pronounced *Kaer Vyl*) or, like some other names of places, from the genitive case, *Kaer-Vyli* That this place was also in the Country of the *Silures*, is not controverted and farther, that it has been a Roman garrison, is so likely, from the stately ruins still remaining, that most persons of Curiosity who have seen it, take it for granted Whereas I cannot learn that any thing was ever discovered at *Bualht*, that might argue it to have been inhabited by the Romans, much less a place of note in their time, as *Bullæum Silurum* must needs have been

On a Mountain called *Kevn Gelli Gaer*, not far from this *Kaer-Phyli*, in the way to *Marchnad y Wayn*, I observed (as it seemed to me) a remarkable Monument, which may perhaps deserve the notice of the curious It is well known by the name of *Y maen hir*, and is a rude stone pillar of a kind of quadrangular form, about eight foot high, with this Inscription to be read downwards Kevn Gelli Gaer

Y maen hir, [illegible] Gelli [illegible]

[illegible]

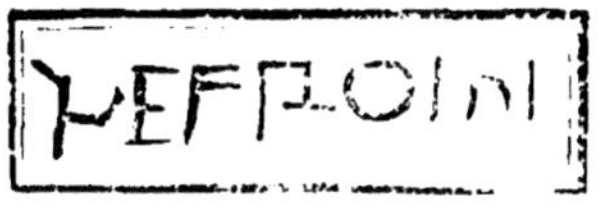

It stands not erect, but somewhat inclining whether casually or that it was so intended is uncertain Close at the bottom of it, on that side it inclines on, there is a small [illegible] or intrenchment including a [illegible] about six yards, and in the middle thereof a [illegible], both which may be better conceived than described

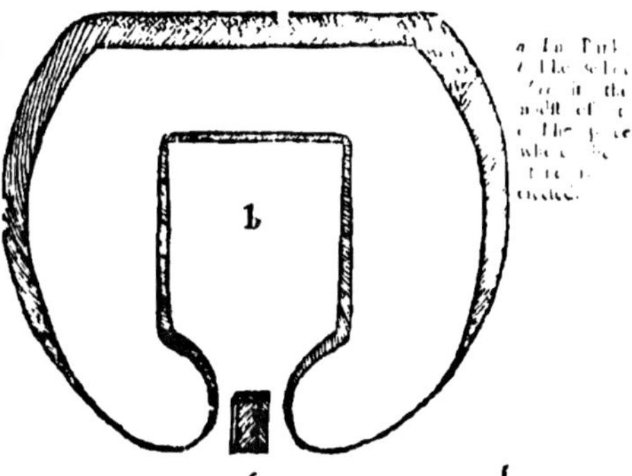

I suppose, that in the bed or Area in the midst, a person has been interred, and that the Inscription must be read *Tefroti* or *Deffroti*, which is doubtless the same with the British proper name *Dyfrod*, expressed otherwise in Latin *Dubrotus* and perhaps *Dubritius*.]

Upon the river *Rhymny* also (tho' the place is uncertain) *Ninnius* informs us, that *Faustus* a pious godly son of *Vortigern* a most wicked father, erected a stately Edifice. Where, with other devout men, he daily prayed to God that he would not punish him for the sins of his father, who, committing most abominable Incest, had begot on him on his own daughter, and that his father might at last seriously repent, and the Country be freed from the Saxon war.

The mouth of Rhatostatius

A little lower, Ptolemy places the mouth of *Rhatostabius*, or *Rhatostibius*, a maimed word for the British *Traeth Taf*, which signifies *the sandy Frith of the river Taf*. For there the river *Taf* coming down from the Mountains, falls into the Sea at *Landaf*, that is, *the Church on the river Taf*, a small place seated in a bottom, but dignified with a Bishop's See (in the Diocese whereof are one hundred fifty four Parishes) and adorned with a Cathedral, consecrated to St *Teliau*, Bishop thereof.

Landaffe

Hist. Landavensis

This Church was then erected by the two Gallick Bishops *Germanus* and *Lupus*, when they had suppressed the Pelagian Heresy which prevailed so much in Britain; and *Dubricius*, a most devout man, was by them first preferred to the Bishoprick, to whom *Meurick* a British Prince granted all the Lands between the rivers *Taf* and *Elei*. From hence *Taf* continues its course to *Caerdiffe*, in British *Kaer Dydo* *, a neat Town considering the Country, and a commodious Haven, fortified with Walls and a Castle by the Conqueror *Fitz-Hamon*, who made it both the Seat of War, and a Court of Justice. Where, besides a standing Army of choice Soldiers, the twelve Knights or Peers were obliged, each of them, to defend their several stations. Notwithstanding which, a few years after, one *Ivor Bach*, a Britain who dwelt in the Mountains, a man of small stature, but of resolute courage, marched hither with a band of Soldiers privately by night, and seized the Castle, carrying away *William* Earl of *Glocester*, Fitz-Hamon's grandson by a daughter, together with his wife and son, whom he detained prisoners till he had received satisfaction for all injuries. But how *Robert Curthose*, eldest son of William the Conqueror (a man in Martial Prowess but too adventurous and fool-hardy) was deprived by his younger brothers of all hope of succession to the Crown, and, being bereft of both his eyes, lived in this Castle till he became an old man, may be seen in our English Historians. Whereby we may also learn, That to be born of the Blood-royal, doth not ensure to us either Liberty or Safety.

Caerdiffe.
* Corruptly, I suppose, for Caer Dydd.

Robert Curthose Duke of Normandy

Scarce three miles from the mouth of the river *Taf*, in the very winding of the shore, there are two small, but very pleasant Islands, divided from each other, and also from the main land, by a narrow frith. The hither-most is called *Sully*, from a Town opposite to it, to which *Robert de Sully* (whether there it was in the Division) is thought to have given name, though we may as well suppose he took his name from it. The farther is called *Barry*, from St *Baruch* who lies buried there, and as he gave name to the place, so the place afterwards gave name to a Family. For that noble family of Viscount *Barry* in Ireland, had its name and original from thence. *In a maritim Rock of this Island*, saith Giraldus, *there is a narrow chink or cleft, to which if you put your ear, you shall perceive such a noise as if Smiths were at work there. For sometimes you hear the blowing of the bellows, at other times the strokes of the hammers, also the grinding of tools, the hissing noise of steel gads, and fire burning in furnaces, &c. These sounds, I should suppose, might be occasioned by the repercussion of the Sea waters into these chinks, but that they are continued at low ebb when there is no water at all, as well as at the full tide.* Nor was that place, which *Clemens Alexandrinus* mentions in the seventh Book of his *Stromata*, unlike to this. *Historians inform us, that in the Isle of Britain there is a certain Cave at the root of a Mountain, and at the top of it a Cleft. Now when the wind blows into the Cave, and is reverberated therein, they hear at the chink the sound of several Cymbals; for the wind being driven back, makes much the greater noise.*

Sully. [illegible]

A remarkable Cave

[But as to the subterraneous noises abovementioned, whatsoever might be heard in this Island in *Giraldus*'s time, it is certain (notwithstanding many later writers have upon his authority taken it for granted) that at present there are no such sounds perceived here. A learned and ingenious Gentleman of this County, upon this occasion writes thus: *I was myself once upon the Island, in company with some inquisitive persons, and we sought over it where such noise might be heard. Upon failure, we consulted the neighbours, and I have since asked elderly and knowing men who lived near the Island, who all owned the tradition, but never knew it made out in fact. Either then the old Avagium is vanished, or the place is mistaken.*

The subterraneous noise at Barry Island contradicted

I shall offer upon this occasion what I think may divert you. You know there is in this channel, a noted point of land, between the Nash-*point in this County, and that of* St Govens *in Pembrokshire, called in the Maps and Charts* Wormshead-point, *for that it appears to the Seamen like a worm creeping, with its head erect. From the main land, it stretches a mile or better into the sea, and at half flood, the Isthmus which joins it to the shore is overflown, so that it becomes then a small Island. Toward the head of it, or that part which is farthest out in the sea, there is a small cleft or crevice in the ground, into which if you throw a handful of dust or sand, it will be blown up back again into the air. But if you kneel or lie down and lay your ears to it, you then hear distinctly the deep noise of a prodigious large bellows. The reason is obvious; for the reciprocal motion of the Sea, under the arched and rocky hollow of this Headland, or Promontory, makes an inspiration and expiration of the Air, through the cleft, and that alternately, and consequently the noise, as of a pair of bellows in motion. I have been twice there to observe it, and both times in the Summer season, and in very calm weather. But I do believe a stormy sea would give not only the forementioned sound, but all the variety of the other noises ascribed to* Barry, *especially if we allow a little advantage and fancy, as they that make such comparisons generally do. The same, I doubt not, happens in other places upon the sea shore, wherever a deep water, and a rocky concave, with proper clefts for conveyance, occur; and in* Sicily *especially, where are* [illegible] sulphur *for the Bellows to work upon,* [illegible] *in those* Vulcano's *to carry off the smoak. But now that this* Wormshead *should be the intended Isle of* Barry, *may seem very unlikely. Here I consider, that* Burry *is the most remarkable river (next that of* Swansy) *for trade, in all* Gower; *and its* Ostium *is close by* Wormshead, *so that who ever*

both his eyes, lived in this Castle till he became an old man; may be seen in our English Historians. Whereby we may also learn, That to be born of the Blood-royal, does not ensure to us either Liberty or Safety.

Scarce three miles from the mouth of the river *Taf*, in the very winding of the shore, there are two small, but very pleasant Islands, divided from each other, and also from the main Land, by a narrow Frith. The hithermost is call'd *Sully,Sully* so call'd perhaps from the *Silures*. from a Town opposite to it; to which *Robert de Sully* (whose share it was in the Division) is thought to have given name; though we may as well suppose he took his name from it. The farthest is call'd *Barry*, from St. *Baruch* who lies buried there; and as he gave name to the place, so the place afterwards gave sirname to its Proprietors. For that noble family of Viscount *Barry* in Ireland, had its name and original from thence. A remarkable Cave. *In a maritim Rock of this Island*, saith Giraldus, *there is a narrow chink or cleft, to which if you put your ear, you shall perceive such a noise as if Smiths were at work there. For sometimes you hear the blowing of the bellows, at other times the strokes of the hammers; also the grinding of tools, the hissing noise of steel-gads, and fire burning in furnaces*, &c. *These sounds, I should suppose, might be occasion'd by the repercussion of the Sea-waters into these chinks, but that they are continu'd at low ebb when there is no water at all, as well as at the full tide*. Nor was that place, which *Clemens Alexandrinus* mentions in the seventh Book of his *Stromata*, unlike to this. *Historians inform us, that in the Isle of Britain there is a certain Cave at the root of a Mountain, and at the top of it a Cleft. Now when the wind blows into the Cave, and is reverberated therein, they hear at the chink the sound of several Cymbals; for the wind being driven back, makes much the greater noise*.

The subterraneous noise at *Barry-Island* contradicted. [But as to the subterraneous noises above-mention'd, whatsoever might be heard in this Island in *Giraldus*'s time; it is certain (not-withstanding many later writers have upon this authority taken it for granted) that at present there are no such sounds perceived here. A learned and ingenious Gentleman of this Country, upon this occasion writes thus: *I was my self once upon the Island, in company with some inquisitive persons; and we sought over it where such noise might be heard. Upon failure, we consulted the neighbours, and I have since ask'd literate and knowing men who liv'd near the Island; who all own'd the tradition, but never knew it made out in fact. Either then that old* Ἀχέμφον *is vanish'd, or the place is mistaken.*

I shall offer upon this occasion what I think may divert you. You know there is in this chanel, a noted point of land, between the Nash-point *in this County, and that of St.* Govens *in Pembrokeshire; call'd in the Maps and Charts* Wormshead-point, *for that it appears to the Sailers like a worm creeping, with its head erect. From the main land, it stretches a mile or better into the sea; and at half-flood, the Isthmus which joyns it to the shore is overflown; so that it becomes then a small Island. Toward the head it self, or that part which is farthest out in the Sea, there is a small cleft or crevise in the ground, into which if you throw a handful of dust or sand, it will be blown up back again into the air. But if you kneel or lie down, and lay your ears to it, you then hear distinctly the deep noise of a prodigious large bellows. The reason is obvious: for the reciprocal motion of the Sea, under the arch'd and rocky hollow of this Headland, or Promontory, makes an inspiration and expiration of the Air, through the cleft, and that alternately; and consequently the noise, as of a pair of bellows in motion. I have been twice there to observe it, and both times in the Summer-season, and in very calm weather. But I do believe a stormy sea would give not only the forementioned sound, but all the variety of the other noises ascrib'd to* Barry; *especially if we a little indulge our fancy, as they that make such comparisons generally do. The same, I doubt not, happens in other places upon the sea-shore, wherever a deep water, and rocky concave, with proper clefts for conveyance, do concur: in* Sicily *especially, where are moreover* fire *and* sulphur *for the Bellows to work upon; and chimneys in those* Vulcano*'s to carry off the smoak. But now that this* Wormshead *should be the intended Isle of* Barry, *may seem very uncouth. Here I consider, that* Burry *is the most remarkable river (next that of* Swansy) *for trade, in all* Gower; *and its* Ostium *is close by* Wormshead, *so that whoever sails to the North-east of* Wormshead, *is said to sail for the river of* Burry.

sails to the North-east of Wormshead *is said to sail for the river of* Burry Wormshead *again is but a late name, but that of* Burry *immemorial Now he that had a mind to be critical, might infer, either that* Wormshead *was of old call'd the Island of* Burry, *or, at least, That before the name of* Wormshead *was in being, the report concerning these noises might run thus, that near* Burry, *or as you sail into* Burry, *there is an Island, where there is a cleft in the ground, to which if you lay your ear, you'll hear such and such noises And* Barry, *for* Burry, *is a very easy mistake*, &c]

Beyond these Islands the shore is continued directly westward, receiving only one river, upon which (a little more within the land) lies *Cowbridge*, call'd by the Britains, from the Stone-bridge, *y Bont vaen* It is a Market town, and the second of those three which the Conqueror *Fitz-Hamon* reserv'd for himself In regard Antoninus places the City *Bovium* (which is also corruptly call'd *Bomium*) in this tract, and at this distance from *Isca*, I flatter'd my self once with an Imagination that this must be *Bovium* But seeing that at three miles distance from this Town we find *Boverton*, which agrees exactly with *Bovium*, I could not, without injury to truth, seek for *Bovium* else where Nor is it a new thing, that places should receive their names from *Oxen*, as we find by the Thracian *Bosphorus*, the *Bovianum* of the *Samnites*, and *Bauli* in Italy, so called *quasi Boalia*, if we may credit *Symmachus* But let this one argument serve for all Fifteen miles from *Bovium*, Antoninus, using also a Latin name, hath placed *Nidum*, which our Antiquaries have a long time search'd for in vain, and yet at the same distance we find *Neath* [in British *Nedh*] a Town of considerable note, retaining still its ancient name almost entire Moreover, we may observe here, at *Lantwit* or St *Iltut's*, a village adjoining the foundations of many buildings, and formerly it had several streets [In the Church-yard at *Lantwit major*, or *Lhan Iltud vawr*, on the North-side of the Church, there are two stones erected, which seem to deserve our notice The first is close by the Church wall, and is of a pyramidal form, about seven foot in height It is adorn'd with old British carving, such as may be seen on the pillars of crosses, in several parts of Wales It is at three several places, and those at equal distance, encompass'd with three circles From the lowest three circles to the ground, it is in grail'd or indented; but elsewhere adorn'd with knots The circumference of it at the three highest circles, is three foot and a half, at the middlemost, above four foot, and the lowest is about five It has on one side, from the top (which seems to have been broken) to the bottom, a notable furrow or *Canaliculus* about four inches broad, and two in depth Which I therefore noted particularly, because upon perusal of a Letter from the very learned and ingenious Dr *James Garden* of *Aberdeen*, to Mr *J Aubrey* R S S I found the Doctor had observ'd, that amongst their circular stone-monuments in *Scotland* (such as that at *Ro'rich*, &c in *England*) sometimes a stone or two is found with a cavity on the top of it, capable of a pint or two of liquor, and such a Groove or small chink as this I mention, continued downwards from this bason so that whatever liquor is pour'd on the top, must run down this way Whereupon he suggests, that supposing (as Mr *Aubrey* does) such circular Monuments to have been Temples of the *Druid*, those stones might serve perhaps for their *Libamina* or liquid sacrifices But although this stone agrees with those mention'd by Dr *Garden*, in having a furrow or crany on one side, yet in regard of the carving, it differs much from such old Monuments, which are generally, if not always, very plain and rude so that perhaps it never belong'd to such a circular Monument, but was erected on some other occasion The other stone is also elaborately carv'd, and was once the shaft or Pedestal of a Cross On the one side it hath an Inscription, shewing that one *Samson* set it up *pro anima ejus*, and another on the opposite side, signifying also that *Samson* erected it to St *Iltutus* or *Iltyd*, but that one *Samuel* was the Carver These Inscriptions I thought worth the publishing that the curious might have some light into the form of our Letters in the middle ages

Cowbridge

Bovium

Neath

From Sir J Stradling

A Pyramidal carv'd Stone

An Inscription

Samson posuit hanc crucem pro anima ejus

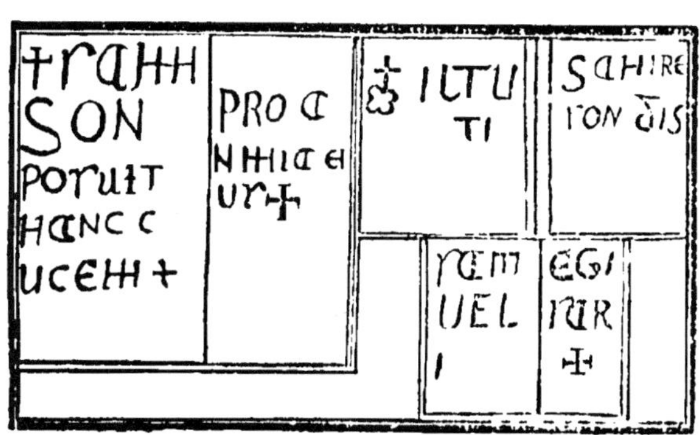

Not far from *Boverton*, almost in the very creek or winding of the shore, stands St *Donat's* castle, the habitation of the ancient and noble family of the *Stradlings*, near which have been dug up several ancient Roman coins, but especially of the thirty Tyrants, and some of *Æmilianus* and *Marius*, which are very scarce A little above this, the river *Ogmor* makes its way into the Sea it falls from the Mountains, and runs by *Kenfig* castle, the seat formerly of the *Turbervils*, afterwards of the *Gamages*, and after that (in right of his Lady) of

St Donat's castle

Roman coins

Sa

Sir *Robert Sidney* Viscount *L'Isle*, and also by *Ogmor*-castle, which devolv'd from the family of the *Londons*, to the Duchy of Lancaster.

Sandford's Well. A Fountain ebbing and flowing contrary to the Sea.

"There is a remarkable Spring within "a few miles of this place (as the learned "Sir *John Stradling* told me by letter) at a "place call'd *Newton*, a small village on the "west side of the river *Ogmor*, in a sandy plain "about a hundred paces from the Severn shore. "The water of it is not the clearest, but pure "enough and fit for use: it never runs over, "and such as would make use of it, must go "down some steps. At full Sea, in Summer "time, you can scarce take up any water in a "dish; but immediately when it ebbs, you "may take what quantity you please. The "same inconstancy remains also in the winter, "but is not so apparent by reason of the ad"ventitious water, as well from frequent "showers as subterraneous passages. This, se"veral of the inhabitants, who were persons "of credit, had assur'd me of. However, be"ing somewhat suspicious of common fame, as "finding it often erroneous, I lately made one "or two journeys to this sacred Spring; for I "had then some thoughts of communicating "this to you. Being come thither, and stay"ing about the third part of an Hour whilst "the Severn *flow'd*, and none came to take up "water, I observ'd that it sunk about three "inches. Having left it, and returning not "long after, I found the water risen above a "foot. The diameter of the Well may be "about six foot. Concerning which my Muse "dictates these few lines;

> *Te Nova Villa fremens, odioso murmure Nympha*
> *Inclamat Sabrina, soloque inimica propinquo,*
> *Evomit infestas rictu violenter arenas.*
> *Damna pari sentit vicinia sorte; sed illa*
> *Fonticulum causata tuum. Quem virgo, legendo*
> *Latus ad amplexus vocitat, latet ille vocatus*
> *Antro, & ludit contra. Namque æstus utrinque est*
> *Continuo motu refluus, tamen ordine dispar:*
> *Nympha fluit propius, Fons defluit; illa recedit,*
> *Iste redit. Sic vota nefas, & pugna perennis.*

> Thee, *Newton*, Severn's noisy Nymph pursues,
> While unrestrain'd th' impetuous torrent flows.
> Her conqu'ring Surges waste thy hated Land,
> And neighbouring fields are burden'd with the Sand.
> But all the fault is on thy fountain laid,
> Thy fountain courted by the amorous Maid.
> Him, as she passeth on, with eager looks
> She calls, in vain she calls, to mutual joys:
> He flies as fast, and scorns the proffer'd love,
> (For both with tides, and both with different move.)
> The Nymph advanceth, strait the Fountain's gone,
> The nymph retreats, and he returns as soon.
> Thus eager Love still boils the restless stream,
> And thus the cruel Spring still scorns the Virgin's flame.

An ebbing and flowing fountain at Cadiz.

Polybius takes notice of such a Fountain at Cadiz, and gives us this reason for it, *viz.* That the Air being depriv'd of its usual vent, returns inwards; by which means the veins of the Spring being stop'd, the water is kept back: and so, on the other had, the water leaving the shore, those Veins or natural Aqueducts are freed from all obstruction, so that the water springs plentifully.

Margan.

From hence, coasting along the shore, you come to *Kenfyg*, the Castle heretofore of *Fitz-Hamon*; and *Margan*, once a Monastery, founded by *William* Earl of Glocester, and now the Seat of the noble family of the Maunsels, Knights [and Baronets: of whom, Sir Thomas Mansel was advanced by her Majesty Queen Anne to the honour of Baron Mansel of this place.] Not far from *Margan*, on the top of a Hill call'd *Mynydd Margan*, is a Pillar of exceeding hard stone, erected for a Sepulchral Monument, of about four foot in height, and one in breadth, with an Inscription, which whoever happens to read, the ignorant common people of that neighbourhood affirm that he shall die soon after. Let the reader therefore take heed what he does; for if he reads it, it is certain death!

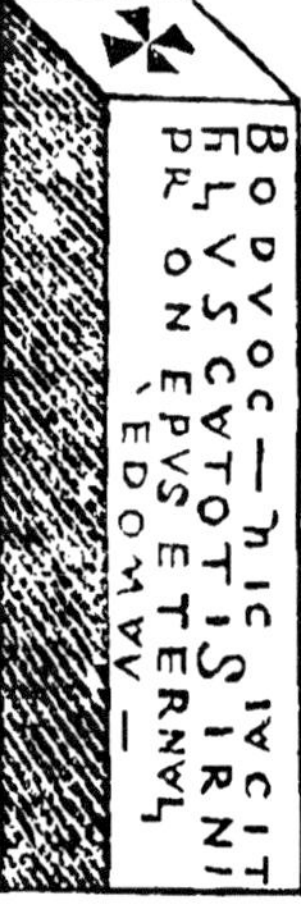

[In old Inscriptions, we often find the Letter V where we use O, as here, *Pronepus* for *Pronepos*:* so that there was no necessity of inventing this character Ɒ (made use of in the former editions) which, I presume, is such, as was never found in any Inscription. In Reinesius, *Syntag. Inscriptionum p.* 700, we find the Epitaph of one *Bodvacus*, dug up at Nimes in France. Whereupon he tells us, that the Roman name *Betulius* was changed by the Gauls into *Bodvacus*. But it may seem equally probable, if not more likely, since we also find *Bodvoc* here, that it was a Gaulish or British name: and the name of the famous Queen of the *Iceni*, *Boadicea*, seems also to share in the same original. Sepulchres are in old Inscriptions often call'd *Domus æternæ*, but *æternalis* seems a barba rous word The laſt words I read *Æternali in Domo*, for in that age Sepulchres were call'd † *Æternales Domus*, or rather *Æternæ*, according to that Dyſtich,

† Reineſ p 716

Docta Lyra grata, & geſtu formoſa puella,
Hic jacet æterna *Sabit humata domo*

The foregoing monument is to be ſeen at the ſame place at this day, exactly according to this new delineation thereof (which is much more accurate than the draughts in former Editions,) and is well known in this part of the Country by the name of *y maen Lhythyrog*]

Betwixt *Margan* and *Kynfyg* alſo, by the way-ſide, lies a ſtone about four foot long, with this Inſcription

PVMPEIVS CARANTORIVS

Which the Welſh (as the Right Reverend the Biſhop of *Landaff*, who ſent me * the Copy of it, informs me) by adding and changing ſome letters, do thus read and interpret, PVMP BVS CAR A'N TOPIUS i e *The five fingers of our friend or kinſman kill'd us* They ſuppoſe it to have been the Grave of Prince *Morgan*, from whom the Country receiv'd its name; who they ſay was kill'd eight hundred years before the birth of our Saviour; but Antiquaries know, that theſe letters are of much later date

* This is not the ſame but more accurate

[The Inſcription is now in the ſame place, and is call'd by the common people *Bêdh Morgan Morganwg*, viz *The Sepulchre of Prince Morgan* which (whatever gave occaſion to it) is doubtleſs an erroneous tradition; it being no other than the tomb ſtone of one *Pompeius Carantorius*, as plainly appears by the ſaid Copy of it, which I tranſcrib'd from the ſtone As for the word *Pumpeius* for *Pompeius*, we have already obſerv'd, that in old inſcriptions the letter V is frequently uſed for O

Bedh Morgan Morganwg

Vid Archæol Brit Vol i p 17 col 2

There is alſo another monument, which ſeems more remarkable than either of theſe, at a place call'd *Panwen Byrdhin*, in the Pariſh of *Kadokſton* or *Lhan Gadok*, about ſix miles above *Neath* It is well known in that part of the County by the name of *Maen dau Lygad yr ych*, and is ſo call'd, from two ſmall circular entrenchments, like cock-pits, one of which had lately in the midſt of it a rude ſtone pillar, about three foot in height, with this inſcription, to be read downwards

Maen dau Lygad yr ych

MCARITIN-FILI BERICCI

which we read *Marci* (or rather perhaps *memoriæ*) *Caritini filii Bericii* But what ſeem'd to me moſt remarkable, were the round *Areæ*, having never ſeen, nor been inform'd of ſuch places of Burial elſewhere So that on firſt ſight, my conjecture was, that this had happen'd on occaſion of a Duel, each party having firſt prepar'd his place of interment and that therefore there being no ſtone in the center of the other circle, this Inſcription muſt have been the monument of the party ſlain It has been lately remov'd a few paces out of the circle, and is now pitch'd on end, at a gate in the high way But that there never was more than one ſtone here, ſeems highly probable from the name *Maen dau Lygad yr ych* whereas had there been more, this place, in all likelihood, had had the name of *Mieneu Lhygaid yr*

On a mountain call'd *Mynydh Gelhi Onnen* in the Pariſh of *Lhan Gyvelach*, I obſerv'd a Monument which ſtood lately in the midſt of a ſmall *Karn* or heap of ſtones, but is now thrown down and broken in three or four pieces, differing from all I have ſeen elſewhere It was a flat ſtone, about three inches thick, two foot broad at bottom, and about five in height The top of it is form'd as round as a wheel, and thence to the baſis it becomes gradually broader On one ſide it is carv'd with ſome art, but much more labour The round head is adorn'd with a kind of flouriſhing croſs, like a Garden-knot below that, there is a man's face and hands on each ſide; and thence, almoſt to the bottom, neat Fretwork; beneath which there are two feet, but is rude and ill-proportion'd (as are alſo the face and hands,) as ſome Egyptian Hieroglyphick

A Monument on Mynydh Gelhi Onnen

Not far from hence, within the ſame Pariſh, is *Karn Lhechart*, a Monument that gives denomination to the Mountain on which it is erected It is a circle of rude ſtones, which are ſomewhat of a flat form, ſuch as we call *Lhecheu*, diſorderly pitch'd in the ground, of about ſeventeen or eighteen yards diameter, the higheſt of which now ſtanding, is not above a yard in height It has but one entry into it, which is about four foot wide and in the center of the Area, it has ſuch a Cell or Hut, as is ſeen in ſeveral places of Wales, and call'd *Kiſt vaen* one of which is deſcrib'd in Brecknockſhire, by the name of St *Ityt*'s Cell This at *Karn Lhechart* is about ſix foot in length, and four foot wide, and has no top-ſtone now for a cover, but a very large one lies by, which ſeems to have ſlipt off *Y Giſt vaen* on a Mountain call'd *Mynydhy Drymmeu* by *Neath*, ſeems to have been alſo a Monument of this kind, but much leſs and to differ from it, in that the Circle about it was Maſon-work, as I was inform'd by a Gentleman who had often ſeen it whilſt it ſtood; for at preſent there is no thing of it remaining But theſe kinds of Monuments, which ſome aſcribe to the Danes, and others ſuppoſe to have been erected by the Britains before the Roman Conqueſt, we ſhall have occaſion to ſpeak of more fully hereafter

Karn Lhechart

Another Monument there is, on a Mountain call'n *Kevn bryn*, in Gower, which may challenge a place alſo among ſuch unaccountable Antiquities, as are beyond the reach of Hiſtory;

Arthur's ſtone in Gower.

story, and of which the same worthy person that sent me his conjecture concerning the subterraneous noise in *Barry*-Island, gives the following account

As to the stones you mention, they are to be seen upon a jutting at the Northwest of Kevn bryn, *the most noted Hill in Gower They are put together, by labour enough, but no great art, into a pile and their fashion and posture is this There is a vast unwrought stone (probably about twenty ton Weight) supported by six or seven others that are not above four foot high, and these are set in a Circle, some on end, and some edge wise, or side long, to bear the great one up They are all of them of the* Lapis-molaris *kind, which is the natural stone of the Mountain The great one is much diminish'd of what it has been in bulk, as having five tons or more (by Report) broke off it to make Mill stones, so that I guess the stone originally to have been between twenty five and thirty tons in weight The carriage, rearing, and placing of this massy Rock, is plainly an effect of human industry and art, but the Pulleys and Levers, the force and skill by which it was done, are not so easily imagin'd The common people call it* Arthur's *stone, by a lift of vulgar imagination attributing to that Hero an extravagant size and strength Under it is a well, which (as the neighbourhood tell me) has a flux and reflux with the Sea, of the truth whereof I cannot as yet satisfy you,* &c There are divers monuments of this kind in Wales, some of which we shall take notice of in other Counties In *Anglesey* (where there are many of them) as also in some other places, they are call'd *Krom-lecheu*, a name deriv'd from *krwm*, which signifies *crooked* or *inclining*, and *llech* a flat stone, but of the name, more hereafter It is generally suppos'd, they were places of burial, but I have not yet learn'd that ever any Bones or Urns were found by digging under any of them]

From Margan the shore runs north east, by

Aber-Avon *Aber-Avon*, a small market town at the mouth of the River Avon (whence it takes its name,) to *Neath*, a River infamous for Quick-sands, upon which stands an ancient town of the same

Nidum Name, in Antonine's Itinerary call'd *Nidum* Which, when Fitz-Hamon subdu'd this Country, fell in the division to *Richard Granvil*; who having built a Monastery under the Town, and consecrated his dividend to God and the Monks, return'd to a very plentiful estate he had in England

Loebor river All the Country from *Neath* to the River *Lo-*

Brit Lhychwr *chor*, which is the Western limit of this Coun-

Gower ty, is call'd by us *Gower*, by the Britains Gwyr, and by Ninnius *Gubir* where (as he tells us) the sons of *Keian*, a Scot, seated and distributed themselves, till they were driven out by *Kynedbav*, a British prince In the Reign of King

Tho Walsingham Henry the first, *Henry* Earl of *Warwick* subdu'd this Country of *Gower*; which afterwards by agreement betwixt *Thomas* Earl of *Warwick*, and King Henry the second, devolv'd to the Crown

Lib Monast Neth 5 Reg Joan But King John bestow'd it on *William de Breos*, *to be held by service of one Knight, for all service*, and his heirs successively held it, till the time of Edward the second For at that time *William de Breos* having sold it to several persons, that he might ingratiate himself with the King, deluded all others, and put *Hugh Spenser* in possession of it And that, among others, was the cause why the Nobles became so exasperated against the Spensers, and so unadvisedly quitted their Allegiance to the King It is now divided into East Gower

East and *West Gowerland* In *East Gowerland*, Swansey

the most noted town is *Sweinsey*, so called by the English from *Porpoises* or *Sea-Hogs*, and by the Britains *Aber-Tawi* (from the River *Tawi*, which runs by it) which was fortify'd by *Henry* Earl of *Warwick* But a more ancient place Loghor

than this, is that upon the River *Logbor*, which Leucarum

Antoninus calls *Leucarum*, and is at this day (retaining its ancient name) call'd *Logbor* [in British *Kas-Lychwr*] Where, about the time of King Henry the first's death, *Hovel ap Mredydb* with a band of Mountaineers, surprized and slew several Englishmen of quality Beneath West Gower

this, lies *West Gower*, which (the Sea making Creeks on each side) is become a *Peninsula*, a place more noted for Corn, than for Towns, and celebrated heretofore for St *Kynedbav*, who led here a solitary life, concerning whom, such as desire a further account, may consult our *Capgrave*, who has sufficiently extoll'd his Miracles Lords of Glamorgan

From the very first conquest of this Country, the *Clares* and *Spensers* Earls of Gloucester (who were lineally descended from Fitz Hamon) were Lords of it Afterwards, the *Beauchamps*, and one or two of the *Nevils*, and by a Daughter of *Nevil* (descended also from the *Spensers*) it came to *Richard* the third King of England, and he being slain, it devolv'd to King *Henry* the seventh who granted it to his uncle *Gasper*, Duke of *Bedford* He dying without issue, the King resum'd it into his own hands, and left it to his Son *Henry* the eighth, whose son *Edward* the sixth sold most part of it to *William Herbert*, whom he had created Earl of *Pembroke*, and Baron of *Caerdiffe*

Of the Off spring of the twelve Knights before mentioned, there remain now only in this County the *Stradlings*, a family very eminent for their many noble Ancestors, with the *Turbervile*, and some of the *Flemmings*, whereof the chiefest dwells at *Flemmingstone*, called now corruptly from them *Flemston* But in England there remain the Lord *St John* of *Bletso*, the *Granvils* in Devonshire, and the *Siwards* (as I am inform'd) in Somersetshire The issue male of all the rest is long since extinct, and their Lands by Daughters pass'd over to other families

[*Edward Somerset*, Lord Herbert of *Chepstow*, Earls of Glamorgan

Ragland and *Gower*, obtain'd of King Charles the first the title of Earl of *Glamorgan*, his Father the Lord Marquiss of *Worcester* being then alive, the Succession of which noble Family may be seen at the end of *Worcestershire*]

Parishes in this County 118

DIME-

DIMETÆ.

THE Remainder of this Tract, which is extended Westward, and is called by the English West-Wales, comprehending Caer-mardhin-shire, Pembrokeshire, and Cardiganshire, was thought by Pliny to have been inhabited by the Silures But Ptolomy, to whom Britain was better known, placed another Nation here, whom he call'd Dimetæ and Demetæ Moreover, both Gildas and Ninnius us'd the word Demetia to signify this Country, whence the Britains call it at this day Dyved, changing the M into V, according to the custom of that Language

West Wales

If it would not be thought a strain'd Piece of Curiosity, I should be apt to derive this name Demetæ, from the words Deheu meath, which signify the Southern Plain, as all this South Part of Wales has been call'd Deheu barth, i e the Southern Part And I find that elsewhere the Inhabitants of a Champain Country in Britain were call'd by the Britains themselves † Meatæ Nor does the situation of this Country contradict that signification, for when you take a prospect of it, the Hills decline gently and gradually into a Plain [But seeing it was the custom among the Romans to retain such names of the places they conquer'd, as the ancient Natives made use of, adding only a Latin Termination, it may seem more probable that Dimetia was made out of the British Name Dyved, than the contrary]

† There is no such word as Meath, for a Champain Country (either in Manuscripts or common use) nor is this Country such as is describ d.

CAER-MARDHIN-SHIRE.

THE County of *Kaer-Vyrdhin*, call'd by the English *Caermardhinshire*, is a Country sufficiently supply'd with Corn, and very well stock'd with Cattel, and in divers places affords plenty of Coal It is bounded on the East with *Glamorganshire* and *Brecknockshire*, on the West with *Pembrokeshire*, on the North it is divided from *Cardiganshire* by the River *Tewi*, and on the South it is bounded with the main Ocean, which encroaches on the Land here, with such a vast Bay, as if this Country out of fear had withdrawn itself In this Bay, *Kydwels* first offers itself, the territory whereof was possessed for some time by the sons of *Keianus* a Scot, till they were driven out by *Kynedhav*, a British Prince But now it is esteemed Part of the Inheritance of the Duchy of Lancaster, by the heirs of *Maurice of London*, or *de Londres*, who removing out of *Glamorganshire*, made himself master of it after a tedious war, and fortify'd *old Kydwels* with Walls, and a Castle, now decay'd with age For the inhabitants passing over the River of *Gwen-draeth-vechan*, built *new Kydwels*, being invited thither by the convenience of a Harbour, which yet at present is of no great use, being choak'd with shelves When Maurice of London invaded their territories, *Gwenlhian* the wife of *Prince Gryffydh*, a woman of invincible courage (endeavouring to restore her Husband's declining state) bravely engag'd him in a pitch'd battle But she with her son *Morgan*, and divers other Noblemen (as Giraldus informs us) were slain in the field

Kydwels

Gwenlhian, a woman of manly courage

By *Hawis*, the Daughter and Heir of Thomas de Londres, this fair Inheritance, with the Title of Lord of *Ogmor* and *Kydwels*, descended to *Patrick Chaworth*, and, by a daughter of his son *Patrick*, to Henry Earl of Lancaster The heirs of Maurice de Londres (as we read in an old Inquisition) *were oblig'd by this Tenure, In case the King, or his Chief Justice, should lead an Army into these Parts of* Kydwels, *to conduct the said Army, with their Banners, and all their Forces, through the midst of the Country of Neath, to Lochor*

Lords of Ogmor and Kydwels

A few miles below Kydwels, the River *Towy*, which Ptolomy calls *Tobius*, is received into the Ocean, having pass'd the length of this County from North to South First, by *Lhan ym Dhyvri* (so call'd, as is suppos'd, from the confluence of Rivers) which, out of malice to the English, was long since demolish'd by *Howel ap Rhys* Afterwards, by *Dinevor Castle*, the Royal Seat of the Princes of South Wales, whilst they flourish'd situated aloft on the top of a Hill And at last by *Caer mardhin*, which the Britains themselves call *Kaer-Vyrdhin* Ptolemy *Maridunum*, and Antoninus *Muridunum*, who continues not his Journeys any farther than this place, and has here been ill us'd by the negligence of the Copyist. For they have carelesly confounded two Journeys the one from *Gauna* to *Isca*, the other from *Maridunum* to *Viroconovium* This is the chief town of the County, pleasantly seated for Meadows and Woods,

The River Towy or Tobius

Dinevor

Maridunum, Caer Mardhin

Woods, and is a place venerable for its Antiquity, excellently *fortified* (saith Giraldus) *with brick-walls, partly yet standing, on the noble river of Towy* which is navigable with ships of small burden, though there is a bed of sand before the mouth of it. Here, our Merlin, the British *Tages*, was born: for as *Tages* was reported to have been the son of a *Genius*, and to have taught his Tuscans Sooth-saying, so our Merlin, who was said to have been the son of an *Incubus*, devised *Prophecies*, or rather mere Phantastical *Dreams*, for our Britains. Insomuch, that in this Island he has the reputation of an eminent Prophet, amongst the ignorant common people. [This *Merlin*, or *Mirdhin Emrys* (for so the British Writers call him) flourished Anno 480. The first of our Historians that mentions him, is * Ninnius, who supposes he was called *Embreys Gluti c*. He says nothing of his being the son of an *Incubus*, but, on the contrary, tells us expressly, his mother was afraid of owning the father, lest she should be sentenced to die for it: but that the boy confessed to King Vortigern, that his father was by Nation a Roman. The same Author informs us, that King Vortigern's Messengers found him *ad campum Electi in regione quæ vocatur Gleuising*, i. e. *at the field of* Electus, *in the Country called Gleuising*, which whether it were at this Town or County, or in some other place, seems very questionable, no places (that I can hear of) being known by such names at present. All the Monkish writers that mention him, make him either a *Prophet*, or *Magician*. But *H. Lhwyd* † a judicious Author, and very conversant in British Antiquities, informs us, that he was a man of extraordinary learning and prudence for the time he lived in, and that for some skill in the Mathematicks, many fables were invented of him by the vulgar, which being afterwards put in writing, were handed down to posterity.]

Merlin or Myrdhin Emri

* Hist. Brit. c. 42. &c.

† Com. Brit. Descript. p. 65.

Soon after the Normans entered Wales, this town fell into their possession, but under whose conduct I know not, and for a long time it encountered many difficulties: having been often besieged, and twice burnt, first by *Gryffydh ap Rhys*, and afterwards by *Rhys* the said Gryffydh's brother. At which time, *Henry Turbervil*, an Englishman, relieved the castle, and cut down the bridge. But the walls and castle being afterwards repaired by *Gilbert de Clare*, it was freed from those miseries, so that being thus secured, it bore the storms of war much easier afterwards. The princes of Wales, eldest sons of the Kings of England, settled here their *Chancery* and *Exchequer* for *South Wales*. Opposite to this city, towards the East, lies *Cantrevbychan*, which signifies the *lesser Hundred* (for the Britains call such a portion of a country as contains one hundred villages, *Kantrev*) where may be seen the ruins of *Kastelh Karreg*, which was seated on a steep, and on all sides inaccessible rock, and likewise several vast caverns, now all covered with green turf (where, in time of War, such as were unfit for arms, are thought [by some] to have secured themselves) *a notable fountain* also, *which* (as Giraldus writes) *ebbing and flowing twice in twenty four hours, imitates the sea-tides*. [Those Caverns are supposed, by inquisitive persons who have often viewed them, rather to have been Copper mines of the Romans. And indeed, seeing it is evident (from some Antiquities found there) that *Kaer-Gai* in Merionydh shire was a Roman Town or Fort, and that the place where these Caves are, is also called *Kaio*, I am apt to infer from the name, that this place must have been likewise well known to the Romans. And that I may note this by the way, I suspect most names of places in Wales, that end in *i* or *o*, such as *Bod-Vari*, *Kevn Kaeroni*, *Kaer-Gai*, *Lhanio*, *Kedic*, and *Kaio*, to be Roman names, these terminations being not so agreeable with the Idiom of the British. But for the Antiquity of this place, we need not wholly rely upon conjectures: for I have lately received from ‖ a curious person these following Inscriptions, which he copied from two stones at a place called *Pant y Polion*, in this parish. The first (being a monument of one *Paulinus*, whence, doubtless, is the name of *Pant y polion*) lies flat on the ground, and is placed cross a gutter: but the other, which seems to be of somewhat later date, is pitched on end, and is about a yard in height, the Inscription whereof is to be read downwards.

Cantrev-bychan

Caverns

‖ Mr. Saunders e Coll. Jesu Oxon.

Pant y Polion

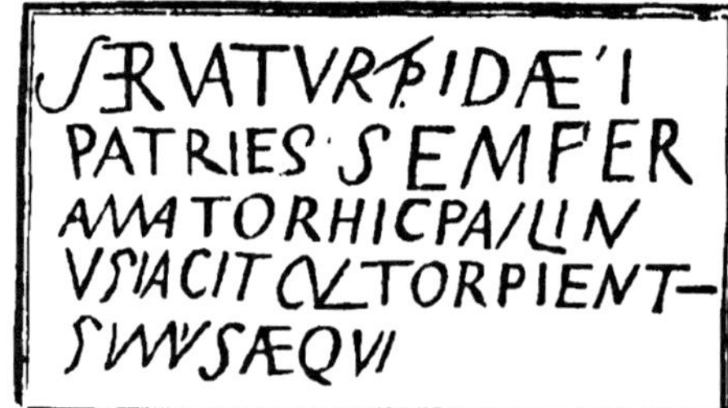

Servator fid..., Patriaque semper amator, hic Paulinus jacet cultor pientissimus æqui.

Whether *Odin* in the several names of places in this neighbourhood be from the same *Advent* (or *Adwen*) whose Monument this was, or some other origin, is recommended to the observation of the Inhabitants However it be, it is certain, there are more of them hereabouts, than in all Wales besides, as, *Gâlbi yr Odyn*, *Pant yr Odyn*, &c]

Cantrev Mawr

To the North is extended *Cantrev Mawr*, or the great Hundred, a safe Retreat heretofore for the *Britains*, as being very woody and rocky, and full of uncouth ways, by reason of the windings of the hills On the South, the Castles of *Talcharn* and *Lhan Stephan* stand on the sea rocks, and are ample testimonies of warlike prowess, as well in the English as Britains

Talcharn. Lhan Stephan

* Brit Tav

Below *Talcharn*, the river * *Taff* is discharged into the sea on the bank of which river, was famous heretofore *Ty gwyn ar Dav*, which signifies, *the white house on the river Taff*, so called, because it was built of white hasel rods for a Summer-house [I cannot conjecture, what might be the original signification of this word *Tav* but it may be worth our observation, that the most noted rivers in South Wales seem to have been thence denominated for besides that there are three or four rivers of that name, the first syllable also in *Tawy*, *Towy*, *Teivi*, and *Dyvi*, seems to me but so many various pronunciations of it and for the latter syllable, I have † elsewhere offered my conjecture, that it only denotes a *River*, or perhaps *Water* Nor would it seem to me very absurd, if any should derive the name of the river *Thames* from the same original For since we find it pretty evident, that the Romans changed *Dyved* (the ancient name of this Country) into *Dimetæ*, and *Kyndav* (a man's name) into ‖ *Cunotamus*, and also that in many words where the Latins use an M, the Britains have an V, as Firmus, *Firv*, Terminus, *Tervin*, Amnis, *Avon*, Lima, *Lliv*, &c it seems not unlikely (considering we find the word *Tav*, usual in the names of our rivers) that the Britains might call that river *Tav*, *Tavwy*, or *Tavwys*, before the Roman Conquest, which they afterwards called *Tamesis* And this seems to be more than a mere conjecture, when we consider further, that the word *Tav* was, according to the old British Orthography, written *Tam*, which shews, not only that *Tav* or *Taff* in Glamorganshire, &c is originally the same word with *Thame* or *Thames*, but also that the Greek ποταμὸς is probably no other]

† Radnorshire

‖ An old Inscription in Pembrokeshire

Archæol. Brit p 4, col 2 & p 268

Here, at the aforesaid *Ty gwyn ar Dav*, in the year of our Lord 914, *Howel*, sirnamed the *Good*, Prince of Wales, in a full Assembly (there being, besides Laymen, one hundred and forty Ecclesiasticks) abrogated the Laws of his Ancestors, and gave [a Body of] new Laws to his people, as the Preface before those Laws testifies, [and yet in an ancient MS Copy of them, to be seen in *Jesus*-College Library in Oxford, fairly writ on parchment, the Preface does not inform us, that *Howel Dha* abrogated all the Laws of his Ancestors, but expresly tells us, that *according to the advice of his Council, some of the ancient Laws be retained, others be corrected, and some be quite disannulled, appointing others in their stead**]

* [illegible]

In the same place, a small Monastery was built afterwards, called *Whitland-Abbey* Not far from whence is *Kilmaen Lhwyd*, where some Country-men † lately discovered an earthen Vessel, that contained a considerable quantity of Roman Coins of embas'd silver; from the time of *Commodus* (who was the first of the Roman Emperors that embas'd their silver) to the fifth Tribuneship of *Gordian* the third; which falls in with the year of Christ 243 Amongst these, were *Helvius Pertinax*, *Marcus Opellius*, *Antoninus Diadumenianus*, *Julius Verus*, *Maximus* the son of *Maximinus*, *Cælius Balbinus*, *Clodius Pupienus*, *Aquilia Severa* the wife of *Elagabalus*, and *Sall Barbia Orbiana* which (as being very rare) were Coins of considerable value among Antiquaries [Anno 1692 there were about two hundred Roman Coins found not far from hence, at a place called *Bronyskawen* in *Lhan Boydy* parish They were discovered by two Shepherd-boys, at the very entry of a spacious Camp call'd *y Gaer*, buried in two very rude leaden boxes (one of which I have caused to be figured in the Table, n 10) so near the surface of the ground, that they were not wholly out of sight They were all of silver, and were some of the ancientest Roman Coins we find in Britain Of about thirty I have seen of them, the latest were of *Domitian* Cos xv An Dom 91 But perhaps a Catalogue of them may not be unacceptable to the curious, though I have only those in my possession, which are thus distinguished with an asterisk *

Whitland Abbey. Kilmaen Lhwyd. Roman Coins.

† So said ann 1607

1 Ant Aug iiivir R P C *Navis prætoria*
  Nf Leg V *Duo vexilla castrensia, cum tertia in medio longe breviori, in cujus summo, aquila alis altius erectis*
2 Ant Aug *Navis prætoria*
  Leg X *Duo signa castrensia cum aquila legionaria* *
3 Ant Aug iiivir R P C *Navis prætoria*
  Leg XIII *Tria vexilla castrensia*
4 ——— *Caput forte Neptuni cum Tridente à tergo*
  Inf Cuc Re *Victoria in dorso Delphini*
  Hic nummus etiam M Antonii videtur
5 Q Cassius Vest *Imago Virginis Vestalis*
  Ac *Templum Vestæ cum sella & urna* *
6 Q Cassius Libert *Imago Libertatis*
  Ac *Templum Vestæ cum sella curuli & urna* *
7 Geta iiivir *Imago Dianæ*
  ——— *Nummus serratus*
8 C Hosidi C F *Aper Venabulo trajectus cum cane venatico*
  Geta iiivir *Imago Dianæ cum pharetra & Arcu* *
9 Marc * *Caput Romæ*
  Roma *Quadrigæ*
10 C iii Næ B *Victoria in Trigis*
  Deæ cujusdam Imago
11 L Procili F *Juno sospita in bigis infra serpens Lanuvinus*
  Junonis sospitæ imago Nummus serratus *
12 M Thoriv Balbu *Taurus decurrens*
  I S.M R *Sospita Juno*
13 . tori *Victoria in quadrigis*
  Sc R *Caput Romæ Nummus serratus* *
14 Cæsar *Elephas cum Dracone*
  Capeduncula, Aspergillum, Securis, & Albogalerus signa Pontificis maximi & Dialis Flaminis *
15 *Caput Augusti, sine Inscriptione*
  Cæsar Divi F *Figura stolata, dextrâ ramum, sinistrâ cornu copiæ* *
16 Ti Cæsar Divi Aug F Aug
  Figura sedens, dextra hastam, sinistra ramum
17 T Claud Cæsar Aug Germ Trib Pot P P
  Agrippinæ Augustæ *Caput Agrippinæ*
18 Nero Cæsar Augustus
  Jupiter Custos *Jupiter sedens, dextra fulmen tenens, sinistra Cathedræ innixa* *

8

19. Nero

19 Nero Cæsar Augustus
Salus *Figura Cathedræ insidens, dextra pateram*

20 Imp Ser Galba Cæs Aug
Salus Gen mini [*forte Generis humani*] *Figura stans coram a a accensa, sinistra temonem, dextro pede globum calcans*

21 Imp M Otho Cæsar Aug Ir P
Securitas P R *Figura stans, dextra coronam, sinistra hastam* *

22 Imp Cæsar Vespasianus August is
Pont Max Tr P Cos V *Caduceum alatum*

23 Cæsar Aug Domitianus
Cos *Pegasus*

24 Imp Cæs Domit Aug Germ Tr P
Imp xxi Cos x. Cens P P P *P... insidens, dextra jaculum, sinistra scutum*

The Camp where these Coins were found, is somewhat of an oval form, and may be at least three hundred paces in circumference. The bank or rampire is near the entry, about three yards in height, but elsewhere it is generally much lower. At the entrance (which is about four yards wide) the two ends of the dike are not directly opposite, the one (at the point whereof the Coins were found) being continued somewhat farther out than the other, so as to render the passage oblique. On each side the Camp, there is an old *Barrow* or *Tumulus*, the one, small, somewhat near it, the other, which is much bigger, at least three hundred yards distant. Both hollow on the top. The leaden boxes wherein these Coins were preserved, are so very rude, that were it not for what they contained, I should never imagine them Roman. For they appear only like lumps of lead ore, and weigh about five pounds, though they contain scarce half a pint of liquor. They are of an orbicular form, like small loaves, and have a round hole in the middle of the lid, about the circumference of a shilling.]

Newcastle It remains now, that I give some account of *Newcastle* (seated on the bank of the river *Teivi*, which divides this County from Cardiganshire for so they now call it, because it was rep... by *Rhys ap Thomas*, a stout warrior, who assisted Henry the seventh in gaining his Kingdom, and was by him deservedly created Knight of the Garter, whereas formerly it * is said by some to have been called † *Emlin*. Which name, if the English gave it from Elm-trees, their conjecture is not to be despised, who are of opinion, that it was the *Lovantium* of the *Dimetæ*, mentioned by Ptolemy, for an Elm is called in British *Llwyfen*. [But it makes against this conjecture, that the old British name of *Emlin*, is *Dinas Emlin*, the most obvious Interpretation whereof (tho' I shall not much contend for it) is *Urbs Æmiliani*, which seems to have no other original, than that a person so named was once the Lord or Proprietor of it. The name (which was common among the Britains anciently, and is partly yet retained) was Roman, and is the same with the *Æmilianus* mentioned in Denbighshire, which the Inscription calls *Æmilini*. I cannot find, that ever it was called *Emlin*, either in Welsh or English, and therefore dare not subscribe to the ‖ foregoing conjecture, that the *Lovantinum* of the *Dimetæ*, mentioned by Ptolemy, was at this place, nor yet that it perished in the lake *Llyn Savadhan*, in Brecknockshire. Indeed the footsteps of several Towns and Forts that flourished in the time of the Romans, are now so obscure and undiscernible, that we are not to wonder if the conjectures of learned and judicious men about their situation, prove sometimes erroneous. I have lately observed in Cardiganshire, some tokens of a Roman Fort, which I suspect to have been the *Lovantinum*, or *Lovantium* of Ptolemy, for which I shall take the liberty of offering my arguments, when we come into that County.

* Was called, C
† Vulgo Emlin
Lovantium
‖ See Brecknockshire and Cardiganshire

In the 19th of King Charles the first, Richard Earl of *Carbery* in Ireland, was advanced to the dignity of a Baron of this Realm, by the title of Lord *Vaughan* of *Emlyn*.

Besides the Inscriptions, which we observed at *Kaio*, there are three or four others in this County which may deserve our notice. The first is not far from *Caer-Mardhin* town, in *Lhan Newydd* parish, which, by the names therein, should be Roman, though the form of some Letters, and the rudeness of the Stone on which they are inscribed, might give us grounds to suspect it the Epitaph of some person of *Roman descent*, but who lived somewhat later than their time. The stone is a rude pillar, erected near the high way, somewhat of a flat form, five or six foot high, and about half a yard in breadth, and contains the following Inscription, not to be read downwards, as on many stones in these Countries, but from the left to the right.

Al. s. *Llan Lhangel y Kreuys*

SEVERINI
FILI SEVERI

Sepulchrum] *Severini filii Severi*

The second is in the Parish of *Hen Lhan Amgoed*, in a field belonging to *Parkeu*, and is almost such a Monument as the former. At present it lies on the ground, but, considering its form, it is probable that it stood heretofore upright, and if so, the Inscription was read downwards.

Parkeu

CMENVENDAN-
FILI BARCUN-

Sepulchrum] [... in Cau ?] *Menvendani filii Barcuni*

Both these names of *Menvendan* and *Barcun* are now obsolete, nor do I remember to have read either of them, in any Genealogical MS. But near this Monument there is a place called *Kevn Varchen*, which may seem to be denominated either from this *Barcun*, or some other of the same name. The third Inscription was copied by my * above mentioned friend, from a polish'd Free-stone at the West-end of the Church of *Lhan Vihangel Jeiwerth*.

* Mr Saunders
Lhan Vihangel Jeiwerth.

HIC IACIT
VLCAGNVS FIUS
SENOMAGL-

Hic iacet Ulcagnus filius Senomagli

The

The fourth (which seems less intelligible than any of the rest) was also communicated by the same hand The stone whence he copied it, is neatly carved, about six foot high, and two foot broad, and has a cavity on the top, which makes me suspect it to have been no other than the Pedestal of a Cross It may be seen at a place denominated from it *Kae'r Maen*, not far from *Aber Sannan*; but for the meaning of the Inscription, if it be any other than the Stone-cutter's name (though I confess I know no name like it) I must leave it to the Reader's conjecture

EIUdon

Lhan Vair y Bryn

In the Parish of *Lhan Vair y Bryn*, we find manifest signs of a place possessed by the Romans For not far from the East-end of the Church, Labourers frequently dig-up bricks, and meet with some other marks of Roman Antiquity, and there is a very notable Roman way of Gravel and small Pebbles, continued from that Church to *Lhan Brân*, the seat of a family of the *Gwyns*, which (as I am told) may be also traced betwixt this *Lhan Vair*, and *Lhan Deilaw Vawr*, and is visible in several other places

This Country abounds with ancient *Forts*, *Camps*, and *Tumuli* or *Barrows*, which we have not room here to take notice of I shall therefore mention only one Barrow, called *Krig y Dyrn*, in the Parish of *Tre'lêch*, which seems particularly remarkable The circumference of it at bottom may be about sixty paces, the height about six yards It rises with an easy ascent, and is hollow on the top, gently inclining from the circumference to the center This *Barrow* is not a mount of Earth, as others generally are, but seems to have been such a heap of stones, as are called in Wales *Karnedheu* (whereof the Reader may see some account in *Radnorshire*) covered with Turf At the center of the cavity on the top, we find a vast rude *Lhecl*, or flat stone, somewhat of an oval form, about three yards in length, five foot over where broadest, and about ten or twelve inches thick A * Gentleman, to satisfy my curiosity, having employed some Labourers to search under it, found it, after removing much stone, to be the covering of such a barbarous Monument, as we call *Kist-vaen*, or *Stone-chest*, which was about four foot and a half in length, and about three foot broad, but somewhat narrower at the East than West-end It is made up of seven stones, *viz* the covering stone, already mentioned, and two side stones, one at each end, and one behind each of these for the better securing or bolstering of them, all equally rude, and about the same thickness, the two last excepted, which are considerably thicker They found, as well within the Chest as without, some rude pieces of brick (or stones burnt like them) and free stone, some of which were wrought They observed also some pieces of bones, but such as they supposed to have been only brought in by *Foxes*, but, not sinking to the bottom of the Chest, we know not what else it may afford

Barrow Tre'lech

* Mr *William Lewes* of *Lhwyn Derw*

Krig y Dyrn (the name of this *Tumulus*) is now scarce intelligible; but if a conjecture may be allowed, I should be apt to interpret it *King's Barrow* I am sensible that even such as are well acquainted with the Welsh tongue, may at first view think this a groundless opinion, and wonder what I aim at, but when they consider that the common word *Teyrnas*, which signifies a *Kingdom*, is only a derivative from the old word *Teyrn* (which was originally the same with *Tyrannus*, and signified a King or Prince,) they will perhaps acknowledge it not altogether improbable And considering the rudeness of the Monument described, and yet the labour and strength required in erecting it, I am apt to suspect it the Barrow of some British Prince, who might live probably before the Roman Conquest For seeing it is much too barbarous to be supposed Roman, and that we do not find in History that the Saxons were ever concerned here, or the Danes any farther than in plundering the Sea-coasts, it seems necessary to conclude it British That it was a Royal Sepulchre I am apt to infer, partly from the signification of the name, which being not understood in these ages, could not therefore be any novel invention of the vulgar, and partly for that (as I hinted already) more labour and strength was required here than we can suppose to be allowed to persons of inferiour quality That it is older than Christianity, there is no room to doubt, but that it was before the Roman Conquest, is only my conjecture, supposing that after the Britains were reduced by the Romans, they had none whom they could call *Teyrn* or King, whose corpse or ashes might be reposited here

Lhan Boudy.

Gwâl y Vilast or *Bwrdh Arthur*, in *Lhan Boudy* parish, is a monument in some respect like that which we have described at this *Barrow*, *viz* a rude stone about ten yards in circumference, and above three foot thick, supported by four pillars, which are about two foot and a half in height

K. l y maen Llwyd

But *Buarth Arthur* or *Meineu Gwyr*, on a Mountain near *Kil y maen lhwyd*, is one of that kind of circular Stone monuments which our English Historians ascribe to the Danes The Diameter of the Circle is about twenty yards The stones are as rude as may be, and pitched on end at uncertain distances from each other, some at three or four foot, but others about two yards, and are also of several heights, some being about three or four foot high, and others five or six There are now standing here, fifteen of them, but there seem to be seven or eight carried off The entry into it for about the space of three yards, is guarded on each side with stones much lower and less than those of the circle, and pitched so close as to be contiguous And over-against this avenue, at the distance of about two hundred paces, there stand on end three other large, rude stones, which I therefore note particularly, because there are also four or five stones erected at such a distance from that circular Monument, which they call *King's stones* near *Little Rolrich*, in Oxfordshire As for the name of *Buarth Arthur*, it is only a nick-name of the vulgar, whose humour it is, though not so much (as some have imagined) out of ignorance and credulity, as a kind of Rustick diversion, to dedicate many unaccountable Monuments to the memory of that Hero; calling some stones of several tun weight his *Coits*, others his *Tables*, *Chairs*, &c But *Meineu gwyr* is so old a name, that it seems scarce intelligible *Meineu* is indeed our common word for large stones, but *gwyr* in the present British signifies only *crooked*, which is scarce applicable to these stones, unless we should suppose them to be so denominated, because some of them are not at present directly upright, but a little inclining

inclining It may be, such as take these circular Monuments for *Druid-Temples* may imagin them so call'd from *bowing*, as having been places of *worship* For my part, I leave every man to his conjecture, and shall only add, that near *Capel Kirig* in Caernarvonshire, there is a stone pitch'd on end, call'd also *Maen gwyr*, which perhaps is the only stone now remaining, of such a circular Monument as this At least-wise it has such a *Kist vaen* by it (but much less) as that which we observ'd in the midst of the Monument, describ'd in Glamorganshire, by the name of *Karn Lhechart*]

Seeing we find it not recorded, which of the Normans first extorted this Country out of the hands of the Princes of *Wales*; Order requires that we now proceed to the description of *Pembrokshire*, [having first observ'd that of late, *Carmarthen* hath given the title of Marquiss to *Thomas Osborn*, Earl of *Danby*, afterwards advanced to the more honourable title of Duke of *Leeds*, which Honours are now enjoy'd by his son] Marquifs of Carmarthen

This County has 87 *Parishes*

PENBROKSHIRE.

THE Sea, now winding it self to the south, and by a vast compass and several Creeks rendering the shore very uneven beats on all sides upon the County of *Penbroke* (commonly call'd *Penbrokshire*, and in ancient Records *The Legal County of Penbroke*, and by some, *West-Wales*, except on the east, where it is bounded with *Caer-mardhin shire*, and the north, where it borders on *Cardiganshire* It is a fertile Country for Corn, affords plenty of *Marl* and such like things to fatten and enrich the Land, as also of Coal for Fuel, and is very well stock'd with Cattel *This Country* (saith Giraldus) *affords plenty of Wheat, and is well serv'd with Sea-fish and imported Wine, and (which exceeds all other advantages) by its nearness to Ireland, enjoys a wholesom Air*

Tenbigh First, on the Southern Coast, *Tenbigh* a neat town, strongly wall'd, beholds the Sea from a dry rock, a place much noted for its harbour and for plenty of Fish (whence in British it is call'd *Dinbech y Pyskod*,) and govern'd by a Mayor and a Bailiff To the west of this place, are seen on the shore the small ruins of *Manober Castl*, call'd by Giraldus *Pyrrhus's* Manober castle *Mansion*, in whose time (as he himself informs us) *it was adorn'd with stately Towers and Bulwarks, having on the west-side a spacious Haven, and under the Wall, to the north and north-west, an excellent Fish-pond, remarkable as well for its neatness, as the depth of its water* The shore being continu'd some few miles from hence, and at length drawing in it self, the Sea on both sides comes a great way into the land, and makes Milford haven that Port which the English call *Milford haven*, than which there is none in Europe, either more spacious or secure, so many Creeks and Harbours hath it on all sides, which cut the banks like so many Fibres, and to use the Poet's words,

> *Hic exarmatum terris cingentibus æquor*
> *Clauditur, & placidam discit servare quietem*

> Here circling banks the furious winds controul,
> And peaceful waves with gentle murmurs rowl

For it contains sixteen Creeks, five Bays, and thirteen Roads, distinguish'd by their several names Nor is this Haven more celebrated for these advantages, than for Henry the seventh of happy memory landing here; who from this place gave England (at that time languishing with Civil Wars) the first Signal of better Times approaching

Penbroke At the innermost and eastern Bay of this Haven, *a long Cape* (saith Giraldus) *which is extended from Milver-dike with a forked head, shews the principal town of this Province, and the Metropolis of* Dimetia, *seated on a rocky oblong Promontory, in the most pleasant Country of all Wales, call'd by the Britains* Penvro, *which signifies the* Cape *or* Sea-Promontory, *and thence in English,* Penbroke *Arnulph de Montgomery, brother to Robert Earl of Shrewsbury, built this Castle in the time of King Henry the first, but very meanly, with Stakes only and green Turf Who returning afterwards into England, he deliver'd it to Girald of Windsor, a prudent man, his Constable and Lieutenant General, who with a small garison was presently besieged therein, by all the Forces of South-Wales* But *Giraldus* and his party made such resistance (tho' more with courage, than strength) that they were forced to retire, without success Afterward, this *Giraldus* fortify'd both Town and Castle, from whence he annoy'd and insulted the neighbouring Countries a great way round And for the better settlement of himself and his friends in this Country, he marry'd *Nest*, the sister of Prince *Gryffyth*, by whom he had a noble Off-spring, *and by their means* saith Giraldus, who was descended from him, *not only the Maritim parts of South Wales were retain'd by the English, but also the Walls of Ireland reduced* For all those noble Families in Ireland call'd *Giralds, Geraldines*, and *Fitz Giralds*, are descended from him Or[illegible] of the [illegible] in Ireland *In regard of the Tenure of this Castle and Town, and the Castle and Town of Tinbigh, and of the Grange of King's Wood, the Commot of Croyteyrath, and Manors of Castle-Martin and Tregent*, Reginald Rotulus [illegible] orum *Grey*, at the Coronation of Henry the fourth, claim'd the honour of bearing the second Sword, but in vain, for it was answer'd, that at that time those Castles and Towns were in the King's hands, as is also at this day the Town of *Pembroke*, which is a Corporation, and is govern'd by a Mayor and two Baylifs

Carew castle On another Bay of this Haven, we find *Carew castle*, which gave both name and original to the illustrious Family of *Carew*, who affirm themselves to have been call'd at first *de Montgomery*, and that they are descended from that *Arnulph de Montgomery* already mention'd

Two Rivers are discharg'd into this Haven, almost in the same Chanel, call'd in the British tongue *Cledheu*, which in English signifie a Cledheu

Sword,

Sword, whence they call it *Aber-dau-Gledheu*, i. e. *the Haven of two Swords* Hard by the more easterly of them, standeth *Slebach*, once a *Commandery* of the Knights of St John of Jerusalem, which, with other Lands, *Wizo* and his son *Walter* settled upon that holy Order, that they might serve, as the Champions of Christ, in order to recover the *Holy*-Land

Slebach

That part of the Country which lies beyond the Haven, and is water'd only with these two rivers, is call'd by the Britains *Rhos* a name, deriv'd from the situation, for it is a large green plain This part is inhabited by *Flemings*, who settled here by the permission of King Henry the first, when the Sea, making breaches in the fences, had drown'd a considerable part of the *Low-Countreys* They are at this day distinguish'd from the Welsh by their speech and customs and they speak a language so much English (which indeed has a great affinity with the Dutch) that this small Country of theirs is call'd by the Britains *Little England beyond Wales* *This* (saith Giraldus) *is a stout and resolute Nation, and very troublesom to the Welsh by their frequent skirmishes a people excellently skill'd in the business of cloathing and merchandize, and always ready to increase their stock at any pains or hazard, by sea and land A most puissant Nation, and equally prepar'd, as time and place shall require, either for the sword or the plow And to add one thing more, a Nation most devoted to the Kings of England, and faithful to the English*, and which, in the time of Giraldus, understood Soothsaying, or the inspection of the Entrails of beasts, even to admiration Moreover, the *Flemings-way*, which was a work of theirs (as they are a People exceeding industrious,) is here extended through a long tract of ground The Welsh, endeavouring to regain their old country, have often set upon these Flemings with all their power, and have ravag'd and spoil'd their borders, but they have always been ready, with great courage, to defend their fortunes, their fame, and their lives Whence William of Malmsbury writes thus of them, and of William Rufus, *William Rufus had, generally, but ill fortune against the Welsh, which one may well wonder at, seeing all his attempts elsewhere prov'd successful But I am of opinion, that as the unevenness of their country and severity of the Climate favour'd their rebellion, so it hinder'd his progress But King Henry, that now reigns, a man of excellent wisdom, found out an art to frustrate all their inventions, by planting* Flemings *in their country, to curb and be a continual guard upon them* And again in the fifth Book, *King Henry, by many expeditions, endeavour'd to reduce the Welsh, who were always prone to rebellion At last, very advisedly, in order to abate their pride, he transplanted thither all the* Flemings *that liv'd in England For at that time there were many of them come over on account of their relation to his mother, by their father's side, insomuch that they were burdensome to the Kingdom wherefore, he thrust them all into* Ros, *a Province of Wales, as into a common shore, as well to rid the kingdom of them, as to curb the obstinacy of his enemies*

Rhos

Flemings, when seated in Wales

Little England beyond Wales

Flemings-way

[To this we may add what Dr *Powel* hath deliver'd upon this occasion, in his * History of Wales

* P 277

In the year 1217 *Prince* Lhewelyn ap Jorwerth *march'd to* Dyved, *and being at* Kevn Kynwarchan, *the* Flemings *sent to him to desire a Peace, but the Prince would not grant them their request Then young* Rys *was the first that pass'd the river* Kledheu, *to fight with those of the town* [*of* Haverford] *whereupon* Jorweth, *Bishop of St David's, with all his Clergy, came to the Prince, to intercede for Peace in behalf of the Flemings, which after long debating was thus concluded First, That all the Inhabitants of* Ros, *and the Land of* Penbroke *should become the Prince's subjects, and ever from thenceforth take him for their liege Lord Secondly, That they should pay him one thousand Marks toward his charges, before Michaelmas next coming Thirdly, that for the performance of these, they should deliver forthwith to the Prince twenty* Pledges *of the best in all the Country*, &c ---And again, *In the year* 1220 Lhewelyn *Prince of Wales led an Army to* Penbroke *against the Flemings, who contrary to their Oath and League had taken the Castle of* Aber Teivi, *which Castle the Prince destroy'd (putting the Garrison to the sword,) and ras'd the Castle, and went thence to the Land of* Gwys, *where he ras'd that Castle, and burn'd the Town Also he caus'd all* Haverford *to be burn'd to the Castle-gates, and destroy'd all* Ros *and* Daugledhau, *and they that kept the Castle sent to him for Truce till May, which was concluded upon Conditions, and so he return'd home*]

P 279

Wiston

On the more westerly of these two rivers call'd *Cledheu*, in a very uneven situation, lies *Harford-west*, call'd by the English formerly *Haverford*, and by the Britains, *Hwlfordh* a town of good account, as well for its neatness, as number of inhabitants It is also a County of it self, and is govern'd by a Mayor, a Sheriff, and two Bayliffs There is a Tradition, that the Earls of *Clare* fortify'd it on the north-side with walls and a rampire, and we have it recorded, that *Richard* Earl of *Clare* made *Richard Fitz-Tankard* Governour of this Castle

Haverford-west

Beyond *Ros*, is a spacious Promontory, extended with a huge front into the Irish Sea, call'd by Ptolemy *Octopitarum*, by the Britains *Pebidiog* and *Kantref Dewi*, and in English St *David's Land* *A Land* (saith Giraldus) *both rocky and barren, neither clad with trees, nor divided with rivers, nor adorn'd with meadows, but exposed continually to the winds and storms* however, it was the retiring-place and nursery of several Saints For *Calphurnius* a British Priest (as some have written, I know not how truly) begat here, in the vale of *Rhôs*, St *Patrick* the Apostle of Ireland, on his wife *Concha*, sister of St Martin of Tours And *Dewi*, a most Religious Bishop translated the Archiepiscopal See from *Kaer Leon* to the utmost corner of this place, viz *Menevia* or *Menevia*, which, from him, was afterwards call'd by the Britains *Ty Dewi*, i e *David's House*, by the Saxons Davidsmynster, and by our modern English, *St David's* For a long time, it had its Archbishops, but the plague raging very much in this Country, the Pall was translated to *Dol* in Little Britain, which was the end of this Archiepiscopal dignity Notwithstanding which, in later Ages, the Britains commenced an Action on that account, against the Archbishop of Canterbury, Metropolitan of England and Wales, but were cast What kind of place St *David's* was heretofore, is hard to guess, seeing it has been so often sack'd by Pirates at present, it is a very mean city, and shews only a fair Church consecrated to St *Andrew* and St *David* Which having been often demolish'd, was built in the form we now see it, in the reign of King John, by *Peter* then Bishop thereof and his successors, in the *Vale* of *Rhos* (as they call it) under the town Not far from it, is the Bishop's Palace and a very fair house, of the Chanter (who is chief next the Bishop, for here is no Dean), the Chancellor, the Trea-

Octopitarum.

St David's Land

St Patrick

St David's

surer,

* 8 Canons. surer, and four Archdeacons, who are * of the Canons (whereof there are twenty-one,) all inclos'd with a strong and stately Wall.

[As to the ancient name of St. *David's*, there is, not far from it, a place at this day call'd Melin Meneu. *Melin Meneu*, wherein is preserv'd the old denomination. But the original signification of the Word *Meneu* is now lost, and perhaps not to be retriev'd. However, I would recommend it to the curious in Ireland and Scotland (where the names of places agree much with those in Wales) to consider whether it may not signify a *Frith* or narrow Sea. For we find the Chanel betwixt *Caernarvonshire* and the Isle of *Anglesey* to be call'd *Aber-meneu*, and there is here also a small *Fretum*, call'd the Sound, betwixt this Place and the Isle of Ramsey; and another place call'd *Meny*, hard by a Frith in Scotland, in the County of *Buquhan*.]

This Promontory is so far extended westward, that in a clear day you may see Ireland, and from hence is the shortest passage into it. Pliny erroneously computed Ireland to be thirty miles distant from the Country of the *Silures*, for he thought their country had extended thus far. But we may gather from these words of *Giraldus*, that this Cape was once extended farther into the Sea, and that the form of the Promontory has been alter'd. Trunks and Stumps of trees in the Sea. *At such time as Henry the second* (saith he) *was in Ireland, by reason of an extraordinary violence of storms, the sandy shores of this coast were laid bare, and the face of the land appear'd which had been cover'd for many ages. Also the Trunks of trees, which had been cut down, were seen standing in the midst of the sea, and the strokes of the axe as fresh as if they had been yesterday, with very black earth, and several old blocks like Ebony. So that now it did not appear like the sea shore, but rather resembled a grove (made by a miraculous Metamorphosis, perhaps ever since the time of the Deluge, or else long after, at leastwise very anciently,) as well cut down, as consum'd and swallow'd up by degrees, by the violence of the sea, continually encroaching upon and washing off the land.* And that saying of *William Rufus*, shews that the lands were not here disjoyn'd by any great sea, who when he beheld Ireland from these rocks, said, he could easily make a bridge of ships, whereby he might walk from England into that Kingdom, as we read in Giraldus.

[Besides this instance of the Sea-sands being wash'd off, we find the same to have happen'd about the year 1590. For Mr *George Owen*, who liv'd at that time, and is † mention'd in this work as a learned and ingenious person, gives us the following account of it in a Manuscript History of this County.

† Pag. 758. See below, at Kemes.

About twelve or thirteen years since, it happen'd that the sea-sands at Newgal, *which are cover'd every tide, were by some extraordinary violence of the Waves so wash'd off, that there appear'd stocks of Trees, doubtless in their native places, for they retain'd manifest signs of the strokes of the axe, at the falling of them. The Sands being wash'd off, in the winter, these Buts remain'd to be seen all the summer following, but the next year the same were cover'd again with the sands. By this it appeareth, that the Sea in that place hath intruded upon the Land. Moreover, I have been told by the neighbours of* Coed Iraeth *near Tenby, that the like hath been seen also upon those Sands,* &c. To this an ingenious and inquisitive Gentleman of this Country, adds, that the same hath been observ'd of late years near *Capel Stinan* or St. *Justinian's*; where were seen not only the roots or stocks of Trees, but also divers pieces of squar'd timber. As for roots or stumps, I have often observ'd them my self at a low ebb, in the Sands betwixt *Borth* and *Aber Dyvy* in Cardiganshire, but remember nothing of any impression of the Axe on them; but on the contrary, that many of them, if not all, were very smooth, and that they appear'd, as to substance, more like the cole-black Peat or Fuel-turf, than Timber.]

There are excellent and noble *Falcons* that breed in these rocks, which our King Henry the second (as the same Giraldus informs us) was wont to prefer to all others. Falcons. And (unless I am deceiv'd by some of that neighbourhood) they are of that kind which they call *Peregrins*. For, according to the account they give of them, I need not use other words to describe them, than the verses of that excellent Poet of † our age, *Jacobus Thuanus Aemerus*, in that golden book which he entitles *Hieracosophion*.

† So said Ann. 1607.

Depressus capitis vertex, oblongaque toto
Corpore pennarum series, pallentia crura,
Et graciles digiti ac sparsi, naresque rotundæ.

Flat heads, and Feathers laid in curious rows
O'er all their parts, hook'd beaks, and slender claws.

The sea with great violence beats upon the land retiring from this Promontory, which is a small region call'd the Lordship of *Kemaes*. Barony of Kemes. In it we first meet with *Fiscard*, Fiscard. seated on a steep rock, and having a convenient harbour for shipping; so call'd by the English from a *Fishery* there, and by the Britains, *Aber Gwain*, which signifies the mouth of the river *Gwain*. Next, is *Newport* on the river *Neverin*, call'd in British *Trev-draeth*, which signifies *the town on the sand*. Newport. This was built by *Martin of Tours*, whose posterity made it a Corporation, and granted it several privileges, and constituted therein a *Portreeve* and Bayliffs, and themselves built a Castle above the town, which was their chief seat. They also founded the Monastery of St. *Dogmael* on the bank of the river *Tivy*, in a Vale encompass'd with hills, from which the village adjoyning (as many other towns did from Monasteries) took its beginning. Dogmael, or St. Dogmael. This Barony was first taken out of the hands of the Welsh, by *Martin of Tours*, from whose posterity (call'd from him *Martins*) it descended by marriage to the Barons *de Audeley*. Kemes. The family of the Martins. They held it a long time, till, in the reign of King Henry the eighth, *William Owen*, descended from a daughter of Sir *Nicholas Martin*, after a tedious suit at law for his right, obtain'd it at last and left it to his son *George*, who (being an exquisite Antiquary,) has inform'd me, that there are in this Barony, besides the three Boroughs (*Newport*, *Fishgard*, and St. *Dogmael*) twenty Knights fees and twenty six Parishes.

More inward, on the river *Tivy* already mention'd, lies *Kil Garan*, Kil Garan. which shews the ruins of a Castle built by Giraldus. But now, being reduced to one street, it is famous for nothing but a plentiful *Salmon Fishery*. For there is a very famous *Salmon Leap*, The Salmon Leap. where the river falls headlong, and the Salmons, making up from the Sea towards the Shallows of the river, when they come to this cataract, bend their tails to their mouths (nay sometimes, that they may leap with greater force, hold it in their teeth,) and then upon disengaging themselves from their

their circle, with a sudden violence, as when a stick that's bent is reflected, they cast themselves from the water up to a great height, to the admiration of the spectators which *Ausonius* thus describes very elegantly

> *Nec te puniceo rutilantem viscere, Salmo,*
> *Transierim, latæ cujus vaga verbera caudæ,*
> *Gurgite de medio summas referuntur in undas*

> Nor thou, red Salmon, shalt be last in fame,
> Whose flirting tail cuts through the deepest stream,
> With one strong jerk the wondring flood deceives,
> And sporting mounts thee to the utmost waves

[There are in this County several such circular stone Monuments, as that describ'd in *Caer-mardhen-shire* by the name of *Meineu gwyr*, and *Karn Lhechart* in Glamorganshire But the most remarkable, is that which is call'd *y Gromlech*, near *Pentre Evan* in *Nevern* Parish, where are seveal rude stones, pitch'd on end, in a circular order, and in the midst of the circle, a vast rude stone placed on several pillars The diameter of the *Area* is about fifty foot The stone supported in the midst of this circle is eighteen foot long, and nine in breadth, and at the one end it is about three foot thick, but thinner at the other There lies also by it a piece broken off, about ten foot in length, and five in breadth, which seems more than twenty Oxen can draw It is supported by three large rude Pillars, about eight foot high, but there are also five others, which are of no use at present, as not being high enough, or duly placed, to bear any weight of the top-stone Under this stone, the ground is neatly flagg'd, considering the rudeness of Monuments of this kind I can say nothing of the number and height of the stones in the circle, not having seen this Monument my self; but this account I have of it, is out of Mr *George Owen*'s Manuscript History above-mention'd, which was communicated to me by the worshipful *John Lewis* of *Manour Nowen*, Esquire And I have also receiv'd a description of it from a person, who at my request lately view'd it, not differing, materially, from that which we find in the Manuscript The name of this Monument seems much of the same signification with *Meineu gwyr*, for *Krwm*, in the Feminine gender *Krom*, signifies (as well as *gwyr*) *crooked* or *bending*, and *Llech*, a *stone* of a *flat* form, more or less, whether natural or artificial And as we have observ'd another Monument in *Caernarvonshire*, call'd *Llech* or *Maen gwyr*, so we meet with several in *Anglesey*, and some in other parts of *Wales* call'd *Kromlecheu* Now, that these Monuments have acquir'd this name from *bowing*, as having been places of worship in the time of Idolatry, I have no warrant to affirm However, in order to farther enquiry, we may take notice, that the Irish Historians call one of their chiefest Idols *Cromcruach*, which remain'd till St *Patrick*'s time in the plain of *Moy-sleucht* in *Brefin* This Idol is describ'd to have been *carv'd, with gold and silver*, and said to be attended with twelve others much less, all of brass, placed round about him *Cromcruach*, at the approach of St *Patrick*, fell to the ground, and the lesser Idols sunk into the earth up to their necks the heads whereof (says one of the authors of the life of St Patrick, cited by *Colganus*) are, in perpetual memory of this miracle, still prominent out of the ground, and to be seen at this day Now altho' we should question the authority of this Writer, as to these miracles, yet if we may be allow'd to make any use at all of such Histories, we may from hence infer, that this circle of stones (which are here mention'd by the name of *Idol*'s heads) was, before the planting of Christianity in this Country, a place of Idolatrous worship And if that be granted, we shall have little reason to doubt, but that our *Kromlech*, as well as all other such circular Stone-monuments in Britain and Ireland (of which, I presume, there are not less than one hundred yet remaining) were also erected for the same use But to proceed farther, this relation of Idolatrous worship at *Crumcruach*, seems much confirm'd by the general Tradition concerning such Monuments in Scotland For upon perusal of some Letters on this subject, from the learned and judicious Dr *James Garden*, Professor of Divinity at Aberdeen, to an ingenious Gentleman of the Royal Society *, (who, for what I can learn, was the first that suspected these Circles for *Temples of the Druids*,) I find that in several parts of that Kingdom, they are call'd Chapels and Temples, with this farther Tradition, that they were places of worship in the time of Heathenism, and did belong to the *Drounich* Which word some interpret *the Picts*, but Dr *Garden* suspects that it might originally denote *the Druids* in confirmation whereof, I add, that a village in Anglesey is call'd *Tre'r Driw*, and interpreted *the Town of the Druid* Now the diminutive of *Driw* must be *Driwin* (whence, perhaps, *Kaer Dreuin* in *Merionydhshire*,) and *ch* is well known to be an usual Irish termination in such Nouns

As for such as contend that all Monuments of this kind, were erected by the Danes, as Trophies, Seats of Judicature, places for electing their Kings, *&c* they will want History to prove, that ever the Danes had any Dominion, or indeed the least Settlement in Wales or the High-lands of Scotland, where yet such Monuments are as frequent, if not more common, than in other places of Britain For although we find it register'd, that they have several times committed depredations on our Sea-coasts, destroying some Maritim places in the Counties of *Glamorgan*, *Pembroke*, *Cardigan*, and *Anglesey*, and sometimes also making excursions into the Country yet we read, that they made no longer stay, than whilst they plunder'd the Religious Houses, and extorted money and provisions from the people Now, if it be demanded, why they might not, in that short stay, erect these Monuments, I have nothing to answer, but that such vast perennial memorials seem rather to be the work of a people settled in their Country, than of such roving Pirates, who for their own Security must be continually on their guard, and consequently have but small leisure, or reason, for erecting such lasting Monuments And, that we find also these Monuments in the Mountains of *Caernarvonshire*, and divers other places, where no history does inform us, nor conjecture suggest, that ever the Danes have been To which may be added, that if we strictly compare the descriptions of the Danish and Swedish Monuments in *Saxo Grammaticus*, *Wormius*, and *Rudbeckius*, with our's in Britain, we shall find considerable difference in the order or structure of them For (if we may place that here) I find none of them comparable to that magnificent, tho' barbarous Monument, on Salisbury Plain, nor any that has such a table in the midst, as our *Kromlech*

* Joh. Aubrey of Easton Pierce in Wiltshire Esq

Y Gromlech

here describ'd; whereas several of ours in Wales have it, though it be usually much less; and very often this Table or a *Kist-vaen* is found without any circle of stones, and sometimes on the contrary circles of stones, without any *Kist-vaen* or other stone in the midst. But this we need not so much insist upon; for tho' they should agree exactly, yet are we not therefore oblig'd to acknowledge that our Monuments were erected by the Danes. For as one Nation since the planting of Christianity hath imitated another, in their Churches, Chapels, Sepulchral Monuments, *&c.* so also in the time of Paganism, the Rites and Customs in Religion must have been deriv'd from one Country to another. And I think it probable, should we make diligent enquiry, that there may be Monuments of this kind still extant in the less frequented places of Germany, France, and Spain, if not also in Italy. But I fear I have too long detained the Reader with probabilities, and shall therefore only add, that whatever else hath been the use of these Monuments, it is very evident they have been (some of them at least) us'd as burial places; seeing Mr *Aubrey* in that part of his *Monumenta Britannica* which he entitles *Templa Druidum*, gives us some instances of human Skeletons, found on the outside of one or two of them in Wiltshire. And Dr *Garden* in his forementioned Letters, affirms that some persons yet living have dug ashes out of the bottom of a little circle (set about with stones standing close together) in the center of one of these Monuments, near the Church of *Keig* in the Shire of *Aberdeen*; and adds farther, that in the Shire of *Inverness*, and Parish of Enner Allen, there is one of these Monuments, call'd the Chapel of *Ti'agorum*, alias *Capel Mac mulach*, which is full of Graves, and was, within the memory of some living, an ordinary place of burial, at least for poor people, and continues to be so at this day for strangers, and children that dye without baptism.

We have not room here to take notice of the other Monuments of this kind, which this County affords; and shall therefore only observe, that in *Newport* Parish there are five of these *Tables* or *Altars* (that we may distinguish them by some name,) placed near each other, which some conjecture to have been once encompass'd with a circle of Stone-pillars, for that there are two stones yet standing near them. But these are nothing comparable in bigness to the *Grom'ech* here describ'd, nor rais'd above three foot high; nor are they supported with pillars, but stones placed edgewise; and so are rather of that kind of Monuments which we call *Kist-vaen* or Stone-chests, than *Krom-lechs*.

I had almost forgot to acquaint the Reader, that there is also in *Nevern* Parish, besides the *Grom'ech*, another Monument call'd commonly

Llech y Drybedh *Llech y Drybedh* i.e. *Tripodium*; and by some the *Altar stone*. It is of somewhat an oval form, and about twelve yards in circumference, and placed on four stones (whereof one is useless, as not touching it) scarce two foot high. At the south end, it is about four foot and a half in thickness, but sensibly thinner to the other end, where it exceeds not four inches; at which end there is cut such a *Ductus* or Conveyance, as might serve to carry off any liquid that should run down; but to what purpose it was design'd, I shall not pretend to conjecture.

Y maen Sigl *Y maen sigl*, or the *Rocking stone*, deserves also to be mention'd here; although (having never seen it myself) I am not fully satisfy'd, whether it be a Monument, or, as Mr *Owen* seems to suppose, purely accidental. But by the account I hear of it, I suspect it rather an effect of human industry, than chance. *This shaking stone* (says he) *may be seen on a Sea-cliff within half a mile of St. David's; it is so vast, that I presume it may exceed the draught of an hundred Oxen; and it is altogether rude and unpolish'd. The occasion of the name is, for that being mounted upon divers other stones, about a yard in height; it is so equally pois'd, that a man may shake it with one Finger, so that five or six men sitting on it, shall perceive themselves mov'd thereby.* But I am inform'd, that since this worthy Gentleman wrote the History of this County (*viz.* in the late Civil wars) some of the Rebel-soldiers looking upon it as a thing much noted, and therefore superstitious, did, with some difficulty, so alter its position, as to render it almost immoveable. There is also a Rocking stone in Ireland in the County of *Dunegal*, and Parish of *Clunmany*, no less remarkable than this, call'd by the vulgar *Magarl Ibin mhic Cuill*, which is describ'd to be of a vast bigness, and somewhat of a pyramidal form, placed on a flat stone, the small end downward; but whether by accident or human industry, I must leave to further enquiry.

In the Church-yard at *Nevern* on the north side, I observ'd a rude stone pitch'd on end, about two yards in height, of a triquetrous form, with another smaller angle, having on the south side this Inscription, which seems older than the foundation of the Church. It was, perhaps, the Epitaph of a Roman Soldier; for I guess it must be read *Vitaliani Emeriti*. Nevern.

In the same Church-yard, on the south side, is erected a very handsome pillar, as the shaft or pedestal of a Cross. It is of a quadrangular form, about two foot broad, eighteen inches thick, and thirteen foot high, neatly carv'd on all sides with certain endless knots, which are about one and thirty in number, and all different sorts. The top is covered with a cross stone, below which there is a Cross carv'd on the east and west sides, and about the midst these Letters

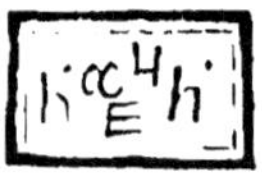

which perhaps are no other than the initial letters of the names of those persons that erected this Cross. But whatever they may signify, the second character is such as I have not met with elsewhere, and therefore I thought it worth the publishing.

There is also an Inscription within this Church, which to me is equally obscure, and seems more like Greek than Roman Characters, of which the following Copy was sent me by Mr *William Gambold* of Exeter College, *Oxon*, who, I presume, hath transcrib'd it with due exactness.

V/OICUNNE

The stone is pitch'd on end, not two foot high, and is round at top (about which these Letters are cut) like the Monument describ'd at *Mynydh Gelhi Onnen* in Glamorganshire

I receiv'd also from the same hand the following Inscription, copy'd from a stone amongst the ruins of the Abbey of St *Dogmael*, which he describes to be seven foot in length, two in breadth, and six inches thick

St Dogmael

SASRANI FILI
CVNOTAMI

The latter of these words [*Cunotami*] I take to be a British name, and the same with what we call *Kynedha* or *Kynedhav*, but the former is a name which I cannot parallel with any that are now us'd, or that are extant in our Genealogical Manuscripts

Barrows.

In this County, are divers ancient *Tumuli*, or artificial Mounts for Urn-burial, whereof the most notable I have seen, are those four call'd *Krigeu Kemaes*, or the Barrows of *Kemaes* One of these, a Gentleman of the neighbourhood *, out of curiosity, and for the satisfaction of some friends, caus'd lately to be dug, and discover'd therein five Urns, which contain'd a considerable quantity of burnt bones and ashes One of these Urns, together with the bones and ashes it contain'd, was presented to the *Ashmolean Repository* at Oxford, by the worshipful *John Philips* of *Dôl Hadh*, Esquire I shall not pretend to determin what Nation these Barrows did belong to, though from the rudeness of the Urns, as well in respect of matter as fashion, some might suspect them rather Barbarous than Roman But we know not how unskilful some Artists amongst the Romans might be, especially in these remote parts of the Province, where probably not many of them, besides military persons, ever settled Another Urn was found not many years since, in a Barrow in the Parish of *Melineu*, and one very lately on a mountain not far from *Kil Rhedyn*

* Mr Lloyd of Kwm Gloin.

But seeing the design of this Work is not confin'd to Antiquities and Civil History, but sometimes, for the Reader's diversion, is extended also to such occurrences in *Nature*, as seem more especially remarkable; I hope it may be excusable if I add here some few observations in that kind and shall therefore communicate part of a Letter from my ingenious Friend, the Reverend Mr *Nicholas Roberts*, A. M Rector of *I han Dhewi Velfrey*, which contains an account of some *migratory* Sea birds that breed in the Isle of Ramsey, with some other relations that seem remarkable

Ramsey-Island

Over against Justinian's *Chapel, and separated from it by a narrow* Fretum, *is* Ramsey Island *(call'd formerly* Ynis Devanog *from a Chapel there dedicated to that Saint, now swallow'd up by the sea) which seems by the proverb* [Stinan a Devanog dau anwyl gymydog] *to have been once part of the* Continent, *if I may properly call our Country so, when I speak of such small Insulets In it there is a small promontory or neck of land, issuing into the sea, which is call'd* Ynis yr hyrdhod *, *whence I presume is the name of* Ramsey *To this Island, and some rocks adjoyning, call'd by the sea men* The Bishop and his Clerks, *do yearly resort about the beginning of April such a number of birds of several sorts, that none but such as have been eye witnesses can be prevail'd upon to believe it, all which, after breeding here, leave us before August They come to these rocks, and also leave them, constantly in the night time for in the evening the rocks shall be cover'd with them, and the next morning not a bird to be seen, so in the evening not a bird shall appear, and the next Morning the rocks shall be full They also visit us commonly about Christmas, and stay a week or more, and then take their leave till breeding time Three sorts of these* Migratory *birds are call'd in Welsh,* Mora, Poeth wy, *and* Pâl; *in English,* Eligug, Razorbil, *and* Puffin, *to which we may also add the* Harry-bird, *though I cannot at present assure you, whether this bird comes and goes off with the rest*

* Id est, Rams Island

The † Eligug *lays but one egg, which (as well as those of the* Puffin *and* Razorbil) *is as big as a Duck's, but longer, and smaller at one end From this egg she never parts (unless forced) till she hatches it, nor then till the young one be able to follow her, being all the while fed by the male This and the* Razorbil ‖ *breed upon the bare rocks, making no manner of nest, and sometimes in such a place, that being frighten'd thence, the egg or young one (which before was upheld by the breast, upon a narrow shelving rock) tumbles into the sea The* Puffin * *and* Harry-bird † *breed in holes, either those of Rabbets (wherewith* Ramsey *is abundantly furnish'd, all black) or such as they dig with their beaks The* Harry birds *are never seen on land, but when taken, and the manner of taking these and the* Puffins, *is commonly by planting nets before their berries, wherein they soon entangle themselves These four sorts cannot raise themselves upon the wing, from the land, but, if at any Distance from the cliffs,* waddle *(for they cannot be well said to go, their legs being too infirm for that use, and placed much more backward than a Duck's, so that they seem to stand upright) to some precipice, and thence cast themselves off, and take wing but from the water they will raise to any height The* Puffin *lays three white eggs, the rest but one, speckled, &c*

† Lomwia Hoieri in Epist ad Clusium In Cornwal it is call'd a *Kiddaw*, and in Yorkshire a *Skout* See Willoughby's Ornithology, pag 324

‖ *Alka Hoieri* in Epist ad Clusium Murre Cornubiens Wil p. 323

* Anas Arctica Clusii, Fratercula Gesneri. Wil p 325

† The Shearwater of Sir Tho Brown Wil p. 334 Tab ult

He adds much more of the other birds that frequent these Rocks; and also gives a short account of several things remarkable in this County; but being confin'd within narrow limits, I shall only select two of them The first is of a narrow deep pond, or rather pit, near the sea side, and some Cliffs which by their noise presage storms, &c whereof he gives the following relation

Near Stack pool Bosher, *otherwise* Bosherston, *upon the sea side, is a pool or pit call'd* Bosherston-mear; *the depth whereof, several that have sounded, have not yet discover'd This pit bubbles and foams, and makes such a noise before stormy weather, that it is heard above ten miles off The banks are of no great circumference at the top, but broader downwards, and from the bottom, there is a great breach towards the sea, which is about a furlong distant So that, considering the bubbling, and the extraordinary noise this pit makes against stormy weather, I am apt to suspect it may have a subterraneous communication with the sea water But there is much more talk'd of this place, than I shall trouble you with at present, because I take some relations of it for fabulous;*

lous; and living remote from it myself, I have had no opportunities of being satisfy'd of the truth from others. Its noise is distinctly known from that of the sea; which also on these coasts often roars very loud And the neighbouring inhabitants to the sea, can give a shrewd guess what weather will ensue by the noise it makes For when it proceeds from such a Creek *or* Haven, *they will expect this or that sort of weather will follow And by these Observations, I have been told the Evening before, what weather we should have next day, which has happen'd very true, and that not once, as by chance, but often*

The other, is a sort of *Food*, made in several parts of this County, of a Sea plant, which, by the description I hear of it, I take it to be the *Oyster green* or *Lectuca marina* This Custom I find obtains also in Glamorganshire (where it is call'd *Laverbread*) as also in several parts of Scotland and Ireland, and probably in some Counties of England

Near St David's (says he) *especially at* Eglwys Abeinon, *and in other places, they gather, in the spring time, a kind of* Alga *or sea-weed, with which they make a sort of food call'd* Lhavan *or* Lhawvin, *in English* Black butter *Having gather'd the weed, they wash it clean from sand and slime, and sweat it between two tile stones, then they shred it small, and knead it well, as they do dough for bread, and make it up into great balls or rolls, which some eat raw, and others, fry'd with oatmeal and butter It is accounted sovereign against all distempers of the liver and spleen and the late Dr* Owen *assured me, that he found relief from it in the acutest fits of the stone*]

Earls of Penbroke.

There have been divers Earls of Penbroke descended from several families As for *Arnulph of Montgomery*, who first conquer'd it, and was afterwards outlaw'd, and his *Castellan Girald* [of *Windsor*] whom King Henry the first made afterwards President over the whole country; I can scarce affirm that they were Earls King Stephen first confer'd the title of *Earl of Penbroke* upon Gilbert *Strongbow* son of Gislebert *de Clare* He left it to his son Richard *Strongbow*, the Conqueror of Ireland; who was (as Girald is has it) *e* Clara Clarensium *familia oriundus*, descended from the famous family of the *Clares* *Isabella* the only daughter of this Earl, brought this title to her husband *William Marshal* (so call'd, for that his Ancestors had been hereditary Marshals of the King's Palace,) a very accomplish'd person, and well instructed in the arts of peace and war Of whom we find this Epitaph in Rudburn's Annals

> *Sum quem Saturnum sibi sensit Hibernia, Solem*
> *Anglia, Mercurium Normannia, Gallia Martem*

> Me *Mars* the French, their *Sun* the English own'd,
> The Normans *Mercury*, Irish *Saturn* found

After him, his five sons were successively Earls of Penbroke, viz *William*, call'd *the younger*, *Richard*, who having rebell'd against Henry the third, fled into Ireland, where he dy'd in battel, *Gilbert*, who at a tournament at *Ware* was unhors'd, and so kill'd, and *Walter* and *Anselm* All these dying in a short space without issue, King Henry the third invested with the honour of this Earldom *William de Valentia*, of the family of *Lusignia* in *Poictiers*, who was his own brother by the mother's side, and marry'd *Joan*, the daughter of *Gwarin de Mont Chensey* by a daughter of William *Marshal* To *William de Valentia* succeeded his son *Audomar*, who was Governour of Scotland under King Edward the first His sister and coheir Elizabeth, being marry'd to *John* Lord Hastings, brought this title into a new family For Lawrence *Hastings* his grandchild by a son, who was Lord of Abergavenny, was made Earl of Penbroke by a Rescript of King Edward the third, a copy of which it may not be amiss to subjoyn here, that we may see what right there was, by heirs female, in these honorary titles *Rex omnibus ad quos, &c salutem Know ye, that the good presages of wisdom and virtue, which we have form'd from the towardly youth and happy beginnings of our well beloved Cousin* Lawrence Hastings, *deservedly induce us to countenance him with our especial grace and favour, in those things which concern the due preservation and maintenance of his honour Whereas therefore, the inheritance of* Aimar *of* Valence, *sometime Earl of* Penbroke *(deceas'd long since without heir begotten of his body) hath been devolv'd upon his sisters, to be proportionably divided among them and their heirs and because we know for certain, that the foresaid* Lawrence, *who succeedeth the said* Aimar *in part of the inheritance, is descended from the eldest sister of* Aimar *aforesaid, and so, by the avouching of the learned, whom we consulted in this matter, the Prerogative both of name and honour is due unto him We deem it just and due, that the same* Lawrence, *claiming his title from the elder sister, assume and have the name of* Earl *of* Penbroke, *which the said* Aimar *had whilst he liv'd Which, as much as lyeth in us, we confirm, ratify, and approve willing and granting, that the said* Lawrence *have and hold the Prerogative and honour of Earl Palatine, in those lands which he holdeth of the said* Aimar's *inheritance, as fully, and after the same manner, as the same* Aimar *had and held them, at the time of his death,* &c *Witness the King at Montmartin, the 13th day of October, in the 13th year of his reign*

This *Lawrence Hastings* was succeeded by his son *John*, who being taken by the Spaniards in a sea fight, and afterwards redeem'd, dy'd in France in the year 1375 To him succeeded his son *John*, who was kill'd in a Tournament at *Woodstock* in the year 1391 And it was observ'd of this family, that (by a certain particular Fate) no father ever saw his son, for five generations He leaving no issue, several considerable Revenues devolv'd to the Crown and the Castle of Penbroke was granted to *Francis At court*, a Courtier of that time in great favour, who, upon this account, was commonly call'd *Lord of Penbroke* And not long after, John Duke of Bedford, and after him his brother *Humfrey* Duke of Glocester, sons of King Henry the fourth, obtain'd the same title After that, *William de la Pole* was made *Marquiss* of Penbroke, upon whose decease King Henry the sixth created *Jasper de Hatfield* his brother by the mother's side, Earl of Penbroke; who, being afterwards divested of all his Honours by King Henry the fourth, was succeeded by *William Herbert*, who was killed in the battel at *Banbury* To him succeeded a son of the same name, whom Edward the fourth, having recover'd his Kingdom, created Earl of *Huntingdon*, conferring the title of Earl of Penbroke on his eldest son *Edward* Prince of *Wales* A long time after that, King Henry the eighth entitled *Anne of Bullen* (whom he had betroth'd) Marchioness of Penbroke At last King Edward the sixth, † in our memory, invested *William Herbert*, Lord of *Caer Diff*, with the same title He was succeeded by his son *Henry*, who was President of Wales under Queen Elizabeth;

† So said anno 1607

* alter

* And now, C
† Enjoys, C

* after whom his son *William*, a person of extraordinary Accomplishments both of body and mind, † enjoy'd that honour [Upon the death of *William*, the honour of Earl of *Penbroke* descended to *Philip Herbert*, who was also Earl of *Montgomery*, and was succeeded by *Philip* his son After whose death, *William* his son and heir succeeded, as did, upon his death, *Philip Herbert*, half brother to the last William, to whom succeeded Thomas his only brother, a person of great Virtue and Learning, who now enjoys the titles of Earl of Penbroke and Montgomery]

This family of the *Herberts* is very noble, and ancient, in these parts of Wales For they derive their pedigree from *Henry Fitz Herbert*, Chamberlain to King Henry the first, who marry'd that King's ‖ Concubine, mother of *Reginald* Earl of *Cornwal*, as I am inform'd by Mr *Robert Glover*, a person of great knowledge in Genealogies, by whose untimely decease Genealogical Antiquities have suffe'd extremely Origin of the Herberts ‖ Amasium.

Parishes in this County 145

CARDIGANSHIRE.

HE Shores, obliquely retiring from *Octopitarum* or St *David's* Promontory toward the East, receive the Sea into a vast Bay, much of the form of a half-moon, on which lies the third Division of the *Dimetæ*, call'd by the English *Cardiganshire*, in British *Sir Aber Tevi*, and by Latin Writers, *Ceretica* If any shall suppose it to be denominated from King *Carattacus*, his conjecture may seem to proceed rather from a fond Opinion of his own, than from any Authority of the Ancients And yet we read, that the same renowned Prince *Caratacus* rul'd in † these parts On the west, towards the Sea, it is a champain Country; as also to the south, where the river *Teivi* divides it from *Caer Mardhin-Shire* But to the east and north, where it borders on *Brecknockshire* and *Montgomeryshire*, there is a continued ridge of Mountains, which however afford good pasture for Sheep and Cattel, and in the valleys whereof are several lakes, or natural ponds That this country was planted formerly, not with Cities but small Cottages, is gathered [by some] from that saying of their Prince *Caratacus*, who when he was a captive at Rome, having view'd the Splendour and Magnificence of that City, said, *Seeing you have these and such like noble structures, why do you covet our small cottages?* [If indeed this was subject to King *Carattacus*, which seems not evident from any place in *Tacitus* or other Author For we find no mention of the names of those Countries under his Dominion, unless we may presume the *Silures*, his Subjects, from these words of Tacitus, *Eum inde in Silures, super propriam ferociam Caractaci viribus confisos* &c From thence to the *Silures*, who besides their own natural fierceness, rely'd on the strength of *Caractacus*, &c Moreover, though we should grant him to have been King of the *Dimetæ*, yet they who are concern'd for the ancient reputation of this Country, may fairly urge, that though they accept of the authority of Zonaras, who liv'd a thousand years after, yet nothing can be collected from that Speech of *Caractacus*, that may prove this Country to have been more poorly inhabited in those times, than other Provinces, seeing it only speaks in general of the Countries in his Dominion, and that we find by his Speech in Tacitus, that he was *plurium Gentium Imperator*, Prince or Sovereign of many Countries] However, let us take a cursory view of such places as are of any Antiquity

King Caractacus

† See below

Zonaras

Annal l 12

The river *Teivi*, call'd by Ptolemy Tuerobius (corruptly for *Dwr Teivi*, which signifies the *Teivi water*,) springs out of the lake *Lhyn Teivi*, under the Mountains already mention'd At first, it is retarded by rocks, and, rumbling among the stones without any chanel, takes its course through a very stony tract (near which the Mountaineers have, at *Ros*, a very great Fair for Cattel,) to *Strat-fleur*, a Monastery heretofore of the *Cluniack Monks*, and encompass'd on all sides with mountains Tuerobius, or Teivi Ros Fair Strat-fleur, Strata florida

From hence, being receiv'd into a chanel, it runs by *Tre' Garon*, and by *Lhan Dhewi Brevi*, a Church dedicated to the memory of St *David* Bishop of *Menevia*, and thence denominated Where in a full Synod, he confuted the Pelagian heresy, at that time reviving in Britain, and that not only out of holy Scripture, but likewise by Miracle, for it is reported, that the ground on which he stood preaching, mounted up to a hillock under his feet Tre Garon. Lhan Dhewi Brevi

[This Synod for suppression of the Pelagian Heresie, was held about the year 522 For we find in some British Records, that St *Dubricius* Archbishop of *Caer Lheon*, having assisted at the Synod, and resign'd his Bishoprick to St David, betook himself that year (together with most of the Clergy who had met on that occasion) to a Monastery at *Ynys Enlhi* *, where being free from the noise of the World, they might, with less interruption, devote the remainder of their Lives to the service of God Of this retirement of St *Dubricius* and his followers, mention is made also by an eminent Poet † of that age, in these words MS. of Mr P. Vaughan of Hengwrt * Bardsey Island

Pan oedh Saint Senedh Brevi,
Drwy arch y prophwydi,
A 'bl grew bregeth Dewi,
In myned i Ynys Enlhi, &c

† Aneurin Gwawdrydh [*Aneurin Gwawdrydh*] Mychdeyrn Beirdh i.e. Aneurin the Sovereign King of Bards

At this Church of *Lhan Dhewi Brevi*, I observ'd an ancient Inscription on a Tomb stone, which is doubtless remov'd from the place where it was first laid, it being now set above the Chancel door

Upon

+ hIC IACET IdNERT FILIVS I.........
QVI OCCISVS FVIT PROPTER P......
SANCTI

Upon a Review of this Monument, it appears that the vacant Spaces at the end of each line, are ſupplied, by adding to the firſt, ACOBI, to the ſecond, REDAM, and to the third DAWID

There is alſo another old Inſcription on a Stone erected by the Church door, on the out ſide, which ſeems (as well as ſome others on Croſſes) to conſiſt wholly of Abbreviations What it may import, I ſhall not pretend to explain, but ſhall add nevertheleſs a Copy of it, leaving the ſignification to the Reader's conjecture

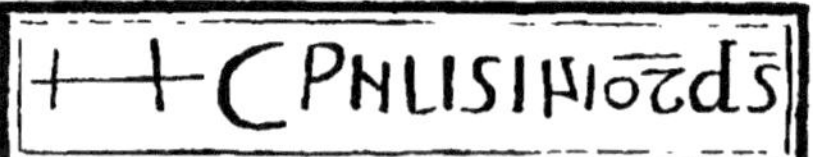

The Sexton of this place ſhew'd me a Rarity by the name of *Matkorn yr ych bannog*, or *Matkorn ych Dewi*, which he told me had been preſerv'd there ever ſince the time of St. *David*, adding the fabulous tradition of the Oxen call'd *Ychen bannog*, which I ſhall not trouble the Reader with, as being no news to ſuch as live in Wales, nor material information to others

This *Matkorn*, however, ſeem'd to me a very remarkable Curioſity For if it be not really (as the name implies) the interiour horn of an Ox, it very much reſembles it, and yet it is ſo weighty that it ſeems abſolutely petrified It is full of large cells or holes, and the circumference of it at the root, is about ſeventeen inches.

Whilſt I was copying the Inſcriptions abovementioned, a Country man told me there was another at a houſe called *Lhannio ijaf*, in this pariſh, diſtant about a mile from the Church Being come thither, I found theſe two Inſcriptions, and was informed that ſeveral others had been diſcovered by digging, but that the ſtones were applied to ſome uſes, and the Inſcriptions not regarded

Mae'r gareg, ir a uwch ben drws y Glowty

ↃARTIↃMↃ
ENNIVS
PRIMVSↃ

ƆVERIONI

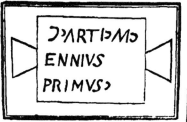

The firſt I read *Caij Artij Manibus* (or perhaps *memoriæ*) *Ennius Primus* From which name of *Primus*, I take the Church of *Lhan Dewi* to have receiv'd the addition of *Brevi*, ſeeing the Latin word *Primus* is commonly expreſſed in Welſh by Priv, and ſo, *Formus*, *Fyrv*, *Turma Twrv*, Terminus, *Tervyn*, &c Another Roman Epitaph, circumſcribed with lines, in the ſame manner as this is, may be ſeen in * *Reineſius* The Letter C reverſed (as in the firſt place of this Inſcription) denotes frequently *Caia*, but ſometimes alſo *Caius*, as may be ſeen in the ſame † Author

* Syntag In ſcr Cl I 31 LXIV

† P 72.

Ↄ SEMPRONIO, &c

This Note or Character [Ↄ] added to the firſt, fifth, ſixth and laſt letters, is ſometimes obſerv'd in other Roman Inſcriptions ‖ As for the ſecond letter of this Inſcription, we have frequent examples, on ſtones and coins, of that form of the letter A In * Reineſius, we find this Inſcription

‖ Reineſ p 755

* Pag 3

HERCVLI ARTIVS, &c

which that learned Critick directs us to read *Herculi Lartius*, but ſeeing we find here alſo the name of *Artius*, peradventure that correction was ſuperfluous

Beſides Inſcriptions of the Romans, they ſometimes find here their Coins, and frequently dig up bricks and large free-ſtone neatly wrought The place where theſe Antiquities are found, is call'd *Kae'r Keſtilh*, which ſignifies *Caſtle Field*, or to ſpeak more diſtinctly, *the Field of the Caſtles*, though at preſent there remains not above ground the leaſt ſign of any building, nor have there been any (for what I could learn) within the memory of any perſon now living in the neighbourhood, or of their Fathers or Grandfathers However, ſeeing it is thus call'd, and that it affords alſo ſuch manifeſt tokens of its being once inhabited by the Romans, we have little reaſon to doubt, but that they had a Fort or Garriſon, if not a conſiderable Town, at this place And that being granted, it will alſo appear highly probable, that what we now call *Lhannio*, was the very ſame with that which Ptolemy places in the Country of the *Dimetæ*, by the name of † *Lo antinum*, or (as it is otherwiſe read) *Lo vantium* If any ſhall urge, that to ſuppoſe it only a Caſtle, and not a City or Town of note,

† See Breknokſhire and Caermarthenſhire

note, is to grant it not to have been the old *Lovantium*; I answer, that perhaps we do but commit a vulgar Error, when we take all the Stations in the *Itinerary*, and Burroughs of Ptolemy, for considerable Towns or Cities, it being not improbable, that many of them were only Forts or Castles with the addition of a few Houses, as occasion required]

† i. e. to Lan deui brevi Lhan-Bedr

Thus † far, and farther, the river *Teivi* runs southward, to *Lhan Bedr*, a small Market town From whence directing it's course to the west, it makes a broader channel, and falling over a steep precipice, * near *Kil Garan*, makes that *Salmon Leap* which I have already † mention'd For this river abounds with Salmon, and was formerly the only river in Britain (as Giraldus supposed) that bred Beavers A Beaver is an *amphibious* animal, having the fore feet like a dog, but footed behind like a goose, of a dark gray colour, with an oblong flat *cartilagineous* tail, which, in swimming, it makes use of to steer it's course *Giraldus* makes several remarks upon the Subtilty of this creature; but at this time they are none of them found here [However, though we may not rely on the authority of Giraldus in many things he relates (as one who wrote in an age less cautious and accurate, and when nothing pleas'd so much as what excited the admiration of the Reader,) yet in this case, the price of a *Beaver's Skin* being mentioned in the Laws of *Howel Dha*, there remains no reason to question his veracity And in case there had been no such proofs that there were formerly Beavers in this Kingdom, there is no room to doubt it, in that there are two or three Ponds or Lakes in Wales, well known at this day, by the name of *Lhyn yr Avangk*, i e Beaver-pool The vulgar of our age, scarce know what creature that *Avangk* was, and therefore some have been perswaded, that it was a *Phantom* or *Apparition* which heretofore haunted Lakes and Rivers As for the name, I take it for granted that it is derived from the word *Avon*, which signifies a River, and suppose it only an abbreviation of the word *Avonog*, i e *Fluviatilis*; as *Lhwynog* (i Fox,) signifies *Sylvaticus*, from Lhwyn, *Sylva* And as for the signification, it is not to be controverted, some old Poets so describing it, that they evidently meant a *Beaver*

** In Pembrokeshire*

Kil Garan

† It is not there, but betwe en Kaermarth and Lhan Dugwyab

Beavers

Beasts in Wales

Besides the *Beaver*, we have formerly had some other Beasts in Wales, which have been long since totally destroyed As, first, *Wolves*, concerning which we read in *Meirionydh shire*, as also in *Derbyshire* and *Yorkshire* Secondly, *Roe Bucks*, called in Welsh *Iyrchod* which have given names to several places, as *Bryn yr Iwrch*, *Phynon yr Iwrch*, *Lhwyn Iwrch*, &c Thirdly, The *Wild-Boar*, of which mention is made by Dr *Davies*, at the end of his Dictionary And lastly, I have offered some Arguments to prove also that *Bears* were heretofore natives of this Island, which may be seen in Mr *Ray's Synopsis Methodica Animalium quadrupedum*]

Pag 213

Cardigan

Scarce two miles from *Kil Gâran*, lies *Cardigan*, called by the Britains *Aber Teivi*, i. e *Teivimouth*, the chief town of this County It was fortified by Gilbert, the son of *Richard Clare* but being afterwards treasonably surrender'd, it was laid waste by *Rhys ap Gryffydh*, and the Governor *Robert Fitz Stephen*, whom some call *Stephanides*, was taken prisoner who after he had remained a long time at the mercy of the enrag'd Welsh, was at length releas'd; but compell'd to resign into their hands all his possessions in Wales Whereupon, he made a descent upon Ireland, and though with a small army, yet very successfully; and was the first of the Normans, who by his valour made way for the English-Conquest of that Kingdom

Fitz Stephen

From the mouth of the *Teivi*, the shore, retiring gradually, is wash'd by several rivulets Amongst them, that which Ptolemy calls *Stuccia*, at the upper end of the County, deserves our notice; the name whereof is still preserved by the common People, who call it *Ystwyth* Near the source of the river, there are Lead-mines, [several of which have been discovered within the memory of man in this part of the County, but the most considerable that has been found in our time (either here, or in any other part of the Kingdom) is that of *Bwlch yr Eskir Hir*, discovered *Ann* 1690, which was lately the possession of Sir *Carbury Pryse* of *Gogerdhan*, Baronet, who dying without issue, and the title being extinct, was succeeded in this estate of *Gogerdhan*, by *Edward Pryse*, son of *Thomas Pryse* of Lhan Vred, Esq The Ore here was so nigh the surface of the Earth, that (as I have been credibly inform'd) the moss and grass did in some places but just cover it, which seems to add credit to that place of Pliny Nat. Hist lib 34 c 17 —— *Nigro plumbo ad fistulas laminasque utimur, laboriosius in Hispania eruto sed in Britannia summo terræ corio, adeo large, ut lex ultro dicatur, ne plus certo modo fiat* —— *in Britain it lies on the Surface of the Earth, so plentifully, that there is a Law, that more shall not be made, than a certain quantity prescribed* But because there is a Map of these Lead-mines, published by Mr *William Waller*, together with a larger account of them than can be expected here, it seems needless to add any more on this subject]

Stuccia, or the river Ystwyth

Bwlch yr Eskir hir

At the mouth of the *Teive*, is the most populous Town of the whole County, call'd *Aber-Ystwyth*, which was also fortified with walls by the above mention'd Gilbert Clare, and defended a long time by *Walter Beck* an English-man, against the *Welsh* Near this place, is *Lhan Badarn Vawr*, i e *Great St Patern's*, who (as we read in his life) *was an Armorican, and govern'd the Church here by feeding, and fed it by governing* To whose memory a Church and Bishop's See was here consecrated But the Bishoprick (as Roger Hoveden writes) fell to decay long since, *for that the People had most barbarously slain their Pastor* At the same place the river *Rheidiol* also casts it self into the Ocean having taken it course from that very high and steep hill, *Plin Lhymmon*, which is the bound of the north part of the County, and gives rise, besides this, to those two noble rivers we have already mention'd, *Severn* and *Wye* Not very far from *Aber ystwyth*, the river *Dyvy*, the boundary betwixt this County and Merionydhshire, is also discharged into the Ocean

Lhan Badarn Vawr

Rheidiol

[There are likewise in this County, several such ancient Stone Monuments as we have observ'd in the preceeding Counties, whereof I shall briefly mention such as I have seen, because they may differ in some respect from those already describ'd

Lhech yr Ast, in the parish of *Lhan Gybmor*, is a vast rude stone of about eight or nine yards in circumference, and at least half a yard thick. It is placed inclining, the one side of it on the ground, the other supported by a Pillar of about three foot high I have seen a Monument somewhat like this near *Lhan Ilern* in Glamorganshire, call'd also by a name of the same

Lhech yr Ast

same signification *Gwâl y Vilast*, which affords no information to the curious; as signifying only the *Bitch-Kennel*, because it might serve for such use *Gwâl y Vilast* is such a rude stone as this, but much longer, and somewhat of an oval form, about four yards in length, and two in breadth, supported at one end by a stone about two foot high, somewhat of the same form (though much more rude) as those we find at the head and feet of graves in Country Churches There is also by this *Llêch yr Ast*, such another Monument, but much less and lower, and five beds (such as we call *Kistieu Maen*, but not cover'd) scarce two yards long of rude stones pitch'd in the ground; as likewise a circular *area* of the same kind of stones, the diameter whereof is about four yards, but most of the stones of this circle are now fallen and, about six yards from it, there lies a stone on the ground, and another beyond that, at the same distance, which doubtless belong to it

Meineu hi[rion] *Meineu hirion* near *Neuodh* (the seat of the worshipful *David Parry* Esq, not many years since High Sheriff of Penbrokeshire) are perhaps some remaining pillars of such a circular stone monument (though much larger) as that describ'd in Caer Mardhin shire, by the name of *Meini gwyr*

Meini Kyv[rivol] *Meini kyvri ol* (or the *numerary Stones*) near the same place, seem to be also the remains of some such barbarous Monument They are nineteen stones lying on the ground confusedly, and are therefore called *Meineu Kyvrivol* by the vulgar, who cannot easily number them, of which two only seem to have been pitch'd on end

[Ll]ech y [G]owres [Gowres] d[ict], *Sax fæminæ* ... *Llêch y Gowres* * a Monument well known also in this neighbourhood) seems much more worthy our observation, being an exceeding vast stone, placed on four other very large pillars or supporters, about the height of five or six foot Besides which four, there are two others pitch'd on end under the top stone, but much lower, so that they bear no part of the weight There are also three stones (two large ones, and behind those a lesser) lying on the ground at each end of this Monument and at some distance, another rude stone, which has probably some reference to it This *Llêch y Gowres* stands on such a small bank or rising, in a plain open field, as the five stones near the circular Monument called *Rolrich stones* in Oxford shire

[M]aen [gwy]dhog [dict] *Co*... *Hir vaen guydhog* †, is a remarkable Pillar about sixteen foot high, and three foot broad, and two thick It is erected on the top of a mountain, in the confines of the parishes of *Kelham* and *Lhan y Krwys*, and is at present (for what end soever it was first set-up) the mere stone or boundary betwixt this County and Caer-Mardhin shire Not far from it, is *Maen y pren vol*, which I have not seen, but suppose, from the name, to be a Monument of the same kind that we call *Kistvaen*; for *Prenvol* in this country (in North-Wales *Prennol*) signifies a small coffer or chest

[Gwe]ly Talie[sin] *Gwely Taliesin*, in the parish of *Lhan-Vihangel gencu'r glyn*, by its name and the tradition of the neighbours concerning it, ought to be the grave of the celebrated Poet *Taliesin ben beirdh*, [Il]l. *Talie[sin]* ... *pretiova* ... who flourished about the year 540 This grave or bed (for that is the signification of the word *Gwely*) seems also to be sort a of *Kist vaen*, four foot in length, and three in breadth; composed of four stones, one at each end, and two side stones; the highest of which is about a foot above ground I take this, and all others of this kind, to be old heathen Monuments, and am far from believing that *Taliesin* was inter'd here.

But to proceed from these barbarous Monuments (which yet I take to be no more rude than those of our neighbour nations, before they were conquer'd by the Romans) to something that was later and more civilized; I shall here add an Inscription which I lately copied from a large rude stone in *Penbryn* Parish, not far from the Church It stood not long since (as I was inform'd) in a small heap of stones, close by the place where it now lies on the ground The stone is as hard as marble, and the letters large and very fair, and deeper inscrib'd than ordinary; but what they signifie, I fear must be left to the Reader's conjecture

I must confess, at first view, I thought I might venture to read it, *Cor Balencii jacit Ordous* and to interpret it, *The heart of Valentius of North-Wales lies here*, supposing that such a person might have been slain there in battel In old Inscriptions we often find the letter B used for V as *Balerius* for *Valerius*, *Bixsit for Vixsit*, *Militabit* for *Militavi*, &c and the word *Ordous* I thought not very remote from *Ordovices* But I am not satisfied with this notion of it my self, much less do I expect that others should acquiesce in it

CORBALENGHACIT
ORDOVS

In this same Parish of *Penbryn*, was found some years since, a British gold coyn, weighing (I suppose) above a Guinea, and belonging to *John Williams*, Esquire, of *Aber Nant bychan*, who was pleas'd to send me the figure of it, that is now inserted amongst some other Antiquities at the end of these Counties of Wales

From this, and many others that are found in several places of this Kingdom, it is manifest the Britains had gold and silver coyns of their own, before the Roman Conquest, unless such as contend for the contrary can make it appear that these coyns were brought in by the Phœnicians, or some other trading Nation, which I think no man has yet attempted For seeing such of these Coyns as want Inscriptions, are always a little hollow on the one side, and have also impressions or characters (if I may so call them) different from those of Roman and all other Coyns, it is very plain, that the art of coyning them was not learn'd of the Romans for if so, we had not met with these unintelligible Characters on them, but Roman letters, such as, by some coyns of † *Cassivelaunus* and *Cunobelin*, we find they make use of after their Conquest] † Brit. Kas[s]wallawn *and* Kynvelyn

The Normans had scarce settled their conquest in Britain, when they assailed this Coast with a Navy, and that with good success For in the time of William Rufus, they got the sea coasts by degrees out of the Welshmen's hands, but granted the greatest part of it to *Kadwgan ap Bledbyn*, a Britain, noted for Wisdom, and of great interest throughout all *Wales*, and at the same time in much favour with the *English* But his son *Owen*, proving a rash youth,

youth, and a hater of Peace, and annoying the English, and the Flemings who had lately settled there, with continual excursions, the unhappy father was depriv'd of his Inheritance, and forced to suffer for the offences of his son, who was also himself constrained to leave his native Country, and to flee into Ireland King Henry the first granted this County of Cardigan to *Gilbert Clare*, who planted Garrisons in it, and fortified several Castles But *Kadwgan*, with his son *Owen*, being afterwards received into favour by the English, had all his Lands restored to him Notwithstanding this, *Owen* returning again to his old ways, and raising new Troubles, was slain by Giarld of Penbroke, whose wife *Nesta* he had * ravished His father being carried prisoner into England, expected for a long time a better change of Fortune, and being at last in his old age restored to his own, was unexpectedly and on a sudden stab'd by his nephew *Madock* After that, Roger *de Clare* received Cardiganshire, by the munificence of King Henry the second but *Richard* Earl of *Clare* (his son, if I mistake not) being slain in his journey hither by land; *Rhys*, Prince of South-Wales, after he had with his victorious Army made a great slaughter of the English, reduced it at last under his subjection However, it fell afterwards by degrees, without any blood shed, into the hands of the *English*

* *Rapuerat*

[*Thomas Brudenel*, Baron Brudenel of *Stougbton*, was created Earl of *Cardigan* by King Charles the second, *April* 20, 1661, upon whose death *Robert* his son succeeded in his estate and titles which *Robert* hath been also succeeded by *George* his Grandson, the present Earl *Francis* Lord *Brudenel* his son, dying in the lifetime of his Father]

Earls of Cardigan

It contains 64 Parish Churches

ORDI-

Minutes of T
Skerries
ST.
Holy Head
HOLY HEAD
TALIBO-
LION HUN
MALTRAETH
HUN
Newborough
OR THE

XVI XV XIV XIII

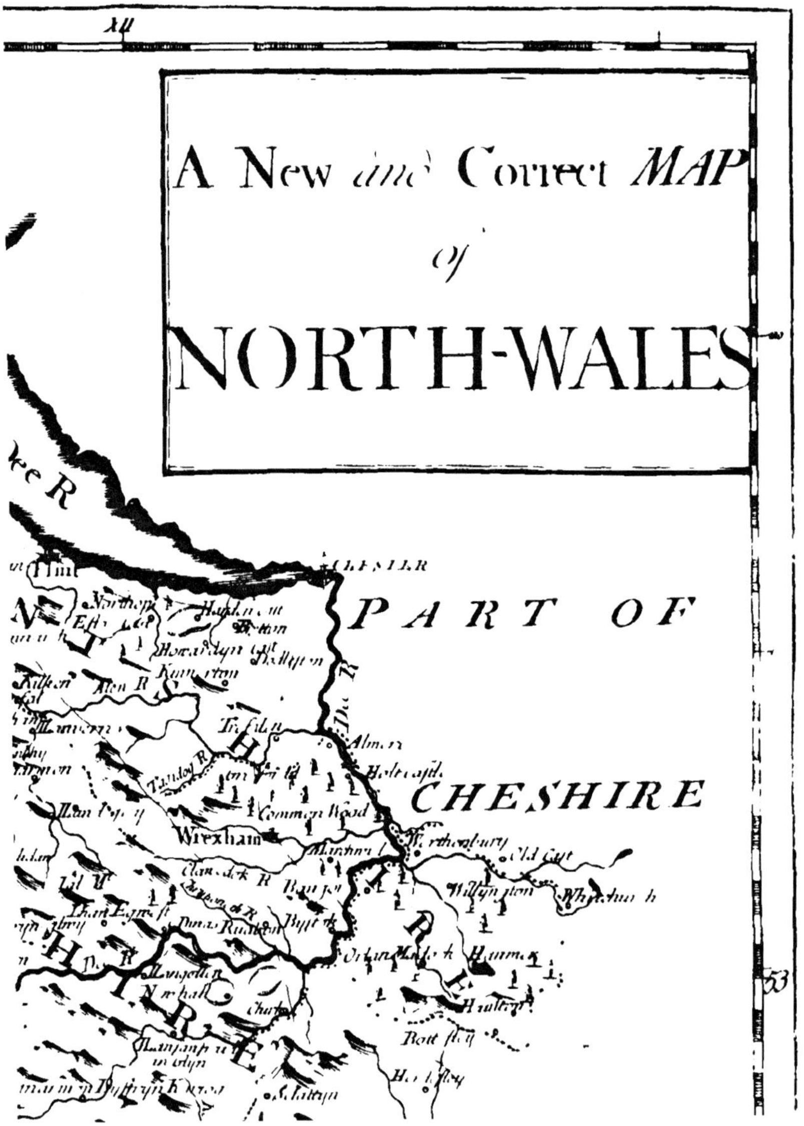

A New and Correct *MAP* of

NORTH-WALES

PART OF

CHESHIRE

Wrexham

Common Wood

Old Cast

53

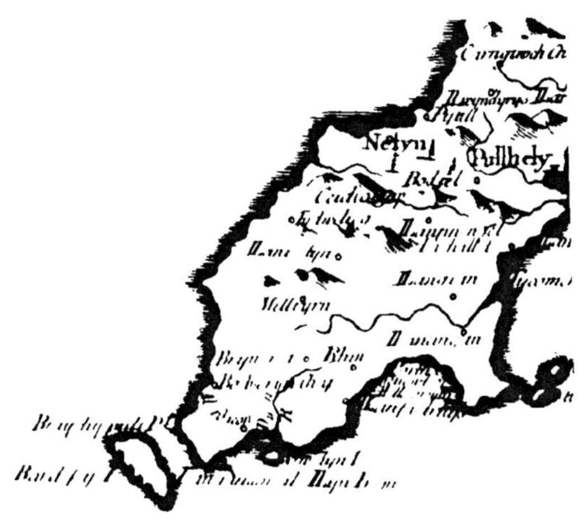

I R I S H S

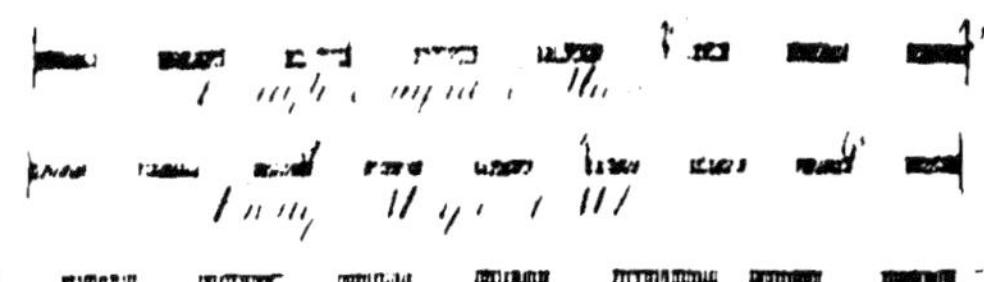

MERIONETH
SHIRE
Harlech
Dogelle
Mathynlleth
MONTGOMERY
SHIR
Plymllymon hill
PART OF
SOUTH WALES
Aberistwith
E A

P. OF SHROP-
SHIRE
Shrewsbury
Welsh Pool
T G O M E R Y
Montgumery
Newtown
P. OF
HEREFORD SHIRE

ORDEVICES.

THose Countries of the Silures *and* Dimetæ *which we have last survey'd, were in after-times, when* Wales *came to be divided into three Principalities, call'd by the Natives* Deheubarth *(or the* Right hand part,) *and in* English, *as we have already observ'd,* South-Wales. *The other two Principalities (which they call* Gwynedh *and* Powys, *and we,* North Wales, *and* Powisland) *were inhabited by the* Ordovices, *call'd also* Ordevices *and* Ordevicæ, *and in some Authors (though corruptly)* Ordolucæ. *A couragious and puissant Nation these were, as being Inhabitants of a mountainous country, and receiving vigour from their native soil, and who continu'd, the longest of any, unconquer'd either by Romans or English. For they were not subdu'd by the Romans, till the time of the Emperor Domitian, when* Julius Agricola *reduced almost the whole Nation; nor were they subjected by the English, before the reign of Edward the first. For a long time they enjoy'd their liberty, confiding as well in their own strength and courage, as in the roughness and difficult situation of their country, which seems to be laid out by nature for Ambuscades, and the prolonging of war.*

To determin the limits of these Ordevices, *is no hard task, but to give a true reason of the name, seems very difficult. However, I have entertain'd a conjecture, that, seeing they are seated on the two rivers of* Dev, *which, springing not far asunder, take their course different ways, and that* * Oar-devi *in the British language signifies,* Upon the rivers of *Devi, they have been thence call'd* Ordevices. *So the* Arverni *receiv'd their name from their situation on the river* Garumna, *the* Armorici *from inhabiting a maritim country, and the* Horesci *from their bordering on the river* Esk.

* Peal [illegible]

Nor is the name of the Ordevices *so entirely extinct in this country, but that there remain some footsteps of it. For a considerable part of it, which lies on the Sea, is at this day call'd by the inhabitants* Ardudwy, *out of which the Romans, by a softer pronunciation, may seem to have coin'd their* Ordovices *and* Ordevices. *But now this whole tract (except one small County) is call'd in Latin* Gwynedhia, *and* Venedotia, *and in British* Gwynedh, *from the* Veneti *in Armorica as some imagin, who (as Cæsar writes) were used to sail often into Britain. And if it were allowable to change one letter, I might suppose that this name was not unknown to the Greeks and to* Pausanias, *who in his* Arcadia *informs us, that* Antoninus Pius *had sufficiently chastis'd our* Brigantes, *for making Inroads into* Genounia, *a Roman Province in Britain. Now if we may be allow'd to read* Genouthia *for* Genounia, *the word comes so near* Guinethia, *and this* Guinethia [*or* Gwynedh] *borders so much on the country of the Brigantes, that unless* Pausanias *meant this country, some Oracle must find out for us what country he meant. To the* Ordovices *belong'd those Countries which are now call'd in English by new names,* Mont Gomery shire, Meirionydh shire, Caernarvon-shire, Denbigh-shire, *and* Flint shire.

Genounia

MONTGOMERYSHIRE.

MOntgomeryshire, call'd in British *Sir Dre' Valdwyn,* from its chief town, is bounded on the south with *Cardiganshire* and *Radnorshire*; on the east with *Shropshire*, on the north with *Denbighshire*, and on the west with *Meirionydshire*. This Shire, though it be mountainous, is yet in general a fertile Country, having fruitful Vales as well for pasture as arable land; and was formerly a breeder of excellent horses, *which* (as Giraldus informs us) *were much esteem'd, as well for their shape and stateliness* †, *as the incomparable swiftness, which nature had given them.*

† Membrorum [illegible]

At the utmost limit of this County, westward, where it ends in a Cone or sharp point, lies *Machynllheth*; the *Maglona* perhaps of the Romans, where, in the time of *Honorius* the Emperor, the Prefect of the *Solensians* lay in garrison under the *Dux Britanniæ*, in order to keep in subjection the inhabitants of that mountanous tract. And at two miles distance, near *Penalht*, [in the County of Meirionydh,] we find a place call'd *Kern Kaer*, or *the back of a city* *, where they sometimes dig up Roman Coins, and where are seen the footsteps of a round wall of considerable extent. [Concerning which ancient place, a Gentleman who has liv'd there many years, adds this further account. The main Fort which was on the highest part of the hill, was built quadrangularly, and encompass'd with a strong wall and a broad ditch, of an oval form, excepting, that towards the valley, it was extended in a direct line. On the out-side of the great ditch next the river *Dyvi*,

Machynllheth

Maglona

* Dorsum urbis

Kern Kaer

Dyvi, the foundations of many houses have been discover'd; and on a lower Mount, there stood a small Fort, which may be suppos'd to have been built of bricks, for that they find there plenty of them. All the out walls were built of a rough hard stone, which must have been carry'd thither by water, there being none such nearer than *Tâl y Gareg*, which is distant from this place about seven miles. From the Fort to the water-side, is a broad hard way of pitch'd pebles and other stones, continu'd in a strait line through meadows and marsh grounds, which may be about two hundred yards in length, and ten or twelve in breadth. It is very evident, that this Fort was demolish'd before the building of the Church of *Penalht*, for that we find in the walls of that Church, several bricks mix'd with the stones, which were doubtless brought thither from this place. Roman Coins have been found here, since those before-mention'd, particularly some silver pieces of *Augustus* and *Tiberius*: and near the main Fort, in a field call'd *Kae Lhwyn y Neuodh* (i. e. *the Court or Palace grove*) a small gold chain was found, about four inches long; and at another time a Saphire stone neatly cut. Some other things of less note have been discover'd in the same place, as, a very large brass Cauldron, us'd since as a brewing vessel at *Kae'r Berlhan*, several pieces of lead, and very odd Glasses of a round form like hoops, which were of various sizes, some about twenty inches in circumference, others much less, &c. These hoop glasses were curiously listed, of divers colours, some of which being broke, it was observ'd, that that variety of colours proceeded from Sands or Powders of the same colours, inclos'd in several Cells within the glass.]

† Vulgo *Plymhymmon*, an rectiùs *Pen Lhuman*, i. e. *Jugum vexillare*? The fountain-head of Severn.

Five miles hence, that mountain of † *Plinlimmon*, which I mention'd, rises to a great height; and on that side where it is the bound of this County, it sends out the river *Sabrina*, call'd by the Britains *Havren*, and in English *Seavern*, which, next to Thames, is the most noble river in Britain. Whence it had that name, I could never learn; for, that a Virgin call'd *Sabrina* was drown'd in it, seems only a Fable of *Jeffrey*'s invention; on whose authority also a late Poet built these verses:

> ———*in flumen præcipitatur Abren,*
> *Nomen Abren fluvio de virgine; nomen eidem*
> *Nomine corrupto, deinde Sabrina dato.*

> Headlong was *Abren* thrown into the stream,
> And hence the river took the Virgin's name,
> Corrupted thence at last *Sabrina* came.

This river has so many windings near its Fountain head, that it often seems to return; but proceeds nevertheless, or rather wanders slowly through this County, *Shropshire*, *Worcestershire*, and lastly *Glocestershire*; and having, throughout its course, very much enrich'd the soil, is at last discharged calmly into the Severn sea. In this County, Severn, being shaded with woods, takes its course northward by *Lhan Idlos*, and *Tre'newydh* or *New town*, and *Kaer Sws*, which is reported to be both ancient, and to enjoy ancient privileges. [That it was a town of considerable note, may be concluded from the street there, and the lanes about it. I cannot learn, that any Roman coins have been discover'd at this place, how-

Lhan Idlos. New town. Kaer Sws.

ever that it was of Roman foundation seems highly probable, for that there have been lately (besides some neat hewn stones for building) several bricks dug-up there, of that kind which we frequently meet with in such ancient Cities as were possess'd by the Romans. It has had a Castle, and at least one Church, and is said to have been heretofore the seat of the Lords of *Aruystli*; but how far this town extended, seems at present altogether uncertain. It has had encampments about it at three several places, *viz*. First, on the north side, on a mountain call'd *Gwyn vynydh*: secondly, eastward, near a place call'd *Rhos dhiaberd*, in the parish of *Lhan Dhinam*, where, besides entrenchments, there is a very large Mount or Barrow. And thirdly, at a place call'd *Kevn Karnedh*, about a quarter of a mile on the west-side of the town. Moreover, about half a mile southward from this *Kevn Karnedh*, on the top of a hill above *Lhan Dhinam* Church, there is a remarkable entrenchment call'd *y Gaer Vechan*, which name may signify either *the lesser City*, or *the lesser Fortification*, but is here doubtless put for the latter.]

Not far from the bank, on the east-side, the *Severn* leaves *Montgomery*, the chief town of the County, seated on a rising rock, and having a pleasant plain under it. It was built by *Baldwin*, Lieutenant of the Marches of Wales, in the reign of King William the first, whence the Britains call it *Tre' Valdwin*, i. e. *Baldwin's Town*; but the English, *Montgomery*, from *Roger de Mont Gomery*, Earl of Shrewsbury, whose inheritance it was, and who built the Castle, as we read in Domesday-book: though Florilegus fabulously tells us, that it was call'd *Mons Gomericus* (from its situation) by King Henry the third, after he had rebuilt it; for the Welsh, putting the garrison to the sword, had demolish'd it in the year 1095, after which it lay a long time neglected. However, certain it is, that King Henry the third granted by Charter, *That the Burrough of Montgomery should have the privilege of a free Burrough, with other Liberties*. Near this town, *Corndon hill* rises to a considerable height; on the top of which are placed certain * stones, in form of a crown (whence [say some] is the name) in memory perhaps of a victory. [But these stones are no other, than four such rude heaps as are commonly known on the Mountains of Wales, by the name of *Karneu* and *Karnedheu*, of which the Reader may find some general account in *Radnorshire*. And to me it seems very probable (seeing these stones can in no respect be compar'd to a Crown) that the name of *Corndon* is deriv'd from this word *Karn* (the singular of *Karneu*) with the addition of the English termination *don*, signifying *Mountain* or *Hill*, as in *Snowdon*, *Huntingdon*, &c. which conjecture is much confirm'd, when we consider, that there are many hills in Wales denominated from such heaps of stones, as *Karn Lhechart* in Glamorganshire, *Karnedh Dhavidh*, *Karnedh Hygin*, and *Karnedh Lhewelyn* in Caernarvonshire, with many more in other Counties.]

Montgomery. Tre' Valdwyn. Anno 11. Corndon hill. * Commonly call'd Migfold.

A little lower, the river *Severn* runs by *Tralhwn*, i. e. *the town by the Lake* (whence the English call it *Welsh Pool*;) [which Etymology is agreeable enough with the situation of this place: otherwise, I should suspect, that the word *Tralhwn* might be the name of a place near this pool, before the town was built, and that the town afterwards took its name from it. For in some parts of Wales, it is a common appellative, for such soft places on the Roads

Welsh Pool. Etymology of the word Tralhwn.

(or

(or elsewhere) as Travellers may be apt to sink into, as I have observ'd particularly in the Mountains of Glamorganshire. And that a great deal of the ground near this place is such, is also very well known. As for the Etymon of the appellative *Tralhwn*, I suppose it only an abbreviation of *Traeth lyn*, i. e. *a Quagmire*.]

Red Castle. Near *Tralhwn*, on the south-side, is a castle, call'd from the reddish stones of which it is built, *Kastelh Kôch*, where, within the same walls, are two castles, one belonging to the *Lord of Powys*, the other to *Baron Dudley*. *Kadwgan ap Bledhyn*, that renown'd Britain mention'd in the last County, who, whilst he was intent on the building of this Castle, was slain by his nephew *Madok*, as we find in the Abridgment of *Kradok* of *Lhan Garvan*. Opposite to this, on the other side of the river, lies

Buttington. *Buttington*, a place noted for the Danes wintering there; whence, as *Marianus* tells us, they were driven by *Adheredus* Duke of *Mercia*, in the year 894. The river *Severn*, having left these places, winds it self by degrees towards the east, that it may the sooner receive a small

* L. Myrnwy. river call'd *Tanat* *, wherewith being united, it enters *Shropshire*.

I am fully perswaded (because it seems a certain truth) that the *Mediolanum* of the *Ordovices*,

Mediolanum. celebrated by *Antoninus* and *Ptolemy*, stood in this Country; the footsteps whereof I have diligently endeavour'd to trace out, tho' with no great success, so far doth age consume even the skeletons and ruins of Cities. However, if we may conjecture from its situation (seeing those Towns which *Antoninus* places on each side, are well known, *viz.* on one side *Bonium*, call'd now *Bangor* by the river Dee, and on the other *Rutunium*, now *Rowton Castle*, for he places it twelve Italian miles from this, and twenty from the other,) the lines of Position, if we may so term them, or rather of Distance, cross each other betwixt *Mathraval* and *Lhan Vylhin*, which are scarce three miles asunder, and in a manner demonstrate to us the situation of our *Mediolanum*. For this method of finding out a third from two known places, cannot deceive us, when there are neither Mountains interpos'd,

† Itinerarum flexus impositus Mathraval. nor † the turnings of roads discontinu'd. This *Mathraval* lies five miles to the west of Severn; and (which in some degree asserts the Antiquity of it) though it be now but a bare name, it was once the Royal Seat of the *Princes* of *Powys*, and is also noted in Authors, who tell us, that

* De recta ponte. Lhan Vylhin. after the Princes left it, * *Robert Vipont* an English man built a Castle there. But *Lhan Vylhin* (i. e. *the Church of Mylhin*) a small market-town, though in respect of distance it be a little further off, is yet, as to the affinity of name, much nearer *Mediolanum*. For the word *Vylhin* is, by an Idiom of the British, only a variation of *Mylhin*, as *Kaer Vyrdhin*, from *Kaer* and *Myrdhin*, and *Ar-von* from *Ar mon*. [and very lately a great many *Roman* Coins have been found here.] Nor is this name of *Mylhin* [or *Mylin*] more remote from *Mediolanum*, than *Millano* in Italy, or *Le Million* in *Xantoigne*, or *Meillen* in the Low Countries, all which (as is generally alow'd) were formerly known by the name of *Mediolanum*. But whether of these conjectures comes nearer the truth, let the Reader determin; for my own part, I do no more than deliver my Opinion. [Only, as to *Lhan Vyllin*, there is this Objection against it, that we do not find it was customary among the Britains, to prefix the word *Lhan* (i. e. *Church*) to the name of Roman Cities; but if any word was prefix'd, it was generally *Kaer* (i. e. a *Fort* or *Fence*) as *Kaer Lheion*, *Kaer Went*, *Kair Vyrdhin*, &c. And tho' we should allow the invalidity of this objection, and suppose the word *Lhan* might be introduced in latter times; yet considering that a learned and inquisitive Gentleman of this Town (who among his other studies, has always had a particular regard to the Antiquities of his Country) has not in the space of forty years met with any Coins here, or other tokens of a place inhabited by the Romans, nor yet discover'd the least signs that this Town was anciently of any considerable note; I think we cannot with safety (barely on account of its name, and vicinity to the situation requir'd) conclude it the

old *Mediolanum*. Therefore it seems convenient to have recourse to the situation assign'd this City by Dr *Powel*; who, in his learned Annotations on *Giraldus*'s Itinerary †, assures us, it was not only the opinion of some Antiquaries, that the ancient *Mediolanum* was seated where the village of *Mervod* stands at present, but also that the same village and places adjoyning afforded in his time several such remarkable Monuments, as made it evident, that there had been formerly a considerable town at that place. Also, this *Mervod* is seated about a mile below *Mathraval*, on the north side of the river *Myrnwy*, and three miles southward of *Lhan Vylhin*. At present, there remains only a Church and a small village, but several yet living have seen there the ruins of two other Churches. I am inform'd, that about a mile from the Church there is a place call'd *Lhwyr Porth*, i. e. the Gate-*acre*, which is suppos'd to have taken its name from one of the Gates of the old City; and, that in the grounds adjoyning to this village, Causeys, Foundations of Buildings, Floors and Hearths are often discover'd by Labourers; but whether any such Monuments, as we may safely conclude to be Roman (as Coins, Urns, Inscriptions, &c.) are found at this place, I must leave to farther enquiry. *Mervod* (as Bishop Usher supposes) is call'd by Nennius *Caer Meguid*, and in other copies *Cair Metguod*, but what the word *Meguid* or *Metguod*, or yet *Mervod* or *Mediolanum*, might signify, is hardly intelligible at present, unless the name be taken from an *Hermitage*, in regard they have a tradition at that place, that a Religious Hermit call'd *Rhys* (corruptly, as some suppose, for *Cyrus*) liv'd there; and the word *Metguod* was the same, according to old orthography, with *Medzod* or *Meudwy-vod*, i. e. a hermitage, from *Meudwy* a hermit, and *bod* an habitation. What confirms this, is, that at *Lhan rhystid* in Denbighshire, there is another *Mevod*, with the very same tradition; and both Churches bear the name of the same Founder, namely, *Tyssilio* the son of *Brochwel Yskithrog*, Prince of Powys, about the year 600.]

If I should affirm, that this our *Mediolanum*, and those other cities of the same name in Gaul, were built either by Duke *Medus* or Prince *Olanus*, or that whilst it was building, *Sus mediatim lanata* [a Sow half clad with wooll] was dug up; should I not seem to grasp at clouds and trifles? And yet the *Italians* tell all these stories of their *Mediolanum*. But being it is most evident that all these were founded by people who spoke the same language (for we have shewn already, that the Gauls and Britains us'd one common tongue,) it seems highly probable, that they had their denomination from one and the same original. Now, our *Mediolanum* agrees in nothing with that of Italy, but that each of them are seated in a

Right margin: Mediolanum. — l. 2. c. 4.

Plain between two rivers, and a learned Italian has from thence deriv'd the name of his, *Mediolanum*, for that it is seated *media inter lanas* which he interprets *betwixt Brooks or small Rivers*

Lane, what it signifies

[*Mathraval* before mention'd, as heretofore the seat of the Princes of Powys, shews at present no remains of its ancient splendour, there being only a small Farm house where the Castle stood *Lhan Vylhin* is a market-town of considerable note, first incorporated by *Lhewelyn ap Gruffydh* Lord of *Mechain* and *Mochnant*, in the time of Edward the second It is govern'd by two Bailiffs, chosen annually, who, besides other Privileges granted to the town by King Charles the second (bearing date March 28 *Anno Reg* 25) were made Justices of the Peace within the Corporation during the time of their being Bailiffs]

Earls of Montgomery
† So said, ann 1607

This County had dignify'd no Earl with its name and title, till † very lately, *Anno* 1605 King James [the first] created at *Greenwich*, *Philip Herbert*, a younger son of *Henry* Earl of *Penbroke* by Mary Sydney, at one and the same time Baron *Herbert* of *Shurland* and Earl of *Montgomery*, as a particular mark of his favour, and for the great hopes he had conceiv'd of his virtuous qualifications

See Penbrokeshire

[Which Philip being also Earl of Penbroke, by the death of his brother without issue, the same persons ever since have enjoy'd both the titles of Penbroke and Montgomery]

Princes of Powys
† From Bledhyn ap Kynvyn Powel 109

The Princes of *Powis*, descended from the third son of *Roderic* the Great †, possess'd this County with some others (only *Roger* and *Hugh* of Montgomery had got away part of it) in a continu'd series till the time of Edward the second For then *Owen* the son of *Gruffydh ap Gwenwynwyn* the last Lord of *Powys* of British Extraction (for the title of Prince was disconti-nu'd long before) left one only daughter, call'd *Hawis*, who was marry'd to *John Charlton* an English-man, the King's *Valett*, and he thereupon was created Earl of *Powys* by King Edward the second His Arms (as I have observ'd in several places) were *Or*, *a Lion rampant Gules* He was succeeded in this title by four Brothers, till the male-line became extinct in *Edward*; who by *Eleanora*, daughter and one of the heirs of Thomas *Holland* Earl of *Kent*, had two daughters, *viz* *Jane* marry'd to Sir *John Grey*, and *Joyce* the wife of John Lord *Tiptoft*, from whom descended the Barons *Dudley* and others This Sir *John Grey*, by his own martial valour, and the munificence of King Henry the fifth, receiv'd the Earldom of *Tanquervil* in *Normandy*, " to him and his heirs-" male, delivering one *Bassinet* at the Castle of " *Roan*, yearly on St George's day" His son was *Henry* Lord Powys, in whose Family the title of Powys continu'd with great honour, till *Edward Grey*, not long before † our time, dy'd without lawful issue [The Lordship of *Powys* was afterwards purchased by Sir *Edward Herbert*, second son of William Earl of *Penbroke*, to whom succeeded his eldest son Sir *William Herbert*, who was created Lord Powys, and was succeeded in the same title by Percy his son, and *William* son of Percy, was first made Earl, and afterwards Marquis of Powys, by King James the second As to the title of Earl of *Tanquervil*, it lay dormant, till *Ford* Lord *Grey* of *Werk* was advanc'd to that honour by King William the third]

Lords of Powys
D Powel.

Dupl Norm 6 Hen 5 Earl of Tanquervil

† So said, ann 1607

Vid *Osulston* in Middlesex

There are in this County 47 Parishes.

MEIRIONYDSHIRE.

BEyond the County of Montgomery, lies *Meirionydhshire*, which the Britains call *Sir Veirionydh*, the Latins *Mervinia*, and Giraldus, *Terra filiorum Conani*, i e the Land of the sons of Conanus It reaches to the crooked bay which I mention'd, and is wash'd by the main Ocean on the west side, with such violence, that it may be thought to have carry'd off some part of it On the south (for some miles) it is divided from *Cardiganshire* by the river *Dyvy*, and on the north, borders on *Caernarvonshire* and *Denbighshire*

Mountains exceeding high

This County hath such heaps of mountains, that (as Giraldus observes) *it is the roughest and most unpleasant County of all Wales For the hills are extraordinary high, and yet very narrow, and terminating in sharp peaks, nor are they thin scatter'd, but placed very close, and so even in height, that the shepherds frequently converse from the tops of them, who yet, in case they should wrangle and appoint a meeting, could scarce come together from morning till night*

[It is (as he observes) generally consider'd, the most mountainous of all the Welsh Counties, though its mountains are not the highest; those of *Snowdon* in *Caernarvonshire* exceeding them in height, and being at least equal to them in rocky precipices But whereas Giraldus calls it the roughest and most unpleasant Country in all Wales, it may be answer'd (if that be worth notice) that for the *pleasing prospect* of a Country, there is hardly any standard, most men taking their measures herein, either from the place of their own nativity and education, or from the profit which they suppose a Country may yield But if (as some hold) variety of objects make a Country appear delightful, this may contend with most; as affording (besides a sea prospect) not only exceeding high mountains, and inaccessible rocks, with an incredible number of rivers, cataracts, and lakes but also variety of lower hills, woods, and plains, and some fruitful vallys Their highest mountains, are *Kader Idris*, *Aren Vowdhwy*, *Aren Benlhyn*, *Arennig*, *Moelwyn*, *Mannod*, &c These maintain innumerable herds of cattel, sheep and goats, and are (in regard they are frequently fed with clouds and rains, and harbour much snow) considerably more fertil, tho' the grass be coarse, than the hills and ridges of lower Countries *Kader Idris* is probably one of the highest mountains in Britain, and (which is one certain argument of its height) it affords some variety of Alpine plants but for mountains so high, and their tops notwithstanding so near, that men may converse from them, and yet scarce be able to meet in a whole day; I presume there are none such in nature and am certain there are not any in Wales, but that men conversing from their top, may meet in half an hour]

Wolves in England destroy'd

Innumerable flocks of Sheep [(as hath been said)] do graze on these Mountains; nor are they in any danger of Wolves, which are thought to have been destroy'd throughout England, when King Edgar impos'd a yearly tribute of three hundred wolves-skins on † *Ludwal* Prince of these Countries. For (as we find in William of Malmesbury) 'When he had performed 'this for three years, he desisted the fourth, al'ledging he could not find one more' However, that there remained some long after, is manifest from unquestionable records The Inhabitants, who apply themselves wholly to the breeding of Cattel, and who feed on Milk-meats, *viz* Butter, Cheese, *&c* (notwithstanding Strabo formerly derided our Britains, as ignorant of the art of making Cheese,) are scarce inferiour to any People of Britain, in stature, clear complexion, comeliness and proportion, but have an ill character, among their neighbours, for incontinency and Idleness

† No Prince of this name in Wales. An leg. Ll-... See Derby shire and Yorkshire

It hath but few towns On the east, where *Dyvy* runs, *Kummwd Mowdhwy* is a place well known, which was formerly the inheritance of *William*, otherwise call'd *Wilcok Mowdhwy*, a younger son of *Grufydh ap Gwenwynwyn*, Lord of *Powis*, and by his son's daughter it descended to *Hugo Burgh*, and again * by daughters of this house, to the honourable families of *Newport Leighton*, *Lingen* and *Mitton*

Mowdhwy

* Per ejusnept ...

Where the river *Avon* runs more westerly, lies *Dôl Gelheu*, a small Market-town, so called from the valley in which it is seated, (or rather, from it's situation in a woody vale, the word *Dôl* being much the same with the English *Dale*, so common in the North of England and in Scotland and * *Kelhe* in the southern dialect *Kelhi*) signifying strictly *a wood where much hazel grows*, and being sometimes us'd for any other wood; though at present there are not so many woods about this town, as were formerly What Antiquity this place is of, or whether of any note in the time of the Romans, is uncertain, however, some of their coyns have been of late years dug-up near a well call'd *Fynon Vair*, within a bow shot of the town two whereof was sent me by the reverend † Rector of the place, which are fair silver pieces of Trajan and Hadrian *viz*

Dol Gelheu

* Idest, The ... Corylitum

† Mr M... Jones

1 IMP TRAIANO AVG GER DAC P M TR P
COS V P P S P Q R OPTIMO PRINC
Trophæum de Dacis

2 IMP CAESAR TRAIAN HADRIANVS AVG P. M TR P COS III
Mars Gradivus cum hasta & spoliis]

1 *Imperatori Trajano Augusto Germanico Dacico Pontifici maximo, Tribunitia potestate, Consuli quinto, Patri Patriæ Senatus populusque Romanus optimo Principi*

Close by the Sea in a small Country of *Arudwy*, stands on a steep rock of the Castle of *Ar lech* (called heretofore *Kaer Kolhwyn*,) which as the Inhabitants report, was built by Edward the first, and took it's name from the situation, for *Ar lech* in British signifies *on a rock*, though some call it *Harlech* †, and interpret it, *A rock pleasantly situated* When England was embroil'd in civil war, *Davidh ap Jenken ap Enion*, a British Nobleman, who sided with the House of Lancaster, defended this Castle stoutly against Edward the fourth, until *William Herbert*, Earl of Penbroke forcing his way through the midst of the Alps of Wales, a very difficult passage, attack'd it with so much vigour, that it was surrender'd into his hands It is almost incredible, what great difficulties he and his Soldiers struggled with in this troublesome journey; when in some places whilst they ascended the mountains, they were forced to creep, and elsewhere in descending, in a manner to tumble down whence the way is called by the neighbours at this day, *Lle Herbert.*

Har lech

† Quasi Hardd-lech

Herbert's way

[This *Harlech* (for that is the right name, and the denomination is probably from a *rock*,) was once call'd *Twr Bronwen*, and afterwards receiv'd the name of *Kaer Kolhwyn* from *Kolhwyn ap Tagno*, who lived there in the time of Prince *Anarawd*, about the year 877, and was Lord of *Ardudwy* and *Evionydh*, and some part of *Llyn*, which countries are yet, for the most part, possess'd by his posterity His Arms were, Sable, a cheveron argent, betwixt three flower-de-luces Notwithstanding *Harlech* might receive this name of *Kaer Kolhwyn* from *Kolhwyn ap Tagno*, yet it seems probable that this place, or some other near it, was call'd *Kaer* before his time For I am assured, that in the memory of some persons yet living, several Roman Coins have been found hereabouts, and that the Britains prefix'd the word *Kaer* to most places fortified by the Romans, is well known to all Antiquaries

Mr Robert Vaughan's MS

In the year 1692 an ancient golden *Torques* was dug-up in a Garden somewhere near this Castle of *Harlech* It is a wreathed bar of gold (or rather perhaps three or four rods joyntly twisted) about four foot long, flexil, but bending naturally only one way, in form of a hat band, hooked at both ends exactly (that I may describe it intelligibly, though in vulgar terms) like a pair of pot-hooks, but these hooks are not twisted as the rest of the rod, nor are their ends sharp, but plain, and as it were cut even It is of a round form, about an inch in circumference, and weighs eight ounces, and is all over so plain, that it needs no farther description It seems very probable, that Roman Authors always intended an ornament of this kind, by the word *Torques*, seeing it is derived from *Torqueo*, and not a chain (composed of links or annulets) as our Grammarians commonly interpret it, and as *Joannes Schefferus* supposes, who in his learned and curious dissertation *de Torquibus*, tells us, that the Torques *were moveable, and made of rings, the Circles solid and round; and the Monilia, a little broader*, &c Moreover, the British word *Torch*, which is doubtless of the same origin as well as signification with the Latin *Torquis*, is never used for a chain, but generally for a wreath, and sometimes, though in a less strict sense, for any collar, or large ring, our word for a chain being *Kadwen*, which agrees also with the Latin Whether the *Torques* here describ'd was British or Roman, seems a question not easily decided; seeing we find, that anciently most Nations that we have any knowledge of, used this kind of ornament And particularly, that the Britains had golden Torques's, we have the authority of *Dio Cassius* †, who in his description of *Boadicea*, or *Bunduica*, Queen of the *Iceni* in the time of Nero, tells us, *she wore a large golden Torques* (στρεπτὸν μέγαν χρυσοῦν ἐφόρει) *that her garments was of divers colours*, *&c* If it be objected, that though she wore such an ornament, yet it might be in use amongst the Britains only since the Roman Conquests; it may be answer'd, that this seems not to have been the sense of the Author, but that he thus describes her for the strangeness of her habit, adding, *that her yellow hair hung loose, and reach'd down to her hips*, &c A farther confirmation, that the

Torques, or Chain

† Hist Rom lib 62

the Britains used golden *Torques's*, is, that they were so common among their neighbour-nation (and probably their progenitors) the Gauls. For Livy tells ‖ us, that Publius Cornelius, when he triumph'd over the *Boii*, produced, amongst other spoils, one thousand four hundred and seventy golden Torques's. And *Britomarus*, a commander amongst the Gauls, who is presumed to have been a Britain, wore such an ornament, as we find in *Propertius* (a)

‖ Lib 36 c 40

If any shall urge farther (notwithstanding this authority of Dio Cassius, which with me is sufficient) that seeing there is no British name for this Ornament (the common word *Torch*, being derived from the Latin *Torquis*,) it follows, that the Britains knew no such thing. I answer (though we need not much insist on that objection) that to me it seems very suspicious, the word was Celtick before it was Roman For though I acknowledge it derived from *Torqueo*, yet we have also the verb *Torchi* in the same sense and seing both the British words *Torch* and *Torchi* are in all appearance deriv'd from the common word *Tro*, i e. *to turn*, and also that Grammarians know not well whence to derive *Torqueo*; I know not but we may find the origin of it in the British *Torch* Nor ought any one to think it absurd, that I thus endeavour to derive Latin words from the Welsh, seeing there are hundreds of words in that Language, that agree in sound and signification with the Latin, which yet could not be borrowed from the Romans, for that the Irish retain the same, who must have been a Colony of the Britains, long before the Roman Conquest and also that the Welsh or British is one Dialect of the old Celtic whence, as the best Criticks allow the Roman tongue borrow'd several words, and I presume, by the help of the Irish, which was never alter'd by a Roman Conquest, it might be traced much farther For instance, we must acknowledge these British words, *Tir*, *Awyr*, *Môr*, *Avon*, *Llwch*, &c to have one common origin with those of the same signification in the Latin, *Terra*, *Aer*, *Mare*, *Amnis*, *Lacus*, but seeing the Irish also have them, it is evident that they were not left here by the Romans; and I think it no absurdity to suppose them used in these Islands before Rome was built

Hib *Tir*, *Aier*, *Muir*, *Avan*, *Loch*

But that we may not digress too far from our subject, it is manifest from what we have alledg'd, that golden *Torques's* were much used by the Gauls; and I think it not questionable, but that they were in use also amongst the Britains before the Roman Conquest but whether this we now speak of, were Roman or British, remains still uncertain To which I can only say, that it seems much more probably to have been British For whereas it is evident from the example of *Boadicea*, *Britomarus*, the Champion that fought with *T Manlius Torquatus*, &c that the great Commanders amongst the Gauls and Britains wore them, I do not know that it appears at all that the Roman Officers did so and unless that be made out, I think we may safely pronounce it British; for no other Roman, but a Soldier could lose it here. As for these honorary rewards presented to * Soldiers of merit, we need not presume them to have been Roman, but rather Spoils taken from the barbarous Nations which they conquer'd. The use of this Ornament seems to have been retain'd by the Britains long after the Roman and Saxon Conquests. for we find, that within these few Centuries, a Lord of *Iâl* in Denbighshire, was call'd *Lhewelyn aur-dorchog*, i e *Leolinus torque aureo insignitus* and it is at this day a common saying in several parts of Wales, when any one tells his adversary, he'll strive hard, rather than yield to him; *mi a dynna'r dorch a chwi*, i e *I'll pluck the* torques *with you*

* Gruter Inscr p 96

This which we have here describ'd, seems by the length of it to have been for use as well as ornament, which perhaps was to hold a Quiver, for that they were apply'd to that use, seems very plain from Virgil's † description of the Exercises of the Trojan Youth

† Æneid. l 5

Cornea bina ferunt præfixa hastilia ferro
Pars leves humero pharetras et pectore summo
Flexilis obtorti per collum circulus auri.

Each brandishing aloft a Cornel Spear
Some at their backs their gilded Quivers bore;
Their Wreaths of burnish'd gold hung down before

But I fear I have dwelt too long on this one subject, and shall therefore only add (for the satisfaction of such as may scruple this relation) that this valuable Monument of British Nobility and Antiquity is now reposited in the hands of Sir *Roger Mostyn* of Mostyn, Baronet

We must not here forget to transmit to Posterity some account of that prodigious fire or kindled exhalation which annoy'd this neighbourhood some years since. There is already a short relation of it publish'd in the Philosophical Transactions ‖, in a Letter from my abovementiond * Friend; but those pieces coming to few hands, I shall make bold to insert it here, with some additions:

Exhalation.

‖ Num. 208.

* Mr Jones. Jan 20 1694.

Sir,

THis Letter contains no answer to your Queries about the Locusts, for I am wholly intent at present upon giving you the best account I can, of a most dismal and prodigious accident at Harlech *in this County, the beginning of these Holydays It is of the unaccountable firing of sixteen Ricks of Hay, and two Barns, whereof one was full of Corn, the other of Hay I call it unaccountable, because it is evident they were not burnt by common fire, but by a kindled exhalation which was often seen to come from the Sea Of the duration whereof I cannot at present give you any certain account, but am satisfied it lasted at least a fortnight or three weeks, and annoy'd the Country as well by poisoning their Grass, as firing the Hay, for the space of a mile or thereabouts Such as have seen the fire, say it was a blue weak flame, easily extinguished, and that it did not the least harm to any of the men who interpos'd their endeavours to save the Hay, tho' they ventur'd (perceiving it different from common fire) not only close to it, but sometimes into it All the damage that was sustain'd, happened constantly in the night I have enclos'd a catalogue of such as I have received certain information of; and have nothing to add, but that there are three small Tenements in the same*

(a) ——— *Vosti parma relata ducis*
Virdomari ———
Illi virgatis jaculantis ab agmine bracbis,
Torquis ab incisa decidit unca gula Lib 4

neigh-

neighbourhood (call'd Tydhin Siôn Wyn) *the Grass of which was so infected, that it absolutely kill'd all manner of Cattle that fed upon it. The Grass has been infectious these three years, but not throughly fatal till this last. Pray send with all convenient speed, your friends thoughts, and your own, of the causes, and if possible also the remedy, of this surprizing* Phænomenon, *&c*

Thus far, Mr. *Jones's* account of this surprizing and unparalleled Meteor; since which time, I received information from him and others, that it continu'd several Months longer. It did no great damage by consuming the Hay, and Corn, besides those of some particular persons; but the Grass, or Air, or both, were so infected with it, that there was all the while a great mortality of Cattle, Horses, Sheep, Goats, *&c*. For a long time they could not trace this fire any further than from the adjoyning Sea shores; but afterwards those who watch'd it (as some did continually) discover'd that it cross'd a part of the Sea, from a place call'd *Morva bychan* in Caernarvonshire, distant from Harlech about eight or nine miles, which it describ'd to be a Bay both sandy and marshy. That winter, it appear'd much more frequently than in the following summer: for whereas, they saw it then almost every night, it was not observ'd in the summer, above one or two nights in a week, and that (which if true, is very observable) about the same distance of time, happening generally on Saturday or Sunday nights: but afterwards it was seen much oftner. They add, that it was seen on stormy as well as calm nights, and all weathers alike: but that any great noise, such as the sounding of Horns, the discharging of Guns, *&c* did repel or extinguish it; by which means it was suppos'd, they sav'd several Ricks of Hay and Corn, for it scarce fir'd any thing else.

This Phænomenon, I presume, is wholly new and unheard of; no Historian or Philosopher describing any such Meteor; for we never read that any of those fiery Exhalations distinguish'd by the several names of *Ignis fatuus*, *Ignis lambens*, *Scintillæ volantes*, &c. have had such effects, as thus to poison the Air or Grass, so as to render it infectious and mortal to all sorts of Cattle. Moreover, we have no examples of any fires of this kind, that were of such consistence as to kindle Hay and Corn, to consume Barns and Houses, *&c*. Nor are there any describ'd to move so regularly as this, which several observ'd to proceed constantly to and from the same places for the space of at least eight months. Wherefore seeing the effects are altogether strange and unusual, they who would account for it, must search out some causes no less extraordinary. But in regard that that may not be done (if at all) without making observations for some time upon the place, we must content our selves with a bare relation of the matter of fact. I must confess, that upon the first hearing of this murrain amongst all sorts of Cattle, I suspected that those Locusts that arriv'd in this Country about two months before, might occasion it, by an infection of the Air; proceeding partly from the corruption of those that landed, and did not long survive in this cold Country; and partly of a far greater number which I suppos'd were drown'd in their voyage, and cast upon these Coasts. For though I know not, whether any have been so curious as to search the Sea weeds for them in this County, yet I am inform'd that a Gentleman accidentally observ'd some quantity of them on the shores of Caernarvonshire near *Aber Dâron*; and that others have been seen on the Sands of the Severn Sea. Now, that a considerable quantity of these Creatures being drown'd in the Sea, and afterwards cast ashore, will cause a Pestilence, we have many instances in Authors*, and particularly one that happen'd in the year 1374, when there was a great mortality of Men and Cattle, on the Coasts of France, occasion'd by Locusts drown'd in our English Channel, and cast upon their shores†. But whether such a contagious vapour, meeting with a viscous exhalation, in a moorish Bay, will kindle, and so perform in some measure, such a devastation of Hay and Corn, as the living Creatures would do (where we may also note that ‖ Pliny says of them, *multa contactu adurunt*, i. e. they burn many things by the touch,) I must recommend to farther consideration. I know there are many things might be objected, and particularly the duration of this fire; but men are naturally so fond of their own conjectures, that sometimes they cannot conceal them, though they are not themselves fully satisfy'd.

* V. Tho. Moufeti [illegible] Insectorum, p. 123

† Otho Frisingensis

‖ Lib. xi. c. 29

About two miles from Harlech, there is a remarkable Monument call'd *Koeten Arthur*. It is a large Stone table somewhat of an oval form, but rude and ill shap'd (as are the rest of these Heathen-Monuments,) about ten foot long, and above seven where it is broadest; two foot thick at one end, but not above an inch at the other. It is placed on three rude Stone-pillars, each about half a yard broad, two of which that support the thick end, are betwixt seven or eight foot; but the third, at the other end, about three foot high.]

V. Llech y Drybedh in Pembrokeshire.

Higher up in the confines of this County and Caernarvonshire, two notable arms of the Sea encroach on the land, call'd *Y Traeth mawr*, and *Traeth bychan*, that is, the *Greater Wash or Frith*, and the *Lesser*. And not far from hence, near a small Village call'd *Festineog*, is a high road or military way of pitch'd stones, which leads thorough these difficult and almost unpassable mountains, and seeing it is called in British *Sarn Helan*, or *Helen's way*, it is but reasonable that we suppose it made by *Helena* the mother of Constantine the Great; whose works were many and magnificent throughout the Roman Empire. [This was probably of a very considerable extent; unless we should suppose the same *Helen* was Author of several other high ways in Wales. For besides the place here mention'd, it is also visible at one end of *Kraig Verwyn*, where it is called *Fordh gam Hel n Luedhog*, i. e. *The crooked Road of* Helen *the great, or puissant*. And I observed a way call'd *Fordh* [or Sarn] *H len*, in the parish of *Lhan Badarn Odyn* in Cardiganshire; as also that a great part of the road from Brecknock to Neath in Glamorganshire, is distinguished by the same name. At this parish of *Festineog*, it is call'd otherwise *Sarn y Dhdal* (a name, whereof I can give no account) for the space of three miles, *viz.* from *Rhyd yr Hâl n** to *Kastelh Dôl Wydhêlen*; and some presume that *Pont aber Glaslyn*, and *y Gymwynas* in Caernarvonshire, is a continuation of the same Road.

Festineog.

Helen's way.

On a Mountain call'd *Mikneint* near *Rhyd ar Halen*, within a quarter of a mile of this Road, are some remarkable Stone monuments, call'd *Bedheu Gwyr Ardudwy*, i. e. *the Graves of the men of* Ardudwy. They are at least thirty in number; and each Grave is describ'd to be

* Q. Whether this Brook (as some others in Wales) was once call'd *Halen*; or whether the true name be *Rhyd ar Halen*, &c with respect to the Road? Mikneint Stone Monuments.

be about two yards long; and to be distinguish'd by four Pillars, one at each corner of a Grave; which are somewhat of a square form, about two or three foot high, and nine inches broad. The tradition is, that these are Sepulchral Monuments of some persons of note slain here, in a battle fought betwixt the men of *Dyffryn Ardudwy*, and some of Denbighshire. That they are indeed the Graves of men slain in battel, seems scarcely questionable; but when, or by what persons, &c. is wholly uncertain. One of the next neighbours informs me, that he saw, amongst other stones brought hence to mend the walls of *Festiniog* Church-yard, one with an Inscription; but at present there remains no account of it. By the description he gives of it, I suppose it Roman. For he says it was a polish'd stone, about two foot long, half a yard broad, and three or four inches thick: whereas all the later Inscriptions that I have seen in Wales, are on large Pillars, which are generally rude and unpolish'd. I am told there are also a considerable number of Graves near this Causey, on the Demeans of *Rhew goch*, in the parish of *Trawsfynydh*: and in the year 1687. I copied this Inscription from a stone call'd *Bédh Porws*, or *Porus's Grave* near Lhêch Idris in the same Parish.

PORIVS
HIC IN TVMVLO JACIT
HOMO -RIANVS FVIT

I found afterwards, it was generally understood, as if this had been the Grave of one of the first Christians in these parts; and that they read it, *Porius hic in tumulo jacit. Homo Christianus fuit*. Being at that time wholly unacquainted with any studies or observations in this kind, perhaps I might not transcribe it with that accuracy I ought; but if it be thus on the Stone (which I must recommend to farther examination) it can never bear that reading, unless we suppose the Letters STI omitted by the Stone-cutter after RI in the last line, which would be such a fault as we have scarce any instance of in those many hundreds of Inscriptions which Authors have publish'd. But howsoever we read the word, —RIANVS, I suppose this Inscription to have been the Epitaph of some Roman, about the second or third Century.]

Sarn Helen. Kaer Gai. Not far from *Sarn Helen*, is *Kaer Gai*, i. e. *Caius's* Castle, built by one *Caius* a Roman, of whom the common People of that neighbourhood report great things, and indeed scarce credible.

The Fountains of Dee. In the east part of the County, the river *Dee* springs from two fountains, whence it is supposed to have deriv'd the name; for they call it *Dwy*, which also signifies the number *two*; though others contend that it took the name from the word *Dwu*, as if a *sacred* river; and some again from *Dû*, which denotes *black*, from the colour of the water. This river after a very short course * is said to pass entire, and unmix'd through a large lake, call'd *Llyn Tegid*, in English *Pimble Mear*, and † *Plenlyn Mear*, carrying out the same quantity of water that it brought in. For neither are the *Gwiniad*, which are a fish peculiar to this lake, found in the *Dee*; nor any Salmons taken in the lake, though common in the river; [but this indeed, may be no conclusive Argument because we find that Fish, as well as Birds and Beasts, have their stations Providentially assigned them, and delight in such places as afford them agreeable feeding, &c. so that the passing of this river through all the lake, unmix'd, may be no more than a frivolous opinion of the Vulgar.] If you please, take here an accurate description of this lake, by an Antiquarian Poet.

(Margin: This river is call'd in Welsh Dowrdwy. See Radnorshire. * Passes. C. † Corruptly for Pen llyn Mear. Gwiniad Fish.)

Hispida qua tellus Mervinia respicit Eurum,
Est lacus antiquo Penlinum nomine dictus,
Hic lacus illimeis in valle Tegeius altâ
Late expandit equas, & vastum conficit orbem
Excipiens gremio latices, qui fonte perenni
Vicinis recidunt de montibus, atque sonoris
Illecebris captas demulcent suaviter aures.
Illud habet certe lacus admirabile dictu,
Quantumvis magna pluvia non æstuat atque
Aëre turbato, si ventus murmura tollat,
Excrescit subito rapidis violentior undis,
Et tumido superat contemptas flumine ripas.

Where eastern storms disturb the peaceful Skies,
In Merioneth famous *Pelin* lies.
Here a vast Lake which deepest Vales surround,
His watry Globe rowls on the yielding ground.
Encreas'd with constant Springs that gently run
From the rough Hills with pleasing murmurs down,
This wondrous property the Waters boast,
The greatest Rains are in it's Channels lost,
Nor raise the flood, but when loud tempests roar,
The rising Waves with sudden rage boyl ore,
And conqu'ring Billows scorn th' unequal Shore.

[As to the *Gwiniad* before mention'd, the word might be aptly render'd in English a *Whiting*, but the fish so call'd is very different from it, being of the Trout kind. A description of it may be seen in Mr. Willoughby's *Ichthyology*, who supposes it the same with what they call (by names of the like signification) *ein Albelen*, and *Weissfisch* in some parts of Switzerland, and the *Ferra* of the Lake of *Geneva*. And here, we may observe the natural agreeableness of those Alpine Lakes with these in our Mountains, in affording the same Species of Fish, as well as of our high Rocks, in producing some variety of Alpine Plants. They are never taken by any bait, but in nets, keeping on the bottom of the Lake, and feeding on small shells, and the leaves of *water Gladiol* *, a Plant peculiar to these Mountain-Lakes.] * Gladiolus lacustris Clusii.

Bala. On the brow of this Lake, lies *Bala*, a small Town with certain Privileges; having but few Inhabitants, and the Houses rudely built, which yet is the chief Market of these Mountaineers.

[The word *Bala*, though now very seldom (if it all) us'd as an Appellative, denotes, as the Author of the Latin British Dictionary † informs us, the place where any River or Brook issues out of a Lake; as *Aber* signifies the fall of one river into another, &c. and hence Dr. *Davies* supposes this Town to be denominated. In confirmation whereof, I add, that near the outlet of the River *Seiont*, out of

† The Gulielmus Vide Davisii Dict.

of *Lhyn Peris* * in Caernarvonshire, there is a place call'd *Bryn* † *y Bala*. Others || contend that *Bala* in the old British, as well as Irish, signifies a Village. I incline to the former Opinion, and imagin, that upon farther enquiry, other instances besides these two might be found, which would make it still more evident. The round Mount or Barrow at this Town, call'd *Tommen y Bala*, as also that other about half a mile from it, call'd *Brynlhysk*, and a third at *Pont Mwnwgl y Lhyn*, in the same neighbourhood, are supposed by their names, form, and situation, not to have been erected for Urn burial, but as Watch mounts to command the road and adjacent places, upon the Roman Conquest of this Country.

* The Lake of St *Peris*.
† *Bryn* signifies a hill.
|| H. Perry, (in Dr *Dav.* Dict.) whom we find too apt to presume *Irish* words to be old *British*.

Not far from hence in the Parish of *Lhan iw' Lhyn*, we find the ruins of an ancient Castle, of which no Author makes mention. It is call'd *Castelh Corndochen*, a name of which I can give no account, and is seated on the top of a very steep Rock, at the bottom of a pleasant Valley. It shews the ruins of a Wall, and, within that, of three Turrets, a square, a round, and an oval one, which is the largest. The Mortar was mix'd with Cockle-shells, which must have been brought hither by Land-carriage, about fourteen miles. It seems probable that this Castle, as also such another (but much less) in *Traws vynydh* Parish, call'd *Castelh Prysor*, were built by the Romans, but nothing certain can be affirm'd herein.

Castelh Corndochen.

We have not room here to take notice of several other places remarkable, and shall therefore only mention a gilt Coffin, and some brass Arms, found there of late years. The Coffin was discover'd about the year 1684, in a Turbery, †, call'd *Mownog ystradgwyn* near *Maes y Pandy*. It was of wood, and so well preserv'd, that the gilding remain'd very fresh; and is said to have contain'd an extraordinary large Skeleton. This is the only instance I know, of burying in such places: and yet they who placed this Coffin here, might have regard to the perpetual preservation of it; seeing we find by daily examples of trees found in Turberies, that such bituminous earth preserves wood beyond all others.

† Boggy or moorish ground, where fuel turfs are dug up.

The brass Arms were found in the year 1688, in a rock call'd *Katreg Dhiwin*, in the Parish of *Bethkelert*. They seem to be short Swords or Daggers, and to have been all cast in molds. They were of different forms and sizes, some of them being about two foot long, others not exceeding twelve inches: some flat, others quadrangular, &c. About fifty of them were found by removing a great stone, so near the surface of the ground, that they were almost in sight. I have been inform'd, that several were gilt: but twenty or thirty that I saw of them when first found, were all cover'd with a bluish scurf. Their handles probably were of wood, for they were all wasted: and there remain'd only (and that but in very few) two brass nails that fasten'd them, which were something of the form of chair nails, but headed or riveted on each side, so that they could not be taken out without breaking the round holes wherein they were placed, which they did not fill up, but hung loose in them. Such weapons have been found elsewhere in Wales; and those were probably of the same kind, which were found at the foot of St *Michael*'s Mount in Cornwall, suppos'd to be British.]

See Fig. 14, 15.

Hugh, Earl of Chester, was the first Norman that seiz'd this Country, and planted garrisons in it, whilst *Grufydh ap* * *Kynan* was his prisoner: but he afterwards recovering this land with the rest of his Principality, left it to his Posterity, who possess'd it till their fatal period in Prince *Lhewelyn*.

* Conanus.

There are in this County 37 Parishes.

CAERNARVONSHIRE.

Above Merionydhshire, lies that County which the Britains call *Sir Gaernarvon*, and the English *Caernarvonshire* (from the chief Town,) and, before the division of Wales into Counties, *Snowdon Forest*: whence in Latin Historians it is call'd *Snaudonia*; as also *Arvonia*, because it lies opposite to the Island of *Mona* or *Anglesey*. The north and west parts of it border on the Sea; the south on *Merionydhshire*; and on the east the river *Conwy* divides it from *Denbighshire*. The maritim part of it is fertile enough, and well peopled; especially that south-west Promontory, which with its crooked shores faces *Octopitarum*, or St *David's Land*, in Penbrokeshire.

Conwy, riv.

But for the inner parts, nature has raised them far and wide into high Mountains (as if she would † condense here within the bowels of the earth, the frame of this Island;) and made a most safe retiring place for the Britains in time of war. For here are such a number of rocks and craggy places, and so many valleys incumber'd with woods and lakes, that they are not only unpassable to an army, but even to men † lightly appointed. We may very properly call these Mountains the British *Alps*; for, besides that they are the highest in all the Island, they are also no less inaccessible, by reason of the steepness of their rocks, than the Alps themselves, and do all of them encompass one hill, which far exceeding all the rest in height, does so towre the head aloft, that it seems, I shall not say, to *threaten* the Sky, but to thrust its head into it. And yet it harbours Snow continually, being throughout the year cover'd with it; or rather with a harden'd crust * of Snow of many years continuance †. And hence the British name of *Kreigieu Eryreu*, and that of *Snowdon* in English; both which [seem to] signify *Snowy Mountains*. So, *Niphates* in Armenia, and *Imaus* in Scythia, as Pliny informs us, were denominated from *Snow*. [But it is observ'd by others, that the British name of these Mountains *Kreigieu'r Eryreu*, signifies *Eagle Rocks*, which are generally understood by the Inhabitants to be so call'd from the

† *Compages hujus Insulæ visceribus ista densaret.*

† *Expediti.*

The British Alps.

* *Nivium senie.*

† In this he was misinformed. See below, p. 797. Snowdon Hills.

the Eagles that formerly bred here too plentifully, and do yet haunt these Rocks some years, though not above three or four at a time, and that commonly one summer in five or six, coming hither, as is suppos'd, out of Ireland. Had the mountains been denominated from *Snow*, the name must have been *Kreigieu'r Eira*, whereas the Welsh always call them *Eryreu*. Nor do the ancientest Authors that mention them, favour that other Etymology; for Giraldus Cambrensis writes it *Eryri* (which differs nothing in pronunciation from the present name,) and Ninnius, who writ *Anno* 858, *Herirl*. However, seeing the English call it *Snowdon*, the former derivation was not without grounds; and it is possible the word *yrbau* might be either the ancient pronunciation, or a corruption of *eira*, and so these Rocks call'd *Kreigiau yr Yrau*, which might afterwards be written *Kreigieu Eryreu*.]

Notwithstanding the Snow, these Mountains are so fertile in grass, that it is a common saying among the Welsh, *That the mountains of Eryreu would, in case of necessity, afford Pasture enough for all the Cattel in Wales*. I shall say nothing of the two lakes on the tops of these Mountains (in one of which there floats a wandering Island, and the other affords plenty of Fish, each whereof has but one eye;) lest I might seem to countenance † Fables; though some, relying on Giraldus's authority, have believ'd both. However, that there are lakes and standing waters on the tops of these mountains, is certain: whence Gervase of *Tilbury*, in his book entitl'd *Otia Imperialia*, writes thus: *In the land of Wales within the bounds of Great Britain, are high Mountains, which have laid their foundations on exceeding hard rocks, on the * tops whereof the ground is so boggy, that where you do but just place your feet you'll perceive it to move a stone's cast off. Wherefore upon any surprise of an enemy, the Welsh by their agility skipping over that boggy ground, do either escape their assaults, or resolutely expect them, while they advance forward to their own ruin.* *Joannes Sarisburiensis*, in his *Polycraticon*, calls the Inhabitants of these Mountains by a new coin'd word *Nivicollinos*; of whom he wrote thus in the time of Henry the second: *Nivicollini Britones irruunt*, &c. *The Snowdon-Britains make inroads; and being now come out of their caverns and woods, they seize the plains of our Nobles, and before their faces, assault and overthrow them, or retain what they have got; because our youth, who delight in the house and shade, as if they were born only to consume the fruit of the land, sleep commonly till broad day*, &c.

† See below.

* This inner ror. See below.

[Amongst these Mountains, the most noted are *Moel y Wydhva*, *y Glyder*, *Karnedh Dhavidh*, and *Karnedh Lhewelyn*; which are very properly call'd the British Alps. For besides their extraordinary height, and craggy precipices, and their abounding with Lakes and Rivers, and being cover'd with Snow for a considerable part of the year; they agree also with the Alps in producing several of the same * Plants, and some Animals; as particularly *Merula Saxatalis Aldrovandi*, call'd here, and in Meirionydhshire, *Mwyalchen y Graig*, i. e. Rock-ouzel, and in Switzerland, Berg Amzel, or Mountain Black-bird; and the *Torgoch*, a Fish †, which Mr. ‖ Ray supposes to be the same with the * *Rootel* of the Alpine Lakes. In these Mountains (as probably in the Alps also, and other places of this kind) the greatest variety of rare Plants are found in the highest and steepest Rocks. The places here that afford best entertainment for Botanists, are, *Klogwyn Karnedh y Wydhva*, call'd commonly *Klogwyn y Garnedh* (which is probably the highest Rock in the three Kingdoms, *Krib y † Distil*, *Trigvylchau*, or as it is generally, and perhaps more truly, pronounced *y Dugyvylche* ‖, and *y Klogwyn dû ymhen y Glyder*, which are all near Lhan Berys, and well known to the Shepherds. Such as have not seen Mountains of this kind, are not able to frame an Idea of them, from the hills of more champain or lower Countries. For whereas such hills are but single heights or storey, these are heap'd upon one another; so that having climb'd upon one Rock, we come to a Valley, and most commonly to a Lake, and passing by that we ascend another, and sometimes a third and a fourth, before we arrive at the highest Peaks.

* See Ray's Synopsis of British Plants.

† Umbla minor Gesneri, p. 1201.

‖ Willough. Ichthyol.

* The word *Rootel* signifies the same with *Torgoch*.

† Call'd so corruptly perhaps for *Krib y Distilh*, for water drops down this precipice continually.

‖ i. e. Treigl-Vylchau.

These Mountains, as well as *Kader Idris* and some others in Meirionydhshire, differ from those by Brecknock, and elsewhere in South-Wales, in that they abound much more with naked and inaccessible Rocks; and that their lower skirts and valleys are always either cover'd, or scatter'd over, with fragments of Rocks of all magnitudes, most of which I presume to have fall'n from the impendent Cliffs. But of this, something more particular may be seen in Mr. Ray's *Physico Theological Discourses*, wherefore I shall mention here only two places, which seem'd to me more especially remarkable. The first, is the summit, or utmost top of the *Glyder* (a Mountain above mention'd as one of the highest in these parts) where I observ'd prodigious heaps of stones, many of them of the largeness of those of *Stone-henge* *, but of all the irregular shapes imaginable, and all lying in such confusion, as the ruins of any building can be suppos'd to do. Now I must confess, I cannot well imagin how this hath happen'd: for that they should be indeed the ruins of some Edifice, I can by no means allow, in regard that most of them are altogether as irregular as those that have fall'n to the Valleys. Let us then suppose them to be the Skeleton of the hill, expos'd to open view, by rains, snow, &c. but how came they to lye across each other in this confusion? some of them being of an oblong flat form, having their two ends (*ex gr.*) east and west, others laid athwart these some flat, but many inclining, being supported by other stones at the one end; whereas we find by Rocks and Quarries, that the *natural* position of stones is much more uniform. Had they been in a valley, I should have concluded, that they had fall'n from the neighbouring Rocks, because we find frequent examples of such heaps of stones augmented by accession of others tumbling on them; but being on the highest part of the hill, they seem'd to me much more remarkable.

Rocks.

Pag. 285.

Glyder.

* See Wiltshire.

The other place, which I thought no less observable, though for contrary reasons (that being as regular and uniform, as this is disorder'd and confus'd) is this. On the west side of the same hill, there is amongst many others one naked Precipice †, as steep as any I have seen; but so adorn'd with numerous equidistant Pillars, and these again slightly cross'd at certain joynts, that such as would favour the Hypothesis of the ingenious Author of the *Sacred Theory*, might suppose it one small pattern of the Antediluvian Earth. But this seem'd to me much more easily accounted for than the former; for it was evident, that the gullets or interstices between the pillars, were occasion'd by a continual dropping of water down this Cliff, which proceeds from the frequent Clouds, Rains

† This *Klogwyn* is near Trigvylchau or is perhaps one of them but distinguish'd by no particular name.

Rains and Snow, that this high Rock, expos'd to a westerly Sea-wind, is subject to. But that the effects of such storms are more remarkably regular on this Cliff than others, proceeds partly from its situation, and partly from the texture or constitution of the stone it consists of. However, we must allow a natural regularity in the frame of the Rock, which the storms only render more conspicuous.

Snow, not constantly here.

That these Mountains are, throughout the year, cover'd either with Snow, or *a harden'd crust of Snow of several years continuance, &c.* is a wrong notion, probably receiv'd from some persons who had never been at them. For generally speaking, there is no Snow here from the end of April to the midst of September. Some heaps excepted, which often remain near the tops of *Moel y Wydhva* and *Karnedh Lhewelyn*, till the midst of June, e'er they are totally wasted. It often snows on the tops of these Mountains in *May* and *June*; but that Snow, or rather Sleet, melts as fast as it falls; and the same shower that falls then in Snow on the high Mountains, is but Rain in the Valleys. As for an incrustation of Snow or Ice of several years continuance, we know not in Wales what it means. Though *Wagnerus* || tells us they are common in the Alps of Switzerland. ——*Tempore æstivo*, &c. *i. e. in summer time the tops of the Alps have perpetual frost, and perpetual snow.* And adds, *there are Mountains crown'd with hillocks or vast heaps of such Ice call'd by them* Firn *or* Gletscher, *which may be presum'd to have continu'd for two or three thousand years, insomuch that so hardness it may seem to be rather* Chrystal *than* Ice, &c.

|| Joan. Jac. Wagneri Hist. Nat. Helvetiæ Curiosa. Sect. 2.

Lakes.

The number of Lakes in this mountainous tract, may be about fifty or threescore. I took a Catalogue of fifteen, visible from the top of *Moel y Wydhva*. These are generally denominated either from the rivers they pour forth, or from the colour of their water; amongst which I observ'd one, under the highest Peak of Snowdon, call'd *Fynon lâs*, that signifies the *Green Fountain*, which I therefore thought remarkable, because Mr *Ray* * observes that the waters of some of the Alpine Lakes, are also inclin'd to that colour. Others receive their names from some Village or Parish Church adjoyning, or from a remarkable Mountain or Rock under which they are situated; and some there are (though very few) distinguished by names scarce intelligible to the best Criticks in the British, as *Lhyn Teirn*, *Lhyn Eigiau*, *Lhyn Lhydaw* †, &c. *Giraldus Cambrensis* (as was before observed) informs us of two Lakes on the highest tops of these Mountains; one remarkable for a wandering Island; and the other for monocular Fish. To this we must beg leave to answer, that amongst all the Lakes in this mountainous Country, there is none seated on the highest part of a hill, all of them being spread in Valleys either higher or lower, and fed by the Springs and Rivulets of the Rocks and Cliffs that are above them. The Lake wherein he tells us there's a wandering Island, is a small Pond, call'd *Lhyn y Dywarchen* (i. e. *Lacus cespitis*,) from a little green moveable patch, which is all the occasion of the Fable of the wandering Island; but whence that other of monocular Fish (which he says were found also at two places in Scotland) took beginning, I have nothing to say, but that it is credibly reported that Trouts having only one eye are sometimes taken at *Lhyn ykwn* near *Lhan Berys*. Most of these Lakes are well stor'd with Fish, but generally they afford no other kinds than Trout and Eel. The *Torgochiaid* or red Charres (if we may so call them) are found in some other Lakes of this County and *Merionydh*, besides *Lhyn Peris*. But this Lake of St Peris affords another kind of Alpine Fish; and by the description I hear of it, I suspect it to be the *Gelt* or *Gilt Charre* of Winandermear in Westmorland, which Mr. *Willoughby* and Mr. *Ray* conclude to be the same with the *Carpio Lacus Benaci* of Rhondeletius and Gesner. The season here for catching both, begins about the eleventh of November, and continues for a month. These Fish, as well as the *Guiniad* of *Lhyn Tegid* in Meirionydhshire, are never taken by bait, but always in nets, near *Pontvawr*, in the river *Seiont*, which issues out of this Lake, and is call'd now corruptly *Avon y Sant*, from St Peris.

* Observations Topographical &c.

† Some might interpret the two former *Kings mear* and *Shoals mear*, the word *Teirn* signifying a King or Prince and *Eigiau* Shoales of fish. *Lhydaw* is the same whereby we call *Armorica* but signifies nothing else that we know of.

I observ'd, that the Inhabitants of these Mountains call any low Country *Hendrev*, which signifies *the ancient habitation*, and that it is a common tradition among them, as also amongst those that inhabit the like places in Brecknockshire and Radnorshire, that the Irish were the ancient Proprietors of their Country. Which I therefore thought remarkable, because it is impossible that either those of South wales should receive it from these, or the contrary; seeing they have no communication, there being a Country of about fourscore miles interposed.]

But let us now descend from the Mountains to the Plains; which we find only by the Sea, and therefore it may suffice if we coast along the shore.

That Promontory which we have observed already to be extended to the south west, is call'd in the several Copies of Ptolemy, *Canganum*, *Janganum*, and *Langanum*. Which is truest, I know not; but it may seem to be *Langanum*, seeing the Inhabitants at this day call it *Lhyn*. It runs in with a narrow and strait Peninsula, having larger Plains than the rest of this County, which yield plenty of Barley. It affords but two small Towns worth our notice: the innermost, at the bay call'd *Pwlh heli*, which name signifies the *Salt Pool*; and the other by the Irish Sea (which washes one part of this Peninsula,) call'd *Nevin*, * a small trading Village; where, in the year 1284 the English Nobility (as Florilegus writes) triumphing over the Welsh, celebrated the Memory of *Arthur the Great* with Tournaments and festival Pomp. If any more Towns flourish'd here, they were then destroy'd, when *Hugh* Earl of Chester, *Robert* of Rutland, and *Guarin* of Salop (the first Normans who advanc'd thus far) so wasted this *Promontory*, that for seven years it lay desolate.

Canganum. Lhyn. Pwlh Eli. * *Vill'm mercatorium* Nevin. *Vita Grufydh ap Conani.*

From *Nevin*, the shore, indented with two or three Promontories, is continued northwards; and then turning to the north east, passes by a narrow firth or chanel call'd *Meneu*, which separates the Isle of *Anglesey* from the firm land. Upon this *Fretum*, stood the City *Segontium*, mention'd by Antoninus, of the walls whereof I have seen some ruins near a small Church built in Honour of St *Publicus*. It took its name from a river that runs by it, call'd to this day *Seiont*, which issues out of the lake *Lhyn Peris*, in which they take a peculiar Fish, not seen elsewhere, call'd by the Inhabitants from its red belly, *Torgoch*. Now, seeing an ancient copy of Ptolemy places the haven of the *Setantii* on this coast, which other copies remove much further off; if I should read it

Menau, or *Menai* Sea. *Pembrokeshire.* Segontium. Lhan Beblic. Torgoch fish. See above *Setantii*.

Segontio

Segontiorum Portum, and should say it was at the mouth of this river, perhaps I should come near the truth; at least, a candid reader would pardon the conjecture Ninnius calls this City *Kaer Kystenydh*, and the author of the life of *Grufydh ap Kynan* tells us, that *Hugh* Earl of Chester built a castle at *Hên Gaer Kystenin*; which the Latin Interpreter renders, *The ancient city of the Emperor Constantine*. Moreover, *Matthew* of Westminster hath recorded (but herein I will not vouch for him) that the body of *Constantius*, the father of *Constantine* the Great, was found here in the year 1283, and honourably inter'd in the Church of the new Town, by command of King Edward the first, who at that time built the Town of *Kaer'n Arvon*, out of the ruins of this City, a little higher, by the mouth of the river, in such a situation, that the Sea washes it on the west and north This, as it took the name from its situation, as *opposite to the Island* Mona, so did it communicate that name to the whole County for thence the English call it *Caernarvonshire* This Town is encompassed with a firm Wall, though of small circumference, and almost of a circular form, and shews a beautiful Castle, which takes up all the west-side of it The private buildings, for the manner of the Country, are neat; and the civility of the Inhabitants much commended They esteem it a great honour, that King Edward the first was their founder, and that his son Edward the second, the first Prince of Wales of English extraction, was born there, who was therefore stiled *Edward of Caernarvon* Moreover, the Princes of Wales had here their Chancery, their Exchequer, and their Justiciary for *North Wales*

Caernarvon

In a bottom seven miles hence on the same *Fretum*, lies *Bangor* or *Banchor*, enclosed on the south-side, with a very steep mountain, and with a Hill on the north-side; so call'd *à choro pulchro*, from a *beautiful Quire*, or as others suppose, *quasi locus chori*, the place of a Quire † It is a Bishop's See, and contains in its Diocese 96 Parishes The Cathedral is consecrated to *Daniel*, once Bishop thereof It is no very fair building, having been burnt by that most profligate Rebel *Owen Glyn Dowrdwy*, who design'd no less than the destruction of all the Cities of Wales It was afterwards * rebuilt in the time of Henry the seventh, by the Bishop thereof, *Henry Deny*; but hath not yet recover'd its ancient splendour Now, it is only a small Town, but heretofore it was so considerable, that for it's *large* extent, it was call'd *Bangor-vawr*, and was fortified with a castle by *Hugh* Earl of Chester, of which (tho' I made diligent enquiry) I could not discover the least footsteps It was seated at the very entrance of this *Fretum* or chanel, where Edward the first attempted in vain to build a bridge, that his Army might pass over into the Island *Mona* or *Anglesey* (of which we shall speak in its proper place) Here also, as we find in Tacitus, *Paulinus Suetonius* pass'd over with the Roman soldiers; the horse at a ford, and the foot in flat-bottom'd boats

Bangor

† See Dr *Davies*'s Welsh Dictionary in the word *Ban*. Others, *quasi Pen Clor*, or chief *Chorus*

* *Ref* [illegible]

Vit Gruf

From hence the shore with a steep ascent passes by a very high and perpendicular rock call'd *Pen maen mawr* which hanging over the Sea, affords Travellers but a very narrow passage; where the rocks on one hand seem ready to fall on their heads; and on the other, is the roaring Sea of a vast depth But having pass'd this, together with *Pen maen bychan*, i e *the lesser rocky Promontory*, a plain extends it self as far as the river *Conwy*, the eastern limit of this County This river is call'd in Ptolemy, *Toisovius* for *Conovius*; an error that has crept into Copies from a compendious way of writing Greek It springs out of a lake of the same name, in the southern limit of the County; and hastens to the Sea, being confin'd within a very narrow and rocky chanel, almost to the very mouth of it This river breeds a kind of *Shells*, which being impregnated with dew, produce Pearl [It is probably one of the noblest streams, of the length, in Europe, for whereas the whole course of it is but twelve miles, it receives so many Brooks and Rivulets from the bordering Mountains of Snowdon, that it bears Ships of burden for eight of them And hence, if I may be free to conjecture, it receiv'd its name; for supposing that *Gwy* (or *Wy*) signifies *a River* ‖; *Kynwy* or Conwy (for in Etymologies we regard the pronunciation, not the orthography) must denote *an extraordinary great or prime river* the Particle *Kyn* prefix'd in compound words, being generally augmentative, or else signifying the first and chief. As *Kyn kan*, extraordinary white; *Kyndyn*, very stiff or obstinate. *Kynvid*, the Antediluvian world, *Kyndhydh*, the dawning of the day, *Kynverthyr*, a Proto martyr, &c And (that we may note this by the way) I suspect the word *Cyn* to have been the same originally with the Irish *Cean*, i e Head, whence *Kyntav* signifies *the first*, quasi *pennav* the chiefest, and Dr *Davies* supposes the word *Kyndhâredh*, i e *Megrim* or *Vertigo*, to be equivalent in signification with *Pendhâredh* If this may be allow'd, I know not but these proper names, *Cungetorix*, *Cunobelinus*, *Cuneglasus*, and *Cunotamus* * (call'd in British *Kyntwrch*, *Kynvelyn*, *Kynglas*, and *Kynedhav* †) might bear the interpretation of *Charocephalus*, *Flavicomus*, *Canus* and *Capito*, or *Bucephalus*, since we find that persons of the greatest dignity were stiled by such sirnames, not only among the Britains, but the Romans also, and probably most Nations in these parts of Europe

Conwy river, call'd Toisovius.

Pearls

‖ See *Radnorshire*

* See the Inscriptions in *Pembrokeshire*

† Hibern *Damh* eu *Dav* Bos

The Pearls of this river are as large and well colour'd as any we find either in Britain or Ireland, and have probably been fish'd for here, ever since the Roman Conquest, if not sooner For it is evident, that Pearls were in esteem amongst the Britains before that time, seeing we read in Pliny †, that Julius Cæsar dedicated a Breast plate to *Venus genitrix*, placing it in her Temple at Rome, all cover'd or studded over with British Pearls: which must have been receiv'd from the Britains, and not discover'd here by his own Soldiers, for he advanced not much nearer than one hundred miles off any river that affords them The British and Irish Pearls are found in a large black Muscle (figured and described by Dr *Lister*,) under the title of *Musculus niger omnium crassissimâ & ponderosissimâ testâ* *; by which it is sufficiently distinguish'd from all other shells. They are peculiar to rapid and stony rivers; and are common in Wales, and in the North of England, and in Scotland, and some parts of Ireland In this Country, they are called by the vulgar *Kregin Dilitw*, i. e Deluge-shells; as if Nature had not intended shells for the rivers; but being brought thither by the Universal Deluge, they had continu'd there, and so propagated their kind ever since They who fish here for Pearls, know partly by the out side of these Muscles, whether they contain any; for generally such as have them, are a little contracted or distorted from their usual shape A curious and

† Nat hist 9 c 35

* Append ad Tract de Animal Angl p 11

Penmaen mawr

and accomplish'd Gentleman lately of these parts * (whose untimely death I have reason, amongst many others, to bewail) shew'd me a valuable Collection of the Pearls of this river; amongst which I noted a stool-pearl, of the form and bigness of lesser button-mold, weighing seventeen grains, and distinguish'd on the convex side with a fair round spot of a Cornelian colour, exactly in the center]

* *Robert Wyn* of Bod Yskalhen, Esq

Conovium

The Town of *Conovium* mention'd by Antoninus, receiv'd its name from the river which Town, though it be now quite destroy'd, and the very name, in the place where it stood, extinct, yet the Antiquity of it is preserved in the present name for † in the ruins of it we find a small Village call'd *Kaer bên*, which signifies the *old City* [It is now called *Kaer Rhûn*, which probably is a corruption of *Kaer bên* unless we should rather suppose it call'd *Y Gayer hyn*, which signifies *the elder Town or City*, with reference to the Town of Conway, which was built out of the ruins of it The common tradition of this neighbourhood is, that it received its name from *Rhûn ap Maelgwn Gwynedh*, who liv'd about the end of the sixth Century, for his Father, whom Gildas calls *Maglocunus* (which word I suppose some Copyist writ erroneously for *Maelocunus*) and, who, by way of Invective, is call'd also *Draco Insularis*, or *Island* Dragon, died about the Year 586 * This I suspect was at first no other than the conjecture of some Antiquary, conceiv'd from the affinity of the names, which being communicated to others, became at length a current Tradition, as we find too many more have, on the like occasion but whether *Rhûn ap Maelgwn* gave name to this place or not, it is certain it was a City long before his time, there being no room to doubt but this was the old *Conovium* of the Romans, mention'd in the Itinerary

† *Kaer ben* is 3 miles above *Conway.*

* Mr *Robert Vaughan's* Ms

Not many years since, there was a Roman Hypocaust discover'd at this place, agreeable in all respects (by the account I hear of it) with those found at *Kaer Lheion ar Wysk*, mention'd by Giraldus, and near *Hope* in Flintshire, as described before in that County So that in all places in Wales, where any Legions had their station, such stoves or hot vaults, &c have been discover'd those at *Kaer Lheion ar Wysk* being made by the Legion *Secunda Augusta*, that near *Hope* by the twentieth Legion (entitled *Britannica Valens Victrix*, which lay at *Kaer Lheion ar Dhowrdwy*, or West-chester,) and this, by the Tenth Legion For I find in some notes of a late * Reverend Divine, that he had seen several Brick-tiles, which were found near this Church of *Kaer hyn*, inscrib'd LEG X Not the *tenth Legion*, which *Julius Cæsar* brought with him (for none ever dreamed that he came thus far,) but the *tenth Legion* called *Antoniana* (which serv'd under *Ostorius*, against the *Silures* and *Ordevices*;) as appears by the following Coin, dug up in Caermarthenshire

* Mr *William Brikdal* Rector of Lhan Rwst Gale, p 122

And as those two places above-mentioned were called *Kaer Lheion* (i e *Urbs Legionum*) from the Legions that had their stations there, with the addition of the names of the rivers on which they were seated, so I suspect this place might be call'd anciently *Kaer Lheion ar Gynwy*, because we find a hill near it, call'd at this day *Mynydh Caer Lheion*, i e *Kaer Lheion Mountain* The late Sir *Thomas Mostyn* Baronet, who may be justly stil'd a Gentleman of exemplary qualifications, shewed me amongst his valuable Collection of Antiquities, some Curiosities which he had received from this place Amongst these, I noted a hollow brick, taken from the Hypocaust above-mention'd, thirteen inches long, and five and a half square, having a round hole in the midst, of about two inches diameter, the thickness of the brick not exceeding three quarters of an inch Of this I thought a figure might be acceptable to the Curious, and have therefore added one at the end of these Welsh Counties *, as also of a round piece of Copper found here, and preserv'd in the same Collection, which I thought very remarkable It is somewhat of the form of a Cake of Wax, even or flat on one side, and convex on the other, about eleven inches over, and forty pounds weight It is uneven in the margin or circumference, and somewhat ragged on each side; and on the flat side hath an oblong square sunk in the midst, with an Inscription as in the figure † This he supposed to have been a piece of rude Copper or Bullion, and that the Inscription was only the Merchant's stamp, or direction to his Correspondent at Rome adding, that there were some signs of a Roman Copper work near *Trevriw*, about three miles hence, and elsewhere in this neighbourhood, whence it was probable they had dug it

* Fig 8

† Fig 10

In the Year 880, a memorable Battel was fought near *Aber Kynwy*, betwixt *Anârawd* Prince of North-Wales, and *Iadred* Duke of Mercia; of which that judicious Antiquary, Mr *Robert Vaughan* of *Hengwyrt*, gives the following account, in some notes he writ on Dr *Powel's* History of Wales

Aber Kynwy Battel

After the death of Roderic *the Great, the Northern Britons of* Stratclwyd *and* Cumberland, *were (as* Hector Boethius *and* Buchanan *relate) much infested and weakened with the daily incursions of Danes, Saxons, and Scots, which made many of them (all that would not submit their necks to the yoke) to quit their country, and seek out more quiet habitations Under the conduct of one* Hobert, *they came to* Gwynedh *, *in the beginning of* Anârawd's *reign, who commiserating their distressed condition, gave them the country from* Chester *to the river* Conwy *to inhabit, if they could force out the Saxons, who had lately possessed themselves thereof Whereupon, these Britons first engaged the Saxons, and, necessity giving edge to their valour, soon drove them out thence, being yet scarce warm in their seats About three years after this,* An Dom 880, *Edryd Walbtbir* †, *King of the Saxons (called by the English Historians* Eadred *Duke of Mercia) made great preparations for the regaining of the said country, but the northern Britons, who had settl'd there having intelligence thereof; for the better securing of their cattel and goods, removed them over the river Conwy In the mean time,* P Anarawd *was not idle; but gather'd together all the strength he could make His army encamp'd near* Conwy, *at a place call'd* Kymryd, *where he and his men making resistance against the assaults of the Saxon power, at length, after a bloody fight, obtain'd a compleat victory This battel was called* Gwaeth Kymryd,

* North Wales

† [illegible]

Konwy, *because it was fought in the Township of Kymryd, hard by Conwy, but* Anârawd *call'd it* Dial Rodri, *because he had there reveng'd the death of his father* Rodri *In this battel,* Tudwal *the son of* Rodri Mawr *receiv'd a hurt in the knee, which made him be call'd* Tudwal Glôf, *or the* Lame, *ever after. His brothers to reward his valour and service, gave him* Uchelogoed * Gwynedh. *The Britons pursuing their victory, chased the Saxons quite out of Wales into Mercia, where having burnt and destroyed the borders, they return'd home laden with rich spoils* Anârawd, *to express his thankfulness to God for this great victory, gave lands and possessions to the Church of* Bangor, *as the Records of that See do testifie, and likewise to the Collegiate Church of* K'lynog *in* Arvon, *as we read in the extent of North Wales After this, the northern Britons came back from beyond the river Conwy, and possessed again the lands assigned them between Conwy and Chester, which for a long time after they peaceably enjoy'd Some English Writers, as* Mat Westminster, &c *not considering, probably, that the Britons had lands in* Lhoegria *and* Albania *after King Cadwalader's time, take those of* Cumberland *and* Stradklwyd *for the Britons of Wales Asser Menevensis, who liv'd* A D 875, *says that* † Halden *the Dane marched into Northumberland, which he subdued, having before conquer'd the Picts and Britons of Stratclud* ——In regionem *Nordan-hymbrorum* perrexit, eamque subjugavit, necnon & Pictos & * Stratcludenses]

* An rectius Uchelgoed.

† Chr Sax *Healfdene*

* The Oxford Edit An 1691 hath *Strecledenses* Chron Sax *Straecledwealas*, and *Straeledwealas Ystrad Klwyd* signifies Cluyd's Dale or the Vale of Cluyd, whence *Strecled*, *Streclet*, and *Straetled*, are so many variations.

Out of the ruins of this City [as hath been intimated] King Edward the first built the new Town at the *mouth* of the river, which is therefore call'd *Aber Conwy*, a place that Hugh Earl of Chester had fortified before This new *Conwy*, both in regard of its advantageous situation, and for its being so well fortified, as also for a very neat Castle by the river side, might deserve the name of a small City rather than a Town, but that it is but thinly inhabited [In the 3d year of King Charles I *Edward* Lord *Conway* of Ragley, was created Viscount *Conway* of Conway Castle, and also afterwards in the 31st of King Charles II *Edward* Lord Viscount *Conway* (who had succeeded to another Edward) was created Earl of Conway, whose adopted heir, *Francis Seymour Conway*, was created Lord Conway, and Baron of Ragley, in the second year of her Majesty Queen Anne]

Opposite to *Conwy* on this side the river (though in the same County) we have a vast Promontory with a crooked elbow (as if nature had designed there an harbour for shipping) call'd *Gogarth*, where stood the ancient City of *Diganwy* on the sea of *Conwy*, which many ages since, was consumed by lightning This I suppose to have been the City *Dictum*, where under the later Emperours, the commander of the *Nervii Dictenses* kept guard As for it's being afterwards call'd *Diganwy* who sees not that *Ganwy* is a variation only of *Conwy* and that from thence also came the English *Ganoc*? for so was the Castle call'd, which in later times was built there by Henry the third

Gogarth Diganwy

Dictum

Ganoc

[About ten years since, there was found at the Castle of *Diganwy* (or very near it) several brass Instruments, somewhat of the shape of axes; but whether they were British or Roman, or what use they were designed for, I must leave to be determin'd by others There were about fifty of them found under a great stone, placed heads and points, whereof some are yet preserv'd in the collection above-mention'd They have been also discover'd in several other parts of Wales; and that, of which I have given a Figure (*numb* 13) is one of seven or eight that were found of late years at the opening of a Quarry on the side of *Moel yr Henlhys* † in Montgomeryshire Dr *Plot*, in his * Natural History of Staffordshire, mentions such brass Instruments found at four several places in that County; which, though they differ something from ours, were yet in all likelihood intended for the same use But that they were Bolt heads of Roman *Catapultae* (as that learned and ingenious Author supposes) seems to me somewhat questionable not only for that we find no mention of brass Arms amongst the Romans, but partly because they seem not large enough for that use, nor well contriv'd either for flight or execution; and partly because Antiquaries take it for granted, that the Britons had no wall'd Towns or Castles before the Roman Conquest, so that such machines as *Catapultae* and *Ballistae* were unnecessary in this Island If it be urged, that they might be of use to cover the passes of rivers or friths ‖, as that into Anglesey out of his County; it is evident, that they were not used here on that occasion for if so the British army had not been posted on the opposite shore to receive the Romans (as * Tacitus expresly tells us they were) but had been compelled to a farther distance It seems very probable, that the brass Axes found at St *Michael's Mount* in Cornwal, were of this kind, because there were found with them certain Arms of the same Metal, like short swords or daggers, such as we find also in these parts, and have mention'd in the last County Of those, the Opinion is, that they were British and indeed it is not to be doubted but that they were so, if the brass Arms there mention'd were really swords (as is supposed,) for no man will imagin that the Romans used swords of that metal and that being granted, it will be scarce questionable but the Axes and Spear-heads which are said to be lodg'd with them, belong'd to the same Nation For my own part, I must confess, that for a long time I suspected these Instruments to be *Roman* (supposing them too artificial to have been made by the Britons before the Romans civiliz'd them.) and that they were not swords, &c but intended for some other uses But seeing they had gold and silver Coins before that time (as all Antiquaries allow) and that it is scarce questionable, but the golden *Torques* described in the last County was theirs, and also that Pliny tells us the Druids cut down their Misseltoe with golden sickles I know not but they might have more arts than we commonly allow them, and therefore must suspend my judgment.

† A Hill so call'd in Dewen parish.

* Pag 403

‖ Tacit Annal lib xiv [illegible]

* Annal lib xiv

See Cornwall

There are in this County (as also in the other Provinces of North-Wales) several remarkable old forts, and such stone monuments as we have noted in the Counties of *Caer Mardhin*, *Penbroke* and *Cardigan*, of which, because I have taken no description my self, I shall here insert, for the satisfaction of the curious, some short notes out of a MS written by a person of Quality in the reign of King Charles the first, and communicated to me by my worthy friend Mr *Griffith Jones*, School-master of *Lhan Rwst*

Sir *John Wynn*, of Gwydyr

On the top of Penmaen, *stands a lofty and impregnable Hill call'd* Braich y Dhinas; *where we find the ruinous walls of an exceeding strong fortification, encompass'd with a treble wall, and within each wall the foundation of at least a hundred towers, all round and of equal bigness, and about six yards*

Braich Dhinas

yards diameter, within the walls. The walls of this Dinas *were in most places two yards thick, and in some about three This Castle seems (while it stood) impregnable, there being no way to offer any assault to it, the hill being so very high, steep, and rocky, and the walls of such strength. The way or entrance into it ascends with many turnings; so that a hundred men might defend themselves against a whole Legion; and yet it should seem that there were Lodgings within these walls for twenty thousand men. At the summit of this rock, within the innermost wall, there is a Well, which affords plenty of water, even in the dryest Summers By the tradition we receive from our Ancestors, this was the strongest and safest refuge or place of defence that the ancient Britons had in all* Snowdon, *to secure them from the incursions of their enemies Moreover, the greatness of the work shews, that it was a princely fortification, strengthen'd by nature and workmanship, seated on the top of one of the highest mountains of that part of* Snowdon, *which lies towards the Sea*

About a mile from this Fortification, stands the most remarkable Monument in all Snowdon, *call'd* Y Meineu hirion, *upon the plain mountain, within the parish of* Dwy Gyvylcheu, *above* Gwdhw glâs *It is a circular entrenchment about twenty six yards diameter, on the out side whereof, are certain rude stone pillars pitch'd on end; of which about twelve are now standing, some two yards, and others five foot high, and these are again encompass'd with a stone wall It stands upon the plain mountain, assoon as we come to the height, having much even ground about it, and not far from it, there are three other large stones pitch'd on end in a triangular form*

Y Meineu hirion

About three furlongs from this Monument, there are several such vast heaps of small stones as we call Karnedheu, *concerning which, the tradition is, that a memorable battel was fought near this place betwixt the Romans and Britons; wherein after much slaughter on both sides, the latter remaining conquerors buried their dead in heaps, casting these stones on them; partly to prevent the wild boars (which in those times were common in these parts) from digging up their bodies, and partly as a memorial to posterity, that the bodies of men lay there inter'd There are also about these heaps or* Karnedheu, *several graves, which have stones pitch'd on end about them, and are cover'd with one or two large ones These are presumed to be the Monuments of the Commanders or greatest persons then slain in battel; but having nothing to inform us herein, we must rely on tradition and conjecture,* &c]

Karnedheu

Soon after the Norman Conquest, this Country was govern'd by *Grufydh ap Kynan* *, who not being able to repel the English-troops which made frequent inroads into Wales, was constrain'd sometimes to yield to the storm And when afterwards by his great Integrity he had gain'd the favour of King Henry the first, he also easily recover'd his lands from the English, and left them to his posterity, who enjoy'd them till the time of *Lhewelyn ap Grufydh* † But he having provok'd his brothers with injuries, and the neighbouring English with incursions, was at length brought to that strait, that he held this mountainous Country (together with the Isle of *Mona* or *Anglesey*) of King Edward the first, as Tenant in fee, paying a thousand Marks yearly. Which conditions when he afterwards would not stand to, but (following rather his own and his perfidious brother's obstinacy, than led on with any hopes of prevailing) would again run the hazard of war, he was kill'd, and so put an end to his own Government, and that of the Britons in Wales

* Conanus.

† An account of the life and death of this excellent Prince may be seen at large in Dr Powel's History of *Wales*, p 314, *&c*

[In the fourth year of King Charles the first, *Robert* Lord *Dormer* of *Wing* was advanced to the title and dignity of Viscount *Ascot* and Earl of *Caernarvon*; and was succeeded therein by *Charles* his son and heir Since which this honourable title hath been confer'd on *James Brydges*, eldest son of *James* Lord *Chandois*, invested for some time with both these Titles, and lately advanced to the higher honour of *Duke* of *Chandois* *]

* See *Glocestershire*

This County contains 68 Parish-Churches.

ANGLESEY.

WE have already observ'd, that the County of *Caernarvon*, which we last survey'd, deriv'd its name from the chief Town therein, and that the Town borrow'd that name from the Island of *Mona*, which lies opposite to it It remains now, that (having heretofore, not so properly plac'd it among the Islands) we restore that tract to its right place, and describe it in order; seeing it also enjoys, and not undeservedly, the title of a County This Island was call'd by the Romans, *Mona*; in British, *Môn* and *Tir Môn*, i e *the Land of Mon*, and *Ynys dowylh* or *the shady Island*; by the old Saxons, Moneg; and in latter times, when reduc'd by the English, Engles ea and Anglesey, i e *the English Island* It is divided from the Continent of Britain by the narrow frith of *Meneu* *; and on all other sides, is wash'd by that raging Irish sea It is of an irregular form, and extended in length from east to west twenty miles †, and where broadest, about seventeen 'This Land (saith 'Giraldus) although as to outward appearance 'it may seem a dry, rocky, and unpleasant 'country, not unlike that of *Pebidiog* near *St 'David's*; is yet, as to the quality of the 'soil, much otherwise, for it is incomparably 'the most fruitful country for wheat, in all 'Wales insomuch that in the Welsh language, 'it is proverbially said of it, *Môn Mam Cymry*, 'i e *Mon the Nursery of Wales* because when 'other Countries fail'd, this alone, by the richness of the soil, and the plentiful harvests it 'produced, was wont to supply all Wales' It is also at this time very rich in cattel, and affords milstones; and in some places a kind of * Alum-earth, of which they † lately began to make *Alum* and *Coperas*; but the project not succeeding, they * desisted

Mona

* St David's in Penbroke shire

† From Beaumaris to Holy head are 24 miles

* Of the *Alumen plumosum* or *Amianthus* in the Parish of *Llanvaing Hornwy*, See Philos Transact n 156

This is that celebrated Island *Mona*, anciently the seat of the Druids; which was attempted first by *Paulinus Suetonius*, and reduced under

† So said, ann 1695

* Have now

under the Roman yoke by *Julius Agricola* *In the reign of Nero, this* Paulinus Suetonius *(as we read in* Tacitus*) prepared for an attempt on the Island* Mona, *a very populous country, and a receptacle of deserters, and to that end, built flat bottom'd vessels, because the shores were but shallow and hazardous Thus, the foot passed over; and the horse follow'd, either at a ford, or else, in deeper waters (as occasion requir'd) swam their horses On the opposite shore, stood the Enemies army, well provided of arms and men, besides women running about with dishevel'd hair like furies, in a mournful habit, bearing torches in their hands About the army, stood the Druids, who (with hands lifted up to heaven pouring forth dreadful Imprecations, so terrify'd the soldiers with the novelty of the sight, that (as if their limbs had been benummed) they expos'd their bodies, like so many stocks, to the strokes of the enemy But at last, partly by exhortation of the General, and partly by encouraging each other not to stand amazed at the sight of distracted women and* ‖ *a company of frantick people, they advanced their ensigns, and trampled down their enemies, thrusting them into their own fires They being thus conquer'd, a garrison was planted there, and their groves cut down, which were consecrated to their cruel superstitions For they held it lawful to sacrifice with the blood of Captives, and to consult their Gods by inspection into human Entrails. But while these things were in agitation, a sudden revolt of the whole Province recall'd him from this enterprise* Afterwards, as the same Author writes, Julius Agricola *resolv'd to reduce the Island* Mona, *from the Conquest whereof* Paulinus *was recall'd (as we have already observ'd) by a general rebellion in Britain but being unprovided of transport Vessels, as it commonly happens in doubtful Counsels, the policy and courage of the General found new means of conveying over his army For, after they had first laid down their baggage, he commanded the choicest of the Auxiliaries (to whom the fords were well known, and whose custom it was in their country, so to swim as to be able to guide themselves and their arms, and horses) to pass over the chanel Which was done in such a surprising manner, that the enemies, who expected a Navy, and watch'd the sea, stood so much amaz'd, that supposing nothing difficult or invincible to men of such resolution, they immediately supplicated for peace, and surrender'd the Island* So Agricola *became famous and great*

‖ Fanaticum agmen

Many ages after, when this Island was conquer'd by the English, it took their name, being call'd formerly by the Saxons Englesea, and now *Anglesey*, which signifies the *English Island* But seeing *Humfrey Lhwid*, in his learned Epistle to that accomplish'd Scholar *Ortelius*, has restor'd the Island to its ancient name and dignity, it is not necessary we should dwell long upon this County

However, we may add, that about the decline of the Roman Government in Britain, some of the Irish Nation crept into this Island For besides certain intrench'd Banks, which they call *Irish Cottages*, there is another place known by the name of *Yn bericy Gwidil*, from some Irish, who under the conduct of one *Sirige*, overcame the Britons there, as we read in the Book of *Triades* [Which words *Yn bericy Gwidil* seem to have been erroneously printed for *Kerig y Gwydhil*, i e *Irish stones*, for we find a place so call'd in the parish of *Lhan Gristiolus* But I think, we may not safely conclude from that name, either that the Irish had any settlement in these parts, or that there was any memorable action here betwixt that Nation and the Britons; seeing it relates only to one person, who perhaps might be buried at that place, and a heap of stones cast on his grave, as has been usual in other places I also make some doubt, whether those Monuments mention'd by the name of *Hibernicorum Casulæ*, or *Irish Huts*, be any proof that ever the Irish dwelt there, for they are only some vast rude stones laid together in a circular order, enclosing an Area of about five yards diameter, and are so ill-shap'd, that we cannot suppose them the foundations of any higher building and as they are, they afford no shelter or other convenience for Inhabitants Those I meant, are to be seen in a Wood near *Lhygwy*, the Seat of the worshipful *Thomas Lloyd* Esq, and are commonly call'd *Kitteu'r Gwydhelod*, i e *Irish Cotts*, whence I infer, that they must be the same which are here call'd *Hibernicorum Casulæ*

A Monument of this kind, though much less, may be seen at *Lhech yr Ast* in the parish of *Lhan Goedmor* near Cardigan, which was doubtless erected in the time of Heathenism and Barbarity, but to what end, I dare not pretend to conjecture The same may be said of these *Kitteu'r Gwidhelod*, which I presume to have been so call'd by the vulgar, only because they have a tradition, that before Christianity, the Irish were possess'd of this Island, and therefore are apt to ascribe to that Nation, such Monuments as seem to them unaccountable, as the Scotish Highlanders refer their circular Stone pillars to the Picts * For we must not suppose such barbarous Monuments can be so late as the end of the sixth Century, about which time, the Irish Commander *Sirigi* is said to have been slain by *Kaswalhaun law hir* (i, e *Cassivelaunus Longimanus*) and his people forced to quit the Island † We have many places in Wales besides these, that are denominated from the Irish, as *Pentre'r Gwydhel* in the parish of *Rhos Golin* in this County, *Pont y Gwydhel* in Lhan Vair, and *Pentre'r Gwydhel* in Lhysvaen-parish, in Denbighshire, *Kerig y Gwydhel* near *Festiniog* in Meirionydhshire, and in Cardiganshire we find *Kwm y Gwydhyl* in Penbryn-parish, and *Karn Philip Wydhil* in Lhan Wennog, but, having no History to back these names, nothing can be infer'd from them

Lhech yr Ast.

* Dr Garden's Letters to Mr Aubrey

† See the Description of Wales before Dr Powel's History

About the year 945 there was a battel fought for the Isle of Anglesey, betwixt Howel Dha *King of Wales, and* Kynan ap Edwal Voel, *wherein Kynan fell Afterwards* Grufudh *his son, renewing the War, was likewise overcome; and Kyngar a potent man, being driven out of the Isle, Howel kept quiet possession thereof*]

Mr Robert Vaughan's Manuscript

Nor was it afterwards harrass'd by the English only, but also by the *Norwegians* and, in the Year 1000, a Navy of King Æthelred sailing round the Island, wasted and consum'd it in a hostile manner After this two Normans of the name of *Hugh*, the one Earl of *Chester*, and the other of *Salop*, oppress'd it in a grievous manner, and, to restrain the Inhabitants, built the castle of *Aber Lhienawg* But *Magnus* the Norwegian coming thither at the same time, shot Hugh Earl of Chester through the body with an arrow, and having pillag'd the Island, departed The English having afterwards often attempted it, at last brought it under their subjection in the time of Edward the first It contain'd formerly three hundred and sixty three Villages, and is a very populous Country at this time

Marianus

The chief Town is *Beaumaris*, built in the east-part of it, in a moorish place, by King Edward the first, and call'd by the name of *Beau marish* from its situation, whereas the place before was call'd * *Bonover* He also fortify'd it with a Castle, which yet seems not to have been

Beaumaris

* This seems not to be a *British* name

† So said ann. 1607

been ever finish'd; the † present Governour whereof is the right worshipful Sir *Richard Bulkley* Knight, whose civility towards me, when I survey'd these Counties, I must always gratefully acknowledge.

Lhan Vaes

Not far from hence, lies *Lhan Vâes*, a famous Cloister heretofore of the *Friers minors*; to which the Kings of England were bountiful Patrons, as well on account of the devout ness and exemplary lives of the Friers who dwelt there, as (that I may speak the language of the Records) *because there were bury'd at that place, a daughter of King John, a son of the King of Denmark, the bodies of the Lord Clifford, and of other Lords, Knights, and Esquires, who were slain in the wars of Wales, in the times of the illustrious Kings of England*.

2 Part Pat. ann. 2 Hen 5

Lhan Idan

On the Frith of Meneu, about half way between Beaumaris and Newburgh, is *Lhan Idan*, between which, and Lhin Vair is Gaer on the other side in Glamorganshire, it is thought that the Romans pass'd the said Frith into the Island * 'Opposite to this suppos'd 'passage, there is a hill call'd *Gwydryn* (a name 'corrupted perhaps from *Gwydh Uryn*, i e. *Conspicuous Hill*, which having two Summits or 'Tops, one of them shews the ruins of an 'ancient Fort, and on the other I observ'd a 'round pit sunk in a Rock, of about nine 'foot diameter, fill'd up with pure Sand What 'may be the depth of it, I cannot at present 'inform you; some who have sounded it for 'three yards, having discover'd no bottom I 'have had some suspicion, that this might be 'the place where the Druids offer'd their cruel 'Sacrifices with the blood of Captives, but 'having nothing out of History to confirm 'my conjecture, I shall not much contend for 'it, but leave it to you and others to consider, what so odd a contrivance was design'd 'for

* A Letter from the Reverend Mr John Davies Rector of Newburgh

'About a mile from the place where we 'suspect the Romans to have landed, we find '*Tre'r Druw*, which doubtless took its name 'from some *Druid*, and may be interpreted '*Druids Town*, seeing we find the adjoyning 'Township is call'd *Tre'r Beirdh*, i e *Bards-Town* And this puts me in mind of a place 'call'd *Maen y Druw*, i e *Druid Stone*, within '*Kommwd* of *Twrkelyn* in *Lhan Elian* pa 'rish, where we need not much question, but 'there was formerly a Sepulchral Monument 'of a Druid, though now it is only the name 'of a house

Tre'r Druw

'Upon the Confines of the Townships of '*Tre'r Druw* and *Tre'r Beirdh*, we meet with a 'square Fortification, which may be suppos'd 'to be the first Camp that the Romans had, 'after their landing here, and opposite to it, 'westward, about the distance of three furlongs, 'there is another strong hold, of a round form 'and considerable height, which probably was 'that of our Ancestors Farther westward, 'under the protection of this Fort, there are 'stones pitch'd on end, about twelve in number, whereof three are very considerable, the 'largest of them being twelve foot in height, 'and eight in breadth where it is broadest, 'for it is somewhat of an oblong oval form 'These have no other name than *Kerig y Bryngwyn* * (or *Bryngwyn stones*) and are so call'd 'from the place where they are erected On 'what occasion they are rais'd, I cannot conjecture, unless this might be the burial place 'of some of the most eminent Druids In '*Bod Owyr*, which lies on the north side of the 'same round Fort, at a farther distance, we

Tre'r Druw and Tre'r Beirdh

* Bryngwyn signifies White hill or White hil

'find a remarkable *Kromlech*, which several, as 'well as my self, suppose to be another kind 'of Sepulchral monument since the time of 'Heathenism These (for we have several 'others in the Island) are compos'd of three 'or four rude stones, or more, pitch'd on end 'as supporters or pillars, and a vast stone of 'several tuns laid on them as a covering; and 'are thought to have receiv'd the name of '*Cromlecheu*, for that the Table or Covering-stone is, on the upper side, somewhat *gibbous* 'or *convex* the word *Krwm* signifying (as 'you know) crooked or bunch-back'd, and '*Llech*, any flat stone † This *Kromlech* at '*Bod Owyr*, is more elegant than any Monument that I have seen of its kind for whereas in all others which I have noted, the top-stone, as well as the supporters, is altogether 'rude and unpolish'd in this it is neatly 'wrought, considering the natural roughness 'of the stone, and pointed into several angles, 'but how many I cannot at present assure you 'We have a tradition, that the largest *Kromlech* in this County, is the Monument of 'Bronwen, daughter to King *Llyr* or *Leirus*, 'who, you know, is said to begin his reign '*Anno Mundi* 3105 But of this, and the rest 'of our *Kromlecheu*, take here the words of 'an ingenious Antiquary whilst living, Mr *John* '*Griffith* of *Lhan Dhyvnan*, in a Letter to Mr 'Vaughan of Hengwrt —— Bronwen Leir *filiam quod attinet*, &c i e *As to the daughter of* Bronwen Leir, *there is a crooked little* Cell of stone *not far from* Alaw, *to the west, where, according to Tradition, she was bury'd But whether there ever was such a King in being, is doubted by many, how justly, will rest upon them to shew Such little Houses, which are common in this Country, you know are call'd, by an apposite name,* Cromlechau *Lastly, this Island, which in those days was almost one continu'd Wood, and, as it were, appropriated to the Druids, abounds with the Graves of Noblemen, who were induced by a Reverence for the Place, to be bury'd here*, &c

† See Pembrokshire

'I know there are some who suppose these 'Monuments, and such like, to have been se 'deral testimonies, but that I take to be a 'groundless conjecture and the opinion of 'their being places of Interment seems much 'confirm'd, for that a Gentleman of my ac 'quaintance remembers that an odd kind of '*Helmet* * was discover'd, by digging about a 'rude stone, which, together with some others, 'is pitch'd on end at a place call'd *Kae y maes mawr* †, in the parish of *Lhan Rhwydrus* [*Of these stones there are but three now standing, and those in a manner triangularly One of them is eleven foot and a half high, four foot broad, and fourteen inches thick, another, about three yards high, and four foot broad, and the third, ten foot high, eight broad, and but six inches thick*]

* I am also inform'd, there was a kind of Spear or Halbert, found by digging near the same place

† Maes signifies properly only a large open field; but I am told, that in the names of places in this Country it is us'd for battel; so that Kae'r maes mawr implies some great battel fought here. A farther Confirmation whereof as also that these stones are Sepulchral Monuments, is, that a small Brook on the South of them is call'd Rhyd y hedhow, i e Graves-ford

'As for inscrib'd Stones, I have noted only 'two in this County one whereof was a 'kind of square pillar in the parish of *Lhan Babo*, of about ten foot in height, one in 'breadth, and near the same thickness I 'never was so curious as to copy the Inscription, and I am told it is now too late, it 'being † broken in several pieces The other 'is in my neighbourhood, but is so obscure, 'that I scarce think it worth while to trouble you with a Copy of it I could read 'only —— *Filius Ulrici erexit hunc Lapidem* —— [*This was perhaps erected by some Dane or Norwegian,* Ulricus *seeming to be rather a Danish name,* than British]

Inscrib'd Stones

† Lhan Baho

† See below

'I can give you no certain information of 'any Coins found here, except a large gold 'Medal of *Julius Constantius* ‖, which was found 'on the plow'd land at a place call'd *Tre' Varthin*, about the year 1680, and was afterwards 'added by the late Sir Thomas Mostyn, to 'his curious Collection of Antiquities ———

‖ Figured Num 20 Tre' Varthin

Thus far Mr *Davies*; since the date of whose Letter I receiv'd a Copy of the Inscription which he mentions at *Lhan Babo*, from the Reverend Mr *Robert Humphreys*, Rector of *Lhan Vechelh* For though the Stone be (as he mentions) broken in two pieces, and remov'd from the place where it stood, the Inscription, whatever it may import, is yet preserv'd which though I understand not my self, I shall however insert here, because I know not but it may be intelligible to several Readers, and so give some light towards the explaining of other Inscriptions

ᕼT_OP ISI HI X ET

Maen Lhanol

This Monument is call'd *Maen Lhanol*, corruptly I suppose for *Maen Lhineol*, i e *Lapis insculptus sive lineolis exaratus*, a Stone graven or written with lines for there is such another, known by that name, at *Penbryn* parish in Cardiganshire It seems scarce questionable, but this Stone, as well as those others above mention'd, was a Sepulchral Monument, and that the words *Hic jacet* end the Inscription But now, to proceed in the description of the more remarkable Towns in this Island]

Newburgh

The Town of *Newburgh*, in British *Rhosir*, is esteem'd next to *Beaumarish*, and distant from it about twelve miles westward; which having struggl'd a long time with the heaps of Sand cast against it by the Sea, has now lost much of its former splendour

[The Welsh name of *Newburg* is so variously written, that it is doubtful which is the right In the description of Wales, before Dr *Powel's* History, it is call'd *Rhossyr*, and in another impression of the same (which was never publish'd, because not compleated) it is written *Rhôs ir*, which either alters the signification, or makes it more distinct In a Manuscript Copy of the same it is call'd *Rhosfir*, which we are to read *Rhosvir*; but Mr *Davies* above mention'd, Rector of the place, informs me, that it ought to be *Rhos Vair*, in confirmation whereof he adds this *Englin*

Mae lhys yn Rhos Vair, mae lhyn,
Mae eur gluch, mae Arglwydh Lhewelyn,
A Gwyr tál yn ei galyn,
Mil myrdh mewn gwyrdh a gwyn

Baron Newburgh

This place hath been honour'd, by giving the title of Baron to *George Cholmondley*, the only surviving Brother to *Hugh* Earl of *Cholmondley*]

Aber Fraw

Aber Fraw, not far from thence, though at present but a mean place, was yet heretofore of much greater repute than any of the rest, as being the Royal Seat of the Kings of *Gwynedh*, or North-Wales, who were thence also styl'd Kings of *Aber Fraw*

Llangudwaladr

[Not far from hence, is *Llangudwaladr*, where, over the Church door, is the following Monument of *Kadran*, who was Prince of North Wales about the middle of the sixth Century

CATAMANUS REX
SAPIENTISIMUS OPI
NATISIMUS OMNIUM
REGUM

To be read thus *Catamanus Rex sapientissimus opinatissimus omnium Regum*]

Holy head
Kaer Gybi

Near the western Cape of this Island, which we call *Holy-head*, there is a small Village call'd in Welsh *Kaer Gybi*; which receiv'd its name from *Kybi* (a devout man, and Disciple of St *Hilary* of Poictiers) who led here a religious life from whence there is a common passage into Ireland [In Mr Aubrey's *Monumenta Britannica* *, I observ'd a note of some remarkable Monument near Holy head, in these words *There is in Anglesey, about a mile from Holy head, on a hill near the way that leads to Beaumaris, a Monument of huge stones They are about twenty in number, and between four and five foot high, at the Northern end of it there are two stones about six foot high They stand upon an hillock in a Farm call'd* Trevigneth, *and have no other name than* Lhecheu †, *whence the field where they are rais'd, is call'd* Kaer Lhecheu]

* Aubr MS

† Id est, Flat stones

Of the Islands adjoyning to Anglesey, see among the British Isles

Earls of Anglesey

The other parts of this Island are well planted with Villages, which afford little worth our notice, and therefore I shall now pass over to the Continent, and take a view of *Denbigh-shire*; [having observ'd (according to the course of this and method of this Work) that the first who took the title of Earl from this Island, was *Christopher Villers*, brother of *George* Duke of Buckingham, created *Sept* 24 1623; who was succeeded by *Charles* his son and heir But he dying in the year 1659 without issue male, it was conferred on *Arthur Annesley*, created Lord *Annesley* of *Newport Pagnel* (in the County of *Bucks*) and Earl of *Anglesey*, *April* 20 1661 In which titles he was succeeded by *James* his Son, and then by a Grandson

son of the same name, who dying without issue-male, was succeeded by *John* his brother, but he dying also without issue-male, this title descended to *Arthur*, the present Earl, brother of the two last Earls; a person of great Eloquence, and distinguish'd Abilities]

There are in this Island 74 Parishes.

DENBIGHSHIRE.

N this side the river Conwy, *Denbigh shire*, call'd in British *Sir Dhinbech*, retires-in from the Sea, and is extended eastward as far as the river *Dee* It is encompass'd on the north for by some space by the Sea, and afterwards by the small County of *Flint*, on the west by Merionydhshire and Montgomeryshire, and on the east by Cheshire and Shropshire

The western part of it is somewharet barren; the middle, where it falls into a Vale, exceeding fruitful, the eastern part next the Vale not so kindly a soil; but towards *Dee*, it is much better. Towards the west (except by the sea-side, where it is somewhat more fruitful,) it is but thinly inhabited, and swells pretty much with bare and craggy hills but the diligence and industry of the husbandmen hath long since begun to conquer the barrenness of the Land on the sides of these Mountains, as well as in other places of Wales For having pared-off the surface of the earth, with a broad iron instrument for that purpose, in thin clods and turfs, they pile them up in heaps, and burn them to ashes, which being afterwards scatter'd on the lands thus pared, does so enrich them, that it is scarce credible, what quantities of Rye they produce Nor is this method of burning the ground any late invention, but very ancient, as appears out of Virgil and Horace

Kerig y Drudion

Amongst these Hills, is a place call'd *Kerig y Drudion*, or Druid stones, [and that it was so denominated from *Druids*, seems highly probable, though not altogether unquestionable for, that the word *Drudion* signifies *Druids*, is, for what I can learn, only presumed from its affinity with the Latin *Druidæ*, and because we know not any other signification of it In the British Lexicon, we find no other word than *Derwydhon* † for *Druids*, which may be fitly render'd in Latin *Quercetani*; *Derw* signifying in Welsh, Oak trees, which, agreeing in sound with the Greek, might occasion * Pliny's conjecture (who was better acquainted with that language, than the Celtic or British) that *Druides* was originally a Greek name The singular of *Derwydhon* is *Derwydh*, which the Romans could not write more truly than *Deruida*, whereof *Druida* seems only an easier variation The word *Drudion* might likewise vary only in dialect from *Derwydhon*, and so the name of this place be rightly interpreted by our Countrymen and others, *Druid stones*; but what stones they were that have been call'd thus, is a question which I could not be throughly satisfy'd in, though I have made some enquiry. The most remarkable stone monuments now remaining in this parish, are two of that kind which we call *Kistieu maen* or *Stone chests*, whereof some have been mention'd in other Counties, and several omitted as not differing materially from those I had describ'd These I have not seen my self, but find the following account of them, in a Letter from an ingenious Gentleman of this neighbourhood *As for ancient Inscriptions, either of the* Druids *or others, I believe it is in vain to glean for them now in these parts Nor can those mention'd at* Voelas *in our neighbourhood (as we may collect from their characters) boast of any great Antiquity for, that they are so obscure and intricate, I impute to the unskilfulness of the stone-cutters, supposing they were not plainly legible in those times that first saw them* ——— *The most remarkable pieces of Antiquity in this parish of* Kerig y Drudion, *are those two solitary prisons, which are generally supposed to have been used in the time of the Druids They are placed about a furlong from each other, and are such huts, that each prison can well contain but a single person One of them is distinguish'd by the name of* Karchar Kynrik Rwth, *or* Kenrik Rwth's *Prison, but who he was, is altogether uncertain The other is known by no particular title, but that of* Kist vaen *or* Stone chest; *which is common to both, and seems to be a name lately given them, because they are somewhat of the form of large chests, from which they chiefly differ in their opening or entrance They stand north and south, and are each of them compos'd of seven stones Of these, four being above six foot long, and about a yard in breadth, are so placed as to resemble the square tunnel of a Chimney a fifth, which is not so long, but of the same breadth, is pitch'd at the south end thereof, firmly, to secure that passage At the north end, is the entrance, where the sixth stone is the lid and especial guard of this close confinement But in regard it was necessary to remove it when any person was imprison'd or releas'd, it is not of that weight as to be alone a sufficient guard of the prisoner, and therefore on the top-stone or uppermost of the four first mention'd, lies the seventh, that is a vast stone, which with much force was remov'd towards the north end, that with its weight it might fasten, and as it were clasp, the door stone These, and the name of our parish, are all the memorials we have of the residence of those ancient Philosophers the Druids; at least wise, all that tradition ascribes to them,* &c

† Used by *Llywarch Brydydh y Moch* who writ An 1240 and *Kyndhelw Brydydh mawr* 1250

* Hist Nat l 16 c 44

Thus far the Letter which makes it very probable, that these are some of the Stones (if not all) whence this parish receiv'd the name of *Kerig y Drudion*; and adds not a little to Mr *Aubrey*'s conjecture, that those rude Stones erected in a circular order, so common in this Island, are also Druid Monuments * seeing that in the midst of such circle, we sometimes find *Stone chests*, not unlike those here describ'd; as particularly, that of *Karn Llechart*, mention'd in Glamorganshire, which, without all doubt, was design'd for the same use with these But that any of them were used as Prisons in the time of the Druids, does not at all appear from this account of them;

* See Pembrokeshire

th re

there being no other argument for it, than that one of them is call'd *Karchar Kynric Rwth*, whereas that *Kynric Rwth*, as I find in an ano-nymous Welſh writer †, was only a tyranni-cal perſon in this neighbourhood (of no anti-quity in compariſon of the Druids) who, ſhut-ting up ſome that had affronted him, in one of theſe Cells, occaſion'd it to be call'd his *Pri-ſon* ever after What uſe they were of in the time of the Druids, we muſt leave to further enquiry; but that they really are ſome of their Monuments, I ſcarce queſtion Whether they were ever encompaſs'd with circles of ſtones, like *Karn Ichart* above-mention'd, or with a wall as the *Kiſt vaen* on *Mynydh y Drymmeu* in the ſame County, is altogether uncertain For in this revolution of time, ſuch ſtones might be carried off by the neighbours, and applied to ſome uſe, as we find has been lately done in other places ‖

† A MS in the hands of *Thomas Price* of Lhan Vyl lin, Eſq

‖ V Ty Ilh tud at Lanhammwlch Brecknockſhire

Theſe Druid ſtones put me in mind of a cer-tain relique of their Doctrine, which I have lately obſerv'd to be yet retain'd amongſt the vulgar (For how difficult it is to get rid of ſuch erroneous opinions as have been once ge-nerally receiv'd, be they never ſo abſurd and ridiculous, may be ſeen at large in the excel-lent Treatiſe written upon that ſubject by Sir *Thomas Brown*) In moſt parts of Wales, and throughout all *Scotland*, and in *Cornwall*, we find it a common opinion of the vulgar, that about Midſummer Eve (though in the time they do not all agree) it is uſual for Snakes to meet in companies, and that by joyning heads together and hiſſing, a kind of Bubble is form'd like a ring about the head of one of them, which the reſt by continual hiſſing blow on till it comes off at the tail, and then it immediately har-dens, and reſembles a glaſs ring; which who-ever finds (as ſome old women and children are perſwaded) ſhall proſper in all his underta-kings The rings which they ſuppoſe to be thus generated, are call'd * *Gleineu Nadroedh*, i e *Gemmæ Anguinæ*, whereof I have ſeen, at ſeveral places about twenty or thirty They are ſmall glaſs Annulets, commonly about half as wide as our finger rings, but much thicker, of a green colour uſually, though ſome of them are blue, and others curiouſly wav'd with blue, red, and white I have alſo ſeen two or three earthen rings of this kind, but glaz'd with blue, and adorn'd with tranſverſe ſtreaks or furrows on the out ſide The ſmalleſt of them might be ſuppoſed to have been glaſs-beads worn for ornament by the Romans, becauſe ſome quantity of them, together with ſeveral Amber-beads, have been lately diſcover'd at a Stone-pit near *Garvord* in Berkſhire, where they alſo find ſome pieces of Roman Coyn; and ſometimes dig up ſkeletons of men, and pieces of Arms and Armour But it may be objected, that a battel being fought there be-twixt the Romans and Britains, as appears by the Bones and Arms they diſcover, theſe glaſs-beads might as probably pertain to the latter And indeed it ſeems to me very likely, that theſe *Snake-ſtones* (as we call them) were uſed as charms or amulets amongſt our Druids of Britain, on the ſame occaſions as the *Snake eggs* amongſt the Gauliſh Druids For Pliny, who liv'd when thoſe Prieſts were in requeſt, and ſaw one of their Snake eggs, gives us the like account of the origin of them, as our common people do of their *Glain Neidr* (a)

* *Gleine*, in the Iriſh ſignifies *Glaſs* In Glamorganſhire and Monmouthſhire theſe Rings are call'd *Maen Magl* and corruptly *Glaim* for *Glain*

Thus we find it very evident, that the opi-nion of the vulgar concerning the generation of theſe *Adder beads* or *Snake ſtones*, is no other than a relique of the Superſtition, or perhaps Impoſture, of the Druids But whether theſe we call Snake ſtones, be the very ſame Amu-lets that the Britiſh Druids made uſe of, or whether this fabulous origin was aſcribed for-merly to ſomething elſe, and in after times ap-plied to theſe glaſs-beads, I ſhall not undertake to determine, though I think the former much more probable As for Pliny's *Ovum anguinum*, it can be no other than a ſhell (either marine or foſſil) of that kind which we call *Echinus marinus*, whereof one ſort (though not the ſame that he deſcribes) is call'd at this day in moſt parts of Wales where they are found, *Wyeu'r môr*, i e Sea-eggs I had almoſt forgotten to add, that ſometimes theſe glaſs Annulets were ſtruck through a larger ring of Iron, and that again through another much larger of Copper, as appears by one of them found in the river *Charwell* near *Hampton Gay* in Oxfordſhire, and figur'd and deſcrib'd by Dr *Plot* in his Natural Hiſtory of that County † To theſe Amulets (but whether Britiſh or Roman I know not) that ſmall braſs Head ‖, figur'd numb 18 muſt be refer'd, which was found in a Well ſome where in this Country, together with certain braſs Snakes, and ſome other figures now loſt, all hung about a wire]

Philoſ Tran N 335

† [illegible] 45

At *Voelas*, there are ſome ſmall Pillars, in-ſcribed with ſtrange Letters, which ſome ſuſ-pect to be the Characters uſed by the *Druids* [But if the following Inſcription be one of thoſe, it will ſcarce be allow'd to be half ſo old as their time The Pillar whence it was copied, is a hard, rough Stone, of ſomewhat a ſquare form, about ten foot in length; and is now to be ſeen at *Voelas* The Copy here in-ſerted was ſent me by a worthy friend Mr *Griffith Jones*, School maſter of *Lhan Rwſt*, who I doubt not hath tranſcrib'd it from the Monument, with great accuracy

(a) —— *Praeterea eſt ovorum genus in magna Galliarum fama, omiſſum Græcis Angues innumeri æſtate convoluti, ſalivis faucium corporumque ſpumis artifici complexu glomerantur, anguinum appellatur Druidæ ſibilis id dicunt in ſublime jactari, ſagoque oportere intercipi ne tellurem attingat Profugere raptorem equo Serpentes enim inſequi, donec arceantur amnis alicujus interventu Experimentum ejus eſſe ſi contra aquas fluitet vel auro vinctum Atque ut eſt Magorum ſolertia occultandis fraudibus ſagax, certa Luna capiendum cenſent, tanquam congruere operationem eam ſerpentium humani ſit arbitrii Vidi equidem id Ovum mali orbiculati modici magnitudine, cruſta cartilaginis, velut acetabulis brachiorum Polypi crebris inſigne Druidis Ad victorias litium ac regum aditus mire laudatur tantæ vanitatis ut habentem id in lite in ſinu equitem Romanum e Vocontiis, a Divo Claudio principe interemptum non ob aliud ſciam, &c* Hiſt Nat l 29 c 3

This

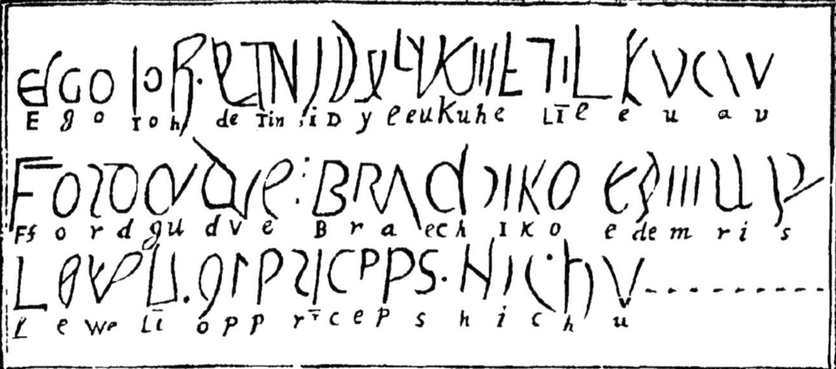

This Inſcription is ſo very obſcure and different from all I have ſeen elſewhere, that it ſeems ſcarce intelligible However, I ſhall take the liberty of offering my thoughts, which, though they ſhould prove erroneous, may yet give ſome hint to others to diſcover the true reading I have added under each Character the Letters I ſuppoſe to be intended, which if I rightly conjecture make theſe words

Ego Job de Tin i Dyleu Kubeli leuav
Iſcrd gudve Braecb i Koed Emris
Leweli op priceps hic bu———

Which I ſuppoſe, according to our modern Orthography, might be written thus

Ego Johannes de Ty'n y Dylau Gwydhelen leuaf
[ar] *ffordd gyddſau braich y coed Emris*——
Levelinus optimus princeps hic humatur ——

The meaning whereof is, That one *John, of the houſe of Dyleu Gwydbelen*, &c. *on the Road of* Ambroſe wood Hill, *erected this Monument to the memory of the excellent Prince, Lhewelin* But who this Lhewelyn was, I muſt leave to be determin'd by others If it was any of the three Princes of that name, recorded in the Annals of Wales, it muſt be the firſt, i e *Lhewelyn ap Sitſylht*, who was ſlain (but where, is not mention'd) by *Howel* and *M'redyd's* the ſons of Edwyn, in the year 1021 For we find that *Lhewelyn ap Jorwerth was honourably buried in the*
* Dr Powel, *Abbey of Conwy, Anno* 1240 * and his Stone
p 298. coffin remov'd, upon the diſſolution, to the Church of *Lhan Rwſt*, where it is yet to be
Ibid p 374 ſeen And, that *Lhewelyn ap Gruffydh*, the laſt Prince of Wales of the Britiſh Race, was ſlain near *Buallt* in Brecknockſhire, ſo that his body was in all likelihood inter'd ſomewhere in that Country, though his head was fixed on the Tower of *London*]

Klokainog Not far from *Klokainog* we read this Inſcription on a Stone, [which is doubtleſs an Epitaph of ſome Soldier of note, who can be but very little, if at all later than the Romans

AIMILINI
TOVISAG

The name *Aimilinus*, we are to underſtand, as the ſame with *Æmilinus*, and that no other than *Æmilianus* Thus, amongſt *Reineſius's* In- Pag 228
ſcriptions, we find M AIMILIVS for *M Æmilius* And in the ſame Author, we have two or three examples of the letter A in the Pag 560.
ſame form with the firſt character of this Inſcription As for the ſecond word, I am in ſome doubt whether we ought to read it *Tovi-ſag* or *Tov ſaci* if the former it is Britiſh, and ſignifies *a Leader* or *General* † and if the lat- † Tywyſog, Dux Princeps, from the Verb Tywyſo to lead; is the Latin Dux from Duco
ter, it ſeems only the ſame word latiniz'd Mr *Lloyd* from whom I receiv'd this more accurate Copy of the Inſcription, than had been printed before) adds that the place where this Stone lies, is call'd *Bryn y Beddeu*, which ſignifies the *Hill of Graves*, and that there is near it an artificial Mount or *Tumulus*, call'd y *Krig-Vryn*, which may be engliſh'd *Barrow hill* ‖ Al- ‖ See Radnorſhire
ſo that on the Hills adjoining there are ſeveral Circles of Stones, and in the ſame neighbourhood, a place call'd *Rhôs y Gadva*, or *Battel field*]

Towards the Vale, where theſe Mountains begin to be thinner, lies *Denbigh*, ſeated on a Denbigh
ſteep rock, and call'd formerly by the Britons *Kledvyrn yn Rhôs*, which ſignifies *the craggy hill in Ros*, for ſo they call that part of the County, which King Edward the firſt beſtow'd, with many other large poſſeſſions, on *Davidh ap Gruffydh*, brother of Prince *Lhewelyn* But he being ſoon after attainted of High Treaſon and beheaded, King Edward granted it to *Henry Lacy* Earl of Lincoln, who fortified it with a very ſtrong wall (though of a ſmall circumference,) and on the ſouth-ſide with a caſtle adorn'd with high towers But his only ſon being unfortunately drown'd in the Caſtle well, he was ſo much griev'd at it, that he deſiſted from the work, leaving it unfiniſh'd After his deceaſe, this Town, with the reſt of his Inheritance, deſcended by his daughter Alice to the houſe of Lancaſter From whom alſo, when that family decay'd, it devolv'd firſt, by the bounty of Edward the ſecond, to *Hugh Spenſer*, and afterwards to *Roger Mortimer*, by covenant with Edward the third For his Arms are ſeen on the chief gate But he being ſentenced to die, and executed, it fell to *William Montacute* Earl of Saliſbury, though ſoon after reſtor'd to the *Mortimers*, and by theſe at length it came to the houſe of York For we read, that out of malice to King Edward the fourth (who was of that houſe) this Town ſuffer'd much by thoſe of the family of

Lancaster Since which time, either because the Inhabitants disliked the situation of it (for the declivity of the place was no way convenient,) or else because it was not well serv'd with water, they remov'd hence by degrees insomuch, that the old Town is now deserted, and a new one, much larger, sprung up at the foot of the hill, which is so populous, that the Church not being large enough for the Inhabitants, they have † now begun to build a new one, where the old Town stood, partly at the charges of their Lord *Robert* Earl of Leicester, and partly with the money contributed for that use by several well-dispos'd Persons throughout England. This *Robert* Earl of Leicester was created baron of *Denbigh* by Queen Elizabeth in the year 1566 Nor is there any Barony in England that hath more Gentlemen holding thereof in Fee

† So said, ann 1607

Dyffryn Clwyd

We are now come to the heart of the County, where nature, having remov'd the Mountains on all hands (to shew us what she could do in a rugged Country) hath spread out a most pleasant vale, extended from south to north seventeen miles and about five in breadth It lies open only to the Ocean, and to * the clearing North-wind; being elsewhere guarded with high mountains, which (towards the east especially) are like battlements or turrets, for by an admirable contrivance of nature, the tops of these mountains seem to resemble the turrets of walls Among them, the highest I call'd *Moel Enlhi* at the top whereof I observ'd a military fence or rampire, and a very clear Spring. This Vale is exceeding healthy, fruitful, and pleasant the complexion of the Inhabitants is bright and chearful, their heads of a sound constitution, their sight very lively, and even their old age vigorous and lasting The green Meadows, the Corn-fields, and the numerous Villages and Churches in this Vale, afford the most pleasant prospect imaginable The river *Clwyd*, from the very fountain-head runs through the midst of it, receiving on each side a great number of rivulets And from hence it has been formerly call'd *Ystrad Klwyd*, for Marianus makes mention of a King of the *Stradcluid* Welsh and at this day it is called *Dyffryn Klwyd*, i e the *Vale of Cluid*, where, as some Authors have told us, certain Britons coming out of Scotland, planted a Kingdom, having first driven out the English which were seated there

* *Serenanti Borea*

Moel Enlhi

Clwyd, riv

See Caernarvonshire

Ruthin

In the south part of this Vale, on the east side of the river, lies the Town of *Ruthin*, in Welsh *Rhuthyn*, the greatest Market in the Vale, and a very populous Town, famous † not long since, for a stately and beautiful Castle, which was capable of a very numerous family Both the Town and Castle were built by *Roger Grey*, with permission of the King, the Bishop of St *Asaph*, and the Rector of *Lhan Rhydh*, it being seated in that parish To this *Roger Grey*, in consideration of his services against the Welsh, King Edward the first granted almost the whole Vale, and this was the seat of his posterity (who flourish'd under the title of Earls of Kent) till the time of *Richard Grey* Earl of Kent and Lord of *Ruthin*, who dying without issue, and having no regard to his brother *Henry*, sold this ancient inheritance to King Henry the seventh; since which time the castle has been uncovered, and has daily decay'd, * Of late, through the bounty of Queen Elizabeth, it † hath belong'd to Ambrose Earl of Warwick, together with large revenues in this Vale

† So said ann 1607

* So said, ann 1607

† *Spectavit*

Ial

Ascending eastward out of this Valley, we come to *Iâl*, a small mountainous tract, of a very high situation, if compared with the neighbouring tract, so that no river runs into it from any other country, though it pours out several By reason of this high situation, it is a very rough, cold, bleak Country I know not whether it might receive it's name from the small river *Alen*, which, springing up in this country, hides it self in one or two places by undermining the earth These mountains are well stored with Oxen, Sheep, and Goats, and the Valleys in some places are pretty fertile in Corn, especially to the east, on this side *Alen* but the western is somewhat barren, and in some places mere heath and desart It hath nothing in it memorable, except the ruins of a small Monastery, seated very pleasantly in a Valley, which, amongst woody hills, is extended in the form of a Cross whence it had the name of *Vale Crucis*, whereas in British it is call'd *Lhan Gwest* Eastward of Iâl, the territory of *Maelor Gymraeg* or *Welsh Maelor*, call'd in English *Bromfield*, is extended to the river *Dee*, a pleasant little Country, and well stored with Lead, especially near *Mwyn glodh*, a small Village, denominated from the Lead mines

Vale Crucis

Bromfield

Lead

Wrexham

In this part lies *Wrexham*, call'd in Saxon Wrıtelesham, remarkable for a very neat tower, and the Organ there, and near this place is *Leonis Castrum*, so call'd perhaps from the *Legio vicesima Victrix*, which kept garrison a little higher, on the other side *Dee* It is now call'd *Holt*, and is supposed to have been repair'd, † more lately by *William Stanley*, and formerly by *John* Earl of Warren, who being guardian in trust to one *Madok* a British Prince, seiz'd for his own use this Province, together with that of Ial From the Earls of Warren, it descended afterwards to the *Fitz-Alans*, Earls of Arundel, and from them to William Beauchamp Baron of *Aber Gavenny* and afterward to *William Stanley*, who being beheaded, this, as well as the rest of his estate, was forfeited to the Crown

Holt

D. Powel

† So said, ann 1607

Chirk

Southward of *Bromfield*, lies *Chirk*, call'd in Welsh *Gwayn*, a Country also pretty mountainous, but honour'd with two Castles, viz *Chirk*, whence it received its name, and which was built by Roger Mortimer and *Kastell Dinas Bran*, seated on the highest top of a sharp hill, whereof there remain at present only some ruinous walls The common People affirm, that this was built and so call'd by *Brennus* General of the Gauls, and some interpret the name, *The King's Palace* for *Bren* in British signifies a King (from whence possibly that powerful Prince of the Gauls and Britons was call'd by way of eminency, *Brennus*) but others will have it to derive the name from the situation on a hill, which the Britons call *Bryn* and this in my opinion, is much more probable In the time of Henry the third, it was the seat of *Gruffydh ap Madok*, who when he sided with the English against the Welsh, was wont to secure himself here But upon his decease, *Roger Mortimer*, who was appointed guardian to his son *Lhewelyn*, seiz'd this [and] *Chirk* into his own hands, as John Earl of Warren, mention'd before, had usurp'd *Bromfield*

Castle Dinas Bran

Brennus

Entrenchments

[There are divers old Forts or Entrenchments in this County, that seem no less remarkable, than that at *Moel Enlhi*, some of which are mention'd in the Letter from the foresaid Mr *Lloyd* As still *Pen y Gaer vawr* on

Pen y Gaer vawr

on Kader Dhimmael, distant about a mile from *Kerrig y Druidon*; which is a circular Ditch and Rampire, of at least one hundred paces diameter. But what seems most remarkable, is, that it is presum'd to have had once some kind of wall, and that the stones have been long since carried away by the neighbours, and applied to some private uses. Secondly, *Kaer Dhynod*, or as others, *Kaer y Dhynod*, which lies (as also *Pen y Gaer*) in the Parish of Lhan Vihangel. This is situate close by the river Alwen, and is rather of an oval form, than circular. The Dike or Rampire consists of a vast quantity of stones, at present rudely heap'd together, but whether formerly in any better order, is uncertain. On the river side, it is about three hundred foot high perpendicularly, but not half that height elsewhere. On the other side the river, we have a steep Hill, about twice the height of this *Kaer Dhynod* (on which lies *Kaer Forwyn*, i. e. *Maiden Fort*, a large circular entrenchment, and much more artificial than the former. This *Kaer Dhynod* (as the said Mr. *Lloyd* supposes) was in all likelyhood a British Camp, seeing it agrees exactly with † Tacitus's description of the Camp of King *Caratacus*, when he engag'd Ostorius Scapula somewhere in this Country of the *Ordovices*——*He chose such a Camp to maintain, as in point of approach, retreat, and all other respects, was difficult to the Enemy, and convenient to themselves. On a high hill, guarded with great Stones in the nature of a* Vallum, *wherever it was accessible; and before it, a River with uncertain fords*, &c. Third-

Kaer Dhynod

Kaer Vorwyn

† Annal. 12. c. 33.

ly, *Dinas Melin y Wyg*, which he supposes to have been a British *Oppidum*, it being much such a place as Cæsar informs us they call'd so, in these words, *The Britains call thick Woods fenced with a* Vallum *and ditch*, a Town; *where they meet to defend themselves as oft as an enemy makes Incursions*.* This place, as the word *Gwyg* implies, is full of Woods, Dingles, &c. The Fortification rises about fifteen or twenty yards where lowest; and is faced for the most part with a craggy Rock, and encompass'd with a deep Trench, having two Entries call'd *y Porth ucha*, and *Borth isa*, or the upper and lower Gates.]

Dinas Melin y Wyg

* Cæs. Com. lib. 5.

When the dominion of the Welsh, by factions among themselves, and invasions of the English, fell to decay, and could now subsist no longer, the Earls of *Chester*, and *Warren*, the *Mortimers*, *Lacy*, and the *Greys* (whom I have mention'd) were the first of the Normans that by degrees reduc'd this small Province, and left it to be possess'd by their posterity. Nor was it made a County before the time of King Henry the eighth, when *Radnor*, *Brecknock*, and *Montgomery*, were likewise made Counties by Authority of Parliament.

[In the year 1622. *William* Viscount *Fielding* and Baron of *Newnham Padox*, was created Earl of Denbigh, and was succeeded in that honour by *Basil* his son (created also Lord St. Liz, in the 16th year of King Charles the second.) To whom succeeded *William Fielding* Earl of *Desmond*, his Nephew, and after him *Basil Fielding* his son, who was father of *William* the present Earl.]

Earls of Denbigh.

It contains 57 Parishes.

FLINTSHIRE.

ON the north of *Denbighshire*, lies *Flintshire*, a very small County of an oblong form, wash'd on the north by the Irish Sea, or rather by a branch of it, which is the chanel of the *Dee*, and bounded on the east by *Cheshire*, and elsewhere by *Denbighshire*.

We cannot properly call it mountainous, for it only rises gently with lower hills, and falls by degrees into fertile plains, which (towards the Sea especially) every third year they are plow'd, bear in some places Barley, in others Wheat, but generally Rye, with at least twenty fold increase, and afterwards Oats for four or five years. On the west, it descends to the maritim part of the Vale of Cluid, and takes up the higher end of that Vale.

In the Confines of this County and Denbighshire, where the Mountains, with a gentle declivity, seem to retire, and afford an easier descent and passage into the Vale, the Romans built, at the very entrance, a small City call'd *Varis*, which *Antoninus* places nineteen miles from *Conovium*. This, without any diminution of its name, is call'd at this day *Bod Fari*, which signifies the mansion of Varus; and shews the ruins of a City, on a small hill adjoyning, call'd *Moel y Gaer*, i. e. the City hill. What the Name signifies is not evident. I have suppos'd in other places, that *Vara* in

[illegible]

the old British signified a *Pass*, and accordingly have interpreted *Durnovaria*, and *Ijannavaria*, The *Passage of the water*, and of *Ijanna*. And the situation of this Town confirms my conjecture, it being seated at the only convenient Pass through these Mountains.

[As to the fore-mention'd *Moel y Gaer*, we cannot doubt but that place receiv'd its name from the fortification or entrenchments that are yet to be seen there; the word *Kaer* (as we have already hinted) strictly signifying only a *Wall*, *Fortress*, or *Enclosure*; which being prefix'd to the names of Roman towns, because fortify'd, has occasion'd several to suppose the genuine signification of it to be *a Town or City*. We have divers Camps on our mountains call'd *Kaeren*, where we have not the least ground to suspect that ever any Cities were founded; and in some places I have observ'd the Church yard-wall to be call'd *Kaer y Vynwent*. Nor does it seem improbable that this *Kaer* was deriv'd originally from *Kau*, which signifies *to shut up, or enclose*. This fortification is exactly round, and about one hundred and sixty paces over. We may frame an idea of it, by supposing a round hill with the top cut off, and so made level. All round it, the earth is rais'd in manner of a Parapet, and almost opposite to the Avenue there is a kind of Tumulus or artificial Mount.

Kaeren

* At this *Moel y Gaer*, *Howel Gwynedh* † (who sided with *Owen Glyndwr* against King Henry

Hugh M...

† Of the tribe of Edwyn ap Gr...

'the fourth) was beheaded. He was one who 'for a long time annoy'd the English of his 'neighbourhood, but being taken at length 'by his enemies of the town of *Flint*, and 'beheaded at this place, his estate was dispos'd 'of to one *Saxton*. Before him, one *Owen ap Aldud* had also oppos'd the English in their 'borders; who by force of arms kept all *Tegaingl* under his subjection for about three 'years, until such time as he had obtain'd full 'pardon.]

Caer wys. Not three miles hence, lies *Kaer-wys*, a name which favours much of Antiquity, but I observ'd nothing there either ancient, or worth notice.

Below this *Vare*, the river Clud runs thro' the *Vale*, and is immediately join'd by *Elwy*, a little river, at the confluence whereof there is a Bishop's See, call'd in British from the name of the river, *Llan Elwy*; in English,

St Asaph. from the Patron, St *Asaph*; and in Historians, *Episcopatus Asaphensis*. Neither the Town is memorable for its neatness, nor the Church for its structure or elegancy; yet in regard of its antiquity, it is requisite we should mention

Capgrave. it. For about the year 560, *Kentigern* Bishop of *Glascow* fleeing from *Scotland*, instituted here an Episcopal See and a Monastery, placing therein six hundred and sixty three Monks, whereof three hundred (being illiterate) were appointed for tilling the Land, the same number for other employments within the Monastery, and the rest for Divine Service: and all these he so distributed into Convents, that some of them were at Prayers continually. Upon his return afterwards into Scotland, he appointed *Asaph*, a most upright and devout man, Governour of this Monastery, from whom it receiv'd its present name. The Bishop of this Diocese has under his jurisdiction about one hundred and twenty eight Parishes, the Ecclesiastical Benefices whereof (when this See was vacant) were, till the time of Henry the eighth, in the disposal of the Archbishop, in right of his See, which is now a Prerogative of the Crown. For so we find it recorded in the History of Canterbury.

Rhudhlan. Higher up, *Rhudhlan*, so called from the reddish bank of the river Clud where it is seated, shews a very fair Castle, but almost decay'd with age. It was built by *Lhewelyn ap Sitsilht*, Prince of Wales, and first taken out of the

* Nephew. Welshmen's hands by Robert de Ruthlan (*nephew of Hugh Earl of Chester,) and fortify'd with new works, by the said Hugh's Lieutenant. Afterwards, as the Abbot *de Monte* informs us, King Henry the second having repair'd this Castle, gave it to Hugh Beauchamp.

At this *Rhudhlan* (though now a mean village) we find the manifest signs of a considerable town ... of the Abbey and Hospital, and of a gate at least half a mile from the village. One of the towers in the Castle is call'd *Twr y Brenin*, i.e. *King's tower*; and below the hill, upon the bank of the river, we find another apart from the Castle, call'd *Twr Silod*. Offa King of Mercia, and Meredydh King of Dyved, dy'd in the battel fought at *Rhudhlan*,

† Vaugh. MS. in the year 794†.]

Below this Castle, the river Clud is discharged into the Sea, and though the Valley at the mouth of that river, seems lower than the Sea, yet it is never overflown; but by a natural, though invisible impediment, the water stands on the very brink of the shore, to our just admiration of the Divine Providence.

Disart. The shore descending gradually eastward from this place, passes first by *Disart* castle, so call'd from its steep situation, or (as others will have it) as being *Desert*, and thence by *Basingwerk*,

Basingwerk. which also Henry the second granted to Hugh Beauchamp. Under this place, I view'd *Holy*

Holy well. *well*, a small Town, where is a Well much

St Winifrid. celebrated for the memory of *Winifrid* a Christian Virgin, ravished here, and beheaded by a Tyrant; as also for the moss it yields, of a very sweet scent. Out of this Well a small Brook flows (or rather breaks forth through the stones, on which are seen I know not what kind of blood red spots,) and runs with such a violent course, that immediately it is able to turn a mill. Upon this very Fountain, there is a Chapel, which with great art was hewn out of the live rock, and a small Church adjoyning thereunto, in a window whereof is painted the History and Execution of St *Winifrid*. Giraldus writes, that in his time there was not far from hence *a rich vein of silver, where, for the sake of that metal, they broke up the bowels of the earth*. [The water of *Holy-well* breaks forth with such a rapid stream, that some ingenious persons have suspected it to be rather a subterraneous rivulet which the miners might turn to that chanel, than a spring, it being their common practice, when they meet with under ground *Currents* in their work, to divert them to some *Swallow*. And this suspicion they confirm with an observation, that after much rain the water often appears muddy, and sometimes of a bluish colour, as if it had wash'd some Lead mine, or proceeded from Tobacco-pipe clay: adding farther, that this seems to have happen'd *since* the time of *Giraldus Cambrensis*, it being not likely that so noble a fountain would have escap'd his observation, had it then existed. But though we should grant that Giraldus might neglect the taking notice of so extraordinary a *Current*; yet we have good grounds to assent to Dr Powel's opinion, that it was not frequented by Pilgrims at that time, nor at all celebrated for miraculous cures, or the memory of St *Beuno* and *Winifrid*, who yet liv'd above five hundred years before||. For seeing we find that Author,

|| D. Powel's Notes ad Giraldi Cambr. Itin. Cambriæ, l. 2. c. 10.

throughout the whole course of his Journey, was particularly curious and inquisitive about miraculous fountains, stones, bells, chains, &c. we have no reason to presume, had this place been noted at that time, either for *Winifrid's* being restor'd to life by St *Beuno* and the miraculous origin of the Fountain thereupon, or for any sovereign vertue of the water in healing Diseases, but he would have taken care to deliver some account of it to posterity; especially, considering that he lodg'd one night at *Basingwerk*, within half a mile of this place. From hence Dr Powel very rationally infers, that the Monks of Basingwerk, who were founded above one hundred years after, were (for their own private ends) the first broachers of these fabulous miracles. For (says he) before the foundation of that Abbey, which was in the year 1312, no writer ever made mention of the Romantick origin and miracles of this Fountain. But I refer the Reader to his own words, more at large, in the place above-cited; being, for my own part, of their opinion who think we pay too much regard to such frivolous Superstitions, when we use arguments to confute them.

Of this St *Beuno*, who was founder of the Abbey of Klynog Vawr in Caernarvonshire, as also of *Ennian* who built the Church of Llan Ennian Vrenin in the same County, I find some account in Mr Vaughan's Annotations on the *History of Wales*, which, though not so pertinent to this place, I shall however add here, as being willing to make use of the least occasion of publishing any Notes of an Author so well acquainted with the Antiquities of his Country

Vaughan's MSS Notes on Dr Powel's History

St Beuno, *to whom the Abbey of* Clynog *was dedicated, was the Son of* Hywgi *ap* Gwynllw *ap* Glywis *ap* Tegid *ap* Cadell, *a Prince or Lord of Glewisig, brother's son to St Cadoc ap Gwynllw, sometime Bishop of* Beneventum *in Italy he was, by the mother's side, Cousin German to Laudatus (or* Lhowdhad) *the first Abbot of* Enlli *(in English, Bardsey) and to Kentigern Bishop of Glascow in Scotland, and of Lhan Elwy in Wales The said Kentigern's Father was* Owen Reged *of Scotland, son of* Urien *king of* Cumbria. *Beuno having rais'd to life, as the tradition goes, St Winifrid (who was put to death by one Cradoc a Lord in North Wales, because she would not yield to his unchast desires) was much respected by King* Cadvan, *who gave him Lands, whereon to build a Monastery Cadwalhon, Cadvan's son, bestow'd also other Lands on him, call'd* Gwredog, *where having begun to build a Church, a woman came to him with a child in her arms, and told him those Lands were the inheritance of that Infant Whereat* Beuno *being much concern'd, gave orders she should follow him to* Caer Seiont *(call'd by the Romans* Segontium, *and now* Caernarvon) *where King Cadwalhon resided When he came before the King, he told him with a great deal of zeal, he had done ill, to devote to God's service such Lands as were not his own lawful possessions, and demanded he would return a golden Scepter he had given him as a consideration for the said Lands, which when the King refus'd, he was excommunicated by him Beuno having pronounced his sentence against him, departed, but* Gwyddaint, *who was Cousin German to this Prince* Cadwalhon, *being inform'd of what had happen'd, follow'd after him, and overtaking him, gave him (for the good of his own soul and the King's) the Township of Clynnoc vawr, which was his undoubted inheritance, where Beuno built a Church about the year of our Lord* 616, *about which time* Cadvan *dy'd, leaving his son Cadwalhon to succeed him Some tell us, Beuno restor'd St Winifrid to life in the year* 644, *but whatever we may think of the miracle, that time is not reconcileable to the Truth of History*

Not long before this time, Einion Phrenin *or* Anianus Rex Scotorum, *a Prince in the North of Britain, having left his Royalty, came to* Lhyn *in* Gwynedd, *where he built a Church, which at this day is call'd from him* Lhan Engan Bhrenin, *where he spent in God's service the remainder of his days King Einion was the son of* Owen Danwyn *ap* Einion Yrth, *ap* Cunedda Wledig *King of* Cumbria, *and a great Prince in the North He was Cousin German to* Maelgwn Gwynedh *King of Britain, whose father was* Caswallon Lawhir *brother to Owen Danwyn The said* Maelgwn *dy'd about the year of our Lord* 586 Medi, *daughter to* Voylch ap Talw trwys *of Nant-conwy, was Maelgon's mother, &c*]

This part of the Country, because it affords the most pleasant prospect, and was long since reduced by the *English*, was call'd by the Britons *Tegengl*, which signifies *Fair England* But whereas a certain Author has call'd it *Tegenia*, and supposes the *Iceni* dwelt there, let the Reader be cautious how he assents to it For that worthy Author was deceiv'd by a corrupt name of the *Iceni*

Flint

Upon the shore at this place, we see *Flint castle*, which gave name to this Country, begun by King Henry the second, and finish'd by Edward the first Beyond that, on the eastern limit of the County, next *Cheshire*, lies *Hawarden-castle*, near the shore, call'd commonly *Harden* *, out of which, when *David* brother of Prince *Lhewelyn* had led captive *Roger Clifford* Justiciary of Wales, he brought a most dismal war on himself and his country men, whereby their Dominion in Wales, was wholly overthrown This castle, which was held by Senescalship to the Earls of Chester, was the seat of the Barons of *Mount-hault*, who became a very illustrious family, and bore azure a Lion rampant argent, and also encreased their honour, by marriage with *Cecilia* one of the daughters of *Hugh D' Albany* Earl of Arundel But the issue male being at last extinct, Robert, the last Baron of this family (as we have mention'd already) made it over to Queen *Isabella*, wife of King Edward the second, but the possession of the castle was afterwards transfer'd to the *Stanleys*, who are now Earls of Derby

* Brit Pen Harddh law g Vaugh MS

Barons of Mont hault or de monte alto

Below these places, the south part of this Country is water'd by the little river *Alen*, near which, on a mountain † in the Parish of *Kilken* there is a spring, which, [as is said] ‖ ebb'd and flow'd at set times like the Sea [But it neither ebbs nor flows at present, tho' the general report is that it did so formerly But whereas Dr Powel supposes this to be the Fountain to which Giraldus Cambrensis ascrib'd that quality; it may perhaps be more probably suppos'd, that Giraldus meant *Fynnon Assav*, a noble spring, to which they also attribute the same Phænomenon * But seeing that Author (though a learned and very curious person for the time he liv'd in) is often either erroneous or less accurate in his Physiological Observations, it is seldom worth our while to dispute his meaning on such occasions]

† At a village call'd C

‖ Ebbs and flows, C

* Girald Cambr lib 2 c 10

Hope castle

On this river Alen, lies *Hope castle*, call'd in Welsh *Kaer Gwrle* (into this, King Edward the first retir'd when the Welsh had surpriz'd his Army) near which there are milstones hewn out of a rock And likewise *Mold*, call'd in British *Y Wydgrug*, the castle, formerly, of the Barons of Monthault, both which shew many tokens of antiquity

Milstones

[The present name of *Mold* I suppose to be an abbreviation of the Norman *Mont hault*, and that, no other than a translation of the British name *Gwydhgrig*, which signifies a *conspicuous Mount* or *Barrow*, for though the word *Gwydh* be not us'd in that sense at present, yet that it was anciently so us'd, is manifest from some names of places, the highest Mountain in Wales being call'd *y Wydhva* *, and the highest Stone-pillar or Monument I have seen there, call'd *Hir-vaen gydhog* †, so that there being a considerable *Krig* at this place (for so they call artificial Mounts or Barrows in South Wales) we may safely conclude it to be thence denominated

* i e locus conspicuus

† Colossus conspicuus See Cardiganshire An hinc forte Gwydhelod Saxonum Gigantes?

Near this Town, as the learned ‖ Usher supposes, was that celebrated victory (which he calls *Victoria alleluiatica*, for that the Pagans were put to flight by the repeated shouts of Allelujah) obtained by the Britons under the conduct of *Germanus* and *Lupus*, against the Picts and Saxons Adding, that in memory of that miraculous victory, the place is call'd at this day *Maes Garmon*, or St *German's Field* * And whereas it may be objected, That seeing it is allow'd St German dy'd in the year 435, it was impossible he should lead the Britons in this Island against the Saxons, for that Hengist and Horsa arriv'd not here till 449] he answers, that long before their time (as appears from *Ammianus Marcellinus*, *Claudian*, &c) the Saxons made frequent inroads into this Island

‖ Usher Prim Eccl Brit

Leefwood Plants in Coal. It will not perhaps be unacceptable to the Curious, if we take notice here of some delineations of the leaves of Plants, that are found upon sinking new Coal-pits in the Township of Leefwood in this parish. These (though they are not much minded) are probably found in most other parts of England and Wales, where they dig Coal; at leastwise I have observ'd them at several Coal-pits in Wales, Glocestershire, and Somersetshire, and have seen considerable variety of them, in that excellent *Musæum* of Natural Bodies, collected by Mr. William Cole of Bristol, as also amongst Mr. Beaumont's curious Collection of Minerals. They are found generally in that black slat, or (as the Workmen call it) the *slag* or *clift* which lies next above the Coal; so that in sinking new Pits, when these mock plants are brought up, they are apt to conclude the Coal not far off. These are not such faint resemblances of leaves, as to require any fancy to make out the comparison, like the *Pietra imboschata*, or *Landskip stone* of the Italians, but do exhibit the whole form and texture more compleatly than can be done by any Artist, unless he takes off their impressions from the life, in some fine paste or clay. I say, *resemblances* of leaves, because amongst all the stones I have seen of this kind, I have hitherto observed none delineated with any roots or flowers, but always either pieces of leaves or whole ones, or else (which happens but seldom) some singular figures which I know not what bodies to compare to. Those I have seen from these Coal-pits (and the same may be said of others in general) do for the most part resemble the leaves of capillary Plants, or those of the fern-kind: but our observations in this part of Natural History, are as yet in their infancy, and we know not but the bowels of the Earth, were it possible to search them, might afford as great variety of these mock-plants, as the surface contains of those we esteem more perfect. However, this I shall venture to affirm, that these Plants (whatever may be their origin) are as distinguishable into *Species*, as those produced in the Surface. For although we find (as yet) no resemblance of flowers or seeds, yet the form and texture of these leaves, which are always constant and regular, will soon discover the Species to such as have any skill in Plants, or will take the trouble to compare them nicely with each others. For example, I have observed amongst the ruble of one Coal pit, seven or eight Species of Plants, and of each Species twenty or more Individuals.

Whoever would prove these *subterraneous Leaves* an effect of the universal Deluge, will meet with the same difficulties (not to mention others) as occur to those who assign that origin to the fossil shells, the teeth and vertebræ of fish, Crabs claws, Corals and Sea mushrooms, so plentifully dispersed not only throughout this Island, but doubtless in all parts of the World. For as amongst the fossil-shells of England, we find the greatest part, of a figure and superficies totally different from all the shells of our own Seas, and some of them from all those which the most curious Naturalists have hitherto procur'd from other Countries: so amongst these Plants, we find the majority not reconcileable with those produced in this Country, and many of them totally different from all Plants whatever, that have been yet describ'd. But that the Reader might not wholly rely on my judgment herein, I have added three figures of such leaves, out of a Coal pit belonging to the *Demeans* of *Eagle*'s Bush near Neath in Glamorganshire.

One represents a Leaf of a Plant which I Fig. 27. presume totally different from any yet describ'd. It is about six inches long (but seems to be broken off at each end) and almost two in breadth. The four ribs are a little prominent, somewhat like that of Hart's-tongue, as are also the three orders of *Characters*, betwixt those ribs, which seem in some sort to answer the seeds of such Plants as are call'd dorsiferous, as those of the *Hart's tongue* or *Fern kind*.

Another resembles a branch of the common Fig. 28. female Fern, and agrees with it in superficies and proportion, as well as figure.

The third expresses the common Polypody, Fig. 29. though not so exactly as the 28th imitates the female Fern. This is an elegant Specimen, having the middle rib very prominent, and that of each leaf rais'd proportionably, four inches long, and an inch and a quarter broad.

I find, these Mineral Leaves are not only produced in the Coal-flats, but sometimes in other Fossils; for I have formerly observ'd some of them in Marle Pits near Kaer-wys in this County, where in some measure they resembled Oak leaves. And amongst that valuable Collection of Minerals reposited in the Ashmolean *Musæum*, by Dr. Robert Plot, I find a Specimen of Iron ore out of Shropshire, delineated with a branch of some undescrib'd Plant, which from the texture of the leaves I should be apt to refer to the capillary Tribe, though the figure (as the Doctor observes in his Catalogue) seems rather to resemble Box-leaves†. But I † Scrin. 1. Caps. 2. num. 34. shall add no more on this subject, as expecting shortly a particular Treatise of the origin of form'd Stones and other Fossils, from an ingenious person, who for some years has been very diligent in collecting the Minerals of England, and (as far as I am capable of judging) no less successful in his Discoveries.]

Near *Hope*, † whilst I was drawing up these † So said ann. 1607. notes, a certain Gardener digging somewhat deep, discover'd a very antient work, concerning which several have made various conjectures: but whoever consults *M. Vitruvius Pollio*, will find it no other than the beginning of a Hypocaust of the Romans, who growing luxurious as their wealth increas'd, us'd Baths very Baths. much. It was five ells long, four broad, and about half an ell high, encompass'd with walls hewn out of the live rock. The floor was of brick set in mortar; the roof was supported with brick pillars, and consisted of polish'd Tiles, which at several places were perforated; on these, were fix'd certain brick tubes, which carry'd off the force of the heat, and thus, as the Poet saith,

——*Vo[illegible] vapore fla[illegible]*,

I. e. The Hypocausts breath'd out a *vaporous* heat.

Now who can suppose but that they were such *Hypocausts*, that Giraldus so much admir'd at *Kaer Lheon* in Monmouthshire, when he wrote thus of the Roman works there: *And which seems more particularly remarkable, you may see there several stoves, contriv'd with wonderful skill, breathing heat insensibly through small pipes*, &c. Whose work this was, appears by an Inscription on some tiles there, LEGIO XX. for the twentieth Legion, which was stil'd *Victrix*, as we have shewn already, lay in garrison at Chester, scarce six miles hence.

Near

Coleshull — Near this river Alen, in a narrow place beset with woods, lies *Coleshull*, call'd by Giraldus *Collis Carbonarius*, or a Cole-hill Where, when King Henry the second had made the most diligent preparation to give battel to the Welsh, the English, by reason of their disorderly Approaches, were defeated, and the King's standard forsaken by Henry of Essex, who, by right of inheritance, was standard bearer to the Kings of England Whereupon, being charged with High treason, and overcome by his adversary in a duel, and his estate forfeited to the crown; he was so much asham'd of his cowardise, that he put on a Hood, and retir'd into a Monastery

English Maelor — There is another small part of this County, on this side *Dee*, which is in a manner wholly divided from the rest, and is call'd *English-Maelor*, whereof we have taken notice in Cheshire, when we gave an account of *Bangor*, and therefore need not repeat what we have said already

Han mere — Nothing else deserves to be mention'd here, except *Han mere*, seated by a lake or mear, whence that antient and honourable family dwelling there, took the name of *Hanmer*

Maen y Chwyvan — [It remains only that we make some mention of that remarkable Monument or carv'd Pillar on Mostyn mountain, which is represented in the Plate by the first and second figures It stands on the cavenest part of the mountain, and is in height eleven foot and three inches above the Pedestal, two foot and four inches broad, and eleven inches thick The Pedestal is five foot long, four and a half broad, and about fourteen inches thick and the Monument being let thorow it, reaches about five inches below the bottom, so that the whole length of it is about thirteen foot

The first figure represents the east side, and that edge which looks to the south, and the second the western side with the north-edge, though the Sculptures on these edges are grav'd as if they were no part of the stone

When this Monument was erected, or by what Nation, I must leave to further enquiry, however, I thought it not amiss to publish those draughts of it, supposing there may be more of the same kind in some parts of Britain or Ireland, or else in other Countries, which being compar'd with this, it might perhaps appear what Nation used them, and upon what occasions [illegible] Dr Plot in his History of Stafford shire, gives us the draughts of a Monument or two, which agree very well with this in the chequer'd carving, and might therefore possibly belong to the same Nation Those, he concludes to have been erected by the Danes, for that there is another very like them at Beau-Castle in Cumberland, inscrib'd with Runick Characters, which is presum'd to have been a Funeral Monument* But the Characters on the east side of ours, seem nothing like the Runic, or any other letters I have seen, but resemble rather the numeral figures 1221, though I confess I am so little satisfy'd with the meaning of them, that I know not whether they were ever intended to be significative Within a furlong or less of this Monument, there is an artificial Mount or Barrow (of which sort there are also about twenty more in this neighbourhood, call'd *y Gorsedheu*) where have been formerly a great many carcases and skulls discover'd, some of which were cut, and one or two particularly had round holes in them, as it pierced with an arrow upon which account this pillar has been suspected for a Monument of some signal victory, and the rather, for that upon digging five or six foot under it, no bones were discover'd, nor any thing else that might give occasion to suspect it Sepulchral

* Phil Tranf Num 178

This monumental Pillar is call'd *Maen y Chwyvan*, a name no less obscure than the History of it, for though the former word signifies a *Stone*, yet no man understands the meaning of *Chwyvan* Were it *Gwyvan*, I should conclude it corrupted from *Gwydhvaen*, i e *the high Pillar* but seeing it is written *Mean y Chusan* in an old Deed bearing date 1388 (which scarce differs in pronunciation from *Chuyvan*) I dare not acquiesce in that Etymology, though at present I can think of none more probable]

Earls of Chester — The Earls of *Chester*, by light skirmishes with the Welsh as occasion and opportunity offer'd, were the first Normans that subdu'd this County Whence in antient Records we read, *The County of Flint appertaineth to the dignity of the Sword of Chester* and the eldest sons of the Kings of England, were formerly stil'd *Earls of Chester and Flint* But when it was added to the Crown,

Policy of Ed — King Edward the first (supposing it of singular use, as well to maintain his own, as to bridle the Welsh) kept this and all the maritim parts of Wales in his own hands, and distributed the inland countries to his Nobles, as he thought convenient Imitating herein the policy of *Augustus Cæsar*, who himself undertook the charge of the outward and most potent Provinces, leaving the rest to the government of *Proconsuls* by lot And this he did with a shew of defending his Empire, but in reality, that he might keep the Armies under his own command

This County hath only 28 Parishes

PRIN-

PRINCES of WALES.

S for the antient Princes of Wales *of British Extraction, I refer the Reader to the* Annals of Wales *already publish'd but for the later Princes of the Royal Line of England, it seems pertinent to our design, that we add here a short account of them.*

Edward the first (to whom, during his minority, his father Henry the third had granted the Principality of Wales) having (when Lhewelyn ap Grufydh *the last Prince of the British blood was slain) cut as it were the* sinews *of the Government of Soveraignty of that Nation, united the same to the Kingdom of England in the 12th year of his reign and the whole Province swore fealty and allegiance to his son Edward of* Caernarvon, *whom he constituted Prince of Wales But Edward the second confer'd not the title of* Prince of Wales *on his son Edward, but only the honour of Earl of* Chester *and* Flint, *as far as I can yet learn out of the Records of the Kingdom Edward the third first solemnly invested his son Edward, sirnam'd* the Black, *with this title, who, in the very height of all his military glory, dy'd an untimely death. After that, he confer'd the same on his son* Richard of Bourdeaux, *heir to the crown, who, being depriv'd of his Kingdom by King Henry the fourth, dy'd miserably, leaving no issue The same Henry the fourth confer'd the Principality of Wales on his eldest son, who was that renowned Prince Henry the fifth His son Henry the sixth, whose father dy'd whilst he was an infant, confer'd that honour (which he never receiv'd himself) on his young son Edward, who being taken in the battle of Tewkesbury, had his brains barbarously dash'd out by the* York-*Party Not long after, King Edward the fourth being settled on the throne, created his young son Edward (afterwards Edward the fifth) Prince of Wales And soon after, his Uncle Richard, having dispatch'd him out of the way, substituted in his place his own son Edward, who had been created Earl of Salisbury before by Edward the fourth, but he dy'd soon after (which I have but lately discover'd) Afterwards Henry the seventh constituted, first, his son Arthur,* Prince of Wales, *and after his decease,* Henry, *famous afterwards under the title of Henry the eighth. On all these the Principality of Wales was confer'd by solemn* Investiture, *and a Patent deliver'd them in these words,* Tenendus sibi & hæredibus Regibus Angliæ, &c *For in those times, the Kings would not deprive themselves of so fair an opportunity of obliging their eldest sons, but thought it prudence to engage them with so great an honour, when it seem'd most convenient*

Mary, Elizabeth, *and* Edward, *the children of Henry the eighth, although they receiv'd not the Investiture and Patent, were yet successively stil'd* Princesses *and* Prince of Wales *For at that time,* 25 Hen 8 *Wales was by Act of Parliament so united and incorporated with England, that they enjoy'd the same Laws and Privileges [But since that time,* Henry, *and after him,* Charles, *the sons of King James the first, and* Charles *eldest son of King Charles the first, were all successively* created *Princes of Wales, by* Patent *As was also his Royal Highness,* George Augustus, *who is the only son of our present Soveraign King* George, *and (which is a Blessing that this Nation hath not known for some ages) hath several Children living, in his* Father's *Reign, to the great happiness of these Kingdoms, and the inexpressible joy of every faithful and loyal Subject]*

But now let us return out of Wales into England, and proceed to the Country of the Brigantes

An INDEX *of the Curiosities represented in the following* TABLE.

Fig 1 2 THE carv'd pillar or monument call'd *Maen y Chwyvan* in Flintshire
3 4 The Pillars describ'd in the Hall at *Kaer-phyli Castle* in Glamorganshire
5 The Alabaster Statue, found near *Porth Shini Kran* in Monmouthshire
6 *Maen y Morynnion* at *Gaer* near Brecknock
7 The chequer'd Pavement discover'd Anno 1692 at *Kaer Lheion* in Monmouthshire
8 A hollow Brick out of a Roman Hypocaust at *Kaer-hyn* in Caernarvonshire
9. The *Phiala* or Bowl describ'd at *Kaer Lheion* in Monmouthshire
10 One of the leaden Boxes mention'd at *Lhan Boydy* in Caermardhinshire
11 12 The same open'd
13 A brass axe found at *Moel yr Henblys* in the Parish of *Dero ven* in Montgomeryshire
14 Part of one of the brass Daggers (if we may so call them) found at *[illegible]* in Meirionydhshire with the nails that fasten'd it to the handle
15 The point of such a Dagger, found at the same place
16 17 The Roman *Fibula*, describ'd at *Kaer Lheion* in Monmouthshire
18 A brass Amulet dug out of a Well somewhere in Denbighshire The other side differ'd not from that which is engraven
19 A cake of Copper describ'd at *Kaer Rhyn* in Caernarvonshire
20 A gold Medal of Julius Constantius, found at *Trewerthin* in Anglesey
21 A British gold coin (such as they used before the Roman Conquest) found at *Penrn* Parish in Cardiganshire
22 23 24 Other British coins of gold, kept in the Ashmolean Repository at Oxford
25 26 The Coins describ'd at *Kaer Phyli* Castle in Glamorganshire
27 28 29 Mock Plants out of a Cole pit near *Neath* in Glamorganshire See a description of them in Flintshire

On the left hand of the Table

a An Adder bead or Glain Neidr of green glass, found at *Aber Ffraw* in Anglesey
b Another of earth, enamell'd with blue, found near *Dol Gelhau* in Meirionydhshire
c A third of glass, undulated with white, red, and blue, found near *Maes y Pandy* in the same County
d Represents one end of the same Of these Adder beads, which are suppos'd to have been Druid Amulets, some account is given at *Kerrig y Drudion*, in Denbighshire

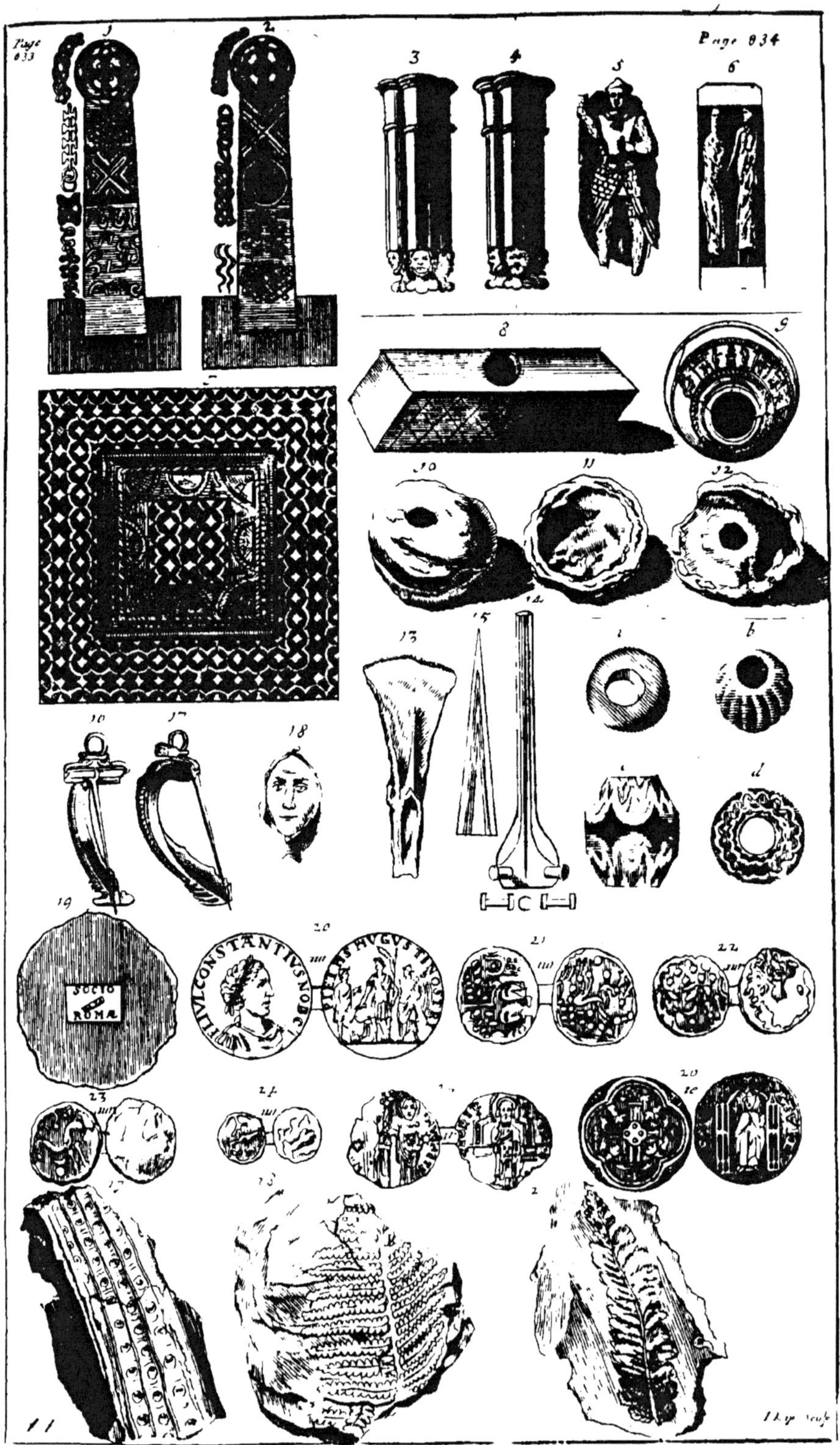

Page 833
Page 834
SOCIO
ROMÆ
FL IVL CONSTANTIVS NOB C

More rare Plants growing in Wales.

Acetosa Cambro britannica montana. *Park.* rotundifolia repens Eboracensis, foliis in medio deliquium patientibus *Moris hist Mountain round-leaved Sorrel of Wales On most high rocks, and by rivulets about Snowdon in Caernarvonshire almost every where, as also by rivulets among the broken rocks of Cader-idris above a certain lake call'd Llin y cau*

Argemone lutea Cambro-britannica *Park* Papaver luteum perenne, laciniato folio Cambro-britannicum *Yellow wild bastard Poppy About a mile from a small village called Abler, and in the midway from Denbigh to Guidar, also near a wooden bridge over the river Dee, near to a village called Bala, also going up the hill that leads to Bangor near to Anglesey,* Park p 270 *But more certainly to be found on Clogwyn y Garnedh, yscolion duon, Dygyvylche, as you ascend the Glyder from Lhanberies, and several other places about Snowdon, most commonly by rivulets, or on moist rocks also beyond Pontvawr very near the bridge, among the stones Mr Lhwyd*

Alsine myosotis lanuginosa Alpina grandiflora, seu Auricula muris villosa flora amplo membranaceo An Caryophyllus holosteus Alpinus angustifolius *C B prod? Hairy mountain Mouse-ear Chickweed with a large flower On the rock called Clogwyn y Garnedh, the highest of all Wales, near Lhanberys in Caernarvonshire plentifully*

Adiantum nigrum pinnulis Cicutariæ divisurâ An Ad album tenuifolium Rutæ murariæ accedens *J. B Fine leaved white Mayden-hair divided like bastord Hemlock On Snowdon-hill.*

Bistorta minima Alpina, foliis imis subrotundis & minutissimè serratis *D Lhwyd* Alpina pumila varia *Park.* pumila foliis variis rotundis & longis *Moris The least mountain Bistort, with round and long leaves In the steep pastures of the high rock called Grib Goch above the lake or pool called Phynon bhrêch near Llanberys Whether this be specifically different from the Westmoreland* Bistor-minor, *I leave to others, upon comparing the plants, to determine*

Bugula cærulea Alpina *Park* Consolida media cærulea Alpina *C B Mountain Bugle or Sicklewort Found on Carnedh Lhewellin in Caernarvonshire by Dr Johnson*

Caryophyllata montana purpurea *Ger emac* montana seu palustris purpurea *Park* aquatica nutante flore *C B* aquatica flore rubio striato *J B Purple Mountain Avens or Water-Avens On Snowdon and other mountains*

Cirsium Britannicum Clusii repens *J B* aliud Anglicum *Park* singulari capitulo magno vel incanum alterum *C B The great English soft or gentle Thistle, or melancholy Thistle As you ascend the Glyder from Lhanberys, and in many other mountainous pastures about Snowdon*

Cirsium montanum humile Cynoglossi folio polyanthemum An Carduus mollis Helenii folio *Park? On Clogwyn y Garnedh, and most other high rocks in Caernarvonshire about Snowdon*

Cirsium montanum polyanthemum Salicis folio angusto denticulato *By a rivulet on Gallt yr Ogo near Capel kirig, and in other places with the precedent, of which perhaps it may be only a variety*

Chamæmorus Cambro-britannica sive Lancastrense Vaccinium nubis *Park The Welsh Knoutberry said to be found in Wales by Dr Lobel We met not with it there It grows abundantly on* Berwyn *mountain, not far from* Lhan Rhaiadar ym moxnant *in Denbighshire, where it is well known by the name of* Moyar Berwyn, *mora montis Berwini*

Cochlearia minor rotundifolia nostras & *Parkinsoni Small round leaved Scurvy grass The lower leaves from the root are round Those on the stalks angular On the coast of Caernarvonshire, and likewise of Anglesey, about Beaumaris*

Cotyledon hirsuta *P B* Saniculæ Alpinæ aliquatenus affinis *J B* forte *Hairy kidney-wort By the rills and on the moist rocks of many mountains in Wales, as Snowdon, Cader idris, Carnedh-Lhewelyn,* &c *abundantly*

Filix Alpina Pedicularis rubræ foliis subtus villosis *D Lhwyd,* pumila, Lonchitidis Maranthæ species Cambro britannica, An Lonchitis aspera Ilvensis *Lugd? ejusd apud Plukenetum in Phytograph Stone-Fern with red rattle leaves, hairy underneath On the moist rocks called Clogwyn y Garnedh, near the top of the mountain Gwy lhva the highest in all Wales It is a rare plant even at Snowdon*

Filicula petræa florida perelegans seu Adiantum album floridum An Adianthum Alpinum crispum Schwenckfeldii *J B? Small flowering Stone fern On Clogwyn y Garnedh, and most other high rocks*

Filix montana ramosa minor argute denticulato *D Lhwyd.* Alpina Myrrhidis facie Cambro-britannica *D Plukenet Phytograph Small-branched Mountain-Fern, with finely indented leaves On the top of the mountain Glyder, where it overhangs the lake or pool called Lhyn Oguan*

Filix marina Anglica *Park* Chamæfilix marina Anglico *J B* Filicula petræa fœmina seu Chamæfilix marina Anglica *Ger emac* Filix petræa ex insulis Stœchadibus *C B Dwarf Sea-fern On the rocks about Presthólm Island near Beaumaris, and on Lhandwyn in the Isle of Anglesey*

Filix saxatilis Tragi *J B Park* Adiantum ἀκρόςιχον seu furcatum *Thal* Filix corniculata *C B On the top of Carnedh Lhewelyn near Lhan Lhechyd in Caernarvonshire Horned or forked white Maiden-hair*

Gnaphalium maritimum *C B* maritimum multis *J B* marinum *Ger* marinum sive Cotonaria *Park Sea Cudweed or Cotton weed On the sand near Abermeney ferry in the Isle of Anglesey plentifully, where the common people call it* Calamus aromaticus, *from its sweet scent*

Gramen sparteum montanum spica foliacea graminea *P B Grass upon grass On the tops of the highest mountains, Snowdon, Cader-idris,* &c *among the stones and moss, where no other Plant grows*

Hipposelinum *Ger emac* Hipposelinum seu Smyrnium vulgare *Park* Macerone, quibusdam Smyrnium, semine magno nigro *J B* Hipposelinum Theophrasti sive Smyrnium Dioscoridis *C B Alexanders On the rocks about Presthólm Island near Beaumaris plentifully*

Hyacinthus stellatus Fuchsii *Ger* stellatus vulgaris sive bifolius Fuchsii *Park parad* stellatus bifolius & trifolius vernus dumetorum flore cæruleo at albo *J B* stellaris bifolius Germanicus *C B Small vernal Star Hyacinth On the coasts of North Wales among the bushes, and in the adjacent Islands, Bardsey,* &c *plentifully*

Juncus acutus maritimus Anglicus *Park English Sea hard Rush On the southern Sea coast of Wales*

Juncus acutus capitulis Sorghi *C B* maritimus capitulis Sorghi *Park* pungens, seu acutus capitulis Sorghi *J B Pricking large Sea Rush, with head like Indian millet On the sandy hills*

hills on the Weſtern ſhore of North-Wales, Merionethſhire about Harlech

Juniperus Alpina *J B Cluſ Park* Alpina minor *Ger emac* minor montana folio latiore, fructuque longiore *C B Mountain Dwarf Juniper On Snowdon hill The Country people call it Savine, and uſe the decoction of it to deſtroy the bots in horſes*

Lamium montanum Meliſſa folio *C B* Meliſſa Fuchſii *Ger* Meliſſophyllon Fuchſii *Park* Meliſſa adulterina quorundam, amplis foliis, & floribus non grati odoris *J B Baulm leaved Archangel, Baſtard-Baulm In the woods about Haverford West in Pembrokeſhire*

Leucoium maritimum ſinuato folio *C B* maritimum Camerarii *J B* marinum maximum *Park* ut & majus *ejuſdem* marinum purpureum Lobelii *Ger emac Great Sea-ſtock-Gillyflower, with a ſinuated leaf On the ſandy ſhores about Abermeney ferry in the Iſle of Angleſey, and at Aberdaren in Caernarvonſhire*

Lychnis Alpina minima Caryophylleus flos 9 Cluſio, Caryophyllus pumilio Alpinus *Ger emac* Lychnis Alpina pumila folio gramineo, ſeu Muſcus Alpinus Lychnidis flore *C B* Muſcus Alpinus flore inſigni dilute rubente *J B* Ocymoides muſcoſus Alpinus *Park The leaſt Mountain Campion or Moſſe-Campion On the ſteep and higher rocks of Snowdon hill in Caernarvonſhire almoſt every where*

Lychnis ſylveſtris viſcoſa rubra anguſtifolia *C B Park* Odontidi ſive Flore cuculi affinis Lychnis ſylv 1 Cluſii in Pannon 4 in Hiſt *J B* Muſcipula anguſtifolia *Ger emac Narrow-leaved red Catchfly On the ſides of* Craig Wreidhin *hill in Montgomeryſhire*

Alſines myoſous facie Lychnis Alpina flore amplo niveo repens *D Lloyd Mountain-Campion with a large white flower, reſembling Mouſe-ear Chickweed By the water-courſes on the ſides of Snowdon hill plentifully*

Lonchitis aſpera *C B* aſpera major *Ger* aſpera major Matthiolo *Park* altera cum folio denticulato, ſive Lonchitis altera Matthioli *J B Rough Spleenwort with indented leaves It ſprings out of the rifts and chinks of the rocks, in the high Mountains of* Snowdon v g Clogwin y Garnedh, y Grib Gôch Trygvylchau

Lithoſpermum majus Dodonæi, flore purpureo, ſemine Anchuſæ *J B* majus *Ger* vulgare majus *Park* minus repens latifolium *C B the leſſer creeping Gromwel On the top of a buſhy hill on the North ſide of Denbigh-town*

Malva arborea marina noſtras *Park Engliſh Sea-Tree Mallow On the rocks of* Caldey *Iſland in* South Wales *plentifully*

Muſcus clavatus ſive Lycopodium *Ger Park Club moſs or Wolves claw On the Mountains every where*

Muſcus terreſtris foliis retro reflexis *J B* Lycopodium elatius Abieti forme Julo ſingulari ipode *D Lhwyd Club moſs with reflected leaves, and ſingle heads, without foot ſtalks It grows together with Cypreſs-moſs on the Mountains of Caernarvonſhire, but more rarely We found it plentifully on the Mountain call'd* Rhwn Glyder *above the Lake* Lhyn y cwn, *and elſewhere on the ſaid Mountain*

Muſcus clavatus foliis Cupreſſi *Ger emac C B Cypreſs Moſs or Heath Cypreſs On Snowdon, Cader Idris, and moſt other of the high mountains among the graſs*

Muſcus erectus Abieti-formis, terreſtris rectus *J B* Selago tertia *Thal Upright Fir-moſs On Snowdon, Cader Idris, and other high Mountains*

Muſcus terreſtris repens, clavis ſingularibus folioſis erectis *Creeping Club moſs with erect heads On moiſt and watery places about ſprings, and in meadows about* Capel Cerig

Muſcus terreſtris erectus minor polyſpermos. *Seeding Mountain moſs In moiſt places and about ſprings on* Snowdon *and other Mountains*

Muſcus Trichomanoides purpureus, Alpinis rivulis innaſcens. *Purple Mountain-water moſs reſembling black maiden-hair In the mountainous rivulets*

Muſcus croceus ſaxigena holoſericum referens, ſeu Byſſus petræus. An muſcus ſaxatilis ſerico ſimilis *Commelini* in *Cat plant Holland? Saffron colour'd ſilken ſtone-moſs Under high rocks where they are prominent.*

Orchis puſilla alba odorata radice palmata. *White-handed muſk Orchies On the ſides of* Snowdon *by the way leading from* Lhanberis *to* Caernarvon

Orobus ſylvaticus noſtras *Engliſh wild Wood-Vetch or bitter Vetch. Below* Brecknock *hills in the way to* Cardiff *and in* Merioneth-ſhire *not far from* Bala

Plantago anguſtifolia montana An Alpina anguſtifolia *J B Narrow leav'd Mountain Plantain On the rocks of* Trigvylchau *above the Lake* Lhyn Bochlyn, *near the Church of St* Peris

Polypodium Cambro britannicum pinnulis ad margines laciniatis *Laciniated Polypody of* Wales *On a rock in a wood near* Denys Powys *Caſtle, not far from* Caerdyff *in* Glamorganſhire

Ranunculus globoſus *Ger Park parad The Globe-flower or Locker-goulens In the mountainous meadows, and on the ſides of the Mountains plentifully*

Rhodia radix omnium Autorum *Roſewort; On the rocks of the high Mountains of* Snowdon *and* Cader idris, *&c plentifully*

Sedum Alpinum Ericoides cæruleum *C B. J B Mountain Heath like Sengreen with large purple flower, On the ſteep and higher rocks of* Snowdon *almoſt every where*

Sedum Alpinum trifido folio *C B Small Mountain-Sengreen with jagged leaves On* Snowdon *and other high mountains, chiefly by the rivulets ſides.*

Sedum ſerratum floſculis compactis non maculatis *Indented Mountain Sengreen with unſpotted flowers growing cloſe together On the higheſt Mountains, it ſprings out of the chinks and commiſſures of the rocks, as in* Clogwyn y Garnedh, Crib y Diſtilh, Clogwyn du ymhen y Glyder, *near* Lhanberys

Thalictrum montanum minus foliis latioribus *The leſſer Meadow rue with broader leaves On the ſteep ſides of the Mountain call'd* Cader-Idris *by* Dolgelli *in Merionethſhire, out of the clefts or chinks of the rock,*

Thalictrum minimum montanum, atro-rubens, foliis ſplendentibus *The leaſt mountainous Meadow rue, with ſhining leaves and dark red flowers On the moiſt rocks, and by the rivulets in the Mountains of* Caernarvonſhire, *Mr* Lhwyd *There are two varieties of this, the one with broader, the other with narrower leaves*

Thlaſpi ſive Lunaria vaſculo ſublongo intorto *Lunar Violet with a wreathen cod On the Mountains of* North-Wales, *obſerv'd by Mr.* Lhwyd *Who alſo found another Plant there on the high rocks call'd* Hyſvæ, *hanging over the valley* Nant Phrancon *in* Caernarvonſhire, *which he intitled* Paronychiæ ſimilis ſed major perennis Alpina repens, *of which, having not ſeen it in the ſeed, he was in ſome doubt, whether it might not be the ſame with the precedent*

Thlaſpi Vaccariæ incano folio perenne *Perennial Mithridate muſtard In the mountainous part of* North Wales

Naſturtium petræum *Johnſoni Merc Bot* part alt *Dr Johnſon's Rock creſs On the high Mountains*

tains of Caernarvonshire *and* Merionethshire, *as* Moelyn rudh *near* Phestiniog, Clogwyn du y yr Ardhus *and* Clogwyn y Garnedh *near* Lhanberys

Bulbosa Alpina juncifolia pericarpio unico erecto in summo cauliculo dodrantali *A certain Rush-leav'd bulbous Plant, having one Seed-vessel on the top of an erect stalk about nine inches high On the high rocks of* Snowdon, *viz* Trigvylcha i y Clogwyn du ymhen y Gluder, Clogwyn yr Ardhu Crib y Distilh, *&c Mr* Lhwyd *It hath three or four more narrow and short leaves upon the stalk*

Subularia lacustris seu Calamistrum herba aquatico Alpina, s Aizoides Fusiforme Alpinorum lacuum *D Lhwyd A Spindle leav'd Water-Sengreen-like Plant, growing in the bottom of a small Lake near the top of* Snowdon-*hill, call'd* Phynon vrêch, *&c*

Graminifolia plantula Alpina capitulis Armeriæ proliferæ, *D Lhwyd A Mountain grass-leav'd Plant with heads like the Cluster-pink In the pastures at the foot of a certain high rock call'd* Clogwyn du ymhen y Glyder *in* Caernavonshire,

Gladiolus lacustris Dormanni *Clus cur post* Glad lacustris Clusii, sive Leucoium palustre flore cæruleo Bauhini *Park Water Gladiole In most of the Lakes in* North-Wales

Graminifolia lacustris prolifera, seu plantulis quasi novis hinc inde cauliculis accrescentibus *A Grass leav'd childing water plant, having young Plants springing from the stalks*

Veronica spicata latifolia *C B Ger* major latifolia, foliis splendentibus & non splendentibus *J B* spicata latifolia major *Park Great broad-leav'd spiked Speedwell or Fluellin On the sides of a Mountain call'd* Craig-Wreidhin *in* Montgomeryshire

Auricula muris pulchro flore, folio tenuissimo *J B Small fine leav'd Mountain-Chickweed with a fair flower On most of the high and steep rocks about* Snowdon

Trichomanes ramosum *J B* aliud, foliis mucronatis profunde incisis *Sibbald Prod Scot Branched English Black Maiden hair On the high rocks about* Snowdon *plentifully*

BRIGAN-

BRIGANTES.

RITAIN, *which has thus far bulg'd out into several large Promontories, coming gradually nearer, on one side to* Germany, *and on the other to* Ireland, *does now (as if it were afraid of the breaking-in of the Ocean) draw it self in on each side, and retire further from its neighbours, and is contracted into a much narrower breadth For it is not above a hundred miles over, between the two coasts, which run northward almost in a streight line as far as Scotland While the Government of the Britains lasted, almost all this tract was inhabited by the* Brigantes *For Ptolemy tells us, that they were possessed of all, from the Eastern to the Western Sea This was a people stout and numerous; and they are very much commended by the best Writers, who all name them* Brigantes, *except Stephanus in his Book of* Cities, *who calls them* Brigæ *What he says of them there, we know not, the place where he speaks about them, being imperfect in the Copies which we have at this day. If I should imagin, that those* Brigantes *were so call'd from* Briga, *which among the old Spaniards signified a* City; *it is a conjecture that I could not acquiesce in, because it is evident from* Strabo *that this is a pure Spanish word Or if I should think with* Goropius, *that these* Brigantes *were deriv'd from a Belgick word* Free-hands (i e. Liberi manibus,) *what were it but to obtrude Dreams upon those who are waking? But whatever becomes of these Opinions; our Britains at this day, if they observe a fellow of a resolute, restless, intruding temper, will twit him by saying that* * he plays the Brigans *and the French at this time call the same sort of men* Brigand, *and Pirate-ships* Brigantin; *which are probably remains of the old Gaulish But whether the word had that signification in the old Gaulish or British languages, and whether our* Brigantes *were of that temper, I dare not affirm. Yet if my memory fail me not, Strabo calls the* Brigantes *(a People of the Alps)* Grassatores, *i. e robbers and plunderers, and* Julius Belga, *a desperately bold youth (who look'd upon Power to be Authority, and Virtue to be no more than an empty name,) is in Tacitus sirnam'd* Briganticus *And our* Brigantes *seem to have been a little guilty in that way, who were so very troublesome to their neighbours, that Antoninus Pius dispossess'd them of a great part of their territories for no other reason; as* Pausanias *tells us in these words,* Ἀπετέμετο δὲ Ἀντωνῖνος ὁ εὐσεβὴς καὶ τῶν ἐν Βριττανίᾳ Βριγάντων τὴν πολλήν, ὅτι ἐπεσβαίνειν καὶ οὗτοι σὺν ὅπλοις ἦρξαν τὴν Γεννουνίαν μοῖραν, ὑπηκόους Ῥωμαίων *i e* Antoninus Pius depriv'd the *Brigantes* in Britain of much of their lands, because they began to make incursions into *Genounia*, a Region under the Jurisdiction of the Romans *I hope none will construe this as a reproach for my part, I should be unlike my self, should I now go to cast a scandal even upon a private person, and much less upon a whole Nation Nor was this indeed any* reproach *in that warlike age, when all Right was in the longest Sword* Robberies *(says Cæsar)* among the Germans are not in the least infamous, so they be committed without the bounds of their respective Cities and this they tell you they practise, with a design to exercise their youth, and to keep them from sloth and laziness. *Upon the like account also, the* Pæones *among the Greeks had that name from being* † Strikers *or* Beaters, *as the* Quadi *among the Germans, and also the* Chaldæans, *had their's from being* ‖ Robbers *and* Plunderers.

Brigæ Brigantes, from whence so call'd.

* Brigantem agit Pasquierus, Les Recherches de France l. 6 c. 40

† Percussores ‖ Grassatores

Reinerus Reineccius

When Florianus del Campo, *a Spaniard (out of vanity and ostentation,) carried the* Brigantes *out of Spain into Ireland, and from thence into Britain, without any manner of ground, but that he found the City* Brigantia *in Spain; I am afraid he very much mistook the mark For if it may not be allow'd, that our* Brigantes *and those in Ireland had the same name upon the same account; I had rather conjecture, with my learned friend Mr* Thomas Savil, *that part of our* Brigantes, *with others of the British nations, retir'd into* Ireland, *upon the coming over of the Romans Some, for the sake of ease and quietness; others, to keep their eyes from being witnesses of the Roman insolence, and others again, because that liberty which Nature had given them, and their younger years had enjoy'd, they would not now quit in their old age However, that the Emperour* Claudius *was the first of all the Romans who made an attempt upon our* Brigantes, *and subjected them to the Roman yoke, may be gathered from these Verses of Seneca*

Some Copies call those in Ireland Brigantes

In *Ludo*

—————Ille Britannos,
Ultra noti littora Ponti, & cæruleos
Scuta *Brigantes*, dare Romuleis colla catenis
Jussit, & ipsum nova Romanæ jura securis
Tremere Oceanum.

'Twas he whose all-commanding yoke
The farthest Britains gladly took,
Him the Brigantes *in blue arms ador'd,*
When the vast Ocean fear'd his power
Restrain'd with Laws unknown before,
And trembling Neptune *serv'd a Roman Lord*

Yet I have always thought, that they were not then conquer'd, *but rather surrender'd themselves to the Romans because what he has mention'd in a* Poetical *manner, is not confirm'd by Historians For Tacitus tell us, that then* Ostorius, *having new conquests in his eye, was drawn back by some mutinies among*
Cartismandua *the* Brigantes; *and that after he had put some few to the sword, he easily quieted the rest At which time, the* Brigantes *were govern'd by* Cartismandua, *a noble Lady, who deliver'd up King* Caratacus *to the*
Se. *The Romans in Britain* *Romans This brought in wealth, and that, Luxury, so that, leaving her husband* Venutius, *she marry'd* Vellocatus *(his armour bearer) and made him sharer with her in the government This Villany was*
Tacitus *the overthrow of her House, and gave rise to a bloody war The City stood up for the Husband, and the Queen's lust and cruelty, for the Adulterer She, by craft and artifice, got* Venutius's *brother and nearest relations to be cut off* Venutius *could no longer brook this infamy, but call'd in succours, by whose assistance partly, and partly by the defection of the* Brigantes, *he reduc'd* Cartismandua *to the utmost extremity The Garrisons, Wings, and Cohorts, with which the Romans furnish'd her, brought her off in several battels, yet so, that* Venutius *kept the* Kingdom, *and left nothing but the* War *to the Romans, who could not subdue the* Brigantes *before the time of Vespasian For then* Petilius Cerealis *came against this People with whom he fought several battels, not without much bloodshed, and either wasted or conquer'd a great part of the* Brigantes *But whereas Tacitus tells us, that this Queen of the* Brigantes *deliver'd Caratacus prisoner to* Claudius, *and that he made a part of* Claudius's *triumph; it is a manifest*
† A mistake in Chronology † *Ἀναχρονισμὸς in that excellent Author, as Lipsius (that great Master of ancient Learning) has long since observ'd. For neither was this* Caratacus *(Prince of the* Silures) *in that triumph of Claudius; nor yet* Caratacus, *son of* Cunobelin *(for so the* Fasti *call the same person, that Dio calls* Catacratus,) *over whom* Aulus Plautius, *if not the same year, at least the very next after,* * *triumph'd by way of* Ovation. * Ovans triumphavit *But these things I leave to the search of others, though something I have said of them before In the time of* Hadrian, *when (as* Ælius Spartianus *has it)* the Britains could no longer be kept under the Roman Yoke, *our* Brigantes *seem to have revolted among the rest, and to have rais'd some very notable commotion Else, why should* Juvenal *(who was a Contemporary) say?*

Dirue Maurorum attegias, & castra Brigantum.

Brigantick forts and Moorish booths pull down

And afterwards, in the time of Antoninus Pius, *they seem not to have been over-submissive; seeing that Emperor (as we observ'd) dispossess'd them of part of their territories, for invading the Province of* Genunia *or* Guinethia, *an Allie of the Romans*

If I thought I should escape the Censure of the Criticks who, presuming upon their wit and acuteness, do now-a days take a strange liberty,) methinks I could correct an error or two in Tacitus, relating to the Brigantes *One is in the 12th book of his* Annals, *where he writes that* Venutius *(the person we just now mention'd) belong'd to the City of the* Jugantes, è civitate Jugantum, *I would read it* Brigantum, *and Tacitus himself, in the third Book of his* History, *seems to confirm that Reading The other is in the Life of* Agricola Brigantes *(says he)* fœminâ Duce, exurere Coloniam, &c *i e the* Brigantes, *under the conduct of a woman, began to set fire to the Colony Here, if we will follow the truth, we are to read* Trinobantes *for he speaks of Queen* Boodicia, *who had nothing to do with the* Brigantes, *whereas, it was she that stir'd up the* Trinobantes *to rebellion, and burnt the Colony* * Camalodunum * Maldon

This large Country of the Brigantes *runs out narrower and narrower, and is cut in the middle (as* Italy *is with the Appennine) by a continu'd ridge of Mountains; and these separate the Counties into which it is at present divided For under these Mountains, towards the East and the German Ocean, lie* Yorkshire *and* the Bishoprick of Durham; *and to the* West, Lancashire, Westmorland, *and* Cumberland *all which Counties, in the infancy of the Saxon Government, were contain'd under the Kingdom of the* Deiri. *For the Saxons call'd these Countries in general,* the Kingdom of Northumberland, *dividing it into two parts* Deira *(call'd in that age* Deir lanb) *which is nearer us, namely on this side the river Tine; and* Bernicia, *the farther, reaching from the Tine* † *to the Frith of Edenburrow, [(though it must* † Fretum Scoticum Usser Primord p 211 *be observ'd, that our Historians very much differ in their accounts concerning the precise* Limits *of these two Divisions)] Which parts, though for some time they had their different Kings, yet at last they came all under one Kingdom And, to take notice of this by the way; where it is said in the* || *life of* Charles *the* || Pag 2-2 Annal Franc octavo *Great,* Eardulphus Rex Nordanhumbrorum, *i e De Irland,* patria pulsus ad Carolum magnum venit, *i. e* Eardulph, *King of the Northumbrians, that is, of* Irland, *being driven out of his own Country, came to Charles the Great; instead of* De Irland, *we are to read* Deirland, *and so to understand it, that he went over to* Charles the Great *out of this Countrey, and not from* Ireland.

YORK-

IX
VIII
P A
The County Stone
Dent
Langstreth Dale
Chase
Ingleborough Hill
Ingleton
Bentham
Clapham
Horton on Ribble
Penigent Hill
STANCLIFE and NEWC ROSS
Settle
WAPENT
Bowland
Forrest
Gisborne
Newhall
Tatham
Waddington

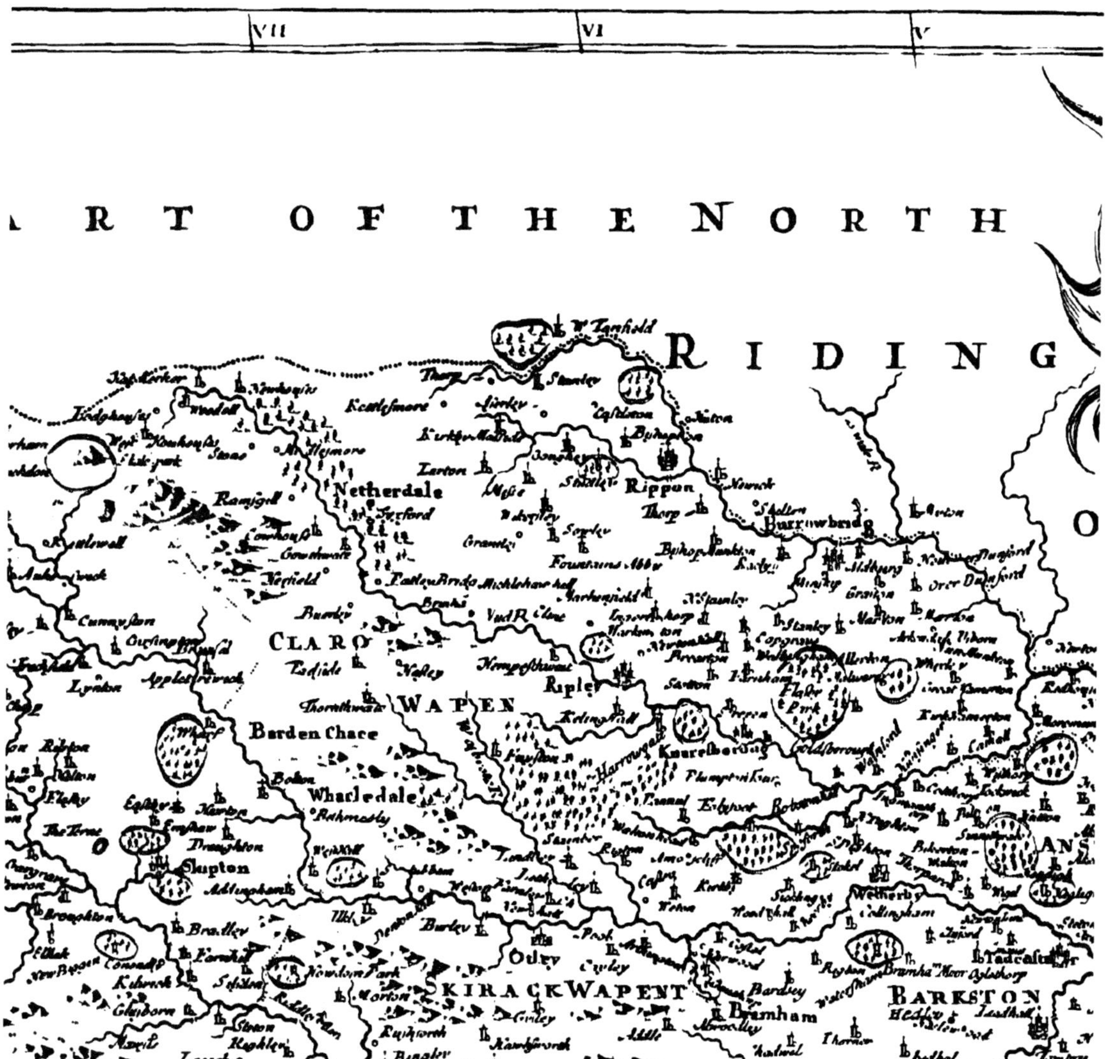

VII VI V

RT OF THE NORTH RIDING

Netherdale

Rippon

CLARO

WAPEN

Ripley

Barden Chace

Wharledale

Knaresborough

Skipton

Wetherby

Otley

SKIRACK WAPENT

Bramham

BARKSTON

Tadcaster

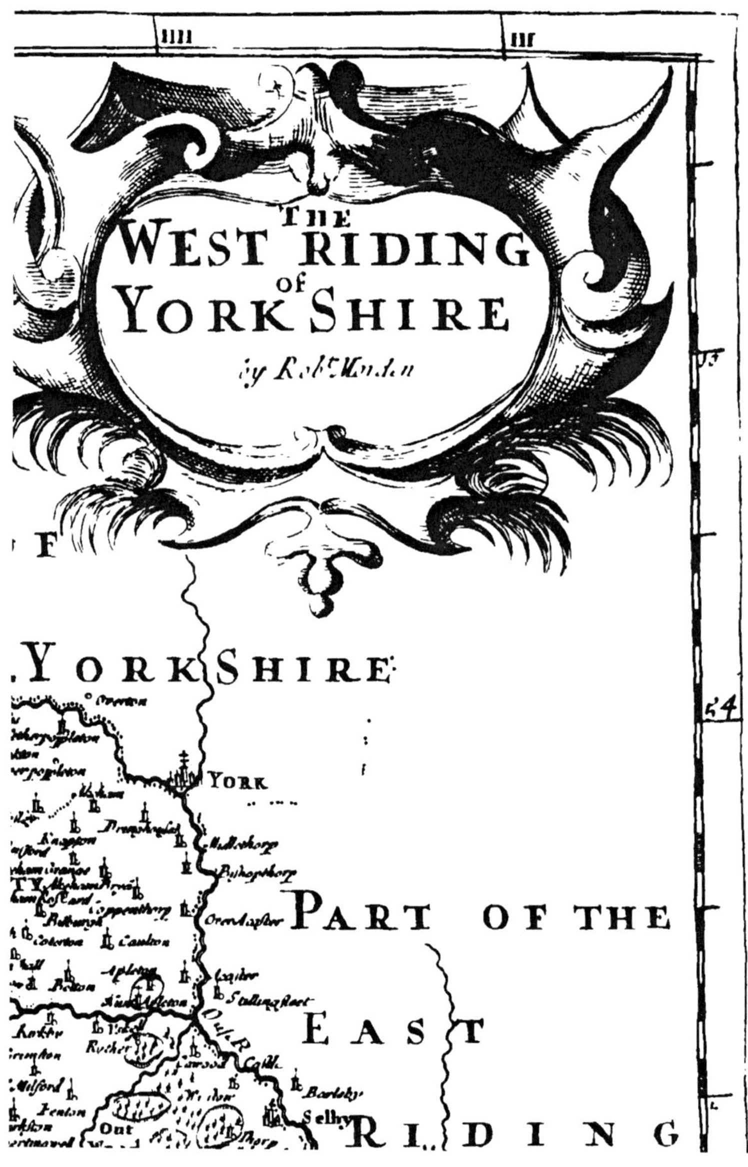
THE WEST RIDING of YORK SHIRE
by Robt. Morden
YORK SHIRE
YORK
PART OF THE EAST RIDING
Selby
54

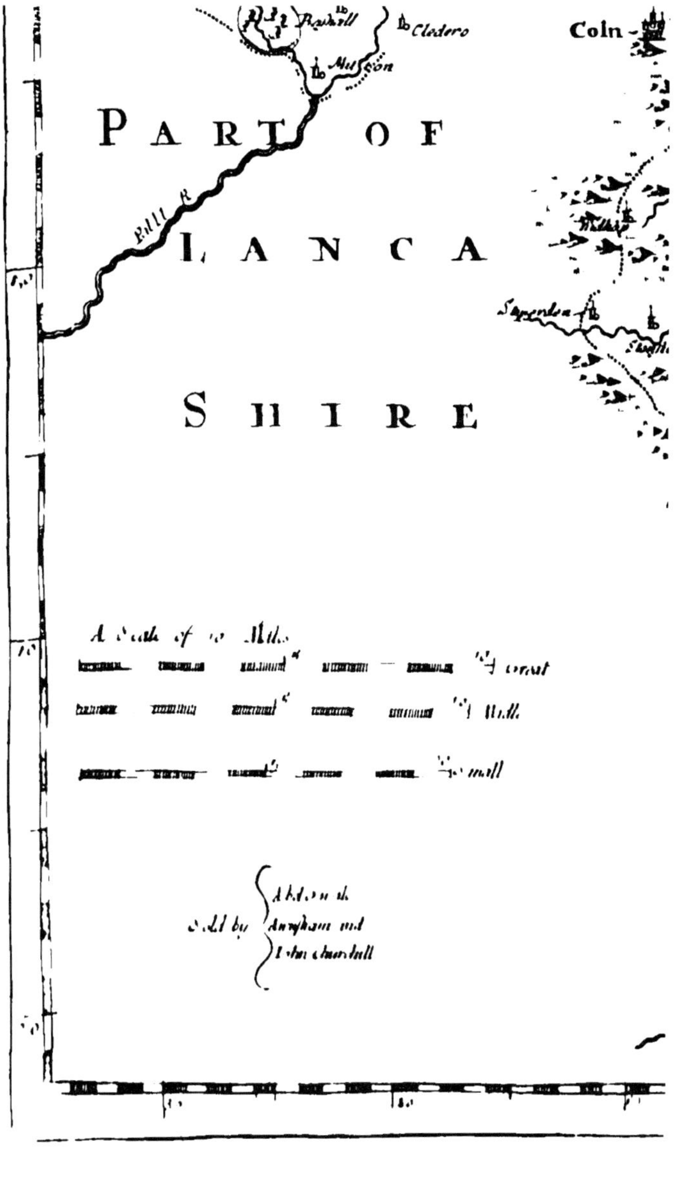
PART OF
LANCA
SHIRE
Coln
Cledero
Ribble R
A Scale of 10 Miles
Sold by
John Churchill

MORLEY
Old Town
Bradforth
Leedes
Calverley
PEN
Blackston Edge
AGBRIDG
WAPENT
Holmforth
STAINCROSS WAP
STRASFORD WAPEN
PART
OF
CHES
SHIRE
PART OF
DARBY SHIRE

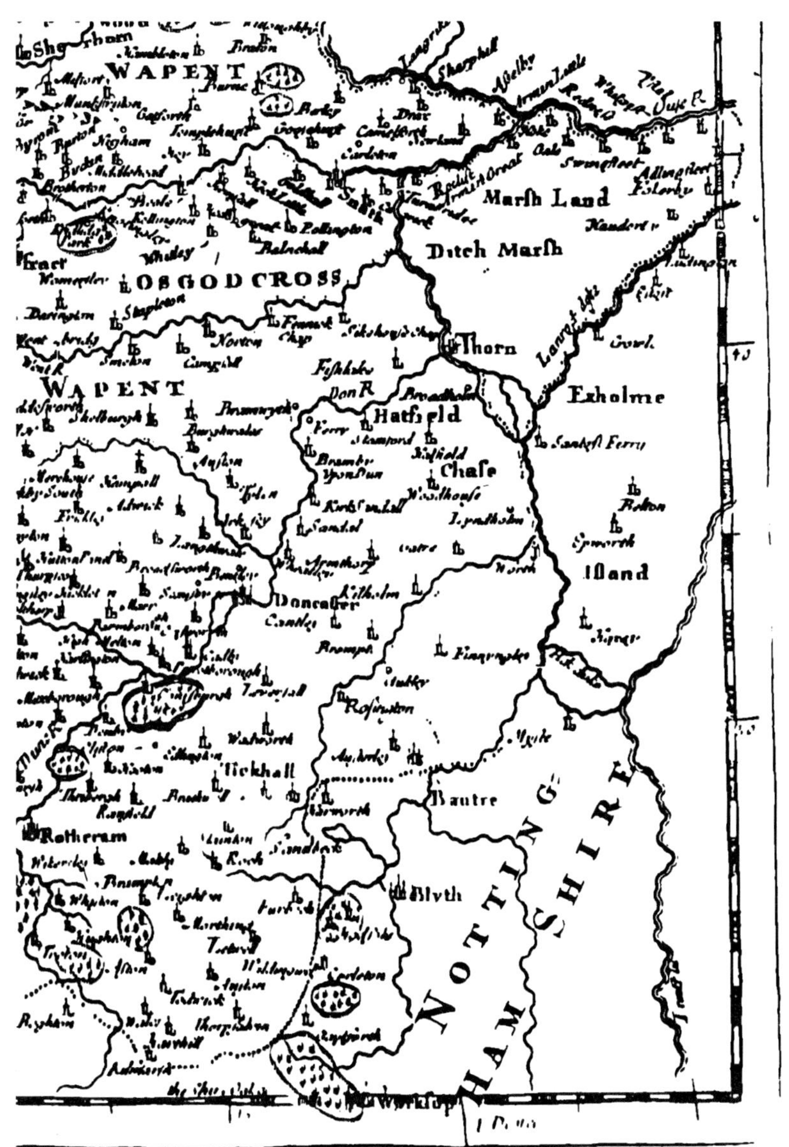

WAPENT
OSGODCROSS
WAPENT
Marſh Land
Ditch Marſh
Thorn
Exholme
Hatfield
Chaſe
Iſland
Doncaſter
Tickhall
Rotheram
Bautre
Blyth
Worksop
NOTTINGHAM
SHIRE

YORKSHIRE.

HE County of *York*, in Saxon [Eoforwicscyre] Euerwicscyre, Evrwicscyre, and Eborarcyre, commonly *Yorkshire*, is by far the largest County in England; and is reckon'd, as to *Fruitfulness*, a mixt kind of soil If in one place it be of a stony, sandy, barren nature, in another it is pregnant and fruitful; and so if it be naked and expos'd in one part, we find it cloath'd and shelter'd with great store of wood in another, Nature using an allay and mixture, that the entire County, by this variety in the parts, might appear more pleasing and beautiful. Towards the west, it is bounded by those hills already mention'd, and by Lancashire, and Westmorland Towards the north, it borders upon the County of Durham, which is separated from it through out by the river *Tees* On the east, it bounds upon the German Ocean The south side is enclos'd, first with Cheshire and Derbyshire, then with Nottinghamshire, and lastly with Lincolnshire, where that noble æstuary the *Humber* breaks-in, the common rendezvouz for the greatest part of the rivers hereabouts The whole County is divided into three parts, denominated from three several quarters of the world, West Riding, East Riding, and North Riding [And this Division by *Ridings*, is only a corruption of the Saxon Đrihing, which consisted of several *Hundreds* or *Wapentakes* Nor was it peculiar to this Country, but formerly common to most of the neighbouring ones, as appears by the * Laws of Edward the Confessor, and † the life of King Alfred] *West Riding* or the West part, is for some space bounded by the river * *Ouse*, by Lancashire, and by the southern limits of the County, and lies towards the south and west *East-Riding* or the east part of the County, lies towards the east, and towards the Ocean, which, together with the river Derwent, encloses it *North Riding* or the north part, fronts the north, and is in a manner surrounded by the rivers Tees and Derwent, and by the long course of the river Ouse From the western mountains, or those that border on the west part of the County, many rivers break forth, which are, every one, at last receiv'd by the Ouse, and so in one chanel flow into the Humber And I do not see any better method in describing this part, than to follow the course of the Dune, Calder, Are, Wherfe, Nid, and Ouse, which issue out of these mountains, and are not only the most considerable rivers, but flow by the most considerable places

Humber

* Cap 13 34

† Pag 74, 75 &c.

West-Riding

* First called *Ure* and *Youre*

Danus, commonly Don and Dune, seems to be so call'd, because it is carry'd in a *low deep* chanel, for that is the signification of the British word *Dan* It first salutes *Wortley*, which has given name to the eminent family of the *Wortleys*, [the issue male of which, expired in Sir *Francis Wortley*, † who devis'd the greatest part of his estate to *Anne Newcomen*, wife of the honourable *Sidney Wortley* Esq; (‖ second son of *Edward Montague* Earl of *Sandwich*, slain in the Dutch wars) who in right of his said wife is Lord of *Wortley*] Then it salutes another place near Wortley, call'd *Wentworth*, from which many Gentry both in this County and elsewhere, as also the Barons of Wentworth, have deriv'd their name and original [Of the family of that name and place, was *Thomas* Viscount *Wentworth*, Lord Lieutenant of Ireland, created Earl of *Strafford*, and Knight of the Garter, who being beheaded on Tower hill, lyeth here inter'd, and was succeeded in his Honours by his son *William* Earl of *Strafford*, and Knight of the said noble Order, who dying without issue, the title was extinct, until it was revived in the person of Thomas Wentworth, the present Earl, who succeeded the last Earl in the Barony of Raby, and was advanced by Queen Anne (by whom he had the honour to be employ'd in divers Embassies abroad, and to be made Knight of the Garter) to the Earldom of Strafford] Next, the Don arrives at *Sheafield*, remarkable, among other little towns hereabouts, for Blacksmiths (great plenty of iron being dug in these parts,) and for a strong old Castle, which has descended by inheritance from the *Lovetofts*, the Lords *Furnival*, and *Nevil* Lord Furnival, to the most honourable the *Talbots*, Earls of Shrewsbury [It is the Staple-town for Knives, and has been so these three hundred years Witness that Verse of Chaucer's,

Don, river

Wortley

† Sid Reports, 315

‖ Dugd Bar 2 Vol p 445 May 28 1672

Wentworth

15 Car I May 12 1641

Sheafield

Furnival

A Sheffield whittle bare he in his hose

Many of the Talbots, Earls of *Shrewsbury*, are here inter'd, particularly, *George* the first of that name, who dy'd the 26th of July, 1538, and his grandson of the same name (to whose custody *Mary* Queen of Scots, was committed) the date of whose death is now inserted upon the Tomb [xviii Novembris, anno redemptionis Christi MDLXXXX] which is the more worthy our observation, because it was deficient in that part, when Sir *William Dugdale* publish'd his * Baronage. His son *Gilbert*, likewise inter'd here, gave 200 *l per Ann* to the poor of *Sheafield*, where his great grandson erected a stately Hospital with this Inscription

* Vol I p 334

The Hospital of the Right Honourable
Gilbert Earl of *Shrewsbury*,
erected and settled by the Right Honourable *Henry*
Earl of *Norwich*, Earl Marshal of *England*,
Great grand child of the aforesaid Earl, in
pursuance of his last Will and Testament,
Anno Dom 1673

The Manour of *Sheafield* is descended from the said Earl Marshal to the present Duke of *Norfolk* The forementioned Castle was built of stone in the time of Henry the third, and was demolish'd (when other Castles also were order'd to be ras'd (after the death of King *Charles* the first. Here it was (or in the Manour house in the Park) that *Mary* Queen of Scots was detained Prisoner in the custody of *George* Earl of Shrewsbury, between sixteen and seventeen years Concerning the vast Oak-tree growing in this Park, the Reader is refer'd to Mr *Evelyn's* account of it; who says, it had above ten thousand foot of board in it, and he adds, concerning another Oak growing in the same Park, that it was so vast, that when cut down, two men on horse-back being on each side of it, could not see the Crowns of each others hats

Sylva, c xxx p 155

Before the river *Don* comes to Rotheram, it passes close by a fair Roman fortification, call'd Temple Brough *Temple-Brough*. The north east corner of it is worn away by the river: the area is about two hundred paces long, and one hundred and twenty broad, besides the *agger*; and without it, is a very large Trench, thirty-seven paces deep from the middle of the Rampire to the bottom. On the outside of it is another large bench, upon which are huge trees: and upon the side of the bench of the high way, there grew a *Chesnut*-tree, that had scarce any bark upon it, but only upon some top branches which bore leaves. It was not tall, but the Bole could scarcely be fathom'd by three men. On the north-side of the river, over-against Winco bank *Temple-brough*, is a high Hill call'd *Winco bank*, from which a large bank is continu'd without interruption almost five miles, being in one place call'd *Danes bank*. And about a quarter of a mile south from *Kemp bank*, (over which this *Bank* runs) there is another *agger*, which runs parallel with that from a place call'd *Birchwood*, running towards *Mexburgh*, and terminating within half a mile of its west-end; a Kemp-bank runs by *Swinton* to *Mexburgh* more north.]

From hence the Dane, under the shade of Rotheram alder, yew trees, and others, flow to *Rotheram*, which glories in having had an Archbishop of York of its own name, viz *Thomas Rotheram*, a very wise and prudent man, born here, and a great benefactor to the place; having founded and endow'd a College with three Schools for instructing boys in Writing, Grammar, and Musick, which are now suppress'd by the wic- * Thr. C ked Avarice of * the last age. [It is also honour'd, by being the birth place of the learned and judicious Dr *Robert Sanderson*, late Lord Thribergh Bishop of Lincoln, according to Mr Walton, the writer of his life, but there is more reason to think that he was born at Sheffield, by the Register there *Robertus filius, Roberti Saunderson, baptizat' 20th Sept.* 1587. Near which, is *Thribergh*, lately the seat of Sir *William Reresby*, Baronet, but since the estate of *John Savil* of Med- Sandbeck ley, Esq; and *Sandbeck*, which hath been honour'd by giving the title of Viscount to the Right Honourable James Sanderson, Viscount Castleton of Sandbeck.] Then the Don runs within Connisborow view of *Connisborow*, an old Castle, call'd in British *Caer Conan*, and situated upon a rock, whither (at the battel of Maisbelly, when Aurelius Ambrosius routed the Saxons and put Florilegus 487 them to a disorderly flight) Hengist their General retir'd, to secure himself, and a few days after, took the field against the Britains, who pursu'd him, and with whom he engag'd a second time, which prov'd fatal both to himself and his army. For the Britains cut off many † *Capitis amputati capite M Westm* of them, and † taking him prisoner, beheaded him, if the authority of the British History is to be prefer'd in this matter before that of the ‖ *It appears not, that any Saxon Annals say so* ‖ Saxon Annals, which report him to have dy'd a natural death, being worn out and spent with fatigue and business. [This Castle hath been a large strong-built Pile, the out walls whereof are standing, situate on a pleasant ascent from the river, but much over-top'd by a high hill on which the town stands. Before the gate is an *agger*, said by tradition to be the burying-place of *Hengist*. In the Church-yard, under the wall, lies a very ancient stone of blue marble, with antique figures upon it; one representing a man with a target encountering a vast winged Serpent, with another bearing a target Fuller's Worth p 91 behind him. It is rigid like a Coffin, on which is engraven a man on horse-back, curiously cut, but very ancient. This place is also famous for being the birth-place of *Richard Plantagenet* Duke of York, grandson to King Edward the third, and grandfather to Edward the fourth, who aspiring too soon to the Crown, was beheaded by King Henry the fifth. Nigh this Town, is *Carhouse*, the seat of *John Gill* Esq, High Sheriff Ca house of the County in the year 1692. And above three miles off, *Aston* the ancient seat of the Aston Lords D'Arcies, now Earls of Holderness.

Not far from Consburgh, is *Edlington*, the Edlington seat of the Lord *Molesworth*; near which place, at *Clifton*, a considerable quantity of Roman Clifton Coins was found in the year 1705, by a labourer, who casually struck his pick-axe into an Urn full of them. Upon further search, there was found a larger *Theca nummaria*, that might contain about two Gallons. They were both full of Copper-Coins of the *Bas-Empire*, *Gallienus*, *Postumus*, &c and some, particularly, of *Quintillus*, who reign'd but seventeen days. A Vid Philos Transf n 303 considerable number of these are now deposited in the Musæum of Mr *Ralph Thoresby* of Leeds.]

After Consburrow, the Done washes *Sprotburg*, Sprotburg the ancient Seat of an ancient Family, the *Fitz Williams*, Knights, ally'd to the best families of England, the ancestors of William *Fitz Williams*, who within the memory of † the † Fitz-Williams † so said, ann 1607 last age was Earl of Southampton; and also of William *Fitz-Williams*, * Lieutenant of Ireland. * Late Lieutenant, C But this is now descended to the *Copleys* (as *Elmsley* and many other estates of their's in these parts, are to the *Saviles*,) [and is made a most delightful seat by Sir *Godfrey Copely*, Baronet, who has greatly adorn'd it, with Canals, Gardens, Fountains, &c.]

From hence the Don, severing into two Chanels, runs to an ancient town, to which it leaves its name, commonly call'd at this day *Doncaster*, Doncaster but by the Scots *Doncastle*, and by the Saxons Dona-ceaster, by Ninnius, *Caer-Daun*; by Antoninus, *Danum*, and so likewise by the *Notitia*, which relates, that the Præfect of the *Crispinian* Horse, under the *Dux Britanniæ*, garrison'd there. About the year 759 it was burnt to the ground by lightning, and so bury'd in its own rubbish, that it has hardly yet recover'd it self. The plot of a large tower is still visible (which they imagine was destroy'd in that fire,) where now stands a neat Church dedicated to St *George*, the only Church in the town. [In this Church is inter'd *Thomas Ellis*, five times Mayor, and founder of an Hospital call'd *St Thomas the Apostle* and one *Byrks* who give *Rossington*-wood to the publick, with this uncouth Inscription upon his Tomb. *Howe Howe Who is heare, I Robin of Doncastere and Margaret my feare; that I spent that I had, that I gave that I have, that I left that I lost* A.D 1579. *Quoth* Robertus Byrkes, *who in this world did reign threescore years and seven, and yet liv'd not one*.

At the end of *Doncaster*, is a memorable old Cross, with this Norman Inscription round it: + ICEST EST LA CRVICE OTL D TILLIAKI· ALME DEU EN FACE. MERCI AM.

This place hath afforded the title of Viscount, to *James Hay* Baron of Sauley, created 16 Jac 1; who afterwards in the 20th year of the same King, was also made Earl of Carlisle, and was succeeded in his estate and titles by James his son, who dy'd without issue. Whereupon, in the 15th of Car 2 James *Fitz Roy* Baron of *Tindale*, was created Earl of *Doncaster*, and Duke of Monmouth.

Thence *Don* runneth by *Wheatley*, the Seat Wheatley of Sir *George Cook*, Baronet, whose uncle *Bryan Cook* Esq; gave by Will the whole Rectory of Ann 1660 *Arksey* to five Trustees for the payment of so

much

much to the Vicar there, as with * his ancient stipend amounts to 100 *l* *per Ann* He gave also 40 *l* *per Ann* to a School master to instruct the poor of the Parish, and 60 *l* for the building of an Hospital for twelve of the ancientest poor, which receive each 5 *l* *per Ann* His brother Sir George Cook Baronet, gave by Will 200 *l* and two Cottages, for building of a fair School house Scarce two miles from *Arksey* lies *Adwick in the street*, memorable on this account, that Mrs *Anne Savill* (a Virgin Benefactor) daughter of *John Savill* of Medley Esq; † purchas'd the Rectory thereof, and settled it in the hands of Trustees for the use of the Church for ever and this from a generous and pious principle, upon the reading of Sir *Henry Spelman*'s noted Treatise, *De non temerandis Ecclesiis* The ‖ Incumbent erected this Inscription over the door of the Parsonage-house, built from the foundation at his own charge *Rectoria de Adwick accessit Clero ex Donatione D^na Annæ Savile, ex Prosapiâ Savillorum de Medbley oriundæ*]

* 121 13 ; 4 d

1683

Adwick

† For about 900 *l*

‖ Mr *Jos* Brook

Scarce five miles from Doncaster, to the south, stands a place which I must not pass by, nam'd *Tickhill* [(so call'd from a Saxon word, signifying *Goats*,)] an ancient town, and fortify'd with an old castle, which is large, but only surrounded with a single wall, and by a huge mount with a round tower on the top of it It was of such dignity heretofore, that all the manours hereabouts appertaining to it, were stil'd, *the Honour of Tickhill* In Henry the first's reign, it was held by Roger *Busly*, but afterwards King Stephen made the Earls of Ewe in Normandy Lords of it Next, King Richard the first gave it to his brother *John* In the Barons war, Robert *de* * *Vipont* took and held it, till Henry the third deliver'd to him the castle of Carlisle, and that County, upon condition that he should restore it to the Earl of Ewe But upon the King of France's refusal to restore the English to the estates they had in France, the King dispossess'd him again, John Earl of Ewe still demanding the restitution of it from King Edward the first, in right of Alice his great grandmother Lastly, Richard the second, King of England, gave it to John of Gaunt Duke of Lancaster Now, the Dan, which rises often hereabouts and overflows its banks, re-unites its divided streams, and runs on in one intire channel by *Hatfield-Chase*, where is most excellent Deer hunting In this place *Cadwallin* King of the Britains (the * printed *Bede* calls him *Carduella*, but *Credwalle* seems to be the right, as it is in a † Manuscript *Bede*) with Penda, the Pagan King of *Mercia*, in a bloody battle slew *Edwyn* the first Christian King of Northumberland, and Prince *Offride* his eldest son, in the year 633 Here also was the birth-place of *Prince William*, second son of King Edward the third, which the rather deserves our mention, because by most Historians it is misplac'd at *Hatfield* in *Hertfordshire*, but that it is an error, plainly appears by the Rolls, which tell us, that Queen *Philippa* gave five marks *per Ann* to the neighbouring Abbot of *Roch*, and five nobles to the Monks there, to pray for the soul of this her son *William de Hatfield*, which summs are transfer'd to the Church of York, where he was bury'd, and are to this day paid by the Earl of Devonshire to the Bishop, and Dean and Chapter of York, out of the Impropriation of the Rectory of *Hatfield* Near the town are many Intrenchments, as if some great army had been there encamp'd It is said that no Rats have ever

Tickhill

Plac An 3 Joan Plac. M 4 H 3

* *Veteri ponte*

Hatfeld Chase

* Lovanii Ann 1556

† Penes R Thoresby

A D 1335

been seen in this town, nor any Sparrows at a place call'd *Lindham*, in the Moors below it; though it is a good earth for corn or pasture, but encompass'd with a morass] After this, the Dan divides it self again, one stream making towards the river *Idel* which comes out of Nottinghamshire, and the other towards the river *Are*, in both which they continue till they fall into the æstury of *Humber* [Near the confluence of *Don* and *Are*, is *Cowick*, the pleasant seat of the ancient family of the *Dawneys* (which name occurs frequently amongst the Sheriffs of this County) of which Sir *John Dawney* was by King Charles the second advanc'd to the degree of Viscount *Downe* in the Kingdom of Ireland] Within the Island, or that piece of ground encompass'd by the branches of these two rivers, are *Diche-marsh* and *Marshland*, fenny tracts, or rather River-islands, about fifteen miles round, which produce a very green rank grass, good for cattle, and are in a manner set round with little villages. [One of these is *Whitgift*, from the family of which name and place, was descended *John Whitgift*, the learned and pious Archbishop of Canterbury] Some of the inhabitants imagin that the whole Island floats upon the water, and that when the waters are increas'd, it is rais'd higher, just like what Pomponius Mela tells us of the Isle of *Antrum* in Gaul [These *Levels* or *Marshes*, especially eastward, and north-east of *Thorn* (a market town,) are generally a Turf moor, but in some places are intermix'd with arable and pasture grounds By reason of the many *Meres*, it was formerly well-stor'd with fresh-water fish (especially Eels) and with fowl But in the reign of King Charles the first several Gentlemen undertook to drain this moorish and fenny country, by drawing some large rivers, with other smaller cuts There is an angle cut from about *Thorne* to *Gowle*, which is ten miles in length, and extraordinary broad As to what is observ'd before, of the ground being heav'd up, several old men affirm'd, that the Turf moor betwixt *Thorne* and *Gowle* was so much higher before the draining (especially in winter-time) than now they are that before, they could see little of the Church steeple, where is now they can see the Church yard wall Under the Turf-earth and other grounds, from one yard to two yards deep, are frequently dug-up great quantities of *Fir wood*, and of other Trees, particularly Oaks, the wood of the last being very black At low water, in the great cut to *Gowlestance*, have been observ'd several roots of trees, some very large, standing upright, others inclining, some of the trees have been found lying along with their roots fasten'd, others seem'd to have been cut or *burnt*, and broke off from the roots Upon the digging of these large rivers, there were found gates, ladders, hammers, shoes, nuts, &c and the land in some places was observ'd to lie in the ridges and furrows, as if it had been plow'd Under some part of the Turf-moor, firm earth was found, but in other places, nothing but sand About fifty years since, they found the entire body of a man at the bottom of a Turf-pit, about four yards deep, with his head northward; his hair and nails not decay'd It is said, that in the cut-river to *Gowle*, there was found a Roman Coin either of *Domitian* or *Trajan*; and it is very † certain, that other Coins of divers of the Roman Emperors, have been since met with From the position of the Trees, Roots, and all other circumstances, it appears evidently that

Cowick.

Marshland

Whitgift

Levels

† Philos Trans n. 275

that those trees grew where they are found lying; of which it is a very ingenious and very probable * account, That this, and the other like places where subterranneous wood is found, were anciently *Forests*, cut down and burnt by the Romans, wherever they were found to be a refuge to the Britains, in their wars against them.]

* Ab de la Pryme Phil Transf n 275

Among other brooks which water this place, I must not forget to mention the *Went*, because it arises from a pool near *Nosthill*, where formerly stood a monastery dedicated to that Royal Saint King *Oswald*, which was repair'd by *A Confessor* to King Henry the first, and hath been the seat of the famous family of the * *Gargraves* Knights. [Not far from *Nosthill* is *Hemsworth*, where *Robert Holgate* Archbishop of York (depriv'd in the first year of Queen Mary, for being marry'd) did found an Hospital for ten poor aged men, and as many women, who have each about 10 *l per Ann* and the Master who is to read Prayers to them, betwixt 50 and 60 *l per Ann*. He was likewise a Benefactor to, if not Founder of, the School there.]

Nosthill
St Oswald
† Is, C
* Now of Sir Rowland Wynne
Hemsworth
Ann 1544

The river *Calder*, which flows along the borders between this and Lancashire, among other inconsiderable little places, runs near [*Stamland*, where have been found several Roman Coins, and] *Gretland*, situated on the very top of a hill, accessible on one side only, where was dug up this *Votive Altar*, sacred, as it seems, to the tutelar God of the city of the *Brigantes*. It is to be seen at *Bradley*, in the house of the famous Sir John Savil, Knight, * Baron of the Exchequer, [whose brother was Sir *Henry Savil*, Warden of Merton College, Provost of Eaton-College, and the learned Editor of St *Cryfostom*.]

Calder, riv
Stamland
Gretland
Bradley
* Ann 1607

Anno Christi 209

DVI CI BRIG	On the other side
ET NVM GG	
T AVR AVRELIAN	ANTONINO
VS DD PRO SE	III ET GET COSS
ET SVIS S M A G S	

Which is to be read, *Dui Civitatis Brigantum & numinibus Augustorum, Titus Aurelius Aurelianus dedicavit pro se & suis*, i e *To the God of the City of the Brigantes, and to the Deities of the Emperors, Titus Aurelius Aurelianus hath dedicated this in behalf of himself and his*. As for the last remaining letters, I cannot tell what they mean. The Inscription on the other side, is, *Antonino tertium & Geta Consulibus*.

Whether this *Dui* be that God which the present Britains call *Diw*, or the peculiar and topical Genius of the *Brigantes*, may be decided by those who are better Judges. But as Symmachus has it, *As the souls are distributed among those that are born, even so are the fatal Genii among Nations. God appoints every Kingdom its respective Guardians*. This was the perswasion and belief of the Ancients in those matters. For, to say nothing of foreign nations, whose Histories are full of such local Deities, the Britains themselves had their *Andates* in Essex, their *Bellatucadrus* in Cumberland, their *Viterinus* and *Mogontus* in Northumberland, as will be more manifest from the Inscriptions, which I shall insert in their proper places. And it is rightly observ'd by *Servius Honoratus*, that these local Gods were never transitory, or removed from one Country to another. [At *Sowerby*, near Gretland, where the Votive Altar was dug up, a considerable quantity of Roman Coins was found in plowing, in the year 1678, but the greatest part thereof was seiz'd and conceal'd by the workmen.]

Dui
Genii of places
Lib 1 Ep 40
Dio
Sowerby,

But to return to the *Calder*: Which, with supplies from other currents, is now become larger, and therefore made passable by a very fine bridge at *Eland*, not far distant from *Grimscar*, where bricks have been dug-up with this Inscription

Grimscar

COH IIII BRE

For the Romans, who were excellent Masters in all the arts of War, wisely took care to preserve their Soldiers from effeminacy and sloth, by exercising them in times of peace, in draining the Country by ditches, mending the high-ways, making bricks, building bridges, and the like.

Vopiscus in Probo

Then, the river *Calder* passing through the Mountains, on the left leaves *Halifax*, a very famous town, situated from west to east upon the gentle descent of an hill. This name is of no great antiquity. Not many ages since, it was call'd *Horton*, as some of the Inhabitants say, who tell us this story concerning the change of the name. A certain Clergy-man of this town, being passionately in love with a young woman, and by no means able to move her to a compliance, grew stark mad, and in that condition villanously cut off her head. Her head was afterwards hung upon an Ew-tree, where it was reputed holy by the vulgar, till quite rotten, and was visited in Pilgrimage by them; every one plucking off a branch of the tree [as a holy relique.] By this means the tree became at last a meer trunk, but still retain'd its reputation of Sanctity among the people, who believ'd that those little veins, which are spread out like hair in the rind, between the bark and the body of the tree, were indeed the very hair of the Virgin. This occasion'd such resort of Pilgrims to it, that *Horton*, from a little village grew up to a large town, assuming the new name of *Halig-fax* or *Halifax*, which signifies *holy hair*. For *fax* is us'd by the English, on the other side Trent, to signify *hair*. And that noble family of *Fairfax* in these parts, are so named from their *fair hair*. And therefore, whoever from the affinity of the names, would have this place to be what Ptolemy calls *Olicana*, are certainly mistaken. This town is no less famous among the common people for a *By-law*, whereby they † behead any one instantly that is found stealing, nor among the Learned, who will have *John de sacro Bosco*, Author of the Treatise *De Sphæra*, to be born in it. But it is more remarkable for the unusual extent and largeness of the Parish, which has under it † twelve Chapels (two whereof are Parochial) and about twelve thousand men in it. So that the Parishioners are wont to say, that they can reckon more *Men* in their Parish, than any kind of animal whatever, whereas in the most fruitful places of *England* elsewhere, one shall find thousands of Sheep, but so few men, in proportion, that one would think they had given place to sheep and oxen, or were devour'd by them. The Industry of the Inhabitants is also admirable, who notwithstanding an unprofitable, barren soil, not fit to live in, have so flourish'd by the Cloath trade (which within these * seventy years they first fell to) that they are very rich, and have gain'd a reputation for it above their neighbours. Which confirms the truth of that old Observation, That a barren Country is a great whet to the industry of the Natives. By which we find, that *Nurenberg* in Germany, *Venice* and *Genoua* in Italy,

Halifax
Some think it was formerly call'd *The Castel in the Grove*
Fax, what it signifies
Halifax law † Ann 1607.
† Eleven, C
* So said, Ann 1607

ly, and lastly *Limoges* in France (all situated in barren soils,) have ever been very flourishing Cities [To this Town and Parish, Mr *Nathaniel Waterhouse*, was an eminent Benefactor † by providing an House for the Lecturer, an Hospital for twelve aged poor, and a Work house for twenty children (the Overseer whereof is to have 45 *l per An*) and a yearly Salary to the preaching Ministers of the twelve Chapelries, which, with moneys for repair of the banks, amounts to three hundred pounds *per Ann* *Brian Crowther* Clothier was a good Benefactor to the Poor, and to the *Free School of Queen Elizabeth* in the Vicarage of Halifax In this Church is inter'd the heart of *William Rokeby* (of the *Rokebys* of *Kirk Sandal* by *Doncaster*, where he was born) Vicar of *Halifax*, and Parson of *Sandall*, afterwards Bishop of Meath and Arch bishop of *Dublin*, where dying he order'd his bowels to be bury'd at *Dublin*, his heart at *Halifax*, and his body at *Sandall*, and over each a Chapel to be built, which was perform'd accordingly

1642 July 1 by Will

† Extract of his Will

To the first 10 *l* to the second 20 *l* per *Ann*

Nov 29 1521

The vast growth and increase of this Town may be guess'd at from this instance, which appears in a Manuscript of Mr *John Brearcliff's*, of one ‖ *John Waterhouse* Esq He was Lord of the Mannour, and liv'd nigh an hundred years, in the beginning of whose time, there were in *Halifax* but thirteen Houses, which in one hundred twenty three years were increas'd to above five hundred and twenty house holders that kept fires, and answer'd the Vicar, *Ann* 1566 It is honour'd by having given title to *George* Lord *Savile* of Eland, Earl and Marquiss of *Halifax*, whose son *William* Lord *Savil*, late Marquiss of *Halifax*, dying without issue, the title of Baron of *Halifax* was conferred by King William the third, upon the honourable *Charles Montague*, a person of great Learning and Eloquence, descended from *Henry*, first Earl of Manchester, and advanced to this dignity (and afterwards by King George to the more honourable title of Earl of *Halifax*) for most eminent Services done to his Prince and Country; particularly, in that most difficult and important Article of *Recoining* the Money of the Nation, the effecting of which, at a very critical juncture, without damage to the Subjects at home or advantage to our Enemies, abroad, was owing to the extraordinary conduct, industry, and penetration of this noble Lord Since whose death, the Honour of Earl of *Halifax* hath been confer'd upon the Right Honourable *George Mountague*, his Nephew and Heir

‖ Born, 1443

This place is also honoured with the nativity of Dr *John Tillotson* late Arch-bishop of Canterbury So that this West riding of Yorkshire had at one time the honour of giving both the Metropolitans to our Nation; Dr *John Sharp* Archbishop of *York*, being born in the neighbouring town and contiguous parish of *Bradford*, where Mr *Peter Sunderland* (of an ancient family at *High Sunderland* nigh *Halifax*) besides other benefactions, founded a Lecture, and endow'd it with 40 *l per Ann*

But nothing is more remarkable, than their method of proceeding against Felons, which was just hinted before, *viz* That a Felon taken within the Liberty, with Goods stol'n out of the Liberties or Precincts of the Forest of *Hardwick*, should after three Markets or Meeting days within the town of *Halifax*, next after his apprehension, be taken to the Gibbet there, and have his head cut off from his body But then the fact was to be certain; for he must either be taken *hand habend*, i e. having his hand in, or being in the very act of stealing, or *back berend*, i e. having the thing stolen either upon his back, or somewhere about him, without giving any probable account how he came by it; or lastly *confession'd*, owning that he stole the thing for which he was accus'd. The cause therefore must be only *theft*, and that manner of *theft* only which is call'd *furtum manifestum*, or notorious Theft, grounded upon some of the foresaid evidences The value of the thing stolen must likewise amount to above 13 *d ob* for if the value was found only so much, and no more, by this Custom he should not die for it. He was first brought before the Bailiff of *Halifax*, who presently summon'd the *Frithborgers* within the several Towns of the Forest and, being found guilty, within a week he was brought to the Scaffold The Ax was drawn up by a pulley, and fasten'd with a pin to the side of the Scaffold If it was an horse, an ox, or any other creature, that was stol'n, it was brought along with him to the place of execution, and fasten'd to the cord by a pin that stay'd the block So that when the time of execution came (which was known by the Jurors holding up one of their hands) the Bailiff or his Servant whipping the beast, the pin was pluck'd out, and execution done But if it was not done by a beast, then the Bailiff or his Servant cut the rope

But the manner of execution will be better apprehended by the following draught of it

A A The Scaffold
B The piece of wood wherein the Axe is fix'd.
C The Axe
D The Pulley by which the Axe is drawn up
E The Malefactor who lies to be beheaded
F The Pin to which the Rope is ty'd that draws up the Axe]

Almondbury Cambodunum Six miles from *Halifax*, not far from the right side of the river *Calder*, and near *Almondbury*, a little village, there is a steep hill, only accessible by one way from the plain, where the marks of an old rampire, and some ruins of a wall, and of a castle well guarded with a round triple fortification, are plainly visible. Some would have it to be the remains of *Olicana*, but it is really the ruins of *Cambodunum* (by a mistake in Ptolemy, call'd *Camulodunum*, and made two words by Bede, *Campo dunum*,) as appears by the distance which Antoninus makes from *Mancunium* on the one hand, and *Calcaria* on the other [It is, in King *Alfred*'s Paraphrase, render'd *Donafelda* A Manuscript Copy of Bede has it, *Attamen in campo dono*, and so it is in the Lovain Edition, whence probably came that mistake of Stapleton, in translating it *Champion, called Down*] In the beginning of the Saxon times, it seems to have made a great figure For it was then a Royal Seat, and graced with a * Church built by *Paulinus* the Apostle of these parts, and dedicated to St *Alban*, whence, for *Albanbury*, it is now [by corruption] call'd *Almonbury* But in those cruel wars that Ceadwall the Britain and Penda the Mercian make upon Edwin the Prince of these Territories, it was burnt down which † hath been thought in some measure to appear in the colour of the stones to this day [It was probably built mostly of wood, there being no manner of appearance of stone or brick The fire that burnt it down seems to have been exceeding vehement, from the cinders which are strangely solder'd together On lump was found, of above two feet every way, the earth being melted rather than burnt But, the conjecture of a burning there, from the *blackness* of the stones in the present buildings, is groundless for the edges of them are so in the Quarry which is half a mile off; and so deep, that for fire to reach them there, is a thing impossible] Afterwards, a Castle was built here, which, as I have read, was confirm'd to *Henry Lacy* by King Stephen

* Basilica

† Appears, C

Whitley Not far from this stands *Whitley*, the Seat of the ancient and famous family of the *Beaumonts* (who are different from that of the Barons and Viscounts *Beaumont*, and flourish'd in England before they came over) [of which, *Richard Beaumont* is lately dead without issue]

Kirkley The *Calder* having passed by these places, runs on to *Kirkley*, heretofore a Nunnery, thence to *Robin Hood's Tomb*, a generous robber, and very famous upon that account and so to *Deusborrough*, situated at the foot of a high Hill Whether this name be deriv'd from *Dui*, the local Deity already mentioned, I cannot determine The name is not unlike; for it resembles *Duis Burgh* in sound, and this Town has been considerable from the earliest date of Christianity, among the English of this Province For I have been inform'd that there was once a Cross here, with this Inscription:

Deusborrough.

PAVLINVS HIC PRÆDICAVIT ET CELEBRAVIT.

That is,

Paulinus *here preached and Celebrated*

[Of which Cross, nothing now appears, either in sight or by tradition; but,] that this Paulinus was the first Archbishop of York, about the year 626, we are assured by the concurring evidence of our Historians. From hence *Calder* goes by *Thornhill*, which from a knightly family of that name descended to the *Savils*, [and became the possession of the Lord Marquis of *Halifax*] and so to *Wakefield* [(to which place from Castleford, it was made navigable in the year 16?8,)] a Town famous for it's Cloath trade, largeness, neat buildings, and great Markets, and for the bridge, upon which King Edward the fourth built a very neat Chapel, in memory of those that were cut-off in the battle here [The carved work hath been very beautiful, but is now much defaced The whole structure is artificially wrought, about ten yards long and six broad] This town belong'd heretofore to the Earls of Warren and Surry; as also *Sandal castle*, hard by, built by John Earl of Warren, whose mind was never at liberty from the slavery of lust, for, being too familiar with the wife of Thomas Earl of Lancaster, his design was to detain her there securely from her husband Below this town, when England was embroil'd with civil wars, Richard Duke of York, and father of Edward the fourth (whose temper was rather to provoke fortune, than quietly to court and expect it,) was here slain amongst many others, by the Lancastrians [And in the very place was found a large antique * gold ring, suppos'd to belong to that Prince Within it, is engraved in the characters of that age, *pour bon amour*, and on the out side, which is very broad, are wrought the effigies of three Saints On the right hand of the high way leading from Wakefield to Sandal, is a small square Plot of ground hedg'd in from a Close, within which (before the war between King Charles and the Parliament) there stood a Cross of stone, where Richard Duke of York was slain The owners are oblig'd by the tenure of the land, to hedge it in from the Close Here, by the noble Charity of the pious Lady *Campden*, is a weekly Lecture, endow'd with fourscore pounds *per Ann* The other (for she left three thousand pounds to Trustees for the founding two Lectures in the north of England) is at *Grantham*]

Thornhill

Wakefield

1460

* In Mr Thoresby's Musæum

The ground hereabouts for a pretty way together, is call'd the Lordship of *Wakefield*, and hath always some one or other of the neighbouring Gentry for its Seneschal or Steward; an Office often administer'd by the *Savils*, a very numerous family in these parts, and † particularly in the hands of Sir J *Savil* Knight, whose * very beautiful seat || was at *Howley*, not far off [This, with several other considerable Lordships, went from the *Savils* to the *Brudenels*, by the marriage of Frances, sister and sole heir to James Earl of Sussex. Two miles from Howley, is *Drighlington*, memorable only for the nativity of Dr James Margetson, Archbishop of Armagh, who founded a School here, with a good * endowment

† At this day, C

* Now demolish'd

|| Is, C Howley

Drighlington

* 60 *l per an*

Darton At some distance from Wakefield, is *Darton*, a seat of a branch of the family of the *Beaumonts* of which Mr *George Beaumont*, a Merchant, left considerable Sums of money to be employ'd in several charitable Uses, *viz* † the founding of a free School at this place of his Nativity, and to || poor Ministers, and to the Poor of * London, † York, and || Hull; besides a considerable estate amongst his relations

† 500 *l*
|| 500 *l*
* 150 *l*
† 50 *l*
|| 30 *l*

Burton grange Farther from the *Calder* lies *Burton-grange*, where the no less religious than honourable Lady *Mary Armyn* daughter of *Henry Talbot*, fourth

fourth son of the illustrious *George Talbot* Earl of *Shrewsbury*, and Relict of Sir William Armyn, Baronet, erected an Hospital for six poor widows, each of which have 40 *s* and a Gown every year She built also and endow'd two other Hospitals in other Counties during her life, and at her death left 40 *l per Ann* for 99 years, to be apply'd to such-like uses More to the south, is *Wurspur*, where *Henry Edmunds* Esq, and others, have generously built a good house for the Minister; and Mr *Obadiah Walker*, late Master of University-College in Oxford, and born here, annex'd a Library to the School and *Stainbrough*, where the Earl of Strafford hath erected a noble seat, which also gives him the title of Baron But to return

Ann 1575

Wurspur

Stainbrough

Between *Wakefield out wood*, and *Thorp on the hill*, at a place call'd *Lingwell-yate*, in the year 1697, were found certain Coining-molds or impressions upon clay, which had been invented for the counterfeiting of Roman Coins, and are accordingly all of such Emperors, in whose times the Roman monies were notoriously adulterated. It is probable enough, that the *Lingones* who were quarter'd at *Ilkley*, were also sometimes encamp'd here, near *Thorp super montem*, as it is written in the Registers; and that the entrenchments there were from them denominated *Ling-well*, the Roman *Vallum* being pronounced *Wallum*]

Lingwell-yate

About five miles from Wakefield, the river Calder loses both its name and waters in the river *Are* Upon the confluence stands *Medley*, formerly Mebeley, so called from its situation, in the middle between two rivers In the † last age, this was the seat of *Robert Waterton*, Master of the Horse to King Henry the fourth, and * afterwards of the famous Sir *John Savil*, a most worthy Baron of the Exchequer, to whose Learning this work, and to whose Civility the Author of it, † was exceedingly engag'd [In this Church, he has a stately monument, which says, that he *was, by the special favour of the King, Justice of Assise in his own County* In the 10th year of King William, an * Act of Parliament pass'd, for making and keeping navigable the two rivers Are and Calder

Medley

† So said, ann 160-

* At present, C

† Is, C

* Stat 10 W 3, c 19

But before we proceed to the Are, we must take notice, that the river *Ribble* runs a course of forty miles in this County, before it enters Lancashire, upon which is *Gigleswick*, where, at the foot of a very high mountain, is the most noted spring in England for ebbing and flowing, sometimes thrice in an hour, and the water subsides three quarters of a yard at the reflux, though thirty miles from the Sea At this town, is a noted School, founded by Mr *Bridges*, and well endow'd, and at *Waddington*, upon the same river, is a noble Hospital for ten poor Widows, and a Chaplain, founded by Mr Robert Parker]

Ribble, riv

Gigleswick

Wadding on

The river *Are* issuing from the root of the Mountain *Pennigent* (which is the highest in these parts,) at first seeming doubtful whether it should run forwards into the Sea, or return to its Spring, is so winding and crooked, that in travelling this way, I had it to pass over seven times in half an hour, upon a strait road Its course is calm and quiet, so easy that it hardly appears to flow, and I am of opinion that this has occasion'd the name. For I have already observ'd that the British word *ara*, signifies *slow and easy* and hence that slow river *Araris* in France, takes its name That part of the Country where the head of this river lies, is call'd *Craven*, possibly from the British word *Crage*, a rock for what with huge stones, steep rocks, and rough ways, this place is very wild and unsightly In the very middle of which, and not far from the *Are*, stands *Skipton*, hid (as it were) with those steep precipices surrounding it, like * *Latium* in Italy, which Varro thinks was so call'd from its low situation under the *Appennine*, and the *Alps* The town is pretty handsome, considering the manner of building in these mountainous parts, and is secur'd by a very beautiful and strong Castle, built by Robert de Rumeley, by whose posterity it came to be the inheritance of the Earls of Albemarle But being afterwards *escheated* (as the Lawyers term it) to the Crown, Edward the second gave it (with other large possessions hereabouts) to Robert *de Clifford* ancestor to the Earls of Cumberland, in exchange for some lands of his in the Marches of Wales [Here lie inter'd several of the *Cliffords*, particularly *George*, third Earl of Cumberland, honour'd with the Garter by Queen *Elizabeth*, and famous for his Sea-services; performing * nine Voyages in his own person, most of them to the *West-Indies*, and being the best born Englishman that ever hazarded himself in that kind He dy'd in the year 1605, leaving one only daughter *Anne*, Countess of *Pembroke*, *Dorset*, and *Montgomery*, an eminent benefactor, born in the year 1589 90. at Skipton castle in Yorkshire, wherein we are the more particular, because Dr Fuller in his Worthies, by a mistake, says it was in *Hertfordshire* She built from the ground, or considerably repair'd, six ancient Castles, one of which, *Brough*, had lain one hundred and forty years desolate after the fire had † consum'd it, another, *Pendragon castle* (of which nothing remain'd above an hundred years since, but the bare name and an heap of stones,) three hundred and twenty years after the invading Scots, under their King *David*, had * wasted it She built also seven Chapels or Churches, with two stately Hospitals richly endow'd, and dy'd in the year 1675 This Country (*Craven*) gave the Title of Earl to *William Craven*; who by King Charles the first was created Baron of *Hampsted Marshal*, and by King Charles the second, in the 16th year of his reign, Earl of Craven

Araris in Gaul

Craven

Skipton.

* *Latere*, to lie hid

* Inscription in Skipton Castle

Ob Ob 30

Jan 30

Com Westm

† Ann 1,20 See *Westmorland*

* Ann 13,1

Mar 22

From hence the *Are* passeth by *Thornton* (the seat of the *Thorntons*,) to *Rawdon*, famous for Sir *George Rawdon* a most accomplish'd person, who with two hundred or fewer British, most valiantly repuls'd Sir *Phelim o Neile*, at the head of an army of about seven thousand Rebels, assaulting *Lisnegarvy* (now *Lisburn*) in Ireland, in that grand massacre 1641, wherein thousands of Protestants were most cruelly murder'd *Henry* (son of *Francis*) *Layton* Esquire, in pursuance of his Father's Will, built here, and endow'd with 20 *l per ann* a Chapel, which was ‡ consecrated by Archbishop *Dolben* In the year 1664, were summon'd out of a small village in *Craven*, call'd *Dent*, two persons as Witnesses in a Cause at York Assises, the father and the son, the first of whom wanted only half a year of 140, and the second was above 100 years of age

Rawdon

‡ May 1684

From Carlton, a town in Craven, the Right Honourable *Henry Boyle*, third son of Charles Lord Clifford of Lanesborough, hath been created a Peer of this Realm by King George, under the title of Baron of Carlton; a person of great Honour and Abilities, and who hath been successively Principal Secretary of State to their Majesties King William and Queen Anne]

Kigbeley

Libera Warrena.

† So said, ann 1607

* Now, C

The *Are* having pass'd *Craven*, is carry'd in a much larger chanel with pleasant fields on both sides, by *Kigbeley*, from which the famous family of *Kigbeley* derive their name One of whom, *Henry Kigbeley* (inter'd here) procur'd from Edward the first, for this his manour, the *privileges of a Market and Fair, and a free Warren, so that none might enter into those grounds to chase there, or with design to catch any thing pertaining to the said Warren, without the permission and leave of the said Henry and his Successors* Which was a very considerable favour in those days and I the rather take notice of it, because it teaches us the nature and meaning of a *Free-Warren* The male-issue in the right line of this family ended in Henry *Kigbeley* of *Inskip*, within the memory of the † present age the daughters and heirs were marry'd, one to *William Cavendish* * then Baron *Cavendish* of *Hardwick*; the other to Thomas *Worseley* of *Boothes*

Cookridge Phil Transf n 316

Adle mill

[At Cookridge, on the way from *Ilkley* to Adle, have been dug-up ancient Roman Coins; and upon the moor, not far from *Adle-mill*, in the year 1702, were discover'd the footsteps of a Roman Town Among the Ruins, are many fragments of their Urns, and others of their Plaisticks, with the remains of a large aquæduct in stones At a little distance, is a Roman Camp, pretty intire, above four Chains broad and five long, surrounded with a single *Vallum* Three monuments have been found there; of which one is but a fragment, but has enough remaining to discover it to have been *Sepulchral* the other is evidently a Funeral monument, and the third, the head of a Statue, found some years before, with a large Inscription, which perish'd by the ignorance of the Labourers

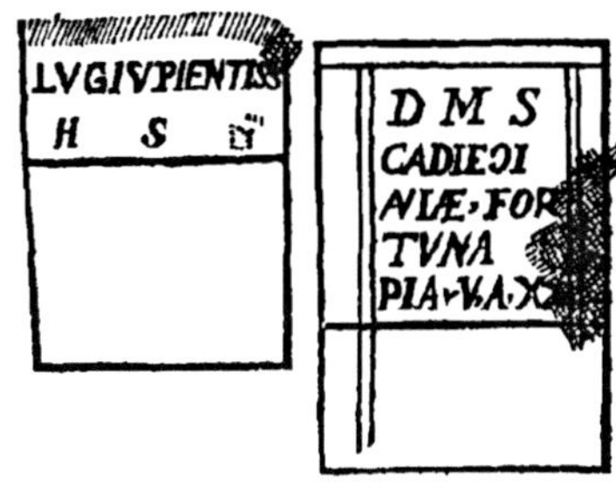

Near Bramham moor, have also been discover'd ancient brass Instruments]

Kirkstall

Leeds

† Jul 30 2 regn

* 80 l per an

† 10 l per an

1569

‖ 80 l per an and 130 l per an for Repairs

From *Kigbley* the river *Are* glides on [by *Bingley*, from which, Robert Benson Esq, was created by Queen Anne Baron of Bingley, and] by *Kirkstall*, a Monastery of good note, founded about the year 1147 by *Henry Lacy* And thence [(being made navigable thus far in the year 1698)] by *Leeds*, in Saxon Loidis, which was made a royal Village when *Cambodunum* was burnt down by the enemy; and now much inrich'd by the woollen manufacture [The name of *Leeds* is possibly taken from the Saxon Leod, *gens*, *natio*, implying it to have been very populous in the Saxon times Which town and parish King Charles the first, by † Letters Patents, incorporated under the government of one chief Alderman, nine Burgesses, and twenty Assistants, Sir *John Savil*, afterwards Baron *Savil*, being the first Alderman, and his Office executed by *John Harrison* Esq, a person to be particularly mention'd here, as a most noble benefactor, and a pattern to succeeding ages 1 He founded and * endow'd an Hospital for relief of indigent persons of good conversation, and formerly industrious, with a † Chapel, for a Master to read Prayers, and to instruct them 2 He built the Free-school (to which *Godfrey Lawson* Esquire, Mayor of the Burrough of *Leeds*, added a Library) placed it upon his own ground, and enclos'd it with a beautiful Wall 3 He built a most noble Church, dedicated to St *John* the Evangelist, and ‖ endow'd it; and provided a house for the Minister 4 He erected a stately Cross for the conveniency of the market When his estate was almost exhausted in acts of charity, he left the remainder for relief of such of his relations as by the frowns of the world should unhappily be reduc'd to poverty, bequeathing an * annual Sum to be manag'd by four Trustees, to put out the males to trades, and to prefer the females in marriage And as these are instances of his charity, so in a Codicil annex'd to his Will, there is a fair testimony of his strict justice and integrity *Whereas I heretofore bought of Richard* Falkingham *Esq, divers lands and tenements, part of which I endow'd the New Church withal, and part I since sold to several persons for a good sum of money more than I purchas'd the same for; I thought my self bound to bestow upon the eldest son of* John Green, *and the eldest son of* John Hemerton, *who marry'd the coheirs of the said Richard* Falkingham, *the surplus of all such moneys as I sold the lands for, over and above what indeed they cost me*, together with a large addition thereunto the product of the whole sum amounting to 1600 *l* which, upon a strict estimate of his whole estate, appears to be a full half He was baptiz'd in St *Peter's* Church at Leeds, and was chief Alderman in the year 1626, and again 1634; in which year the new Church of his own foundation was † consecrated by *Richard Neile*, then Archbishop of York He dy'd ‖ at seventy-seven years of age, and lies inter'd under an Altar tomb of black marble in the said Church, over which is the well painted effigie of this Benefactor (in his *scarlet-gown*,) the gift of the reverend Mr *Henry Robinson*, the present Incumbent, who is perhaps the single instance of one that enjoys a Church both founded and endow'd by his own Uncle, and from whom there is a fair and near prospect of some exemplary acts of publick piety.

* 30 l per an

Aug 16 1579

† Sept 21

‖ Oct 29 1656

By

By a second Patent, bearing date 2 Nov 18 Car 2, the government of *Leeds* was alter'd to a Mayor, twelve Aldermen, and twenty four Assistants This place was also honour'd by giving the title of Duke, to the right honourable Thomas Lord Marquis of Caermarthen, to which dignity he was advanc'd, for his personal merits and eminent Services to the Crown, in the sixth year of King William and Queen Mary, and was succeeded in those titles by his son and heir

Temple Newsome

From *Leeds*, *Are* passeth by *Temple Newsome*, of old a Commandery belonging to the *Knights Templars*, the seat of the right honourable *Rich* Lord *Ingram*, Viscount *Irwin*, in the Kingdom of Scotland]

In these parts, *Oswy* the Northumbrian routed *Penda* the Mercian, *to the great advantage*, says Bede, *of both people, for it both secur'd his own nation from the inroads of the Pagans, and was the occasion of converting the Mercians to the Christian Faith* The very spot where this engagement was, goes by the name of *Winwidfield* in our Historians I suppose, deriv'd from the *victory* it self, as when *Quintilius Varus* and his Legions were cut off in Westphalia, the place of Action was call'd in High Dutch *Winfield (the field of victory,)* as the most learned, and my most worthy friend, *Abraham Ortelius*, has observ'd [It is at this day call'd *Winmore*, and is four miles from *Leeds* in the road to *York* But all the difficulty is, to find out the right *Winwid flu*[illegible] of *Bede* (in the *Lovain* edition mis-printed *Innet*, whence probably *Speed*'s *Innet*, but a very old Manuscript has it *Winwed*, as that also which *Wheelock* us'd,) and the Winpiðstream of King *Alfred* For a † very curious Enquirer declares, that after many years search, and frequent traversing the ground, he cannot find or hear of either great or small Brook, that carries a name any thing akin to *Winwed*, which he now concludes to be our river *Are* And indeed, there is no river besides, that seems to have the least probability of being it *Wherf* cannot pretend to it, because the *Mercians*, upon their defeat, would certainly flee homewards *Calder* is too remote from the place of Battel, which was *in regione Loidis* All the difficulty (for the Inclosures between the present *Winmore* and *Leeds* may well enough be concluded of a modern standing, and consequently the old *Winwid field*, the nigher *Are*) is, the different names, and yet the matter may be thus solv'd, That the Christian Saxons, in memory of so signal a deliverance from their Pagan Enemies, who threaten'd the extirpation of their whole race, might endeavour to change the British *Are* into the Saxon Winpið, and *Bede*, who was a Northern man, and wrote his History presently after, might accordingly celebrate it under that name, though in a few ages the old name seems to have reverted Now, that British names sometimes give place to Saxon, *Somner* himself admits, in his Treatise of the Roman Ports, where he concludes *Sandwich* to have let go its British *Rutupium*, for the Saxon Lundenpic and *Limene* and *Rother* he positively asserts to be different names of the same *Romney water* As to the Etymon, I fansy it to be from pin victory and pið *broad*, as is observ'd before; and so it had need have been for so vast an army, where thirty cyne bearna, *Captains of the Blood Royal*, with their forces, were slain on one side, or rather drown'd in the Winpiðstream, for *Bede* puts the accent upon that, *l 3 c 4 That the river* Winwid, *having overflow'd the banks, by reason of excessive rains, many more were drown'd in the flight, than kill'd in the field* And, methinks, our modern *Winmore* and *Broad Are* agree very well with the old *Winwid-field* and *Winwid stream* And I am very apt to think, that even when the old British name reverted, it hence got that universal Epithet of *broad*, which is to this day so generally us'd, or rather incorporated into the very name of the River, that the common people can scarce pronounce the one without the other And why (except from this memorable Victory, which was chiefly owing to the water) it should be *Broad Are*, rather than *Broad Ouse* or *Calder*, I cannot conceive And I am rather induc'd thus to take pið appellatively, both because the place of battel is call'd *Winmore*, not *Winwidmore*, and because Winpiðream is synonymous to Brabant, i e *Broadwater*, which was so nigh akin to the old name, that nothing is more easy, than the change of Brab ea to Brad are]

Penes R Thoresby

† Mr Thoresby, Antiq Leeds

Winwidfield

The Country, for some little way about Winwidfield aforesaid was anciently call'd *Elmet*, [i e a grove of Elms,] which Edwin King of Northumberland, son of Ella, brought under his own dominion, by the conquest of *Cereticus* a British King, An Dom 620 † Bede says, that out of the Fire which burnt the Royal Villa *Donafeld*, one Altar was sav'd, being of stone, and was kept in the Monastery of Abbot *Thrythwulf*, in the wood *Elmete*, which Monastery might possibly be placed at * *Berwick* in Elmet] Here, in Elmet, Lime stone is plentifully dug up they burn it at *Brotherton* and *Knottingly*, and at certain seasons convey it in great quantities, for sale, to *Wakefield*, *Sandal*, and *Standbridge* from thence it is sold into the western parts of this County, which are naturally cold and mountainous, and herewith they manure and improve the soil But leaving these things to the Husbandmen, let us return

Elmet

Nennius

† L 2 c 14

* Vid infra

Lime stone

The *Calder* above mention'd, is at last receiv'd by the *Are* and near the Confluence stands the little village *Castleford*, but call'd by Marianus *Casterford*, who tells us, that the Citizens of York slew great numbers of Ethelred's army there, pursuing them in a disorderly flight, at the time when he infested this Country, for their treachery and breach of Leagues Yet the older name of this place is that in Antoninus, where it is call'd *Legeolium* and *Lagetium*, which, among other plain and remarkable remains of antiquity, is confirm'd by these great numbers of Coins (call'd by the common people *Sarasins heads*) dug-up here in *Beanfield*, a place near the Church, and so call'd from the beans growing there Also, by the distance of it from *Danum* and *Eboracum* on each side not to mention its situation by a Roman way; nor that *Hoveden* expresly calls it a City [*Thomas de Castleford*, a Benedictine, who flourish'd Anno 1326, wrote the History of Pontefract, from *Ask*, a Saxon, first owner thereof to the *Lacies*, from whom that large Lordship descended to the Earls of Lancaster Not far from hence is *Ledston hall*, formerly the seat of the ancient family of the *Witham*s but late of Sir *John Lewis* Baronet, who [illegible] his estate during his [illegible] year [illegible] for the East India Company (much [illegible]ted by the Jewels presented him by the King of Persia, who much delighted in [illegible] company) dy'd here without Issue male in the year 1671 He * erected a curious Hospital, and endow'd it, for the maintenance of ten aged poor people, who by his Will are requir'd religiously to observe

Castleford

Legeolium

Fuller's Worthies

Ledston hall

* Aug 14 [illegible]

[illegible] 60l per an

serve the Sabbath day, and to be present at Church in time of Divine-Service and Sermon. At present, Ledston hall is the seat of the Lady *Elizabeth Hastings*, daughter of Theophilus Earl of Huntington, by the eldest daughter and coheir of Sir John Lewis; which said Elizabeth (a true pattern of Piety and Charity) hath greatly improv'd and adorn'd this Seat.]

Brotherton

* His second wife

The river *Are*, now enlarged by the confluence of the *Calder*, leaves *Brotherton* on the left, where * *Margaret* wife of King Edward the first took up as she was a hunting, and was brought to bed of her son Thomas, sirnam'd *de Brotherton* from this place, who was afterwards Earl of Norfolk, and Marshal of England. [He was born in the year † 1300, having his Christian name from St *Thomas* of Canterbury, whom his mother in her extremity pray'd to for ease. Not far from the Church, is a place of twenty acres, surrounded with a trench and a wall, where (as tradition saith) stood the House in which Queen Margaret was deliver'd; and the Tenants are oblig'd by the tenure of their Lands, to keep it surrounded with a wall of stone.] Somewhat below this town, the river *Are* is join'd by the *Dan*, and then runs into the river *Ouse*. On the right, there is found a *yellow marle* of such virtue, that the fields once manur'd with it prove fruitful many years after. And not far from the banks of the river, is *Pontfract* (or, *Broken bridge*) commonly call'd *Pomfrett*, which arose out of the ruins of *Legeolium*. In the Saxon times, the name of this town was *Kirkby*, which was changed by the Normans into *Pontfract*, because of a broken bridge there. The story is, that here was a wooden bridge over this river, when William Archbishop of York, who was sister's son to King Stephen, return'd from Rome; and that he was welcom'd here with such a crowd of people, that the bridge broke, and many fell into the river, but that the Archbishop wept and pray'd so fervently, that not one of them was lost. [But this account is inconsistent with the Records of the place, especially in point of time. At first, as hath been said, it was call'd *Kirby*, for in the Charter made by Robert *de Lacy*, son of *Hildebert*, to the Monks of St *John* the Evangelist, they are stil'd *Deo servientes de Kirkby*, and this, he says, he did by advice of T. Archbishop of York. Yet the same *Robert* by another Charter (to which are the same witnesses, except that T. Archbishop of York is added) confirms other Lands and Churches *Deo & S. Johanni & Monachis meis de Pontefract*. By this account, it is plain, that in the time of T. Archbishop of York, it had both the names of *Kirkby* and *Pontefract*. Now this T. could be no other than the first *Thomas*, who came to the Archbishoprick about the eighth of the Conqueror, and continu'd in it till about the beginning of Henry the first whom he crown'd, and soon after dy'd. For *Robert*, who granted these Charters, was banish'd in the 6th of Henry the first, for being at the battel of *Tenercebray*, on behalf of *Robert* Duke of Normandy against King Henry, and dy'd the year after; which was before any other Archbishop succeeded in that See, to whose name the initial *T* will agree. *Thomas* the second indeed came presently after (Anno 1109) but this St. *William* (to whom the Miracle is attributed) was not possess'd of it before 1153. From which it is evident, that the town was call'd *Pontefract* at least fifty two years before the miracle, and how much longer, we know not.

A yellow Marle

Pontfreit

T. de Castleford

S. Gulielmus Eboracensis

Monast. Angl. vol.

† June 1

Below the Church and a water mill (call'd *Bongate mill*) there is a level ground nam'd the *Wash*, the road from *Pontefract* to *Knottingley*, and the directest way from *Doncaster* to *Castleford*. By this *Wash*, the current of waters, flowing from the springs above and supplying two mills, passes into the river at *Knottingley*. But it retains not that name above a large bow-shot, being terminated by a place call'd *Bubwith Houses*, where by an Inquisition taken in the reign of Edward 2, it appears that one *John Bubwith* held the eighteenth part of a Knight's fee *juxta veterem pontem de Pontefract*, i. e. near the old bridge of Pontefract. Which must have been over this *Wash*, as will be made more probable, if we consider that even now upon any violent rains, or the melting of snow, it is so overflow'd as to be scarce passable, and that formerly, before the conveyance of the waters into chanels to serve the mills, and the drains made from hence to *Knottingley*, the passage must have been much more difficult, and by consequence did the rather require a bridge. So then, from the probability of a bridge over this *Wash*, and the Record making the *Pons de Pontefract* to be near *Bubwith houses* hard by, and there appearing no necessity of a bridge in any other part of the town, it follows that the bridge which was broken, must have been here. And the occasion of it being, no doubt, very considerable, it was natural enough for the Norman Lords (who knew what number of places took their name from *Bridges* in their own country) to lay hold on this opportunity of changing the name, especially when that former one of *Kirkby*, upon the building of more *Churches* round it, grew less emphatical, and less distinguishing. And so much for the occasion of the name.]

The town is sweetly situated, and is remarkable for producing *Liquorish* and *Skirworts* in great plenty: the buildings are neat, and secur'd by a castle which is very stately, and strongly founded upon a rock, and not only fortify'd, but also beautify'd, with many outworks. It was built by *Hildebert Lacy* a Norman, to whom William the Conqueror gave this town, and the grounds about it, after he had dispossess'd *Alric* a Saxon. [though some question, whether the Castle was first built by *Alric* the Saxon, or by *Hildebert*. In the history of the *Lacies* indeed, the latter is said to have caus'd a Chapel to be erected in the Castle of Pontfract, which he had built. But since it's being demolish'd of late years (among several others throughout England) it is observ'd that the round-tower stood upon a rais'd hill of very hard fat clay which looks as if it had been of those sort of fortifications that the Saxons call'd *Keeps*, and might, from a fortification of earth, be built of stone by the said *Hildebert*.] *But Henry Lacy* † *his nephew* (as the *Pleadings* of those times tell us) *being in the battel of Trenchbrey against Henry the first, was disseis'd of his Barony of Pontfract, and then the King gave the honour to Wido de la Val, who held it till King Stephen's time, when Henry de Lacy re-enter'd upon the said Barony; and, by the King's intercession, the difference was adjusted with Wido for 150 l.* This Henry had a son *Robert*, who dy'd without issue, leaving *Albreda Lisours*, *his sister by the mother's side, his heir; for there was no one else so nearly related to him: so that by the decease of Robert, both the Estates, that of the Lacies by her brother, and that of the Lisours by her father, descended to her.* This is word for word out of the Register of *Stanlow* Monastery. She was marry'd to Richard *Fitz Eustach* Constable

Lacy

Monast. Angl. vol. 2

† Nepos. Placit. 11 Hen.

Lib. Monast. de Stanlow

stable of Chester, whose posterity took the name of *Lacy*, and were honour'd with the Earldom of Lincoln The Daughter of the last *Lacy* of this family convey'd that fair inheritance * by a short Deed to the Earls of Lancaster; who enlarg'd the Castle very much it was afterwards repair'd, at great expence, by Queen Elizabeth, who began a fine Chapel here This Castle has been fatal to great men. it was first stain'd with the blood of *Thomas* Earl of Lancaster, who held it in right of his wife, and was the first of this family that possess'd it He was justly beheaded here by King Edward the second, who hop'd, by that example, to free himself from future Rebellions and Affronts however, he was afterwards Sainted by the people Here also King Richard the second (depos'd by Henry the fourth) was barbarously destroy'd with hunger, cold, and other unheard-of torments Here, *Anthony* Earl Rivers, Uncle to Edward the fifth, and Sir *Richard Grey* Knight, brother by the mother's side to the said King *Edward*, were both put to death (notwithstanding their innocence) by King Richard the third For this tyrant was jealous, that men of such spirits and honour as these were, might check his designs of tyranny and ambition As for the Abbey founded here by the *Lacies*, and the Hospital by the bounty of *R Knolles*, I industriously omit them, because † now the very ruins of them are hardly to be seen

* *Formula transcriptionis*

Thomas Earl of Lancaster

† So said ann 16.7

From *Legeolium* we pass by *Shirborn*, a populous small town (which takes the name from the clearness of the little river there, and was given by Athelstan to the Archbishops of York [It is now chiefly famous for the benefaction of *Robert Hungate* Esquire, a most zealous Protestant, who by Will ordain'd the erection of an Hospital and School, with convenient Lodgings, &c for twenty four Orphans, who have each 5 *l per ann* allow'd for their maintenance there from seven to fifteen years of age, and then a provision for binding them Apprentices, or finding them to the University This, with the Salaries of the † Master, (who is also to catechize them,) and of the ‖ Usher, and * of a man and his wife who are to make suitable provisions of meat and apparel for the Orphans, and forty marks *per ann* for four poor scholars in St *John's* College Cambridge, &c amounts in all to 250 *l per ann*]

Shirborn

† 30 *l per an*
‖ 10 Marks
* 10 Marks.

From Shirborn, we travel upon a Roman way, very high rais'd, to *Aberford*, a little town situated hard by that way, and famous for its art of *pin making*; the pins made here being in particular request among the Ladies Under the town lies the course of the river Cock (or as it is in Books *Cocarus*; between which and the town, the foundation of an old Castle (which they call *Castle Cary*) is still visible Scarce two miles from hence, where the *Cock* springs, stands *Berwick in Elmet*, which is said to have been the royal seat of the Kings of Northumberland It has been walled round, as the remaining rubbish shews On the other side stands *Hessell wood*, the chief seat of that famous and very ancient family the *Vavasors*, who have their name from their Office (being formerly the King's *Valvasors*,) and towards the end of Edward the first's reign, we find by the Writs of those times, that *William Vavasor* was summon'd to Parliament among the other Barons of this Kingdom Under the town is the remarkable Quarry, call'd *Petres Post*, because the stately Church at York dedicated to St *Peter*, was built with the stones hew'd out here, by the bounty of the *Vavasors* [This Town has a pleasant prospect the two Cathedrals of *York* and *Lincoln*, sixty miles asunder, may thence be discover'd, and *Tonstal* Bishop of Durham affirm'd to King Henry the eighth (when he made his progress to York,) that the Country within ten miles, was the richest valley that ever he found in all his travels through Europe, there being one hundred sixty five manour-houses of Lords, Knights, and Gentlemen of the best quality, two hundred seventy five several Woods (whereof some contain five hundred acres) thirty two Parks, and two Chases of deer, one hundred and twenty rivers and brooks, whereof seven are navigable, well stor'd with Salmon and other Fish, seventy six water mills for Corn, twenty five cole mines; three forges for making of Iron, and stone enough for the same, within those limits also as much sport and pleasure for hunting, hawking, fishing, and fowling, as in any part of England]

Aberford

Cary castle

Berwick in Elmet

Hesselwood

Valvasors or Vavasors

Petres Post

Ann 1541.

From *Aberford* the *Cock* runs somewhat slowly to the river *Wherf*, as if it were melancholy, and detested Civil Wars, ever since it flowed with the English blood formerly shed here For upon the very bank of this river, not far from *Towton*, a small country Village, was the true *English Pharsalia* Here was the greatest Engagement of Nobility and Gentry, and the strongest Army that ever was seen in England, no fewer than an hundred thousand fighting Men, who under the conduct of two daring and furious Generals, engaged here upon Palm-Sunday, in the year 1461 The Victory continued doubtful for a long time, but at last the Lancastrians proved the weakest, by their being too strong For their numbers proved cumbersome and unweildy; which first caused disorder, and then flight The York party gave the chase briskly; which, together with the fight, was so bloody, that no less than thirty five thousand English were cut off, and amongst them a great many of the Nobility Somewhat below this place, near *Shirburn*, at a Village call'd *Huddleston*, there is a noble *Quarry*; out of which when the Stones are first cut, they are very soft, but by being in the air, they presently consolidate and harden.

Towton bat[tle]

Huddleston Quarry

Out of the foot of *Craven hills*, springs the river *Wherf* or *Wharf*, in Saxon Guerf, the course of which, for a long way, keeps at an equal distance from the *Are* If one should derive the name of it from a British word *Guer*, *swift*, the nature of the river would favour him, for it's course is swift and violent, fretful and angry, as it were, at those stones which obstruct its passage; and it rolls them along in a very surprising manner, especially when it is swell'd by the winter rains However, it is dangerous and rapid even in the summer time, as I am sensible by experience, who in my last travels this way run no small risk in passing it For it has such slippery stones, that a horse's foot cannot fix on them; or else the current itself is so strong, that it drives them from under his feet Though the whole course of it be long (no less than fifty miles, computing from the first rise to its joyning the *Ouse*) yet there are no considerable Towns upon it It runs down by *Kilnsey Cragge* (the highest and the steepest [illegible] that I ever saw,) to *Burnsal*, where Sir *W[illegible]* *Craven*, Alderman of London, was born, and * built a stone bridge [illegible], out of a pious con[cern] for the good of his own Country, [illegible] founded and endowed a Free School [illegible]

Wharf riv[er]

[illegible]

[He built also a Church there, and encompass'd it with a Wall at great * expence. He built in all † four Bridges and a ‖ Causeway He gave one thousand Pounds to Christ's Hospital in London, and the Royalties of *Creek*, with the perpetual donation of the Parsonage to St John's College in Oxford *William*, his eldest Son, much affecting Military Discipline, was sent to the Wars of Germany under *Gustavus Adolphus*, the famous King of *Sweden*, and after into the *Netherlands* under Henry Prince of Orange, by King Charles the first *] Then the *Wherf* runs to *Barden towre*, a little tower belonging to the † Earls of Cumberland, noted for the good hunting thereabouts and so to *Bolton*, where stood formerly a little Monastery, [and now is a Free-School, the noble † Benefaction of the Honourable *Robert Boyle*,] and to *Bethmesley*, the seat of the famous family of *Claphams*, of which was *J Clapham*, an eminent Soldier in the Wars between York and Lancaster Hence it passes by *Ilekely*, which I imagin to be the *Olicana* in Ptolemy, both from its situation in respect of *York*, and the resemblance of the two names It is, without question, an ancient Town, for (not to mention those engrav'd Roman Pillars, lying now in the Church-yard and elsewhere,) it was rebuilt in *Severus*'s time by ‖ *Virius Lupus*, Legate and Propraetor of Britain, as we are informed by an Inscription lately dug up near the Church

* 600 *l*
† One 500 *l* another 250 *l*
‖ 200 *l*
* See before, at *Craven*
Barden-towre
† So said ann 1607
Bolton
† To the value of 1100 *l*
Bethmesley
Ilekely
Olicana
‖ Mention'd by Ulpian lib 2 de *Vulgari & Pupillari substitutione*

IM SEVERVS
AVG ET ANTONINVS
CAES DESTINATVS
RESTITVERVNT, CV-
RANTE VIRIO LVPO
* LEG EORVM ‖ PR PR

* *Legato*
‖ *Pro Praetore*

That the † second Cohort of the *Lingones* quartered here, is likewise attested by an old Altar which I have seen there, now put under a pair of stairs, and inscribed by the * Captain of the second Cohort of the *Lingones*, to *Verbeia*; perhaps she was the Nymph or Goddess of the *Wherf* (the river) and call'd *Verbeia*, I suppose, from the likeness of the two words

† First
* Praefect

VERBEIAE SACRVM
CLODIVS FRONTO
PRAEF COH † II LINGTON

Verbeia fl. vel Nympha
† P

For Rivers, says Gildas, *in that age had divine honours paid them by the ignorant Britains* And Seneca tells us of Altars dedicated to them; *We worship the heads of great rivers, and we raise altars to their first springs* And Servius says, *that every river had its Nymph presiding over it* [But it seems rather to have been the first *Cohort*, the last line of that Inscription being not II LINGON but P LINGON in the original, as appears from Mr *John Thoresby*'s Papers late of *Leeds*, an eminent Antiquary, who accurately transcrib'd it, being very critical in his Observations upon Inscriptions and original Coins, of which he had a valuable Collection Besides his own, he purchas'd those of the Reverend Mr *Stonehouse*, and the Right Honourable *Thomas* Lord *Fairfax* This *Musaeum* is very much improv'd, and still growing, by the curiosity and industry of Mr *Ralph Thoresby*, an excellent Antiquary, who has obliged the Publick with the Particulars contained in it, in his late curious History of *Leeds*

Epist 41

The original Altar above-mention'd, is remov'd to *Stubham* the new one erected at *Ilkley*, had this Inscription erected upon the Reverse

Stubham.

GVILM MIDLETON
ARM ME FECIT AD
IMAGINEM ANTI
QVISS LAPIDIS HIC
REPERTI 1608]

In the Walls of the Church there is this imperfect Inscription

——— ——— ———
RVM CAES
AVG ———
ANTONINI
ET VERI
JOVI DILECTI
CAECILIVS
PRAEF COH

I found nothing in my search up and down the Church for pieces of Roman Antiquity, but the Portraicture of Sir *Adam Middleton*, armed and cut out in stone, who seems to have lived in Edward the first's reign His posterity remain still in the neighbourhood, at a place called *Stubham*

[At some distance from hence is *Bramhope*, the Seat of the ancient family of the *Dinelys*, of which *Robert Dinely* Esq; (deceas'd not many years since in a good old age, having seen four generations of most of the neighbouring Nobility and Gentry) erected a Chapel, with a competent endowment]

Bramhope

Somewhat lower stands *Otley*, which belongs to the Archbishops of York, memorable for nothing but its situation under a huge craggy Cliff called *Chevin* For the ridge of a mountain is in British *Chevin*, and so, that long ridge of Mountains in France (where they formerly us'd the same language with our Britains) is called *Gevenna* and *Gebenna* From hence, the river flows in a chanel bank'd on both sides with *Lime stone*, by *Harewood*, where stands a tolerably neat and strong Castle, which has had † successively a variety of Masters It was formerly the *Curcies*, but passed from them, with *Alice* the heiress of that family, to *Warren Fitz Gerold*, who married her, and had issue *Margery*; who being one of his heirs, and a great fortune, was first married to *Baldwin de Ripariis*, son to the Earl of Devonshire, who died before his father, and then, by the favour of King John, to *Falcatius de Brent*, for his great service * in pillaging Afterwards, *Isabel de Ripariis*, Countess of Devonshire, dying without issue, this Castle fell to *Robert de Lisle*, the son of *Warren*, as a relation, and one of her heirs. At last, by those of *Aldborough*, it came to the *Rithers*, as I learn'd from *Fr. Thinn*, who with great judgment and diligence * has been long enquiring into the Antiquities of this Kingdom [This Castle was reduc'd to a skeleton in the late Civil wars In the Church are several curious Monuments of the owners of it, and the *Gascoyns*; of whom the famous Judge, Sir *William Gascoyne*, is the most memorable, for committing the Prince (afterwards King Henry the fifth,) prisoner to the Kings-Bench, till his Father's pleasure was known; who being inform'd of it, gave God thanks, for

Otley
Chevin what it signifies
Gevenna
Harewood
† *Pro temporum vicissitudine*
Placit 1 Jo an Rot 10 in D Moulte le droit 3, Ed 1
* *In Direptionibus*
Lords *de Insula*, or *Lisle*
* So said, ann 1607

for having given him, at the same instant, a Judge who could administer, and a Son who could obey, justice He was made Judge in the year 1401, and dy'd in † 1412, as appears by their Pedigree curiously drawn by that accomplish'd Antiquary Mr *Richard Gascoyne*, and it is the rather mention'd here, because most Histories are either deficient, or mistaken therein This great Manour of *Harewood*, has eight or nine dependant Constabularies, wherein are many Antiquities; and the present generous and charitable * Lord thereof hath been a considerable Benefactor to the Church and Poor] Nor must I forget to take notice of a place hard by, called *Gawthorp*, remarkable for that ancient, virtuous and warlike family the *Gascoigns*, [just now mention'd,] and descended very probably from *Gascoigne* in France [This place, called *Gawthorp hall*, hath been lately raised out of it's Ruins by the present owner, the Lord of the Manour of *Harewood* before-mention'd, and from a place only venerable for it's Antiquity, hath made it a most pleasant and delightful Seat]

† Dec 17

* *John Boulter*, Esq.

Gawthorp.

Gascoigns

Hence the course of the river *Wherf* is by *Wetheroy*, a noted trading Town, which has no remains of Antiquity, but only a place below it call'd *Helensford*, where a Roman military way lay through the river [Thence *Wherf* passeth by *Wighill*, the Seat of an ancient family of the *Stapletons*, of which, Sir *Robert* being Sheriff 23 *Eliz* met the Judges with sevenscore men in suitable Liveries For a Person well spoken, comely, and skill'd in the Languages, he is said to have had scarce an equal (except Sir *Philip Sidney*,) and no superiour, in England Not far from it is *Helaugh-manor*, which belong'd to the honourable and ancient family of the *Whartons*, in the Church whereof is the Monument of Sir *Thomas Wharton*, Lord Warden of the West-marches, who gave so great a defeat to the Scots at *Solemn moss*, An 1542, that their King, James the fifth, soon after dy'd of grief With three hundred men, he not only defeated their Army, but took * above a thousand prisoners, for which good service he receiv'd several marks of honour]

Wetherby

Helensford

Wighill

Helaugh manour

Nov 24

* Herbert Hen 8 p. 484.

Then *Wherf* passeth by *Tadcaster*, a very small Town, which yet I cannot but think was the same with *Calcaria*, both from the distance, the name, and the nature of the soil, especially, since it is agreeable to the opinion of Mr *Robert Marshal* of *Bickerton*, a person of excellent judgment For it is just nine Italian miles from York, which is the distance in Antoninus And *Limestone* (which is the main ingredient in mortar) is hardly to be found all about, but plentifully here; from whence it is convey'd to York, and all the Country round, for building. This *Limestone* was call'd by the Britains, the Saxons, and the Northern English, after the manner of the Latins, *Calc* (' for ' that imperious City not only impos'd her ' Laws upon those she had subdu'd, but her ' Language too,)' and *Calcarensis* in the *Theodosian Code* is used to denote them who burnt this Limestone, from whence one may, not improbably infer, that this Town had the name *Calcaria*, from Lim stone, like the City *Chalcis* from χαλκός *brass*, *Ammon* from ἄμμος *sand*, *Ptelion* from πτελέαι, *elms*, and perhaps the city *Calcaria* in *Cirve* from the word *Calx* Especially, considering that *Bede* calls it *Calca cester*; who tells us farther, that *Heina*, the first woman of this Country that turned Nun, came to this City, and lived in it. [(Some Copies of Bede call her *Heru* and *Hegu*, but others more truly *Begu* and *Bega*, being the † S *Bega* from Ireland, who built her first Monastery at St *Bege's* in Cornwall; her second at *Heruty* or *Hartlepool*, and her third, here But this by the way)] Again, here is by the Town, a hill called *Kelcbar*, which still retains something of the old name The other proofs of Antiquity (not to mention its situation near a Roman Consular way,) are the many Coins of the Roman Emperours dug up here, the marks of a trench quite round the Town, and the platform of an old Castle, out of the ruins of which, a bridge was made over the *Wherf*, not many years ago [But there are others, who place the Roman *Calcaria* at *Newton Kyme*, in the Water fields, near St *Helens ford*; for many Roman Coins have been plowed up there, particularly of *Constantius*, *Helena*, and *Constantine*, also, an Urn or Box of Alabaster, with only ashes in it, melted Lead and Rings, one of which had a Key of the same piece joined with it And as the Coyns, so the Roman High-way makes for this Opinion For it goes directly to *Roadgate*, and crosses the river *Wharfe* at St *Helens ford*, so call'd from *Helena* mother of Constantine the Great, unless we should say, with Dr *Gale*, that it is a contraction of *Nebalenn's-ford*, the Goddess *Nebalennia* being the Patroness of the *Chalk* workers) Also, the passage from that to York, is firmer ground by much than that from Tadcaster; which would hardly be passable, were it not for the Causey made over the Common, between *Tadcaster* and *Bilburgh* Now, this Ford dividing the Roman *Agger*, gives just reason to expect a Roman City or Station, rather near this, than any other place Nor ought it to be objected, that there is at present no passage for it had formerly a bridge of wood, the sills whereof yet remain, but when that was broken down, and the Wharf was not fordable, they found a way by *Wetherby* Nor is there any thing said in favour of *Tadcaster*, but what is equally, if not more, applicable to *Newton Kyme* The distance holds more exactly, the hill call'd *Kelc bar* is at *Smawe*, which is nearer *Newton* than Tadcaster, and as to *Heina*, who remov'd to *Calca cester*, it is possible enough there might in those early times be a Religious House consecrated to the memory of the pious *Helena*, about St *Helens ford* At *Calcaria* liv'd also *Adaman*, (who was afterward *Abbot* of *Hue*, or *Huensis*, and dy'd *Octob* 23 *An* 704) of whose name there seem to be some remains, in that place at *Newton Kyme* call'd *Adaman-grove* The present name (which carries in it something *new* and modern) ought not to be any prejudice to it For since it is back'd with such infallible proofs of Antiquity, this conclusion is very natural, that it was call'd *New town*, when new buildings began to be erected upon the foundations of the old town But, of these two Opinions, the Reader is left to chuse which he pleases] Not far from the forementioned bridge, the *Wherf* glides gently into the *Ouse* And really, considering the many currents that fall into it, this so shallow and easie stream under the Bridge, is very strange, and might well give occasion to what a certain Gentleman, who passed it in the Summer time, said of it

Tadcaster

Calcaria

Calcarienses De Decurionibus l 27 Roman Language in the Provinces Augustin l 19 de Civit Di

† Monast Ang p 393

> *Nil* Tadcaster *habet Musis vel carmine dignum*
> *Præter magnifice structum sine flumine pontem*

Itinerary of J Lel.

Nothing

Nothing in *Tadcaster* deserves a name,
But the fair Bridge that's built without a stream

But if he had travell'd this way in winter, he would have thought the bridge little enough for the river For (as Natural Philosophers know very well) the quantity of water in springs and rivers ever depends upon the inward or outward heat and cold

[Here, at *Tadcaster*, Dr *Owen Oglethorp* (a native of *Newton Kime*) Bishop of Carlisle, who crown'd Queen Elizabeth (the See of Canterbury being then void, and York refusing it,) founded, and endowed a Free school, as also an Hospital for twelve poor people with a suitable Revenue Near *Tadcaster* is *Bramham moor*, where, at *Bramham Park*, the Lord Bingley hath built a stately House]

* 40 *l* per ann

Bramham moor

Nid, riv

Nidherdale

Ripley

Somewhat higher the river *Nid*, issuing from the bottom of *Craven hills*, is carried in a muddy channel by *Nidherdale*, a valley so call'd from it, and thence under the cover of woods on both sides, by *Ripley*, a Market Town, where the family of the *Inglebeys* have flourish'd with great Antiquity and Reputation [This was the birth place of Sir *George Ripley*, famous for his study after the Philosopher's Stone, whom we are the rather to mention, because he hath been falsly plac'd at *Ripley* in *Surrey*] Then it goes on to *Gnaresburgh*, commonly *Knarsborrow*, a Castle situated upon a craggy rock (from whence it took its name) and surrounded by that deep river It is said to have been built by *Serlo de Burgh*, uncle by the father's side to *Eustace Vescy*; afterwards, it came to be the Seat of the *Estotevilles*, and now it belongs to the Dutchy of Lancaster Under it, there is a fountain, which does not issue from the bowels of the Earth, but distills, in drops, from the rocks hanging over it, and so is call'd *Dropping Well* if a piece of wood be put in it, it is in a little time crusted over with a stony substance, and by degrees turned into stone [The Castle is now demolish'd, so that it is chiefly famous for our medicinal Springs nigh unto it, and possibly *England* cannot produce a place, that may truly boast of four, so near in situation, and yet of very different operations 1 The *Sweet-Spaw* or *Vitrioline well*, discover'd by Mr *Slingsby* about the year 1620 2 The *Stinking* or *Sulphur well*, said to cure the Dropsie, Spleen, Scurvy, Gout, *&c* so that what formerly was call'd *the dishonour of Physick*, may be call'd *the honour of the Knaresborow Spaw*, the late way of *bathing* being esteem'd very soveraign 3 St *Mongahs* (not *Magnus*, *amangus*, *mungus* or *mugnus*, as frequently miscall'd) or *Kentigern*'s, a Scotish Saint, much honour'd in these parts, whom his Tutor *Servanus* Bishop of *Orkney*, lov'd beyond others, and us'd to call him *Mongah* †, in the Norish tongue, a *dear friend* The fourth, *viz* the *Dropping Well* before-mention'd, is * the most famous of all the *petrifying Wells* in England; and the ground upon which it drops from the spungy porous rock above twelve yards long is all become a solid Rock, from whence it runs into *Nid*, where the spring water hath made a rock, that stretches some yards into the river Yet it must be confess'd to fall short of that stupendous Spring in *Clermont* in *Auvergne*, a Province in France, where the Lapidescent is so strong, that it turns all its substance into stone, and being put into a glass will turn presently into a stone of the same form And † *Petrus Johannes Faber*, a French Physician, reports, that they make bridges of it, and it to pass into their gardens over the river that comes from it for by placing timber, and then pumping up the water upon it, they have a compleat stone-bridge in 24 hours Nor must St *Robert's Chapel* be forgot, being a Cell hewn out of an entire Rock, part whereof is form'd into an Altar which yet remains, and three heads, which (according to the devotion of that Age) might be design'd for the *Holy Trinity* The said *Robert*, Founder of the Order of the *Robertines*, was the son of one *Flower*, who was twice Mayor of *York*; * where he was born, and forsaking his fair Lands, betook himself to a solitary life among the Rocks here, where he dy'd about the year 1216]

Knarsborrow Castle

Dropping well

A fountain that converts wood into Stone

† Spotswood Hist of the Church of Scotland, pag 11

* Dr Wittie's Answ to Dr Tonstall

† Hydrocr Spag l 2 c 11

St Robert's Chapel

* Legend of the life and death of St Robert

In the adjacent fields, *Liquorish* grows plentifully, and they find a yellow soft *marl* which proves an excellent rich manure The office of Ranger of the Forest here, belong'd formerly to one *Gamellus*, whose posterity took the name of *Screven*, from *Screven* the place of their habitation From them are descended the *Slingsbeys*, who were made Rangers of this Forest by King *Edward* the first, and live here to this day in a very flourishing condition [Of this family was the Loyal Sir *Henry Slingesby*, who was beheaded for his Fidelity to King Charles the second Upon the Forest, was lately found a large stately † Medal, inscrib'd, JO KENDAL. RHODI TVRCVPELLERIVS *Rev* TEMPORE OBSIDIONIS TVRCHORVM MCCCCLXXX + Which is the more remarkable, because it expresseth the presence of our Country-man *Kendall* (with his image and arms) in that famous siege of *Rhodes*, when the great *Mahomet* was worsted

Slingsbey

† In Mr Thoresby's Museum

Ribston hall

East from *Knaresbrough* stands *Ribston hall*, the pleasant Seat of the *Goodricks*, of whom, Sir *Henry* was Ambassadour from King Charles the second to the King of Spain, and also Privy Councellor, and Lieutenant of the Ordnance of the Tower of London; and dying without issue, was succeeded by his Nephew, of both his names At *Copgrave*, to the north, is a memorable Epitaph of *John Wincupp* Rector thereof for 54 years, pious, charitable and peaceable, never su'd any, nor was su'd, liv'd 52 years with his wife, had six children and a numerous family (boarding and teaching many of the Gentry) out of which not one dy'd in all that time, himself was the first, the 8th of July, *A D* 1637, in the 86th year of his age Northward from *Knaresborough*, is a most noble Hall, built by Sir *Edward Blacket*, with delicate Gardens adorn'd with Statues] The *Nid*, having pass'd these places, runs but a little way, before it falls into the *Ouse*, not far from *Allerton*, the Seat of an ancient and famous family, the *Malliverers*, Knights, who in old writings are call'd *Mali Leporarii*, [and whose name occurs in the List of the Sheriffs of the County, since the 8th year of Henry the fifth]

Copgrave

Allerton

Out of these Western Mountains springs likewise the river *Ure*, but in another part of the Country (namely in the *North riding*) which still retaining this name, and watering the North part of the County, a little before it reaches *Rippon*, becomes the boundary between the North and the West-riding This *Rippon*, in Saxon Һrippun, is situated between the *Ure* and the little river *Skell*, and owes it's greatness to Religion, especially to a Monastery built by *Wilfrid* Archbishop of York, in the infancy of the English Church, *which was wonderful*, says Malmesbury, *for its arched vaults, its fine pavements,*

Ure, riv

Rippon

ments, and winding Entries But this was entirely demolish'd (together with the whole town) by the *Danes*, whose outrage and cruelty knew no distinction between things sacred and prophane. After that, it was rebuilt by *Odo* Archbishop of Canterbury, who being a most religious observer of holy Rites, transferred the Reliques of St *Wilfrid* from hence to *Canterbury* [But *before* the time that Wilfrid came hither, there was a Monastery of Scots at Ripon, as † Bede acknowledgeth, and ‖ he tells us also, who those Scots were, namely, *Eata* Abbot of Mailros, and his Monks] However, this Town was never so considerable as since the Norman Conquest, when, as one tells us, greater plenty of Monasteries began to be built Then, this Monastery also began to encrease and flourish under the patronage of the Archbishops of York, and the Town too, under it's Governour, call'd in Saxon *Wakeman*, that is to say *Watchman*, and by their diligence in the Woollen Manufacture, which is now slackened The Town is adorn'd with a very neat Church, built by the contributions of the Gentry hereabouts, and of the Treasurer of the Town, having three Spire steeples, which welcome Strangers at a distance, and vie with the rich Abbey of *Fountain*, built within Sight of it, by *Thurstin* Archbishop of York, [and favourably valued at the Dissolution, at 1173 *l* 0 *s* 7 *d ob* In the Minster yard, is this modest Inscription for a two thousand-pound Benefactor, *Hic jacet Zacharias Jepson, cujus ætas fuit* 49 *Perpaucos tantum annos vixit*] On one side of the Church, stands a little College † for Singing men, founded by * *Henry Bolb* Archbishop of York; on the other side, a great earthen Mount, call'd *Hilshaw*, cast up, as they say, by the Danes Within the Church, *Wilfrid's Needle* was mighty famous in the last age The business was this; there was a strait passage into a room close and vaulted, under ground, whereby trial was made of any woman's *chastity* if she was chast, she pass'd with ease, but if otherwise, she was, by I know not what miracle, stop'd, and detain'd there [At this Town, in the year 1695 was found a considerable number of Saxon Coins, namely, of their brass *Stica's*, whereof there were eight to a Penny. They were of the later race of the Kings of Deira, or rather the *Subreguli*, after Egbert had reduc'd it to be part of his Monarchy]

† Eccl Hist l 3 c 25 l. 5 c 20
‖ Life of S Cuthbert, cap 7, 8
Wakeman
† Cantorum
* So in the Text.
St Wilfrid's Needle

The Monastery of *Fountain* is delicately situated, in a fruitful soil, wherein are veins of Lead; and had its original from twelve Monks of York, who affecting a more rigid and strict course of life, left their Cloisters, and, after a great deal of trouble and hardship, were setled here by *Thurstin* Archbishop of York, who founded it for that purpose However, I should scarce have taken notice of them, but that St *Bernard* in his Epistles has so much commended their Order and Discipline

Fountain

Not much lower, upon the river *Ure*, is *Burrowbridge*, a little Town so call'd from the bridge there, which is made of stone, and is very high and stately; but in Edward the second's time it seems to have been only a wooden one For we read, that while the Barons harass'd that King and the whole Kingdom, *Humphrey de Bohun* Earl of Hereford, in passing over it, was run up the groin quite through the body by a Soldier who lay under the bridge, and took the advantage of pushing through a chink Just by the bridge, in three little fields to the Westward, I saw * four huge Stones, of a pyramidal form, very rough and unpolish'd, and placed as it were in a straight line one from another The two middle Stones (one of which was lately displaced in hopes of finding Money) almost touch'd one another, the outer ones standing at some small and equal distance from them As for the design or meaning of them, I have nothing to say, but that my Opinion is agreeable with some others in this point, That it was a Roman Trophy rais'd by the high way, which runs along here As for the silly stories of their being those bolts which the Devil shot at some Cities hereabouts, and so destroy'd them, I think it not worth while to mention them Thus much however is observable, that many, and those learned men, are of opinion, that the Stones are not natural, but an artificial compound of fine *Sand*, *Lime*, and *Vitriol* (for of this they fansy it has some grains,) as also of an oily unctuous Matter Much like those Cisterns at Rome, which Pliny tells us were made of Sand and hot Lime, so very compact and firm, that one would have taken them for real stone [This Opinion that they are *artificial*, may seem to receive support from the like Stones in Oxfordshire, call'd the *Devils coits*, which Dr Plot affirms to be made of a small kind of stones cemented together, whereof there are great numbers in the fields thereabouts But others think it evident, that they are *natural*, and not fictitious, and that they are made of one of the most common sort of Stone, viz a coarse Rag or Milston grit, alledging, that the remains of the Gates of York, and a Roman Head, and two Roman Altars, in Yorkshire, are plainly of that kind of Stone, and the same with these And against the imagined impossibility of bringing Stones of that bigness from any considerable distance, they alledge, the vast pile at *Stonehenge*, supposed to have been brought from *Rockley*, twenty miles from the place, whereas above *Ilkley*, a Roman Station within sixteen miles of *Burrowbridge*, is a solid bed of Stone, that would yield Obelisks thirty foot long

Burrow bridge
* Now 3 Pyramids
Devils bolts
Hist Oxford p 343
Philosoph Collect N 4 P 90, 91

Whether the foregoing conjecture of their being set up as Trophies by the Romans, may be allow'd, is not so certain A * later Antiquary seems inclin'd to conclude them to be a British work; supposing, that they might be erected in memory of some battel fought there but he is rather of opinion, that they were *British Deities*, agreeing with the Learned Dr *Stillingfleet*, and grounding upon the custom of the Phœnicians and Greeks Nations undoubtedly acquainted with *Britain*, before the arrival of the Romans) who set up unpolish'd stones instead of images, to the honour of their Gods And another, † yet later, thinks they are those *Mercuries*, describ'd by the Ancients, which were usually placed where four ways met (as they did here,) and that the head of the Mercury on the top of the stones, and the Inscriptions, may be worn off by Time,

* Hist Staff p 398
† Gale, Itinerar p [illegible]

In the Garden wall of Sir William Tancred's house at Burrowbridge, is an imperfect Inscription, which seems to have been sepulchral

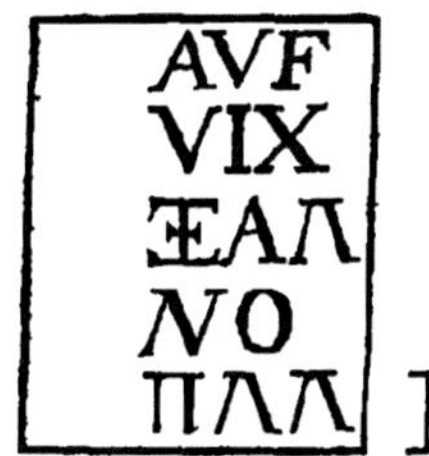

]

Somewhat Eastward from the bridge before-mention'd, stands *Isurium Brigantum*, an ancient city, which took its name from the *Ure* running by it; but has been entirely demolish'd many ages since There is still a Village upon the same spot, which carries Antiquity in its name, being call'd *Ealdburg* and *Aldborrow*, that is to say, *an old Burrough*; where are now few or no signs remaining of a City, the plot thereof being converted into arable and pasture ground, So that the evidence of History itself would be suspected, in testifying this to be the old *Isurium*, if the name of the river *Ure*, the Roman coins continually dug up, and the distance between it and York, according to Antoninus [*viz* sixteen miles] were not convincing and undeniable Proofs

Isurium

Aldborrow

Letters from Mr Morr Minister there

[But to be somewhat more particular in the description of this Place, and the remains of Antiquity they meet with The ancient Town (as appear'd by a late Survey) contain'd within the walls, sixty Acres; being almost a direct square, upon a declining hill towards Ure on the north side Road gate, leading to the old *Cataractonium*, went through it to Milby, and the way through the meadows may yet be discover'd, bearing the name of *Brig-gates*, near half a mile east of the present Bridge Under the South-wall, there seems to have been an old Camp, of about two acres, the only place, on the outside, where Coins are found The old Walls were about four yards thick, founded upon large pebles laid on a bed of blue Clay, four or five yards deep The soil is black; which makes the tradition probable, that it was burnt by the Danes when York was almost destroy'd by them, and also, upon opening the ground, Bones are seen half burnt, with other black Ashes Here have been found also fragments of Aquæducts cut in great stones, and cover'd with Roman tyles; and in the late Civil wars, as they were digging a Cellar, they met with a sort of Vault, leading, as it is said, to the river if it was of Roman work (for it has not yet met with any one curious enough to search it) it might probably be a Repository for the Dead The Coins (generally of brass, but some few of silver) are rarely elder than *Claudius*, yet some there are of *Augustus Cæsar*, and so down to the Antonines, with *Carausius* and *Alectus*, and two of the thirty Tyrants, *viz Posthumus* and *Tetricus*, but those of *Constantine* are most common They meet also with little Roman heads of brass, and have formerly found coin'd pieces of gold, with chains of the same metal; but none of late Here have likewise been found, within the circuit of the old walls, about twenty little polish'd Signet stones, of divers kinds and cuts, particularly one had a horse upon it, and a stamp of Laurel shooting out five branches another, a Roman sitting, with a sacrificing dish in one hand, and resting his other on a spear a third, a Roman (if not *Pallas*) with a spear in one hand, wearing a helmet, and a shield on the back, or on the other arm; and under that something like a quiver hanging to the knee a fourth (of a purple colour) has a Roman head like *Severus* or *Antonine* a fifth, hath the head of Jupiter *Ammon*, a sixth, an *Eagle*, with a Civick Crown in its Bill, a seventh, a winged *Victory* crowning a Trophy Several Pavements have been found about a foot under-ground, and compass'd with stones of about an inch square, but within are little stones of a quarter that bigness, wrought into knots and flowers, after the Mosaick-fashion No Altars are met with, but pieces of Urns and old Glass are common and they have also found several Vessels of red earth, wrought with knots, flowers, heads, birds, and beasts; and lately, a lamp of earth, and a *Cothon* or *Poculum Laconicum*, which the Soldiers did use, in their marches, for clearing of water, by passing it into several Concavities made therein In the Vestry wall of the Church, is plac'd a figure of *Pan* or *Silvanus*, in one rough stone nyched]

6

By that time the *Ure* (which from henceforward the Saxons call'd *Ouse*, because the *Ouseburne*, a little brook, falls into it here) has run sixteen Italian miles further, it arrives at the City *Eboracum* or *Eburacum*, which † Ptolemy calls *Brigantium*, * if the Book be not faulty, and that mistake have not risen from its being the Metropolis of the *Brigantes*, [Spartian, simply and by way of excellency, *Civitas*, a* City;] *Ninnius*, *Caer-Ebrauc*, the Britains *Caer Effroc*, the Saxons Euoꞃ-ꝩic, and Eoꝼoꞃ-ꝩic, [Eoꝼoꞃꝩic-ceaꞅꞇeꞃ, and sometimes simply Ceaꞅꞇeꞃ,] and we at this day, *York* The British History derives the name from the first founder, King *Ebraucus* But with submission to better judgments, my opinion is, that the word *Eburacum* comes from the river *Ure*, implying its situation to be upon that river Thus the *Eburovices* in France were seated by the river *Ure*, near *Eureux* in Normandy, the *Eburones* in the Netherlands, near the river *Ourt*, in the Diocese of *Liege*, and *Eb-lana* in Ireland, by the river *Lefny* York is the second City in England, the finest in this County, and the great defence and ornament to those northern parts It is pleasant, large, and strong, adorn'd with fine buildings (public and private,) populous, rich, and an Archbishop's See The river *Ure*, which now has the name of *Ouse*, runs gently (as I said) from north to south, quite through the City, and divides it into two parts, joyn'd by a Stone bridge, which, among others, has one of the largest Arches I ever saw The west-part of the City, is less populous, and lies in a square form, enclos'd with stately walls, and with the river, and has but one way to it, namely by *Mikell barr*, which signifies a *great Gate*. From whence a long fair-built street on both sides, leads to the very bridge, with fine Gardens behind them, and the fields, for Exercises, extended to the very walls In the south-angle of which, form'd by them and by the river, I saw a mount that has probably been cast up for some Castle to be built there, now call'd the *old Bale*, which *William Melton* the Archbishop (as we find it in the Lives of the Archbishops) *first us'd first with thick planks eighteen foot long, and afterwards with a stone wall*; of which nothing now remains

Eboracum. York

† Lib 2

* Mag Con struct

* Gale Itinerar p 19.

The

The east-part of the City (where the buildings are thick, and the streets but narrow) is shap'd like a lentil, and strongly wall'd On the south east it is defended by a *Foss* or Ditch, very deep and muddy, which runs by obscure ways into the very heart of the City, and has a bridge over it so set with buildings on both sides, that a stranger would mistake it for a street after which, it falls into the *Ouse* At the confluence, over-against the Mount before-mention'd, William the Conqueror built a very strong Castle, to awe the Citizens But this, without any care, has been left to the mercy of time, ever since fortify'd places have grown into disrepute among us, as only fit for those who want courage to face an enemy in the field On this side also, to the north east, stands the *Cathedral*, dedicated to St *Peter*, a magnificent and curious fabrick, near which, without the walls, was a noble Monastery, surrounded with the river and its own walls, nam'd St *Mary*'s This was founded by *Alan* the third, Earl of *Bretaign* in *Armorica* and of *Richmond* here in England, and plentifully endow'd by him, [being valu'd at the Dissolution at above two thousand Pounds] But, † after that, it was converted into a Royal Palace, and is commonly call'd the *Manour*, [and it is now divided into lesser Houses]

Foss river

† Now it is C The Manour

As for the original of York, I cannot tell whence to derive it, but from the Romans, seeing the British towns before the coming in of the Romans were only woods fortify'd with a ditch and rampire, as Cæsar and Strabo (who are Evidences beyond exception) assure us Nor to mention the story of King *Ebraucus* (a word form'd from the name *Eboracum*) who is grossly feign'd and believ'd to be the founder of it, this is certain, that the *sixth Legion*, call'd *Victrix*, and sent out of Germany into Britain by Hadrian, was in garrison here and, that this was a Roman Colony, we are assur'd both by *Antoninus* and *Ptolemy*, and by an old Inscription, which I myself have seen in the house of a certain Alderman of this City

M VEREC VIP COL
EBORIIT MO MORT CIVESBITVRIX
CABVS HAEC SIBI VIVVS FECIT

And also from Severus the Emperor's Coins, which have this Inscription on the reverse,

COL EBORACVM LEG VI VICTRIX

[It seems also plain, that the ninth Legion resided here, from an Inscription upon a funeral Monument for the Standard-bearer thereof, which was found in Trinity-yard in Micklegate, under his Statue in bass-relieve, and is now in the Gardens at Ribston, the seat of the Goodricks

L DVCCIVS
L.VOT. RVFI
NVS. VIEN
SIGN. LEG.VIIII.
AN.XXIIX.
H. S. E.

Philosoph Trans N 305

That this ninth Legion was in Britain in Galba's time, and that it was also call'd *Hispaniensis*, appears from the notes of the Learned Sir *Henry Savil* at the end of his Edition of Tacitus; but that it was still'd *Victrix*, as well as the sixth and twentieth, and that its station was at York, hath no been observ'd before; and yet both are evident from this Inscription upon a Roman brick found there

LEG IX VIC

Philosoph Trans N 305

Other remains of Roman Antiquity have been also discover'd from time to time in this place For (not to mention the *old Arch* in the Bar leading to *Micklestreet*, and several parts of the City walls, and a multangular tower in *Coningstreet*, all of Roman work,) there was lately found, in digging a Cellar in Coningstreet, a Monument dedicated to the *Genius*, or tutelar Deity of the place, which is thus inscrib'd,

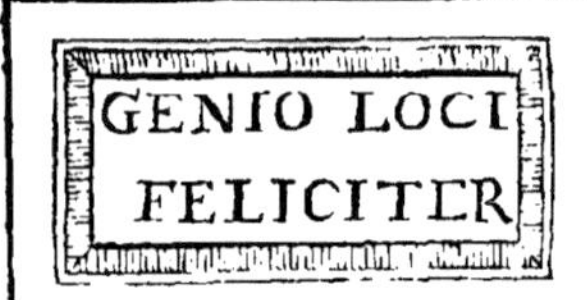

Philosoph Trans N 30

Also, a little without *Boutham Bar*, was the Roman burying place, where have been found considerable numbers of their Urns, with their burnt Bones and Ashes, *bouth*, or *boetham*, being so call'd, probably, from these burnings of the Romans, for *boeth* in British signifies what is *burnt with fire* Here was also dug up an old *Roman Coffin*, of red Clay above fourteen inches long; and a Lead Coffin, seven foot long, inclos'd in a prodigious strong one of Oak Planks, within which, the Bones were entire, though probably inter'd near fifteen hundred years ago, after the Antonines had introduc'd the Custom of *Burying* the dead, instead of *Burning*

Philosoph Trans N 244 296.

In the year 1638 in a house near Bishop-hill, was found this Altar, which is, or lately was, at the Duke of Buckingham's house in York

I O M
DIS DEABVSQVE
HOSPITALIBVS PE
NATIBVSQ OB CON
SERVATAM SALVTEM
SVAM SVORVMQ
P AEL MARCIAN
VS PRAEF COH
ARAM SAC F NCD

In the Church wall, in All Saints-street, is this Monument of *Conjugal Affection*

Philosoph Trans N 145

Not

A
AE AN
S SEC
ENEM
I ANTO
CONVGI

Not many years since, in digging for the foundation of a new house, † were discover'd a great number of *Norman* Coins, mostly of William the Conqueror]

† Phil Transf n 303

The same *Victor* that was lately publish'd by *Andr Scottus*.

Upon what grounds, *Victor*, in his History of the *Cæsars*, calls York a *Municipium*, when it was a Colony, I cannot readily tell, unless the Inhabitants might desire, as the *Prænestines* did, to be chang'd from a Colony to a *Municipium* For Colonies were more obnoxious and servile, being not left to their own Liberty, as Agellius tells us, but govern'd by the Roman Laws and Customs. Whereas, the *Municipia* were allow'd the free use of their own Constitutions, and enjoy'd those honourable offices which the Citizens of Rome did, without being ty'd to any other duties, and therefore it is not strange that a Colony should be converted into a *Municipium*. But to what purpose is this nicety? For the difference between those two words is not always precisely observ'd in the History of the Emperors, but sometimes both *Colonia* and *Municipium* are promiscuously apply'd to one and the same place Yet, from the Coins before mention'd, I dare hardly affirm this Colony to have been planted here by *Severus*, seeing Ptolemy tells us, that in the time of the *Antonines*, this was the station of the sixth Legion However, we read that Severus had his Palace here, and that he dy'd in this city, uttering these words with his last breath, *The Commonwealth was disorder'd in all the parts when I receiv'd it, yet leave I it in peace, even to the* Britains His Corps was also brought out after the Roman manner by the Soldiers, and committed to the flames, and the day was solemniz'd with races by his sons and soldiers, at a certain place below the town, to the west, near *Ackham*, where stands a huge mount, which Radulphus Niger tells us, was, in his time, call'd *Sivers* (as it is also by some at this day) from *Severus* His ashes were preserv'd in a golden Urn, or a vessel of *Porphyrite stone*, which was carry'd to *Rome*, and laid in the monument of the *Antonines* I must not forget to take notice, that there was in this City a Temple dedicated to *Bellona*, for Spartian speaking of the City, says, *That* Severus *coming into it, and intending to offer sacrifice, was first conducted to the Temple of* Bellona *by the mistake of an ignorant Augur* And, that it was then so happy, as to have justice administer'd in it by that great Oracle of the Law, *Æmilius Paulus Papinianus*, Forcatulus has told us From this City, the Emperors *Severus* and *Antoninus*, upon a question arising about the sense of the Law, directed their Rescript *de Re Vindicatione* About a hundred years after the death of Severus, *Flavius Constantius*, surnam'd *Chlorus*, an Emperor endow'd with all moral and Christian Virtues, *came to this City* (as the Panegyrist speaks,) *the Gods calling him hither, as to the remotest part of the world* Here he dy'd likewise, and was afterwards deify'd, as appears by the old Coins And though *Florilegus* tells us, that his Tomb was found in Wales, as I have already observ'd; yet I have been inform'd by credible persons, that at the suppression of Monasteries in the † last age, there was found a Lamp burning in the vault of that little Chapel, wherein *Constantius* was thought to be bury'd *Lazius* tells us, that the ancients had an art of dissolving gold into a fat liquor, and of preparing it so, that it would continue burning in the Sepulchres for many ages Constantius, by his first wife *Helena*, had issue *Constantinus Maximus*, stiled in Inscriptions *Romanæ Urbis Liberator*, *Quietis fundator*, and *Reipublicæ instaurator*, who here receiv'd the last breath of his dying father, and was immediately declar'd Emperor *The soldiers* (as the Panegyrist says) *regarding rather the benefit of the State, than their own private interests, cast the Robes upon him, whilst he wept and spur'd his horse, to avoid the importunity of the army, attempting at that instant to make him Emperor, but at last his modesty gave way to the Happiness of the State* And therefore he exclaims at last, *O fortunate Britain, now bless'd above all Nations for having first seen Constantine Emperor* Again —— *Liberavit ille Britannias servitute, tu etiam Nobiles illic oriendo fecisti* i e *He rescu'd the Britains from slavery, but thou hast ennobled them by being born there* Which passage, in the judgment of the learned *Baronius* and others, refers to the native Country of Constantine But I will not here repeat, what I have † already said

Severus

Bellona's Temple

Constantius Chlorus

Municipium Colonia

† So said, anno 1607

Constantine the Great

† Pag xcii

From all this it may be infer'd, what figure *Eboracum* then made in the world, seeing it was the Seat of the Roman Emperors Our own Historians tell us †, that it was made an Episcopal See by Constantius But that Taurinus the Martyr, Bishop of the *Eburovices* or *Evreux*, presided in this See I am not inclin'd, with others, to believe, since *Vincentius*, by whom they were led into this error, wou'd confute me with his own words When the Romans withdrew themselves, and left Britain a prey to the barbarous Nations; such a large share of those miseries fell upon this City, that towards the end of the Scotch and Saxon wars, it was nothing but the Shadow and Echo of what it had been For when Paulinus preach'd Christianity to the Saxons of this Province, it was reduced so low, that the whole City could not afford so much as a small Church wherein to baptize King *Edwin*, who, in the year 627, rais'd ‖ a fabrick of wood for Divine Service, and, intending after that to build another of stone, he had scarce laid the foundation, but he dy'd, leaving the work to be finish'd by his successor King Oswald From this time, the City began to be great in Ecclesiastical Dignity Pope Honorius sent it a *Pall*, and it was made a *Metropolitan* City; with the *Primacy*, not only over twelve Sees here in England, but over all the Bishopricks of Scotland But Scotland hath disown'd its Prerogative many years since, and itself hath swallow'd up several small inconsiderable Bishopricks hereabouts, so that the whole Province is now reduc'd to the four Sees of *Durham*, *Chester*, *Carlisle*, and *Man* (or *Sodor*) in the Isle of Man Egbert, Archbishop of this See, who liv'd about the year 740, *founded a noble Library here* (these are the words of Malmsbury,) *a Treasury and Cabinet, if I may so express myself, enrich'd with all*

† The truth of this is questiond See Full Hist ann 305

Vincentii *Speculum Historiale*

‖ *Oratorium*

Scotland formerly subject to the Archbishop of York

See in Scotland

The Library

all Arts and Sciences Of which also, Alcuinus of York (who was Tutor to *Charles* the great, and the first Founder of an Academy at Paris, and also the great glory of this City) makes mention in his Epistle to the same *Charles* the great *Give me such excellent and learned Books of Scholastick Divinity, as I have seen in my own Country, collected by the useful and pious industry of Egbert, Archbishop And if it seem good to your Wisdom, I will send some of your own servants, who may copy out of them such things as be necessary, and so transplant the flowers of Britain into France, that this garden may no longer be confin'd to York, but some bing of that Paradise may be brought to Tours*, [where, by the way, Alcuinus dy'd anno 780, and was bury'd in a small Convent appendant to the Monastery of St *Martin*, of which he was Abbot] The Church of York was by the Princes of that time endow'd with many large possessions, especially by *Ulphus* the son of Torage, which I the rather note from an old book, that a strange way of *Endowing* heretofore, may be observ'd *This Ulphus govern'd in the west parts of Deira, and by reason of a difference like to happen between his eldest son and his youngest, about † his Estate after his death, he presently took this course to make them equal Without delay he went to York, and taking with him the Horn, wherein he used to drink, he fill'd it with wine, and kneeling upon his knees before the Altar, bestow'd upon God and the blessed St Peter, Prince of the Apostles, all his Lands and Revenues* This Horn was kept there to the * last age, as I have been inform'd, [and having been lost or stolen, for a long time, it was recover'd by Henry Lord Fairfax, and remains in the Minster at this day]

Flaccus Albinus, or Alcuinus, flourish'd about 780

Bale

† Dominia

* Godwin, ann 1600

It would seem to reflect upon the Clergy, if I should relate the secret emulations and open quarrels which ambition has rais'd between the two Sees of York and Canterbury, whilst, with great expence of money, but more of reputation, they warmly contended for Pre-eminence For (as one relates it) *the See of York was equal in Dignity, though it was the younger, and too eager for a d bishop gra... d to the same power that the See of Canterbury was, and having its Privileges confirm'd by the same Apostolical Authority*, took it very heinously to be made *subject* by the decree of Pope Alexander, which declares, *that the Archbishoprick of* York *ought to yield to that of* Canterbury, *and pay an obedience to her Archbishop, as Primate of all Britain, in all matters relating to Religion* [Which Controversy was determin'd in the time of Archbishop *Thoresby*, anno 1353, at the special solicitation of King Edward the third (who earnestly excited the two Archbishops to Peace and Concord) so as the Archbishops of York might lawfully write themselves *Primates of England*] It falls not within the compass of my design, to treat of the Archbishops of this See, though many of them have been persons of great virtue and piety It is enough for me to observe, that from the year 622, when *Paulinus* the first Archbishop was consecrated, there † succeeded in it threescore and five Archbishops, to the year 1606 In which Dr *Tobias Matthews*, Venerable for his virtue and piety, for his learned eloquence, and for his indefatigable Preaching, was translated hither, from the Bishoprick of Durham, [since which, ten others having been added, raise the number of Archbishops of York to seventy five] The wife of the foresaid Archbishop *Matthews*, a prudent Matron, daughter of Bishop Barlow (a Confessor in Queen Mary's time was a great Benefactress to this Church, bestowing upon it the Library of her husband, which consisted of above three thousand Books She is memorable likewise for having a Bishop to her father, an Archbishop (Matthew Parker of Canterbury) to her father-in-law, four Bishops to her brethren, and an Archbishop to her husband]

† Hobbes

Angl Sacr vol 1 p 71

† Ive fuc wde C

This City flourish'd very much for some time under the Saxon Government, till those Danish storms came from the North, and spoil'd its beauty again, by great ruins and most dismal slaughter Which Alcuin in his Epistle to Egelred King of the Northumbrians seems to have foretold *What (says he) can be the meaning of that shower of blood, which in Lent we saw at York, the Metropolis of the Kingdom, near St Peter's Church, descending with great terror from the roof of the north part of the House in a clear day? May not we imagine that this foreboded destruction and blood among us from that quarter?* For in the following age, when the Danes laid every thing waste, this City was involv'd in very great and very terrible Calamities *In the year 867* the walls of it were so shaken by the many assaults made upon them, that *Osbright* and *Ella* Kings of Northumberland, as they pursu'd the Danes in these parts, easily broke into the City, and after a bloody conflict in the midst of it, were both slain, leaving the victory to the Danes, who had retir'd hither Hence that of William of Malmesbury, *York, ever most obnoxious to the fury of the northern nations, hath sustain'd the barbarous assaults of the Danes, and groan'd deeply under the miseries which it hath suffer'd* But, as the same Author informs us, King Athelstan took it from the Danes, and demolish'd that castle with which they had fortify'd it Nor in after-ages was it quite deliver'd from the calamities of War, in that age especially, which was so noted for the subversion of Cities

But the Normans, as they put an end to these miseries, so they almost brought destruction to York For when the sons of Sweyn the Dane arriv'd here with a fleet of two hundred and forty sail, and landed hard by, the Normans, who kept garrison in two castles in the City, fearing lest the houses in the suburbs might be serviceable to the enemy for filling up the trenches, set them on fire, which being so encreas'd and dispers'd by the wind, that it presently spread over the whole City, and set it all on fire In this distraction, the Danes took the town, putting many of the People to the sword, and reserving *William Malet* and *Gilbert Gant*, two principal men, to be *Decimated* among the soldiers afterwards For every tenth prisoner of the Normans on whom the lot fell, was executed Which so exasperated William the Conqueror, that (as if the Citizens had sided with the Danes) he cut them all off, and set the City again on fire and (as Malmesbury says) *so spoil'd all the adjacent territory, that a fruitful Province was become a prey, and the country for sixty miles together lay so much neglected, that a stranger would have lamented the sight (considering its once fine cities, high towers, and rich pastures,) and no former inhabitant could so much as know it* The ancient grandeur of the place may appear from Domesday book *In the time of Edward the Confessor, the City of York contain'd six Shires or Divisions, besides the Shire of the Archbishop One was wasted for the castles, in the five remaining Shires there were one thousand four hundred and seventy eight houses inhabited, and in the Shire of the Archbishop two hundred houses inhabited* After all these Overthrows, *Neckam* sings thus of it

Ord of Vit in the ... of ... Raleigh, Treatise of England

\ Decimation

Visito quam fælix Ebraucus condidit urbem,
Petro se debet Pontificalis apex,
Civibus hæc toties viduata, nov sque repleta,
Diruta prospexit mœnia sæpe sua
Quid manus hostilis queat, est experta fre quenter,
Sed quid? nunc pacis otia longa fovent.

There happy *Ebrauk's* lofty towers ap pear,
Which owe their mitre to St *Peter's* care
How oft in dust the hapless town hath lain?
How oft its walls hath chang'd? how oft it's men?
How oft the rage of sword and flames hath mourn'd?
But now long peace, and lasting joy's re turn'd

For in his days, these troublesome times be ing follow'd with a long and happy peace, it began to revive, and continu'd flourishing, tho' often mark'd out for destruction by our own Rebels, and the Scots Yet in King Stephen' time, it suffer'd extremely by a casual fire, which burnt down the *Cathedral*, St *Mary's* Monastery, and other *Religious* houses, and al so, as it is suppos'd, that excellent Library which *Alcuin* tells us was founded by his Ma ster Archbishop Egbert The Monastery of St Mary did not lie long, till it rose again to its former splendor; but the Cathedral lay neglected till King Edward the first's time, and then it was begun by *John Roman*, Treasurer of this Church, and brought to that beautiful Fabrick we now see it, by his son *John*, *William Melton*, and *John Thoresby*, all Archbishops, together with the contributions of the Gentry thereabouts Especially of the *Percies* and the *Vavasors*, as the Arms of those families in the Church, and their portraictures in the gate, do shew, the *Percies* with a piece of timber, and the *Vavasors* with a stone, in their hands; in memory of the one's having contributed *stone*, and the other *timber*, to this new Fabrick [Archbishop *Thoresby* was a very great benefactor to it, and on the 29th of July 1361 laid the first stone of the new Quire, to which, at sixteen payments, he gave so many hundred pounds, besides many other less sums for particular uses, towards carrying on that work As he was Archbishop of York, so was he also Lord Chancellor of England, and Cardinal (which I the rather take notice of here, because he is omitted by *Onuphrius*,) as the Inscription of his seal testifies *S Jobis tit Sci P ad vincula Presbyteri Cardinalis*]

Spelm Glof in Cancellarius

Comment Pii P P lib 1

This Church (as we are told by the Author of the Life of *Æneas Silvius*, Pope *Pius* the se cond, as he had it from the Pope's own mouth) *is famous for its wonderful magnificence and workmanship, and for a lightsome Chapel with glaz'd walls united by small thin wasted pillars* This is the beautiful Chapter house, where the following verse is written in golden Letters

Ut Rosa flos florum, sic est Domus ista Domorum

The chief of Houses, as the Rose of flowers

[The dimensions of this Cathedral were exactly taken by an ingenious Architect, and are as follows

	Feet.
Length beside the buttresses	524 ½
breadth of the east-end	105
breadth of the west-end	109
breadth of the Cross from north to south	222
breadth of the Chapter-house	58 ½
height of the Chapter house to the Canopy	86 ½
height of the body of the Minster	99
height of the Lanthorn to the Vault	188
height to the top-leads	213]

About the same time, the Citizens began to fortify themselves with new walls, adding many towers for their further security, and made excellent laws for the government of the City. King Richard the second made it a *County incorporate*, and Richard the third began to raise a new Castle in it, from the ground; [near which, stands the shell of *Clifford's tower*)] and that nothing might be wanting, King Henry the eighth in the † last age establish'd a Council or Senate here, not unlike the Parliaments in France, who were to judge of all Causes arising in these northern parts, and to decide them by the rules of Equity The Court consisted of a President, and what number of Counsellors the King * pleas'd, with a Secretary and Under officers, [but it is now taken away, and entirely abolish'd]

† So said ann 1607 The Council establish'd in the North

Consists, I

* Pleases C

This ancient and noble City might, e're this time, have stood in a more clear and agreeable light, if Sir *Thomas Widdrington*, a person accomplish'd in all Arts, as well as his own Profession of the Laws, after he had written an entire History of it, had not upon some disgust, prohibited the publication The original Manuscript of this History, is, or was lately, in the possession of *Thomas Fairfax* of *Menston* Esquire]

Our Mathematicians have settled the Longitude of York to be 22 degr and 25 scr. the Latitude 54 degr and 10 scr

Thus far we have been describing the west part of this County, and the City of *York*, which neither belongs to this nor any other part of the Shire, but enjoys its own Liberties, and a jurisdiction over the neighbourhood on the west-side, call'd the *Liberty of Ansty* which some derive from *Ancienty*, to denote its Antiquity; and others more probably from the German word *Anstossen*, imp'ying a bound or limit I will conclude what I have said of this City with these Verses written * some time since by *J Jonston* of *Aberdeen*

Ansty

* So said ann 1607

Præsidet extremis Artoæ finibus oræ
Urbs vetus in veteri facta subinde nova,
Romanis Aquilis quondam Ducibusque superba,
Quam post barbaricæ diripuere manus
Pictus atrox, Scotus, Danus, Normannus, & Anglus,
Fulmina in banc Martis detonuere sui
Post diras rerum clades, totque aspera fata,
Blandius aspirans aura serena subit
Londinum *caput est, & regni urbs prima Britanni*;
Eboracum *à primâ jure secunda venit*

O'er the last Borders of the Northern land,
York's ancient Towers (tho' oft made new) command
Of *Rome's* great Princes once the lofty seat,
Till barbarous foes o'erwhelm'd the sinking state

The

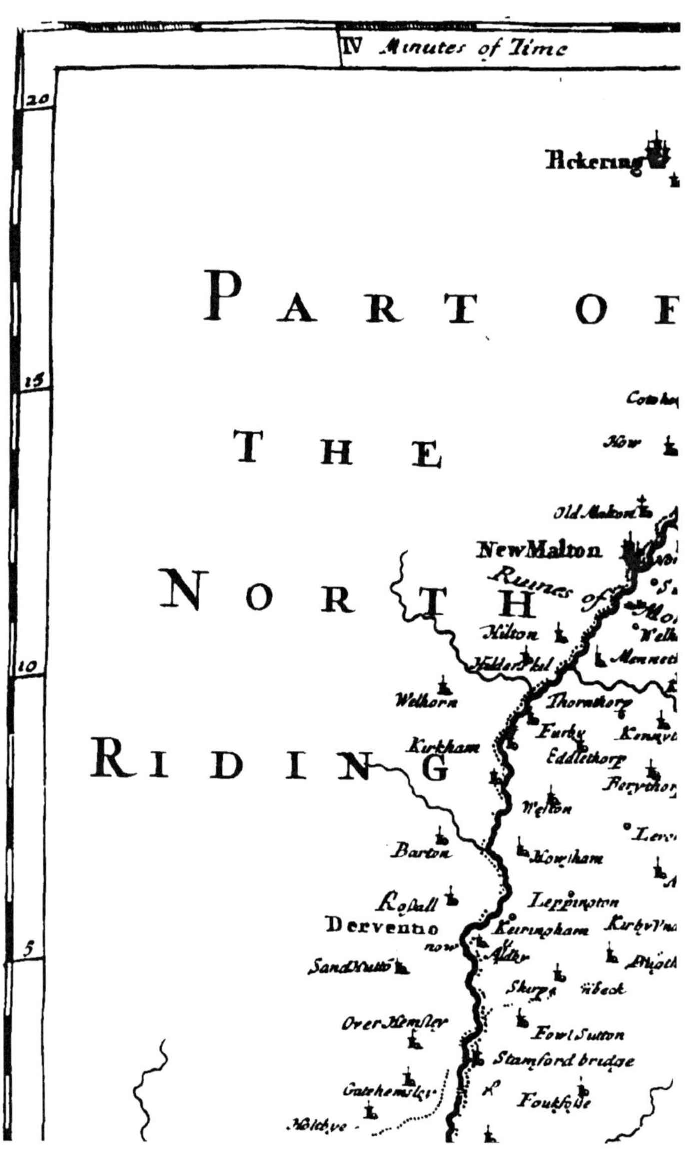

IV Minutes of Time
20
15
10
5
Pickering
PART OF
THE
NORTH
RIDING
New Malton
Old Malton
Runes of
Kilton
Welhorn
Kirkham
Thornthorp
Eddlethorp
Barton
Howsham
Leppington
Derventio
now
Aldby
Sand Hutton
Over Helmsley
Stamford bridge
Fowl Sutton
Foukfolde

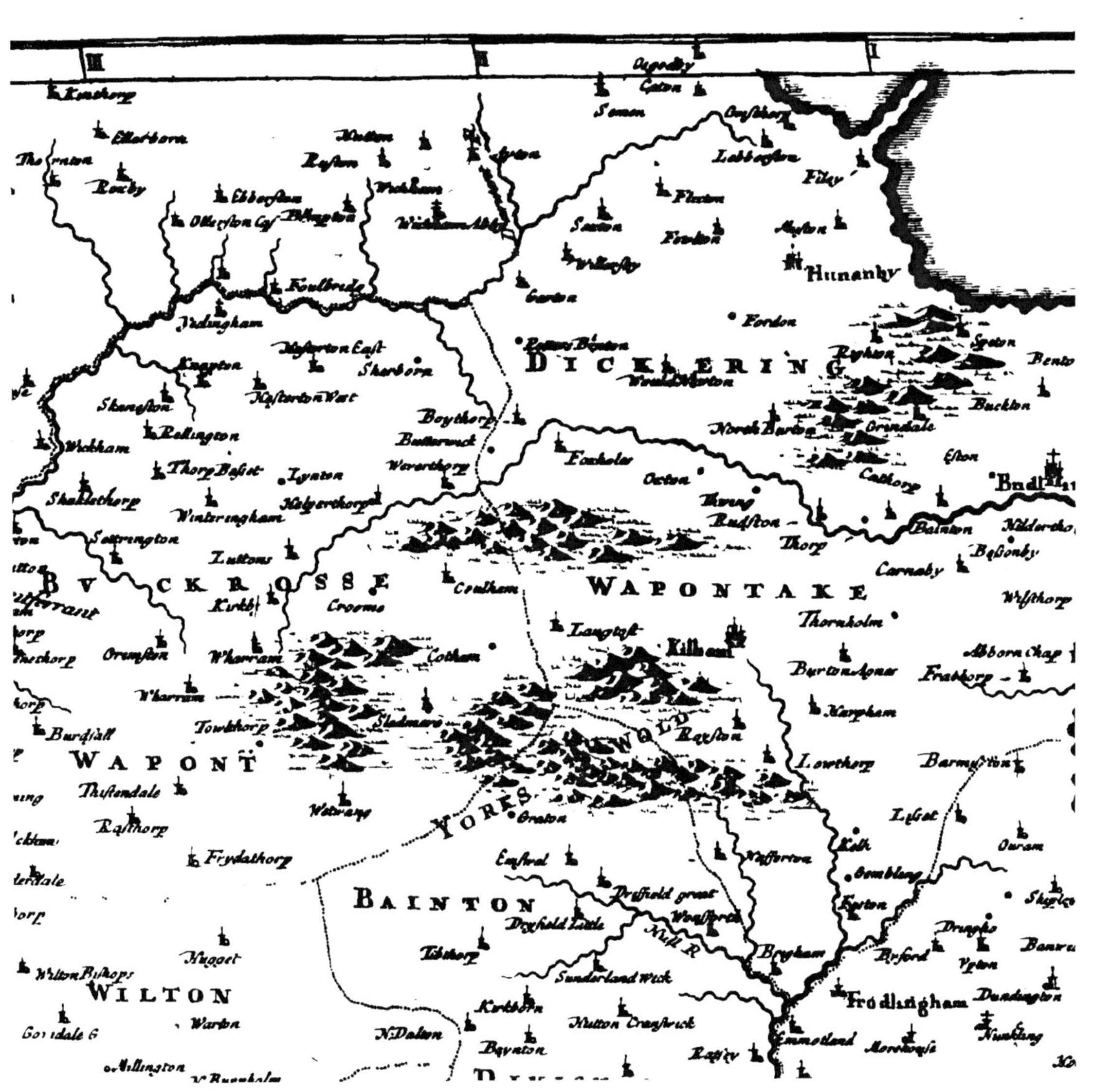

Hunanby
DICKERING
WAPONTAKE
BVCKROSSE
WAPONT
WOLD
YORKS
BAINTON
WILTON
Frodingham
Filey
Fordon
Langtoft
Kilham
Sledmere
Cotham
Brigham
Driffield great
Dryfield Little
Sunderland Wick
Emmotland
Nafferton
Lowthorp
Barmston
Kelk
Carnaby
Thornholm
Bainton
Grindale
Buckton
Boython
Butterwick
Foxholes
Wharram
Towthorp
Thistendale
Frydathorp
Burdsall
Settrington
Wintringham
Rillington
Thorp Basset
Knapton
Wickham
Yedingham
Kirkburn
Tibthorp
Hutton Cranswick
Wilton Bishops
Huggot
Warton
Canton
Fordon
Sherborn
Lebberston
Gunsthorp
Muston
Flixton
Folkton
Willersby
Garton
Reighton
Speton
North Burton
Bridlington
Rudston
Thorp
Bessingby
Wilsthorp
Burton Agnes
Haryham
Lissett
Ouram
Skipsey
Dringho
Brigham
Dunnington
Beswick
Baynton
N.Dalton
Watton
Kirkby
Croome
Cowlam
Ormston
Weaverthorp
Helperthorp
Lutton
Sherborn
Lynton
Wold Newton
Potter Brompton
Ebberston
Allerston
Roxby
Ellerburn
Malton
Wickham Abby

THE
EAST RIDING
of
YORK SHIRE
by
Robert Morden
the Tower
Flamborough
Suerby
GABRANTOVICORUM
Atwick
15
10
5
54

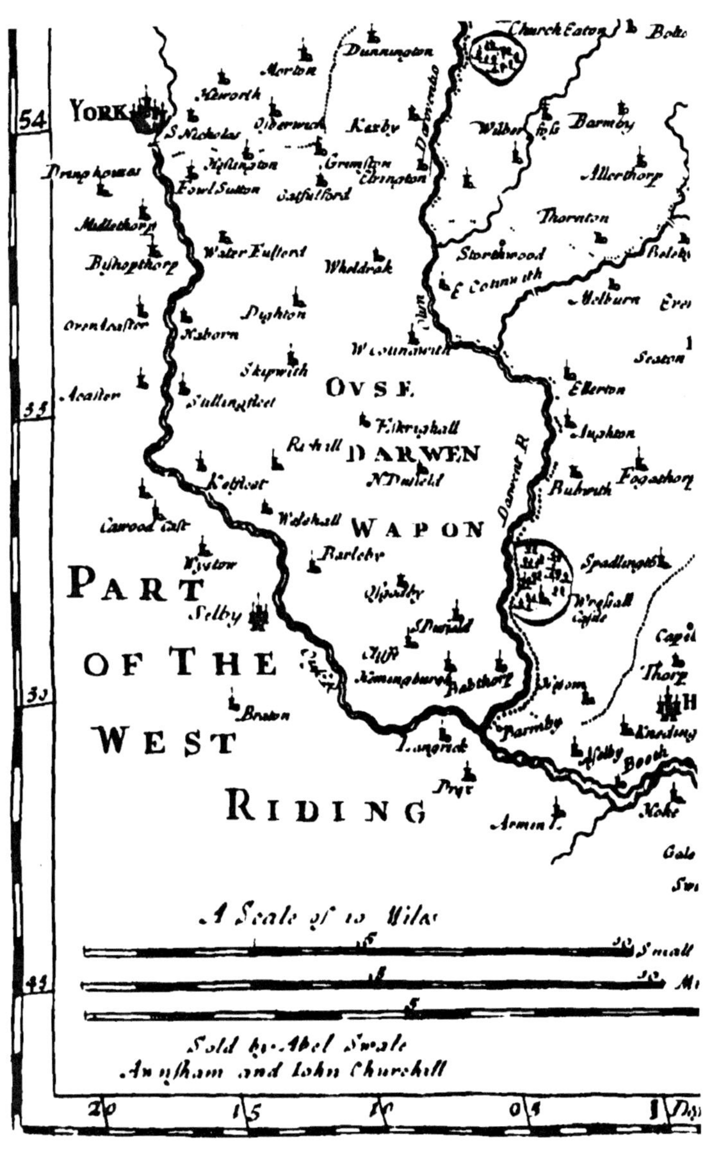

Church Eaton
Dunnington
Morton
Heworth
YORK
S Nicholas
Kexby
Wilberfoss
Barmby
Dringhouses
Fowl Sutton
Allerthorp
Middlethorp
Thornton
Water Fulford
Storthwood
Bishopthorp
Wheldrak
E Cottingwith
Melburn
Dighton
Naborn
W Cottingwith
Seaton
Skipwith
Acaster
Ellerton
OVSE
Stillingfleet
Aughton
Riccall
DARWEN
Kelfleet
Bubwith
Foggathorp
Derwent R
Cawood Cast
WAPON
Barleby
Wistow
Spaldington
PART
Selby
Wresshall Castle
OF THE
Hemingburgh
Babthorp
Breton
Barmby
WEST
Langrick
Asselby
RIDING
Armin
A Scale of 10 Miles
Small
Sold by Abel Swale
Awnsham and Iohn Churchill
54
55
50
45
20
15
10
05

DIVISION
HART HILL
HOLME
WAPONT DIVISION
Pocklinton
Beverly
Wighton ol Delgovitia
HUNSLEY DIVISION
HOLDE
WAPON
Kingston Super Hull
Humber
PART OF LINCOLN SHIRE
Barton
Barrow

Hornsey
Mapleton
Great Hatfield
Wetherwick
Aldborough
Morton
RNES
Humbleton
Sprotley
Garton
Grimstongarth
Hilton
Burtonpidsey
Preston
Rosse
Overthorn
HOLDERNES
Halsham
Thorngumbold
Paulholm
Winsted
Pretorium
now Patrington
Ottringham
Welwick
Norton
Skeffling
Easington
BUS ÆSTVARIUM
Sunk Island
the Den
Grimsby
Ocellum prom now Spurn head
55
50
45

The *Picts*, the *Scots*, *Danes*, *Normans*, *Saxons*, here
Discharg'd the loudest thunder of the War
But this once ceas'd, and every storm o'er-blown,
A happier gale refresh'd the rising Town
Let *London* still the just precedence claim,
York ever shall be proud to be the next in fame

The *Ouse* leaving York, begins here and there to be disturb'd with eddies (that whirl of waters, call'd *Higra*, and so marches by *Bishops-Thorp*, that is, the Bishop's Village; formerly called S *Andrew's Thorpe*, till *Walter Grey* Archbishop of York purchased it, and (to prevent the mischief usually done to Bishop's Lands and Goods by the King's Officers, as oft as any See is vacant,) gave it to the Dean and Chapter of York, upon condition that they should always yield it up to his Successors Of whom, *Richard le S rope*, Archbishop of York (a hot furious man, and a lover of Innovations) was in this very place found guilty of High Treason by King Henry the fourth, for raising a Rebellion

Bishop's Thorp.

1405

[Southward from *York*, is *Nun Apleton*, so call'd from a Nunnery founded there by the Ancestors of the Earls of Northumberland, afterwards it was remarkable for being the seat of *Thomas Lord Fairfax*, General of the Parliament-Army, who merits a memorial here upon account of the peculiar respect he had for Antiquities As an instance whereof, he allow'd a considerable pension to that industrious Antiquary Mr *Dodsworth*, to collect those of this County, which else had irrecoverably perish'd in the late wars For he had but just finish'd the transcripts of the Charters and other Manuscripts then lying in St Mary's tower in York, before the same was blown up, and all those sacred remains mix'd with common dust He preserved the Cathedral at York, when that Garrison was surrender'd to the Parliament; and when * Oxford was in the like state, he took great care for the preservation of the Public Library, and bequeathed to it many Manuscripts, with the Collections aforesaid, which of themselves † amounted to one hundred twenty two Volumes at least]

Nun Apleton

* Fasti Oxon part 2 p 7 8

† Ibid p. 699

Upon the same river *Ouse*, stands *Cawood*, a Castle of the Archbishops, which King Athelstan gave to the Church, as I have been informed Over-against it, on the other side the river, is seated *Rical*, where *Harold Haardread* landed with a numerous Fleet of the Danes. From hence the *Ouse* runs to *Selby*, a pretty populous little town, and famous for the birth of Henry the first Here, William the first, his father, built a Church in memory of St *German*, who extirpated the Pelagian Heresie in Britain; notwithstanding that, Hydralike, it had frequently reviv'd The Abbots of this, and of St *Maries* at York, were the only Abbots of these northern parts who had places in Parliament [Part of the ancient and beautiful Church here, with half of the Steeple, fell down suddenly, in the year † 1690, about six a Clock on the *Sunday morning*, but is since rebuilt] At last the *Ouse* runs to the *Humber*, [leaving *Escricke*, which gave the title of Baron to Sir *Thomas Knevet* He was Gentleman of the Privy Chamber to King James the first, and the Person intrusted to search the Vaults under the Parliament-house, where he discover'd the thirty six barrels of Gun-powder, with the person who was to have fired the train, which Sir *Thomas* dying without issue, the title of Lord *Howard* of *Escrick* was conferred upon Sir *Edward Howard*, son of *Thomas Howard* Earl of *Suffolk*, who had married the eldest daughter and coheir of Sir *Henry Knevet*; and having been enjoy'd successively by his two sons, descended from them to *Charles* his grandson, the present Lord Then it runs] by *Drax*, a little Village, formerly famous for a Monastery, where *Philip de Tollevilla* (*William Newbrigensis* is my Author) had a Castle, strongly situated, in the midst of rivers, woods and marshes, which he, relying on the courage of his men, and the great store of arms and provisions in the place, held against King Stephen; but it was quickly taken and reduced by the King [Here, the benefaction of *Charles Read* Esq; (a native of the place, and a Judge in Ireland) ought not to be omitted, he having erected an Hospital, as also a School house, and endowd them with one hundred Pounds *per Ann*]

Cawood

Rical

Selby

† March 30

Baron of Escricke

Drax

EAST-RIDING.

East Riding, or the east part, where the *Parisi* are seated by Ptolemy, makes the second division of this County; lying East of York The north and west sides of it are bounded by the winding course of the river *Derwent*; the south by the æstuary of *Humber*; and the east by the German Ocean That part of it towards the sea and the river *Derwent*, is pretty fruitful; but the middle is nothing but a heap of Mountains, called *Yorkes wold*, that is, [as some interpret it] *Yorkshire hills*, [and yet *wolb* in Saxon, properly signifies a *large Plain without Woods*] The river *Derventio*, or as we call it *Derwent*, rises near the shore and runs first to the west, but then turns again to the south, and passes by *Aiton*

Fast Riding *Parisi*

Derwent, riv

and *Malton*; which, because they belong to the North-Riding of this County, I shall reserve to their proper places As soon as the river has enter'd this Division, it runs on not far from the remains of that old castle *Montferrant*, which belonged formerly to the *Fossards*, men of great Honour and Estate But *William Fossard* of this family being in ward to the King, and committed to the guardianship of *William le Grosse* Earl of Albemarle, enraged the Earl so, by debauching his sister, though he was then but very young, that in revenge he demolished this castle ['which Leland says, in his time, was clearly defaced, so as bushes grew where it had formerly stood,')] and also forced the noble young Gentleman to forsake his country Yet after the death of the Earl, he recovered his state; and left an only daughter, married to

Montferrant Histor. Meauxensis.

R de

R. de Tornham, by whom ſhe had a daughter, afterwards married to *Peter de Malo-lacu*; whoſe poſterity, being enriched with this eſtate of the *Foſſards*, became very famous Barons. [Of this family *de Malo-lacu* (or as Leland calls them, *Mauley*) there were eight who ſucceſſively enjoyed the Eſtate, all *Peters*, but the laſt of theſe leaving only two daughters, the one was married to *Bygod*, and the other to *Salwayne*, though the Records of the Family of *Fairfax* give us an account ſomewhat different, That *Conſtantia*, daughter of *Peter* the 7th, and ſiſter and co-heir of *Peter de Malo lacu*, the 8th and laſt Baron, was firſt married to *William Fairfax* Eſq, by whom he had iſſue *Thomas*, Anceſtor to the Lords of that name, and after his death to Sir *John Bygod* Knight.]

Kirkham Not far from hence, ſtands a place ſeated upon the bank of the river, called *Kirkham*, i. e. *the place of the Church*, for here was a College of Canons, founded by *Walter Eſpec*, a very great man, whoſe daughter brought a vaſt eſtate by marriage to the family of the *Roſſes*. Next, but ſomewhat lower upon the *Derwent*, there ſtood a city of the ſame name, which Antoninus calls

Derventio *Derventio*, and makes it ſeven miles diſtant from York. The Notitia mentions a Captain over

‖ *Numeri Derventienſis* ‖ the Company of the *Derventienſes* under the General of Britain, that quarter'd here: and in the time of the Saxons it ſeems to have been the Royal Village ſituated near the river *Derventio* (ſays Bede,) where Eumer, that Aſſaſſin (as the ſame Author has it) made a puſh with his Sword at Edwin King of Northumberland, and had run him through, if one of his retinue had not interpos'd, and ſav'd his maſter's life with the lo's of his own. But this place I could never have diſcover'd, without the light which I received from that polite and accurate ſcholar *Robert Marſhall*. He ſhewed me, that at the diſtance from York which I mention'd, there is a little Town ſeated upon the *Derwent* call'd

Auldby *Auldby*, which ſignifies in Saxon, *the old habitation*; where ſome remains of Antiquity are ſtill to be met with, and, upon the top of the hill towards the river, the rubbiſh of an old Caſtle: ſo that this cannot but be the *Derven-*

* Gale Itinerar. p. 24. *tio*. [A late * learned Author makes it alſo the *Petuaria* of Ptolemy, which he ſuppoſes to have been added by him and by the *Notitia* (where they ſpeak of *Peturienſe Derventione*) to diſtinguiſh this from the other *Derventio's*: and, as it appears that neither Ptolemy nor Ravennas, who mention *Petuaria*, do ſay any thing of *Derventio*, ſo it is certain that in Ravennas, this *Petuaria* ſtands in the very place that *Derventio* doth in Antoninus, i. e. between *Eboracum* and *Delgovitia*. And whereas the termination *Varia* always implies a *ford* or *paſs*, it is plain, that there hath been ſuch an one near this *Auldby*.]

From hence the river flows through *Standford bridge*, which from a battel fought there, is alſo call'd [by writers, but not by the common

Battel bridge. Monaſt. Angl. Tom. 1. p. 331. people,] *Battle bridge*. [So we find it named in an Inſtrument concerning the Tranſlation of *Oſwin*; which ſpeaking of this place, adds, *Nunc verò* Pons Belli *dicitur*, i. e. at preſent it is call'd *Pons Belli* or *Battel Bridge*.] For here, Harold *Haardread* the Norwegian (who with a Fleet of two hundred ſail had annoy'd this Kingdom, and from his landing at *Richal* had marched thus far with great outrage and devaſtation) was encounter'd by King Harold of England: who, in a pitch'd battel here, ſlew him and a great part of his army, and took ſo much gold among the ſpoil, that twelve young men could hardly bear it upon their ſhoulders, as we are told by *Adam Bremenſis*. This engagement was ſcarce nine days before the coming-in of William the Conquerour; at which time the diſſolute luxury of the Engliſh ſeems to have foretold the deſtruction of this Kingdom. But of this we have ſpoken already.

The *Derwent* (which, as oft as it is encreas'd with rains, is apt to overflow the banks, and lay all the neighbouring Meadows a-float) In the general Part, ſub tit. *Normans*.

paſſes from hence to *Wreſhil*, a Caſtle neatly Wreſhil built and fortified by *Thomas Percy* Earl of Worceſter, [which deſerves to be remember'd here, not only for its ſtately building, of Square-ſtone (ſaid to be brought from France,) which Leland commends as one of the moſt *proper buildings* north of Trent; but chiefly for a Study in an eight ſquare, called *Paradiſa*, which he found furniſhed with choice Books, and convenient Deſks.] Thence it runs more ſwiftly below *Babthorpe*, which has given both ſeat Babthorpe and name to a famous family of Knights there; and from thence into the *Ouſe*. A father and ſon, both of this family (I muſt not forget to be juſt to their memories, who have been ſerviceable to their King and Country) were ſlain in the battel of St. *Albans*, fighting for Henry the ſixth, and lie buried there with this Epitaph:

Cum patre Radulpho Babthorpe jacet ecce Radulphus
Filius, hoc duro marmore preſſus humo.
Henrici ſexti dapifer, pater Armiger ejus,
Mors ſatis id docuit, fidus uterque fuit.

The two *Ralph Babthorps*, father and his ſon,
Together lie inter'd beneath this ſtone:
One Squire, one Sew'r to our ſixth *Henry* was,
Both dy'd i'th' field, both in their maſter's cauſe.

Now the Derwent, [(for the making of which navigable to the river of Ouſe, an Act of Parliament paſs'd in the firſt year of the reign of Cap. xx. Queen Anne,)] glides on with a larger ſtream near *Howden*, a market-town, remarkable neither for neatneſs nor reſort, but for giving name Howden. to the neighbouring territory, which from it is call'd *Howdenſhire*; and † not long ſince, for a † So ſaid Ann. 1607. little Collegiate Church of five Prebendaries, to which a houſe of the Biſhops of Durham adjoins, who have large poſſeſſions hereabouts. Walter *Skirlaw*, one of them, who flouriſh'd about the year 1390 (as we find in the book of Durham) *built a very tall ſteeple to this Church, that in caſe of a ſudden inundation, the inhabitants might ſave themſelves in it*. [It was formerly call'd *Hovedene*, as is plain from ſeveral Records in the time of Edward the ſecond and Edward the third, as alſo from * Leland's calling the * Itin. MS. firſt Canon of the place *John Hovedene*. Here the bowels of Walter *Skirlaw* Biſhop of *Durham* were bury'd, ‖ as appear'd by the Inſcription on ‖ Ibid. a very fair ſtone *varii marmoris*, as Leland calls it. The ſame perſon had good cauſe to build that high Belfrey, in order to ſecure them againſt Inundations, inaſmuch as the ſeveral Commiſſions which have been iſſu'd out for repairing the banks thereabouts, argue the great danger they were in: and within theſe few years, the Ebb, by reaſon of great freſhes coming down the *Ouſe*, broke through the banks, and did conſiderable damage both to *Howden* and the neighbouring parts. Here, the Londoners

doners keep a Mart every year, beginning about the fourteenth of September, and continuing about nine days; where they furnish, by whole-sale, the Country Tradesmen with all sorts of Goods.]

Metham.

Not far from hence is *Metham*, which gave name and seat to the ancient and famous family of the *Methams*. [Upon the Moors in this neighbourhood, hath been discover'd a Roman Pottery, where their Urns were made, about a mile from the military High-way; and pieces of broken Urns, and cinders, are found up and down there. And at *Youle*, nigh the meeting of Dun and Humber, have been dug up subterraneous Trees, suppos'd to be *Firrs*, which appear, by the remaining roots and other circumstances, to have been natives of the Place.]

Phil. Transf. n. 228

Æstuary of Abus

Humber

The *Ouse*, grown more spacious, runs with a swift and violent stream into the Æstuary *Abus*, the name by which it is express'd in Ptolemy: but the Saxons, and we at this day, call it *Humber*, and from it, all that part of the country on the other side, was in general call'd *Nordan Humbria*. Both names seem to be derivatives from the British *Aber*, which signifies *the mouth of a river*, and was perhaps given to this by way of excellence, because the *Urus* or *Ouse*, with all those streams that fall into it, and many other considerable rivers, discharge themselves here. [But although the *Abus* and the Humber be generally look'd on as one and the same, yet Ptolemy's [illegible] seems to be a corrupt Greek reading of the old name *Ouse*, rather than to have sprung from the British *Aber*. It is plain, however, by that expression, [illegible], i. e. *the emptying of the river Abus*, that he meant, the river had that name before ever it came to the Out-let.] It is, without question, the most spacious Æstuary, and the best stor'd with fish, of any in that Kingdom. At every tide, it flows as the sea does, and at ebb returns its own waters with those borrow'd from the Ocean, with a vast force and noise, and not without great danger to sailors and passengers. Hence Necham:

Fluctibus equoreis Nautis suspectior Humber
Dedignans urbes visere, rura colit.

Humber, whom more than seas the Pilots fear,
Scorning great towns, doth through the country steer.

The same Author, following the British History, as if the Humber deriv'd this name from a King of the Hunns, continues:

Hunnorum princeps ostendens terga Locrino,
Submersus nomen contulit Humbris aquæ.

The Hunne's great Prince by *Locrin*'s arms subdu'd,
Here drown'd, gave name to *Humber*'s mighty flood.

Another Poet also says of the same river:

Dum fugit, obstat ei flumen, submergitur illic,
Deque suo tribuit nomine nomen aquæ.

Here stopt in's flight by the prevailing stream,
He fell, and to the waters left his name.

In Necham's time, there were no Towns upon this Æstuary; though before, and in after-ages, there flourish'd one or two in those parts. In the Roman times, not far from its bank up on the little river *Foulnesse* (where *Wighton*, a small town, but well-stock'd with husbandmen, now stands,) there seems to have formerly stood *Delgovitia*, as is probable both from the likeness and the signification of the name, without drawing any further proof from its distance from *Derventio*. For the British word *Delgwe* [or rather *ddelw*,] signifies the Statues or Images of the Heathen Gods, and in a little village not far off, there stood an Idol-Temple, which was in very great honour even in the Saxon times, and, from the Heathen Gods in it, was then call'd *God mundingham*, and now in the same sense, *Godmanham*. Nor do I question, but here was some famous Oracle, even in the British times, when blindness and ignorance had betray'd all Nations into these superstitions. [A late learned Author thinks it was a Temple of the *Druids*, such as *Weighteburg* in Germany, and that in the wood *Derwald* (which he derives from *Deruen* an Oak), were their Groves.] But after Paulinus had preach'd Christ to the Northumbrians, *Coyf*, who had been a Priest of these heathen Ceremonies, and was now converted to Christianity, first *prophaned this Temple, the House of impiety* (as Bede tell us,) * *by throwing a spear into it, nay destroy'd, and burnt it, with all its † fences*. [But here it is to be observ'd, that proper *cover'd* Temples appear not to have been erected for the service of those Pagan-Idols, which the Saxons here worship'd. *Polluit & destruxit eas, quas ipse sacraverat, ædes*, says the Latin * Bede, speaking of his *Coyf*, (i. e. he polluted and destroy'd the Temple which himself had consecrated,) where the Saxon-Paraphrase uses the word pigbeo, or (as some Copies have it) peopede þæp hƿepenan gylɒep, implying not a *Temple*, but an *Altar*, as is evident from the Saxon Translation of the † Gospels. No, they were only surrounded with a hedge to defend their ditches from the annoyance of cattel, as is sufficiently intimated by another expression in the same Chapter, [illegible], i. e. *with the hedges wherewith they were surrounded*.

Wighton

Delgovitia

Bede

Godmanham

A Temple of the Gods

* Injecta lancea.

† Septis.

* Lib. 2. c. 13.

† Mat. v. 23. xxiii. 18, 19.

Holme

Not far from *Wighton*, is *Holme*, from which the Loyal Sir *Marmaduke Langdale*, had the title of Baron Langdale of Holme, confer'd upon him during the Exile of King Charles the second; being the first Englishman that was advanced to the dignity of a Peer by that Prince. Also *Londesburgh*, in this neighbourhood, gives the title of Baron Clifford of *Lansborough* to the Earl of Burlington, who has here one of the noblest seats in this part of South Britain. Elizabeth, Countess of Burlington (daughter and sole heir of Henry Earl of Cumberland,) founded and endow'd here an Alms-house for twelve aged persons, being decay'd Farmers, &c.]

Londesburg.

Driffeld

Leckenfeld

Garthum

Somewhat more eastward, the river *Hull* runs into the Humber: the rise of it is near a village call'd *Driffeld*, remarkable for the monument of *Alfred*, the most learned King of the Northumbrians; and likewise for the many Barrows rais'd hereabouts. The same river runs with a swift course, not far from *Leckinfield*, a house of the *Percies* Earls of Northumberland; near which, at a place call'd *Scorburg*, is the habitation of a truly famous and ancient family, the *Hotkams*, and at *Garthum*, the ruins of an old castle, which belong'd to P. de *Mauley*.

Beverley

The river Hull begins now to approach *Beverley*, in Saxon Beuer-lega, (which Bede seems to call *Monasterium in Deirwaud*, that is, the Monastery in the *wood of the Deiri*,) a town, large and very populous From its name and situation, one would imagin it to be the * *Petuaria Parisiorum*; though it pretends to nothing of greater antiquity, than that *John* sirnam'd *de Beverley*, Archbishop of York (a man, as Bede represents him, both devout and learned) when, out of a pious aversion to the world, he renounced his Bishoprick, retir'd hither; where, about the year 1721, he died The memory of this man was so sacred among our Kings (particularly *Athelstan*, who honour'd him as his Guardian-Saint after he had defeated the Danes,) that they endow'd this place with many considerable Immunities They granted it the privilege of a *Sanctuary*, to be an inviolable protection to all Debtors, and persons suspected of Capital Crimes Within it stood a Chair of stone, with this Inscription

Petuaria. * Vid Auldby, before

Life of Jo de Beverley

Asylum

HÆC SEDES LAPIDEA Freedstooll DICITUR, i e PACIS CATHEDRA, AD QVAM REVS FVGIENDO PERVENIENS OMNIMODAM HABET SECVRITATEM

That is,

This Stone seat is call'd Freedstool, *i e. the Chair of Peace, to which what Criminal soever flies, has full protection*

By this means, the Town grew to a considerable bigness, strangers throng'd thither daily, and the Towns-men drew a chanel from the river *Hull*, for the conveyance of foreign commodities by boats and barges The Magistrates were first, *twelve Wardens*, which were after that chang'd to *Governors* and *Wardens* But at this day, by the favour of Queen Elizabeth, the Town has a *Mayor* and *Governors* [The place was call'd formerly *Beverlac*, *quasi locus vel lacus* Castorum, à Castoribus *quibus Hulla aqua vicina abundabat* (says Leland * from an old Anonymous Manuscript concerning the Antiquities of *Beverolac* or *Beverley*,) i e from *Castors*, with which that river abounds, and the same Manuscript informs us, that it had a Church before the time of *John* of *Beverley*, dedicated to St *John* the Evangelist; which that Archbishop converted into a Chapel for his new erected Monastery

The river *Hull*

* Vid Monast Angl t. 1 p 170

Sept 13.

In the Year 1664 upon opening a Grave, they met with a Vault of squared free stone, fifteen foot long, and two foot broad at the head, but at the feet a foot and a half broad Within it, was a sheet of lead four foot long, and in that, the ashes, and six beads (whereof three crumbled to dust with a touch; and of three remaining, two were suppos'd to be *Cornelians*) with three great brass pins, and four large iron nails Upon the sheet, lay a leaden Plate, with this Inscription.

+ ANNO AB INCARNATIONE DOMINI MCLXXXVIII COMBVSTA EST HÆC ECCLESIA IN MENSE SEPTEMBRI, IN SEQVENTI NOCTE POST FESTVM SANCTI MATHÆI APOSTOLI ET IN AN MCXCVII VI IDVS MARTII FACTA FVIT INQVISITIO RELIQVIARVM BEATI JOHANNIS IN HOC LOCO, ET INVENTA SVNT HÆC OSSA IN ORIENTALI PARTE SEPVLCHRI ET HIC RECONDITA, ET PVLVIS CEMENTO MIXTVS IBIDEM INVENTUS EST ET RECONDITVS.

In English thus.

In the year of our Lord 1188 this Church was burnt in the Month of *September*, on the night following the Feast of St *Matthew* the Apostle, and the year 1197, on the sixth of the Ides of *March*, Inquisition was made after the Reliques of St *John* in this place, and these bones were found in the east part of the Sepulchre, and were buried here, and there also, Dust mixed with Mortar, was found, and buried

Cross over this, lay a box of lead, about seven inches long, six broad, and five high, wherein were several pieces of bones, mix'd with a little dust, and yielding a sweet smell, as also a knife, and beads All these things were carefully re inter'd in the middle Alley of the body of the Minster, where they were taken up. But a *Seal*, which was also found therein, was not re-inter'd with the rest, but came into the possession of a † private hand Which account agrees not with what Bishop *Godwin* has left us about this Saint, namely, that he was bury'd in the Church-porch For though what is mention'd in the Inscription was only a *Re interment* upon the Inquisition made, yet it looks a little strange, that they should not lay the Reliques in the same place where they found them unless we solve it this way, that but part of the Church was then standing, and they might lay him there with a design to remove him when it should be rebuilt, but afterwards either neglected or forget it

† Marmaduke Nelson

The *Minster* here, is a very fair and neat Structure, and the roof, an arch of Stone In it, are several Monuments of the *Percies* Earls of Northumberland, who have added a little Chapel to the Quire, in the window whereof are the Pictures of several of that family, drawn in the glass At the upper end of the Quire, on the right side of the Altar place, stands the *Freed-stool* beforementiond, made of one entire stone (said to have been remov'd from *Dunbar* in Scotland,) with a Well of water behind it. At the upper end of the body of the Church, next the Quire, hangs an ancient Table with the pictures of St *John* (from whom the Church is nam'd) and of King *Athelstan* the founder of it and, between them, this Inscription;

As fre make I the,
As hert may thynke,
Or eyh may see

Hence, the Inhabitants of *Beverley* pay no Toll or Custom in any Port or Town in England; to which Immunity (I suppose) they owe in a great measure their riches and flourishing condition For indeed, one is surpris'd to find so large and handsome a Town within six miles of *Hull* In the body of the Church stands an ancient Monument, which they call the *Virgins Tomb*, because two Virgin sisters lie buried there, who gave the Town a piece of Land, into which any Free man may put three milch kine from *Lady day* to *Michaelmas* At the lower end of the body of the Church, stands a fair large Font of Agate stone Near the *Minster*, on the south side, is a place named

Hall garth,

Hall-garth, wherein they keep a Court of Record call'd *Provost's Court*. In this, may be try'd *Causes for any Sum*, arising within its *Liberties*, which are very large, having about a hundred towns and parts of towns in *Holderness* and other places of the *East-Riding* belonging to it. It is said to have also a *Power* in Criminal Matters, though at present that is not us'd. But to come to the condition of the Town. It is above a mile in length, being of late much improv'd in its buildings, and has pleasant Springs running quite through it. It is more especially beautified with two stately Churches, and has a Free-school, that is improv'd and encouraged by two Fellowships, six Scholarships, and three Exhibitions in St. John's College in Cambridge, belonging to it, besides six Alms-houses, the largest whereof was built by the Executors of *Michael Wharton* Esq; who by his last Will left one thousand Pounds for that use. The Mayor and Aldermen (having sometimes been deceiv'd in their choice) admit none into their Alms-houses, but such as will give Bond to leave their effects to the poor when they die: which is mention'd here, as a good example to other places.

The principal Trade of the Town, is, making of Malt, Oat-meal, and Tann'd-leather; but the poor people mostly support themselves by working of *Bone-lace*, which of late has met with particular encouragement, the children being maintain'd at School, to learn to read, and to work this sort of lace. The Cloth trade was formerly follow'd in this Town,

† Itin. MS.

but † *Leland* tells us, that even in his time it was very much decay'd. They have several Fairs; but one more especially remarkable, beginning about nine days before Ascension, and kept in a Street leading to the Minster-garth call'd *Londoner street*. For then the Londoners bring down their Wares, and furnish the Country Tradesmen by whole-sale.

About a mile from *Beverley* to the east, in a Pasture belonging to the Town, is a kind of Spaw; tho' they say it cannot be judg'd by the taste whether or no it comes from any Mineral. Yet, taken inwardly, it is a great dryer, and being wash'd in, it dries scorbutick scurf, and all sorts of scabs, and also, very much helps the King's Evil.]

Regist. Mon. de Meaux.

More to the east, flourish'd *Meaux Abbey*, so nam'd from one *Gamell* born at *Meaux* in France, who obtain'd the Place of William the Conqueror for a Seat. Here *William le Gross*, Earl of Albemarle, founded a Monastery for Monks of the Cluniack Order, to compound for a vow which he had made, to go in pilgrimage to Jerusalem. Somewhat lower, stands

Cottingham.

Cottingham, a long Country town, where are the ruins of an old Castle, built (with King John's

Estotevill.

permission) by Robert *Estotevill*, who was descended from Robert *Grundebeofe* a Norman Baron, and a man of great note in those times, whose estate came by marriage to the Lords de *Wake*, and afterwards by a daughter of *John de Wake* to Edmund Earl of Kent, from whom descended *Joan*, wife to Edward the warlike Prince of Wales, who defeated the French in so many Engagements. The river *Hull*, about six miles from hence, falls into the Humber. Just at its mouth, stands a Town, call'd from it

Kingston upon Hull.

Kingston upon Hull [in all writings of concernment,] but commonly, *Hull*. The Town is of no great antiquity; for King Edward the first, whose royal virtues deservedly rank him

Plac. an. 44 Ed. 3 Libor 14.

among the greatest and best of Kings, having observ'd the advantagious situation of the place (which was first call'd *Wik*) obtain'd it, by way of exchange, of the Abbot *de Meaux*; and instead of the *Vaccaries* and *Bercaries* (that is, as I apprehend, *Cribs for Cows* and *Sheepfolds*) which he found there, he built the Town call'd *Kingston*, that is, the *King's Town*, and *there* (as the words of the Record are) *he made a harbour and a free burgh, making the inhabitants of it free burgesses, and granting them divers liberties*. [The walls, and town ditch were made by leave from King Edward the second, but Richard the second gave them the present harbour. In the 33d year of King Henry the eighth, a special Act of Parliament passed concerning the privileges of *Kingston upon Hull*; and in the 37th year of the same Prince, it was by Act of Parliament also erected into an *Honour*, and in the 9th year of King William, the inhabitants were enabled, by the same Authority, to erect work-houses, and houses of Correction, for the employment and maintenance of their poor.]

Cap. 33. Cap. 18. Cap. 47.

By degrees it has grown to such a Figure, that for stately buildings, strong forts, rich fleets, resort of merchants, and plenty of all things, it is the most celebrated Mart-town in these parts. All this increase is owing, partly to *Michael de la Pole*, who, upon his advancement to the Earldom of Suffolk by King Richard the second, procur'd them their privileges, and partly to their trade of *Iseland fish* dry'd and harden'd, and by them call'd *Stock fish*, which has strangely enrich'd the Town. Immediately upon this their rise, they fortify'd the place with a brick wall and many towers on that side where they are not defended by the river; and brought in such a quantity of stones for ballast, as was sufficient to pave all the parts of the Town very beautifully. As I have been inform'd by the Citizens, they were first govern'd by a *Warden*, then by *Bailiffs*, and after that by a *Mayor* and *Bailiffs*, and at last they obtain'd of Henry the sixth, that they should be govern'd by a *Mayor* and *Sheriff*, and that the City should be a County *incorporate* of it self. Concerning the first Mayor, let it not be tedious to relate this passage, from the Register of the Abbey *de Melsa* or *de Meaux*, tho' the stile be barbarous. *William de la Pole, Knight, was first a Merchant at Ravens rod, skilful in the arts of trade, and inferior to no English Merchant whatever. Afterwards, living at King-ston upon Hull, he was the first Mayor of that Town, and founded the Monastery of St. Michael, which now belongs to the Carthusian Monks, near the said Kingston. His eldest son Michael de la Pole, Earl of Suffolk, caus'd the said Monastery to be inhabited by that Order. William de la Pole aforesaid lent King Edward many thousand pounds of gold, during his abode at Antwerp in Brabant. In consideration whereof, the King made him chief Baron of his Exchequer, gave him by Deed the Seigniory of* Holderness, *with many other Lands then belonging to the Crown, and made him a Baneret.* If any one question the truth of this, the Records of the Tower will, I hope, satisfy him: there, it is expresly, William *de la Pole dilectus, valectus, & mercator noster*. Now *Valectus* (that I may observe it once for all) was then an honourable title both in France and England, but afterwards came to be apply'd to servants; upon which, the Nobility dislik'd it, and the title was changed, and he was call'd Gentleman of the Bed-chamber. It is a Town, as hath been said, very considerable for Merchandise (being the Scale of trade to *York*, *Leeds*, *Nottingham*, *Gainsborough*, and several other places) as also for importing goods from beyond sea. And (to speak now of

Stock fish. Coblestones. De la Pole. Cl. 5 R. 2 m. 8. Valectus or Valettus, Talius.

of its more modern improvements) they have, for the better convenience of managing their Trade, an Exchange for Merchants, built in 1621, and much beautify'd in 1673 Above that, is the *Custom house*, and near these the *Wool house*, made use of formerly, without all doubt, for the selling and weighing of Wool, as well as Lead; but now only for the latter, when it is to be sold or ship'd here On the east-side of the river, is built a strong Citadel, begun in the year 1681, and including the Castle and south Block house It hath convenient Apartments for lodging a good many Soldiers, with distinct houses for the Officers; it has also an engine for making salt-water fresh, and is well furnish'd with Ordnance But yet the strength of the Town consists not so much in it's walls or fortifications, as it's situation for all the Country being a perfect level, by cutting the sea-banks they can let in the flood, and lay it under water five miles round

The Town hath two Churches, one call'd *Trinity* (or the *High Church*) a very spacious and beautiful building, on the south side of the Quire whereof is a place now alter'd from a Chapel into a neat Library, consisting mostly of modern Books For before the Reformation, it had twelve Chantries or private Mass Chapels on the north and south-sides of the Quire, and at the west end of the Church yard, is a row of houses, twelve in number, which to this day retains the name of *Priest-row* The other Church is St *Mary* (or *Low-Church*) supposed to have been the Chapel Royal, when King Henry the eighth resided here, and the Steeple whereof the same Prince is said to have order'd to be pull'd down to the ground, because it spoiled the prospect of his house over
Ann 1538 against it, wherein he had his residence for some months, but it is now of late rebuilt, at the charge of the Inhabitants Near the *High Church*, is the Free school, first founded by *John Alcock* Bishop of Worcester, and then of Ely; and in the year 1583 built by Mr *William Gee* with the *Merchants Hall* over it North-west of the said Church, is the *Trinity house*, begun at first by a joint contribution of well dispos'd Persons, for the relief of distressed Sea men and their wives But afterwards, a Patent was obtain'd from the Crown with several privileges, by the advantage of which they maintain many distressed Sea men, with their widows, both at *Hull*, and other places, members of the Port of *Hull* The Government consists of twelve elder brethren, with six Assistants out of the twelve, by the majority of them and of the six Assistants, and the younger brethren, are annually chosen two Wardens; and two Stewards out of the younger brethren These Governours have a power to determine matters, in Sea Affairs, not contrary to Law, chiefly between Masters and Sea-men; and also in Tryals at Law, in Sea-Affairs, their judgments are much regarded But here, take an accurate description of this House, as it was
* Mr Ray given by a curious and ingenious * Person, who actually view'd it 'The *Trinity House* 'belongs to a Society of Merchants, and is endow'd with good revenues. There are maintain'd thirty poor Women call'd *Sisters*, each 'of whom hath a little chamber or cell to live 'in. The building consists of a chapel, two 'rows of chambers beneath stairs for the 'sisters, and two rooms above stairs; one, in 'which the brethren of the Society have their 'meetings; and another large one, wherein 'they make Sails, with which the Town drives 'a good trade In the midst of this room, 'hangs the effigies of a native of *Greenland*, 'with a loose skin-coat upon him, sitting in a 'small boat or *Canoe* cover'd with skins; and 'having his lower part under deck. For the 'boat is deck'd or cover'd above with the same 'whereof it is made, having only a round hole 'fitted to his body, through which he puts 'down his legs and lower parts into the boat. 'He had in his right hand (as I then thought) 'a pair of wooden oars, whereby he rowed 'and managed his boat, and in his left, a dart, 'with which he struck fishes But it appearing by the Supplement to the *North-East* '*Voyages* lately publish'd, that they have but '† *one* oar about six foot long, with a paddle six † This had but one long Oar, which was broken.
'inches broad at either end, I am inclin'd to 'think, that, the boat hanging so high, I 'might be mistaken The same Book hath 'given us an account of their make, to which 'I refer you This, on his forehead had a 'bonnet, like a trencher, to fence his eyes from 'sun or water Behind him lay a bladder or 'bag of skins, in which I suppose he bestow'd 'the fish he caught Some told us, it was a 'bladder full of oyl, wherewith he allured the 'fish to him This is the same individual '*Canoe* that was taken in the year 1613 by '*Andrew Barker*, with all its furniture, and the 'boat-man The Groenlander that was taken, 'refus'd to eat, and dy'd within three days after I have since seen several of these boats 'in publick Town houses and Cabinets of the '*Virtuosi* Here, I cannot but reflect upon and 'admire the hardiness and audaciousness of 'these petty water-men, who dare venture out 'to sea single in such pitiful vessels as are not 'sufficient to support much more than the 'weight of one man in the water, and which 'if they happen to be overturn'd, the rower 'must needs be lost And a wonder it is to 'me, that they should keep themselves upright, 'if the sea be ever so little rough It is true, 'the dashing of the waves cannot do them 'much harm, because the *Canoe* is cover'd 'above, and the skin coat they have upon them 'keeps off the water from getting in at the 'round hole, receiving and encompassing their 'body

A little above the bridge (which consists of fourteen arches, and goes over into *Holderness*) stands the *Greenland house*, built in the year 1674 at the joint charge of several Merchants; but by reason of the bad success of that trade, it is now only employ'd for the laying up of corn and other merchandise At a little distance from this, is *God's house*, which, with God's house
the Chapel over-against it to the north, was pull'd down in the late Civil wars, for preventing inconveniences when the Place was besieg'd But now both are built again, and the house is enlarg'd; and the Arms of the *De la Poles*, being found among the rubbish cut in stone, are now set over the door, with this Inscription, *Deo & pauperibus posuit D Michael de la Pole A D* 1384 i. e Michael de la Pole founded this for God and the Poor, A D 1384 The Chapel over against it is built on the old foundation, with this Inscription over the door; *Hoc sacellum Deo & pauperibus posuit D Mich de la Pole An Do* 1384 *quod ingruente bello civili dirutum* 1643 *tandem auctius instauratum fuit* 1673 *Ricardo Kitson S T B Rectore domus Dei super Hull*, i e Michael de la Pole built this Chapel for God and the Poor A D 1384, which, at the beginning of the Civil wars

Ann.

Ann 1643 was pull'd down, but rebuilt in a more stately manner Ann 1673 Richard *Kitson*, S T B being Rector of God's-house above Hull Near this Chapel, to the east, is built a new Hospital for the better reception of the poor belonging to this house, the other being not large enough to contain all the poor, together with the Master and his family This new one hath over the door, *Deo & pauperibus posuit Michael de la Pole Hæc omnes reparata domus perduret in annos W Ainsworth, Rector, An Dom 1663* i e Michael de la Pole built this for God and the Poor Being thus repair'd, may it for ever stand W Ainsworth, Rector, A. D 1663

Without the walls, westward of the town, stands the *Water house*, which at first came from *Julian-Well*, it appearing by an Inquisition made in the 3d of Henry the fourth, that the drawing a new *Sewer* from thence to the town through the meadows and pastures of *Anlabie*, would be no damage to the King or any other person But in the latter end of the said King's reign, upon a motion to supply the town from thence, it was consider'd, that part of the spring descending from the Priory of *Haltemprise*, it could not be done without licence from the Pope, and so the Grant thereof was seal'd to the town from Rome in the year 1412 under the hands and seals of three Cardinals After ward, the course of that spring altering, and running into the grounds of Sir *John Barrington*, the town was forc'd to come to a composition with him

The Mayor of this town hath two swords, the one given by King Richard the second, and the other, which is the larger, by King Henry the eighth, yet but one is born before him at a time also a Cap of maintenance, and another Ensign of honour, viz an Oar of *Lignum vitæ* wood, which is a badge of his Admiralty with in the limits of the Humber The Poor are extraordinarily provided for in this place there being several considerable Hospitals erected by private Benefactors, besides the two famous ones of *Trinity* and *Charter-house*

The town hath given the honourable title of Earl to *Robert Pierpoint* of *Holme*, Viscount *Newark*, created July 25 4 Car 1 who was succeeded by *Henry* his son, created also Marquis of Dorchester, March 25 1645 during life only Which Henry, dying without issue male, was succeeded in the Earldom, by Robert Pierpoint, son of Robert, the son of William Pierpoint of *Thoresby*, who dying unmarry'd, left this honour to William his brother and heir, and he also dying without issue, it descended to *Evelyn* his brother, who hath been further advanced to the higher Honours of Marquis of Dorchester, and Duke of Kingston]

From Hull, a large promontory shoots out into the Sea, call'd by Ptolemy *Ocellum*, and by us at this day *Holderness* A certain Monk has call'd it *Cava Deira*, that is to say, *the hollow County of the Deiri*, in the same sense that *Cœlosyria* is so call'd, that is, the *hollow Syria* [It hath afforded the title of Earl, first to *John Ramsey* Viscount *Haddington*, created Dec 30 18 Jac 1 who dying without issue, the title was confer'd Jan 24 1643 upon Prince *Rupert* Count Palatine of the Rhine Since which time, the right honourable *Conyers D'Arcie* hath been created Earl of *Holderness*, in which title he was succeeded by *Robert* his grandson The true ancient writing of the name is Holdern-nesse, as much as to say, *the promontory of Holderne*, so call'd to distinguish it from Deira- *palo*, now the *Wolds* Though, after all, the Country may seem rather to have had this name of distinction given it from the river *Hull*, which passes through it, than (as *Holland*, both in Lincolnshire, and beyond sea) from *hol*, *cavus* or *hollow* The Seigniory of *Holderness* belongs to the right honourable *Robert* Viscount *Dunbar*; and the town of *Hedon* finds him a prison for those who are taken in the Liberty of Holderness, till they can be sent to the Castle of York The same town finds him a Hall, wherein he holds a Court call'd *Wapentak Court*, for tryal of Actions under forty shillings]

Ocellum Holderness

The first place we come to, on a winding shore, is the fore mention'd *Headon*, which formerly (if we believe fame, that always magnifies) was a very considerable place for merchants and shipping For my part, I have faith enough to believe it [(there being the remains of two Churches, besides the one which they still have,)] notwithstanding it is now so decay'd (partly by its nearness to Hull, and partly because the Harbour is block'd up) that it has not the least shew of the grandeur it pretends to have had, which may teach us, that the condition of Towns and Cities is every jot as unstable as that of Men King John granted to Baldwin *Earl of Albemarle and Holderness*, [illegible] *free burgage* [illegible], *so that the Burgesses might hold* [illegible] *by the same customs with York and* [illegible] [In St Nicolas, Austin's, the present Church, are the pictures of a *King* and a *Bishop*, with this Inscription much the same as that, which we meet with at *Beverley*,)

Headon

Als free make I thee,
As heart may think or eigh fe]

At this present, the Town begins to flourish again, and has some hopes of attaining by degrees its former greatness [The old Haven nigh the town, being grown up, there is a new cut made on the south east, which helps to scowre that part of the Haven now left, but without any hopes of rendring it so useful as formerly it was In the year 1656 a great part of the Town was consum'd with fire, and not many years since, several houses in the market-place suffer'd the same fate but now the greatest part is rebuilt, and the town thereby render'd much more beautiful Of late years they have grown in wealth more than formerly, which is suppos'd to be owing principally to the several Fairs procur'd for them The Inhabitants have a tradition, that the Danes destroyed this town, and there is a Close belonging to it, call'd *Dane field* to this day]

Somewhat farther on the same Promontory, stands an ancient Town call'd *Prætorium* by Antoninus, but by us, *Patrington*, as the Italians call'd *Patrecina* from the Town *Prætorium* That I am not mistaken here, the distance from *Delgovitia*, and the name still remaining, do both shew; which also seems to imply, that this is the * *Petuaria* that is corruptly so call'd in the Copies of Ptolemy, for *Prætorium* But whether it took the name from the *Prætorium*, which was then Court of Justice, or from some large and stately edifice (for such all the Romans call'd *Prætoria*) does not appear [Besides these two [illegible] of *Prætorium*, there is a third, which [illegible] the most probable reason why Antoninus should call our Patrington *Prætorium* [illegible] *in their ordinary encampments*, in which [illegible] the most learned

Prætorium Patrington

* Vid [illegible]

5

† De Milit. Rom. lib. 5. p. 40, 41.
* Gale, Itin. p. 20.

learned † *Lipsius* has shown it to be us'd And this may seem to some more agreeable to the Roman affairs in Britain, than either of the other two significations, but * a late judicious Author still believes it most probable, that it was a Place where Justice was done between Merchant and Merchant]

The Inhabitants boast of their antiquity, and of the former excellence of their harbour, nor may they less glory in their situation, having a very pleasant prospect on one side, as looking toward the Ocean, and on the other, as surveying the *Humber* and the shores about it, together with the green skirts of Lincolnshire The Roman way from the Picts wall, which Antoninus the Emperor first trac'd out, ends here So Ulpian tells us, that High ways of that kind do end at the sea, or at a River, or at a City Somewhat lower stands *Winsted*, the Seat of the *Hildeards*, Knights and a little higher, *Rosse*, which gave both name and seat to that famous race of Barons *de Rosse* and upon the sea, *Grimston garth*, where the *Grimstons* long flourish'd At a little distance from hence, stands *Rise*, formerly the seat of those Noble men, who were call'd *de Faulconberge* On the very tip of this Promontory, where it draws most towards the Point, and is call'd *Spurnhead*, stands the little village *Kellnsey*, which name shews plainly that this is the *Ocellum* in Ptolemy for as *Kellnsey* comes from *Ocellum*, so without doubt *Ocellum* is deriv'd from *Y kill*, which signifies in British a *Promontory*, or *a narrow slip of ground*, as I have already said [Upon the *Spurnhead* (the utmost part of the Promontory) call'd by some *Conny hill*, is a Light house built in the year 1677 by one Mr *Justinian Angil* of London, who had a Patent for it from King *Charles* the second, and in the year 1684 a *Day* mark was also erected, being a Beacon with a barrel on the top of it]

Winsted
Barons of Rosse
Grimston
Ravenspur and Ravensburg
Kellnsey

From *Ocellum*, the shore draws back gradually, and with a small bending runs northward, by *Overthorne* and *Witberensey*, two little Churches, call'd from the sisters who built them, *Sisters-kirks*, and not far from *Constable Burton*, so nam'd from the Lords of it, who by marriages are ally'd to very honourable families, and flourish in great splendour at this day Robert of this family (as we find it in the book of Meaux Abbey) *was one of the Knights of the Earl of Albemarle, who being old and full of days, took upon him the Cross, and went with King Richard to the Holy Land* Then, by *Skipsey*, which *Drugo* the first Lord of Holderness fortify'd with a Castle Here the shore begins to shoot again into the Sea, and makes that Bay, which is call'd in Ptolemy † Εὐλίμενος *Gabrantovicorum*, and which some Latin Translators render *Portuosus sinus*, and others *Salutaris* Neither of them expresses the sense of the Greek word better than that little town in the return of it, call'd *Suerby* For that which is safe and free from danger, is by the Britains and Gauls call'd *Seur*, as we also call it in English, deriving it probably from the Britains There is no reason therefore why we should question, whether this was the very Εὐλίμενος of the *Gabrantovici*, a People that liv'd in this neighbourhood [In these parts of Holderness, there have been several towns swallow'd up by the *Humber* and the Sea *Frismerk* particularly, which, upon the grant of a *tenth* and *fifteenth* to the King about the 18th of Edward the third, represented to the King and Parliament how much they had suffer'd by the Sea and River, breaking in upon them, and petition'd

Sisters Kirks
Constable
Skipsey
† Εὐλίμενος in some Copies
Sinus Salutaris
* Recessu
Suerby
Gabrantovici
Frismerk

to have a proportionable deduction made in the Rating Whereupon, Commissioners were appointed to make enquiry concerning it, who certify'd that a third part of their lands were totally destroy'd by the tides and thereupon, the King issued out his Precept to the Assessors and Collectors *to supersede*, &c and they were assess'd according to their moveables at *1 l 6 s 8 d* for each of the two years He also sent his Mandate to the Barons of the Exchequer, commanding that neither then, nor on the like occasion for the future, they should be rated at any greater summ The like Mandate was directed to the Collectors of Wooll in the *East Riding*, for a proportionable abatement to the Inhabitants of the town of *Frismerk*

In the 16th of Edward the third, among other Towns in *Holderness* bordering on the Sea and Humber, mention is made of *Tharlethorp*, *Redmayr*, and *Pensthorp* but now not one of them is to be heard of At what time precisely they were lost, does not appear, but about the 30th of Edward the third, the tides in the rivers of *Humber* and *Hull* flow'd higher by four foot than usual, it is likely, therefore, that they might then be overflow'd Probably also, about the same time, *Ravensere* (which seems to be the same with *Ravenspur*, and *Ravensburg*) was much damnify'd, and not long after totally lost The Inhabitants hereabouts talk of two other towns, *Upsall* and *Potterfleet*, which are quite destroy'd About the 38th of Edward the third, the Lands and Meadows between *Sudcote fleet* and *Hull* were much overflow'd; when probably *Ravensere* was greatly damnify'd, as it was afterwards entirely lost, and the town of *Drypool*, with the adjoining grounds, were also very much damnify'd at which town, it is said they of *Ravensere* design'd to settle, but were forc'd to go to *Hull* Likewise before, about the 30th of Edward the third, the High way betwixt *Anlaby* and *Hull*, as also the Grounds and Pastures lying between both these places and *Hesse*, were all drown'd, but the said King by his Letters Patents order'd several persons to see that an old ditch thereabouts should be deepen'd, and a new one (twenty-four foot broad) should be made, and the way rais'd higher, which was accordingly effected]

Near this Bay, is *Bridlington* a town famous for John *de Bridlington* a Monkish Poet, whose rhyming prophecies, which are very ridiculous, I have seen, [and yet he has to this day in all that neighbourhood, the reputation of a Saint And very justly too, if all the mighty things were true of him which *Nicholas Harpsfield* in his Ecclesiastical History has related with great gravity and assurance Mr *William Hustler* (grandfather to Sir *William Hustler*) was a considerable Benefactor to this Town, and in the 16th of Charles the second *Richard Boyl* Baron *Clifford*, &c was created Earl of *Bridlington* or *Burlington*, in which title he was succeeded by Charles his grandson, and it is now enjoy'd by a great grandson of both his names, the right honourable Richard Earl of Burlington For repair of the Piers of this place, two several Acts of Parliament have been obtain'd, in the reigns of King William and King George]

Not far from hence, for a great way towards *Drifield*, a ditch was drawn by the Earls of Holderness to divide the Land, call'd *Earls dike* But why this little People was call'd *Gabrantovici*, I dare not so much as conjecture, unless perhaps the name was taken from *Goats*, which the Britains call *Gafr*, and of which

there

there are not greater numbers in any part of Britain, than in this place Nor is this derivation to be look'd on as absurd, seeing that *Ægira* in Achaia has its name from *Goats*, *Nebrodes* in Sicily, from *Deer*, and *Bœotia* in Greece, from *Oxen* The little Promontory which by its bending makes this Bay, is commonly call'd *Flamborough head*, but by Saxon Authors Fleamburg, who write that *Ida* the Saxon (he who first subdu'd these parts) landed here Some think it took the name from a Watch tower, in which were Lights for the direction of Sailors into the Harbour For the Britains still retain the Provincial word *Flam*, and the Mariners paint this Creek with a flaming head, in their Sea Charts Others are of opinion, that this name came into England out of *Angloen* in Denmark, the ancient Seat of the *Angli*, there being a town call'd *Flemsburg*, from whence they think the English gave it that name, as the Gauls (according to Livy) nam'd *Mediolanum* in Italy, from the town *Mediolanum* which they had left in *Gaul* For a little village in this Promontory is call'd *Flamborough*, which give original to another noble family of *Constables*, by some deriv'd from the *Lacies* Constables of Chester [Going from *Bridlington* we come to the *Mair*, a water pretty deep and always fresh, about a mile and a half long, and half a mile broad, well-stor'd with the best Pikes, Perches, and Eels Whether it has been caus'd at first by some Earth-quake with an overflow that might follow it, is hard to say, but they tell you, that there have been old trees seen floating upon it, and decay'd nuts found on the shore And it is certain, that in the Sea cliffs against *Hornsey*, both have been met with at present also there is (or was, not long since) a vein of wood, looking as black as if it had been burnt, which possibly has been occasion'd by the Sea-water, as preserving wood better than fresh-water, and by its saltness (and consequently greater heat) helping to turn it black Upon the Coast of the German Ocean is *Hornsey*, the Church steeple whereof, being a high broach or spire, is a notable Sea mark, though now it is much fallen to ruin, and the Inhabitants are scarce able to repair it Not many years ago, there was a small street adjoyning to the Sea, call'd *Hornsey beck*, which is now wash'd away, except one or two houses, and about *Skips* below mention'd, a few miles north of *Hornsey*, they have a tradition, of a town call'd *Hide* being devour'd by the Sea More inward into the Land, is *Rudston*, where, in the Church yard, is a kind of Pyramidal stone of great height Whether the name of the town may not have some relation to it, can be known only from the private History of the place, but if the stone bear any resemblance to a *Cross*, Rod in Saxon doth imply so much]

Flamborough head. Ida.

Constables of Flamborough. Marr.

Hornsey.

Rudston.

Upon my enquiries in these parts, I heard nothing of those Rivers (call'd *Vipseis*) which *Walter de Hemingburgh* tells us, flow every other year from unknown Springs, and with a great and rapid current run by this little Promontory to the Sea However, take what *William* of *Newborough* (who was born there) has said of them *These famous waters commonly call'd* Vipseis, *break out of the earth at several sources, not incessantly, but every other year, and having made a strong current, run through the lower grounds into the Sea When they are dry'd, it is a good Omen, for the flowing of them is truly said to forbode the misery of an approaching famine* [Concerning these, take the account of the pious Mr *Ray* "These Gipseys, or sudden eruptions of water —— "whether the word in *Newbrigensis* were by "mistake of the Scribe, and change of a letter, "put in stead of *Gipseys*, or whether *Vipseys* "were the original name, and in process of "time chang'd into *Gipseys*, I know not, certain it is, they are this day call'd *Gipseys* of "which Dr *Witiey* in his *Scarborough Spaw* "writes, that they break out in the wolds or "downs of this Country, after great rains, "and jet and spout up water to a great heighth "Neither are these eruptions of Springs, proper and peculiar to the wolds of this Country, but common to others also, as Dr *Childrey* in his *Britannica Baconica* witnesseth in "these words Sometimes there breaks water, "in the manner of a suddain Land-flood, out "of certain stones that are like rocks standing "aloft in open fields, near the rising of the river *Kinet* in *Kent*, which is reputed by the "common people a fore runner of dearth and "*Newbrigensis* saith the like of the *Gipseys*, that "the flowing of them is said infallibly to portend a future famine So, we see, these "Gipseys do not come at set times, every other "year, as *Newbrigensis* would make us believe, "but only after great gluts of rain, and lasting "wet weather, and never happen but in wet "years and moreover, that they always portend a dearth, not as a Divine indication "or forewarning, but by a natural significancy "it being well known, that cold and wet "Springs and Summers mar the Corn, and do "almost constantly and infallibly induce a "dearth thereof in England, which a drought, "how lasting soever it be, hath never in my "memory been observed to do

Vipsei.

"If any be so curious as to enquire, how a "glut of rain comes to cause such a springing "up of waters? I answer, that there are hereabouts, in the wolds, and in like places "where such jets happen, great subterraneous "basins or receptables of water, which have "issuing out from their bottoms, or near them, "some narrow small veins or chanels reaching "up to the surface of the earth So, the water in the basin lying much higher than the "place of eruption, by its weight forces that "in the veins upward, and makes it spout up "to a great height, as is evidently seen in "the *Lacus Lugeus*, or *Zirchnitzer Sea* in "which this spouting up of water happens "every year after the rains are fallen in the "Autumn These suddain and intermittent "fountains or eruptions of water have a particular name in Kent as well as Yorkshire, "being there call'd *Nailbourns*]

As the Shore winds it self back from hence, a thin slip of land (like a small tongue thrust out) shoots into the Sea, such as the old English call'd *File*, from which the little village *Filey* takes its name More inward stand *Flixton*, where a Hospital was built in the time of Athelstan, for defending *Travelers from Wolves* (as it is, word for word, in the * Publick Records, *that they should not be devoured by them* This shews, that in those times, Wolves infested this tract, which now are to be met with in no part of England, not so much as in the frontiers of Scotland, although in that Kingdom they are † very numerous

This small territory of *Holderness* was given by William the first to *Drugo de Beurere* a Fleming, upon whom also he had bestow'd his niece in marriage, but she being poison'd by him, he was forc'd to fly for his life, and was succeeded by *Stephen* the son of *Odo*, Lord of Albemarle in Normandy, descended from the family

* Rot. in Arch. Turr. Lond.

Wolves.

† Both Wolves and Bears have long since been wholly destroyed in that Kingdom.

Holderness. Drugo de Beurere. [illegible] Albemarle. [illegible]

SCARCE two miles above the Promontory of *Flamburow*, begins the North-part of this Country or the *North-riding*; which makes the frontier to the other parts. From the Sea it extends it self in a very long but narrow tract, for threescore miles together, as far as *Westmorland*, to the west; being bounded on one side, by the river *Derwent*, and for some space by the *Ure*; and on the other side, all along, by the course of the river *Tees*, which separates it from the Bishoprick of *Durham* to the North. This Riding may not unfitly be divided into the following parts, *Blackamore, Cliveland, Northalvertonshire*, and *Richmondshire*.

That which lyeth East and towards the Sea, is call'd *Blackamore*, that is, a land *black* and *mountainous*, being all over rugged and unsightly, by reason of craggs, hills, and woods. The Sea-coast is eminent for *Scarborough*, a famous Castle, formerly call'd Sceap-bupg, i.e. *a Bourg upon a steep Rock*: Take the description of it from the History of William of Newburgh. *A rock of wonderful height and bigness, and inaccessible by reason of steep craggs almost on every side, stands into the Sea; which quite surrounds it, except in one place, where a narrow slip of land is the entrance to it on the West. It has on the top a pleasant plain, grassy and spacious, of about * * See below.sixty acres or upwards, and a little* † † See below.*well of water, springing from a rock. In the very entrance, which one is at some pains to reach, stands a* ¦ ¦ *Turris regia.stately tower; and beneath the entrance the City begins, spreading its two sides South and North, and carrying its front Westward, where it is fortified with a wall; but on the East it is fenc'd by that rock where the Castle stands; and lastly, on both sides by the Sea. William, sirnam'd* le Grosse, *Earl of Albemarle and Holderness, observing this place to be fitly situated for a Castle, encreased the natural strength of it by a very costly work, having enclosed all that plain upon the rock with a wall, and built a Tower in the entrance. But this being decay'd and fallen through age, King Henry the second commanded a great and noble Castle to be built upon the same spot.* For he had now reduc'd the Nobility of England, who during the loose reign of King Stephen, had impair'd the revenues of the Crown; but especially this William of Albemarle, who had lorded it over all these parts, and kept this Place as his own.

[The Town, on the North-east, is fortified with a high and inaccessible rock, stretch'd out a good way into the Sea (as *Newbrigensis* says,) and containing at the top about eighteen or twenty acres of good Meadow; and not near *sixty*, as the same Writer adds. Whether the difference lie in the several measures of Acres; or the greater part of it be wash'd away by the Sea; or the number be false, and owing to an error of that Historian; I shall not dispute, since the matter of fact is plain. * * Dr. *Wittie*'s Description of *ScarboroughSpaw*.The Spaw-well is a quick Spring, about a quarter of a mile South from the Town, at the foot of an exeeding high cliff; arising upright out of the Earth like a boyling pot, near the level of the Spring-tides, with which it is often overflown. It is of that sort of *Springs*, which Aristotle calls πηγὰς ἀενάας, which in the most droughty years are never dry. In an hour, it affords above twenty four gallons of water: for the stones through which it flows, contain more than twelve gallons, and being emptied every morning, it will be full within half an hour. It's virtue proceeds from a participation of *Vitriol, Iron, Alum, Nitre* and *Salt*: to the sight it is very transparent, inclining somewhat to a sky-colour; it hath a pleasant acid taste from the *Vitriol*, and an inky smell. This Town drives a good trade with Fish taken in the Sea hereabouts, with which they supply the City of York, though thirty miles distant. Besides *Herrings*, they have *Ling, Codfish, Haddock, Hake, Whiting, Mackrel*, and several other sorts, in great plenty. From this place, *Richard* Viscount *Lumley* hath his title of Earl of

is (or was, not long since) a vein of wood, looking as black as if it had been burnt; which possibly has been occasion'd by the Sea-water, as preserving wood better than fresh-water, and by its saltness (and consequently greater heat) helping to turn it black. Upon the Coast of the German Ocean is *Hornsey*,Hornsey. the Church-steeple whereof, being a high broach or spire, is a notable Sea-mark; though now it is much fallen to ruin, and the Inhabitants are scarce able to repair it. Not many years ago, there was a small street adjoyning to the Sea, call'd *Hornsey-beck*, which is now wash'd away, except one or two houses; and about *Skipsie* before-mention'd, a few miles north of *Hornsey*, they have a tradition, of a town call'd *Hide* being devour'd by the Sea. More inward into the Land, is *Rudston*,Rudston. where, in the Church-yard, is a kind of Pyramidal-stone of great height. Whether the name of the town may not have some relation to it, can be known only from the private History of the place; but if the stone bear any resemblance to a *Cross*, Roð in Saxon doth imply so much.]

Upon my enquiries in these parts, I heard nothing of those Rivers (call'd *Vipseis*)Vipseis. which *Walter de Heminburgh* tells us, flow every other year from unknown Springs, and with a great and rapid current run by this little Promontory to the Sea. However, take what *William* of *Newborough* (who was born there) has said of them: *These famous waters commonly call'd* Vipseis, *break out of the earth at several sources, not incessantly, but every other year, and having made a strong current, run through the lower grounds into the Sea. When they are dry'd, it is a good Omen, for the flowing of them is truly said to forbode the misery of an approaching famine*. [Concerning these, take the account of the pious Mr. *Ray*.

"These *Vipseys*, or suddain eruptions of water— whether the word in *Newbrigensis* were by mistake of the Scribe, and change of a letter, put in stead of *Gipseys*; or whether *Vipseys* were the original name, and in process of time chang'd into *Gipseys*, I know not; certain it is, they are this day call'd *Gipseys*: of which Dr. *Wittey* in his *Scarborough-Spaw* writes, that they break out in the wolds or downs of this Country, after great rains, and jet and spout up water to a great heighth. Neither are these eruptions of Springs, proper and peculiar to the wolds of this Country, but common to others also, as Dr. *Childrey* in his *Britannica Baconica* witnesseth in these words. Sometimes there breaks water, in the manner of a suddain Land-flood, out of certain stones that are like rocks standing aloft in open fields, near the rising of the river *Kinet* in *Kent*; which is reputed by the common people a fore-runner of dearth: and *Newbrigensis* saith the like of the *Gipseys*, that the flowing of them is said infallibly to portend a future famine. So, we see, these *Gipseys* do not come at set times, every other year, as *Newbrigensis* would make us believe, but only after great gluts of rain, and lasting wet weather; and never happen but in wet years: and moreover, that they always portend a dearth, not as a Divine indication or forewarning, but by a natural significancy: it being well known, that cold and wet Springs and Summers mar the Corn, and do almost constantly and infallibly induce a dearth thereof in England; which a drought, how lasting soever it be, hath never in my memory been observed to do."

"If any be so curious as to enquire, how a glut of rain comes to cause such a springing up of waters? I answer, that there are hereabouts, in the wolds, and in like places where such jets happen, great subterraneous basins or receptables of water, which have issuing out from their bottoms, or near them, some narrow small veins or chanels reaching up to the surface of the earth. So, the water in the basin lying much higher than the place of eruption, by its weight forces that in the veins upward, and makes it spout up to a great height; as is evidently seen in the *Lacus Lugeus*, or *Zirchnitzer-Sea*: in which this spouting up of water happens every year after the rains are fallen in the Autumn. These suddain and intermittent fountains or eruptions of water have a particular name in Kent as well as Yorkshire, being there call'd *Nailbourns*".]

As the Shore winds it self back from hence, a thin slip of land (like a small tongue thrust out) shoots into the Sea, such as the old English call'd *File*; from which the little village *Filey* takes its name. More inward stands *Flixton*, where a Hospital was built in the time of Athelstan, for defending *Travellers from Wolves* (as it is, word for word, in the * * *Regiis Archivis*.Publick Records) *that they should not be devoured by them*. This shews, that in those times, WolvesWolves. infested this tract, which now are to be met with in no part of England, not so much as in the frontiers of Scotland; although in that Kingdom they are † † Both *Wolves* and *wild Boars* are long since totally destroyed in that Kingdom. *Sibbald. Nun. Scot. Brit.* p.2. 9.very numerous.

This small territory of *Holderness* was given by William the first to *Drugo de Bruerer* a Fleming, upon whom also he had bestow'd his niece in marriage; but she being poison'd by him, he was forc'd to fly for his life, and was succeeded by *Stephen* the son of *Odo*,Earls of *Albemarle* and *Holderness*. Genealogiæ Antiquæ. Lord of Albemarle in Normandy, descended from the family of the Earls of *Champaigne*, whom William the first (his nephew by a half sister on the mother's side) is said to have made Earl of *Albemarle*; and his posterity retain'd that title in England, notwithstanding *Albemarle* is a place in Normandy. He was succeeded by his son *William*, sirnam'd * * Le Gross.*Crassus*. His only daughter *Avis* was married to three husbands successively: to *William Magnavill* Earl of Essex, to *Baldwin de Beton*, and to *William Forts*, or *de Fortibus*. By this last husband only she had issue, *viz. William*, who left also a son *William* to succeed him. His only daughter *Avelin*, being married to Edmund ¦ ¦ Gibbosus.Crouchback Earl of Lancaster, dy'd without issue. And so (as it is said in the Book of Meaux-Abbey) *for want of heirs, the Earldom of Albemarle and the Honour of Holderness were seized into the King's hands*. Yet, in after-times, King Richard the second created *Thomas de Woodstock* his Uncle, Duke of Albemarle; and afterwards *Edward Plantagenet*, son to the Duke of York, in the life-time of his father. Henry the fourth also made his son *Thomas*, Duke of Clarence and Earl of Albemarle; which title King Henry the sixth added afterwards as a farther honour to *Richard Beauchamp* Earl of Warwick. [After the said *Richard de Beauchamp*, the title lay vacant, till, upon the Restoration of King Charles the second, *George Monk* (who had been the chief Instrument therein) was advanc'd to the Honours of Baron Monk of *Potheridge, Beauchamp*,12 Car.2. and *Teyes*, as also*July* 7. of Earl of *Torrington* and Duke of *Albemarle*. Who departing this Life in 1669, was succeeded in his Estate and Titles by *Christopher* his son and heir. But he dying without issue, King William the third bestow'd the title of Earl of *Albemarle*, upon *Arnold Joost van Keppel*, descended from an ancient Family of the Nobles of *Gelderland*; whose Son and Heir doth now enjoy that Honour.]

Scarborough; to which he was advanced in the second year of King William and Queen Mary.]

North Riding of York Shire

It is not to my purpose, to relate the desperate boldness of *Thomas Stafford*, who (that he might fall at least from *great* attempts) surpriz'd this Castle in Queen Mary's reign, with a very small

family of the Earls of *Champaigne*, whom William the first (his nephew by a half sister on the mother's side) is said to have made Earl of *Albemarle*, and his posterity retain'd that title in England, notwithstanding *Albemarle* is a place in Normandy. He was succeeded by his son *William*, sirnam'd * *Crassus*. His only daughter *Avis* was married to three husbands successively, to *William Magnavill* Earl of Essex, to *Baldwin de Beton*, and to *William Fortis*, or *de Fortibus*. By this last husband only she had issue, *viz William*, who left also a son *William* to succeed him. His only daughter *Avelin*, being married to Edmund || Crouchback Earl of Lancaster, dy'd without issue. And so (as it is said in the Book of Meaux-Abby) *for want of heirs, the Earldom of Albemarle and the Honour of Holderness were seized into the King's hands*. Yet, in after-times, King Richard the second created *Thomas de Woodstock* his Uncle, Duke of Albemarle, and afterwards *Edward Plantagenet*, son to the Duke of York, in the life-time of his father. Henry the fourth also made his son *Thomas*, Duke of Clarence and Earl of Albemarle, which title King Henry the sixth added afterwards as a farther honour to *Richard Beauchamp* Earl of Warwick. [After the said *Richard de Beauchamp*, the title lay vacant, till, upon the Restoration of King Charles the second, *George Monk* (who had been the chief Instrument therein) was advanc'd to the Honours of Baron Monk of *Potheridge*, *Beauchamp*, and *Teyes*, as also of Earl of *Torrington* and *Duke of Albemarle*. Who departing this Life in 1669, was succeeded in his Estate and Titles by *Christopher* his son and heir. But he dying without issue, King William the third bestow'd the title of Earl of *Albemarle*, upon *Arnold Joost van Keppel*, descended from an ancient Family of the Nobles of *Gelderland*, whose Son and Heir doth now enjoy that Honour.]

* Le Gross.
|| Gibbosus.
12 Car. 2. Jul. 7.

NORTH-RIDING.

North Riding.

SCARCE two miles above the Promontory of *Flamburow*, begins the North-part of this Country or the *North riding*; which makes the frontier to the other parts. From the Sea it extends it self in a very long but narrow tract, for threescore miles together, as far as *Westmorland*, to the west, being bounded on one side, by the river *Derwent*, and for some space by the *Ure*, and on the other side, all along, by the course of the river *Tees*, which separates it from the Bishoprick of *Durham* to the North. This Riding may not unfitly be divided into the following parts, *Blackamore*, *Cleveland*, *Northalvertonshire*, and *Richmondshire*.

That which lyeth East and towards the Sea, is call'd *Blackamore*, that is a land *black* and *mountainous*, being all over rugged and unsightly, by reason of craggs, hills, and woods. The Sea-coast is eminent for *Scarborough*, a famous Castle, formerly call'd Skeerburg, i. e. *a Bourg upon a steep Rock*. Take the description of it from the History of William of Newburgh. *A rock of wonderful height and bigness, and inaccessible by reason of steep craggs almost on every side, stands into the Sea, which quite surrounds it, except in one place, where a narrow slip of land is the entrance to it on the West. It has on the top a pleasant plain, grassy and spacious, of about * sixty acres or upwards, and a little † well of water, springing from a rock. In the very entrance, which one is at some pains to reach, stands a || stately tower, and beneath the entrance the City begins, spreading its two sides South and North, and carrying its front Westward, where it is fortified with a wall, but on the East it is fenc'd by that rock where the Castle stands, and lastly, on both sides by the Sea. William, sirnam'd* le Grosse, *Earl of Albemarle and Holderness, observing this place to be fitly situated for a Castle, encreased the natural strength of it by a very costly work, having enclosed all that plain upon the rock with a wall, and built a Tower in the entrance. But this being decay'd and fallen through age, King Henry the second commanded a great and noble Castle to be built upon the same spot.* For he had now reduc'd the Nobility of England, who during the loose reign of King Stephen, had impair'd the revenues of the Crown, but especially this William of Albemarle, who had lorded it over all these parts, and kept this place as his own.

* See below.
† See below.
|| Turris regia.

[The Town, on the North-east is fortified with a high and inaccessible rock, stretch'd out a good way into the Sea (as *Neubrigensis* says,) and containing at the top about eighteen or twenty acres of good Meadow, and not near *sixty*, as the same Writer adds. Whether the difference lie in the several measures of Acres, or the greater part of it be wash'd away by the Sea, or the number be false, and owing to an error of that Historian, I shall not dispute, since the matter of fact is plain. * The Spaw-well is a quick Spring, about a quarter of a mile South from the Town, at the foot of an exceeding high cliff, arising up out of the Earth like a boyling pot, near the level of the Spring-tides, with which it is often overflown. It is of that sort of *Springs*, which Aristotle calls [illegible], which in the most droughty years are never dry. In an hour, it affords above twenty four gallons of water, for the stones through which it flows, contain no more than twelve gallons, and being emptied every morning, it will be full within half an hour. It's virtue proceeds from a participation of *Vitriol*, *Iron*, *Alum*, *Nitre* and *Salt*; to the sight it is very transparent, inclining somewhat to a sky-colour; it hath a pleasant acid taste from the *Vitriol*, and an inky smell. This Town drives a good trade with Fish taken in the Sea hereabouts, with which they supply the City of York, though thirty miles distant. Besides *Herrings*, they have *Ling*, *Codfish*, *Haddock*, *Hake*, *Whiting*, *Mackrel*, and several other sorts, in great plenty. From this place, *Richard* Viscount *Lumley* hath his title of Earl of *Scarborough*, to which he was advanced in the second year of King William and Queen Mary.]

* The Spaw-well [illegible]

It is not to my purpose, to relate the desperate boldness of *Thomas Stafford*, who (that he might fall at least from great attempts) surpriz'd this Castle in Queen Mary's reign, with a ve-

VIII
VII
Part of
Weſt
moreland
Bauderdale
Lune Forreſt
Lune R.
Depe Dale
Barnard
Caſtle
Bowes
GILLING

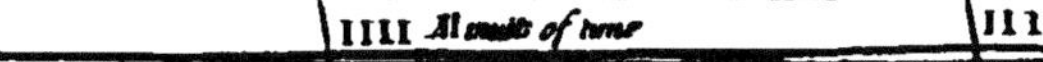

PART OF

HE BISHOPRICK

F DURHAM

Darlington

Standrop

Gisborough

Cleveland

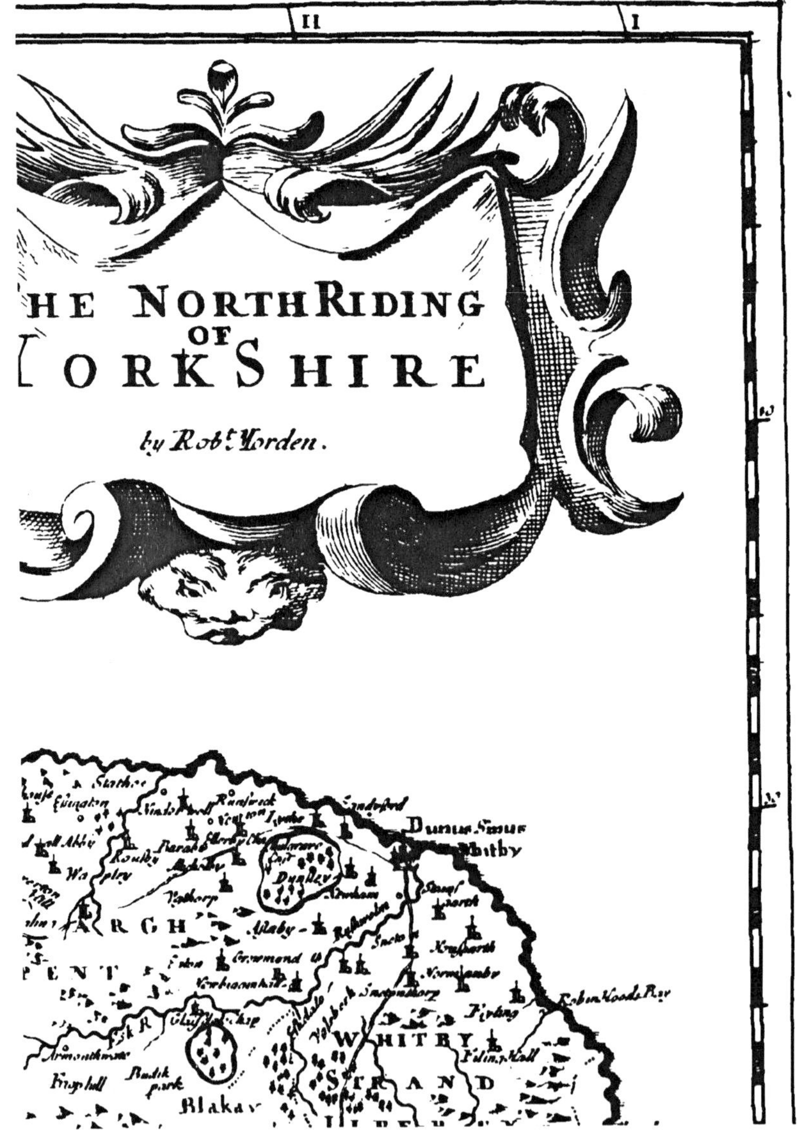

II
I
HE NORTH RIDING
OF
ORK SHIRE
by Robt. Morden.
Dunus Sinus
Whitby
WHITBY
STRAND

Applegarth Forrest
Swaledale Forrest
Bishop dale Chace
PART

OF
THE
RIDING
YORK
HALLIKELD
BVRDFORTH
WAPENT
Rippon
Malham

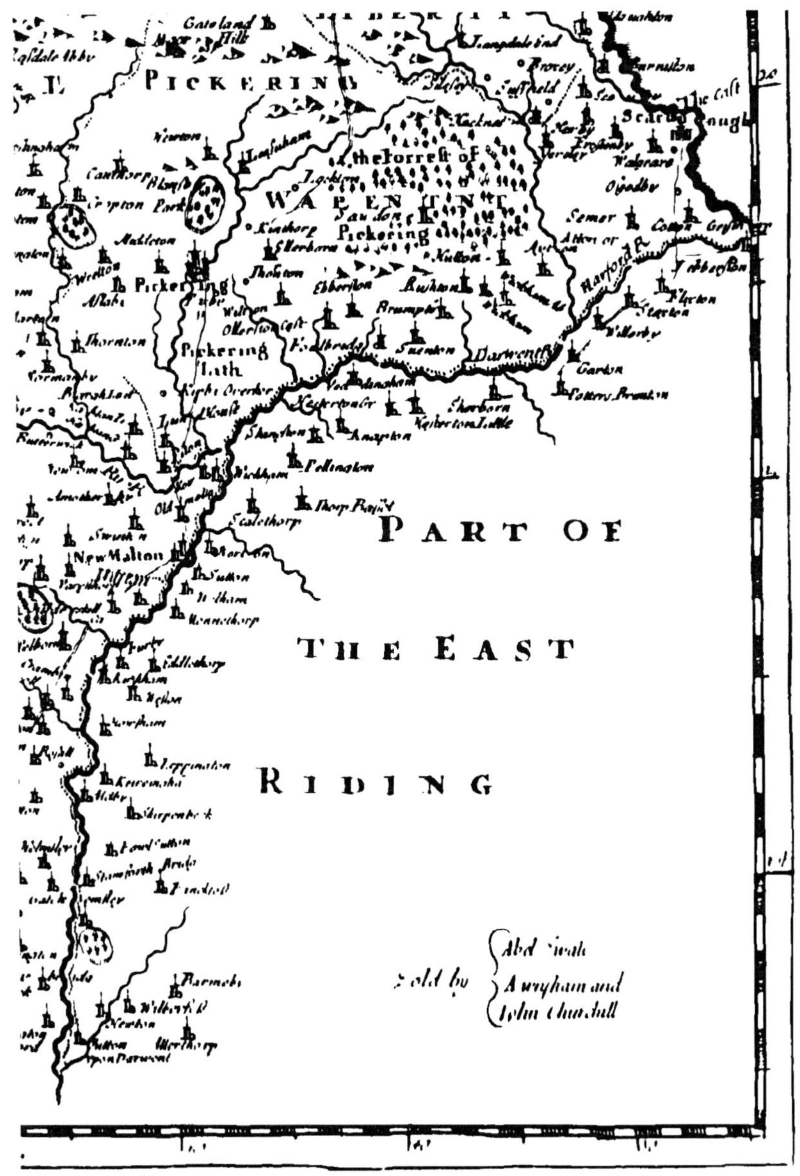

PICKERING
the Forrest of
Pickering
New Malton
Darwent R.
PART OF
THE EAST
RIDING

ry small number of French, and kept it for two days: nor yet of *Oberleis*, a noble French man of the same company, who was arraign'd for High Treason, although a foreigner, *because he had acted contrary to the duty of his Allegiance*; Vid. Dier 144 there being then a Peace between the Kingdoms of England and France. These things are too well known in the world, to need further light from me, [especially, since the Castle itself is now in Ruins, having been demolished in the time of the great Rebellion.] It is worth remarking, that those of Holland and Zealand carry on a very great and gainful trade of fishing in the Sea here for Herrings (call them in Latin *Haleces*, *Leucomenidæ*, *Chalcides*, or what you please,) after they have, according to ancient Custom, obtain'd Licence for it from this Castle. For the English always granted leave for Fishing, reserving the Honour to themselves, but out of a lazy humour resigning the gain to others. It being almost incredible, what vast gains the Hollanders make by the Fishery on our Coast. These Herrings (pardon me if I digress a little, to shew the goodness of God toward us) which in the time of our † Grandfathers swarm'd only about Norway, do now, in our times, by the bounty of divine Providence, swim in great shoals round our coasts every year. About Midsummer, they draw from the main Sea towards the coast of Scotland, at which time they are immediately sold off, as being then at their best. From thence they arrive on our coasts, and from the middle of August to November, there is excellent and most plentiful fishing for them, all along from *Scarborough* to the Thames mouth. Afterwards, by stormy weather they are carried into the British Sea, and are there caught till Christmas, thence having ranged the coast of Ireland on both sides, and gone round Britain, they return into the Northern Ocean, where they remain till June, and after they have cast their spawn, return again in great shoals. This relation puts me in mind of what I have formerly read in St Ambrose. *Fish, in prodigious numbers, meeting as it were by common consent out of many places from several creeks of the sea, do in one united body make towards the Coasts of the* * *North-east wind, and by a kind of natural instinct swim into the northern seas. One would think, when he sees them as it were climb the main, that mountains were approaching, with such violence do they rush on and cut the waves as they go through* Propontis *to the Euxin Sea*. But to return.

The gainful trade of Herring-fishing

† So said ann. 1607.

Hexameron, [illegible]

* [illegible]

[Whitby and Hull being the only Ports short of Yarmouth, where Life and Goods can be secured in stress of weather, the Peer here is maintain'd at the publick charge by an imposition upon Coals from *Newcastle* and *Sunderland*. And the Mariners have erected a Hospital for the Widows of poor Seamen, which is well maintain'd by a rate on Vessels, and by certain deductions out of the Seamen's wages.

At *Harwood dale*, near *Scarborough*, Sir *Thomas Posthumus Hobby*, Lord of the Manour, and *Margaret* his wife, built a handsome Chapel, and endow'd it with the great and small Tythes, which the Minister now enjoys.]

From hence the shore is craggy, and bends inward as far as the river *Teise*, and by its winding, there is made a bay about a mile broad, which is call'd *Robin Hoods Bay*, from that famous Outlaw *Robin Hood*. He liv'd in the reign of Richard the first, as *Jo Major* a Scotchman informs us, who stiles him *the Prince of Robbers*, and *the most kind and obliging robber*. [Upon the adjacent Moor, are two little Hills

Teise, riv.

Robin Hood's Bay.

a quarter of a mile asunder, which are called his *Butts*. This noted robber lies buried in the Park near *Kirk-lees* Nunnery, in the West-riding, under a Monument which remains to this day.]

From hence the shore, immediately going back on both sides, shews us the Bay *Dunus sinus*, mention'd in Ptolemy, upon which is seated the little village *Dunesly*, and hard by it, *Whitby* [a commodious harbour, which hath sixty Ships of eighty Tuns or more, belonging to it; with a Peer, for the rebuilding and repairing of which, an Act of Parliament was pass'd in the first year of Q. Anne. It is call'd] in the Saxon tongue ƿyꞃeaneꞅ-ꞅealc, [and ƿyꞃco-neꞅꞅeal,] which Bede renders, *the bay of the Watch tower*. I will not dispute this interpretation of it, tho' in our language it seems so plainly to intimate a *bay of Safety*, that I should certainly have said it was the *Sinus Salutaris*, if its situation (as the Geographer makes it) did not perswade me to the contrary. [But others observe, that it is call'd in Saxon, not ƿyꞃeaneꞅ-ꞅealc, but ƿyꞃeoneꞅ-ꞅalꞅ, as it is in the Saxon Paraphrase of Bede, and also in the best Latin Copies. And therefore Mr *Junius* in his Gothick Glossary, under the word *Alb*, seems to hit the true original, when he fetches it from the Saxon ꞅæl, ꞅal, or ꞅealꞅ, (call'd by Cædmon *alb*) which, like our Northern word *Hall* still in use, signifies *any eminent building*. Hence the name of the Pagan God *Woden's Valhol* (or *Valhaul*,) so frequently mention'd in the *Edda*, and other old Cimbrian Writers. and Crantzius fetches the name of the City of *Upsal* from the same original.]

Dunum sinus

Duneesley

Whitby

Here are found certain Stones, resembling the wreaths and foldings of a Serpent, these strange frolicks of nature, which (as one says) she forms for her diversion, after a toilsome application to serious business. For one would believe that they had been Serpents, crusted over with a cover of stone. Fame ascribes them to the power of *Hilda*'s prayers, as if she had transform'd them. [Dr *William Nicholson*, the present learned and worthy Bishop of *Derry* in Ireland and late of *Carlisle* (who has made large Observations upon the Natural Rarities of these parts) affirms them to be the same with those which the Modern Naturalists call *Cornua Ammonis*. Whether they be original productions of Nature, or petrify'd Shell fishes of the *Nautilous* kind, has been very much controverted by several Learned men on both sides. But he is of opinion, that they are rather spiral petrifications produc'd in the Earth by a sort of fermentation peculiar to Alum mines. Hence, they are plentifully found in the Alum pits at *Rome*, *Rochel*, and *Lunenburg*, as well as in those of this Country. and it may be, that *Keinsham*, and other parts of England, where these Stones are found, would afford likewise good store of *Alum*. The particular *method* of making it in this place, is fully describ'd by Mr *Ray*, in his † *Collection of English words*.]

Stony Serpents

Hilda

† Pag. 201

The forementioned *Hilda*, in the infancy of the Saxon Church, withstood, to the utmost of her power, the Tonsure of the Clergy, and the celebration of Easter after the Roman manner, in a Synod which met about these matters, *An.* 664, and was held in the Abbey which she had founded in this place, of which herself was the first Governess, [if indeed such a Synod was really held here, which the silence of King Alfred's Paraphrase, and of the Saxon Chronicle, renders suspicious.] It is also ascribed to the sanctity of *Hilda*, that those wild Geese (which

Geese dropping down

in winter flie in great flocks to the unfrozen lakes and rivers in the southern parts,) to the great amazement of every body, fall down suddenly upon the ground, when they are in their flight over certain neighbouring fields hereabouts a relation that I should not have given, if I had not received it from several very credible persons But they who are less inclin'd to superstition, attribute it to some occult quality in the ground, and to somewhat of † antipathy between it and the Geese, such as they say is between Wolves and Scylla roots For, that such hidden tendencies and aversions as we call *Sympathies* and *Antipathies*, are implanted in many things by nature for their preservation, is a point so evident, that every body readily allows it *Edelfleda*, daughter of King Oswin, afterwards enriched this Abbey with very large revenues, and here also she buried her father But at length, in the time of the Danish Ravages, it was utterly destroyed; and although *Serlo Percius* (who presently after the Conquest was made Governour of it) rebuilt it, yet at this day it has hardly the remains of its ancient greatness [In the Church yard, are a vast number of ancient funeral Monuments, (some Statues, others with plain Crosses upon them) which were removed from the adjoyning Abbey]

† Dissensum

Sympathy and Antipathy

Hard by, upon a steep Hill near the Sea (which yet is between two that are much higher) a Castle of *Wada* a Saxon Duke is said to have stood, who (in that confused Anarchy of the Northumbrians, so fatal to the petty Princes) having combined with those that murder'd King *Ethered*, gave battel to King *Ardulph* at *Whalley* in Lancashire, but with such ill success, that his Army was routed, and himself forced to fly Afterwards, he fell into a Distemper which kill'd him, and was inter'd on a hill here between two solid Rocks about seven foot high, which being at twelve foot distance from one another, occasions a current Opinion, that he was of a gyant-like stature A long time after, *Peter de Malo lacu* built a Castle near this place, which from its *grace* and beauty he nam'd in French *Moulgrace* (as we find it in the History of *Meaux*,) but because it became a *beavy* grievance to the neighbours thereabouts, the people (who have always the right of coyning words) by changing one single letter, call'd it *Moulgrave*, by which name it is every where known, though the reason thereof is little understood This *Peter de Malo lacu*, commonly called *Mauley* (that I may satisfy the curious in this point) was born in *Poictou* in France, and married the only daughter of *Robert de Turnham* in the reign of Richard the first, in whose right he came to a very great inheritance, enjoyed by seven *Peters*, Lords *de Malo lacu* successively, who bore for their Arms, *a bend sable in an Escocheon Or* But the seventh dying without issue, the inheritance was divided by sisters, between the Knightly families of the *Salvains* and *Bigo's* [*Mulgrave* hath given the title of Earl to *Edmund* Lord *Sheffield* of *Butterwick*, who was Lord President of the North, and created Earl of this place *Feb* 7 in the first year of K Charles the first He was succeeded by *Edmund*, his grandchild by Sir *John Sheffield* his second son; to which *Edmund*, *John* his son and heir succeeded, who hath been further honoured with the titles of Marquis of *Normanby* and Duke of the County of *Buckingham*, and *Normanby*]

Duke *Wada*, from whom the family of the *Wardes* derive their pedigree

7 8

Walesgrave

Mulgrave Castle

Peter de Malo lacu

Near this place, and elsewhere on this shore, is found *Black Amber* or *Geate* Some take it to be the *Gagates*, which was valued by the Ancients among the rarest stones and jewels It grows upon the rocks, within a chink or cliff of them, and before it is polish'd, looks reddish and rusty, but after, is really (as Solinus describes it) Diamond-like, black and shining Of which, Rhemnius Palæmon, from Dionysius, writes thus

Geate Gagates

Others are opinion that Pitch is a sort of Gagates

> ——— *Præfulget nigro splendore Gagates,*
> *Hic lapis ardescens austro perfusus aquarum*
> *Ast oleo perdens flammas, mirabile visu,*
> *Attritus rapit hic teneras, ceu succina, frondes*

> All black and shining is the Jeat,
> In water dip'd it flames with sudden heat
> But a strange coldness, dip'd in Oyl, receives,
> And draw, like Amber, little sticks and leaves

Likewise *Marbodæus* in his Treatise of Jewels

> *Nascitur in Lycia lapis, & prope gemma Gagates,*
> *Sed genus eximium fæcunda Britannia mittit,*
> *Lucidus & niger est, levis & levissimus idem*
> *Vicinas paleas trahit attritu calefactus,*
> *Ardet aqua lotus, restinguitur unctus olivo*

> Jeat stone, almost a gemm, the *Lybians* find,
> But fruitful *Britain* sends a wondrous kind,
> 'Tis black and shining, smooth and ever light,
> 'Twill draw up Straws, if rubb'd till hot and bright,
> Oyl makes it cold, but water gives it heat

Hear also what Solinus says *In Britain, there is great store of* Gagates *or* Geate, *a very fine Stone If you ask the Colour*, † *it is black and shining, if the quality, it is exceeding light if the nature, it burns in water, and is quenched with oyl, if the virtue, it has an attractive power when heated with rubbing* [All along these shores, the people are observed to be very busie in making of *Kelp*, which they do in this manner They gather the Sea-wrack, and lay it on heaps; and when it is dry, they burn it While it is burning, they stir it to and fro with an Iron rake and so it condenses and cakes together into such a body as we see *Kelp* to be, which is of use in making of *Alum* If they should not stir it, it would burn to ashes as other combustible bodies do]

† Nigerrimus

From *Whitby* the shore winds back to the westward, and near it stands *Cleveland*, so called, as it should seem, from precipices, which we call *Cliffs*, for it is situated by the side of several steep hills, from the foot of which the Country falls into a plain even fertile ground [The Soil is exceeding clayie, which hath occasioned this Rhyme among them;

Cleveland

> *Cleveland in the clay*
> *Bring in two Soles, and carry one away*

The

This tract has given the title of Earl to *Thomas* Lord *Wentworth*, created *Feb* 7. 1 Car 1, who dy'd without issue male, his Son *Thomas* Lord *Wentworth* dying the year before him. In the 22d year of K. Charles the second, the title of Dutchess of *Cleveland* was conferred upon *Barbara Villiers*, daughter to the Lord Viscount *Granadson*, and, at her death, descended to *Charles*, the present Duke.]

Skengrave

Upon the shore, *Skengrave*, a small Village, thrives by the great variety of Fish which it takes, where, it is reported that * seventy years ago they caught a † *Sea-man*, who lived upon raw fish for some days, but at last, taking his opportunity, he made his escape into his own element. When the winds are laid, and the sea is in a calm, the waters being spread (as it were) into a plain, a hideous groaning is oft times heard in these parts on a sudden, and then the fishermen are afraid to go to Sea, who, according to their poor sense of things, believe the Ocean to be a huge Monster, which is then hungry, and eager to glut itself with the bodies of men. Beneath *Skengrave* stands *Kilton*, a Castle, with a Park round it this belonged formerly to the famous family of the *Thwengs*, whose estate descended to the Barons of *Lumley*, *Hilton*, and *Daubeney*. Very near this place is *Skelton castle*, [heretofore] belonging to the antient family of the Barons *de Brus*, who are descended from *Robert Brus* a Norman. He had two Sons, *Adam* Lord of *Skelton*, and *Robert* Lord of *Anan-dale* in Scotland, from whom sprang the Royal Line of Scotland. But *Peter Brus*, the fifth Lord of *Skelton*, died without issue, and left his sisters heirs, *Agnes*, married to *Walter de Falconberg*, *Luce*, married to *Marmaduke de Thwenge*, from whom the Baron *Lumley* is descended, *Margaret*, married to *Robert de Roos*, and *Laderina*, married to *John de Bella aqua*, all, men of great honour and esteem in that age. The Posterity of *Walter de Falconberg* flourish'd a long time, but at last the estate came by a female to *William Nevil*, famous for his warlike valour, and honour'd with the title of *Earl of Kent* by King Edward the fourth. His daughters were married to *J. Conyers*, *N. Bethowing*, and *R. Strangways*. [*Robert Bruce*, Earl of Elgin in Scotland, was by King Charles the second, in the year 1663, advanced to the title of Earl of *Ailesbury* and Baron *Bruce* of *Skelton*.]

* So said, ann 1607.
A Sea man
† *Hominem marinum.*
Kilton
Skelton castle
Brus of Skelton
Barons Falconberg

Kirk Letham

Near the mouth of the *Tees*, is *Kirk Letham*, where Sir *William Turner* (Lord Mayor of *London* in the year 1669) built a most stately Hospital, at this place of his Nativity, and endowed it generously for the maintenance of forty poor people (aged, and children,) with liberal Salaries also to a Chaplain, a Master and Mistress. To which, at his death, he added a benefaction of five thousand Pounds for the erecting a Free School, and the purchasing of plentiful Salaries.]

† Toth Master, 1607
[illegible]
Huntcliff
Sea calves

Near *Huntcliff*, on the shore, when the tide is out, the rocks shoot up pretty high, and to these the *Sea-calves* (which we by contraction call *seals*, as some think for *Sea veals* or *Sea calves*) come out in great droves, and there sleep and sun themselves. Upon one of the rocks nearest the shore, some one of them stands *centry* as it were, and when any body comes near, he either pushes down a stone, or with great noise throws himself into the water, to alarm the rest, that they may provide for themselves, and get into the Sea. Their greatest fear is of Men, and if they are pursued by them, and cannot reach the Sea in time, they often keep them off, by casting up sand and gravel with their hinder feet. They are not in such awe of Women; so that the *Men* who would take them, disguise themselves in Womens habit. Here are upon this Coast yellowish and reddish Stones, and some crusted over with a brinish substance, which by their smell and taste resemble Coperas, Nitre, and Brimstone and also great store of *Pyrites*, in colour like Brass.

Huntly Nabb

Near, at *Huntly Nabb*, the shore (which for a long way together has lain open) now rises into high rocks, and here and there, at the bottoms of the rocks, lie great stones of several sizes so exactly form'd round by nature, that one would think them bullets cast by some Artist for the great Guns. If you break them, you find, within, stony Serpents wreathed up in Circles, but generally without heads. Hence we see *Wilton castle*, formerly belonging to the *Bulmers*. Higher up, at *Dobham*, the river *Tees* rolls into the Sea, having [visited *Cleasby*, where Dr *Robinson*, Envoy for many years to the Court of *Sweden*, and now Bishop of *London*, hath rebuilt and endowed a Chapel (with a convenient House for the Minister) at this his native place, and also] receiv'd many small rivulets, the last whereof is a nameless one, which enters it near *Yarum*, noted for its Market, and washes *Stokesley*, a small Market town likewise, which * remain'd long in the hands of the famous family *de Eur*, [of which, was Sir *William Eure*, whom King Henry the eighth advanced to the degree of a Baron of this Realm, but this honour expir'd, *ann.* 1707 in *Ralph* Lord *Eure*.] Below these, stands *Wharlton-castle*, which formerly belonged to the Barons *Meinill*, and *Harlsey*, to the family of *Hotham*, but afterwards to the *Strangwayes*, [and now to the *Lawsons*] both of them old and ruinous.

Round Stones
Wilton castle
Cleasby
Yarum
Stokesley
* *Jam du...*
Wharlton-castle
Harlsey

The mouth of the [forementioned] *Tees*, was hardly trusted by Mariners heretofore, but now is found to be a safe Harbour; and to direct the entrance, there were Light-houses made on both sides of it, within the memory of † the present age. Four miles from the mouth of this river, *Gisburgh* stands upon a rising ground, at present a small Town, but formerly very famous for a beautiful and rich Monastery, built about the year 1119 by *Robert de Brus* Lord of the Town. It has been the common burial-place for the Nobility of these parts, and produced *Walter de Hemingford*, no unlearned Historian, [and the Abbey Church, by the ruins, seems to have been equal to the best Cathedrals in *England*.] The place is really fine and may, in point of pleasantness, and a grateful variety, and other advantages of Nature, compare with *Puteoli* in Italy; and in point of healthfulness, it far surpasses it. [The Inhabitants are observed by Travellers to be civil and well bred, cleanly in their diet, and neat in their houses.] The coldness of the air, which the Sea occasions, is qualified by the hills between; the Soil is fruitful, and produces grass and fine flowers a great part of the year; it abounds with veins of Metal and *Alum* earth of several colours (but especially with those of *ocher* and *murray*) from which they now † begin to extract the best sort of Alum and Coperas. This was first discover'd a few years since by the admirable sagacity of that learned Naturalist Sir *Thomas Chaloner*, Knt (to whose tuition, * his Majesty [King James the first] committed the delight and glory of Britain, his Son Prince *Henry*,) by observing that the leaves of

† So in 1607.
Gisburgh
† An 1607.
Alum
Coperas
* His present Majesty hath.

This tract has given the title of Earl to *Thomas* Lord *Wentworth*, created *Feb*. 7. 1. Car. 1, who dy'd without issue-male, his Son *Thomas* Lord *Wentworth* dying the year before him. In the 22th year of K. Charles the second, the title of Dutchess of *Cliveland* was conferred upon *Barbara Villiers*, daughter to the Lord Viscount *Grandison*, and, at her death, descended to *Charles*, the present Duke.]

Upon the shore, *Skengrave*,Skengrave. a small Village, thrives by the great variety of Fish which it takes; where, it is reported that * * So said, ann. 1607.
A Sea-man.seventy years ago they caught a † † *Hominem marinum.Sea-man*, who lived upon raw fish for some days; but at last, taking his opportunity, he made his escape into his own element. When the winds are laid, and the sea is in a calm, the waters being spread (as it were) into a plain, a hideous groaning is oft-times heard in these parts on a sudden, and then the fishermen are afraid to go to Sea; who, according to their poor sense of things, believe the Ocean to be a huge Monster, which is then hungry, and eager to glut it self with the bodies of men. Beneath *Skengrave* stands *Kilton*,Kilton. a Castle, with a Park round it: this belonged formerly to the famous family of the *Thwengs*, whose estate descended to the Barons of *Lumley, Hilton*, and *Daubeney*. Very near this place is *Skelton-castle*,Skelton-castle. [heretofore] belonging to the ancient family of the Barons *de Brus,Brus* of Skelton. who are descended from *Robert Brus* a Norman. He had two Sons, *Adam* Lord of *Skelton*, and *Robert* Lord of *Anan-dale* in Scotland, from whom sprang the Royal Line of Scotland. But *Peter Brus*, the fifth Lord of *Skelton*, died without issue, and left his sisters heirs; *Agnes*, married to *Walter de Falconberg*; *Lucie*,Barons Falconberg. married to *Marmaduke de Thwenge*, from whom the Baron *Lumley* is descended; *Margaret*, married to *Robert de Roos*; and *Laderina*, married to *John de Bella aqua*; all, men of great honour and esteem in that age. The Posterity of *Walter de Falconberg* flourish'd a long time; but at last the estate came by a female to *William Nevil*, famous for his warlike valour, and honour'd with the title of *Earl of Kent* by King Edward the fourth. His daughters were married to *J. Coigniers, N.Bedhowing*, and *R. Strangwayes*. [*Robert Bruce*, Earl of Elgin in Scotland, was by King Charles the second, in the year 1663, advanced to the title of Earl of *Ailsbury* and Baron *Bruce* of *Skelton*.

Near the mouth of the *Tees*, is *Kirk-Letham*,Kirk-Letham. where Sir *William Turner* (Lord Mayor of *London* in the year 1669.) built a most stately Hospital, at this place of his Nativity, and endowed it generously for the maintenance of forty poor people (aged, and children,) with liberal Salaries also to a Chaplain, a Master and Mistress. To which, at his death, he added a benefaction of five thousand Pounds for the erecting a Free-School, and the purchasing of plentiful † † To the Master, 100 *l. per ann.*
To the Usher 50 *l*.Salaries.]

Near *Hunt-cliff*,Hunt-cliff. on the shore, when the tide is out, the rocks shoot up pretty high; and to these the *Sea-calves* (which we by contraction call *Seales*, as some think for *Sea-veals* or *Sea-calves*)Sea-calves. come out in great droves, and there sleep and sun themselves. Upon one of the rocks neerest the shore, some one of them stands *centry* as it were; and when any body comes near, he either pushes down a stone, or with great noise throws himself into the water, to alarm the rest, that they may provide for themselves, and get into the Sea. Their greatest fear is of Men; and if they are pursued by them, and cannot reach the Sea in time, they often keep them off, by casting-up sand and gravel with their hinder feet. They are not in such awe of Women; so that the *Men* who would take them, disguise themselves in Womens habit. Here are upon this Coast yellowish and reddish Stones, and some crusted over with a brinish substance; which by their smell and taste resemble Coperas, Nitre, and Brimstone: and also great store of *Pyrites*, in colour like Brass.

Near, at *Huntly Nabb*,Huntly Nabb. the shore (which for a long way together has lain open) now rises into high rocks; and here and there, at the bottoms of the rocks,Round Stones. lie great stones of several sizes so exactly form'd round by nature, that one would think them bullets cast by some Artist for the great Guns. If you break them, you find, within, stony Serpents wreathed up in Circles, but generally without heads. Hence we see *Wilton-castle*,Wilton-castle. formerly belonging to the *Bulmers*. Higher up, at *Dobham*, the river *Tees* rolls into the Sea, having [visited *Cleasby*,Cleasby. where Dr. *Robinson*, Envoy for many years to the Court of *Sweden*, and now Bishop of *London*, hath rebuilt and endowed a Chapel (with a convenient House for the Minister) at this his native place; and also] receiv'd many small rivulets; the last whereof is a nameless one, which enters it near *Yarum*,Yarum. noted for its Market; and washes *Stokesley*,Stokesley. a small Market-town likewise, which * * *Jam diu spectavit*.remain'd long in the hands of the famous family *de Eure*, [of which, was Sir *William Eure*, whom King Henry the eighth advanced to the degree of a Baron of this Realm; but this honour expir'd, *anno* 1707. in *Ralph* Lord *Eure*.] Below these, stands *Wharlton*-castle,Wharlton-castle. which formerly belonged to the Barons *Meinill*; and *Harlsey*,Harlsey. to the family of *Hotham*, but afterwards to the *Strangwayes*, [and now to the *Lawsons*:] both of them old and ruinous.

The mouth of the [foremention'd] *Tees*, was hardly trusted by Mariners heretofore; but now is found to be a safe Harbour: and to direct the entrance, there were Light-houses made on both sides of it, within the memory of † † So said, ann. 1607.the present age. Four miles from the mouth of this river, *Gisburgh*Gisburgh. stands upon a rising ground; at present a small Town, but formerly very famous for a beautiful and rich Monastery, built about the year 1119. by *Robert de Brus* Lord of the Town. It has been the common burial-place for the Nobility of these parts, and produced *Walter de Hemingford*, no unlearned Historian; [and the Abbey-Church, by the ruins, seems to have been equal to the best Cathedrals in *England*.] The place is really fine, and may, in point of pleasantness, and a grateful variety, and other advantages of Nature, compare with *Puteoli* in Italy; and in point of healthfulness, it far surpasses it. [The Inhabitants are observed by Travellers to be civil and well-bred; cleanly in their diet, and neat in their houses.] The coldness of the air, which the Sea occasions, is qualified by the hills between; the Soil is fruitful, and produces grass and fine flowers a great part of the year; it abounds with veins of Metal and *Alum*-earth of several colours (but especially with those of *ocher* and *murray*) from which they now † † Ann. 1607.begin to extract the best sort of AlumAlum. and CoperasCoperas.. This was first discover'd a † few years since by the admirable sagacity of that learned Naturalist Sir *Thomas Chaloner* Kt. (to whose tuition, * * His present Majesty hath, C.his Majesty [King James the first] committed the delight and glory of Britain, his Son Prince *Henry*;) by observing that the leaves of trees were * * *Magis subvirere*.of a more weak sort of Green here than in other places; that the oaks shoot forth their roots very broad, but not deep; and that these had much strength but little sap in them; that the soil was a white clay, speckled with several colours, namely, white, yellowish, and blue; that it never froze; and that in a pretty-clear night it shin'd and sparkled like glass, on the road-side. [Here are two Alom-works; one belonging to the *Chaloners*, the other to the *Darcies*; but both have been laid aside for some years. Possibly, *Whitby* lying more conveniently, and having plenty of the Mine at hand, may have drawn the Trade from them.]

* Magis sub virere

of trees were of a more weak sort of Green here than in other places, that the oaks shoot forth their Roots very broad, but not deep, and that these had much strength but little sap in them; that the soil was a white clay, speckled with several colours, namely, white, yellowish, and blue, that it never froze; and that in a pretty-clear night it shin'd and sparkled like glass, on the road-side [Here are two Alom works; one belonging to the *Chaloners*, the other to the *Darcies*, but both have been laid aside for some years. Possibly, *Whitby* lying more conveniently, and having plenty of the Mine at hand, may have drawn the Trade from them]

Ounesbery or Rosebery Topping.

Next, *Ounesbery-Topping*, a steep Mountain and all over green, riseth so high, as to appear at a great distance; and it is the land-mark that directs Sailors, and a prognostick of weather to the neighbours hereabouts For when it's top begins to be darkened with clouds, rain generally follows Near the top of it, there issues from a huge rock, a fountain, very good for sore eyes And from hence, the valleys round it, the grassy hills, green meadows, rich pastures, fruitful corn-fields, rivers full of fish, the creeky mouth of the *Tees*, shores low and open, yet free from inundation, and the Sea with the Ships under sail, do render the prospect very agreeable and entertaining Beneath this, stands *Kildale*, a Castle belonging to the *Percies* Earls of Northumberland, and more to the east, *Danby*, which came from *Brus*, by the *Thwengs*, to the Barons *Latimer*, from whose heir are descended the *Willoughbies* Barons *Broke* But this *Danby*, among other estates, was sold to the *Nevils*, of whom, *George Nevil* was summon'd among the Barons, to Parliament, by Henry the sixth, under the title of Lord *Latimer*; in whose posterity that Honour remain'd to the † present age [Since which *Danby* hath afforded the title of Earl to *Henry* Lord *Danvers* of *Dantsey*, created *Feb* 7. 1 Car 1. but he dy'd without issue in the year 1643 In 1674. *June* 27 the title of Earl of *Danby* was conferred upon *Thomas Osborn*, a very able Statesman in his time, who was created before Baron of *Kiveton*, and Viscount *Latimer*, and was afterwards advanced to the dignity of Marquiss of *Caermarthen*, and Duke of *Leeds*]

Kildale

Danby

Barons Latimer

† So said, ann 1607

I have nothing more to observe here, but that the Baron *de Meinill* held some lands in this County, of the Archbishops of Canterbury, and that the *Coigniers* and *Strangwaies*, with some others descended from them, are obliged to be attendant, and to pay certain military services to the Archbishops, for the same And whereas *the King of England, by his Prerogative* (these are the very words of the Statute) *shall have the Ward of all the lands of such as hold of him in chief by Knights service, whereof the tenants were seized in their demesne as of fee at the day of their death, of whomsoever they hold else by like service, so that they held in ancient time any land of the Crown, till the heir come to his lawful age* Yet these fees are excepted, and others of the Archbishop of Canterbury and the Bishop of Durham, *so that they shall have such Wards, tho' they held of the King in some other Place.*

The History of Canterbury

Prerog. Reg.

Wardship

More inward, among the Mountains of *Blackamore*, there is nothing remarkable (besides some rambling brooks and rapid torrents, which take up all the vallies hereabouts;) unless it be *Pickering*, a pretty large Town belonging to the Dutchy of Lancaster, seated up on a hill, and fortified with an old Castle, to which many neighbouring villages belong; so that the adjacent territory is commonly called *Pickering Lith*, *the Liberty of Pickering*, and *the Forest of Pickering*; which Henry the third gave to *Edmund* his younger son, Earl of Lancaster In this, upon the Derwent, *Atton* is situated, which gave name to the famous family of the *Attons* Knights, descended from the Lords de *Vescy*, whose estate was divided by daughters between *Edward de St John*, the *Euers*, and the *Coigniers* From this *Edward de St John*, a great part of it came by a daughter to *Henry Bromflet*; who was summon'd to Parliament in the following manner (no where else to be met with among the Summons to Parliament;) *We will that both you and the heirs males of your body lawfully begotten, be Barons of Vescy* Afterwards, this title came by a daughter to the *Cliffords*. On the other side, four miles from *Pickering*, near *Dow* (a little rapid river) is *Kirby-Morside*, none of the most inconsiderable Market-towns, formerly belonging to the *Estotevills*, and situate near hills, from which it takes the name.

Blackamore

Pickering

Atton

27 Hen 6 Bromflet Lord Vesy

Kirkby Morside

After these, westward, stands *Rhidale*, a very fine vale, pleasant and fruitful, and adorned with twenty three Parish-Churches, and the river *Rhy* running through the midst of it *A place* (says Newbrigensis) *of vast solitude and horror*, till *Walter Espec* gave it to the Cluniack Monks, and founded a Cloister for them. In this Vale is *Elmesly*, which (if I mistake not) Bede calls *Ulmetum*, where *Robert*, sirnamed *de Ross*, built the Castle of *Fursan*; near which, the river *Recall* hides it self under Ground Lower down upon this river, stands *Riton*, the ancient * estate of an ancient family the *Percihaies*, commonly called *Percyes*

Rhidale

Elmesley call'd also Hamlak

* Now Baronus

[At a little Village named *East-ness* in *Rhydale*, was found the following Sepulchral Inscription upon a Stone-Monument, which was full of bones

East ness

TITIA' PINTA' VIXIT' ANN'
XXXVIII' ET' VAL' ADIVTORI'
VIXIT' ANN' XX' ET' VARIOLO'
VIXIT' ANN' XV' VAL' VINDI
CIANVS' CONIVGIE' T' FILIS'
F C]

From hence the *Rhy*, with many waters received from other currents, rolls into the *Derwent*, which washes *Malton* in this Vale, a Market-town, famous for its vent of Corn, Fish, and † Country utensils [For the making of the said river navigable to this place, and from hence to its joining with the river *Ouse*, an Act of Parliament pass'd in the first year of Queen *Anne*] Here [at *Malton*,] the foundation of an old Castle is still visible; which formerly, as I have heard, belonged to the *Vesceys*, Barons of great note and eminence in these parts. Their pedigree (as appears from the Records) is derived from *William Tyson*, Lord of *Malton* and *Alnewick* in *Northumberland*, who was cut off in the battle of *Hastings*, against the Normans His only daughter was married to *Ivo de Vescy* a Norman, who likewise left one only daughter *Beatrice*, married to *Eustachius*, son of *John Monoculus*, who in the reign of King Stephen founded two religious houses, at *Malton* and *Watton* for his second wife (daughter to William Constable of Chester) was Lady of *Watton* *William*, son of Eustachius by his wife Beatrice, who was ripped out of his mother's womb, took the name *Vescey*, and

Malton

† Instrumenta Rustica

Baron Vescy

Arms of the Vescies *Matth. Paris MS*

ard for Arms, *A Cross, Argent, in a field, Gules* This William, by B daughter to Robert Estotevill of Knaresburgh, had two sons; *Eustace de Vescey*, who married Margaret, daughter of William King of Scots; and *Guarin de Vescey* Lord of *Knapton* *Eustace* was father to *William*, who had a son, *John*, that died without issue, and *William*, famous for his exploits in Ireland, and who changed the old Arms of the family into *a Shield, Or, with a Cross, Sable* William, (whose lawful son, *John*, dy'd in the wars of Wales) gave some of his lands in Ireland to King Edward, on condition, that his

Lib. Dunelm

natural son called *William de Kildare*, might inherit his estate, and made *Anthony Bec* Bishop of Durham, his Feoffee in trust to the use of his son, who did not acquit himself over-fairly in that part of his charge relating to *Alnwick, Eltham* in Kent, and some other estates, which he is said to have converted to his own use This natural son, aforesaid, was slain at the Battle of *Sterling* in Scotland, and the title came at last to the family of the *Attons*, by *Margaret* the only daughter of *Guarin Vescey*, who was married to *Gilbert de Atton* But enough of this, if not too much, and besides, it has been spoken of before

1st pag printed *Newborrow*

Near this Vale, stands *Newborrow*, to which we owe *William of Newborrow*, the English Historian, a learned and diligent Writer now it is the Seat of the famous family *de Ballasise*, who came originally from the Bishoprick of Durham, [and are honoured with the title of Viscounts *Falconberge*, the Earldom being extinct, by the death of *Thomas* Earl of Falconberge without issue] Near the same Vale,

Biland

stands *Bellaland*, commonly called *Biland* this, and Newborrow, were two famous Monasteries,

Family of the Mowbrays

both founded and endowed, by *Roger Mowbray* The family of the *Mowbrays* was very considerable for Power, Honour, and Wealth possessing very great Estates, with the Castles of *Slingesby*, *Thresk*, and others, in these parts The rise of the family was in short thus *Roger de Mowbray* Earl of Northumberland, and *R de*

** In another place call'd De Fronte Bovis*

* *Grandebeofe*, being depriv'd of their estates for Disloyalty, King Henry the first gave the greatest part of them to *Nigell de Albenie* (descended from the same family with the *Albenies* Earls of Arundell) a person of very noble extraction

The Register of Fountains Abby

among the Normans He was Bow bearer to William Rufus, and was enrich'd to that degree by Henry the first, that he had in England 140 Knights fees, and in Normandy 120. His son Roger was also commanded by him to take the name of *Mowbray*, from whom the *Moubrays* Earls of Nottingham, and Dukes of Norfolk, were descended To these *Mowbrays*

Gilling castle

also *Gilling-castle*, a little way from hence, did formerly belong, but now it is in the hands of that ancient and famous family, which from

Fairfax *Fix*

their *fair hair*, have the name of *Fairfax* for *fax* in Saxon signifies *hair*, or *the hairs of the head*, upon which account they call'd a Comet

Faxed star

or Blazing-star a *Faxed star*, as also the place before spoken of, *Haly-fax*, from *holy hair*

The Forest of Galtres

Below this, to the South, lies the *Calaterium nemus*, commonly call'd *The Forest of Gaultres*, which in some places is thick and shady, and in others flat, wet, and boggy [This Forest extended to the very walls of the City of York, as appears by a Perambulation made in the 28th

A Horse race An. 1607 [illegible]

year of Edward the first] At present it is famous for a yearly Horse race, wherein the prize for the horse that wins, is a little golden bell It is hardly credible, how great a resort of people there is to these races from all parts, and what great wagers are laid. In this Forest

Creac

stands *Creac*, which Egfrid King of Northumberland in the year * 685 gave, with the ground

+ 684 C contrary to the original Charter

three miles round, to S *Cuthbert*, by whom it came to the Church of Durham

Sherry hutton

Scarce four miles from hence, *Sherry hutton*, [heretofore] a very neat and beautiful Castle, built by *Bertrand de Bulmer*, and repair'd by *Ralph Nevill* first Earl of Westmorland, is pleasantly situated among the woods; [but now has little more remaining, than the Shell] Near

Hinderskel *|| Centum fontes*

which is *Hinderskell*, a Castle built by the Barons of Greystock, which others call || *Hundred Skell*, from the many fountains that spring there [Here, the Right Honourable *Charles Howard*, Earl of Carlisle, hath built a most noble and beautiful seat, call'd *Castle Howard*, in-

Castle Howard

stead of the old Castle, which was burnt down

Stitenham

In this neighbourhood, is *Stitenham*, the ancient Seat of a Knightly Family, of which was the famous Poet Sir *John Gower* and of the same family is the present *John* Lord *Gower*, Baron of *Stitenham*]

North Allerton

Behind the hills to the Westward, where the Country spreads it self into a level, and into fruitful fields, lies *Alvertonshire*, commonly *North-Allerton*, a small territory, water'd by the little river *Wiske* It takes its name from the Town of *Northalverton*, called formerly Ealfertun, which is nothing but a long street, yet, the throngest Beast fair on St Bartholomew's day, that I ever saw *William Rufus* gave this place, with the fields about it, to the Church of Durham, to the Bishops whereof it is much oblig'd For *William Comin*, who forcibly possess'd himself of the See of *Durham*, built the Castle here, and gave it to his nephew, which is

** Quondammodo disparuit* *Cap 1.6*

now * almost quite gone The Bishops likewise, his Successors, endow'd it with certain priviledges For in the Book of *Durham*, we find, *that* Hugh de Puteaco, *Bishop of Durham, fortified the Town, having obtain'd this favour of the King, that of all those † unlawful Castles, that*

† Adulterina *1137*

were order'd to be destroy'd throughout England, this alone should still be permitted to remain, which, notwithstanding, the King afterwards commanded to be rased and laid even with the ground Near this

The Battel of Standard *Hoveden*

was fought the Battel, commonly call'd, *The Standard* [from which, one part of the History written by *Richard Prior* of *Hexham*, bears the title *De Bello Standardi*,)] wherein David King of Scots, who, by his unheard of Cruelties had made this Country a Desolation, was put to flight, and that with such slaughter, that the English themselves thought their revenge compleated For what Ralph the Bishop said in his Exhortation to the English before the fight, was fully effected *A multitude without discipline is an encumbrance to it self, either to hurt when they conquer, or to escape when they are conquer'd* This was call'd the *Battle of Standard*, because the English, being rang'd into a body round their Standard, did there receive and bear the first onset of the Scots, and at last routed them This *Standard* (as I have seen it painted in old books) was a huge Chariot upon wheels, with

** Malus* *Carrocium*

a * *mast* of great heighth fix'd in it, on the top whereof was a cross, and under that, a banner This was a signal, us'd only in the greatest Expeditions, and was look'd upon as a kind of sacred Altar; being indeed the very same with the *Carrocium* among the Italians, which was never to be used but when the very Government lay at stake

Thresk

There is further remarkable in this division, a place call'd *Thresk*, commonly *Thrusk*; which had formerly a very strong Castle, where *Roger de de Mowbray* began his rebellio, and call'd in the King of Scots to the destruction of his Country, King Henry the second having very unadvisedly *dug his own grave*, by taking his Son into an equal share of the Government. But this Sedition was at last, as it were *quench'd and extinguish'd* with blood, and the Castle utterly demolish'd; so that I could see nothing of it there, besides the rampire. Another flame of Rebellion likewise broke out here, in King Henry the seventh's reign; when the lawless Rabble, repining grievously at a small subsidy laid on them by Parliament, drove away the Collector, and forthwith (as such madness upon the least success, drives on, without end or aim) fell here upon *Henry Percie* Earl of Northumberland, who was † Lieutenant of this County, and kill'd him, and then, under the conduct of *John Egremond* their Leader, took up Arms against their King and Country. Yet it was not long before they were brought to condign punishment. Hard by, stands *Scureby* and *Brakenbak*, belonging to the ancient and famous family of *Lascelles*; and more to the south, *Sezay*, formerly the estate of the *Darells*; and after that of the *Dawnies*, who † flourish'd long under the title of Knights, [till Sir *John Dawnie* was by King Charles the second advanced to the dignity of Viscount *Downe*, in the kingdom of Ireland.]

Earl of Northumberland slain by the Rebels.

† *Provinciæ præfuit.*

Scureby. Brakenbak. Lascelles. Sezay.

† Have flourish'd, C.

Earls and Dukes of York.

An. 1. R. 1. Hoveden.

The first and only Earl of Yorkshire (after William *Mallet*, and one or two *Estotevills*, both of Norman extraction, whom some reckon hereditary Viscounts;) was *Otho*, son of *Henry Leon* Duke of Bavaria and Saxony, by Maud the daughter of Henry the second King of England. He was afterwards saluted Emperor by the name of *Otho the fourth*. From his brother *William* (another son by Maud) the Dukes of Brunswick and Lunenburgh in Germany, are descended; who, in testimony of this their relation to the Kings of England, bear the same Arms with our first Kings of Norman descent, namely, *two Leopards or Lions, Or, in a Shield, Gules*. Long after this, King Richard the second made *Edward of Langley*, fifth Son of King Edward the third, Duke of York, who by one of the daughters of Peter, King of Castile and Leon, had two sons: *Edward*, the eldest, in the life time of his father, was first Earl of Cambridge, after that, Duke of Albemarle, and last of all, *Duke of York*, who dy'd valiantly in the battel of Agincourt in France, without issue. *Richard*, the second son, was Earl of Cambridge, he marry'd *Ann*, sister of Edmund Mortimer Earl of March, whose grandmother likewise was the only daughter and heir of *Leonel* Duke of Clarence; and, attempting to set the Crown upon the head of his wife's brother *Edmund*, he was presently discover'd, and beheaded, as if hired by the French to take away the life of King Henry the fifth. Richard his son, in the sixteenth year after, was by the great, but unwary, generosity of Henry the sixth, fully restor'd, *as son of Richard, the brother of Edward Duke of York, and Cousin German to Edward Earl of March.* And now being Duke of *York*, Earl of *March* and *Ulster*, and Lord of *Wigmore*, *Clare*, *Trim*, and *Conaght*, he grew to that pitch of boldness, that whereas formerly he had sought the Crown privately by indirect practices, as complaining of male-administration, dispersing seditious rumors and libels, entring into secret combinations, and raising broils and factions against the Government, at last he claim'd it publickly in Parliament, against Henry the sixth; as being son of Ann Mortimer, sister and heir to Edmund Earl of March, descended in a right line from *Philippa* the daughter and sole heir of Leonel Duke of Clarence, third son of King Edward the third; and therefore in all justice to be prefer'd in the succession to the Crown, before the children of *John of Gaunt*, the fourth son of the said Edward the third. And when it was answer'd, That the Nobles of the Kingdom, and the Duke himself, had sworn Allegiance to the King, that the Kingdom by Act of Parliament was conferr'd and entail'd upon Henry the fourth and his heirs, that the Duke, who derived his title from the Duke of Clarence, never took the Arms of the said Duke, and that Henry the fourth was possess'd of the Crown by the right he had from Henry the third: All this he easily evaded; by replying, that the said Oath sworn to the King, being barely a human Constitution, was not binding, because it was inconsistent with truth and justice, which are of Divine appointment, That there had been no need of an Act of Parliament to settle the Kingdom in the line of Lancaster, neither would they have desir'd it, if they could have rely'd on a just title. That as for the Arms of the Duke of Clarence, which of right belong'd to him, he had in prudence declin'd the using them, as he had done the entring his claim to the Crown, till that moment. and, That the title deriv'd from Henry the third, was only a ridiculous pretence to cloak the Injustice, and was exploded by every body. Tho' these things, pleaded in favour of the Duke of York, shew'd his title to be clear and evident, yet upon a wise foresight of the dangers that might ensue, the matter was so adjusted, That Henry the sixth should possess and enjoy the Kingdom for life, and that Richard Duke of York should be appointed his heir and successor in the Kingdom, with this proviso, that neither of them should attempt or contrive any thing to the prejudice of the other. However, the Duke was so far transported with ambition, as to endeavour to anticipate his hopes, and raise that dreadful War between the Houses of York and Lancaster, distinguish'd by the *white* and the *red* Roses; which in a short time prov'd fatal to himself at *Wakefield*. King Henry the sixth was four times taken prisoner, and at last depriv'd of his Kingdom and his Life. Then, Edward Earl of March, son of Richard, obtain'd the Crown; and though he was depos'd, yet he recover'd it: thus did Fortune, inconstant and freakish as she is, sport her self with the rise and fall of Princes. In the mean time, many of the Blood royal and of the greatest of the Nobility were cut off, those hereditary and rich Provinces of the Kings of England in France were lost, Ireland was neglected, and relaps'd to its old wildness, the wealth of the Nation was wasted, and the harass'd people were oppress'd with all sorts of misery. Edward being now settled in his Throne, as the fourth King of that name, bestow'd the title of Duke of York upon Richard his second son; who, with the King his brother, was destroy'd, very young, by that Tyrant *Richard* their Uncle. Next, Henry the seventh confer'd it upon his younger son, who was afterwards crown'd King of England by the name of Henry the 8th. And † K. James [the 1st] invested his second son *Charles* (whom he had before, in Scotland, made *Duke of Albany, Marquiss of Ormond, Earl of Ross*, and *Baron Ardmannoch*) Duke of York, 1604
by girding him with a Sword (to use the words of the form) *and putting a Cap and Coronet of* Gold

Dukes of *Brunswick*.

Parl. 10 H. 6.

Parl. Rolls, 39 H. 6.

Wars between the House of York and Lancaster, between the *Red rose* and the *white*.

† Now very lately, C.

Gold upon his head, and delivering to him a Verge of Gold, after he had the day before, according to the usual manner, created both him and eleven others of noble and honourable families, Knights of the Bath [And as James the first created *Charles* his second son Duke of York, so Charles succeeding his father in the Throne, declar'd his second son James (afterwards King *James* the second) Duke of the same place whereupon, at his birth he receiv'd that title, but was not created till the 27th of Jan. 1643, being the 19th year of his father's reign Since the accession of King George to the Throne, his Majesty hath been pleas'd to confer the same High Title upon Ernest Augustus, his brother, who is Knight of the most Noble Order of the Garter, and also Duke of York and Albany, and Earl of Ulster]

There are in this County 459 Parishes; with very many Chapels under them, which for number of Inhabitants are equal to great Parishes

RICHMONDSHIRE.

THE rest of this County, which lies to the North west, and is of large extent, is call'd *Richmond shire*, or *Richmountshire* The name is taken from a Castle built by *Alan* Earl of Bretagne in Armorica, to whom William the Conqueror gave this Shire (which belong'd to Edwin, an English-man) by a short Charter in these words *I William, sirnam'd Bastard, King of England, do give and grant to thee my nephew Alan Earl of Bretagne, and to thy heirs for ever, all the villages and lands which of late belong'd to Earl Eadwin in Yorkshire, with the Knights fees and other Liberties and Customs, as freely and honourably as the same Edwin held them Dated from our Siege before York*

By reason of craggy Rocks and vast Mountains, this Shire is almost one continu'd eminence the sides of them here and there yield pretty good grass, and the bottoms and valleys are not unfruitful The hills afford great store of Lead, Pit Coal, and also Brass In a Charter of Edward the fourth, there is mention made of a Mineral or Mine of Copper near *the very city of Richmond* But covetousness, which makes men dig even to Hell, has not yet mov'd them to sink into these Mountains, being diverted perhaps by the difficulties of the Carriage

Brass, Lead, and Pit-coal

On the tops of these Mountains, as likewise in other places, there have been found stones resembling Sea cockles and other Water animals; which, if they are not Miracles of Nature, I cannot but think, with Orosius a Christian Historian, to be certain tokens of the universal Deluge in the time of Noah *The Sea* (as he says) *being in Noah's time spread over all the earth, and a deluge pour'd forth upon it (so that the whole world was overflow'd, and the Sea, as heaven, surrounded the earth;) all mankind was destroy'd, but only those few sav'd in the ark for their Faith, to propagate posterity; as is clearly taught by the most faithful Writers That this was so, those persons have also been witnesses, who, knowing neither past times, nor the Author of them, yet from the signs and indications of those stones (which we often find on mountains distant from the Sea, but overspread with cockles and oysters, yea oft times hollow'd by the water) have learn'd it by conjecture and inference* [As to these stones like *Cockles*, a diligent Observer of these Curiosities affirms, that he cou'd never hear of any that were met with lying single and dispers'd; but that plenty of them, as well here as in other places in the North, are found in firm rocks and beds of Lime-stone; sometimes at six or eight fathom within ground Whence the Miners call them *Run Limestone*; they supposing these figures to be produced by a more than ordinary heat, and a quicker fermentation than they allow to the production of the other parts of the quarry And this, perhaps, is as rational an account of these sports of Nature (supposing them such) as any that our modern Virtuosi have hitherto pitch'd upon]

Stone cockles

Where this Shire touches upon the County of Lancaster, the prospect among the hills is so wild, solitary, and unsightly, and all things are so still, that the neighbouring Inhabitants have call'd some brooks there, *Hel becks*, that is to say, *Hell* or *Stygian Rivulets*, especially *that*, at the head of the river *Ure*, which, with a bridge over it of one entire stone, falls so deep, that it strikes one with horror to look down Here is safe harbour in this tract, for goats, deer, and stags, which for their unusual bulk and branchy heads are very remarkable and extraordinary

Hell becks.

The river *Ure*, which we have often mention'd, has its rise here out of the western mountains, and first runs through the middle of the vale *Wensedale*, sufficiently stock'd with cattel, and in some places with lead Not far from its spring, while it is yet but small, it is encreased by the little river *Bairt* from the south, which issues from the pool *Semur* with a strange murmur At the confluence of these two streams (where are some few cottages, call'd from the first bridge over the Ure, *Buntbrig*) there was formerly a Roman garrison, of which some remains are still to be seen For upon the hill (which from the burrough, they now call *Burgh*) there are the ground works of an old fortification, about five acres in compass, and under it, to the east, the tracks of many houses are still visible Where, among several proofs of Roman Antiquity, I lately saw this fragment of an old Inscription, in a very fair character, with a *winged Victory* supporting it

Wensedale

Bracchium

IMP

IMP CÆS. L. SEPTIMIO
PIO PERTINACI AVGV.–
IMP CÆSARI. M AVRELIO A-
PIO FELICI AVGVSTO—

The name of Geta eras'd.

- - - - - - - - - - - - - -
- - - - - - - - - - - - - - -

BRACCHIO CÆMENTICIVM -
VI NERVIORVM SVB CVRA LA
SENECION AMPLISSIMI
OPERI L. VI SPIVS PRÆ-
- - - - LEGIO - - - -

From whence we may conjecture, that this Fort at *Burgh*, was formerly call'd *Bracchium*, which before had been made of turf, but then was built of stone and mortar; and that the sixth Cohort of the *Nervii* garrison'd here, who also seem to have had a Summer camp upon that high entrench'd Hill, hard by, which is now call'd *Ethenbury* It is not long, since a Statue of *Aurelius Commodus* the Emperor, was dug-up here, who (as Lampridius has it) was stil'd by his flatterers *Britannicus*, even when the Britains were for chusing another Emperor against him This Statue seems to have been set up, when, through an extravagant Esteem of himself he arriv'd to that pitch of folly, as to command every one to call him, *The Roman Hercules, son of Jupiter* For it is in the habit of *Hercules*, with his right-hand arm'd with a club, and under it (as I am inform'd) was this broken and imperfect Inscription, which had been ill copy'd, and was lost before I came hither

Statue of *Commodus* the Emperor

——CÆSARI AVGVSTO
MARCI AVRELII FILIO

SEN IONIS AMPLISSIMI
VENTS PIVS.

Nappa
The numerous family of *Medcalf*

This was to be seen at *Nappa*, a house built with turrets, and the chief seat of the *Medcalfs*, which is counted the most numerous family this day in England For I have heard that Sir *Christopher Medcalf* Knight, and chief of the family, being † lately Sheriff of the County, was attended with three hundred Horse, all of this family and name, and all in the same habit, to receive the Justices of Assize, and conduct them to York From hence the *Ure* runs very swiftly, with abundance of *Crey fish*, ever since C *Medcalf*, within the memory of * this age, brought that sort of fish hither from the south parts of England; [(which, however, he might have had much nearer hand; the rivers of *Kent*, *Lowther*, &c in the County of Westmorland, being plentifully stock'd with them)] And, between two rocks (from which the place is called *Att-scarre*) it violently rolls down its channel, not far from *Bolton*, the ancient seat of the Barons *de Scrope*, and a stately Castle which *Richard* Lord *le Scrope*, Chancellour of England in Richard the second's time, built at a very great charge [This place is now honoured, by giving the title of Duke, to *Charles Powlet*, Lord Lieutenant of Ireland; whose Ancestors for many generations have enjoy'd the Titles of Earl of Wiltshire, and Marquiss of Winchester, and whose Father was advanced to this higher dignity, in the first year of King William and Queen Mary. In the Parish, not long since, lived one *Henry Jenkins*, a much more noted instance of Longævity, than the famous *Par*; as dying (*Dec* 8. 1670) at the age of 169 years He could easily remember the Dissolution of Monasteries, and hath given Evidence of ancient customs, in Courts of Justice, for above 140 years After he was past the age of 100, he used frequently to swim in rivers. He had been Butler to the Lord *Coniers*, and after that, a Fisherman, and at last, a Beggar.]

† So said, ann. 1607.

Crey fish
* So said, ann 1607

Bolton.
Barons le *Scrope*

Philosoph Tranf N 221, 228

Ure, taking its course eastward, comes to the Town of *Midelham*, the *Honour* of which (as we read in the Genealogy of the *Nevils*) *Alan* Earl of Richmond gave to his younger brother * *Rinebald*, with all the lands, which before their coming had belong'd to *Gilpatrick* the Dane His grandchild by his son *Ralph*, called *Robert Fitz-Ralph*, had all *Wensledale* bestow'd on him by *Conanus* Earl of Bretagne and Richmond, and built a very strong castle at *Midleham* Ranulph his son built a small Monastery for Canons at *Coverham* (now contracted into *Corham*) in Coverdale, and his son *Ralph* had a daughter *Mary*, who being married to *Robert* Lord *Nevill*, brought this large estate, for her portion, to the family of the *Nevills* This Robert Nevill, having had many children by his wife, was taken in adultery, unknown, and had his privy members cut off by the adultress's husband in revenge, which threw him into such an excess of grief, that he soon after dy'd

Midleham

* By others *Ribald*

Lords of Midleham.

An ancient Genealogy.

[Near *Midleham*, is *Thoresby*, the Seat of an ancient Family of that name, of which was *John Thoresby* Archbishop of York and Chancellor of England; and of which also (being the eldest branch) was Mr *John Thoresby* late of Leeds, an eminent Antiquary, and famous for his *Musæum*, which is now possess'd and very much augmented by his son Mr *Ralph Thoresby*, a person excellently skilled in the subject of Antiquities]

Thoresby

From *Midleham*, the *Ure* having pass'd a few miles, washes *Jervis* or *Jorvalle*-Abbey, which is now reduced to ruins; and then runs by *Masham*, which belonged to the *Scropes* of Masham (who, as they are descended from the *Scropes* of *Bolton*, so are they again grafted into the same Family by marriage,) [but now to the *Danbies*] On the other side of this river, but more inward, stands *Snath*, the chief seat of the Barons *de Latimer*, whose noble extraction is from *G Nevill*, younger son of Ralph Nevill first Earl of Westmorland, who had this honourable title confer'd on him by King Henry the sixth, when the elder family of the *Latimers* ended in a female and so they flourish'd in a continu'd succession, till * our time, when for want of heirs male of the last Baron, this noble inheritance was parted among his daughters, who were married into the families of the *Percies*, *Cecils*, *D'anvers*, and *Cornwallis* There is no other place in these parts remarkable upon the *Ure*, but *Tanfield*, formerly the seat of the *Gernegans* Knights, from whom it descended to the *Marmions* the last of these, left *Amice*, his heir, second wife of John Lord Grey of Rotherfield; whose two children, taking the name of *Marmion*, were heirs to their mother; and one of them left an only daughter and heir, *Elizabeth*, the wife of Fitz Hugh a famous Baron

Jorvalle Abbey
Masham
Snath
Barons Latimer
* So said, ann 1607
Tanfield
Marmion Inq 6 H 6

The *Ure* now receives the *Swale* (so call'd, as *Tho. Spot* has* it, from its swiftness) which joins it with a great *leaping of the waters* This also rises out of the western mountains, scarce five

Swale, a sacred river.

five miles above the head of the river *Ure*, and runs to the east. It was very sacred among the Saxons, because when they were first converted to Christianity, there were baptiz'd in it in one day, by Paulinus Archbishop of York (to their great joy) above ten thousand men, besides women and children. The course of the *Swale* lies through a pretty broad vale, which from thence is called *Swaldale*, and has grass enough, but wants wood; first, by *Marricke*, where stood a Cloister built by the *Askes*, a Family of great note heretofore: then by *Mask*, where there is great store of lead: from thence, by *Richmond*, the chief City of this Shire, enclos'd with walls of a small compass, yet, by the suburbs, which shoots out in length to the three gates, it is pretty populous. It was built by *Alan* the first Earl (who did not dare to rely upon *Gilling*, his village or *manour* hard by, to withstand the assaults of the Saxons and Danes, whom the Normans had strip'd of their inheritances) and honoured by him with this name, which signifies a *Rich Mount*, and fortify'd with walls and a very strong castle situated upon a rock, from whence it looks down upon the river *Swale*, which with a terrible noise seems to *rush*, rather than *run*, among the Rocks. The village *Gilling* was more holy on account of Religion, than strong in respect of Fortifications, ever since *Oswin* King of Northumberland, by the treachery of his † Host, was slain in this place, which is call'd by Bede *Getling*. To expiate whose murder, a Monastery was built here, which was highly esteem'd and honour'd by our Ancestors. More to the north, stands *Ravenswath*, a Castle encompass'd with a pretty large wall, but now ruinous, which belong'd to the Barons call'd *Fitz-Hugh* (descended from those *Saxons* that were Lords of this place before the Norman Conquest) who flourish'd till the time of *Henry* the seventh, being enrich'd with great estates by marriages with the heirs of the famous families of the *Forneaux* and *Marmions*, which came at last by females to the *Fienes* Lords Dacre in the South, and to the *Parrs*.

[Margin: Swaldale. Marricke. Mask. Richmond. Gilling. † Hospitis. Ravenswath. Baron Fitz Hugh.]

Three miles below Richmond the *Swale* flows by that ancient City which Ptolemy and Antoninus call *Caturactonium* and *Catarracton*, but Bede * *Catarracta*, and in another place the village near *Catarracta*, which makes me think the name was given it from a Catarract, seeing here is a great fall of water hard by, though near *Richmond*, where (as I before observ'd) the *Swale* rather *rushes* than *runs*, its waters being *dash'd* and *broken* by the Rocks in its way. And why should he call it a village near *Catarracta*, if there had been no *catarract* of waters there? That it was a city of great note in those times, may be inferr'd from Ptolemy, because an Observation of the Heavens was made there. For in his *Magna Constructio* he describes the 24th parallel to be through *Cataractonium* in Britain, and makes it to be distant from the æquator, 57 degrees. Yet in his Geography he defines the longest day to be 18 Equinoctial hours; so that according to his own calculation, it is distant 58 degrees. But at this day (as the Poet says) *it has nothing great, but the name*. For it is a very small village, call'd *Catarrick*, and *Catarrick bridge*; yet remarkable for its situation by a Roman high-way, which crosses the river here; and those ‖ heaps of rubbish here and there, which carry a face of antiquity: especially near *Kettericksvart*, and *Burghale*, which are at some distance from the bridge; and more eastward, hard by the river, where I saw a huge mount with the appearance of four bulwarks, cast up with great labour to a considerable height. [Tho' therefore the name of the old *Caturactonium* be left in *Catarick*, yet are the remains of it met with about three flight shots from the bridge, at a farm house call'd *Thornburgh*, standing upon a high ground, where, as well as at *Brampton* upon *Swale* on the other side of the river, they have found Roman Coins. Upon the bank of the river (which here is very steep,) are foundations of some great walls, more like a castle than a private building, and the large prospect makes it very convenient for a Frontier-garrison. It is credibly reported, that about a hundred years ago, these walls were dug into, out of hopes of finding some treasure, and that the workmen at last came to a pair of Iron gates. Overjoy'd at this, and thinking their end compass'd, they went to refresh themselves; but before their return, a great quantity of hanging ground had fall'n in, and the vast labour of removing the rubbish discouraged them from any further attempt.

[Margin: Catarractonium. Catarricke. * Dr Gale thinks this was [illegible] three miles off. Lib. 2. c. 6. Magnum nil nisi nomen habet. Catarrick bridge. ‖ Rudera.]

The level plot of ground upon the hill adjoyning to the Farm-house, may be about ten acres, in several parts whereof Roman Coins have been plow'd up, one particularly of gold, with this Inscription, *Nero Imp Cæsar*: and on the Reverse, *Jupiter Custos*. Within this compass also, they have met with the bases of old pillars, and a floor of brick with a pipe of lead passing perpendicularly down into the earth, which is thought by some to have been a place where sacrifice was done to the Infernal Gods, and that the blood descended by those pipes. Likewise heretofore, in plowing, the Plow-share stuck fast in the ear of a great brass pot, which, upon removing the earth, they observ'd to be cover'd with flat stones, and, upon opening, found it (as it is receiv'd from our Ancestors by tradition) to be almost full of Roman Coins, mostly copper, but some of silver. Great quantities have been given away by the Predecessors of Sir *John Lawson* (to which family the Estate came by marriage,) and he himself gave a good number, to be preserv'd among other Rarities, in King Charles's Closet. The Pot was redeem'd at the price of eight Pounds, from the Sequestrators of Sir *John Lawson*'s Estate in the late Civil War, the Metal being an unusual sort of composition. It was fix'd in a Furnace to brew in, and contains some twenty four gallons of water.

Further, very lately (*anno* 1703) some of the Inhabitants, digging the ground to make a Lime kiln (on the higher-bank of the river, scarce a hundred paces below the bridge,) met with a *Vault*, fill'd with five *Urns*, viz. a large one in the middle, encompass'd with two on each side which were less. And to this place also belongs the following Inscription.

[Margin: Dr Gale, Funeral p. 13]

DEO QVI VIAS
ET SEMITAS COM
MENTVS EST. T IR
DAS.S C. F V L L.M
Q. VARIVS. VITA
LIS ETECOS ARAM
SACRAM RESTI
TVIT
APRONIANO. ET BRA
DVACOS

Now, from all this, why should not we conclude that *Thornburrow*, belonging to *Burgh hall*, was the *Vicus juxta Catarractam*, since *Catarick*-bridge, and the grounds adjoining, belong not to *Catarrick*, but to *Brough*? In this place, we will also add the following Inscription,

Upon the South end of the bridge, stands a little Chapel of stone, where tradition says, Mass was formerly said every day at eleven a clock, for the Benefit of Travellers, who would stay and hear it]

What it suffer'd from the Picts and Saxons, when they laid waste the Cities of Britain with fire and sword, we have no certain account; yet after the Saxon Government was establish'd, it seems to have flourish'd (tho' Bede always calls it a *village*,) till in the year 769 it was burnt by *Eanredus* or *Beanredus* the tyrant, who † destroy'd the Kingdom of Northumberland But immediately after, he himself was miserably burnt, and *Catarractonium* began to raise its head again for, in the 77th year after, King Ethelred solemniz'd his marriage with the daughter of Offa, King of the Mercians, in this place Yet it did not continue long in a flourishing condition, for in those Devastations of the Danes which follow'd, it was utterly destroy'd

† *Convulsit*

The *Swale*, after a long course (not without obstructions) flows pretty near *Hornby*, a castle of the family of S *Quintin*, which afterwards came to the *Cogniers*; and, except pleasant pastures and country villages, sees nothing but *Bedal*, situate upon another little river that runs into it, which in the time of King Edward the first glory'd in its Baron *Brian Fitz-Alan*, of a very ancient Family, being descended from the Dukes of Britain and the Earls of Richmond but, for want of issue-male, this inheritance came by daughters to the *Stapletons*, and the *Greys* of *Rotherfeld*

Hornby. Bedal. Fitz-Alan.

The *Swale* being now past Richmondshire, draws nearer to the *Ure*, where it sees *Topcliffe*, the chief seat of the *Percies*, call'd by Marianus Taban-clipe, who says, that in the year 949 the States of Northumberland took an oath of Allegiance there, to King Eldred the West Saxon, brother to Edmund, [But Ingulphus, who had better opportunities than Marianus to know that matter, says, it was done by Chancellor *Turketyl* at York] At the very confluence of the two rivers, stands *Mitton*, a very small village, but memorable for no small slaughter there For, in the year 1319, when England was extremely weaken'd by a Plague, the Scots continu'd their Ravages to this place, and easily routed a considerable body of Priests and Peasants, which the Archbishop of York had drawn together against them But to return From *Catarractonium*, the military way falls into two roads That towards the north lies by *Caldwell*, and by *Aldburgh* (that is, *an old burgh*) By what name this formerly went, I cannot easily guess It seems to have been a great City from its large ruins, and near it, through a village called *Stanwig*, lies a ditch about eight miles long, drawn between the *Tees* and the *Swale* The Way running to the † north west, twelve miles off, comes to *Bowes*, at present a little village, and sometimes writ *Bough*, where, in former ages, the Earls of Richmond had a small castle, and a tribute call'd *Thorough-Toll*, and their Gallows But more anciently, it was call'd in Antoninus's Itinerary *Lavatræ* and *Levatræ*, as both the distance and the situation by a military way (which is here visible by the ridge) do plainly demonstrate The Antiquity of it is further confirmed by an old Stone in the Church us'd * not long ago for a Communion-table) with this Inscription in honour of Hadrian the Emperor

Topcliffe. Mitton. Caldwell. Aldburgh. † Cir um. Bowes. Lavatr. * So fuit anno 1 o

IMP CÆSARI DIVI TRAIANI PARTHICI Max filio
DIVI NERVÆ NEPOTI TRAINO Hadria
NO AVG PONT MAXM - - - - - - -
COS I - - - - P P COH IIII F - -
IO SLV

This fragment was also dug-up there

- - - - - - - - - - -
- - - - - - - - -
NO L CAE
FRONTINVS
COH I THRAC
- - - - - -

In Severus's reign, when *Virius Lupus* was Legate and Proprætor of Britain, the first Cohort of the *Thracians* was garrison'd here, to which he restored the *Balineum* or Bath (called also *Balneum*,) as appears from this Inscription, which was remov'd hence to *Connington*, the house of the most famous and learned Sir *Robert Cotton*, Knight.

Balineum, or Balneum

DAI IORTVNÆ
VIRIVS LVPVS
LEG AVG PR PR
BALINEVM VI
IGNIS EXVSI
VM COH I THR-
ACVM REST-
ITVIT CVRANTI
VAL FRON
TONE PRÆF --
EQ ALAL VETTO

Inscriptio Dr...

Here, I must correct an errour in those, who, from a false draught of this Inscription which has it *Balingium* corruptly for *Balineum*, imagine the place to have been call'd *Balingium*; for upon a nearer inspection, it plainly appears to be

Balineum

Balneum in the stone. A word, used for *Balneum* by the ancients, as the learned very well know; who are not ignorant, that *Baths* were as well us'd by Soldiers as any other persons, both for the sake of health and cleanliness (for in that age, they were wont to wash every day, before they eat;) and also that Baths, both publick and private, were built in all places at such a lavish rate, that *the man thought himself poor and mean, who had not the walls of his Bath shining with great and costly* * *Bosses*. In these, men and women wash'd promiscuously, though that was often prohibited, both by the Laws of the Emperours, and by Synodical Decrees.

Seneca, See Flint shire

* Orbibus

In the decline of the Roman Empire, a † Band of the *Exploratores*, with their Præfect under the command of the * Governour of Britain, had their Station here, as is manifest from the *Notitia*, where it is nam'd *Lavatres*. Now, seing these Baths were also call'd *Lavacra* by the Latins, perhaps some Critick will imagin that this place was call'd *Lavacra* instead of *Lavatræ*, yet I should rather derive it from that little river hard by, which I hear is call'd *Laver*. This modern name *Bowes* (seeing the old Town was burn'd down, according to a tradition among the Inhabitants) seems to me to be deriv'd from that accident. For that which is burn'd with fire, is call'd by the Britains, *Boeth*, and so the Suburbs of Chester beyond the Dee, which the English call *Hanbridge*, is called by the Welsh or Britons, from its being burn'd down in a Welsh in-road, *Treboth*, that is, *a little burnt Town*.

† Numerus Exploratorum

* Ducis Britanniæ

Greata-bridge.

[Not far from Bowes, is *Greata-bridge*, where has been a Camp of the Romans, and their old Coins are often found here, and of late also an Altar with this Inscription,

DEAE NVM
ERIAE NV
MINI BR
IG ET
IAN . . .

Rookby

And at *Rookby*, in the neighbourhood of *Greata bridge*, an Altar with the following Inscription was dug up in the year 1702.

Eggleston Abbey

In this Tract also, hard by, is *Eggleston*, where Conan Earl of Richmond built a Monastery (which hath by several Writers been misplaced at *Eggleston* in the Bishoprick of Durham, about five miles higher, on the *Tees*,) where also, out of the Rocks, they hew Marble.]

Camd Speed Harpsfield

Stanemore

Little on Stanemore.

Here begins that mountainous and vast tract, always expos'd to wind and weather, which being rough and *stony* is call'd by the Inhabitants, *Stanemore*. It is desolate and solitary throughout, except one Inn in the middle for the entertainment of Travellers, near this, is the remainder of a Cross, which we call *Rere cross*, and the Scots, *Rei Cross*, that is, *a Royal Cross*. Hector Boetius, the Scotch Historian says, that this Stone was set for a boundary between England and Scotland, when William the first gave Cumberland to the Scots, upon this condition, that they should hold it of him by fealty, and attempt nothing to the prejudice of the Crown of England. Somewhat lower, just by the Roman Military way, was a small Roman Fort of a square form, which is now call'd *Maiden castle*. From hence, as I had it from the Borderers, this Military Roman way ran with many windings to *Caer Voran*.

Rere cross.

Maiden-castle

Earls of Richmond

As the favour of Princes vary'd, there have been several Earls of Richmond, and of different families, of whom I will give you the Succession, with all the accuracy and certainty that I can. *Alan Rufus*, Earl of Britain in Armorica, *Alan Niger*, to whom William the Conqueror gave this County, *Stephen* Earl of Britain his brother, *Alan* Earl of Britain, his son, of *Stephen*. *Conanus* Earl of Britain, the son, who by the assistance of Henry the second King of England, recover'd Britain from his Father-in law the Sheriff of *Porhoet*, who had seis'd it. *Geoffry Plantagenet*, son of Henry the second King of England, whose first wife was *Constantia*, only daughter of Conanus. *Arthur* his son, who is said to have been made away by King *John*. Upon this account King *John* was certainly impeach'd by the French as Duke of Normandy, and they pass'd Sentence upon him, tho' he was absent, unheard, had made no confession, nor was convict, and yet they ad judg'd him depriv'd of Normandy and his hereditary Lands in France. Whereas he had publickly promis'd to answer before the Judicature at *Paris* concerning the death of *Arthur*, who, as his Subject, had taken an oath of Allegiance to him, and yet had broken the same, and raised a rebellion, and was taken prisoner in the course of the war. At that time, a question was rais'd, Whether the Peers of France could sit Judges upon a Crown'd head, that is, upon their Superiour; seeing *every greater dignity, as it were, drowns the less*, and the King of England and Duke of Normandy at that time was the self same person. But to put an end to this digression. After *Arthur*, there succeeded

About this time, *Overus de St Martino* is mention'd as Earl of Richmond

Normandy taken from the King of England

ceeded in the Earldom of Richmond, *Guy* Viscount of Thouars, second husband of *Constantia* aforesaid; *Ranulph* the third, Earl of Chester, third husband of the said Constantia *Peter de Dreux*, descended from the Blood royal of France, who marry'd Alice only daughter of Constantia by her husband *Guy of Thouars* *Peter of Savoy*, Uncle of Eleanor, Consort to King Henry the third, who finding the Nobility and Commons of England much incens'd against Foreigners, voluntarily renounc'd this honour, *John* Earl of Britain, Son of *Peter de Dreux* *John* the first Duke of Britain, and son of him who marry'd Beatrice daughter of Henry the third King of England He had issue, *Arthur* Duke of Britain, who, according to some Writers, was also Earl of Richmond Certain it is, that *John* his younger brother, presently after the death of his father, enjoy'd this honour; who added to the ancient Arms of Dreux, with the Canton of Britain, *the Lions of England in bordure* He was * Governour of Scotland under Edward the second, where he was kept prisoner three years, and at last dy'd without issue in the reign of Edward the third, and *John* Duke of Britain his Nephew, the son of *Arthur*, succeeded in this Earldom He dying without issue, at a time when the Dutchy of Britain was warmly † contended for, Edward the third, to advance his Interest in France, gave to John Earl of Montford (who had sworn fealty to him for the Dutchy of Britain) all this Earldom, till such time as he should recover his Lands in France, he seeming preferable to the daughter of his brother deceas'd, as he was a Man, as he was nearer ally'd, and as he had a better title in Law His lands being at length regain'd by means of the English, the same King gave this to *John of Gaunt* his son, who at last restor'd it to the King his father for other Lands in exchange The King forthwith created John Earl of Montford (the second duke of Britain, sirnam'd the *Valiant*, to whom he had marry'd his daughter) Earl of Richmond, that he might oblige him to his interest by the strongest ties, being a warlike man, and an inveterate enemy to the French Yet, by Authority of Parliament, in the 14th year of Richard the second, he was depriv'd of this Earldom, for adhering to the French against the English However, he retain'd the title, and left it to his posterity The Estate belonging to the Earldom was given by the King to *Joan* of Britain his sister, widow of *Ralph Basset of Drayton* After her death, first *Ralph Nevil* Earl of Westmorland, by the bounty of Henry the fourth, had the Castle and Country of *Richmond* for *term of Life*; and then, *John* Duke of Bedford Afterwards, Henry the sixth confer'd the title of *Earl of Richmond* upon *Edmund de Hadham* his brother by the mother's side, with this peculiar privilege, *That he should take place in Parliament next to the* Dukes To him succeeded *Henry* his son, afterwards King of England by the name of Henry the seventh But while he was in exile, *George* Duke of Clarence, and Richard duke of Glocester, had this County bestow'd upon them by King Edward the fourth their brother Next, *Henry*, a natural Son of Henry the eighth, was by his father invested Duke of Richmond; but in the year of our Lord 1535 he dy'd without issue.

Robert de *Arthur* was not Earl of *Richmond* (as Froissardus has it) but of *Bellomont* Lib Feod Richmondiæ

* Custos

† Between *John de Montefortis*, and *Joan Claudia* wife of *Charles* of *Blois*

Duke of Richmond

[Next after *Henry Fitz-Roy*, *Lodowick*, Duke of Lenox, was created Earl of *Richmond*, 11 Jac I Oct 6 and afterwards in 1623 Duke of *Richmond*. After him, *James Stewart*, Duke of *Lenox* and Earl of *March*, was created Duke of Richmond by King Charles the first, Aug. 8 1661, and was succeeded by his Son *Esme*, who, dying young in the year 1660, was succeeded by Charles Earl of Lichfield his Cousin german Which said *Charles* dying without issue, *Charles Lenox* natural Son of King Charles the second, was created, Aug 9 1675. Baron of *Setrington*, Earl of *March*, and Duke of *Richmond*]

They are reckon'd in this County 104 great Parishes, besides Chapels of Ease.

More rare Plants growing wild in Yorkshire

Allium montanum bicorne purpurem proliferum. *Purple flower'd mountain Garlick On the scars of the Mountains near Settle See the description of it in* Synopsis method stirpium Britannicarum

Alsine pusilla pulchro flore, folio tenuissimo nostras *Small fine Mountain chickweed with a milk-white flower In the Mountains about Settle plentifully*

Bifolium minimum *J B* Ophris minima *C B* *The least Twayblade On the Heaths and Moors among the Furze in many places As on Blackaymoor in the way to Gisburgh near Scaling damm, and in the Moor near Almondbury*

Calceolus Mariæ *Ger* Damasonii species quibusdam seu Calceolus D Mariæ *J B* Elleborine major seu Calceolus Mariæ *Park* *Ladies slipper At the end of Helks-wood near Ingleborough*

Campanula cymbalaria foliis *Ger Park* *Tender Ivy-leav'd Bell-flower I have observed it in watery places about Sheffield*

Cannabis spuria flore luteo amplo, labio purpureo *Fair-flow'd Nettle-hemp In the mountainous parts of this Country, among the Corn plentifully.*

Carum seu Careum *Ger* Carum vulgare *Park* *Caraways In the pastures about Hull plentifully, so that they gather the Seed there for the use of the shops*

Caryophyllata montana purpurea *Ger emac* montana seu palustris purpurea *Park* aquatica nutante flore *C B* aquatica, flore rubro striato *J B* *Purple Avens In the Mountains near the Rivulets and Water courses about Settle, Ingleborough, and other places in the West and North ridings of this County* *Mr* Lawson *hath observed this with three or four rows of leaves in the flower*

Caryophyllus marinus minimus *Ger* montanus minor *C B* *Thrift or Sea-Gillyflower Mr* Lawson *found this in Buckbarry-gill at the head of Stockdale-fields not far from Settle so that it may not improperly be call'd mountainous as well as maritime*

Cerasus avium nigra & racemosa *Ger* racemosa fructu non eduli *C B* avium racemosa *Park* racemosa quibusdam, aliis Padus *J B* *The Wild-cluster cherry, or Birds-cherry In the mountainous parts of the West-riding of this County*

Christophoriana *Ger* vulgaris *Park* Aconitum racemosum, Actæa quibusdam *J B* racemosum, an Actæa Plinii l 27 c 7 *C B* *Herb-Christopher or Baneberries In Haselwood woods near Sir Walter Vavasor's Park-pale, also among the Shrubs by Malham Cave.*

Cirsium Britannicum repens Clusii *J B* aliud Anglicanum *Park* singulari capitulo squamato, vel incanum alterum *C B* *The great English soft or gentle Thistle, or Melancholy Thistle In the Moun-*

Mountains about Ingleborough and elsewhere in the West riding of Yorkshire

Cochlearia rotundifolia *Ger* folio subrotundo *C B* *Common round leav'd Scurvy grass This, though it usually be accounted a Sea plant, yet we found it growing plentifully upon Stanemore near the Spittle; and upon Penigent and Ingleborough hills; in which places, by reason of the coldness of the air it is so little, that it hath been taken for a distinct Species, and call'd* Cochlearia minor rotundifolia; *but its Seed being taken and sown in a warm Garden, it soon confesses its Species, growing to the dimensions of the common Garden Scurvy-grass*

Conyza Helenitis foliis laciniatis. *Jagged-leav'd Fleabane-mullet About a stones-cast from the East end of Shirley-Pool near Rushy-moor P B This hath been already mention'd in several Counties*

Erica baccifera procumbens nigra *C B* *Black-berried heath, Crow berries, or Crake berries On the boggy mountains or moors plentifully*

Fucus sive Alga tinctoria *P B* *Diers wrack. It is often cast on the shore near Bridlington*

Fungus piperatus albus, lacteo succo turgens *C B* *Pepper Mushrome with a milky juice Found by Dr Lister in Marton woods under Pinno moor in Craven plentifully*

Geranium batrachioides montanum nostras An batrachiodies minus seu alterum *Clus hist?* batrachioides minus *Park?* batrachioides folio Aconiti *C B* ? batrach aliud folio Aconiti nitente Clusii *J B* ? *Mountain Crowfoot-Cranesbill In the mountainous meadows and bushets in the West-Riding*

G Geranium moschatum *Ger Park* *Musked Cranes bill, commonly called Musk or Muscovy It is to be found growing common in Craven Dr Lister is my Author*

G Gnaphalium montanum album sive Pes cati *Mountain Cudweed or Cats foot Upon Ingleborough and other hills in the West Riding also in Sculby leas near Doncaster*

Helleborine foliis longis augustis acutis *Bastard Hellebore with long narrow sharp pointed leaves Under Bracken brow near Ingleton At the end of a wood near Ingleborough, where the* Calceolus Mariæ *grows*

Helleborine altera atro rubente flore *C B* Elleborine flore atro rubente *Park* *Bastard Hellebore with a blackish flower In the sides of the mountains near Malham, four miles from Settle plentifully, especially at a place call'd Cordil or the Whern*

Hieracium montanum Cichorei folio nostras An Hieracium Britannicum *Clus* *Succory leav'd mountain Hawkweed In moist and boggy places in some woods about Burnley*

Hordeum polystichon *J B* polystichon hybernum *C B* polystichon vel hybernum *Park* *Winter or square Barley, or Bear barley, called in the North country Big This endures the winter, and is not so tender as the common Barley; and is therefore sown instead of it in the mountainous part of this country, and all the North over*

M Lilium convallium *Ger* *Lilly convally or May lilly On Ingleborough and other hills*

Lunaria minor *Ger Park* botrytis *J B* racemosa minor vel vulgaris *C B* *Moon-wort Tho' this grows somewhere or other in most Counties of England; yet have I not found it any where in that plenty, and so rank and large, as on the tops of some mountains near Settle*

Lysimachia Chamænerion dicta latifolia *C B* Chamænerion *Ger* Chamænerion flore Delphinii *Park* minus recte *Rose bay Willow herb In the meadows near Sheffield, and in divers other places*

Lysimachia lutea flore globoso *Ger Park* bifolia flore globoso luteo *C B* altera lutea Lobelii, flore quasi spicato *J B* *Yellow loose strife, with a globular spike or tuft of flowers Found by Mr Dodsworth in the East Riding of this County*

M Muscus clavatus sive Lycopodium *Ger Park* *Club-moss or Wolfs claw*

Muscus clavatus foliis Cupressi *C B* *Ger emac* clavatus cupressiformis *Park* terrestris ramosus pulcher *J B* Sabina sylvestris *Trag* Selaginis Plinianæ prima species *Thal* *Cypress-moss or Heath cypress*

Muscus terrestris repens, clavis singularibus foliosis erectis *Smaller creeping Club-moss with erect Heads*

Muscus erectus Abietiformis *nobis* terrestris rectus *J B* S lago 3 *Thalii* *Upright fir moss*

Muscus terrestris rectus minor polyspermos *Seeding mountain mosse All these sorts are found upon Ingleborough hill The last about springs and watery places The first and third are common to most of the moors and fells in the north of England*

Ornithogalum luteum *C B* *Park* luteum seu Cepe agraria *Ger* Bulbus sylvestris Fuchsii flore luteo, seu Ornithogalum luteum *J B* *Yellow Star of Bethlehem In the woods in the northern part of Yorkshire by the Tees side, near Greata bridge and Bignall*

Pentaphylloides fructicosa *Shrub Cinquefoil On the south bank of the river Tees below a village called Thorp as also below Eggleston Abbey At Mickle Force in Teesdale there are thousands of these plants.*

Pentaphyllum parvum hirsutum *J B* *Small rough Cinquefoil In the pastures about Kippax, a village three miles distant from Pontefract*

Pyrola *Ger J B* nostras vulgaris *Park* *Common Winter green We found it near Hallifax, by the way leading to Kighley, but most plentifully on the moors south of Heptenstall in the way to Burnly for near a mile's riding*

Pyrola folio mucronato serrato *C B* serrato *J B* tenerior *Park* Secunda tenerior Clusii *Ger* *Sharp pointed Winter green with serrate leaves. In Haselwood woods near Sir Walter Vavasor's park*

Polygonatum floribus ex singularibus pediculis *J B* latifolium flore majore odoro *C B.* majus flore majore *Park* latifolium 2 Clusii *Ger* *Sweet smelling Solomon's seal, with flowers on single foot stalks On the ledges of the scars or cliffs near Settle and Wharf*

Primula veris flore rubro *Ger Clus* Paralysis minor flore rubro *Park-parad* Verbasculum umbellatum Alpinum minus *C B* *Birds-eyn In the mountainous meadows about Ingleborough and elsewhere in moist and watery places*

Pyrola Alsines flore Europæa *C B* *Park.* Herba trientalis *J B* *Winter-green with Chickweed flowers At the east end of the Rumbles-mear near Helwick*

Pyrola Alsinis flore Brasiliana *C. B* *prod.* *Winter green Chickweed of Brasil Found near Gisburgh Cleveland, as was attested to me by Mr. Lawson.*

Ranunculus globosus *Ger Park* *parad* flore globoso, quibusdam Trollius flos *J B* montanus Aconiti folio, flore globoso *C B* *Indeed it ought to be entitled an Aconite or Wolfsbane with a Crowfoot flower The Globe-flower or Locker gowlons In the mountainous meadows, and by the sides of the mountains and near water courses plentifully*

Ribes vulgaris fructu rubro *Ger* vulgaris acidus ruber *J B* fructu rubro *Park* Grossularia sylvestris rubra *C B* *Red Currans In the woods in the northern part of this County, about Greatabridge, &c*

Ribes Alpinus dulcis *J B* *Sweet Mountain Currans Found in this County by Mr Dodsworth.*

Rhodia radix omnium Autorum Telephium roseum rectius. *Rosewort On the rocks on the north side of Ingleborough hill plentifully*

Rosa Sylvestris pomifera major nostras Rosa pomifera major *Park parad The greater English Apple Rose In the mountainous parts of this County it is very frequent*

Rosmarinum sylvestre minus nostras *Park* Ledum palustre potiùs dicendum *Wild Rosemary or Marsh Holy Rose On Mosses and moorish grounds*

Rubus saxatilis *Ger* Alpinus saxatilis *Park* Alpinus Humilis *J B* Chamærubus saxatilis *C B The stone-Bramble or Raspis On the sides of Ingleborough hill, and other hills in the West Riding*

Salix folio laureo seu lato globro odorato *Bay leav'd sweet Willow In the mountainous parts of the West-riding, by the rivers and rivulets*

Salix pumila montana folio rotundo *J B Round leav'd mountainous dwarf Willow On the rocks upon the top of Ingleborough hill, on the north side and on an hill called Whernside over-against Ingleborough on the other side of the subterraneous river*

Sedum Alpinum ericoides cæruleum *C B J B Mountain Sengreen with Heath like leaves, and large purple flowers On the uppermost rocks on the north-side of Ingleborough*

Sedum minus Alpinum luteum nostras *Small yellow mountain Sengreen On the side of Ingleborough hill about the rivers and springing waters on the north-side of the hill plentifully*

Sedum Alpinum trifido folio *C B* Alpinum laciniatis Ajugæ foliis *Park* Sedis affinis tri sulca Alpina flore albo *J B Small mountain-Sengreen with jagged leaves On Ingleborough and many other hills in the north part of this County*

Sedum purpureum pratense *J B* minus palustre *Ger* arvense seu palustre flore rubente *Park* palustre subhirsutum purpureum *C B Small Marsh-Sengreen On the moist Rocks about Ingleborough hill, as you go from the hill to Horton in Ribbles dale in a ground where Peat is got in great plenty.*

Sideritis arvensis latifolia hirsuto flore luteo *Broad-leav'd rough Field Ironwort with a large flower. In the West riding of Yorkshire about Sheffield, Darfield, Wakefield,* &c *among the Corn plentifully.*

Thrachelium majus Belgarum *Giant Throatwort. Every where among the Mountains*

Thalictrum minus *Ger Park. C B The lesser Meadow rue Nothing more common on the Rocks about Malham and Wharfe*

Thlaspi foliis Globulariæ *J B* montanum Glasti folio minus *Park C B opp In the mountainous pastures going from Settle to Malham, plentifully*

Thlaspi vel potiùs Leucoium sive Lunaria vasculo sublongo intorto *Lunar Violet with an oblong wreathen cod. On the sides of the Mountains, Ingleborough and Hinckel haugh, in moist places, and where waters spring*

Vaccinia Nubis *Ger* Chamæmorus *Clus* Anglica *Park* item Cambro britannica *ejusdem* Rubo Idæo minori affinis Chamæmorus *J B.* Chamæmorus folio Ribes Anglica *C. B Cloud-berries, Knot berries, or Knout-berries This I found plentifully growing and bearing fruit on Hinckel-haugh near Settle I have found it also in Ingleborough and Pendle hills, but not in flower and fruit Both Gerard and Parkinson make two Plants of it*

Valeriana Græca *Ger Park* Græca quorundam, colore cæruleo & albo *J B* cærulæa *C B Greek Valerian, which the vulgar call Ladder to Heaven, and Jacob's Ladder Found by Dr Lister in Carleton beck in the falling of it into the river Are but more plentifully both with a blue flower and a white about Malham-cove, in the Wood on the left hand of the water as you go to the Cove plentifully, as also at Cordill or the Whern, a remarkable Cove, where there comes out a great stream of water near the said Malham*

To these I shall add a Plant, which tho' perchance it be not originally native of this County, yet is planted and cultivated in large Gardens at Pontefract for sale, and hath been taken notice of by Camden *and* Speed, *that is,*

Glycyrrhiza volgaris *Ger* emac vulg. siliquosa *Park* siliquosa vel Germanica *C B* radice repente, vulgaria Germanica *J B Common Liquorice. The quality of this Plant in taking away the sense of hunger and thirst, we have taken notice of in Cambridgeshire Catalogue*

The BISHOPRICK *of* DURHAM.

HE Biſhoprick of *Durham* or *Dureſme*, lies north of *Yorkſhire*, and is ſhaped like a Triangle; the * top whereof lies to the weſt, being made there by the meeting of the north boundary and the *Tees* head That ſide of it towards the South, is bounded all along by the courſe of the river *Tees* The other which lies Northward, runs in a ſhort line from the top of the Triangle to the river *Derwent*, and thence is bounded by the Derwent it ſelf, till it receives the little river *Chopwell*; and after that, by the river *Tine* The baſis of this triangle which lies Eaſtward, is formed by the Sea-ſhore, which the German Ocean beats upon with great rage and violence

* Apex

In that part where it is contracted into the top angle, the fields are naked, the woods few, and the hills bald, but not without veins of Iron; but the Vales produce graſs pretty well (for the *Appennine* of England, which I have already ſpoken of, cuts it at this angle) But on the Eaſt part, or the baſis of this triangle, as alſo at the ſides of it, the ground is made very fruitful by tillage, and the returns are anſwerable to the pains of the huſbandman; being enamell'd with Meadows, Paſtures, and Corn-fields, and thick ſet with Towns in all parts of it, and abounding in Coal; which is uſed for fewel in ſo many places Some would have this Coal to be a black earthy bitumen, others to be *Jeat*, and others the *Lapis Thracius*; all which that great Maſter of Mineral learning, *Georgius Agricola*, proves to be the very ſame For certain, this of our's is nothing but bitumen, harden'd and concocted by the heat under ground, for it has the ſame ſmell with bitumen † and if water be ſprinkled on it, it burns the hotter and the clearer; but whether or or no it is quenched with oyl, I have not try'd If the *Lapis Obſidianus* be in England, I ſhould take

Coal

† This is proper to *English Jeat*; but the *Coal* here is quenched with water, and flames with Oyl

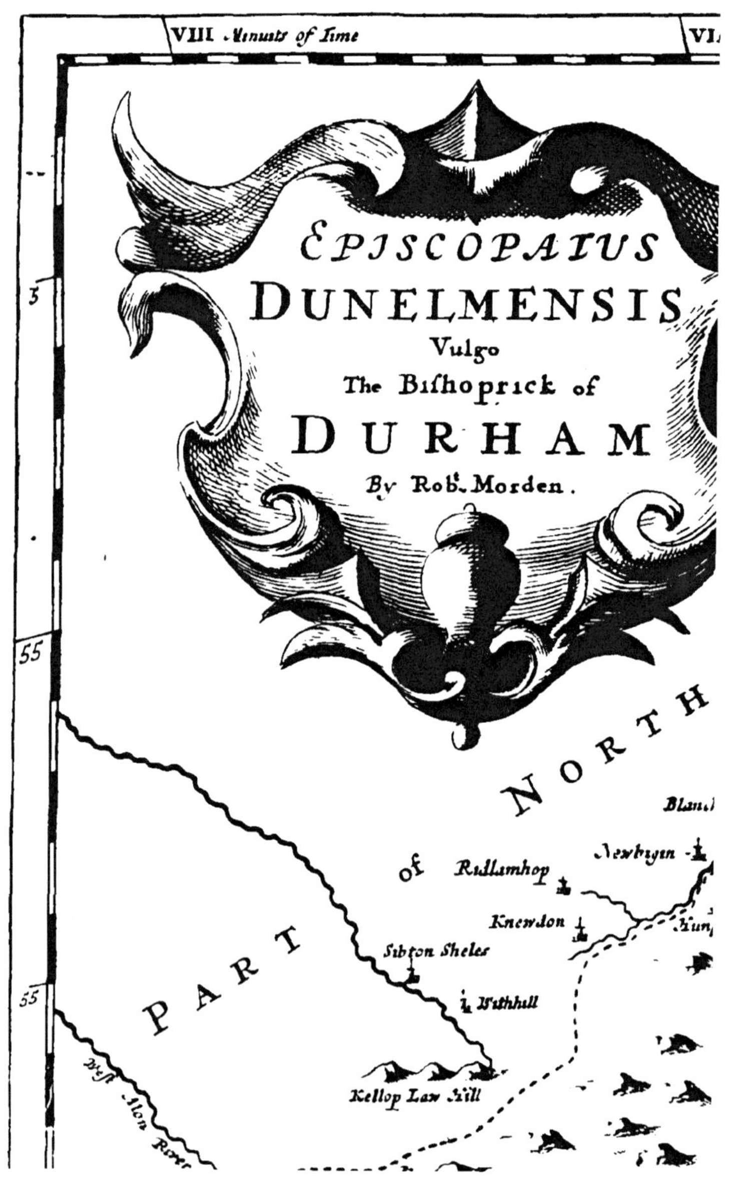

VIII Minuts of Time
EPISCOPATUS
DUNELMENSIS
Vulgo
The Bishoprick of
DURHAM
By Robt. Morden.
55
55
PART of NORTH
Ridlamhop
Newbigen
Knewdon
Sibton Sheles
Kellop Law Hill

VI
V
Tinmouth Castle
LAND.
Willington
Walker
Heddon
Thorkley
Wawbottel
Houghton
The Close
Newburne
Benwell
Biker
Hebborn
Newcastle
Wilam
Owingham
Ovington
Prudo Castle
Bywel Castle
Tyne River
Ryton
Stellaw
Blaydon
Crawcroke
Swalwel
Whickham
Gateshead
Thorneley
Hedley
Aperley
Chopwell
Spen
Axwell
Gibside
Ravensworth
Kibblesworth
Black Hall
Whitton Stall
Ebchester
Pan Sheals
Shotley
Shotley bridg
Darwen River
Biersyde
Lanfield
Collierly
Pontop Pike
Shildraw
Standley
Lamesley
Great Usworth
Little Usworth
Follonsby
Birtley
Urpath
Lambton
Pelton
Chester in y Street
Whitwell
Lumley Castle
Lumley
UMBER
CH
TER
Benfield Side
Consett Hall
Edmondbiers
Pedumside
Greencroft
The Mannor
Waldridg
Plausworth
Nettleworth
Lanchester
Newbiggin
Langley
Foulforth
Newton
The Grange
Kipper
Ush
Ushaw
Bear Park
Cornsey
Satley Chap
Flasse
Enthank
Haughall
Durham
Shuckley
WARD
Roman way

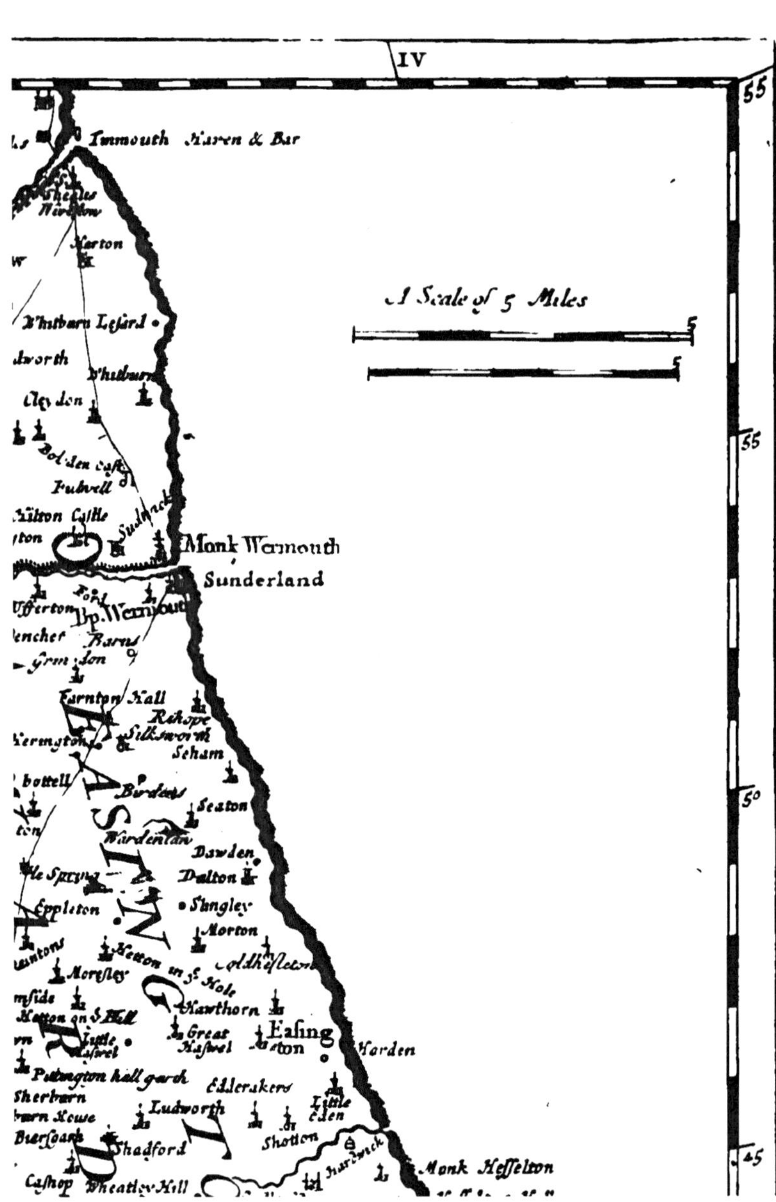

IV
55
Tinmouth Haven & Bar
Harton
Whitburn Lesard
Whitburn
Monk Wearmouth
Sunderland
Bp. Wearmouth
Silksworth
Seham
Seaton
Dawden
Dalton
Morton
Hawthorn
Easington
Horden
Ludworth
Shadford
Shotton
Sherburn
Wheatley Hill
Monk Hesselton
A Scale of 5 Miles
5
5
55
50
45

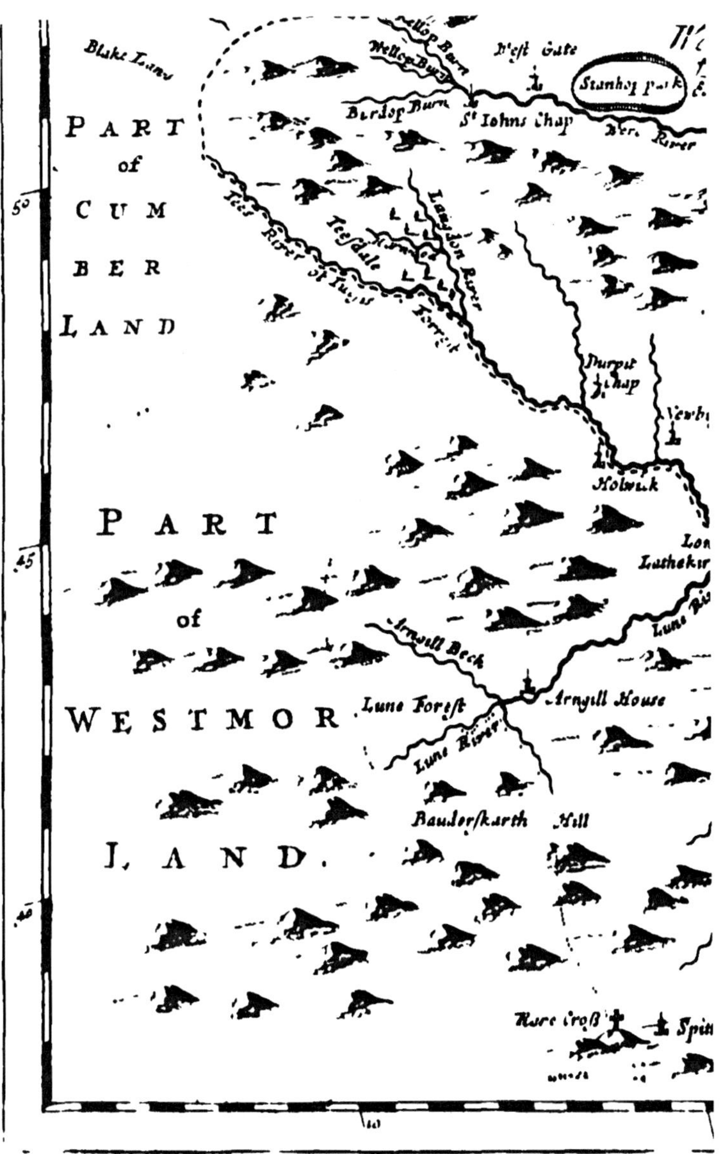

PART of CUMBER LAND
PART of WESTMOR LAND.
Stanhop park
West Gate
St Iohns Chap
Holwick
Arngill House
Lune Forest
Lune River
Arngill Beck
Bauderskarth Hill
Rere Cross
Tees River
Durpit Chap
50
45
40

DERLINGTON WARD
Stanhope
Unthank
Wolsingham
Bradley Hall
Brandon West
Brandon East
Little Burn
Brandipeth Castle
East Park
West Park
Whitworth
Willmoton
Black Hall
Beachbarn
Landew
Mill Houses
Bollop
Bedburn Park
Harpers Hall
Hamsterley
Witton Castle
Escomb
Aukland Bishops
Aukland St. Helens
Aukland St. Andrewes
Aukland West
Cundon
Windleston
Great Chilton
Hayland
Gaunlesse River
Evenwood West
Thickley West
Shildon
Thickley East
Windridg
Redworth
Schole Acley
Heighington
Bolam
Walker Field
Cock Field
Shotton
Eglestone
Myckleton
Rumbald Kirk
Cudderston
Shopley
Marwood Hag
Langley Hall
Raby Castle
Ingleton
Morton
Houghton
Graystone
Cotham
Beamont Hill
Kiverby
Denton
Langton
Staindrop
Snotterton
Streitlam
Medlam
Newton
Thornton
Cockerton
Cletlam
Gainford
Somer house
Piersbridg
Derlington
Over Cunsley
Nether Cunsley
Blackwell
Selaby
Winston
Hurworth
Bernard Castle
Westwick
Wharlton
Craig
Stratford
Egleston
Rokebye
Orinton
Wickliff
Thorpe
Mansfield
Cleesby
Stapleton
Croft Bridg
Stanmore
Bowes
Gretabridge
Dawton
Degrees West
50
40
30

Thornley
Kedlam
Thorp Bulmer
Windgate
Kellow
Hutton Henry
Nesbit
Hart
Hartle Pool
Shoroton
Throstons
Hurworth
Trimdon
Elwick
Tunstall
The Raw
Mortons
Daulton
Stranton
Garmondsway
Fishburn
STOCKTON
Brearton
Seaton
Stotfold
Owston
Butterwick
Elmedon
Claxton
Gretham
Old Akers
Bruntoft
Sedgfield
Newton Harford
Newton Beauley
Bradbury
Hardwick
Layton
Wynyard
Cowpon
The Isle
Shotton
Foulthorp
Holm
Mordon
Beauley Grange
Foxton
Grindon
Thorp
Bellosyse
Billingham
Tees Mouth
Elstob
Whitton
Stillington
Norton
Midlesburgh
Carleton
Arsham
Great Stamton
Redmershill
Stockton
Newport
Brafferton
Bishopton
Hartburn
Ketton
Little Stainton
Acklam
WARD
Elton
Barnton
Thornabye
Little Burdon
Preston
Newton Long
Great Burdon
Sadberge
Cotham
Barwick
Haughton
West Hartburn
Eglescliff
Aslaby
Midleton George
Newsham
Yarum
Midleton Ero
Worsall
Nether Dittensdale als Dinsdale
Over Dittensdall als Dinsdale
Nesham
Sockburn
Eriholm
Grisbye
Sold by Abel Swale Awnsham & John Churchil
35
30
20
10

it for that which is found in other parts of the Kingdom, and commonly goes by the name of *Canole Coal* for that is hard, shining, light, and apt to cleave into thin flakes, and to burn out as soon as kindled. But let us leave these points to such persons as pry into the secrets of nature.

This whole County, with others bordering upon it, is call'd by the Monkish Writers *The* St. Cuthbert's Patrimony *Land or Patrimony of St. Cuthbert.* For so they call'd all that belong'd to the Church of *Durham*, of which Cuthbert is esteemed Patron; [and so, *Creke* in Yorkshire, *Bedlington*, *Northam*, and *Holy Island*, Shires in Northumberland, are to this day parts of the County Palatine, and as such have the benefit of the Courts at *Durham*.] St Cuthbert, in the very infancy of the Saxon Church, was Bishop of *Lindesfarne*, and led such a holy and upright Life, that he was kalendar'd for a Saint. And our Kings and Noblemen (believing him to be their Guardian Saint against the Scots) have not only gone often in pilgrimage to his Body, which continued long entire and uncorrupted, as some Writers would perswade us, but also endow'd his Church with very great possessions, and many immunities. King Egfrid gave large Revenues in the very City of York, and also *Creake*, which I have spoken of, and the City *Luguballia* or *Carlisle*, to Cuthbert himself in his life time, as it is in *the History of Durham.* [But yet his Charter (be it true or counterfeit) mentions no such thing. *Simeon Dunelmensis* indeed (or rather Abbot *Turgot*, tells us, that *Creake* was given him by this King, *That in his way to and from* York, *he might have a Mansion to rest at.* But this only intimates, that St *Cuthbert* might have frequent occasions to travel to York, probably, to attend the Court, which the Historian supposes to have been most commonly resident in that City.] King *Alfred*, and *Gutburn* the Dane Malmes l. 1 p. 25 b. * See below (whom he * set over the Northumbrians) afterwards gave all the Land *between the River Were, and the Tine* (these are the words of an old Book) *to Cuthbert, and to those that should minister in that Church, for ever, that they might not be in want, but have enough to live upon: moreover, they made his Church an* Asylum *or* Sanctuary *for fugitives, that whosoever upon any account should fly to his Body, should have peace there for thirty seven days, not to be violated on any pretence whatsoever.* [As to *Gutbrun* before-mentioned (whom our Historians call also *Gutbredus*, *Cutbredus*, *Gormo*, and *Gurmundus*) however it is said, that he was *Lieutenant* to the great King Ælfred in the Kingdom of Northumberland, yet according to others, he was no more so, than Ælfred was his Deputy in that of the West-Saxons. For they two seem by compact to have divided the whole Kingdom betwixt them, and to have jointly enacted Laws, which were to be mutually observ'd both by the English and Danes. And hence, some Monks have taken occasion to unite them falsly, in granting Charters to Monasteries, &c. But this by the way.] King Edward and Athelstan, and Cnuto or Canutus the Dane (who went barefoot to Cuthbert's Tomb, [from a place called Garmondsway, about five miles from *Durham*,)] not only confirm'd these Laws and Liberties, but also enlarg'd them. Nor did William the Conqueror less, from whose time it was reckon'd a County Palatine; and some of the Bi- A County Palatine shops, as Counts Palatine, have grav'd in their Seals a Knight arm'd, sitting upon a horse with trappings, with one hand brandishing a *Sword*, and the other holding out the *Arms of the Bishoprick.* The Bishops have also had their Royalties, so that the Goods of Outlaws were forfeited to *them*; and not to the King: nay the common people, insisting upon privilege, have refus'd to go to the wars in Scotland under the *King. For they pleaded* (these are the words of the History of Durham) *that they were Haliwerke folks,* i. e. *register'd or enrolled for holy work. That they held their Lands to defend the body of St* Cuthbert, *and that they ought not to march out of the confines of their Bishoprick, namely beyond the Tine and the Tees, either for the King, or for the Bishop.* But Edward the first abridged them of these liberties. For he (voluntary interposing himself as mediator between *Anthony Bec* Bishop, and the Prior, who had then a sharp contest about certain Lands, and at last would not stand to his determination; [or, as others will have it, provoked by that Bishop's siding with the Earls Mareschal and Hereford.)] *seized* (as my Author says) *the Liberty of the Bishoprick into his own hands, and then were many things searched into, and their privileges abridg'd in many particulars.* However, the Church recover'd its Rights afterwards, and [(excepting certain Liberties taken away by Statute, 27 Hen. 8 and annexed to the * Crown] held them without diminution till Edward the sixth's time, to whom (that Bishoprick being dissolv'd) the Parliament gave all its Revenues and Immunities. But immediately after, Queen Mary had this Act of Parliament repealed, and [(except the foresaid Liberties)] restor'd all entire to the Church; which it enjoys at this day. For *James Pilkington*, Bishop, commenced a suit with Queen Elizabeth, for the Lands and Goods of *Charles Nevil* Earl of Westmorland, and other out-laws in this County, who had been in actual rebellion and had prosecuted the suit, if the Parliament had not interposed, and for that time (so the words are) adjudged it to the Queen, in consideration of the great charge she had been at, in rescuing both the Bishop and the Bishoprick from the rebels.

[The *Palatine* Right of the Bishops of *Durham* Its Palatine Rights is founded upon Prescription Immemorial, because there is no Record of its being granted by any Princes before the Conquest or since, wherein it is not supposed to have been granted also by their Predecessors. It proceeded at first from a principle of Devotion to St Cuthbert, that whatever Lands were given to him, or bought with his money, he should hold them with the same freedom that the Princes who gave them, held the rest of their Estates. But this piety to the Saint was not without its *Prudential purposes* all along, both for the service of the Crown in the wars in Scotland, and also for the service of the Country, because of its distance from the Courts of Law above.

It consisted of all manner of Royal Jurisdicti- Its Jurisdiction on, both Civil and Military, by Land and by Water. For the exercise of which, the Bishops had their proper Courts of all sorts held in their Name, and by their Authority; their Chancery, Exchequer, and Court of Pleas, as well of the Crown as of the Country, and all other Pleas, and Assises, Certifications and Juries, whatsoever; and all Officers belonging to them, as Chancellor, Justices, High Sheriff, Coroners, Escheator, and other Ministers, as well such as the Kings have been wont to have elsewhere in the Kingdom, as such as the said Kings have been wont to depute according to the exigency of emergent Cases, or for the special execution of Acts of Parliament. Thus, by themselves and their Officers, they did justice to all Persons in all Cases, without either the King, or any of his Bailiffs or Officers interfering ordinarily

in

in any thing. Whatever occasion the King had within this Liberty, his Writs did not run here; they were not directed as to his own Officers in other Counties, but to the Bishop himself, or, in the vacancy of the See, to the proper Officers of the Palatinate. When King Henry the second sent his Justices of Assize hither upon an extraordinary occasion of Murthers and Robberies, he declared by his Charter, That he did it with the Licence of the Bishop, and *pro hac vice* only, and that it should not be drawn into Custom either in his time, or in the time of his Heirs, not being done but upon absolute necessity, and that he would nevertheless have the Land of St. Cuthbert to enjoy its Liberties and ancient Customs as amply as ever.

By virtue of these Privileges, there issued out of the Bishop's Courts all sorts of Writs, Original, Judicial, and Common; Writs of Proclamation upon the Exigent for Outlawries from six weeks to six weeks, and Letters of Peace upon the Return and Appearance of the Persons, and Writs *de Excommunicato capiendo* upon Certificates directed from the Bishops Spiritual Capacity to his Temporal.

As all Writs went out in his name, so he had a Register of Writs, of as much authority as that in the King's Courts, and all Recognizances enter'd upon his Close Rools in his Chancery, and made to him, or in his Name, were as valid within the County, as those made to the King without.

* Cap. 42. But now the * Act of the 27th of King Henry the eighth, for the *Recontinuing of certain Liberties taken from the Crown*, directs, That all Writs, Indictments, and all manner of Process in Counties Palatine, shall be made only in the King's name, since which time, all the difference that is in the Style of Proceedings in this Country from others, is, that the *Teste* of the Writs is in the name of the Bishop, according to the directions of that Act. Still he is perpetual Justice of Peace within his Territories, as is also his Temporal Chancellor, because the chief Acts of the Exempt Jurisdiction used to run through his Court. All the Officers of the Courts, even the Judges of Assize themselves, have still their ancient Salaries from the Bishop, and all the standing Officers of the Courts are constituted by his Patents. When he comes in person to any of the Courts of Judicature, he sits Chief in them, those of Assize not excepted: and even when Judgment of *Blood* is given, though the Canons forbid any Clergyman to be present, yet the Bishops of Durham did, and may sit in Court in their purple Robes upon the Sentence of Death; whence it used to be said *Solum, Dunelmense Stola jus dicit & Ense*. All Dues, Amerciaments, and forfeited Recognizances in the Courts of the Palatinate, belong to the Bishop; as also, all Deodands. If any Forfeitures are made, either of War, or by Treason, Outlawry, or Felony, even although the Soil be the King's, they fall to the Bishop here, as to the King in other places. And though the first great wound that the Palatinate receiv'd, was occasioned by the Alienation of *Bernard-castle* and *Hartlepole*, upon the forfeitures of *Baliol* and *Bruce*, yet the Bishop's right to them was declared upon full hearing; and tho' the possession of them could not be retrieved, yet they still resort to the Courts of *Durham* as other parts of the County do. Indeed all the Tenures of Land in this County do spring originally from the Bishop, as *Lord paramount in Capite*. From hence proceeded his giving of Charters for the erection of Burroughs and Incorporations, Markets and Fairs; for the inclosure of Forests, Chases, and Warrens; Licences to build Chapels, to found Chanteries and Hospitals; and Dispensations with the Statute of Mortmain; all these things being within his property. From hence it is, that if there be any Moors or Wastes in the County, to which no other can make title, they fall to him, and even inclosed Estates also in that case escheat to him, it being implied, that they could not have been inclosed without his Grant. If any Estates here fall to Lunaticks or Idiots, the Bishop grants the custody of them, as the King does elsewhere, and whilst there was such a thing as Wards and Liveries in the Kingdom, if any Person left his Child a Minor, the custody of him was in the Bishop. Besides the dependance of those that hold of him by Lease or Copy of Court-roll, if any Freeholders alienated their Lands without his leave, they were obliged to sue to him for his Patent of Pardon; and to this day, all the silver paid for Licences of Alienation of Lands by Fines or Recoveries which belongs to the King at *Westminster*, belongs to the Bishop here.

As for the *Military* power, the Bishop of Durham had his Thaines anciently, and afterwards his Barons and others, who held of him by Knights Service, as the rest of the *Haliwerkfolk* held of them, by inferior Tenures. Upon occasions of Danger, he called them together in the nature of a Parliament, to advise and assist with their Persons, Dependents, and Money, for the publick service, either at home or abroad. And when Men and Money were to be levied, it was not done here as in other places, but by the Bishop's Commissions, or Writs in his name, out of the Chancery at *Durham*: for as he had power to coin Money, so he had power to levy Taxes also, and to raise defensible persons within the Bishoprick from sixteen to sixty years of age, and to arm and equip them for service. He himself us'd often to go at the head of them; however, the Officers by whom they were led, acted by Commission under him, and were accountable to him for their duty, as he was to the King. According as he found their strength, he had power to go out against the Scots, or make Truces with them. One of the Bishops built a strong Castle in his Territory, upon the Border, to defend it against them, though, at the same time, if any other person would have done such a thing in any part of his Territory, they must have had his leave: not the greatest man of the Palatinate could build or embattle his Castle or Manor house without Licence from the Bishop. As they depended upon him in these things, so were they free from every body else; insomuch, that when the Lord Warden of the Marches would have summoned some of the Bishop's People to his Courts, a letter was sent from the King to forbid him upon the penalty of a thousand pounds. But now the *Militia* of this County has been, of long time, upon the same foot with the rest of the Kingdom, under a Lord Lieutenant from the King; only with this distinction, That the Lieutenancy has been here, for the most part, though not always, in the hands of the Bishop.

This Royal Jurisdiction extends also to the *Sea coasts*, and Waters that lie within, or adjoyning to the County Palatine, or any of its Dependencies; wherein the Bishop of *Durham* has all along had a distinct Admiralty, and held his Admiralty Courts by proper Judges according to the Maritime laws; appointing, by his Patents, a Vice-Admiral, Register, and Marshal

shal or Water-bailiff, and having all other Officers requisite to that authority, and all the Privileges, Forfeitures and Profits incident thereunto, as Royal-fishes, Wrecks of the Sea, Duties for Ships applying to his Ports, Anchorage, Beaconage, Wharfage, Moorage, Butlerage, Ulnage, Metage, and other such like advantages; Keys for Balast or Merchant Goods, Ferry-boats, Fishings, and Dams over the Rivers, Houses also and Shops to the Midstream that borders upon his County, as on the South-side of Tine bridge To him also belongs the Conservation of the Waters within his Royalty; in pursuance of which, he used to issue out Commissions for the prohibition, limitation or abatement of Yares and other Erections in prejudice of his Rivers When any Ships of War were to be set forth and array'd within the Ports of the County Palatine, it was always done by the Bishop's Commissions and Writs to his High Sheriff. And when the King issued out his Orders from his Admiralty to the High-Sheriffs of other Maritime Counties, there came none from thence to this County, but there was a particular Letter from the King to the Bishop for his concurrence; whereupon the Bishop gave his Commission to his own High-Sheriff, with express command, 'That nothing should be done by the King's Commissioners without him' It is but very lately, that any instance was known of the Admiralty's being separated from the Bishoprick, and it is now again restor'd, though with some diminution in the Honour

This is some account of the Palatine Rights of this Bishoprick, so far as the nature of this Work would allow If they have been formerly or of late contested or abridg'd, or given, or taken away, or alter'd, by violence, or by authority, or by time, it is no wonder; considering the changes that have been in this Kingdom, not only in the Tenures of the Subjects, but also in the Royalties of the Crown it self

The great privileges of this Church in Temporal Jurisdiction, do easily lead us to suppose that it had some extraordinary *Spiritual* Immunities also. After *Paulinus*'s departure from *York*, the Bishops, who restor'd Christianity among the *Northumbers*, placed their See at *Lindisfern*, tho' not with the title of Metropolitan, yet with all the Ecclesiastical power that was then in these Countries. This occasion'd a great veneration for their Successors among the Saxons, besides the particular reverence that was paid to St Cuthbert. When the See was establish'd at *Durham* in the time of the Conqueror, Thomas the Elder, then Archbishop of York, having been miraculously recover'd of a Fever at the Shrine of that Saint, granted several Immunities to this Church, with relation to Jurisdiction, Visitations, Attendance upon Convocations, &c And these having been confirmed by the King, and Parliament, and Pope, and also by several of his next Successors, could never be recall'd afterwards: but after many struggles and contests, too long to be here set forth, the old Pleas still obtain'd, and, so far as the state of things requires, are to this day upheld] But leaving these matters, let us now proceed to the description of places

Tee Twesis

The river which bounds the South part of this County, is call'd by the Latins *Teisis* and *Teisa*, and commonly *Tees*; by Polydore an Italian (who was certainly thinking of *Athesis* in his own Country) without any grounds, *Athesis*; by Ptolemy it seems to be call'd ΤΟΥΑΣΙΣ and *Tuesis* but I am of opinion, that by the heedlessness of Transcribers, it is misplac'd in him For whereas he makes the *Tuesis* and *Tina* to be in the remoter parts of Britain, now inhabited by the Scots; and the *Tees* and *Tine* are the boundaries to this County if I durst criticise upon this ancient Geographer, I would recall them hither to their proper place, and, as I hope, without offence to the Scottish Nation, who have no rivers, to which they can truly apply these names; [unless Sir *George Mackenzy*'s Conjecture be good, that Ptolemy's Ταιΐα εἴσχυσις is now the *March of Angus*, being the Frith or Out-let of the river *Tay*; and so the Τύαυσις (or as some Books have it Τύεσις) εἴσχυσις of the same Ptolemy, may be left to the River of *Tees*; and this, upon supposition, that in those Tables they are misplaced]

Defence of the Royal Line, p 79

The *Tees* rises † in *Crosse-fell* [upon the very point of Cumberland, dividing the Bishoprick, from Westmorland first, and then from Yorkshire; tho' anciently in the upper-parts of this river, the Bishop's Royalty extended three miles beyond it to the south, and six miles to the west Among the rocks, at the bottom of *Teasdale*, alias *Langden-forest*, near Dirtpeth Chapel (which is now demolished) there is a remarkable Cataract in the river, where the Water falls near twenty yards And about two miles above it, there is as remarkable a stand of water, where the river forms it self into a narrow Lake of about half a mile long It is called to this day by the old Saxon name, *The Weel*, and is noted for plenty of Trouts]

† In that stony ground called *Stanemore*, C

The *Tees*, together with the many currents joyning it on both sides, flows through rocks; out of which, at * *Eggleston*, they hew Marble, [and in its course, receives the river *Bauder*; above which, in the year 1689, about Midsummer, there happen'd an Eruption of Water on the *Mosses*, and the earth which was broken thereby, is computed to be about one hundred and sixty yards long, and in some places three, in others fourscore yards broad, and about six or seven deep Which great quantity of Earth being most of it carried down by the flood of water into a neighbouring brook, and so into the river *Bauder*, did great damage by overflowing the Meadows, and leaving behind it vast quantities of Mud, which the Inhabitants were forced to dig up, and cast into the river, lest it should spoil the ground It poison'd all the fish, not only in the foresaid Brook, and the Bauder, but also in the Tees for many miles] Then the *Tees* runs by *Bernard castle*, built by *Bernard Baliol*, great grand-father to John Baliol King of Scots, and so named from him [The same Bernard created Burgesses also in this Town, with the same liberty and freedom, as those of Richmond] But John Balliol, whom Edward the first had declared King of Scots, lost this, with other possessions in England, for falling from the Allegiance that he had sworn to King Edward At which time, the King, being displeas'd with *Anthony* Bishop of Durham (as the History of that place tells us) *took this Castle with all its appurtenances from him, and confer'd it upon the Earl of Warwick.* * Hert and Hertnes, *he bestow'd upon Robert Clifford*, and Kewerston *upon Galfrid de Hertlpole, which the Bishop had, as forfeited by J de Baliol, R de Brus, and Christopher de Seton* But some few years after, *Ludovicus de Bellomonte* the Bishop, descended from the Royal Line of France (who yet, as it is written of him, was a perfect stranger to all matters of Learning) went to law for this Castle and other Possessions, and carry'd the Cause; Sentence being given in these words, *The Bishop of Durham*

Eggleston
* Vid *Egleston* in Richmondshire; as to the Monastery plac'd here by Mr. *Camden*

Bernard castle.

* Herks, C.

ham ought to have the forfeitures in war within the liberties of his Bishoprick, as the King hath them without [In the fourteenth year of King Henry the third, an Hospital was erected in this place by John Baliol, and dedicated to St John Baptist. Also Richard Duke of Glocester (whose Cognisance, the *Boar*, yet remains in several parts of the Town) founded a College of Secular Canons within the Castle; and for the Lands and Advowsons to be settled on them, he had a Licence of Mortmain in the 14th year of Edward the fourth. In whose time, there was likewise erected an Hospital, consisting of a Master or Warden, and three poor Women]

Stredham. Bowes.

Near this, stands *Streilham*, which hath been a long time the Seat of the famous and knightly family of the *Bowes* or *De Arcubus*, who have done great Service to their King and Country in the most difficult times Their pedigree is from *W de Arcubus*, to whom (as I have read) *Alanus Niger*, Earl of Britain and Richmond, gave it in these words, *That he should bear for his Arms the Scutcheon of Britain, with three bent* Bowes *in it* [Yet others say, that *Streilham* came to the Bowes by marrying the heiress of Sir *J. Frain*, as he had it by marrying the heiress of *Ralph de la-bay* Lord *Piercy* of *Stainton in the Street*, to whom Bernard Baliol gave it with his Niece

This name of *Streilham*, and *Stainton in the Street* about half a mile off, directly in the way to Bernard-castle, answering to Stratford on the other side of it, seems to point out to us a branch of the Roman high-way, which, from Greta-bridge, and Bowes, and Brough, meeting at Stratford, and passing over the river at Bernard Castle, runs by Stainton, Streilham, and Stanethrop, to Binchester There, it meets with the High Roman way to Lanchester on the left hand, but there also did probably run another way directly forwards by Sunderland-bridge, and Chester in the Street, to *Gabrosentum* or Newcastle A very great Antiquary placed *Condercum* at Sunderland, and the name may seem to favour it, and as for *Chester*, the very title of the Street, meeting us again there, and several Coins lately found in the place (whatever its *name* was) shew it to be Roman As Streilham answers this passage of the Tees at Bernard castle, so *Stratwich* answers another passage over it, above, at *Egleston*, from Westmorland to Newcastle, by Wolsingham and Lanchester There, meeting again with the Roman Highway, it either turned on the left hand to Ebchester, and Corbridge, or went directly forward by Wrecansdike to Gate side, and so on to Shields About four miles below Bernard castle, stands

Winston

Winston, where the learned Dr *Gale* places another passage of the Roman way, from Catarick to Binchester. But to return]

S andrope

At less than five miles distance from *Streilham*, and somewhat farther from the *Tees*, is *Standrope*, (which is also call'd *Staintborp*, that is, *A stony village*,) [heretofore] a small Market-town, where stood a Collegiate Church built by the *Nevills*, which was also a burial place to the Family

Rabye castle

Near this, is *Rabye*, which King Canutus the Dane gave to the Church of Durham, with the County about it, and *Stantborpe, to have and to hold freely for ever From which time* (as my

The Family of the Nevill

Author has it) *the family of the Nevils, or* de Nova villa, *held* Rabye *of the Church, by a yearly rent of four Pounds and a Stag*, [(which Stag was used to be constantly presented on St *Cuthbert's* day, till there arose contests about the Ceremony, and the Monks chose rather to forego the Present, than be at the expence and trouble of receiving it)] This Family is descended from *Walthoef* Earl of Northumberland; of whose Posterity, *Robert* the Son of *Maldredus*, and Lord of *Rabye*, having marry'd the daughter of *Geffrey Nevill* the Norman (whose grandfather *Gilbert Nevill*, is said to have been Admiral to King William the first,) their Posterity took the name of *Nevill*, and grew to a most numerous and powerful family They built here a very spacious Castle, which was their principal and chief Seat [but, ever since the reign of King James the first, it hath belong'd to the ancient Family of the *Vanes*, lately made noble under the title of Lord *Bernard* of Bernard-Castle And as to *Raby*, it gave the title of Baron to Sir *Thomas Wentworth*, created Earl of Strafford and Baron of Raby, in the 15th year of King Charles the first,] These two places, *Staintborpe* and *Raby*, are separated only by a little river, which after some few miles falls into the Tees near *Selaby*, where † was the Seat of the family of the *Brakenburys*, eminent for their Antiquity, and their marriages with the heirs of *Denton* and *Witcliff*

Selaby

† Is, C

[At the falling of this little river into the Tees, lies *Gainford*, an ancient Manour, and of a large territory, mentioned by old Historians, as taking up all that side of the Country The Danes first, then the Earls of Northumberland, and afterwards William Rufus, seised these parts He, being displeas'd at William de S Karilefo, gave the Forest of Teasdale, and Marwood, together with the Manours of Middleton and Gainford, to Guy Baliol and tho', upon John's forfeiture, the Bishop's Right after much opposition was formally allowed, yet the settled Possession could never be obtained. The Church of Gainsford is still the mother to Bernard-castle, and was originally so to Middleton too; but the Rectory was given by Guy Baliol to the Abby of St *Mary* in York, and doth now belong to Trinity-College in Cambridge

Gainford

Percebridge

Next, upon the same river, lies *Percebridge*, which, in the old Map of the North riding of Yorkshire, is called *Presbrigge*, and, according to Tradition, should be called *Priestbridge*, from two neighbours of that *Order*, who built it of Stone, it having been of Wood before, or from the Priests appointed to serve the Devotion of Travellers, as well as of the neighbourhood, in a Chapel, the ruins of which remain hard by the Bridge At this place was dug-up an Altar with the following Inscription

Here, it is generally taken for granted, that the High Roman way from *Catarick* enter'd this County,

County, being fairly to be traced ſtrait along to Binchester, and many other marks of Antiquity being found here, beſides the foreſaid Altar wherein the diſtinct mention of *Condati*, would tempt us at firſt ſight to believe, that this was the ancient *Condate*, placed hitherto at *Congleton* in Cheſhire, but the courſe of the Itinerary, and the Diſtances on each hand, will by no means give us leave to remove it from thence, and much leſs to bring it into this County

Joyning to the Bridge, is a large ſquare-Incloſure, about the uſual bigneſs of the Roman Fortifications in theſe parts. A Gentleman of good underſtanding, in this neighbourhood, ſpeaks of an Idol that he ſaw himſelf, which fell into his Father's hands; who, through exceſs of Zeal, cauſed it to be cruſh'd to pieces It is certain, that ſeveral Urns have been found, and many Coins, and, in the neighbourhood, many years ago, the Plowers ſtruck upon a large Stone-coffin, with a Skeleton in it, in a field adjoyning to the yard of the foreſaid Chapel, and which in all likelyhood was formerly part of it North from

Heighington

hence is *Heighington*, where *Elizabeth Jenſon* founded a School in the 43d year of Queen Elizabeth, to which Mr *Edward Kirby*, late Vicar of the place, left a handſom Legacy

Walworth

Hard by, is *Walworth*, anciently a Seat of the *Nevils*, from whom it paſſed, by the marriage of an heireſs, to the *Hanſards*, one of the Baron-Families of the Biſhoprick, from them it paſſed in the ſame manner to the *Aſcoughs*, and ſeveral other great Families, and being adorn'd by one of the late Owners with a good houſe, it is at preſent the Seat of the *Jenſons*

The *Tees*, not far from this place, receives the river *Skern*, famous for its Pikes, near the

Fiſhburn

Midleham

head of which, is *Fiſhburn*, part of the ancient Eſtate of the *Claxtons*; and hard by, *Midleham*, where was formerly a Caſtle of the Biſhops, built moſtly by *Richard de Kellow* and *Lewis Beaumont* At ſome diſtance from the ri-

Sedgfield

ver, is *Sedgfield*, a Market Town, which was firſt made ſo by grant from Biſhop *Richard de Kellow*, anno 1312 with a Fair for five days, to be held on the Eve and day of Edmund Archbiſhop of Canterbury, and on the three days following This was for ſome time neglected but is now revived Here is a good Alms-houſe, well endowed, for ten poor People Lower

Acley

down, is *Acley*, where (as Sir *Henry Spelman* conjectures) two ancient Saxon Councils were held, about the years 782, and 789 Then,

Haughton

Haughton, the mother-Church to *Sadberge*, which notwithſtanding the old general Grants, was with-held from the Church, till Biſhop Hugh purchaſed it of King Richard the firſt, in exchange for other Manours in Lincolnſhire Hence it is ſtill diſtinctly named with Durham, in the title of a County Palatine, as a ſeparate *Wapentake*, which formerly comprehended moſt of the Eaſt ſide of the County]

Derlington

Next, is *Derlington*, a throng Market town, which † *Seir* a Saxon, the ſon of Ulphus, with King Etheldred's leave, gave to the Church of Durham; and *Hugh de Puteaco* or *Pudſey* adorn'd with a [Collegiate] Church and other Buildings [This was one of the four Ward-Towns in this County, and the Church, one of the three Churches appointed to receive the Secular Prieſts, when the Monks enter'd into their places, in the Church of Durham By being thus made Collegiate (of a Dean and four Prebendaries,) it was expoſed to be alienated in King Edward the ſixth's time; and a ſmall Penſion only was reſerved to the Miniſter out of it There were alſo Chantry-Lands in ſeveral Places, which were partly aſſigned for the maintenance of a Free-School in this place Here are ſtill ſome remains of an Epiſcopal Houſe, which, being rather a burden to the See, than any convenience to the Biſhop, has been a long time neglected.]

† Sym. Dunelm [illegible]

In a Field belonging to this place, there are three Wells of great depth, commonly called *Hell kettles*, or the Kettles of *Hell*, becauſe the water by an *Antiperiſtaſis* (or reverberation of the cold Air) is † heated in them The more thinking ſort reckon them to have been ſunk by an Earth quake, and probably enough For we find in the Chronicle of *Tinmouth*, *That in the year of our Lord 1179 on Chriſtmas day, at Oxenhall in the out fields of Darlington in the Biſhoprick of Durham, the Earth rais'd it ſelf up to a great height like a lofty tower, and remain'd ſo all that day till the evening, as it were fix'd and unmoveable, but then it ſunk down again with ſuch a horrible noiſe, that it terrified all the neighbourhood; and the Earth ſuck'd it in, and made there a deep pit, which continues as a teſtimony hereof to this day*

Hell Kettles

† This confuted below

[Concerning theſe Pits, take the following account, as I had it in a Letter from a very * ingenious Gentleman, who view'd them.

* Dr Kay

ACcording to the promiſe which I made you, I went to ſound the depth of Hell Kettles *near* Darlington *The name of bottomleſs* Pits *made me provide my ſelf with a line above two hundred fathoms long, and a lead weight conſiderable, of five or ſix pounds weight, but much ſmaller preparations would have ſerved: for the deepeſt of them took but fifteen fathoms, or thirty yards of our line I cannot imagine what theſe* Kettles *have been, nor upon what grounds the people of the Country have ſuppos'd them to be* bottomleſs *They look like ſome of our old wrought Coal-pits, that are drown'd but I cannot learn that any Coal, or other Mineral, has ever been found thereabouts They are full of water* (cold, *and not* hot, *as hath been affirmed) to the very brim, and almoſt the ſame level with the* Tees *which runs near them; ſo that they may have ſome ſubterraneal communication with that river But the water in the* Kettles *(as I was inform'd) is of a different kind from the river-water for it curdles Milk, and will not bear Soap But this I did not try*]

That there are ſubterraneous paſſages in theſe Pits, and a way out of them, was firſt diſcover'd by *Cuthbert Tunſtall* the Biſhop, * who found a Gooſe in the *Tees*, which he had mark'd, and put into the greater of them, for an experiment From *Derlington*, the *Tees* has no place of note upon it, [except *Neſham*, where was a Nunnery founded by the Anceſtors of the Lord *Dacres* At this place, is the uſual ford over the river from the South, and therefore here commonly is perform'd the Solemnity of meeting the Biſhop at his firſt coming The Lord of *Sockburn* (whoſe Seat is a little below upon the river) being at the head of the Gentlemen of the Country, ſteps forward with his Faulchion to the middle of the Stream, and there preſents it to the Biſhop, who returns it to him again, and thereupon is conducted along with loud Acclamations A little lower, is *Sockburn* before mentioned, the Houſe of that ancient and noble Family of *Conyers*, from whom are deſcended the Barons *Conyers* of *Hornby*, whoſe eſtate being much enlarged by marriages with the heirs of *Darcy* of *Menill*, and

* There is no Tradition of this Story hereabouts

Neſham

Sockburn.

and of *William Nevill* Earl of Kent and Lord *Fauconberg*, came in the last age save one to the *Alberstons* and the *Darcies* In a window of *Sockburn* Church is painted the Faulchion we just now spoke of, and it is also cut in Marble, upon the Tomb of the great Ancestor of the *Coigniers*, together with a Dog, and a monstrous Worm or Serpent lying at his feet, of his own killing, of which the History of the Family gives an account. They were Barons of the Palatinate, and Lords of *Sockburn* from the Conquest and before, till the Inheritance was carried lately, by the marriage of the heiress, into the family of the Earl of Shrewsbury From her daughter, the Manours of *Sockburn*, *Girsby*, and *Bishopton*, passed by Sale to Sir *William Blacket*, Baronet, whose Son Sir *Edward*, now enjoys them *Cuthbert*, second Son of the last Sir *John Conyers*, purchased *Layton*, near *Sedgfield*, where the *Sockburn* family hath for several descents been seated Below *Sockburn*, is *Yarum*, bigger and better built than *Darlington*, and a considerable Market]

From *Derlington*, the *Tees* winding on by green fields and country *villages*, [and by the Town of
Stockton. *Yarum* just now mention'd ; runs to *Stockton*, which is one of the four Ward towns of this County, and the Port of the river *Tees*, and a Corporation govern'd by a Mayor and Aldermen Of late years, it is much increased in Trade, and in the number of Inhabitants, which hath made it necessary to erect a new
Stat 12 Ann 1 Geor Church, instead of the little ancient Chapel that they had before It is also an Episcopal Borough ; and here was formerly a House of
Those Gentlemen call'd *Sur-Tees* (i.e. upon the *Tees*) formerly flourish'd upon it the Bishops The *Tees* having pass'd *Stockton*,] throws it self at last out of a large mouth into the Ocean, where begins the basis of the Triangle towards the Sea-coast

The shore runs hence northward (being di-
Gretham. vided only by one or two brooks) near *Gretham*, where Robert Bishop of Durham founded a noble Hospital, after the Manour had been bestow'd on him by the Lord of it, *Peter de Montfort*, [whose Father had indeed forfeited it to the Bishop] Next, stands *Claxton*, which gave name to a famous family in these parts ; and I the rather take notice of it, because *T Claxton*, a great admirer of Antiquities, was a branch thereof From hence the shore starts out in one only little Promontory (scarce seven miles above the mouth of the river *Tees* ;) up-
Hartlepole on which stands *Hartlepole*, † a famous Market,
† Ann 1607 and a safe harbour, very commodiously situated Bede seems to call it Heoртu (which Huntingdon renders *Cervi insula*, or the Island of a Hart,) and tells us that *Heiu*, a religious woman, formerly built a Monastery there, if *Heortеu* be not rather the name of that small *territory*, as the Durham book intimates, which also in some places calls it *Heortnesse*, because it shoots out pretty far into the Sea [This is an ancient Corporation ; but is now much fallen to decay, and subsists only by the fishing trade] From this place, for fifteen miles together, the shore, with towns here and there upon it, affords an entertaining prospect to those that sail
Esington by ; [who see *Esington*, a Ward Town, and a
Horden Capital Manour of the Bishop ; *Horden*, anciently a Seat of the *Claxtons*, but since, for seve-
Dalden ral Descents, of the *Coniers* ; *Dalden*, formerly the Seat of a Family of the same name, but now the possession of the Milbanks. *Warden-*
Warden Law *Law*, which St *Cuthbert's* Legend hath render'd famous, for the holding his Body, immoveable, till a Revelation directed the bringing it to Durham]

The Shore continues uninterrupted, till it opens a passage for the river *Vedra* ; for so it is Vedra call'd by Ptolemy ; but in Bede *Uiurus*, in Saxon [Wire, Wira,] Weorg, and by us *Were* This Were river rises in the very top of the triangle (namely, in the utmost part of the County westward) from two small streams, *Kellhop* and *Burnhop* ; which, being united in o one current, takes this name, and runs swiftly to the east, through vast heaths, and large Parks belonging to the Bishop ; [by *Stanhope*, which, together with *Wolsingham*, a little lower on the same river, and *Aukland*, did hold of the Bishop by *Forest-Services*, besides Demesnes, and other Tenures Particularly, upon his great Huntings, the Tenants in these parts were bound to set up for him in a *Field house*, or Tabernacle, with a Chapel, and all manner of Rooms and Offices ; as also to furnish him with Dogs and Horses, and to carry his Provision, and to attend him during his stay, for the supply of all Conveniencies But now, all Services of this kind are either let fall by disuse, or changed into Pecuniary Payments

The western Mountains here, are all along full of Minerals ; and the works of Nature under-ground are very curious, as, besides the Ore it self, the various Incrustations of the Sparr into infinite Forms and Colours, the petrifactions which hang from the tops of Grotts and Caverns, and the several Coats of them into which the Distillations are hardened

At *Stanhop* aforesaid, was the ancient Seat or Stanhop. Hall of the Family of *Fetherstonhaugh*, for many Generations ; the last of whom was slain at the battel of *Hockstet*, and the Estate was purchased by the Earl of *Carlisle* And, near Bradley-hal *Walsingham* aforesaid, is *Bradley hall*, an ancient Seat of the *Eurys*, but since of the *Bowes* ; for the battlementing of which, a Licence was obtained of the Bishop in the year 1431] Next, the *Were* runs by *Witton*, a Castle of the Lords Witton *d' Euers*, an ancient and noble Family of this Barons Eur or de Eure County (as being descended from the Lords of *Clavering* and *Warkworth*, as also by daughters from the *Vescies* and the *Attons* Barons) who, as Scotland can testifie, have been famous for their warlike Gallantry For *Ketenes*, a little Town in the further part of Scotland, was bestow'd upon them by King Edward the first for their great services ; and in the * last age Henry the * So said, ann 1607 eighth honoured them with the title of Barons. [*Ralph* of this family, being created Baron *Eure* of *Witton* From them, it passed by Sale to the *Darcies*, in whose possession it now remains] After this, the *Were*, some few miles lower, receives *Gaunless* a little river, from the south, [at the head of which, is *Evenwood*, a Barony Evenwood and Capital Manour of the Bishop, held of him formerly by the *Hansards*, who had one of their chief Seats here ; from whence it runs to *West-Aukland*, formerly the Estate of the *Daltons*, West Aukland but now, by marriage, the Seat of the *Edens* ; and St *Helen Aukland*, the Seat of the *Cars*] St. Helen.

At the very confluence of the *Were* and *Gaunless*, upon a pretty high hill, stands *Bishops-Aukland*, so nam'd (as *Sarron* in Greece Aukland Bishops Aukland was) from the *Oaks* ; where we see a fair built house of the Bishop, with turrets, magnificently repair'd by *Anthony Bec* , and a very noble bridge, built by *Walter Skirlaw*, Bishop, about the year 1400, who also enlarged this house, and made a bridge over the *Tees* at *Yarum* [It was formerly call'd *North-Aukland*, and sometimes *Market-Aukland*, and now *Bishop-Aukland*, from the Bishop's house here ; which was pulled down in the Great Rebelli-

on

on by Sir *Arthur Hasterig*, who built a new house out of the materials. At the Restoration, Bishop *Cosins* pull'd down the new House, and built a large Apartment to what remained of the old one, joyning the whole to a magnificent Chapel of his own erecting, in which he lies buried What remained unfinish'd, hath been carried on by the present Bishop, to very great Advantage, for the convenience and ornament of the Place The said Bishop *Cosins* founded and endowed here an Hospital for two men and two women The Church of St *Andrew*, near this place (the mother Church to all this district, which goes by the name of *Aukland-shire*) was anciently Collegiate, under the Vicar, but the forementioned Bishop, *Anthony Bec*, gave him the title of Dean, with twelve Prebendaries under him, and *Thomas Langley* regulated them to an equality, and restored the Solemnity of their Service, and got his Appointment confirmed by King Henry the sixth]

From hence the *Were* (that it may water this County the longer) turns to the north, and soon comes within sight of the remains of an old City upon the top of a hill, which is not in being at this day, nor has been for many ages, call'd by Antoninus *Vinovium*, and by Ptolemey *Binovium*, in which last Author it is so misplac'd, and seated as it were under another pole, that I could never have discover'd it, but by Antoninus's direction At present, it is call'd *Binchester*, and consists but of one or two houses, yet much taken notice of by the neighbours thereabouts, for the rubbish, and the ruins of old walls, and also for the Roman Coins often dug-up in it, which they call *Binchester-pennies*, and for Roman Inscriptions, one of which, cut out thus in an Altar there, I lately met with.

Vinovium

Binchester

Of the *Mother Goddesses*, see Lancashire In the year of Christ 236

DEAB
MTRQ·QLO
TCLQWI
TINS·ACS
VSLM

Votum solvit lubens merito

Another Stone was lately dug-up here, very much defaced with gaps, with yet, upon a narrow view, shews this Inscription

- - - - - - -
- - - - - - - - -

TRIB COHOR I
CARTOV- - -
MARTI VICTORI
GENIO LOCI
ET BONO
EVENTVI

[The Antiquities of this place have been carefully search'd for by the present Owner, Mr *Charles Wren*, who, among other Curiosities, discover'd a Cornelian; and in another part, a fair Urn, shut up in a round Wall, and within that a Vessel of Wood]

I have heard nothing else relating to this place, but what is mention'd in an old Book, That the Earls of Northumberland † did rend this, with other villages, from the Church; when that cursed Thirst after Gold swallow'd up the Lands and Patrimony thereof.

† This still holds of the Bishop, as anciently

On the other side of the *Were* [is *Hunwick*, noted for its Wells, both sulphureous and sweet, to which there is great Resort; and] among the hills, we see *Branspeth-Castle*, built by the *Bulmers*; and by a daughter of * *Bertram Bulmer* (marry'd to ‖ *Robert Nevill*,) added with other great possessions to the family of the *Nevills*

Hunwick.

Branspeth-castle

* Bernard, C Dugd

‖ Galfrid, C

[Upon the forfeiture of the *Nevils*, it was bought of the *Londoners*; and lately sold to Sir *Henry Bellasis* In this Parish, lies *Hairebolme*, commonly *Hairum*; whither, it is reported, some of the murderers of *Thomas Becket* fled after the fact, and built a Chapel there to his memory Not far from whence, on the other side of the river, is *Whitworth*, an ancient manour of a family of that name, but now the Seat of the *Shaftoes*, and below it, *Crokestell*, commonly *Croxdale*, where the ancient family of the *Salvins* hath been settled for several Descents]

Hairum

Whitworth

Crokestell

A little below *Branspeth*, the *Were* has many huge stones in its chanel, never cover'd but when the river is overflow'd by rains upon these, if you pour water, and it mix a little with the stone, it becomes brackish; a thing which happens no where else Nay, at *Butterby*, a little village, when the river is shallow and sunk from those stones in the summer time, there bursts out of them a reddish salt water, which grows so white and hard, by the heat of the Sun, [as hath been thought,] that they who live thereabouts use it for Salt [But, that the *Saltness* itself proceeds not from the heat of the Sun, is plain by experience, in that which is most saltish, and issues out of a rock; insomuch as if all the water be laved out of the place, there immediately bubbles, out of the body of the rock, a water as salt as the former, and besides, the rock out of which it issues, is a *Salt* rock, of a sparkling substance On the other side of the *Were*, there is also a *Medicinal* Spring of strong Sulfur, and, above it, towards *Durham*, is a Mineral water, upon which Dr *Wilson* wrote his *Spadacrene Dunelmensis* On the same River, is *Old Durham*, from the name of which one would conjecture, either that the Monks had first come thither with St *Cuthbert's* Body, or that there had been a Town of that name before their coming But both these things are unwarranted from History At present, it is the Seat of the *Tempests*]

Butterby

Salt Stones.

Philosoph Trans N 163

Old Durham

Now, the river (as if it design'd to make an Island) almost surrounds the chief City of the County, seated on a *hill*; upon which account it was call'd *Dunholm* by the Saxons For, as we gather from Bede, they call'd a hill *Dun*, and a River-Island *holme* Out of this, the Latins fram'd *Dunelmum*, which [the Normans calling *Duresme*,] the common people afterwards corrupted into *Durham* The Town stands high, and so is very strong; but of no great compass It lies in a kind of oval form, enclos'd by the river on all sides except the north, and fortify'd with walls In the south part, almost where the river winds it self back again, stands the Cathedral Church, which with its spires and tower steeple makes a noble show In the heart of the town, stands the Castle almost in the middle between two stone bridges, one

Dunholm, Durham, or Duresme

one over the river on the east side, the other over the same river on the west. From the Castle northward lies the Market place, and S. *Nicholas's Church*, from whence, for a good way, there shoots out a Suburbs to the north east, within a winding of the river; as do others on both sides beyond the river, which lead to the bridges; and each Suburbs has its particular Church. The original of this Town is not very ancient. For when the Monks of Lindisfarn were disquieted in the Danish wars, and forc'd to wander up and down with the reliques of S. *Cuthbert*; at last being admonish'd by an oracle (if you will believe it) they fix'd and settl'd here about the year of Christ 995.

Sim. Dunelm. X Script. p. 28. But take this relation from my *Durham-Author* himself. *All the people following the corps of our most holy father* Cuthbert, *came to* Durham, *a place strong by nature, and scarce habitable, being overspread with a very thick wood; only, in the middle, there was a small plain, which they us'd to plough and sow, where Bishop Aldwin afterwards built a pretty large Church of stone. The said Prelate therefore, with the help of all the people, and the assistance of Utbred Earl of the Northumbrians, cut down and rooted up all the wood, and in a short time made the place habitable. In short, from the river* Coqued *to the* Tees, *the People, to a man, came in readily, both to help forward this work, and afterwards to build the Church; and so devout were they, that till it was finish'd, they ceas'd not to lend a helping hand. The wood being thus rooted up, and every one having a house assign'd him by Lot, the foresaid Bishop, out of a zeal to Christ and S.* Cuthbert, *began to build a pretty large and handsome Church, and endeavour'd with great application to finish it.* Thus far my Author, [and, to omit the many pretended Miracles, and other passages of less moment, he says further, that the first Church erected at *Dunholm* by Bishop *Aldwin*, was, *facta citissimè de virgis Ecclesiola*, a little Church, quickly made, of Rods; just such another Structure, as that which is said to have been first built at *Glassenbury*, whereof Sir *Henry Spelman* has given us a draught.]

Concil. T. 1. p. 11. Not many years after, those of the English who could not endure the Norman Yoke, trusting to the strength of this place, made it the seat of war, and from hence gave William the Conqueror no small disturbance. For *Gulielmus Gemeticensis* writes, *That they went into a part of the County, inaccessible by reason of woods and waters; building a Castle, with a strong rampire round it, which they call'd* Dunholm. *Out of this, they made frequent sallies, and for some time kept themselves close there, waiting for the coming of King Sueno the Dane.* But things not happening as they had expected, they betook themselves to flight; and William the Conquerour, coming to Durham, granted many Privileges whereby to secure and confirm the liberties of the Church, and built the Castle already mention'd higher upon the hill, which afterwards became a habitation for the Bishops; and the Keys of it, when the See was vacant, by an old custom were wont to be hung up at St. *Cuthbert's* Tomb. [This Castle was beautified, and a noble Library erected and furnished with Books, at great expence, by Dr. *John Cosins*, the learned and pious Bishop of this place; who also built here an Hospital for poor People.]

When the Castle was built, William of Malmesbury, who liv'd about that time, gives us this description of the City. *Durham is a hill rising by little and little from the valley, by an easie and gentle ascent, to the very top; and notwithstanding, by its rugged situation and craggy precipice, the access to it be cut off on all sides, yet lately they have built a Castle upon the hill. At the bottom of the foundation of the castle, runs an excellent river for fish, especially Salmon.* [but this excellency is very much impaired by the heightening of the Dams, which have given a check to the fish.] Almost at the same time, as that ancient book has it, *William de Carelepho* the Bishop, who resettl'd Monks here (for their Cloisters had been every where demolished by the Danes,) having pull'd down the Church, which Aldwin built, began another more noble, which * is said to have been finished by Radulph his successor, and was enlarged by *Nicholas Fernham* the Bishop, and *Thomas Melsamby* the Prior, in the year 1242. * Was, C.

A good while after, William *Skirlaw*, Bishop, rais'd a neat building on the west part of the Church, which they call'd *Gallilee*, whither they remov'd the marble tomb of Venerable Bede. Gallilee

In which place, *Hugh de Puteaco* formerly begun a Building; where *Women* (these are the words of an old book) *might lawfully enter; and they who might not personally view the secrets of the holy places, might at least have some comfort from the view and contemplation of the Saints.* The same Bishop Ralph (as our Historian relates) *converted all that space between the Church and the Castle (where many houses stood) into a plain field, lest the Church should either be defil'd by the dirt, or endanger'd by the fire of the town. And although the city be naturally strong; he increased both the strength and state of it, by a wall, for he built one, all along, from the Chancel of the Church to the tower of the castle;* which by degrees † was sinking under the weight of age; [but hath been effectually rescued from ruin by the present Bishop, who hath also been a great Benefactor to both his Castles of Durham and Aukland.] It never did, that I know of, suffer from an enemy. For when *David Brus* King of Scots destroy'd all with fire and sword as far as *Beaupark* or *Berepark* (a Park just under the city) whilst Edward 3. was at the siege of Calais in France, *Henry Percy*, and *William Zouch* Archbishop of York, with such troops as they could raise on a sudden, encounter'd the Scots, and charg'd them with that heat and bravery, that they cut off the first and second ‖ Ranks almost to a man, took the King prisoner, and put the third into such terror, that the fled with great precipitation; their fears carrying them over the steepest precipices, till they got into their own country. This was a noble engagement, to be always reckon'd among the many bloody defeats we have given the Scots; and is call'd by us *The Battel of Nevill Cross*. For the best of the Scotch Nobility being slain here, and the King himself taken, they were forced to give up much ground hereabouts, and yield many Castles into our hands. And this may suffice for *Durham*; to which, with the Reader's leave, I will add a Distich of *Necham's*, and an Hexastich of *Jonston's*, and then I have done.

† Is now, C.

Berepark

17 Oct. 1346.

Battel at Nevil's-Cross.

‖ Aciem

Arte, situque loci munita Dunelmia, salve,
Qua floret sanctæ religionis apex.

Hail, happy Durham! Art and Nature's care,
Where Faith and Truth at th' noblest height appear.

Vedra *ruens rapidis modò cursibus, agmine lenis,*
Seque minor celebres suspicit urbe viros,

Quos

Quos dedit ipsa olim, quorum & tegit ossa sepulta ;
Magnus ubi sacro marmore Beda *cubat*
Se jactent aliæ vel relligione, vel armis ;
Hæc armis clara, hæc relligione potens

Unequal *Were*, as by her walls it runs,
Looks up, and wonders at her noble sons,
Whom she gave life, and now their death does mourn,
And ever weeps o'er *Beda*'s sacred urn
Let others boast of piety or war,
While she's the care of both, and both of her

* The two Archdeacons were before the Monks

As for the Monks being turn'd out, and twelve Prebendaries * with two Archdeacons substituted in lieu of them; and also the Style of Prior being changed into that of Dean I need say nothing of them, being things sufficiently known to every body It stands in 22 degrees, Longitude, and in 54 degrees, 57 minutes, Latitude

† Below, C
Shirburn Hospital
‖ *De Puteaco*
* See another like instance at *Jarrow*

† Near Durham (not to omit this) there stands to the east a very noble Hospital, founded by *Hugh* ‖ *Pudsey* (an extraordinary rich Bishop, and for a little time Earl of Northumberland) *for Lepers, and* (as Newbrigensis says, [with too great * severity, if not injustice, to the Founder,)] *at great cost and expence, yet upon some accounts not very honourable For, to advance this charitable design, he made use of his power to extort supplies from others, when he was not willing to allow a competent share of his own towards the work* However, he settled a very good allowance for the maintaining of sixty five Lepers, beside Mass-priests; [and the † Hospital, after several Regulations, is settled by the name of Christ's Hospital, for a Master and thirty Brethren]

† Stat 27 El.

Finchale.
‖ Mat Par p 98
* *Ecclesiola*
Chron Sax
Sim. Dun. p 114

From hence the *Were* is carry'd in a streighter course toward the north, by *Finchale*, where in the reign of Henry 2d, Godric, ‖ a man of true ancient Christian simplicity, and wholly devoted to God and Religion,, led and ended a solitary life, and was here buried in the same place, *where* (as William of *Newburrow* says) *he was wont in his devotion to prostrate himself, or in sickness to lie down* This man became so much admir'd for his holy simplicity, that R brother to that rich Bishop *Hugh Pudsey*, built a * Chapel to his memory [*Finchale* (call'd in Saxon Pincanheal, by Henry Huntingdon *Wincanhale*, by Hoveden *Phincanhal*, and by others *Finchale*, which difference has risen from the likeness of the Saxon p, p, and) is supposed to be the place, where two Synods were held in the Saxon times, one in the year 788, the other in the year 798 It was a Cell to the Church of Durham; having a Prior, and an uncertain number of Monks. Near this place, is *Houghton le Spring*, where is a Free School, and an Hospital competently endowed]

Houghton le Spring

Lumley
Barons Lumley

Then, the *Were* runs by *Lumley*, a castle with a Park round it; the ancient seat of the *Lumleys*, descended from *Liulphus* (a Nobleman of great figure in these parts, in Edward the Confessor's time) who married *Aldgitha*, daughter of Aldred Earl of Northumberland Of these, *Marmaduke* took his mother's Coat of Arms; in whose right he came to the large Estate of the *Thwengs* The Arms were, *In a field argent a fess Gules between three Poppinjays Vert*, whereas, before that, the *Lumleys* bore for their Arms, *Six Poppinjays argent in a field Gules* For she was the eldest daughter of *Marmaduke Thweng* Lord of Kilton, and Coheir of *Thomas Thweng* her brother. But Ralph the son of this Marmaduke, was made the first Baron of Lumley by Richard the 2d Which honour, *John*, the ninth from him, * enjoy'd, a person of entire virtue, integrity and innocence, and, † in his old age, a compleat pattern of true Nobility [But this Honour being extinct in him, was not revived, till Richard, the present Earl of Scarborough, was created by King Charles the second, Baron *Lumley* of *Lumley-castle*; and by King William and Queen Mary, first Viscount, and then Earl thereof; who hath repair'd and adorn'd this Seat of his Ancestors, with all the Advantages that modern Art can give it At the Town of *Lumley*, is an Hospital, erected by Sir *John Duck* Baronet, for twelve poor women and a Chaplain; to which the whole Town, being far from the Parish-Church, have also the convenience of resorting.]

† Now in his old age, C.

Chester upon the Street
Condercum
‖ More probably *Benwall* in *Northumberland*, which see.

Opposite to this Town, and not far from the River, on the other side, stands *Chester upon the street*, that is, a castle or little city by the highway; call'd in Saxon Concerceſt for which reason I have thought it the *Condercum* ‖, where *upon the line of the* Vallum, the first wing of the *Astures*, kept garrison in the Roman times, as the *Notitia* tells us For it is but some few miles from the *Vallum* (of which I shall particularly treat hereafter,) [and several pieces of Roman Coin have been found here; and the rivulet which runs by it from the west, is call'd *Conkburn*.] The Bishops of Lindisfarn lived retiredly in this place, for 113 years, with the body of St *Cuthbert*, in the time of the Danish wars And, whilst *Egelric* Bishop of Durham, in memory thereof, was laying the foundation of a new Church there, he dug up such a prodigious sum of Money, that he quitted his Bishoprick, as being now rich enough and so, returning to Peterborough, where he was Abbot before, he made Causeys through the fens, and did several other good works, at very great expence. Long after this, *Anthony Bec* Bishop of Durham founded here a Collegiate Church, consisted of a Deanery and seven Prebends In this Church, *John* Baron *Lumley*, just now mention'd, placed the Monuments of his Ancestors, in order as they succeeded one another, from *Liulphus* down to our * own times; which he had either pick'd out of the demolish'd Monasteries, or made new [This is the fourth Ward-Town of the County, and is the Habitation of the family of *Hedworth*, who are of long standing in this County, taking their Rise from the Town of that name] More inward, and almost in the middle of the triangle, stands another small village, † heretofore noted for it's College of Dean and Prebendaries, founded by the said *Anthony* The name of the place is *Lanchester*, which I once thought to be the old *Longovicum*, [* and the Antiquity of it is further confirmed from divers Inscriptions found near it, within these few years

* So said, ann 1607
† Lately, C
Lanchester
* Phil Trans N 166

IMP· CAES·M·ANT· GORDIA
NVS·P·F·AVG·BALNEVM·CVM
BASILICAM SOLO INSTRVXIT
PREGNLVCILANVM LEG. AVG
PR·PR·CVRANTE M·AVR·
QVIRINO PRE· COH I LEG P

FORTVNAE
AVG· SACR
P·AEL ATTI
CVS·R AFF
VSLM

MAR
TI

DEO
MARCAV
RSVSVOT

GENIO PRAETORI
CL·EPAPHRODITVS
CLAVDIANVS
TRIBVNVS CHO
I LING·V·L·P·M

C O H T

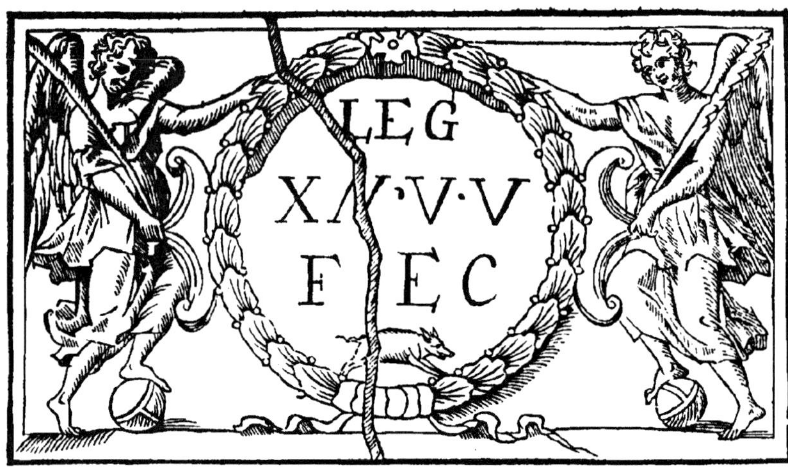

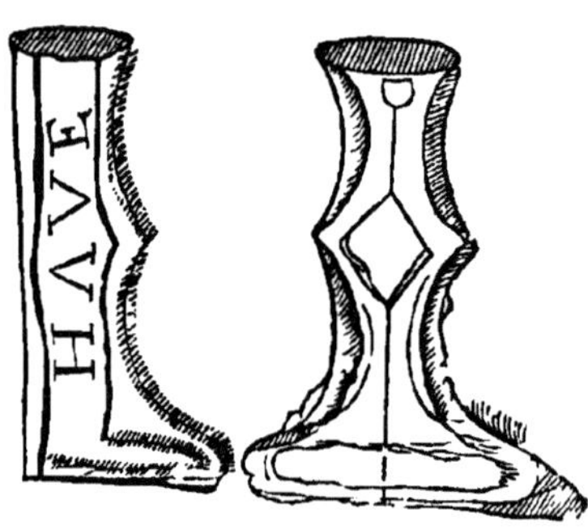

Add to this, that the High way runs directly to it from *Binchester*, by the name of *Watling street*; and that there has been a square Inclosure of Aisler work, with a broad ditch.]

Hilton Castle — But to return to the *Were*, which at last winds about to the east, and runs by *Hilton*, a castle of the *Hiltons*, [an ancient Family, wherein is preserved to this day the title of the Bishop's *Barons*. The Gate house, which is all that remains of the old Castle, shews how large it hath been, with the Chapel, a fine Structure, wherein there were Chaplains in constant Attendance, it being the burying place of the Family. Then the *Were*] falls into the Sea at Wiran-muth (as Bede calls it, [in Saxon *Wiremutha*)] but now *Monks-were mouth*, that is, the mouth of the *Were*, belonging to the Monks. Of which mouth, *William* of *Malmesbury* writes thus: *The* Were *flowing into the Sea here kindly receives the Ships brought in with a gentle gale upon each bank thereof, Benedict the Bishop built* Bishop Benedict *a Church, and likewise in the same places founded two Monasteries, one to* St. Peter, *another to* St. Paul. *Whoever reads the life of this man, will admire his industry in furnishing this place with great store of books, and being the first that brought* Glaziers first in England *Masons and Glaziers into England.* [But as to the two Churches being built upon the banks of the river, it is a manifest mistake. For St. *Paul's* was at *Girwy* or *Jarrow*, some miles distant from *Weremuth*, as appears from all the rest of our Historians, and also from an Inscription which will follow hereafter in this County. On the Southern bank of the *Were* stands *Sunderland*, a handsome populous Town, Sunderland built in the last age, and very much enrich'd by the Coal-trade. If the Harbour were so deep, as to entertain Ships of the same burthen, that the river doth, it would be no small loss to *Newcastle*. As to the name, the reason of it may well be gather'd from Bede, compared with the Saxon Translation. Bede tells us, that he was born in the territory of *Jarrow*, and the Saxon has it, in the sundorlande of that Monastery, which word denotes any particular Precinct, having certain Freedoms within it self, and such, this place is. It gave the title of Earl to *Emanuel* Lord Scrope of *Bolton*, created June 19. 3 Car. 1. who dying without issue, *Henry* Lord Spencer of *Wormleighton* was honour'd with the title of Earl of Sunderland by King Charles the first, and being slain the same year in the Service of his Royal Master, at the first battel at Newbury, was succeeded by *Robert* his son and heir, to whom, in the year 1702, succeeded Charles the present [illegible] whose excellent Endowments of Nature, [illegible] proved by long Study and Experience in publick Affairs, have already carry'd him, with great reputation and honour, through the most important Offices in the State. Near *Whitburn*, not far from this place, Copper Coins were taken up some years since, mostly of *Constantine*, with the Sun on the Reverse, and these words *Soli invicto Comiti*. One also was of *Maxentius*, with something like a Triumphal Arch on the reverse, and these words, *Conservatoris Urbis*. There were likewise one or two of *Licinius*, and one or two of *Maximianus*.]

Five miles above *Sunderland*, the *Tine* comes to its mouth, which for some way (as we have observ'd) made the north-side of our triangle, together with the *Derwent*. Upon the *Derwent*, which rises near the top of this triangle, nothing is eminent, unless it be *Ebchester* (as they now call it,) a small village, so named from *Ebba* the Virgin, descended from the blood-royal of the Northumbrians; who flourish'd about the year 630, with such reputation for Sanctity, that she was solemnly canoniz'd for a Saint, and has many Churches dedicated to her in this Island, which are commonly call'd St *Tabb's*, for St *Ebb's*. [Here not many years since, was observ'd a *Roman Station*, about two hundred yards square, with large Suburbs; and here also, together with divers ancient Monuments, hath been found the following Altar;

Ebchester

St Ebba

S Tabl's Pl I Jun [illegible] N 2-8

and also an Urn of a very uncommon shape, near a yard high, and not above seven inches wide, with a little cup in the heart of it; perhaps for an Oblation of Tears, or of Wine and Milk, such as the Romans used at the burying of their dead. Also, the High-way goes along from *Lanchester* to this place, and to *Corbridge* from it, and the *Epiacum* of Ptolemy, answers to it in sound, and is not inconsistent with it in situation. This river, *Derwent*, is clad all the way down, with Mills, Furnaces, and Forges, for the smelting of lead and silver, and for the manufactures of Iron and Steel.]

The first place remarkable upon the *Tine*, is *Gateshead*, called in Saxon Gaetſheveð, and in the same sense by our Historians, *Capræ caput*, i. e. Goats-head; which is a kind of Suburb to Newcastle on the other side the *Tine*, and was annex'd to it by Edward the sixth, when he had dissolved the Bishoprick; but Queen Mary soon after restor'd it to the Church. This place is commonly believ'd to be of greater Antiquity, than Newcastle it self. And if I should say further, that this and Newcastle (for they seem formerly to have been one Town parted by the river) was that Frontier garrison which in the times of the later Emperors was call'd *Gabrosentum*, and was defended by the second Cohort of the *Thracians*; and that this hath retain'd it's old name in sense and signification, notwithstanding *Newcastle* has chang'd

Gateshead

Gabrosentum

its name once or twice; I hope it would not be at all inconsistent with truth. For *Gaffr* is us'd by the Britains for a *Goat*, and *Hen* in † compounds for *Pen*, which signifies a *head*: and in this very sense it is plainly call'd *Capræ Caput*, or Goats-head, by our old Latin Historians: as *Brundusium*, in the language of the *Messapii*, took its name from the head of a Stag. And I am apt to fansy, that this name was given the place from some Inn which had a *Goats-head* for the sign; like the *Cock* in Africa, *The three Sisters* in Spain, and *The Pear* in Italy, all of them mention'd by Antoninus; which (as some of the Learned think) took their names from such Signs. As for our Historians, they unanimously call it *Capræ caput*, when they tell us that *Walcher* Bishop of Durham (who was constituted by William the Conquerour, Governour of Northumberland with the authority of Earl,) was slain in this place by the rabble, for his tyrannical proceedings.

† 8 rmon. contexts

1080

Below this village, almost upon the very mouth of the *Tine* stands *Girwy*, now *Jarrow*, where venerable Bede was born, and where a little Monastery heretofore flourished. When, and by whom, it was founded, may be learnt from this Inscription, which is fairly legible to this day in the Church wall.

Girwy, Jarrow

DEDICATIO BASILICAE
SCI PAVLI VIIII KL: MAI
ANNO XVI ECFRIDI REG.
CEOLFRIDI ABB: EIVSDEM
Q; ECCLES: DO: AVCTORE
CONDITORIS ANNO IIII.

[In this Inscription, the XVI should be XV. For King Egfrid reigned no more than fifteen years, and so Sir *James Ware* has given it in his Notes upon Bede's History of the Abbots of Wiremuth. But it ought not to be infer'd from the Inscription, that *Ceolfrid* was the Founder of this Monastery; since it appears from Bede's account, that he was only constituted first Abbot of the place by *Benedictus Biscopius*, who sent him hither (with a Colony of about seventeen Monks) from *Weremuth*.]

The greater Churches, when the saving light of the Gospel began to shine in the world (let it not be thought impertinent to note thus much,) were call'd *Basilicæ*, because the *Basilicæ* of the Gentiles, namely those stately Edifices where the Magistrates held their Courts of Justice, were converted to Churches by the Christians. (Whence Ausonius, *Basilica olim negotiis plena, nunc votis*; i. e. The *Basilica, once fill'd with business, now with devotion*.) Or else, because they were built in an oblong form, as the *Basilicæ* were.

Basilicæ

Here, our Bede, the glory of England (for his eminent piety and learning, sirnam'd *Venerable*) apply'd himself, as he says, to the study of the Scriptures; and, in the times of greatest barbarity and ignorance, wrote many learned Volumes. *With him* (as William of Malmesbury says) *almost all knowledge of History from thence to our times went to the grave*. For

Bede.

while

while one succeeded laxer than another, the spirit of study and industry was extinct all over the Island. The Danes had so harrass'd this Religious place, that, in the beginning of the Norman times, when some had revived the Monastick Order in these parts, and Walcher the Bishop had assign'd them this place; *the walls* (says my Author) *stood without a roof, and with very small remains of their ancient splendour however, having cover'd them with rough unhew'n wood, they thatch'd them with straw, and began to celebrate Divine Service in them* [Here, and at *Wermouth*, the Monks continued, till the year 1083, when Bishop *William de S Kerlefo* translated them to *Durham*, to attend the Body of St. *Cuthbert*; from which time, *Wermouth* and *Jarrow* became Cells to Durham

Some years since, upon the bank of the river *Tine*, was discover'd a Roman Altar; the figure whereof take here, as it was deliver'd to the Royal Society by the ingenious and learned Dr. *Lister*, together with his description of it, in a Letter to the said Society.

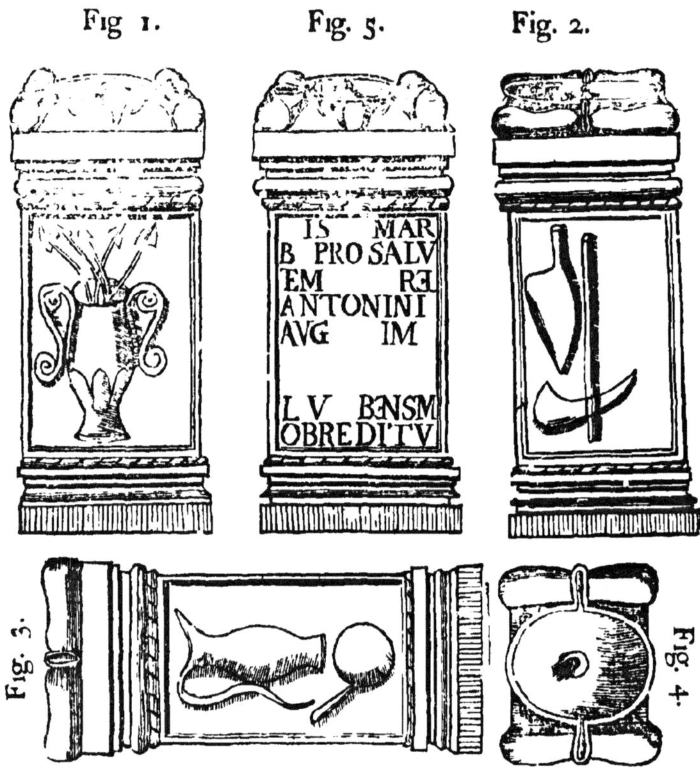

Dr *Lister's* Letter

" I have with much trouble got into my " hands a piece of Roman Antiquity, which " was but a very few years ago discover'd upon " the south bank of the river *Tine*, near Shields " in the Bishoprick It is a very large and " fair Roman Altar, of one entire stone But " after all my cost and pains, I am very sorry " to find the Inscription very ill defaced, that " much of it is not legible And I believe it " hath been also misshandled by those who have " endeavoured to read it; whereas if the re- " mainder of the Letters had been exactly mea- " sured, and the face black'd and lightly " wash'd off again, as in prints, some things " more might have been spelled

" As to the nature of the stone it self, it is " of a coarse Rag, the same with that of the " Pyramids at Burrow Briggs It is four foot " high, and was ascended to by steps; which " appeareth, in that all the sides, but the front " have two square holes near the bottom, " which let in the irons that joyn'd it to the " steps

" I have carefully designed it in all it's sides, " and have given the plan of the top also; " which if you please, we will survey in or- " der

1 " The backside, opposite to the Inscrip- " tion; on which is engraven, in bass-relief, a " Flower-pot, furnished, I suppose, with what " pleased the Stone-cutter · for these men need- " ed not to be more curious than the Priests " themselves, who were wont to make use " of herbs next at hand to adorn the Altars, " and therefore *Verbena* is put for a kind of " herb yet if we will have it resemble any " thing with us, I think it most like, if not " truly, the *Nymphæa*, a known and common " river Plant.

2 " One

2 "One of the sides, which is somewhat "narrower than the front or back on this are "engraved in Bass-relieve, the Cutting-knife "(Secespita) and the Axe (Securis) The Knife "is exactly the same with that on the other "Altar formerly by me mention'd in the Phi "losophical Collections of Mr Hooke but the "Axe is different, for here it is headed with "a long and crooked point, and there the head "of the Axe is divided into three points.

3 "The other side, on which are engraved, "after the same manner, an Ewer (*Urceolus*) "and a Ladle, which serve for a *Sympulum* "This I call rather a Ladle than a Mallet, it "being perfectly Dish-wise and hollow in "the middle, although *Camden* is of another "opinion, in that elegant Sculpt of the Cum "berland Altar And the very same Utensil I "have seen and noted on the *Ickley* Altar, which "is yet extant at *Middleton-Grange* near that "town, but the stone which *Camden* say "supports a pair of stairs there (as at this day "it does in the very road) is but an ill copy of "it, and not the original

4 "The plane of the top which is cut in "the figure of a Bason (*discus* or *lanx*) with "Ansæ on each side, consisting of a pair of "links of a chain, which rest upon and fall "over two rowles and this was the *Harth*

5 "The Front, which hath an Inscription "of nine lines in Roman letters, each letter a "very little more than two inches deep of our "measure, now remaining as in the prefix'd "sculpture, Fig. 5 which I would read thus "*Dis deabusque Matribus pro Salute M Aurelii* "*Antonini Augusti Imperatoris*——*votum solvit* "*lubens meritò ob reditum*

"The *Deæ Matres* are well interpreted by "*Selden* It is much, that his Safety and Re- "turn both vowed, should be so separated in "the Inscription, but I have not *Gruter* by me "to compare this with the like *Caracalla*, say "the Historians *, after his father's death at "York, took upon him the command of the "army alone, and the whole Empire; he went "alone against the enemy, who were the *Cale* "*donii* inhabiting beyond the wall which his "father had built; he made peace with them, "received their hostages, slighted their fortified "places, and returned And this seems to be "confirmed by the Inscription; for undoubted- "ly, upon this his last expedition alone, with "out his brother *Geta* and mother, was this "Altar erected to him alone, at a place about "two Stations on this side the wall So that "the vow might be as well understood of his "return from this expedition, as for his safety "and return to *Rome*, which methinks should "be true, or his mother and brother *Geta* "would scarce have been left out, at least so "early For yet the Army declared for them "both, according to their Father's will

* *Xiphilinus, Herodianus, &c*

"Further, it seems also to have been erected "by those who flatter'd him, and who were "afterwards killed by him and for this reason "the persons names who dedicated it, seem to "me to be purposely defaced, the sixth and "seventh lines of the Inscription being design "edly cut away by the hollowness of them, "and there not being the least sign of any letter "remaining And this, I suppose, might be "part of their diligence; as it was usual to de "face and break the Statues and Monuments of "persons executed, of which this monster made "strange havock

"But since worn Inscriptions admit of va "rious readings, because some letters are worn "out, and some more legible, whereby unpre- "judiced people may conceive them diversly "I will therefore tell you another reading of "part of the two first lines, which I do not "disallow, but that it will agree well enough "with the history of *Severus*, though his *Apo-* "*theosis*, or solemn deification, was not per- "formed till he came to Rome, in the manner "of which funeral-pomp *Herodian* is very large. "It was the Reading of that excellent Anti- "quary Dr *Johnson* of *Pomfret*

CONSERVATO
RI B PROS, &c

The rest as follows in mine

"Which shews the height of flattery of those "times. So that they paid their vows to the "lately dead father the Conservator of Britain, "for the safety of the son and the story tells "us how gladly he would have had him "made a God long before, even with his own "hand

Along the river *Tine*, are several Houses for the making of *Glass*; for which use also one House hath been erected upon the river *Were* The workmen are Foreigners, but know not well from whence they came only, they have a Tradition of their being Normans, and that they came from *Sturbridge*, and removed from thence hither, in the reign of Edward the sixth or Queen Elizabeth At *Shields*, upon the mouth of the *Tine*, is a Manufacture of *Salt*, in above two hundred Pans]

It is not necessary, that I give a Catalogue of all the Bishops of *Durham*, who are like- wise Counts Palatines It may suffice to ob- serve in short, that from the first foundation of this Bishoprick in the year 995 to our times, there have been † forty Bishops of this See The most eminent, were these four, *Hugh de Puteaco* or *Pudsey*, who for * 1013 *l* ready mo- ney, purchas'd of Richard the first the Earldom of Northumberland for his own life, and *Sath- bregia* to him and his Successors for ever; and founded a very noble Hospital, as I observed before Between him and the Archbishop, there happen'd a most grievous contest, while (as a certain writer words it) *one would be superiour, the other would not be inferiour, and neither would do any good* Next, *Anthony Bec*, Patriarch of Jerusalem, who spent vast sums of money in extravagant buildings, and splendid furniture *Thomas Wolsey*, Cardinal, who wanted nothing to compleat his happiness, but moderation of mind his Story is well known And *Cuthbert Tunstall*, who dy'd about the beginning of ‖ the last age, and for Learning and Piety was (with- out envy be it spoken) * equal to them all, and a very great Ornament to Britain

Bishops of Durham

† 3, C.

* 000 Marks

See the Earls of Northumberland

‖ Th . C

* [illegible]

There are in this County and Northumberland 118 *Parish Churches, besides a great many Chapels*

More rare Plants growing in the Bishoprick of Durham

Buphthalmum vulgare *Ger* Dioscoridis *C B* Matthioli sive vulgare millefolii foliis *Park* Chamæmelum chrysanthemum quorundam *J B* *Common Ox eye. I found this on a bank near the*

XII Minuits of Time XI X

PART OF WESTMORELAND

PART OF CUMBERLAND

Amblesyde

Hawkeshead

Fourness

Kendall

Black Hall

Rusel and

New Brig

Cartmell Hall

Sedgwick

Levens bridge

FOURNESS HUNDRED

Broughton

LOY DALE

Ulverston

Cartmel

Frith hall

Holker

Flookburton

Humphrey head

Dalton

Aldingham

Leven Sand

Lancaster Sands

Ken Sand

Pile of Foudray

Foulney I.

Pile Sands

Burton

Farleton

Betham

Kirkby Lan

Whettington

Bolton

Hest bank Passage

Bare

Caton

Claughton

Hornby

Longovicum

Lancaster

Scotford

Cloughho

Wiersdale

Middleton

Overton

Sunderland Point

Thurnham

Cokerham

Garstang

Kirkland

Garstang Church

Greenhalgh Castle

Bowla

Claughton Hall

The Launs

Ken R

To Carlisle

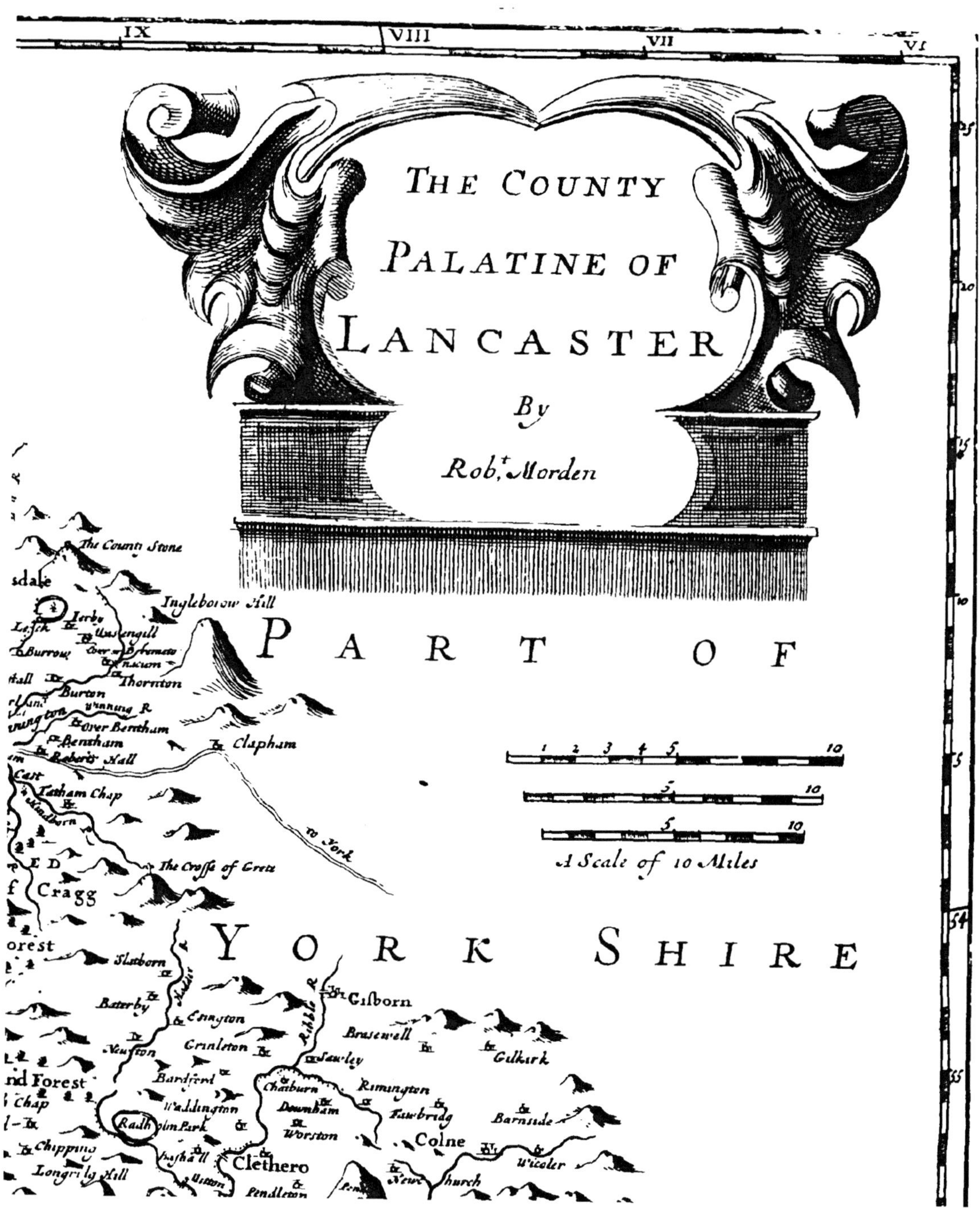

IX
VIII
VII
THE COUNTY PALATINE OF LANCASTER
By
Rob.t Morden
The County Stone
Ingleborow Hill
PART OF
Burton
Thornton
Over Bentham
Bentham
Clapham
Tatham Chap
to York
A Scale of 10 Miles
The Crosse of Grete
Cragg
YORK SHIRE
Slatborn
Gisborn
Baterby
Bracewell
Gilkirk
Grinleton
Sawley
Bardsend
Chatburn
Rimington
Waddington
Downham
Barnside
Worston
Colne
Clethero
Pendleton
Chipping

THE
IRISH
SEA
Preston Sand
PART
Sold bi Abel Swale Aun_sham
& Iohn Churchill
Barton
Preston
Kirkham
Penwortham
Walton Hall
Langton Chap
The Moss
Laland
LAYLAND
Ormskirck
WEST DARBYE HUNDRED
Raynford Chap
the Brigant
Prescot
St Helens
Leverpole
Toxteth Park
Appleton
Garston
Speak
Mersey R

Burnley
Blackburn
Haslingden
BLACK BURN HUN
Accrington
Rossendale
Bacup
Todmorden
Widdop Head
Stiperden
Whaley
Padiham
Gawthrop
Marshden
Tockholes
Darwen
Rochdale
Littleborough
Whitworth
Milnrow
Taume
Saddleworth
Bury
Bolton
SAL FORD
HUNDRED
Wigan
Leigh
Chorley
Manchester or Mancunium
Denton
Gorton
Ashton Underline
Oldham
Chatterton
Middleton
Heaton
Blackely Chap
Dunkenfeld
Motteram
Shawlay Hall
The Wood Head
Melehurst
Stopford
Altrincham
Warberton
Flixton
Partington
Carrington
Sale
Northen
Chedle
Redish
Harden
Gorthall
Marpull
Meller Chappel
Beardhall
PART OF DARBY SHIRE
The Chappel in y Firth
Wyllay Brdg
Erdley Hall
Bollen R
Goyt R
To Derby
To York
The Batinges
Edg Hill
Chatmoss
Newton Chap
Warrington
Thelwall
Lum
Sankey
The Pele
To Darliston & London
From Chester
CHESHIRE

river Tees, not far from Sogburn in this Bishoprick

Cerasus sylvestris septentrionalis, fructu parvo serotino *The wild northern Cherry-tree, with small late ripe fruit On the banks of the river Tees, near Bernards-castle in the Bishoprick plentifully.*

Ribes vulgaris fructu rubro *Ger* vulgaris acidus ruber *J B Red Currants. In the woods as well in this Bishoprick of Durham, as in the northern parts of Yorkshire, and in Westmorland.*

Pentaphylloides fruticosa. *Shrub-Cinquefoil This is also found in this County.*

Muscus Coralloides ramosus, capitulis magnis, *N D Upon Rocks in this County, Yorkshire and Northumberland.*

Equisetum nudum *Ger Frequent in this County and Northumberland in dry sandy ground.*

Camæfilix marina Anglica, *J B. Common in the Rocks on this Coast near Esington*

Vicia pratensis verna seu præcox Solomensis semine cubico, seu Hexaëdron referente moris Vicia minimia Rivini *On Blunt's Key near New-castle*

Alsine nemorosa maxima montana. *Common on the shady banks of the river Were, as near the New bridge at Durham, and several other places*

Pseudo-Asphodelus palustris Scoticus minimus Raij *On a fell in this County about a mile East from Birdale in Westmorland*

Betula rotundifolia nana *N D On a moss near Birdale*

LANCASHIRE.

I Must now strike into another Road, and proceed to the remaining part of the *Brigantes*, who settl'd beyond the Mountains towards the Western Ocean And first, of those of *Lancashire*, whom I approach with a kind of dread may it forebode no ill! But I fear I shall be so far from satisfying the Reader, that I shall not satisfie my self For after I had survey'd the far greater part of this County, I found very few Discoveries to my mind, the ancient names seem'd every where to be so much obscur'd and destroy'd by age. However, that I may not seem wanting to this County, I will run the hazard of the attempt, hoping that the Divine assistance which hath favour'd me in the rest, will not fail me in this

Under the Mountains (which, as I have often observ'd, run through the middle of England, and, if I may so say, make themselves *Umpires*, and distinguish the several Tracts and Counties) lyes the County of *Lancaster* on the West, call'd in Saxon Loncaster scyre, and commonly *Lonka-shire*, *Lancashire*, and the County Palatine of *Lancaster*, because it is dignified with the title of *Palatine* It lies pent up between York-shire on the East, and the Irish Sea to the West, but on the South-side towards *Cheshire*, it is broader, and by little and little, as it shoots out to the North, where it borders upon Westmorland, it grows narrower And there, by the breaking in of the Sea, it is divided by an Arm thereof so as a considerable part lies beyond the Bay, and joins to *Cumberland*

County Palatine See the beginning of *Cheshire*

Where this County is plain and level, it yields Barley and Wheat pretty well, at the foot of the hills, Oats grow best The Soil is every where tolerable, except in some moist and unwholsome places, call'd *Mosses*; which notwithstanding make amends for these inconveniences, by Benefits that very much over balance them For the surface of them being par'd off, makes an excellent fat *Turf* for fuel, and sometimes they yield Trees, that have either grown under-ground, or lain long buried there Lower down, in some parts, they find great store of *Marle* to manure their ground, whereby that soil which was reckon'd uncapable of Corn, is so kindly improv'd, that we may rather suppose Mankind to blame for their Idleness, than the Earth for Ingratitude But as for the goodness of this Country, we see it in the very complexion of the Natives, who are exceeding well-favour'd and comely, nay, and if we will observe it, in the Cattle too For in the *Oxen* (which have huge horns, and * compact bodies) you miss nothing of that perfection, which *Mago* the Carthaginian, in *Columella*, requires

Mosses

Turf

Lancashire Oxen

* Composito corpore

On the South, it is divided from Cheshire by the river *Mersey*; which springs out of the middle of the Mountains, and becomes the boundary as soon as it is got a little from its rise, and runs with a gentle stream towards the West, as it were *inviting* other rivers (to use the words of the Poet) *into his azure lap*, and forthwith receives the *Irwell* from the North, and with it all the rivers of this Eastern part The most noted is the river *Roch*, upon which in a valley, stands *Rochdale*, a market town of no small resort, as also *Bury* upon the *Irwell* it self, a market-town no way inferiour to the other [The first of these gives the title of Biron to the *Lord Byron*, whose ancestor, Sir *John Byron*, was, for his great valour, and eminent loyalty to King *Charles* the first, created Lord *Byron* of Rochdale] Near *Bury*, while I sought for *Coccium* mentioned by Antoninus, I saw *Cockley* a wooden Chapel set round with Trees, *Turton-Chapel*, situate in a dirty steep place *Turton-tower*, and *Entweissel* † neat and elegant houses The latter of which belong'd formerly to an honourable Family of the name, the former ‖ was the seat of the famous family of the *Orells*, [and now of the *Cheethams*] Where the Irk runs into the *Irwell*, on the left-hand bank (which is a kind of reddish stone) and scarce three miles from the Merfey, stands that ancient Town, called in *Antoninus*, according to different copies, *Mancunium* and *Manutium*; which old name it has not quite lost at this day, being now call'd *Manchester* This surpasses all the Towns hereabouts in building, populousness, woollen-manufacture, market place, and Church; and in its College, which was founded in the reign of *Henry* the fifth, by *Thomas* Lord *La-Ware*, who was in Orders, and was the last heir male of the family He was descended from the *Greleys*, who were, by report, the ancient Lords of the Town. [(That stately stone-building is now wholly employ'd

Rochdale

Cockle

Turton

† So said, Ann 1607

‖ Is at this day. C

Mancunium

Manchester

ploy'd for the use of the Hospital and Library)] But in the * last age, this place was much more eminent for its Woollen-cloth or *Manchester Cottons*; and also for the privilege of a Sanctuary, which by Act of Parliament in Henry the eighth's time was transferr'd to *Chester* [But the growth of this place, in this and the last age, having been so considerable, and what has set it so far above its neighbours in all respects, it may deservedly claim a particular account to be given of its present state For although it is neither a Corporation, nor does it send Burgesses to Parliament; yet perhaps, as an in-land town, it has the best trade of any in those Northern parts The Fustian Manufacture, call'd *Manchester Cottons*, still continues there, and is of late very much improv'd by some modern inventions of dying and printing; and this, with the great variety of other manufactures, known by the name of *Manchester-Wares*, renders not only the town it self, but also the Parish about it, rich, populous and industrious Eighty years ago, there were computed near 20000 Communicants in the Town and Parish, since which time the inhabitants are much more numerous, proportionable to the increase of trade, and, of late, the Town hath been much improved by the building of many fair and stately Houses, which make a very handsom Street At the end of this, a beautiful Church hath also been lately erected, by the voluntary Contributions of the Inhabitants, and others, for which end, we find a Statute pass'd in Parliament, in the seventh year of her Majesty Queen Anne

* So said, ann 1607 and it is so still Manchester Cottons

Churches

Chap 6

The Collegiate Church (which was built in the year 1422) is also a very large, beautiful, and stately edifice, and the Quire is particularly remarkable for its neat and curious carv'd work The Town is likewise beautify'd with three remarkable Foundations, a *College*, a *Hospital*, and a *Publick School*, the following account whereof we owe to the late worthy Warden of this place

College

The College was founded A. D 1421 by *Thomas de la Ware*, at first Rector of the said Parish Church, and brother to the Lord *de la Ware*; to whom he succeeded in the estate and honour, and then founded a College here, consisting of one Master or Keeper, eight Fellow Chaplains, four Clerks, and six Choristers, in honour of St *Mary* (to whom the said Parish Church was formerly dedicated) and of St *Dennis* of France, and St *George* of England This foundation was dissolved 1547, in the first year of King Edward the sixth, and the lands and revenues of it were taken into the King's hands, and by him demised to the Earl of Derby; and the College-house and some lands were sold to the said Earl The College was re founded by Queen Mary, who restored most of the lands and revenues; only the College it self, and some of its revenues, remain'd still in the hands of the Earl of Derby It was also founded a new by Queen Elizabeth A D 1578, by the name of *Christ's College* in *Manchester*, consisting of one Warden, four Fellows, two Chaplains, four Singing men, and four Choristers; the number being lessen'd, because the revenues were also lessen'd, chiefly by the covetousness and false-dealing of *Thomas Herle* then Warden, and his Fellows, who sold away, or made such long leases of the revenues, as could never yet, some of them, be retriev'd. It was, last of all, re founded by King Charles the first, A D 1636, constituting therein one Warden, four Fellows, two Chaplains, four Singing men, and four Choristers, and incorporating them by the name of the Warden and Fellows of *Christ's College* in *Manchester*, the Statutes for the same being drawn up by Archbishop *Laud*

Hospital.

The Hospital was founded by *Humphrey Chetham* Esquire, and incorporated by King Charles the second, being designed by the said bountiful Benefactor for the maintenance of forty poor boys, out of the Town and Parish of Manchester, and some other neighbouring Parishes But since, it is enlarged to the number of sixty by the Governours of the said Hospital, to be taken-in between the age of six and ten, and there maintained with meat, drink, lodging, and cloaths, to the age of fourteen, and then to be bound Apprentices to some honest trade or calling at the charge of the said Hospital For the maintenance whereof, he endow'd it with * a large yearly revenue, which is since † much improved by the care and good husbandry of the Feoffees or Governours, who laid out || a large sum in the purchase of lands, which was saved out of the yearly income over and above the maintenance of the poor children, and others belonging to the said Hospital, wherein there are annually near seventy persons provided for

* 420 l per ann
† To 517 l 8 s 4 d per ann
Ann 169, || 182 l

Library

Within the Hospital, and by the bounty of the said Founder, is also erected a very fair and spacious Library, already furnished with a competent stock of choice and valuable books, and daily encreasing, with * a large yearly income settled upon the same by the said worthy benefactor, to buy Books forever, and to afford a competent salary for a Library-keeper There is also a large School for the Hospital-boys, where they are daily instructed, and taught to write and read

* 116 l per ann

School

The *Publick School* was founded A D 1519, by Hugh Oldham D D and Bishop of Exeter, who bought the Lands on which the School stands, and took the Mills there in † lease of the Lord *De la Ware*. Afterwards, with the Bishop's money, *Hugh Bexwick*, and *Joan* his sister, purchased of the Lord *De la Ware* his Lands in *Ancoates*, and the Mills upon Irk, and left them in Feoffment to the said Free school for ever Which Revenues are of late very much encreas'd by the Feoffees of the School, who, out of the improvements, have considerably augmented as well the Masters salaries, as the Exhibitions annually allowed to the maintenance of such scholars at the University, as the Warden of the College and the high Master shall think requisite, and have besides, for some years past, added a third Master, for whom they have lately erected a new and convenient School at the end of the other

† For 60 years.

Besides these publick Benefactions and Endowments, there have been several other considerable sums of money, and annual revenues, left and bequeated to the Poor of the said Town; who are thereby, with the kindness and charity of the present inhabitants, competently provided for, without starving at home, or being forced to seek relief abroad

The Town gives title to an honourable family; *Henry Montague* (Lord Montague of Kimbolton and Viscount Mandevil) having been created Earl of Manchester by King Charles the first, A D 1625; who was succeeded therein by *Edward* his son and heir, Lord Chamberlain of the Houshold to King Charles the second To him succeeded in the same Titles, first, *Robert* his son and heir; and then, *Charles* his Grandson, who hath been Ambassador Extraordinary to *Venice*, and to the French Court, and was soon after constituted one of the Principal Secretaries of State; and who also, in conside-

consideration of these and the like Services to his Country, hath been advanced by King George, to the higher honour of Duke of *Manchester*]

In a neighbouring Park, [heretofore] belonging to the Earls of Derby, call'd † *Alparc*, I saw the foundation of an old square Fort, which they call *Mancastle*, where the river Medloc joins the Irwell I will not say, that this was the ancient *Mancunium*, the compass of it is so little, but rather that it was some Roman station Here I saw an ancient Stone with this Inscription,

† Aldport, Leigh Mancastle

ↃCANDIDI
FIDES XX
IIII

This other was copied for me, by the famous Mathematician, *J Dee* Warden of *Manchester* College

COHO I FRISIN
Ↄ MASAVONIS
P XXIII

They seem to have been erected to the memory of those Centurions, in consideration of their approved loyalty for so many years

[Another Inscription was dug up at the same place, by the river *Medlock*, in the year 1612,

FORTVNAE
CONSERVA
TRICI
L SENECIA
NIVIS MAR
TIVS ϶ LEG
VI VICT

The Stone is three quarters long, fifteen inches broad, and eleven thick; and is preserv'd entire in the garden at *Hulme*, the seat of the *Blands*, Lords of the Town of *Manchester* by marriage with the heiress of the *Moseleys* "It seems to "be an Altar dedicated to *Fortune* by *L. Senecianus Martius*, the *third* Governour or Commander in the sixth Legion, which remain'd at "York in the time of Severus's being there, after he had vanquish'd *Albinus* General of the "Britains, and reduc'd their State under his "obedience It was sirnam'd *Victrix*, and is "plac'd by *Dio* in *Lower Britain*, and the 20th "Legion, sirnam'd also *Victrix*, remain'd at "Chester, which he placeth in higher Britain, "This division, it seemeth, was made by the "same *Severus*" So saith a Manuscript, written by Mr *Hollingworth* (once Fellow of the Collegiate Church here,) and now preserv'd in the Publick Library at *Manchester* But as to *Senecianus*'s being third Governour or Commander; it is a way of expressing the particular station of a single person in the army, which is hardly to be met with in their Inscriptions Besides, their Numerals, both in Coins, Medals, and Inscriptions, were always express'd by Capital Figures, and not in that abbreviated way which we use now a-days. So that one would rather imagine, that what he calls 3, was designed to express the Office which he bore in that Legion]

Lib. 55 p 645, 646 Edit Steph 1592

In the year 920, *Edward* the elder, as Marianus says, sent an Army of the Mercians into Northumberland (for then this belong'd to the Kings of Northumberland) *that they should repair the City of Manchester, and put a Garrison in it* [This passage, Marianus had from the Saxon Chronicle, and Florence of Worcester transcrib'd it from him, and so it was handed down as current to the rest of our Historians. Which consent hath induc'd some more modern Writers to close with the receiv'd Opinion But in the Saxon Annals (which are the original of this story) we are told, that *An 922 Edward* repair'd manige ceaſter, by which a * learned Antiquary (taking it appellatively) will have only *multæ civitates*, *many Cities*, to be meant, without confining it to any particular one And this opinion is confirm'd, not only by the writing of the Copies (for they make them two distinct words,) but also by the deriving of the present name from the old *Mancunium*, whereby the relation that it might seem to have to the Saxons, and the supposition of its Original from thence, is made of no force]

* Bishop N. [illegible]

This Town seems to have been destroy'd in the Danish wars, and because the Inhabitants behav'd themselves bravely against them, they will have their Town call'd *Manchester*, that is, as they explain it, *a City of men* and of this notion they are strangely fond, as seeming to contribute much to their honour But these well meaning people are not sensible, that *Mancunium* was the name of it in the British times, so that an original fetch'd from our English tongue, will by no means hold And therefore I had rather derive it from the British word *Main*, which signifies a *stone* For it stands upon a *stony hill*, and beneath the Town at *Colyhurst*, there are noble and famous *Stone-Quarries*

Colyhurst

But to return The *Mersey*, now enlarged by the river Irwell, runs towards the Sea, by *Trafford*, which hath given both name and habitation to the famous family of the *Traffords* and by *Chatmoss*, a wet marshy ground of great extent, a considerable part whereof, in the memory of † our Fathers, was wash'd away by a river flood, not without great danger to the neighbours, causing also a corruption of the waters, which destroy'd abundance of the fish in those rivers In this tract there is now a Valley water'd by a small river, and * Trees have been discover'd lying flat in the ground From whence one would think, that (while the earth lay uncultivated, and the ditches unscour'd in these low plains, and, either by neglect or depopulation, the water passages were stop'd up,) those grounds that lay lower than the rest, turn'd into such boggy *Mosses*, or else into standing Pools If this be true, there is no reason to admire, that so many Trees in places of this nature all over England, but particularly in this County, do lie bury'd in the ground For when the roots of them were loosen'd by the too great moisture of the earth, it was impossible but they should fall, and so sink and be drown'd in such a spungy Soil The People hereabouts use poles and spits to discover where they lie, and having found the place, they dig for them, and use them for firing For they burn as bright and clear as a Torch; which perhaps is caused by the bituminous earth that they have laid in For this reason, the common people think they have been *Firr trees*, which Cæsar denies to have grown in Britain I know the Opinion generally receiv'd, is, that these have remain'd here ever since the Deluge, and were then beaten down by the violence of the waters and [illegible] rather, because they are sometimes dug up in the higher grounds However they deny not, but these higher grounds they speak of, are wet and quaggy This kind of huge Trees is likewise often found in Holland and in Germany; which

Trafford
Chatmoss
† So said ann 1607
Mosses how they come
* See Leig. [illegible]
Trees under ground
No Firr in Britain in Cæsar's day

which the learned there suppose, either to have been undermin'd by the Waves on the Sea shore, or blown down by Storms, and so carry'd into these low washy places, and there sunk into the ground But these Points are more proper to be consider'd by a College of *Virtuosi*

[As to that Opinion of Cæsar, that no Firtrees ever grew in Britain, it is not only confuted by Firs lying under ground, but, as Sir *Robert Sibbald* tells us, by whole forests of those trees in the north of Scotland And * *Speed* gives us this memorable passage, That at *Lough-Argick* in the north-west of that Kingdom, there grew Firs of great height and thickness At the root they bore twenty eight handfuls about, and the bodies mounted to ninety foot in length, bearing twenty inches diameter throughout This, he tells us, was certify'd to King James the first, by Commissioners who were sent purposely to enquire for such timber, for masts Nay, and it is demonstrable, that most of our *Moss-wood* is of this kind In this very County also, at *Hey* (formerly a seat of the *Heys*) these Trees grow in great abundance, by the industry and contrivance of *Thomas Brotherton* Esq, to whom the world is indebted for many curious Observations and Experiments concerning the growth of *Trees* And to shew that Fir-trees grew in these parts *anciently*, as well as now, in the draining of a large Meer, they have found not only *Fir-Stock* but *Fir-apples* also and however the Wood might be altered into something like Firr by the *bituminous* matter it lay in, it is certain, the Apples could not belong to a Tree of any other kind]

* Chron p 160.

Hey

Phil Transf N 16 Leigh, l 1 p -1

Next to *Chatmoss*, we see *Holcroft*, which gave both seat and name to the famous family of the *Holcrofts*, formerly enriched by marriage with the Coheir of *Culchit* For this place stands hard by; which Gilbert de Culchit held *in fee* of Almarick Butler, as Almarick held it in Fee of the Earl *de Ferrariis* in Henry the third's time Whose eldest daughter and heir being marry'd to *Richard* the son of *Hugh de Hindley*, he took the name of *Culchit*; also *Thomas* his brother, who marry'd the second daughter, was call'd from the estate, *Holcroft*, another, for the same reason, took the name of *Peasfalong*, and the fourth, that of *de Riseley* Which I mention, for a testimony, that as our Ancestors were grave and settl'd in other things, so in rejecting old and taking new names from their Estates, they were very light and changeable And this was a thing commonly practis'd heretofore, in other parts of England Hereabouts, are many little Towns (as also through this whole County, and *Cheshire*, and other Northern parts) which have given names to famous Families, and continue in the hands of those of the name to † this very day As *Aston* of *Aston*, *Atherton* of *Atherton*, *Tillesley* of *Tillesley*, *Standish* of *Standish*, *Bold* of *Bold*, *Hesket* of *Hesket*, *Worthington* of *Worthington*, *Torbeck* of *Torbeck*, &c It would be endless to reckon up all, and it is not my design to give an account of eminent Families, but to survey Places of Antiquity Yet, as these and such like families in the northern Counties (that I may observe it once for all,) rose by their Bravery, and improv'd in Wealth by their frugality and by the good old self contented plainness and simplicity; so, in the South parts of England, Luxury, Usury, Debauchery, and Cheating, have undone the most flourishing families in a short time; insomuch that many complain, how fast the old race of our Nobility † fades and decays.

Holcroft Lib Inq in Scaccar

Variety of names.

† Ann 1607

† So said, ann. 1607

Let us now go on with the *Mersey*, which runs by *Warrington*, remarkable for its Lords the *Butlers*, who obtain'd for it the privilege of a Market, from Edward the first [Here is a fine bridge over the *Mersey* The Town is pretty large and its Market considerable In the second year of King William and Queen Mary, *Henry Booth* Lord *Delamere* of *Dunham-Massey* (son of the eminently loyal Sir *George Booth*) was created Earl of Warrington, which title is enjoy'd at present by *George*, his son] Hence, northward, at no great distance, stands *Winwick*, [suppos'd by some to be the City *Caer Guntin* among the Britains; which is call'd by Ninnius *Caer Guinguic*, and is] famous for being one of the best * Benefices in England Here, in the uppermost part of the Church, are these Verses in an old barbarous character, concerning King Oswald

Warrington

Winwick

Usher Primord p 3..

* *Sacerdotia*

> *Hic locus*, Oswalde, *quondam placuit tibi valde*,
> *Northanhumbrorum fueras Rex, nuncque Polorum*
> *Regna tenes, loco passus* Marcelde *vocato*

> This happy Place did holy *Oswald* love,
> Who once *Northumbria* rul'd, now reigns above,
> And from *Marcelde* did to Heaven remove

From *Warrington*, the *Mersey* grows broader, and soon after contracts again, but at last opens into a wide mouth very commodious for trade, and then runs into the Sea near *Litherpoole*, in Saxon Lirenpole, commonly *Lirpoole*, so call'd (as it is thought) from the water spread there like a Fen. It is the most convenient and usual place for setting sail into Ireland, but not so eminent for Antiquity, as for neatness and populousness [Such persons as are free of this Town, have the benefit of being Free-men, also of *Waterford* and *Wexford* in that Kingdom, as also of *Bristol* in this To this (with their trade to the *West-Indies*, and the several Manufactures in the parts adjacent) is probably owing the vast growth of the Town, of late years Insomuch, that its buildings and people are more than doubly augmented, and the Customs eight or tenfold encreas'd, in the present age They have built a Town-house plac'd on pillars and arches of hewn stone, with a publick Exchange for the Merchants underneath it, and a publick Charity-School, which is a large and beautiful Structure It is principally indebted to the *Mores* of *Blankhall*, chief Lords and Owners of the greatest part of it, by whom it was beautified with goodly buildings of hewn stone so that some of the streets are nam'd, from their relation to that Family In the tenth year of the reign of King William, a Statute was passed to enable them to build a Church and endow the same, and to make the Town and Liberties thereof a Parish of itself distinct from *Walton* And in the eighth year of Queen Anne, was pass'd another Law, for making here a convenient Dock or Bason, for the Security of all Ships trading to and from this Port; and a third, the same year, for bringing fresh water into the Town, for the convenience of the Inhabitants They have a Free-School, which was formerly a Chapel; at the west end whereof,

Litherpoole.

of, next the river, there stood the statue of St *Nicholas* (long since defac'd and gone) to whom the Mariners offer'd, when they went to Sea. To add to the reputation of this Town, it hath had several Mayors who where persons of the most considerable families in this County, both before and since the Restoration.]

The name is not to be met with in old Writers, but only that Roger of *Poictiers*, who was Lord *of the Honour of Lancaster* (according to the language of those days) built a Castle here; the Government whereof was enjoy'd for a long time by the noble family of the *Molineaux*, Knights, [and now Lords *Molineaux*,] whose chief Seat is hard by at *Sefton*, which the same Roger de *Poictiers* bestow'd upon Vivian de *Molineaux*, a little after the coming in of the Normans, for all the Land between the *Ribell* and the *Mersey*, belong'd to the said Roger, as appears by Domesday. [Their ordinary Residence is at a House newly built, about *three miles from this place*.

Molineaux

Sefton

Near *Sefton*, is *Crosby magna*, where they have a Grammar-School, founded by one *Harrison* a native of the place. It is a fair building of free stone, and † well endow'd, besides * a provision for Repairs and Visitations. At a little distance is *Crosby parva*, within which Lordship, in a place call'd *Harkirke*, several Saxon Coins have been dig up, the portraictures whereof were printed in a Copper-plate by *William Blundel*, Esquire.]

Crosby-magna

* 50 l. per ann.

† 7 l. or 8 l. per ann.

Near *Sefton* aforesaid, the little river *Alt* runs into the Sea, leaving its name to *Altmouth* a small village at the mouth of it, and running at a little distance from † *Formby*, where, in the mossy grounds, they cast up *Turves*, which serve the Inhabitants both for fire and candle. Under the Turf there lies a blackish dead water, which has a kind of oily fat substance floating upon it, and little fishes swimming in it, which are taken by the Diggers *, so that we may say, we have Fish dug out of the ground in England, as well as they have about *Heraclea* and *Tius* in Pontus. Nor is this strange, since in very places of this nature, the fish following the water, often swim under ground, and so men are forc'd to *fish* for them with spades. But, that in Paphlagonia many fish are dug-up, and those good ones too, in places not at all watery, has somewhat of a peculiar and more hidden cause in it. That of Seneca was pleasantly said, *What reason is there why fish should not travel the Land, if we traverse the Sea?* [As to the oily matter abovementioned, a Chymist in the neighbourhood extracted from it an Oyl extraordinary Sovereign in Paralytick Distempers, having first congealed it into a turf.]

† Ferneby C. Formby

Fishes dug up

* Nothing like this is to be seen or heard of, at present.

From hence the shore is bare and open, with a very great winding. More inward from the Sea, stands *Ormeskirke*, a Market town, remarkable for being the burial place of the *Stanlys*, Earls of Derby, whose chief Seat was *Latham* hard by, a House large and stately, which from the time of Henry the fourth * had been continually enlarging. At that time, Sir *John Stanley* Knight (father of *John* Lord Lieutenant of Ireland, descended from the same stock with the Barons of *Audley*) marry'd the daughter and heir of *Thomas Latham* an eminent Knight, to whom this great Estate, with many other, had come in right of his wife. From that time the *Stanleys* liv'd here, of whom *Thomas* (son of Thomas *Lord* Stanley) was made Earl of Derby by King Henry the seventh, and had by *Eleanor Nevill*, daughter to the Earl of Salisbury, *George* Lord *Le Strange*. For he had marry'd *Joan*, the only daughter and heir of *John* Baron *Le Strange* of *Knockin*, who dy'd during the life of his father, leaving a son *Thomas*, the second Earl of Derby. He by his wife *Ann*, daughter of Edward Lord Hastings, had a son, *Edward*, the third Earl of Derby, who by *Dorothy*, the daughter of *Thomas Howard* Duke of Norfolk, had *Henry*, the fourth Earl; whose wife was *Margaret*, daughter of *Henry Clifford* Earl of Cumberland, and mother of *Ferdinand* the fifth Earl, and of *William* the sixth Earl, † who succeeded his brother [and whose son was *James*, the seventh Earl, a person of eminent Loyalty and Valour; father of *Charles* the eighth, and of *James* the ninth Earl, who at present enjoys the honour.

Ormeskirke

Is C. Latham

* Has, C.

Stanleys Earls of Derby

† Who dy'd lately, C.

This place is memorable, as for its Earls, so also for that personal and successful defence of it, made by *Sherlotta* the loyal Countess of Derby, against a close and long siege of the Parliament Army in the year 1644. For a more particular account of her bravery, the Reader is referred to Sir *William Dugdale's* account of this Action, in his *Baronage*. However, this ancient House of *Lathom*, after a second siege, was laid almost flat in the dust, and the head of *James*, that heroick Earl of Derby, was cut off at *Bolton* in this County, Octo. 15. 1651. by the prevailing power of the Parliament. Near *Lathom* Park, is a Mineral water or Spaw, as deeply impregnated with the *Iron* and *Vitriol* Minerals, as any either in this County, or in Yorkshire. The want of convenient Lodging and other Accommodations, make it less frequented; but it is certain, it has done some notable Cures. On each side of the Bay, which divides the shore, was a large Meer, known by the name of *Martin meer*. the larger of which was drained some years since, and in draining it, they found no less than eight *Canoos*, which, in figure and dimension, were not much unlike those that are us'd in America.]

L. h. l. t. 18

Here *Duglesse*, a small brook, runs with a still gentle stream, near which our *Arthur* (as Nennius tells us) defeated the Saxons in a memorable battel. Near the rise of it, stands *Wiggin*, a Town (as they say) formerly called *Wibiggin*. I have nothing to say of the name, but that in *Lancashire* they call buildings *Biggin*, nor of the place, but that it is neat and plentiful, and a Corporation *consisting of a Mayor and Burgesses*; also, that the Rector of the Church is (as I have been told) Lord of the Town. Hard by, stands *Holland*, from which the Hollands, a famous family (who were Earls of Kent and Surrey, and Dukes of Exeter) took their name in Original. The daughter and heir of the eldest Brother (who flourished here with the degree and title of Knights, being at last marry'd to the *Lovels*, brought them both the Estate and the Arms of this Family, namely, *In a field Azure* * *florete Argent a Lion rampant gardant Arg.*

Duglesse river

Wiggin

Biggin, what

Family of Hollands

Arms of the Holland

* With flowers de Lys

[In *Haigh*, near *Wiggin*, are very plentiful and profitable Mines of an extraordinary Coal. Besides the clear flame it yields in burning, it has been curiously polish'd into the appearance of black marble, and form'd into large Candlesticks, Sugar boxes, and Spoons, with many other such sorts of Vessels, which have been presented as Curiosities, and met with good acceptance, both at home and abroad. North from hence lies *Whittle*, near *Chorley*, where a Mine of Lead has been lately found, and wrought with good success, possibly, the first that has been wrought in this County. And near the same place is a plentiful Quarry of *Mill-stones*, no less memorable than those

Haigh

Whittle

which are mentioned before in the *Peake* of Derby. Within a mile and half of *Wiggin*, is a Well (Burning Well) which does not appear to be a spring, but rather rain-water. At first sight, there is nothing about it that seems extraordinary; but upon emptying it, there presently breaks out a sulphureous vapour, which makes the water bubble up as if it boyl'd. When a Candle is put to it, it presently takes fire, and burns like brandy. The flame, in a calm season, will continue sometimes a whole day, by the heat whereof they can boyl eggs, meat, &c. tho' the water it self be cold. By this bubbling, the water does not encrease, but is only kept in motion by the constant Halitus of the vapours breaking out. The same water *taken out* of the Well, will not burn, as neither the mud upon which the Halitus has beat. * and this shews, that it is not so much the *water* that takes fire, as some *bituminous* or *sulphureous* fumes that break out there.]

* Philosoph. Transf. N. 26

Near the mouth of the *Duglesse*, lies *Merton* (Merton), a large broad lake, that empties it self into this river, which, at the mouth or bay, is joyn'd by the river *Ribell*. After the *Mersey*, this is the next river that falls into the Ocean: the old name whereof is not entirely lost, for Ptolemy calls the Æstuary here, *Bellisama* (Bellisama), and we *Ribell*, perhaps by joyning to it the Saxon word *Rhe*, which signifies a *river*. This river, running with a very swift stream from Yorkshire-hills, first passes southward, by three high mountains, *Ingleborrow hill* (Ingleborrow hill), near the head of it; which is a wonderful sight, for it shoots out in a vast ridge rising gradually to the westward, and towards the end mounts up as if another hill were laid upon the back of it. *Penigent* (Penigent), so call'd perhaps from it's white and snowy head, for that is the signification of *Pengwin* in British. It is a huge mountain, but not so high as the other. Where the *Ribell* enters Lancashire (for the two that I have mention'd, are in Yorkshire) stands *Pendle hill* (Pendle hill), of great height, and which, on the very top, produces * a plant, call'd *Clowdesberry*, as if it were the off-spring of the *Clouds*. [Some of our Botanists have given it the name of *Vaccinia nubis*, but the more common, and the truer, is *Chamæmorus*; for it is a Dwarf mulberry. It is not peculiar to *Pendle hill*, but grows plentifully on the boggy tops of most of the high mountains both in England and Scotland. In *Norway* also, and other Northern Countries, it is plentiful enough. Instead of Gerard's mistaken name of *Clowdberry*, the Northern Peasants call it *Cnout berry*, and have a tradition that the Danish King Knute, being (God knows when) distress'd for some time in these walls, was reliev'd, by feeding upon these dainties. I know not whether it will countenance the story, to observe, that this King's name is in our ancient Records † sometimes written *Knout*. But this berry is not the only edible that bears his name to this day; for in this County, it is said that they have a Bird of a luscious taste, ‖ which (in remembrance of King Cnute) they call *Knot-bird*. But to return.] This hill is chiefly famous for the great damage done to the lower grounds heretofore, by a terrible fall of water which it sent down, and for being an infallible prognostick of rain, when the top of it is in a cloud. I the rather make mention of these, both because they are the highest hills in our English *Appennine* (and therefore it is commonly said,

* A peculiar Plant, C. Clowdesberry.

† See Selden's Titles of Honour, p. 501.

‖ Drayt. Polyolb. p. 112.

Ingleborrow, Pendle, and Penigent,
Are the highest hills between Scotland and Trent.)

and also, that what I have already observ'd may be the better understood, *viz.* How the highest *Alps* come to be call'd *Penninæ* (Alpes Penninæ), and the very top of a hill, *Pennum*, and why the *Appennines* were so called by the old Gauls. For *Pen* in British signifies the tops of mountains. (Pen, what in British.)

[Not far from this hill, is *Colne* (Colne), where Roman Coins are frequently dug-up, but without any other appearance of a Roman *Town* or *Station* here, such as Fortifications, Altars, Boundaries, or the like: which makes the Learned Antiquary and Historian of this County, conclude those Coins to have been hid there by some of the Roman Soldiers, upon a foresight of their falling into the Enemies hands, or upon some other accidental occasion.] (Dr. Leigh, p. 12.) At the bottom of *Pendle hill* stands *Clithero-castle* (Clithero-castle), which was built by the *Laceys*, at a small distance from the Rhibell, and near it, *Whaley* (Whaley), in Saxon Walleg, remarkable for a Monastery built by the *Laceys*, which was translated from *Stanlaw* in the County of Chester, in the year 1296. And in the year 798 Duke *Wada* was defeated in a Battel, by *Ardulph* King of the Northumbrians, here at *Billangho*, now by contraction call'd *Langho*. [Not far from *Whaley* to the west, is *Brunly*, † in which Parish have been found several ancient Roman Coins, many of them Consular, with the antique form of the *Caput Urbis*, without Inscription instead of the Emperor's head.]

† Philosoph. Transf. N. 244

The Rhibell turning short to the west, gives name to a village call'd at this day *Rible chester* (Riblechester), where so many marks of Roman Antiquity, as Statues, Coins, Pillars, Pedestals, Chapiters, Altars, Marbles, and Inscriptions, are commonly dug-up, that this hobbling ryhme of the Inhabitants does not seem to be altogether groundless.

It is written upon a wall in Rome,
Ribchester *was as rich as any Town in Christendome.*

Moreover, two Military-ways led hither; one, which is plain by it's high causey, from York, the other from the north through *Bowland*, a large forest, and this also appears very plain for several miles together. But the Inscriptions are so defac'd by the country-people, that though I met with many, I had much ado to read one or two of them. At *Salesbury Hall* (Salesbury hall), hard by, [heretofore] the Seat of the noble and ancient family of the *Talbots*, on the pedestal of a Pillar, I saw this Inscription;

DEO
MARTI, ET
VICTORIÆ
DD. AVGG.
ET CC—NN.

In the Wall adjoyning, there is another Stone with the portraicture of *Cupid* and another little Image, and from the back part of it this Inscription was copy'd for me. After a great deal of study, being able to make no sense of it, I have here subjoyn'd it, that others also may try their skill.

SFOE-

SEOESAM
ROLNASON
OSALVEDN
AL. Q Q SAR
BREVENM
BEDIANIS
ANTONI
VS MEG VI
IC. DOMV
ELITER

For my part, I have no Conjecture to offer, but that many of the words are the British names of places hereabouts In the year 1603 when I came a second time to see this place, I met with an Altar, the largest and the fairest that I ever saw, with this Inscription,

In the house of *Thomas Rhodes* Ann 1607

DEIS MATRIBVS
M. INGENVI-
VS ASIATICVS
* DEC. AL. AST.
SS. LL. M.

* Perhaps *Decurio Alæ Asturum susceptum solvit (sc votum) libens lubens merito*

† *Juno & Diana*, Leigh

Upon enquiry who † these *Deæ Matres* are, I can find nothing (for among all the Inscriptions in the world, except in one other found here in Britain, there is not the least mention of them,) but only that *Enguium*, a little town in Sicily, was famous for the presence of the *Mother Goddesses*, where some spears and brass-helmets were shown, which had been consecrated to those Goddesses by *Metio* and *Ulysses*

Deæ Matres Vid Bishop of Durham *Pref in M Marcello*

I saw also another little Altar cast out among the rubbish, with this Inscription,

PACIFE
ROMARTI
ELEGAVR
BA POS
VIT EX VO
TO

This is so small, that it seems to have been the portable Altar of some poor man, only for the offering of incense, or salt flour, whereas that other of a much greater size, must have been us'd in the sacrificing of larger beasts These things were certainly done by after-ages, in imitation of *Noah*, even when they had revolted from the worship of the true God Nor was it to the Gods only that they rais'd these Altars, but, out of a servile flattery, to their Emperours likewise, under the impious title of NVMINI MAJESTATIQVE EORVM At these, they fell on their knees, and worship'd; these they embrac'd and pray'd to, before these they took their Oaths; and to be short, in these and their Sacrifices, the whole of their Religion consisted So that those among them who had no Altar, were suppos'd to have no Religion, and to acknowledge no Deity.

The Heathen Altars *Gen* viii

Here was also lately dug-up, a Stone with the Portraicture of a naked man on horseback, without saddle or bridle, brandishing his spear with both hands, and insulting over a naked man prostrate, who defends himself with something in the form of a square Between the horse and the person prostrate, stand the letters D M Under the prostrate man, are * GAL. SARMATA The other letters, (for there were many more) are so defaced, that they cannot be read; and I shall not venture to guess at them It should seem, both from the Inscription before, and this which many years ago was found hard by, that a wing of the *Sarmatæ* had their station here

* Possibly, C Al for *Centurio Alæ Sarmatarum*

HIS TERRIS TEGITVR
AEL. MATRONA QV - --
VIX AN XXVIII M II D VIII
ET M IVLIVS MAXIMVS FIL
VIX. AN VI M III D XX ET CAM
PANIA DVBBA MATER
VIX ANI IVLIVS MAXIMVS
-- ALAL SAR CONIVX
CONIVGI INCOMPARABILI
ET FILIO PATRI PIENTIS
SIMO ET SOCERAE TENA
CISSIMAE MEMORIAL P

Out of the Papers of *William Lambard*

[Another Altar hath been also found, with this Inscription,

DEO MARTI ET
VICTORIÆ DEC
ASIATIC AL SARMAT.
SS LL M IT CC NN

'This (saith Dr *Leigh*) seems to be an Altar 'dedicated to *Mars* and Victory, the *Genii* of 'the place, by one of the Decuriones by birth 'an Asiatick, commanding in a wing of the '*Sarmatæ*, and the six last Letters may be *Im*'*peratori Triumphanti Cæsari Coccio Nervæ*, from 'whom this place was by Antoninus called '*Coccium* Pag 8

'There was, also, one eminent piece of Antiquity dug up here, *viz* a large Stone, now 'a corner stone in *Salisbury hall*, which, (as hath 'been said) did anciently belong to the *Tal*'*bots*, on one side, is *Apollo* with his quiver 'on his shoulder, leaning on his *plectrum* or 'harp, with a loose mantle or *velamen*, and on 'the other side, two of his Priests in the same 'habit, with an Ox's head in their hands, 'sacrificing to him, also, the heads of various 'Animals, lying prostrate at his feet' Pag 9

Likewise, at a Fortification call'd *Anchorhill*, and at other places in and about this ancient Station, have been found Roman Coins, Platters, Tyles, and Bricks, with an ancient Pavement of Bricks, and a Pillar about seventeen inches diameter, but the Inscription not legible All which demonstrate it to have been a place of great note and consideration in the Roman times] See Leigh, p 6 7

None of these afford any [clear] light, whereby to discover the ancient name of the place, for which we are utterly at a loss, except it has changed the name, a thing, not at all unusual for *Ptolemy* places *Rigodunum* hereabouts, and if we may suppose *that* to be a corruption of *Ribodunum*, it is not altogether unlike *Riblechester*; [(unless *Rixton* or *Rishton* in this neighbourhood may rather be supposed to have some Remains of *Rigodunum*, the common Reading)] and at the same distance from *Mancunium* or Manchester, *viz* eighteen miles, Antoninus fixes *Coccium*, which is also read *Coccium* in some copies

Ribodunum

Coccium

When

When this City came to its fatal Period, and was destroy'd either by wars, or (as the common people believe) by an earthquake, some what lower where the tide flows up the *Ribell*, and is call'd by the Geographer *Belisama Æstuarium*, near *Penworth* (where was a castle in the Conqueror's time, as appears by the records of that King) there sprang out of the ruins of Riblechester, *Preston*, a large Town, handsom and populous for these parts, and so call'd from the *Religious*, for the name in England signifies *Priest's town*. Below it, the *Ribell* is joyn'd by the *Deruen*, a little river, which runs first by *Black burne* a Market town, so call'd from the *blackness* of the water. It belong'd formerly to the Lacies, and has given the name of *Blackburneshire* to a small neighbouring Tract. From hence it runs by *Haughton Tower*, which gave name to an eminent family that has long dwelt there, and by *Walcton*, which William Lord of Lancaster, King Stephen's son, gave to *Walter de Walcton*: afterwards, it belong'd to the famous family of the *Langtons*, who are descended from the *Waltons*. But to return.

Penworth, otherwise call'd *Penverdant*. Preston.
Black burne
Haughton Tower
Walcton

Preston, just now mention'd, is commonly call'd *Preston in Andernesse*, instead of *Acmundesnesse*, for so the Saxons called this part of the Country, because, between the rivers *Ribell* and *Cocar*, it hangs out for a long way into the Sea like a *Nose*. It was also afterwards called *Agmondernes*. In William the Conqueror's time, *there were in it only sixteen villages, inhabited, the rest lay wast*, as we find in Domesday: *and it was possess'd by Roger of Poictiers*. Afterwards, it belong'd to *Theobald Walter* (from whom the *Butlers* of Ireland are descended,) for so we read in the Charter of Richard the first: *Know ye, that we have given, and by this present Charter confirm'd, to* Theobald Walter, *for his homage and service, all* Agmondernes, *with the appurtenances thereunto belonging, &c.* This Soil bears oats pretty plentifully, but is not so good for barley; it is excellent pasture, especially towards the Sea, where it is partly champain, whence a great parcel of it is call'd the *File*, as one would guess, for the *Field*. Yet in the records of the Tower, it is express'd by the latin word *Lima*, which signifies a *File*, the Smith's Instrument, wherewith Iron and other things are polish'd. In other places it is fenny, and therefore counted unhealthful. The *Wyr*, a little river, † touches here, which coming from *Wierdale*, a solitary and dismal place, runs with a swift stream by *Grenhaugh* castle, built by *Thomas Stanley*, the first Earl of Derby of that family, while he was under apprehension of danger from certain of the Nobility of this County, who had been outlaw'd, and whose estates had been given him by Henry the seventh: for they made several attempts upon him, and many Inroads into his grounds, till at last these feuds were extinguish'd, by the temper and prudence of that excellent person.

Andernesse
The File
Wyr river.
† *Hinc etiam perstringit*
Wierdale
Grenhaugh castle

In many places along this coast, there are heaps of sand, upon which they pour water from time to time, till they grow brackish, and then, with a turf fire, they boil them into a white salt. Here are also *Quick sands*, very dangerous to those travellers, who when the tide is out take the shortest cut, and who had need be very careful, lest (as *Sidonius* expresses it) *they be shipwrack'd at land*. Especially, near the mouth of the *Cockar*, where, *in a field of quick-sands*, stands *Cocka sand-Abbey*, formerly a small Monastery for Canonick Monks, founded by *Ranulph de Meschines*. It lies expos'd to the winds, between the mouth of the *Cockar* and the *Lune*, commonly call'd the *Lone*; with a large prospect into the Irish Sea.

A new way of making Salt, of which see Mr Ray, *Northern words* p. 209.
Quick sands.
Syrticus Ager

The *Lone*, commonly call'd *Lune*, which has its rise among the mountains of Westmoreland, runs southward within uneven banks, and in a crooked chanel, by which the Current is much hinder'd. To the great gain of the neighbouring Inhabitants, it affords store of *Salmon* in the Summer season; for this sort of Fish, taking great delight in clear water, and particularly in sandy fords, come up in great shoals into this and the other rivers on the same coast. As soon as the *Lone* enters Lancashire, the *Lac*, a little river, joyns it from the east. In this place stands *Overburrow*, a small country village, but that it was formerly a great City upon a large plot of ground between the *Lac* and the *Lone*, and being besieg'd, was forc'd to surrender by famine, is what the Inhabitants told me, who have it by tradition from their Ancestors. And certain it is, that the place makes proof of its own Antiquity, by many ancient Monuments, Inscriptions, chequer'd Pavements, and Roman Coins; as also by this modern name, which signifies a *Burrow*. If it ever recover its ancient name, it must owe it to others, and not to me; though I have sought it with all the diligence imaginable. And indeed, we are not to reckon, that the particular name of every place in Britain is set down in *Ptolemy*, *Antoninus*, or the *Notitia*, or mention'd in *Classick* Authors. If I may have the liberty of a conjecture, I must confess I should take it to be *Bremetonacum* (which was a distinct place from *Brementuracum*, as *Jerom Surita* a Spaniard has well observ'd, in his notes on Antoninus) upon account of its distance from *Coccium* or *Riblechester*.

Lune, river
Salmon.
Over burrow
Bremetonacum

From this *Burrough*, the river *Lone* runs by *Thurland-Tunstalls*, a fort built in Henry the fourth's time by Sir *Thomas Tunstall* Knight; the King having granted him leave *to fortifie and kernel his mansion*, that is, to embattel it; and then by *Hornby*, a noble Castle, which glories in its founder *N. de Mont Begon*, and in its Lords the *Harringtons*, and the *Stanleys* Barons of *Mont Eagle*, descended from *Thomas Stanley* the first Earl of Derby. *William Stanley*, the third and last of these, left Elizabeth his only daughter and heir, who was marry'd to *Edward Parker*, Lord Morly, and was mother of *William Parker*, who was restor'd by King James [the first] to the honour of his ancestors, *the Barony of Mont-Eagle*, and must be acknowledg'd, by us and our posterity for ever, to have been a wonderful Blessing to these Kingdoms: for, by an obscure Letter privately sent to him, and produced by him in the very nick of time, the most horrid and detestable Treason that Hell it self could project, was discover'd and prevented, when the Kingdom was upon the very brink of ruin; while a wicked Generation, under the execrable masque of Religion, stood ready to blow up their King and Country in a moment, with a great quantity of Gun powder, lodg'd under the Parliament house for that purpose.

Thurland Tunstals.
What it is to kernel
Hornby-castle
Barons Mont eagle
Gun powder Plot

The *Lone*, after it has got some miles further, sees *Lancaster* on its south bank, the chief Town of the County, which the Inhabitants call more truly *Loncaster*, and the Scots *Loncastell*, from the river *Lon*. Both the present name, and that of the river, seem to mark it out for the old *Longovicum*, where, under the Lieutenant of Britain (as the *Notitia* informs us) a Company of the *Longovici*, who took that name

Lancaster

name from the place, were in garriſon. Though * at preſent the Town is not populous, and the Inhabitants thereof are all huſbandmen (for the grounds about it are well cultivated, open, and freſh, and without any want of wood) yet, in proof of its Roman Antiquity, they ſometimes meet with Coins of the Emperors, eſpecially where the Fryers had their cloyſter For there (*as they report*) was the Area of an ancient City; which the Scots (who, in a ſudden inroad in the year 1322, deſtroy'd every thing they met with) burnt to the ground From that time they began to build nearer a green hill, by the river, upon which ſtands a Caſtle, not very great nor ancient, but fair and ſtrong; and on the very top of the hill, a Church, the only one in the town, where was heretofore a Cell of Monks-Aliens Below this, near a very fine bride over the *Lone*, on the ſteepeſt part of the hill, there hangs a piece of a very ancient wall which is Roman they call it *Wery wall*, probably from the later Britiſh name of the town, who call'd it *Caer Werid*, that is, a *green City*, in all likelyhood from the green hill; but I leave the further diſcovery of this to others [Lately, in digging of a Cellar, were found ſeveral Roman *Diſci*, and *Sympuria*, or Cups uſed in Sacrifice, with the figures of various Creatures on the ſides, and *Julius Flavius* in letters On the bottom of one of them, appeared very legibly theſe Letters *Regina I* which (ſaith Dr *Leigh*) we may eaſily interpret a *diſcus* uſed in Sacffice to *Juno*, as ſhe was ſtiled *Regina Cæli*]

[left margin:] ... ſtud. ... 167 ... now, a ... ing ... wn and ... t

[left margin:] ...igh p 10

[left margin:] Ibid

John Lord of Morton and Lancaſter, who was afterwards King of England, *confirm'd by Charter, to his Burgeſſes of Lancaſter, all the liberties which he had granted to the Burgeſſes of Briſtow* Edward the third, in the 36th year of his reign, *granted to the Mayor and Bailiffs of the village of* Lancaſter, *that Pleas and Seſſions ſhould be held no where elſe, but there* The latitude of this place, (not to omit it) is 54 degrees 5 minutes, and the longitude 20 degrees 48 minutes

From the top of this hill, while I look'd round to ſee the mouth of the *Lone* (which empties it ſelf not much lower,) I ſaw *Forneſs* the other part of the County, to the weſt, which is almoſt ſever'd from this part by the Sea for whereas the ſhore lay out a great way weſtward into the Ocean the Sea (as if enrag'd at it) ceas'd not to ſlaſh and mangle it Nay, it has ſwallow'd the ſhore quite up, at ſome boiſterous tide or other; and thereby has made three large bays, namely, *Kentſand* (which receives the river *Ken*) *Levenſand*, and *Duddenſand* [Theſe three Sands are very dangerous to Travellers, both by reaſon of the uncertainty of the Tides (which are quicker and ſlower, according as the Winds blow more or leſs from the Iriſh ſea;) and alſo of the many quick ſands, which are caus'd principally by much rainy weather Upon this account, there is a guide on horſe-back appointed to each *Sand*, for the direction of ſuch perſons who ſhall have occaſion to paſs over; and each of the three has a yearly Sallary paid him out of his Majeſty's revenue] Between theſe, the land ſhoots ſo much like a *Promontory* into the Sea, that this part of the County takes its name from it; (for *Forneſs* and *Foreland* ſignifie the ſame with us, which *Promontorium anterius*, that is, a *Fore promontory*, does in Latin;) [unleſs we ſhould rather chuſe to derive the name from the *Furnaces* there, which in old time were numerous, as the Rents and Services paid for them do teſtifie (For many Tenants in this County do ſtill pay a rent called *Bloom Smithy Rent*) In the ſame manner, *Foulney* hath its name from the great ſtore of *Fowl* uſually there]

[left margin:] ...rneſs

[left margin:] ...entſand ...evenſand ...uddenſand

[right margin:] Bloom Smithy-Rent Foulney

The whole tract, except by the Sea-ſide, is all high mountains and great rocks (they call them *Forneſs-fells*,) among which the Britains liv'd ſecurely for a long time, relying upon theſe fortifications wherewith nature had guarded them, but nothing prov'd impregnable to the Saxon Conqueror For, that the Britains lived here in the 228th year after the coming of the Saxons, is plain from hence, that at that time Egfrid King of the Northumbrians gave to St *Cuthbert* the land called *Carthmell*, and all the Britains in it; for ſo it is related in his life Now *Carthmell*, every one knows, was part of this County, near *Kentſand*, and a little Town in it keeps the name to this day, wherein *William Mareſchal* the elder, Earl of Pembroke, built and endowed a Priory If, in Ptolemy, one might read *Setantiorum* λίμνη (*a lake*) as ſome books have it, and not *Setantiorum* λιμὴν (*a haven*,) I would venture to affirm, that the Britains in theſe parts were the *Setantii*, for among thoſe Mountains lies the greateſt lake in England, now call'd *Winander-mere*, in Saxon Winpabnemen, perhaps from its winding Banks, about ten miles in length, the bottom pav'd, as it were, with one continued rock, wonderful deep in ſome places (as the neighbouring Inhabitants tell you,) and well ſtored with a ſort of Fiſh [commonly ſaid to be] bred no where elſe, which they call *Chare* [But this is a ſort of golden *Alpine* Trout, and to be had in other of the Northern Lakes, as *Ulleswater*, *Butter-meer*, &c as well as here They have alſo the ſame fiſh in ſome parts of North-Wales, where it is called *Tor goch* or *Red-belly*] Upon this Lake ſtands a little Village of the ſame name, where in the year 792 *Eathred*, King of the Northumbrians, † is ſaid to have ſlain the ſons of King *Elfwold*, after he had taken them from York, that, by his own wickedneſs and their blood, he might ſecure himſelf in the Kingdom [But as to the truth of this Story, it is the leſs probable, becauſe this Eathred was himſelf King Elfwold's Son]

[right margin:] Forneſs Fells

[right margin:] Carthmell

[right margin:] Setantiorum Lacus

[right margin:] Winander mere

[right margin:] Chare a fiſh

[right margin:] Hiſtory of Mailros

[right margin:] † Slew C.

Between this Lake and the river *Dudden*, is the Promontory which we commonly call *Forneſs*; with the Iſland *Walney* like a Counterſcarp before *it*, *for a long way together*, and a ſmall arm of the Sea between The Entrance is defended by a fort called *The Pile of Fouldrey*, ſituate upon a rock in the middle of the water, and built by the Abbot of *Forneſs* in the firſt year of King Edward the third, [but now quite ruinated]

[right margin:] The Pile of Fouldrey

Upon the Promontory there is nothing to be ſeen, but the ruins of *Forneſs Abbey*, which Stephen Earl of Bullen, afterwards King of England, built in the year 1127 in a place formerly call'd *Bekenſgill*, or rather *tranſlated* it, from *Tulket* in *Anderneſs* Out of the Monks of this place, and no other (as themſelves relate) the Biſhops of the Iſle of Man, which lies over againſt it, were wont, by ancient cuſtom, to be choſen this being the mother of ſeveral Monaſteries both in that Iſland and in *Ireland* More to the Eaſt, ſtands *Aldingham*, the ancient eſtate of the family of the *Harringtons*, to whom it came from the *Flemings* by the *Cancefelds*; and whoſe inheritance went by a daughter to *William Bonvill* of Devonſhire, and by him at laſt to the *Greys* Marquiſſes of Dorſet [With in the Mannour of *Aldingham* is *Gleſton Caſtle*, which has been very large and firm, having four ſtrong Towers of a great height, beſides many other

[right margin:] The Forneſs ...

[right margin:] Aldingham ... [illegible]

[right margin:] Gleſton Caſtle

other buildings with very thick walls. To observe it here once for all, many persons of quality, especially towards Scotland, had either Castles or Towers to dwell in, to defend themselves and their Tenants from the inroads of the Scots. Anciently, they had their houses kernell'd, fortify'd, or embattel'd, and divers Commissions have been awarded (in pursuance of an Act of Parliament made in the † reign of Philip and Mary) unto certain persons, to enquire how many and which Castles, Fortresses, &c. have been decay'd, which were fit to be re-edify'd, and how many new ones necessary to be erected. This of *Gleston* is seated in a fertile vale amongst rich meadows, and shelter'd from the Sea by fruitful hills, all which render it one of the most pleasant Seats in this County.]

† 1 & 2 Phil. & Mar. c. 1

Ulverston

Somewhat higher, lies *Ulverston*, memorable upon this account, that Edward the third gave a moiety of it to *John Coupland*, one of the most warlike men of that age, whom he also advanced to the honour of a *Banneret*, for taking David the second, King of Scots, prisoner, in the battel of Durham. After his death, the said King gave it, with other great estates in these parts, and with the title of Earl of Bedford, to *Ingelram Lord Couchy*, a French man; he having marry'd his daughter *Isabella*, and his Ancestors having been possess'd of great Revenues in England, in right of *Christiana de Lindsey*. [In this corner, round *Ulverston*, lie the following Places, which deserve our notice. *Kirkby-Ireleth*, the Manour-house whereof (*Kirkby-Cross-house*, so call'd from a *Cross* plac'd before the gates, the top of which was broken off, as is said, by Archbishop Sandy's order) is a stately Seat, giving name to the *Kirkbys*, the Lords of it from the time of the Conquest. *Broughton*, formerly the chief seat of a family of that name, till in the reign of Henry the seventh, it was forfeited for Treason by Sir *Thomas Broughton* Knight, who then took part with the counterfeit *Plantagenet* that landed in *Fourness*. And here it may not be improper to observe a mistake in the History of that King's reign, where it is affirmed that Sir *Thomas Broughton* was slain at *Stokefield*, whereas, in truth he escap'd from that battel, to *Witherslack* a Manour then belonging to him in the County of Westmorland. Here he liv'd *incognito* a good while among his Tenants, here also he dy'd and was bury'd, and his grave is known, and is to be seen, at this day. *Coniside*, anciently call'd *Conyngesheved*, heretofore an Hospital, or Priory, founded by *William de Lancaster*, Baron of Kendal, and formerly the possession of the *Sandys*. It is said, that *Edward Sandys*, Archbishop of York, was born here. *Scartmoor*, so call'd from *Martin Swart* (who came in with the counterfeit *Plantagenet* at the Pile of Fouldrey, in King Henry the seventh's time.) Here it was also that *Anno* 1652 *George Fox* and some of his fellow Quakers, first shew'd themselves in this Country. *Plumpton*, where were formerly *Mines* and a *Forge*, from whence a pretty way to the North, is *Conniston*, a Manour plac'd between *Conningston Fells* (very high Mountains, wherein are many Mines of Copper, Lead, &c.) and *Conniston water*, a lake five miles long, and near a mile broad. This Town is sometimes call'd *Fleming Conningston* (to distinguish it from another lying on the contrary side of the Lake, nam'd *Monk Conningston* as formerly belonging to the Abbey of *Furness*.) For in the reign of Henry the third, it came by marriage from the *Urswicks* to Sir *Richard le Fleming* of Caernarvon-Castle, and has been ever since enjoy'd by his heir-males, Sir *William Fleming* of *Rydal hall* in the County of Westmorland Knight, being the present owner. This Manour of *Rydal* came to them by Sir *Thomas le Fleming*'s marrying *Isabel*, one of the daughters and coheirs of Sir *John de Lancaster* of *Rydal* and of *Hoighl castle* in the same County, Knight. The Chapel here was made Parochial, among divers others in this Country, by *Edwin Sandys*, Archbishop of York. By the Sand-side is *Wraysholme tower*, near which was not long since discover'd a Medicinal Spring of a brackish taste. The Water is now drunk by many, every Summer; being esteem'd a very good remedy for *Worms*, *Stone*, *Gout*, *Itch*, and several other Distempers.]

Kirkby Ireleth

Kirkby Cross house

Broughton

Coniside

Scartmoor

Plumpton

Conningston

Wrays holme tower

As for those of the Nobility, who have born the title of *Lancaster*; there were three in the beginning of the Norman Government, who had the title of *Lords of the Honour of Lancaster*. Roger of *Poictou*, son of Roger *Montgomery*, sirnam'd *Pictavensis* (as William of Malmesbury says,) because he had marry'd a wife out of *Poictou* in France. But he being depriv'd of that honour for his disloyalty, King Stephen confer'd it upon his own son *William*, Earl of *Moriton* and *Warren*. Upon whose Death, Richard the first bestow'd it on *John* his brother, who was afterwards King of England. For thus we find it in an ancient History, *King Richard shew'd great affection to his brother John. For, besides Ireland and the Earldom of Moriton in Normandy, he made such mighty additions in England, that he was a kind of* Tetrarch *there. He gave him Cornwal, Lancaster, Nottingham, and Derby, with the adjacent Country, and many others.* A good while after, King Henry the third, son of King John, did first advance *Edmund Crouchback* his younger son (to whom he had given the estates and honours of Simon Montfort Earl of Leicester, *Robert Ferrars* Earl of Derby and *John of Monmouth*, for their rebelling against him,) to the Earldom of Lancaster, giving, in these words, *The Honour, Earldom, Castle, and Town of Lancaster, with the † Cow pastures and Forests of Wiresdale, Lownsdale, Newcastle under Lime, and the Manour, Forest, and Castle of Pickering, the Manour of Scaleby, the Village of Gumecestre, and the Rents of the Town of Huntendon*, &c. after he had lost the Kingdom of *Sicily*, with which the Pope, by a ring, invested him in vain, and (which made the English the Scoff and Laughter of the World) had caus'd pieces of gold to be coin'd with this Inscription, AIMVNDVS REX SICILIÆ; having first chous'd the credulous King of great sums of money upon that account. The said *Edmund* (his first wife dying without issue, who was the daughter and heir of the Earl of *Albemarle*; yet by her last Will made him her heir) had by his second wife *Blanch* of Artois of the * Royal Family of France, *Thomas* and *Henry*, and *John* who dy'd very young. *Thomas* was the second Earl of Lancaster, who married *Alice* the only daughter and heir of Henry Lacy Earl of Lincoln. She convey'd this and her mother's estate, who was of the family of the *Long Espee's* Earls of Salisbury (as her father *Henry Lacy* had also done with his own Lands, in case Alice should die without issue, as it afterwards happened) to the family of Lancaster. But this Thomas, for his Insolence towards *Edward* the second, and for embroiling the State, being taken prisoner, was beheaded, and left no issue. However, the Sentence in virtue of which he was executed, was afterwards revers'd by Act of

Lords of Lancaster

Gualter de Hemingford
R. Hoveden p. 373 b

Earl of Lancaster.

† *Vaccaria*

* *Domo Francica*

of Parliament, because he was not try'd by his Peers, and so his brother Henry succeeded him in his estate and honours. He was also enrich'd by his wife *Maud*, daughter and sole heir of Patrick Chaworth, and that not only with her own, but also with great estates in Wales, namely, of *Maurice* of *London*, and of *Siward*, from whom she was descended. He dying, left one only son *Henry*, whom Edward the third advanc'd from the title of Earl to that of Duke, and he was the second of our Nobility, who bore the title of *Duke*. But he dy'd without issue male, leaving two daughters *Mawd* and *Blanch*, between whom the Estate was divided. Mawd was married to William of *Bavaria*, Earl of Holland, Zeland, Friseland, Hanault, and of Leicester too in right of his wife. But she dying without issue, *John of Gaunt* (so called because he was born at Gaunt in Flanders) fourth son of Edward the third, came to the whole Estate, by marriage with *Blanch* the other daughter of Henry. And now being equal to many Kings in wealth, and created Duke of Lancaster by his father, he also obtain'd the Royalties of him, the King advancing the County of Lancaster into a *Palatinate* by † a Patent, wherein he declares the great service that he had done to his Country, both at home and abroad, and then adds, *We have granted for us and our heirs to our son aforesaid, that he, during the term of life, shall have, within the County of Lancaster, his Chancery, and his Writs to be issued under his own Seal belonging to the Office of Chancellor, his Justices likewise, as well for Pleas of the Crown, as for other Pleas relating to Common Law, to have cognisance of them, and to have power of making all Executions whatsoever by his Writs and Officers. And to have all other Liberties and Royalties of what kind soever appertaining to a County Palatine, as freely and as fully as the Earl of Chester within the said County is known to have*, &c. Nor was he only Duke of Lancaster, but also, by marriage with *Constantia*, daughter of Peter King of Castile, had for some time the title of *King of Leon and Castile*. But by agreement, he parted with this title, and in the thirteenth of King Richard the second, was created by consent of Parliament, *Duke of Aquitain*, to the great dissatisfaction of that Country. At that time, his titles were, *John, son to the King of England, Duke of Aquitain and Lancaster, Earl of Derby, Lincoln, and Leicester, and high Steward of England.*

Dukes of Lancaster

† Rescriptum

John of Gaunt K. of Castile.

After *John*, Henry de Bullingbroke his son succeeded in the Dutchy of Lancaster; who having deposed Richard the second, and obtain'd the Crown, confer'd this honour upon Henry his son, afterwards King of England. And that he might entail it upon him and his heirs for ever, he had an Act of Parliament made in these words: *We being unwilling, that our said Inheritance, or its Liberties, by reason of our taking upon us the Royal state and dignity, would be any way chang'd, transferr'd, diminish'd, or impair'd, do declare, that our said Inheritance, with its rights and liberties aforesaid, in the same manner and form, condition and state, wherein they descended and came to us, and also with all and singular liberties, franchises and other privileges, commodities, and profits whatsoever with which our Lord and Father in his life time had and held it for term of life by the grant of the late King Richard; shall be wholly and fully preserv'd, continued and enjoy'd by us and our heirs, as specified in the said Charters. And by the tenor of these presents, we do, upon our certain knowledge, and with the consent of this our present Parliament, grant, declare and ordain, for us and our heirs, that as well our*

K. Henry the fourth

*Dutchy of Lancaster, as all and singular Counties, Honours, Castles, Mannors, Fees, Advowsons, Possessions, Annuities, and Seigniories whatsoever, which descended to us before we were rais'd to the Royal Dignity, how or in what place soever, by right of inheritance, * in the hands of our Tenant, or in reversion, or by any other way, do remain to us and our said heirs, as specified in the Charters abovesaid, after the said manner and form, for ever.* Afterwards, Henry the fifth by Act of Parliament annex'd a very great estate to this Dutchy, which had come to him in right of his mother, who was the daughter and coheir of *Humphry Bohun*, Earl of Hereford. And in this state and condition it remain'd from that time, saving that Edward the fourth, in the first year of his reign, when he had attainted Henry the sixth in Parliament for High Treason, *annex'd it to the Crown*, that is, to him and his heirs Kings of England. However, Henry the seventh presently broke this Entail, and to † at this day it has its particular Officers, namely, *a Chancellor, Attorney, Receiver, Clerk of the Court, six Assessors, a Messenger, two Auditors, three and twenty Receivers, and three Supervisors.*

* In nomine Servis.

† Ann. 1 H. 7.

There are reckon'd in this County (besides several Chapels) † 60 Parishes, but those very large, and such as, for numbers of Parishioners, do far exceed the greatest Parishes any where else.

† Only 36.

More rare Plants growing wild in Lancashire.

Asphodelus Lancastriæ verus *Ger. emac. descr.* Pseudo asphodelus palustris Anglicus *C. B.* *Lancashire Asphodel, or Bastard English Asphodel.* This being a Plant commonly growing in mosses or rotten boggy grounds in many Counties of England, I need not have mentioned here, but that our English Herbarists have been pleased to denominate it from this County, as if it were peculiar to it. Lobel saith, they call it *Maiden-hair, because the Women here about were wont to colour their hair with the flower of it.*

Britannicum minimum. *The least Tway blade. Observed upon Pendle hill among the Heath.* See the *Synonymes in Yorkshire.*

Cerasus Sylvestris fructu minimo cordiformi *P. B. Wild Heart cherry tree, commonly call'd the Merry-tree. About Bury and Manchester.* See *Westmorland.*

Cochlearia minor foliis angulosis parvo *D. Lawson. Small Sea Scurvy-grass with a corner'd leaf. In the Isle of Walney. I take this to be the same with the Cochlearia rotundifolia minor nostras & Park and the Thlaspi hederaceum Lob.*

Conyza helenitis folio laciniato. *Jagged Fleabane-Mullet, or Marsh Fleabane. In the ditches about Pillingmoss plentifully.*

Carduus spinosum Ger. marinum spinosum C. B. maritimum spinosum, seu Pastinaca marina Park. Pastinaca marina, quibusdam Secacul & Crithmum spinosum J. B. *Prickly Sampire or Sea Parsnep. Observed by Mr. Lawson at Roosbeck in Low Furness.*

Echium marinum P. B. Buglossum dulce ex insulis Lancastriæ Park. *Sea Bugloss. Over against Bigger in the Isle of Walney plentifully.*

Eruca Monensis laciniata lutea *Cat. Ang.* Antirrhinum Sylvestris minor lutea Bursa pastoris folio C. B. *Small jagged yellow Rocket of the Isle of Man. Between Marsh Grange and the Wheel-ferry.*

Geranium hæmatodes Lancastrense, flore eleganter striato. *Bloody Crane's-bill with an elegant striated flower. In the Isle of Walney near Sandsele. Innumerable Sea-shore.*

Lotus

Juncus Alpinus cum cauda leporina *J B Hares tail-Rush, Moss crops, upon the Mosses, of which there are plenty in this County.*

Rosmarinum purpureum *Purple-Goats beard On the banks of the river Chalaer, near the Lady Hesketh's house, two miles from Whalley, P B This, Mr Fitz-Roberts, a skilful Herbarist, affirms himself to have found wild, but not in the place mentioned*

Tormentilla quadrifolia radice rotunda *Merret Pin Near Wigan in Lancashire*

Sambucus foliis laciniatis. *Elder with jagged leaves In a hedge near Manchester I suspect that this was no native, but industriously or accidentally planted there*

WESTMORELAND.

TO the utmost bounds of Lancashire on the North, joyns another small tract of the *Brigantes*, call'd in Latin *Westmorlandia*, in English *Westmoreland*, and by some modern Writers *West maria* On the West and North, it is bounded by Cumberland, and on the East, by Yorkshire and the Bishoprick of Durham * From its situation among high Mountains (for here our *Appennine* runs out broader and broader) and from its lying generally uncultivated, it [seems to have] had this name For the North parts of England call wild barren places, such as are not fit for tillage, by the name of *Mores*, so that *Westmoreland* implies *an uncultivated tract lying towards the West* Let then that idle story about King *Marius* (whom some of our Historians affirm to have conquer'd the *Picts*, and to have call'd this County after his own name) be banished for ever out of the School of Antiquities, [unless, as to the History it self, the truth of it may in some measure be retrieved, or stand doubtful at least, by what the learned Primate of *Armagh* has said in favour of it But before we go further, it is to be observed, that the forementioned description of the County in general, answers but *one* part of it, viz from Lancaster, through the Barony of *Kendal*, to *Workington* in Cumberland, where Travellers meet with little in their road, besides mountains, with here and there a Valley between, and so take an estimate of the whole from that part; imagining probably, that that more *southerly* corner is like to be as good at least, if not better than the rest But if they go directly northward, they will find reason to change their opinion, the *Barony* of Westmorland (commonly call'd the *bottom of Westmorland*, from its low situation) being a large open champain country, in length not less than twenty miles, and in breadth about fourteen And so far is it from being *uncultivated*, that it affords great plenty of arable grounds; and those good store of corn Nor do *Mores* in the northern parts signifie *wild barren mountains*, but generally *Common of Pasture*, in opposition to Mountains or Fells So that in the Barony of *Kendal* (where they have most Mountains) there are few or no Mores, their *Commons* being generally call'd *Fells*, and in the bottom of Westmorland there are few mountains (except that ridge which bounds the Country like a rampire or bulwark,) but very many Mores which yet are so far from being uncapable of improvement, that most of them have been formerly plow'd, as the ridges appearing do assure us If the whole Country therefore were to be derived from barren mountains, we might say with more reason, that it had the name from lying westward of that long ridge of hill, which is call'd the *English Appennine*.

* This is a mistake, vide infra

Antiq Eccl Brit p 302

The Gentlemens houses in this County, are large and strong, and generally built Castle-wise, for defence of themselves, their Tenants, and their goods, whenever the Scots should make their inroads, which before the time of King James the first were very common

It is divided into the Barony of *Kendal*, and the Barony of *Westmorland*, as we have before hinted And these two parts belong to two several Dioceses, the former to *Chester*, the latter to *Carlisle* In each we find (with two *Wards*,) several *Deaneries*, *Parishes*, and *Constablewicks*, but no *Hundreds* possibly, because in ancient times these parts paid no Subsidies, being sufficiently charg'd in the *Border service* against the Scots]

The South part of the County (which for some space is pent up in a narrow compass between the river *Lone* and *Winander mere*) is pretty fruitful in the Vallies, thought not without rocks, rough and smooth, and is called by one general name, *The Barony of Kendal* or *Candal a*, signifying *a Vale upon the Can* This it took from the river *Can*, which runs along the valley in a stony Chanel, and has upon its Western bank a very populous town, call'd *Candale*, or *Kirkby Candale*, i e *a Church in the valley, upon Can*, [which Dr Gale will have to be the *Brovonaca* of Antoninus] It has two Streets crossing each other, is very eminent for the woollen manufacture, and for the industry of the inhabitants, who trade throughout *England* with their woollen cloth [And as early as Richard the second and Henry the fourth, we find special Laws enacted on purpose for the regulating of *Kendal Clothes* Queen Elizabeth, in the eighteenth year of her reign, erected it into a Corporation, by the name of Aldermen and Burgesses But afterwards King *James* the first incorporated it with a Mayor, twelve Aldermen, and twenty four Burgesses] Their greatest honour is, that *Barons*, *Earls*, [and *Dukes*,] have taken their titles from the place The Barons were of the family of *Ivo Taleboys*, of whose posterity, *William*, by consent of King Henry the second, call'd himself *William of Lancaster* His * niece and heir was marry'd to Gilbert, son of *Roger Fitz-Reinfrid*, by whose daughters (upon the death of *William* his son) the estate came to *Peter Brus* the second Lord of *Skelton* of that Christian name, and to *William Lindsey*, from whom, on the mother's side, *Ingelram* Lord of *Coucy* in France deriv'd his pedigree, as I understood by the History of *Fourness Abbey* By the daughter of this *Peter Brus*, sister and heir to *Peter Brus* the third, the Barony descended to the *Rosses* of *Werk*; and from

Barony of Kendal

Kendal

Candale

Page 39

13 R 2 c 1

9 H 4 c

Lords of Kendal

* Neptis Family of Lancaster

History of Furness Abbey

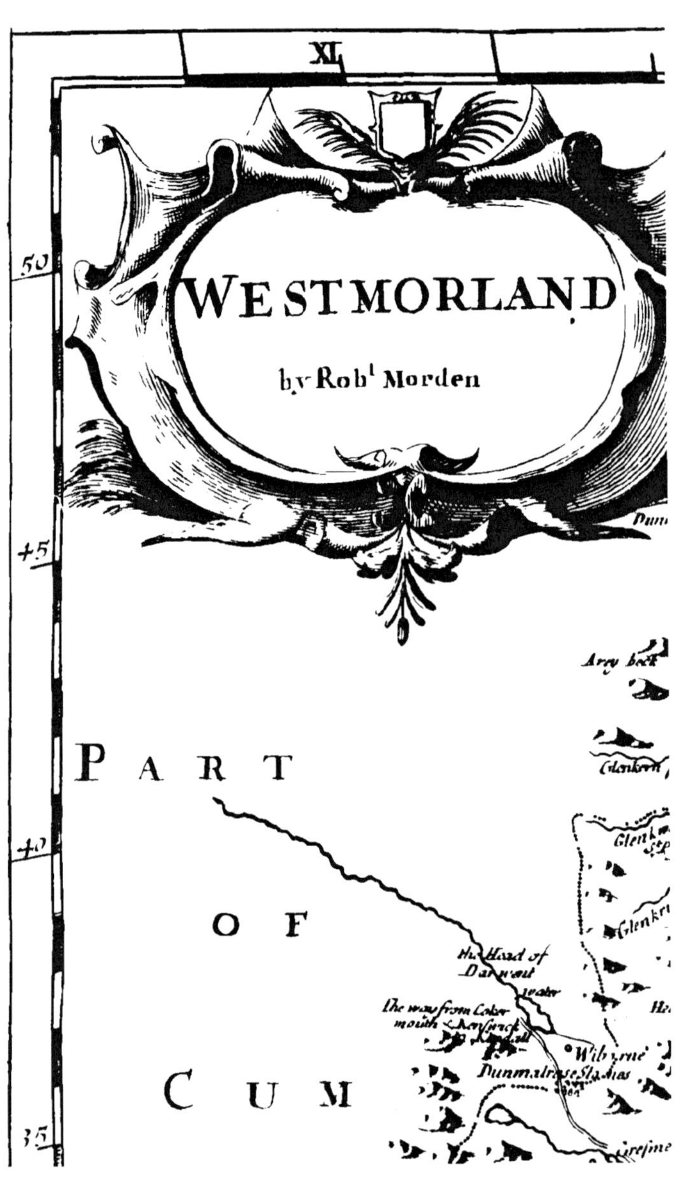
XL
WESTMORLAND
by Robt Morden
50
45
40
35
PART
OF
CUM
The Head of Darwent water
The way from Cokermouth to Kerswick

X
IX
VIII
Milburne Forrest
Kirkland
Blenkern
Edenhall
Hornby
Penrith Beacon
The military way from Carlile
Penrith
King Arthurs round Table
Dalemaine
Daker castle
Barton
Pooley
Barton Park
Martindale Forrest
Broader water
Brougham Cast
Whinfeld Forrest
Cleborne
Clifton
Lowther
Askham
Thrimby
Shap
Morland
Strickland Hall
Newby
Hardendale
Reagill
Crosby
Orton
Temple sowerbye
Kirby Thure
Newbiggin
Knock
Dufton
Dufton Pike
Murton pike
Murton
Bolton Chaple
Crakenthorp
ABALLABA
Apalby
Langton
Sandford
Great Ormside
Flakebridge
Melton
Brackenburgh
Drueners
Gathorn Hall
Great Ashby
Little Ashby
Whitwall
Parke
Odlleten
Haberin
Wiberslack
Soulby
Rawenstonedale or Russendale
Shales
Cottesflat
Kellath
New Begin
Raysbeck
Tunthwaite
Kathey

VII
PART
OF
YORK
Birkdale
Stanemore
Forrest
Helbeckfell
Kirkby Steven
Wauthy
Hughs Head

BER
LAND
PART

Kendall
Kirkby Lonsdale
Burton
Kentale castle
Crostwhate
Hawgill
Delake
Holme
Warton
Barwick Hall
Underley
Skelsmere
Winander mere
New Bridg
Mansergh
OF
LANCASHIRE
From Lancaster to Kendall and Apulby

S H I R E
the County Stone
Sold by
John Churchill

from them the honour was devolv'd by Inheritance upon the *Parrs*, whose Castle over-against the town, is ready to drop down with age. It has had three Earls; *John* Duke of Bedford, who was advanc'd to that honour by his brother King Henry the fifth, *John* Duke of Somerset, and *John de Foix*, descended from the noble family of the *Foix* in France, whom King Henry the sixth advanc'd to this Dignity, for his faithful services in the French wars. Upon which account, possibly, it is, that some of this family of *Foix* in France, have still the sirname of *Kendal*. [The first *Duke* of this place, was *Charles Stuart* (third Son of *James* Duke of York, afterwards King *James* the second) who was declared Duke of *Kendal* in the year 1664. Since which, his Royal Highness Prince *George* of Denmark, at the same time that he was created Duke of Cumberland, was also created Earl of Kendal. And, lately, Melusina Erengart Schulenberg, who had been before created Dutchess of Munster in Ireland, hath been honour'd with the title of Dutchess of Kendal, together with the titles of Baroness of *Glassenbury*, and Countess of *Feversham*.]

Earls of Kendal.

I know no other mark of Antiquity, that *Kendal* can boast of. Once indeed I was of opinion that it was the old Roman station, *Concangii*, but time has inform'd me better. [Below Kendal, is *Water Crook* (so call'd from a remarkable *crooking* in the river,) where, on the east side of that river, is an old square fort, the banks and ditches whereof are still visible. That it was Roman, the discovery of *Coins*, broken *Altars*, and other pieces of *Antiquity*, will not give us leave to make the least doubt: which seems to some, to fix the *Concangii* rather here, than in any other place, because in the *Notitia* it is plac'd as it were in the very middle of the Northern Stations. For whereas between *York* and *Derwent*, the *Notitia* speaks of fourteen Stations, the *Concangii* is the seventh, and the very next that come after it are *Lavatræ* (Bowes,) *Verteræ* (Brough,) and *Brovonacum* (Browham;) the two last in this County, and the first upon the edge of it. But, after all, this *Concangii*, which the *Notitia* makes the Station of the *Præfectus Numeri Vigilum*, is most probably to be sought for nearer the Wall, and perhaps (as * Dr Brady has observed) on the north-side of that Fortress.

Water Crook.

* Hist. p. [illegible]

Lower in the river *Can*, there are † two *Water falls*, where the water is tumbled headlong with a hideous noise, one at a little village call'd *Levens*, another more Southward near *Betham*. From these, the neighbours form their prognostications of the weather: for when the Northern one sounds clear, they make themselves sure of fair weather; but when the Southern, of rain and mists. [At *Levens* is a fair stone bridge over the river *Kent*, on the south side of which river, are still to be seen the ruins of an ancient round building (now called *Kirks head*) which is said to have been formerly a Temple dedicated to *Diana*. And not far from it, there appear the ruins of another building, which seems to have belong'd to the same place. In the Park (well stor'd with fallow deer, and almost equally divided by the river Kent) is a Spring call'd the *Dropping Well*, that petrifies moss, wood, leaves, &c. West from hence, lies *Witherslack*, in which Manour, not long since, a fair *Parochial Chapel* was built and endowed by Dr *John Barwick* late Dean of St Paul's, a native of the place, and consecrated by Dr *Wilkins* late Bishop of Chester, and

[illegible] The Forces. † On [illegible] Betham river above Milthrop. Leven. Betham.

Witherslack.

dedicated to St *Paul*. The Charity was so much the greater, because of its remoteness from *Betham*, the Parish Church. Below this, at the mouth of the river, is *Milthrop*, the only Sea town in this County, and the Commodities which are imported, are brought hither only in small Vessels from *Grange* in Lancashire.]

Milthrop.

And thus much of the Southerly and more narrow part of this County, which is bounded on the West with the river *Winster*, and the spacious Lake we mention'd but now, call'd *Winander-mere*, and on the east, with the river *Lone* or *Lune* †. [But it is to be observed, before we leave it, that this doth wholly take in the great Lake *Winander mere*. For all the Isles (or *Holmes*, as they call them) that are in it, are own'd to be in the County of Westmorland: all the Fishing belongs to *Ipelthwaite* in Winandermere-Parish in the said County, and all the Tithe-fish to the Rector thereof, who has a Pleasure-boat upon the said Lake, and a Prescription of so much a boat, in lieu of the Tithe of all the Fish that are taken in it. Nor is it of any moment, that the Abbey of *Furness* had two boats upon it, since that was the gift of *William de Lancaster* Baron of Kendal.]

Winander-mere.

† It goes beyond the river.

At the upper corner of the Lake *Winandermere*, lies the *carcass*, if I may so say, of an ancient City, with large ruins of walls, and without the walls, the rubbish of old Buildings, in many places. The Fort has been of an oblong figure, fortify'd with a ditch and rampire, in length, one hundred thirty two Ells, and in breadth, eighty. That it was a work of the Romans, the British bricks, the mortar temper'd with small pieces of bricks, the little Urns, the Glass Vials, the Roman Coins commonly met with, the round stones like Mill stones (of which, * solder'd together, they us'd formerly to make Pillars,) and the pav'd ways leading to it, are all undeniable testimonies. But the old name is quite lost, unless one should imagine from the present name *Ambleside*, that this was the *Amboglana* mention'd by the *Notitia*. [But there are two things which stand in our way: the first, that we are directed by the *Notitia* to seek [illegible] *Irthing*; the second, that without all doubt, the *Cohors prima Ælia Dacorum*, [illegible] at [illegible] in Cumberland, as appears from several Inscriptions which have been found at a little distance on the other side of the river. These two Opinions, then, can perhaps be [illegible] reconciled, [illegible] this *Ambleside* might be [illegible] quarters, and [illegible] the other [illegible] *ward*, [illegible] the *Romans*, [illegible] bridge there over the river [illegible] defend) [illegible] the Fort [illegible] when they were called [illegible] upon [illegible] occasions to defend the *Pass* [illegible]. It is not to be doubted, but [illegible] had [illegible] from the *Glen* of *Cambeck* near Willowford, [illegible] the many Roman Monuments, found [illegible] neighbourhood, do [illegible] prove [illegible] unless, but that the Troops which were quartered [illegible] to keep the Enemy [illegible] their [illegible] *Pass* [illegible] employment [illegible] went [illegible] *Pass* [illegible] It will be observed, that the *Notitia* [illegible] *Aliana*, [illegible] but [illegible] to [illegible] is not [illegible] to [illegible] the [illegible] of the Wall [illegible] the *Line* of

* Cæmentia.

* Ambleside Amboglana.

Commu-

Communication which several *Auxiliaries* had with those who were quarter'd upon the *Picts-wall* Among other pieces of Antiquity, discover'd about this old Work at *Ambleside*, were several *Medals* of gold, silver, and copper, some of which are in that Collection which Mr *Thomas Braithwate* of Ambleside gave by † Deed to the Library of the University of Oxford A little mile north of Ambleside, is *Ridal* hall, a convenient large ancient house in which Lordship is a very high Mountain call'd *Ridall-head*, from the top whereof one has a large prospect, and, if the day be clear, may see Lancaster Castle, and much farther The Manour anciently belong'd to the Family of *Lancaster*, from whom it descended in the reign of Henry the fourth to the *Flemings*, who have been Lords of it ever since, and the late Sir *Daniel Fleming* ought to be particularly mention'd, as a great lover of ancient Learning, and to whom this Work is oblig'd for several useful Informations in *Westmorland* and *Lancashire*

† Nov 26 1674

Ridal hall

Towards the East, the river *Lone* is the limit; and gives its name to the adjoyning tract, *Lonsdale*, i e *a Vale upon the Lone*, the chief Town whereof is *Kirkby Lonsdale*, whither the neighbouring Inhabitants resort to Church and Market [This hath been honoured by giving the title of Viscount, to Sir *John Lowther*, who was created Baron of *Lowther*, and Viscount *Lonsdale*, a person of great Accomplishments, who hath been succeeded in these Titles by his two Sons, *Richard* and *Henry*] Above the head of the *Lone*, the Country grows wider, and the Mountains shoot out with many windings and turnings, between which there are exceeding deep Vallies, and several places hollow'd, like so many dens or caves [But, as we caution'd before, this is only to be understood of one part of it, the Barony of Westmorland being an open champain Country, of Corn fields, Meadows, and Pastures, mix'd with woods, and as it were hemm'd in by a wall of high Mountains

Lonsdale

The river *Lune* rising a little above *Rissendale*, runs by *Lang gil*, where the learned Dr *Barlow* late Bishop of *Lincoln* was born; famous for his great Reading, and his Zeal against Popery Afterwards, receiving the river *Birkbeck*, it runs down by a field call'd *Gallaber*, where stands a * red Stone, about an ell high, with two Crosses cut deep on one side The tradition among the Inhabitants is, that formerly it was the Mere stone between the *English* and *Scots* How true it may be, I dare not affirm but shall only observe, that it is about the same distance from Scotland that *Rere cross* upon *Stanemore* is; and to what end that was erected, hath been † already observ'd To prevent also the Incursions of that people, there is an artificial Mount call'd *Castle how*, near Tebay (where is a Free School endow'd by Mr *Adamson*, born at *Rownthwait*, who was likewise a great Benefactor to the Church of *Orton*,) and another at *Greenholme*, which two Mounts command the two great Roads

Lang gill.

* Brandreth stone

† In Richmondshire

A little above *Rownthwait*, on the north side of Jeffrey mount, is a small Spring call'd *Goud sike*, which continually casts up small silver like pieces resembling spangles what the cause is, must be left to Naturalists to determine This Parish of *Orton*, in the year 1612 purchas'd very honourably all the Tithes belonging to the Rectory, for the use of the Incumbent, with the Advowson and Patronage of its Vicaridge, for ever For which they paid a considerable * Sum, subscrib'd by the Parishioners Hereabouts, they commonly dig up in their wet Mosses such *Subterraneous Trees*, as are met with in other parts of England]

Goud sike

* 570 l

The noble river of *Eden*, call'd by Ptolemy *Ituna*, rises in † Westmorland, [at a place called *Hugh-seat Morvill*, or *Hugh-Morvils* hill, from one of the name, sometimes Lord of Westmorland; out of which hill also run two other great Rivers on Yorkshire-side, *Eure* and *Swale*,] It has at first only a small stream; but increases by the confluence of several little rivers, and finds a passage through these Mountains to the North west, by *Pendragon Castle* [The walls, being four yards in thickness (with battlements upon them) † were standing, till the year 1660, when the most noble Lady *Ann Clifford*, Countess Dowager of *Pembroke*, *Dorset*, and *Montgomery*, repair'd this ancient house of her Ancestors, with three more Castles which she had in this County; and, removing frequently from one to another, kept hospitality, and diffus'd her Charity all over the Country This Castle is wash'd on the East by the river *Eden*, and on the other sides are great trenches, as if the first builder had intended to draw the water round it But the attempt prov'd ineffectual, from whence they have an old rhyme hereabouts,

Eden, riv

† Yorkshire, C

Hugh-Morvils hill

Pendragon Castle

† To which Age has left nothing, but the name, and a heap of great Stones, C.

> *Let Pendragon do what he can,*
> *Eden will run where Eden ran*]

Then this River runs by *Wharton hall*, the seat of the Barons of *Wharton* [of which Manour the present Family have been Proprietors beyond the date of any Records extant, and have likewise been Lords of the Manour of *Croglin* in Cumberland, and Patrons of the Rectory there, more than four hundred years past] The first Baron was *Thomas*, advanced to that honour by King Henry the eighth, [for his surprising conduct and success in the entire defeat of the Scots at *Solom-moss* Which Victory, in all its circumstances, was perhaps one of the most considerable that the English ever obtained over the forces of the neighbouring kingdom And therefore King Edward the sixth, in recompence of that eminent Service, granted to the said Lord an augmentation of his Paternal Coat of Arms, *viz* a *Border engrailed*, Or, *charged with Legs of Lions in Saltire*, Gules, *Armed*, Azure] To him succeeded his son of the same name; who was succeeded by *Philip* *, a person of great honour, [and he by *Philip* his grand-child (son of Sir *Thomas* his eldest son who dy'd in his father's life time,) whose son *Thomas* Lord *Wharton*, in consideration of his great Abilities and Services, was further advanced to the Honours of Viscount *Winchendon* and Earl of *Wharton*, as his only son hath since been, to the yet higher honour of Duke of *Wharton*]

Wharton hall

Lords of Wharton

Regstr Halton Ep Carl p 154

* The present Lord, C

Next, *Eden* goes to *Kirby Stephen*, or *Stephen's Church*, a noted Market; [where is a Free School, founded and endowed by the Family of *Wharton*,] and so by two little villages call'd *Musgrave*, which gave name to the warlike Family of the *Musgraves*, [unless one may say, with greater probability, that the Towns had their name from the Family For the name of *Musgrave* is to be reckon'd among those, which have been taken from Offices, and Civil or Military Honours, and is of the like original as *Landtgraff*, *Markgraff*, *Burggraff*, &c among the Germans And indeed, this name and *Markgraff* (now turn'd into *Marquis*) are probably the same The signification of both, is *Dux Limitaneus*, and anciently *Musgrave*, or *Mosgrave*,

Kirby Stephen

Musgrave

Mosgrave, was all one as in our later language, *a Lord Warden of the Marches*] Of this family, *Thomas Musgrave*, in the time of Edward the third, was summon'd to Parliament among the Barons their seat was *Heartly-Castle*, hard by

Heartley Castle

Here the *Eden* seems to stop its course, that it may receive some rivulets, upon one of which, scarce two miles from *Eden* itself, stood *Verteræ*, an ancient Town mention'd by *Antoninus* and the *Notitia* From the latter of these we learn, that in the decline of the Roman Empire, a Præfect of the Romans quarter'd there with a band of the *Directores* The Town it self is dwindl'd into a village, which is defended with a small Fort, and the name is now *Burgh*; for it is call'd *Burgh under Stane more*, i e a Burrow under a stony Mountain [It is divided into two, the *Upper*, otherwise, *Church-Brough*, where the Church standeth, of which *Robert Eglesfield*, Founder of Queen's-College in Oxford, was Rector, and procur'd the appropriation thereof from King Edward the third to the said College Here also stands the Castle of *Brough*, and a tower call'd *Cæsar's tower*, or the Fort before mention'd the Castle, having been raz'd to the ground, was rebuilt not long since by the Countess of Pembroke Near the bridge, is a Spaw-well, which hath not been long discover'd The other village is call'd *Lower-Brough* from its situation, and *Market-Brough* from a Market held there every Thursday] In the time of the later Emperours (to observe this once for all) the little Castles, which were built for the emergent occasions of war, and stor'd with provisions, began to be call'd *Burgi*, a new name, which, after the translation of the Empire into the East, the Germans and others seem to have taken from the Greek πύργος And hence the *Burgundians* have their name from inhabiting the *Burgi*, for so that age call'd the Dwellings planted at a little distance one from another along the Frontiers I have read no more concerning this place, but that in the beginning of the Norman Government, the English form'd a Conspiracy here against William the Conquerour I dare be positive, that this *Burgh* was the old *Verteræ*, both because the distance, on one side from *Lavatræ*, and on the other from *Brovonacum*, if resolv'd into Italian miles, exactly agrees with the number assign'd by Antoninus, and also because a Roman military Road, still visible by its high ridge, runs this way to *Brovonacum*, by *Aballaba*, mention'd in the *Notitia*; the name whereof is to this day kept so entire, that it plainly shews it to be the very same, and leaves no ground for dispute For instead of *Aballaba*, we call it at this day, by contraction, *Apleby* Nothing is memorable about it, besides it's antiquity and situation for under the Romans it was the Station of the *Mauri Aureliani*, and it is seated in a pleasant field, and almost encompass'd with the river *Eden* But it is † so slenderly peopl'd, and the buildings are so mean, that if Antiquity did not make it the chief Town of the County, and the Assizes were not held * in the Castle, which is the publick Gaol for Malefactors; it would be but very little above a village, [tho' the best Corn-market in these Northern Parts]) For all its beauty consists in one broad street, which runs from north to south with an easie ascent; at the head of which is the Castle, ‖ almost surrounded with the river, [and trenches, where the river comes not But it hath several testimonies of its ancient splendour

Verteræ

Burgh under Stanemore

Church Brough

Lower Brough

Market Brough

Veget. l. 4 c. 10

OroGus

Aballaba Apleby

† Infrequens

* They are held in the Town hall and the Gaol is now at the end of the Bridge

‖ Entirely, C

Henry the first gave it privileges equal to *York*, that City's Charter being granted (as it is said) in the fore noon, and this in the afternoon Henry the second granted them another Charter of the like Immunities; and Henry the third (in whose time there was an Exchequer here, call'd *Scaccarium de Apleby*) a third Which were *in all things like York*; and were confirm'd by the succeeding Kings of England When it was first govern'd by a Mayor, does not appear, but it is certain that in the reign of Edward the first, they had a Mayor and two Provosts (who seem to have been formerly men of principal note, i e Sheriffs, or the same as we now call *Bailiffs*, and who sign'd the publick Acts of the Town together with the Mayor *, though at present they only attend the body of the Mayor with two Halberds) Brompton makes mention of *Apleby-schire*, which should seem to imply, that at that time it had Sheriffs of its own, as most Cities had, though we now call them Bailiffs For in the second year of Edward the first, in a Confirmation-Charter to *Shap-Abbey*, we find this Subscription, *Teste Thomâ filio Johannis, tunc Vice Comite de Apleby* Unless one should say, that *Westmorland* was call'd the *County of Apelby*, or *Apelby schire*, as indeed *Brompton* seems to intimate But the Scotch wars by degrees reduc'd this Town to a much lower condition † In the 22d of Henry the second, it was set on fire by them, and again, in the 11th of Richard the second, when of 2200 Burgages (by due computation of the Fee farm-rents, there remain'd not above a tenth part, as appears by Inquisitions in the Town-chest Since which, it never recover'd it self, but lay as it were dismember'd and scatter'd one street from another, like so many several villages; and one could not know, but by Records, that they belong'd to the same body For though *Burgh gate* only is spoken of above, as the principal street, yet *Bongate*, *Battle burgh*, *Dungate*, *Scattergate*, are all of them members of it, and probably the *Burrals* also, which may be an evidence of its having been wall'd round (that word implying *Burrow-wall*,) and the rather, because at *Bath* in Somersetshire, they call the town walls by the same name of *Burrals* Concerning the condition and misfortunes of this place, take the following *Inscription*, which is placed in the Garden belonging to the School-house

* E Chartis Machellorum de Crakenthorp.

† See the Inscription a little below

ABALLABA QVAM C C
FLVII ITVNA STATIO FVIT
RO TEM MAVR AVREL
HANC VASTAVIT TI
GVIL R SCOT 1176
HIC PESTIS SÆVIT 1598
OPP DESERT MERCATVS
AD GILSHAVGHLIN F

DEVM TIME

The CC in the first line, is *Circumfluit* the FV in the fourth, *Funditus* and the F in the end, *Fuit* So that here we have its situation, its Roman Antiquity, and the devastations made in it by *War* and *Pestilence*, together with the remove of the Market to *Gilshaughlin*, four or five miles north west of the town]

At the lower end, is the Church, and a School built by *Robert Langton* and *Miles Spencer* Doctors of Law, [and, since that time, much improved and augmented by Benefactors, the chief of whom

whom was Dr *Thomas Smith* late Bishop of Carlisle.] The worthy Master hereof, *Reginald Bainbrigg*, a very learned Person, courteously transcrib'd for me several ancient Inscriptions, and has remov'd some into his own garden, [where also (as we have said) is to be seen the Inscription of a more modern date, which describes the Misfortunes and Calamities of this place] It was not without good reason, that *William* of *Newburrow* call'd this place and the foremen tion'd *Burgh*, * *Royal Forts*, where he tells us that William King of Scots took them by surprise, a little before himself was taken at *Alnewick* Afterwards, they were recover'd by King John, who gave them to *John de Veteri ponte* or *Vipon*., as a reward for his good services; [and the *Viponts*, and *Cliffords* (the Ancestors, by the mother's side, of the Earls of *Thanet*) have been Lords of this Country, and flourish'd at this place, for above five hundred years]

* Regias munitiones

From hence the river posts to the north-west, by *Buley-Castle*, belonging to the Bishop of Carlisle [It is said to have been erected at several times by two or three Bishops, and there is still in being an account of several Ordinations held here

Buley castle

Next, *Eden* runs to *Crakenthorp hall*, a pleasant seat on the East side of it, where the chief branch of the *Machels* (a family of good note in this Country) † have always resided, from the Conquest downwards, to this very day; nor do any Records afford an account how much longer they have flourish'd here And as the place is memorable on account of this uninterrupted succession for so many ages, so is it also for the wonderful Camps which lie near it, and the Antiquities discover'd thereabouts, which (with others found in these parts) were carefully collected and preserv'd by Mr *Thomas Machel* (brother to *Hugh Machel* Lord of this Manour, and late Minister of *Kirkby-Thore*) in order to his intended *Antiquities* of this County]

Crakenthorp hall

† Gwillam's Heraldry

Then, it runs to *Kirkby-Thore*, below which appear the vast ruins of an ancient Town where also Roman Coins [and Urns] are now and then dug up, and not † long ago, this Inscription

Kirkby Thore

† So said ann 1607

DEO BELATVCAD-
RO LIB VOTV
M FECIT
IOLVS

Time has quite worn out the old name, and they call it at this day * *Whelp-Castle* If it might be no offence to the Criticks in Antiquity, I should say that this was the *Gallagum* mention'd by Ptolemy, and call'd by Antoninus *Gallatum* Which conjecture, as it agrees with the distances in the Itinerary, so is it partly favour'd by the present name For such names as in British begun with *Gall*, the English turn'd into *Wall* Thus, *Guana* was call'd Wallingford, *Gal Sever*, Wall of Sever, &c This was, without doubt, a place of considerable note, seeing an old causey (commonly call'd *Maiden-way*) runs almost directly from it to *Caer-Vorran* (near the *Picts Wall*) along moorish hills and mountains, for some twenty miles Upon this, I am enclin'd to believe, the old *Stations* and *Mansions* mention'd by Antoninus in his ninth *Iter*, were settl'd, though no one has pointed out the particular places For indeed how should they? when Time (which consumes and destroys every thing) has been, as

* Wheallep, C Whelp castle

Gallatum

Maiden way

it were, preying upon them for so many years

[Dr *Gale* (in his Notes upon Ninnius, cites an old Manuscript fragment in *Cotton's* Library, which seems to intimate something of a quarrel betwixt *Ambrosius* and *Guitolinus* and his son *Marchantius*, at *Catguoloph*. This, he fansies, is the same that is now call'd *Whellop* or *Whallop*-Castle, and he believes the neighbouring ruins of *Marchantonsby* (carrying such evident remains of *Marchantius*) a great support to his Opinion But what if there should be no such place as *Marchantonsby*? It is certain, there is no such thing appears at this day, as the hanging walls mention'd to be there Besides, I see no reason, why *Catguoloph* in one of the *Appendices* of that learned person, may not be the same with either *Catgabail*, *Catgubail*, *Cotgualat*, or *Catgublaum*, in the other and those are manifestly the names of men, and not of places

Pag. 133

Whether this place was the ancient *Gallagum*, or not; the old Saxon God *Thor* (from whom our *Thursday* is call'd) seems to have had a Temple here, which is imply'd in the present name of *Kirbythure*, writen in old Records *Kirkbythore*, and sometimes *Kirkby Thor* Of the manner of Worship, and magnificence of the Temple of this God *Thor* among the Saxons, we need not be particular, because it is already done to our hands ‖ But a new discovery having been lately made of a curious Rarity relating to this Idol, and communicated by an ingenious * Antiquary to some learned Gentlemen, for their Opinion, we cannot but observe something of it, and of their thoughts concerning it The shape is this

‖ Sc Sheri, Antiq

* Mr *Hugh Thoresby*

It is a Coin about the bigness of a silver Groat but the best Danish Antiquaries are of opinion, that no current money was ever minted in these Northern Kingdoms till the *Runick* Character was laid aside So that, though it be true that they sometimes meet with pieces of Silver, of the like fashion with this before us, *Ast ego* (says *Tho Bartholine* [illegible] who speaks the sense of all the rest) *Amuletorum quoddam genus*, &c [illegible] *But for my part, I look upon them to have been a sort of Amulets, us'd as Magical Spells having learnt from our Antiquities, that our Pagan Ancestors had certain portable pieces of gold or silver, with their Gods represented upon them in a human face* [illegible] *they foretold what was to come, and look'd on them as their Tutelar Deities, which (so long as they kept them) would assure them of safety and prosperity* Now, it is probable, that this may prove one of these *Amulets* For the imagery gives us a human visage with a glory surrounding the head, [illegible] And the account which † [illegible] (with some others of his learned Country men) has left us of their God *Thor*, is this, That (in the posture they worshipp'd him) he had *Caput flammis circumdatum*, &c [illegible] *his head surrounded with a flame, like the Sun, as Painters us'd to adorn the heads of their Gods* [illegible] *and the print a Scepter, or* [illegible] ‖ Malcolm

† Not [illegible] [illegible] [illegible]

[illegible] son,

fcription, fo agreeable (at firft fight) to the figure reprefented, that it could not have been more exact, though copy'd from this Original But the *Runick* Characters on the Reverfe go yet further, if they are to be read thus,

+ Thur gut Luetis i e

Thoris Dei facies (*feu effigies*)

The face or effigies of the God *Thor*

The figures of the Half moon and Stars may feem alfo to confirm the fame opinion For the old Gothic Nations had the fame notion of their mighty God *Thor*, as the Phœnicians had of their *Sun*, their μόνος οὐρανοῦ θεὸς, *cujus nutum Planetæ reliquaque fidera obfervabant*, the only God of Heaven, to whofe direction the Planets and other Stars, were fubject, and this was the Deity that the old Pagan Saxons ador'd, above all other Gods

D *Andr Fountaine* Differt ad Numb Sax. p 165 The learned Dr Hickes is of opinion, that the words *Thur Gut Luetis* in this curious Coin (fuppofing them to be the true reading) ought rather to be render'd *Thor Deus patrius*

But N Keder, a worthy member of the College of Antiquaries at Stockholme, publifhed a critical difcourfe upon it at Leipfick, A D 1703 wherein he endeavours to fhew, that the Legend has no relation to the northern God *Thor*, though he acknowledges, that the additional embroidery of the *Moon* and *Stars*, fuits well enough with that account which their Writers have given of this Deity He thinks it probable, that the Imagery reprefents our Saviour, as *King of Kings*, according to the practice of other Nations in the early times of Chriftianity, and that *Thurgut* on the reverfe, is the proper name of the Mint-mafter; which is agreeable to the ufage obferved in moft of the Coins of our *Saxon* Kings, as he proves by feveral inftances For *Luetis* he reads *Luntis*, by which word he believes that the piece was coined at *London*; but whether in the City of that name here in England, or in that of *Schonen*, in the dominions of his own Soveraign, he refers to the determination of his Readers

Another Opinion, is that of the famous G *Leibnitz*, who believes that this is a Medal ftruck in honour of *Thurgut*, the Admiral and General of thofe *Danifh* Pirates, who (in the year 1016) block'd up our great City of *London*, whofe name (for our *Englifh* Hiftorians fay nothing of him) he learns from the Saxon Hiftory of *Ditbmar*, Bifhop of Merfeburg

Not. G *Wotton* in *Hicke* Thefaur To the feveral Conjectures and Opinions concerning this famous and moft valuable Coin, I will fubjoin what is faid of it by a learned perfon, and an excellent Judge of thefe matters, Sir *Andrew Fountaine*; *Numifmatum omnium, quæ aut Anglo Saxonibus aut Anglo-Danis, in ufu fuiffe videntur, nullum notatu dignius eft, quàm id Literis* Runicis *infcriptum, quod poffidet Vir genere & ingenio clarus*, Radulphus Thorefbeius *Leodienfis*; i e Of all the Coins, which feem to have been in ufe, either among the Anglo-Saxons or Anglo-Danes; there is none that more deferves our Notice and Regard, than that, with a *Runick* Infcription, which is in the poffeffion of *Ralph Thoresby* of Leeds, a perfon of an ancient Family, and an excellent Genius Differt Epift. ad Com Pemb

As to the forementioned Roman *Way*, it may not be amifs to give you here the courfe of it through this County, at one view Firft then, it paffes through a large Camp where the ftone of King *Marius* formerly ftood; inftead of which there is another erected call'd *Rere-Crofs* Thence, through *Maiden-Caftle*, a fmall fquare fort, in which has been found Roman mortar next, it runs quite through *Market-Brough*, over *Brough-Fair-hill*, on which are fome *tumuli*, *barrows*, or ancient burying-places Then, leaving *Warcop* (a pretty village which gave name to the *Warcops*,) on the left-hand it paffes along *Sandford-moor*, and fo down a delicate horfe-race to *Cowplanbeck-brig*, where, on the right, are the ruin'd foundations of a noble round tower, and near it on the left, *Ormfide-hall*, the feat of the ancient family of *Hiltons*, Ormfide-hall Then by *Apleby* to the Camps upon *Crackenthorp-moor*, fo, through the Down-end of *Kirkby-Thore*, and through *Sawerby*, a village of the *Dalftons* of *Akernbank*. then all along by the fide of *Whinfeld-Park* to Hart-horn-tree, which may feem to give name to *Hornby-hall*, a feat of the *Dalftons*, and to have borrow'd its own from a *Stag* which was cours'd by a fingle Grey-hound to the *Red Kirk* in Scotland, and back again to this place, where, both being fpent, the Stag leapt the pales, but dy'd on the other fide, and the Grey hound, attempting to leap, fell, and dy'd on this fide Whence they nail'd up their heads upon the tree; and (the dog's name being *Hercules*) they made this rhyme upon them

Hercules kill'd Hart-a greefe,
And Hart a greefe kill'd Hercules

In the midft of the Park, not far from hence, is the *three brether tree* (fo call'd becaufe there were three of them, whereof this was the leaft) thirteen yards and a quarter in circumference, a good way from the root From Hart-horn-tree, the way goes directly weftward to the *Countefs pillar*, erected by *Anne* Countefs Dowager of *Penbroke*, and adorn'd with *Coats of Arms*, *Dials*, &c with an *Obelifk* on the top colour'd with black, and this Infcription in brafs, declaring the occafion and meaning of it

THIS PILLAR WAS ERECTED ANNO 1656
BY THE RIGHT HONO ANNE COUNTESS DOWAGER OF
PENBROKE AND SOLE HEIR OF THE RIGHT
HONORABLE GEORGE EARL OF CUMBERLAND, &c
FOR A MEMORIAL OF HER LAST PARTING IN THIS PLACE
WITH HER GOOD AND PIOUS MOTHER THE RIGHT HONORABLE
MARGARET COUNTESS DOWAGER OF CUMBERLAND
THE SECOND OF APRIL 1616 IN MEMORY WHEREOF
SHE ALSO LEFT AN ANNUITY OF FOUR POUNDS
TO BE DISTRIBUTED TO THE POOR WITHIN THIS
PARISH OF BROUGHAM EVERY SECOND DAY OF APRIL
FOR EVER UPON THE STONE TABLE HERE BY

LAUS DEO

Broughamcastle — From this Pillar, the *Way* carries us to *Brougham castle*, mentioned below, and from thence, directly to *Lowther-bridge*, and so over *Emot* in to Cumberland]

Crawdundale waith — Hard by *Whelp castle*, at *Crawdundale waith*, there appear ditches, rampires, and great mounts of earth cast up, among which was found this Roman Inscription, transcrib'd for me by the above-mention'd *Reginald Bainbrig* School master of *Appleby* It was cut in a rough sort of rock, but the fore part of it was worn away with age

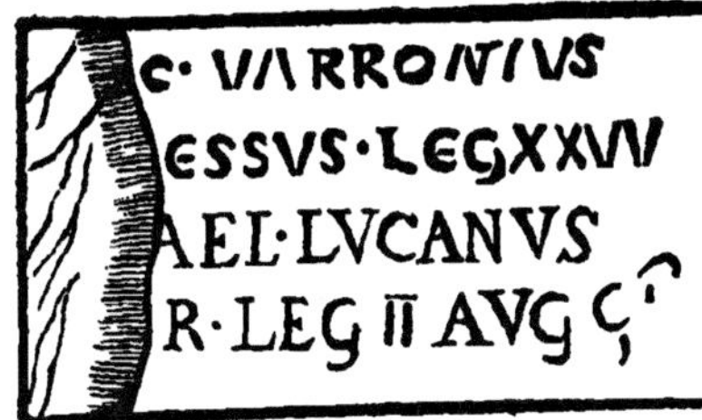
C· VARRONIVS
ESSVS·LEGXXVV
AEL·LVCANVS
R·LEG II AVG

i e (as I read it) *Varronius Præfectus legion s vicesimæ Valentis victricis —— Aelius Lucanus Præfectus legionis secundæ Augustæ, castrametati sunt*, or some such thing [The two upper lines are cut very deep, but the two lower with a lighter hand, and in a much finer and more polite Character For which reason, one may conclude them to be different Inscriptions, and the rudeness of the Characters in the first, must needs argue it to be of much greater Antiquity And what may the more induce us to believe them two distinct Inscriptions, is the writing of the letter A, which in *Varronius* wants the cross stroke, whereas all the three in the two last lines are according to the common way of writing] The *Legio Vicesima Valens Victrix*, garrison'd at *Deva* or West Chester, as also the *Legio secunda Augusta*, which was in garrison at *Isca* or *Caer Leon* in Wales, being both detach'd against the enemy in these parts, seem to have fix'd, and pitch'd their camps for some time in this place, and it is probable that the Offi ers, in memory thereof, might engrave this in the rock [Or, what if one should say, that this was the place which afforded the Romans a supp'y of Stones for their building hereabouts, and that upon this account the Inscriptions were left here? The truth of the fact appears from the Stones dug up out of the Foundations at *Kirkby-thore*, most of which did certainly come from hence, and that upon those occasions they us'd to leave Inscriptions behind them, is confirm'd by the like instances both in *He'beck Scar*, by the river *Gelt*, and on *Leuge Crag* near *Naward Castle* in Gilsland, from whence they had their stone for the *Picts wall* Doubtless there have been more Letters here, though now defac'd Also, the forementioned Mr *Maclel* discover'd the following Inscription, not observ'd before (Kirkby thore)

LEG II AVG XXIN

(This was, ...) When these were done, is hard to determine though, to signify the time, these words were engraven in large Characters, and are still to be seen in a rock near it, CN OCT. COT COSS But I do not find in the *Fasti*, that any two of that name were Consuls together This Observation however I have made, that from the age of *Severus* to that of *Gordianus* and after, the Letter A in all the Inscriptions found in this Island, wants the cross-stroke, and is engrav'd thus, Λ, [as it is in the first of those Inscriptions] (Λ for A)

From hence the *Eden* runs along, not far from *Howgil*, a castle of the *Sandfords*, but the Roman Military way runs directly west through * *Whinfeild* (a large Park thick set with trees) to *Brovomacum*, twenty Italian miles, but seventeen English, from *Verteræ*, as Antoninus has fix'd it He calls it also *Brocovum*, as the Notitia *Brocomacum*, from which we understand that the † Company of the *Defensores* had their abode here Though Age has consum'd both it's buildings and splendour, the name is preserv'd almost entire in the present one of *Brougham*, [the Antiquity whereof hath been further confirm'd of late years, by the discovery of several Coins, Altars, and other testimonies] (Howgil; * See above *Whin* in the North is the same as a *Furz*; Brovonacum; † *Numerus*; Brougham)

Here the river *Eimot* (which runs out of a large Lake, and is for some space the border between this County and Cumberland) receives the river *Loder*; near the head of which, at *Shap*, formerly *Hepe* (a small monastery built by *Thomas Fitz-Gospatrick*, the son of *Orm*) there † was a *Well*, which, like *Euripus*, ebb'd and flow'd several times in a day, [Which *intermittent* Springs are no rarities in hollow and rocky Countries, though perhaps not so commonly observ'd, as they might be The cause of this unconstant breaking-out of their streams, is purely fortuitous, and therefore the effect is not always very lasting, nor is there any ebbing-fountain at present to be heard of near *Shap*] Here are large Stones in the form of Pyramids (some of them nine foot high and fourteen thick) almost in a direct line, and at equal distances, for a mile together. They seem design'd to preserve the memory of some Action or other but time has put it beyond all possibility of pointing out the particular occasion Upon *Loder* is [*Bampton*, where is a good Free-School, built and endowed by Dr. *John Sutton*, a worthy Divine in his time, and also] a place of the same denomination with the river, which as likewise *Strickland*, not far off) hath given name to an ancient and famous family, [the *Lowthers* This is one of those English Sirnames, concerning which Sir *Henry Spelman*, at the request of Sir *Peter Osburn*, desired the thoughts of the learned *O Wormius*, who observes it to be amongst the most ancient names of the Kings of Denmark, and (deriving it from the words *Loth* and *Er*) makes it to carry a *fortunate* stock of *boneur*, in its very Etymology The conjecture of this excellent Antiquary seems to be further strengthen'd by the name of *Lotharius*, which we meet with so frequently among the Emperors and other Princes of Germany And yet, after all this, it is perhaps more agreeable to truth, to believe that both the seat and family of *Lowther* in this County (as *Lauder*, and *Lauderdale* in *Scotland*) have their names from that neighbouring river, which in the old * British language signifies *water* that is *clear*, *limpid*, and *without mud*, all, very proper Epithets to this river The now *noble* family of *Lowther* hath made a great figure in this County for many generations, (Loder, riv; Shap; † Is, C; Bampton; Strickland; Mon Dan p ..., &c; * Gladdwr)

tions; and the late Sir *John Lowther* was Keeper of the Privy Seal, and one of the Lords Justices of England during the absence of King William; and was, for his many eminent Services and great Abilities, advanced to the dignity of Baron of *Lowther* and Viscount *Lonsdale* Here, he erected a noble Seat, adorn'd by him with curious Paintings, and rich Furniture; which hath been lately burn'd down

A little before *Loder* joins the *Emot*, it passes by a large round entrenchment, with a plain piece of ground in the middle, and a passage into it on either side; the form of which is this

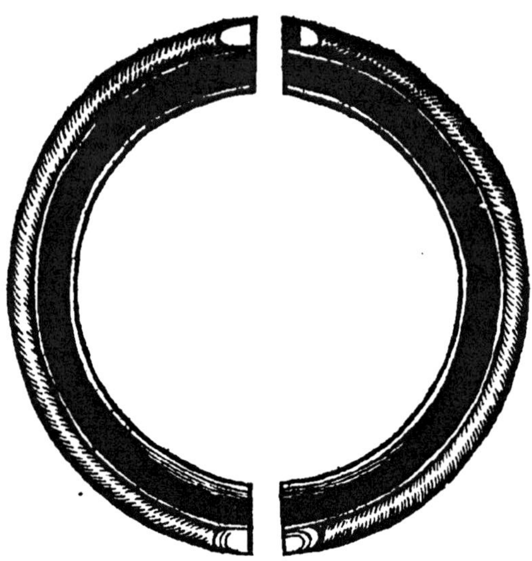

It goes by the name of King *Arthur's Round Table* and it is possible enough, it might be a *Justing-place* However, that it was never design'd for a place of strength, appears from the trenches, being on the inside Near this, is another great Fort of Stones, heap'd up in form of a horse-shoe, and opening towards it, call'd by some King *Arthur's* Castle, and by others *Mayburgh*, or *Maybrough*

Emot may be called the *Ticinus* of the two Counties of Westmorland and Cumberland (falling in a clear and rapid stream, out of *Ulleswater*, as the *Tesin* doth from the *Lago Maggiore*,) and will yet be more remarkable on account of this and the neighbouring remains of Antiquity upon its banks, if we believe them to be, as I think we may, Monuments of that treaty of Peace and Union, which was finish'd by King Æthelstan, in the year 926, with *Constantine* King of Scots, *Haeval* King of the Western Britains or Stratcluid-Welsh, *&c* of which St *Dunelmensis* (and, from him, *R Hoveden* in the same words) gives us this account, *Hi omnes*, &c *All these, finding that they could not make head against him, and desiring Peace of him, met together on the 4th of the Ides of July, in the place which is called* Eamotum, *and enter'd into a League, that was confirmed by the said Oath* The very name also of Mayburg extremely favours this

Wolufpa, St. 1 and 51

Opinion For in the old Islandick Writers, we have *Mogur*, and *Mogu*, in the plural, for *Son* and *Sons* But in the Islandick Lexicon of

† Gram Sax p. 108, 109 111

* Goth Glos sar in voc Magus

G. Andreas, *Mogr* is render'd by *Affinis*, *Gener*, *Socer*; *and Magel* is *Affinitas* The same thing † Dr *Hickes* observes of the Saxon words Mago, Magu, *&c.* * and saith Junius, *Ab hoc nexu*, &c *From this relation of blood, the word came to degrees to be transferr'd to any* intimate union *or* friendship *among Men* or *Societies*, where he observes, that in the old Cimbrian or Runick Language, *Mag* signifies *Socius*, a Companion So that *Mayburg* seems to have been (on occasion of the forementioned Treaty) so called, as if one should say, *The Fort of Union* or *Alliance* Would *M Zeiller*, and the rest of the German Geographers give me leave, I should willingly fetch the name of the famous City of *Magdeburgh* from the same Original, since *Magde*, in the Teutonick, signifies *kindred*, as well as a *Girl*, or *Virgin*; and *Irenopolis* might found as well as *Parthenopolis*, as they love to call it The fable of the Image of *Venus* anciently worship'd there (supported by the Arms of the Town) is of the like authority with our ‡ *Llan Dian*] ‡ Middlesex

Lower down, at the confluence of *Loder* and *Eimot*, was dug up (in the year 1602) this Stone, set up in memory of *Constantine* the Great

IMP
C VAL
CONSTA-
NTINO
PIINT
AVG

[Here, the *Loder* joyns *Eimot*, which runs by *Barton*, a very large Parish, reaching from the bounds of *Rydal* and *Ambleside* on the south to the river *Loder* on the north They have a School well endow'd by that learned and great man, Dr *Gerard Langbain*, Provost of *Queen's* College in Oxford, who was a native of this Barton

parish;

parish, as was also Dr *William Lancaster* the late Provost, who was a considerable Benefactor to the said School]

Isanparles

After *Eimot* has been for some space the boundary between this County and *Cumberland*, near *Isanparles*, a rock well known in the neighbourhood, which Nature hath made of a very difficult ascent, with several caverns and windings, as if she design'd it for a retreat in troublesome times, it empties its own waters, with those of other rivers, into *Eden*, a few miles below having first receiv'd the little river *Blencarne* (the boundary on this side between Westmoland and Cumberland,) upon which I understood there were vast ruins of a Castle, by the name of the *Hanging Walls of Marcantonby*, that is (as they tell you) of *Mark Antony*, [nothing whereof now remains]

Hanging walls of *Mar a nto-nby*

† *Ralph Meschines*, and *Hugh de Morvil*, are said to have been Lords thereof, before

Arms of the *Veponts*

Pin Term Mich R 6 H 8

The † first Lord of Westmorland that I know of, was *Robert de Veteri ponte* or *Vipont*, who bore *in a shield gules six Annulets Or* For King John gave him the *Bailwick and Rents of Westmorland, by the service of four Knights* Whereupon the *Cliffords* his successors, [and after them the *Tufions*,] have holden the *Sheriffdom of Westmorland*, down to this time For *Robert* the last of the *Vipons*, left only two daughters, *Sybil* wife of *Roger* Lord *Clifford*, and *Idonea* wife of *Roger de Leyburne* A long time after, King Richard the second created *Ralph de Nevil* or *New-Ville* (Lord of *Raby*, and a person of a very noble and ancient English Pedigree, being descended from Uhtred Earl of Northumberland) first Earl of Westmorland, whose posterity by his first wife *M* daughter of the Earl of *Stafford*, enjoy'd this honour, till *Charles*, hurry'd on by a boundless Ambition to violate his duty to Queen Elizabeth and his Country, brought an eternal infamy upon this noble family, and a foul blemish upon his own honour, so that, leaving his native Country, he liv'd and dy'd miserably in the *Netherlands* His issue by the second wife *Katharine*, daughter of *John* of *Gaunt* Duke of Lancaster, became so famous and numerous, that, almost at the same time, there flourish'd of that Family, the Earl of *Salisbury*, the Earl of *Warwick*, the Earl of *Kent*, the Marquiss of *Montacute*, Baron *Latimer*, and Baron *Ivergevenny*

Earls of Westmorland

[From the year 1584 this Honour lay dead, till King James the first, in the year 1624, advanced *Francis Fane* (as a Descendant of the said *Nevil*) to the dignity of Earl of Westmorland, who was succeeded in that Honour by *Mildmay* his Son and *Charles* his Grandson Which *Charles*, dying without issue, was succeeded by his brother *Vere Fane*, father of *Vere Fane*, who died unmarried, and of *Thomas* the present Earl]

* 26 C

In this County are * 32 *large Parishes*; [*besides a great number of* Chapels *of Ease*]

More rare Plants growing in Westmoreland

Adiantum petræum perpusillum Anglicum foliis bifidis vel trifidis *Small rock Maiden hair whose leaves are divided into two or three segments Found by Mr Newton and Mr Lawson on Buzzardrough crag near Wrenose Dr Plukenet in his Phytography hath figured this, and entitled it* Adiantum radicosum [illegible], foliis minus bisectis, cæteris vero integris [illegible] *distinguishing it from that found by Mr. George Daire near Tunbridge in Kent*; *which he calls* Adianthum radicosum globuliferum, humi sparsum *I am now of opinion, that neither of them are any species of* Adiantum, *but mere mosses*

Allium sylvestre amphicarpon, foliis porraceis, floribus & nucleis purpureis An Allium seu Moly montanum primum *Clus? Broad leav'd mountain Garlick with purple flowers In Troutbeck-holm by great Strickland*

Bistorta minor nostras *Park.* Alpina minor *C B.* minima *J B Small Bistort or Snakeweed In several places of this County, as at Crosby Ravensworth See Yorkshire*

Cratæogonon foliis brevibus obtusis Westmorlandicum *Eye bright Cow-wheat with short blunt leaves Near Orton beside a rivulet running by the way that leads thence to Crosby*

Cerasus avium sive Padus Theophrasti *Birds Cherry common among the mountains as well in this Country as in Yorkshire, where see the Synonymes*

Cerasus sylvestris fructu minimo cordiformi *P B The least wild Heart cherry-tree, vulgarly called the Merry-tree About Rosgill*

Chamæcistus seu Helianthemum folio Pilosellæ minoris Fuchsii *J B (The* Pilosella minor Fuchsii *is nothing but Mountain Cudweed or Catsfoot) Hoary dwarf mountain Cistus or Holy-rose, with Cats-foot leaves Found by Mr Newton on some rocks near Kendale*

Gentianella fugax verna seu præcox *Dwarf Vernal Gentian Found by Mr Fitz-Roberts on the backside of Helse-fell-nab near Kendall, as also in the Parks on the other side of Kendall on the back of Birkbeg It begins to flower in April, and continues to flower till June*

Geranium batrachoides flore eleganter variegato. *Crow foot Cranesbill with a party-coloured flower In old Deer park by Thornthwait This, though it may be but an accidental variety, yet is so ornamental to a garden, that it deserves to be taken notice of*

Geranium batrachoides montanum nostras *Mountain Crowfoot-Cranesbill In the hedges and among the bushes in the mountainous meadows and pastures of this County no less than in Yorkshire*

Filix saxatilis caule tenui fragili Adiantum album folio Filicis *J B Stone Fern with slender brittle stalks and finely cut leaves On old stone walls and rocks plentifully*

Filicula petræa crispa seu Adiantum album floridum perelegans *Small flowering Stone fern At the bottom of stone walls made up with earth in Orton parish and other places plentifully*

Filix ramosa minor *J B* Saxatalis ramosa, nigris punctis notata *C B* Pumila saxatilis prima Clusii *Park* Dryopteris Tragi *Ger The lesser branched fern On the sides of the mountains, in shady places especially*

Gladiolus lacustris Dortmanni *Clus cur post* Leucoium palustre flore subcœruleo *C B* Gladiolus lacustris Clusii sive Leucoium palustre flore cœruleo Bauhini *Park Water Gladiole In a pool call'd Huls-water, and in Winander mere plentifully*

Gramen sparteum spica foliacea graminea majus *P B Grass upon grass In an Isle call'd House holm in Huls water*

Gramen junceoides lanatum alterum Danicum *Park* Item Gr junceum montanum spica subcœrulea Cambro-Britannicum *ejusdem* Juncus Alpinus cum cauda leporina *J B.* Alpinus capitulo lanuginoso sive Schœnolaguros *C B Hare tail rush or Moss crops On Mosses and boggy places*

Hellebo-

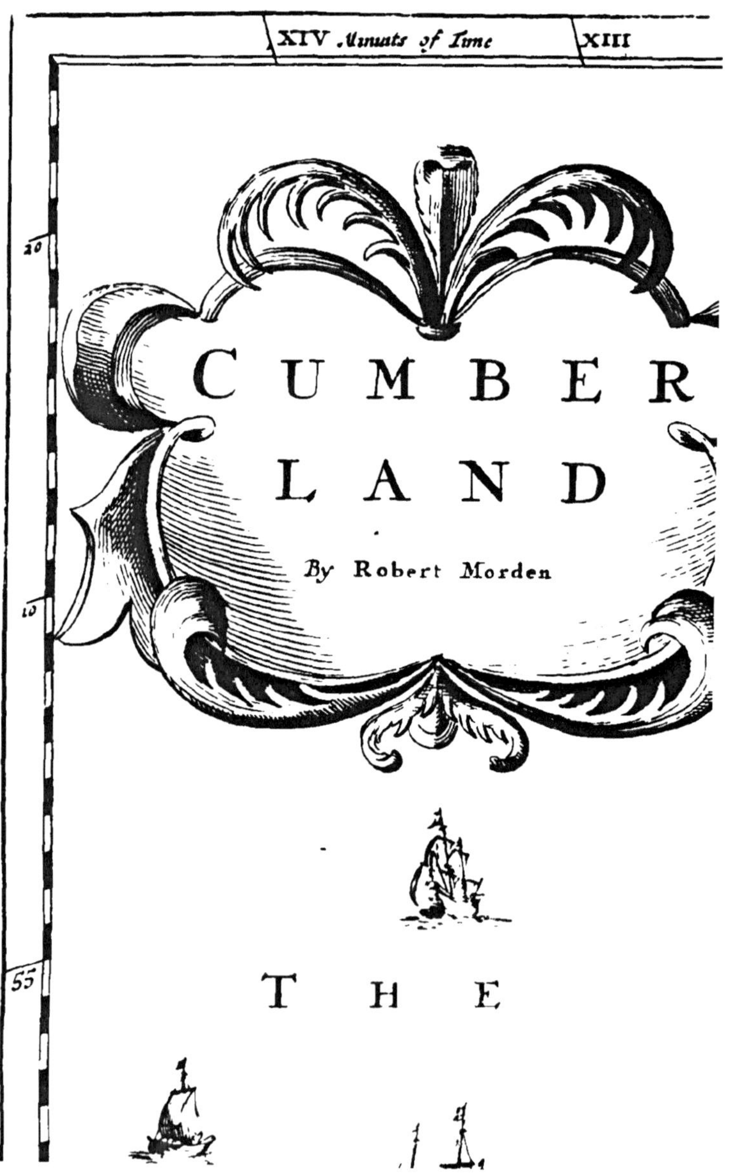
XIV Minuts of Time
XIII
20
10
55
CUMBER
LAND
By Robert Morden
THE

XII
XI
X
IX
PART of SCOTLAND.
Harelaw
Stangertick Side
Lothel
Kings Field
Cannobye
Kinment
Kirkanders
The Mote
The Masthorn
Buckness
Sowport
DALE
ESH
Nether by
Gretney Kirk
Durno Kirk
The Red Kirk
Anand Castle
Tordoff
West Mill
Solway Frith or Ituna Flu now Eden R.
Bowness
Glason
Drumbugh Cast
Cardornack
Whitrede
Moricambo
Chappel of y Grune
Skinburnes
Silloth
Wulsty Castle
Holm Cultrum
NORTH
Sowterfield
Mawborow Old
Dubmill
Newton in Ardale
ALLERDALE
Allonby
Crosby
Alwarby
Canonby
Birkby
Elne R
Dereham
Gilcrost
Wardal
Newton Beacon
Redmaine
Sunderland
Bothell
The Mines
Bolton
Ulldale
Torpenhow
Plumland
Blennerhasset
Brumfield
Crokedake
Alhallows
Wigton
West Ward
Forest
Rose Castl
Castra exploratorum
Warnel
Sebraham
Heskett
Cardew
Dalston
Thursby
Crofton
Orton
Fingland
Kirk Andrews
Burgh
CARLISLE
Stanwich
Rowcliff
Houghton
Tarraby
Scalby Cast
Newtown
Kirk Levington
Arthur et
Brakenhill
WARD
Skutterby
Harper Hill
Staple ton
Bew Castle
Spade Adam
Kirk Cambeck
Askerton Castle
Trettermane
Lanercost
Denton Over
Denton Nether
Naworth Castle
Brampton
Farlam
Crosby
Newby
Corby Castle
Wetherall
Cumrew
Ainstable
Croglin
Armanthwate Cast
Barrock Wood
Inglewood
Forest
Raughton
Highgate Castle
Brathwate
Hutton
Skelton
Lazonby
Kirk Oswald
Glassonby
Langanby
Culgarth
Hornby
Unthank
Lamonby
Johnby
Graystoch castle
Penrith
Threlkeld
Newbiggin
Thwates
Grysdall Chap

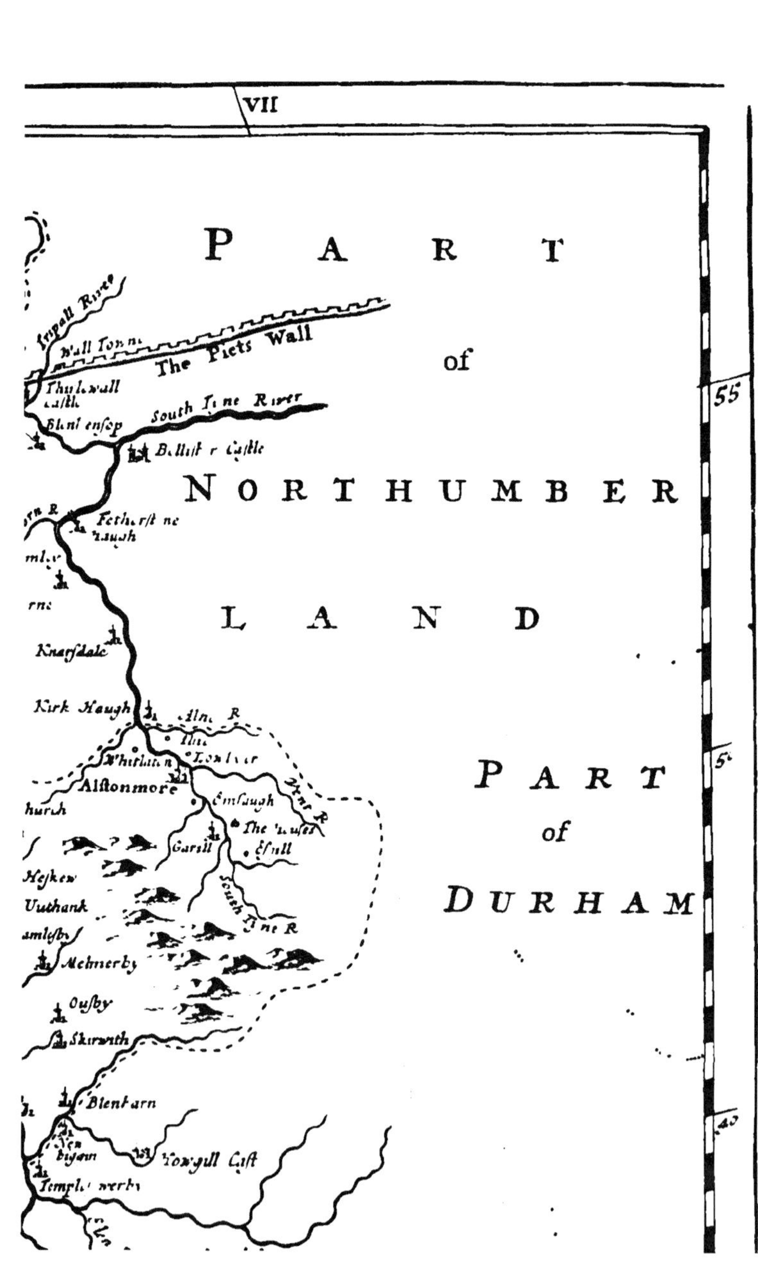

VII
PART
of
NORTHUMBER
LAND
The Picts Wall
South Tine River
55
Knarsdale
Kirk Haugh
Alstonmore
South Tine R
PART
of
DURHAM
Uuthank
Ousby
Skirwith
Blenkarn

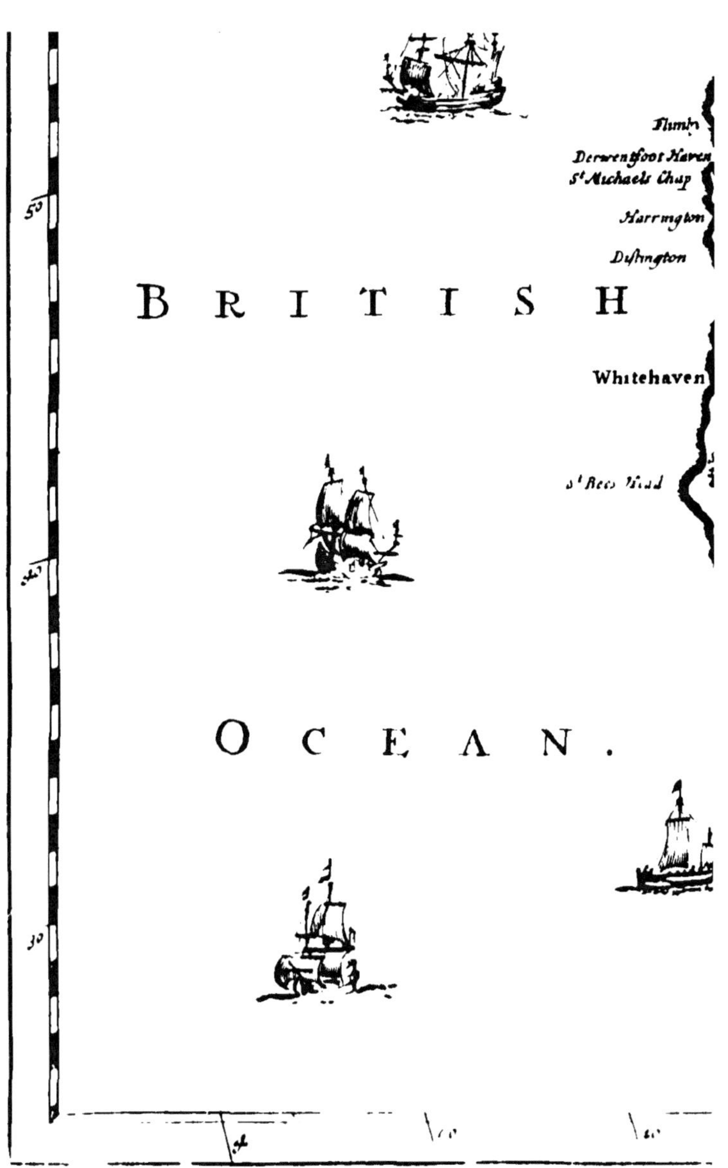
Derwentfoot Haven
St Michaels Chap
Harrington
Distington
BRITISH
Whitehaven
OCEAN.
50
30

Armanthwate
Pap Castle
Bride Kirk
Isle
Tallantire
Camerton
Ribton
St Lawrence
Devonby
Satmurther
Cockermouth
Bassing thwate
Skiddow Hill
Crosthwate Church
Keswick
The Mines Royal
Threlkeld
Matteraale
Wathermulach
Douthwate
St Johns
Fornside
Glenkwren R.
Glenkroden R.
Patterdale
Penrodock
Thakthwate
Dacor castle
Dalemain
Barton
Pole
Askham
Crostermond
Markendale Chap
Bridgham
Workington
Dean
Eglesfield
Embleson
Thornthwate
Lorton
Brathwate
Ullock
Bradsay Hall
Brakenthwate
Portinscal
Lampley
SOUTH
Newland Chap
Grange
Armeboth
Legburg thwate
Arladon
ALLERDALE
WARD
Oswald How
COPELAND
Enerdale
Cleator
Dent Hill
Copeland Forest
Borrodale
Derwent R.
Dunbalrase Stones
Gresmere
WESTM
Egremont
Hale
Warsdale Chap
Hard Knot Hill
Great Langdale
Amble Side
Troutbeck
St Johns
Bekermet
Calder
Nether Warsdale
Little Langdale
Shire Stones
Upon Wrenest
St Brides
Ponsonby
Sello field
Gosforth
Miterdale
Eskdale
Hawks head
Cowgarth
Dale Garth
PART
LAN
Irton
P Drigg
Black Hall
Carlton
Moncaster
Esk R.
Four neß Fels
of
Irt R.
Raven glas
Wawburthwate
St Johns
Duddon R.
Corno
Newbridge
Seaton
Park
LANCA
Bootell
Whidbeck
Broughton
Whittecham
SHIER.
Ullum
Kirkby
3 Degrees

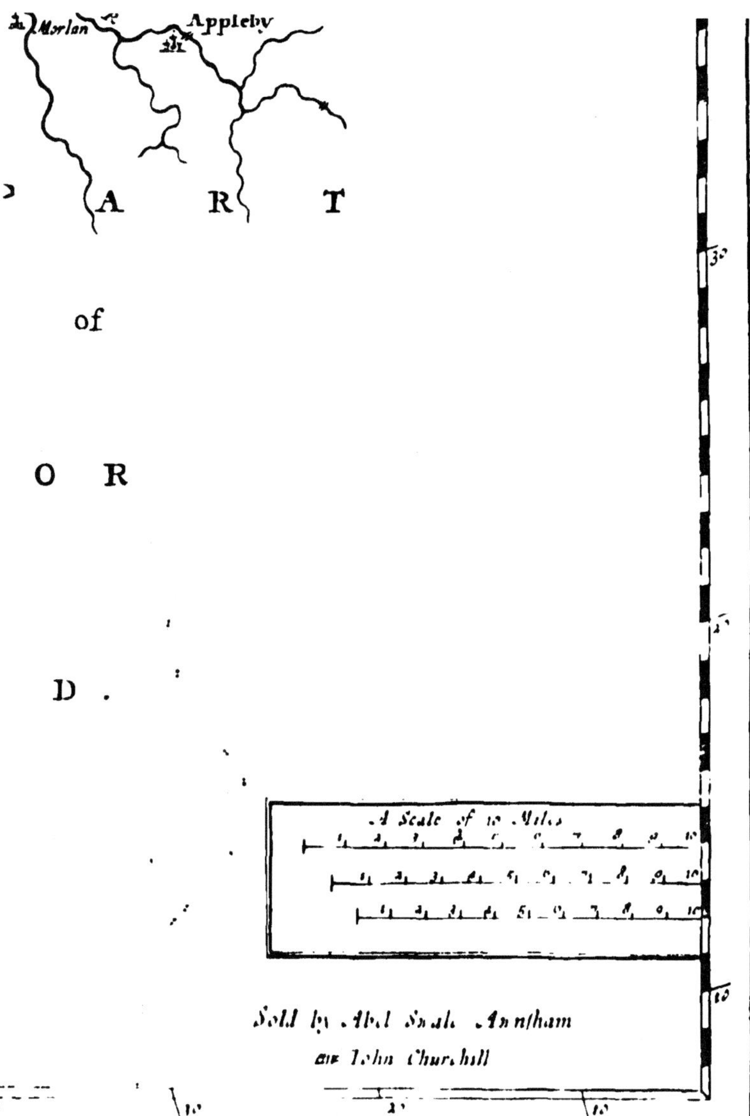
Morlan
Appleby
A R T
of
O R
D .
A Scale of 10 Miles
Sold by Abel Swale Awnsham
and John Churchill

Helleborine minor flore albo *Park.* *The lesser white flower'd bastard Hellebore. In Sir John Lowther's Wood, directly against Askham hall*

Hieracium fruticosum latifolium glabrum *Park* *The smoother broad leav'd bushy Hawkweed Near a Lake call'd Huls-water*

Hieracium macrocaulon hirsutum folio rotundiore *D Lawson* An Hierac fruticosum folio subrotundo *C B* *Round-leav'd rough Hawkweed with a long stalk. By Bucbarrow well in long Sledale*

Hieracium [illegible] hirsutum folio rotundiore *D Lawson* *On the rocks by the rivulet between Shap and Anna-well.*

Juncus parvus calamo seu scapo supra paniculam compactam longius producto *Newtoni* *Small rush with the shaft produced to a great length above its compact panicle Not far from Ambleside*

Juniperus Alpina *J B* *Clus* *Park* *Mountain dwarf Juniper, call'd by the Country people Savine, as well here as in Wales Upon the tops of the Mountains*

Lilium convallium angustifolium *D Lawson* *Narrow leav'd Lily convally By Water-fall-bridge and elsewhere in this County*

Meum *Ger* vulgatius *Park* foliis Anethi *C B* Meu vulgare, seu Radix ursina *J B* *Common Spignell or Meu About two miles from Sedberg in the way to Orton abundantly in the meadows and pastures, where it is known to all the Country-people by the name of Bald money, or (as they pronounce it) Bawd money, the reason of which name I could not fish out*

Oxalis seu Acetosa rotundifolia repens Eboracensis folio in medio deliquium patiente *Moris Hist* *Round-leav'd Mountain-sorrel Observ'd by Mr Lawson on the Mountains of this County, and by Mr Fitz Roberts in Long Sledale near Bucbarrow-well, and all along the rivulet that runs by the Well for a mile or more This never degenerates into the common Roman or French Sorrel*

Persicaria siliquosa *Ger* Noli me tangere *J B* Mercurialis sylvestris, Noli me tangere dicta, sive Persicaria siliquosa *Park* Balsamine lutea, sive Noli me tangere *C B* *Codded Arsmart, Quick in hand, Touch me not I observ'd it growing plentifully on the banks of Winander-mere near Ambleside, and in many other places*

Rubia erecta quadrifolia *J B* *Cross-wort-madder Near Orton, Winander mere, and elsewhere in this County plentifully*

Salix folio laureo sive lato glabro odorato *P B* *Bay-leav'd sweet Willow Frequent by the river sides in the meadows among the Mountains*

Tormentilla argentea *Park* Alpina folio sericeo *C B* Pentaphyllum seu potius Heptaphyllum argenteum flore muscoso *J B* Pentaphyllum petrosum, Heptaphyllum Clusii *Ger* Vera & genuina Alchymillæ species est *Cinque foil Ladies-mantle On the rocks by the side of the Lake call'd Huls-water, or as some write it Ulles-water*

To these I might add, Lunaria minor ramosa, & Lunaria minor foliis dissectis, *That is, branched Moon wort, and cut leav'd Moon-wort, both observ'd by Mr Lawson at Great Strickland, though they be (I suppose) but accidental varieties*

Vitis Idæa magna, sive Myrtillus grandis *J B* *The great Billberry Bush. In the forest of Whinfield. Mr Lawson,*

CUMBERLAND.

BEfore Westmorland, to the West, lies *Cumberland*, in Latin *Cumbria*, [and in Saxon Cumbꞃa-land, and Cumeꞃ land,] the furthest County in this part of England, as being bounded by Scotland on the North It is encompass'd by the *Irish Sea* to the South and West, and on the East, above Westmorland, it borders upon Northumberland It had the name from the Inhabitants; who were the true and genuine Britains, and call'd themselves in their own language *Kumbri* or *Kambri* For, that the Britains, in the heat of the Saxon wars, posted themselves here for a long time, we have the authority of our Histories, and of Marinus himself, who calls this County *Cumbrorum terra*, i e the Land of the *Cumbri* Not to mention the many names of places purely British, such are, *Caer-luel*, *Caer-dronoc*, *Pen rith*, *Pen rodoc*, &c which are plain evidences of the thing, and a pregnant proof of what I assert [And yet the opinion of a learned * Writer is different from this, viz that it is derived from our English *Cumber*, with relation to the lakes and mountains that *encumber* it, and make it difficult for travellers to pass] * Sommer's Glossar

Though the Northern situation renders the Country cold, and the Mountains are rough and uneven; yet it has a *Variety* which affords a very agreeable Prospect For after swelling rocks, and crowding mountains, big as it were with Metals (between which, are Lakes stored with all sorts of wild Fowl,) you come to rich hills cloath'd with flocks of sheep, and below these are spread out pleasant large plains, which are tolerably fruitful The Ocean also which beats upon this shore, affords great plenty of the best Fish, and as it were upbraids the Inhabitants for their idleness, in not applying themselves more closely to the fishing trade Varietas

The South part of this County is call'd *Copeland* and *Coupland*, because it rears its head in sharp mountains, call'd by the Britains *Kopa*; (or as others will have it) *Copeland*, as if one should say, *Copperland*, from the rich veins of *Copper* In this part, at the sandy mouth of the river *Duden*, by which it is divided from Lancashire, is *Millum*, a Castle of the ancient family of the *Hodlestons* [The first Lords whereof stil'd themselves *de Millum*, as *William de Millum*, and *Henry de Millum* about Henry the first's time But in the time of Henry the third, the heiress of *Adam de Millum* transferr'd it by marriage to her husband *John Huddleston*; whose posterity doth now enjoy it] From hence, the shore wheeling to the North, comes to *Ravenglas*, a harbour for ships, and commodiously surrounded with two rivers, where (as I am told) there have been found Roman Inscriptions Some will have it to have been formerly called *Aven glas*, i e an * *azure sky coloured river*; and tell you abundance of stories about King *Eveling*, who had his Palace here Copeland Millum Castle Ravenglas * Cæruleus here One of these rivers, *Esk*, rises at the foot of *Hardknott*, a steep ragged mountain; on the top of which were lately dug-up huge stones, and the foundation of a Castle; which is very strange, considering the mountain is so steep, that one can hardly get up it [These stones are possibly the ruins of some Church or Chapel, which was built upon the mountain For *Wormius* in his *Danish Monuments* gives instances of the like in Denmark; and it was thought an extraordinary piece of devotion, upon the planting of Christianity in these parts, to erect *Crosses* and build Chapels in the most eminent places, as being both nearer Heaven, and more conspicuous: they were commonly dedicated to St *Michael* That large Tract of Mountains on the East side of the County, call'd *Cross Fells*, had the name given them upon that account, for before, they were call'd *Fiends-Fell*, or *Devils-Fell*, and *Dilston* a small town under them, is contracted from *Devil's-Town*] Higher up, the little brook *Irt* runs into the Sea, [on the bank of which is the Manour and Town of *Irton*, or *Irtindale*, now in the possession of an ancient family of that name; of which *Radulphus de Irton*, Bishop of Carlisle, A D 1280 was a branch] In this brook, the shell fish, eagerly sucking in the dew, *conceive* and *bring forth* Pearls, or (to use the Poet's word) * *Shell berries* These the Inhabitants gather up at low water; and the Jewellers buy them of the poor people for a trifle, but sell them at a good price. Of these, and such like, *Marbodæus* seems to speak in that verse,

Hard Knott

Dilston

Irt, river

Irton

* *Baccas concheas* Pearls See Pliny

Gignit & insignes antiqua Britannia baccas

And *Britain's* ancient shores great Pearls produce

[The *Muscle-Pearls* are frequently found in other rivers hereabouts, as also in Wales and foreign Countries Sir *John Narborough*, in his late Voyage to the *Magellanick Straits*, A D 1670 tells us, he met with many of them there *Abundance of Muscles* (says he) *and many Seed-pearls in every Muscle* And Sir *Richard Hawkins*, who had been there before him, affirms the same thing in his † *Observations*, adding also, that *the Muscles are very good Diet* There was, not long since, a Patent granted to some Gentlemen and others, for *Pearl-fishing* in this river, but whether it will turn to any account, is uncertain for they are not very plentiful here, and if they are a valuable commodity, they might be had in abundance, and at no extraordinary charge, from the *Straits of Magellan* Tacitus (in the Life of *Agricola*) takes notice, that the British Pearls are *subfusca ac liventia*, of a dark brown and lead colour; but that character ought not to have been given in general terms Bede's account is more just; where he says, they are of all colours Those that are not bright and shining (and such indeed are most of what we meet with in *Irt*, *Inn*, &c) are usually call'd *Sand pearl*, which are as useful in Physick as the finest, though not so valuable in beauty The great Naturalist of our Age, Dr *Lister*, says, he has found sixteen of those in one Muscle; and asserts of them all, that they are only *Senescentium Musculorum vitia*; or, the Scabs of old Muscles]

Page 7

† Printed Ann 1622 p 88

Hist Eccl l 1 c 1

De [illegible]

From hence, the shore goes out by degrees to the west, and makes a small Promontory, commonly call'd S *Bees*, instead of S *Bega* For *Bega*, a pious and religious Irish Virgin, led a solitary life there and to her sanctity they ascribe the Miracles, of taming a Bull, and of a deep Snow that by her Prayers fell on Midsummer day [Here also, the same holy Virgin is said to have founded a Nunnery; but it appears not that it was ever endow'd, or that it continued for any time a voluntary Society It is probable enough, that it was ruin'd and dispers'd in the civil wars before the Conquest, and that the Priory of *Benedictines*, built and endow'd afterwards by *William de Meschin*, was in the same place Here is a good Grammar-School, founded and endow'd by *Edmund Grindal* Archbishop of Canterbury, who was born at this place. It has a Library belonging to it, and is much improv'd by the munificence of Dr *Lamplugh* late Archbishop of York, Dr *Smith* late Bishop of Carlisle, Sir *John Lowther* of *Whitehaven*, and others The right of presenting a Master is in the Provost and Fellows of Queen's College in Oxford, to which Society its founder was also a considerable Benefactor] Scarce a mile from hence, is *Egremont*-Castle, seated upon a hill, formerly, the seat of *William de Meschines*, upon whom King Henry the first bestow'd it, to hold *by the service of one Knight, who should be ready, upon the King's Summons, to serve in the wars of Wales and Scotland* He left a daughter, the wife of William Fitz Duncan, of the Blood Royal of Scotland, by whose daughter also the estate came to the family of the *Lucies* and from them, by the *Multons* and *Fitz Walters*, the title of *Egremont* descended to the *Radcliffs* Earls of Sussex Notwithstanding, *Th Percy*, by the favour of King Henry the sixth, enjoy'd that title for some time, and was summon'd to Parliament by the name of *Thomas Percy of Egremont* [Below S *Bees*, is *White-haven*, so call'd from the *white* rocks and cliffs near it It is chiefly beholden for its improvement, to Sir *John Lowther*, who took his title of distinction from it, and whose son now enjoys a considerable estate there]

S Bees

See Stat 3 Jac 1 N 37

Egremont Castle

Close of [illegible] Lib Inq

White haven

From S *Bees* the Shore draws-in by little and little, and (as appears by the ruins) was fortify'd by the Romans in all such places as were convenient for landing For this was the utmost bound of the Roman Empire, and the Scots, when like a deluge they pour'd out of Ireland into our Island, met with the greatest opposition upon this coast It is very probable, that the little village *Moresby*, where is now a harbour for Ships, was one of those Forts There are many remains of Antiquity about it in the Vaults and Foundations of Buildings; several *Caverns*, which they call *Picts-holes*, and several pieces of stones dug up, with Inscriptions Upon one of them is, LVCIVS SEVERINVS ORDINATVS Upon another, COH VII And I saw this Altar (* lately dug-up there) with a little horned image of *Silvanus*;

The Shore fortify'd

Moresby

Picts-holes

* So said ann 1607

DEO SILVAN— —
COH II LING
CVI PRÆES— —
G POMPEIVS M—
SATVRNIN— —

To the God Silvanus the second Cohort of the Lingones under the command of G Pompeius M Saturninus

As also this fragment, which was copy'd out and sent me by J Fletcher, Lord of the Place

OB

....

....

OB PROSPE
RITATEM
CVLMINIS
INSTITVTI

But there has been no Inscription yet found, to encourage us to believe, that this was the *Morbium*, where the *Equites Catapbractarii* quarter'd; though the present name seems to imply it. Nor must I omit the mention of *Hay-Castle*, which I saw in the neighbourhood, very venerable for its antiquity, and which, the Inhabitants told me, belong'd formerly to the noble families of *Moresby* and *Distinton*.

Mori 31 — Hay Castle

After this, the river *Derwent* falls into the Ocean; which rising in *Borrodale* (a Vale surrounded with crooked hills) creeps among the mountains call'd *Derwent-fells*, in which, at *Newlands* and other places, some rich veins of Copper, not without a mixture of Gold and Silver, were discover'd † in our age, by *Thomas Thurland* and *David Hochstetter* a German of Augsburg, though known many ages before, as appears from the Close Rolls of Henry the third. About this, there was a memorable Trial between Queen *Elizabeth*, and *Thomas Percie* Earl of Northumberland and Lord of the Manour, but, by Virtue of the Prerogative Royal (it appearing that there were also veins of gold and silver) it it was carried in favour of the Queen. So far is it from being true, what Cicero has said in his Epistles to Atticus, *It is well known, that there is not so much as a grain of silver in the Island of Britain*. Nor would Cæsar, if he had known of those Mines, have told us, that the Britains made use of *imported* Copper, when these and some others afford such plenty, that not only all England is supply'd from them, but great quantities are yearly exported. Here is also found abundance of that Mineral-earth, or hard shining Stone, which we call *Black lead*, that is us'd by Painters in drawing their Lines, and † shading their pieces in black and white. Which, whether it be *Dioscorides*'s *Pnigitis*, or *Melanteria*, or *Ochre* (a sort of earth burnt black) for, was wholly unknown to the Ancients,] is a point that I cannot determine, and so shall leave it to the search of others. [The people thereabouts call it *Wadd*. It is much us'd in cleansing rusty Armour, having a particular virtue for that purpose. It is said, there is a Mine of it in the West Indies; but there is no need of importing any, for, as much may be dig here in one year, as will serve all Europe for several years. By the descriptions which the ancient Naturalists give us of their *Pnigitis*, it does not seem, as if that and our Black lead were the same; for theirs agree better with the composition of that black chalk mention'd by Dr Plot. It may perhaps be allow'd to fall rather under the Catalogue of *Earths*, than either *Metals* or *Minerals*. But then a Ruddle is acknowledg'd to be an Earth strongly impregnated with the Steams of Iron; so is this with those of Lead; as may be made out from its weight, colour, &c. Dr *Merret* gives it the name of *Nigrica fabrilis*, telling us, that it wanted a true one, till he bestow'd this on it at *Keswick*; and he further adds, that it is the peculiar product of Old and New England.]

Copper Mines — † So faid anno 1567 — Numb. 18 — Veins of gold and silver — Black lead — † Monochromata — Wadd — Oxford. p. 56. — Pinax. Nat. p. 18

The *Derwent*, falling through these mountains, spreads into a spacious Lake, call'd by Bede *Pragrandis stagnum*, i. e. a vast Pool, wherein are three Islands; one, the seat of the Knightly family of the *Ratcliffs*; another, inhabited by German Miners; and a third, suppos'd to be that wherein Bede tells us St *Herbert* led a Hermit's life. [The story of St *Herbert*'s great familiarity with St. *Cuthbert*, and their endearments at Carlisle, with their death on the same day, hour, and minute, &c. we have at large in Bede. All which are repeated in an old Instrument of one of the Bishop of Carlisle's Register-books, whereby *Thomas de Apulby* (Bishop of that See, A. D. 1374.) requires the Vicar of Crosthwait to say a yearly Mass in St *Herbert*'s *Isle*, on the thirteenth of April, in commemoration of these two Saints, and grants forty days Indulgence to such of his Parishioners as shall religiously attend that Service.] Upon the side of this Lake, in a fruitful field, encompass'd with wet dewy mountains, and protected from the north-winds by *Skiddaw*, lyes *Keswick*, a little market-town, a place long since noted for ‖ Mines (as appears by a certain Charter of Edward the fourth) and at present inhabited by Miners. The privilege of a Market was procur'd for it of Edward the first, by *Thomas* of *Derwent-water*, Lord of the place, from whom it descended hereditarily to the *Ratcliffs*, [who were ennobled by King James the second (*regn.* 3.) in the person of Sir *Francis Ratcliffe* of *Dilston* in Northumberland, under the title of Baron of Tindale, Viscount Ratcliffe and Langley, and Earl of Derwentwater. To *Keswick* and the Parish of *Crosthwait* (in which it lies) was given a considerable benefaction for the erecting of a Manufacture house, and maintaining the Poor, by Sir *John Banks* Knight, Attorney General in the reign of King Charles the first, who (as I take it) was born here. The Charity is still preserv'd, and well disposed.] The *Skiddaw*, just now mention'd, mounts up to the Clouds with its two tops, like another Parnassus, and views *Scruffel*, a mountain of Galloway in Scotland, with a kind of emulation. From the Clouds rising or falling upon these two mountains, the Inhabitants judge of the weather, and have this rhyme common among them:

Eccl. Hist. l. 4. c. 29. Vit. S. Cuthb. c. 28. Regist. Apulb. p. 261 — Keswick — ‖ Æraria Sectura — Skiddaw, a very high mountain — Anandale, C.

— *If Skiddaw hath a cap,*
Scruffel wots full well of that.

As also another, concerning the height of this and two other mountains in those parts:

Skiddaw, Lauvellin, and Casticand,
Are the highest hills in all England.

From thence the Derwent, sometimes broad and sometimes narrow, rowls on to the North in great haste, to receive the river *Cokar*. Which two rivers at their meeting do almost surround *Cokarmouth*, a populous well traded market town, where is a Castle, [heretofore] of the Earls of Northumberland, [and now of the Duke of Somerset.] It is a town neatly built, but of a low situation, between two hills: upon one is the Church, and upon the other over-against it [which is evidently artificial,] a very strong Castle, on the gates whereof are the Arms of the *Moltons*, *Humfranvills*, *Lucies*, and *Percies*; [and for the better prospect of which the forementioned Mount was raised.] Over against this, on the other side of the river, † at about two miles distance, are the ruins of an old Castle, call'd *Pap Castle*, the Roman Antiquity whereof is attested by several Monuments. Whether this be the *Gnaf-*

Cokarmouth — † Ad alterum milliare — Pap Castle — Gnasmonemonis *merie*, which Nennius tells us was built by King *Guortigern* near *Lugabellia*, and that it was by the old Saxons call'd *Palm castle*, I shall not determine. Here, among other Monuments of Antiquity, was found a large open vessel of greenish stone, with little images curiously engraven upon it which, whether it was an *Ewer* to wash in, or a *Font* (call'd by S Ambrose *Sacrarium Regenerationis*, the sacred Laver of Regeneration) to which use it is now employ'd at *Bridekirke* (i e the Church of St *Bridget*) hard by, I cannot say Only, we read that *Fonts* were anciently adorn'd with the pictures of Holy Men, whose Lives were propos'd as a pattern to such as were baptiz'd Besides the pictures, there are these strange Characters visible upon it. *Paulinus*

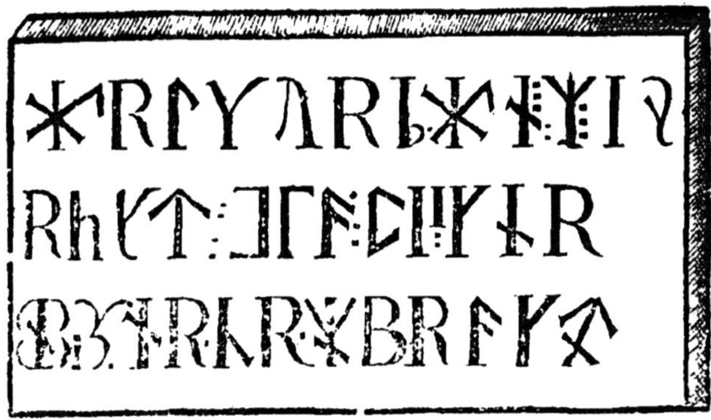

But what they mean, and to what nation they belong, let the learned determine, for it is all mystery to me The first and eighth are not much unlike that, whereby the Christians, from the time of Constantine the Great, express'd the name of Christ The rest, in *shape*, not in *power*, come nearest to those upon the tomb of *Gormon* the Danish King at *Jelling* in Denmark, which Petrus Lindebergius publish'd in the year 1591 [Upon a later view of this, it seems very plain that the figures are no other than the Pictures of S *John Baptist*, and our Saviour baptized by him in the river *Jordan* the descent of the Holy Ghost in the shape of a Dove, is very plain, and as to the Inscription, it has been in great measure cleared by the learned Bishop *Nicholson*, in the following Letter, sent many years since to Sir *William Dugdale*

Carlisle, Nov 23 1685

Honour'd Sir,

MY worthy and good Lord, our Bishop, was lately pleased to acquaint me, that you were desirous to have my thoughts of the Inscription on the Font at *Bridekirk* in this County I am, Sir, extremely conscious of the rashness of bringing any thing of mine to the view of so discerning an Antiquary; but, withal, very tender of disobeying so great and worthy a person I know you were pleased to make your own observations upon it, in your Visitation of these parts, when *Norroy* and I shall hope that you will give me an opportunity of rectifying, by your's, my following conjectures

1 The Fabrick of this Monoment does, I think, fairly enough evince, that it is Christian; and that it is now used to the same purpose for which it was at first designed Mr *Camden* (though not acquainted with the Characters of the Inscription, yet) seems to fansy thus much and, for proof of his Opinion, brings a notable quotation out of S *Paulinus*'s Epistles But he needed not to have sent us so far off for a Voucher, if he had taken good notice of the Imagery on the East side of this Stone, as I doubt not, Sir, but you have done. We have there, fairly represented, a person in a long Sacerdotal Habit dipping a Child into the water, and a Dove (the Emblem, no doubt, of the *Holy Ghost*) hovering over the Infant Now, Sir, I need not acquaint you, that the Sacrament of Baptism was anciently administer'd by plunging into the water, in the Western as well as Eastern parts of the Church, and that the *Gothic* word **ΔΑΠΠϹΑΝ**, the *German* word **dauffen**, the *Danish* **Dobe**, and the *Belgic* **doopen**, do as clearly make out that practice, as the *Greek* word Βαπτίζω Nor, that they may all seem to be deriv'd from [Δύπτω] another word of the same Language and signification, and are evidently a kin to our *English* **Dip**, **Deep**, and **Depth**. Indeed, our *Saxon* Ancestors expressed the Action of Baptism by a word of a different import from the rest For, in the fore-mention'd place of St *Mark*'s Gospel, their Translation has the Text thus ic eop fullge on pætepe, he eop fullað on halgum gaste, i e *Ego vos aquis Baptizo; ille vos Spiritu Sancto Baptizabit* Where the word fullian or fullgean signifies only simply *Lavare* Whence the *Latin* word *Fullo*, and our *Fuller* have their original But to conclude from hence, that the *Saxons* did not use dipping in the Sacrament of Baptism, is somewhat too harsh an argument *Mark*, 1 8 *Luke* and 1-

2 There are other Draughts on the North and West-side of the Font, which may very probably make for our purpose but with these (as not thoroughly understanding them, and having not had an opportunity of getting them drawn in Paper) I shall not trouble you at present

3 On the South-side of the Stone we have the Inscription, which I have taken care accurately to write out; and it is as follows

[illegible]

Now, these kinds of Characters are well enough known (since *Ol. Wormius*'s great Industry in making us acquainted with the *Literatura Runica*) to have been chiefly used by the *Pagan* Inhabitants of *Denmark*, *Sweden*, and the other Northern Kingdoms, and the *Danes* are said to have swarmed mostly in these parts of our *Island*. Which two considerations, seem weighty enough to persuade any man at first sight to conclude, that the Font is a *Danish* Monument. But then on the other hand, we are sufficiently assured, that the Heathen *Saxons* did also make use of these *Runæ*, as is plainly evident from the frequent mention of Run cræftigen and Run reafar in many of the Monuments of that Nation, both in Print and Manuscript, still to be met with. Besides, we must not forget that both *Danes* and *Saxons* are indebted to this Kingdom for their Christianity and therefore thus far their pretensions to a *Runic* (Christian) Monument may be thought equal. Indeed some of the Letters (as Ð, Ʒ and 7) seem purely *Saxon*, being not to be met with among *Wormius*'s many Alphabets and the words themselves (if I mistake them not) come nearer to the ancient *Saxon* Dialect, than the *Danish*. However, let the Inscription speak for itself and I question not but it will convince any competent and judicious Reader, that it is *Danish*. Thus therefore I have ventur'd to read and explain it;

> *Er Ekard han men egrosten, and to dis men red wer Taner men brogten*, i e
>
> Here *Ekard* was converted; and to this Man's example were the *Danes* brought.

There are only two things in the Inscription (thus interpreted) that will need an Explanation.

1 Who this *Ekard* was. And this is indeed a Question of that difficulty, that I confess I am not able exactly to answer it. The proper name itself is ordinary enough in the Northern Histories, though variously written as, *Echardus*, *Echinardus*, *Eginardus*, *Ecardus*, and *Eckhardus*. It is certainly a name of Valour, as all others of the like termination; such as *Bernhard*, *Everhard*, *Gothard*, *Reinhard*, &c. So that it may well become a General, or other great Officer in the *Danish* Army and such we have just reason to believe him to have been, who is here drawn into an example for the rest of his Countrymen. Our Historians are not very particular in their accounts of the several Incursions and Victories of the *Danes*, and their own writers are much more imperfect and therefore, in cases of this nature, we must content our selves with probable conjectures.

2 *Han men egrosten*, which, render'd *verbatim*, is *Here men turn'd*, i e was turn'd. A phrase, to this day, very familiar in most dialects of the ancient *Celtic* tongue, though lost in our *English*. In the High *Dutch* it is especially obvious, as, *Man Saget*, *Man hat gesagt*, *Man lobet*, &c and the *French* impersonals (*On dit*, *On fait*, &c) are of the same strain; and evident Arguments that the *Teutonick* and *Gaulish* Tongues were anciently near akin.

The Characters ᛏᛏ and ᛉ are manifest Abbreviations of several Letters into one, of which sort we have great variety of examples in several of *Wormius*'s Books. And such I take the Letter Ð to be, instead of ᛁ and Þ; and not the *Saxon* Ð. I must believe 7 to be borrowed from the *Saxons*; and Ʒ I take to be a corruption of their Ƿ or W. The rest has little of difficulty in it. Only the Language of the whole seems a mixture of the *Danish* and *Saxon* Tongues, but that can be no other than the natural effect of the two Nations being jumbled together in this part of the World. Our Borderers, to this day, speak a leash of Languages (*British*, *Saxon*, and *Danish*) in one; and it is hard to determine which of those three Nations has the greatest share in the Motly Breed. Thus far the foresaid learned Person.

The places last mentioned, with the fourth part of the Barony of *Egremond*, *Wigton*, *Leuse-water*, *Aspatric*, *Uldal*, &c were the large inheritance of *Maud Lucy*, heir of *Anthony Molton* or *de Lucy* her brother, which she gave to *Henry Percy* Earl of Northumberland, her husband. For tho' she had no issue by him, yet she left the family of *Percie* her heir, upon condition that they should bear the Arms of the *Lucies*, namely, *Three pikes* or *Lucy fish in a field gules*, quarterly with their own, or, to use the words of the original Instrument, *Upon condition of bearing her Arms* in a field gules three Pikes or Lucies, *quarter'd with those of the Percies* Or, a Lion azure, * *and the condition was enforced by a* Fine. Arms of the *Lucies* and *Percies*. * *Per finem Levata.*

After these rivers are united, the *Derwent* falls into the Sea at *Wirkington*, famous for the Salmon-fishing. It is now the seat of the ancient knightly family of the *Curwens*, descended from *Gospatrick* Earl of Northumberland, who took that name, by covenant, from *Culwen* a family of *Galloway*, the heir whereof they had marry'd. Here they have a stately castle-like seat; and from this family (excuse the vanity) I my self am descended by the mother's-side. Wirkington. Culwen commonly Curwen.

Some are of opinion, that from hence *Stilico* carry'd a Wall some four miles, for defence of the Coast in such places as were most convenient for landing, at what time the Scots from Ireland infested those parts. For thus *Claudian* makes *Britain* speak of her self: Under Honorius and Arcadius.

> *Me quoque vicinis pereuntem gentibus, inquit,*
> *Munivit Stilico, totam cum Scotus Hibernem*
> *Movit, & infesto spumavit remige Tethys.*

> And I shall ever own his happy care,
> Who sav'd me sinking in unequal war
> When *Scots* came thund'ring from the *Irish* shores,
> And th' Ocean trembled, struck with hostile oars.

And pieces of broken walls continue to the mouth of *Elen*, now *Elne*; which, within a little of its head, hath *Ireby*, a tolerable Market. I am of opinion, that this was the *Arbeia* where the *Barcarii Tigrienses* were garrison'd. At its mouth it has *Elenborrough*, i e a *burrough upon the Elen*, where the first Cohort of the *Dalmatians*, with their Commander, was garrison'd. It was seated on a pretty high hill, from whence is Ireby. Arbeia. Elenborough.

is a large prospect into the Irish-sea; but now Corn grows where the Town stood. Yet there are still plain remains of it; old Vaults are open'd, and several Altars, Inscriptions, and Statues, are dug-up. All which, that worthy Gentleman *J Senhous* (in whose Fields they * were dug-up) † kept very religiously, and plac'd them regularly in the walls of his house. In the middle of the yard, stands a beautiful square Altar of red Stone, the work of which is old and very curious; it is about five foot high, and the characters upon it are exceeding fair. But take the figure of it on all sides, as it was curiously drawn by Sir *Robert Cotton* of *Connington* Knight, a great admirer of Antiquities; when he and I, to discover the Rarities of our native Country, took a survey of these parts, with great pleasure and satisfaction, in the year of our Lord 1599. I could not but make an honourable mention of the * Gentleman I just now spoke of; not only because he entertain'd us with the utmost civility, but also because he † had a veneration for Antiquities (wherein he ‖ was well skill'd,) and with great diligence * preserved such Inscriptions as these, which by other ignorant people in those parts are presently broken to pieces, and turn'd to other uses, to the great detriment of these studies.

* Are, C
† Keeps, C.
* Mr ... house
† Has, C
‖ Is, C
* Preserves, C

In the Inscription every thing is plain: only, in the last line but one, ET and ÆDES have two letters joyn'd in one. At the bottom, it is imperfect; possibly to be restor'd thus, DECVRIONVM ORDINEM RESTITVIT, &c. These *Decuriones* were the same in the *Municipia*, as *Senators* were at Rome and in the Colonies. They were so call'd from *Curia* the Court, wherein they presided; from whence also they were nam'd *Curiales*, as having the chief management of all *Court* or Civil Affairs.

Decuriones Isidor l 9 c. 4.

On the back-side of this Altar, and the upper edge, you see there is VOLANTII VIVAS. Which two words puzzle me, and I can make nothing of them, unless the *Decuriones*, *Equites*, and the *Plebs* (of which three the *Municipium* consisted) did erect it to *G Cornelius Peregrinus* (who restor'd the *Houses*, *Temples*, and the *Decurio's*) by way of Vow or Prayer that this their Benefactor might live at *Volantium*. From which I would conclude (if allowance may be made for a conjecture) that this place was formerly call'd *Volantium*. Underneath it, are engraven sacrificing Instruments, * a sort of axe, and a long chopping knife. On the left side, a mallet and a jugg; on the right, a pa-

Volantium.
* Dolabra, Secespita

a *patera* or gobblet, a dish, and a pear (if I judge aright,) though others will have it to be a Holy-water-pot For these were the vessels us'd in their sacrifices; besides others, such as the *Cruet*, *Censer*, the *Open-pot*, the *Miter*, &c which I observ'd to be engraven upon other Altars in those parts. The second Altar delineated here, was dug-up at *Old Carlisle*, and † remain'd in the house of the *Barbouses* [now the *Kirkbys*,] at *Ilkirk*; [but is, I believe, removed to *Drumbugh* in this County] It had many Ligatures, or connexions of Letters; which the Engraver has given you pretty exactly. It seems to be read thus

Simpulum, Thuribulum, Futile, apex Sacerdotalis Pagan Altars † Is now, C

Jovi Optimo Maximo Ala Augusta ob virtutem appellata, cui praeest Publius Ælius, Publii filius Sergia Magnus de Mursa ex Pannonia inferiore Praefectus Aproniano (and perhaps) *Bradua Consulibus*

The third Altar, inscrib'd to the Local Deity *Belatucadrus*, is to be read thus

Under *Commodus*, in the year of our Lord 193

Belatucadro Julius Civilis Optio (i e * Captain of the Guard) *votum solvit libens merito*

* *Excubiis Praefectus*

The fourth (which is the fairest) has nothing of difficulty in it It is to be read thus

Diis, Deabusque Publius Posthumius Acilianus Praefectus Cohortis primae Delmatarum.

Such *Altars* as these (for we may make our Observations upon those Rites, though Christianity has happily abolish'd them) as also their victims, and themselves too, they us'd to crown with Garlands, and to offer frankincense and wine, and slay their sacrifices upon hem, and to anoint the very Altars Of the demolishing of which, upon the prevailing of Christianity, *Prudentius* writes thus:

Gentile Altars

Exercere manum non paenitet, & lapis illic
Si stetit antiquus, quem cingere sueverat error
Fasciolis aut gallinae pulmone rigara,
Frangitur. ———

Nor spar'd they pains if thus their zeal they show'd,
If in their way some ancient Altar stood,
Oft deck'd with ribbands, sprinkled oft with blood,
Down went the sacred Stone. ———

At the same place, I saw also the following Inscriptions:

PROSA - - - - - - - - - - - - - - - - - -
ANTONINI AV-PII F- - -
P AVLVS * PF. PALATINA
POSTHVMIUS ACILIANVS
PRÆF COH. I DELMATAR.

* *Publii filius*

* D M
INGENVI AN X
IVL SIMPLEX PATER
* F C

* *Diis Manibus*

* *Faciendum curavit*

D M
MORI REGIS
FILII HEREDES
EIVS SVBSTITVE
RVNT VIX A LXX.

HIC EXSEGERE FATA
- - ENVS SC GERMA -
- - S REG VIX AN - - -
S VIX AN — —
— — IX — — — —

D M
LVCA VIX
ANN
IS XX

D M
IVLIA MARTIM
A VIX AN
XII III D XX H.

There is also a Stone very curiously engraven, upon which are two winged *Genii*, supporting a *Garland*, in this manner

i. e. *Victoriæ Augustorum Dominorum nostrorum*

After the Shore has run a little way in a streight line from hence, it bends in with a winding and crooked bay, which therefore seems to be the *Moricambe*, that Ptolemy fixes hereabouts such agreement there is between the nature of the place and the name For this æstuary is *crooked*, and *Moricambe* signifies in British a *crooked Sea* Upon this, is the *Abbey of Ulme*, or *Holme Cultraine*, founded by David the first, King of Scotland but *Vulsty*, a Fort hard by, was built by the Abbots, for the securing of their Treasure, their Books, and their Charters, against the sudden incursions of the Scots. Here, they say, * were long preserved the Magick-Books of *Michael Scot*, † till they were mouldering to dust He was a Monk of this place about the year 1290, and apply'd himself so closely to the Mathematicks, and other abstruse parts of Learning, that he was generally look'd on as a *Conjurer* and a vain credulous humour has handed down I know not what Miracles done by him Below this Monastery, the bay receives the little *Waver*, encreas'd by the *Wize*, a small river; at the head of which the melancholy ruins of an ancient City teach us, That nothing in this world is out of the reach of Fate. By the neighbouring Inhabitants it is call'd *Old Carlisle*, but what its ancient name was, I know not, unless it was the *Castra Exploratorum* The distance in Antoninus (who gives us the most considerable places, but does not always go to them by the shortest way) both from *Bulgium* and *Lugu vallum*, exactly answers For spying of an Enemy, you could not have a more convenient place, for it is seated on a high hill, which commands a free prospect round the Country However, it is very certain, that the *Ala* or Wing (nam'd *Augusta*, and *Augusta Gordiana*,) did quarter here in the time of *Gordianus*; as appears by those Inscriptions which I saw in the neighbourhood

Moricambe. — Holme-Cultraine — * Are still, C — Michael Scot — † But now, C — Castra Exploratorum. Of the ... see more under the Picts Wall — Ala Augusta Gordiana. At Ilkirk.

* *Jovi optimo maximo*

*I O M	D M
ALA AVG OB	MABLI
— —RTVT APPEL CVI	NIVS SEC
PRÆEST TIB CL TIB F P	VNDVS
IN· G· N IVSTINVS	EQVIS
PRAEF FVSCIANO	ALE AVG
II SILANO II COS.	STE STIP

I O M
PRO SALVTE IMPERATORIS
M ANTONI GORDIANI PF
INVICTI AVG ET SABINIAE TR
IAE TRANQVILE CONIVGI EIVS TO
TAQVE DOMV DIVIN EORVM A-
LA AVG GORDIA OB VIRTVTEM
APPELLATA POSVIT CVI PRÆEST
AEMILIVS CRISPINVS PRAEF
EQQ NATVS IN PRO AFRICA DE
TVIDRO SVB CVR NONNII PHI
LIPPI LEG AVG PROPRETO — —
ATTICO ET PRÆTEXTATO
COSS.

Anno C 243

And the Altars were brought from hence, which * were set up in the High-way at *Wigton*; on the sides whereof one sees a † Chalice, a Melter, a Mallet, a Platter, &c. sacrificing vessels but Age has so entirely worn out the Inscriptions, that there is no appearance of Letters And not far from hence, upon the Military way, was dug up a Pillar of rude stone, which ‖ was to be seen at *Thoresby*, with this Inscription

* Are, C Wigton — † *Simpulum, Fusile, Malleus, Patera* — ‖ Is, C Thoresby

IMP

IMP CAES
M IVL.
PHILIPPO
PIO FELI
CI
AVG
ET M. IVL PHI
LIPPO NOBILIS
SIMO CAES
TR P. COS.

This also, among others, was copy'd out for me by * *Oswald Dykes*, a very learned Divine, and is now at *Wardal*, the seat of his brother *T Dykes*, a Gentleman of great note.

* Ann 1607 Wardal

DEO
SANCTO BELA
TVCADRO
AVRILIVS
DIATOVA † ARAE
X VOTO POSVII
LL. MM

† Fit Aram a voto

And to another Local Deity was found this Inscription annex'd,

DEO
CEAIIO AVR
MRII ET MS
ERVRACIO PRO
SE ET SVIS V S.
LL M.

Besides these, an infinite number of *little Images*, *Statues on horseback*, *Eagles*, *Lyons*, *Ganymeds*, with many other evidences of Antiquity, are daily dug-up. A little higher, there jets out a small Promontory, below which is a large arm of the Sea, the boundary at present of England and Scotland, but formerly, of the Roman Province and the Picts. Upon this little Promontory, is that old Town *Blatum-Bulgium* (possibly from the British *Bulch*, signifying a *partition* or *divorce*) from which, as the place most remote, and the Limit of the Province of Britain, Antoninus begins his *Itinerary*. The Inhabitants at this day call it *Bulness*, and though it is but a very small village, yet has it a Fort, and (as a testimony of its antiquity) besides the tracks of streets and pieces of old walls, it has a harbour, now choak'd up; and they tell you, a pav'd Causey ran along the shore, from hence, as far as *Elenborrow*. [Here are also frequently found Roman Coins and Inscriptions; and not long since, was dug up a small brazen figure of a *Mercury*, or a *Victory*; which came into the possession of *John Aglionby* Esq, a curious preserver of all such valuable remains of Antiquity.] A mile beyond this (as appears by the Foundations at low water) begins the *Picts wall*, that famous work of the Romans, which was formerly the boundary of the Province, and was built to keep out the Barbarians, who in those parts were (as one expresses it) continually * *barking and snarling* at the Roman Empire. I was amaz'd at first, why they should be so careful to fortifie this place, when it is fenced by a vast arm of the Sea, which comes up some eight miles; but now I understand, that at low-water it is so shallow, that the Robbers and Plunderers made nothing of fording it. That the figure of the Coast hereabouts has been alter'd, appears plainly from roots of Trees cover'd over with Sand at a good distance from the shore, which are often discover'd when the Tide is driven back by strong Winds. I know not whether it be worth while to observe, what the Inhabitants tell you, of *Subterraneous* Trees without boughs, which they commonly dig up, discovering them by the Dew, which never lies upon the ground that covers them.

Solway Frith, by the Scots. Prom Bulgium. Bulness. Munimentum. * Circumlatraverunt. Trees under ground.

Upon the same Frith, a little more inward, is *Drumbough* Castle, of † late days the possession of the Lords of *Dacre*, [and at present of the Lord Viscount *Lonsdale*,] but formerly a Station of the Romans. Some will have it to be the || *Castra Exploratorum*, but the distances will by no means allow it. [Here are many Roman Monuments, which were collected by *John Aglionby* above mention'd.] There was also another Roman Station, which by a change of the name is at present call'd *Burgh upon Sands* [(to distinguish it from *Burgh* under Stanemore in Westmorland)] from whence the neighbouring tract is call'd the *Barony of Burgh*. This, by *Meschines*, Lord of Cumberland, was bestow'd upon *Robert de Trivers*, and from him came to the * *Morvills*, the last of whom, *Hugh*, left a daughter, who by her second husband *Thomas de Molton* had *Thomas Molton*, Lord of this place, and father of that *Thomas*, who by marriage with the heir of *Hubert de* † *Vallibus*, joined *Gillesland* to his other possessions; all which were carry'd by *Maud Molton* to *Ranulph de Dacre*. But this little Town is noted for nothing more, than the untimely death of King Edward the first, after he had triumph'd over his enemies on all sides. He was a Prince exceeding glorious, in whose valiant breast the spirit of God as it were pitch'd his Tent, and as by his courage, and wisdom of mind, so also by his gracefulness of body, he arose to the highest pitch of Majesty. Providence exercis'd his youth with constant wars and difficulties, to fit him for the Government of England; which, after he came to it, he administer'd so nobly, by conquering the Welsh, and subduing the Scots, that he justly deserves the Character of one of the greatest Glories of Britain. [At the very place where this brave and valiant King expir'd (the memory whereof had been preserv'd by some great stones roll'd upon it) is erected a very fair square Pillar, nine yards and a half in height. On the West side of it is this Inscription, in large Roman Letters.

Drumbough-castle. † So said, ann 1607. || Dr Gale, p. 36 makes these the same with Blatum-Bulgium. Burgh upon Sands. 1307. * The Morvils call'd de Burgh super Sabulones. Lib Inq. † Vaulx. Edw 1.

Memoriæ æternæ Edvardi I Regis Angliæ longè clarissimi, qui in Belli apparatu contra Scotos occupatus, hic in Castris obiit, 7 Julii, A D 1307

On the South-side

Nobilissimus Princeps, Henricus Howard, *Dux Norfolciæ, Comes Mareschall Angliæ, Comes Arund &c ab Edvardo I Rege Angliæ oriundus P. 1685*

On the North side

Johannes Aglionby *J C F C* [i. e. *Jurisconsultus, fieri fecit*.]

That

That is,

To the eternal memory of *Edward* the first, the most famous King of England, who amidst his warlike Preparations against the Scots, died here in the Camp, 7 July, A. D 1307.

The most Noble Prince, *Henry Howard*, Duke of Norfolk, Earl Marshal of England, Earl of Arundel, *&c* ——descended from Edward the first, King of England, placed this Monument, 1685

John Aglionby, a Lawyer by Profession, caus'd it to be made

The Inhabitants say, that under the foresaid *Burgh*, in the very æstuary, there was a Sea-fight between the Scotch and English; and that † when the Tide came in, the dispute was managed by the Horse which seems no less strange than what Pliny relates, with great admiration, of such another place in *Caramania* This æstuary is call'd by both Nations *Solway-Frith*, from *Solway*, a Town of the Scots that stands upon it But Ptolemy calls it more properly *Ituna*, for the *Eden*, a very noble river, which winds by Westmoreland and thro' the inner parts of this County, falls into it with a vast body of waters, still remembering the obstructions it met with from the carcasses of the Scots in the year 1216, when it drown'd them, with their loads of English spoils, and swallowed up that plundering Crew

† Reverso æstu

Solway Frith

Ituna
Eden, riv.

Hist Mail ros

The *Ituna* or *Eden*, as soon as it enters this County, receives from the west the river *Eimot*, flowing out of the Lake call'd *Ulse* (or *Ulse-water*) which I mention'd before Near the bank of which, upon the little river *Dacor*, is *Dacre-castle*, noted in latter ages for giving name to the family of the Barons *de Dacre*, and mention'd by Bede as having a Monastery in his time; as also by Malmesbury, for being the place where *Constantine* King of the Scots, and *Eugenius* King of Cumberland, put themselves and their Kingdoms under the protection of the English King *Athelstan* [Here is a Castle standing, which hath formerly been a magnificent Building, and a seat of the Family; but no remains of a Monastery nor doth it appear by any Records to have been standing since the Conquest Near *Dacre*, is *Dalemayn*, the Mansion house of the *Hassels*, and holden of the Barony of Graystock in *Cornage*]

Eimot, riv

Dacre-Castle

Barons Dacre

Dalemayn

Somewhat higher, at a little distance from the confluence of *Eimot* and *Loder* (at which is the round trench call'd * *King Arthur's Table*) stands *Penrith*, in British *a red hill or head*; for the ground hereabouts, and the stone of which it is built, are both *reddish* [This, according to Dr. *Gale*, is the *Voreda* of Antoninus.] It is commonly call'd *Perith*, and is a noted little market town; fortify'd on the west with a Royal Castle, which, in the reign of Henry the sixth, † was repair'd out of the ruins of *Maburg* a ‖ Danish Temple hard by, [and is now in ruins it self] It is adorn'd with a pretty handsome Church, and has a large Market place with a Town-house of wood for the convenience of the Market people, which is beautify'd with *Bears climbing up a ragged staff*, the Device of the Earls of Warwick Formerly,

* See *Westmoreland*

Perith

† This is a mistake *Ep Carl Ms Northumb* MS par 6

‖ Roman Fort, C

it belong'd to the Bishops of Durham, but when *Anthony Bec*, Bishop of that See, was grown haughty and insolent by reason of his excessive wealth, *Edward the first* (as we read in the book of Durham) took from him *Werk in Tividale, Perith, and the Church of Simondburne* For the benefit of the Town, *W Strickland* Bishop of Carlisle, descended from a famous family in those parts, did at his own charge draw hither a Chanel or Water-course, from *Peterill*, or the *Little River Peter*; [which falls from the *Peat*-Mosses in the Fells about Graystock, and is so called from them In the Church-yard at *Penrith*, on the North-side of the Church, are erected two large Pillars of about four yards in height each, and about five yards distant one from the other It is said, that they were set in memory of one Sir *Ewen Cæsarius* Knight, in old time a famous warriour of great strength and stature, who liv'd in these parts, and kill'd wild Boars in the forest of *Englewood*, which much infested the Country He was bury'd here, they say, and was of such a prodigious stature, as to reach from one pillar to the other, and they tell you that the rude figures of *Bears* which are in stone, and erected, two on each side of his Grave, between the Pillars, are in memory of his great Exploits upon these Creatures On the North out side of the Vestry in the wall, in rude Characters, is this writing, for a Memorandum to posterity *Fuit pestis*, &c i e *There was a plague, A D* 1598, *of which there died at* Kendal 2500, *at* Richmond 2200, *at* Penrith 2266, *and at* Carlisle 1196 And the Church Register, in the neighbouring Parish of *Edenhal*, takes notice also of forty two persons dying the same year of the Plague, in that little Village These instances are the more remarkable, because none of our Historians speak of any such general Distemper in the Kingdom, at that time]

Upon the bank of *Peteril*, lay † *Plompton Park*, very large, and formerly set apart by the Kings of England for the keeping of Deer, but by King Henry the eighth prudently planted with men; being almost a frontier between England and Scotland [Not, that King Henry the eighth first of all *peopled* it; he only gave greater freedom and liberty to the Inhabitants, by disforesting it, and there were as many Parishes and Townships in it before his time, as are since *Hutton* and *Edenhall* were Parishes in the time of Henry the first, and given by him to the Cathedral of Carlisle, and so was *Wedderhall*, *Warwick*, *Lazonby*, *Skelton*, *Sowerby*, St *Maries*, St *Cuthbert's*, *Carliol* and *Dalston*, all, Parishes, at or near the time of the Conquest, and all in the forest of *Englewood*, or bordering very near upon it. It was sixteen miles in length, reaching from *Penrith* to *Carlisle*, ‖ and Edward the first, when he was hunting in this forest, is said to have kill'd two hundred Bucks in one day] Near this, I saw several remains of a demolished City, which, for its nearness to *Perith*, they call *Old Perith* I should rather take it to be the *Petriana* For, that the *Ala Petriana* was quarter'd here, is plain from the fragment of an old Inscription which one Ulpius Trajanus, † a Pensionary of the same *Ala* *Petriana*, set up But take this, with some others which I copy'd out here;

† Call'd in *Hist.* Plompton Park.

‖ Chron Lanerc

Petriana

† Emeritus

GADV

D M.

AICETVOS MATER
VIXIT † A XXXXV
ET LATTIO FIL-VIX
A XII. LIMISIVS
CONIV ET FILIÆ
PIENTISSIMIS
POSVIT

† Annos.

GADVNO
VLP TRAI
EM AL. PET
MARTIVS
* F P C

* Haply, Faciendum procuravit

D M.

FL MARTIO SEN
IN † C CARVETIOR
QVESTORIO
VIXIT AN XXXXV
MARTIOLA FILIA ET
HERES PONEN
‖ ———— CVRAVIT

† Possibly, in Caboste

‖ Dum

DM CROTILO GERMANVS VIX
ANIS XXVI GRECA VIX ANIS IIII
VINDICIANVS * FRA ET FIL TIT PO

* Fr[atri] & fi[lio] ... titulum posuit

A Grotto. [Half a mile above the confluence of *Eden* and *Eimot*, on the very bank of the former, is a G*otto* of two rooms, dug out of the rocks, and call'd *Isis Parlish*, to which there is a difficult and perillous passage In former times it was certainly a place of strength and security, for it had Iron gates belonging to it, which were standing not many years since]

After *Eden* has received the *Eimot*, it hastens to the north, by little inconsiderable villages and Forts, to the two *Salkelds* At Little *Salkeld* there is a circle of Stones, seventy seven in number, each ten foot high, and before these, at the entrance, is a single one by it self, fifteen foot high This the common people call *Long Megg*, and the rest *her daughters*, and within the circle are two heaps of stones, under which they say there are dead bodies bury'd And indeed it is probable enough, that this has been a Monument erected in memory of some victory [But, as to those heaps in the middle, they are no part of the Monument, but have been gathered off the ploughed Lands adjoyning, and (as in many other parts of the County) thrown-up here, in a waste corner of the Field And as to the *occasion* of it, both this, and *Rolrich-stones* in Oxfordshire, are supposed by many to have been Monuments erected at the solemn Investiture of some Danish Kings, and of the same kind as the *Kong stolen* in Denmark, and *Moresteen* in Sweden; concerning which, several large † Discourses have been written]

Salkelds

Long Megg

† [illegible] ... Not ad Sax Gram ... Meier Parg ... The at ... Ox ... p 356

From thence the *Eden* passes by *Kirk Oswald*, dedicated to St *Oswald*, and formerly the possession of that *Hugh Morvil*, who with his Accomplices murder'd Thomas Archbishop of Canterbury, in memory of which fact, the sword he then us'd was preserv'd here for a long time. Then, by *Armanthwayte*, [not long since] the Castle of the *Skeltons*; and *Corby*, a Castle [heretofore] of the noble and ancient family of the *Salkelds* (which was much enrich'd by marriage with the heir of *Rosgil*, [but now of the *Howards*] Then, by *Wetherall*, formerly a little Monastery [the daughter of St *Mary's* in York,) where you see a sort of houses dug out of a rock, that seem to have been design'd * for an ascending place; [if not, for some Hermits to lodge in, being near the Monastery These Caves are in a rock of difficult Access, and are two rooms, one within the other, each about five or six yards square] Next, *Eden* runs by *Warwic*, which I take to be the old *Virosidum*, where the sixth Cohort of the *Nervii* formerly kept garrison along the *Wal*, against the *Picts* and *Scots* In the † last age, there was built here a very strong stone bridge, at the expence of the *Salkelds* and *Richmonds* And so, by *Linstoc*, a castle of the Bishops of Carlisle within the Barony of *Crosby*, which *Waldeve*, son of Earl *Gospatrick* and Lord of *Allerdale*, gave to the Church of Carlisle The present name (I fansy) is a remain of *Olenacum* For, the *Olenacum*, where the *Ala prima Herculea* lay in garrison against the Barbarians, seems to have been along the Wall

Kirk Oswald

Arman thwaite

Corby Castle

Wetherall

* In recessum ... [illegible]

Warwic Virosidum.

† So said, ann 1607.

Linstoc

Crosby

Olenacum

And now *Eden*, ready to fall into the *Æstuary*, receives two little rivers almost at the same place *Peterill* and *Caude*, which run parallel from the south Upon the *Peterill*, besides the *Petriana* already spoken of, is *Greystock*, the Castle of a family which has been long famous, deriving its original from one *Ralph Fitz Walter* Of whose posterity, *William de Greystock* marry'd *Mary* daughter and coheir of *Roger de Merley* Lord of *Morpath* He had a son, *John*, who having no issue, obtain'd Licence of King Edward the first, to make over his estate to his * Cousin *Ralph de Granthorpe* son of *William*, whose posterity for a long time flourish'd here in great honour But about the reign of Henry the seventh, that family expir'd, and the estate came by marriage to the Barons of *Dacre*, the heirs *general* of the last of whom, were marry'd to two sons of *Thomas Howard*, † late Duke of Norfolk

Peterill and Caude, rivers.

Greystock

* Ex amita natus

† So said, ann 1607

[Below *Graystock*, upon the banks of *Peteril*, lies *Blencow*, belonging to an ancient and worthy family of that name Here is a very good Grammar School, founded and endow'd by *Thomas Bourbank*, a person of piety and learning, who was born in the Town, and had himself been a School master]

Blencow

20 Eliz

Near the *Caude*, besides the Copper mines at *Caudebec*, is *Highyate*, a Castle of the *Richmonds*, [From

Higyate

[From whence the river runs to *Hutton-hall*, anciently the possession of a family of that name; of whom it was purchas'd by the *Fletchers*, who have so much improv'd it in buildings, walks, gardens, &c that now it is one of the pleasantest seats in this Country It was lately the dwelling-place of Sir *George Fletcher*, Baronet, to whose care and contrivance it is chiefly beholden for its Improvements The estate is within the *Haia de Plompton*, and † held of the King by this Service amongst others, that the Lord of *Hutton*, shall *Tenere stappam sellæ Domini Regis, dum equum suum in Castro suo Carlioli scanderit*, i e hold the King's Stirrup, when he mounts his horse in his Castle of Carlisle] Near the *Caude*, also, * is a beautiful Castle of the Bishops of Carlisle, call'd *The Rose-Castle* this seems to have been the old *Congavata*, where the second Cohort of the *Lergi* were in garrison; for *Congavata* signifies in British, *a Vale upon the Gavata*, which name is now contracted into *Cauda*. But I have not yet been able to mark out the exact place where it was seated [In the time of the Civil wars, this Castle was burn'd down by order of Collonel *Heveringham*. What was standing of it at the Restoration, Dr. *Stern*, then Bishop, repair'd, and made habitable Dr *Rainbow* his successor, built a Chapel, and put the House in a much better condition Dr *Thomas Smith*, the late Bishop added a new Tower to the former building, and by the great expence he was at in altering and beautifying, has made it a very convenient House but it is still far short of its former magnificence King Edward the first in his expedition against *Scotland* lodg'd here, and dated his Writs, for summoning a Parliament, *apud la Rose*]

† Escaet de An 5 H 7

* Nitidum

Rose Castle

Congavata

Ann 1652

Between the confluence of those rivers, the ancient City of *Carlile* has a delicate pleasant situation, bounded on the north with *Eden*, on the east with *Peterill*, and on the west with *Caude*; and besides these natural fences, it is fortify'd with a strong stone wall, a castle, and a citadel It is of an oblong form, from west to east to the west is a pretty large castle, which [† was built by William the second, and probably repair'd by Richard the third, as it should seem by the Arms] Almost in the middle of the City, stands the Cathedral Church; the upper part whereof (being newer) is a curious piece of Workmanship, built by King Henry the eighth; but the lower is much more ancient. [The lower west part is the Parochial Church, and as old, as St *Cuthbert*; or, as *Walter*, who came in with the Conqueror, was a Commander in his Army, rebuilt the City, founded a Priory, and, turning Religious, became himself the first Prior of it The Chancel was built by Contributions about the year 1350, and the Belfrey was rais'd, and the Bells placed in it, at the charge of *William de Strickland*, Bishop, in the year 1401] On the east, the City is defended by a *Cittadel*, very strong, and fortify'd with * several *Orillons* or *Roundels* The Romans and Britains call'd it *Lugu-vallum* and *Lugu-ballium*, or *Lugu balia*, the Saxons (as Bede witnesses) *Luel*; Ptolemy (as some think) *Leucopibia* [which yet seems rather to be a corruption of Λευκοικίβια, i e white houses, and to be *Candida Casa*, or *Whitern*, in Galloway;)] Nennius, *Caer Lualid*; the ridiculous Welsh Prophecies, *The City of Dubalus*; we, *Carlile*; and the Latins, from the more modern name, *Carleolum* For, that *Lugubalia* and Carlile are the same, is universally agreed by our Historians. But as to the Etymology, what pains has our Countryman *Leland* taken about it! and at last he is driven upon this shift, that *Ituna* might be call'd *Lugus*, and that *Ballum* came from *Vallis*, a valley; and so makes *Lugu vallum* as much as *a valley upon the Luge* But (to give my Conjecture also) I dare affirm that the *Vallum* and *Vallia* were deriv'd from that famous military *Vallum* of the Romans, which runs hard by the City For Antoninus calls *Lugu-vallum*, *Ad vallum*; and the *Picts-wall*, which was afterwards built upon the Wall of *Severus*, is to be seen at *Stanwicks*, a small village, a little beyond the *Eden*, over which there is now a wooden bridge It pass'd the river over-against the Castle, where, in the very chanel, the remains of it (namely, great stones,) appear to this day. Also, Pomponius Mela has told us, that *Lugus* or *Lucus* signify'd a *Tower* among the old *Celtæ*, who spoke the same Language with the Britains For, what Antoninus calls *Lago Augusti*, is in him *Turris Augusti*, so that *Lugu-vallum* both really is, and signifies, *a tower or fort upon the wall or vallum* Upon this foundation, if the French had made their *Lugdunum* signifie a *tower upon a hill*, and their *Lucotetia* (so the Ancients called what we call *Lutetia*) *a beautiful tower* (for the words import so much in the British;) they might possibly have been more in the right, than by deriving the latter from *Lutum* dirt, and the former from one *Lugdus* a fabulous King [As to the present name, *Carlisle*, the original of this is plain enough, from the British *Caer* a City, and *Luel*, *Luel*, *Luguabal*, *Leil*, or *Luil* (according to the several appellations, ancient and modern,) importing as much as *the Town or the City of Luul*, &c.]

Carlile

† By the Arms, appears to have been built by Richard the third, C

* Varia pro pugnacula

Lugu-vallum

Lucus and Lugus what they signified among the ancient Britains and Gauls

Lugdunum Lucotecia Lutetia in France an old Etymology ... that Lugdunum signifies a tower in the mountain

That this City flourish'd in the time of the Romans, appears plainly enough from the several evidences of Antiquity which they now and then dig up, and from the frequent mention made of it by the Writers of those times And even after the ravages of the Picts and Scots, it retain'd something of its ancient Splendour, and was accounted a *City* For in the year of our Lord 619 Egfrid King of Northumberland † gave it to the famous St Cuthbert in these words *I have likewise bestow'd upon him the* City *call'd* Luguballia, *with the lands fifteen miles about it* At which time also it was wall'd round *The Citizens* (says Bede) *carry'd Cuthbert to see the* Walls *of the City, and a* Well *of admirable workmanship built in it by the Romans* At which time, *Cuthbert* (as the Durham-book has it) *founded a Religious-house for Nuns, with an Abbess, and Schools* Afterwards, being most grievously shatter'd by the Danes, it lay bury'd about two hundred years in it's own ashes till it began to flourish again by the favour and assistance of William Rufus, who built it a new with a Castle, and plac'd a Garrison in it, first of *Flemings* (whom, upon better consideration he quickly remov'd into [*North wales and the Isle of Anglesey)] and then of the southern English. [For the Saxon Chronicle relating this matter, has it Cyrlisceo folc, which at first sight should seem to be an error for Englisceo; but, in truth, this seems rather to be an error of the Librarian for Cyrlisceo, and on that supposition the words will imply, That a great number of *Husbandmen* were sent thither, and not *English men*; for *before* that time, the Inhabitants of Carlisle were *English* And, what follows in the Saxon Chronicle þæt lanð to tilianne, strengthens the conjecture, as expressing the errand upon which they were sent; *viz to cultivate those parts* To this Co-

† See Simeon Durham de Donation larga

* Wales C

lony

lony it is, that all the Records ascribe the first tillage that was known thereabouts It is certain, the whole forest of Inglewood lay uncultivated for many years after] At that time (as Malmsbury has it) *was to be seen a Roman* Triclinium *or dining-room, of stone, arch'd over; which neither the violence of* Weather, *nor* Fire, *could destroy On the front of it was this Inscription*, MARII VICTORIÆ. Some will have this *Marius* to be *Arviragus* the Britain; others, the *Marius* who was saluted Emperor in opposition to *Gallienus*, and is said to have been so very strong, that Authors tell us he had only nerves, and no veins, in his fingers. Yet I have heard, that some Copies have it, not *Marii Victoriæ*, but *Marti Victori* which latter may probably be favour'd by some, as seeming to come nearer the truth.

Lugubalia, now grown populous, had (as they write) its Earl or rather Lord, *Ralph Meschines* or *de Micenis*, from whom descended the Earls of Chester, and being about the same time honour'd with an Episcopal See by Henry the first, it had *Athulph* for its first Bishop This, the Monks of Durham look'd upon as an injury to their Church *When Ralph* (say they) *Bishop of Durham was banish'd, and the Church had none to protect it, certain Bishops joyn'd* Carleil *and* Tividale *to their own Dioceses* How the Scots in the reign of King Stephen took this City, and Henry the second recover'd it, how Henry the third committed the Castle of Carlisle, and the County, to *Robert de Veteri ponte* or *Vipont*, how in the year 1292 it was † burn'd down, with the Cathedral and Suburbs, how *Robert Brus* the Scot, in the year 1315, besieg'd it, without success, &c all these matters are treated of at large in our *Histories* But it may be worth our while to add two Inscriptions which I saw here, one in the House of *Thomas Aglionby* near the Citadel, † but not ancient.

Bracden.

† Vid Chron. de Lanercost, of the violence of that Fire

† *Deterioris seculi*

DIIS MANIBV
S MARCI TROIANI
AVGVSTINANI * TVM FA
CIENDVM CVRAVIT
AFEL AMMILLVSIMA
CONIVX † KARISS

* *Tumulum*

† *Carissima.*

To which is joyn'd the effigies of an armed Horse man, with a Lance

The other, in the Garden of *Thomas Middleton*, in a large and beautiful Character

L E G. VI
VIC. P. F.
G. P R. F.

That is, (as I suppose) *Legio Sexta Victrix, Pia, Felix* The interpretation of the rest, I leave to others

Carlisle had only one Earl [in ancient times,] viz *Andrew de Harcla*, whom Edward the second (to speak from the original Charter of Creation) *for his good services against Thomas Earl of Lancaster, and his Adherents, and for subduing the King's Subjects who were in rebellion, and delivering them prisoners to the King*; did by the girding of a Sword *create Earl*, * *under the honourable title of Earl of* Carleol But the same person afterwards prov'd ungrateful, and villanously perfidious to his King and Country, and being taken, was punish'd with such Ignominy as his Treachery and Ingratitude had deserv'd *For being degraded, he had his spurs cut off with a hatchet, then his sword-belt was taken from him, next his shoes and gloves were pull'd off; after which, he was drawn, hang'd, beheaded, and quarter'd* [Upon the restoration of King Charles the second, this place gave the honourable title of Earl to *Charles* (son of Sir *William*) *Howard*, who in the † 13th year of that reign, was created Lord *Dacres* of Gillesland, Viscount *Howard* of *Morpeth*, and Earl of *Carlisle*; for his having been highly instrumental in that happy Restoration In which Honours he was succeeded by *Edward* his son, father of the right Honourable *Charles*, the present Earl]

Andrew Harcla Earl of Carlisle

* *Sub honore & nomine*

Th Avensbury

† *April* 2.

Lugubalia or Carlisle is 21 degrees 31 minutes, in Longitude, and 54 degrees, 55 minutes, in Latitude I will now bid adieu to it, in that encomium of *J Johnston*

CARLEOLUM

Romanis quondam statio tutissima signis,
Ultimaque Ausonidum meta, labosque Ducum,
E specula latè vicinos prospicit agros,
Hinc ciet & pugnas, arcet & inde metus
Gens acri ingenio, studiis asperrima belli,
Doctaque bellaci figere tela manu
Scotorum Reges quondam tenuere beati,
Nunc iterum priscis additur imperiis
Quid? Romane, putas extrema hic limina mundi?
Mundum retro alium surgere nonne vides?
Sit vidisse satis, docuit nam Scotica virtus
Immensis animis hic posuisse modum

CARLISLE

Where the bold Eagles stop'd their noble course,
The latest labour of the *Roman* force
On subject Fields from her high Rock looks down,
Thence galls her foes, and thence secures her own
Her People sharp, and ever fam'd in war,
Fights are their study, and their only care
In ages past she serv'd the *Scottish* crown,
And now her ancient Lord again does own
Romans, how thought you here the world could end,
When you might see another World beyond?
Yet only see the *Scot*'s victorious hand
Here fix'd the limits of your wide command

[Over the river *Eden* is *Stanwicks*, or *Stanewegges* (i e a place upon the *Stony way*) a Town in the time of Henry the first, who gave the Appropriation of it to the Church of *Carlisle* The Picts wall is very visible here; and at *Drawdykes*, a seat of the *Aglionby*'s, is a Roman Altar with this Inscription

Stanwicks

I O. M. ALA AVG O B VRI APPIA
IVL. PVB PS T TB CETBERI------]

Rowcliffe. Then you see *Rowcliffe*, just upon the bank, a little Castle, built * not long since by the Lords *Dacres*, for their own private defence. Above this, two rivers *Esk* and *Leven*, being first joined, enter the æstuary of *Ituna* at the same mouth *Esk* comes out of *Scotland*, but for some miles owns itself of *England*, and receives the river *Kirsop*; where were fix'd, † not long since, the limits between the English and Scots tho' it ‖ was not so much the water that * kept them within bounds, as a mutual dread (having had sufficient experience of each others valour; [and now, a mutual Love, as being entirely united into one kingdom] Upon this, where we see *Netherby*, a little village of two or three cottages, the ruins of some ancient City are so very wonderful and great, and the name of *Esk* running by them does so well concur; that I imagine the old *Æsica* stood there, in which formerly the Tribune of the first Cohort of the *Astures* was in garrison against the Barbarians It is now the seat of the Head of the Family of *Grayham*, very famous among the Borderers for their great valour; and in the walls of the house is this Roman Inscription, set up in memory of *Hadrian* the Emperour, by the *Legio Secunda Augusta*

* So said ann. 1607
† So said, ann 1607
‖ Is, C.
* Keeps, C
Netherby
The Grayham

IMP. CÆS. TRA.
HADRIANO
AUG.
LEG. II. AVG. F.

[Besides this, there are several others, collected, and carefully placed in order, by Sir *Richard Grahame* Knight and Baronet, Grandfather to the honourable *Richard* late Viscount *Preston* Here was found lately a gold Coin of *Nero* of good value, and two Stones with the following Inscriptions The one, IMP COMM COS i e *Imperatori Commodo Consuli*, which (I suppose) was erected in the year of Christ 184, when that Emperour was saluted by the title of *Imperator Britannicus* The other,

DEO MARTI
BELATVCADRO
RO VR RP CAII
ORVSII M

Whereby it appears that *Belatucadrus* was the same with *Mars*, under a more terrible name It is probable, it comes from *Bel*, *Baal*, and *Belinus*, the great Idol of the Assyrians, which Cedrenus says was the same with *Mars*; and which the *Roman* and *German* Soldiers might like better, under a more harsh and round termination]

Barony of Liddell. Where the *Lid* joins the *Esk*, stood formerly *Liddel*, a Castle (as I have been told) and a Barony of the *Estotevills*, *who held Lands in Cornage*, *which Earl Ranulph* (as we read in an old Inquisition) *gave to Turgis Brundas* From Estotevill it descended by Inheritance to the *Wakes*, and by them to the Earls of Kent *John* Earl of Kent granted it to King Edward the third; and King Richard the second, to *John of Gaunt*, Duke of Lanca-

Lidersdal
An 1 R 2

ster Beyond the Esk also, the Country for some miles is reckon'd English ground; in which compass is *Sollom-moss*, noted for the taking great numbers of the Scotch Nobility, prisoners, in the year 1543 For when the Scots were ready to attack the English (who were commanded by *Th. Wharton*, Lord Warden of the Marches,) and found that *Oliver Sinclar*, a person whom they despis'd, was appointed General; each look'd upon it as an affront to himself, and they were so incens'd, as to revenge the *injury* (such was the construction they put upon it) with their own disgrace and damage. for they fell into mutinies, broke their ranks, and put all in disorder The English, who were posted upon the higher ground, observing that, fell upon them, and put them to flight. Great numbers were taken; for they threw down their Arms, and submitted generally to the English and the Moss-troopers; so that only a soldier here and there was kill'd This, James the fifth King of Scotland, laid so much to heart, that he dy'd of grief The neighbouring lands are call'd *Batable-ground*, or *The ground in debate*, because the English and Scots * could not agree about it For the Inhabitants on both sides, as living upon the Frontiers, * were a swift, subtil, and nimble sort of Soldiers; being train'd up to it by frequent skirmishes [This was the former state, but since the happy Union of the two Kingdoms in King James the first, and much more since that under her Majesty Queen Anne, all these Feuds and Quarrels upon the Borders are ceased; and one lives there with as much security, as in any other place whatsoever]

The Battel of Sollom-moss.
Batable ground
* Cannot, C
* Are C
Lewiano

Leven, riv. *Leven*, the other of the rivers which I mentioned, arising in the very limits of the two Kingdoms, runs by nothing memorable, besides *Beucastle* (as they commonly call it,) a Castle of the Kings, which in those solitary parts † was defended by a small Garrison In the publick Records it is written *Bueth-Castle*; so that the name seems to be deriv'd from that *Bueth*, who about Henry the first's time had almost got the entire government of those parts However, it is certain that in Edward the third's reign, it belong'd to *John* Baron *Strivelin*, who marry'd the daughter and coheir of *Adam de Swinborn* In the Church, † now almost in ruins, there lies instead of a Grave-stone, this Inscription, which has been brought from some other place

Beu-Castle
† Is, C
Baron Strivelin
† So said, ann 1607

LEG II AVG
FECIT

In the Church yard, is a Cross, of one entire square stone, about twenty foot high, and curiously wrought; there is an Inscription too, but the ‖ letters are so dim, that they are not legible But seeing the Cross * is of the same kind, as that in the Arms of the *Vaux*, we may suppose that it has been erected by some of that Family

[The letters of this Inscription appear still legible upon a later view A few of them were copied (but unskilfully) A D 1618, as ‖ Sir *Henry Spelman* witnesses Others are explain'd in a Letter to Mr *Walker*, sent him by the same learned, and now ‖ right Reverend person, who communicated his thoughts of that at *Bridekirk* to Sir *William Dugdale* For your satisfaction, be pleased to take his account at large

‖ ...
* ... Is the ...
‖ Ad Olai Wormii Mon Dan pag 161
‖ Bishop Nicolson

SIR,

Carliſle, Nov. 2 1685.

SIR,

IT is now high time to make good my promiſe of giving you a more perfect account of our two *Runic* Inſcriptions at *Beau-caſtle* and *Bridekirk*. The former is fallen into ſuch an untoward part of our Country, and ſo far out of the common Road, that I could not much ſooner have either an opportunity or the courage to look after it. I was aſſur'd by the Curate of the place (a perſon of good ſenſe and learning in greater matters) that the Characters were ſo miſerably worn out ſince the Lord *William Howard*'s time (by whom they were communicated to Sir *H. Spelman*, and mention'd by *Wormius*, *Mon. Dan.* p. 161.) that they were now wholly defac'd, and nothing to be met with worth my while. The former part of this Relation I found to be true: for (though it appears that the forementioned Inſcription has been much larger than *Wormius* has given it, yet) it is at preſent ſo far loſt, that in ſix or ſeven lines none of the Characters are fairly diſcernible, ſave only ᛞᚨᛏᚺᚱ: and theſe too are incoherent, and at great diſtance from each other. However, this *Epiſtylium Crucis* (as Sir *H. Spelman* in his Letter to *Wormius* has called it) is to this day a noble Monument, and highly merits the view of a curious Antiquary. The beſt account, Sir, I am able to give you of it, be pleas'd to take as follows.

It is one entire Free-ſtone, of about five yards in height, waſh'd over (as the Font at *Bridekirk*) with a white oily Cement, to preſerve it the better from the injuries of time and weather. The figure of it inclines to a ſquare Pyramid, each ſide whereof is near two foot broad at the bottom, but upwards more tapering. On the weſt-ſide of the Stone we have three fair Draughts, which evidently enough manifeſt the Monument to be Chriſtian. The loweſt of theſe repreſents the Portraicture of a Layman, with a Hawk or Eagle perch'd on his Arm. Over his Head are the forementioned ruins of the Lord *Howard*'s Inſcription. Next to theſe, the Picture of ſome Apoſtle, Saint, or other Holy man, in a ſacerdotal habit, with a Glory round his Head. On the top ſtands the Effigies of the B. V. with the Babe in her Arms, and both their Heads encircled with Glories, as before.

On the North we have a great deal of Chequer work, ſubſcribed with the following Characters fairly legible.

‖ᚺᚢᚴ ᚼ ᛒᚢᚱᚢ ᛯ‖

Upon the firſt ſight of theſe Letters, I greedily ventured to read them *Rynburu*, and was wonderfully pleaſed to fanſy, that this word thus ſingly written, muſt neceſſarily betoken the final extirpation and burial of the Magical *Runæ* in theſe parts, reaſonably hop'd for upon the converſion of the *Danes* to the Chriſtian Faith: for that the *Danes* were anciently, as well as ſome of the *Laplanders* at preſent, groſs Idolaters and Sorcerers, is beyond Controverſie; and I could not but remember, that all our Hiſtorians tell us, that they brought Paganiſm along with them into this Kingdom. And therefore it was not very difficult to imagine, that they might for ſome time practiſe their *Hocus* tricks here in the North, where they were moſt numerous and leaſt diſturbed. This conceit was the more heightened, by reflecting upon the natural ſuperſtition of our borderers at this day, who are much better acquainted with, and do more firmly believe, their old Legendary Stories of Fairies and Witches, than the Articles of their Creed. And to convince me yet further, that they are not utter ſtrangers to the *Black Arts* of their forefathers, I accidentally met with a Gentleman in the neighbourhood, who ſhew'd me a Book of Spells and Magical Receipts, taken (two or three days before) in the Pocket of one of our *Moſs-Troopers*; wherein, among many other conjuring feats, was preſcrib'd a certain Remedy for an Ague, by applying a few barbarous Characters to the Body of the party diſtemper'd. Theſe, methought, were very near akin to *Wormius*'s RAM RUNER, which, he ſays, differ'd wholly in figure and ſhape from the common *Runæ*. For though he tells us, that theſe *Ramruner* were ſo call'd, *Eo quod moleſtias, dolores, morboſque hiſce inſligere inimicis ſoliti ſint Magi*; yet his friend *Arng. Jonas*, more to our purpoſe, ſays, That —— *His etiam uſi ſunt ad benefaciendum, juvandum, medicandum tam animi quam Corporis morbis, atque ad ipſos Cacodæmones pellendos & fugandos*. I ſhall not trouble you with a draught of this Spell, becauſe I have not yet had an opportunity of learning whether it may not be an ordinary one, and to be met with (among others of the ſame nature) in *Paracelſus* or *Cornelius Agrippa*.

If this conjecture be not allowable, I have, Sir, one more, which (it may be) you will think more plauſible than the former. For if, inſtead of making the third and fourth Letters to be two ᚴ.ᚴ. N N we ſhould ſuppoſe them to be ᛯ.ᛯ. E E the word will then be *Ryeeburu*, which I take to ſignifie, in the old *Daniſh* Language, *Cæmiterium* or *Cadaverum Sepulchrum*. For, though the true old *Runic* word for *Cadaver*, be uſually written ᚼᚱᛆᛯ *Hrae*; yet the *H* may, without any violence to the Orthography of that tongue, be omitted at pleaſure, and then the difference of ſpelling the word, here at *Beau-Caſtle*, and on ſome of the ragged Monuments in *Denmark*, will not be great. And for the countenancing of this latter Reading, I think the above-mentioned *Chequer-work* may be very available: ſince in that we have a notable Emblem of the *Tumuli*, or burying places of the Ancients. (Not to mention the early cuſtom of erecting Croſſes and Crucifixes in Church-yards: which perhaps, being well weigh'd, might prove another encouragement to this ſecond Reading.) I know the Chequer to be the Arms of the *Vaux's*, or *De Vallibus*, the old Proprietors of this part of the North; but that, I preſume, will make nothing for our turn. Becauſe this, and the other carved work on the Croſs, muſt of neceſſity be allow'd to bear a more ancient date than any of the Remains of that name and Family; which cannot be run up higher than the Conqueſt.

On the Eaſt we have nothing but a few Flouriſhes, Draughts of Birds, Grapes and other Fruits; all which I take to be no more than the Statuary's fancy.

On the South, flouriſhes and conceits as before, and towards the bottom, the following decay'd Inſcription.

‖ᛉᚾ ᚢᛒ⁝ ⁝ ᚾᚱᛗᛏ ⁝‖

The

The Defects in this short piece are sufficient to discourage me from attempting to expound it. But (possibly) it may be read thus:

Gag Ubbo Erlat, i. e.

Latrones Ubbo Vicit,

I confess this has no affinity (at least, being thus interpreted) with the foregoing Inscription: but may well enough suit with the manners of both ancient and modern Inhabitants of this Town and Country.

† Hist MS. Northumb. Par 6

Thus far, of that ancient Monument; besides which, there is a large † Inscription on the west; and on the south side of the Stone, these Letters are fairly discernable,

IIYRAMIRMIT

Gillesland. * Ita impedita.

More to South and West, and further in the Country, lies *Gillesland*-Barony: a tract * so cut and mangled with the brooks (which they call † *Gilles*,) that I should have thought, it had taken the name from them; if I had not read in the book of *Lanercost*-Church, that one *Gill* the son of *Bueth* (call'd also *Gilbert* in a Charter of *Henry* the second) was formerly possess'd of it: so that probably it had this name from him. [It might also take it from *Hubert de Vallibus* (or *Vaux*;) since *de Vallibus* and *Gills* signifie the same thing: and it is offer'd to consideration by others, whether it might not after all, be so call'd from the river *Gelt*, which runs along the middle of it.] Through this tract, *Severus's* wall (that famous monument of Britain) runs from Carlisle to the East, almost in a streight line, by *Stanwicks*, a little village, and *Scalby*, a Castle formerly belonging to the *Tilliols* (once a famous Family in those parts) from whom it came to the *Pickerings*. [At this Castle (the seat of the *Gilpins*) are preserv'd three Altars, which were dug up in those parts: One, not far from the Castle, found in the river *Irdin*, on a stone colour'd with a sort of yellow, and of this figure:

† The being wherein the brook runs the Gi.

Scalby Castle.

The second was dug-up at *Cambeck*, in the ruins of an old stone-wall, and is of this form,

This

This third is imperfect, and in what place it was found I cannot positively say,

DEO COCIDI
COH I AEL--
- - - - - - - - - - - -
- - - - - - - - - - - -
- - - - A - - - V S]

Then the *Wall* is crofs'd by the little river *Cambeck*, upon which the Barons *Dacre* built *Askerton* (Akerton Castle) a small Castle, wherein the Governour of *Gillesland* (call'd commonly *Land Sergeant*) kept Garrison Below the *Wall*, it joyns the river *Irthing*, where is *Irthington* (Irthington), the *Capital Manour* of the Barony of *Gillesland* · and here, at *Castlested*, appear very great ruins Hard by, is *Brampton* (Brampton), a little market-town, [where is an Hospital for six poor men, and as many poor women, with a Salary for a Chaplain; founded and endow'd by the Right Honourable Elizabeth Countess Dowager of *Carlisle*, mother to the present Earl of *Carlisle*] This I take to be the *Bremeturacum along the Wall* (Bremeturacum ad lineam valli.) (for it is scarce a mile from the Wall,) where, formerly, the first Cohort of the *Tungri* from Germany, and (Cohors I Tungrorum.) in the decline of the Roman Empire, the *Cuneus Armaturarum*, under the Governour of Britain, were in Garrison Those *Armaturæ*, were (Armaturæ. Veget l 2 c 7) Horse arm'd *Cap-a-pee* · but whether they were *Duplares* or *Simplares*, my Author has not told us. The *Duplares* were such as * had a *double* allowance of Provision, the *Simplares*, such as had a *single* allowance Nor must I omit, that at *Brampton* there is a high hill call'd the *Mote*, ditch'd round at the top; from whence is a large prospect into all the Country round Below this, and at *Castle-steeds*, i e the place of a Castle, as also at *Trederman* hard by, were found these Inscriptions, which the Right Honourable *William* Lord *Howard* of *Naworth*, third son of his Grace † *Thomas* Duke of Norfolk, copy'd out for me with his own hand a person admirably well vers'd in the study of Antiquities, and a peculiar favourer of that study, who in right of his wife, the sister and coheir of the last Lord Baron *Dacre*, came to a large estate in those parts; [which his Posterity still enjoy.]

* Binas consequebantur annonas

† Ann 1607.

This alſo was found there in an old Vault, in which the name of the Emperour's Lieutenant and Proprætor in Britain, is unluckily worn out.

Near *Brampton*, runs the little river *Gelt*, on the bank of which, in a rock call'd *Helbeck*, is this gaping Inſcription, ſet up by an Enſign of the ſecond Legion call'd *Auguſta* (poſſibly *Optio*) under *Agricola* the Proprætor; with ſome others, of which time has depriv'd us.

In

Perhaps Propraetore.

In the same rock also, we read in a more modern character,

OFICIVM ROMANORVM.

Irthing, riv. Naworth-Castle. † Now belonging, C. ‖ Is repairing, C. * So said an. 1607

Here, the *Gelt* empties it self into the river *Irthing*, which runs with a violent rapid stream by *Naworth-Castle*, † belonging to *William Howard* before-mentioned, who ‖ repair'd it but lately to the Barons of *Dacre*, the last of whom * some years ago dy'd young, and *Leonard* his Uncle (chosing rather to try for the Estate, with his Prince in War, than with his Nieces in Law) seiz'd upon this Castle, and got together a company of seditious Rebels But the Lord *Hunsdon*, with the garrison of *Berwick*, easily defeated them, putting a great many to the sword, and the rest (among whom was *Leonard* himself) † to flight [It is now in the possession of the Right Honourable *Charles Howard* Earl of Carlisle (great great grandson to the Lord *William* before mentioned) who has repair'd the Castle, and made it fit for the reception of a Family Here is a Library, formerly well furnished with Books, and there are still in it † many Manuscripts of value, relating chiefly to Heraldry and English History In the Hall, are the Pictures of all the Kings of England, down from the Saxon times; which were brought from *Kirk-Oswald Castle*, when that was demolish'd, above a hundred years ago In the garden wall, are a great many stones with Roman Inscriptions, which were collected and placed there by this Family Some of them are not legible, but others are On one is,

† Fuga effusiori

† Catal Lib MS Oxon

IVL AVG DVO M SILV. . VM

On another,

I O M II ÆL DAC C P PST
ÆRELIVS FA L S TRIB PEI VO COS

On a third,

LEG II AVG

On a fourth,

COH I ÆL DAC CORD ALEC PER ...

With some others, which are evidently the same with those that were copied out in the last age and represented before, and which in all likelyhood were brought hither from *Willyford*.]

Nearer the Wall, stood the Priory of *Lanercost*, founded by *R de Vallibus*, Lord of Gillesland. [Not far from whence is a medicinal spring, which issues out of a rock, the water is impregnated with *Sulphur*, *Nitre*, and *Vitriol*, and is said to be very good for the Spleen, the Stone, and all Cutaneous distempers In the summer time, it is much frequented both by the Scotch and English] Upon the wall, is *Burd Oswald*, and below this, where the Picts-Wall pass'd the river *Irthing* by an arch'd bridge, at a place now call'd *Willoford*, was the Station of the *Cohors prima Ælia Dacorum*, as appears by the *Notitia*, and by several Altars which were erected by that Cohort, and inscrib'd to *Jupiter Optimus Maximus* Some of them I think proper to give you, though much defac'd, and worn with age; Burd-Oswald.

† Jovi optimo Maximo

† I O M
COH I AEL.
DAC CVI
PRAE ||||
IG ||||||
||||||
||||

I O M
DH I AEL DA
C - C - A GLTA
IRI LSAVRNES
---- ---- --
------ ----
------- .

I O M
COH I AEL
DAC C P
STATVI oN
GINVS, TRIB

PRO SALVTE
F N MAXIMIANO
‖ IOR - - - CAE
VA - - - - - -
- - - - - - -
- - - - - - - - OALD

‖ Fortissimo Caesari

LEG.

LEG. VI.
VIC. P. F.
F.

I. O M.
COH I AEL. DAC
TETRICIANORO
--- C P P. LVTIC
---- V. S. DESIG
NATVS
TRIB.

I. O M
COH I. AEL.
DAC. GORD
ANA. C P --
EST.

I. O M
---- H I AEL DAC.
---- C PRAEESI ---
---- FLIUS FA
---- S TRIB ----
---- PETVO ------ --
----- COS

[In those parts, are many rivulets, called by the name of *Glen* or *Glyn*, from whence the *Amblogana ad lineam Valli*, mentioned in the *Notitia*, might, not improbably, take the name, * supposing it to be rightly fix'd at this place, or the neighbourhood of it.]

* V *Amble-side*, in Westmorland

Lords of *Gilsland* Out of an old Missal *R. Cooke* Clarenceux, calls him *Ralph*; as also the MSS of *Fountain* and *Holme*-Abbies

The first Lord of *Gillesland* that I read of, was *William Meschines*, brother of *Ralph* Lord of *Cumberland*, (not that *William* who was brother of *Ranulph* Earl of Chester from whom sprang *Ranulph de Ruelent*, but the brother of *Ralph*,) who was not able to get it out of the hands of the Scots for *Gill* the son of *Bueth*, held the greatest part of it by force of Arms; [(though this could be but for a little while for the father was banished into Scotland in Earl Randolph's time, and the Son *Gillesbueth* (as he was called) was slain by *Robert de Vallibus*, at a meeting for Arbitration of all differences, so that that Family seems never to have claimed it after The murther was barbarous, and *Robert*, to attone for it, built the Abbey of *Lanercost*, and gave to it the Lands which had caused the quarrel But this by the way)] After his death, King Henry the second bestow'd it upon *Hubert de Vallibus*, or *Vaulx*, whose Coat Armour was *Chequey*, *Argent and Gules* His son Robert founded and endow'd the abbey of *Lanercost* But the Estate, within a few years, came by marriage to the *Moltons*, and from them by a daughter to Ranulph Lord *Dacre*, whose posterity have flourished in great honour down to our time [However, it is to be observ'd, that in the account of the Lords of *Gillesland*, the Chronicles differ very much For, according to others, *Ranulph* and *Radulph* are the same name, and *Ranulph de Mechines* is call'd indifferently by these two names Then *Ranulph de Micenis*, who was Lord of Cumberland by Grant from the Conqueror, was the very same who was afterwards Earl of Chester by descent, after the death of his Cousin german *Richard*, second Earl of Chester, who was son to *John Bohun* and *Margaret* his wife, sister to *Hugh Lupus* first Earl of Chester Again, *William de Micenis*, brother to *Randolph de Micenis*, was Lord of *Coupland*, but not of *Gillesland*; for upon *Randolph*'s resignation of the County of Cumberland into the hands of King Henry the first, *Randolph* had given *Gillesland* to *Hubert de Vallibus*, which Grant the King confirm'd to him, and his Successors enjoy'd it. The Right Honourable *Charles Howard* present Earl of Carlisle, and Lord of *Gillesland*, claims descent from him by the mother's side, according to the pedigree of the Family, which is to be seen in the Chapel at *Naworth Castle*.]

Chron Cumbriæ Dugd Mon vol 1 p 400 Id Bar v 1 p 525

Having thus taken a Survey of the Sea coast and inner parts of *Cumberland*, we must pass to the East (a lean, hungry, and desolate Country;) though it afford nothing remarkable besides the head of *South Tine* in a wet spungy ground, and an ancient Roman stone Causey, * above ten yards broad. It is call'd the *Maiden way*, and comes out of Westmoreland and, at the confluence of the little river *Alon* and the *Tine*, on the side of a gentle ascent, there are the remains of a large old Town; which to the North has been fortify'd with a fourfold Rampire, and to the West † with one and a half The place is now call'd *Whitley-castle*; and, as a testimony of it's Antiquity, shows this imperfect Inscription ‖ compendiously written with the Letters link'd one in another from which we learn, that the third Cohort of the *Nervii* built a * Temple here to Antoninus the Emperour, Son of Severus

* 8 Ulnæ. Maiden-way.

† Sescuplo. Whitley Castle

‖ *Compendiose scribendi ratione literis implexis*

* Ædem.

IMP. CAES Lucii Septimi Severi Ara-
BICI, ADIABENICI, PARTHICI,
MAX. FIL DIVI ANTONINI Pii Germanici
SARMA NEP. DIVI ANTONINI PII
PRON
DIVI HADRIANI ABN DIVI TRAIANI
PARTH. ET DIVI NERVÆ ADNEPOTI.
M AVRELIO ANTONINO PIO
FEL AVG GERMANICO PONT MAX.
TR POT -- X -- IMP -- COS. IIII P. p. --
PRO PIETATE AEDE -- VOTO -
COMMVNI CVRANTE ---------
-------- LEGATO AVG
PR -- COH III NERVIO---------
RVM - - G R POS.

Now, seeing the third Cohort of the *Nervii* was quarter'd in this place, seeing also the *Notitia* sets them at *Alione*, as Antoninus does at *Alone*, and a little river running under it is call'd *Alne*, if I should think this the very *Alone*, I could not indeed deliver it for a positive truth, because the injuries of time, and the violence of wars, have long since obscur'd and obliterated these things; but it would at least amount to a probability

Upon the decay of the Roman Power in Britain, though this Country was cruelly harrass'd by the Scots and Picts, yet did it keep its original Inhabitants the Britains, longest of any, and fell late under the power of the Saxons But when the Danish wars had well nigh broken the Saxon government, it had its petty Kings, stil'd Kings of *Cumberland*, to the year of our Lord 946 *At which time* (as *Florilegus* tells us) *King Edmund, by the assistance of* Leolin *King of South Wales, spoil'd Cumberland of all its riches, and having put out the eyes of the two sons of* Dummail *King of that Country, granted that Kingdom to* Malcolm *King of Scots, to hold of him,* and

Kings of Cumberland

and to protect the North-parts of England by Sea and Land against the incursions of Enemies. Upon which, the eldest sons of the Kings of Scotland, as well under the Saxons as Danes, were stil'd *Governours of Cumberland.* But when England had yielded to the Normans, this County submitted among the rest, and fell to the share of *Ralph de Meschines*, whose eldest son *Ranulph* was Lord of *Cumberland*, and at the same time, in right of his mother and by the favour of his Prince, Earl of *Chester*. However, King Stephen, to ingratiate himself with the Scots, restor'd it to them, to † hold of him and his Successors Kings of England But his immediate Successor Henry the second, considering what prejudice this profuse Liberality of Stephen was like to prove both to him and his Kingdom, demanded back from the Scots, *Northumberland*, *Cumberland*, and *Westmorland*. *And the Scotch King*, (as Neubrigensis has it) *wisely considering, that since the King of England had both a better title, and was much stronger in those parts (though he could have alledg'd the oath which was said to have been made to his grandfather* David, *when he was knighted by him,) did very fairly and honestly restore the foresaid bounds, at the King's demand, and in lieu of them had* Huntingdonshire *restor'd, which belong'd to him by ancient right*

Earls of Cumberland. *Cumberland* had no Earls before Henry the eighth's time; who created *Henry Clifford*, descended from the Lords *de Veteri ponte* or *Vipont*, first Earl of Cumberland He, by *Margaret's*, daughter of *Henry Percy* Earl of Northumberland, had *Henry* the second Earl, who by his first wife, daughter of *Charles Brandon* Duke of Suffolk, had *Margaret* Countess of Derby; and by his second wife, daughter of Baron *Dacre* of *Gillesland*, had two sons, *George* and *Francis*. *George* the third Earl, famous for his Naval Exploits, and a person undaunted and indefatigable, dy'd in the year 1605, leaving one only daughter *Anne* *Francis* his brother, the fourth Earl, succeeded him; in whom [even when young] ‖ appeared a strong inclination to Virtue, becoming the issue of such honourable Ancestors; [who dying in the year of our Lord 1641, was succeeded by his only son *Francis*, who dy'd at York, 1643, leaving issue one only daughter; so that the male line of that most ancient and noble family is now extinct Of later years, his Royal Highness Prince *George* of Denmark (a Prince of known Valour, and a great example of Prudence, Wisdom, and Conjugal Affection,) honour'd this County, by having the title of Duke of *Cumberland*; which had been also enjoy'd before him, by Prince *Rupert*, Prince Palatine of the Rhine, a person of great Courage and Bravery]

‖ Appears, &c.

This County has 58 Parish-Churches, besides Chapels.

VALLUM;

OR,

The *PICTS WALL.*

THAT famous *Wall*, which was the boundary of the Roman Province, call'd by ancient Writers, *Vallum Barbaricum*, *Prætentura*, and *Clusura*, i. e. the *Barbarous Wall*, the *Line*, the *Fence* or *Hedge*, by Dio διατείχισμα, or *Thorough-wall*, by Herodian χῶμα, or *A vast Ditch*; by Antoninus, Cassiodorus, and others, *Vallum*, by Bede *Murus*, by the Britains *Gual Sever*, *Gal-Sever*, and *Mur-Sever*, by the Scots *Scottish-waith*, by the English and those that live about it, *the Picts-wall*, or *the Pehits-wall*, also *the Keepe-wall*, and by way of eminence, *The Wall* crosses the *upper part* of Cumberland, and is not by any means to be pass'd over in silence [(The *upper-part* (I say) if we express it according to the custom of the Latins, who call the more northern tract of any Country, *Pars superior*, but otherwise, more justly called by the neighbouring Inhabitants, the *Low-land*.)]

The Fences in the Frontiers of the Provinces are call'd *Clusuræ* ab *excludendo*, from shutting out the enemy, and *Prætenturæ* a *prætendence*, from being stretched out against the enemy. See F. Pithæus in Advers. l. 1. c. 14.

When, by the Providence of God, and their own Valour, the affairs of the Romans had succeeded beyond expectation, and the ambitious bravery of that people had so enlarg'd their Conquests on all sides, that they began to be jealous of their own greatness, the Emperors thought it most advisable to set some bounds to their Dominions. For, like prudent Politicians, they observ'd that *Greatness ought to have its bounds*; *just as the Heavens keep their exact compass, and the Seas are toss'd about within their own limits.* Now these bounds were either *natural*, as the Sea, the larger Rivers, Mountains, Deserts, or *artificial*, viz. Fences placed on purpose for that end, such as Ditches, Castles, Towers, * Barricadoes of Trees, and Walls of Earth or Stone, with Garrisons planted along them to keep out the Barbarians. Whereupon, it is said in Theodosius's *Novels*, *By the contrivance of our Ancestors, whatever is under the power of the Romans, is defended against the incursions of Barbarians, by a Boundary Wall.* In times of peace, the Frontier garrisons were kept along the Line, in Castles and Cities, but when they were apprehensive of the incursions of their neighbours, then part of them, for the defence of their own, pitch'd their Tents in the Enemies Country, and part made excursions into the Enemies quarters, to observe their motions, and to engage, if they could, upon an advantage.

Limits or bounds of the Empire

* Concædes

Tit. 43

Hence we meet with *Stationes Agrariæ* in Vegetius.

In this Island, particularly; when they found, that those more remote parts of Britain had nothing agreeable either in the Air or the Soil, that they were inhabited by that barbarous crew, the Caledonians, and that the advantages of subduing them would not answer the trouble; they did at several times contrive several Fences, to bound and secure the *Province*. The first of that kind seems to have been made by *Julius Agricola*, when he placed Garrisons along that narrow slip of ground between * *Edenborrow-Frith* and *Dunbritten Frith*, which was afterwards fortify'd, as occasion requir'd. [But we are not to suppose, that this *Prætentura* of Agricola, had any thing of Walls or Rampires; since the learned † Archbishop *Usher* has prov'd out of Tacitus, that *Agricola* only *garrison'd* the Frontiers at this place, without contriving any other fence. It is likely, that according to the Roman custom, he plac'd some of his troops within the limits of the Barbarians Country, *intra fines Horestorum*: for these *Horesti* were not the inhabitants on the river Esk, near the borders of *England* (as hath been asserted) but those of *Angus* and *Mernes*, as the Scotch Historians sufficiently evidence, particularly the learned ‖ Sir *George Mackenzie*. * Not but the foundation of the name may, for all that, stand good, and the *Horesti* be deriv'd from *Ar-Esk*, considering there is a *South* as well as a *North Esc*.]

The first *Prætentura*

* Bodotria & Glotta.

† Ant. Eccl. Brit. p. 316.

‖ Defence, p. 79.

* See in Scotland.

Hadrian, for whom the God *Terminus* retreated, made the second Fence, after he had retir'd about eighty miles, either out of envy to the glory of *Trajan* (under whom the Empire was at it's utmost extent,) or out of fear. *He* (says Spartian) *drew a Wall of eighty miles in length, to divide the Barbarians and the Romans!* which one may gather, from what follows in Spartian, *to have been made in fashion of a* † *Mural hedge, being large stakes fix'd deep in the ground, and fasten'd together.* And this is it which we are now speaking of, for it runs along, eighty miles together; and upon it, are the *Pons Ælia*, [(which by the sound should seem to be *Pont-Eland* in Northumberland,)] *Classis Ælia*, *Cohors Ælia*, *Ala Sabiniana*, which took their names from *Ælius Hadrianus* and *Sabina* his wife. And the Scotch Historian, who wrote the *Rota Temporum*, tells us, *That Hadrian did first draw a Wall of a prodigious bigness made of Turfs (of that height that it looks like a mountain, with a deep ditch before it) from the mouth of the Tine to the river Eske, i. e. from the German to the Irish Ocean.* Which Hector Boetius delivers in the very same words.

The second *Prætentura*

† *Murali sepe*. Some read *Muris*.

Rota Temporum.

[With reference to the forementioned retreat of the God *Terminus*, it may be observed here, that not many years ago, was found (on the ruins of the Wall, a little below Carlisle) a small wing'd image of brass, somewhat more than half a foot in length, well agreeing with the description which some of the ancients have given us of the God *Terminus*.]

The God *Terminus*.

Lollius Urbicus, Lieutenant of Britain under Antoninus Pius, did by his great success remove the Bounds again to the place where Julius Agricola had first set them, and rais'd a Wall there, which was the third Fence or *Prætentura*. *He* (says Capitolinus) *conquer'd the Britains, and driving back the Barbarians, made another Wall of Turf*, i. e. distinct from that of Hadrian. The honour of Lollius's success in Britain was by Fronto (as the Panegyrist has it)

The third *Prætentura*

it) *given entirely to* Antoninus *the Emperour*; *affirming, that though he liv'd quietly in his Palace at Rome, and had only given out a Commission to the Lieutenant, yet he had merited all the glory*; *as a Pilot steering a large Ship deserves the whole honour of the expedition* But, that this Wall of *Antoninus Pius*, and of his Lieutenant *Lollius Urbicus*, was in Scotland, shall be shewn hereafter

The fourth Prætentura

When the Caledonian Britains, under *Commodus* the Emperour, had broke thorow this: *Severus* neglecting that farther Wall, and that large Country between, drew a Wall cross the Island, from *Solway Frith* to *Tinmouth* And this (if I judge aright) was along the very same ground, where Hadrian had before made his of stakes In which I have the Opinion of Hector Boëtius on my side *Severus* (says he) *order'd Hadrian's Wall to be repair'd, and Stone-fortresses to be built upon it, and Turrets at such a distance as the sound of a Trumpet, against the wind, might be heard from one to another* And elsewhere *Our Annals tell us, that the Wall which was begun by Hadrian, was finish'd by Severus* The learned Spaniard also, Hieronymus Surita, tells us, that *Hadrian's Fence was* * *carry'd on and compleated with vast works, by* Septimius Severus, *and had the name of* Vallum *given it* Guidus Pancirolus likewise affirm, that Severus only *repair'd* Hadrian's Wall, which was fall'n *He* (says Spartian) *secur'd Britain by a Wall cross the Island, from sea to sea, which is the great glory of his Government whereupon he took the name of* Britannicus *He clear'd Britain* (says Aurelius Victor *of the enemy, and fenc'd-in as much of it with a Wall, as was judg'd for his interest* Which also we meet with in Spartian And Eutropius, *That he might make the utmost provision for the security of the Provinces he had got, he drew a Wall, for thirty five miles together* (read eighty) *from sea to sea And he found it necessary* (says Orosius) *to separate with a Wall that part of the Island which he had possess'd himself of, from the other Nations that were unconquer'd For which reason, he drew a great Ditch, and built a strong Wall fortify'd with several Turrets, from sea to sea, one hundred twenty two miles in length* Bede agrees with him, but is not willing to believe that Severus built a Wall, urging, that a *Murus* or *Wall* is made of stone, but a *Vallum* of pales (call'd *Valli*) and turf, (notwithstanding which, it is certain that *Vallum* and *Murus* are promiscuously us'd) However, Spartian calls it *Murus*, and hints that Severus built both a *Murus* and a *Vallum*, in these words, *Post Murum apud Vallum in Britannia missum* But one may gather from Bede, that this *Vallum* was nothing but a Wall of turf, and it cannot be affirmed with any truth, that Severus's Wall was of stone However, take Bede's own words *Severus having quieted the Civil Commotions (at that time very high) was forc'd over into Britain by almost a general defection of his Allies. There, after several great and difficult engagements, he thought it necessary to separate that part of the Island which he had recover'd from the other Nations that were unconquer'd, not with a* Murus, *as some think, but with a* Vallum *Now a* Murus *is of stone; but a* Vallum, *such as they made round a Camp to secure it against the attacks of the enemy, is made of turf cut regularly out of the ground, and built high above ground like a Wall, with the Ditch before it, out of which the turf has been dug* † *and strong* * *Stakes of wood all along the brink* Severus *therefore drew a great Ditch, and built a strong earthen Wall, for tify'd with several Turrets, from sea to sea* Nor is it express'd by any other word than *Vallum*, either in *Antoninus* or the *Notitia* and in British it is call'd *Guall Sever* [The Royal † Paraphrast upon Bede, says it was mid dice and mid eorþ-wealle, i e. *with a ditch, and a turf of Earth*; and afterwards, speaking of a later fabrick of Stone in the same place, he says, it was built ðær Severus se Casere iu þer dician eorð wall gewircan, i. e. *where* Severus *the Emperor commanded a ditch and a turf wall to be made*] Take also what Ethelwerd (the most ancient Writer we have, next Bede) has said of Severus *He drew a Ditch cross the foresaid Island from sea to sea, and within it, built a* * *Wall with Turrets and Forts* This he afterwards calls *Fossa Severia*, as do also our ancient Saxon-Annals, Severus Brytenland mid dic forgyrde fram sæ oð sæ, i e *Severus girt in Britain with a* dike *from sea to sea* And other Annals of later date, Severus on Brytene geworhte weal of turfum fram sæ to sæ, i e *Severus made a Wall of turf* (or a Vallum) *from sea to sea* Malmesbury also calls it *the eminent and famous Ditch* In the place whereof, a Wall of Stone was built about two hundred years after; of which we shall have occasion to speak by and by

* Longius protractum ...

Murus & Vallum

Gul Malmsb

† Sude.

† Eccl Hist l. 1 c 5

L 1 c 12

* Murum

[There are some of Severus's Coins yet extant with this Inscription, VICTORIÆ BRIT and on the Reverse, the figure of *Victory*, holding a Trophy in her left hand, and dragging a Captive in the right Others have the portraiture of *Severus* on Horseback trampling upon his Enemies And lately, it is said, there was found, not far from Carlisle, near the *Vallum*, a stone with this Inscription, *Sept Severo Imp qui Murum hunc condidit*)]

Vaillant Numism p 2,7, 2,9

As to Eutropius's making the length thirty five miles, and Victor thirty two, and other Authors one hundred thirty two I fansy, this difference must have risen from a corruption in the Numerals For the Island is not one hundred thirty two miles broad at this place, even though you reckon the winding course of the Wall with the ascents and descents, and tho' you take your computation according to the Italian miles, you'll make it amount to little more than eighty, as Spartian has truly stated the account [Let us then try, how far these differences may be reconciled Eutropius sets it at XXXII, and if some others have XXXV, it is easie to imagine, that a little inadvertency in the Transcriber might chang II into V Thus far the Account seems to make for *Buchanan*, that Severus's fortification was really between the two Friths of *Edenburrow* and *Dumbritton* And *Paulus Orosius* (who computes its length at CXXXII miles) goes so far beyond the extent of that which reach'd from *Solway* to *Tinmouth*, that thence no true estimate is to be had But it is most likely, that this whole difference is to be stated from *Spartian*, who (rightly) asserts, that the extent of *Hadrian's* ditch was LXXX miles Out of this number, probably (by the heedless change of L into C) the copyers of Orosius made CXXX, and by a careless dropping of the same Letter, the transcribers of *Eutropius* turn'd it into XXX]

A few years after, they seem to have begun to neglect this Wall. But when the Emperour Alexander Severus (as we read in *Lampridius*) *had given such Lands as were taken from the Enemy, to the Frontier garrisons and their Officers, so as all was to be theirs, upon condition that their heirs too were brought up in the service of the Empire, and never put under the command of private persons, reckoning they would be more diligent and courageous when they fought for their own* (I desire, particular notice may be taken of this, because here we have either the original of *Feudal tenures*, or

Why the grounds [a long the Frontiers] were granted to the Commanders there.

Original of Feudal Tenures

at least a species of them.) Then the Romans pass'd the Wall, and fixing in the Country of the Barbarians, built and mann'd garrisons, and by degrees carried the bounds of the Empire as far as *Bodotria*. Nor but the Barbarians by sallies and skirmishes, drove them back, now and then, to *Severus*'s Wall. Dioclesian took great care to keep his ground, under whom the government of Britain was granted to *Carausius*, as a person every way fit to engage such a desperate People; and he (as we shall observe in its proper place) ‖ restor'd the old Barrier between *Glotta* and *Bodotria*. Constantine the Great is the first, whom we find censur'd for neglecting this Boundary. For Zosimus says, *That when the utmost bounds of the Roman Empire were by the wise conduct of Dioclesian, fortify'd with Towns, Castles and Burrows, wherein all our Troops were garrison'd; it was not possible for the Barbarians to make inroads, their Enemy being planted in all parts to receive them. But Constantine, quitted that custom of Forts and Garrisons, remov'd the better half of the Soldiers from the Frontiers, into Towns which had no occasion for them, and so at the same time, expos'd the Marches to the inroads of the Barbarians, and pester'd the Cities, that had liv'd quietly and undisturb'd, with quartering of Soldiers, by which means several of them were left desolate without Inhabitants. The Soldiers themselves be effeminated with shews and pleasures, and in a word, laid the first foundation of that gradual decay and ruin, which is at this day so visible in the Empire.*

‖ Restituit

Lib. 2.

The decay of the Roman Empire.

Marcellin. l. 38. About the year 367.

The Country between the two Frontier-fences was so entirely recoverd by *Theodosius*, father of Theodosius the Emperour, that he built Cities in it, and garrison'd the Castles, and fortify'd the Borders with Watches and Barriers; and having thus recover'd it, he so compleatly reduc'd it to the former condition, as to set over it a * lawful Governour; and it was call'd *Valentia*, in honour of *Valentinian*. Also, Theodosius his son, when his signal courage had promoted him to the Empire, took particular care of the Frontiers, and commanded that the *Magister Officiorum* (or *Scout-Master-General*) should every year signifie to the Emperour, how the Soldiery stood, and what care was taken of the Castles and Fences. But when the Affairs of the Empire began visibly to sink, and the Picts and Scots, breaking through the Turf-wall at Bodotria, made havock of all these parts; the Roman Legion under *Gallio of Ravenna*, was sent to their assistance, and repuls'd the Barbarians. But they being recall'd for the defence of Gaul, advis'd the Britains (take it in the very words of Gildas and Bede) *to build a Wall cross the Island, between the two Seas, which might secure them against the Incursions of the Enemy; and so they return'd home, in great triumph. But the Islanders building this Wall *, not of stone but of turf, (as wanting skilful hands to carry on such a great work) it signified nothing, in point of Safety.* So Gildas tells us, *that being built of turf, not of stone, and that by an unskilful rabble, without any Director, it stood them in no stead.* Concerning the place where this Wall was built, Bede goes on thus. *Now, they made it between the two arms or bosoms of the Sea, for a great many miles together; that where the Waters did not defend them, the Wall might be a security against the Incursions of the Enemy.* (Such a Wall as this, of a vast length, defended Assyria against foreign Invasions, as Marcellinus has told us. And the | *Chinese* at this day (as we read in Osorius) fence their Valleys and Plains with Walls, to assist them in keeping out the Scythians.) *Of which work, i. e. of an exceeding broad and high Wall, the footsteps are very visible at this day. It begins almost two miles from the Monastery* Abercurnig *to the East, in a place call'd in the language of the Picts* Penuahel, *but in that of the English* Penueltun; *and so, running Westward, ends hard by the City* Alcluith. *But their old Enemies, understanding that the Roman Legion was gone, presently set sail, threw down the bounds, put all to the sword, (and as it were) mow'd them like ripe Corn, and trampl'd them under foot, and overran all in their way. Upon this, they send Ambassadours to Rome once more, who in a most mournful address desire assistance; that their miserable Country may not be utterly ruin'd, and the name of a Roman Province (which had so long flourish'd among them) be brought under contempt by the insolence of foreign Nations. A Legion is again sent over, which, coming over in Autumn (when they did not dream of them) slew great numbers of the Enemy, and drove back such as could make their escape, over the arm of the Sea: whereas, before that, they us'd to cross that arm and keep their set times of Invasion and Plunder every year, without any manner of disturbance.*

* Restorem legitimum. *Valentia.* Codex Theodosii.

Blondus.

The fifth *Praetentura.*

* Non tam lapidibus quam cespitibus.

| Seres.

The Wall between Edinburgh-Frith and Dunbritton-Frith.

And now the Romans retir'd to Severus's Wall; and (as the *Notitia* has it, which was written about the latter end of Theodosius the younger) along the *Linea Valli*, i. e. all-along the wall, on both sides, there lay in garrison five ‖ wings of Horse, with their *Praefects*, fifteen Cohorts of Foot with their *Tribunes*, one * band, and one † squadron. But of these we have spoken in their proper places, and shall have occasion to speak of them again. Concerning what follow'd, Bede goes on thus. *Then the Romans told the Britains once for all, that they would not any more harrass themselves with such toilsome expeditions for their defence, but advis'd them by all means to betake them to their Arms, and to dispute the cause with the enemy; suggesting, that they wanted nothing to be too hard for them, but only to quit that lazy way of living. The Romans also (hoping that that might be of consequence to their Allies, whom they were now forc'd to leave) built a strong * Wall of Stone from Sea to Sea, directly by those Cities which had been settled there for fear of the enemy (where also Severus had formerly made his † Wall.)* I will likewise set down Gildas's words, from whom Bede had this. *The Romans, at the publick and private expence, joyning to themselves the assistance of the miserable Inhabitants, rais'd a* Wall *in a direct line from Sea to Sea, (not like that other, but according to their usual manner of building) along the Cities that had been contriv'd here and there for fear of the enemy.* But to return to Bede. *Which Wall, so much talk'd of, and visible at this day, and built at the publick and private expence, by the joint labour of the Romans and Britains, was eight foot broad and twelve high, running in a direct line from east to west; as is plain at this day to any that shall trace it.* From which words of Bede, it is evident that a certain learned man, instead of hitting the mark, put out his own eyes, when he affirm'd with so much zeal and eagerness against *Boetius*, and the other Scotch writers, that Severus's Wall was in Scotland. Does not Bede, after he has done with that *Vallum* at *Abercurning* in Scotland, expresly tell us of a wall of stone built in the place of Severus's turf-wall? and where, I pray, should this stone-wall be, but between *Tinmouth* and *Solway-frith*? and was not Severus's *Vallum* there too? The remains of a Wall are all along so very visible, that one may follow the track; and in the ‖ *Wastes* I my self have seen pieces of it for a long way together standing entire, except the battlements only, which are thrown down

About the year of our Lord 430. Alciatus calls it *Theodosius's Breviary.*

‖ *Alae.*

Soldiers garrison'd along the Wall.

* *Numerus.*

† *Cuneus.*

A wall of stone, the sixth *Praetentura.*

* *Murum.*

† *Vallum.*

‖ *In Vastis.*

[And

* Usc. p. 317

[And yet * Archbishop *Usher*, notwithstanding all this, enclines rather to the other Opinion, that it was at *Grimesdike*, and thinks this conjecture supported by Gildas's saying, that it was built *recto tramite*, which (says he) that betwixt *Bowness* and *Tinmouth* is not With the Archbishop agrees our late learned Bishop of *Worcester*, in his † historical account of *Church-government*, &c And it is certain, that along *Grimesdike*, are here and there (as hath been observed by the * *Gordons*,) several ruins of Stone-buildings: nor can we doubt, but there were Forts of stone erected at due distances along that Rampier But it is also certain, that in most places there appear no manner of remains of a *stone building*; whereas a continu'd stone-wall is easily follow'd from *Carlisle* to *New castle* As for Ninnius's story, it is so full of contradictions, that it is not to be regarded and after all the stress that is laid upon Gildas's expression, one shall hardly find the same number of miles that the Picts Wall makes, in any great road in England, which goes more (*recto tramite*) in a streight line, than that does]

† Pag 4

* Blaeu's Atlas.

Hist Brit. cap 19.

I have observ'd the track of it running up the mountains, and down again, in a most surprising manner where the fields are plain and open, there lies a broad and deep ditch along the outside of it, only, in some places it is now fill'd up, and on the inside a Causeway or Military way, but very often broken and discontinu'd It had great numbers of Turrets or little Castles a mile one from another, call'd now *Castle steeds*, and on the inside a sort of fortify'd little Towns, which they call to this day *Chesters*, the foundations whereof, in some places, appear in a square form These had Turrets between them, wherein the Soldiers were always in readiness to receive the Barbarians, and in which the *Areans* (whom the same Theodosius, we just now mention'd, remov'd for their treachery) had their stations *These* Areans *were an order of men instituted by the ancients, whose business it was* (as Marcellinus tells us) *to make excursions into the enemy's country, and give intelligence of their motions to our Officers* So that the first founders seem to have follow'd the counsel of him, who wrote a Book to Theodosius and his sons, concerning the *Arts of War* For thus he has it *One of the great interests of the Common wealth, is the care of the Frontiers, which would be better secur'd by good numbers of castles, built at a mile's distance from one another, with a firm wall and strong towers Not at the publick charge, but by the contributions of such as have lands in the neighbourhood, who are to keep watch and ward in these, and the fields all about; that the quiet of the Provinces (girt as it were round, and circled in) may be preserved without the least disturbance* The Inhabitants tell you, there was a brazen * Trumpet or Pipe (whereof they now and then find pieces,) so artificially laid in the wall between each castle and tower, that upon the apprehension of danger at any one place, by the sounding of it notice might be given to the next, and then to the third, and so on Such a wonderful contrivance as this, Xiphilin mentions out of Dio, speaking of the Towers at Constantinople, in the Life of Severus But now, though the Walls be down, and no such thing as a *Trumpet* to be met with, yet several hereabouts hold manours and lands of the King in *Cornage* (as the Lawyers word it,) that is, on condition to give their neighbours notice of the incursion of the enemy by *sounding of a horn*; which some imagine to be a remain of the old Roman custom They were also bound *to serve in the Scotch wars, upon the King's summons* (as it is express'd in the publick Records;) *in their march thither, in the van, at their return, in the rear*

Castle-steeds

Chesters.

Areani Exploratores

* Tubulus A Trumpet to convey the voice

Cornage

The track of the Wall

But to mark out the track of the *Wall* somewhat more accurately it begins at *Blatum Bulgium*, or *Bulness*, upon the Irish Sea; so keeps along the side of the *Frith of Eden* by *Burg upon Sands*, to *Luguvallum* or *Carlisle*, where it passes the *Ituna* or *Eden* Thence it runs along with the river *Irthing* below it, and passes the winding little river of *Cambeck*, where are the marks of a vast Castle Afterwards, passing the rivers *Irthing* and *Poltrosse*, it enters Northumberland, and through those crowding mountains runs along with the river call'd *South Tine* without any interruption (save only at *North Tine*, over which it was formerly continu'd by a bridge) to the very German ocean, as I shall shew in the proper place, when I come to *Northumberland*

But this Structure, however great and wonderful, was not able to stop the incursions of the enemy, for no sooner had the Romans left Britain, but the Picts and Scots surprize them, make an attempt upon the wall, pull down the Guards with their crooked weapons, break through the fortifications, and make a strange havock of Britain, well-nigh ruin'd before with civil wars and a most grievous famine But let *Gildas* a Britain, who liv'd not long after, describe to you the deplorable Calamities of those times; *The Romans being drawn home, there descend in great crowds from their* * Caroghes, *(wherein they were brought over the* † *Stitick Vale, about the middle of summer, in a scorching hot season,) a duskish swarm of vermine out of their narrow holes, or a hideous crew of Scots and Picts, somewhat different in manners, but all alike thirsting after blood, &c Who finding that the old Confederates* [the Romans] *were march'd home, and refus'd to return any more, put on greater boldness than ever, and possess'd themselves of all the north, and the remote parts of the Kingdom, to the very wall To withstand this invasion, the towers* [along the wall] *are defended by a lazy garrison, undisciplin'd, and too cowardly to engage an enemy; being enfeebled with continual sloth and idleness In the mean while, the naked enemy advance with their hooked weapons, by which the miserable Britains are pull'd down from the tops of the walls and dash'd against the ground Yet they who were destroy'd, had this advantage in an untimely death, that they escaped these miseries and sufferings, which immediately besel their brethren and children To be short, having quitted their Cities and the high Wall, they betook themselves to sligh, and fell into a more desperate and hopeless dispersion than ever Still the Enemy gave them chase; still more cruel slaughters overtook them; as Lambs by the bloody Butcher, so were these poor Creatures cut to pieces by their enemies So that they may justly be compar'd to herds of wild beasts; for these miserable people did not stick to rob one another for supplies of victuals; and so, inbred dissensions enhanc'd the misery of their foreign sufferings, and brought things to that pass by spoil and robbery, that meat (the support of life) was wanting in the Country, and no comfort of that kind was to be had, but by recourse to hunting*

* The highlanders call their little ships at this day *Caroches*

† *Stitica Vallis* in the text, but the Paris edition reads *Scythica Vallis*, possibly the Scotch Sea

The prudence of the Romans in contriving the Wall

Thus much is farther observable, That the wisdom of the Romans did so contrive this *Wall*, as to have on the inside of it two great rivers (the *Tine* and *Irthing*, divided only by a narrow slip of land) which might be as it were another fence; so the cunning Barbarians, in their attempts upon it, commonly made choice of that part of the wall between the rivers, that after th y had broke thorow, they might have no rivers in their way, but have a clear passage into the heart of the Province, as we will shew by and by in *Northumberland* As for the stories of the common people concerning this Wall, I purposely omit them but one thing there is, which I will not keep from the Reader, because I had it confirm'd by persons of very good credit. There is a general perswasion in the neighbourhood, handed down by Tradition, that the Roman garrisons upon the frontiers, set in these parts abundance of Medicinal Plants for their own use. Whereupon the Scotch Surgeons come hither a Simpling every year in the beginning of Summer; and having by long experience found the virtue of these Plants, they magnifie them very much, and affirm them to be very soveraign [But, of late years, most diligent search hath been made along the Wall by a curious Botanist, who could never meet with any sort of Plants there, which are not as plentiful in some other part of the Country] Medicinal Plants

[*Observations upon the* PICTS WALL, *in a Journey made between* Newcastle *and* Carlisle, *in the Year* 1708, *on purpose to Survey it.*

Stanwick FROM the foot of the Bank of *Stanwick*, a little Village (where the Wall crosses the Eden, and so runs directly West to *Blatum Bulgium*) it runs directly East through a pleasant level Country (curiously embellished with great plenty of Corn, Meadow, and Pasture-grounds) for eight miles together, in all which space the Wall is for the most part quite taken away for the building of the neighbouring houses, only, one observes where the Ridge of it has been, and also the Trench all the way before it on the North, as also some of their little Towers or mile-Castles on the South-side

Naworth castle Hence, it runs up a pretty high Hill, which lies directly north of *Naworth* Castle, and so continues for about two miles, but still in inclosed grounds, in this space, all the middle part of the wall is still standing

Irthing Hence, to the crossing of the Irthing, for above three miles, it runs through a large Waste for the most part, where generally you see the whole breadth of the wall entire, *i e* eight foot, and five foot, and, in some places, about six foot high Also, in several places you see a fair front of *Ashlers* for little spaces together, which is generally more visible on the North side than the South, by reason the front on this side is for the most part taken away for the building of the neighbouring houses, whereas on the North side there are nothing but great Wastes Half a mile on this side the river *Irthing*, at a place called *Burdissel*, adjoyning to the Wall, is to be seen the foundation of a very large Castle about one hundred and forty yards square, the thickness of the Walls about four foot and a half, and a deep Vallum or Trench round it Burdissel

Where the Wall crosses *Irthing* is a very high and deep Gill; and hard by, is *Willowford*, where the *Cohors prima Ælia Dacorum* had their station Willowford

Hence, it runs through pretty high inclosed grounds, till it crosses the river *Tippall* at *Thirlewall Castle*, which is close by the North side of the wall, and is all standing, except part of the outside leaf of the top of the north side of it, which is fallen; the Structure is square, and has been curiously vaulted underneath, and the walls are about six foot thick; it has six little Turrets on the top, the West and East end has each of them two, and the South and North side each of them one, in the middle; the length of the Castle is about twenty yards, the breadth twelve, including the thickness of the Walls. Thirlwall castle

From the top of the *Thirlewall*-bank, to *Seaven-Shale*, for eight or nine miles together, the Wall runs over the summits of steep, ragged, bare, and inaccessible rocks on the north-side, being built only at eight, six, five, four, and very often at scarce two yards distance from the very precipice. The highest part of the Wall, that ever I saw standing any where betwixt *Newcastle* and *Carlisle*, is at about half a mile's distance from *Caervorran* (which stands on *Thirlewall* bank head,) and there I observed it to be very nigh three yards high The rest of it, to *Seaven-Shale*, is often quite taken away almost to the very foundation In other places, it stands about a yard high or more, and here and there, for little spaces, one sees the front of *Ashlers* on the North side of it; most of the neighbouring places on the South side having been built out of the Stones dug out of the Wall This is a very dismal Country, but more especially on the North side, being all wild Fells and Moors, full of Mosses and Loughes Seavenshale Caervorran

Caer Vorran above-mentioned has been a square Roman City, with a deep Vallum or Trench round it, one hundred and twenty yards one way, and one hundred and sixty, or one hundred and seventy yards the other Great Ruins of old House steeds are very visible, with the tracks of the Streets; and without the South side Trench, are likewise several long streets, and foundations of houses

At a place called the *Chesters*, two miles East of *Caer Vorran*, are the Ruins of another square City, much about the compass of the above-mentioned *Caer-Vorran*, where are likewise abundance of old House-steeds, and tracks of houses, to be discerned, as there are likewise on the South side Vallum of it Chesters

At three miles distance from the *Chesters*, above, is a place called *Little Chesters*, to distinguish them from the other, but at a mile's distance Little chesters stance from the Wall, Southward, with a square Vallum round it, and full of rubbish of old houses: abundance of stones with Inscriptions have been found here; but as I was told, through the ignorance of the Country people they have been all employed to mean uses.

But along the Wall, and about a mile west of *Seaven Shale*, are the largest Ruins that I observed any where; the name of the place is *House steeds*; and I believe is exactly in the midst of the Island betwixt the two Seas. The extent of this City, is, as they told me, and as I guessed also by my eye, almost seven hundred yards one way, and about four hundred from south to north the other. It lies all along the side of a pretty steep Hill, but that part of the City, where the Vallum or square Trench seems to have been, is not by far so large. Vast quantities of Roman Altars with Inscriptions have been here dug-up, as also abundance of Images of their Gods, several Coins, *&c.* Seven or eight Roman Altars are standing there now, being lately dug-up, three or four of which have their Inscriptions very plain and legible; one is dedicated to *Hercules*, another to *Jupiter & Numinibus*, others to other Deities, and all by the *Cohors prima Tungrorum*, which kept garrison here, so that consequently the name of this place must be *Bremeturacum*, for at that place this Cohort kept garrison. I saw there also a great number of *Statues*, as first, the Pedestal of one that had been erected to *Mars*, but there was nothing left but part of the Feet, and on one of the sides of the Pedestal it was inscribed *Marti*. This Pedestal might be two foot long, and eighteen inches broad. A second Statue was very entire, all the parts of the body being cut in full proportion out of one entire stone: the face was young, it had wings upon the Shoulders, a sort of Covering like a Mantle upon the body, and the feet rested upon a large Globe; so that I took it for a Statue of Mercury, for there was no inscription. A third was also out of one entire stone, drawn at full length in the habit of a man, with a different Mantle from the former, and in the left hand had something resembling a staff, in some parts of it streight, but in other parts bending inwards and crooked. Whether this Statue was of *Jupiter* (for I saw no Inscription) holding a Thunderbolt in his hand, or what else, I must leave to others to determine. There were also three Statues all cut out of one stone, and in a sitting posture, but they wanted the heads and shoulders. The bodies, thighs, and legs which remain'd, were very bulky, so as they might be so many Statues of *Bacchus* by their size. Two or three others there were of men and women naked.

Nigh the place where all these and other rarities were found, there was also a Column above two yards in length, and two foot diameter, lying sunk in the ground at one end. The people of the place have a *tradition* of some great house or palace that was at this place. This is at the Southermost part of the East side of the City, in a bottom; three hundred yards West of which, upon a little eminence, are to be seen the foundations of a Roman Temple, and the Inhabitants do still call it the *Chapel-steed*. Here lie two Roman Altars; one whereof is a very fair one, inscribed to *Jupiter & Numinibus*, as above. They told me they had also a Statue drawn in the portraicture of a Priest, with a Sash or Girdle about him, but being at a little distance, I did not see it; probably it might be of one of the Priests or Flamins. It is very surprizing to see the vast rubbish of old buildings that yet remains here, with the tracks of the Streets, *&c.*

House steeds

Chapel steed

At *Seaven-Shale* on the north side of the Wall, the greatest part of a square Roman Castle is still to be seen, standing, and curiously vaulted underneath, as that at *Thirle wall* is.

Seaven Shale

From *Seaven Shale* to *Carrow-Brough*, the Wall runs through a level and better Country for a mile and a half. At this place, is a square Roman City with a Vallum about it, the square one hundred and twenty yards every way. Here is much Rubbish, with many foundations of houses, and tracks of streets, to be seen.

Carraw Brough.

From this place, for two miles and half, the Wall runs over pretty high ground to *Choller ford*, and in most of this space, the true Wall is to be seen standing, with a front of Ashler both inside and outside. It is in many places here, about two yards high, and the breadth eight foot, as *Bede* describes it; and here, the Country is more pleasant and fertile, as it is likewise on the other side of the Ford, being, after we come to *Portgate*, for the most part all inclosed and pleasant grounds, as far as *New castle*.

Chollerford

At this place hath been fixed the fort *Gallana*, and here we find the name of the two *Chesters*, the *Great* and *Little*. In the *Great Chesters* I could observe nothing, but in the *Little Chesters* which join upon *North Tine*, I observed a large Fort one hundred and fifty or one hundred and sixty yards square, with a Vallum about it. In this there were several heaps of rubbish, but probably the place has been some large Castle, rather than any fortified City, inasmuch as the manner of the rubbish did not so much countenance the latter.

At *Walwick-Grange* hard by, I saw a very large and fine Statue of a naked man on horse-back, brandishing a Sword in his hand, and under it was written, *Magnus*, or *A*[illegible]*lius victor vix An xxx.* There was also a Statue of a woman, drawn down as low or lower than her breasts, and under it an Inscription, which I could not very well read, but however so much I read of it, as to find she was daughter of such a one, wife to another, lived so many years, *&c.*

Walwick-Grange

From *Choller ford* to *Portgate*, which is about three miles and half distant, the true Wall it self in some places is to be seen standing, just as I described it on the other side of the *North-Tine*. At this *Portgate*, there seems to have been great ruins of old buildings, and there is a square old Tower still standing, now converted into a dwelling-house. From *Portgate* to *Halton-Sheeles*, at a mile and half's distance, there is nothing but the rubbish of the Wall to be observed.

Portgate

Halton Sheels

From *Halton Sheeles*, along the Moor for two miles East (till we come opposite to *Waltown*) the breadth of the Wall (which is still eight foot) is very discernible, as is also for a little way, in some places, the *Ashler* front thereof, namely, two, three, or four sets of *Ashler* above one another; for the stones above those courses, do very often seem rather to have been set up lately.

Waltown.

At this *Waltown* (which is supposed to be *Bede's Ad Murum*) I conversed with a very intelligent man of ninety years of age, and something read in History; yet I do not find that they have the least tradition of its being a Royal Vill in the time of the Kings of Northumberland, or, of either King *Peada's*, or

Sigb rt's

Sigbert's King of the *East-Angles*, being baptized there by *Finan* Bishop of *Lindisfarne* But there is a place called *Waltown*, a mile East of *Caer-Vorran*, in the way to the *Chesters* above-mentioned, where is part of a square little Fort standing, and where they have a tradition of a certain King's being baptized in a Well hard by, which they shewed me; but then it by no means agrees with the distance of twelve miles from the Sea, which *Bede* makes *Ad Murum* to be.

From this *Waltown* (which stands half a mile within the Wall) for eight miles together all the way to *Newcastle*, the Wall runs over the top of a great deal of very high ground, but all finely inclosed, and the Country on both sides yields a pleasing prospect, by the great plenty and variety of Corn, Meadow, and Pasture-grounds For six miles of this space, the inner part of the Wall is generally discernible by its high ridge, the outer leafs on both sides having long since probably been taken away but, for the latter two miles, from the foot of *Benwell* hills to *Newcastle*, it runs along the High street to West gate in *Newcastle*, and were it not for the Ditch on the north-side, which runs generally through the Inclosures, and may be traced exactly within little more than a quarter of a mile's distance from Westgate, it could hardly be discovered

Old Winchester At *Old Winchester*, or *Vindolana*, seven miles west of *Newcastle*, are the ruinous Walls of an oblong square Fort to be discerned the walls seem to have been five foot or more in thickness, with a Trench or Vallum round about This Fort stands at a quarter of a mile's distance, on the north-side

Ruchester At *Ruchester*, within half a mile of *Vindolana*, but on the south side of the Wall, are visible ruins of a very large square Roman Castle, with foundations of several houses in the middle of the *Area*: the square, as nigh as I can guess, may be about one hundred and fifty yards; and at the west part of the square are three or four plots of ground in the very Wall (which seems to have been five or six foot thick) for little Towers. This has also a Vallum round it, and joins close to the wall.

Benwel hills The last great Fort that I observed, is upon the top of *Benwell* hills; square, and considerably larger than *Rutchester*, with a Vallum also round it By the heaps of rubbish, it appears to have been some very large and considerable Castle, rather than a City; though in one place, something like a track of a Street, with foundations of houses on both sides, is pretty observable.

Besides all these greater Forts, and fortified Cities above-mentioned; throughout all the extent I have been speaking of, are great numbers of little Forts or Castles, which the Inhabitants thereabouts generally call *Mile-Castles*, as built at every mile's end; and so I believe they really were, for, at that distance, I have observed several They are always either exact or oblong squares; but their size or largeness is pretty different Some I have observed thirty yards square, several of them twenty five, or twenty six yards from South to North, and fifteen or sixteen from West to East, including the thickness of the walls, which is likewise often different; others of them again are twenty yards from North to South, and nine or ten yards from West to East, with the thickness of the Walls

Ditch before the Wall All this space, betwixt *Newcastle* and *Carlisle*, there lies a deep and broad ditch before the Wall to the North, even upon the highest hills, excepting only the space afore-mentioned between *Caer-vorran* and *Seaven-Shale*; where the vast and horrid steepness of the Rocks to the North, is more than a sufficient security to it This ditch I generally found to be twelve yards broad at least, and every where very visible, except in some little spaces in Cumberland nigh *Carlisle*, where it is almost level with the rest of the ground; but any where else, the least depth is one yard and half from the North bank of the ditch; in many places, two, three and four yards; and in some it is five or six yards deep, hewn out of the solid Rock The first six yards next the North bank of the ditch generally (in the soft and even grounds) go all level, to the same depth The other six rise up gradually to the foundation of the Wall in form of a Counterscarp But upon the Hills, or in rocky and stony ground, very often only two or three yards rise up next the Wall, so as to admit the Conveniency of a walk, next the north side of the Wall For by the tradition of the Inhabitants thereabouts, there have been many gates fixed in the Wall, and so consequently there must have been a sort of Parade or Walk next the Wall

Throughout all this length, the ground, whereon the Wall runs, is admirably well chosen; for it is all along built upon the highest ground, and sometimes makes little turnings on purpose to take it in, so as the Country on both sides generally falls lower from the Wall. And it is wonderful to observe the many great and towring mountains it runs up and down; in which respect the advantages it has are many and considerable, compared with the *Mud* and *Earthen* wall of *Adrian* and *Severus* For that is generally carried along through bottoms and low grounds (as being more convenient for the digging of that stuff and matter, whereof it was composed;) whereby it had this vast disadvantage, especially in *Northumberland*-wastes, that the Enemy, by possessing the Hills, which adjoin and over-top it, might thence easily annoy the Roman Garrisons on the South-side Wall built upon high Grounds

The Wall we have hitherto been speaking of, is, very little of it (contrary to what *Bede* hath intimated) built *upon* that of *Severus* Indeed, for about four or five miles directly East from *Stanwick* nigh *Carlisle*, it seems to be built upon the same ground; but at that distance from *Irthington-moor* it takes a quite different rout, and the very parting of the Mud or Earthen wall from it I fairly traced And, from that place, I question much, whether ever it joined the Stone-wall again; if it did, it must be within four or five miles of *Newcastle*, but that it did so, I could not discover This Mud or Earthen wall (for so all the people, that live about them, call it) keeps a parallel course with the Stone-wall itself. In *Cumberland*, after the parting abovesaid, I observ'd it for about a mile and half to run to a quarter of a mile's distance or more, but after that I saw no more of it till I came to *Caer-Vorran*; and thence, all along the Wastes, I observed it in the low bottoms at half a mile's distance from the Stone-wall. But afterwards, for a great many miles together, it runs within one hundred and twenty or one hundred and thirty yards of the Stone-wall, and so, either at a lesser or greater distance, I continued to observe it till within four or five miles of *Newcastle*; and whether thereabouts, it came into the Stone-wall, I am wholly uncertain. This Mud-wall has every where a deep Not built upon Severus's Wall

Trench

Trench before it to the North, but generally not above seven or eight yards broad.

Causway on the inside of the Wall.

All along the inside of the Wall, there seems a military Stone-Causway to have run at twenty or thirty yards distance. betwixt *Portgate* and the *Carraw* one sees it pretty entire in the Wastes, I saw little of it, and but one or two pieces of it nigh *Irthing*

Pight-Wall

The Wall is generally called by all the Inhabitants that live nigh it, the *Pight* or *Peaght*-Wall, gutturally, and with an aspiration, scarce pronouncing the *t*

The old man before-mentioned at *Waltown* or *Al Murum*, told me that in the middle part of the Wall, and nigh the foundation, there was lately found a concavity of nine inches square, and in it some pieces of lead-pipe, as there had several times been before in the like places And the tradition is current, through all the whole extent of the Wall, of a certain sort of Pipes or Tubes they had, whereby, as they tell you, in an hour's time any momentous matter might be communicated from Sea to Sea

Pipes or Tubes from Sea to Sea.

Thickness of the Wall

As to *Bede*'s observation of the *thickness* of the Wall (*viz* eight foot) it seems generally to hold (for both on hills and in valleys, where it was any thing entire, or where the foundation could be observed, I found it of that thickness) except upon those steep and ragged hills in the Wastes, where it was little above five foot, or however not full six, thick

Present condition of the Wall

As to the present condition of the Wall; by much the greater part of it has been carried off to build houses, and Stone-walls about Inclosures, which are very common in some parts of the Wall As to what remains, and is not upon Wastes and Moors, it serves either as a hedge between Pasture and Corn, or Pasture and Meadow-ground, or else to distinguish possessions; so that in these inclosed grounds, where it has been too much taken away, so as not to be a sufficient fence against Beasts, one may observe it to be rough cast up by the Husbandmen themselves for great spaces together upon the old foundations I observed a great number of houses, and sometimes whole Towns themselves, to stand at this time upon the very foundation of the Wall

---

Observations upon that part of the PICTS WALL, *which lies betwixt* Newcastle *and the Wall's-end; in a second Journey, begun* May *the 25th,* 1709.

Newcastle Pandon gate Keelmen's Hospital Red barns

FROM West-gate in *Newcastle*, the Wall seems to have continued its course directly through the present Town of *Newcastle* to *Pandon-gate*, so, through a piece of ground, whereon stands the *Keelmen*'s *Hospital*, thence under a House called the *Red barns*, and so for about two miles and an half partly by the road-side (which leads to *N Sheeles*) but for the greater part through delicate inclosed grounds, to its utmost period, which is nigh the town called *Wall's-end* As on the other side of *Newcastle*, so likewise on this, the Wall has met with the like, or rather worse, treatment, by reason of the vast improvements and inclosures that have been made; and the old Inhabitants thereabouts still tell you of vast quantities of Stones that have in their remembrance been dug out of it, and carried away to build houses, &c However the Wall it self is still very discernible, as is likewise the Vallum on the North-side

Wall's end

See p. 1058

Godmundingaham.

The Idol Temple

The place where the Pagan Temple stood, at *Godmundingabam*, seems to be an exact semicircle (whose diameter is two hundred and fifty or two hundred and sixty yards) being distinguish'd into a great many parts or portions, whereof some seem to be more peculiarly designed for the worship of the Idol, the rest to be Offices or Appendices for the reception of such persons as came there to worship, and others again appear probably to have been the places where the Victims themselves were slain and offered, and where all their necessary Utensils, &c were deposited Subservient to this later purpose, is a place, in length one hundred and fifty yards, in breadth twelve or fourteen, and about eight yards deep, except on the East, where from this bottom there rises a hill at least eight or nine fathom perpendicular, whence one easily surveys the whole Area, and which seems to have been more particularly set apart for the worship of the chief Idol For this hill (as the Minister of the place, a very intelligent man, assured me) was artificial, and probably made of the rubbish which was dug out from below. This hollow and deep place seems also to have been proportioned into two squares, a small space being only left betwixt them Besides this hill, there seem to be but two other places more immediately set apart for worship, each whereof may be about sixty yards or upwards one way, and about twelve or fourteen the other But what I call *Offices*, are very numerous over the whole plot, though of very different sizes and forms As to the form, they tend mostly to a round or oval, and some few, square; but the size is vastly different, some being only six, seven, or eight yards in circumference; others again twelve, fifteen, or twenty I was informed that good quantities of Stone had been dug out in many places, and another place was shown me, where several rows of *Ashlers* had been found, a course of sandy metal lying betwixt every row This heretofore fam'd place goes now by the name of *The Howes*, and close adjoyning thereto on the South, is a pretty large piece of ground of ten or twelve Acres, now a Corn field, called *Chapel Garth Ends* The foundations of a Wall are to be seen on the North side, where it unites the two extremities of the semi circle; but all the semi-circular

Howes

cular part seems to have been secured by a mount of Earth.

Castles from Newcastle to the end of the Wall.

In this compass, from *Newcastle* to the end of the Wall, I could observe only three of their Castles; two whereof were of the common size, but the last (which stands within one hundred and twenty yards of the Wall's end) was pretty large, being from West to East about twenty three or twenty four yards long, and from North to South at least sixty. To the extremity of the South-walls whereof on either side, there evidently appeared to me to have been a double Wall or Flanker of Stone joined (though the Area within was much short of the breadth of the Castle) and thence to have been continued at least sixty yards lower down the Hill, and in all probability to the very brink of the river *Tine*, which is not at more than fourscore yards distance from the lowest and farthest place I could trace this Flanker to, and not above two hundred yards from the Wall itself. And this ground being at the bottom of the Hill, and withal soft and spungy, it may pretty reasonably be concluded, that the foundation of the Wall, during this long tract of time, may have sunk in, and so lie under.

Flankers of Stone.

From the Castle to the Wall's-end, is (as I said) a space of about one hundred and twenty yards. there also I observed the plain *Vestigia* and Foundations of a considerable Flanker of Stone, turning from the utmost point of the Wall, directly Southwards, for at least one hundred yards, in length, partly upon the top, and partly upon the declivity of the Hill. And though I could not observe it farther, by reason of the soft and spungy nature of the soil; yet I do not at all doubt but it was extended into the *Tine* it self, which flows but one hundred or one hundred and twenty yards lower than where I could trace it to. And to strengthen this conjecture the more, there are the evident marks of a large Vallum or Ditch, still fairly to be discerned without, upon the East side.

Wall's-end.

Between the Castle and the Wall's-end, and upon the top of the Hill, the Inhabitants have a tradition, that the old town of *Wall's-end* or *Vindobala*, formerly stood (though what is now so called, stands at somewhat more than a quarter of a mile's distance to the North from the Wall itself,) and accordingly they tell you, that vast quantities of Stone have formerly been dug out of that space. The ground where the Wall is terminated, is called the *Well laws*

Well Laws.

(as the Inhabitants think, from some *Well* that was formerly there, and which, after much endeavour, they were never able to discover) but in my opinion, from Wealþ or *Wall*, and læ??e pascuum, as if the Saxons called it the *Wall-pasture*, by way of eminence, for the Inhabitants say, it is the richest ground in that part of the Country; (but it is now meadow). This seems to be the most rational Etymology of the word, unless any body had rather derive it from Wall, and hlæpe or hleap, a rampire, or hill, in respect to the high situation of the Wall in this place, in comparison of the ground and the river below.

The Wall ended 4 miles short of the Sea.

I spoke with several old people who had lived hereabouts for thirty, forty and fifty years, and upwards, and who had likewise (as they told me) spoken with others, that were long since dead, of eighty and a hundred years of age, who all unanimously agreed, that neither the Wall nor the Ditch went further than this place, nor could they ever meet with the *Vestigia* of them in the roads to *Sheelds* or *Tinmouth*, which lay in a direct line from the Walls-end, and were at about half a mile's distance from the *Tine*. Nor indeed could I find the least appearance either of Wall or Ditch, though I sought very diligently through several fields, so that I am entirely satisfied, that the *Romans* thought the breadth and depth of the *Tine* (which is now within four miles of the Sea, and no where fordable) a sufficient security.]

[*An Account of the* (a) *Division of* Cumberland *by* William *the Conquerour amongst his Followers; taken out of two ancient Latin Manuscripts in the Library of the Dean and Chapter of* Carlisle, *carefully Collated by the Reverend Dr.* Hugh Todd.

KING *William*, sirnam'd the Bastard, Duke of *Normandy*, Conqueror of *England*, gave all the Lands of the County of *Cumberland* to *Ranulphus de Meschins* and to *Galfridus*, Brother to the said *Ranulphus*, he gave the whole County of *Chestre* and to *William* another brother, he gave all the Land of *Coupland*, between *Duden* and *Darwent*.

Ranulphus de Meschins infeoffed *Hubbertus* (b) *de Vaux* in the Barony of *Gilsland*; and *Ranulphus* his brother, in *Sowerby*, *Carlaton*, and *Hubbrightby*. And *Robert* the third brother, in the Barony of *Dalston*. He infeoffed also *Robert De Strivers* in the Barony of *Burgh*, and *Richerus de Boyvile* in the Barony of *Levington*; and *Odardus de Logis* in the Barony of *Stanyton*. He infeoffed also *Waldevus*, son of *Gospatricius* Earl of *Dunbar* in *Scotland*, in all the Barony of *Allerdale* between *Wathenpole* and *Darwent*.

The aforesaid *William de Meschins* Lord of *Coupland*, infeoffed *Waldevus* son of *Gospatricius*, in all the Land that lies between *Cocar* and *Darwent*, and also in these five Townships, *Brigham*, *Eglysfeld*, *Dene*, *Braithwaite*, and *Grisothen*, and in the two *Cliftons* and *Staneburne*. He infeoffed also *Odardus le Clerk* in the fourth part of *Crostwaite*, *pro Custodia Asturcorum* (c) *suorum*, i. e. for keeping his Goshawkes.

Galfridus de Meschins Earl of *Chester* dy'd without issue and thereupon *Ranulphus de Meschins* became Earl of *Chestre*; and surrender'd to the King all the County of *Cumberland* on this

(a) It is call'd *Distributio Cumbriæ ad Conquestum Angliæ inter Gentes*. Sir *William Dugdale* calls it *Chronicon Cumbriæ*; and so the Lord *William Howard* has stiled it in one of the Manuscripts, but it is a mistake; for that piece of Antiquity, if it be extant, was of another nature, and writ by one *Everardus* Abbot of *Holme Cultram*, tempore H. 2. It was said to be in the Library of *Sir Thomas Gower* Baronet; but upon search it could not be found.

(b) Vaux MS B.

(c) Austurcorum, MS B.

this condition, That all those who held Lands of him *in Fee*, should hold of the King *in Capite*.

The foresaid *Waldevus*, son of Earl *Gospatricius*, infeoffed *Odardus de Logis*, in the Barony of *Wygton*, *Dondryt*, *Waverton*, *Bleucogo*, and *Kirkbride*. which *Odardus de Logis* founded the Church of *Wygton*; and gave to *Odardus* son of *Liolfe*, *Talentyre* and *Castlerige*, with the Forest between *Caltre* and *Greta* and to the Prior and Convent of *Gisburne* he gave *Appleton* and *Bridekirk*, with the Advowson of the Church there He gave also to *Adam* son of *Liolfe*, *Ulsdendale* and *Gilcruce* and to *Gemelius* son of *Brun*, *Bothill*; and to *Waldevus* son of *Gilemimus*, with *Ethreda* his sister, he gave *Brogham*, *Ribton*, *Broughton* and *Little Brogham*, and *Donwaldese* and *Bowaluese*, *ad unam Logiam*, for a Lodge or House for a Ranger He gave also to *Ormus* son of *Ketellus*, *Seton*, *Camberton*, *Flemingby*, *Craiksothen*, in marriage with *Gunwelda* his sister And to *Dolfinus* son of *Alwaldus*, with *Matilda* another sister, he gave *Applethwaite* and *Little Crosby*, *Langrige* and *Brigham*, with the Advowson of the Church there He gave also to *Melbeth* his Physician, the Town of *Bromfeld*, saving to himself the Advowson of the Church there

Alanus, son and heir of the said *Waldevus*, gave to *Ranulphus Lyndsey*, *Bienerhasset* and *Ukmanby*, with *Ethereda* his sister To *Uthredus*, son of *Fergus* Lord of *Galloway*, in marriage with *Gurnelda* (d) his other sister, he gave *Torpenhow*, with the Advowson of the Church there He gave also to *Catellus de Spenser* (e), *Threpeland* He gave also to *Herbert* the Manour of *Thuresby*, for the third part of a Township He gave also to *Gospatricius*, son of *Ormus*, *High Ireby* for the third part of a Township He gave also to *Gamelius le Brun*, (f) *Rughtwaite*, for a third part of a Township He gave also to *Radulphus Engaine*, *Isell*, with the appurtenances, and *Blencrake* with the Service of *Newton* And the same *Alanus* had one Bastard-brother nam'd *Gospatricius*, to whom he gave *Boulton*, *Bastinthwaite* and *Esterholme* And to *Odardus* he gave *Newton*, with the Appurtenances And to his three Huntsmen, *Sleth* (g), and his Companions, *Hayton* To *Uchtredus* he gave one Carrucat of Land in *Aspatrike*, on condition that he should be his Summoner (*Summonitor*) in *Allerdale* He gave also to *Delfinus* six Bovates or Oxgang of Land in *High Crosby*, that he should be *Serviens D Regis*, the King's Serjeant in *Allerdale* And to *Simon de Shestelyngs* he gave one Moiety of *Deram* And to *Dolfinus*, son of *Gospatricius*, the other Moiety He gave also to *Waldevus*, son of *Dolfinus*, *Brakanthwaite* And to the Priory of St *Bega*, he gave *Stainburne* And to the Priory of *Carliol*, he gave the body of *Waldevus* his son, with the Holy Cross, which they have yet in possession; and *Crosby*, with the Advowson of the Church there, with the Service that *Uthredus* owed him and also the Advowson of the Church of *Aspatrike*, with the Service of *Alanus de Brayton* He gave them also the Advowson of the Church of *Ireby*, with the Suit and Service of *Waldevus de Langthwaite*

The same *Alanus* son of *Waldevus*, gave to King *Henry* (h) the Fields of the Forest of *Allerdale*, with liberty to hunt, whenever he should lodge at *Holme Cultrane* To this *Alanus* succeeded *William* son of *Duncane* Earl of *Murrayse*, Nephew and Heir to the said *Alanus*, as being son to *Ethreda*, sister to his father *Waldevus*

The foresaid *William*, son of *Duncanus*, espoused *Alicia* daughter of *Robert de Rumeney*, Lord of *Skipton* in *Craven* which *Robert* had married a daughter of *Meschines* (i) Lord of *Coupland*. This *William* had by this *Alicia* his wife, a son call'd *William de Egremond* (who dy'd under age) and three daughters The eldest, nam'd (k) *Cecilia*, being a Ward, was married by King *Henry* to *William le Gross* Earl of *Albemarle*, with the Honour of *Skipton* for her Dower The second, nam'd *Amabilla*, was married to *Reginald de Luce*, with the Honour of *Egremond*, by the same King *Henry* And the third, nam'd *Alicia de Romelic*, was married to *Gilbert Pipard*, with *Aspatrike*, and the Barony of *Allerdale* and the Liberty of *Cokermouth*, by the said King *Henry* and afterwards by the Queen, to *Robert de Courtney* but she dy'd without heirs of her body.

William le Gross, Earl of *Albemarle*, had by his wife *Cecilia*, *Harwisia* (l), to whom succeeded *William de Fortibus*, Earl of *Albemarle* to whom succeeded another *William de Fortibus*, to whom succeeded *Avelina*, who was espoused to Lord *Edmond*, brother to King *Edward*, and dy'd without heirs, &c

Reginald de Luce by *Amabilla* his wife, had (m) *Alicia*. To *Amabila* succeeded *Lambert de Multon* To him succeeded *Thomas Multon de Egremond* And to *Alicia* succeeded *Thomas de* (n) *Luce*, to whom succeeded *Thomas* his son, who was succeeded by *Anthony* his Brother]

More rare Plants growing wild in Westmoreland *and* Cumberland

Lan Eruca Monensis laciniata lutea *Jagged yellow Rocket of the Isle of Man In Sella fields Sea bank, found growing abundantly by Mr* Lawson

Echinum marinum P B *Sea-Bugloss On the Sea shore near White haven plentifully, Mr* Newton

W Gladiolus lacustris Dortmanni *Clus cur post Water Gilly flower or Gladiole In the Lake call'd Hulls-water, which parteth Westmoreland and Cumberland*

Orobus sylvaticus nostras *English Wood vetch At Gamblesby about six miles from Pereth in the way to New castle, in the hedges and pastures plentifully*

Vitis Idæa magna quibusdam, sive Myrtillus grandis *J B* Idæa foliis subrotundis ex albidis *C B* Idæa foliis subrotundis major *Ger* Viccinia nigra fructu majore *Park* *Great Bilberry-bush In the same place with the precedent, but where the ground is moist and marshy*

An Additional Account of some more rare Plants observ'd to grow in Westmoreland *and* Cumberland, *by Mr* Nicholson, *Arch deacon of* Carlisle, *and now Lord Bishop of* Derry

Cannabis spuria fl magno albo perelegante *About* Blencairn, *in the parish of* Kirkland, *Cumberland*

Equisetum nudum variegatum minus *In the meadows near Great* Salkeld, *and in most of the like sandy grounds in Cumberland*

Geranium Batrachoides longius radicatum, odoratum *In* Mardale *and* Martindale, *Westm*

Hesperis Pannonica inodora *On the banks of the Rivulets about* Dilehead *in Cumberland, and* Grassmire *in Westmoreland*

Orchis palmata palustris Dracontias *Upon the old Mill-race at little* Salkeld, *and on* Langwathby *Holm, Cumberland*

2 Cyno-

(d) Gunilda MS B (e) le Despenser MS B (f) Ind & Rugl MS B (g) Seleth, MS B (h) D H Regi Scoti MS B (i) Willielmi de Meschines, MS B (k) Ceff MS B and Scotia (l) Hatewisia (m) Richardum de Luey Amabiliam & Aliciam (n) Quæ sequuntur, desunt MS B

Cynoforchis militaris purpurea odorata. *On* Lance-Moor *near* Newby, *and on* Thrimby-*Common, Westmorland*

Serratula foliis ad summitatem usque indivisis. *Found first by* Reginald Harrison, *a Quaker, in the Barony of* Kendal, *Westmorland.*

Thlaspi minus Clusii. *On most Limestone pastures in both Counties*

Tragopogon Purpureum. *In the fields about* Carlisle *and* Rose-Castle, *Cumberland.*

Virga aurea latifolia serrata C B *It grows as plentifully in our fields at* Salkeld *as the* Vulgaris; *which is as common as any Plant we have*

N B The natural Products of the two mountainous Counties, of *Cumberland* and *Westmorland*, are generally much of the same kind with those of the *Alpine* parts of *Switzerland*; as appears from the accurate Account which has been given, not long since, of that Country by Dr. *Scheuchzer*, a learned Physician at *Zurich*, and Fellow of our Royal Society. Amongst the many curious Observations made by this industrious Author, his Discoveries in *Botany* are not the least valuable And, in these, he shews, that not only the choicest Mosses and other imperfect Plants, which Mr. *Ray* and his Followers had reckon'd to be properties of our Northern *British* Hills, are likewise *Helvetick*; but that some others of a more noble kind (such as the *Acetosa rotundifolia repens* Eboracensis, *Alchemilla Alpina pentaphyllos* Raij, *Bistorta Alpina pumila* Morisoni, *&c*) whose very names bespoke them to be the natural *Indigenæ* of this Island, are not so confin'd as we thought they have been These therefore, being as well Natives of *Switzerland* as *Great Britain*, may induce our Naturalists to make a more strict Enquiry, whether they have more of the same Neighbours, in both Countries, than has hitherto been observ'd Whether (for example) the *Trifolium Alpinum* Rhæticum, and the *Euphrasia* Helvetiorum *lutea*, be not as well to be found amongst our Mountains, as the *Lancashire* and *Scotch Asphodels* are upon those of the *Swiss* and *Grisons?*

OTTA-

OTTADINI.

NEXT after the Brigantes, Ptolemy *places those, (who, according to the various readings of several Copies) are call'd* Ottalini, Ottadeni, *and* Ottadini *[All the Copies which Dr* Gale *had perused, read* Ὠταδηνοὶ, Ὠταλινοὶ, &c *with a single* τ, *and* Selden's *Manuscript contracts the word (as it doth most others of the like kind) into* Ὠταδινοὶ *] Instead of all which, I would willingly, with a very easie alteration, read* Ottatini, *that so the word might signifie* beyond *or upon the river* Tyne *Thus, the name of the Inhabitants would exactly agree with the situation of their Country For this People were seated beyond the* Tyne *and our modern* Britains *call that Country in* Wales *which lies beyond the river* Conway, Uch Conway, *that, beyond the Mountains,* Uch Mynyth, *beyond the Wood,* Uch-Coed, *beyond the River* Gyrway, Uch-Gyrway *Nor could it be at all improper, if, by the same rule, they nam'd this Country that is beyond the* Tyne, Uch-Tin; *out of which, by a little disjointing and mellowing of the word, the* Romans *seem to have form'd their* Ottadini *Yet since (as* Xiphiline *reports out of* Dio Nicæus) *all the* Britains *that dwelt near the forementioned Wall, were call'd* Μαιάται *or* Mæatæ, *it is reasonable to believe that our* Ottadini *(living on the Wall) were some of those* Mæatæ, *who, in that remarkable Revolt of the* Britains, *wherein the* Caledonians *were brought into the Confederacy, took up Arms when the Emperour* Severus *gave orders to his Soldiers to give no Quarter to the* Britains, *in those words of* Homer, See the Gale, in Scotland. Mæatæ.

——— Μήτις ὑπεκφύγειν αἰπὺν ὄλεθρον
Χεῖρας θ' ἡμετέρας, μηδ' ὅν τινα γαστέρι μήτηρ
Κοῦρον ἐόντα φέροι, μηδ' ὃς φύγοι αἰπὺν ὄλεθρον Iliad 3

——— None our Arms shall spare,
None shall escape the fury of the War,
Children unborn shall die ———

[Humphrey Lhuyd *places these People about* Lothian *in* Scotland *and herein he is not contradicted by* Buchanan, *who never fails of contradicting him, when he can have an opportunity All agree, that they were* Picts, *and therefore, if they did inhabit some part of this County, it must have been beyond the Wall Possibly,* Næatæ *is the true reading, and then, they are more probably placed near the Wall or Rampire, for* Naid *or* Nawd, *in the old British, signifies a Defence or Security And why might not the Transcribers of* Dio *(for he is the only person of Antiquity that mentions these People) turn his* Næatæ *into* Mæatæ, *as well as the transcribers of* Marcellinus *have made* Attigotti, *and* Catacotti, *and* Catiti, *out of his* Attacotti?

But to return] The storm of that Rebellion was calm'd by the death of Severus, *who dy'd at* York, *in the midst of his preparations for war A good while after, this Country seems to have been part of* Valentia *for so* Theodosius *nam'd it, in honour of the Emperour* Valentinian, *after he had vanquish'd the Barbarians, and recover'd this lost Province But, in the* Saxon *wars, these ancient names grew out of date, and all those Counties which lie North of the Frith of* Humber, *took the* Saxon *Name of* Norðan-humbra ric, *i e the Kingdom of the* North Humbrians *And yet even this name is now lost in the other Counties being only retain'd in this of* Northumberland *Which we are now to visit* Valentia.

NORTH-HUMBER-LAND.

NOrthumberland, call'd by the Saxons Nopðan-humbeplonb, lies enclos'd in a sort of Triangle, but not Equilateral On the South, towards the County of *Durham*, it is bounded with the river *Derwent* running into *Tine*, and with *Tine* it self The East-side is wash'd with the *German* Ocean The West (reaching from South-west to North-east) fronts [*Cumberland* for more than * twenty miles together, and then] *Scotland*; and is first bounded with a ridge of Mountains, and afterwards with the river *Tweed* Here were the Limits of both Kingdoms over which (in this County) two Governours were appointed, whereof the one was stil'd Lord Warden of the *Middle* Marches, and the other of the † *Eastern* The Country it self is mostly rough and barren, and seems to have harden'd the very carcasses of its Inhabitants whom the neighbouring Scots have render'd yet more hardy, sometimes inuring them to war, and sometimes amicably communicating their customs and way of living; whence they are become a most war like people and excellent horse-men And, whereas they have generally devoted themselves to war, there is not a man of fashion among them but has his little Castle and Fort, and so the Country came to be divided into a great many *Baronies*, the Lords whereof were anciently (before the days of *Edward* the first) usually stil'd *Barons*, though some of them men of very low Fortunes But this was wisely done of our Ancestors, to cherish and support Martial Prowess, in the borders of the Kingdom, at least with Honours and Titles, [and very good Baronies they were, according to the old and true import of the word For the Civilians define a Barony to be, *Merum mistumque Imperium in aliquo Castro, Oppidove, con cessione Principis* Such a Jurisdiction it was requisite the Men of rank should have here on the Borders and upon obtaining the Grant, they were properly *Barones Regis & Regni* All Lords of Manours are also to this day legally nam'd *Barons*, in the Call and Stile of their Courts, which are *Curiæ Baronum*, &c] However, this Character of Baron they lost, when (under Edward the first) the name began to be *appropriated* to such as were summoned by the King to the High Court of Parliament [Not but before King Edward the first's time, the name of *Barones* was occasionally apply'd to the Peers in Parliament Thus, in the famous Contest about the Votes of Bishops in Criminal Matters, in the reign of *Henry* the second, we have this decision of the Controversie, *Archiepiscopi, Episcopi, &c sicut cæteri* Barones, *debent interesse judiciis Curiæ Regis cum* Baronibus, *quousque perveniatur ad diminutionem Membrorum vel ad mortem* i e Archbishops, Bishops, &c in like manner as the rest of the *Barons*, ought to be present at the Judgments in the King's Courts together with the *Barons*, until it come to diminution of Members, or to death And many other like Instances might be given] On the Sea-Coasts, and along the river *Tine*, the ground (with tolerable husbandry) is very fruitful but elsewhere, much more barren and rugged In many places the Stones *Lithanthraces*, which we call *Sea-Coals*, are dug very plentifully, to the great benefit of the Inhabitants

Margin notes: * From above *Garyhill* to the river *Kelsop*. — Wardens of the Marches Ranke Riders. — † Western, C. — So, Ann 1607 — Many Baronies in *Northumberland* — Alciat de Sing Cert c 32 — Spelm Gloss *Baro* Seld Tit p. 2 c 5. — A. D 1163 — Matt Par p 101 — Sea-coal.

The nearer part, which points to the South-west, and is call'd *Hexamshire*, had for a long time the Archbishop of *York* for its Lord, and challeng'd (how justly I know not) the Rights of a County Palatine but when † lately it became part of the Crown Lands, by an exchange made with Archbishop *Robert*, it was, by Act of Parliament, annex'd to the County of *Northumberland*, being subjected to the same Judicature, and the Writs directed to the Sheriff thereof [Which is to be understood only of *Civil* matters, for it's Ecclesiastical Jurisdiction is not the same with the rest of the County, it being still a *Peculiar* belonging to the Archbishop of York]

Margin notes: Hexamshire — † So said, Ann 160-

South Tine (so call'd, if we believe the Britains, from its being narrowly pent up within its banks, for so much *Tin* signifies, say some, in the British Language) rising in *Cumberland* near *Alstenmoor*, where there is an ancient Copper Mine, runs by *Lambley* (formerly a Nunnery built by the *Lucies*, but now much worn away by the floods,) and *Fetherston haugh*, the seat of the ancient and well descended Family of the *Fetherstons*, [(who being extinct, the Lands fell into the possession of *Fetherston Dodson*,)] and, being come to *Bellister-Castle*, it turns Eastward, keeping a direct course, along with the Wall, which is no where three miles distant from it

Margin notes: South Tine — Lambley — Fetherston

For the Wall, having left *Cumberland*, and cross'd the little river of *Irthing*, carry'd an Arch over the rapid brook of *Poltross*, where I saw large Mounts cast up within the Wall, as if design'd for watching the Country Near this place stands *Thirlwal castle* (no large structure) which gave seat and sirname to an ancient and honourable family, that had formerly the name of *Wade* Here, the *Scots* forc'd a passage, betwixt *Irthing* and *Tine*, into the Province [of *Britain*] And the place was wisely enough chosen, as having no rivers in the way to obstruct their inroads into the bowels of *England* But the Reader will the better understand this matter and the name of the place, from *John Fordon* the *Scotch* Historian, whose words, since his book is not very common, it may not be amiss to repeat *The* Scots (says he) *having conquer'd the Country on both sides the Wall, began to settle themselves in it, and summoning-in the Boors (with their mattocks, pickaxes, rake, forks, and shovels) caus'd wide holes and gaps to be made in it, through which they might readily pass and repass From these gaps, this indented part got it's present name for in the English tongue the place is now call'd* Thirlwall, *which, render'd in Latin, is the same as* Murus perforatus From hence, southward, we have a view of *Blenkensop*, which gives name and dwelling to an eminent family, and was anciently part of the Barony of *Nicholas* of *Bolteby*, and is situated in a Country pleasant enough [Here, not many years since, was found a Roman Altar, with the following Inscription

Margin notes: Picts-Wall — Irthing riv. — Poltross — Thirlwall — Scholefield, P... — Scots Forc... — Blenkensop — Phil Trans N 3[...]

Beyond

IX
West VIII Minuts
VII
NORTHUMBERLAND.
A Scale of Miles
5
10
56
SCOTLAND
Mordington
Fouldon
Claribald
Paxton
Huton
Hornden
Ladykirk
Norham C
Newbiggens
Grotchugh
Wessel
Tillmouth
Caldstreame
Cornwale
Spaylaw
Long Bridgham
Warke C
Learmouth
Rydam
Carram
Graydon
W Newton
The Hanging stone
The Coklaw hill
Haden hill Crosse
The Black Brous
Coket R
Capup
Tweed R

THE BRITISH or GERMAN OC
50
40
30
20
Barwick upon Twede
the Spittle
Holy Iland
Old Fort
Farne Ilands
Farne I
Belforde
Lowick
Detchin
Newlands
Chillingham
Wooll
Fowberry
Newtown
Ellingham
Newstead
Preston
Newton
Dunstan
Alnewick
Lesbury
Aylmouth
Wooden
Coquet R
Coket I
Seaton house
Boxmere
Houghton
Stamford
Crofter
Rugley
Brandon
Ilderton
Middleton hall
Rodham
Bewick
Bewick M
Titlington
Bowton
Glanton
Alnham
Callaly
Prendik
Roseley
Hartside
Ingram
Newenham
Swinhoe
Nopton
Bednel
Sunderland
Shotton
Elsford
Burton
Spittleston
Bradford
Beadle
Middleton
Esington
Rosse
Buckton
Fenwick
Ryle
Lowlyn
Barrington
Barmore
Kyloe
TTADINI

PART OF
REDES DALE
TYN DALE
PART OF
CUMBER
LAND
VALLUM SEVERI
The Wall of the Picts
Longtowne
Carlisle
Brampton
Haltwe
Alstenmore
Kemblespethe hall
The Read Squire
The Whele Park
The Whele Fell
Tynehead
Flightes Chap
Whithaugh tower
Kirk Andrews
Kirfop foot
Bellingham
Whitchester
Chesterwood
Black hall
Whitfield hall
Permandley
Knaresdale
Williamston
Kirkhaugh
Thornhope
Rosebarne
Blakelaw
Charleton
Leame
Corsenside
Old Towne
Troughwhen
The Rottenraw
Smalhope
Rollinhead
Grenehaugh

EAN.
Rothbury
Morpeth
Ellesdon
Newbiggin
Newcastle
Hexham
Corbridge
Tinmouth Castle
Tinmouth Bar
Sunderland
Whickham
Seaton Delaval
Hartley
Kirkwhelpinton
Capheaton
Bolam
Ryton
The New Chap
Sheales
Bishopwearmouth
Monkwearmouth
Whitburne
Slakborne
PART OF THE BISHOPRICK OF DURHAM.
Sold by Abel Swale Awnsham & Iohn Churchil
Kelloplaw hill
Whitley sheale
West 2 Degrees
55
50
10

DEABVS NYM
PHIS VETS
MANSVETAE
CLAVDIAE VRB
NHI AEMIVS

]

Beyond *Thirlwall*, the wall opens a passage for the rapid river of *Tippall*, where, on the descent of a hill, a little within the wall, may be seen the draught of a square *Roman* Fort, each side of which is one hundred and forty paces in length the very foundations of the houses, and tracks of the streets, being yet fairly discernible The *Wardens men* report, that there lay a high Street-way, paved with Flint and other Stone, over the tops of the mountains, from hence to *Marden-Castle* on *Stanemoor* It is certain, it went directly to *Kirkbythor*, already mention'd An old woman, who dwelt in a neighbouring cottage, shew'd us a little ancient consecrated Altar, thus inscrib'd to *Vitirineus*, a tutelar God of these parts

DEO
VITI
RINE---
.---LIMEO
ROV
* P L. M.

* Posuit libens merito.

This place is now call'd *Caervorran* how it was anciently nam'd, I am not able to determine, since the word hath no affinity with any of the Stations that are mention'd along the Wall, and none of the Inscriptions afford us any discoveries [It may, not improbably, be † *Glanoventa*, for there is a place near it, which is still call'd *Glenwelt* The distance from hence to *Warwick* will suit well enough with the Itinerary, and it is not the first Elbow which *Antoninus* has made, in his Roads, through this part of the Country Thus, by fetching-in *Castra Exploratorum*, he makes it twenty four miles from *Blatum Bulgium* to *Luguvallium* whereas, by the common Road, it is only ten very short ones] But whatever it was, the Wall near it was built much higher and firmer than elsewhere, for within two furlongs of it, on a pretty high hill, it is still standing, fifteen foot in height, and nine in breadth, on both sides * *Ashler*, though Bede says, it was only twelve foot high, [which Account may yet be fair and true in general For in some places on the Wastes, where there has not been any extraordinary Fortification, several fragments come near that height, and none exceed it His breadth also (at eight foot) is accurate enough. For, wherever you measure it now, you will always find it above seven] * Quadrato lapide

From thence the Wall bends about by *Iverton*, *Forsten*, and *Chester in the Wall*, near *Busy-gapp*, noted for robberies, where we heard there were forts, but durst not go and view them, for fear of the *Moss-Troopers* This *Chester*, we were told, was very large, insomuch as I guess it to be the station of the second Cohort of the *Dalmatians* which the *Notitia* calls *Magna* where may be read the following Inscription Iverton Forsten Chester in the Wall Busy gapp

PRO SALVTE
DI SIDILNIÆ
IIANI PRÆ
II SVA S
POSVIT VOT
AO SOLVIT LIBE
NS TVSCO ET BAS
SO COSS

In the year of Christ 259

This imperfect Altar was also brought from thence; which is now at the little Hamlet of *Melkrigg*

These two Inscriptions are now in the house of Sir *Robert Cotton* of Conington.

DEAE SVRI
AE SVB CALP
VRNIO AG--
ICOLA LEG AVG
PR PR A LICINIVS
LEMENS PRAEF
--III A IOR----- --
- - - - - - - - - - - - - -

Dea Suria some will have her to be *Juno*, others *Venus*.

Which, if I might, I would gladly (and the characters seem to allow it) read thus *Deæ Suriæ, sub Calphurnio Agricola Legato Augusti Proprætore, Licinius Clemens Præfectus* Now *Calphurnius Agricola* was sent against the *Britains* by *M Antoninus* the *Philosopher*, upon the breaking out of the *British* wars, about the year of our Lord 170 At which time, some Cohort under his command erected this Altar to the Goddess *Suria*, who was drawn by Lions, with a Turret on her head and a Taber in her hand (as is shewn at large by *Lucian*, in his Treatise *de Dea Syria*;) and whom *Nero*, as fondly as he treated all Religion, very zealously worship'd for some time; and afterwards slighted her to that degree, as to piss upon her [As to the last line of this Inscription, others give it more fully thus, COH I HAMIOR

Besides these, at a place call'd the *House-steeds*, hard by, have been found of late years abundance of Roman Monuments For instance,

NI VENO RI
G OFERSIONIS
ROMVLOALIMAHI
MANSVETIOSENICIONI
RF VINCF QVARIIONIS
ERESIPROCVRAVII DELF
VSRAVTIONIS EXGS

Some years ago, also, on the West side of this Garrison, was discover'd, under a heap of Rubbish, a square Room strongly vaulted above, and paved with large square Stones, and under this, a Lower room, the roof of which was supported by rows of square pillars, about half a yard high]

Willimoteswick. From hence we had a view of *Willimoteswicke*, [heretofore] the seat of the worshipful family of the *Ridleys* [but now belonging to the family of the *Blacketts*,] and of the river *Alon*, which empties itself into *Tine* with a pompous rattle, both the *Alons* being now met in one chanel On *East Alon* stands a village, now call'd *Old-Toun*, [which seems more likely to be the *Alone* of *Antoninus* (call'd in the *Liber Notitiarum*, *Alione*) than any other place which has hitherto been thought of It answers best the distances, both from *Galana* and *Galacum*, and many Roman Antiquities, which have been found there, strengthen the conjecture The name of the river also, whereon it is seated, argues as strongly for this place, as *West-Alon* can do for *Whitley*, where Dr *Gale* and others fix it]

Alon, riv.

Old Town

But to return to the Wall The next station on the Wall, beyond *Busy gap*, is now call'd *Seaven shale*, which name if you allow me to derive from *Sabiniana*, or rather *Sabiniana ala*, I will roundly affirm this place to be that *Hunnum* where the *Notitia Provinciarum* tells us the *Sabinian* Wing were upon duty Then, beyond *Carrow* and *Walton*, stands *Walwick*, which some have fansy'd to be the *Gallana* of *Antoninus* in all which places there are evident remains of old fortifications [Between *Carrow* and *Walwick*, the Wall hath been repaired, and fronted with its old Stones again, upon which have been observ'd the following Inscriptions,

Seavenshale

Gallana

Here,

North Tine. Here, *North Tine* croſſes the Wall It riſes in the mountains on the borders of *England* and *Scotland*, and firſt, running Eaſtward, waters *Tindale* (which has thence it's name, [and was by Act of Parliament made part of the County of Northumberland, in the reign of King Henry the ſeventh,)] and afterwards receives the river *Read*, which falling from the ſteep hill of *Readſquire* (where was frequently the *True-place*, that is, *the place of conference*, at which the Lords Wardens of the Eaſtern Marches of both Kingdoms uſually determin'd the diſputes of that part of the borders,) gives its name to a valley very thinly inhabited by reaſon of the robberies

Tindale. 11 H 7 c 9. Read riv. True place.

Both theſe Dales breed moſt notable Bog-Trotters, and both have ſuch boggy-top'd mountains, as are not to be croſs'd by ordinary horſemen In theſe, one would wonder to ſee ſo many great heaps of ſtones (*Lawes* they call them,) which the neighbourhood believe to have been thrown together in remembrance of ſome perſons there ſlain [Nor are theſe the only Monuments which thoſe Waſtes afford There are alſo large ſtones erected at ſeveral places, in remembrance (as is fanſied) of ſo many battels or ſkirmiſhes, either anciently betwixt the *Britains* and the *Picts*, or (of later times) betwixt the *Engliſh* and *Scots* Particularly, near *Ninwick*, in the Pariſh of *Simondburn*, four ſuch ſtand ſtill erected and a fifth lies fallen to the ground] There are alſo, in both the Dales, many ruins of old forts In *Tindale*, are *Whitcheſter*, *Delaley*, and *Tarſet*, which formerly belong'd to the *Comyns* In *Rheades dale*, are *Rocheſter*, *Greencheſter*, *Rutcheſter*, and ſome others, whoſe ancient names are now ſwallow'd up by time

Lawes.

Rocheſter. [At *Rocheſter* was found a Roman Altar with this Inſcription,

Phil Tranſ N 2 I

D M
CIVL FL
INGEN
MI LEG
VIV F

]

And ſince at the ſame *Rocheſter*, which is ſcated near the head of *Rhead*, on the riſing of a rock that overlooks the Country below (whence it may ſeem to have had this new name,) another ancient Altar was alſo found among the rubbiſh of an old Caſtle, with this Inſcription,

i. e. Dupliares Numeri Exploratorum Bremenii Aram inſtituerunt Numini ejus, Cæpione Charitino Tribuno votum ſolverunt Libentes merito

D. R. S.
DVPL. N. EXPLOR.
BREMEN. ARAM.
INSTITVERVNT
N̄ EIVS C CAEP
CHARITINO TRIB
V S L M

may we not hence conjecture, that here was that *Bremenium*, ſo induſtriouſly and ſo long ſought for, which *Ptolemy* mentions in theſe parts, and from which *Antoninus* begins his firſt journey in *Britain*, as from its utmoſt limit For the bounds of the Empire, were, (as, great rivers, mountains, deſart and unpaſſable countries (ſuch as are in this part) ditches, walls, empalures, and eſpecially caſtles built in the moſt ſuſpected places, of the Remains of which there is great plenty here Indeed, ſince the Barbarians, having thrown down *Antoninus Pius's* Wall in *Scotland*, ſpoil'd this Country, and ſince *Hadrian's* Wall lay unregarded till *Severus's* time, we may believe the limits of the Roman Empire were in this place and hence the old Itinerary, that goes under the name of *Antoninus*, begins here, as it ſeems *a Limite*, i e at the furtheſt bounds of the Empire But the addition * of *i e à vallo* † ſeems to be a gloſs of the tranſcriber, ſince *Bremenium* lies fourteen miles northward from the Wall, unleſs we take it to be one of thoſe Field-ſtations, already mention'd to have been built beyond the Wall in the Enemy's Country] But notwithſtanding the great encouragement which the Inſcription gives to the placing of *Bremenium* at *Rocheſter*, * others are of opinion, that *Brampton* in *Gilleſland* was the place, the diſtance from this *Brampton* to *Corbridge* being as agreeable, as from *Rocheſter*, and they think it ought to be well prov'd, before the weight of the Objection can be taken off, that the words [*id eſt*, *a vallo*] are an Interpolation of the Tranſcribers Nor are they ſatisfy'd, that the bare mention of *Bremenium* in a Monument found at *Rocheſter*, is ſufficient of itſelf to determine it to that place, ſince at *Riſingham* in this very Country, an Inſcription was found, that makes as expreſs mention of the *fourth Cohort of the Gallick Troops*, whoſe Station was *Vindolana*, which yet is ſettled as far diſtant from thence, as Old *Wincheſter*

Bremenium. * [illegible] † [illegible] —Sir Robert [illegible] Pur[illegible] in Scot[illegible]

Add to this (what they think of ſome moment) that [illegible] not *Bremenium*, but [illegible] and [illegible] Manuſcript, *Bræmenio*, to which place alſo is ſuppos'd to belong this Roman Altar, dug up at *Lowther* in Weſtmorland,

Gale, p 7

DEABVS MATRIBVS
TRAMAI VEX GERMA
P. V. R D PRO SALVTE
R FVS L M

the true reading of the ſecond line being ſuppoſed to be, BRAMAI VEXILLATIO GERMANORVM, and to ſignify that thoſe Soldiers, having erected it at *Bramenium* to the honour of the *Deæ Matres*, carried it back with them, in their retreat, leſt it ſhould fall into the hands of the Enemy]

To the ſouth, within five miles lies *Otterburn*, where a ſharp engagement happen'd between the *Scots* and *Engliſh*, Victory three or four times changing ſides, and at laſt fixing with the *Scots* For *Henry Percy* (for his youthful forwardneſs, nick-nam'd *Whot ſpur*) who commanded the *Engliſh*, was himſelf taken priſoner, and loſt fifteen hundred of his men, and *William*

Battel of Otterburn, 1388

liam Douglas the Scotch General fell, with a great part of his Army so that never was there a more pregnant instance of the martial prowess of both Nations [We may be allow'd to remark here what a person of great honour and skill in our English Antiquities has noted before, that the old Ballad of *Chevy Chase* (Sir *Philip Sidney*'s Delight) has no other foundation for its story, save only the Battel of *Otterburn* There was never any other *Percy* engag'd against a *Douglas*, but this *Henry* who was indeed Heir to the Earl of *Northumberland*, but never liv'd to enjoy the Honour himself Sir *John Froisart* (who liv'd at the time) gives the fullest account of this Battel, but says it was Earl *James Douglas* who was the Scottish General]

A little lower, the river *Rhead* washes (or rather has almost wash'd away) another Town of great Antiquity, now call'd *Risingham*, which, in the old English and High Dutch, signifies as much as *Giants Town*, as *Risingberg* in *Germany* is *Giants-hill* [And yet it may be, the name of this place imports no more than its situation on a high and *rising* ground Most of the Villages in these parts were anciently so placed, though afterwards the Inhabitants drew down into the Valleys] Here are many evident remains of Antiquity The Inhabitants report, that the place was long defended by the God *Magon*, against a certain *Soldan* or Pagan Prince Nor is the Story wholly groundless; for that such a God was worship'd here, appears from these two Altars † lately taken out of the River, and thus inscrib'd Risingham.

† So said, an. 1607

Deo Mogonti Cadenorum & Numini Domini nostri Augusti M G Secundinus Beneficiarius Consulis Habitancii Primas tam pro se & suis posuit

DEO
MOGONTI CAD
ET N DN AVG
M G SECVNDINVS
BF COS HABITA
NCI PRIMAS TA -
PRO SE ET SVIS POSVIT

DEO
MOVNO CAD
INVENTVS DO
V S.

From the former of these, a conjecture may be made, that the place was called *Habitancum*, and that he who erected it was * Pensioner to a Consul, and † Governour of the Town (For that the chief Magistrates of Cities, Towns and Forts were call'd *Primates*, is very plain from the *Theodosian Code*) Whether this God was the tutelar Deity of the *Gadeni*, whom *Ptolemy* makes next neighbours to the *Ottadini*, I am not yet able to determine, let others enquire. Here were also found the following Inscriptions, for which, as also for others we are indebted to the famous Sir *Robert Cotton* of *Connington*, Knight, who * very lately saw and copy'd them

* *Beneficiarius*

† *Primatum Primates*

* So said, ann. 1607

D. M
BLESCIVS
DIOVICVS
FILIAE
SVAE
VIXSIT
ANI ET
DIES XXI

- - - - - - - - - - - -
CVI PRAEFEST M
PEREGRINIVS
SVPER TRIB

COH I VANG
FECIT CVRANTE
IVL PAVLO TRIB

DEAE TER
TIANAI SA
CRVM AEL.
TIMOTHEA - - - P
V. S LL M.

HERCV
LI IVL
PAVLLVS
TRIB.
V. S.

AVR.

AVR ANTONI
NI PII AVG. M
MESSORIVS
DILIGENS TRI-
BVNVS SACRVM

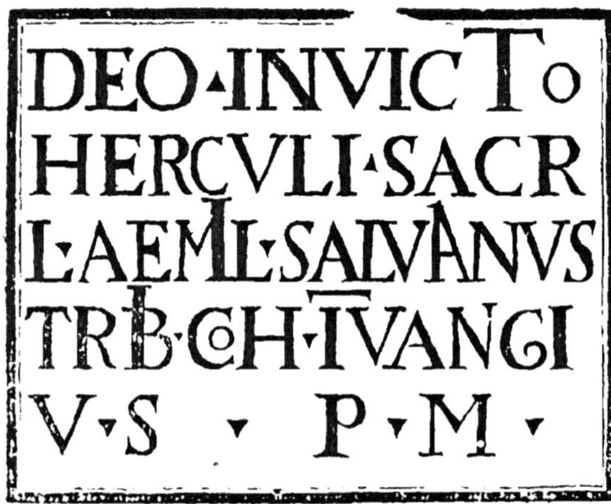

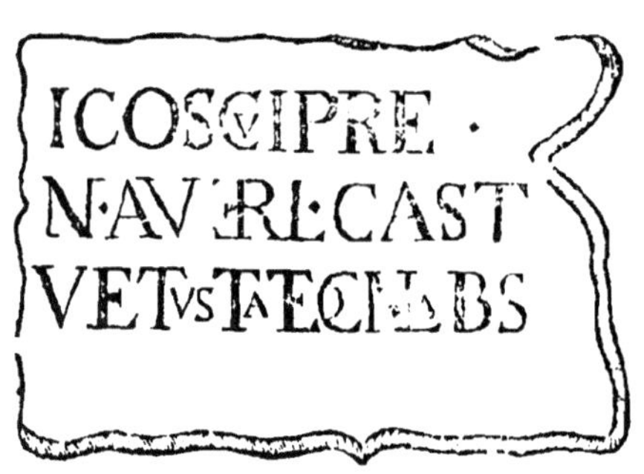

Also, what exceeds all the rest in finery of Work, a long Table curiously engraven, and by the † fourth Cohort of the *Gallic* Troops dedicated to the Sacred Majesty of the Emperours.

† Their Sta[illegible]

But to return A little lower, *Rhead*, with several other brooks that have joyn'd it, runs into *Tine* And so far reaches *Rhedesdale*; which (as Domesday-Book informs us) *the Umfranvils held in Fee and Knights Service, of the King, for guarding the Dale from Robbers*

Wastes All over the *Wastes* (as they call them,) as well as in *Gillesland*, you would think you see Nomades. the ancient *Nomades*; a Martial sort of people, that from *April* to *August*, lie in little Hutts Sheils (which they call *Sheals* and *Shealings*) here and there, among their several Flocks From hence, Chipches. *North-Tine* passes by *Chipches*, a little Fort formerly belonging to the *Umfranvils*, and then to the *Herons*, [whose Ancestors have for very many Generations been of eminent note in this County We meet with their name variously spell'd in our Histories and Records; as *Hairun*, *Heyrun*, *Hairun*, &c Amongst whom, *William Heyrun* was for eleven years together Sheriff of this County in the reign of *Henry* the third, and some of our Histories seem to hint, that he was well enrich'd by the Preferment The Family afterwards was branch'd out into the *Herons* of *Netherton*, *Meldon*, &c] From thence it runs, not far from the small Castle of *Swinborn*, which Swinborn. gave name to a Family of note, and was sometime part of the Barony of *William Heron*, and afterwards the seat of the *Woderingtons*, and so comes to the Wall, which it crosses below *Collerford* by a Bridge with Arches; where are still to be seen the ruins of the large Fort of *Wallwick*. [At this place was found, not many years Phil. Tra. since, a Roman Altar, with the following In N 231 scription,

2

If

FORTVNAE
COHIBATAVOR
CVIPRAEEST
MELACCINIVS
MARCELLVSPRÆ

Cilurnum If *Cilurnum* (where the second wing of the *Astures* lay in garrison) was not here, it was in Scilcester the neighbourhood at *Scilcester* on the Wall, Hoveden where, after *Sigga* a Nobleman had treacherously slain *Elswald* King of *Northumberland*, the Religious built a Church, and dedicated it St Oswald to *Cuthbert* and *Oswald*; which last has so far out done the other, that, the old name being quite lost, the place is now call'd St *Oswald*'s. This *Oswald*, King of Northumberland, being *See p. 1083 ready to give Battel to * *Cedwall* the *Britain* (so Cedwalla or Caswallo *Bede* calls him, whom the British Writers name *Caswallon*, and who was King, as it should seem, of Cumberland, erected a Cross, and on his knees begg'd of Christ that he would afford his heavenly assistance to those that now call'd on his name, and presently with a loud voice thus ad- Bede l. 3. c. 2. About the year 634 Christianity first profess'd in Northumberland dress'd himself to the Army. *Let us all on our knees beseech the Almighty, Living and True God, mercifully to defend us from our proud and cruel Enemy. And we do not find* (says *Bede*,) *that any Banner of the Christian Faith, any Church, any Altar, was ever erected in this Country, till this new General, following the dictates of a devout Faith, and being to engage a most inhumane Enemy, set up this Standard of the Holy Cross.* For after *Oswald* had in this Battel experienc'd that effectual assistance of Christ which he had pray'd for, he immediately turn'd Christian, and sent for *Aidan a Scotchman* to instruct his people in the †See p. 108 Christian Religion†. The place where the Victory was obtain'd, was (if we may trust the Heavenfield, now Halton Monks) afterwards call'd [illegible], or *Heavenfield*, which now in the same sense (as some will have it) is nam'd *Halton*. Upon which, *Oswald*'s Life gives us the following piece of Metre.

Tunc primùm scivit causam cur nomen haberet
Heafenfeld, *hoc est, cælestes Campus, & illi*
Nomen ab Antiquo dedit appellatio gentis
Præteritæ, tanquam belli præsaga futuri
Nominis & Caussam mox assignavit ibidem
Cælitus expugnans cælestis turba scelestam.
Neve senectutis ignavia posset honorem
Tam celebris delere loci, tantique Triumphi,
Ecclesiæ Fratres Haugustaldensis *adesse*
Devoti, Christumque solent celebrare quotannis
Quoque loci persistat honos, in honore beati
Oswaldi *Regis ibi confluxere Capellam*

And now he understood whence *Heavenfeld* came,
Call'd in old time by that prophetick name
For now the reason of the Name was given,
When Hell's vile Troops were overcome by Heaven
But lest devouring Ages should deface
The glorious triumph of the sacred place,
The monks of old *Haugustald* every year
Do meet and joyn in their devotions here
And that great *Oswald*'s fame should never die,
They've rais'd a Chapel to his Memory

And another in his Commendation (well enough for the barbarous Age he liv'd in) writes thus

Quis fuit Alcides? Quis Cæsar Julius? *Aut quis Magnus* Alexander? Alcides *se superâsse*

Fertur, Alexander *Mundum*, *sed* Julius *hostem*
Se simul Oswaldus, *& Mundum vicit*, *& hostem.*

Cæsar and *Hercules* applaud thy fame,
And *Alexander* owns thy greater name,
Tho' one himself, one foes, and one the world o'recame
Great Conquests all! but bounteous Heav'n in thee,
To make a greater, joyn'd the former three

[As to this Story of *Oswald*, *Bede* indeed seems to say, the Battel was against *Cedwall*, but *Matthew* of *Westminster* says, it was fought against *Penda* King of the *Mercians*, who was at that time General of *Cadwallin's* Forces, and the Story of setting up the Banner of the Christian Faith, must be understood to be *in Berniciorum Gente*, as *Bede* says in the place cited, if it have any truth in it, for Christianity was, some years before, planted in the Kingdom of *Northumberland* by *Paulinus*, and a Church was built at *York* by King *Edwin*, *Oswald's* Predecessor But (after all) this remark is not in the Saxon Paraphrase of *Bede's* History, so that we have reason to look upon it as a spurious Corruption It does, indeed, contradict the account that himself elsewhere gives, of *Paulinus's* baptizing great numbers in these very parts, which surely was *Fidei Christianæ signum*, i e a Sign of the Christian Faith Nor was *Heavenfield* the place where the Battel was fought, and the Victory obtain'd, for that was at another place in the neighbourhood, which *Bede* calls *Denises burna*, suppos'd to be *Dilston* The Writer of *Oswald's* Life, it is true, supposes this to have been the Scene of the Action, tho' *Bede* only says, that here was the Cross erected, and here (afterwards) the Chapel built It is no wonder to find a number of Poets (and a great number they are) who have written in praise of St *Oswald* His introducing of Christianity was not the thing that rais'd his credit (for so much King *Edwin* had done before him) but his chief stock of Merit consisted in his bringing in Monkery along with it It was this, that gave him so considerable a figure amongst the men of the Cloister, and advanced him to a like honour with what his name-sake-Saint of *York* attain'd to afterwards]

See *Irvin*

Below St *Oswald's*, both the *Tines* meet, after *South Tine* (which goes along with the Wall, at about two miles distance from it) has pass'd by *Langly*-Castle, where formerly, in the reign of King John, *Adam de Tindale* had his Barony, which afterwards descended to *Nicholas de Boltely*, and was lately in the possession of the *Percies*,) and has slid under a tottering and crazy wooden Bridge at *Aidon* And now the whole *Tine*, being well grown, and still encreasing, presses forward in one Chanel for the Ocean, by *Hexam*, which *Bede* calls *Hangustald*, and the *Saxons* pextolderham That this was the *Axelodunum* of the *Romans*, where the first Cohort of the *Spaniards* were in garrison, the name implies; and so does its situation on a rising hill, for the Britains call'd such a Mount *Dunum* But take an account of this place from *Richard* its Prior, who liv'd about five hundred years ago *Not far from the Southern bank of the river Tine, stands a Town of small extent indeed at present, and but thinly inhabited, but (as the remaining marks of its ancient state will testifie) heretofore very*

Langley-Castle
Testa Nevill
Hexam
Axelodunum
Dunum

large and magnificent This place is call'd Hextoldersham, *from the little rivulet of* Hextold, *which runs by, and sometimes suddenly overflows it In the year* 675 Etheldreda *wife to King* Egfrid *assign'd it for an Episcopal See to* St Wilfrid; *who built here a Church, which for the curiousness and beauty of the Fabrick, surpass'd all the Monasteries in* England [Moreover, the same Prior is very particular in his description of the Church's Fabrick, in its Walls, Roof, Cieling, Stairs, Pillars, *&c* and (at last) concludes, *That no such stately structure was, at that time, to be met with on this side the Alpes* He likewise informs us, at large, what Immunities and Privileges were granted by our Saxon Kings to this Church, how well they were secur'd to her, how far the bounds of her *Fridstol* or Sanctuary extended, *&c*] Take also what *Malmesbury* has written of it *This was Crown Land, till Bishop* Wilfrid *gave other Lands for it to Queen* Etheldreda *It was wonderful to see what towering Buildings were there erected, how admirably contriv'd with winding stairs, by Masons, brought (in prospect of his great Liberality) from* Rome *Insomuch that they seem'd to vie with the* Roman *pomp, and did long out-struggle even Age it self* At which time King *Egfrid* made this little City a Bishop's See, [whereunto St *Cuthbert* himself was both elected and consecrated, though he did not think fit to take the charge upon him] But that Honour, after the * twelfth Bishop, was wholly lost, the Danish wars prevailing Afterwards, it was only reckon'd a Manour of the Archbishops of *York*, till they parted with their right, in an exchange made with Henry the eighth It is also famous for the bloody Battel in which *John Nevil* Lord *Montacute* very bravely engaged, and as fortunately vanquish'd the Generals of the House of *Lancaster*, and, for so doing, was created Earl of *Northumberland* by *Edward* the fourth At present, its only glory is the old Monastery, part whereof † was turn'd into the fair house of Sir *J Foster* Knight, [and was since the Estate of Sir *John Fenwick*, from whom it came by sale to Sir *William Blacket*, Baronet] The West-end of the Church is demolish'd The rest stands entire, and is a very stately Structure in the Quire whereof is an old Tomb of a Person of Honour (of the Martial Family of the *Umfranvils*, as his coat of Arms witnesses,) lying with his Legs across By the way, In that posture it was then the custom to bury such only, as had taken the Cross upon them, being under that Banner, engag'd in the *Hoy War*, for the recovery of the Holy Land out of the Hands of the *Mahometans* Near the East end of the Church, on a rising brow, stand two strong Bulwarks of hew'n stone, which, I was told, belong to the Archbishop of *York*

* Eight. C
† Is, C
Ma[illegible]

From hence Eastward, we pass'd on to *Dilston*, the Seat of the *Ratcliffs*, call'd in old Books *Divelston*, from a small brook which here empties it self into the *Tine*, and which *Bede* names *Devil's burn* where (as he writes) *Oswald*, arm'd with Christian Faith, ‖ in a fair field, slew *Cedwall* the Britain, that wretched Tyrant, who before had slain two Kings of *Northumberland*, and miserably wasted their Country [Only, it is to be observed, that the Latin Copies of *Bede* say, *Oswald's* victory was *in loco qui lingua Anglorum* Denises burna *vocatur*, In the place which is call'd by the English *Denises burna* And the Saxon Copies of King *Ælfred's* Paraphrase have [illegible], [illegible] and [illegible] burna, but the Saxon Chronicle has not recorded this story Sir *Francis Ratcliff*

Dilston
‖ [illegible] Bede, l 3

Baronet

Baronet (late Proprietor of this place) was made Baron of *Dilston*, Viscount *Langley*, and Earl of *Derwent water*] On the other bank of *Tine* Ninius calls it Curia stands *Curia Ottadinorum*, mention'd by *Ptolemy*, which (by the distances) should seem to be *Antoninus's Corstopitum*, [or rather *Corstopilum* (for so saith the Edition of *H Surita*, both in the Text and the Comment)] It is now call'd Corbridge. *Corbridge* (from a Bridge built here,) by *Hoveden*, *Corobridge*, and by *Huntingdon*, *Cure* At this day it has nothing remarkable but a Church, and near it, a little Tower-house built and inhabited by the Vicars of the place Yet there are many ruins of ancient buildings, amongst Treasure sought in vain Hoveden Tacitus. which King *John* search'd for some old hidden treasure but Fortune favour'd him no more in this vain quest, than she did *Nero*, in his enquiries after the conceal'd Riches of *Dido* at *Carthage* For he found nothing but stones mark'd with Brass, Iron, and Lead [But although King *John* could meet with no Discoveries at *Corbridge*, there was a considerable one accidentally made here not many years ago The bank of a small Torrent being worn by • See below some sudden showers, the Skeleton of a • Man appear'd, of a very extraordinary and prodigious size The length of its thigh-bone was within a very little of two yards, and the skull, teeth, and other parts, proportionably monstrous So that, by a fair computation, the true length of the whole body has been reckon'd at seven yards Some parts of it † were † Ann 169, in the possession of the right honourable the Earl of *Derwent-water*, at *Dilston*, but his Lordship, having had no notice of the thing, till it was (in a great measure) squander'd and lost by the unthinking discoverers, the Rarity is not so compleat, as whoever sees the remains of it, will heartily wish it were But since there was Phil Trans N 330 not found here an *entire* Skeleton, but great numbers, or *Strata*, of Teeth and Bones of a very extraordinary size, and withall a sort of Pavement or Foundation of Stone, running along with these *Strata*, and since here hath been dug up an Altar inscribed to *Hercules*, which we shall subjoin, what if we should say, that these are the Teeth and Bones of Oxen, and other like Creatures, which were sacrific'd at some Temple, in this Place? The like Bones are reported to have been frequently discover'd on the shore near *Alnmouth* in this County, all of them at a greater depth in the ground than they can well be imagin'd ever to have been buried] Whoever views the neighbouring heap of rubbish, which is now call'd Colecester *Colecester*, will readily conclude this *Corbridge* to have been a *Roman* Fort

[The Altar above-mentioned which, many years since, was found here, hath this Inscription

Phil Trans N 2 8

As the Roman Street runs from *Ebchester* to *Corbridge*, so from *Corbridge* to *Resingham*, a mile Resingham. south from whence, is a Pillar about eight foot long, which has stood by the way-side, but is now fallen, and at the place it self, in a wall on the inside of a House, is this Inscription,

Phil Trans N 278

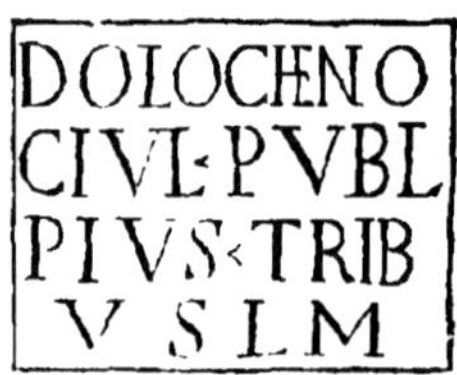

]

Upon the same bank, I saw the fair Castle of *Biwell*, which in the reign of King *John*, was Biwell the Barony of *Hugh Balliol*, *for which he stood oblig'd to pay to the Ward of Newcastle upon Tine, thirty Knights Services*

Below this Castle, there is a most beautiful A Weare Weare for the catching of Salmon, and, in the middle of the river, stand two firm Pillars of Stone, which formerly supported a Bridge Hence *Tine* runs under *Prudhow* Castle (in old Prudhow writings *Prodhow*,) which is pleasantly seated on the ridge of a hill This, till I am better inform'd, I shall guess to be *Protolitia*, which is Protolitia also written *Procolitia*, and was the station of the first Cohort of the *Batavi* It is famous for gallantly maintaining it self (in the days of *Henry* the second) against the siege of *William* King of *Scots*, *who* (as *Neubrigensis* expresses it) *toil'd himself and his Army to no purpose* Afterwards it belong'd to the *Umfranvils*, an eminent Umfranvils Family, one of whom, Sir *Gilbert* (a Knight in the reign of Edward the first) was, in right of his wife, made Earl of *Angus* in *Scotland* [Before which, in the reign of Henry the third, we find honourable mention made of *Gilebert de Humfranvilla* as dying in the year 1245, whom the Historian calls *a famous Baron, the Keeper as well as Ornament, of the Northern Parts of England* Sir *Robert Umfranvil* was Sheriff of the County in the 46th and 51st years of Edward the third, and in the 2d and 6th of Henry the fourth And another Sir *Robert* (a younger son, I think, to the said Sheriff) was Vice Admiral of England in the year 1410, and brought such plenty of *Prizes* (in Cloth, Corn, and other valuable Commodities) from Scotland, that he got the nick name of *Robin Mend market*] The true heiress *of the blood* (as our Lawyers express it) was at length married into the family of the *Talboys*, and, after that, this Castle was (by the King's bounty) bestow'd upon the Duke of *Bedford*

But, to return to the Wall Beyond St *Oswald's*, the Foundations of two Forts which they call *Castle steeds*, are to be seen on the Wall, Castle steeds and then a place call'd *Portgate*, where (as the Portgate word in both Languages fairly evinces) there See above, p 1054 was formerly a Gate [or Sally port] through it Beneath this, and more within the Wall, stands *Halton Hall*, the present seat of the an- Halton Hall cient and warlike Family of the *Carnabies*, (who have been a great while in this County; *William Carnaby* Esq, having been Sheriff of it in the 7th year of King Henry the sixth It is probable, they came hither from *Carnaby* near *Bridlington* in the East Riding of Yorkshire]

and,

and, hard by, *Aidon-Castle*, which was part of the Barony of the forementton'd *Hugh Balliol*. Now, since a great many places on the Wall bear the name of *Aidon*, and the same word (in the British tongue) signifies * a Military Wing or Troop of Horse, many whereof were (as the *Liber Notitiarum* teaches us) placed along the Wall, let the Reader consider, whether these places have not thence had their names, as other Towns had that of *Leon*, where *Legions* were quarter'd. However, near this place was dug up a piece of an old Stone, wherein was drawn the pourtraiture of a Man lying on his bed (leaning upon his left hand, and touching his right knee with his right hand,) with the following Inscriptions.

Aidon
* *Ala militaris*.

NORICI AN XXX
—ESSORVS MAGNVS
FRATER EIVS
DVPL ALAE
SABINIANAE

M MARI
VS VELLI
A LONG
VS AQVI
S HANC
POSVIT
V S L M

Beyond the Wall, rises the river *Pont*, which running down by *Fenwick-hall*, the seat of the eminent and valiant family of the *Fenwicks*, for some miles goes along with the Wall, and had its banks guarded by the first Cohort of the *Cornavii* at *Pons Ælii*, which was built by *Ælius Hadrianus*, and is now called *Pont-Eland*. Here *Henry* the third concluded a Peace with the King of *Scots*, in the year 1244, and near it the first Cohort of the *Tungri* lay at *Borwick*, which the *Notitia Provinciarum* calls *Borcovicus*. From *Portgate*, the Wall runs to *Waltown*, which (from the name, and its twelve miles distance from the eastern Sea) I take to be the same Royal Borough which *Bede* calls *Ad murum*, [and the Saxon Translation æt walle,] † where *Segebert*, King of the *East-Saxons* was baptiz'd by * *Finanus*, [who also (at the same place) baptized *Peada* King of the *Mercians*, together with his whole train of Courtiers and Attendants.] Near this, is a Fort call'd *Old Winchester*, which I readily believe to be *Vindolana*, where, as the *Liber Notitiarum* says, the fourth Cohort of the *Galli* kept a Frontier-garrison. Thence we went to *Routchester*, where we met with evident remains of a square Camp joyning close to the Wall. Near this is *Headon*, which was part of the Barony of *Hugh de Bolebec*, who, by the mother, was descended from the noble Barons of *Mont Fichet*, and had no issue but Daughters, who were marry'd to *Ralph* Lord *Greystock*, *J. Lovell*, *Huntercomb*, and *Corbet*.

Fenwick
Pons Ælii.
Pont Eland
Borwick
Borcovicus
Waltown
See above, p. 1054
Ad murum
† See Observations on the *Picts Wall*
* *Paulinus*, C. Bede l. 3. c. 21
Old Winchester
Vindolana
Routchester
See above, p. 1055
Headon
Barony of Bolebec

[In an original Charter dated the first year of King Stephen) we have, among many Barons, *Signum Walteri de Bol bec*, and one *Isabel de Bolebec* Countess of Oxford, first founded a Convent of Dominicans in that City.] Nearer to *Newcastle*, stands *Benwall*, where were lately found several Urns, with Coins in them, which were broken and squander'd about by the ignorant Diggers; but one of the Urns being preserv'd, was given to the Library at *Durham*, where it remains very entire. Some there are, who have chosen to place the ancient *Condercum* here, rather than at *Chester upon the Street*, by reason of the Antiquity of *Benwall*, and its nearness to the Wall; the *Notitia* describing *Condercum*, as upon the line of the Wall.]

Seld. Tit. Hon. par. 2. c. 5. p. 571
Benwall

And now, near the meeting of the Wall and *Tine*, stands *Newcastle*, the glory of all the Towns in this Country. It has a noble Haven on the *Tine*, which is of such a depth as to carry Vessels of a very good burthen, and of that security, that they are in no hazard of either storms or shallows. [Almost to the Bar of *Tinmouth* (which is a Sand that lies cross the river's mouth, not above seven foot deep at low water) the channel is good and secure: but there, you meet with a number of Rocks, which they call the *Black Middins*, very dangerous. To prevent much of the mischief that might happen among these, in the night time, there are two Light-houses maintain'd by the Trinity house in *Newcastle*, and near these was built *Clifford's* Fort, in the year 1672, which effectually commands all Vessels that enter the River.]

Newcastle upon Tine.

The situation of the Town is climbing and very uneven, on the north bank of the river, which is cross'd by a very fair bridge. As you enter the Town from hence, you have, on the left hand the Castle overtopping you, and after that a very steep brow of a hill. On the right, you have the Market place, and the best built part of the Town; from which to the upper and far larger part, the ascent is a little troublesome. It † was heretofore beautified with four Churches; [but now there are, besides St. *Nicholas* (the Parochial or Mother Church) six other Churches or Chapels, whereof one was rebuilt at the publick charge of the Corporation, A. D. 1682, and endow'd with sixty Pounds *per Annum*, one half of which is for the maintenance of a Catechetical-Lecturer, who is to expound the Catechism of the Church of England every *Sunday*, and to preach a Sermon every first *Wednesday* in the Month. Twenty Pounds are assign'd to a School master, and ten to an Usher, who are to prepare the Children of the Parish for the said Lecture. Besides which, the *Town* very honourably pays five hundred and eighty Pounds a year towards the maintenance of their Vicar, and those Lecturers and Curates who are under him, a pattern, very fit to be imitated by other Towns and Cities.] It is defended by exceeding strong Walls, wherein are seven gates, and a great many turrets upon it. What it was anciently, is not yet discover'd. I am very inclinable to think, it was *Gabrosentum*, since *Gateshead* (which is, as it were, its suburbs) is a word of the same signification with that British name which is deriv'd from *Goats*, as has been already mention'd. Besides, the *Notitia Provinciarum* places *Gabrosentum* (and in it the second Cohort of the *Thracians*) * within the very range of the Wall. And it is most certain, that the Rampire and [afterwards] the Wall pass'd through this Town, and at *Pandon-gate* there still remains, as it is thought, one of the little Turrets of that very Wall. It is indeed different from the rest, both in fashion and masonry, and seems to carry a very great age. The name of *Monkchester* is also an argument of its being a garrison'd Fort; for so it was call'd, from the *Monks*, about the time of the Conquest. Soon after, it got the modern name of *Newcastle*, from that new Castle which was here built by

† I. C.
Gateshead
Gabrosentum
* *Ail* ...
Pandon gate

Robert

Robert son of *William* the Conquerour, and with in a while was mightily enlarg'd and enrich'd by a good trade on the coasts of *Germany*, and by the sale of its Sea-coal (whereof this Country has great plenty) into other parts of *England* In the reign of *Edward* the first, a very rich Burger being carry'd off prisoner by the *Scots* out of the middle of the Town, and having pay'd a round ransom for himself, began the first fortifications of the place The rest of the townsmen, mov'd by his example, finish'd the work, and entirely encompass'd themselves with good stout Walls since which time, this place has so securely manag'd its Trade, in spight of all the attempts of enemies and the many neighbouring thieves, that it is now in a most flourishing state of wealth and commerce (upon which account *Henry* the sixth made it a Country *incorporate of it self*) [Both these are wonderfully encreas'd in this last age The Coal-trade is incredible; and for other Merchandise, *Newcastle* is the great *Emporium* of the northern parts of *England*, and of a good part of *Scotland* The publick Revenue is also very much advanc'd of late year for which the Town is in great measure indebted to the provident care and good management of its two great Patriots Sir *William Blacket* Baronet, and *Timothy Davison* Esquire, Aldermen] It lies in 21 degrees and 30 minutes longitude, and in 54 and 57 of northern latitude We have already treated of the suburbs call'd *Gateshead*, which is joyn'd to *Newcastle* by the bridge, and belongs to the Bishop of *Durham* This Town, for its situation and plenty of Sea-coal (so useful in it self, and to which so great a part of *England* and the *Low Countries* are indebted for their good fires) is thus commended by *Johnston* in his Poems on the Cities of *Britain*.

NOVUM CASTRUM.

Rupe sedens celsa, rerum aut miracula spectat
Naturæ, aut solers distrahit illa aliis
Sedibus Æthereis quid frustra quæritis ignem?
Hunc alit, hunc terra suscitat ista sinu
Non illum torvo terras qui turbine terret,
Sed qui animam Terris, detque animos animis
Eliquat hic ferrum, æs, hic aurum ductile fundit
Quos non auri illex conciet umbra animos?
Quin (aiunt) auro permutat bruta metalla,
Alchimus hunc igitur prædicat esse Deum
Si deus est, ceu tu dictas, divine magister,
Hac quot alit? Quot alit Scotia *nostra Deos?*

NEW-CASTLE.

From her high Rock great Nature's works surveys,
And kindly spreads her goods through Lands and Seas.
Why seek you fire in some exalted sphere?
Earth's fruitful bosom will supply you here
Not such whose horrid flashes scare the plain,
But gives enliv'ning warmth to earth and men.
Ir'n, brass, and gold its melting force obey;
(Ah! who's e'er free from gold's almighty sway?)
Nay, into gold 'twill change a baser ore,
Hence the vain Chymist deifies its power.
If 't be a god, as is believ'd by you,
This place and *Scotland* more than Heaven can shew

[At *Fenham*, a little village in the parish of *Newcastle*, there are some Coal-pits which were burning several years; and are suppos'd to be still on fire The Flames of this subterraneous fire were visible by night; and in the day time the track of it might easily be follow'd by the Brimstone that lay on the surface of the Earth Fenham.

Newcastle has afforded the title of Earl to *Lodowick Stewart* (Duke of Lennox, and Earl of Richmond) created, May, 1604 But in the year 1627 this title was conferr'd upon *William Cavendish*, Viscount *Mansfield* and Baron *Ogle*, who was afterwards, in 1643, created Marquis of *Newcastle*, and the year following Duke of *Newcastle* In 1676 he was succeeded by his son *Henry Cavendish* Since which, the right honourable *John Holles*, Earl of Clare, was created Duke of this place by his Majesty King William the third, and, he dying without issue male, the same honour hath been conferr'd by his Majesty King George upon *Thomas*, Son of *Thomas* Lord *Pelham*, by a Sister of *John* the last Duke, which *Thomas*, the present Duke of *Newcastle*, became Heir to a vast Estate, left by his said Uncle, and hath, on many occasions, discover'd an early and most steady zeal for the honour and interest of his Country]

Scarce three miles hence (for I pass by *Gosseford*, which was the Barony of *Richard Sur-Tees*, or *Upon the Tees*, a person of great repute under *Henry* the first,) stands a little village called *Walls end* The very signification of the word proves this to have been the station of the † first Cohort of the *Frixagi*, which in the *Liber Notitiarum* is call'd *Vindobala*, and by *Antoninus*, || *Vindomora* [for the latter seems, in the provincial language of the Britains, to have signified the *Walls end*, and the former the *Rampier's end*, since they anciently call'd a Wall *Mur*, and a Ditch or Rampier *Gual* [By the way, there is an ill contrived and incoherent Interpolation in *Bede*, wherewith *Buchanan*, and some other Scotch Writers, seem to be mightily pleased, which, if it proves any thing at all, shews, that *Vindobala* was by the Britains called *Penvabel*] Gosseford. Barony Sur-Tees. Walls-end. † Second Cohort of the [illegible] but that was at G[illegible] [illegible] || D Gale places it at [illegible]

As to the Ditch and the Wall, it is not likely that they went any further, since they are not to be traced beyond this place, and *Tine* (being now near the sea) carries a chanel so deep, as to be equal to the strongest Fort Yet some will needs maintain, that only the Ditch, and not the Wall, reach'd as far as *Tinmouth*, which, they assert, was call'd *Pen-ball-crag*, that is, the *Head of the Rampier in the Rock* This opinion I shall not gainsay; however, I dare be confident, that this place was, in the time of the *Romans*, call'd *Tunnocellum*, which signifies as much as the *Promontory of Tunna* or *Tina*, where the first Cohort *Ælia Classica* (that was rais'd, as the name probably imports, by *Ælius Hadrianus*) was in pay for Sea service for the Romans had their *Naves Lusoriæ*, or light Frigats, in their border rivers, both to prevent the excursions of the neighbouring Enemy, and to make incursions upon them, as may be seen in the *Codex Theodosii*, under the title *De Lusoriis Danubii* Under the Saxon Heptarchy, it was called Tinmouth. Tunnocellum. Naves Lusoriæ.

Lib 4 c 2 2

Tunnacestceni; not, as *Bede* affirms, from Abbot *Tunna*, but from the river Here was also a little Monastery, which was frequently plunder'd by the *Danes*, [and, after the Conquest, became a Cell of St Alban] It is now call'd *Tinmouth-castle*, and glories in a stately and strong Castle, which, says an ancient Author, *is seated on a very high rock, inaccessible towards the Ocean on the east and north, and elsewhere so well mounted, that a slender garrison will make it good* For this reason, *Robert Mowbray*, Earl of *Northumberland*, chose it for his chief hold, when he rebell'd against *William Rufus* but, as is usual, matters succeeded not well with this Rebel, who being here brought into distress by his besiegers, retir'd to the adjoyning Monastery, which was esteem'd an inviolable sanctuary Nevertheless, he was thence carried off, and had afterwards the just reward of his Treason in a long and noisom Imprisonment [Within this Castle, the Ruins of the forementioned Monastery are still to be seen Here was also, formerly the Parish-Church, but (that being gone much to decay, and the Parishioners, in the late Civil Wars, often debarred the liberty of a free resort to it) another was begun to be built in the year 1659, which was afterwards finished, and consecrated by Bishop *Cosins*, in the year 1668]

Seton

Seghill

Segedunum

† Fourth, Gale's *Notitia*

* *Vallum*

Belsey

Barons of Ogle

I must now coast it along the shore Behind the Promontory whereon *Tunnocellum* or *Tinmouth* is seated (near *Seton*, part of the Barony of *De la vall* in the reign of *Henry* the third) stands *Seghill*, call'd *Segedunum*, the station of the † third Cohort of the *Lergi*, on the * Wall, and indeed *Segedunum* in the British tongue signifies the same thing, as *Seghill* in the English A few miles from hence, the shore is cut by the river *Blythe*, which (having pass'd by *Belsey*, the ancient inheritance of the *Middletons*; and *Ogle-Castle*, belonging to the Barons of *Ogle*) does here, together with the river *Pont*, empty it self into the sea The *Ogles* were honour'd with the title of Barons from the very beginning of *Edward* the fourth's reign, having enrich'd themselves by marrying the heirs of *Bertbram de Bothal*, *Alan Heton*, and *Alexander Kirkby* The male issue of these Barons was lately extinct in *Cuthbert*, the seventh Baron, who had two daughters, *Joan*, marry'd to *Edward Talbot* a younger son of *George* Earl of *Shrewsbury*, and *Catherine*, marry'd to Sir *Charles Cavendish*, Knight [By reason whereof, Sir *William Cavendish* was created first Baron, and, afterwards Earl of *Ogle*]

Wentsbeck

Barony of *Mitford*

Rutarii or *Ruptarii*

‖ Or, *de Breant*

A little higher, the river *Wentsbeck* falls into the sea It runs by *Mitford*, which was burnt down by King *John* and his *Rutars*, when they so miserably wasted this Country That age call'd those foreign Auxiliaries and Free-booters *Rutars*, who were brought out of the Low-Countries and other places to King *John*'s assistance, by *Fulques* ‖ *de Brent* and *Walter Buc* [Which *Rutarii* or *Ruptarii* are not only mention'd by our Historians in the reign of King *John*, but, before his time also, in the reign of *Henry* the second, and after it under *Henry* the third By all the accounts which we have of them, it appears they were mercenary German Troops Now, in the High Dutch, *Rott* (whence our English *Rout*) is a Company of Soldiers; *Rotten* or *Rottiren*, to muster; *Rottmeister*, a Corporal, *&c* That from hence we are to fetch the true original of the word, we are sufficiently taught by *Will Neubrigensis*, who lived and wrote his History in the times of these *Rutars*. *Rex*, says he, *stipendiarias Brabantionum copias, quas Rutas vocant, accersivit*; i e the King sent for the

Lib 2 c 27

Stipendiary Troops of *Brabant*, which they call the *Rutes* Dr *Wats* (in his Glossary) derives the name from the German *Reuter*, a Trooper or Horseman But this by the way As to the forementioned *Brent* and *Buc*,] *Brent* being a * cruel desperate fellow, was afterwards banish'd the Kingdom [(our Historians call him a *most wicked Robber*, and a thousand hard names besides, because he used to make free with the Monasteries, and their Treasures, as they lay in his way)] But *Buc*, a person of more sobriety, having done the King good service, had confer'd on him by Royal Bounty, Lands in *Yorkshire* and *Northamptonshire*, where his Posterity flourish'd, down to *John Buc*, who was attainted under *Henry* the seventh, Great grandson to this *John*, † is that person of excellent learning Sir *George Buc* Knight, Master of the Revels, who (for I love to own my Benefactors) remark'd many things in our Histories, and courteously communicated his observations to me This was formerly the Barony of *William Bertbram*, whose line soon fail'd in *Roger* his grandson, the three co heirs being marry'd to *Norman Darcy*, *T Penbury*, and *William de Elmeley*

* *Homo ferratus*

† So Gale ...

Morpeth

After this, *Wentsbeck* runs through the famous little Town of *Morpeth*, for [the body of] the Town is seated on the northern bank of the river, and the Church on the southern Near which stands also, on a shady hill, the Castle, and this, together with the Town, came from *Roger de Merlac* or *Merley* (whose Barony it was) to the Lords of *Greystock*, and from them to the Barons *Dacre* of *Gillesland* [This *Roger* (I suppose) is he of whom * *Matth Paris* makes mention, as a person of great note] I meet with nothing anciently recorded of this place, save only that in the year of our Lord 1215 the Towns men themselves burnt it, in pure spight to King *John* [But of later years, it came, together with *Gillesland*, *&c* by *Elizabeth*, sister and co heir of *George* the last Lord *Dacre*, to (her husband) the Lord *William Howard* of *Naworth*, third son to the Duke of *Norfolk*, whose grandson *Charles*, was, soon after the Restauration of K *Charles* the second, created Earl of *Carlisle*, and Viscount *Morpeth* Which Honours were inherited by his son *Edward*, and are now enjoy'd by his grandson *Charles*, the third Earl of *Carlisle* of this Family, a person of great wisdom and honour] From hence *Wentsbeck* runs by *Bothal Castle*, anciently the Barony of *Richard Bertbram*; from whose Posterity it descended to the Barons of *Ogle* [Sir *John Bertbram* was several times Sheriff of *Northumberland* in the reign of King Henry the sixth; and the Christian Name of *Bertbram* (out of which, some think, the Christians have made their *Ferdinando*) is still very common in these Northern Parts] Upon the bank of this river, as I have long fancied (whether upon judgment or opinion I know not) was the seat of *Glanoventa*, where the Romans plac'd a Garrison of the first Cohort of the *Morini*, for the defence of the Marches This, the very situation of the place seems to argue; and the name of the river, with its signification, may be a further evidence of it For it is ‖ upon the range of the Wall or Rampire, as the *Liber Notitiarum* places that Fort; and the river is call'd *Wents beck* Now *Glanoventa* in the British tongue signifies the *shore* or *bank of Went* whence also *Glanon*, a Maritime Town in France (mention'd by *Mela*) may probably have had its name]

* Ann 1215

Hist Major

Bothal Castle

Glanoventa

Not

Not far from hence (to omit other less con
siderable Turrets) stands, on the shore; the old
Withrington Castle of *Withrington* or *Woderington*, in the Saxon
Language Wiðrington; which gave name to
the eminent and knightly family of the *Wi
thringtons*, who have frequently signaliz'd their
valour in the Scotish wars; [and were after
* Now, for wards advanced to the dignity of * Barons]
ferred by Near this, the river *Coqued* or *Coquet* falls into
Alaunder the Sea, which, rising among the Rocks of
Coquet *Cheviot hills*, has near its Head *Billesdun*, from
Billesdun whence are descended the worshipful family of
the *Selbies*, and (lower, to the South) *Harbottle*,
in Saxon Þerbottle, i e the *Armie's station*,
Harbottle whence, the Family of the *Harbottles*, of good
‖ So said note in the ‖ last age. [From the reign of
ann 1607 *Henry* the fourth, to that of *Richard* the third,
several of this name were Sheriffs of Northumberland] Here was formerly a Castle, which
was demolish'd by the Scots in the year 1314
[The Saxon termination botl (of the like im
port with by, ham, and tun) is not only to
be observed in the name of this Village, but
also in *Larbottle*, *Shilbottle*, and others of less
Halyston note in this County] Hard by, stands *Halyston*
or *Holy stone*, where, in the infancy of the Eng
lish Church, *Paulinus* is said to have baptized
many thousands Upon the very mouth of *Coquet*, the shore is guarded by the fair Castle of
Warkworth *Warkworth*, belonging to the *Percies*; wherein is
a Chapel admirably cut out of a Rock, and fully
Parl Rolls, finish'd without Beams or Rafters. This, King
5 Edw 3 Edward the third gave to *Henry Percy*, together
with the manour of *Rothbury* It was formerly
the Barony of *Roger Fitz Richard*, being given
to him by Henry the second King of England,
Clavering who also bestow'd *Clavering* in *Essex* on his son
Whereupon, at the command of King *Edward*
the first, they took the sirname of *Clavering*,
leaving the old fashion of framing sirnames out
of the Christian name of their Father for so,
anciently, acording to the several names of
* The Son their Fathers, men were call'd *Robert* * *Fitz-
Roger*, *Roger Fitz-John*, &c Part of this Inheritance fell, by Fine and Covenant, to the
Nevils, afterwards Earls of *Westmoreland*
and another share of it to a daughter call'd *Eve*,
married to *Th Ufford*, from whose Posterity it
descended hereditarily to the *Fienes* Barons of
Dacre But from the younger sons, branched
out the Barons of *Euers*, the *Euers of Axholme*,
the *Claverings* of *Ca'aly* in this County, and
Morwic others In the Neighbourhood, is *Morwic*,
which may also boast of its Lords, whose Male
issue was extinct about the year 1258 The
Inheritance was convey'd by daughters to the
Lumleys, *Seymours*, *Bulmers*, and *Roscells*.

Alaunus Then the shore receives the river *Alaunus*
which, having not yet lost the name whereby it
Alne was known to *Ptolemy*, is still briefly called *Alne*
Twiford On its banks, are *Twyfford* or *Double Ford* (where
a Synod was held under King *Egfrid* [At this
Synod S *Cuthbert* is said to have been chosen Bi
shop By the account that *Bede* (and especially
his Royal Paraphrast) gives of the matter, it
looks more like a Parliament than a Synod; for
the Election is reported to have been mid
anmodne geþaþunge ealra þæra pitena, i e
with the unanimous consent of all the *Witena*
Bede l 4 Now pitena, in the Language of those times,
c 28 signifies *Senators* or *Parliament-men*, who, it
seems, unanimously chose him Bishop; or at
least approv'd the choice The meeting is in
deed said to have been on the river *Alne*, and
yet it is very much to be doubted, whether this
Twiford be in *Northumberland*, and whether Arch
bishop *Theodore* ever came so far north There
are a great many *Twifords* in the south of *England* the Legend of S *Cuthbert* says, that this Page 17
Synod was held at *Twiford* upon *Slu*] Next, is Eslington
Eslington, the seat of the *Collingwoods*, men of re
nown in the wars; [and who still continue here]
as also, *Alanwick* (call'd by the Saxons Ealnpic, Alanwick
and now usually *Anwick*,) a Town famous for
the victory obtain'd by the English; when our
brave Ancestors took *William* King of Scots, 1174
and presented him a prisoner to *Henry* the second
It is defended with a goodly Castle, which 1037
Malcolm the third King of *Scotland* had so straiten'd by siege, that it was upon the very point of
surrender when presently he was slain by a
Soldier, who stabb'd him with a Spear, on the
point whereof he pretended to deliver him the
Keys of the Castle His son *Edward*, rashly
charging the Enemy, to revenge his father's
death, was also mortally wounded, and dy'd
soon after This was formerly a Barony of the
Vescies for *Henry* the second gave it to *Eusta
chius Fitz John*, father of *William Vescie*, in Te- [illegible]
nure of twelve Knights Services *John Vescie*
returning from the Holy War, [is said to have]
first brought *Carmelites* into England, and to Carmelites
have built a Convent for them here at *Holm*, a
solitary place, and not unlike Mount *Carmel* in
Syria [But, in truth, there never was any Convent or Monastery founded at *Alnwick*, or near
it, by *John Vescie* There was indeed a Monastery of the Order of the *Præmonstratenses* founded
by *Eustachius Fitz John*, Father of *William de
Vescie*, who had that sirname from his Mother,
an Heiress But this was done in the year 1147,
long before the Carmelites were heard of in
England *John Bale* (who was sometime a Carmelite himself) tells us, that the first Convent
of that Order was founded at *Holm* (*Hull* they
now call it' near *Alnwick*, by *Ralph Fresburn*, a
Gentleman of Northumberland, who dy'd *A D.*
1274, and was buried in this Convent *Eustachius's* Abbey is still to be seen, at half a mile's
distance from the Convent of *Hull*, down the
river] *William*, the last of the *Vescies*, made
Anthony Bec, Bishop of *Durham*, Trustee of this *Hist Dunelm*
Castle and the Demesn-lands belonging to it, for
the use of his natural son, the only Child he
left behind him But the Bishop, basely be-
traying his trust, alienated the Inheritance, selling it for a present sum of money to *William
Percie*, since whose time it has always been in
the possession of the *Percies*

From hence the shore, after a great many In Dunstaburg
dentings, passes by *Dunstaburge*, a Castle belong
ing to the Dutchy of *Lancaster*, [within the Circuit of which, there grew not long since two hundred and forty *Winchester* Bushels of Corn, besides
several Cart loads of Hay It is now famous for
Dunstaburgh Diamonds, a sort of fine Spar, which
seems to rival that of St *Vincent's* Rock near
Bristol] This Castle some have † mistaken for † [illegible]
Bebban, which stands further North, and, in [illegible]
stead of Bebbanburg, is now call'd *Bamborrow* Bebban
Our Country man *Bede*, speaking of the Castle's Bamborrow.
being besieg'd and burnt by *Penda* the Mercian,
says it had this name from Queen *Bebba* [But
yet it may be question'd, whether *Bede himself*
ever gave out this Etymology No mention of
it is in the Saxon but it is there call' [illegible]
byrig, *i e* a Royal Mansion; and it is also
said, that it was miserably wasted by *Penda*, [illegible]
the Pagan King of the Mercians; who had cer- [illegible]
tainly burnt it, had not the Prayers of Bishop
Aidan happily interpos'd *Florence of Worcester*
seems to have been the first contriver of this
story of queen *Bebba*;] but *Matthew of Westminster*
tells us it was built by *Ida* the first King of

Nor-

Northumberland, who fenc'd it with a wooden Empalure, and afterwards with a Wall (Take *Roger Hoveden*'s description of it *Bebba*, says he, *is a very strong City, not exceeding large, but containing two or three acres of ground It has one hollow entrance into it, which is admirably rais'd by steps On the top of the hill stands a fair Church; and on the Western point of it is a Well, curiously adorn'd, and of sweet and clear water*) [It was, afterwards, totally ruined and plundered by the Danes, in the year 933] At present, it is rather reckon'd a Castle than a City; though of that extent, that it rivals some Cities Nor was it look'd upon as any thing more than a Castle, when King *William Rufus* built the Tower of *Male-veisin* over-against it, the better to engage the Rebel *Mowbray*, who lurk'd here, and at last stole off and fled [After *Mowbray*'s flight, and his being taken at *Tinmouth*, the Castle of *Bamborrow* was stoutly maintained by *Moral*, his Steward and Kinsman, till the Earl himself was, by the King's Order, brought within view of the Fort, and threatened with the having his eyes put out, in case the besieged held out any longer Whereupon, it was immediately surrender'd, and *Moral*, for his bravery, was received into the King's Court and Favour] A great part of its beauty was afterwards lost in the Civil Wars, when *Bressie* the valiant Norman, who fought for the House of *Lancaster*, dealt very unmercifully with it Since that time, it has been in a continual struggle with Age, and the Wind, which latter has, through its large windows, drifted up an incredible quantity of Sea-sand in its several Bulwarks; [yet, as ruinous as it now is, the Lord of the Manour still holds here, in a corner of it, his Courts of Leet and Baron] Near this is *Emilden*, sometime the Barony of *John le Viscont*, but *Rametta*, the heir of the family, sold it to *Simon de Montfort* Earl of *Leicester* [In this neighbourhood, the improvements in Tillage, and in Gardening and Fruitery, by the *Salkelds*, (in this Parish of *Emilden*,) ought here to be mentioned, as *Fineries* hardly to be equall'd on the North-side of *Tyne* The latter is the more observable, because an eminent Author of this Age will hardly allow any good *Peaches, Plumbs, Pears*, &c to be expected beyond *Northamptonshire*, whereas Fruit is produced here in as great variety and perfection as in most places in the South] In this Barony was born *John Duns*, call'd *Scotus*, because descended from Scotish Parents, who was educated in *Merton* College in *Oxford*, and became an admirable proficient in Logick and School Divinity but was so scrupulous and sceptical, that he obscur'd and perplex'd the great Truths of Religion He wrote many things with that profound and wondrous subtlety (though in an obscure and unpolish'd stile) that he got the name of *Doctor Subtilis*, and had a new Sect called *Scotists*, from his name [This study of School Divinity was mightily in fashion about *Scotus*'s time, and especially in the University of *Oxford*, where the petulant humours of the *Dominicans* put the Students upon all sorts of wrangling Hence, that place has afforded more men of eminence in that way, than (perhaps) all the other Universities of *Europe* and these have marshalled themselves under the pompous Epithets of *Subtilis, Profundus, Irrefragabilis*, &c] As to *Scotus*, he dy'd miserably being taken with an Apoplectic fit, and too hastily buried for dead For, Nature having too late wrought through the Distemper, and brought him to life, he vainly mourn'd for assistance, till (at last) beating his head against the * Tomb stone, he dash'd out his brains, and so expir'd Whereupon a certain *Italian* wrote thus of him

Tower of *Male-veisin*

Sax Chron Ann 1095

Emildon Viscounts

Doctor Subtilis liv'd A D 1300

P... Jovius in Eleg Doct

* Sepulchri lapide

> *Quaecunque humani fuerant, jurisque Sacrati,*
> *In dubium veniunt cuncta vocante* Scoto
> *Quid? quod & in dubium illius sit vita vocata,*
> *Morte illum simili ludificante strophâ*
> *Quum non ante virum vita jugulârit adempta,*
> *Quam vivus tumulo conditus ille foret*

> What sacred Writings or prophane can show,
> All Truths were (*Scotus*) call'd in doubt by you
> Your Fate was doubtful too Death boasts to be
> The first that chous'd you with a Fallacy
> Who, lest your subtle Arts your Life should save,
> Before she struck, secur'd you in the grave

That he was born here in *England*, I affirm upon the authority of his own Manuscript Works in the Library of *Merton*-College in *Oxford*, which conclude thus, *Explicit Lectura Subtilis*, &c *Here ends the Lecture of* John Duns, *call'd* Doctor Subtilis, *in the University of* Paris, *who was born in a certain Hamlet of the Parish of* Emildun, *call'd* Dunston, *in the County of* Northumberland, *and belonging to the House of the Scholars of* Merton Hall *in* Oxford [It was usual in those days for the Oxford-Scholars to spend some time at *Paris*, but our Englishmen then did as seldom reap any real advantage by their French Education, as they commonly do now]

Hist & Ant. Oxon l 1 ann 1682.

Upon this shore there is nothing further worth the mentioning (except *Holy Island*, of which in its proper place) till we come to the mouth of the *Twede*, which for a long way divides *England* from *Scotland*, and is call'd the *Eastern March* Upon which, thus our Countryman *Necham*

Twede

> *Anglos a Pictis sejungit limite certo*
> *Flumen quod Tuedam pristina lingua vocat.*

> The Picts are sever'd from the English ground
> By *Twede* (so call'd of old) a certain bound

This river rises in a large stream out of the Mountains of *Scotland*, and afterwards takes a great many turns among the Mos Troopers and * Drivers (to give them no worse names,) who, as one expresses it, ‖ determined all Titles by the Sword's point When it comes near ‖ the village of *Carram*, being encreas'd with many other waters, it begins to be the Bound of the two Kingdoms and having pass'd *Werk Castle*, which was sometime enjoy'd by the *Rosses*, and † afterwards by the *Greys* (who have been long a Family of great reputation for valour) and was frequently assaulted by the Scots; is inlarg'd by the river of *Till* [Of the last mention'd Family, Sir *William Grey*, in the time of King James the first, was advanced to the honour of a Baron, by the title of Lord *Grey* of *Werk*] The river *Till* has two names.

* S... ‖ Ann 10 ‖ Drivers. Carram. Werk. † Now, G

names For, at its rise (which is further within the body of this County) it is call'd *Bramish*, and on it stands *Brampton*, a little obscure and inconsiderable Village, [but noted for one of the prettiest Houses in this part of the County, a seat of the *Collingwoods*, who are a branch of the House of *Eslington*] Hence it runs Northward by *Bengely*, which, together with *Brampton*, *Bremdun*, *Rodam* (which gave name to a Family of good note in these parts) *Edelingham*, &c was the Barony of *Patrick* Earl of *Dunbar*, in the reign of *Henry* the third The *Book of Inquisition*, among the Records, says, He was *Inborow* and *Outborow* betwixt *England* and *Scotland*, that is, if I understand it right, he was, here, to watch and observe the *ingress* and *egress* of all Travellers between the two Kingdoms For, in the old English Language, In borou is an Ingress or Entry More North, upon the river, stands *Chevelingham* or *Chillingham*, which was a Castle that belong'd to one Family of the *Greys*, as did *Horton*-Castle, at a little distance, to another, but those two are now match'd into one [in the Hall, at *Chillingham Castle*, there is a Chimney piece with a hollow in the middle of it, wherein (it is said) there was found a live Toad, at the sawing of the Stone The other part of it is also still to be seen (with the like mark upon it, and put to the same use) at *Horton Castle*]

Near this, is the Barony of *Wollover*, which King *Henry* the first gave to *Robert de Muscocampo* or *Muschamp*, who bare Azure, three Butterflyes, Argent From him descended another *Robert*, who, in the reign of *Henry* the third, was reckon'd the mightiest Baron in all these Northern parts But the Inheritance, soon after was divided and shared among women one of whom was marry'd to the Earl of *Strathern* in *Scotland*, another to *William de Huntercombe*, and a third to *Odonel de Ford* [This *Wollover*, call'd usually *Wooler*, is now a little inconsiderable Market town, with a thatch'd Church, and some other marks of the Poverty of the Inhabitants]

Soon after, *Till*, is encreas'd by the river of *Glen*, that gives the name of *Glendale* to the Valley through which it runs Of this rivulet *Bede* gives us the following account, *Paulinus coming with the King and the Queen to the Royal Mannor of* Ad gebrin (now call'd *Yverin*) *stay'd there with them six and thirty days, which he spent in the Duties of Catechising and Baptizing From morning till night his whole business was to instruct the Country People, that flock'd to him from all places and villages round, in the Principles of Christianity, and, after they were so instructed, to baptize them in the neighbouring river of* Glen *This Manour house was disus'd by the following Kings, and another erected in its stead at* Melmin, *now* Melfeld [The Saxon Paraphrase gives us a further direction (besides what we have from the river *Glen*) for finding out the place there mention'd, by telling us, that *those places are in the Country of the Bernicians*, which is a full refutation of what *Bede* is made to say before, that King *Oswald* first brought Christianity into that Kingdom]

Here, at *Bramford*, near *Brumridge*, King *Athelstan* fought a pitch'd Battel against *Anlaf* the Dane, *Constantine* King of Scots, and *Eugenius* petty King of Cumberland, wherein he had such success, that the Engagement is describ'd by the Historians and Poets of that Age in extraordinary Raptures of Wit and Bombast [From a passage in *Florence* of *Worcester*, one may probably conjecture, that *Brunanburgh* (for so all our Historians, but *Ingulphus*, call it) must have been some where nearer the *Humber* Tho', perhaps, it will be more difficult to carry the great *Constantine*, of *Scotland*, and the little King of *Cumberland*, so high into *Yorkshire*, than to bring *Anlaf* thus far down into *Northumberland*] At this place, the name of *Bramish* is changed into *Till*, which first passes by *Ford Castle* (heretofore the property of the valiant Family of the *Herons*, now of the *Carrs*,) and *Etal*, formerly the Seat of the Family of *Manours* or *de Maneriis*, which was long since of a knightly rank, and from which the present Right Honourable * Earls of *Rutland* are descended [By Deeds in the hands of the family of *Collingwood* of Brankerton, it appears that this *Etal* was in the possession of their Ancestors of the same name, in the reign of Edward the sixth] I wittingly omit many Castles in this Country for it were endless to recount them all, since it is certain, that in the days of *Henry* the second, there were eleven hundred and fifteen Castles in England

Over against this *Ford*, Westward, rises the high Mountain of *Floddon*, famous for the overthrow of *James* the fourth King of Scots and his Army, who, while King *Henry* the eighth lay at the seige of *Tournay* at *France*, did with great Courage and greater Hopes (for, before they began their March, they had divided our Towns among them) invade *England* Here *Thomas Howard* Earl of *Surrey*, with a good Army, bravely receiv'd him The Dispute was obstinate on both sides, till the night parted them, unable as yet to determine which way the Victory inclin'd But the next day discover'd both the Conquerour and the Conquer'd, and the King of Scots himself, being mortally wounded in several places, was found among the heaps of the slain Whence a new Addition was given to the Arms of the Howards

Twede, encreas'd by *Till*, runs now in a larger stream by *Norham* or *Northam*, which was formerly call'd *Ubban ford* The Town belongs to the Bishops of *Durham* For Bishop *Egfrid* [who was a mighty Benefactor to the See of *Lindisfarn*] built it [and the Church,] and his Successor *Ralph* erected the Castle on the top of a steep rock, and moted it round, [for the better security of this part of his Diocese against the frequent incursions of the Scottish Mosstroopers] On the utmost Wall, and the largest in Circuit, are placed several Turrets on a Canton towards the river, within which there is a second Enclosure much stronger than the former, and, in the middle of that again, rises a high Keep But the well establish'd Peace of our times has made these Forts to be long neglected, notwithstanding they are plac'd upon the very Borders Under the Castle, on a Level Westward, lies the Town, and the Church, wherein was buried *Ceolwulph*, King of *Northumberland*, to whom Venerable *Bede* dedicated his Books of the Ecclesiastical History of *England*, and who afterwards, *renouncing the World, took upon him the habit of a Monk in the Church of* Lindisfern, *and listed himself a Soldier of the Kingdom of Heaven his body was afterwards translated to the Church of* Northam [It was dedicated to St *Peter*, St *Cuthbert*, and St *Ceolwulph*, that religious King of *Northumberland*; who was the first of our Princes, that retir'd from a Throne to a Monastery His body being deposited here by the same Bishop, the Monks of the following Age took care to bring-in the Country round to pay their Devotion (and

(and Tribute) to their Royal Brother, who always oblig'd his visitants with some Miracle or other.] When also the Danes had miserably wasted the *Holy Island*, in which St *Cuthbert* (so much magnified by *Bede*) was Bishop, and lay buried, some endeavour'd, by a religious stealth, to convey his body beyond Sea: but, the winds standing contrary, *they with all due reverence, deposited the sacred Body at* * Ubbanford *(whether a Bishop's see or no, is uncertain) near the river* Twede, *where it lay for many years, till the coming of King* Ethelred. This, and other matters, were taught me (for I shall always own my Instructors) by *George Carlton* born at this place, being son to the Keeper of *Norham Castle*, ‖ whom, for his excellent Proficiency in Divinity (whereof he is Professor) and the other polite parts of Learning, I love, and am lov'd by him: and I were unworthy of that love, if I should not acknowledge his Friendship. The old people told us, that at *Killey*, a little neighbouring Village below *Norham*, were found (within the memory of † our Grandfathers) the studs of a Knight's Belt, and the hilt of a Sword of massy Gold, which were presented to *T. Ruthall* Bishop of *Durham*.

* The printed Books have (corruptly) *Bul befurd*. Will. Malmesb. de Gest. Pont. lib. 1.

‖ This said, ann. 1607.

Killey.

† So said, ann. 1607.

A golden Hilt.

A little lower you have the mouth of *Twede*, on the farther bank of which stands *Berwick*, the last Town in *England*, and [once] the best-fortify'd in all *Britain*, [but it is now much outdone, in strength and regular fortifications, by *Portsmouth*, *Hull*, *Plymouth*, and other Forts in *England*, and is chiefly strong in the present happy Union of the two Kingdoms.] Some derive the name of this Town from one *Berengarius*, a Romantick Duke; *Leland* fetches it from *Aber*, the British word for the mouth of a river, and so makes *Aberwick* to signifie a Fort built upon such a mouth. But they will best understand the true etymology of it, who know what is meant by the word *Berwicus* in the Charters of our Kings: wherein nothing is more common than *I give the Townships of C. and D. cum suis Berwicis*. For my part, what it should mean I know not, unless it be a Hamlet or some such dependency upon a place of better note. For, in the Grants of *Edward* the Confessor, *Totthill* is call'd the *Berwicus* of *Westminster*, *Wandlesworth* the *Berwicus* of *Patricksey*: and a thousand of the like. [In old Records, we find it variously written, *Berewica*, *Berewiba*, *Berwichus*, *Berewich*, *Berewita*, and *Berwita*, of all which, Instances may be seen in Sir *Henry Spelman*'s Glossary. It may be, the most suitable derivation of it (for our present purpose) is what *Mr Tate* has given us in his Manuscript Exposition of the hard words in Domesday Book: *Berewica*, says he, is a *Corn Farm*, which Etymology agrees well with the plenty of grain about the Town of *Berwick*.] But, why all this pains? which is but lost labour, if (as some maintain) the *Saxons* call'd it anciently *Bernica-pic*, that is, the *Town of the Bernicians*; for, that this part of the Country was call'd *Bernicia* we have already noted, and the thing is too well known to be here repeated. But (whencesoever it had its name) its situation carries it a good way into the sea; so that that and the *Twede* almost incircle it. Being seated betwixt two mighty Kingdoms (as *Pliny* observes of *Palmyra* in *Syria*) it has always been the first place, that both Nations, in their wars, have had an eye on; insomuch, that ever since *Edward* the first took it from the Scotch, the English have as often retaken it as the *Scots* have ventur'd to take it. But, if the Reader pleases, we will here give him a summary abstract of its History. The oldest account that I find of *Berwick*, is, that *William* King of *Scots*, being taken prisoner by the *English*, pawned it for his ransom to our *Henry* the second, * redeemable only within such a time. Whereupon, says the *Polychronicon* of *Durham*, *Henry* immediately fortify'd it with a Castle. But *Richard* the first restor'd it to the *Scots*, upon their payment of the money. Afterwards King *John* (as the History of *Melross* reports) *took the Town and Castle of* Berwick, *at the same time that he burnt* Werk, Roxburgh, Mitford, *and* Morpath, *and (with his* Rutars) *wasted all* Northumberland; *because the Barons of that County had done homage to* Alexander *King of* Scots, *at* Feltun. Many years after this, when *John Baliol* King of *Scotland* had broken his Oath, *Edward* the first reduc'd *Berwick* in the year of our Lord 1297. But soon after, the fortune of war favouring the Scots, our men quitted it, and they seiz'd it: but the English forthwith had it surrender'd to them again. Afterwards, in the loose reign of *Edward* the second, *Peter Spalding* surrender'd it to *Robert Brus* King of Scots, who warmly besieg'd it, and the English vainly attempted it's recovery, till (our *Hector*,) *Edward* the third bravely carry'd it, in the year 1333. In the reign of *Richard* the second, some Scottish Moss-Troopers surpriz'd the Castle, which, within nine days, was recover'd by *Henry Percie* Earl of *Northumberland*. Within seven years after this, the Scots regain'd it, but by purchase, not by their valour. Whereupon the said *Henry Percie* (being then Governour of the Town) was accus'd of High-Treason: but he also corrupted the Scots with money, and so got it again. A long time after this, when *England* was almost ruin'd by civil wars, *Henry* the sixth (who had fled into *Scotland*) deliver'd it up to the King of Scots, the better to secure himself in that Kingdom. Two and twenty years after, *Thomas Stanley*, with great loss, reduc'd it to the obedience of *Edward* the fourth. [In the same reign, a Statute was enacted for the enlargement of the Privileges of Berwick, in point of Trade and Merchandise.] Since which time, the Kings of *England* have fortify'd it with new works, but especially Queen *Elizabeth*, who (to the terrour of the enemy, and security of the Burghers) drew it into a less compass than before, and surrounded it with a high stone wall of firm Ashler work, which is again strengthen'd with a deep ditch, bastions, and counterscarp, so that its * fortifications are so strong and regular, that no besiegers can hope to carry it hereafter. († Not to mention the valour of the Garrison, and the surprizing plenty of Ammunition and all warlike stores.) Be it also remember'd, that the Governor of this place was always a person of the greatest wisdom and eminence among the English Nobility; and was also Warden of these eastern Marches. The Mathematicians have plac'd this Town in 21 degrees, and 43 minutes of longitude, and in 55 and 48 of northern latitude. So that the longest day, in this climate, consists of seventeen hours and 22 minutes; and its night only of 6 hours and 38 minutes. So truly has *Servius Honoratus* written of this Country. *Britain*, says he, *has such plenty of day, that she has hardly any room for night*. Nor is it a wonder that the Soldiers of this Garrison are able to play all night at Dice, without a candle, if we consider their continued twilight, and the truth of *Juvenal*'s expression.

Berwick.

Ingulphus ren. de s Berwicis a Manour.

* Matt. Paris says it was about this time made over.

22 Edw. 4. 8.

* Sc. 1600, 1 99.

† Ann. 1607.

Berwick's Plenty of Day.

—— *Minimâ*

——— *Minimâ contentos nocte Britannos.*

Britains with shortest nights content

Take, at parting, *J Johnston's* Verses upon *Berwick*

Scotorum *extremo sub limite, Meta furoris*
Saxonidum *gentis par utriusque labor,*
Mille vices rerum, quæ mille est passa ruinas,
Mirum, qui potuit superesse malis
Quin superest, quin extremis exhausta ruinis,
Funere sic crevit firmior usque suo
Oppida ut exæquet jam munitissima Civis
Militis & censum, & munia Martis obit
Postquam servitio durisque est cuncta periclis,
Effert lætitiæ signa serena suæ
Et nunc antiquo fœlix se jactat honore,
Cum reddit debita jura suo
Cujus ab Auspiciis unita Britannia *tandem*
Excelsum tollit libera in astra caput.

Bound of the *Scottish* and the *English* Land,
Where both their realms and both their labours end,
After a thousand turns of doubtful state,
She yet outbraves the vain assaults of Fate
A happy Port in all her storms hath found,
And still rose higher as she touch'd the ground
Surpass'd by none her stately Forts appear,
Her Sons at once inur'd to Trade and War
Now all her storms and all her fears are gone,
In her glad look returning joys are shown
Now her old honours are at last restor'd,
Securely now she serves her ancient Lord
Bless'd with whose care united *Britain* rears
Her lofty head among the rival Stars

It may not be amiss to add here the account which *Æneas Silvius* or Pope *Pius* the second (who came Legate into *Scotland* about the year 1448) gives of the Borderers in this Country, in his Life, written by himself; since their manners † still continue the same

The Commentaries of Pius 2 published under the name of Gobelinus.

† Now greatly changed.

*A certain * River, falling from a high mountain, parts the two Kingdoms over which Æneas ferry'd, and coming to a large village about Sun set, he alighted at a country-man's house, where he sup'd with the Curate of the place and his host The table was plentifully furnish'd with pottage, hens, and geese; but nothing of either wine or bread appear'd All the men and women of the town flock'd in, as to some strange sight and, as our country men use to admire the Æthiopians or* Indians, *so these people star'd at Æneas, asking the Curate, what country man he was what his errand could be and, whether he were a Christian or no? But Æneas, being aware of the scarcity he should meet with on this road, had been accommodated by a Monastery with a runlet of red wine and some loaves of bread When these were brought to the table, they were more astonish'd than before, having never seen either wine or white bread Big belly'd women, with their husbands, came to the table-side, and handling the bread and smelling to the wine, beg'd a taste so that there was no avoiding the dealing of the whole amongst them. After they had sate at supper till two hours within night, the Curate and the Landlord (with the children and all the men) left Æneas, and rub'd off in haste They said, they were going to shelter themselves in a certain tower, at a good distance, for fear of the* Scots, *who (at low water) us'd to cross the river in the night, for plunder They would by no means be perswaded to take Æneas along with them, tho' he very importunately entreated them to do it Neither carry'd they off any of the women, though several of them, both wives and maids were very handsome for they believe the enemy will not harm them, not looking upon whoredom as any ill thing Thus Æneas was left alone (with only two Servants and a Guide) amongst a hundred women, who sitting in a ring, with a fire in the middle of them, spent the night sleepless, in dressing of hemp, and chatting with the Interpreter When the night was well advanced, they heard a mighty noise of dogs barking and geese gagling, whereupon the women slip'd off several ways, and the guide ran away, and all was in such confusion, as if the enemy had been upon them But Æneas thought it his wisest course to keep close in his Bed-chamber (which was a Stable) and there to await the issue, lest, running out, and being unacquainted with the Country, he should be robb'd by the first man he met Presently, both the women and the guide return, acquainting them that all was well, and that they were Friends (and no Enemies) who were arriv'd* [But whatever roughness might be in the Manners of the People of *Northumberland*, at that time, it is certain that the Description which *Æneas Silvius* gives of them, is not their due at this day Their Tables are as well stock'd as ever, with Hens and Geese, and they have also plenty of good bread and beer Strangers and Travellers, are no novelties to them, the roads betwixt *Edinburgh* and *Newcastle* being as much frequented by such (of all Nations) as almost any others in the Kingdom *Wine* is a greater rarity in a Country man's house in *Middlesex*, than on the borders of *Northumberland*, where you shall more commonly meet with great store of it, than in the Villages of any other County in *England* and, that Wine is not the *constant* drink of the Country, ought no more to be remark'd as a thing extraordinary, than that *Yorkshire-Ale* is not common in *Italy* The Moss-Trooping Trade is now very much laid aside, and a small Sum will recompense all the Robberies that are yearly committed in this County, where men's persons are as safe, and their goods as secure, as in the most civiliz'd Kingdoms of *Europe* Whoredom is reckon'd as scandalous a Vice here, as elsewhere, and it may be truly said, far more scandalous, than in the Southern parts of the Kingdom In a word, the Gentry of *Northumberland* are generally persons of address and breeding, and preservers of the true old English Hospitality in their Houses And the Peasants are as knowing a people, and as courteous to strangers, as a man shall readily meet with in any other parts]

* Tweede.

Manners of the Borderers.

There were * in this Country certain petty Nations who were call'd *Sevenburgenses* and *Fifburgingi*; but so dark is the account we have of them, that I † am not able to ascertain the true place of their residence, nor tell you whether they were Danes or English *Florence* of *Worcester* (publish'd by the right honourable the Lord *William Howard*) says, that *whilst the Parliament sate at* Oxenford, Sigeferth *and* Morcar

* This conjectured to be our Sevenburg or ... Fifburg ...

† So Camden, 1607

1013

(two

(two eminent and powerful Ministers of the Seovenburgenses) *were privately murder'd by* Edrick Streona. *And that Prince* Edmund, *contrary to the good liking of his father, marry'd* Alfrith *the wife of* Sigeferth *and, taking a progress as far as the* Fifburgingi, *invaded* Sigeferth's *Territories, and subdu'd his People.* || [Upon furtder enquiry, these *Fifburgingi* (or *Fifburhingan*, as the Saxons called them) appear to have been the Danish Inhabitants of the five Towns of *Leicester, Lincoln, Nottingham, Stamford*, and *Derby*. To these were afterwards added the Cities of *York* and *Chester*, and then the same People (for the like reason) were called *Seofenburgenses*. Of these *Sigeferth* and *Morcar* were (as *Florence* expresses it) *Ministers*, and (as the Saxon Chronicle) *Thanes*, which being interpreted according to the old Danish *Diagn*, doth import *Government* and *Power.*]

Prince of the Fifburgingi.
|| But let others make a further Enquiry into these matters, &c.

This Province was first brought under the *Saxon* yoke by *Osca*, brother of *Hengist*, and his son *Jebusa*, and was for some time under the government of Dukes, who were homagers to the Kings of *Kent*. Afterwards, when the Kingdom of the *Bernicians* (whom the *Britains* call *Guir a Brinaich*, that is, *Mountaineers*) was erected, the best part of it lay between the *Tees* and * *Edinburgh* Frith, and this was subject to the Kings of *Northumberland*. When these had finish'd their fatal period, all beyond *Twede* became part of *Scotland*; and *Egbert* King of the *East Saxons* had this County surrender'd to him, and annex'd it to his own Dominions, [so far, as that *Eanred* King of the Northumbrians, became Tributary to him; but *Northumberland* continued a Kingdom, long after that.] *Alfred* afterwards assign'd it to the *Danes*, [(or rather was under the necessity of coming to terms with them,)] and they, within a few years, were thrown out by *Athelstane*. Yet, even after this the People made *Eilric* the *Dane* their King, who was forthwith expell'd by King *Ealdred*. Henceforward, the name of King was no more heard of in this Province; but its chief Magistrates were call'd Earls, of whom, these that follow are successively reckon'd by our Historians, *Osulph, Oslac, Edulph, Waldeof* the elder, *Uchtred, Adulph, Alred, Siward, Tostius, Edwin, Morcar*, and *Osculph*. Amongst these, *Siward* was a person of extraordinary valour, who, as he liv'd, so he chose to dye, in his Armour. *His County of* York *was given to* Tostius *Brother to Earl* Harold, *and the Counties of* Northampton *and* Huntingdon, *with his other lands, were bestow'd on the noble Earl* Waldeof, *his Son and Heir*. I have here given you the very words of *Ingulphus*, because there are some who deny that he was Earl of *Huntingdon*. To this let me also add what * I have met with on the same subject, in an old Parchment Manuscript in the Library of *John Stow*, a most worthy Citizen, and industrious Antiquary, of the City of *London*. *Copsi* being made Earl of *Northumberland* by *William* the Conqueror, dispossess'd *Osculph*, who neverthe less slew him within a few days. Afterwards, *Osculph* himself was stabb'd by a Robber, and dy'd of the wound. Then *Gospatrick* bought the County of the Conqueror, by whom he was also presently divested of the Honour, and was succeeded by *Waldeof* the son of *Siward*. He lost his head, and was succeeded by *Walcher* Bishop of *Durham*, who (as well as his successor *Robert Comin*) was slain in an insurrection of the Rabble. [This *Walcher* was a most vile Oppressour, and scandalous Wordling. He bought the Earldom of *Northumberland*, and resolv'd to make the people pay for it. But they, at last, being wearied with daily extortion, and reduc'd almost to beggary, unanimously fell upon him, and slew him, at a County-Court, which he used always to attend himself in person, the better to secure the Fees and other Perquisites. (And, at that time, these were considerable, since the Sheriffs of *Northumberland* never accounted to the King, before the third of *Edward* the sixth.) Their Foreman gave the word, which most of our old Historians have thought worth the recording to Posterity,

Kings, Dukes and Earls of Northumberland.
Bernicians.
* Scoticum fretum.
Ingulph. p. 511. b. An. 1056.
* Scu. ... d ... ann. ...

Short red, good red, slea ye the Bishop.]

The Title was afterwards conferred on *Robert Mowbray*, who destroy'd himself by his own wicked Treason. Then (as the *Polychronicon of Durham* tells us) King *Stephen* made *Henry*, son of *David* King of *Scots*, Earl of *Northumberland*; and his son *William* (who was also himself afterwards King of *Scots*) wrote himself *William de Warren* Earl of *Northumberland*, for his mother was of the family of the Earls of *Warren*, as appears by the Book of *Brinkburn-Abbey*. Within a few years after, *Richard* the first sold this County to *Hugh Pudsey* Bishop of *Durham*, for life: but when that King was *imprison'd by the Emperour in his return from the Holy War, and* Hugh *advanced only two thousand pounds in silver towards his ransom, the King took this slender contribution so ill (knowing that under colour of this ransom he had rais'd vast sums,) that he depriv'd him of the Earldom.* L. S. Dunelm.

* Afterwards, that Honour was enjoy'd by the family of the *Percies*, who being descended from the Earls of *Brabant*, got both the sirname and the inheritance of the *Percies* when *Josceline* (the true off-spring of *Charles* the Great, by *Gerberg* daughter to *Charles* younger brother of *Lotharius*, the last King of *France* of the *Caroline* stock) the younger son of *Godfrey* Duke of *Brabant*, marry'd *Agnes* daughter and sole heir of *William Percie*. This *William*'s great grandfather (call'd also *William Percie*) came into *England* with William the Conquerour, who bestow'd on him large possessions in *Tatcaster, Linton, Normanby*, and other places. The said *Agnes* and *Josceline* covenanted, that he should take upon him the name of *Percie*, but still retain his ancient Arms of *Brabant*, which were, a Lion *Azure* (chang'd afterwards by the *Brabanters*) in a Field *Or*. The first of this family that was made Earl of *Northumberland*, was *Henry Percie*, the son of *Mary*, daughter of *Henry* Earl of *Lancaster*; who, on account of his noble Birth, and warlike exploits, had large Possessions bestow'd upon him in Scotland, by Edward the third. He was very much enrich'd by his second wife *Matilda Lucy*, by whom he had no child, but she oblig'd him to bear the Arms of the *Lucies*; and *Richard* the second created him Earl of *Northumberland*. His behaviour afterwards was very ungrateful to this his great Benefactor; for he deserted him in his straits, and help'd *Henry* the fourth to the Crown. He had the *Isle of Man* bestow'd on him by this King, against whom he also rebell'd; being prick'd in Conscience at the unjust deposing of King *Richard* by his means, and vex'd at the close confinement of

* Percies descended from Charles the Great.

of (the undoubted Heir of the Crown) *Edmund Mortimer* Earl of *March*, his kinsman. Hereupon, he first sent some Forces against him under the command of his brother *Thomas* Earl of *Worcester*, and his own forward son *Henry*, sirnam'd *Whot spur*, who were both slain in the battle at *Shrewsbury*. Upon this, he was attainted of High-Treason; but was presently receiv'd again into the seeming favour of the King, who indeed stood in awe of him. He had also his estate and goods restor'd to him, except only the *Isle of Man*, which the King took back into his own hand. Yet, not long after, this popular and heady man did again proclaim war against the King as an Usurper, having call'd in the Scots to his assistance. And now, leading on the Rebels in person, he was surpriz'd by *Thomas Rokesby*, High Sheriff of *Yorkshire*, at *Barham-moor*; where, in a confused skirmish, his Army was routed, and himself slain, in the year 1408. Eleven years after, *Henry* the fifth (by Act of Parliament) restor'd the Honour to *Henry Percie*, his Grandchild by his son *Henry Whot spur*, whose mother was *Elizabeth*, daughter of *Edmund Mortimer* the Elder, Earl of *March*, by *Philippa*, daughter of *Lionel* Duke of *Clarence*. This Earl resolutely espoused the interest of *Henry* the sixth against the House of *York*, and was slain in the Battel of St *Albans*. His son *Henry*, the third Earl of *Northumberland* (who married *Eleanor* the daughter of *Richard* Baron of *Poynings*, *Brian*, and *Fitz-Pains*) lost his life in the same Cause, at *Towton*, in the year 1461. When the House of *Lancaster*, and (with it) the Family of the *Percies*, was now under a cloud, King *Edward* the fourth created *John Nevil*, Lord *Montacute*, Earl of *Northumberland*: but he quickly resign'd that Title to the King, being made Marquiss *Montacute*. After which, *Edward* the fourth graciously restor'd to his father's Honours *Henry Percie*, son of the foremention'd *Henry*; who, in the reign of *Henry* the seventh, was slain by a rabble of the Country-People, in a Mutiny against the Collectors of a Tax impos'd on them by Act of Parliament. To him succeeded *Henry Percie*, the fifth Earl. From him (who was himself the son of a Daughter and Co-heir of *Robert Spenser*) and *Eleanor*, Daughter, and Co heir, of *Edmund Beaufort* Duke of *Somerset*, descended *Henry*, the sixth Earl. He having no Children (and his brother *Thomas* being executed for rebelling against *Henry* the Eighth in the beginning of the Reformation) squander'd away a great part of his fair Estate, in Largesses upon the King and others, as looking on his Family to be now reduc'd to a final period. A few years after, *John Dudley*, Earl of *Warwick*, got the Title of Duke of *Northumberland*, when, in the Non age of *Edward* the sixth, the Ring-leaders of the several Factions shared the Titles of Honour among themselves and their Abettors. This was that Duke of *Northumberland*, who for some time (like a Whirlwind) troubled the Peace of his Native Country; by endeavouring to exclude *Mary* and *Elizabeth*, the Daughters of *Henry* the eighth, from their lawful Right of Succession; having design'd (by the countenance of Lawyers, who are inclinable to serve the purposes of Great men) to settle the Crown on *Jane Grey*, to whom he had married his son. Hereupon, being convicted of High Treason, he lost his head; and on the Scaffold openly own'd and profess'd the Popish Religion, which (either in good earnest, or seemingly and to serve a turn) he had, for a good while before, renounc'd. [He exhorted the People, to stand to the Religion of their Ancestors, to reject all Novelties, and to drive the Preachers out of the Nation; and declar'd that he had temporiz'd against his Conscience, and that he was always of the Religion of his Fore-fathers.] Upon his death, Queen *Mary* restor'd *Thomas Percie*, Nephew to *Henry*, the sixth Earl, by his brother *Thomas*; creating him at first Baron *Percie*, and (soon after, by a new Patent) Earl of *Northumberland*, *To himself and the Heirs-male of his Body; and for want of such, to his Brother* Henry *and his Heirs-male*. But this *Thomas*, the seventh Earl, under pretence of restoring the Romish Religion, rebelled against his Prince and Country, and so lost both his Life and Honour in the year 1572. Yet, by the special bounty of Queen *Elizabeth*, his brother *Henry* (according to the Tenor of Queen *Mary*'s Patent) succeeded him as the Eighth Earl, and dy'd in Prison in the year 1585. He was succeeded by his son *Henry*, the ninth Earl of *Northumberland* of this Family; who was son of *Katharine*, eldest Daughter, and one of the Heirs, of *J. Nevil* Baron *Latimer*. [This Earl was a great Patron of Learned men, especially Mathematicians, with whom he kept a constant familiarity and correspondence. Soon after the discovery of the Powder-Plot, he was committed Prisoner to the *Tower*, upon suspicion of his being privy to that part which his kinsman *Thomas Percie* had, in the Conspiracy. He was succeeded by his son *Algernoon*, whose son *Joceline* (the last Earl of this Family) dy'd at *Turin*, A. D. 1670, leaving only one daughter, *Elizabeth*, the present Dutchess of *Somerset*. Upon his death, the Honour of Duke of Northumberland was given by King *Charles* the second to his own natural Son *George Fitz-Roy*, by whose death the title is now become vacant.]

Duke of Northumberland

3 & 4 Phil. & Mary

More rare Plants growing wild in Northumberland.

Chamæpericlymenum *Park Ger* Periclymenum humile *C B* parvum Prutenicum Clusii *J B* *Dwarf Honey-suckle* *On the West-side of the North-end of the highest of Cheviot-hills in great plenty*

Echium marinum *B P.* *Sea-Bugloss.* *At Scrammerston hill between the Salt pans and Barwick, on the Sea-bank, about a mile and a half from Barwick*

Lysimachia siliquosa glabra minor latifolia. *The lesser smooth broad-leav'd codded Willow-herb On Cheviot-hills by the Springs and Rivulets of water*

Pyrola Alsines flore Europæa *C B. Park* Herba trientalis *J B* *Winter green with Chick-weed flowers* *On the other side the Picts-wall five miles beyond Hexham Northwards* *And among the Heath upon the moist Mountains not far from Harbottle westward*

Raphanus rusticanus *Ger Park C B* sylvestris sive Armoracia multis *J B* *Horse-radish We observ'd it about Alnwick and elsewhere in this County, in the ditches and by the water sides, growing in great plenty*

Eryngium vulgare *J B* vulgare & Camerarii *C. B* mediterraneum *Ger* mediterraneum seu campestre *Park* *Common Eryngo of the Midland* *On the shore call'd Friar goose near Newcastle upon Tine*

THE

THE
UNION
OF
ENGLAND
AND
SCOTLAND.

THE UNION OF ENGLAND AND SCOTLAND.

Miseries of England and Scotland, in a disjointed state.

WHoever hath perused the Histories of England and Scotland, under two Independent Monarchs, and beheld there the terrible Destructions and Devastations of Fire, Sword, and Rapine; the vast consumption of Blood and Treasure, in maintaining the Borders on both sides; and the frequent Advantages accruing to Foreign Enemies from those terrible Hostilities between the Inhabitants of the same Island; must readily acknowledge, that an *entire* and *perpetual* Union of the Estates of those two Kingdoms under the same Monarch, and with the same *Legislature*, was one of the greatest Blessings to both, that Heaven could send; especially, at a time when there was so much cause to dread a *Return* to that ancient state of *Entire Separation* and *Independence*.

An Union attempted by K. Henry 8 and Edw. 6

It was in a sense of these dreadful Calamities, that King Henry the eighth (to go back no further) did so earnestly labour a match between the daughter of James the fifth of *Scotland*, and his own son Edward; which proceeded so far, as to be ratified in the Parliament of Scotland, and to have Hostages sent from thence to the English Court for performance of Articles. But these Proceedings were zealously and openly opposed by the French, whose influence in the Scotch Counsels was at that time so powerful and prevailing, that the projected Match was broken off, and King Henry (disappointed of the hopes which he had conceived, of laying the foundation of a lasting Union, and growing infirm, and dying not long after) could only leave it in charge with his Council, to prosecute that Point by force of Arms to the last, if the Scots would not be induced by fair means to consent to the Match, according to the National Engagement which they had passed. Pursuant to this charge, the Duke of Somerset, Protector of the Kingdom under Edward the sixth, marched into Scotland at the head of an Army, and having first by message proposed a Treaty about the Match, but in vain, he afterwards defeated them in the memorable Battel of *Musselburgh*. Whereupon, the Scots cast themselves upon the Protection of France, whither the young Queen was conveyed, and many years after married to the Dauphin

Union of England and Scotland under one Head, in K. James I.

But what neither the Counsels nor Arms of England could effect, was brought about by Divine Providence, without the intervention of either, in half a Century after; in which time, Edward the sixth and his two sisters dying without issue, and a son being born to the Queen of Scots, and succeeding to that Kingdom by the name of James the sixth, He, upon the death of Elizabeth Queen of England (the last of King Henry's issue, that wore the Crown) succeeded also to the Kingdom of England, by the name of James the first, *as lineally, rightfully, and lawfully descended of the body of the most excellent Lady* Margaret, *eldest daughter of the most renowned King Henry the seventh and the High and Noble Princess Queen* Elizabeth *his Wife, eldest daughter of King* Edward *the fourth, the said Lady* Margaret *being eldest Sister of King Henry the eighth, father of the High and Mighty Princess of famous memory,* Elizabeth *late Queen of England*, according to the language of an Act of Parliament in England, solemnly recognizing his Right and Title to the Crown

A further Union attempted in vain by K. James I.

The King having thank'd the Parliament for this so ready and chearful Recognition of his Right, did immediately move for an *Union* between the two Kingdoms, *that, as they were made one in the Head, so among themselves they might be inseparably conjoined, and all memory of by past Divisions extinguished* Whereupon, an Act of Parliament was passed in England, presently, and also a like Act in the Parliament of Scotland, some months after, by which Acts, Commissioners of the two Kingdoms, respectively, were empowered to meet and treat concerning Articles of Union, to be laid before the Parliaments of both Nations In virtue of those Powers, they accordingly met at Westminster, *Octob* 20 1604, and agreed upon the following Articles.

Articles of Union, *temp Jac* I. Hostile Laws extinguished

'It is agreed by the Commissioners of *England* and *Scotland* to be mutually propon'd to 'the Parliament of both Realms at the next 'Sessions, That all Hostile Laws made and conceived expresly, either by *England* against '*Scotland*, or *Scotland* against *England*, shall in the 'next Sessions be abrogated and utterly extinguished

The name of Borders abolished

'It is also agreed, that all Laws, Customs, 'and Treaties of the Borders betwixt *England* 'and *Scotland* shall be declared by a general Act 'to be abrogated and abolished, and that the 'subjects on either part shall be governed by the 'Laws and Statutes of the Kingdoms where 'they dwell, and the name of the Borders extinguished

Order for Sentences not satisfied

'And because by abolishing the Border-Laws 'and Customs, it may be doubted, that the 'Executions shall cease upon those Sentences 'that have heretofore been given by the opposite Officers of those Borders, upon wrongs 'committed before the death of the late Queen 'of happy memory; it is thought fit that in 'case the Commissioners or Officers to be appointed by his Majesty before the time of the 'next Sessions of Parliament shall not procure 'sufficient redress of such filed Bills and Sentences, that then the said Parliaments may 'be moved to take such order as to their 'wisdoms shall seem convenient, for satisfaction of that which hath been decerned by 'some Officers; as also how disorders and insolencies may be hereafter repressed, and the 'Country which was lately of the Borders kept 'in peace and quietness in time to come. As 'likewise to prescribe some order, how the pursuits of former wrongs, preceding the death 'of the late Queen and since the last Treatise 'of the Borders in the years 1596 and 1597, 'which have never yet been moved, may be 'continued and prosecuted to a definitive Sentence

Participation of Commodities to be mutual.

'And forasmuch as the next degree to the 'abolition of all memory of Hostility is the 'participation of mutual Commodities and 'Commerce; It is agreed, First, concerning 'importation of Merchandise into either Realm 'from foreign parts, that whereas certain Commodities are wholly prohibited by the several 'Laws of both Realms to be brought into 'either of them by the Natives themselves 'or by any other, the said Prohibitions shall 'now be made mutual to both, and neither an '*English*-man bring into *Scotland*, or a *Scotch*-man into *England*, any of these prohibited 'Wares and Commodities Nevertheless, if the 'said Commodities be made in *Scotland*, it 'shall be lawful to bring them out of *Scotland* 'to *England*; and so reciprocally of the Commodities made in *England*, and carried to '*Scotland*.

Inequality of Privilege, in trade.

'Whereas a doubt hath been conceived against the equal communication of Trade betwixt *English* and *Scottish* subjects in matter 'of Importation, grounded upon some Inequality of Privileges which the *Scots* are reported 'to have in foreign parts, and namely in *France*, 'above the *English*, whereby the *English* might 'be prejudged; and that after a very deliberate 'consideration had of the said supposed Inequalities, both private and publick examination of divers Merchants of either side touching all Liberties, Immunities, Privileges, Imposts and Payments on the part of the *English*, and on the part of the *Scottish*, either 'at *Bordeaux* for their trade of Wines, or in '*Normandy* or any other part of *France* for other 'Commodities, it appeared that in the Trade 'of *Bourdeaux* there was and is so little difference, in any advantage of privileges or immunities, or in the imposts and payments, 'all being reckoned and well weighed on either 'side, as it could not justly hinder the communication of Trade in the trade of *Normandy* 'likewise, or any other parts of *France*, the 'advantage that the *Scottish* subjects by their 'privilege is acknowledged to have is such, as 'without much difficulty may be reconciled and 'reduced to an equality with the *English*, by 'such means as is hereafter declared, It is 'agreed, that the *Scottish*-men shall be free for 'the transporting of Wine from *Bordeaux* into '*England*, paying the same Customs and Duties that the *English* men do pay, and the '*English*-men shall be likewise free for transporting of Wine or other Commodities from '*Bordeaux* into *Scotland*, paying the same Customs and Duties that the *Scottish*-men do pay 'there.

Impositions to be free to both People.

'And likewise for clearing and resolving the 'doubts touching the advantage that the *Scots* 'are supposed to have above the *English* in buying and transporting the Commodities of *Normandy*, and of other parts of the Kingdom of '*France* (excepting the buying of Wine in *Bordeaux*, which is already determined,) It is 'agreed, that there shall be sent some meet 'and discreet persons into *France*, two for 'either side, to take perfect notice of any such 'advantage as either the *English* have above the *Scots*,

'*Scots*, or the *Scots* above the *English*, in the buy-'ing or transporting of any Commodities of '*Normandy* or any parts of *France* (excepting the 'Wine of *Bordeaux*) and as the said persons shall 'find the advantage to be, so for making the 'Trade equal, the Custom shall be advanced to 'the King in *England* and *Scotland* And for 'the part of those that have the advantage, and 'according to the proportion of the said ad-'vantage, the advancement of the Custom to 'continue no longer than the privilege of having 'such advantage shall continue, and that ge-'nerally for all other Trade from any parts 'the *English* and *Scottish* Subjects, each in others 'Country, shall have liberty of Importation as 'freely as any of the native Subjects themselves 'having special Privilege

Exportation of Goods prohibited made unlawful to both.

'Next, concerning Exportation, It is agreed 'that all such Goods as are prohibited and for-'bidden to *Englishmen* themselves to be trans-'ported forth of *England* to any foreign part, 'the same shall be unlawful for any *Scottishmen* 'or any other to transport to any foreign Na-'tion beyond sea, under the same penalties and 'forfeitures that the *English* are subject unto, 'and reciprocally that forth of *Scotland*, no *En-glishmen* shall transport to any foreign part 'the Goods or Commodities that are prohibi-'ted in *Scotland* to *Scottish-men* themselves Ne-'vertheless such Goods and Commodities and 'Merchandises as are licensed to *Englishmen* to 'transport out of *England* to any foreign part, 'the same may be likewise transported by '*Scottish-men* thither, they certifying their go-'ing into foreign parts, and taking a Cocquet 'accordingly, and paying the ordinary Custom 'that *Englishmen* do pay themselves at the ex-'porting of such Wares The like liberty to be 'for *Englishmen* in *Scotland*

Order for Native Commodities.

'As for the Native Commodities which ei-'ther of the Countries do yield, and may serve 'for the use and benefit of the other, It is a-'greed that mutually there may be transported 'forth of *England* to *Scotland*, and forth of *Scot-land* to *England*, all such Wares as are neither 'of the growth or handy-work of either of 'the said Realms, without payment of any im-'post, custom or exaction, and as freely in all 'respects as any Wares may be transported ei-'ther in *England* from part to part, or in *Scot-land* from part to part, excepting such parti-'cular sorts of Goods and Merchandises as are 'hereafter mention'd, being restrained for the 'proper and inward use of each Country And 'for that purpose it is declared, That both in 'this communication of benefit and participa-'tion of the native Commodities of the one 'Country with the other, there shall be speci-'ally reserved and excepted the sorts hereafter 'specified; That is to say, Wool, Sheep, Sheep-'fell, Cattel, Leather, Hides and Linnen yarn, 'which are specially restrained within each 'Country, not to be transported from the 'one to the other, excepting also and reserving 'to the *Scottish men* their trade of Fishing with-'in their Loches, Forthes and Bayes, within-'land, and in the Seas within fourteen mile 'of the Coasts of the Realm of *Scotland*, where 'neither *Englishmen* nor any Strangers have used 'to fish, and so reciprocally in the point 'of Fishing on the behalf of *England* All 'which exceptions and restrictions are not to 'be understood or mention'd in any sort for a 'mark or note of separation or disunion, but 'only as matters of policy and conveniency for 'the several estate of each Country

Order for Custom

'Furthermore it is agreed that all foreign 'Wares to be transported forth of *Scotland* to '*England*, or out of *England* to *Scotland*, by 'any of the Kings subjects of either King-'doms, having at their first entry once paid 'custom in either of the Kingdoms, shall not 'pay outward custom therein afterwards, save 'only inward custom at that Port whereunto 'they shall be transported But the owner of 'the Goods, or the Factor or Master of the ship, 'shall give Bond not to transport the same in-'to any foreign part

Scots may be associated in English Companies.

'It is also agreed that *Scottish-men* shall not be 'debarred from being associates unto any *Eng-lish* company of Merchants, as Merchant ven-'turers or others, upon such conditions as 'any *Englishman* may be admitted; and so re-'ciprocally for *Englishmen* in *Scotland*

Order for transportation

'It is nevertheless agreed by mutual con-'sent, and so to be understood, that the mutu-'al liberty aforesaid of Exportation and Trade 'in each part from the one to the other shall 'serve for the inward use only of either Realm, 'and order taken for restraining and prohibi-'ting the transportation of the said Commo-'dities into foreign parts, and for due punish-'ment of those that shall transgress in that be-'half

Punishment of such as shall transgress

'And for the better assurance and caution 'herein it is agreed that every Merchant so 'offending shall forfeit his goods, the Ships 'wherein the said Goods shall be transported, 'confiscated, the Customers, Searchers, and 'other Officers of the Custom whatsoever, in 'case of consent or knowledge on their part, 'to lose their Offices and Goods, and their 'bodies to be imprisoned at his Majesties plea-'sure Of which Escheats and Forfeitures 'two parts shall appertain to his Majesty, if 'the Customs be unfarmed, and the third to 'the Informer and if the Customs be farmed, 'one third of the Forfeiture shall belong to 'his Majesty, a third to the Farmers of the 'Customs, and the other third to the Informer 'The trial of the offence to be summar in ei-'ther Country in the Exchequer Chamber by 'Writ, sufficient Witnesses or Oath of party, 'or before the Justice by Jury or Assize, and 'his Majesties Officers in either Country to 'convene with the Complainers that interest in 'the pursuit

Caution to be given by the Owners and Masters of Ship

'As also for the more surety that there shall 'be no transportation of such Goods it is a-'greed that the shipping of all such native 'Commodities there be taken by the Custo-'mer of the Port where the Goods or Wares 'are imbarked, a Bond or Obligation sub-'scribed by the Owner of the said Goods, and 'Master of the Ship; by the Owner, if he be 'present, and in case of his absence, by the 'Master of the Ship, and Factor or Party that 'ladeth the same Which Bond shall contain 'a sum of money answerable to the value of the 'Goods, with condition of relieving the party 'obliged, and discharging him of the said Bond 'in case return be made of a due Certificate 'to the Custom where the Goods were la-'den, from any part within *England* or *Scot-land* The Certificate to be subscribed and 'sealed by the Officers of the Customs of the 'part where the said Goods shall arrive, and be 'unladen, or if there be no such Officers there, 'by the chief Magistrate and Town Clerk 'of that Harbour or Town, under their Hand 'and Seal

Indifferency of fraighting

'It is further agreed touching the indifferent 'fraighting of Commodities either in *English* 'or *Scottish* Bottoms, that Englishmen and Scot-

tishmen

tishmen fraight and lade their goods each in others Ships and Bottoms indifferently, paying only *English* and *Scottish* custom, not withstanding any contrary laws or prohibitions And that a Proposition be made to the Parliament of *England* for establishing some good orders for upholding and maintaining the great Fishing of *England*, as likewise that a Proposition be made to the Parliament of *Scotland* for the making of their Shipping more proportionable in burthen to the Shipping of *England*, the better to serve for equality of trade, and a common defence for the whole Isle

Postnati declared free

‘ And because it is requisite that the mutual communication aforesaid be not only extended to matter of Commerce, but to all other benefits and privileges of natural born subjects, It is agreed that an Act be proponed to be passed in manner following That all the subjects of both Realms born since the decease of the late Queen, and that shall be born hereafter under the obedience of his Majesty and of his Royal Progeny, are by the common Laws of both Realms and shall be for ever enabled to obtain, succeed, inherit and possess of all goods, lands and chattels, honours, dignities, offices, liberties, privileges and benefices Ecclesiastical or Civil, in Parliament and all other places of the Kingdoms, and every one of the same, in all respects and without any exception whatsoever, as fully and amply as the subjects of either Realm respectively might have done, or may do in any sort within the Kingdom where they are born

Exception for Offices of the Crown

‘ Farther, whereas his Majesty out of his great jugment and providence hath not only professed in public and private speech to the Nobility and Council of both, but hath also vouchsafed to be contented that, for a more full satisfaction and comfort of all his loving subjects, it may be comprised in the said Act, that his Majesty meaneth not to confer any Office of the Crown, any Office of Judicature, place, voice, or Office in Parliament of either Kingdom upon the subjects of the other, born before the decease of the late Queen, until time and conversation have encreased and accomplished an Union of the said Kingdoms, as well in the hearts of all the people and in the Conformity of Laws and Policies in these Kingdoms, as in the knowledge and sufficiency of particular men, who being untimely employed in such authorities could no way be able, much less acceptable, to discharge such duties belonging to them, It is therefore resolved by us the Commissioners aforesaid, not only in regard of our desires and endeavours to farther the speedy conclusion of this happy work intended, but also as testimony of our love and thankfulness for his gracious promise, on whose sincerity and benignity we build our full assurance, even according to the inward sense and feeling of our own loyal and hearty affections, to obey and please him in all things worthy the subjects of so worthy a Soveraign, that it shall be desired of both the Parliaments, to be enacted by their Authority, that all the subjects of both Realms, born before the decease of the late Queen, may be enabled and capable to acquire, purchase, inherit, succeed, use and dispose of all lands, goods, inheritances, offices, honours, dignities, liberties, privileges, immunities, benefices and preferments whatsoever, each subject in either Kingdom, with the same freedom and as lawfully and peaceably as the very natural and born subjects of either Realm, where the said rights, estates or profits are established, notwithstanding whatsoever Law, Statute, or former Constitutions heretofore in force to the contrary other than to acquire, possess, succeed or inherit any Office of the Crown, Office of Judicatory, or any voice, place or Office in Parliament, all which shall remain free from being claimed, held, or enjoyed by the subjects of the one Kingdom within the other, born before the decease of the late Queen, notwithstanding any words, sense or interception of the Act, or any circumstance thereupon depending, until there be such a perfect and full accomplishment of the Union as is desired mutually by both the Realms. In all which points of reservation, either in recital of the words of his Majesties sacred promise, or in any clause or sentence before specified from enabling them to any of the aforesaid places or dignities, it hath been and ever shall be so far from the thoughts of any of us, to presume to alter or impair his Majesties Prerogative Royal (who contrariwise do all with comfort and confidence depend herein upon the gracious assurance which his Majesty is pleased to give in the declaration of his so just and Princely care and favour to all his people) as for a farther laying open of our clear and dutiful intentions towards his Majesty in this and in all things else which may concern his Prerogative, we do also herein profess and declare, that we think it fit there be inserted in the Act to be proponed and passed, in express terms, a sufficient reservation of his Majesties Prerogative Royal to denizate, enable and prefer to such offices, honors, dignities and benefices whatsoever in both the said Kingdoms, and either of them, as are heretofore excepted in the preceding reservation of all *English* and *Scottish* subjects born before the decease of the late Queen, as freely, soveraignly and absolutely, as any of his Majesties most noble progenitors or predecessors, Kings of *England* or *Scotland*, might have done at any time heretofore, and to all other intents and purposes in as ample manner as no such Act had ever been thought of or mentioned

Reservation of his Majesties Prerogative

Remanding of Malefactors

‘ And forasmuch as the several Jurisdictions and Administrations of either Realm may be abused by Malefactors, by their own impunity, if they shall commit any offence in the one Realm, and afterwards remove their persons and abode unto the other; it is agreed, that there may be some fit course advised of by the wisdoms of the Parliaments for tryal and proceeding against the persons of offenders remaining in the one Realm, for and concerning the crimes and faults committed in the other Realm And yet neverthelesss that it may be lawful for the Justice of the Realm where the fact is committed, to remand the offender remaining in the other Realm to be answerable unto Justice in the same Realm where the fact was committed, and that upon such remand made, the offender shall be accordingly delivered, and all farther proceeding, if any be, in the other Realm shall cease, so as it may be done without prejudice to his Majesty or other Lords in their Escheats and Forfeitures With provision nevertheless, that this be not thought necessary to be made for all criminal offences, 'but in special cases only; as namely in the 'cases of wilful Murther, falsifying of Moneys, 'and forging of Deeds, Instruments and Wri'tings, and such other like cases as upon far'ther advice in the said Parliament may be 'thought fit to be added.

The consideration of the Articles delayed

By the tenor of the Acts made in the Parliaments of both Kingdoms, to empower Commissioners to meet and agree, as aforesaid, the consideration of the Articles agreed on, was expresly limited to the *next Session* of each Parliament; and the *next* in England (being the Parliament which was destined to destruction by that hellish Contrivance of the Gun powder Plot, and abundantly employed in detecting and prosecuting the Traitors, and making provision against any future Attempts of the Papists;) did only pass an Act to *extend* the time for considering the said Articles, to any *other* Session of that Parliament Accordingly, in the next Session, which begun the 18th day of *November* in the year 1607, the Articles were taken into consideration by the Parliament of *England*, but met with so many and great obstructions, that nothing was brought to effect upon any head, except that one of abolishing all memory of Hostilities between the two Nations And this was done, by the repeal of divers *hostile* Laws which had been made from time to time, and the establishing, as much as might be, the Peace and Tranquility of the Borders, by a certain method of trying such Offences as should be committed by the English in *Scotland*, and by the Scots in *England*, in case the persons, after such offences committed, did escape into their own Kingdom All this was provided for in a separate Act, which was to take place, as soon as the like Provisions should be made on the other part, by the Parliament of *Scotland*

The Articles not confirm'd by Parliament

The Articles confirmed in the S[illegible] Parliament,

The King was exceedingly grieved, to see himself in great measure disappointed in an Affair of such Consequence, and which he had laid so much to heart And, to try whether the disappointment might not be repaired, and his design compassed by *beginning* in *Scotland*, he summoned a Parliament of that Kingdom to meet the *August* following, in the year 1608 In this, all the Articles which had been agreed upon by the Commissioners, were allowed and ratified, on condition that the Parliament of *England* should do the same, and should make special Declaration, that the Kingdom of Scotland *should remain an absolute and free Monarchy, and the fundamental Laws receive no Alteration*

— but not in the English

But the English Parliament (for what reasons, and upon what grounds, is not certainly known) silently drop'd the Articles, and never took them into consideration again By which means, the two Kingdoms, though under a Succession of the same Monarchs, and (through the interest of those Monarchs in both) preserved in a state of Peace, Friendship and Correspondence, did, notwithstanding two subsequent Attempts towards a *closer* Union in the reigns of K Charles the second and Queen Anne, still remain separate and independent in point of Constitution and Commerce, till, in the year 1706 (the 5th of Queen Anne) this mighty Work, which had been so often attempted in vain, was most happily accomplished; and is deservedly reckoned among the most glorious and most *important* Successes of Her Majesty's Reign

An Attempt of [illegible] by K Charles the 2d

The importance and necessity of an Union, temp. Annæ Reginæ,

The great *Importance* of this Work, will appear by the unhappy Condition which this Island must have been reduced to, had this last Attempt proved *Abortive*, as so many others had done before It was now about a hundred years, that the two Nations had been united under one and the same head and however a *nearer* Union had been always wished, as evidently tending to the strength and interest of both Kingdoms, yet, as long as that *Union in one and the same Prince* should continue, they were sure at least to live in *peace*, and could be under no apprehension of returning to their ancient state of Hostility But *William* Duke of *Glocester*, a youth of incomparable Parts, who promised whatever a Nation could wish or desire, being taken away at 12 years of age, and being also the only remaining issue of her then Royal Highness, and afterwards our gracious Soveraign Queen Anne; there was no apparent hope of an *uninterrupted* Succession of Protestant Princes and therefore the King and the Estates of the Realm (convinced by the unhappy reign of King James the second, that this Protestant Kingdom can have no Security of its Laws, Liberties, and Religion, under the Government of a Popish Prince, passed an Act for the Succession of the Crown of *England* in the *Protestant* Line Which Act, being made only in the Parliament of *England*, and neither that nor any of the like nature received or passed in the Parliament of *Scotland* the Scotch Nation did not understand themselves in the least obliged, after the decease of the Queen, to acknowledge or regard the Protestant Successor, who was by such Act entitled to the English Crown The consequence of which was, that nothing but the life of her then Majesty Queen Anne, stood between Us, and an entire Separation, or, in other words, between Us, and a Return to that Rapine, Bloodshed, and Misery, which fill the Histories of the two Kingdoms for so many hundred years, during that former Independent State

— to prevent an entire disunion of the two Nations

Commissioners appointed to treat of an Union 1 Ann

In this view of approaching Misery to both Nations, it pleased Her Majesty in the first year of her reign, to appoint Commissioners of both (pursuant to the Authority vested in her, by two Statutes made in the respective Parliaments,) to meet and treat of an *Union* between the two Kingdoms, who met accordingly, but, as I intimated before, without effect From which time, the Dangers and Calamities of a *disunited State*, were perpetually hanging over our heads, till her Majesty (empower'd by both Parliaments as before, and with better *prospect* of Success,) did in the sixth year of her Reign, appoint and nominate Commissioners anew Whose great Knowledge, Wisdom, and Temper, having surmounted all difficulties, and, with the addition of Parliamentary Sanctions, having established us in an united State *for ever*, their Names ought to be honour'd, to all Posterity, as the chief Instruments, under our then gracious Soveraign, of laying this lasting foundation of the Peace and Prosperity of the Island of GREAT BRITAIN

— and again, 5 Ann

Commissioners for ENGLAND.

Thomas Lord Archbishop of *Canterbury*
William Cowper, Lord Keeper
John Lord Archbishop of *York*
Sidney Lord *Godolphin*
Thomas Earl of *Pembroke* and *Montgomery*.
John Duke of *Newcastle*
William Duke of *Devonshire*
Charles Duke of *Somerset*.
Charles Duke of *Bolton*
Charles Earl of *Sunderland*
Evelin Earl of *Kingston*
Charles Earl of *Carlisle*
Edward Earl of *Orford*
Charles Viscount *Townshend*
Thomas Lord *Wharton*
Ralph Lord *Grey*
John Lord *Poulett*
John Lord *Sommers*
Charles Lord *Halifax*
John Smith, Esq;
William Marquiss of *Hartington*
John Marquiss of *Granby*.
Sir *Charles Hedges*
Robert Harley, Esq,
Henry Boyle, Esq,
Sir *John Holt*
Sir *Thomas Trevor*
Sir *Edward Northey*
Sir *Simon Harcourt*
Sir *John Cook*
Stephen Waller

Commissioners for SCOTLAND.

James Earl of *Seafield*, Lord Chancellor.
James Duke of *Queensberry*
John Earl of *Marr*
Hugh Earl of *Loudoun*.
John Earl of *Sutherland*
James Earl of *Morton*
David Earl of *Wemyss*.
David Earl of *Leven*.
John Earl of *Stair*
Archibald Earl of *Roseberie*.
David Earl of *Glasgow*
Lord *Archibald Campbell*.
Thomas Viscount *Duplin*.
William Lord *Rosse*
Sir *Hugh Dalrymple*
Adam Cockburn
Robert Dundas
Robert Stewart
Francis Montgomery
Sir *David Dalrymple*
Sir *Alexander Ogilvie*
Sir *Patrick Johnston*
Sir *James Smollett*.
George Lockhart
William Morison
Alexander Grant
William Seton
John Clerk
Hugh Montgomery
Daniel Steuart
Daniel Campbell.

Commissioners meet and finish the Articles and lay them before the Queen

The Lords Commissioners of *England* and *Scotland*, thus appointed, met at a place called the *Cock-pit*, near *Whitehall*, *Westminster*, on the 16th day of *April*, in the year 1706, and pursu'd that great and important Work with so much zeal and assiduity, that the Articles of Union were *signed* and *sealed* by the Commissioners of both Nations on the 22d day of *July* following, and on the 23d of the same month, one Copy or Instrument thereof, was (according to the tenor of both Commissions) presented to her Sacred Majesty, who accepted it, with expressions of great Thanks for the pains they had taken in the Treaty, and with a declaration of her own earnest desire to see *so great a Security and Advantage to both Kingdoms, accomplished in her Reign*

and before the Parliament

By the tenor of the Commissions, the Articles of Union, being signed and sealed by the Commissioners, were in like manner to be laid before the Parliaments of both Kingdoms, which was accordingly done the winter following; and (the doctrine, worship, discipline, and government of both Churches, as established in the respective Kingdoms, having been first unalterably secured by Acts of Parliament in each,) the said Articles, with some Additions and Alterations, were ratified and approved in both Parliaments The tenor of which is as follows

ARTICLE I

The two Kingdoms united for ever by the name of Great Britain

'That the Two Kingdoms of *England* and *Scotland* shall, upon the First Day of *May*, which 'shall be in the Year One thousand seven hundred and seven, and for ever after, be United into One Kingdom by the Name of *Great Britain*, and that Ensigns Armorial of the 'said United Kingdom be such as Her Majesty shall Appoint, and the Crosses of St *George* and St *Andrew* be Conjoyned in such 'manner as Her Majesty shall think fit, and 'used in all Flags, Banners, Standards and 'Ensigns, both at Sea and Land

ARTICLE II

'That the Succession to the Monarchy of 'the United Kingdom of *Great Britain*, and of 'the Dominions thereunto belonging, after Her 'most Sacred Majesty, and in default of Issue of 'Her Majesty, be, remain, and continue to the 'most Excellent Princess *Sophia*, Electoress and 'Dutchess Dowager of *Hanover*, and the Heirs 'of Her Body, being Protestants, upon whom 'the Crown of *England* is settled by an Act of 'Parliament made in *England* in the Twelfth 'Year of the Reign of His late Majesty King '*William* the Third, Intituled, *An Act for the further Limitation of the Crown, and better Securing the Rights and Liberties of the Subject* 'And that all Papists, and Persons Marrying 'Papists, shall be Excluded from, and for ever 'incapable to Inherit, Possess, or Enjoy the 'Imperial Crown of *Great Britain*, and the 'Dominions thereunto belonging, or any Part 'thereof And in every such case, the Crown 'and Government shall from time to time 'descend to, and be enjoyed by such Person, 'being a Protestant, as should have Inherited and Enjoyed the same, in case such Papist, or Person Marrying a Papist, was Na'turally

'turally Dead, according to the Proviſion for 'the Deſcent of the Crown of *England*, made 'by another Act of Parliament in *England*, in 'the Firſt year of the Reign of Their late 'Majeſties King *William* and Queen *Mary*, Intituled, *An Act declaring the Rights and Liberties of the Subject, and Settling the Succeſſion of the Crown*

ARTICLE III

One Parliament

'That the United Kingdom of *Great Britain*, be Repreſented by one and the ſame 'Parliament, to be Stiled, *The Parliament of* 'Great Britain

ARTICLE IV

Intercourſe of Trade and Navigation

'That all the Subjects of the United Kingdom of *Great Britain* ſhall, from and after 'the Union, have full Freedom and Intercourſe 'of Trade and Navigation to and from any 'Port or Place within the ſaid United Kingdom, and the Dominions and Plantations 'thereunto belonging, And that there be a 'Communication of all other Rights, Privileges and Advantages, which do or may 'belong to the Subjects of either Kingdom, 'except where it is otherwiſe expreſly Agreed 'in theſe Articles

ARTICLE V

Ships of Scotland to be deem'd Ships of Great Britain

'That all Ships or Veſſels belonging to Her 'Majeſties Subjects of *Scotland*, at the time of 'Ratifying the Treaty of Union of the Two 'Kingdoms in the Parliament of *Scotland*, 'though Foreign Built, be deemed, and paſs 'as Ships of the Built of *Great Britain*, the 'Owner, or where there are more Owners, 'one or more of the Owners, within Twelve 'Months after the Firſt of *May* next, making 'Oath, that at the time of Ratifying the 'Treaty of Union in the Parliament of *Scotland*, the ſame did, in whole or in part, belong to him or them, or to ſome other 'Subject or Subjects of *Scotland*, to be particularly Named, with the Place of their reſpective Abodes, And that the ſame doth 'then, at the time of the ſaid Depoſition, 'wholly belong to him or them, And that no 'Foreigner, Directly or Indirectly, hath any 'Share, Part or Intereſt therein, which Oath 'ſhall be made before the Chief Officer or 'Officers of the Cuſtoms, in the Port next to 'the Abode of the ſaid Owner or Owners, 'And the ſaid Officer or Officers ſhall be Impowered to Adminiſter the ſaid Oath, and 'the Oath being ſo Adminiſter'd ſhall be Atteſted by the Officer or Officers, who Adminiſter'd the ſame, And being Regiſter'd 'by the ſaid Officer or Officers, ſhall be delivered to the Maſter of the Ship for Security 'of her Navigation, and a Duplicate thereof 'ſhall be tranſmitted by the ſaid Officer or 'Officers, to the Chief Officer or Officers of 'the Cuſtoms in the Port of *Edinburgh*, to be 'there enter'd in a Regiſter, and from thence to 'be ſent to the Port of *London*, to be there enter'd in the General Regiſter of all Trading 'Ships belonging to *Great Britain*

ARTICLE VI

Both Kingdoms ſhall be under the ſame Regulations, as to Trade

'That all Parts of the United Kingdom for 'ever, from and after the Union, ſhall have 'the ſame Allowances, Encouragements, and 'Draw backs, and be under the ſame Prohibitions, Reſtrictions and Regulations of Trade, 'and liable to the ſame Cuſtoms and Duties 'on Import and Export And that the Allowances, Encouragements, and Draw backs, Prohibitions, Reſtrictions, and Regulations of 'Trade, and the Cuſtoms and Duties on Import and Export ſettled in *England*, when the 'Union commences, ſhall, from and after the 'Union, take place throughout the whole 'United Kingdom; Excepting and Reſerving 'the Duties upon Export and Import, of ſuch 'particular Commodities, from which any 'Perſons, the Subjects of either Kingdom, are 'ſpecially Liberated and Exempted by their 'Private Rights which after the Union, are 'to remain Safe and Entire to them in all 'Reſpects, as before the ſame And that from 'and after the Union, no *Scots* Cattle carried 'into *England*, ſhall be liable to any other 'Duties, either on the Publick or Private Accompts, than thoſe Duties to which the Cattle of *England* are, or ſhall be liable within 'the ſaid Kingdom And ſeeing by the Laws 'of *England*, there are Rewards granted upon 'the Exportation of certain kinds of Grain, 'wherein Oats Grinded or Ungrinded, are not 'Expreſſed, that from and after the Union, 'when Oats ſhall be ſold at Fifteen Shillings 'Sterling *per* Quarter, or under, there ſhall 'be paid Two Shillings and Six Pence Sterling for every Quarter of the Oat meal Exported in the Terms of the Law, whereby 'and ſo long as Rewards are granted for Exportation of other Grains, and that the Bear 'of *Scotland* have the ſame Rewards as Barley, 'And in reſpect the Importations of Victual 'into *Scotland*, from any Place beyond Sea, 'would prove a Diſcouragement to Tillage, 'therefore that the Prohibition as now in Force 'by the Law of *Scotland*, againſt Importation 'of Victuals from *Ireland*, or any other Place 'beyond Sea into *Scotland*, do, after the Union, 'remain in the ſame Force as now it is, until 'more proper and effectual Ways be provided 'by the Parliament of *Great Britain*, for Diſcouraging the Importation of the ſaid Victuals 'from beyond Sea

(Some Exceptions and Explanations)

ARTICLE VII

Exciſe of Liquors, the ſame

'That all Parts of the United Kingdom be 'for ever, from and after the Union, liable to 'the ſame Exciſes upon all Exciſeable Liquors, 'Excepting only that the Thirty four Gallons, '*Engliſh* Barrel of Beer or Ale, amounting to 'Twelve Gallons *Scots* preſent Meaſure, ſold 'in *Scotland* by the Brewer at Nine Shillings 'Six Pence Sterling, excluding all Duties, and 'Retailed, including Duties and the Retailers 'Profit at Two Pence the *Scots* Pint, or Eighth 'part of the *Scots* Gallon, be not after the Union liable, on accompt of the preſent Exciſe 'upon Exciſeable Liquors in *England*, to any 'higher Impoſition than Two Shillings Sterling, upon the foreſaid Thirty four Gallons, '*Engliſh* Barrel, being Twelve Gallons the 'preſent *Scots* Meaſure And that the Exciſe 'ſettled in *England*, on all other Liquors, when 'the Union commences, take place throughout the whole United Kingdom

ARTICLE

ARTICLE VIII.

'That from and after the Union, all Foreign Salt which ſhall be Imported into *Scotland*, ſhall be Charged at the Importation there, with the ſame Duties as the like Salt is now charged with, being Imported into *England*, and to be Levied and Secured in the ſame manner But in regard the Duties of great Quantities of Foreign Salt Imported may be very heavy upon the Merchants Importers, that therefore all Foreign Salt Imported into *Scotland*, ſhall be Cellar'd and Locked up under the Cuſtody of the Merchants Importers, and the Officers employed for Levying the Duties upon Salt, and that the Merchant may have what Quantity thereof his Occaſion may require, not under a Wey or Forty Buſhels at a time, giving Security for the Duty of what Quantity he receives, payable in Six Months But *Scotland* ſhall, for the ſpace of Seven Years from the ſaid Union, be Exempted from Paying in *Scotland*, for Salt made there, the Duty or Exciſe now payable for Salt made in *England*, but from the Expiration of the ſaid Seven Years, ſhall be ſubject and liable to the ſame Duties for Salt made in *Scotland*, as ſhall be then payable for Salt made in *England*, to be Levied and Secured in the ſame manner, and with proportionable Draw-backs and Allowances as in *England*, with this Exception, That *Scotland* ſhall, after the ſaid Seven Years, remain Exempted from the Duty of Two Shillings Four Pence a Buſhel on Home-Salt impoſed by an Act made in *England*, in the Ninth and Tenth of King *William* the Third of *England*; And if the Parliament of *Great Britain* ſhall, or at before the Expiring of the ſaid ſeven Years, ſubſtitute any other Fund in Place of the ſaid Two Shillings Four Pence of Exciſe on the Buſhel of Home-Salt, *Scotland* ſhall, after the ſaid ſeven Years, bear a Proportion of the ſaid Fund, and have an Equivalent in the Terms of this Treaty, And that during the ſaid ſeven Years, there ſhall be paid in *England* for all Salt made in *Scotland*, and Imported from thence into *England*, the ſame Duties upon the Importation, as ſhall be payable for Salt made in *England*, to be Levied and Secured in the ſame manner as the Duties on Foreign Salt are to be Levied and Secured in *England* And that after the ſaid ſeven Years, as long as the ſaid Duty of Two Shillings Four Pence a Buſhel upon Salt is continued in *England*, the ſaid Two Shillings and Four Pence a Buſhel ſhall be payable for all Salt made in *Scotland*, and Imported into *England*, to be Levied and Secured in the ſame manner, and that during the Continuance of the Duty of Two Shillings Four Pence a Buſhel upon Salt made in *England*, no Salt whatſoever be brought from *Scotland* to *England* by Land in any manner, under the Penalty of Forfeiting the Salt, and the Cattle and Carriages made uſe of in bringing the ſame, and paying Twenty Shillings for every Buſhel of ſuch Salt, and proportionably for a greater or leſſer Quantity, for which the Carrier as well as the Owner ſhall be liable, joyntly and ſeverally, and the Perſons bringing or carrying the ſame to be Impriſoned by any one Juſtice of the Peace, by the ſpace of ſix Months without Bail, and until the Penalty be paid And for Eſtabliſhing an Equality in Trade, that all Fleſh Exported from *Scotland* to *England*, and put on Board in *Scotland*, to be Exported to Parts beyond the Seas, and Proviſions for Ships in *Scotland*, and for Foreign Voyages, may be ſalted with *Scots* Salt, paying the ſame Duty for what Salt is ſo employed as the like Quantity of ſuch Salt pays in *England*, and under the ſame Penalties, Forfeitures and Proviſions for preventing of Frauds, as are mentioned in the Laws of *England*. And that from and after the Union, the Laws and Acts of Parliament in *Scotland* for Pining, Curing and Packing of Herrings, White Fiſh and Salmon for Exportation with Foreign Salt, only, without any mixture of *Britiſh* or *Iriſh* Salt, and for preventing of Frauds in Curing and Packing of Fiſh, be continued in Force in *Scotland*, ſubject to ſuch Alterations as ſhall be made by the Parliament of *Great Britain* And that all Fiſh Exported from *Scotland* to Parts beyond the Seas, which ſhall be Cured with Foreign Salt only, and without mixture of *Britiſh* or *Iriſh* Salt, ſhall have the ſame Eaſes, Præmiums, and Draw-backs, as are or ſhall be allowed to ſuch Perſons as Export the like Fiſh from *England*; And that for Encouragement of the Herring-Fiſhing, there ſhall be Allowed and Paid to the Subjects, Inhabitants of *Great Britain*, during the preſent Allowances for other Fiſh, Ten Shillings Five Pence Sterling for every Barrel of White Herrings which ſhall be Exported from *Scotland*, and that there ſhall be allowed Five Shillings Sterling for every Barrel of Beef or Pork ſalted with Foreign Salt, without mixture of *Britiſh* or *Iriſh* Salt, and Exported for Sale from *Scotland* to Parts beyond Sea, alterable of the Parliament of *Great Britain* And if any Matters of Fraud relating to the ſaid Duties on Salt ſhall hereafter appear, which are not ſufficiently provided againſt by this Article, the ſame ſhall be ſubject to ſuch further Proviſions as ſhall be thought fit by the Parliament of *Great Britain*

Duties upon Salt

ARTICLE IX

'That whenever the Sum of One Million nine hundred ninety ſeven thouſand ſeven hundred and ſixty three Pounds, Eight Shillings, and Four Pence half penny, ſhall be Enacted by the Parliament of *Great Britain* to be Raiſed in that part of the United Kingdom now called *England*, on Land and other Things uſually Charged in Acts of Parliament there, for Granting an Aid to the Crown by a Land Tax, that part of the United Kingdom now called *Scotland* ſhall be Charged by the ſame Act, with a further Sum of Forty eight thouſand Pounds free of all Charges, as the *Quota* of *Scotland* to ſuch Tax, and ſo proportionably for any greater or leſſer Sum raiſed in *England* by any Tax on Land, and other Things uſually Charged together with the Land, And that ſuch *Quota* for *Scotland*, in the caſes aforeſaid, be Raiſed and Collected in the ſame manner as the Ceſs now is in *Scotland*, but ſubject to ſuch Regulations in the manner of Collecting, as ſhall be made by the Parliament of *Great Britain*.

Proportion of publick Tax

ARTICLE

ARTICLE X.

Duties upon Stamp'd Paper

'That during the Continuance of the reſpective Duties on Stamp Paper, Vellum and Parchment, by the ſeveral Acts now in Force in *England*, *Scotland* ſhall not be Charged with the ſame reſpective Duties.

ARTICLE XI.

—Windows

'That during the Continuance of the Duties payable in *England* on Windows and Lights, which determine on the Firſt Day of *Auguſt*, One thouſand ſeven hundred and ten, *Scotland* ſhall not be Charged with the ſame Duties.

ARTICLE XII.

—Coals

'That during the Continuance of the Duties payable in *England* on Coals, Culm and Cynders, which determine the Thirtieth Day of *September*, One thouſand ſeven Hundred and ten, *Scotland* ſhall not be Charged therewith for Coals, Culm and Cynders conſumed there, but ſhall be Charged with the ſame Duties as in *England* for all Coals, Culm and Cynders not conſumed in *Scotland*.

ARTICLE XIII.

—Malt

'That during the Continuance of the Duty payable in *England* upon Malt, which determines the Twenty Fourth Day of *June*, One thouſand ſeven hundred and ſeven, *Scotland* ſhall not be Charged with that Duty.

ARTICLE XIV.

Scotland not to be charged with Duties already laid by the Parliament of *England*

'That the Kingdom of *Scotland* be not Charged with any other Duties laid on by the Parliament of *England* before the Union, except theſe Conſented to in this Treaty, in regard it is agreed, That all neceſſary Proviſion ſhall be made by the Parliament of *Scotland*, for the Publick Charge and Service of that Kingdom, for the Year One Thouſand ſeven hundred and ſeven. Provided nevertheleſs, That if the Parliament of *England* ſhall think fit to lay any further Impoſitions by way of Cuſtoms, or ſuch Exciſes, with which, by virtue of this Treaty, *Scotland* is to be Charged equally with *England*, in ſuch caſe *Scotland* ſhall be liable to the ſame Cuſtoms and Exciſes, and have an Equivalent to be ſettled by the Parliament of *Great Britain*. With this further Proviſion, That any Malt to be made and conſumed in that part of the United Kingdom now called *Scotland*, ſhall not be Charged with any Impoſition on Malt, during this preſent War. And ſeeing it cannot be ſuppoſed that the Parliament of *Great Britain* will ever lay any ſort of Burthens upon the United Kingdom, but what they ſhall find of neceſſity at that time for the Preſervation and Good of the Whole, and with due regard to the Circumſtances and Abilities of every Part of the United Kingdom; therefore it is Agreed, That there be no further Exemption inſiſted upon for any part of the United Kingdom, but that the Conſideration of any Exemptions beyond what are already agreed on in this Treaty, ſhall be left to the Determination of the Parliament of *Great Britain*.

ARTICLE XV.

Equivalent of *Scotland*, for contributing to Debts contracted by *England*, before the Union

'That whereas by the Terms of this Treaty, the Subjects of *Scotland*, for preſerving an Equality of Trade throughout the United Kingdom, will be liable to ſeveral Cuſtoms and Exciſes now payable in *England*, which will be applicable towards payment of the Debts in *England* contracted before the Union, It is agreed, That *Scotland* ſhall have an Equivalent for what the Subjects thereof ſhall be ſo charged towards payment of the ſaid Debts of *England*, in all particulars whatſoever, in manner following, *viz.* That before the Union of the ſaid Kingdoms the Sum of Three hundred ninety eight thouſand and eighty five Pounds, ten Shillings, be Granted to Her Majeſty by the Parliament of *England*, for the Uſes after-mentioned, being the Equivalent to be anſwered to *Scotland*, for ſuch parts of the ſaid Cuſtoms and Exciſes upon all Exciſeable Liquors, with which that Kingdom is to be Charged upon the Union, as will be applicable to the payment of the ſaid Debts of *England*, according to the Proportions which the preſent Cuſtoms in *Scotland*, being Thirty thouſand Pounds *per Annum*, do bear to the Cuſtoms in *England*, computed at One million three hundred forty one thouſand five hundred and fifty nine Pounds *per Annum*, And which the preſent Exciſes on Exciſeable Liquors in *Scotland*, being Thirty three thouſand and five hundred Pounds *per Annum*, do bear to the Exciſes on exciſeable Liquors in *England*, computed at Nine hundred forty ſeven thouſand ſix hundred and two Pounds *per Annum*. Which Sum of three hundred ninety eight thouſand eighty five Pounds ten Shillings, ſhall be due and payable from the time of the Union. And in regard that after the Union, *Scotland* becoming liable to the ſame Cuſtoms and Duties payable on Import and Export, and to the ſame Exciſes on all exciſeable Liquors as in *England*, as well upon that Accompt, as upon the Accompt of the encreaſe of Trade and People (which will be the happy conſequence of the Union) the ſaid Revenues will much Improve beyond the before mentioned Annual Values thereof, of which no preſent Eſtimate can be made, Yet nevertheleſs, for the Reaſons aforeſaid, there ought to be a proportionable equivalent anſwered to *Scotland*, It is agreed, That after the Union there ſhall be an Accompt kept of the ſaid Duties ariſing in *Scotland*, to the end it may appear, what ought to be Anſwered to *Scotland*, as an Equivalent for ſuch proportion of the ſaid Encreaſe, as ſhall be applicable to the payment of the Debts of *England*. And for the further and more effectual Anſwering the ſeveral Ends hereafter-mentioned, It is Agreed, That from and after the Union, the whole encreaſe of the Revenues of Cuſtoms, and Duties on Import and Export, and Exciſes upon exciſeable Liquors in *Scotland*, over and above the Annual Produce of the ſaid reſpective Duties, as above ſtated, ſhall go and be applied, for the

—before the Union

—after the Union

'Term of ſeven Years, to the Uſes hereafter mentioned, and that, upon the ſaid Accompt there ſhall be Anſwered to *Scotland* Annually from the end of Seven Years after the Union, an equivalent in proportion to ſuch Part of the ſaid encreaſe, as ſhall be applicable to the Debts of *England*, And generally, That an equivalent ſhall be anſwered to *Scotland* for ſuch parts of the *Engliſh* Debts, as *Scotland* may hereafter become liable to pay by reaſon of the Union, other than ſuch for which Appropriations have been made by Parliament in *England*, of the Cuſtoms, or other Duties on Export and Import, Exciſes on all exciſeable Liquors, in reſpect of which Debts, Equivalents are herein before provided And as for the Uſes to which the ſaid Sum of Three hundred ninety eight thouſand eighty five Pounds Ten Shillings, to be Granted, as aforeſaid, and all other Monies which are to be Anſwered or Allowed to *Scotland*, as aforeſaid, are to be Applied, It is Agreed, That in the firſt place, out of the aforeſaid Sum, what Conſideration ſhall be found neceſſary to be had for any Loſſes which private Perſons may ſuſtain by Reducing the Coin of *Scotland* to the Standard and Value of the Coin of *England*, may be made good, in the next place, That the Capital Stock, or Fund of the *African* and *Indian* Company of *Scotland*, advanced together with Intereſt for the ſaid Capital Stock, after the rate of Five *per Centum per Annum*, from the reſpective Times of the payment thereof, ſhall be paid, Upon payment of which Capital Stock and Intereſt, It is Agreed, the ſaid Company be diſſolv'd and ceaſe, and alſo, that from the time of paſſing the Act of Parliament in *England*, for raiſing the ſaid Sum of Three hundred ninety eight thouſand eighty five Pounds Ten Shillings, the ſaid Company ſhall neither Trade, nor grant Licence to Trade, Providing, That if the ſaid Stock and Intereſt ſhall not be paid in Twelve Months after the Commencement of the Union, That then the ſaid Company may from thenceforward Trade, or give Licence to Trade, until the ſaid whole Capital Stock and Intereſt, ſhall be paid And as to the Overplus of the ſaid Sum of Three hundred ninety eight thouſand eighty five Pounds Ten Shillings, after payment of what Conſideration ſhall be had for Loſſes in repairing the Coin, and Paying the ſaid Capital Stock and Intereſt, and alſo the whole encreaſe of the ſaid Revenues of Cuſtoms, Duties and Exciſes, above the preſent Value which ſhall ariſe in *Scotland*, during the ſaid Term of Seven Years, together with the Equivalent which ſhall become due upon the Improvement thereof in *Scotland* after the ſaid Term, And alſo, as to all other Sums, which, according to the Agreements aforeſaid, may become payable to *Scotland* by way of Equivalent, for what that Kingdom ſhall hereafter become liable towards Payment of the Debts of *England*, It is Agreed, That the ſame be applied in manner following, *viz* That all the publick Debts of the Kingdom of *Scotland*, as ſhall be adjuſted by this preſent Parliament, ſhall be paid And that two Thouſand Pounds *per Annum*, for the ſpace of Seven Years, ſhall be applied towards encouraging and promoting the Manufacture of Coarſe Wooll within thoſe Shires which produce the Wooll; and that the firſt Two thouſand Pounds Sterling be paid at *Martinmas* next, and ſo yearly at *Martinmas*, during the ſpace aforeſaid; and afterwards the ſame ſhall be wholly applied towards the encouraging and promoting the Fiſheries, and ſuch other Manufactures and Improvements in *Scotland*, as may moſt conduce to the general good of the United Kingdom And it is Agreed, That Her Majeſty be Impowered to appoint Commiſſioners, who ſhall be accomptable to the Parliament of *Great Britain*, for Diſpoſing the ſaid Sum of Three hundred ninety eight thouſand and eighty five Pounds Ten Shillings, and all other Monies which ſhall ariſe to *Scotland*, upon the Agreements aforeſaid, to the Purpoſes before mentioned Which Commiſſioners ſhall be Impowered to call for, receive and diſpoſe of the ſaid Monies, in manner aforeſaid, and to Inſpect the Books of the ſeveral Collectors of the ſaid Revenues, and of all other Duties, from whence an Equivalent may ariſe And that the Collectors and Managers of the ſaid Revenues and Duties be obliged to give to the ſaid Commiſſioners ſubſcribed Authentick Abbreviates of the Produce of ſuch Revenues and Duties ariſing in their reſpective Diſtricts And that the ſaid Commiſſioners ſhall have their Office within the Limits of *Scotland*, and ſhall in ſuch Office keep Books containing Accompts of the Amount of the Equivalents, and how the ſame ſhall have been diſpoſed of from time to time, which may be inſpected by any of the Subjects who ſhall deſire the ſame

Application of the Equivalent

Commiſſioners for diſpoſing of the Equivalent.

ARTICLE XVI.

Coin of the ſame Value and Standard in both Kingdoms

'That from and after the Union, the Coin ſhall be of the ſame Standard and Value throughout the United Kingdom, as now in *England*, and a Mint ſhall be continued in *Scotland*, under the ſame Rules as the Mint in *England*, and the preſent Officers of the Mint continued, ſubject to ſuch Regulations and Alterations, as Her Majeſty, Her Heirs or Succeſſors, or the Parliament of *Great Britain* ſhall think fit.

ARTICLE XVII

Weights and Meaſures to be the ſame in both Kingdoms

'That from and after the Union, the ſame Weights and Meaſures ſhall be uſed throughout the United Kingdom, as are now eſtabliſhed in *England*, and Standards of Weights and Meaſures ſhall be kept by thoſe Burghs in *Scotland*, to whom the keeping the Standards of Weights and Meaſures, now in uſe there, does of ſpecial Right belong All which Standards ſhall be ſent down to ſuch reſpective Burghs, from the Standards kept in the Exchequer at *Weſtminſter*, ſubject nevertheleſs to ſuch Regulations as the Parliament of *Great Britain* ſhall think fit

ARTICLE XVIII.

Laws of Trade *&c* to be the ſame in *Scotland*, as in *England*

'That the Laws concerning Regulation of Trade, Cuſtoms, and ſuch Exciſes to which *Scotland* is, by Virtue of this Treaty to be liable, be the ſame in *Scotland*, from and after the Union, as in *England*; And that all

other

— but all other Laws of Scotland, to remain as before.

'other Laws in use within the Kingdom of 'Scotland, do after the Union, and notwithstanding thereof, remain in the same Force as 'before (except such as are contrary to, or inconsistent with this Treaty) but alterable by 'the Parliament of *Great Britain*, with this 'Difference betwixt the Laws concerning Publick Right, Policy, and Civil Government, 'and those which concern private Right, that 'the Laws which concern publick Right, Policy, and Civil Government, may be made 'the same throughout the whole United Kingdom But that no Alteration be made in 'Laws which concern private Right, except 'for evident Utility of the Subjects within '*Scotland*

ARTICLE XIX

Court of Session to continue,

'That the Court of Session, or College of 'Justice, do after the Union, and notwithstanding thereof, remain in all time coming 'within *Scotland*, as it is now constituted by 'the Laws of that Kingdom, and with the 'same Authority and Privileges as before the 'Union, subject nevertheless to such Regulations for the better Administration of Justice, 'as shall be made by the Parliament of *Great Britain*, And that hereafter none shall be 'named by Her Majesty, or her Royal Successors, to be Ordinary Lords of Session, but 'such who have served in the College of Justice as Advocates, or Principal Clerks of 'Session for the space of Five years, or as 'Writers to the Signet for the space of Ten 'years, with this Provision, that no Writer to 'the Signet be capable to be admitted a Lord 'of the Session, unless he undergo a Private and 'Publick Trial on the Civil Law, before the 'Faculty of Advocates, and be found by them 'qualified for the said Office, two years before 'he be named to be a Lord of the Session; yet 'so as the Qualifications made, or to be made, 'for capacitating persons to be named Ordinary Lords of Session, may be altered by 'the Parliament of *Great Britain* And that 'the Court of Justiciary do also after the Union, and notwithstanding thereof, remain in 'all time coming within *Scotland*, as it is now 'constituted by the Laws of that Kingdom, 'and with the same authority and Privileges 'as before the Union, subject nevertheless to 'such Regulations as shall be made by the Parliament of *Great Britain*, and without prejudice of other Rights of Justiciary, and that 'all Admiralty Jurisdictions be under the Lord 'High-Admiral, or Commissioners for the Admiralty of *Great Britain*, for the time being, and 'that the Court of Admiralty now Established 'in *Scotland* be continued, and that all Reviews, 'Reductions, or Suspensions of the Sentences 'in Maritime Cases, competent to the Jurisdiction of that Court, remain in the same 'manner after the Union, as now in *Scotland*, 'until the Parliament of *Great Britain* shall 'make such Regulations and Alterations, as 'shall be judged expedient for the whole United Kingdom, so as there be always continued in *Scotland* a Court of Admiralty, such 'as in *England*, for Determination of all 'Maritime Cases relating to private Rights in '*Scotland*, competent to the Jurisdiction of the 'Admiralty Court, subject nevertheless to such 'Regulations and Alterations, as shall be thought 'proper to be made by the Parliament of *Great Britain*, And that the Heretable Rights of 'Admiralty and Vice Admiralties in *Scotland* 'be reserved to the respective Proprietors as 'Rights of Property, subject nevertheless, as 'to the manner of exercising such Heretable 'Rights, to such Regulations and Alterations, 'as shall be thought proper to be made by the 'Parliament of *Great Britain*; and that all 'other Courts now in being within the Kingdom of *Scotland* do remain, but subject to Alterations by the Parliament of *Great Britain*, 'and that all inferior Courts within the said 'Limits do remain subordinate, as they are 'now, to the supreme Courts of Justice within the same, in all time coming, and that no 'Causes in *Scotland* be cognoscible by the Courts 'of *Chancery*, *Queen's-Bench*, *Common-Pleas*, or 'any other Court in *Westminster Hall*, and that 'the said Courts, or any other of the like nature, after the Union, shall have no Power to 'cognosce, review, or alter the Acts or Sentences of the Judicatures within *Scotland*, or 'stop the Execution of the same, and that 'there be a Court of Exchequer in *Scotland* after 'the Union, for deciding Questions concerning 'the Revenues of Customs and Excises there, 'having the same Power and Authority in such 'cases, as the Court of Exchequer has in *England*, and that the said Court of Exchequer 'in *Scotland* have power of passing Signatures, 'Gifts, Tutories, and in other things, as the 'Court of Exchequer at present in *Scotland* 'hath, and that the Court of Exchequer that 'now is in *Scotland* do remain, until a new 'Court of Exchequer be settled by the Parliament of *Great Britain* in *Scotland* after the 'Union; And that after the Union, the 'Queen's Majesty, and her Royal Successors, 'may continue a Privy Council in *Scotland*, for 'preserving of Publick Peace and Order, until 'the Parliament of *Great Britain* shall think fit 'to alter it, or Establish any other effectual 'method for that end.

— and Rules concerning it. Court of Justiciary to continue. Court of Admiralty to continue. Proviso, for all Heretable Rights of Admiralty and Vice-Admiralty. All other Courts in Scotland, to remain; — and no Causes in Scotland, to be cognisable by the Courts of Westminster-hall in England. A Court of Exchequer to be erected in Scotland; — and Privy Council to continue, if the Queen please.

ARTICLE XX

Proviso, for Heretable Offices

'That all Heretable Offices, Superiorities, 'Heretable Jurisdictions, Offices for Life, and 'Jurisdictions for Life, be reserved to the 'Owners thereof, as Rights of Property, in 'the same manner as they are now enjoyed by 'the Laws of *Scotland*, notwithstanding this 'Treaty

ARTICLE XXI

Proviso, for the Rights of Royal Burghs

'That the Rights and Privileges of the 'Royal Burghs in *Scotland*, as they now are, 'do remain entire after the Union, and notwithstanding thereof

ARTICLE XXII.

Sixteen Peers, and forty five Commoners, from Scotland, to sit in the Parliament of Great Britain

'That by virtue of this Treaty, of the 'Peers of *Scotland*, at the Time of the Union, 'sixteen shall be the Number to Sit and Vote 'in the House of Lords, and Forty five the 'Number of the Representatives of *Scotland* 'in the House of Commons of the Parliament 'of *Great Britain*, and that when Her Majesty, Her Heirs or Successors, shall declare 'Her or their Pleasure for holding the first 'or any subsequent Parliament of *Great Britain*, until the Parliament of *Great Britain* 'shall make further Provision therein, a Writ 'do issue under the Great Seal of the United 'Kingdom, directed to the Privy Council of *Scotland*

Manner of Electing them

'*Scotland*, commanding them to cauſe ſixteen 'Peers, who are to ſit in the Houſe of Lords, 'to be ſummoned to Parliament, and forty five 'Members to be elected to ſit in the Houſe of 'Commons of the Parliament of *Great Britain*, 'according to the Agreement in this Treaty, 'in ſuch manner as by an Act of this preſent 'Seſſion of the Parliament of *Scotland* is or ſhall 'be ſettled; which Act is hereby declared to be 'as Valid as if it were a part of, and in 'groſſed in this Treaty And that the Names 'of the Perſons ſo ſummoned and elected ſhall 'be returned by the privy Council of *Scotland* 'into the Court from whence the ſaid Writ did 'iſſue And that if her Majeſty, on or be 'fore the Firſt Day of *May* next, on which 'Day the Union is to take place, ſhall declare 'under the Great Seal of *England*, That it i 'expedient that the Lords of Parliament o '*England*, and Commons of the preſent Par 'liament of *England*, ſhould be the Member 'of the reſpective Houſes of the firſt Parli 'ment of *Great Britain*, for and on the pa 'of *England* then the ſaid Lords of Parlia 'ment of *England*, and Commons of the pre- 'ſent Parliament of *England*, ſhall be the Mem 'bers of the reſpective Houſes of the firſt Par- 'liament of *Great Britain*, for and on the part 'of *England* And her Majeſty may, by Her 'Royal Proclamation, under the Great Seal of '*Great Britain*, appoint the ſaid firſt Parlia 'ment of *Great Britain* to meet at ſuch Time 'and Place as Her Majeſty ſhall think fit 'Which Time ſhall not be leſs than fifty days 'after the date of ſuch Proclamation, And the 'Time and Place of the Meeting of ſuch Par 'liament being ſo appointed, a Writ ſhall be 'immediately iſſued under the Great Seal of '*Great Britain*, directed to the Privy Council 'of *Scotland*, for the ſummoning the ſixteen 'Peers, and for electing forty five Members 'by whom *Scotland* is to be repreſented in the 'Parliament of *Great Britain* And the Lords 'of Parliament of *England*, and the ſixteen 'Peers of *Scotland*, ſuch ſixteen Peers being 'ſummoned and returned in the manner agreed 'in this Treaty, and the Members of the 'Houſe of Commons of the ſaid Parliament 'of *England*, and the forty five Members for '*Scotland* ſuch forty five Members, being elected 'and returned in the manner agreed in this 'Treaty, ſhall aſſemble and meet reſpectively, 'in the reſpective Houſes of the Parliament 'of *Great Britain*, at ſuch time and place as 'ſhall be ſo appointed by Her Majeſty, and 'ſhall be the two Houſes of the firſt Parlia 'ment of *Great Britain*, and that Parliament 'may continue for ſuch time only, as the 'preſent Parliament of *England* might have 'continued, if the Union of the two King- 'doms had not been made, unleſs ſooner diſ 'ſolved by her Majeſty And that every one 'of the Lords of Parliament of *Great Britain*, 'and every Member of the Houſe of Commons 'of the Parliament of *Great Britain*, in the 'firſt and ſucceeding Parliaments of *Great* '*Britain*, until the Parliament of *Great Britain*, 'ſhall otherwiſe direct, ſhall take the reſpective 'Oaths appointed to be taken, inſtead of the 'Oaths of Allegiance and Supremacy, by an 'Act of Parliament made in *England* in the firſt 'year of the Reign of the late King *William* 'and Queen *Mary*, Intituled, *An Act for the* '*abrogating of the Oaths of Supremacy and Alle-* '*giance, and appointing other Oaths*, and make, 'ſubſcribe, and audibly repeat the Declaration 'mentioned in an Act of Parliament made in '*England* in the thirtieth year of the Reign of 'King *Charles* the ſecond, intituled, *An Act for* '*the more effectual preſerving the King's Perſon and* '*Government, by diſabling Papiſts from ſitting in* '*either Houſe of Parliament*; and ſhall take and 'ſubſcribe the Oath mentioned in an Act of 'parliament made in *England*, in the firſt year 'of Her Majeſty's Reign, intituled, *An Act to* '*declare the Alterations in the Oath appointed to be* '*taken by the Act*, intituled, *An Act for the fur-* '*ther Security of His Majeſty's Perſon, and the ſuc-* '*ceſſion of the Crown in the Proteſtant Line, and for* '*extinguiſhing the hopes of the Pretended Prince of* '*Wales, and all other Pretenders, and their open* '*and ſecret Abettors, and for declaring the Aſſo-* '*ciation to be determined*, at ſuch time and in 'ſuch manner as the Members of both 'Houſes of Parliament of *England* are, by the 'ſaid reſpective Acts directed to take, make, 'and ſubſcribe the ſame, upon the Penalties 'and Diſabilities in the ſaid reſpective Acts 'contained And it is declared and agreed, 'That theſe words, *This Realm*, *The Crown of* *this Realm*, and *The Queen of this Realm*, men- 'tioned in the Oaths and Declaration con- 'tained in the aforeſaid Acts, which were in- 'tended to ſignifie the Crown and Realm of '*England*, ſhall be underſtood of the Crown and 'Realm of *Great Britain*, and that in that ſenſe 'the ſaid Oaths and Declaration be taken and 'ſubſcribed by the Members of both Houſes 'of the Parliament of *Great Britain*

Parliament not to meet till 50 days after Proclamation

ARTICLE XXIII

'That the aforeſaid ſixteen Peers of *Scotland* 'mentioned in the laſt preceding Article, to ſit 'in the Houſe of Lords of the Parliament of '*Great Britain*, ſhall have all Privileges of Par- 'liament, which the Peers of *England* now 'have, and which they or any Peers of *Great* '*Britain* ſhall have after the Union, and par- 'ticularly the Right of Sitting upon the Trials 'of Peers And in caſe of the Trial of any 'Peer, in time of Adjournment, or Proroga- 'tion of Parliament, the ſaid ſixteen Peers ſhall 'be ſummoned in the ſame manner, and have 'the ſame Powers and Privileges at ſuch Trial, 'as any other Peers of *Great Britain*, and that 'in caſe any Trials of Peers ſhall hereafter hap- 'pen, when there is no Parliament in being, 'the ſixteen Peers of *Scotland*, who ſat in the 'laſt preceding Parliament, ſhall be ſummoned 'in the ſame manner, and have the ſame 'Powers and Privileges at ſuch Trials, as any 'other Peers of *Great Britain*, and that all 'Peers of *Scotland*, and their Succeſſors to their 'Honours and Dignities ſhall from and after 'the Union, be Peers of *Great Britain*, and 'have Rank and Precedency next and imme- 'diately after the Peers of the like Orders 'and Degrees in *England* at the time of the 'Union, and before all Peers of *Great Britain* 'of the like Orders and Degrees, who may be 'created after the Union, and ſhall be Tried 'as Peers of *Great Britain*, and ſhall enjoy all 'Privileges of Peers, as fully as the Peers of '*England* do now, or as they, or any other 'Peers of *Great Britain* may hereafter enjoy 'the ſame, except the Right and Privilege 'of ſitting in the Houſe of Lords, and the 'Privileges depending thereon, and particular- 'ly the Right of Sitting upon the Trials of 'Peers

The ſixteen Peers ſhall have all the Privileges of Parliament.

—particularly, at the Trial of Peers

Peers of Scotland ſhall enjoy all Privileges of Peers of Great Britain

—and ſhall be tried as Peers of Great Britain

ARTICLE

ARTICLE XXIV.

One Great Seal of *Great Britain*.

'That from and after the Union, there be 'one Great Seal for the United Kingdom of '*Great Britain*, which shall be different from 'the Great Seal now used in either Kingdom, 'and that the Quartering the Arms, and the 'Rank and Precedency of the Lyon King of 'Arms of the Kingdom of *Scotland*, as may 'best suit the Union, be left to her Majesty 'And that in the mean time, the Great Seal 'of *England* be used as the Great Seal of the 'United Kingdom, and that the Great Seal 'of the United Kingdom be used for Sealing 'Writs to Elect and Summon the Parliament 'of *Great Britain*, and for Sealing all Treaties 'with Foreign Princes and States, and all pub 'lick Acts, Instruments and Orders of State, 'which concern the whole United Kingdom, 'and in all other Matters relating to *England*, 'as the Great Seal of *England* is now used, 'and that a Seal in *Scotland* after the Union, 'be always kept and made use of in all things 'relating to private Rights or Grants, which 'have usually passed the Great Seal of *Scotland*, 'and which only concern Offices, Grants, 'Commissions, and private Rights within that 'Kingdom, and that until such Seal shall be 'appointed by her Majesty, the present Great 'Seal of *Scotland*, shall be used for such Pur'poses, and that the Privy Seal, Signet, Casset, 'Signet of the Justiciary Court, Quarter-Seal, 'and Seals of Courts now used in *Scotland* be 'continued, But that the said Seals be altered 'and adapted to the State of the Union, as 'Her Majesty shall think fit, and the said 'Seals, and all of them, and the Keepers of 'them, shall be subject to such Regulations as 'the Parliament of *Great Britain* shall here'after make And that the Crown, Scepter, 'and Sword of State, the Records of Parlia'ment, and all other Records, Rolls and Re'gisters whatsoever, both Publick and Private, 'General and Particular, and Warrants thereof, 'continue to be kept as they are within that 'part of the United Kingdom now called '*Scotland*, and that they shall so remain in all 'time coming, notwithstanding the Union

—except in Matters which concern each Kingdom separately

Crown, &c to be kept in *Scotland* as at present

ARTICLE XXV

All Laws, contrary to these Articles, to be void

'That all Laws and Statutes in either King'dom, so far as they are contrary to, or in'consistent with the Terms of these Articles, 'or any of them, shall, from and after the 'Union, cease and become void, and shall be 'so declared to be, by the respective Parlia'ments of the said Kingdoms

Thus, was compleated a Work of equal *Difficulty* and *Importance*, viz the *perpetual Union* of England and Scotland, in the same *Prince*, the same *Parliament*, the same Name of *Great Britain*, and the same Privileges of *Trade* and *Commerce*

The Union made more *entire*, by several Acts since

Since which time, several Acts have been made by the Parliament of *Great Britain*, to render the Union of the two Kingdoms more *entire* and *complete* By one of those Acts, it is provided, That there shall be but one Privy Council for the Kingdom of *Great Britain*; and, That Justices of Peace shall be appointed in *North Britain*, with the addition of all Powers used and practised by those in *South Britain* And by another, That the Laws relating to *Treason*, and *Misprision of Treason*, and the *Trial* thereof, in the two United Kingdoms, shall be the very same

Stat 6 Ann' c 6

Stat 7 Ann' c 21

May the God of Peace and Concord prosper and establish this happy Union, and also improve it more and more, as shall be most for his Glory, the Honour of our Gracious Sovereign, and the Strength and Interest of this most potent and flourishing Island]

SCOTLAND,

[O R,

NORTH-BRITAIN.]

THE

GENERAL HEADS

IN

SCOTLAND,

[OR,

NORTH-BRITAIN.]

The General Heads in SCOTLAND.

SCOTLAND.

N*OW I am bound for* SCOTLAND, *whither I go with a willing mind: but I ſhall paſs it over lightly, and with gentle touches; not forgetting that ſaying,* Minus notis minus diu inſiſtendum, *the leſs we know things, the leſs we are to dwell upon them, and that advice of the* Grecian, Ξένος ὢν, ἀπράγμων ἴσθι, Be not too buſie, where thou art not acquainted. *For it would be great imprudence, to pretend to ſpeak copiouſly, where our notices have been but few But ſince this* Country *is alſo honour'd with the name of* BRITAIN, *I will take the liberty, with all due reſpect to the* Scottiſh Nation, *in purſuance of my bold Deſign of illuſtrating* BRITAIN, *to proſecute that Undertaking; and, drawing aſide the* Veil *of dark Antiquity, to point out, as far as I am able, the Places of ancient note For this, I aſſure my ſelf of pardon, both from the good nature of the People themſelves, and in regard of the extraordinary Happineſs of* [a] *our* Times, *when, by divine Providence,* That *is* *fallen into our hands, which we durſt hardly hope for, and which our* Anceſtors *ſo often and ſo earneſtly wiſh'd to ſee; namely, That* BRITAIN, *which for ſo many Ages had been divided in it ſelf, and been a kind of* unſociable *Iſland, ſhould (like one uniform City,) be joined in one entire Body, under* [b] *one moſt* Auguſt Monarch, *the founder of an* ever-laſting Peace. *Who, being through the propitious goodneſs of Almighty God,* appointed, *and* born, *and* preſerved, *for the common good of both Nations, and a prince of ſingular wiſdom,*

[a] So ſaid, ann. 1607.

[b] K. James, the 6th of Scotland, and firſt of England

singular wisdom, and fatherly affection to all his Subjects; [a] *did so cut off all occasions of fear, hope, revenge, and complaint, that the fatal* Discord, *which* [b] *had so long engaged these* Nations, *otherwise invincible, in mutual Wars,* [c] *was now stifled, and suppressed for ever;* and Concord *exceedingly* [d] *rejoiced, and even* [e] *Triumph'd; because, as the Poet sings,*

[a] doth, C
[b] hath, C
[c] is, C.
[d] rejoyces, C
[e] Triumphs, C.

Jam cuncti Gens una sumus,
Now all one Nation, we're united fast.

To which we answer by way of Chorus,

Et simus in ævum.
And may that Union *for ever last.*

But before I enter upon Scotland, *I think it not amiss to advertise the Reader, that I leave the first Original of the* Scottish *Nation, and the Etymology of the Name (discarding all* Conjectures *of others, which, as well in former Ages as in these our days, have ow'd their birth either to Credulity, or Supineness) to be discussed by their own Historians, and the Learned of that Nation. And, following the same method that I took in* England, *I shall first say something in short touching* [Scotland *in general, with*] *the* Division of it; *as also of the* States of the Kingdom, *and the* Courts of Justice; *and shall then briefly touch upon the Situation and Commodities of every particular County; shewing, which are the Places of greatest Note, and what Families are most eminent, and have flourish'd with the title and honour of* [Dukes,] Earls, [Viscounts,] *and* Barons of Parliament, *so far as by reading and enquiry I could possibly procure information. And this I shall do very cautiously, taking all imaginable care, by an ingenuous and sincere regard to truth, not to give the least offence to the most Censorious and Critical; and, by a compendious brevity, not to prevent the curious diligence of those, who may possibly attempt all this in a more full, polite, and elegant way.*

OF

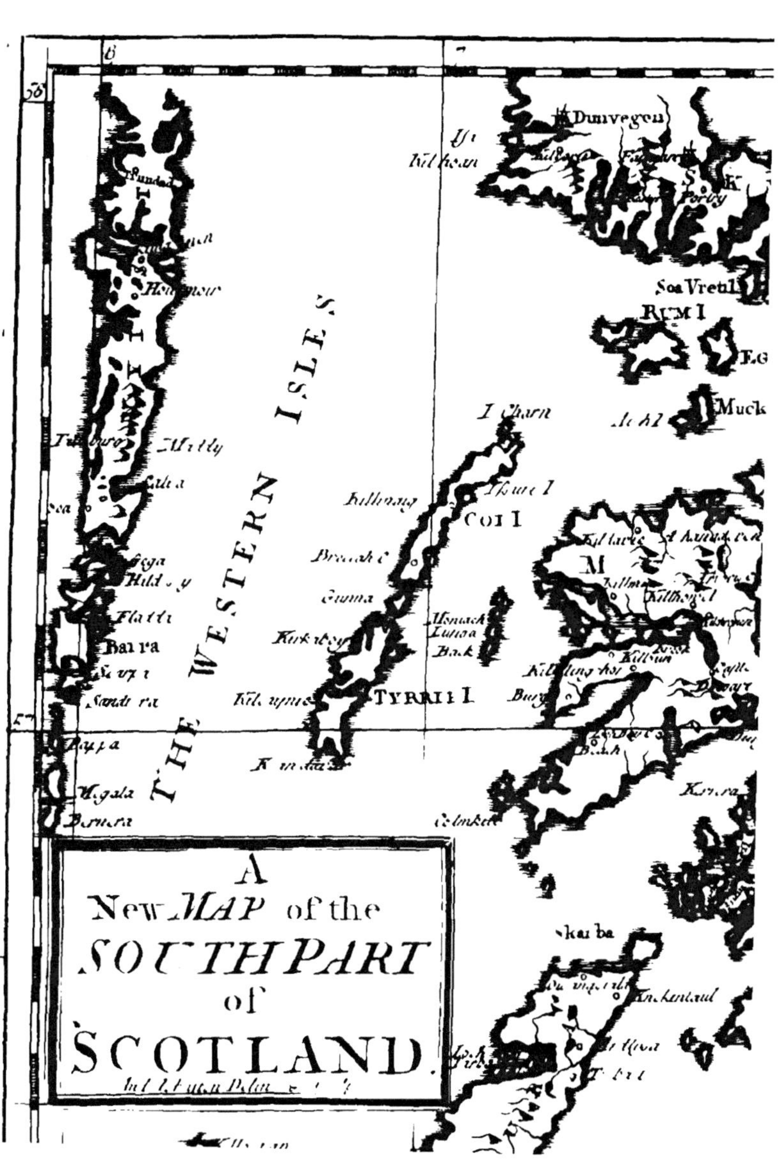
A
New MAP of the
SOUTH PART
of
SCOTLAND.
THE WESTERN ISLES
Dunvegen
Barra
COL I
TYRRII I
Muck
Soa Vretil
Skarba

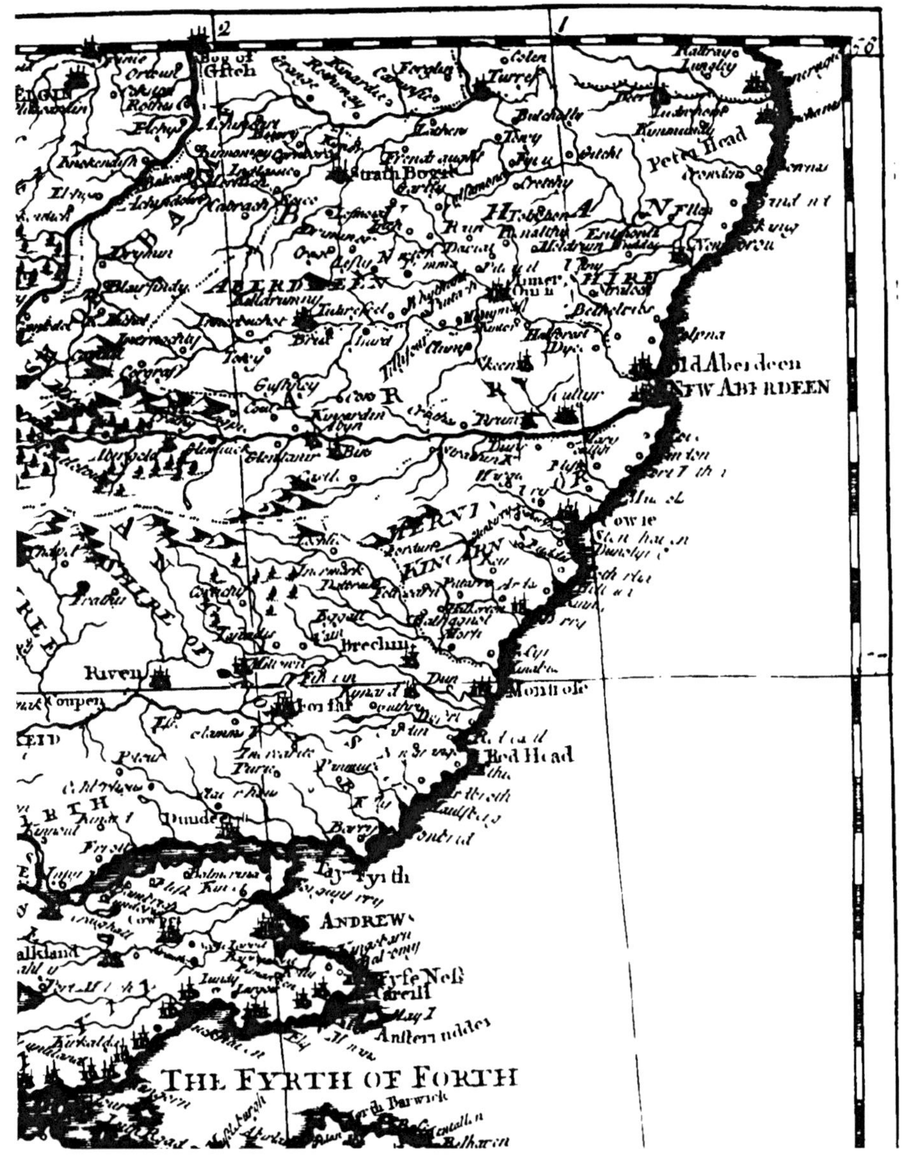

Bog of Gitch
Turreff
Strath Bogie
Peter Head
ABERDEEN
Old Aberdeen
NEW ABERDEEN
KINCARDIN
Brechin
Riven
Montrose
Red Head
Dundee
Tay Fyrth
ANDREWS
Fyfe Ness
Anstermddes
THE FYRTH OF FORTH
North Barwick

Collansa
Orvonlà
Coleraine
Londonderry
PART OF IRELAND

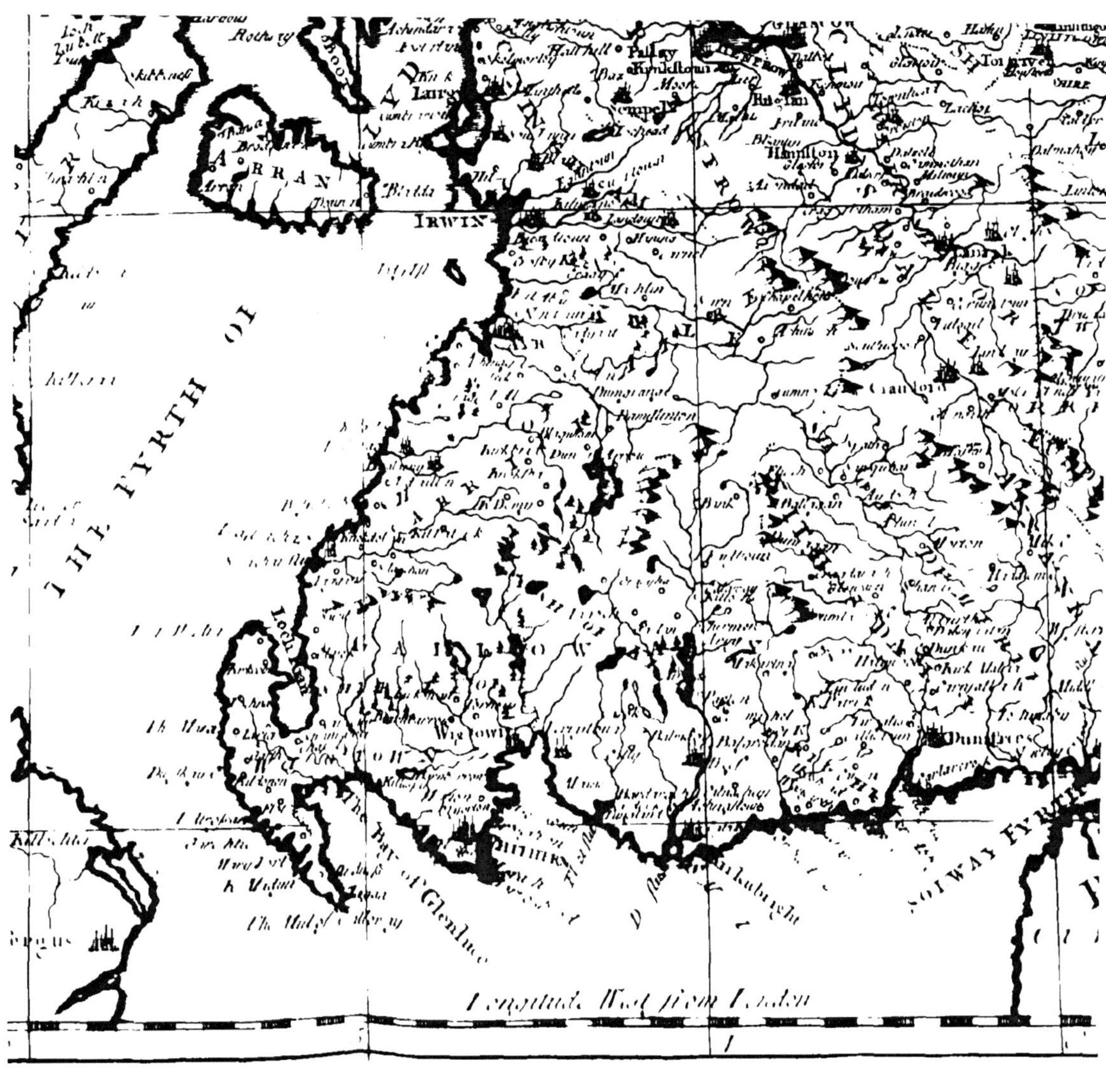

ARRAN
IRWIN
THE FYRTH OF
Paisley
Hamilton
Craufurd
Wigtown
Dumfries
Loch Ryan
The Bay of Glenluce
SOLWAY FYRTH
Longitude West from London

Broxmouth
Coldingham
BARWICK
The Staple
PART OF
CARLILE
DURHAM

OF SCOTLAND, in general.

Albania

S *Albion* was the first and most ancient name of *Great Britain*, that we meet with in the Greek and Latin Authors, so was *Albania*, of that northern part, which lay beyond the *Humber* and the *Deva* Learned men have delivered various reasons, why it should be so call'd, but the most probable of them is, from the ancient Inhabitants calling themselves *Albanich*, who likewise call'd their Country, *Albin*, and their posterity, the *High landers*, do still retain the name in a part of their Country call'd *Braid-Albin*

This Country, which, till our late Union, was known under the name of the Kingdom of *Scotland*, is divided from England by the Water of Tweed, to *Carboom*, then by *Keddon-burn*, *Haddon-rigg*, *Black down-hill*, *Morsla-hill*, *Battinbush hill*, to the risings of the rivers *Keal* and *Ted*, after, by *Kersop burn*, *Lider-water*, *Esk*, to the *Tod hills*, the *Marchdike*, to *White-sack* and *Solloway frith* On the west, it hath the *Irish Sea*, on the north, the *Deucaledon an*, and on the east, the *German* Ocean On all which sides bordering upon the Sea, it hath several Isles belonging to it

From the Mule of *Galloway* in the south, to *Dungsbay head* in the east point of *Cathness* in the north, it is about two hundred and fifty miles long, and betwixt *Buchan ness* on the east sea, and *Ardnamurcham*-point on the west, one hundred and fifty miles broad The most southerly part of it, about *Whitern*, is fifty four degrees, fifty four minutes in Latitude, and in Longitude, fifteen degrees, forty minutes The northermost part, the above mentioned *Dungsbay head*, is fifty eight degrees, thirty two (some say thirty) minutes in Latitude, and seventeen degrees, fifty minutes in Longitude The longest day is about eighteen hours and two minutes, and the shortest night five hours and forty five minutes

The air temperate

It was not without reason, that Cæsar said of Britain, *Cælum Gallico temperatius*, i e a Climate more temperate than that of Gaule, for even in North Britain, the Air is more mild and temperate than in the Continent under the same Climate, by reason of the warm vapours from the sea upon all sides, and the continual breezes of the wind from thence The heat in Summer is no way scorching The constant winds purifie the air and keep it always in motion, so that there is seldom any Epidemick disease rages here

Hills in Scotland

The nature of the Country is for the most part hilly and mountainous, there being but few plains, and they of no great extent Those they have, are generally by the Sea-side, and from thence the ground begins to rise sensibly, the farther in the Country the higher so that, the greatest hills are in the middle of the Kingdom These hills, especially upon the Skirts of the Country, breed abundance of Cows, which not only afford store of butter and cheese to the Inhabitants, but likewise considerable profit by the vent of their hides and tallow, and the great numbers that are sold in South Britain The size of these (as also of their *sheep*) is but small, but the meat of both is of an exceeding fine taste, and very nourishing The High-Lands afford great Flocks of *Goats*, with store of Deer, and are cleared from *Wolves* The whole Country has good store and variety of fowl, both tame and wild

Quality of the Soil

The Quality of the soil, compared in general with that of South Britain, is not near so good It is commonly more fit for pasture, and is very well watered for that purpose Where the surface is leanest, there are found Metals, and Minerals, and considerable quantities of Lead are exported yearly there is also good Copper, but they will not be at the pains to work it But in much of the in land Country, especially where it lyeth upon some of the *Friths*, the soil is very good, and there, all sorts of grain do grow, that are usual in the South parts of Britain The *Wheat* is frequently exported by Merchants to Spain, Holland, and Norway *Barley* grows plentifully, and their *Oats* are extreme good, affording bread of a clean and wholsom nourishment In the Low grounds they have store of *Pease* and *Beans*, which, for the strength of their feeding, are much used by the labouring-People In the skirts of the Country, which are not so fit for Grain there grow great Woods of Timber, to a vast bigness, especially *Fir Trees*, which are found to thrive best in stony grounds

Springs of *Mineral* waters (which the people find useful in several Diseases,) are common enough No Country is better provided with Fish Besides flocks of smaller Whales, with the *Porpess*, and the Meerswine, frequently cast in; great *Whales* of the *Baleen* or *Whale bone* kind, and of the *Sperma Ceti* kind, are cast now and then upon several parts of the shore.

Besides the grain and other commodities already named, the Merchants export alabaster, linnen, and woollen cloath, freezes, plaids, plaiding, stuff, stockings, malt and meal, skins of rabbets, hares, *&c* fishes, eggs, oker, marble, coal, and salt

Christianity early in North Britain The Christian Religion was very early planted here; for Tertullian's words, *Britannorum inaccessa Romanis loca*, Christo *verò subdita*, i e Places in Britain, inaccessible to the Romans, but subdu'd by *Christ*, must be understood of the north part of the Island, possessed by the Scots, and separated by a wall from that part which was subject to the Romans The Religion of the Kingdom established by Law, is that which is contained in the *Confession of Faith*, authoriz'd in the first Parliament of King James the sixth, and defined in the nineteenth Article of the said *Confession*, to be *That* which is contained in the written word of God

For the promotion of Learning, they have four Universities, St. *Andrews*, *Glasgow*, *Aberdeen*, and *Edenburgh*; wherein are Professors of most of the Liberal Arts, endowed with competent Salaries. Learning in North Britain

THE

THE DIVISION OF SCOTLAND.

ALL the North part of the Island of *Britain*, was anciently inhabited by the Picts, who were divided into two Nations, the *Dicalidonii* and *Vecturiones*, of whom I have spoken already, out of *Ammianus Marcellinus*. But when the Scots had got possession of this Tract, it was shared into seven parts, among seven Princes, as we have it in a little ancient Book *Of the Division of Scotland*, in these words

> The first part contained *Enegus* and *Maern*.
> The second, *Atheodl* and *Goverin*,
> The third, *Stradeern* with *Meneted*
> The fourth was *Forthever*
> The fifth, *Mar* with *Buchen*
> The sixth, *Muref* and *Ross*
> The seventh, *Cathness*, parted in the middle by the *Mound*, a mountain which runs from the Western to the Eastern Sea

After that, the same Author reports, from the Relation of Andrew Bishop of Cathness, that the whole Kingdom was divided likewise into seven Territories

> The first from *Fryth* (so termed by the *Britains*; by the Romans *Werid*, now *Scottwade*,) to the River *Tae*
> The second, from *Hilef*, as the Sea fetches a reach, to a mountain in the North-east part of *Sterling*, named *Athran*
> The third, from *Hilef* to *Dee*
> The fourth, from *Dee* to the River *Spe*
> The fifth, from *Spe* to the Mountain *Brunalban*
> The sixth, *Mures* and *Ross*
> The seventh the Kingdom of *Argathel*
> This is as it were the *Border* of the Scots, who were so called from *Gathelgas* their Captain

With respect to the [a] *manners* and *customs* of the People, it is divided into the *High-land men* and *Low-land men*. These are more civilized, and use the language and habit of the English, the other, more rude and barbarous, and use that of the Irish, as I have already mentioned, and shall more largely hereafter observe. Out of this Division I exclude the *Borderers*, because they, by the blessed and happy [b] Union, enjoying the *Sun-shine* of peace on every side, are to be look'd on as living in the very midst of the British Empire, and (being sufficiently tir'd with war) [c] begin to grow acquainted with, and to have an inclination to Peace

[a] *Habitudo*. *High-land-men*. *Low land-men*. *Borderers*.
[b] Of King *James* the first.
[c] So said, ann 1607.

With respect to the situation of the Places, the whole Kingdom is again divided into two parts, the *Southern*, on this side the river Tay, and the *Northern*, beyond the River Tay, besides a great many Islands lying round. In the South part, these Countries are most remarkable

Teifidale
Merch
Lauden
Liddesdale
Eskdale
Annandale
Niddesdale
Galloway
Carrick
Kyle
Cunningham
Arran
Cluydesdale
Lenox
Stirling
Fife
Stratbern
Menteith
Argile
Cantire
Lorn

In

In the North part, are reckon'd these Countries

Loquabar
Braidalbin
Perth
Athol
Angus
Mern
Marr
Buquhan
Murray
Ross
Sutherland
Cathness
Strathnavern

These are subdivided again, with respect to the Civil Government, into *Sheriffdoms, Stewarties, and Bailliaries*

[a] The Sheriffdoms are,

[a] *Dugdale* (in his List of the Shires) makes them 33 reckoning the Stewarty of *Kircudbright*, as one; as also *Hadington*, *Ross*, *Stirling*, *Cathness*, and *Sutherland*, and leaving out *Forres*, which is reckon'd one here

Edenburgh
Linlithquo
Selkirk
Roxburgh
Peeblis
Berwick
Lanerick
Renfrew
Dumfreis
Wigton
Aire
Bute
Argyle and
Tarbet
Dunbarton
Perth
Clackmannan
Kinross
Fiffe
Kincardin
Forfar
Aberdene
Bamff
Elgin
Forres
Narne
Innerness
Cromartie
Orknay and
Shetland

Stewarties

Menteith
Strathern
[b] *Kircudbright*
Annandale
Orkney
Falkland

[b] This contains the East part of *Galloway*

Bailliaries

Kile
Carrick
Cunningham
Lauderdale

Constablery.

Haddington

Besides these Divisions, there are four other taken from the *Rivers*, the *Mountains*, the quality of the *Soil*, and the ancient *Inhabitants*

1 The Rivers divide it by three *Isthmus's*, into so many Peninsula's, one to the south, one in the middle, and one to the north The rivers on each side running far into the Country, are hinder'd from meeting, by a small tract of ground; and if that were removed, they would make three Islands of that which is now the Continent or main-land of North-Britain.

1 Peninsul

The first Peninsula is to the south, divided from South Britain by the river of *Tweed*, and where it faileth, by a line drawn to *Solloway-Frith*, which reacheth far up into the adjacent country, and towards the north, from the rest of the continent by the *Firth*, and river of *Forth*, and a short line over land to *Clide*, by which, and its Firth, it is separated from the north-west part, and the rest of the continent. This comprehendeth the following Counties, *Merse*, *Teviotdale*, *Forrest*, and *Etterick*, *Annandale*, and *Nithisdale*, *East-Lothian*, *Mid-Lothian*, and *West Lothian*, *Lauderdale*, *Tweedale*, *Stirling shire*, *Renfrew*, *Cliddisdale*, *Cunningham*, *Kyle*, and *Carrict*, *Galloway*, which containeth the Stewarty of *Kircudbright*, and Shire of *Wigton*

2 Peninsula

The middle Peninsula hath to the south, the *Firth* and river of *Forth*, and the line betwixt it and the river and Firth of *Clide*, to the west and east, the ocean, and to the north, it is separated from the rest of the continent of Scotland, by the *Loch* and water of *Lochly*, and a line through a short neck of land to the rise of *Loch Nesse*, and then by the *Loch* and river of *Ness* to the place where that River runneth into the sea, it containeth these Counties, *Fyfe*, *Kinrossshire*, *Clackmannanshire*, *Menteith*, *Lennox*, *Argyle*, *Lorn*, *Cantyre*, *Perthshire*, *Angus*, *Mernes*, *Aberdeenshire*, *Bamf-shire*, all *Badenoth*, part of *Lochaber*, and much of the Shire of *Inverness*

3 Peninsula

The northern Peninsula hath, to the south, the *Loch* and water of *Lochly*, and a short line from thence to *Lochness* and the water of *Ness*, and to the west, north, and east, it hath the Ocean, and containeth these Counties, *Ross*, *Sutherland*, *Strathnavern*, and *Cathness*, and that part of *Lochaber*, and *Inverness-shire*, that lyeth to the north of the *Loch*, and water of *Ness*

Grantzbain hills

2 It is divided by the *mons Grampius*, or the *Grantzbain hills*, which run through it from the west to the east, rising near *Dumbarton*, and running to the town of Aberdeen, into the south and north parts; tho' this division is not so equal as the former

High-lands and Low-lands

3 By the quality of the soil, it is divided into the *High-lands* and *Low-lands*, For the people who affected pasture and hunting, betook themselves always to the hills, as most proper for them, and were of old called *Brigantes*, *Scoto-Brigantes*, and *Horesti*, ὀρεσαι, that is *Highlanders* and *Braemen*, as they are called to this day And the rest, who gave themselves to the culture of the lands, and affected more of a civil life, betook themselves to the low grounds, towards the sea, and were called of old *Picts* and *Meatæ*, *Vecturiones*, and *Peahts* and by some of the Roman writers *Caledonii*; while those who did inhabit the mountains, were called *Dicaledones*, and as some read it *Duncaledones* In others of the Romans, the word *Caledonia* comprehendeth the Country possessed by both

4 It was divided into the two Kingdoms of the *Scots* and *Picts* The *Scots* were possessed of all the Western-Isles, and the skirts of the Country towards the west the *Picts* had all

that which lay upon the German Ocean The Romans breaking in upon them, gain'd a large tract, which contain'd all the ground between the two *Walls*; and which they erected into a Province called *Valentia*

The particular Shires, with their extent, are as follows,

Shires and their Extent

The Shire of	Contains
Edenburgh	Midlothian,
Mers	Mers and Lauderdale
Peebles	Tweedale
Selkirk	Etterick and Forrest
Roxburgh	Teviotdale, Liddisdale, Eskdale and Eusdale
Dumfries	Nithisdale and Annandale,
Wigton	The west part of Galloway
Aire	Kyle, Carrict, and Cunningham
Renfrew	The Barony of Renfrew
Lanerick	Cledsdale
Dumbron	Lenox
Bute	The Isles of Bute and Arran
Innerara	Argyle, Lorn, Kintyre, most part of the west Isle, as Ila, Jura, Mul, Wyst, Terrii, Col, Lismore
Perth	Menteith, Strathern, Balwhidder, Glenurghay, Stormont, Athol, Gource, Glenshee, Strattardill, Braid-Albin, Raynock
Striveling	Much of the ground that lyeth close upon both sides of Forth
Linlithgow	West-Lothian
Kinros	That part of Fyfe lying between Lochleven and the Ochill hills
Clackmannan	A small part of Fyfe lying on the river of Forth towards Strvelling
Couper	The rest of Fife to the east of Lochleven
Forfar	Angus with its pertinents, *Glen Ila*, *Glen Esk*, *Glen prossin*
Kinkardin	The Mernis
Aberdeen	Mar with its pertinents, as Birs, Glen-Tanner, Glen-Muick, Strath-dee, Strathdon, Brae of Mar and Cromar, and most part of Buchan, Fourmartin, Gareock, and Strath-Bogie-Land
Bamff	A small part of Buchan, Strath-dovern, Boyn, Finzie, Strath Awin, and Balvenie
Elgin	The East part of Murray
Nairn	The West part of Murray
Inverness	Badenoch, Lochabir, and the South part of Ross
Cromartie	A small part of Ross, lying on the South side of Cromartie-Frith
Tayn	The rest of Ross, with the Isles of Sky, Lewis, and Herris
Dornoch	Sutherland and Strathnavern
Wike	Cathness]

Dioceses.

Concerning the Administration of Church affairs As the rest of the Bishops of the world had no certain *Dioceses*, till Dionysius Bishop of Rome, about the year 268, set out distinct *Dioceses* for them, so the Bishops of Scotland exercised their Episcopal Functions indifferently wherever they were, till the Reign of Malcolm the third, that is, about the year of our Lord 1070 At which time, the Dioceses were confined within their respective bounds and limits Afterwards in process of time, this Hierarchy was established in Scotland There [d] were two Archbishops, of *St Andrews*, and *Glasco*, the first [e] was *Primate of all Scotland*, and [f] had under his Jurisdiction [g] nine Bishopricks

Archbishopricks and Bishopricks

[d] Are, C

[e] Is, C

[f] Hath, C,

[g] Eight C

[h] Added by K Ch I

[h] *Edinburgh*
Dunkeld
Aberdeen
Murray
Dumblane
Brechen
Ross
Cathness
Orkney

Under the Archbishop of *Glasco*, [e] were only [d] three

[d] Are C

Galloway
Lismore and
The Isles

[But to give the Reader a more distinct view of the several Dioceses, and their respective bounds, we will add the following Scheme

Diocese of	Contains
St Andrews	Part of Perthshire, and part of Angus and Mernes
Glasgow	The shires of Dunbarton, Ranfrew, Air, Lanerick, part of the shires of Roxburgh, Dumfreis, Peblees, and Selkirk
Edinburgh	The shires of Edinburgh, Linlithgow, part of Strivelingshire, Berwickshire, the Constabularie of Hadington, and Bailliary of Lauderdale
Dunkeld	The most part of *Perthshire*, part of Angus, and part of West-Lothian
Aberdeen	Most part of Bamf-shire, and part of Mernis
Murray	The shires of Elgin, Nairn, and part of Inverness and Bamf-shire
Brichin	Part of Angus and Mernis
Dumblane	Part of Perth, and Striveling-shires
Ross	The shire of Tain, Cromertie, and the greatest part of Inverness shire
Caithness	Cathness and Sutherland
Orkney	All the Northern Isles of Orkney and Zetland
Galloway	The shire of Wigton, the Stewartie of Kircudbright, the Regality of Glentrune, and part of Dumfries-shire
Argyle	Argyle, Lorn, Kintyre, and Lohabar, with some of the West Isles
The Isles	Most of the West Isles

Church Government under *Episcopacy*

Under this Constitution, the Government was thus 1 In every Parish, the cognizance of some Scandals belong'd to the *Session* (a Judicature compos'd of the greatest and worthiest persons in each Parish,) where the Minister presided, *ex officio* 2 But if the Case prov'd too intricate, it was referred to the *Presbyterie*, a superior Judicature, consisting of a certain number of Ministers, between 12 and 20, who met almost every fortnight The *Moderator* was nam'd by the Bishop, and, besides the censures which they inflicted, it was by them, that such as enter'd into Orders, were solemnly examined

Provincial Synod

3 Above this, was the *Provincial-Synod*, which met twice a year in every Diocese, and had the examination of such cases as were referred to them by the Preysbteries Here, the Bishop presided *ex officio* 4 Above all, was the *Convocation*, when the King pleas'd to call it, wherein the Archbishop of *St Andrews* presided And besides these, every Bishop, for the Causes of *Testaments*, &c had his Official or Commissary, who was judge of that Court within the Diocese Of these, *Edenburgh* had four, the rest, one

Episcopacy abolished and *Presbytery* established

Thus stood the Constitution of the Church of Scotland, in the State of *Episcopacy*, which continued till the year of our Lord 1689 But since that time, the Ecclesiastical Constitution of Scotland hath been alter'd by several Acts pass'd in the Parliament there, one, by which the Estate of Bishops, being the third Estate of Parliament, is abolished; another, by which Presbyterian Church Government is settled, and the Nobility (who consisted before, of the greater Barons or Lords, and the lesser Barons or Freeholders) are divided into *two* Estates

Under the State of *Presbyterie*, the Church Government is thus

Government under *Presbytery*

1 They also have their *Parochial Sessions*; but with this difference, that though the Minister presides, yet a Lay man (a *Bailie*) ordinarily *assists* 2 In their *Presbyteries*, they chuse their own Moderator to preside 3 They have their *Synod*, or *Provincial Assembly*, but without a constant head; for, every time they meet, they make choice of a new Moderator 4 Their *General Assembly*: this consists of two members from every Presbytery, and one Commissioner from each University The King too has his Commissioner there, without whose consent no Acts can pass, and before they are in force, they must be also ratify'd by the King

The Presbyteries, are these that follow,

Presbyteries.

Dunce
Chernside.
Kelso
Ersilton
Jedburgh
Melross
Dumbar
Hadington
Dalkeith
Edinburgh
Peebles
Linlithgow
Perth
Dunkeld
Auchterarder
Striveling
Dumblane
Dumfreis
Penpont,
Lochmabane
Midlebie
Wigton
Kircudbright
Stranraver
Aire
Irwing
Pastlay
Dumbarton
Glasgow
Hamilton
Lanerick
Biggar
Dunnune
Kinloch

Inerary

Inerary
Kilmore
Sky.
St Andrews
Kirkaldy
Cowper
Dumfermelin.
Meegle.
Dundee.
Arbroth
Forfar.
Brichen
Mernis.
Aberdeen.
Kinkardin.
Alfoord
Gareoch.
Deir

Turref
Fordyce
Ellon
Strathbogie.
Abernethie
Elgin
Forres
Aberlower
Channie
Tayn
Dingwell
Dornoch.
Week
Thurso.
Kirkwal.
Scaloway
Colmkill]

THE

THE States or Degrees, OF SCOTLAND.

THE Government of the Scots, as that of the English, consists of a *King*, *Nobility*, and *Commonalty*

King

The King (to use the words of their own Records) is, *directus totius Dominii Dominus*, direct Lord of the whole Dominion or Domain, and hath Royal Authority and Jurisdiction over all the States of his Kingdom, as well Ecclesiastick, as Laick Next to the King, is his Eldest Son, stiled *Prince of Scotland*, and by birth Duke of *Rothsay*, and Steward of *Scotland* But the rest of the Kings Children are called simply, *Princes*

Thanes

Among the *Nobles*, the greatest and most honourable in old Times, were the *Thanes*, that is (if I judge aright) those who were ennobled only by the office they bore, for the word in the ancient Saxon signifies *The King's Minister* Of these, they of the higher rank were called *Ab thanes*, they of the lower, *Under Thanes* But these Names by little and little have grown out of use, ever since King Malcolm the third conferred the Titles of *Earls* and *Barons* (borrow'd out of England from the Normans) upon such Noblemen as had merited them Since when, in process of time, new Titles of Honour have been much taken up, and Scotland, as well as England, hath *Dukes*, *Marquisses*, *Earls*, *Viscounts*, and *Barons* As for the Title of *Duke*, the first who brought in into Scotland was *Robert* the Third, about the year of our Lord 1400, as the honourable titles of *Marquiss* and *Viscount*, were [a] lately brought in by our most gracious Sovereign, King *James* the sixth These are accounted Nobles of a *higher* degree, and have [b] place and Voice in *Parliament*, and by special right are called *Lords*, [c] as the Bishops also were

Dukes Marquisses Earls, Viscount, Baron

Amongst the Nobles of a *lower* degree, in the first place are *Knights*, who are certainly created with greater Solemnity here, than any where else in Europe, by taking of an Oath, and being proclaimed publickly by the Heralds [In the year 1621 was instituted the hereditary Order of *Knights Baronet*, for advancing the plantation of *Nova Scotia* in America, with precedency of all ordinary Knights, lesser Barons or Lairds, of which Order there is a great number, but the ancient great Lairds, Chiefs of Clans or Families, have not generally yielded precedency to them] In the second rank, are those who are called *Lairds*, and commonly without any addition *Barons*, amongst whom none were anciently reckon'd, but such as held *Lands* immediately of the King *in Capite*, and had the [d] *Jus Furcarum* In the third place, are such as being descended of Honourable Families, and dignify'd with no certain title, are term'd *Gentlemen* All the rest, as *Citizens*, *Merchants*, *Artificers*, &c are reckon'd among the Commonalty

[a] So said ann [illegible]

[b] In person, or by proxy [illegible] since [illegible] on

[c] Together with the B. [illegible]

Knights

Knights Baronet

Lairds

[d] Power to hang

Gentlemen

Commonalty

THE

THE JUDICATORIES, OR COURTS of Justice.

The Parliament

b Now made one with the Parliament of England by the Union [illegible] in whom this and the next Paragraph run in the present tense

c So said, ann 1607

d Deputes

THE [a] Supreme Court, as well in dignity as authority, [b] was the *Assembly of the States of the Kingdom*, which was called a *Parliament*, by the same name as it is in England, and had the same absolute Authority It consisted of three Estates, of the *Lords Spiritual*, that is, the Bishops, Abbots, and Priors, of the *Lords Temporal*, viz Dukes, Marquisses, Earls, Viscounts, and Barons; and the *Commissioners for the Cities and Boroughs* To whom where joined, [c] not long since, for every County, two [d] *Commissioners*, [and in the reign of King William the third, by act of Parliament, certain Shires, and the Stewartie of *Kirkcudbright*, were allowed an *additional* Representation of Commissioners in Parliament, whereby, of the greater Shires, some were allow'd four, some three, according to the *largeness* and *extent* of the Lands]

It was called by the King at pleasure, allowing a certain time for notice before it was to sit When they were convened, and the causes of their meeting were declar'd by the King and the Chancellour, the Lords Spiritual retired apart, and chose eight of the Lords Temporal, and the Lords Temporal, likewise, as many out of the Lords Spiritual Then, all these together nominated eight of the Knights of the Shires, and as many of the Burgesses, which, in all made thirty two, and were called *Lords of the Articles*, and, with the *Chancellour*, *Treasurer*, *Privy-Seal*, the *King's Secretary*, &c admitted or rejected such matters as were offer'd to be propos'd to the *States*, after they had been first communicated to the King Being approved by the whole Assembly of the *States* they were throughly examined, and such as pass'd by a majority of Votes, were presented to the King, who by touching them with his Scepter signified the confirming or vacating of them But if the King disliked any thing, it was first rized out

[This was the ancient method of proposing and finishing the Affairs of Parliament, but in the reign of William the third, the Committee of Parliament was abrogated by a particular Law, and the Parliament was empower'd to appoint Committees of what number they pleas'd, and equally of Noblemen, Barons, or Burgesses, to be chosen out of each Estate by it self, for preparing all motions and overtures first made in the House, with a power in the Parliament to alter the Committees so appointed, and (if they thought fit) to conclude such Business as should be proposed, without appointing any Committees]

The College of Justice

a Takes, C

b Think, C

Next to the Parliament (which is now made one with the Parliament of England,) is the *College of Justice*, or, as they call it, the *Session*, which King James the fifth instituted, *An* 1532 after the manner of the *Parliament* at *Paris*, consisting of a *President*, *fourteen Senators*, seven of the *Clergy*, and as many of the *Laity* (to whom was afterwards added the *Chancellor*, who [a] took place first, and three or four other [a] *Senators*,) with three *principal Clerks*, and as many *Advocates* as the Senators [b] thought convenient [Thus stood the *Session* in its original Institution, but now, the distinction of half *Spiritual*, half *Temporal*, is laid aside, and the Lords are all of the Temporalty, and in the reign of King James the seventh, an Act of Parliament pass'd, allowing two persons to be conjoined in each of the three Offices of Ordinary Clerks of Session, so that now there are six Clerks The proper Title of those who compose the Session, is *Lord*, and by an Act of Parliament in the year 1661 the President is declared to have Precedency of the Lord Register and Advocate]

The Session administers justice (not according to the Rigour of the Law, but according to reason and equity) every day except Sunday and Monday, [anciently] from the first of November to the fifteenth of March, and from Trinity Sunday to the first of August [But as Law and Custom have now settled it, the *Session* sitteth from the first of November to the last of February (the *Yule Vacance* excepted, viz from c ... 10 Dec 20 to Jan 10) and from the first of June Ann c 13 to the last of July inclusive] All the space between, as being the times of sowing and harvest, is *Vacation*, or an Intermission of Suits and Matters of Law They give judgment according to Act of Parliament [and the Municipal Laws,] and where they are defective, according to the Civil Law

The Inferiour Courts

There are besides in every County, inferiour *Civil Courts*, wherein the Sheriff or his deputy decides controversies amongst the Inhabitants, about Ejectments, Intrusions, Damages, Debts, *&c* from whom, upon suspicion of hardship, partiality or alliance, they appeal sometimes to the *Session* These Sheriffs are for the most part hereditary For the Kings of Scotland as well as England, to bind the better sort of Gentlemen more closely to them by their favours, did in old time make their *Sheriffs* hereditary and perpetual But the Kings of England, soon perceiving the inconveniences happening thereupon, changed them into annual There are Civil Courts held also in the several Regalities, by their respective Baillies, to whom the King graciously granted Royal privileges; as they are also held in free Boroughs and Cities, by their Magistrates.

Commissariat

There are likewise Judicatories, that are called *The Commissariat* the highest of which is kept at *Edenborough* wherein, before four Judges, Actions are pleaded concerning matters which relate to Wills, Advowsons, Tythes, Divorces, *&c* and other Ecclesiastical Causes of like nature But in almost all the other parts of the Kingdom, there sits but one Judge on these Causes

Court at *Edenborough* g Hath for some time, been, C

In Criminal Causes, the King's Chief Justice holds his Courts generally at *Edenborough*; which Office[g] was heretofore executed by the Earls of *Argyle*, who deputed two or three Lawyers to take cognizance of Actions of life and death, loss of limbs, or of goods and chattels [But by an Act of Parliament in the reign of King Chares the second, concerning the *Justice Court*, it is now made to consist of the Lord Justice General, and the Lord Justice Clerk (both of the King's nomination,) to whom are added five of the Lords of the Session, who are supply'd from time to time by the King, and are called Lords of the Justiciary] In this Court, the Defendant is permitted, even in case of High-Treason, to retain an Advocate to plead for him

Special Commissions

Moreover, in criminal Matters, *Justices* are sometimes appointed by the King's Commission, for deciding this or that particular cause

Stat 6 Ann c. 23

[And, since the late Union of the two Kingdoms, special Provision hath been made by Parliament, for the trying of Peers in North Britain, for Treason, Murder and Felony, by Commission under the Great Seal of *Great Britain*, and in such manner as is usual upon Indictments taken before the Justices of Oyer and Terminer in South-Britain.]

Sheriff.

Also, the Sheriffs in their territories, and Magistrates in some Boroughs, may sit in judgment of *Man-Slaughter*, in case the Man-slayer be apprehended in the space of 24 hours; and having found him guilty by a Jury, may put him to death But if that time be laps'd, the cause is referr'd to the King's Justice, or his Deputies The same privilege also some of the Nobility and Gentry enjoy against Thieves, taken within their own Jurisdictions There are those likewise, who have such Royalties, that in criminal Causes they exercise Jurisdiction within their own limits, and in some cases call those who dwell within their own Liberties, from before the King's Justice; with this proviso, that they judge according to *Law*

Pomponius Mela

h K James I

These Matters (as having had but a transient view of them) I have just touched upon *What manner of Country* Scotland *is, and what Men it breeds* (as of old that excellent Geographer writ of Britain) *will in a little time more* certainly *and* evidently *be shown, since the*[h] *greatest of Princes hath opened a passage to it, which had been so long shut up* In the mean time, I will proceed to the *Places*, which is a subject that I am more immediately concern'd in

GADENI

GADENI or LADENI.

UPON *the* Ottadini, *or Northumberland, bordered the* ΓΑΔΕΝΟΙ (Gadeni) *who, by the turning of one letter upside down, are called in some Copies of Ptolemy* Laden, *and were seated in the Country lying between the mouth of the River* Tweed *and* Edenborough-Frith, *which is now cantoned into many smaller Countries The principal of them are* Teifidale, Twedale, Merch, *and* Lothien, *in Latin* Lodenium *under which general name the Writers of the middle age comprised them all* Joh Skene, *de verborum significatione*

[*But yet we must observe, that it is a point not universally agreed on, that the People inhabiting those four Counties were called* Gadeni *and* Ladeni *For some are of opinion, that they are no other than those call'd (according to different Copies)* Ottadini, Ottadeni, *and* Ottalini, *and by that learned Gentleman* Drummond, *of* Hawthernden, Scottedeni; *upon a supposition that the initial letters* Sc *were probably either quite gone, or so obscur'd as not to be legible; by which means the Transcribers might be drawn into an error However, that they are to be carried farther Northward than* Northumberland *(to which they have been hitherto confin'd) is plain from* Ptolemy's *fixing that* Curia *(the place remarkable amongst them) in the fifty ninth degree of Latitude And in a village in* Mid Lothian *call'd* Cutrie, *there seem to be plain Remains of the old* Curia, *as there are of the* Ottadeni, Scottedeni, &c *in* Caer Eden, *now called* Carriden, *in* West Lothian, *where was found a Medal of* Titus Vespasian *in gold, with some Roman Urns, and a Stone with the Head of an Eagle engraven upon it* Dun-Eden *also, the ancient Name of* Edenburgh, *seems to point out to us that ancient People, and to prove that their bounds extended as far as the Water of* Eden, *called yet by some* Eden-water *About the mouth whereof, at a place call'd* Inner-Even, *are yet to be seen some remains of ancient buildings*]

TEIFIDALE.

T*Eifidale*, that is to say, the Valley or Dale by the River *Tesy* or *Teviot*, [(which divides that part properly called *Teviotdale*, into north and south)] lies next to England, amongst cliffs of craggy hills and rocks It is inhabited by a [a] warlike people, who by reason of the frequent encounters between the Scots and English in former ages, [b] were always very ready for service and sudden invasions

[a] So said, ann 1607
[b] Are, C

[It comprehends under it *Ladesdale*, *Eusdale*, and *Eskdale*; and is in length, from Reddenburn on the east to Annandale on the west, about thirty miles, and in breadth, from the border to the blue *Cairn* in *Lawdermoor*, about fourteen or fifteen It is a good soil, extraordinary well mix'd with Grass and Corn, and water'd with several rivulets which run into *Tiot* and *Tweed* The Vallies abound with Corn, short of few Shires in North Britain for the goodness of the grain; so that great quantities of it are frequently transported into South Britain Free stone and Lime they have in great abundance The high grounds are furnish'd with excellent grass and produce great store of cattel of all kinds, and of the best broods in Scotland, both for largeness and goodness Nor does this County want it's remains of Roman Antiquity for here are some footsteps of their Encampments, and a military way runs from *Hounam* to *Tweed*, call'd the *Roman Causey*, and by the vulgar, the *Rugged Causey*.

The *Mountains* most eminent in it, are *Cokraw*, from which there runs a tract of hills westward, dividing Scotland from England, and it is passable only at some places There is another tract of hills going from *Harewell*, which run along to *Craucross*, being twelve miles, and in the body of the Shire, are *Rucburgh Law*, *Mynto-hill*, and *Hadington hills*

They have the Regalities of *Jedburgh forest* belonging to the Duke of Douglas, the Regality of *Hawick*, belonging to Buccleugh; and the Regality of *Melross*, in the person of the Earl of Hadington Regalities

The Sheriffdom (for it is governed by a *Sheriff*) is in a branch of the House of *Douglas*, who are *hereditary* Sheriffs They have also three Presbyteries, *Jedburgh*, *Kelso*, and *Melross*]

The first place we meet with, is *Jedburgh*, a Borough pretty well inhabited and frequented, standing near the confluence of the *Tesy* and *Jed*, Jedburgh.

from

from whence it takes its name, [as it gives title to the Laird of *Fernherst* of the Family of *Ker*, created by King James the sixth Lord *Jedburgh*, which Peerage was resigned in favour of William Lord Newbottle, eldest Son to the then Earl, since Marquis of Lothian, so that (what is peculiar to the Marquis of Lothian's family) both the Father and Son are *Peers* Not far from whence, is *Ancrum*, honour'd, in the reign of K Charles the first, by giving the title of Earl to Sir *Robert Ker*, of the Family of *Fernherst*; of whom the Earl of *Lothian* is descended; as *Teviot* was also dignify'd by giving the title of Earl to Lieutenant General *Thomas Rotherford*, in the reign of King Charles the second, who had before been advanced by the said Prince to the title of Lord Rutherford, with the remarkable Privilege of *assigning* that honour to whomsoever he should name at his death, which he accordingly devised by Will to *Thomas Rotherford* of Hunthill Afterwards in the reign of King James the seventh, *Teviot* gave the title of Viscount to Robert Lord Spencer, eldest Son of Robert Earl of Sunderland, in England, and, after that, to Sir Thomas Levingstoun, in the reign of King William the third]

Ancrum

Teviot

Mailros

Then, *Mailros*, a very ancient Monastery, where, in the infancy of the Church, were Monks of that ancient institution, who gave themselves to prayer, and earn'd their living with the labour of their hands, [which holy King David restor'd and replenish'd with *Cistercian* Monks] More Eastward, where the *Twede* and the *Tefy* join, is *Roxburgh*, called also *Roxburgh*, and in antient times *Marchidun*, from its being seated in the *Marches*, where stands a Castle, that by its natural situation, and tower'd fortifications, was in times past exceeding strong Which being surpriz'd and held by the English; while King James the second of Scotland was besieging it, he was untimely slain in the flower of his age, by a piece of Cannon that casually burst; and was exceedingly lamented by all his Subjects. The Castle was surrender'd, and being mostly demolish'd, is now scarce to be seen [The Royalty also of this place is transmitted to *Jedburgh*, the chief Burgh Royal of the Shire] But the adjacent Territory (called from it *the Sheriffdom of Roxborough*) hath an hereditary Sheriff of the family of *Douglass*, who is called *the Sheriff of Teviotdale* And [c] afterwards *Roxborough*, by the favour of King James the sixth, [d] was also made a Barony, in the person of *Robert Kerr*, of the house of the *Kerrs*, a very eminent and numerous family in this tract; from which descended the *Fernhersts*, and others, who being educated in the school of *Arms*, have render'd themselves very illustrious [The said *Robert* was created, first, Lord *Ker* of *Cesford*, upon his attending K James the sixth in the year 1603, to take possession of the Crown of England, and afterwards in the year 1616 *Earl of Roxburgh*, whose descendant, *John*, Earl of *Roxburgh*, one of the Principal Secretaries of State, and a person of great Honour, Merit, and Fidelity to his Prince and Country, hath been advanced to the higher title of Duke of *Roxburgh*

Roxburgh

Sheriffdom of Roxborough Hereditary Sheriffs

[c] Now, C

[d] Is, C

In the fifth year of the reign of Queen Anne, the Lord *Henry Scot*, second Son of *James* Duke of *Monmouth*, was advanc'd to the dignity of Lord *Scot* of *Goldy lands*, Viscount of *Hermitage*, and Earl of *Deloraın*, all in the District of *Roxburgh*

[* TWEDALE or PEBLES.

* Camden joins this to *Tefsdale*

HE Shire of *Pebles*, or *Tweedale*, is so call'd from the river *Tweed*, which runs east, the whole length of the Shire, and for the most part with a swift stream It is bounded on the east with *Etrick* forest, on the south with Part of the forest of *St Mary Lough*, and *Annandale*, on the west with the overward of *Cludesdale*, and on the north with part of *Caldermoor*, the head of *North Esk*, and *Mid-Lothian*. In length it is twenty six miles, and where broadest does not exceed sixteen In which compass are seventeen Parish Churches, that make up a Presbytery, call'd *The Presbytery of Peebles* The Country is generally swell'd with hills, many of which are green and grassy, with pleasant and fertil valleys between, well watered and adorned with Gentlemen's houses Their grain is generally oats and barley; and as for planting, they have little of it, except about the houses of the Gentry]

Tweedale

Tweed aforesaid [as hath been observ'd] runs through the middle of this Valley or Dale, which takes its name from it, abounding in sheep, whose Wool is much priz'd This is a very noble River; which, having [*] its source among the hills more inwardly to the West, runs in a straight Channel by *Drumlar-Castle*, and by *Pebles*, a Market-Town, [a Burrough Royal, and the head Burrough of the County, seated in a pleasant plain on the side of the river, with a stately bridge of five arches over the *Tweed*, and a fine Church] It [b] had for its Sheriff Baron *Yester*, [Earl of *Tweedale*, who sold his Estate in that Shire, and the Sheriffship, to his Grace the Duke of Queensbury As to Antiquity; the place called *Randall's* trenches seems to have been a Roman Camp, and there is a Causey leads from it, for half a mile together, to the town of *Lyne* In this shire, Sir *John Stewart*, Laird of Traquair, was by K Charles the first created Lord *Stewart* of Traquair, and in the year 1633 was advanced to the higher honour of Earl of Traquair]

* At Tweeds Cross,

Pebles

[b] Has, C

Randal's trenches

Next to *Pebles* is *Selkirk*, a Sheriffdom, called otherwise *The Sheriffdom of Etrick forest*, because formerly it was wholly covered with Woods, which were well furnish'd with Harts, Hinds, and Fallow Deer, but now they are in great measure destroyed On the north, it is bounded partly by *Tweedale*, and partly by the Regality of *Stow* in Mid Lothian, on the east and south by *Teviotdale*, and on the West, partly by *Teviotdale*, and partly by *Annandale* It is very near Quadrangular, and the Diameter every way about sixteen miles The Inhabitants have generally strong bodies, being sober and frugal in their diet, and living mostly by feeding of Cattle whereby they do not only support them-

Selkirk

themselves, but maintain a good Trade in England with their *Wooll*, *Sheep*, *Cows*, &c. The chief Town of this Sheriffdom is] *Selkirk* [which hath a weekly market, and several Fairs. It is the head Burgh of the Shire, and the Seat of the Sheriff and Commissary Courts; it is also a Burgh-Royal, and] hath a Sheriff out of the Family of *Murray* of Falahill, [an ancient Family designed of *Philippaugh*, famous for the defeat of the Army of the great Marquiss of Montross. In the year 1646 the Lord William Douglas, Son to the Marquiss of Douglas, was created Earl of Selkirk, and having marry'd *Anna* Dutchess and Heiress of Hamilton, he was advanc'd to the dignity of Duke of Hamilton by King Charles the second, and did also, in his life-time, by the favour of King James the seventh, convey the title of Earl of *Selkirk* to Charles his second son, now Earl of *Selkirk*.

Bucleugh. At some distance from hence, to the north-west, is *Bucleugh*, which, in the reign of King James the sixth, gave the title of Baron, and afterwards of Earl, to the ancient family of *Scot*; and, in the reign of King Charles the second, the title of Dutchess, to *Anna* daughter of *Francis* the last Earl, who was marry'd to *James* Duke of Monmouth (natural son to King Charles the second,) and also Duke of Bucleugh, whose second son, Lord *Henry Scot*, was in the fifth year of Queen Anne, advanc'd to the honour of Earl of Delorain.]

Lauder. The Twede receives the little river *Lawder*, upon which is *Lauder*, [a Royal Burgh and the seat of a Bailliary, belonging to the Family of Lauderdale, within the Sheriffdom of Berwick. Here, the late Duke of Lauderdale built a well contrived handsom Church, consisting of four Isles, and a large Steeple in the middle.] Near it is *Thirlestan*, where John Maitland, * Chancellor of Scotland (for his singular prudence and wisdom, created by King James the sixth Baron of Thirlestan,) † had a very beautiful seat, [adorned, of late years, with Avenues, Pavilions, Out-Courts, and other beauties required to the making of a compleat seat, by his Grace the Duke of Lauderdale. *John* his son was created Viscount of Lauderdale, and afterwards Earl of Lauderdale by King James the sixth, whose son, *John*, being Secretary of State to King Charles the second, was in the year 1672 created Duke of Lauderdale, with whom the title of Duke being extinct, his brother *Charles Maitland* succeeded in the dignity of Earl of *Lauderdale*.] Thirlestan * Not long since, C. † Hath, C.

Then the *Tweed*, increased by the accession of the River *Teviot* beneath Roxburgh, watereth the Sheriffdom of *Berwick*, which is most of it the Estate of the *Humes*, wherein the Head of that Family now exerciseth the Jurisdiction of a Sheriff: and then running under *Berwick*, the ‡ best fortified Town in Britain (of which I have already spoken) with a prodigious plenty of *Salmon*, it emptieth itself into the Sea. [Of which family of *Hume*, Sir *Patrick*, in consideration of his own great merit, and eminent Services to the Protestant Cause against the attempts of Popery, was advanced by King William and Queen Mary to the honour of Lord *Polwarth* of *Polwarth*, an ancient Barony in this Tract, and, a few years after, to the higher honour of Earl of Marchmont. ‡ So said ann. 16[illegible]

In the year 1646 *John Hay*, Lord *Yester*, was created Earl of Twedale: whose Son of the same name was Lord High Chancellor of Scotland, and in the year 1694 was advanced to the higher honour of Marquiss of Twedale.]

MERCHIA, *MERCH*, or *MERS*.

MERCH, which is next, and so named because it is a *March* Country, lieth wholly upon the German Ocean. [And as it hath its present name from being the boundary or *march* between England and Scotland, so was it also called *Berwick-shire*, because the town of *Berwick* was formerly the chief burrough thereof, which was afterwards given away by King James the third upon capitulation, for Redemption of *Alexander* Duke of Albany. But (if we may believe some Scotch Authors) a name more ancient than either of these, was *Ordolucia*, and that of the Inhabitants *Ordolutæ*, a branch of the *Scottidani*.

It is the south-east Shire of all *Scotland*, bordering upon the sea, and divided from Berwick by the Bound-rod, and from Northumberland, by the river Tweed, running between them for about eight miles. This river is one of the three that rise out of the same tract of hills; *Clide* runs west towards *Dumbarton*, *Anand*, south towards *Solway sands*; and this, east, towards *Berwick*. It is of a swift course, environ'd with hills, running through *Tweedale* forest, and *Teviotdale*, before it go into the Ocean. It's current is above fifty miles, in all which compass it hath only two bridges, one at *Peebles* of five arches, and another at *Berwick* of fifteen. It had one at *Melross*, the pillars whereof are yet standing.

The length of this County is twenty miles, from *Lamberton* to *Ridpeth* on the south side, and from *Cockburns path* to *Secum* [illegible] *hill* kirk on the north side. But take the length angle-wise, it is from *Lamberton* to *Lenthugh*, direct east and west, twenty four miles. It's breadth is about fourteen miles, whether you take it on the west end, south end, or middle of the Shire.

It is divided into three parts, *Mers*, *Lammermoor*, and *Lauderdale*. The *Mers* is a pleasant low ground, lying open to the influence of the sun, and guarded from storms by *Lammermoor*. So that the soil is fertil, and affords great plenty of oats, barley, wheat, pease, &c. with abundance of hay. *Lammermoor* is a great tract of hills on the north-side of the Shire, above sixteen miles in length, and six at least in breadth, abounding with moss and moor. The west end of them, for four miles together, belongs to *Lauderdale*, the rest of it [illegible] is almost equally parted between *Lauderdale* and *Mers*. The peculiar use of this tract is Lammermoor pasturage in the summer time, and the game it affords by the abundance of *Partridge*, *Moor-fowl*, *Plover*, &c But the product of these parts is not reckon'd so good as of others, being generally sold at a lower rate *Lauderdale* is a tract of ground lying on each side of the water of *Leider*, abounding with pleasant haughs, green hills, and some woods; well stor'd also with corn and pasturage

Lauderdale

The Judicatories in this Shire are, 1 The Sheriff-Court, which sits at the town of *Duns* 2 The Commissariat, which sits at *Lauder* 3 The Regality of *Thirlstan*, belonging to the Earl of *Lauderdale* 4 The Regality of *Preston*, and Forest of *Dye*, belonging to the Marquiss of *Douglas* 5 The Lordship of *Coldingham* and Stewarty of *March*, belonging to the Earl of *Hume*, who was Sheriff, and has his residence at *Hirsell*] Which Office is since conferred on the Earl of Marchmont

Judicatories

Here *Hume Castle* first presents its self, the ancient possession of the Lords of *Home* or *Hume*, who being descended from the Earls of *Merch*, have spread themselves into a numerous and noble family Of which, *Alexander Hume*, who was before Primier Baron of Scotland, and Sheriff of Berwick, was [h] advanced by *James* the first King of Great Britain, to the title of *Earl of Hume* [But the Castle was demolished by the English in the late Wars] Below this lieth *Kelso*, formerly famous for a monastery founded by King *David* the first, with thirteen more, for the propagation of God's glory, but, in the consequence, to the great impairing of the Crown Lands [This is a Burgh of Barony, and a large beautiful Town]

Hume-castle

[h] Lately C

Earl Hume

Kelso.

Thence we have a prospect of *Coldingham*, called by Bede *Coldana*, and *Coludi urbs*, perhaps the *Colania* of Ptolemy, and, many Ages since, a famous House of Nuns, whose Chastity is recorded in ancient Writings, for their cutting off (together with *Ebba* their Prioress) their Noses and Lips, chusing to secure their Virginity from the Danes, rather than preserve their Beauty but they, notwithstanding that, burnt them, together with their Monastery Hard by, is *Fast-Castle*, [heretofore] belonging to the *Humes*; so called from its strength, and situated near the Promontory of *S Ebbe*, who, being the daughter of *Edelfrid* King of Northumberland, when her Father was taken Prisoner, seized a Boat in the Humber, and passing along the tempestuous Ocean, landed in safety here, and became famous for her sanctity, and left her name to the place [Besides these there are in this Shire, *Duns*, a Burgh of Barony, standing upon a rising ground in the midst of the Shire Every Wednesday, it has a great market of Sheep, Horses, and Cows, and is *reputed* by some the birth-place of *Joannes Duns Scotus* *Eymouth*, the only port in the Shire for shipping, which was fortified by the French in Queen Mary's minority, and from which place, Colonel *John Churchill*, afterwards Duke of Marlborough in England, was created by King Charles the second, Lord *Churchill* of *Eymouth* *Ersilton* or *Earlstown*, famous for the birth of *Thomas Lermouth*, called *Thomas the Rymer*, *Caldstream*, a market town lying close upon Tweed *Greenlaw*, a burgh of Barony, with a weekly market *Fouldon*, a large town *Rosse*, famous for its harbour and plenty of fish. *Aton*, situate upon the water of *Ey* *White-coat*, where is a harbour for herring fishing

Coldingham

Colania

Fast castle

Duns

Vide Northumberland, p 109,

Eymouth

Ersilton

Caldstream

Greenlaw

Rosse.

White coat.

Sir *James Douglas*, second Son to *William* Earl of Angus, marrying *Anne*, only daughter and heir of *Lawrence* Lord Oliphant, was by King Charles the first created Lord *Mordington*, with precedency of the Peerage of Oliphant

Lord Mordington

At *St Germans*, the Templars, and after them the Knights of *Rhodes* and *Malta* had a Residence [i]

[i] St Germans is in Lothien.

About *Bastenrig* on the east-hand, and the *Moristons* and *Mellerstoun* downs on the west, they frequently take the *Dotterel*, a rare Fowl, towards the latter end of April and beginning of May]

Eastenrig

Dotterel

But *Merch* is much more celebrated in History for its Earls, than Places, who were renown'd for their Martial Courage They were the descendants of *Gospatrick* Earl of Northumberland, who, after being driven out of his Country by William the Conqueror, was entertain'd by *Malcolm Conmer*, that is, *Great-head*, King of Scotland, and honour'd by him with *Dunbar*-Castle and the Earldom of *Merch* His Posterity, besides very large possessions in Scotland, held (as appears by an old Inquisition) the Barony or *Bengeley* in Northumberland, on condition that they should be *Inborrow* and *Utborrow*, between England and Scotland What the meaning should be of these terms, let others guess, what my conjecture is, I have told you already But in the Reign of King James the first [of Scotland,] *George of Dunbar*, Earl of Merch, by authority of Parliament, and upon account of his Father's Rebellion, *lost the propriety and possession of the Earldom of Merch, and the Segniory of Dunbar* And when he proved by undeniable Evidence, that his Father had been pardon'd that fault by the Regents of the Kingdom, he was answered, that it was not in the Regents power to pardon an offence against the State, and that it was provided by the Laws, that the Father's transgression should succeed to the Children, lest at any time being Heirs to their Father's Rashness as well as Estate, they should, out of a vain opinion of their power, plot against their Prince and Country The Title of *Earl of Merch* was afterwards, amongst other honourable Titles, confer'd on *Alexander* Duke of Albany And in our [k] memory, this Title of honour was revived in *Robert* the third, Brother of Matthew Earl of Lenox, who being from Bishop of Cathness made Earl of Lenox, soon after resign'd that Title to his Nephew (created *Duke of Lenox*,) and received of the King, by way of recompence, the name and style of *Earl of Merch* [But he dying without issue, the title of Earl of *Merch* lay vacant, till it was confer'd on the Lord *William Douglas*, second Son of *William* first Duke of Queensberry, by King William the third]

Earls of Merch

In Northumberland at Brampton, p 1097

143-

[k] Sound ann 160

LAUDEN,

LAUDEN, or LOTHIEN.

Lauden

OTHIEN, called also *Lauden*, and anciently, from the Picts, *Pictland*, shoots out from *Merch* as far as the Scottish Sea, or the *Frith*, having many hills, and little wood, but for its excellent Corn-lands, and the civility of the People, [as also for the number of Towns and Seats of the Nobility and Gentry,] it is distinguished, above any County in Scotland About the year of our Lord 873, Edgar King of England (between whom and Keneth the third, King of Scotland, there was a strict alliance against the Danes, the common Enemy) resigned up his right in this *Lothian* to him, as Matthew Florilegus tells us, and, to tie him the closer to his Interest, *He bestowed upon him many Houses in the way, wherein both he and his Successors, in their coming to the Kings of England, and return homewards, might be entertained, which, till King Henry the second's time, remained in the hands of the Kings of Scotland* [It hath *Mers* to the east, part of Lammermoor, and part of Lauderdale, with the Forest, and Tweedale, to the south part of Cliddesdale and Stirlingshire to the west, and to the north the *Firth* or *Forth* It is in length from *Cockburns-path* in the east, to the Shire of Clidesdale, about fifty seven miles, and where it is broadest, between sixteen and seventeen miles over It is divided into three distinct Tracts, called *East-Lothian*, *Mid Lothian*, and *West-Lothian*

East Lothian

East-Lothian or the Constablery or Shire of *Hadington* (so called from Hadington, one of the three Burghs-Royal, and seat of the Courts) is in length about twenty two, and in breadth about twelve miles, bounded by the *Firth* on the north and east, by a tract of hills called *Lammermoor* on the south, and by *Mid Lothian* on the west It abounds with corn of all sorts, and has good store of grass, with some considerable woods, as *Prestmennan*, *Colston*, *Humbie*, and *Ormestan*, and abundance of Coal, and Lime-stone It has good store of *Sheep*, especially towards the hills of *Lammermoor*, and by west *Lammerlaw* and from the west part to the sea all along to the east, it abounds with Conies It hath many Salt pans, wherein much white *Salt* is made, and at *New Milns* there is a considerable manufactury of *Broad-cloth* The sea coast is accomodated with many convenient harbours, and has the advantage of several Fishery towns, particularly, at *Dumbar*, and on the coast thereabout, every year after Lammas is a Herring-fishing, where they take great numbers, not only to serve the Inhabitants, but also for exportation

Mid Lothian

The Sheriffdom of *Edenburgh*, commonly call'd *Mid Lothian*, is the principal Shire of the Kingdom, and is in length twenty or twenty one miles, the breadth of it is different according to the several parts, in some sixteen or seventeen miles, in others not above five or six On the south, it is bounded with the Sheriffdom of *Hadington*, on the east with the Bailliary of Lauderdale, on the south with the Sheriffdom of *Tweedale*, on the south west with the Sheriffdom of *Lanerick*, and on the west by the said Sheriffdom, on the north west with the Sheriffdom of *Linlithgow*, and on the north with the *Firth* or *Forth*

This tract is abundantly furnished with all necessaries, producing a great deal of corn of all sorts, and affording good pasture for cattle It has very much coal and lime-stone, as also a sort of soft black marble, and some few miles from *Edenburgh*, near the water of *Leith*, they have a Copper mine

West Lothian

The Shire of *Linlithgow*, called *West-Lothian*, takes it name from *Linlithgow*, the head burgh, and has on the north the *Forth*, and is divided from *Mid Lothian* towards the south and east by the waters of *Almond* and *Breichwater* to the north west, it meets with part of *Stirling-shire*, and to the west with part of *Clidesdale* It is in length fourteen miles, and in breadth about nine It affords great plenty of Coal, Lime-stone, and White Salt, and in the reign of King James the sixth, a silver Mine was found in it, out of which they got a great deal of silver]

Dunbar

In this *Lothian*, the first place that presents it self on the Sea-shore is *Dunbar*, a Castle in ancient times very strongly fortify'd (the seat of the Earls of Merch before mentioned, thence commonly called Earls of *Dunbar*) and often taken by the English, and recover'd by the Scots But in the year 1567 it was demolished by order of the States, to prevent its being a retreat for Rebels King James, in the year 1515, conferred the title and honour of Earl of *Dunbar*, upon *Geo Hume*, for his approved Loyalty, whom he had created before Baron *Hume* of Berwick, *to him, his Heirs, and Assigns* [After which, the same King conferr'd the dignity of Viscount of *Dunbar* upon Sir *Henry Constable*, an English Gentleman, whose heirs do at present enjoy it Not far from hence, is *Dungla*, a pleasant seat on the sea coast, which formerly belonged to the Earls of *Hume* In the time of the Civil Wars, a garrison was kept there by the Earl of *Hadington*, for the Army, who (with thirty Knights and Gentlemen of the name of *Hamilton*, besides several other considerable persons) perished in the ruins of this house For it was designedly blown up in the year 1640, by *Nathanael Paris* an Englishman, one of his own servants, while the Earl was reading a Letter in the Court, which he had then received from the Army, with all the Gentlemen about him Only four, of the whole Company, escaped, who by the force of the powder were thrown to a great distance from the house It hath been since repaired, and adorned by Sir [illegible] *Hall*, with curious Gardens, spacious Courts, and a large and pleasant Avenue They had there a Collegiate Church, a goodly large building, and vaulted, but it is now ruinous Along the Coast, to [illegible], is a pleasant Country, the most fruitful in the Kingdom, especially in *Wheat* and *Barly* South-east of *Dunbar* aforesaid, is *Dunbill*, memorable for the victory obtained over the Scotch army under *Lesly*, by [illegible] 1650 a handful of men and those tooke the field, under the command of *Cromwell* Which miscarriage (if some ingenious persons, who were in the Action, may be believed) was rather owing to the treachery of [illegible] men, than the conduct or bravery of the Enemy]

Earls of Dunbar

Baron Hume or Hume of Berwick

Dunglas

Hard by *Dunbar*, the little River *Tine*, after a short course, falleth into the Sea, near the source whereof stands *Tyle*, which hath a very

Baron of the Family of the *Hays* Earls of Arroll, who is likewise hereditary Sheriff of the little Territory of *Tweedale*, or *Peblis* [This place hath been extraordinarily improv'd and beautified with planting and enclosing]

Hadington

Upon the same rivulet, some few miles higher, in a large plain, lies *Hadington* or *Hadina*, fortified by the English with a deep and large ditch, and a four-square turf-wall without, also four bulwarks at the four corners, and as many more upon the Inner wall It was valiantly defended by Sir *George Wilford* an Englishman, against Monsieur *Dessie*, who fiercely attack'd it with ten thousand French and Germans, till the Plague growing hot and lessening the garrison, *Henry* Earl of Rutland came with a great Army and rais'd the siege, and having levell'd the Works, conducted the English home And King James the sixth brought into the number of the Nobility of *Scotland* Sir *John Ramsey* as a reward of his Loyalty and Valour (his *RIGHT HAND being* [a] *the DEFENDER OF HIS PRINCE AND COUNTRY*, in that horrid Conspiracy of the *Gowries*) under the honourable title of Viscount *Hadington* [It was afterwards erected into an Earldom in the person of Sir *Thomas Hamilton* (a Gentleman of great honour and wealth) in the reign of King James the sixth, he exchanging that title for his other of Earl of *Melros*]

[a] *Vindex*

Viscount Hadington.

Of this *Hadington* J Johnston hath these Verses;

Planities prætensa jacet prope flumina Tinæ,
Fluminis arguti clauditur ista sinu
Vulcani & Martis quæ passa incendia, fati
Ingemit alterno vulnere fracta vices
Nunc tandem sapit ista Dei præcepta secuta
Præsidio gaudet jam potiore poli

Near *Tine's* fair stream a spatious plain is shown,
Tine's circling arms embrace the hapless town
Where *Mars* and fiery *Vulcan* reign'd by turns
With fatal Rage, whose dire effects she mourns
By sad experience now at last grown wise
She slights their fury and their power defies
Contemns the dangers that before she fear'd,
And rests secure when mighty Heav'ns her guard

Athelstanford

A little way from Hadington, stands *Athelstanford*, so named from *Athelstan*, an English Commander, who was slain there with his men, about the year 815; but, that this was *Athelstan* the Warlike King of the West-Saxons, must be utterly denied, if we have any regard to the time, or manner of his Death [From Ellibank, in this tract, *Patrick Murray*, was, for his approved Loyalty, advanced to the honour of Lord Ellibank, by King Charles the first]

Tantallon

Above the Mouth of the *Tine*, upon the doubling of the Shore, stands *Tantallon* Castle; from whence *Archibald Douglas*, Earl of Angus, gave great disturbance to James the fifth, King of Scotland Here, by the winding of the shores on both sides, room is made for a very noble Arm of the Sea, well furnish'd with Islands, and, by the influx of several rivers, and the tides together, extended to a mighty breadth Ptolemy calls it *Boderia*; *Tacitus*, *Bodotria*, from its depth, as I conjecture, the Scots, the *Forth* and *Frith*, we, *Edenborough Frith*; others, *Mare Fresicum*, and *Mare Scoticum*, and the Eulogium, *Morwiridh* [*Patrick Ruthven*, General to King Charles the first (having been first created Lord *Estrick*, from the name of a Rivulet) was created Earl of *Forth*, which title was extinct in him]

Bodotria

Upon the *Frith*, after you are past *Tantallon*, are seated, first *North Berwick*, anciently famous for a Nunnery, and then *Dirlton*, which formerly belonged to the eminent family of the *Haliburtons*, and [b] afterwards by the favour of King James the sixth, [c] gave the title of Baron to *Thomas Ereskine*, Captain of his Guards, as *Fenton*, hard by, [d] gave the Honourable Title of Viscount to the same person; who was the first that had the style and dignity of a *Viscount* in Scotland [Afterwards, Sir *James Maxwell* was created by the same King Lord *Elbotle* and Earl of *Dirlton* Upon which coast, is *Belhaven*, dignified by giving the title of Viscount to a Gentleman of the name of *Douglas*, and (that honour being extinct) the title of Lord, to Sir *James Hamilton*, in the reign of King Charles the first]

Dirlton

Fenton

Viscount Fenton

Belhaven

Over against these, in the sea, near the shore, lies the *Bass*, an Island which rises as it were in one continued craggy rock, inaccessible on every side, yet it has upon it a Fort, a fountain, and pasture grounds, but is so hollow'd and undermined by the waves, that it is almost wrought through What prodigious flights of sea-fowl, especially of those *Geese* which they call *Scouts* and *Soland Geese*, do at certain times flock hither (for by report, their number is so great as to darken the Sun at Noon day,) what multitudes of Fish these Geese bring (so as one hundred Soldiers in Garrison here, liv'd upon no other Provision but the fresh fish brought hither by them, as they report,) what quantities of sticks they convey for the building of their nests (so that by their means the inhabitants are abundantly provided with firing,) what vast profit also their Feathers and oyl bring in These are things, so incredible, as no one can well believe, but he who has seen them [This Garrison of the *Bass* having stood out long against King William the third, and at last surrender'd, the fortifications thereof were order'd to be slighted]

The Bass

Scouts

Seton

Then, as the shore draws back, *Seton* appears, which seems to take its name from the situation upon the Sea, and hath given name to the Honourable House of the *Setons*, descended from an English Family, and the sister of King *Robert Bruce*, of which the Marquiss of *Huntley*, Robert Earl of *Wintoun*, and Alexander Earl of *Dunfermeling* (all advanced to honours by King *James* the sixth) [e] were Branches [This, together with Wintoun, another Seat of the Earls of Wintoun, *Brocksmouth*, a Seat of the Duke of Roxburgh, and *Tiningham*, the residence of the Earl of Hadington, are the most considerable Seats in this Country]

Brocksmouth

Tiningham

Then, the River *Esk* is discharged into the *Frith*, having run by *Borthwic* (which [f] had its Barons so sirnamed, of Hungarian extraction, but now extinct ;)] by *Newbottle*, that is, *the new building*, formerly a little Monastery, and [g] afterwards made a Barony, in the person of *Mark Ker*, by *Dalkeith*, [h] heretofore a pleasant seat of the Earls of *Morton*, [but now belonging to the Dutchess of Bucleugh, from whence her eldest Son takes the title of Earl] and by *Musselburgh*

Newbottle

Dalkeith

Musselburgh

rough, below which (upon *Edward Seymour* Duke of Somerset's entring Scotland with a powerful Army, to challenge the Performance of Articles for the marrying *Mary* Queen of Scotland to *Edward* the sixth King of England,) there happened a most dismal Day to the youth of the noble Families of Scotland, who fell there in great numbers

I must not pass by an Inscription, which as *J Napier*, a learned person, informs us in his Commentaries on the *Apocalyps*, was dug up here, and which the eminent Sir *Peter Young* Knight, King *James* the sixth's Tutor, did thus more truly delineate,

APOLLINI
GRANNO
Q LVSIVS
SABINIA
NVS
PROC
AVG
*V S S L V M

* Votum sol- vitum libens merito

Who this *Apollo Grannus* was, and whence he had that name, no one Antiquary, to the best of my knowledge, has ever told us But if I, one of the lowest fourm, may give my sentiments, I should say that *Apollo Grannus* amongst the Romans, was the same with the Grecian Ἀπολλων ακερσεκομης, that is, *long lock'd* For Isidore calls the long hair of the Goths, *Granni* But this may be reckon'd foreign to my business

Cranston [In these parts, is *Cranston*, the Seat of a Family of the same name, to whom, by the favour of King *James* the sixth, it gave the title of Lords *Cranston*, *Presteun*, on the sea side, from which Sir *Richard Graham* had the title of Viscount conferr'd upon him by King Charles the second, the Castle of *Dalhousie*, belonging to the ancient family of *Ramsay*, created by King James the sixth Lords *Ramsay*, and by King Charles the first honoured with the title of Earls of *Dalhousie* and nigh to Edenborough, the Castle of *Marchistoun*, which belong'd to the *Napers*, of whom Sir *Archibald Naper* was created Lord *Naper* in the reign of King Charles the first also, from *Oxenford*, in East Lothian, Sir *James Macgill* had the title of Viscount conferr'd upon him by King Charles the second and Sir *James Primrose* was created by Queen Anne Lord Primrose of *Castlefield* and Viscount *Primrose*]

Prestoun

Dalhousie

Marchistoun

Oxenford

Lord Primrose

Edenborough

Lower, near the Scottish Frith, stands *Edenborough*, called by the Irish Scots *Dun Eaden*, that is, *Eaden Town*, which, without doubt, is the same that Ptolemy calls Στρατοπεδον πτερωτον, that is, the winged Castle For *Edenborough* signifies the same as *Winged Castle*, *Adain* in the British denoting a *Wing*, and so *Edenborough* (from a word compounded of the British and Saxon Tongue) is nothing else but the *Winged Borough* From *Wing* therefore we are to derive its name, which may be done, either from those Squadrons of horse call'd *Wings*, or from those *Wings* which the Greek Architects call *Pteromata*, that is (as Vitruvius tells us) two walls so rising up with the same height, that they bear a resemblance of Wings For want of these, a certain City of Cyprus was anciently (as we read in the Geographers) called *Apteron*, that is, *Wingless* But if any one has a mind to believe, that it took the name from *Etank* a Britain, or from *Heth* a Pict, let him enjoy his own fancy, I shall not oppose him

This City, in regard of its high situation, the goodness of the air, and fertility of the soil, so many Seats of the Nobility lying round it, its being water'd with excellent Springs, and reaching from East to West a mile in length, and half so much in breadth, is, upon these accounts, justly esteem'd the Metropolis of the whole Kingdom It is strongly walled, and adorned with publick and private buildings, and well peopled and frequented, for the advantage of the Sea, which the neighbouring Port at *Leith* affords And as it is honoured with the King's residence, so is it the sacred repository of the Laws, and the chief Tribunal of Justice For the high Court of Parliament * was generally held here for the making and repealing of Laws; as the Session, and the Court of the *King's Justice*, and of the Commissariat (of which I have already spoken,) are also settled in this place On the East side stood Holy Rood Monastery, founded by King David the first, and made a Royal Palace by King James the fifth, over which, within a Park well stor'd with Deer, Conies, and Hares, hangs a mountain, called *Arthur's Chair*, from Arthur the Britain On the West side, there mounts up a rock to a mighty height, steep and inaccessible on all sides but that which looks towards the City, upon which stands a Castle, so strongly fortified with a great number of Towers, that it is look'd upon as impregnable This, the Britains called *Castle Myned Agned*, and the Scots the *Maidens Castle*, and the *Virgins Castle*, because the Maiden Princesses of the Blood-Royal of the Picts were kept here, and the same may, easily, be look'd upon as the *Castrum Alatum*, or *Winged Castle*, abovementioned [But to speak of this place as particulary as it deserves

* Is, C

The first building of a Fort here, seems to have given rise to the town, and to have encouraged the neighbours to fix under the protection of it So that the houses and inhabitants by little and little increasing, it is brought down to the very foot of the ascent toward the east, and is become an entire *Scotch* mile in length, and half of it in breadth The ascent upon which the City stands, has on the north-side a pool call'd the *North Loch*, and was formerly guarded by another on the south, call'd the *South Loch*, as appears from the leases of some houses of S *Ninian's* Row, which are let with the privilege of a Boat annex'd But this is drain'd many years ago, and upon the banks of it are built two several tracts of houses The City has six Gates, the principal whereof to the east, was magnificently rebuilt in the year 1616, and adorned with Towers on both sides Two streets run along, the whole length of the town The *High-street* from the Castle to the Abby (said to be the broadest in Europe) is of late years built of hewn stone, since, by an Act of the Town Council, they were prohibited to build any more of Timber either in the City or Suburbs, upon account of the many *Fires* which had happened

About forty years ago, the Magistrates were at great expence to bring one of the best springs of *Scotland* into the City, which they did by leaden Pipes, from a Hill at above three miles distance And to make it more convenient, they have erected several stately Fountains in the middle of the *High street*, to serve the town with water

As the *private* Buildings, so much more the *publick* do greatly exceed those in other parts of *North Britain* In the middle of the City, is St Giles's Church, a Cathedral, built of hewn stone, and Publick Buildings Churches and adorned with stone *pillars* and *vaultings* It is so large, as to be divided into three Churches, each

Grey Friars whereof has its Parish Besides this, they have the *South-Church*, in the Church-yard of which, amongst many other monuments, is that of the learned Sir *George Mackenzy* The *Trone*-Church, built in 1641 The Collegiate Church of the Sacred *Trinity*, built by Mary of *Gueldres*, King James the second's Queen The Lady *Yester's* Church, built and endow'd by one of the Lady *Yesters* and another very beautiful one, built not many years since To these, we must add two Chapels, *St Magdalen's* and *St Mary's*, with another at the foot of the *Canon Gate*

Hospitals Next to these, we are to mention the Hospitals, *viz St Thomas's* and *Heriot's* Hospital In the first, the poorer sort of Inhabitants are maintained very handsomly, and have their own proper Chaplain The second (so called from the founder *George Heriot*, Jeweller to King James the sixth) is a stately Fabrick, like a Palace In the inner Frontispiece, is erected the Statue of the Founder, and round about the houses are pleasant Gardens, adorned with large Walks and Greens It is a Nursery for Boys, wherein the children of the poorer Citizens, to the number of a hundred and up wards, have their education, till they be fit for the publick Schools and Colleges

Parliament-House Near the Cathedral-Church, is the *Parliament-house*, with other rooms adjoining for the Session, and above stairs for the Exchequer, &c It stands in a great Court, which on one side is enclosed with the upper and lower Exchange, and with a tract of very stately buildings Here is one of the highest houses perhaps in the world, mounting seven stories above the Parliament Court, and, being built upon the descent of a hill, the back-part is as much below it; so that, from the bottom to the top one stair-case ascends fourteen stories high In the middle of the Court, is the Statue of King Charles the second, in brass, erected upon a stately *Pedestal* at the charge of the City

College On the South-side, is the College of King James the sixth, founded in the year 1580, and endowed with all the Privileges of an University The Precincts are very large, and the whole is divided into three Courts, adorned on all sides with excellent buildings, two *lower*, and one *higher*, which is as large as both the other They have their publick *Schools*, and a *Common hall*, wherein *Divinity*, *Hebrew*, and *Mathematicks* are taught The Library is well stor'd with printed books, and has some Manuscripts under which is the King's *Printing* house The Students have very good accommodation, and the Professors neat and handsom Lodgings, with very good Gardens for their recreation

Palace The *Royal-Palace* (which was burnt by Oliver Cromwel, but nobly re edified by King Charles the second, and of which his Grace the Duke of *Hamilton* is hereditary Keeper,) hath four Courts The Outer Court, which is as big as all the rest, has four principal Entries It is on all hands bounded with lovely Gardens, and on the south, lies the *King's Park*, which hath great variety of medicinal plants The Entry of the Palace is adorned with great pillars of hewn stone, and a *Cupola*, in fashion of a Crown, above it The fore part is terminated by four high towers The Inner Court has *Piazza's* round it, of hewn stone But, above all, the *[illegible] Gallery* is most remarkable, being adorned with the pictures of all the Kings of Scotland

from *Fergus* the first From the Palace here erected, *John Bothwel* (one of the honourable persons who attended King James the sixth to England) had confer'd upon him the style and title of Lord of *Holy rud-house*, which honour is now extinct

College of Justice Here is also a *College of Justice*, which hath its Dean of faculty They try their intrants, or Candidates, and have a Library well furnished with Books of Law and History

Bishop. This City was further honour'd by King Charles the first, by erecting it into an Episcopal See in the year 1633, the Bishop of which was made Suffragan to the Archbishop of St *Andrews*, and to take place of the Bishop of Dunkeld

King Charles the second did likewise erect at *Edinburgh* a College of Physicians, giving them, by Patent under the Great Seal, an ample Jurisdiction within this City and the Liberties thereof, and appointing the Judicatures to concur to the execution of their Decreets By a latter Grant, they have the Faculty of professing Physick They have their Conferences once a month for the improvement of Medicine, and have begun to erect a Library]

How *Edenborough*, by the vicissitudes of war, has been subject, sometimes to the Scots, and sometimes to the Saxons (who inhabited this Eastern part of Scotland) till it became wholly under the Dominion of the Scots, about the year of our Lord 960, when the English Empire, terribly weaken'd by the Danish Wars, lay as it were expiring How likewise (as it is in an old Book *Of the Division of Scotland*, in the Library of the Right Honourable the Lord *Burleigh*, [k] Lord High-Treasurer of England) *in*[k] *the Reign of Indulph*, Eden-*Town was*[l] *quitted*,[l] *and is abandoned to the Scots to this present day*, and what different turns of fortune it felt afterwards These things, the Historians relate at large, and from them you may be informed concerning them In the mean time, read, if you please, the ingenious J Johnston's Verses, in praise of *Edenborough*

Margin: Lat. C / Vacatum

Monte sub acclivi Zephyri procurrit in auras,
Hinc Arx celsa, illinc Regia clara nitet
Inter utramque patet sublimibus ardua tectis
Urbs armis, animis clara, frequensque viris
Nobile Scotorum caput, & pars maxima regni,
Pæne etiam gentis integra Regna suæ
Raræ artes & opes, quod mens optaverit, aut hic
Invenias, aut non Scotia tota dabit
Compositum hic populum videas, sanctumque senatum,
Sanctaque cum puro lumine jura Dei
An quisquam Arctoi extremo in limite mundi,
Aut hæc aut paria his cernere posse putet?
Dic, Hospes, postquam externas lustraveris urbes,
Hæc cernens, oculis credis an ipse tuis?

Beneath a Western hill's delightful brow,
The Castle hence, and hence the Court we view
The stately Town presents it self between,
Renown'd for arms, for courage, and for men
The kingdom's noblest part, the lofty head,
Or the whole kingdom of the *Scottish* breed

Wealth,

Wealth, arts, and all that anxious minds desire,
Or not in *Scotland*, or you meet with here
The people sober, grave the Senate show,
The worship pure, the faith divinely true.
In the last borders of the Northern coast
What rival land an equal sight can boast?
These Glories, Trav'ler, when at last you see,
Say if you don't mistrust your wond'ring eye
And think it transport, all, and extasy!

Brughton [Near Edinburgh, is *Brughton*, which belong'd to the family of the *Ballendens*, of which Sir *William Ballenden* was made Lord *Ballenden* of *Brughton* by King Charles the second, but afterwards, the Honour, together with the Estate, was convey'd to *John Ker*, second son of William Earl of Roxburgh, who thereupon changed his name into *Ballenden* An English Gentleman, Sir *Thomas Fairfax*, Grandfather of the famous General of that name, had the honour of a Baron conferred upon him by King Charles the first, under the title of Lord *Cameron* And Sir *George Forester* had the title of Lord Forester of Corstorphine conferr'd upon him by the same King Also, *Archibald Primrose*, son of *Archibald* Lord *Dalmeny*, was created by King William the third, Viscount Roseberry, and by Queen Anne was advanced to the higher honour of Earl of Roseberry

Rosberry

As this part has at present several considerable Houses (whereof *Hawthorenden* is famous for its caves hewn out of the rock, and *Roslin* for the [m] stately Chapel,) so can it produce some remains of Antiquity For near the Town of *Cramond* (at which Salmon and several other Fish are taken,) many stones have been dug up with Roman Inscriptions Also, in the grounds of *Inglistown*, belonging to *Hugh Wallace*, were found, not many years since, two stones, parts of a Pillar upon one of which is a Lawrel-Crown, upon the other (the longest of the two) there is, on each side, the Roman *Securis* The name of the Emperor is broken off, but by the progress of the Roman arms, as described by Tacitus, it appears to have been set up in the time of *Julius Agricola's* government And since only the Emperor's name is struck off and it appears that by order of the Senate the Statues and Inscriptions of *Domitian* were defaced, we may probably conclude, that it was erected in honour of that Emperor What remains of it is this

Hawthorn den

[m] Vide Thea trum Scotiæ

Cramond

Inglistown

AVG COS IV
GERMANICUS
PONTIFEX MAX

These Stones are to be seen in the Garden at *Edmonstoun*, belonging to Sir *Robert Sibbald*, Doctor of Physick

Also, not far from *Edinborough*, is a Pictish Monument called by the common People *Ket Stean* which is to be read thus; *In oc tumulo jacet Vetta f Victi*

Ketstean

Next to [illegible] [n] that noted spring two miles South of *Edinburgh*, deserves our notice The name of it is *St Catherine's Well*, though it is commonly call'd *The Oily Well*, because it sends up along with the water, an *Oyl* or *Balm*, which swims upon it It is found by experience to be exceeding good, not only for the cure of Scabs, but also of any pains proceeding from cold, and also for strengthening and putting life into any decay'd part]

[n] Sibbald's Prodr Cap 10 p 21.

A mile from *Edinburgh* lieth *Leith*, an excellent Haven upon the River *Leith*, which, after Monsieur *Dessie* had fortified it with works to secure *Edinborough*, did, by the conflux of people thither, grow from a mean village to a large Town Again, when the French King, Francis the second, had married Mary Queen of Scotland, the French (who then made themselves sure of Scotland, and began now to gape after *England*) in the year 1560 strengthened it with more fortifications But Queen Elizabeth of England, upon the solicitation of the [o] Reformed Nobility of that kingdom to side with them, effected, by her wisdom and authority, their return into France, and these their fortifications were levell'd with the ground, and Scotland, ever since, hath stood clear of all apprehensions from the French [At present it hath in it several Manufactures Near this place, is *Newhaven*, which hath given the title of Viscount to an English family, the *Cheneys*, rais'd to that honour by King Charles the second]

Leith

[o] Qui puriorem Religionem amplexi

Newhaven

In the midst of this Frith, where it begins by degrees to contract itself, there stood (as Bede noteth) the City *Caer Guidi*, which seems to be *Inch Keith Island* Whether this be the *Victoria* mentioned by Ptolemy, I will not now dispute, though it is natural to believe, that the Romans might turn this *Guith* into *Victoria*, as well as our Isle of *Guith* or *Wight*, into *Vectesis* or *Vecta* [p] Certainly, since both these are broken from the shore, there is the same reason for the name in both languages For Ninnius informs us, that *Guith* in the British Tongue signifies a *breaking off* or *separation* Upon the same Frith, more inward, lies *Abercorne*, a famous Monastery in Bede's time, and by the favour of King James the sixth, [q] it gave the title of Earl to *James Hamilton* Hard by, [r] stands *Blackness Castle*, and beneath that, southward, the ancient City of *Lindum*, which Ptolemy takes notice of, and by the learned is still call'd *Linlithquo*, but by the common people *Lithquo*, adorn'd with a fair House of the Kings and a noble Church, [(which stands upon a level with the Palace, and is curious work of fine Stone,)] and a Lake plentifully stock'd with Fish, from which *Lake* it seems to derive its name, for *Lin*, as I observed before, signifies in British a *Lake* [This Town is a Royal burgh, well built and is accommodated with *Fountains* which furnish water to the Inhabitants, and with a stately Town house for the meeting of the Gentry and Citizens, and with a harbour at *Blackness* The King's house before mentioned stands upon a rising ground, which runs almost into the middle of the *Loch*, and looks like an Amphitheater, having Terras walks (as it were) and a descent from them, but upon the top where the castle stands, it is a Plain The Court has Apartments like towers, upon the four corners, and in the midst of it a stately fountain adorned with several curious statues, the water whereof rises to a good height The *Levingstons* Earls of this place are Hereditary Keepers of it, as they are also hereditary Bailiffs of the King's Bailiary and hereditary Constables of the King's Castle of *Blackness*] This District had formerly an Hereditary Sheriff of the House of *Hamilton* of *Peyle*, but its first Earl [s] was *Alexander Levingston*, advanced by King James the sixth from the dignity of a Baron (which his Ancestors had long been honour'd with) to that of Earl, [t] and his second Son, Sir *James Levingston*, was created

Caer Guidi

[p] See the Discourse of the *Roman Wall* in Scotland

[q] Now gives.

[r] Earl of Abercorne

Blackness

Linlithquo

The Town Scot r

Earl of Linlithquo

[s] In our memory C

[t] Now forfeited by Attainder

ted Earl of Calendar by King Charles the first

Peyle of Levingston

In the same Shire, is the *Peyle of Levingston*, which was burnt by *Oliver Cromwel*, and did anciently belong to the family of *Levingston* aforesaid

Calder

Nigh to this, is the Castle of *Calder*, anciently belonging to the family of *Sandilands*, of which, Sir James Sandilands, Preceptor of *Torpichen*, was in the year 1563 created Lord *Torpichen*

Borrostoness

Nor ought we to omit *Borrostoness*, north from *Linlithquo*, upon the sea coast, erected into a burgh of Regality by the Duke of Hamilton, who hath in the neighbourhood his castle of *Kineil*, adorned with large Parks and stately Avenues

Torphichen

Torphichen, to the south of Linlithgow, doth also deserve our Notice, as being a burgh of Regality, and once the residence of the Knights of *Malta* but since, as we said, hath given the title of Lord to the chief of the name of *Sandilands*

Bathgates

And *Bathgate*, the parish whereof is erected into a Sheriffdom by it self

And as the Towns, so also some Houses of note require our notice

Nidry

Nidry Castle, south west from Linlithgow, upon a river, the possessor of which Manor is hereditary Bailiff of the Regality of *Kirkliston*, and, by the Barony of Abercorn, is hereditary Sheriff of the Shire

Dundass

And north from thence, *Dundass*, formerly a fortification, which, with the Lands, hath belong'd for six hundred years past to a very ancient Family of the same name

Livingston

At some distance from whence, is *Levingston*, a fine seat, adorned with parks and gardens, wherein are many curious plants, by the care of that worthy Gentleman, *Patrick Murray*, the late owner thereof, who, whilst he lived, was the Ornament of his Country, and

Bins

Bins, adorned by General *Dalzell* with Avenues, large Parks, and fine Gardens After he had procured himself a lasting name in the Wars, here it was that he rested his old Age, and pleased himself with the culture of curious Flowers and Plants

Medop

And upon the same coast, *Medop*, the residence of the Earl of *Linlithgow*, famous likewise for its fine Gardens, enclosed with high walls, and furnish'd with Orange trees, and such like curious Exoticks

West-Lothian hath also its Antiquities

Kipps

At the east end of the enclosure of the *Kipps*, south from *Linlithgow*, there is an ancient Altar of great stones, unpolished, and so placed, that each of them doth support another, and so as no one could stand without leaning upon another Hard by it, are several great stones set in a Circle, and, in the two adjacent hills, the remains of old Camps, with great heaps of stones and ancient Graves

Queens ferry

Some miles also to the west of *Queens-Ferry* upon the sea coast (supposed to be so call'd from *St Margaret*, Queen to King Malcolm Canmore, as the shortest passage over the Forth to *Dumfermling*, where she resided much, and began to build a Monastery,) and near *Abercorn*-Castle, Bede tells us that the Roman wall be

Roman wall

gan One may trace it towards *Cariddin* where a figured stone is to be seen, and a gold Medal was found In a line parallel, about a mile to the south of this, there is a Village which preserves the remains of the old wall, being called *Walltoun*

Walltoun

From the name, and the artificial Mount cast up there, one would think it to be the very place, which Bede calls *Penvalltoun* The track of the wall appears in several places, between this and *Kinneall*, and from thence to *Falkirk*]

ᶜ A little after, C

ᶜ In the year 1606, *Mark Ker*, Baron of *Newbottle*, was advanced to the title of Earl of Lothian, [whose Grandchild *Anna*, Countess of Lothian, being married to Sir *William Ker*, eldest Son of *Ancrum*, King Charles the first created him Earl of Lothian, and *Robert* his Son was advanced by King William the third to the higher honour of Marquis of Lothian]

SEL-

SELGOVÆ.

ENEATH the Gadeni *to the South and West (where now lie the small Territories of* Liddesdale, Eusdale, Eskdale, Annandale, Niddisdale, [*and* Wachopdale,] *all so call'd,* [*except the last,*] *from the names of the Rivulets running through them, which all lose themselves in* Solway Frith,) *were anciently seated the* Selgovæ, *the footsteps of whose name seem to me, whether to others too I know not, to remain in the name* Solway.

LIDDESDALE, EUSDALE, ESKDALE.

Liddesdale. Armitage.

N *Liddesdale*, we have a prospect of *Armitage*, seated on high, and so called because it was anciently dedicated to a solitary life. But now it is a very strong Castle, which belonged to the *Hepburnes*, who deduce their Original from a certain English Captive, whom the Earl of *March* did greatly enrich, for delivering him out of an imminent Danger. They were Earls of *Bothwell*, and

Hepburnes Earls of Bothwell.

for a long time Admirals of Scotland by inheritance: but by a sister of James Earl of *Bothwell* (the last of the *Hepburnes*) who was married to *John Prior* of Coldingham a natural son of King James the fifth, who had several such issue, both title and estate devolved to their son, [who forfeited for his treasonable design of seising the King's Person in his own Palace of *Holyrood House*, in the year 1593, and passed the remainder of his days beyond the Seas.] Hard by, is *Brakensey*, the seat of the

Brakensey. Lord Buccleugh.

warlike Family of *Buccleugh*, surnamed *Scot*, with many little Forts of military men, up and down the Country.

Eusdale. Uzelum.

In *Eusdale*, I should be apt to think, from the affinity of the name, that the ancient *Uzelum* mentioned by Ptolemy, lay upon the River *Euse*.

Eskdale. Horesti.

In *Eskdale*, some are of opinion that the *Horesti* dwelt, into whose borders Julius Agricola, after he had subdued the Britains inhabiting this Tract, led the Roman Army; especially, if we read *Horesti* for *Horesti*. For the British *Ar Esk* signifies a place by the river *Eske*. (As for *Uxelum* in *Eskdale*, I have spoken of it before in England, and need not repeat what I have said.)

[But as to the conjecture concerning the seat of the *Horesti*, it is not by any means probable, if we consider the circumstances of that Action. It was in the latter end of his Government, that he led his Forces against *them*; whereas, we find, that even in his fourth year, all to the south of that neck of land between the two *Friths*, was added to the Roman Province, so that we must go further north to seek for them. And Tacitus himself, in effect, forbids us to look after them hereabouts, when he says, that the people against whom Agricola was then fighting, were the *Populi Caledoniam incolentes*, and *Novæ Gentes*, namely, those beyond the *Friths*, who by the fortification of that neck of land, were *Submoti velut in aliam insulam*, i. e. Driven as it were into another Island. (So that if the relation which the *Horesti* may have to *Esk*, be of any moment, it would better suit the people dwelling between *South Esk*, and *North Esk* in *Angus*. But that name really seems to imply no more than *Orea-ai*, the *Mountaineers* or *High-landers*.) Add to this, what Tacitus further says, 'That Agricola having beat Galgacus near the Grampian hills, 'brought back the Roman Army to the borders of the *Horesti*, and having received Hostages from them, he ordered the Commanders of the Roman Fleet to sail about the 'Isle.' Which cannot agree to *Eskdale*, a small inconsiderable Country, surrounded with others, and not bordering on the sea, but seems to be most properly applicable to the Mouth and Firth of *Tay*, and the Country of Angus and Mernis situate thereupon, where the Roman Navy landed their Men, and remained there to receive them at the end of the Expedition. Besides, from this Port to the Grampian Hill, through the large Country of Strathmore, there are still the evident Remains of a great Highway, along which, we may suppose, they marched their Army and Carriages, and by the same way returned to their Ships But there is no direct continued way between the Grampian Hills and Eskdale, nor could an Army, with such great Carriages, march between those two places]

ANNANDALE.

[HE Shire of *Dumfrise* contains *Annandale*, *Wachopdale*, and *Niddisdale* It takes its name from the chief Burgh of the Shire On the west it hath *Galloway* and *Kyle*, on the east it is bounded with *Solway Frith*, and the March of Scotland and England, on the north with part of *Clidsale*, *Tweedale*, and *Teviotdale*, and on the south with the Irish-sea From west to south east, it is about fifty miles long, and in breadth about thirty four The Inhabitants were a stout warlike People, and in former times the bulwark of the Kingdom The soil, generally, is not so good for Corn, as for Pasturage, so that they deal mostly in *Cows* and *Sheep*, which turn to considerable gain]

Annandale. Joined to *Eskdale* on the west side, lies *Annandale*, that is, the Valley or Dale upon the river *Annan*, into which the access by land is very difficult [It runs in a streight line from west to east, about twenty four miles in length, and fourteen in breadth The places of greatest note are these A Castle upon *Lough Maban*, which is three parts surrounded with water, and strongly walled Their tradition about this *Lough-Maban*, that a Castle stood formerly in the *middle* of it that which now stands upon the brink, is going to decay The Town of *Logh Maban*, a Royal burgh, situate upon the south side of the water of *Anan*, in the middle of the Country Near the source of which river, stands *Moffet*, famous for its Medicinal well] *Annandale* Town is almost upon the very mouth of the river *Annan*, divested of all its glory by the English War in the reign of Edward the sixth [Afterwards, it gave the title of Viscount to Sir *John Murray*, whom King James the sixth did also create Earl of *Annandale*]

Logh Maban.

Moffet.

The *Jonstons*. In this Territory of Annandale, the *Jonstons* are men of greatest name, a family born for War, between whom and the *Maxwells* (who by ancient right preside over the *Stewarty*, for so it is term'd) there * hath been too long an open enmity and defiance, even to blood-shed [The Laird of *Johnstoun* was created Lord *Johnstoun* by King Charles the first, and Earl of *Hartfield* by the same King, which title was changed by King Charles the second into that of Earl of *Annandale*, and this, by the favour of King William the third, into that of Marquiss of *Anandale*, in the person of *William*, son of the said Earl, who also in the next reign, was deservedly honour'd with the Offices of President of the Council, and Secretary of State] This Valley, *Edgar* King of Scots, upon his restoration to the Kingdom by the Auxiliaries that he had out of England, gave, for his good services, to *Robert Brus*, Lord of *Cleaveland* in the County of York, who bestowed it, by the King's permission, upon *Robert* his younger son, being unwilling himself to serve the King of Scots in his Wars From him, are branched the *Bruses* Lords of *Annandale*, of whom, *Robert Bruse* married *Isabella*, daughter of *William* King of Scots by the daughter of *Robert Avenel* his son likewise, *Robert* the third of that name, married the daughter of *David* Earl of *Huntingdon* and *Garioch*, whose son *Robert* surnamed the *Noble*, upon failure of the issue of Alexander the third, King of Scotland, did in right of his mother challenge the Kingdom of Scotland, before Edward the first King of England (*as direct and superior Lord of the Kingdom of Scotland*, so the English say, or, *as an Honorary Arbitrator*, as the Scots will have it, *as being more nearly ally'd in degree and blood to King Alexander the third, and to Margaret daughter of the King of Norway*, although a second sister's son Who soon after resigning his right, *granted and gave over* to his son *Robert Brus Earl of* Carrick, *and to his heirs* (I speak out of the Original Record) *all the right and claim which he had or might have to the Kingdom of Scotland* But the point was determined in favour of *John Baliol* (who sued for his right, *as descended from the eldest sister, though in a more remote degree*) in these words, *Because the person more remote in the degree descending in the first line, is to be preferred before a nearer in the second line, in the Succession of an inheritance that cannot be parted*

The Stewartry of *Annandale*.

* So said, ann 1607

The *Brus*.

Nevertheless, the said *Robert*, son to the Earl of Carrick, by his valour possess'd himself of the Kingdom, and establish'd it in his posterity. A Prince, who as he was illustrious for his great Exploits, so did he triumph over Fortune (so often his Adversary) with invincible courage and constancy of mind

Wachopdale. [Between *Anandale* and *Eskdale* lieth *Wachopdale*, so called from the water of *Wachop* running through it, and is much of the same nature with the adjacent Counties already described The most ancient Monument remarkable hereabouts, is St *Ruth's* Church, where is a Pillar curiously engraven, with a Danish Inscription upon it Near this place, the people have a way of making Salt of Sea sand the Salt is something bitterish, which probably proceeds from the nitre in it]

St *Ruth's*.

NIDIS-

NIDISDALE.

CLOSE to *Annandale* on the West, lies *Nidisdale*, tolerably stock'd with arable and pasture grounds, and so named from the River *Nid*, by Ptolemy falsely written *Nobius*, for *Novius* or *Nidius*, of which name there are other Rivers in Britain, [a] full of muddy shallows, as this *Nid* is [It is encompassed with a ridge of Hills on all sides, and in the bottoms has abundance of Corn It is divided into the *Overward*, containing the Parishes in the Presbytery of *Pempont*, and the *Netherward*, containing those of Dumfrise Presbytery]

The River Nid.

[a] *Vadosi et faculenti*

The *Nid* springs out of the Lake *Lough-Cure*, upon which stood anciently *Corda*, a Town of the *Selgovæ* It takes its course first by *Sauqubar*, a Castle of the *Creightons*, who were long honoured with the Title of Barons of *Sauquar*, [(and advanced by King James the sixth to the dignity of Viscounts of *Air*, and by King Charles the first to that of Earls of *Dumfreis*,)] and were also honoured with the authority of hereditary Sheriffs of *Nidisdale* Next, it runs by *Morton*, which [b] hath given the Title of Earl to a branch of the family of *Douglass*, of whom, others are seated at *Drumlanrig* upon the same River, [which gave the title of Viscount to the Laird thereof, by the favour of King Charles the first, and now the eldest son to the Duke of *Queensberry* hath the title of Drumlanrig, at which place, the late Duke hath built a noble Seat For, to the said title of Drumlanrig, was added by King Charles the first, the honour of Earl of *Queensberry*, which was afterwards changed by King Charles the second into the more honourable titles, first of Marquiss, and then of Duke, of *Queensberry*]

Corda

The *Creightons* Barons of *Sauquhar*

[b] Ann. 1457

Earls of *Morton*

Drumlanrig

See *Dover*, in *England*

Near the mouth of the river, stands *Dunfreys* between two Hills, the most flourishing Town of this Tract, which still shews its ancient Castle The Town is famous for its Woollen Manufacture, and remarkable for the murder of *John Commin*, a person exceeding all others in Interest amongst the Scots, whom *Robert Brus*, lest he should oppose his coming to the Crown, ran through in the Church, and easily got a pardon of the Pope for a murther committed in a *sacred* place [Here, over the *Nith*, is a stone bridge of nine Arches The Streets are large, and the Church and Castle very stately, For the convenience of Trade (which is much help'd by the Tide flowing up to the Town, and making an Harbour) they have also an *Exchange* for Merchants]

Dunfreys

Nearer to the Mouth of the *Nith*, *Solway*, a Village, still retains somewhat of the old name of *Selgovæ* Upon the very mouth, is situated *Caer Laverock*, Ptolemy's *Carbantorigum*, a Fort look'd upon as impregnable, till King Edward the first, accompanied with the flower of the English Nobility, besieged and took it But [c] now it is a weak Mansion House of the Barons *Maxwell*, who, being of ancient Nobility, were long *Wardens* of these Western Marches, and were [d] lately advanced by marriage with a Daughter and Coheir of the Earl of *Morton*, on which account *John* Lord *Maxwell* was declared Earl of *Morton*, as also with the Daughter and Heir of *Hereis* Lord *Tericles*, whom J a second son, took to wife, and had by her the title of Baron *Hereis* [Afterwards the title of Earl of Morton came to the Lairds of *Lochleven*] In this Valley also, upon the Lake, lies *Glencarn*, of which the *Cunninghams* (to be spoken of under another head) have long born the title of Earl, [being advanced to that honour, in the person of *Alexander* Lord of *Kilmaures*, by King James the third, in the year 1488]

Caer Laverock

[c] Ann 1607

[d] Ann 1607

Barons *Hereis*

Glencarn

This *Nidisdale*, together with *Annandale*, breeds a warlike sort of people, but [e] infamous for their depredations For they dwell upon *Solway*, a fordable Arm of the Sea, through which they often made excursions into England for booty, and in which the Inhabitants on both sides (a pleasant sight [f]) *hunt Salmons* (of which there is great plenty) with spears on horseback, or, if you had rather call it so, *fish* for them [From this territory, the Lord *Maxwel* was created by King James the sixth Earl of *Nithsdale*, the heirs of whose eldest son failing in the reign of King Charles the second, the Lord *Hereis*, of the second branch, became Earl of *Nithsdale*]

[e] so said, Ann 1607

Salmons

What manner of *Cattle stealers* they [f] were that inhabit these Valleys in the Marches of both Kingdoms, *John Lesley*, a Scotchman himself, and Bishop of *Ross*, will inform you *They sally out of their own borders in the night, in troops, through unfrequented ways, and many intricate windings All the day, they refresh themselves and their Horses in lurking holes which they had pitch'd upon before, till they arrive, in the dark, at the places they have a design upon As soon as they have seized the booty, they in like manner return home in the night, through blind ways, and fetch long compasses The more skilful any Captain is to pass through those wild Desarts, crooked turnings, and deep precipices, in the thickest mist and darkness, his reputation is the greater, and he is looked on as a man of an excellent head And they are so very cunning, that they seldom have their booty taken from them, unless sometimes, when by the help of Blood hounds following exactly in the same track, they chance to fall into the hands of their adversaries When, being taken, they have so much persuasive Eloquence, and so many smooth insinuating words at command, that if they do not move their Judges, nay and even their Adversaries (notwithstanding the greatest severity of nature) to mercy, they at least move them to admiration and compassion*

Cattle-stealers Are, C

NOVAN-

NOVANTES.

NEXT to Nidiſdale, the Novantes inhabited that tract in the Valleys, which ſpreads a great way towards the Weſt, yet is ſo indented with Creeks, that in ſome places it is narrow, but towards the end grows wider again, whence ſome have call'd it the Cherſoneſſus, or *Peninſula, of the* Novantes But now their Country contains, Galloway, Carick, Kyle, *and* Cunningham

GALLOWAY.

Galloway

GALLOWAY, call'd in Latin writers of the middle age, *Galwallia* and *Gallovidia* (taking its name from the Iriſh, who were its ancient Inhabitants, and who call themſelves, in their own language for ſhortneſs-ſake, *Gael*,) is a hilly Country, better for feeding of Cattle than bearing of Corn [It hath upon the ſouth, the *Iriſh Sea*, upon the weſt, the *Frith of Clyde*, upon the north, *Carick* and *Kyle*, and to the north eaſt the river of *Nith* It is in length, from North-eaſt to South-weſt, about ſeventy miles, in breadth, from North to South, in ſome places twenty four miles, in others twenty, and in others only ſixteen It is divided into the *Higher* and *Lower* Country The *Higher* lies between the water of *Cree* and the point or *Mule*, making the Sheriffdom The *Lower* takes up the reſt, namely, all upon the water of *Cree*, making the Stewartry of *Kilcumbright* The plenty of paſtures, induces them to keep vaſt flocks of *Sheep* as alſo of *Cows*, which they ſend into England in great numbers] The Inhabitants follow Fiſhing, as well in the Sea round about as in the rivers and loughs that are every where under the hills, in which, about *September*, they catch in incredible number of [a] excellent well-taſted Eels in their [b] *Weeles*, by which they are no leſs gainers, than by their little truſs Niggs, which, upon account of the compactneſs of their bodies, and their enduring of labour, are bought up here in great numbers

[a] *Sapidiſſimarum*
[b] *Excipulis*
Galloway Naggs

Among theſe, the firſt place that preſents it ſelf upon the river *Dea* (mentioned by Ptolemy, and which yet keeps its name, being call'd *Dee*) is *Kircowbright*, the moſt convenient harbour of this Coaſt, and one of the *Stewarties* of Scotland, belonging to the *Maxwells*, [Earls of *Nithſdale* The ancient family of *Maclellan* was dignify'd by King Charles the firſt, with the title of Lord *Kircudbright*] Then *Cardines*, a Fort upon the river *Fleet*, built upon a craggy and high rock, and fortify'd with ſtrong Walls Hard by, the river *Ken* (call'd by Ptolemy *Jena*, but corruptly) falls into the Sea [On this river, ſtands *Kenmure*, from whence the family of the *Gordons* had the name of Viſcount of *Kenmure* confer'd on them by King Charles the firſt near which, is *New Galloway*, a Burgh Royal]

Dee in Kirkcowbright
Cardines
Kenmure
New Galloway

Next, *Wigton*, a Port with a very narrow entrance between the two ſtreams, *Blaidnoo* and *Crea*, reckoned among the *Sheriffdoms*, over which [c] *Agnew of the Iſle* preſides It formerly had for its Earl, *Archibald Douglas*, famous in the French Wars, and [d] after that (by the favour of King James [the ſixth] *John* [e] *Fleming*, who derived his pedigree from the ancient Earls of *Wigton*, [and whoſe poſterity doth ſtill enjoy that honour]

Wigton
[c] *Agnew of Insula*
Earls of Wigton
[d] Now C
[e] Dec

Near this, Ptolemy fixes the City *Leucophibia*, which I know not where to look for Yet by the circumſtances of the place, it ſhould ſeem to be that Epiſcopal See of *Ninian*, which Bede calls *Candida Caſa*, and the Engliſh and Scots in the ſame ſenſe *Whit herne*, [and the Saxons, before them Ƿꝩıꞇ ǣꞃne, the latter part of which name ſignifies any ſort of [f] *Veſſel*] What then, if Ptolemy (as his way was) tranſlated *Candida Caſa*, which was the name the Britains gave it, into Λευκ οικίδια in Greek, that is, *white Houſes*, inſtead of which, the Tranſcribers have obtruded upon us *Leucophibia* In this place, *Ninia* or *Ninian*, the Britain, a holy man (the firſt who inſtructed the Southern Picts in the Chriſtian Faith, in the reign of Theodoſius the Younger) had his reſidence, and built a Church, which was dedicated to St *Martin*, the form whereof (as Bede obſerves) was different from that of the Britiſh buildings The ſame Author tells us, that the Engliſh in his time were poſſeſs'd of this Country, and that, when the number of the *Faithful* encreaſed

Leucophibia
[f] The word ... is called in the north ...
S Ninian

encreased, an Episcopal See was erected at this *Candida Casa* A little higher, is a Peninsula (the Sea insinuating it self on both sides,) which by a narrow neck is joined to the main land This is properly call'd *Novantum Chersonesus* and *Promontorium*, but commonly the *Mull of Galloway*

Novantum Promontorium

Beyond this, Northward, is an open Bay, full of Islands, and of a mighty compass; into which abundance of rivers on all sides empty themselves But first of all, at the very point of the Promontory, is *Abravanus*, which, being a little misplaced, is so termed by Ptolemy, for *Aber ruanus*, that is, the mouth of the river *Ruan* For at this day, it is call'd the river *Rian*, and the like out of which it runs, *Lough-Rian*, and is admirably well stock'd with Herrings, and a sort of * Gudgeons [On this Lake standeth *Stranrawer*, a Burgh Royal The Promontory or Point by which it entereth into the Sea, is called the Point of *Corsehill*, stretching to *Cantyre*, and on the other side is *Port Patrick*, a known Sea port, which is opposite to *Donaghadee*, in Ireland, and from thence runs Southward to the point of the Mule The Land betwixt the two points of *Corsehill* and the *Mule*, is called the *Rinnes of Galloway* (perhaps, because the points *run* out narrow, a great way into the Sea) and are twenty four miles distant To the South of *Lochrian*, is another Bay, called the Loch or Bay of *Luce*, running betwixt the points of the *Mule* and *Whitehern* opposite to the Isle of Man The neck of Land between the Lakes joining the *Rinnes* to the main Land, is six miles broad, and near the midst in a little rising ground standeth the Castle of the *Inch*, among the Lakes On this Bay, is the Vale or *Glen* of *Luce*, where was an Abbey founded by Rolland Lord of Galloway, father to Allan, and confirm'd by the King with a Regality, whereof the Family of *Staire* is hereditary Baillie]

Abravanus

* Saxatiles pisces

Stranrawer

Corsehill

Port Patrick

Rinnes of Galloway

Bay of Luce

Castle of the Inch

Lords of Galloway

Galloway had its own Princes and Lords in ancient times, of whom, the first recorded in History, was *Fergus*, in the reign of Henry the first of England, who gave for his Arms, *A Lion Rampant Argent, crown'd* [Or] *in a Shield Azure* After many Disturbances which he had raised, he was driven to such straits by King Malcolm, as to give his Son *Uchtred* for an hostage, and, being grown weary of the world, to take upon him the habit of a Canon at *Holy rood* House at Edenborough As for *Uchtred*, Gilbert his younger brother took him Prisoner in Battle, and after he had cut out his Tongue, and pulled out his Eyes, most cruelly deprived him both of life and estate But within a few years, after Gilbert was dead, *Roland* the Son of Uchtred recovered his father's inheritance, who, of a sister of William Morvill, Constable of Scotland, begat *Alan*, Lord of Galloway, and Constable of Scotland Alan, by Margaret, the eldest daughter of David Earl of Huntingdon, had *Dervolgilda*, the wife of *John Balliol*, and mother of *John Balliol*, King of Scotland, who contended with *Robert Brus* for that Kingdom, and by a former Wife, as it seems, had *Helen*, married to *Roger Quincy*, an Englishman, Earl of Winchester, who upon that account was Constable of Scotland as was likewise *William Ferrers*, of Groby, grand son of the said Roger, by a daughter and coheir But these English soon lost their inheritance in Scotland, as also the dignity of Constable, which the *Commins* Earls of Bughuan had (as decended likewise of a daughter of *Roger Quincy*) till it was transferred to the Earls of *Arrol* But the title of Lord of *Galloway* fell afterwards to the Family of Douglass, [and since to the family of *Stuart* of Garleis, which being first dignify'd by King James the sixth with the title of Lord of Garleis, was further rais'd by the same King to the dignity of Earl of *Galloway*, on account chiefly of their descent from the illustrious Family of *Lennox*

THE Second part of the *Novantes* is said to be the Sheriffdom of *AIRE* (so called from the Town of [b] *Aire*, the head Burgh of the Shire,) though the north part of this tract seems rather to have belonged to the *Damnii* The Country is bounded on the north by the Shire of *Rainfrew*, on the south with *Galloway*, on the east with *Cl.dsdale*, and on the west with the Frith of *Clyde* It generally produces good store of Corn and Grass, and is very populous, and the Inhabitants of it are exceeding industrious

Sheriffdom of Aire

[b] Of his, see Ayr, afterward

It is divided into three *Bailliaries*, viz *Carick Kyle*, and *Cunningham* The most considerable Loch in it, is that of *Dun*, six miles in length, and two in breadth, with an Isle in it, upon which is an old house, call'd *Castle-Dun* Upon the Water *Down*, is a bridge of one arch, ninety foot long]

CARRICT.

ARRICT comes next; a Country fruitful in Pasture, and abundantly furnished with Commodities both by Sea and Land. Here Ptolemy places both *Rerigonium* a creek [(probably the same with the bay of *Glenluce*,)] and *Rerigonium* a Town. For which, in a very ancient Copy of Ptolemy, printed at Rome in 1480, we have *Berigonium*. So that I cannot chuse but think, it was that which is now called *Bargeny*. It * had a Lord of the Family of the *Kennedyes* (which came out of Ireland in the reign of *Robert Brus*,) a Family, noble, numerous, and powerful, in all this tract. [But the Lands of Bargeny being purchased by Sir *John Hamilton*, natural son of *John* Marquiss of *Hamilton*, his son was created Lord *Bargeny* by King Charles the first.] The head of it, is Earl of *Cassils* (the name of a Castle upon the river Dun, which is his seat,) [the Family of *Kennedy* being first advanced to that honour by K. James the fourth, in the year 1509.] Upon the banks of the same river, he had another call'd *Dunnur Castle*; and he is likewise hereditary Bailiff of this Province. For this, with *Kyle* and *Cunningham*, are the three *Ballairies* of Scotland, so call'd, because they who govern these with ordinary power and Jurisdiction, are stiled *Bailiffs*, a word coined in the middle age, which signifies amongst the Greeks, Sicilians, and French, a *Conservator* or Keeper.

Bengonium

Bargeny

* Has. C. The *Kennedyes*

Earls of *Cassils*

Dunnur, Castle

But *Carrict*, in former times, had its Earls. Not to mention Gilbert of Galloway's Son (to whom King *William* gave *Carrict* entire, to be possess'd for ever) we read that Adam of Kilconah, about the year 1270 was Earl of *Carrict*, and died in the Holy War, whose Widow Margaret fell in love with *Robert Brus*, a beautiful young Gentleman, as she saw him a hunting, and, making him her Husband, brought him the title and estate of Earl of *Carrict*, and bore him *Robert Brus*, the renown'd King of Scotland, and founder of the royal Line. But the title of Earl of *Carrict*, being for some time left to the younger Sons of the Family of *Brus*, afterwards became an addition to the other Honours of the Princes of Scotland, [and King Charles the first conferred this title upon *John Stuart*, descended from King James the fifth, by a natural Son.]*

Earls of Carrict. *Lib. Malros.*

KYLE.

YLE is next, lying more inward upon the Bay, a plentiful Country, and well inhabited. In Bede's *Auctarium* (or Supplement) it is call'd *Campus Cyel*, and *Coil*, where it is recorded, that *Eadbert, King of the Northumbers, added this, with other Territories, to his Kingdom.* [This Country lies between the river of *Dune*, which separates it from *Carrick*, and the river of *Irwine*, which separates it from *Cunningham*. It is divided into *Kings-Kyle*, under the Jurisdiction of the Sheriff; and *Kyle Stewart*, which belong'd anciently to the *Stuarts* of Scotland, and since, to the Prince, the King's eldest Son.]

An. 750

In Ptolemy's time, *Vidogora* was a place of note, [now possibly *Locbrian*; or] perhaps *Aire*, which is a Sheriffdom, a Market [formerly] but little,] and a well known Port upon a small river of the same name. [It is now the chief Market town, in the west of Scotland. Its situation is in a sandy plain; yet hath it pleasant and fruitful fields, with *Greens* which afford a good prospect both winter and summer. The Church is stately enough, and there is a bridge of four arches which joins it to the *New Town*, seated on the north side of the water. The ancient name of this *Aire* was St. *John's Town*, but that is now lost. By the King's Patent, it is the Sheriff's Seat, and hath within its Jurisdiction thirty two miles. A mile north of the town, not far from the Sea shore, there is a *Lazar house*, commonly call'd the King's Chapel, which King *Robert de Brus* set apart for the maintenance of *Lepers*.]

Vidogora. Aire.

Concerning *Aire*, * these Verses sent me by *J. Johnston*, may be well worth the inserting.

* I can meet with no lines better worth the inserting, than——C.

Parva urbs, ast ingens animus in fortibus hæret,
Inferior nulli nobilitate virum.
Aëris e campis haurit purissima cœlum,
Incubat & miti mollior aura solo.
Aeria hinc, non *Æria prius, credo, illa vocata est,*
Cum duris quid enim mollia juris habent?
Infera cum superis quod si componere fas est,
Aurea *fors dici debuit illa prius.*

Small is the Town, but of great Souls is proud,
For Courage fam'd, and Sons of noble blood.
From th' happy Clime, pure draughts of air descend,
And gentle breezes bless the fruitful Land.
Old times (if Poets have a right to guess)
Not *Æria*, but *Aeria* call'd the place:
Rough brass could ne'er such soft delight express.
If I so high might raise my noble theme,
I'd swear that *Aurea* was the ancient name.

* The title given to John Stuart, was from a place in the Orknies.

Besides the River *Aire*, there are two other Rivulets which water this small Territory, having many little Villages scatter'd upon their banks *Lougar*, upon which the *Crawfords*, and *Cesnock*, upon which the *Cambells*, have their residence (noted families in this tract) On the bank of the same river, is also *Ucbiltre-Castle*, the Seat of the *Stewarts*, of the blood Royal, as descended from the Dukes of Albany, hence [heretofore] stiled Barons of *Ucbiltre*, of which House was that *Robert Stewart*, who was the inseparable companion of the Prince of *Conde*, and kill'd with him in a battle in France [In the year 1651, King Charles the second advanced Sir *Robert Colvil* to the honour of a Peer, by the stile and title of Lord *Colvil* of *Ocbiltree* Near this place, to the west, is *Stair*, which, by the favour of King William and Queen Mary, gave the title of Viscount, to Sir *James Dalrymple*, whose Inheritance it was; and afterwards, the title of Earl, to *John* Viscount *Stair*, by the favour of Queen Anne, whose Son of the same name, the present Earl, hath greatly distinguish'd himself by his gallant and wise Conduct, in the Camp, and in the Court.

Crawfords Cambells

Ucbiltre, or Ocbiltre

The chief messuage of the Stewartry of *Kile*, was *Dundonald*, purchased by Sir *William Cochran*, who was created Lord Cochran by King Charles the first, and by King Charles the second, Earl of *Dundonland*] *Cambel* of *Louden* enjoys the honour of Hereditary Bailiff of *Kyle*

Dundonald.

CUNNINGHAM.

O *Kyle*, upon the West and North, is joined *Cunningham*, which so hems in and contracts the Bay, that it makes it much narrower than hitherto it has been The name signifies as much as the *King's habitation*, whence you may imagin how pleasant it is It is water'd by the *Irwin*, that divides it from Kyle, at the head almost of which river, [we see *Lowdoun*, the ancient seat of the *Crawfords*, which, coming by marriage to the *Campbels*, was rais'd to the dignity of a Barony by K James the sixth, in the person of Sir *Hugh Campbel*, and to the higher honour of an Earldom, by K Charles the first, in the person of Sir *John Campbel*, upon his marriage with the grand daughter of the said *Hugh* Next, on the same river, not far from the head,] we have a sight of *Kilmarnock*, the Seat of the Barons *Boids* In the reign of King James the third, *Thomas*, one of these, * was, by a gale of Court favour, advanc'd to the authority of Regent, and *Robert* his Son to the Honour of Earl of *Arran* and a marriage with the King's Sister But the same gale blowing contrary, they were adjudged enemies to the State, *Robert* had his Wife taken from him, and given to *James Hamilton*, and their Estates were confiscated, and being by the inconstancy of fortune strip'd of all, they died in exile Yet their Posterity recover'd the ancient honour of Barons, and ' continued to enjoy it, [and were, moreover, dignify'd with the title of Earl of *Kilmarnock* by King Charles the second]

Lowdoun

Kilmarnock Barons *boids*

' Enjoy it at this day, C (ie 1607)

Upon the mouth of the river *Irwin*, stands *Irwin*, a Borough, with a Port so choaked upon with Banks of sand, and so shallow, that it is only capable of small Vessels [By the favour of King Charles the first, *James*, Brother to the Earl of Argyle, was created Earl of *Irwin*, which title being extinct, Sir *Arthur Ingram* of *Temple Newsom* in the County of York, was created Viscount of *Irwin* by King Charles the second] Higher up, over the Bay, stands *Ardrossan*, a Castle of the Montgomeries, an ancient and noble family, which can shew, as a proof of their Warlike Valour, *Poununy Castle*, built out the ransom-money of *Henry Percy*, surnamed *Hotspur*, whom *J Montgomery* took with his own hands in the Battle at *Otterburne*, and brought him away Prisoner Not far from *Ardrossan*, is *Largis*, embru'd in the blood of the Norwegians by King Alexander the third From whence, following the winding of the shore, we meet with *Eglington* Castle, once possessed by Gentlemen of that name, from whom it descended to the *Montgomeries*, who took from hence the title of Earls of *Eglington* But whence this Surname came, is hard to guess, That, out of Normandy it came into England, and that there were several Families of that name, I am satisfied But the Family in *Essex*, from which Sir *Thomas Montgomery*, Knight of the Garter in the reign of King Edward the 4th, was descended, gave Arms but a little different from these However, this noble House hath enlarg'd itself very much, and out of those of *Gevan*, was that *Gabriel de Lorges*, called Earl of Montgomery, and Captain of the Scotch Guard du Corps (instituted by Charles the fifth, King of France, for a Guard to him and his Successors, as a signal mark of their fidelity and favour to him,) who in a Tournament slew Henry the second King of France with a Splinter of his Spear, which (his Beaver chancing to be up) penetrated through the eye into his brain Afterwards siding with the *Huguenots* in the Civil Wars of France, he was taken, and beheaded

Irwin, riv

Ardrossan Castle

Largis

Montgomeries Earls of Eglinton

The Scotch Guard du Corps in France

But the Family of the *Cunninghams* is accounted more numerous in this Tract, the head whereof, the Earl of *Glencairn* hath a Seat at *Kilmaurs*, and derives his descent out of England, viz from an English Gentleman, who, together with others, murdered *Thomas* Archbishop of Canterbury How true this is, I know not, but perhaps it may be grounded upon a probable conjecture, taken from an Archbishop's Pall, which they give in their Coat of Arms

Cunninghams [illegible]

* This is differently related by others viz That *Thomas* Son of Robert married the King's [illegible] That her Marriage with James Hamilton was not till after the Death of her first Husband and [illegible] James Boyd, her Son

The

The Island *GLOTTA,* or *ARRAN.*

Glotta Ithin sight of *Cunningham*; amongst many other Islands, *Glotta* is of greatest eminence; and Island mentioned by Antoninus, in the very Frith of the river *Glotta* or *Clyde*, and called [a] at this day from a Castle of the same name, *Arran*. The innermost parts are wholly mountainous, but the bottoms along the shore are well inhabited. The first Earl it had, that I read of, was [b] *Thomas Boyd*, whose Wife and Earldom together, upon *Boid's* being banished the Kingdom, *James Hamilton* (as I mentioned before) obtain'd; and his Posterity enjoy'd the same, saving [c] that *James Steward*, appointed Guardian to *James Hamilton* Earl of *Arran* (who was so defective in his understanding, that he could not manage the Estate,) took this Title in the Right of being *Guardian*.

[a] Ann 1607.

[b] *Robert*, C. Earls of *Arran*.

[c] That of late, C.

Buthe Near this, stands *Buthe*, nam'd from a little Religious Cell founded by *Brendanus* (for so in Scotch they call a *Cell*,) which has a Sheriff of the Family of the *Stewards*. In this Island is *Rothesay* [Town and] Castle, which gives the Title of Duke to the eldest Son of the King of Scotland (who is born *Prince of Scotland, Duke of Rothsay*, and *High Steward of Scotland*,) ever since King Robert the third invested *David* his eldest Son with the Dukedom of *Rothsay*, who was the first in Scotland that was honoured with the Title of *Duke*. With which Title Queen Mary honoured *Henry* Lord *Darnley*, before she took him to be her Husband. Rothesay

After this, in the same Bay, we have *Hellan*, antiently *Hellan-Leneow*, that is, (according to *J. Fordon's* interpretation,) *The Saints Island*, and *Hellan Tinoc*, that is, *the Island of Hogs*, with many other of less note. [These Islands are erected into a Sheriffdom, and the Stewards of *Bute*, descended of a son of King *Robert* the second, are *Heretable* Sheriffs thereof. Also, in the year 1703, *Bute* was erected into an Earldom, in the person of Sir *James Steuart*, which is now enjoy'd by his son and heir.] Hellan.

DAMNII.

DAMNII.

BEYOND the Novantes, *but somewhat more inward along the River* Glotta *and* Cluyde, *and farther up even to the very Eastern Sea, dwelt the* Damnii; *and (if I judge aright (for who can be certain at such a distance from our own times, and in so much obscurity?)* in Cluydesdale, the Barony of Renfraw, Lenox, Sterling, Menteith, *and* Fife.

CLUYDESDALE.

Cluydesdale. CLUYDSEDALE (called also the Sheriffdom of *Lanrick*, from the Town of *Lanrick*, where the Sheriff keeps his Courts) is bounded on the South-East with the Stewartry of *Annandale*, on the South with the Sheriffdom of *Dumfrise*, on the South-west with that of *Aire*, on the North-west with that of *Ranfreu*, on the North with that of *Dumbarton*, on the North-east with that of *Sterling*, on the East with that of *Linlithgow*, and a little to the South-east, with that of *Mid Lothian*. It is in length about forty miles, in breadth, where broadest, some twenty four, and where narrowest, sixteen miles. The country abounds with *Coal*, *Peets*, and *Lime-stone*, but what turns to the greatest account, is the *Lead Mines*. It is divided into two *Wards*, the *Over-ward* and *Nether-ward*; this, hilly and full of heaths, and fit for pasturage, the other, plain and proper for grain. It is watered with the pleasant river of *Cluyde*, which gives name to the Shire. The rise of it is *Errickstir*, and, running quite through the County, glideth by many pleasant Seats of the Nobility and Gentry, and several considerable Towns, till it fall into its own Frith at *Dunbarton*.]

Crawford Moor. Near the head of the *Cluyde*, in *Crawford Moor*, among the wastes, the Husbandmen of the Country, after violent Rains, found a sort of shavings of Gold, which hath long given hopes of great Wealth, more especially, [a] since *B. Bulmer* undertook with great application to find out a Mine of Gold. They certainly dig up daily [b] the *Lapis Lazuli* with little or no labour. [and near this place are the Lead mines belonging to the Earl of *Hopton*.]

[a] In our times, (A Gold Mine.)
[b] Azurium.

Crawford-Castle, together with the title of Earl of Crawford, was [*] confer'd by King Robert the second, on *James Lindesay*, who in a single Combat with Baron *Welles* an Englishman, got much praise and commendation for his valour. The *Lindsays* have deserved exceeding well of their Country, and are of ancient Nobility, ever since *William Lindesay* married one of the Heirs of William de Lancaster, Lord of Kendal in England, whose [c] great grand daughter was married into the honourable family of *Coucy* in France. The Cluyde, after it hath, with much struggling, forced its way Northward by the [d] seat of Baron *Somervill*, [call'd *Carnwath* (which being purchased by the family of *Dalziel*, who where created by King Charles the first Lords *Dalziel*, did, in the same reign, give the [e] title of Earl to the same family) receives from the West the river *Duglas* or *Douglas*, so called from its dark greenish water. This river gives name to the Valley through which it runs, called *Douglasdale*, and to the Castle thereon, which in turn gives its name to the family of *Douglas*. This family is very ancient, but hath been most eminent ever since *James Douglas* adhered firmly to King *Robert Bruce*, and was ever ready with extraordinary courage, and singular prudence, to assist him, while he claim'd the Kingdom in those troublesome times. To him it was, that the same *Robert* gave his Heart in charge, to be convey'd to the Holy Land, for the performance of his Vow; in memory whereof, the *Douglasses* have added a Man's Heart, in their Coat of Arms. Since when, this family hath grown up to such mighty power and greatness (especially after *William's* being created Earl of *Douglass* by David the

The *Lindesays* Earls of *Crawford*.
[c] *Abneptis*.
[d] Ann. 1607. Baron *Somervill*. Carnwath.
[e] Now forfeited by Attainder.
Douglass or Duglass.
The Douglasses.

[*] The Barony of Crawford ... Crawfords to the Lindesays by Marriage, and the first Earl, Ann. 1399, was ... David Lindesay.

second,) that they have awed even the Kings themselves for almost at one and the same time, there were six Earls of it, by the titles of *Douglas*, *Angus*, *Ormond*, *Wigton*, *Murray*, and *Morton*, amongst whom, the Earl of *Wigton*, for his Martial valour, and good services, was honour'd by King Charles the seventh of France, with the Title of Duke of *Tourain*, and left the same to two Earls of *Douglass*, his heirs [But upon the forfeiture of the Earl of *Douglass* in the reign of King James the second, the Earl of Angus got the Castle and Country of *Douglass*, whose descendant *William* Earl of *Angus* was created Marquiss of *Douglass* by King Charles the first To which noble Family was added by Queen Anne, in the ninth year of her reign, the higher honour of Duke of *Douglass* In *Cydsdale*, is also the seat of the Lairds of *Carmichael*, of which family, Sir *James* was created by King Charles the first, Lord *Carmichael*]

Dukes of Tours or Tourain

Above the confluence of the *Douglas* and the *Cluyde* lies *Lanerick*, the hereditary Sheriffdom of the *Hamiltons*, who owe their name to *Hamilton Castle*, seated somewhat higher upon the Cluyd's bank, in a place extremely pleasant and fertile [It is a Seat of the Duke of *Hamilton*, [a] the Court whereof is on all sides adorned with very noble buildings It has a magnificent Avenue, and a Frontispiece towards the East of excellent workmanship On one hand of the Avenue, there are very fair large Gardens, well furnished with fruit trees and flowers The Park (famous for its tall Oaks) is six or seven miles round, and has the Brook *Aven* running through it Near the Palace, is the Church, the Vault whereof is the burial place of the Dukes of Hamilton] Their original is from England, as themselves affirm, *viz* from a certain Englishman surnamed *Hampton*, who taking part with *Robert Brus*, received from him large possessions in these Parts Their Estate was much augmented by the bounty of King James the third, who gave his own eldest Sister (after he had taken her from *Boid*) to *James Hamilton*, in marriage, together with the Earldom of *Arran* As their Honours were augmented by the States of the Kingdom, who, after the death of King James the fifth, ordained *James Hamilton*, this Lord's Grandson, Regent of Scotland (who was likewise made Duke of *Chasteau Herault* in Poictou, by Henry the second King of France,) as also by King James the sixth, who created his son *John*, Marquiss of *Hamilton*, a title wholly new, and never us'd before in Scotland [Afterwards, his grandson *James* Marquiss of Hamilton, was created Duke of Hamilton by King Charles the first, and his younger brother, *William* (Secretary to the said King) Earl of *Lanrick*, from the head burrough of the Shire, who after the Death of his brother Duke *James*, was also Duke of Hamilton, but both these dying without issue male, the Honour descended to the Lady *Anne*, eldest daughter to Duke *James*, who marry'd *William* Earl of Selkirk, created afterwards Duke of Hamilton Also, the Lord *John Hamilton*, third son of *William* Duke of Hamilton, was created Earl of *Ruglen* by King William the third]

Sheriffdom of Lanerick

Theatrum Scotiae

The Hamiltons

Duke of Chasteau Herault Marquiss of Hamilton

Earl of Ruglen

The *Glotta* or *Cluyde* runs hence by *Bothwell*, proud of its Earls, viz *John Ramsay*, who was too much a creature of King James the third, to his own and the Prince's ruin, and the *Hepburns* of whom we have spoken before [Near the place is *Blantyre*, from which, *Walter*, Prior of *Blantyre*, was created Lord *Blantyre* by King James the sixth] Then, it runs streight through *Glasgow*, antiently a Bishop's See, but long discontinued, till restor'd by King David the first [b] Now, it is an Archbishoprick, and an University, founded by Bishop *Turnbull*, who for the advancement of Religion, built a College here It is the most celebrated Mart of this Tract, and much commended for its pleasant situation and [c] plenty of Fruit, having also a handsome Bridge supported with eight Arches [In respect of largeness, buildings, trade and wealth, it is the chief City in the Kingdom, next *Edinburgh* The river carries Vessels of small burthen up to the very town, but *New Glasgow*, which stands on the mouth of *Clyde*, is a haven for Vessels of the largest size Most part of the City stands on a Plain, and is almost four square In the middle of it (where is the *Tolbooth*, a very stately building of hewn-stone) four principal Streets cross each other, and divide the City as it were into four equal parts In the higher part, stands the Cathedral Church, commonly called St *Mungo's*, consisting indeed of *two* Churches, one whereof is over the other The Architecture of the pillars and towers, is said to be very exact and curious Near the Church is the Archbishop's Castle, fenced with a wall of hewn-stone but its greatest ornament is the College, separated from the rest of the Town by an exceeding high wall, the Precincts whereof have been enlarged with some Acres of ground, purchased not many years since, and the Buildings repaired and adorned, by the Care and prudent administration of the late Principal, the Learned Doctor *Fal'* In the year 1699 *John Boyle* of Kelburn was created Lord *Boyle* by King William the third, and his Son David was afterwards advanced to the higher honour of Earl of *Glasgow* by her Majesty Queen Anne]

Earls of Bothwel

Blantyre.

Glasgow

[b] Ann 1601 Anno 1151

[c] *Pomiferis Arboribus*

Of this Place, thus *J Johnston*,

Non te Pontificum luxus, non Infula tantum
Ornavit, dirti quæ tibi causa mali,
Glottiade, quantum decorant Te, Glascua, Musæ,
Quæ celsum attollunt clara sub astra caput
Glotta, decus rerum, piscosis nobilis undis,
Finitimi recreat jugera læta soli
Ast Glottæ decus, & vicinis gloria terris,
Glascua fecundat flumine cuncta suo.

Not haughty Prelates e'er adorn'd thee so,
Nor stately Mitres, cause of all thy woe,
As Cluyd's Muses grace thy blest abodes,
And lift thy head among the deathless gods
Cluyd, great flood! for plenteous Fish renown'd,
And gentle streams that cheer the fruitful ground
But happy *Glasgow*, *Cluyd's* chiefest pride,
Glory of that and all the World beside,
Spreads round the riches of her noble tide

[Nor does this tract want remains of Roman Antiquity For from *Errick stone* in the one end, to *Mauls Mire* in the other, where it borders upon *Renfraw*, there are evident footsteps of a Roman Causey or Military way, called to this day

Roman High way

day the *Watlin street* This in some parts is visible for whole miles together, and the people have a tradition, that another Roman *Street* went from *Lanrick* to the Roman Camp near *Falkirk*

Lismehago

At *Lismehago*, a Town in this Shire, was a Priory and Convent of the Monks of the order of *Vallis Caulium*, a sort of Cistercians, founded by King David the first]

Barons Reinfraw

On the hither bank of the Cluyde, lies the Barony of *Reinfraw* [separated from the shire of *Dumbarton* on the West by the River *Clyde* (which carries up ships of great burden for ten miles) On the East, it is joined to the Shire of *Lanrick*, and on the West and South to the Sheriffdom of *Aire* It is in length twenty miles, and in breadth eight, but where broadest thirteen That part which lyeth near *Clyde* is pleasant and fertil, without mountains, only, has some small risings but that to the South, South west, and West, is more barren, hilly, and moorish The Nobility and Gentry of this Tract, keep up almost a constant relation, by marriage one with another The convenience of the Frith of *Clyde* (the Coast whereof is all along very safe to ride in) hath caused good Improvements in these parts]

Randvara

The Barony is so called from its principal Town, which seems to be Ptolemy's *Randvara*, and lies on the River *Cathcart*, upon which the

Barons Cathcart

antient Barons of *Cathcart* have their habitation Near adjoining (for this little Province

Cruikston

is full of Nobility) lies *Cruikston*, antiently the seat of the Lords of *Darnley*, to whom the Right to the Earldom of *Lennox* came by marriage with a Daughter of Duncan Earl of Lennox

Halkead Barons of Roos

Then, *Halkead*, the residence of the Barons of *Ros*, [who have been Lords of Parliament ever since the reign of King James the fourth, and are] descended originally of English Blood, as deriving their Lineage from that *Robert Roos* of *Warke*, who left England, and came under the Allegiance of the King of Scots [Besides these,

Gourock

at the west end of a fair Bay, stands *Gourock* Town and Castle, where is a good road and harbour lately contrived, and a village built

Greenock

More inward, stands *Greenock*, a good road, and well built town, of best account on all this Coast It is * the chief seat of the Herring-fishing, and the Royal Company of Fishers have built a House at it, for the convenience of trade In the second year of Queen Anne, *John Crawford* was advanced by Her Majesty to the Honour of Viscount *Mount-Crawford*, which he afterwards changed again to the title of † *Garnock*

Crawfird Dyke

Near this, is *Crawfird Dyke*, where are well-built houses and a little more to the South,

New work

New work, where the Town of *Glasgow* hath

Por Glasgow

built a new Port, and called it *Port Glasgow*, with a large Publick House Here is the Custom house for all this Coast, and the Town of *Glasgow* hath obliged the Merchants to load

Paslay

and unload here] *Paslay*, [in these parts,] was formerly a famous Monastery, founded by ‹ *Alexander* the second, High Steward of Scotland, and was inferior to few, in a noble Church, and rich Furniture But, by the favour of King

Gives, C

James the sixth, it * gave a seat, and the title of Baron, to *Claud Hamilton*, a younger son of the Duke of *Castle Herald* [The Abbey and Church, with fair Gardens and Orchards, and a little Park for Fallow deer, are all enclosed with a stone wall, about a mile in circuit The Monastery here was of the Order of the *Clunacks* The Nave of the Church is yet standing, where lie buried Robert the third, and his grand mother At this Town, is a large Roman Camp the *Praetorium* is at the West end on a rising Ground, upon the descent whereof the Town of *Pasly* stands This *Praetorium* is not large, but has been well fortified with three fosses and *dykes* of earth, of which so much is still remaining, that one on horseback cannot see over them It seems to have inclos'd all that ground on which the Town stands, and may have been about a mile in compass When you tread upon the ground of the *Praetorium*, it gives a sound as if hollow, occasioned, probably, by some Vaults underneath, such as are at *Camelon* and *Airdoch*, two others of their Camps About a quarter of a mile from this, are two other risings, one to the South, and the other to the West, which, with this, make a triangular form By the footsteps remaining, they seem to have been little larger than the *Praetorium* of the first, without any fortifications, save a single *Fosse* and a *Dyke* of the same form It is probable enough, that these might be the Stations for the outer guards At

Langside

Langside also there is the appearance of an old Camp on the top of the hills Here, a battle was fought between Queen *Mary* and the Earl of *Murray*, call'd *the Field of Langsyde*

And (to give the Reader the Remains of Roman Antiquity in this Tract, at one view) there were found opposite to *Erskin*, upon the river *Clyde* the two following Inscriptions

2

* The Royal Society for Herring Fishing is dissolved
† Garnock is a River in Cunningham, in the Viscount's Estate

These

IMP.C.T.AELIO
HADRIANO.ANTO
NINO.AVG.P.P.
VEX.LEG.VI.VIC.
P.F.OPVS.VALLI.
P.∞.∞.∞.∞.C.XLI.

MP.C.T.AE
ADRIANO.
NTONINO.
G.PIO.P.P.
EG.XXVV.
D.XI.

These are now placed, among others, in the Library at *Glasgow*

Ebbing-Spring

In the Lands of New yards, near *Pasly*, is a remarkable Spring, which is observed to ebb and flow with the tide, tho' on a far higher ground than any place where the tide comes The water of the River *Whyte-Cart* (upon which *Paslay* stands) is commended for its largeness, and the fineness of the *Pearls* that are frequently found hereabouts and three miles above They fish for them mostly in summer-time, and meet with them at the bottom of the water in a fish-shell, much larger than the ordinary Muscle]

Barons Sempill

Not far from *Paslay*, is *Sempill*, whose Lord is Baron *Sempill*, [(advanced to that Dignity by King James the fourth,] and, by ancient right, Sheriff of this Barony But I have read, that the title of Baron *Reinfraw* by special right belongs to the Prince of Scotland

LENNOX.

LENNOX.

On the other side of the *Cluyd*, above Glascow, *Levinia*, or *Lennox* runs out a long way Northward, amongst a continued knot of hills [It is also called *Dumbartonshire*, from *Dumbarton*, a Burgh Royal and chief Town in the Shire, and is made a part of the *Damnii*, though some learned men, according to the division of it into the *High* country and the *Low*, have thought it more convenient to make the latter, part of the *Gadeni*, and the former, the seat of the *Vacomagi*, the remains of which name they observe in a village upon *Loch-lomond*, called *Blowvochie* It is bounded on the South, with the river *Clyde* and its *Firth*, on the West it hath *Logh-Long*, and a water of the same name which falleth into it, on the North it hath the *Grampion hills*, and on the East, the water of *Blane* divides it from *Stirlingshire* Its length is about twenty four miles, and its breadth about twenty The *Lower* part lies to the East, and is very fertil in corn, especially towards the Rivers The *Higher* is hilly, moorish, and more fit for pasture, especially where the *Grampion mountains* begin The country is very well furnished with Gentlemens seats, particularly, here is the Castle of *Mugdock*, the residence of the Duke of Montross It is surrounded with hills on all sides, except the South, and is full of Isles, some whereof are cultivated and inhabited]

See *Angus*

This Tract takes its name from the River *Levin*, Ptolemy's *Lelanonius*, which falleth into the Cluyde, out of *Logh Lomund*, a Lake that spreads itself under the Mountains, [a] twenty [four] miles in length, and eight in breadth It is excellently well stocked with Fish, especially with one sort that is peculiar to it (they call it *Pollac*) It hath likewise several Islands in it, concerning which there are many Traditional stories amongst the ordinary sort of people As for the *Floating-Island* here, I shall not call the truth of it in question, for what should hinder a body from swimming, that is dry and hollow like a pumice, and very light, and so, Pliny tells us, that certain green Islands cover'd with reeds and rushes, float up and down in the lake of *Vadimon* But I leave it to the Neighbours, who know the nature of this place, to be Judges, whether this old Distich of our *Necham* be true,

Lelanonius Logh Lomund

[a] Twenty, C

Pollac fish

Lib 8 Epist o

> *D tatu flu-nt Ph n t, fa i i'ent*
> *Dat Lomu i l mul a fr gid te po rs*

> Scotland's enrich'd with Rivers, Timber, thrown
> Into cold Lomund's waters, turns to Stone

There are many Fishermens Cottages round about, upon the banks of the *Logh*, but nothing worth our notice, except *Kilmaronock*, a beautiful House of the [b] Earl of *Cassil*, seated upon the East-side, which hath a delicate prospect into the *Logh* But at the influx of the *Levin* out of the Logh into the Clyde, stand *Al-Cluyd*, so called by the antients Bede observes, that it signifies *the Rock Cluyde*, but I know not in what language *Ar Cluid* in the British certainly signifies *upon Cluid*, and *Cluid* in old English signify'd a *Rock* Succeeding ages call'd it [c] *Dunbritton*, that is, the *Britains Town* (and corruptly by a transposition of letters, *Dunbarton*,) because the *Britains* held it longer than any other place, against the Scots, Picts, and Saxons For both by nature and situation, it is the strongest Castle in all Scotland, seated at the confluence of two rivers, in a green plain, on a craggy two headed rock Upon one of the heads, stands a high Watch-Tower, upon the other, which is somewhat lower, many strong Towers It hath but one ascent to it, and that on the North side, between the two heads, having scarce room enough to pass one by one, (by steps cut out of [d] the rock,) crosswise, with a world of labour Upon the west side, the *Levin*, upon the South, the *Cluyde*, serve instead of ditches Eastward lies a Morass, which, at every tide, is wholly under water Towards the North, it is very well secur'd by the steepness of its situation. Here, some remains of the Britains (who, as Gildas writes, *generally retreated for shelter, to the tops of craggy inaccessible mountains, to thick Forests, and to Rocks upon the sea shore*,) presuming upon the natural strength of the place, and their own Courage, defended themselves after the departure of the Romans, for three hundred years, though in the very midst of their Enemies For in Bede's time (as he himself writes,) it was the best fortify'd City that the Britains had But in the year 756 *Eadbert* King of Northumberland, and *Oeng* King of the Picts, with their joint Forces shut it up on every side, and reduced it to such extremity, that it surrender'd, upon Articles From this place, [which, as we have said, is a Burgh Royal, and chief town of the Shire] the Territory round about is called the *Sheriffdom of Dunbarton*, and hath long had the Earls of *Lennox* for its Sheriffs, by inheritance [It was erected into an Earldom by King Charles the second, in the person of *George Douglas* one of the youngest Sons of William Marquis of Douglass, who, besides his high birth, render'd himself very eminent by his military Services]

Al-cluid

[c] See the Discourse of the Roman Wall in Scotland

Dunbritton. Britannodunum

[d] Obliquam rupem

R Hoveden

As for the Earls of *Lennox*, not to mention the more ancient, one *Duncan* was Earl of Lennox in the reign of Robert the second He dying, left two only Daughters behind him, one of which was marry'd to *Alan Stewart*, who was descended from Robert, a younger son of Walter the second, High Steward of Scotland, and Brother of Alexander Stewart the second, founder of the Royal line of Scotland For this illustrious Family took its name from that Honourable Office of *Steward* of the Kingdom, that is, the person who had the charge of the Revenues of the Crown This *Alan* had issue *John* Earl of Lennox, and *Robert* who was made Captain of the Scotch Guard *de Corps* first established by the French King, Charles the sixth in recompence of the good service which that nation had done the Crown of France)

The Earls of Lennox

Stewart

as also Lord of *Aubigny* in *Auvergne*, by the same King, as a reward of his valour John had issue, *Matthew* Earl of Lennox, who marry'd the daughter of *James Hamilton* by *Mariona*, daughter to King James the second, by whom he had *John* Earl of Lennox, who, taking up Arms to deliver King James the fifth out of the hands of the *Douglasses* and *Hamiltons*, was kill'd by his Uncle the Earl of Arran This John had issue, *Matthew* Earl of Lennox, who, after many troubles in France and Scotland, found fortune more favourable in England, under the patronage of King Henry the eighth, who bestow'd upon him his sister's daughter in marriage, with a large estate The issue of this happy match were *Henry* and *Charles*, Henry, by Mary Queen of Scots, had James the sixth, King of Great Britain, born by the propitious favour of heaven, at a most lucky juncture, to unite in one Imperial Body the British World, divided before as well in itself, as from the rest of mankind, and (as we [e] hope and pray) to lay a sure foundation of Peace and Security for childrens children, for ever As for *Charles*, he had issue, one only daughter, *Arabella*, a Lady who made a progress in learning, so much beyond her Sex, and was so much improved thereby in all virtuous Accomplishments, that she might well be compar'd with the Ladies of ancient days When Charles was dead, and the Earldom of Lennox (of which he stood enfeoffed) was by authority of Parliament [f] resumed in the year 579, and his Uncle *Robert*, Bishop of Cathness, had born this title for some time (in lieu whereof he had of the King the honour of Earl of *March*,) King James [the sixth] conferr'd the title of Duke of Lennox upon *Esme Stewart*, son of John Lord D'Aubigny, second Brother of Matthew Earl of Lennox aforesaid, which his son *Lodowick* (or *Lewis*) [g] enjoy'd after him For since the reign of Charles the sixth, there were of this line, Lords of *Aubigny* in France, the said *Robert* before named, and *Bernard* or *Eberard* (under Charles the eighth and Lewis the twelfth) whose memory hath been transmitted to posterity by Paulus Jovius, with much commendation for his valiant Exploits in the War of Naples He was a most faithful Companion of Henry the seventh when he came for England, and used for his Device *a Lion* [h] *between buckles*, with this motto, *Distantia jungit*, because by his means the Kingdoms of France and Scotland, so far distant, were joyned together in a strict league of Friendship As likewise *Robert Stewart*, Lord D'Aubigny of the same family, a Marescal of France under Lewis XI, did for the same reason use the Royal Arms of France with *Buckles Or* in a Bordure *Gules*, which were from that time born by the Earls and Dukes of Lennox

James King of Great Britain

[e] So said, ann 1607

[g] Enjoys at this day, c Lords of Aubigny

[h] Inter fibulas Paradinus

[The race of the Dukes of Lennox aforesaid, being extinct, by the Death of Charles Duke of Lennox and Richmond, Ambassador from King Charles the second to the King of Denmark, and the Estate falling to the King by Succession, his Majesty conferr'd the title of Duke of Lennox upon Charles his natural Son, about the same time that he advanced him to the honour of Duke of Richmond in England]

STERLING Sheriffdom.

Sterlingshire borders to the North east upon Lennox, and is so named from its principal town For fruitfulness of soil, and the number of Gentry, it is outdone by no County in Scotland [It is usually reckoned within the bounds of the ancient *Damnii*, but it hath been the opinion of one, who hath considered these matters very accurately, that this, as well as the adjacent part of *Dumbartonshire*, belonged to the *Gadeni*, a name, referring to this narrow neck of land It is encompassed to the west with *Dunbartonshire*, to the South with part of *Clydesdale* and part of *Dunbarton shire*, to the East with the shire of *Linlithgow*, and to the North with the *Firth* and river of *Forth* where it is longest, it is about twenty miles, and where broadest, twelve miles over The South part is high hilly ground, somewhat moorish, and fit for pasture, but that which lies upon the *Firth* of *Forth* is very fertil, and abounds with Coal]

Here is that narrow neck of Land [aforesaid,] by which *Glotta* and *Bodotria*, or (to use the language of these times) *Dunbritton Frith*, and *Edenborough Frith*, Arms of different seas, which come a great way up into the Country, are kept from joining This, *Julius Agricola*, who went thus far and further, first observed, and fortified the streight with Garrisons, by which means, all Britain on this side was then in the possession of the Romans, and their Enemies removed as it were into another Island, so that Tacitus was right in his Judgment, that no other Bound of Britain was to be sought for. Nor indeed, in after times, did either the Valour of their Armies, or the Glory of the Roman name (which could scarce be stopped) carry the limits of their Empire farther in these parts, although they harrassed them, now and then, with inrodes But after this glorious expedition, Agricola was recall'd, and *Britain* (as Tacitus says) *lay neglected*, nor did they keep their possession thus far For the *Caledonian* Britains drove the Romans back as far as the River Tine, insomuch, that Hadrian who came into Britain about forty years after, and reformed many things in it, made no farther progress, but commanded that the God *Terminus* (who was wont to give ground to none) should yield to Hadrian, and retire backwards out of this place, as he had done in the East to this side Euphrates Whence that of St Augustine, *The God* Terminus, *which gave not place to Jove, yielded to the will of* Hadrian, *yielded to the rashness of* Julian, *yielded to the necessities of* Jovian So that Hadrian contented himself to make a *Turf-wall* between the rivers Tine and Esk, one hundred miles on this side *Edinborough-Frith* But Antoninus Pius (who being adopted by Hadrian, bore his name, and was stiled *Titus Ælius Hadrianus Antoninus Pius*) did again, under the conduct of *Lollius Urbicus*,

The God Terminus

Aug de Civ Dei, l 4 c 29

[f] It was not *resumed*, but Robert resigned it to his great Nephew

whom

whom he sent his Lieutenant into Britain, repel the Barbarians beyond Edingborough Frith, and build another Wall of Turf, besides that of Hadrian, according to *Capitolinus*. To prove which wall to be in the very place we are now treating of (and not drawn by Severus, as is commonly believed,) I will produce no other Witnesses than two ancient Inscriptions dug up here, one of which is fixed in the wall of a house at *Calder*, and informs us, that the *Legio Secunda Augusta* built the wall for three miles and more, the other is in the Earl Marshal's House at *Dunotyr*, which hints, that a party of the *Legio Vicesima Victrix* made it for three miles more. But take them here, as *Servatius Ribelius* a Silesian Gentleman, who made curious observations upon these Countries, copied them for me.

Antoninus Pius's wall

IMP CAESARI
T AELIO HADRI
ANO ANTONINO
AVG PIO P P
VEXILLATIO
LEG XX VAL VIC F.
PER MIL P III

IMP CAES TIT IO AELIO
HADRIANO ANTON
AVG PIO P P LEG II AVG
PER M P III D CIXVIS

At *Calder*, where the latter Inscription is, there is another stone to be seen, on which, within a Laurel Garland supported by two little *Victories*, we read thus,

And in a Village, called *Minaburch*, this Inscription was removed out of the Minister's house, into a [i] Gentleman's [k], then in building.

[i] Nobilis
[k] Ædificatur

D M
C JULI
MARCELLINI
PRAEF
COH I HAMIOR

Cohors prima Hamiorum

But when, in the Reign of Commodus, the barbarous nations had pass'd the wall, and harrass'd the country, Severus (as I have already said) repaired the Wall of *Hadrian*. But afterwards, the Romans, again, brought under their subjection all the Country between. For (as Ninius has told us) *Carausius* under Dioclesian repaired this Wall, and fortified it with seven castles. Lastly, the Romans fortified this place in the reign of *Theodosius* the younger, under the conduct of *Gallio* of Ravenna.

Now (saith Bede) they made a Turf wall to no purpose, building it not so much with stones as with turfs (as having no artificer that understood so great a work) between two Friths or arms of the sea, for many miles together, that, where the fence of water was wanting, there, by the help of a wall, they might defend their Marches *from Incursions of the Enemy. Of which work (that is to say, of a very broad and high wall) the plain footsteps are to be seen at this day.* This wall began (as the Scots report) at the River *Aven*, which falls into *Edinborough Frith*, and having passed over the little River *Carron*, reaches to *Dunbritton*. But Bede, as I have said but now, affirms that it begins in a place called *Penvael*, that is, in the Pictish tongue, *the head of the wall*, in the British *Pen gual*, in the English *Pen-walton*, in the Scotch *Cevall* (all which names are undoubtedly derived from the Latin *Vallum*,) and that the place is almost two miles from *Abercurvig* or *Abercurning*. It ends (as the common people think) at *Kirk-Patrick*, the birth place of St *Patrick* the Irish Apostle, near *Clyde*, but according to Bede, at *Alcluyd*, and, as Ninnius tells us, at the City *Pen-Aldort*, which may seem to be but one place. But this *Wall* is commonly called *Graham's Dyke*, either from *Graham*, a valiant Scot who signalized himself in breaking through it, or from the mountain *Grampius*, at the foot whereof it is visible. The Author of *Rota Temporum* calls it the *Wall of Abercorneth*, that is, of the mouth of the River *Corneth*, where, in Bede's time, *was a famous Monastery* (as he tells us) *on the English side of the Pale, but near the Frith, which divided the English Lands from those of the Picts.*

Ninnius. Abercorn. Graham's Dyke

Hard by this wall of turf, where the River *Carron* cuts Sterlingshire in two, to the left are two Mounts cast up, which they call *Duni Pacis*, and almost two miles lower, an ancient round piece of building, twenty four Cubits high, and thirteen broad, open in the top, and framed of rough stones without lime, and having the upper part of each stone so tenanted into the nether, that the whole work rising narrower and narrower, supports it self by mutual interlacings.

Duni pacis

Some

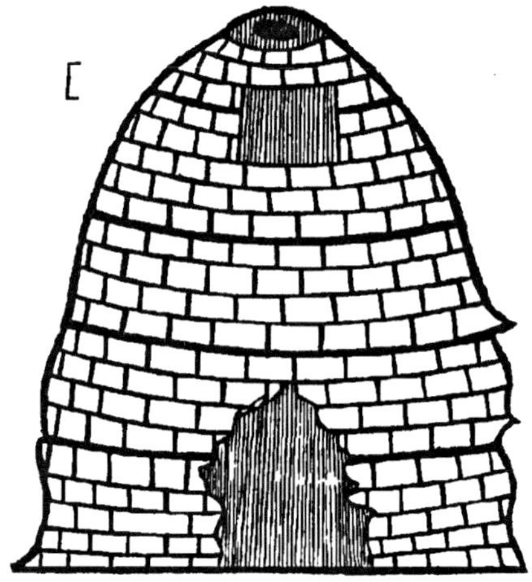

[l] See Buchan l. 4. in Reg. Donald.

Arthur's Oven.

Some call this the temple of the God [l] *Terminus*, others, who father every thing that is magnificent upon Arthur, *Arthur's Oven*, others also call it *Julius Hoff*, and suppose it was built by *Julius Cæsar* but I should rather have thought, by *Julius Agricola*, who fortified this part, had not Ninnius informed me, that *Carausius* erected it for a triumphal Arch *For he* (as Ninnius writes) *built upon the bank of* Carron *a round house of polished stone, erecting a Triumphal Arch in memory of a Victory, and rebuilt the Wall, and fortified it with seven Castles.* [so that what Hector Boethius tells us from Veremundus, That it was evident from an Inscription taken away by King Edward the first, that it was a Temple dedicated by Vespasian to the honour of Claudius, must probably be a mistake.]

Lib. 3.

In the middle, between *Dun pacis* and this piece of building, on the right hand bank of *Carron*, there is yet a confus'd Appearance of a little ancient City, where the common people believe there was formerly a Road for Ships, [(and it is true, that some years ago an Anchor was found, a little to the west of *Dun Pacis*.)] They call it *Camelot* (a name often used in King *Arthur's* story,) and contend, but in vain, that it is the *Camalodunum* mentioned by Tacitus. From the name of the River Carron, that runs under it, it may rather seem to be the [m] *Coria Damniorum*, mentioned by Ptolemy [The footsteps of the Streets, and some Vaults, are still to be seen.] And now take the Verses of Buchanan, that incomparable Poet, upon this boundary of the Roman Empire at *Carron*.

Coria Damniorum.

[m] See Discourse of the *Roman Wall* in Scotland.

> *Roma securis pr etendit mænia Scotis,*
> *Hic spe progressus posita, Carronis ad undam*
> *Terminus Ausonii signat divortia Regni*

> A frontier wall against the *Scottish* force
> The *Romans* rais'd, nor farther urg'd their course,
> Content to keep their own, on *Carron's* shore
> They fix'd the Bounds of their resisted pow'r

[Nigh the *Dun Pacis* beforementioned, is *Kilsyth*, belonging to an ancient Cadet of the Family of the *Levingston*, who in the year 1606 was a Lord of the Session, and his Successor was by King Charles the second, in the year 1661, created Viscount of *Kilsyth* Here the Marquis of Montross obtained a signal Victory.] Kilsyth.

[n] Now forfeited by Alexander.

In this *Sterlingshire*, on the East side, we have a prospect of *Callendar Castle*, belonging to the Barons of *Levingston*, [which, with the Lands of Almond, were purchased by James, second Son to Alexander the first Earl of *Linlithgow*, who by King Charles the first was created Lord Almond, and then Earl of Callendar, in the year 1641.] And at *Cumbernald*, hard by, dwells the family of the Barons *Fleming*, which Seat was bestowed upon them by King *Robert Brus*, for their good Service, in valiantly and loyally defending their country, on which account they had also conferred upon them the honour of Hereditary *Chamberlains* of Scotland. And this family [who had enjoyed the Dignity of Barons from the time of King James the second,] [o] was, by the favour of King James the sixth, farther honoured with the title of Earl, upon his creating 7 Baron *Fleming* Earl of *Wigton*. In the neighbourhood stands *Elphingston*, honoured with its Barons, who were advanced to that dignity by King James the fourth, [and whose residence this is, adorned with a large wood, of Firs, &c.] And, upon the crooked windings of the *Forth* (where it is capable of a bridge) stands *Sterling*, commonly called *Striveling*, and *Sterling Borough*, which is over-top'd by a strong Castle of the Kings, standing upon the brow of a steep rock, and was beautified with new buildings by King James the sixth. It [p] was long under the command of the Lords of *Areskin*, as Castellans; who had often had the charge and tuition of the Princes of Scotland, during the Minority. But they are much mistaken, who think that

Callendar. Barons Levingston.

Cumbernald.

[o] Vere the 7. C.

Fleming, Earl of Wigton.

Firth of Edin.

[p] High Steward.

Sterling money. ¹ *Vid. Som. Gloss. Easterlingus*

our *good and lawful money of England,* commonly called *Sterling-money*, takes its name from hence ¹ for that came from the Germans, who were termed *Easterlings* by the English, from their living *Eastward*, and who were first called-in by King John, to reduce the Silver to its due fineness and such money in antient writings is always called *Easterling* But Johnston's verses upon *Sterling* shall supply the rest

Regia sublimis celsa despectat ab arce
Pendula sub biforis mœnia structa jugis
Regum augusta parens, Regum nutricula natis,
Hinc sibi Regifico nomine tota placet
Hospita sed cuivis quovis sub nomine, amicus
Sive est, seu non est, hospes an hostis item
Pro lucro cedit damnum Discordia tristis
Heu quoties procerum sanguine tinxit humum!
Hoc uno infelix, at felix cætera, nusquam
Lætior aut cæli frons, geniusve soli

The lofty palace with proud state looks down
On circling walls that grace the subject town
Mother and Nurse to Prince's dearest cares,
And ever proud of the great name she bears
But ah! too fondly kind to friends and foes,
While none her hospitable seats refuse
Such gains too oft' to fatal losses turn
What fewds, what slaughters must she ever mourn?
Hapless in this all other joys attend,
No purer air she owns, no richer land,
And wealth and pleasure wait at her command

Banocburn.

About two miles hence, the river *Banoc* runs between very high banks on both sides, towards the *Forth*, with a stream which in the winter is very ᵐ rapid, famous for as glorious a victory as ever the Scots obtained, when Edward the second King of England was put to flight, and forc'd to save himself in a Boat, and the finest Army that England had ever sent out, was routed by the Valour and conduct of King *Robert Brus* Insomuch, that for two years after, the English did not in the least disturb the Scots A neighbouring Field is infamous for the murder of *James* the third, slain here by certain Noblemen of *Scotland*, who had arm'd the Son against the Father [Whether the Fault was more his than their's, I know not, but this I am sure of, the Example was very pernicious

ᵐ *Rapidus* but in the Errata, *trepidus*

Alauna. ⁿ See Discourse of the *Roman Wall* in Scotland

Ptolemy seems to place his ⁿ *Alauna* some where about *Sterling*, and it was either upon *Alon*, a little River that runs here into the *Forth*, or at *Alloway*, a seat of the *Erskines*, [heretofore] hereditary Sheriffs of all the County without the Borough, (which Office belongs at present to the Earls of Callender

Falkirk.

Besides *Sterling*, here is *Falkirk*, a Burgh of Barony, well built upon arising ground, and much beautified with buildings by the first Earl of *Kalendar*, brother to the Earl of *Linlithgow*, a person famous for his valour and conduct

Cambuskenneth

Near *Sterling* also, stands the Abbey of *Cambuskeneth*, which belonged to the monks of the Order of St *Augustin*, and was founded by King David To which we will add, *Emanuel* a Nunnery of the Cistertian Order, founded by Malcolm the fourth, and standing upon *Avonwater*]

Emanuel

I have not read of any one honoured with the title of *Earl of Sterling*, [till Sir *William Alexander* (the King's Lieutenant in *Nova Scotia*, and who had precedency of all those Baronets) was created, first Viscount, and then Earl of Sterling, by King Charles the first]

CALEDONIA.

Caledonia

ALL that part of Britain, which lies Northward beyond Graham's Dyke, *or the forementioned Wall of* Antoninus Pius, *and jets out on both sides, is called by Tacitus* Caledonia, *and the People,* The Britains inhabiting Caledonia *Ptolemy divides them into many Nations, viz the* Caledonii, Epidii, Vacomagi, &c *All these were afterwards, from their retaining that custom of painting their bodies, called* Picts *by the Romans and Provincials They are divided by Ammianus Marcellinus into two Nations, the* Dicaledones, *and* Vecturiones, *which have been treated of before* [*The* Dicaledones *seem to have possessed the Countries of* Argile, Perthshire, *and part of Loughaber, with the mountainous part of Angus, and the* Vecturiones, *the rest of Scotland, north of the* Firth *of* Forth] *But, in Classick Authors, they all go under the name of* Caledonii, *who, I should think, were so called of* Kaled, *a British word, signifying* hard, *which in the Plural number is* Kaledion, *whence* Caledonii, *that is, a people* hardy, rough, unciviliz'd, wild *and* rustick, *such as the Northern People generally are; of a fierce temper, from the extream coldness of the climate, and bold and forward, from their abundance of blood And besides their climate, the nature of the country contributes to it, rising up every where in* rough *and* rugged *mountains, and Mountaineers are known by all to be a* hardy *and* robust *People. But whereas Varro alledges out of* Pacuvius, *that* Caledonia breeds men of exceeding large Bodies, *I should rather think it meant of that part of* Epirus *called Caledonia, than of our's, although our's too may justly challenge this commendation Among these, was the* Sylva Caledonia, *called by Lucius Florus* Saltus Caledonius, *spread out to a vast compass, and by reason of the thickness of trees, impassable, and, divided by the Mountain* Grampius, *now called* Grantzbaine, *that is, the crooked Mountain Solinus tells us,* It is plain, that *Ulysses* arrived in *Caledonia,* by a votive Altar inscribed with Greek Characters *But I should rather think, it was set up in honour of* * Ulysses, *than by* Ulysses *himself Martial also in this verse mentions the* Caledonian Bears

Sylva Caledonia

Ulysses's Altar

* Concerning his being in Britain and his Altars in several Nations, see the *General Part*, pag xliv

> Nuda Caledonio sic pectora præbuit urso.
>
> *His naked breast to* Caledonian *bears*
> *He thus expos'd* ———— ——

Plutarch also writes, that they transported Bears *from Britain to Rome, where they had them in great admiration, but Britain has bred none for many ages What sort of Monster that should be, which is mentioned by* Claudian,

> ——Caledonio velata Britannia monstro,
>
> *With* Caledonian *monsters cover'd o'er*
> *Great* Britain *next appears;* ———

Caledonian Bulls

I cannot really tell It certainly bred in ancient times abundance of wild milk white Bulls, with thick manes like Lions; but it breeds few now a days, and those very cruel and fierce, having such an aversion to mankind, that for some time they cannot endure any thing handled or breathed upon by them, nay, they value not the baiting of dogs, though Rome *in former ages wonder'd at the fierceness of* Scottish Dogs, *to such a degree, that they thought they were brought over in cages of Iron However, this word* Caledonii *grew so common among the Roman writers, that they made use of it to express all Britain, and all the Forests of Britain Hence Florus tells us, that Cæsar pursued the Britains as far as the* Caledonian Forests, *and yet he never saw them Hence also Valerius Flaccus addresses himself thus to* Vespasian,

Caledonius

——Caledonius postquam tua Carbasa vexit
Oceanus ——————

When Caledonian *waves your streamers bore,*

That is, the British Sea. *Hence likewise* Statius *addresses his verses to* Crispinus, *concerning* Vectius Volanus, *his Father, and Proprætor of Britain about* Vitellius's *time.*

Quanta Caledonios attollet gloria campos,
Cum tibi longævus referet trucis incola terræ,
Hic suetus dare jura parens, hoc cespite turmas
Affari, ille dedit, cinxitque hæc mœnia fossa,
Belligeris hæc dona deis, hæc tela dicavit,
Cernis adhuc titulos, hunc ipse vacantibus armis
Induit, hunc regi rapuit thoraca Britanno.

What glories Caledonian *plains shall boast,*
When some rude native of the barb'rous coast
Salutes you thus,—Here, Sir, with awful state
Your noble father oft in Judgment sate
On this small hill I've seen the Heroe stand,
While willing Legions heard his just command
These walls, these ditches, own his mighty hand
These Arms (their old inscriptions yet appear,)
He fix'd, glad trophies to the God of War;
This sumptuous Corslet for the fight put on,
And this from Britain's *Prince in combat won.*

But in these, as in other things,

Crescit in immensum facunda licentia vatum.

Nor laws nor bounds poetick licence owns.

For neither Cæsar nor Volanus ever so much as knew the Caledonians. *In Pliny's time (as himself witnesses) which is almost thirty years after* Claudius, *the Romans, with all their expeditions, had carried their victories in Britain no farther than to the Neighbourhood of the* Caledonian Forest. *For* Julius Agricola, *under* Domitian, *was the first that enter'd* Caledonia, *which was then under the government of* Galgacus *(called in the* Triadum Liber, *amongst the three Worthies of Britain,* Galauc ap Liennauc*) a Prince of mighty spirit and courage, who having routed the ninth Legion, did with an undaunted resolution charge the Romans, and with the utmost bravery defended his country, till fortune, rather than his own valour, fail'd him. For then (as he saith)* these Northern Britains were the utmost bounds both of land and liberty. *And they certainly were the* utmost *Inhabitants of this Island;* as *Catullus calls the Britains the* utmost Inhabitants of the world, in his verses to *Furius.*

Galgacus the Britain.

Cæsaris visens monumenta magni,
Gallicum Rhenum, horribilesque ulti-
mosque Britannos.

To view the noble marks of Cæsar's *power,*
The Gallick Rhine, *and* Britain's *farthest shore.*

Argetecoxus.

In the time of Severus (as we read in Xiphiline) Argetecoxus, a petty King, reigned over this Tract, whose wife, being reproached as an Adulteress by Julia *the Empress, frankly made this answer,* We British Dames have to do with the bravest men, but you Roman Ladies with every base lewd fellow, in private.

THE.

FIFE.

Clackmans. Kinross. [a] I, C. Clackmananshire.

IN this large Country of the *Caledonians*, beyond Sterlingshire (of which I treated last) are two little Governments or Sheriffdoms, *Clackmans*, of which a Knight named *de Carss*, and *Kinross*, of which the Earl of *Morton*[a] was Sheriff, [but the first hath been purchased by Bruce of Clackmannan, and the second by Sir William Bruce.) *Clackmananshire* (so called from the head burgh of it, *Clackmanan*) is bounded to the North by the *Ochil hills*, to the south by the Firth of Forth, to the east with part of Perthshire, and to the west with part of *Sterlingshire*. It is about eight miles in length, and where broadest, but five. Towards the *Firth* it is a plain Country, and a fertile soil, the rest is fitter for pasture, but that below the *Ochill hills* abounds both with grain and pasture. About *Alloa* and *Clackmanan*, they have great store of Coal-pits, the Coal whereof, together with their *Salt*, furnish a foreign trade. It is watered with the river *Devan*, which runs six miles through the shire.

Clackmanan. Alloa.

Clackmanan is seated on a rising ground, the Castle whereof is a stately dwelling, with fine gardens and good Inclosures. *Alloa* is a pleasant little town, with a small harbour for ships, where is a Castle, which hath been the chief residence of the Earls of *Marr*, hereditary Governours of *Sterling*-Castle. It is also adorned with fine Gardens and inclosures.

Kinross shire.

Kinrossshire is another little tract, lying to the north, so called from a Town seated in the middle of the shire, not far from a Loch, about four miles in length, and as many in breadth, which abounds with *Pykes*, *Trouts*, *&c.* and with all sorts of water fowl. It has one Island, upon which the Castle stands, and another, wherein are to be seen the ruins of the Priory of *Portmolloch*, which belonged to monks of St. *Augustine's* Order. It is called *St. Serf's inch*, and was anciently the residence of some of the *Kuldees*. Out of this Loch flows the water of Levin. Between the town and the Loch, is a pleasant plain, where a stately house hath been built by Sir *William Bruce*, which for the goodness of the stone, the curious Architecture, and the avenues, gardens, and inclosures, together with the pleasant prospect of the Lough and the Castle, gives place to few seats in Scotland.]

Fife.

Beyond these Sheriffdoms, lies *Fife*, a very fine Peninsula, wedged in as it were between two Arms of the Sea, the *Forth* and the *Tay*, and shooting out a long way to the East. The land yields great plenty of Corn, Forage, and Pit Coal: the Sea, besides other fish, yields abundance of *Oysters* and *Shell-fish*: and the coast is well planted with little towns, that breed good store of lusty Seamen. [This Sheriffdom was anciently called *Ros*, the remains of which name are still preserved in *Culross*, i. e. the back or lower part of *Ross*, and *Kinross*, i. e. the head of *Ross*.] The name of *Fife*, it had from *Fifus*, a Nobleman, to whom it was given by King Kenneth [illegible] for his great service against the Picts. The *Macduffs* of [illegible], for more than a hundred years, were hereditary Sheriffs of [illegible], and upon the failing of that family, the Sheriffdom was transferred to the Ea[rls]

mily of *Rothess*. To the north, it is divided from Angus by the Firth of *Tay*, to the north-west, from part of Perthshire by the same Firth of Tay, meeting also with part of Strathern, to the west, it hath the Ochil hills, Kinross-shire, and part of Perthshire, to the south, the Firth of Forth, dividing it from the Lothians, and to the east, the German Ocean. It is in length, thirty two miles, and about seventeen wide. To the west it is more mountainous, to the east much plainer. The north and south parts are very fertile in corn, and full of Towns with good bays and harbours, but the middle is more proper for pasture. On the south side also, there is much coal, and many salt-pans, where very good salt is made. They have a quarry at *Dalgaty* of excellent free-stone, employ'd in the best pieces of Architecture, and near the water of *Ore* they find Lead, as also many fine Crystals of several colours at the *Bin* and at *Orrock*. They have likewise several Mineral Waters, as, the Spaw at *Kinghorn*, and *Ballgrigie*.]

In the south side hereof, upon the *Forth*, we first have a sight, Westward, of *Culross* aforesaid, seated on a descent, the chief Commodities of which are Salt and Coals. Its greatest ornament, is the stately building of the Earl of *Kincardin*, with the Gardens and Terrace-walks about it, which a pleasant prospect to the very mouth of the River *Forth*.] This is a late erected Barony in the person of *James Colvil*. [Near *Culross*, to the north west, is *Kincardin*, of which Edward Bruce of Carnock was created Earl by King Charles the first.] Then, we see *Dunfermling*, seated on an Eminence, and a famous Monastery in former times, which was built by King *Malcolm* the third, and was also the place of his Burial.[e] It gave the style and title of Earl, to that wise Statesman *Alexander Seton*, who was deservedly advanced from Baron of *Fyvy*, to be Earl of *Dunfermling*, and was also made Chancellor of the Kingdom of Scotland, by James [the sixth] King of Great Britain. Then, upon the *Forth* stands *Kinghorn*, from which *P[atrick] Lyon*, Baron *Glamys*, by the favour of King James the sixth, [d] received the title and honour of Earl, [and they are also Earls of *Strathmore*.] After this, upon the shore, is *Dysert*, situate on the foot of a rising ground, with an open heath of the same name stretch'd out before it. Here is a good large place, which they call the *Coal pot*, that hath great plenty of an earthy Bitumen, part whereof is on fire, not without damage to the neighbours. [It hath a harbour, and much trade in Coal and Salt, and the residence of the Lords *Sinclare*. [illegible] of the family of *Tullibardin*, was by King Charles the first created Earl of Dysert, which title of *Dysert* was also conferr'd on his daughter and heirs, and from her conveyed to her son [illegible], [illegible] Near *Dysert*, lies *Ravensheugh* [illegible], the [illegible], the seat of the Barons *St. Clair*, or *Sinclairs*, [who were advanced to the honour of Peerage by King James the fourth.] Above this, the River *Levin* buries it self in the *Forth*, which River runs out of the Lake *Levin*, wherein stands a Castle sometime belonging to the Douglas's, Earls

Dunferm ling. Now [illegible]. Earl of Kinghorn. [d] [illegible]. Dysert. Sinclair. The River Levin.

Earls of Morton, and which now belongs to Sir Thomas Bruce [Sir Alexander Lesly, General of the *Scots* forces, was by King Charles the first created Earl of *Levin*, in the year 1641] The Fourth hath at its mouth *Wemmis Castle*, the seat of a noble family of that surname, who were advanced to the dignity of Barons by King James the sixth, [and in the year 1633, to the dignity of Earls, to whom belongs the new built Haven, very commodious for Shipping]

Wemmis-Castle

Lately, C

From hence, the shore bends inwards, with many windings and turnings, as far as *Fif-ness*, that is, the Promontory or *Nose* of *Fife* Above it, St *Andrews*, an Archiepiscopal City, hath a fine prospect into the open Sea [It takes the name, from St *Andrew* (whose bones are said to have been brought over hither from *Patras* in *Peloponnesus*, by Regulus a Grecian Monk, in the year 368) and was the principal See of the old *Culdees*] The more ancient name of this place was *Regimund*, that is, St *Regulus's Mount*, as appears by certain old Evidences, in which we read, *Oengus or Ungus, King of the Picts, granted unto God and St Andrew, that it should be the Head and Mother of all the Churches in the Picts Dominions* And then an Episcopal See was placed here, whose Bishops, as all the rest of the Kingdom of Scotland, were consecrated and confirm'd by the Archbishop of York, till, at the intercession of King James the third, by reason of the frequent Wars between the Scots and English, Pope *Sixtus* the fourth constituted the Bishop of St *Andrews* Primate and Metropolitan of all *Scotland*, and Pope Innocent the eighth bound him and his successors to the *imitation* of the Metropolitan of *Canterbury*, in these words, *That in matters concerning the Archiepiscopal state, and the offices of Primacy and Legatine power, with their rights, and the free exercise thereof, and the honours, charges, and profits, they should follow, keep, and inviolably observe the laudable customs of the famous Metropolitan Church of Canterbury, whose Archbishop is Legate born of the Kingdom of England*, &c But before this, *Lawrence Lundoris* and *Richard Corvil*, Doctors of the Civil Law, reading publick Lectures in this place, had laid the Foundation of an University, which is now grown famous for the many learned men it hath produced, and for its three Colleges, and, in them for the *Regius-Professors* [The City lies towards the east, with a pleasant prospect to the Ocean, as hath been said, and has a harbour for Ships It had formerly a very strong Castle, some remains whereof are yet to be seen upon the rocks to the north, and the ruins of the Cathedral Church and Monastery show their ancient Magnificence The chief Church is that called *the New Church* (not far from the *New College*) wherein is a very stately Monument of Archbishop *Sharp*, they have also another Church, which is called St *Leonard's* But their greatest ornaments, are the three Colleges before-mentioned; 1 St *Salvator*, commonly called the *Old College*, founded by *James Kennedy*, Bishop of St Andrews, together with a Church, wherein he hath a curious monument Dr *Skene*, Principal, repair'd and augmented it, and also founded a Library, which is now very well furnished with Books 2 St *Leonard's* College was founded by *James Hepburn*, Prior of St *Andrews*, in which is a principal, who is always Doctor of Divinity, and the four Professors of Philosophy; to whom Sir *John Scot* added a *Philology Professor*, with a liberal Salary, and augmented the Library with the gift of several considerable Volumes; since encreased by the great Collection of Books left to it by Sir *John Wedderburne*. 3 The *New College* was founded by *James Beaton*, Archbishop, wherein are two Professors, always Doctors of Divinity, the one stiled *Principal Professor of Theology*, the other only *Professor of Theology* To these was added a Professor of Mathematicks, for the improvement of which Science, the first Professor, Mr *James Gregory*, procured an *Observatory* to be erected in the College garden, and also furnished it with many Mathematical Instruments] In commendation of this place, *J Johnston*, Regius Professor of Divinity there, hath these Verses,

Fif-ness

St Andrews

St Regulus

Ex Can. Apostolical 24

FANUM REGULI,

Sive

ANDREAPOLIS.

Imminet Oceano, paribus descripta viarum
Limitibus, pingui quam bene septa solo?
Magnificis opibus, staret dum gloria prisca
Pontificum, hic fulsit Pontificalis apex
Musarum ostentat surrecta palatia cœlo,
Delicias hominum, deliciasque Deûm
Hic nemus umbriferum Phœbi, Nymphæque sorores
Candida quas inter prænitet Urame
Quæ me longinquis redeuntem Teutonis oris
Suscipit, excelso collocat inque gradu
Urbs nimium fœlix, Musarum si bona nôsset
Munera, & ætherei regna beata Dei
Pelle malas pestes urbe, & quæ noxia Musis,
Alme Deus, coeant Pax Pietasque simul

In equal Streets the beauteous Structures run,
And tower'd the Ocean stretch the spacious Town
While *Rome* and Mitres aw'd the easy Seat,
Here the great Prelate kept his splendid Seat
In lofty Courts the gentle Muses reign,
And cheer with heavenly numbers Gods and Men
While tuneful *Phœbus* charms the sounding groves,
And wond'ring Nymphs repeat his sacred loves
Here me, returning from the *German* Coast
To those dear Comforts I so long had lost,
Me *Phœbus* blest with his peculiar care,
Me in his honours gave the largest share
Too happy Town, did she but rightly know
The gifts that Heaven and Heaven's dear tribe bestow
Far hence, ye guardian powers, all dangers chase,
But crown the Muses and the sacred place
With constant joys of piety and peace.

Falkland. Strutbers. Cupre.

Hard by, the little river *Eden* or *Ethan* hath its entrance into the Sea, which rises near *Falkland*, formerly belonging to the Earls of *Fife*, but now a Royal Retirement, and excellently well seated for the pleasures of hunting [It was built by King James the fifth, and the Duke of *Athol* is Hereditary Keeper of it It is particularly famous for giving the title of Viscount to the Family of *Cary*, in *England*, of which was *Lucius* Lord *Falkland*, a person of excellent Parts and Learning, and eminent for his Loyalty to King Charles the first] From thence *Eden* runs (under a continued ridge of hills, which cuts this Country in the middle,) by *Strutbers*, so called from the abundance of *Reeds* that grow there, and a Castle of the Barons *Lyndsay*, [of whom was descended *John* Lord *Lyndsay*, created by K Charles the first Earl of *Lindsay*] Next, *Eden* runs by *Cupre*, a noted Borough, where the Sheriff keeps his Court Upon which *J Johnston* hath these Verses,

CUPRUM FIFÆ.

Arva inter, nemorisque umbras & pascua læta
Lene fluens vitreis labitur Eden aquis
Huc veniat siquis Gallorum a finibus hospes,
Gallica se hic iterum forte videre putet
Anne etiam ingenium hinc & fervida pectora traxit?
An potius patriis hauserat illa focis?

By fields, by shady woods, by flow'ry meads,
His crystal stream the gentle *Eden* guides
To these blest seats should *Gallick* strangers come,
They'd find no change, but think themselves at home
Did that kind neighb'ring country lend the town
The wit and courage she so oft hath shown?
Or was she better furnish'd from her own?

Bolmerinock. Lundoris. * Now, L. Banbrich.

The shore now turns towards the North, and upon the æstuary of *Tay*, stood two famous Monasteries, *viz* *Bolmerinock*, built by Queen *Ermengerd*, wife to King William, and daughter of Viscount Beaumont in France, and proud of its Baron *James Elphinston*, [who was created in the year 1604 by King James the sixth, and whose Descendants do still enjoy the same honour] and *Lundoris* founded amongst the Woods by *David* Earl of *Huntingdon*, and * the Barony of *Patrick Lesly*, [who was created Lord *Lundoris* about the year 1600, and whose Descendant is the present Lord Lundoris] Between these two, lies *Banbrich*, a seat of the Earls of *Rothes*, strongly built in form of a Castle But concerning the Towns of *Fife*, lying along the shore, take, if you please, these verses of *J Johnston*

Oppida sic toto sunt sparsa in littore, ut unum
Dixeris, inque uno plurima juncta eadem
Littore quot curvo Forthæ volvuntur arenæ,
Quotque undis refluo tunditur ora salo;
Pene tot hic cernas instratum puppibus æquor,
Urbibus & crebris pene tot ora hominum
Cuncta operis intenta domus, fœda otia nescit;
Sedula cura domi, sedula cura foris
Quæ maria, & quas non terras animosa juventus
Ah! fragili fidens audet adire trabe?
Auxit opes virtus, virtuti dura pericla
Juncta etiam lucro damna fuere suo
Quæ fecere viris animos, cultumque dedere,
Magnanimis prosunt, damna, pericla, labor.

O'er all the shore so thick the towns are shown,
You'd think them thousands, and yet all but one
As many sands at *Forth's* great stream can hide,
As many waves as swell the rising tide,
So many vessels cut the noisy flood,
Such numerous tribes the scatter'd hamlets crowd
On land some ply their work, and some on seas,
And scorn the pleasures of inglorious ease
Through what strange waves, to what forsaken shores,
The lab'ring youth still urge their slender oars?
Thus riches come, and happy plenty flows,
But riches still to accidents expose,
And he that gains must ever fear to lose
Thus bred in hardships and inur'd to care,
They trust their courage and forget to fear
Loss, pains, and all that angry fate can send,
Prove but incentives to a noble mind

Thane. Earls of Fife. Cross Mac duff. * Colpindach.

The Governor of this County, as likewise of all the others in the Kingdom, was in ancient times a *Thane*, that is, in the old English tongue, the *King's Minister*, as it is also in the Danish at this day but Malcolm Canmore made *Mac-duff*, who was Thane of *Fife* before, the first hereditary Earl of *Fife*, and, in consideration of his good services, granted that his posterity should place the King (at his Coronation) in the chair, and lead the van guard in the King's Army, and if any of them should by chance kill either a Gentleman or a Commoner, he should compound for the murder with money. Not far from *Lundoris*, stands a stone-cross, which is a boundary between *Fife* and *Stratbern*, with old barbarous verses upon it, and it had thus far the Privilege of a Sanctuary, that any Manslayer ally'd to *Mac-duff*, Earl of Fife within the ninth degree, if he came to this cross, and gave nine cows, with a * *Heifer*, he should be acquitted of the manslaughter When his Posterity lost this title, I cannot learn, but it appears by the the Records of the Kingdom, that K David the second gave this Earldom to *William Ramsay*, with all and every the immunities, and the Law which is called *Clan Mac duff* And it is look'd upon as undeniable, that the families of *Wemes* and *Douglass*, and that great Clan *Clan Hatan*, whose head is *Mac Intoskech*, descended from them I find also by the learned *J Skene*, Clerk Register of Scotland, in his *Signification of words*, that *Isabella*, daughter and heir to Duncan Earl of Fife, granted the Earldom of Fife upon certain conditions to Robert the third, King of Scotland, in trust for Robert Steward, Earl of Menteith, who being afterwards Duke of *Albany*, and ambitiously aspiring to the Crown, put *David*, the King's eldest son, to the most miserable of deaths, that of hunger But his son *Murdac* suffered the punishment due to the wickedness both of his father and his own sons, being put to death by King James the first, at which time, a Decree passed, *That the Earldom of Fife should for ever be united to the Crown* But the authority of Sheriff

Earl of Rothes. Sheriff of Fife belongs by inheritance to the Earl of *Rothes*.

Balfours. [In this Shire, several other persons of note have been advanced to the dignity of Lords. Sir *Michael Balfour* of Balgarvie, was created Lord [1] Burghlie by King James the sixth, and Sir *Robert Melvil*, Lord *Melvil*, by the same King, of which family, *George* Lord Melvil was created Earl of Melvil by K. William and Q. Mary. Lindsays. Sir *David Lindsay* was created Lord Balcarras by King Charles the first, and his Son *Alexander*, afterwards, Earl of Balcarras by King Charles the second. Sir *Thomas Erskine*, who had before been advanced to the dignity of Viscount Fentoun by King James the sixth, was created by the said King, *anno* 1619 Earl of Kelly. Fentouns. Sir *James Levingston* of Kinnaird was created Lord *Newburgh* by King Charles the first, and Earl of *Newburgh* by King Charles the second. Levingstons. *Sandilands*, Laird of St Monans, was created Lord Abercromby by King Charles the first, and Lieutenant General Lesly, Son to the Lord *Lundoris*, was created by King Charles the second, Lord Newark. Sandilands. Newark. And from Kingstown in Lothian, Sir Alexander *Seaton*, younger son of George Earl of Winton, received the title of Viscount from King Charles the first.]

[1] Now, forfeited by Attainder. Melvils.

Now forfeited by Attainder.

STRATHERN.

Strathern Stewartry.

As far as the Æstuary of Tay, which is the bound of Fife on the North side, *Julius Agricola*, the best of all the Propraetors of Britain, under Domitian the worst of the Emperors, carried his victories, in the third year of his Expedition, having wasted the Kingdom so far. Into this Æstuary, falls the noted River of *Ern*, which running out of a Logh of the same name, bestows it on the Country that it runs through, for it is call'd *Strathern*, which in the ancient British, signifies *a Valley upon Ern*. [This Stewartry seems to be the *Ierne*, mentioned by Roman Writers. For in it are many Roman Camps, one particularly at *Ardoch* very remarkable, the figure and description whereof is in the account of the [a] *Thule*. Besides which, there is a *Via Militaris*, or Roman high-way, towards *Perth*. Several Roman Medals have also been found, and not many years since, two *Fibulae* curiously enamell'd, with a Sepulchral stone [b].

The River Ern.

[a] See, at the end.

The *Ochil hills*, which run along the South parts of this Shire, abound with metals and minerals, particularly, they find good Copper, and the *Lapis Calaminaris*, and, in *Glen Devon*, they meet with Lead. Here is great want of Coal, but their excellent Peats, and the abundance of wood, supply that defect.]

[b] Ibid.

Drummen Baron Drummond. The banks of the *Ern* are adorned with *Drummen Castle*, belonging to the family of the Barons of *Drummond*, who have been advanced to great honours, since King *Robert Stewart* the third married a Wife out of this family. For the Women of that family have been, for charming beauty and complexion, beyond all others, insomuch that they have been most delighted in by the Kings. [Of the said family, James Drummond was created by King James the sixth, Earl of Perth, from the head burgh of the Shire. Also, James, a Son of the same family, was created, by King James the sixth, Lord *Maderty*; and Lieutenant General *William Drummond*, was by King James the seventh created Viscount of *Strathallan*.]

Earl of Tullibardin. And upon the same bank, *Tullibardin* Castle shews itself aloft, and that, with greater honour since, by the favour of King James the sixth, *John Murray* Baron of *Tullibardin*, was advanced to the title and dignity of Earl of *Tullibardin*, [whose Son *William* having married the eldest of the Coheirs of Stuart Earl of Athol, his Son John succeeded to the dignity of Earl of Athol, and Sir *Patrick Murray* his brother, became Earl of Tullibardin, whose Son James dying without issue, the Estate and Dignity fell to John Earl of Athol.] See Perth-shire. Upon the other bank, lower, stands *Duplin Castle*, the Seat [heretofore] of the Barons *Oliphant*, which still remembers how great an overthrow (not to be equalled in former Ages) the English, who came to assist King *Edward Baliol*, gave the Scots there. Insomuch, that the English Writers of that time, attribute the victory wholly to the power of God, and not to the valour of man, and the Scots report, that there fell of the family of *Lindsay* eighty persons, and that the name of *Hays* had been quite extinct, had not the head of the family left his Wife big with child at home. [The Lands of Duplin were purchased by Sir *George Hay*, who was first created Viscount Duplin, and afterwards Earl of Kinnoul, by King Charles the first.] Not far off, lies *Inermeth*, well known for its [ancient] Lords the *Stewards*, of the family of *Lorn* [who were advanced by King James the sixth to the honour of Earls of Athol.]

Duplin Baron Oliphant. Created ann. 1470.

Lords of Inermeth.

But after the conflux of *Ern* and *Tay*, the *Tay*, now become a broader, sees above it upon the bank, *Abernethy*, anciently the Royal Seat of the Picts, and a populous city, which (as we read in an old fragment) *Nectanus King of the Picts, gave to God and S. Brigid, till the day of judgment, together with the bounds thereof, which lie from a stone in Apurfeirt, to a stone near* Cairful, *that is* Loghtol, *and from thence as far as* Athan. But a long time after, it came into the possession of the *Douglasses*, Earls of Angus, who are called Lords of *Abernethy*, and are some of them there interred.

Abernethy.

The first Earl of *Strathern* that I read of, was *Robert Steward*, in the year 1380. Then, *David*, a younger Son of King Robert the second, whose only daughter being given in marriage to *Patrick Graham*, was mother of *Malisse* or *Melisse Graham*, from whom King James the first took the Earldom as escheated, after he had found by the Records of the Kingdom, that it had been given to his Mother's Grandfather, and his Heirs Male. This Territory (besides *Menteith* adjoyning) was under the government of the Baron *Drummond*, hereditary Stewards of it, [but now the Lord Drummond is Earl of

Earls of Strathern. 1380.

Men,,

Murray) are hereditary Stewards of the Jurisdiction of Menteith]

Menteith Stewarty

Menteith, as they say, hath its name from the River *Teith*, called also *Taich*; and thence in Latin they call this little Territory, *Taichia* Upon the bank of which, lies the Bishoprick of

Dunblain

Dunblain, erected by King David the first of that name [This is a pleasant little town, where the ruins of the Bishops, and Regular Canons houses, are to be seen Here was also a Church of excellent workmanship, part of which remains entire In the ruins of it, is an ancient Picture, representing the Countess of Strathern with her children, kneeling and asking a blessing from St *Blanus*, who is cloathed in his Pontifical habit Not long since, *Robert Leighton* was Bishop of this place, a man of an exemplary Life and conversation At his death, he left all his Books, both Manuscripts and others, to the use of the Diocese of *Dumblane*, and amortiz'd a sum for erecting a Library, and a Salary for a Library-keeper was amortiz'd by the same Bishops sister's son It gives the title of Viscount of *Dumblane* to his Grace the Duke of *Leeds*, in England The Lord *William Drummond*, Viscount of *Strath-allan*, hath here a very fine Dwelling, and considerable revenues in the Country all round]

Theatrum Scotiæ, p. 38

Kirk bird

At *Kirk-Bird*, that is, St. *Brigid's-Church*, the Earls of *Menteith* [g] had their principal residence, as also the Earls of *Montross* of the same family, not far off at *Kin kardin* This *Menteith* (as I have heard) reaches to the Mountains that enclose the East side of *Logh lomond*. [The Laird of *Dincrub* was, by King Charles the second when in Scotland, created Lord *Rollo*, from his surname

[g] Have, ...

Dincrub

Cardross.

Near these places is *Cardross*, which King James the sixth erected into a temporal Lordship, in the person of *Henry Erskin* Earl of Mar

Ardoch

In this Country, about the mid way between Dumblain and the Castle of Drummond, is the house of *Ardoch*, where are the footsteps of a large [h] Roman Camp, enclosed on some sides with treble trenches Here, at several times, Roman Medals have been found, and from hence there is a great Road which leads towards St *Johnstoun* or *Perth* (causey'd in many places,) and so on, through Strathmore, towards Angus This Encampment is believed to have been made by *Julius Agricola*, being near to the Grampian Hills, where he defeated the Scots and Picts

[h] See the ... count of *Thule*

Within the Camp, was found a square stone, which hath been kept at the Castle of Drummond, with the following Inscription,

DIS MANIBVS
ANTONIVS
DAIMONIVS
COHORTIS I
LEGIONIS
XVII HISPANORVM
HEREDES
F C]

Earls of Menteith.

The ancient Earls of *Menteith* were of the family of *Cumen*, formerly the most numerous and potent in all Scotland, but ruin'd by it's own greatness The later Earls have been of the House of *Graham*, ever since *Malisse Graham* attain'd to the honour of Earl, until William, the last Earl, died without issue in the year 1694, having conveyed his Estate to James, then Marquiss, and now Duke, of Montross]

AR-

Its chief town is *Innererra,*Innererra. a Burgh-Royal, near which is the Castle, the chief residence of the Earl of Argile, adorn'd with fine gardens standing upon the water of *Eira*, where it falls into *Lochfyne*. And from *Melfort*Melfort. in this Country, did *John Drummond* of Lundin, second Son of James Earl of Perth, by grant from King James the seventh, take the title of Viscount, and afterwards of Earl of Melfort.]

King James the fourth, with consent of the States of the Kingdom, enacted, that Justice should be administer'd to this Province by the Justices Itinerant at *Perth*, whensoever the King should think convenient. But the Earls themselves have in some cases their *Jura Regalia*; who are persons of very great authority, and of a mighty interest, deriving their pedigree from the ancient petty Kings of *Argile*, through an infinite series of Ancestors, and taking their sirname from their Castle *Cambel*; [if it may not be said, with greater truth, that the Castle had the name from the Family: for it is said in the *Black Acts*, that the name was *Castle Gloune* before it came to this Family, and that it was afterwards changed into *Castle Campbel*.] But they are obliged to King James the second forEarls of Argile. the honour and title of Earl; who (as it is recorded) created *Colin* Lord *Campbel* Earl of *Argile*, in regard to his own personal worth and valour, and the dignity of his Family. Whose Posterity, by the favour of their Kings, have been a good while *General Justices of the Kingdom of Scotland*, or (according to their way of expressing it) *Justices generally constitute*, and † † *Præfecti*.Stewards of the King's Houshold. [*Archibald* Earl of Argile, was created Marquis of Argile, by King Charles the first; and he being *forefaulted* by King Charles the second, his Son Archibald Lord Lorn was restored to the dignity and precedency of the Earl of Argile, in the first year of King William and Queen Mary, and created Duke of Argyle in the year 1701; whose son, *John*, succeeded him in these high Honours, and, in consideration of his great Merits and Abilities, was also made a Peer of England, before the Union, under the title of Earl of Greenwich;*Vid.* Greenwich, in *Kent*. which hath been since changed by King George into the more honourable title of *Duke* of Greenwich.]

THE Shire of *Argile* and *Perth*, with the Countries adjacent seem to have been formerly inhabited by the *Horesti*, Ὀρεσαὶ, or *Mountaineers*, mention'd by Tacitus, *viz*. the true ancient Scots, who came from Ireland, and possess'd themselves of the West-Isles, and of these Countries. For distinction's sake, they were called the *Northern Picts*, and are the same with Ammianus Marcellinus's *Dicalidones*, which Buchanan (agreeably to the meaning of *Horesti*, and the *Highlanders*) reads *Duncaledonii*. By the Panegyrist Eumenius, they are called *Hiberni, soli Britanni*; and by the Writers of the middle age, their Country is call'd *Hibernia*, as is proved in the Description of * * See at the end.*Thule*. These two Counties, with the Western Isles, made up the Kingdom of the Scots, whilst the rest of Scotland was under the *Romans* and *Picts*. Afterwards, the whole Country came under one King, namely, *Kenneth* the second, who was called *Rex Scotorum*.]

Beyond *Logh-Lomond*, and the western part of Lennox, near Dunbritton-Forth,Argile. *Argile* spreads out it self; call'd in Latin *Argathelia* or *Argadia*, and commonly *Argile*, but more truly *Argathel*, and *Ar-Gwithil*, that is, *near to the Irish*, or as some old Records explain it, *the brink, or edge of Ireland*; for it lies towards Ireland, whose inhabitants the Britains call *Gwithil* and *Gaothel*. A Country, running out to a great length and breadth, and all mangled with Lakes well stock'd with fish, and rising in some places into mountains very commodious for feeding of cattle; wherein also wild Cows and Deer range up and down. But along the coast, what with rocks, and what with blackish barren mountains, it makes a horrid appearance. In this tract, as Bede observes, *Britain received (after the* Britons *and* Picts) *a third Nation, viz. the* Scots, *into the* Picts *territories; who coming out of Ireland with* Reuda *their Leader, got, either by force or friendship, the habitation, which they still keep; from which leader they are to this day call'd* Dalreudini,Dalreudini. *for in their language* DalDal. *signifies a part*. And a little after, *Ireland* (says he) *is the proper Country of the Scots; and they being departed thence, added to the Britons and Picts a third Nation in Britain. There is a very great Arm of the sea, or bay, that anciently divided the Nation of the Britons from the Picts; which from the West breaketh a great way into the Land; and there, to this day, standeth the strongest City of the Britons, call'd* Alcluith. *In the Northern part of which bay, the Scots (whom I now mentioned) coming over, got themselves room to settle in.* Of that name *Dalreudin*, there are no remains that I know of, nor any mention of it in Authors, unless it be the same with *Dalrieta*. Dalrieta. For in an old little book *of the Division of Albany*, we read of one *Kinnadius* (who it is certain was a King of Scotland, and subdu'd the Picts) in these very words, *Kinnadius, two years before he came into Pictavia* (so it calls the country of the *Picts*) *enter'd upon the government of* Dalrieta. Also, there is mention made, in a more modern History, of *Dalrea*,Dalrea. hereabouts; where King *Robert Brus* unsuccessfully fought a battle.

[The Shire of *Argile* had formerly two Sherifdoms, *Argile* and *Tarbert*; but now they are united into one, which comprehends *Kantyre, Knapdale, Askeodnish, Cowell* (in which is *Denoun* the Bishop of Argile's seat,) *Lorne*, and many of the western Isles. To the east, it is joyned to Perthshire, to the north-east it touches upon Lochaber, to the north-west it hath several Isles, and to the south the Irish-sea, and the Firth of *Clyde*. In length, it is about six score miles, and in breadth about forty. The sea in many places runs up a great way into the land, in long bays which they call *Loughs*. The Tract properly called *Argile* lies between *Loch-fyne*, wherein is a great Herring-fishing, and *Loch-Aw*, a fresh water Loch, twenty four miles long, and one broad; out of which the River of *Aw* runs for some six or seven miles, and then enters *Loch-Ediff*. The whole shire is mountainous, and the Inhabitants, who speak the Irish, live mostly by their hunting and fishing.

ARGATHELIA, or *ARGILE*.

THE Shire of *Argile* and *Perth*, with the Countries adjacent, seem to have been formerly inhabited by the *Horesti*, *Orestæ*, or *Mountaineers*, mentioned by Tacitus, *viz* the true ancient Scots, who came from Ireland, and possess'd themselves of the West Isles, and of these Countries For distinction's sake, they were called *Northern Picts*, and are the same with Ammianus Marcellinus's *Dicalidones*, which Buchanan agreeably to the meaning of *Horesti*, and the *Highlanders*) reads *Duncaledonii* By the Panegyrist Eumenius, they are called *Hiberni*, *soli Britanni*, and by the Writers of the middle age, their County is call'd *Hibernia*, as is proved in the Description of *[*] Thule* These two Counties, with the Western Isles, made up the Kingdom of the Scots, whilst the rest of Scotland was under the *Romans* and *Picts* Afterwards, the whole Country came under one King, namely, *Kenneth* the second, who was called *Rex Scotorum*]

[*] See at the end

Argile — Beyond *Logh Lomund*, and the western part of Lennox, near Dunbritton Forth, *Argile* spreads out itself, call'd in Latin *Argathelia* or *Argadia*, and commonly *Argat*, but more truly *Argathel*, and *Ar-Gwithil*, that is, *near to the Irish*, or as some old Records explain it, *the brink, or edge of Ireland*, for it lies towards Ireland, whose inhabitants the Britains call *Gwithil* and *Gaothel* A Country, running out to a great length and breadth, and all mangled with Lakes well stock'd with fish, and rising in some places into mountains very commodious for feeding of cattle, wherein also wild Cows and Deer range up and down But along the coast, what with rocks, and what with blackish barren mountains, it makes a horrid appearance In this tract, as Bede observes, *Britain received (after the* Britons *and* Picts *a third Nation, viz the* Scots, *into the* Picts *territories, who coming out of Ireland with* Reuda *their Leader, got, either by force or friendship, the habitation, which they still keep, from which leader they are to this day call'd* Dalreudini, *for in their language* Dal *signifies a part* And a little after, *Ireland* (says he) *is the proper Country of the Scots, and they being departed thence, added to the Britons and Picts a third Nation in Britain There is a very great Arm of the sea, or bay, that anciently divided the Nation of the Britons from the Picts, which from the West breaketh a great way into the Land, and there, to this day, standeth the strong[e]st City of the Britons, call'd* Alcluith *In the Northern part of which bay, the Scots (whom I now mentioned) coming over, got themselves room to settle in* Of that name *Dalreudin*, there are no remains that I know of, nor any mention of it in Authors, unless it be the same with *Dalrieta* For in an old little Book of *the Division of Albany*, we read of one *Kinnadius* (who it is certain was a King of Scotland, and subdued the Picts) in these very words, *Kinnadius, two years before he came into Pictavia* (so it calls the country of the *Picts*) *enter'd upon the government of* Dalrieta Also, there is mention made, in a more modern History, of *Dalrea*, hereabouts, where King *Robert Brus* unsuccessfully fought a battle

Dalreudini Dal

Dalrieta

Dalrea

[The Shire of *Argile* had formerly two *Sheriffdoms*, *Argile* and *Tarbert*, but now they are united into one, which comprehends *Kantyre*, *Knapdale*, *Askeodnish*, *Cowell* (in which is *Denoun* the Bishop of Argile's seat,) *Lorne*, and many of the western Isles To the east, it is joined to Perthshire, to the north-east it touches upon Lochaber, to the north-west it hath several Isles, and to the south the Irish-sea, and the Firth of *Clyde* In length, it is about six score miles, and in breadth about forty The sea in many places runs up a great way into the land, in long bays which they call *Loughs* The Tract properly called *Argile* lies between *Loch fine*, wherein is a great Herring-fishing, and *Loch Aw*, a fresh water Loch, twenty four miles long, and one broad, out of which the River of *Aw* runs for some six or seven miles, and then enters *Loch Edisff* The whole shire is mountainous, and the Inhabitants, who speak the Irish, live mostly by their hunting and fishing

Its chief town is *Inveraria*, a Burgh Royal, near which is the Castle, the chief residence of the Earl of Argile, adorn'd with fine gardens standing upon the water of *Fine*, where it falls into *Loch-fyne* And from *Melfort* in this Country, did *John Drummond* of Lundin, second Son of James Earl of Perth, by grant from King James the seventh, take the title of Viscount, and afterwards Earl of Melfort] Inveraria Melfort

King James the fourth, with consent of the States of the Kingdom, enacted, that Justice should be administer'd to this Province by the Justices Itinerant at *Perth*, whensoever the King should think convenient But the Earls themselves have in some cases their *Jura Regalia*, who are persons of very great authority, and of a mighty interest, deriving their pedigree from the ancient petty Kings of *Argile*, through an infinite series of Ancestors, and taking their surname from their Castle *Cambel*, [It may not be said, with greater truth, that the Castle had the name from the Family for it is said in the *Black Act*, that the name was *Caple Gloure* before it came to this Family, and that it was afterwards changed into *Castle Campbel*] But they are obliged to King James the second for the honour and title of Earl who [illegible] created *Colin* Lord *Campbel* [illegible] Earl of [illegible] gard to his own personal worth and valour, and [illegible] the dignity of his Family Whose Posterity by the favour of their Kings, have been a good while *General Justices of the Kingdom of Scotland*, or according to [illegible] *Justices* [illegible] and [illegible] of [illegible] the King Household [illegible] Earl of Argile, was created Marquis of [illegible] by King Charles the first and he being [illegible] King Charles the second, [illegible] Lord Lorn was restored to the [illegible] precedency of the Earl of Ar[illegible] year of King William and Queen [illegible] created Duke of Ar[illegible] whose son, [illegible] succeeded [illegible] Honours, and in consideration of his Merits and Abilities, was [illegible] England, before the Union, under [illegible] Earl of G[illegible] which [illegible] changed by King G[illegible] into the [illegible] honour [illegible] able title of *Duke* of G[illegible]]

CANTIRE.

Logh Finn  Ogh-Finn, a Lake which in the proper season produces incredible sholes of *herrings*, divides *Argile* from a promontory, which for about thirty miles together, grows by little and little into a sharp point, and thrusts itself with such a seeming earnestness towards Ireland (separated from it by a narrow streight of scarce thirteen miles) as if it would call it over to it Ptolemy calls this the *Promontory of the Epidii* between which name, and the Islands *Ebudæ* (opposite to it) me thinks there is some affinity It is now called in Irish (which language they use in all this Tract) *Can-tyre*, that is, the *Land's head* [and (as hath been said) is about thirty miles long, and eight or nine broad, and hath in it a Burgh of Barony, situate upon the Lough of *Kilkerran*, call'd *Campell-Town*, where is a safe harbour for Ships, having an Island in the mouth of the Bay]

Epidium

This tract is inhabited by the family of *Mac-Conell*, who are very powerful here; but yet at the command of the Earl of Argile They, sometimes, in their * little Vessels, make excursions for booty into Ireland, and have possess'd themselves of those little Provinces, which they call *Glines* and *Rowte* This Promontory lieth close to *Knapdale*, with so small a neck of land (being scarce a mile over, and sandy too) that the Seamen, by a short cut, as it were *transport* their vessels over land Which one would sooner believe, than that the *Argonautes* laid their *Argos* upon their shoulders, and carried it along with them five hundred miles This place gave, first, the title of Lord, to a brother of the Earl of Argile, and afterwards, when the Head of that Family was created Marquis, he was made *Earl of Cantyre* Sept 1211

* Mi..paron es

LORN.

 Omewhat higher, towards the North, lies *Lorn*, a Country producing the best Barley, and divided by *Logh-Leave*, a vast Lake, upon which stands *Berogomum* a Castle, wherein the Courts of Justice were antiently kept and not far from it, *Dunstafag*, that is *Stephen's Mount*, antiently a seat of the Kings; above which, is *Logh-Aber*, a Lake that insinuates itself so far into the Land out of the Western Sea, that it would meet the Lake of *Ness*, which empties, itself into the Eastern Ocean, did not the hills, which lie between, separate them by a very narrow neck The chief place in this tract, is *Tarbar* in *Logh-Kinkeran*, where King James the fourth, by authority of Parliament, constituted a *Justice* and *Sheriff*, to administer Justice to the Inhabitants of the Southern Isles, [but now the Shires of *Argile* and *Tarbar* are joined into one]

Berogonum

Dunstafag

Logh Aber

Tarbar 1503

These Countries, and the others beyond them were in the year of our Lord 605 held by those *Picts*, which Bede calls the *Northern Picts* where he tells us, that in the said Year, Columbanus *a Priest and Abbot, famous for the profession of Monkery, came out of Ireland into Britain* to instruct those in the Christian Religion, *who by the high and fearful ridges of Mountains, were sequester'd from the Southern Countries of the Picts*, and that they in requital, granted him the Island *Hii*, lying over-against them, now [said to be] *I-comb kill*, of which in its proper place [But against the supposing this to be *I comb-kill*, it is alledged, that it appears not that the *Western Isles* belonged to the Picts at that time (so that they could not dispose of any part of them,) and that it was more probably *Hoia*, one of the *Orkney Isles*]

Lib 3 c 4

Its Stewards, some ages since, were the Lords of *Lorn*, but now by an heir female it is come to the * *Dukes* of *Argyle*, who always use this, among their other titles of honour

* Earl

BRAID

BRAIDALBIN.

MORE inward, among the high and craggy ridges of the Mountain *Grampius*, where they begin a little to slope and settle downwards, lies *Braid Albin*, that is, *the highest part of Scotland*, (for the true genuine Scots, call Scotland in their Mother-Tongue, *Albin*,) and that part where it rises up highest, *Drum Albin*, that is *the Ridge of Scotland* But in a certain old Book it is read *Brun-Albin*, where we find it thus written, *Fergus the Son of Erc was the first of the seed of Chonare, that enter'd the Kingdom of Albany, from Brun-Albain to the Irish sea, and* [a] *Inch Gall And after him the Kings of the race of Fergus reigned in Brun-Albain or Brunhere, unto Alpinus the son of Eochal* But this *Albany* is better known for its Dukes, than for the Produce of the ground The first Duke of Albany that I read of, was *Robert* Earl of Fife, who was advanced to that honour by his Brother King Robert the third of that name, yet he, spurr'd on by Ambition, most ungratefully starved to death *David* his Son, the next heir to the Crown But the punishment due to this wicked fact, which himself by the forbearance of God felt not, came heavy upon his son *Mordac*, second Duke of Albany, who was condemned for Treason and behead-ed, after he had seen his two sons executed in like manner, the day before The third Duke of Albany was *Alexander*, second son of King James the second, who being *Regent of the Kingdom, Earl of March, Marr* and *Garioth*, and *Lord of Annandale* and *Man*, was outlaw'd by his brother James the third, and after many strugglings with the World and the difficulties of it, happen'd in the end, as he stood by to see a Tournament at Paris, to be wounded by a splinter of a broken Lance, and so died His son *John*, the fourth Duke of Albany, who was also Regent, and appointed Guardian to King James the fifth, being charm'd with the pleasures of the French Court (as having married a daughter and coheir of *John* Earl of *Bologne* and *Lauragne*, died there without issue Whom, out of respect and deference to the blood Royal of Scotland, Francis the first King of France, honour'd so far, as to allow him a place in France, between the Archbishop of *Langres*, and the Duke of *Alencon*, Peers of the Realm After his death, there was no Duke of Albany, till Queen Mary conferred this honour upon Henry Lord *Darnley*, whom, in a few days after, she made her Husband, and King James the sixth granted the same to his second son, *Charles* an Infant, [b] afterwards Duke of York, [and then King After whose Restoration, *James* Duke of York, afterwards King *James* the seventh, enjoy'd the title of Duke of *Albany*, by creation, during the life of his elder brother King *Charles* the second]

These parts are inhabited by a People, uncivilized, warlike, and very mischievous, commonly called *Highland men*, who being the true race of the ancient Scots, speak Irish, and call themselves *Albin nich* A People they are of firm and compact bodies, of great strength, swift of foot, high minded, inur'd to the exercises of War, or rather Robbery, and desperately bent upon revenge They wear, after the manner of the Irish, [c] strip'd Mantles of divers colours, with their hair thick and long, living by hunting, fishing, and stealing In war, their armour is an iron head piece, and a coat of Mail, and their arms, a bow, barbed arrows, and a broad back sword And, being divided into Families, which they call *Clanns*, what with plundering and murdering, they commit such barbarous outrages, that their savage cruelty hath made this Law necessary, That, if one of any *Clann* hath committed a trespass, whoever of that Clan chances to be taken, shall repair the damage, or suffer death

[In the reign of King Charles the second, Sir *John Campbel* of *Glenurchie* Baronet, an ancient and powerful Cadet of the Family of *Argile*, was created Earl of *Bredalbin*, about the year 1681, and this Family are hereditary Bailies the cof]

Albin

a The Hebudæ

Dukes of Albany

Title

b Now, C

High land-men

c Plaids

Parliam. 1581

PERTH-

PERTHSHIRE.

The River Tay.

OUT of the very bosom of the Mountains of *Albany*, issues the *Tay*, the greatest river in all Scotland, and rolls along violently through the Fields, till widening it self into a Lake full of Islands, it there restrains its course After this, being kept within bauks, it waters *Perth*, a large, plentiful, and rich Country, [so called from *Perth*, a Burgh Royal, and the head burgh of the County,) which to the north and north west hath *Badenoch* and *Lochabire*, to the north east is bounded with *Mari*, to the west with *Argileshire*, to the south-west with *Dumbartonshire*, and to the south with *Clackmananshire*, part of *Sterlingshire*, and the river and firth of *Forth*, to the south east, it hath *Kinrosshire* and *Fife*, and to the east, *Angus* The length of it from east to west is above fifty two miles, the breadth about forty eight The high grounds are good pasture, and the low very fruitful in Corn]

Perth

Amund, riv

The *Tay* receives the *Amund*, a little River coming out of *Athol* This *Athol* (to make a short digression,) is infamous for *Witches*, but a country fruitful enough, having woody vallies, where once the *Caledonian Forest* (dreadful for its dark intricate windings, and for its denns of Bears, and its huge wild thick-maned Bulls, which we have mentioned before) extended it self far and near in these parts As for the Places herein, they are of little account, but the Earls are very memorable *Thomas*, a younger Son of *Rolland* of *Galloway*, was, in right of his Wife, Earl of Athol, whose son Patrick was murder'd at Haddington in his Bed-chamber, by the *Bissets*, his Rivals, and they immediately set the house on fire, that it might be supposed he perished casually in the flames In the Earldom succeeded *David Hastings*, who had married *Patrick's* Aunt by the mother's side whose son that *David* (surnamed of *Strathbogy*) seems to have been, who a little after, in the reign of Henry the third of England, was Earl of Athol, and married one of the daughters and heirs of Richard, base son to King John of England, and had a very noble Estate with her in England She bore him two Sons, *John* Earl of Athol, who being very unsettled in his allegiance, was hanged on a Gallows fifty foot high and *David* Earl of Athol, who by marriage with one of the daughters and heirs of *John Comin* of *Badzenoth* by one of the heirs of Aumar de Valence, Earl of Pembroke, came to a mighty Estate He had a son *David*, who, under King Edward the second, was sometimes summoned to Parliament amongst the English Earls and being made, under King *Edward Baliol*, Lieutenant General of Scotland, was conquer'd by the valour of *Andrew Murray*, and slain in a battle in *Kelblen* Forest, in the year 1335 His son *David* had only two daughters, *Elizabeth*, married to *Thomas Percy*, from whom the Barons *de Burrough* derive their original, and *Philippa*, married to Sir *Thomas Halsham*, an English Knight Then the title of Athol fell to that *Walter Stewart*, son to King Robert the second, who barbarously murder'd James the first, King of Scotland, and was punish'd suitably to so execrable a piece of cruelty insomuch that *Æneas Sylvius*, then Nuncio in Scotland to Pope Eugenius the fourth, is reported to have said, *That he could not tell whether he should give them greater commendations who reveng'd the King's death, or punish them with sharper censures and invectives, who polluted themselves with so heinous a Parricide* After an interval of some few years, this honour was granted to *John Stewart* of the house of *Lorne*, son of *James*, surnamed the *Black Knight*, by *Joan*, the widow of King James the first, daughter of *John* Earl of Somerset, and * neice to *John of Gaunt* Duke of Lancaster, whose Posterity enjoy it at this day [That is to say, by the marriage of *Dorothea Steuart*, eldest daughter of the last Earl of Athol, with *William Murray* Earl of *Tullibardin*, whose Descendants have been successively advanced to the higher honours, first of Marquis, and then of Duke, of *Athol* Lord *Charles Murray*, second son to the Marquiss of *Athol*, was by King James the seventh created Earl of *Dunmore*, and *William*, the fourth son of the said Marquiss, and his descendants, became vested with the title of Lord *Nairn*, by marriage with the only daughter of *Robert* Lord *Nairn*]

The Caledonian Forest

Earls of Athol]

Chronicon Mailross

* Ne

Now the *Tay*, being enlarged by the Influx of the *Almund*, makes for *Dunkeld*, adorned by King David with an Episcopal See This, on account of the name, is look'd upon by most as a Town of the *Caledonians*, and those persons interpret it, *The h l of Hazels*, who will have it to take the name from the *Hazels* of the *Caledonian Forest* [It is surrounded with pleasant woods, at the foot of the *Grampian* hills, on the north-side of *Tay* The ruins of the Cathedral Church are still to be seen It is the chief Market Town of the High lands, and is of late very much adorned with stately buildings, erected by the Duke of *Athol* Sir *James Galloway*, Master of Requests to King James the sixth and King Charles the first, was by the latter created Lord *Dunkeld* In these parts lies *Gillicbrankie*, remarkable of late days for the defeat of the King's Forces, by the late Viscount *Dundee* and his Associates, himself being killed in the Action]

Dunkeld

Gillicbrankie Ann 1689

From hence the *Tay* takes its course by the ruins of *Berth*, a little desolate City, not forgetting what calamity it brought upon it in times past, when with an impetuous torrent it overflow'd the pasture and corn-ground and destroyed all the labours of the Husbandmen, and swept away this poor City, with a Royal Infant, and all the Inhabitants Instead of which, King *William* built *Perth*, much better situated, and this presently grew so rich, that Necham, who lived in that age, made this Distich upon it,

Berth

> *Transis, ampla Tai, per rura, per oppida, per Perth,*
> *Regnum sustentant illius urbis opes.*

> Great *Tay* through *Perth*, through Towns, through Country flies
> *Perth* the whole Kingdom with her Wealth supplies.

P t

But posterity hath named it, from a Church founded in honour of St *John*, *St John's Town* (St John's Town). And the English, in the heat of the war between the *Bruses* and the *Baliols*, fortified it with large Bulwarks, the greatest part of which the Scots afterwards demolished. It is nevertheless a neat little City, pleasantly seated between two Greens, and although some of the Churches are defaced, yet wants it not its beauties: and it is so divided, that almost every street is inhabited by a several trade apart, and is furnished by the *Tay* every tide with Commodities from Sea, in their light Vessels. Upon it, *J. Johnston*, so often mentioned, hath these Verses:

PERTHUM.

Propter aquas Tai liquidas, & amœna vireta,
Obtinet in medio regna superba solo
Nobilium quondam Regum clarissima sedes,
Pulchra situ, & pinguis germine dives agri.
Finitimis dat jura locis, moremque modumque
Huic dare, laus illis hæc meruisse d[illegible]
Sola inter patrias incincta est mœnibus urbes,
Hostibus assiduis ne vaga præda foret.
Quanta virum virtus, dextræ quæ præmia norunt
Cimber, Saxo ferox, & genus Hector dam
Felix laude nova, felix quoque laude vetusta,
Perge recens, priscum perpetuare decus.

Near *Tay's* great stream, amongst delightful plains,
Mucstick *Perth* in royal splendor reigns.
For lofty Courts of ancient Kings renown'd,
Fair is the site, and ever rich the ground.
Hence Laws and Manners neighb'ring parts receive,
Their praise 'tis to deserve, and her's to give.
No Walls like her, her Sister Towns can show,
Which guard her riches from the ford'ring foe.
How stout her Knights, what noble spoils they won,
The *Britains*, *Saxons*, and the *Danes* have known.
Renown'd in eld[illegible] and in latest day[illegible],
Oh! may her glor[illegible] with [illegible] years encreafe,
And new deferts [illegible] ance her [illegible] ncient pride.

King James the sixth [illegible] advanced *Perth* to [illegible] Earldom, upon his creating *[illegible]* Baron Dromond, *Earl of Perth*.

Near *Perth* is *M[illegible]*, which Margaret of England, Dowager to K. James the 4th, purchased with a Sum of mon[illegible], for her third husband *Henry St[illegible]art* of the Blood Royal and his Heirs, and did withal obtain for him, of her son *James* the fifth, the [illegible] of a Baron. A little lower is *Ruthven*, a Castle of the *Ruthvens*, a name to be [illegible], and [illegible] out of all Memorials, since the States of the Kingdom pass'd a Decree, that all of that name should lay it down, and take a new one, after that the *Ruthvens*, Brothers [illegible] in an execrable and horrid Conspiracy, had plotted the murther of the best of Princes, *James* the sixth, who had created their father *William*, Earl of *Gowry*, but did afterwards (upon his insolently prescribing Laws to his Sovereign, and being convicted of high Treason) behead him. But I may seem to have said too much of persons condemned to eternal oblivion, and yet the mentioning such wicked generations, may be in useful caution to posterity. [Sir *Thomas Ruthven* of *Freeland*, descended of this Family, was created by King Charles the second, Lord *Ruthven*. Not far from hence, is *Duncrub*, from which place Sir *Andrew Rollo* was created Lord *Rollo*, by King Charles the first.]

- Very fit[illegible]ly call[illegible]
- Earl of Perth
- Baron Methven
- Ruthven or Reuven

As for *Gowry*, so much celebrated for its Corn fields, and the fertility of the Soil, it lies along the other side of the *Tay*, and is a more level Country. In this Tract, over-against *Perth*, on the further side of *Tay*, stands *Scone*, a famous Monastery in times past, and honoured with the Coronation of the Kings of *Scotland*, ever since King *Kenneth*, having hard by made a general slaughter of the Picts, placed a Stone here, enclosed in a wooden Chair, for the Inauguration of the Kings of Scotland. It was transported out of Ireland into *Argile*, and King Edward the first of England caused it to be convey'd to *Westminster*. Concerning which, I have inserted this Prophesy, so common in every man's mouth, since it hath [c] proved true, as few of that sort do.

- Gowry
- Scone
- [c] Now, C.

Ni fallat fatum, Scoti quocunque locatum
Invenient lapidem, regnare tenentur ibidem.

Or Fate's deceiv'd, and Heaven decrees in vain,
Or where they find this Stone the *Scots* shall reign.

By the special favour of King James [the sixth,] *Scone* [d] gives the title of Baron to *David Murray*, [created afterwards by the same King Viscount of *Stormmouth*, which is the Upper Part of the Country of *Gowry*.]

- [d] Gives, C.

Where the *Tay*, now grown larger, spreads itself, *Arrol* hangs over it, the seat of the noble Earls of *Arrol*. They have been hereditary Constables of Scotland ever since the time of the *Bruses*, and deduce their original (which is exceeding ancient) from one *Hay*, a very stout and valiant man, who, together with his sons, in a dangerous battle against the Danes at *Longcarty*, catching up an Ox yoke, did, by fighting bravely himself, and encouraging others, rally the retreating Scots, so as they got the day. Which Victory and Deliverance, the King and the States ascrib'd to his singular valour. Whereupon, several excellent Lands were assign'd in this place to him and his posterity, who in testimony of this action have a *Yoke* for their Crest over their Coat of Arms. [From this Family was descended *John* Earl of *Arrol*. Near to which lived Sir *George Kinnaird* of *Rossie*, who was created Lord *Kinnaird* in the year 16[illegible].] As for *Huntly Castle*, hard by, I have nothing to write of it, but that it has given name to a very great and honourable family, since, perhaps, the title of Earl of *Huntly* was taken from a place in the *M[illegible]*, called by that name, which is part of the Barony of *Gordon*, the ancient Inheritance

- Arrol
- Earls of Arrol
- Huntley Castle

tance of this Family *Huntley Castle* is one of the dwelling-houses of the Earl of *Strathmore*, and now passeth under the name of *Castle-Lyon*, and is well planted and pleasantly situate As to *Antiquities* in this Shire, at the *Meagle*, there is an ancient Monument of Stone, cut with several figures, said to be the burial place of Queen *Vanera*, who had her dwelling three miles north, upon a hill called *Barray*, where are the ruins of a great building]

ANGUS.

Angus

UPON the Æstuary of the *Tay*, and a little way within it, along the *North Eske*, lies *Angus*, called by the genuine Scots *Æneia*, extending it self into Fields very fruitful in wheat and all other sorts of grain, with large hills, lakes, forests, pastures and meadows, and beautified with very many forts and castles [From the head Town hereof, *Forfar*, it is likewise called the Shire of *Forfar*, and is always so named in the Rolls of Parliament Is is bounded upon the South with the Ocean and the Firth of Tay, upon the West and North-west, it is divided from *Perthshire* by a line twenty seven miles long, towards the North, the ridge of *Binchinnin*-mountains parts it from the *Brae* of *Marr*, and to the East it is separated from the *Mernes* by the water of *Tarf*, and a line drawn from it to the water of *North Eske*, which to its mouth continues to divide this Shire from the *Mernes* It is in length about [a] twenty eight miles, and in breadth about [b] twenty and in circumference about ninety It was anciently divided between the *Scots* and *Picts* the *Picts* possess'd the low Champain Part lying next the Sea, and the *Scots* inhabited that Part of the *Gramian* Mountains which lie in this Shire But, upon the Subversion of the *Pictish* Monarchy in the reign of *Kenneth* the second, King of Scotland, it came to be wholly possess'd by the Scots

Forfar

[a] Others, 32
[b] Others, 28

They have, in this County, several Quarries of free stone, and much slate, with both which they drive a good trade Near the Castle of *Invermarke*, there are Lead mines, and they find great plenty of Iron ore near the wood of *[illegible]* The higher ground, called the *Brae*, abounds with Hart, Hind, Roe-buck, Roe, and Fowl, and their Salmon trade turns to good account

Where this Shire joins to that of *Perth*, lieth the Town of *Coupar*, surrounded with large Corn fields Here, *Malcolm* the fourth, King of Scotland, founded an Abbey of Cistercian Monks, in the year 1174, and, upon the dissolution of Religious Houses at the Reformation, King James the sixth erected the Abbey into a temporal Lordship in favour of *James Elphinston*, second son of *James* Lord *Balmerino*, but he dying without issue, the Honour was swallowed up in the title of *Balmerino*]

Coupar

At the first entrance into this County from *Gowry*, stands *Glamis*, a Castle and Barony of a Family sirnamed *Lyons*, which have been famous ever since *[illegible]*, a great favourite of King Robert the second, received this and the dignity of a Baron with the King's daughter in Marriage, and therewith as I find it written, the [illegible] of *Lyon* with a *Lyon* in his [illegible] [illegible] the [illegible]

Baron Glamis

The shield [illegible] [illegible] [illegible] the flower [illegible]

themselves bear, but in different colours [c] *Patrick Glamis* obtain'd [d] the honour of Earl of *Kinghorn* from King *James* the sixth, [which title hath been changed from *Kinghorn* to *Strathmore*, as being the largest Strath in Scotland, running through *Perthshire* and *Angus*, where the Estate of the said Earl, for the greatest part, lies]

[c] Now living, C
[d] Very lately, C

At a little distance, is *Forfar*, where Justice is administer'd by the Barons *Greys*, hereditary Sheriffs, who are descended from the *Greies* of *Chillingham* in *Northumberland*, and [[e] are said to have first come] into Scotland with King James the first, when he returned out of *England* Upon [f] one of whom, nam'd *Andrew*, the King bountifully conferr'd the Lordship of *Foulis*, with [g] *Helena Mortimer* for his Wife [The said Sir *Andrew Gray* of *Foulis* made a very bright figure in the times of King James the first and second, and was in that reign one of the great Barons, who were fixed Hereditary Lords And true it is, that by this marriage the Family was greatly enriched, but it is also true, that a person of both the names, who was also Son of the Lord *Gray*, came into *Scotland* long before, *viz* in the reign of King *Robert Bruce*; and had from that Prince, in consideration of his great Services, a Grant of all the Lands which had appertain'd to Sir *Edmund de Hastings*, lying in this County Sir *Walter Ashton*, an English Gentleman, was created Lord *Forfar* by King Charles the first, and *Archibald Douglass*, brother to *James*, Marquiss of *Douglass*, was, by King Charles the second, created Earl of *Forfar*]

Sheriffdom of Forfar
Baron Grey
[e] Came, C
[f] The first, C
[g] *Janet*

Near the *Tay's* mouth, is *Dundee*, which the ancients called *Alectum*, and others *Taodunum*, [a Town (of great note, good trade, and well built,] whose Constable, by special privilege, is Standard bearer to the Kings of *Scotland* Hector Boetius, who was borne here, expounds the name *Dundee*, by allusion, *Donum Dei*, or the gift of God This person, in the age when Learning reviv'd, wrote an elegant History of Scotland, out of Monuments of Antiquity so ancient, that *Paulus Jovius* wonder'd, there should be in his writings concerning these remote parts of the World, the *Hebrides*, and the *Orcades*, Records of above one thousand years standing, when in Italy (the nurse of excellent wits) there was, for so many ages after the expulsion of the Goths, such a scarcity of writers [The name seems to be derived from *Dun*, a hill and the river *Tay*, on the north side whereof it is situated ; It stands in a pleasant Plain, and (besides the advantages just now mentioned) had two Churches, a very high Steeple, and a harbour for Ships of burthen The Inhabitants are generally rich, and those who fall to decay, have a large Hospital provided for them Sir *James*

Dundee
J Skene de verb signif
Hector Boetius

James Scrimgeor, of the ancient Family of the *Scrimgeors* of *Dudop*, and Constables of *Dundee*, was first created by King Charles the first, Viscount of *Dudop*, and by King Charles the second Earl of *Dundee*, Which title being extinct, King James the seventh created Colonel *John Grahme* of *Claverhouse*, Viscount of *Dundee*, who was slain at the battle of *Gillinchrankie* in the year 1689]

But upon this place *Johnston*, who was born not far from hence, hath these Verses,

TAODUNUM.

Or

DEIDONUM.

Qua Notus argutis adspirat molliter euris,
Hic placide coeunt Taus & Oceanus
Hic facili excipiens venientes littore puppes,
Indigenis vasti distrahit orbis opes
Sæpe dolis tentata, & belli exercita damnis,
Invictis animis integra præstat adhuc
Fama vetus crevit cum Religione renata,
Lucis & hinc fulsit pura nitela aliis
Alectum *dixere prius, si maxima spectes*
Commoda, forsDonum dixeris esse Dei
Tu decus æternum gentisque urbisque Boeti,
Cætera dic patriæ dona beata tuæ

Where the calm South with gentle murmurs reigns,
Tay with the Sea his peaceful Current joyns
To trading ships an easy port is shown,
That makes the riches of the World its own
Oft have her hapless sons been forc'd to bear
The dismal thunder of repeated War,
Yet unsubdu'd their noble souls appear
Restor'd Religion hath advanc'd her height,
And spread through distant parts the sacred light
Alectum once 'twas nam'd, but when you've view'd,
The joys and comforts by kind heav'n bestow'd,
You'll call it *Donum Dei*, Gift of God
Boetius, honour of the Realm and Town,
Speak thou the rest, and make thy mother's honours known

Brochty Crag 154. Hence, we have a sight of *Brochty craig* a Fort defended by a Garrison of English for many months together, when, out of an earnest desire of a perpetual peace, they sued for a Marriage between *Mary* of *Scotland* and *Edward* the sixth of England, and, upon promise thereof, demanded the performance by force of arms but the Garrison at length abandon'd it [About four miles north-east from this, stood the old Castle of *Panmure*, which was gallantly defended by *Robert Maule*, of *Panmure* (a strenuous opposer of the said Match,) against the English Garrison of *Brochtycraig*, but it still was forced to surrender Which Castle was afterwards demolished, and now, about half a mile from it, stands the new House of *Panmure*, a very noble Structure, built since the Restoration of King Charles the second, and adorn'd with fine Gardens and large Inclosures Of this family (descended from the Lords *de Moulin* in Normandy,) *Patrick* was created by King Charles the first [a] Earl of *Panmure*] (Panmure)

[a] Now forfeited by Attainder

Then, to the open Sea lies *Aberbroth*, by contraction *Arbroth*, [(a Royal Burgh and a Harbour, and of old)] a place consecrated to Religion by King *William*, in honour of St *Thomas* of *Canterbury*, and endow'd by him with large Revenues [Here he lies interred, and hath a stately Monument Here also is a famous Mineral Water, which is very much frequented for various Diseases] (Arbroth) Near *Aberbroth*, the *Red head* shoots out into the Sea, a Promontory to be seen at a great distance (Red head) Hard by, *South-Eske* enters the Ocean, which flowing out of a Lake, passes by *Finnevin-Castle*, much fam'd for being the seat of the *Lindsays*, Earls of *Crawford*, of whom I have spoken already (South Eske; Finnevin-Castle; The Lindsays) [Beneath, on the same river, stan[d]eth *Kinnaird*, the Inheritance of the *Karnagies*, who, by being Members of the College of Justice, did greatly advance their Fortunes, and of whom, Sir *David* was created Lord *Carnagy* by King James the sixth, and afterwards, by King Charles the first, Earl of [b] *Southesk*, also, Sir *John Carnegie* was by King Charles the first created Lord *Lour*, and afterwards Earl of *Ethie*, which titles his eldest son *David* exchanged, by permission of King Charles the second, for those of Earl of *Northesk*, and Lord *Rosehill*, as being more agreeable to the title of Earl of *Southesk*, the chief of the Family] (Kinnaird)

[b] Now forfeited by Attainder

Then, *Brechin* stands upon the same River, which King David the first adorned with a Bishop's See [It is a Royal Burgh of great Antiquity, and a Market Town, considerable for Salmon, Horses, Oxen and Sheep It has a stately bridge over the River Esk, and shows the ruins of the Bishop's Palace, and of the Canons houses It is likewise famous for a memorable slaughter of the Danes not far from it On the South-side of the Town, stood the old Castle of *Brechin*, famous for the brave and heroic defence of it by Sir *Thomas Maule*, against Edward the first, King of England, in the year 1303 Where this Castle stood, a very stately new House hath been built, which is one of the finest and most pleasant Seats in these parts] (Brechin)

At the very mouth of *South Esk*, is *Montrose*, that is, *The Mount of Roses*, a Town anciently called *Celurca* (risen out of the Ruins of another of the same name, and situated between the two *Eskes*,) which gives the title of [c] Duke to the family of *Graham* [King James the fourth conferred the title of Earl of *Montrose*, upon *William* Lord *Graham*, in the year 1504, and afterwards *James* Earl of *Montrose* was created Marquis by King Charles the first, being the person so much celebrated in our Histories, for his glorious Actions in the Civil Wars Whose Descendant, the present Inheritor of this antient Title and Estate, a person of great Honour and Wisdom, and highly deserving of his Country, was further advanced by Queen Anne to the dignity of Duke of *Montrose*] (Montrose)

[c] Earl C.

Upon this Town, *Johnston* writes thus

CELURCA,

CELURCA,

Or

MONS ROSARUM

Aureolis urbs picta rosis mons molliter urbi
Imminet, hinc urbi nomina facta canunt
At veteres perhibent quondam dixisse Ce lurcam,
Nomine sic prisco & nobilitata novo est
Et prisco atque nova insignis virtute, virûmque
Ingentis, Patriæ qui peperere decus

A leaning Mount which golden roses grace
At once adorns and names the happy place
But ancient times *Celurca* call'd the Town,
Thus is it proud of old and late renown,
And old and late brave sons, whose wit and hand
Have brought new Trophies to their native Land

Boschain. Barons Ogilvy

Not far from hence, is *Boschain*, belonging to the Barons of *Ogilvy*, who are of very ancient Nobility, as being descended from that *Alexander*, Sheriff of Angus, who was slain in the bloody battle at *Harley* against the Macdonalds of the Isles

Airlie

[In this Shire, is also *Airlie*, which was the first title of the Lord *Ogilvie* of *Airlie*, and *James* Lord *Ogilvie* was created by King Charles the first Earl of *Airlie*; the seat of which family is at *Cortochie*, in this County, at the foot of the *Grampian* hills

Cortochie

Before we conclude, we must observe, that in this Shire it was, that the General of the *Danes* was kill'd by the valiant *Keith*, who thereupon was advanced to great honours by King Malcolm the second, who was present at the battle Upon the General's Grave, there was a high Stone erected, which carries the name of *Camus's Cross* And about ten miles distant from this, at *Aberlemno*, is another Cross, erected upon some of the Danes kill'd there Both these have some antique Pictures and Letters upon them In this river, below the Castle of *Brechin*, are found Pearls, some of which are so fine and large, that they may be compared with many that are Oriental]

Earls of Angus

As for the Earls of Angus, *Gillebred*, and his son *Gilchrist*, of *Angus* (a person illustrious for his brave exploits under Malcolm the fourth,) [l] were the first [m] Earls of Angus that I read of About the year 1242 *John Comin* was Earl of Angus, who died in France, and his Dowager (perhaps heiress of the Earldom) was married to *Gilbert Umfravile*, an Englishman For both he and his heirs successively were summoned to the Parliament of England till the third year of King Richard the second, under the title of *Earls of Angus* But the English Lawyers refused in their Instruments to stile him *Earl* because *Angus* was not within the Kingdom of *England*,) till he produced in open Court the King's Writ, whereby he was summoned to Parliament under the name of *Earl of Angus* In the reign of *David Brus*, [n] *Alexander Steward* was Earl of Angus, who took *Berwick* by surprize, but presently lost it again, and a little after, died miserably in prison at *Dumbritton* The *Douglasses*, Men of noble brave Spirits and invincible Courage, have been Earls of *Angus*, ever since the reign of Robert the third (after that *George Douglass* had married the King's Daughter,) and are reputed [o] the chief and principal [p] Earls of Scotland, whose Office it is to carry the Regal Crown before the King's, at all the solemn Assemblies of the Kingdom The sixth Earl of *Angus* of this race, was *Archibald*, who married *Margaret*, daughter to Henry the seventh of England, and mother to James the fifth of Scotland, by whom he had issue *Margaret*, Wife to *Matthew Steward* Earl of Lennox She, after her brother's death without issue, willingly resigned her right to this Earldom (with the consent of her husband and sons) to *David Douglass* of *Petendreich*, her Uncle's son by the father's side, to the end that by this obligation she might engage that Family (already the nearest in Blood) more closely to her At the same time, her son Henry was about to marry Q Mary From which marriage, King *James* [the 6th,] Monarch of *Great Britain*, was happily born for the general good of these Nations, [and from the Earls of *Angus* and *Douglass*, the Duke of *Douglass* is lineally descended]

[l] Wa C
[m] Earl, C
[n] *Thomas*, C *Scotochronicum*
[o] *Prima Scotica* C m t
[p] Now Duke

MERNIS.

These parts were in Ptolemy's time inhabited by the *Vernicones*, the same perhaps with Marcellinus's *Vecturiones*. But that name is now quite lost, unless we can imagine a little piece of it to remain in *Mernis*. For oft-times (in common discourse) in the British tongue *V* is changed into *M*.

This little County of *Mernis*, butting upon the German Ocean, is a rich soil, and a pretty plain and level country. [It is so named from *Mearn*, a valiant Gentleman, to whom it was given by *Kenneth* the second, and is called also the shire of *Kincarden*, from the ancient town of *Kincarden*. To the east, it is bounded with the sea, to the south, with the water of *North-Esk*, to the west, with the *Gransbain hills*, and to the north, with the River of *Dee*. In length, it is about twenty six, or (as some say) twenty eight miles, and in breadth, about twenty. Upon the sea-coasts, they have several convenient Creeks, and some good harbours, of which *Stone hive* is one of the best, and, for its greater safety, the Earl Marshal (who has a Salmon fishing upon the north side of the harbour) did some years since raise a Pier of stone.

Mearns

Where the water of Cowy falls into the sea, stands *Cowy*, a free burgh. Beneath the town, are to be seen the ruins of a Castle, built (as is reported) by *Malcom Kenmore*, who made the town a free Burgh. On the Lands of *Ardutbie* and *Ridcloak*, are some trenches to be seen, which were cast up by the Danes at one of their Invasions made upon those parts, and round the hill of *Urie*, is a deep ditch, where the Scots encamped. But] the most memorable place in this Tract is *Dunnotyr*, a castle advanced upon an high and inaccessible rock, from whence it looks down on the sea beneath, being fortified with strong walls, and with towers at certain distances. [This rock is washed by the sea on three sides, and joined to the Land only by a narrow neck. Towards the entrance of the Gate, is a huge rock near forty ells high, which one would think was always ready to fall. The Court is a large plot of green ground, and the old buildings, seven story high, have exceeding thick walls, and it had once a Church, which was demolished in the late Civil wars. In the new buildings, there are some rooms very stately, and a Closet wherein is a Library. Within the Close, there is a large Cistern, about thirty cubits about. St Padie's Church here, is famous for being the burial place of St *Palladius*, and not far from this place is a dropping Cave, where the water petrifies.]

Cowy

Dunnotyr

This Castle hath long been the seat of the *Keiths*, a very ancient and noble family, and they, in consideration of their great valour, have long been hereditary [a] Earls Marshal of the Kingdom of Scotland, as they have also been Sheriffs of this County. In a Porch here, is to be seen that ancient Inscription abovementioned, of a [b] *Company* belonging to the *XXth Legion*, the letters whereof the most honourable the [c] present Earl, a great admirer of Antiquity, hath caused to be gilded. Somewhat farther from the sea, stands *Fordon*, to which it is some honour, that *John de Fordon* was born here, who with great industry compiled the *Scotochronicon*, and to whose Labours the modern Scotch Historians are very much indebted. But *Fordon* was much more honour'd in ancient times by St *Palladius's* reliques, formerly (as it is thought) deposited here, who in the year 431 was sent by Pope Cælestine to preach the Gospel to the Scots.

Keith

[a] Now forfeited by Attainder. Earls Marshal. Sheriffdom of *Kincardin* or *Mernis*.

[b] *Vexillatio*.

[c] So said, ann. 1607.

Fordon

St *Palladius*

In this Shire, the Laird of Arburthnet, of an ancient Family, was created *Viscount Arburthnet* by King Charles the first. As also, Sir *Alexander Falconer* of Halcertoun, was by King Charles the first created Lord Halcertoun, and Lieutenant General *Middletoun*, of an ancient family of that surname, was by King Charles the second created Earl of *Middletoun*.

Arburthnet

Halcertoun

Middletoun

Also, in this Shire, are to be seen two large and remarkable Monuments of Antiquity, at a place called *Auchincochtie*, five miles from Aberdeen. One of these, is two Circles of Stones, the *outward* Circle consisting of thirteen great ones (besides two that are fallen, and the broad-stone towards the South,) about three yards high above ground, and between seven and eight paces distant one from another; the Diameter of which is twenty four large paces. The *inward* Circle is about three paces distant from the other, and the stones thereof three foot high above ground. Towards the East from this Monument, at twenty six paces distance, is a large stone, fast in the ground, and level with it, wherein is a Cavity, partly natural and partly artificial, which (supposing this a Temple) may be imagined to have served for washing the *Priests*, the *Sacrifices*, and other things that were esteemed sacred among the Heathens.

Auchincochtie

Dr Garden's Letter to Mr Aubrey

The other Monument (which is full as large, if not larger than that already described, and distant from it about a Bow-shot) consists of three Circles, having the same common Center. The stones of the greatest Circle are about three yards above ground, and those of the two lesser Circles, three foot, the innermost Circle being three paces Diameter, and the stones standing close together. One of the Stones of the largest Circle on the east side of the Monument, hath upon the top of it (which is but narrow, and longer one way than the other) a hollowness about three inches deep, in the bottom whereof, is cut out a trough one inch deep and two inches broad (with another short one crossing it) that runs along the whole length of the Cavity, and down by the side of the stone a good way, so that whatever Liquor is poured into the Cavity upon the top of the stone, doth presently run down the side of it by this trough, and it should seem, that upon this stone they poured forth their *Libamina*, or liquid Sacrifices. There is also another stone in the same circle, and upon the same side of the Monument (standing nearest to the broad stone on edge, which looks towards the South) with a Cavity in the upper end, cut after the fashion of the cavity in the top of the other stone already described, and a natural fissure, by which all the Liquor poured into the Cavity, runs out of it to the ground.

Stone Monuments

The general Tradition throughout the Kingdom, concerning this kind of Monuments, is, that they were places of Worship and Sacrifice in the Heathen-times In this part of the Country, they are commonly called *Standing-stones*, and in the High-lands, where the Irish is spoken, thep call them *Caer*, which signifies a *Throne*, an *Oracle*, or a place of *Address*, and they have such a superstituous Veneration for them, that they will not meddle with any of the Stones, nor apply them to another use Some of them are called, in their language, by the name of Chapels, and others by the name of *Temples*, and as to this *Auchincochtie* in particular, the tradition is, that the Pagan-Priests dwelt here, there being yet to be seen, at a little distance from one of the Monuments, the foundation of an old House From another of those Monuments, a place in the Shire of Aberdeen and Parish of Ellon, is called *Focbel* (i e below the Chapel,) from a third, a place in the Shire of Bamf and Parish of Aberlowr is called *Leachel beandich* (i e the blessed Chapel,) from a fourth, in the same Shire, another place is called the *Chapel-den* Again, other Places where these Monuments remain, are called *Temples*, so, in the Parish of *Strathawen*, within fourteen miles of Aberdeen, there is a place called *Temple town*, from two or three of this kind, that stand upon the bounds of it, and those two which we have described before, are called by the neighbours *Temple* stones. All which instances do sufficiently prove, that they were places of *Worship*, and the same is confirmed by Groves near them, which we may well judge, from the superstitious Veneration that is still paid them, to have been formerly held sacred One in the Parish of Killernen, in the Shire of Nairn, another in the Parish of Enerallen in the Shire of Invernes, and a third, in the Parish of *Dutkel* in the same Shire]

MARR.

Aberdeen-shire

[ABERDEENSHIRE (so called from the chief burgh in it,) contains the Countries of *Marr*, *Fourmanteen*, *Garioch*, *Strathbogie*, and that part of *Buchan* which lieth south of the water of *Ugie* To the South, it is bounded with the River *Dee* and the *Granjbain* mountains, to the north west and west it hath *Banf-shire* and the river of *Doverne*, to the east, the Ocean, and to the north, part of Murray-Frith In length it is about forty six miles, and in breadth twenty eight The Inhabitants are generally very civil and polite They find here a spotted sort of Marble, and much Slate, and in the waters, abundance of Pearls, some of them very big, and of a fine colour They have Deer in great abundance, and the Eagles have their Nests upon the Craigs of Pennan]

Above *Mernes*, *MARR*, lies farther in from the sea, a large midland Country, spreading about sixty miles To the west, where it is broadest, it swells up in mountains, except where the rivers *Dee* (Ptolemy's *Diva*) and the *Done*, open themselves a way, and make the champagne ground very fruitful Upon the bank of the *Done* stands *Kildrummy*, a great ornament to it, the ancient seat of the Earls of *Marr* Not far off, is the residence of the Barons *Forbois*, of a noble and ancient Stock, who took this surname (being before called *Bois*) upon the Heir of the Family's valiantly killing a huge mighty *Boar* But at the very mouth of the river are two towns that are a greater ornament to it, which from the said mouth (called in British *Aber*,) do both borrow the same name, and are divided only by a little field that lies between The hithermost of them, which stands nearer the river *Dee*, is much enobled by the honour of a Bishop's See (which King David the first translated hither from *Murthlake*, a little village, and also by the fine houses of the Canons, and an Hospital for the Poor, with the publick School founded by *William Elphingston* Bishop of this place in the year 1480, and is called *New Aberdene* The other beyond it, named *Old-Aberdene*, is very famous for the Salmon taken there [But to treat of these more particularly, *Old Aberdeen* hath a Cathedral Church, commonly called St *Machars*, large and stately, which hath been built by several Bishops of this See In this Church was formerly a Library, but about the year 1560, it was almost wholly destroyed, so that now only the ruins remain The *King's* College (so called from King James the fourth, who assumed the Patronage of it) is seated on the south side of the town, and for neatness and stateliness much exceeds the rest of the houses One side is covered with Slate, the rest with Lead The windows of the Church (wherein is a fine monument of Bishop *Elphingston* the Founder) were formerly very remarkable for their painted glass, and something of their ancient splendor still remains The Steeple, besides other Bells, hath two of a very extraordinary bigness The top is vaulted with a double cross Arch, above which is a King's crown, having eight corners upheld by as many pillars of stone, and a round globe of stone, with two gilded crosses closing the crown Hard by the Church, is a Library well stock'd with Books, enlarged not many years since by those which Doctor *Henry Scougal*, Professor of Divinity there, and his Father, Bishop of *Aberdeen*, gave to it The College has a primate or Principal, a Professor of Divity, a Professor of the Civil Law, a Professor of Physick, a Sub-Principal, who is also Professor of Philosophy, with three other Philosophy Professors, and a Professor of the Languages

Kildrummy

Barons *Forbois* or *Forbes*

Aberdeen

Theatrum Scotiæ, p 28

New Aberdeen,* about a mile from the *Old*, as it is the Capital of the Sheriffdom of *Aberdeen*, and the Seat of the Sheriff for tryal of causes; so doth it much exceed the rest of the Cities in the north of Scotland, in bigness, trade and beauty The air is wholsome, and the Inhabitants well bred The Streets are paved with flint, or a very hard sort of stone like it; and the houses very beautiful; generally, four Stories high or more, which, having

New Aberdeen

* *Theatrum Scotiæ*

for the most part Gardens and Orchards behind them, make the whole City at a distance look like a Wood In the *High-street*, is a Church of *Franciscans*, of free-stone, begun by Bishop *Elphingston*, and finished by *Gavin Dumbar*, Bishop of the place The same *Gavin* built also a bridge of seven Arches over the river *Dee*, about a mile from the City But the greatest ornament to this City, is its Colledge called the *Mareshallian Academy*, as being founded by *George Keith*, Earl Marshal, in the year 1693, which the City of *Aberdeen* hath very much adorned with several additional buildings Besides a Primary Prtoessor (who is called *Principal*) it has four Professors of Philosophy, one of Divinity, and one of Mathematicks There is also a famous Library founded by the City which hath been supplied with Books by the benefactions of several learned Men, and is well furnished with mathematical Instruments This College, with that in the *New Town*, make up one University, called the University of King *Charles* Add to these, the School house (founded by Dr *Dune*) which has one head Master and three Ushers as also a Musick School St *Nicholas's* Church (the Cathedral) is built of Free-stone, and cover'd with Lead Formerly it was divided into three Churches, the biggest was called the *Old Church*, another the *New Church*, and a third the *Arch'd Church* They have also an Alms house for the maintenance of such Inhabitants as are old and poor, with three Hospitals, founded by several Persons

The City is built upon three hills, but the greatest part, upon the highest The outer parts are spread out upon the plain, from whence there is an easie access, by an ascent every way It had formerly a Mint, as appears by silver Coins stamped there with this Inscription, *Urbs Aberdeæ*, which are still preserved in the Closets of the curious

At the West end of the City, is a little round hill, at the foot of which there breaks out a fountain of clear water And in the middle, another Spring bubbles out, called the *Aberdonian Spaw*, and coming near the Spaw-water in the Bishoprick of Liege, both in taste and quality] *J Johnston*, a native, has described *Aberdeen* in these verses

ABERDONIA

Ad Boream porrecta, jugis obsessa superbis
Inter connatas eminet una Deas
Mitior algentes Phœbus sic temperat auras
Non æstum ut rabidum, frigora nec metuat
Fœcundo ditat Neptunus gurgite, & amnes
Piscosi, gemmis alter adauget opes
Candida mens, frons læta hilaris, gratissima tellus
Hospitibus morum cultus ubique decens
Nobilitas antiqua, opibus subnixa vetustis,
Martiaque invicto pectore corda gerens
Justitiæ domus, & studiorum mater honoris,
Ingenio ars, certant artibus ingenia
Omnia ei cedunt, meritos genitricis honores
Pingere non ulla Ars, ingeniumve valet

ABERDEEN,

With circling cliffs her lofty turrets vie,
And meet her rival sisters of the sky
So gentle *Phœbus* warms the sharper air,
Nor cold nor heat's extream her people fear
Great *Neptune* and his sons for fish renown'd
With useful floods enrich the fertile ground
In one fair current pretious gems are found
True hearts and pleasant looks, and friendly cheer,
And honest breeding never fail you here
Old their estates, old is their noble blood;
Brave are their souls, and scorn to be subdu'd
Here steddy justice keeps her aweful seat,
Wit strives with art, and art contends with wit
But my great Mother's worth and matchless praise
Nor art, nor wit can ever hope t' express

[Sir *George Gordon* of Haddo, Baronet, was created Earl of Aberdeen, by King Charles the second, in the year 1682 Also from *Glasford*, in the Shire of Lanerk, Francis Abercromby was created Lord Glasford by King James the seventh And from Portmore, Sir David Collier, for his military Services, was created a Baron by King William the third, and was by Queen Anne advanced to the higher honour of Earl of Portmore]

Glasford

Portmore

It is almost incredible, what abundance of *Salmon* there are, as well in these rivers, as in others on both sides of Scotland, a fish unknown to Pliny (unless it was the [b] *Esox* of the Rhine,) but very common and well known in those northern parts of Europe, [c] *being* ([d] as one says) *of a bright scarlet all within* They breed in Autumn in little rivers, and mostly in shallows, where they cover their spawn with sand; at which time they are so very poor and lean, that they are scarce any thing but bones Of that spawn in the spring following, comes a fry of small fish, which going to the sea, in a little time grow to their full bigness, and then making back again to the rivers which they were bred in, struggle against the force of the stream; and where-ever any heighth obstructs their passage, they will with a jerk of their tail (a certain [e] *leap*, whence probably they have the name of [f] *Salmons*) whip over, to the amazement of the spectators; and they keep themselves within these rivers, till they breed During which time, there is a Law against taking them, that is, from the eighth of September to the first of December And it should seem, that they were reckoned among the best commodities of Scotland, since it hath been provided by a Law, that they should be sold to the English for nothing but *English Gold* But these matters I leave to others

[b] Bede and our Writers call it in Latin, *Isicii*

[c] *Puniceo rutilans viscere*

[d] *Ut inquit ille*

[e] *Saltu*

[f] From *salio* to leap

[Besides Aberdeen, *Kintor* (as hath been said) is a Burgh Royal upon the Don, and *Inerurie* was erected into a Burgh-Royal by King *Robert Bruce*, upon account of his having gain'd a signal victory at it Sir *John Keith*, of Keith-hall, Knight Mareschal, and son to *William* Earl Mareschal, was by King Charles the second created Earl of *Kintore*, whose second title is Lord *Inverurie* On the South side of the water of Ugie, stands *Peterhead*, which has a Road that will contain some hundred of ships, and at this place, it is high water when the Moon is directly South

Kintor

Inerurie

Peterhead

In several places also there are *Obelisks*, some with figures upon them, such as one would imagine had been set up for monuments of battles

Obelisks

Cairns of Stones

battles And they have likewise several *Cairns* of stones, some whereof are upon the tops of mountains In some of these, bones have been found, and in one they met with the head of an Ax of Brass, which seems to have been employed in their sacrifices

The dropping Cave of *Slains*, is also very remarkable of the petrified substance whereof, they make excellent Lime

Pitsligo Forbes Baron of *Pitsligo* was by King Charles the first created Lord *Pitsligo*, in the year 1633

Fraser And *Fraser* of Stony wood or Muchill, was at the same time created Lord Fraser Charles, fourth son of the Marquis of Huntley, was created Earl of

Aboyn *Aboyn*, by King Charles the second Sir James

Frendraught Crighton, Laird of *Frendraught*, was by King Charles the first created Vicount of *Frendraught* Lieutenant General King, was created Lord

Ythan *Ythan* by King Charles the first, from a River of the same name in this Shire, in whom the title was extinct]

Earls of Marr As for the Earls of *Marr*, In the reign of Alexander the third, *William* Earl of *Marr* is named among those who were enemies to the King Whilst David Brus reigned, *Donald* was Earl of Marr, and Protector of the Kingdom, and was murder'd in his bed before the battle at Dyplin, by *Edward Ba'liol* and his English Auxiliaries whose daughter *Isabella* King Robert Brus took to his first wife, and had by her *Marjorie*, mother to Robert Stewart King of the Scots Under the same David, there is mention made of *Thomas* Earl of Marr, who was banished in the year 136 And under Robert the third, mention is made of *Alexander Stewart* Earl of Marr, who was slain in the battel at *Harley* against the Islanders in the year 1411 In King James the first's time, we read in the *Scotochronicon Alexander Earl of Marr died in the year 1435, natural son of Alexander Stewart Earl of Buchan, son of Robert the second King of Scotland, to whom (as being a bastard) the King succeeded in the Inheritance John* [a] a younger son of King James the second, afterwards bore this title, who being convicted of attempting by art Magick to take away his Brother's life, was bled to death And after him, *Robert Cockeran* was advanced from a [b] Mason to this dignity, by King James the third, and was soon after hang'd by the Nobility From that time it was discontinued, till Queen *Mary* advanced her Bastard Brother James to this honour, and not long after (upon finding that by ancient right the title of Earl of Marr belonged to John Lord *Ereskin*) in lieu of *Marr* she conferred on him the honour and title of Earl of *Murray*, and created *John Ereskin* (a person of ancient Nobility) Earl of Marr, whose son of the same Christian name [c] enjoyed the dignity, and [d] was in both Kingdoms one of his Majesty's Privy Council, [and in which Family this honour continued, through several Successions, till it became forfeited and extinct, by the Treason of *John* late Earl of Marr, against his Majesty King George]

Scoto. Chron lib 12 cap 3

a Natu minor

b Latomus

c Now enjoys it

d Is it

BUQUHAN.

Here now *Buquhan* (in Latin *Bogbania* and *Buchania*) shoots, above the River *Done*, into the Ocean, were anciently seated the *Taizali* Some derive this later name from *Boes* (Oxen,) whereas the ground is fitter for the feeding of sheep, whose wool is highly commended Notwithstanding, that the Rivers in this Coast breed abundance of *Salmon*, this fish never enters into the River *Ratra*, as Buchanan hath told us, (and let it not be to my disadvantage, if I cite this Testimony, although his books were prohibited by authority of Parliament in the year 1584, *because many passages in them were fit to be dash'd out*) He reports also, *That on the bank of* Ratra, *there is a Cave, near* Stany's Castle, *the nature of which seems to be worth our taking notice of The water distilling by drops out of a natural Vault, is presently turned into pyramidal stones, and if people did not take the pains to clear the cave now and then, the whole place in a little time would be filled up to the top of the vault The stone thus made, is of a middle nature between Ice and Rock, for it is friable and never arrives to the solidity of Marble* It is hardly worth while, to mention the *Clayks*, a sort of Geese, which are believed by some (with great admiration,) to grow upon trees on this coast and in other places, and when they are ripe, to fall down into the sea, because neither their nests nor eggs can any where be found But they who saw the ship, in which Sir *Francis Drake* sailed round the world, when it was laid up in the river Thames, [a] could testifie, that little birds breed in the old rotten keels of ships, since a great number of such, without life and feathers, stuck close to the outside of the keel of that ship Yet I should think that the generation of these birds was not from the logs of wood, but from the sea, term'd by the Poets the *Parent of all things* [b]

The River Ratra

A strange water

Clayks, a sort of Geese

A mighty mass likewise of *Amber*, as big as the body of a Horse, was ([c] not many years since) cast upon this shore This, the learned call *Succinum*, *Glessum*, and *Chryso electrum*, and *Sotacus* was of opinion, that it was a juice, which amongst the Britains distill'd from trees, and ran into the sea, and was there harden'd Tacitus expresses the same sentiments of it, in this passage of his, [d] *I should believe, that as there are trees in the secret parts of the east, which sweat out frankincense and balm, so in the Islands and other countreys of the west, there are woods of a more fat substance, which melting by the hot beams of the neighbouring Sun, run into the sea hard by, and being driven by tempestuous weather, float to the opposite shores* But Serapio and the modern Philosophers will have it to work out of a bituminous sort of earth, under the sea, and by the sea side, and that the waves in stormy weather cast part of it upon the shore, and that part of it is devoured by the fish But I have digressed too far, and will return, hoping that my ingenuous confession will obtain me pardon

a Camd

b Vid Sib bald's illustrat where But this is not herein shown But he is now convinced that they are no ... [illegible]

c So said, ann. 16.. [illegible]

d De moribus Germanorum

In

Earls of Buquhan.

In the reign of Alexander the second, *Alexander Comin* enjoy'd the honour of Earl of *Buquhan*, who married a daughter and one of the heirs of *Roger de Quincy* Earl of Winchester in England, and his grand daughter by his son brought the same title to Henry Beaumont her husband For he, in the reign of Edward the third, sat in the Parliament of England under the name of *Earl of Buquhan* Afterwards, *Alexander Stewart*, son to King Robert the second, was Earl of this place; and was succeeded by *John*, a younger son of Robert Duke of Albany, who being sent for into France (with seven thousand Auxiliary Scots) by the French King, Charles the seventh, did extraordinary services against the English, and had so great a reputation there, that, having killed *Thomas* Duke of Clarence, King Henry the fifth's brother, at *Baugy*, and got as great a victory as ever was obtained over the English, he was made *Constable of France* But three years after, when the fortune of the war turned, he with other valiant Commanders, *Archibald Douglas*, Earl of Wigton, and Duke of Tourain, &c was routed at *Vernoil* by the English, and there slain Whom yet as the Poet said——

The valour of the Scots in the Wars of France

——*Æternum memorabit Gallia cives*
Grata suos, titulos quæ dedit & tumulos.

Those grateful *France* shall ever call her own,
Who owe to her their graves and their renown

The French cannot but confess that they owe the preservation of France and recovery of Aquitain (by forcing out the English in the reigns of Charles the sixth and seventh) in a great measure to the fidelity and valour of the *Scots* Afterwards, King James the first, out of compassion to *George of Dunbar*, whom by authority of Parliament he had before divested of the Earldom of March for his father's crimes, gave him the Earldom of *Buquhan* And not long after, James son of *James Stewart* of Lorn, surnamed the *Black Knight*, whom he had by *Joan Somerset*, obtained this honour, and left it to his posterity, but [f] not long since, for default of heirs male, it went by a daughter to *Douglas*, a younger brother of the House of *Lochlevin* [As the Scotch Historians report it, Christiana daughter and sole heir of John Stewart, Earl of Buchan, married Robert Douglas, Brother of William Earl of Morton, and, being in right of her, afterwards Earl of Buchan, he had by her James Earl of Buchan, whose only daughter Mary, marrying *James Erskin*, eldest son, of the second marriage, of James Earl of Marr, carried the title of Buchan into that noble family, in which it still remains]

[f] So said, ann 1607

Boen

Beyond *Buchan*, in the bending back of the shore northwards, lies *Boen*, and *Bamff*, a small Sheriffdom [It comprehends that part of *Buchan* which lies north of the river Ugie, with the Countries of *Strathaverne*, *Boin*, *Inzie*, *Strathaven*, and *Balveine* To the South, it is separated from that part of *Buchan* which belongeth to *Aberdeenshire*, by the water of *Ugie* · to the East it hath the water of *Doverne* to the West the water of *Spey*, to the South-west it hath *Badenoch* and the *Brae* of Marr, and *Murray-Frith* on the north The length from west to east, is about thirty two miles, and the breadth about thirty In *Balvenie* is found the stone of which Alom is made; and in the country of *Boin*, great quarries of spotted marble have been discovered of late The country is generally well furnished with grass and corn

Bamff

Bamse, a Burgh-Royal, is seated at the mouth of *Doverne* in the *Boine*; where the Sheriff hath his Courts; and it shows the Ruins of an old Castle The country about it is very fertil, and the Salmon-fishing very advantageous. Near this, is the Abbey of *Deer*, which belonged to the Cistercians, and was founded by *William Cumin*, Earl of *Buchan*. At the *Bogchill*, resides the Duke of *Gordon*, whose seat is adorned with excellent gardens, enclosures, and woods of oak, surrounding it In this Shire and the Parish of *Aberlowr*, is a place called (in their language) *the Blessed Chapel*, from a Monument of stones, which stood there, but is now demolished, such as are spoken of in the County of *Mernis*, and supposed there to be Heathen-Temples And in the same Shire, in the Parish of *Aberchinder*, is another of the same kind, called *Cairnedum*, or *Cairnedewn*, the first part of the name being probably derived from *Cairn*, a heap of stones, which is usually to be found within such Monuments]

Deer

Stone Monuments

Near *Bamff*, is *Aunza* a little tract of less note, as also *Rothmy* Castle, the seat of the Barons of *Salton*, surnamed *Abernethy* [f] [Sir *Alexander Fraser* of Philorth, in right of his mother, daughter to the Lord *Saltoun*, was declared Lord *Saltoun*, and approved in Parliament upon the death of *Alexander Abernethy* last Lord Saltoun of that surname] Beneath these lies *Strathbolgy*, that is, *the Valley upon the Bolgy*, formerly the Seat of the Earls of Athol, who were surnamed from thence, but [g] now the chief residence of the Marquiss of *Huntley* For, this title King James the sixth conferred upon *George Gordon* Earl of *Huntley*, Lord *Gordon* and *Badzenoth*, eminent for his ancient Nobility, and his numerous Dependance Whose Ancestors are descended from the *Setons*, and by authority of Parliament took the name of Gordon (upon *Alexandar Seton's*, marrying the daughter of Sir *John Gordon*, with whom he had a very noble estate,) and received the honour of Earl of *Huntley* from King James the second, in the year 1449, [of which family, *George* Marquis of *Huntley* was advanced to the honour of Duke of Gordon by King Charles the second In this Shire, did also reside the *Ogilvies* of Findlater, of whom Walter Ogilvie was created by King James the sixth, Lord *Deskford*, and his son by King Charles the first, Earl of *Findlater*, whose descendant is *James*, the present Earl, a Person of great Eloquence and Ability Also Sir *George Ogilvie* was by King Charles the first created Lord *Bamff*]

Barons *Salton*

[f] Now *Fraser*

Strathbolgy

[g] So said ann 1607

Marquiss of Huntley

Ogilvies

MURRAY.

Vacomagi Sinus Vararis Murray-Frith

Beyond the mountain *Grampius*, (which by a continual range of neighbouring hills, extends its ridge with many risings and sinkings as far as this country) the *Vacomagi* in ancient times had their habitation, upon the Bay of *Vararis*, where now *Murray* lies, in Latin *Moravia*, noted for its fertility, pleasantness, and the profitable product of fruit-trees [It comprehends the Shires of *Elgin* and *Nairn* Upon the north, it hath, *Murray firth* and the water of *Nesse*, which separates it from the shire of *Innernesse*, to the east, it is separated from *Bamf-shire* by the River of *Spey*, to the South it hath *Badenoch*, and to the west, part of *Lochabyr* It is about thirty miles long, and twenty broad The shire of *Elgin* comprehends all that part which lieth to the east of the River *Findorne*, and the shire of *Nairne*, that which is upon the West-side of the said River They have an *air* very wholsom, and *winters* mild the Low country bears very much Corn, which is soon ripe, but the High-country is fitter for pasture They have many great woods of *Firs* and other trees, especially upon the river of *Nairne*]

The *Spey*, a noble river, [famous for the incredible number of Salmon taken in it,] opens a passage through this country into the sea, wherein it lodges it self, after it hath watered *Rothes*-Castle, whence the Family of *Lesly* derive their title of Earl, ever since King James the second advanced *George Lesly* to the honour of Earl of *Rothes*, [of which Family John, Earl of Rothes, High Commissioner for King Charles the second to the Parliament, was created Duke of Rothes by the said King, to him, and the heirs male of his Body, for want of which the Dukedom expired, but the title of Earl still remains] Of the river *Spey*, thus our Poet Necham

Spey loca mutantis praeceps agitator arenae
Inconstans certas nescit habere vias
Officium lintris corbis subit, hunc regit audax
Cursus taventis nauta fluenta sequens

Great Spey drives forward with impetuous force
Huge banks of sand, and knows no certain course
Here for a boat an Osier pannier, row'd
By some bold peasant, glides along the flood

Loxa The river *Loxa*, mentioned by Ptolemy, and now call'd *Losse*, hides itself hard by in the sea

Elgin Near this, we have a sight of *Elgin*, [a Royal Burgh, where are the ruins of an ancient Castle, as also of one of the most stately Churches in the Kingdom] In this Town (as also in *Forres* adjoining) *J Dunbar* of Cumnock, descended from the House of the Earls of March, administered justice as hereditary Sheriff, [whose descendant, is *Alexander Dunbar* of Westfield, Sheriff of Murray, the title of Cumnock being left, upon selling the Barony thereof about the year 1600, which now belongs to the Countess of Dumfries] But when the *Losse* is ready to enter the sea, it finds a more plain and soft soil, and spreads itself into a Lake well stored with *Swans*, wherein the Herb *Olorina* grows plentifully Upon it, stands *Spiny-Castle*, of which, *Alexander* of the House of *Lindsay* was the first Baron, [but the title is now extinct] As also *Kinloss*, a near neighbour, and formerly a famous Monastery (call'd by some *Kill flos*, from certain flowers miraculously springing up on a sudden, when the Corps of King *Duff*, murdered and hidden there, was first found [b] ;) which [c] had for its Lord, *Edward Brus*, Master, of the Rolls in England, and of his Majesty's Privy Council, created by King James the sixth Baron *Brus* of *Kinloss*, [whose Son was created by King Charles the first Earl of *Elgin*, and his Son, by King Charles the second, Earl of *Ailesbury* in England In this Shire also, Sir *Alexander Sutherland* of Duffus, an ancient Cadet of the family of Sutherland, was created [d] Lord *Duffus*, in the beginning of the reign of King Charles the second

* Administrator, C

Baron Spiny

Baron Kinloss

b In the year 972

c Hath, C

Duffus

d Now forfeited by Attainder

Not far from hence, is an *Obelisk* of one Stone, a Monument of the fight between King Malcolm, Son of Keneith, and Sueno the Dane

This much for the shore More inward, where *Beon* Castle now stands, (thought to be the *Banatia*, mentioned by Ptolemy) there was found in the year 1460, a Marble Vessel very finely engraved, and full of Roman Coins Hard by, is *Nardin* or *Nairne*, [a Royal Burgh, and] an Hereditary Sheriffdom of the *Cambells* of Lorn, where in a Peninsula, stood a Tower of mighty height, and with wonderful works, and formerly held by the Danes [From this place, *Robert Nairn* was advanced by King Charles the second to the honour of Lord Nairn, whose only daughter marrying the Lord William Murray, this title descends to the issue of the said Marriage In the Parish of *Killernen* and Shire of *Nairne*, is a Grove, enclosed with a Trench or dry Ditch, having two Entries to it All who live near it, account it *sacred*, and will not so much as cut a rod out of it, and it is observable, that in a field hard by, are several large stones, fallen down and lying out of order; such, as those Monuments (that are elsewhere conjectured to have been *Heathen Temples*) did use to consist of]

Banatia

Nairne Sheriffdom

Killerner

A little way from Nairn, is *Legh-Nesse*, a very large lake, three and twenty miles long, the water whereof is so warm, that even in this cold climate, it never freezes, [as neither doth the water of *Nesse*] From that, by a very small Isthmus of hills, the *Logh Lutea* or *Lothea* (which by *Aber* lets itself into the western Ocean) is divided Upon these lakes, stood anciently two noted fortifications, called, from the Loghs, one *Innernesse*, the other *Innerlothy* Innerness hath the [e] Duke of Gordon for its hereditary Sheriff, who hath a large Jurisdiction hereabouts [The Sheriffdom comprehends *Lochaber Badenoch*, and the South part of *Rosse* To the South it hath the *Brae of Marr* and *Athol*, to the West, the Western sea, to the North *Rosse*; and to the East, part of *Murray frith* The length of it from *Innerlochy* to

Logh Nesse

e Marquess of Huntly, C

to

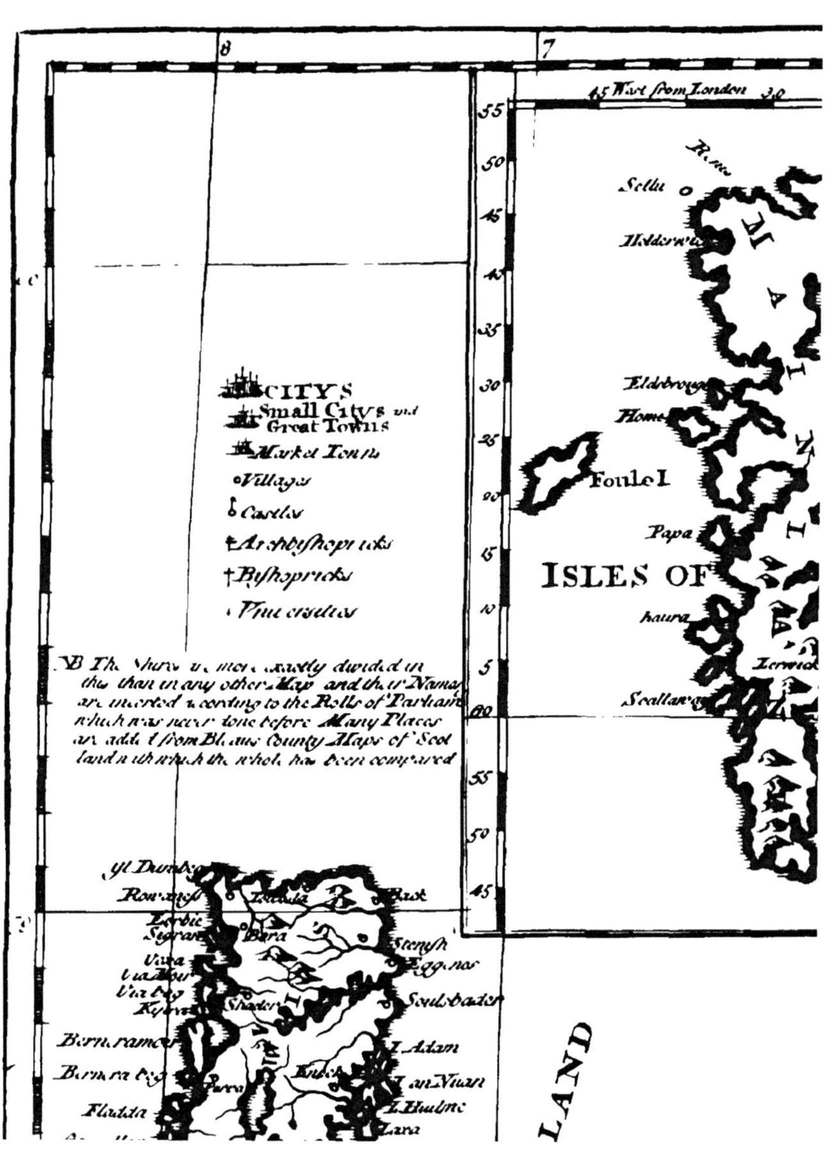

45 West from London 30
CITYS
Small Citys and Great Towns
Market Towns
Villages
Castles
Archbishopricks
Bishopricks
Foule I
ISLES OF
Papa
Scallaway
LAND

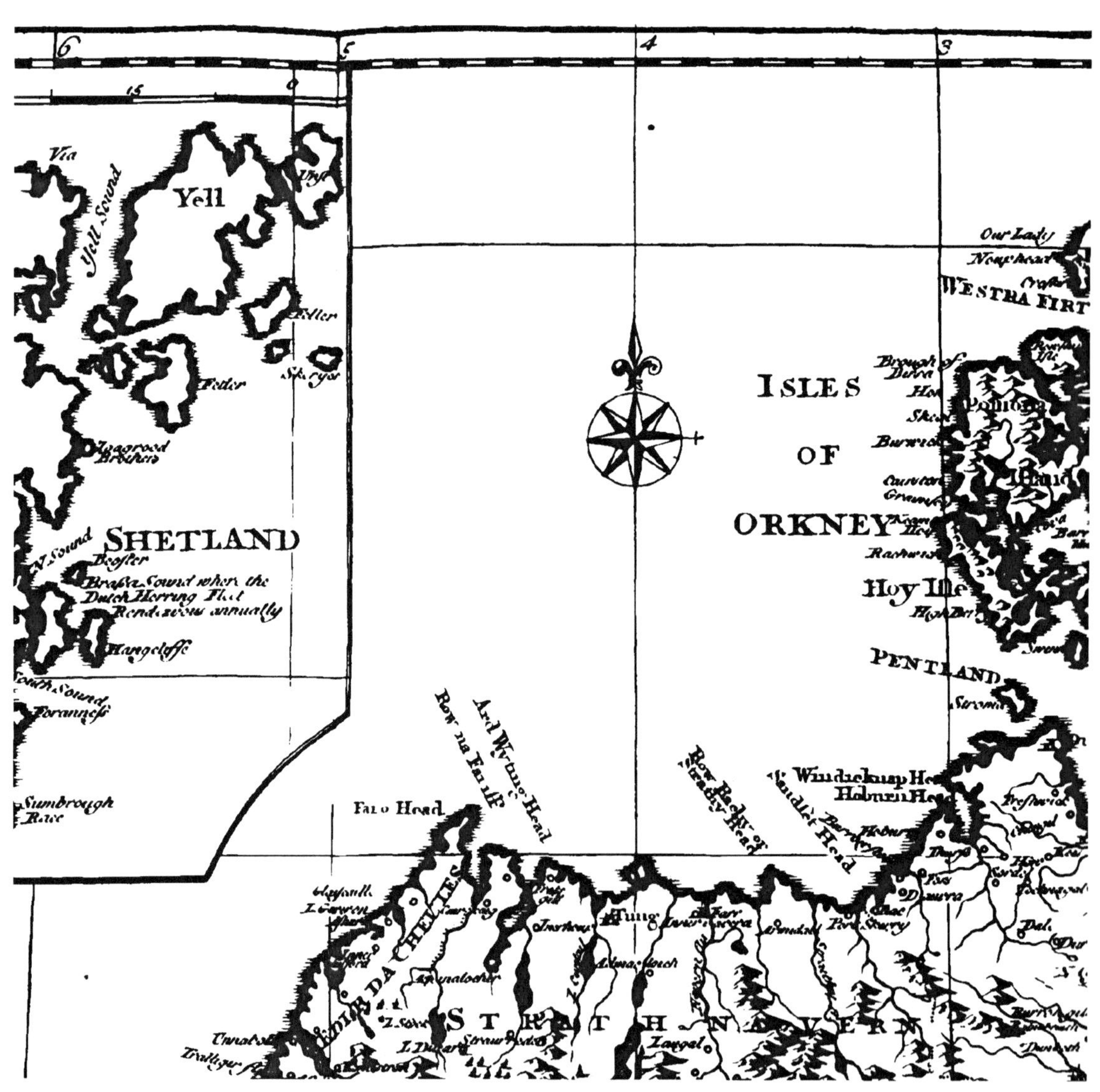

6
5
4
3
Yell
Yell Sound
SHETLAND
Brassa Sound where the Dutch Herring Fleet Rendezvous annually
Sumbrough Race
ISLES OF ORKNEY
WESTRA FIRTH
Hoy Isle
PENTLAND
Faro Head
STRATHNAVERN

A
New MAP of the
NORTH PART
of
SCOTLAND.
North Ronalsha
Start
Auskerry
FIRTH
FIRTH
Nose Head
Wick
59

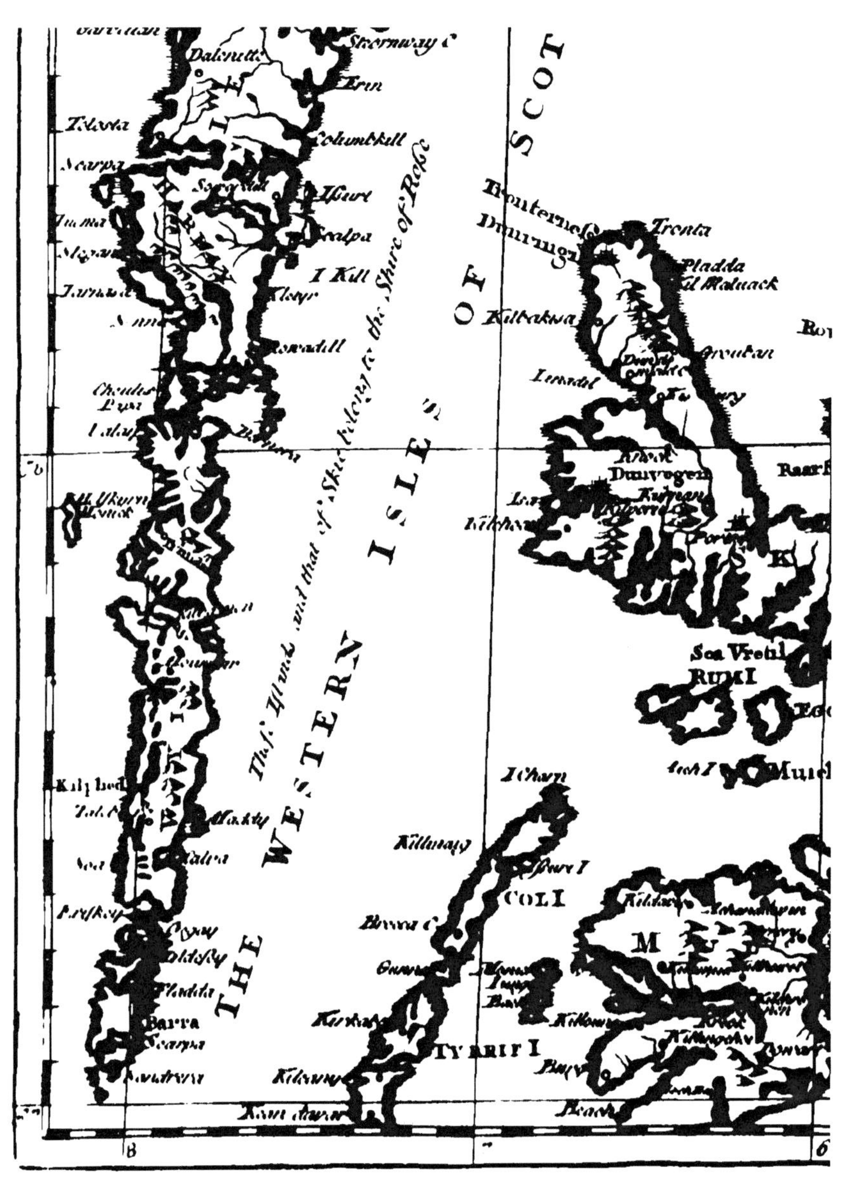

THE WESTERN ISLES OF SCOT
These Islands and that of Skie belong to the Shire of Rosse
Stornway C
Erin
Columbkill
Scalpa
I Kill
Tronta
Pladda
Dunvegen
RUMI
COLI
Barra
Scarpa
Pladda

Row na Broig
Row na Haid
Point Cannord
Row na Ra
Coygach
SOUTHERL
Tayne
Ardmeanach
Dunakin
Slate
Culloden

The Ord Head
MURRAY FYRTH
Kynnard-head
Cullen
Peter Head
Old Aberdeen
NEW ABERDEEN
Drum
Brechin

[As to the *Loch-ness* beforementioned; upon it stood the famous Castle of *Urqhart*, consisting of seven great Towers, said to be built by the *Cumines*, and overthrown by King Edward the first. About four miles to the westward of which Castle, on the very top of a high hill, two miles perpendicular, is a Lake of cold fresh water, about thirty fathom in length, and six in breadth; no Stream running to it or from it. It could never yet be fathomed; and at all Seasons of the year, it is equally full, and never freezes; as on the contrary, about seventeen miles to the west, on the north-side of a Mountain called *Glen-in-tea*,Glen-in-tea. there is a Lake called *Lochan-wyn* or *Green-lake*,Green-lake. which is always covered with Ice, Summer and Winter; as is also the Lake *Straglash*Phil. Trans. N.114. at *Glencanich*, in the middle. Straherrick. Another Lake there is in *Straherrick*, which never freezes all over (in the most vehement frosts) till *February*; after which, one night will freeze it all over, and two nights make it of a considerable thickness. The same thing hath been observed also in two other Lakes, one of which is called *Loch-Monar*.

West from the end of the river *Nesse*, is an Arm of the Sea called *Beaulie-Frith*,Beaulie-Frith. which undoubtedly was heretofore firm Land, inasmuch as near the middle of it are found long oaken Trees, under the Sand, with the roots: and in it also are three great heaps of Stones, called *Cairns*; the greatest of which, being accessible at Low-water, appears to have been a Burial-place, from the Urns that are sometimes discovered in it.

Dr. *Garden*, to Mr. *Aubrey*. In this Shire, are many of the Stone-Monuments, spoken of more at large in the County of *Mernis*. And one of them, in the Parish of *Enerallen*,Enerallen. is full of Groves, and was, within the memory of the last age, an ordinary place of burial, at least for poor People; and continues to be so at this day, for Children who die without Baptism, and for Strangers. Another, in the Countrey of *Strathspey*, and Shire of *Inverness*, and Parish of *Duthell*,Duthell. consists of two Circles of Stones, and is called *Chapel-Piglag*,Chapel-Piglag. from a Lady of that name, who used to repair thither for the exercise of her devotion, before a Church was built in that part of the Country. Within half a mile of which, is a *Bush* or *Grove* of Trees, of no great bigness, which is reputed so *Sacred*, and held in such Veneration, that no body will cut a branch out of it; and the Women who dwell near, when they recover out of Child-bed, go thither to return their Thanks to God, as in other places of the Kingdom they repair to Churches for that end. This Grove is called, in their language; *the Bush of the Chapel*, and, *the Bush belonging to Piglag*; in the midst of which, is a Well or Fountain, call'd *the Well of the Chapel*; and this also is esteem'd Sacred.]

Earls of *Murray*. In the reign of King *Robert Brus, Thomas Randolph*, his sister's son (a person that took infinite pains in the service of his Country, and met with great oppositions) was very famous under the title of Earl of *Murray*. In the reign of King Robert the second, *John de Dunbar* took the King's daughter in marriage, as an amends for her lost virginity, and had with her the Earldom of *Murray*. Under King James the second, *William Creichton*, Chancellor of the Kingdom, and *Archibald Douglass*, had a violent contest for this Earldom; when, against the Laws and ancient Customs of the Realm, *Douglass*, who had married the younger daughter of *James de Dunbar* Earl of *Murray*, was prefer'd before *Creichton*, who had married the elder;

Barony thereof about the year 1600; which now belongs to the Countess of Dumfries.] But when the Losse is ready to enter the sea, it finds a more plain and soft soil, and spreads it self into a lake well stored with *Swans*, wherein the Herb *Olorina* grows plentifully. Upon it, stands *Spiny-Castle*, of which, *Alexander* of the House of *Lindsay*Barons Spiny. was the first Baron, [but the title is now extinct.] Baron Kinloss. As also *Kinloss*, a near neighbour, and formerly a famous Monastery (call'd by some *Kill-flos*, from certain flowers miraculously springing up on a sudden, when the Corps of King *Duff*, murdered and hidden there, was first found ** In the year 972.;) which † † Hath, C.had for its Lord, *Edward Brus*, Master of the Rolls in England, and of His Majesty's Privy Council; created by King James the sixth Baron *Brus* of *Kinloss*, [whose Son was created by King Charles the first Earl of *Elgin*, and his Son, by King Charles the second, Earl of *Ailsbury* in England. In this Shire also, Sir *Alexander Sutherland* of Duffus,Duffus. an ancient Cadet of the family of Sutherland, was created ¦¦ Now forfeited by Attainder.Lord *Duffus*, in the beginning of the reign of King Charles the second.

Not far from hence, is an *Obelisk* of one Stone; a Monument of the fight between King Malcolm, Son of Keneth, and Sueno the Dane.]

Thus much for the shore. More inward, where *Bean* Castle now stands, (thought to be the *Banatia*,*Banatia*. mentioned by Ptolemy) there was found in the year 1460, a Marble Vessel very finely engraved, and full of Roman Coins. Hard by, is *Nardin* or *Nairne*,Nairne Sheriffdom. [a Royal Burgh, and] an Hereditary Sheriffdom of the *Cambells* of Lorn; where, in a Peninsula, stood a Tower of mighty height, and with wonderful works, and formerly held by the Danes. [From this place, *Robert Nairn* was advanced by King Charles the second to the honour of Lord Nairn; whose only daughter marrying the Lord William Murray, this title descends to the issue of the said Marriage. Killernen. In the Parish of *Killernen* and Shire of *Nairne*, is a Grove, enclosed with a Trench or dry Ditch, having two Entries to it. All who live near it, account it *sacred*, and will not so much as cut a rod out of it; and it is observable, that in a field hard by, are several large stones, fallen down and lying out of order; such, as those Monuments*Vid.* Mernis. (that are elsewhere conjectured to have been *Heathen-Temples*) did use to consist of.]

A little way from Nairn, is *Logh-Nesse*,Logh-Nesse. a very large lake, three and twenty miles long; the water whereof is so warm, that even in this cold climate, it never freezes; [as neither doth the water of *Nesse*:] From that, by a very small Isthmus of hills, the *Logh Lutea* or *Lothea* (which by *Aber* lets it self into the western Ocean) is divided. Upon these lakes, stood anciently two noted Fortifications; called, from the Loghs, one *Innerness*, the other *Innerlothy*. Innerness hath the * * Marquiss of *Huntley*, C.Duke of Gordon for its hereditary Sheriff; who hath a large Jurisdiction hereabouts. [The Sheriffdom comprehends *Lochaber, Badinoch*, and the South part of *Roffe*. To the South it hath the *Brae of Marr* and *Athol*; to the West, the Western-sea; to the North, *Rosse*; and to the East, part of *Murray-frith*. The length of it from *Inverlochee* to *Invernesse*, in a streight line, is fifty miles. It has plenty of *Iron-Ore*; and great woods of *Firr*, ten miles long; with some large woods of *Oak*: and that part called *Badenoch*, has many Deer.

murray 1270

to *Invernesse*, in a streight line, is fifty miles It has plenty of *Iron-Ore*; and great woods of *Firr*, ten miles long; with some large woods of *Oak* and that part called *Badenoch*, has many Deer

Invernesse. [f] Theatr Scotiæ, p. 44.

Invernesse [f] is the head town of this Sheriff-dom, and the Sheriff's seat, where he keeps his Court It is commodiously situated upon the South side of the River Nesse, on the very bank of it, which renders it exceeding convenient for commerce with the neigbouring places. It was formerly the seat of the Kings of Scotland, and has a Castle standing on a pleasant hill, with a fine prospect into the fields and town Near the Castle, there is a Bridge built over the water of *Nesse*, consisting of seven Arches, all of hewn stone It hath a harbour for smaller vessels There are in it two Churches, one for the *English*, and the other for the *Irish* Near the town of *Innerlochie*, is a fort with a garrison, upon the bay of *Lochyol*]

But take here what *J Johnston* writes upon these two places

INNERNESS,

And

INNERLOCHY.

Imperii veteris duo propugnacula quondam,
Primaque regali mœnia structa manu,
Turribus oppositis adverso in limine spectant
Hæc Zephyrum, Solis illa orientis equos
Amnibus hinc atque hinc cincta, utisque piscibus amnes
Facundi, hæc portu perpete tuta patet
Hæc fuit, at jacet heu, jam nunc sine nomine tellus,
Hospitaque Regum, est hospita facta feris.
Altera spirat adhuc tenuis sufflamina vitæ,
Quæ dabit & fati turbine victa manus
Dic ubi nunc Carthago potens? ubi Martia Roma?
Trojaque & immensæ ditis opes Asiæ?
Quid mireris enim mortalia cedere fatis
Corpora? cum videas oppida posse mori.

Two stately Forts the Realm's old guardians stood,
The first great walls of royal builders prov'd
Their lofty turrets on the shores were shown,
One to the rising, one the setting sun
All round, well stock'd with fish, fair rivers lay,
And one presents a safe and easie bay
Such once it was, but now a nameless place,
Where Princes lodg'd, the meanest cattel graze
T'other survives, and faintly breaths as yet,
But must e're long submit to conqu'ring fate
Where's haughty *Carthage* now with all her power?
Where's *Rome*, and *Troy* that rul'd its great before?
Where the vast riches of the *Asian* shore?
No wonder then that we frail men should die,
When towns themselves confess mortality

[As to the *Loch-ness* beforementioned, upon it stood the famous Castle of *Urqhart*, consisting of seven great Towers, said to be built by the *Cummins*, and overthrown by King Edward the first. About *four miles* to the westward of which Castle, on the very top of a high hill, two miles perpendicular, is a Lake of cold fresh water, about thirty fathom in length, and six in breadth; no Stream running to it or from it It could never yet be fathomed, and at all Seasons of the year, it is equally full, and never freezes, as on the contrary, about seventeen miles to the west, on the north side of a Mountain called *Glen-in tea*, there is a Lake called *Lochan wyn* or *Green-lake*, which is always covered with Ice, Summer and Winter; as is also the Lake *Straglash* at *Glencanich*, in the middle Another Lake there is in *Straberrick*, which never freezes all over (in the most vehement frosts) till *February*, after which, one night will freeze it all over, and two nights make it of a considerable thickness The same thing hath been observed also in two other Lakes, one of which is called *Loch-Monar*

Phil Trans N 254

Glen in tea Green Lake.

Phil Trans N 114 Straberrick

West from the end of the River *Ness*, is an Arm of the Sea called *Beau'-Frith*, which undoubtedly was heretofore firm Land, inasmuch as near the middle of it are found long oaken Trees, under the Sand, with the roots and in it also are three great heaps of Stones, called *Cairns* the greatest of which, being accessible at Low water, appears to have been a Burial-place, from the Urns that are sometimes discovered in it

Beaulie Frith

In this Shire, are many of the Stone Monuments, spoken of more at large in the County of *Mernis* And one of them, in the Parish of *Enerallen*, is full of Groves, and was, within the memory of the last age, an ordinary place of burial, at least for poor People, and continues to be so at this day, for Children who die without Baptism, and for Strangers Another, in the Countrey of *Strathspey*, and Shire of *Invernes*, and Parish of *Duthell*, consists of two Circles of Stones, and is called *Chapel Piglag*, from a Lady of that name, who used to repair thither for the excercise of her devotion, before a Church was built in that part of the Country Within half a mile of which, is a *Bush* or *Grove* of Trees, of no great bigness, which is reputed so *Sacred*, and held in such Veneration, that no body will cut a branch out of it, and the Women who dwell near, when they recover out of Child bed, go thither to return their Thanks to God, as in other places of the Kingdom they repair to Churches for that end This Grove is called, in their language, *the Bush of the Chapel*, [illegible] *lag*, in the midst of which, is a Well or Fountain, call'd *the Well of the Chapel*, and this also is esteem'd Sacred]

Dr G[illegible] to Mr *Aubrey*

Enerallen

Duthell Chapel Piglag

In the reign of King *Robert Bruce*, [illegible] *Randolph*, his sister's son (a person that took [illegible] finite pains in the service of his Country [illegible] met with great opposition) w[illegible] under the title of Earl of *Murray* In the [illegible] of King Robert the second, [illegible] took the King's daughter in [illegible] mends for her lost virginity, and had with her the Earldom of *Murray*, Under King James the second, [illegible] Chancellor of the Kingdom, and [illegible] *Douglas*, [illegible] lent contest for this Earldom, when, against the Laws and ancient Customs of the Realm, *Douglass*, who had married the younger daughter of *James de Dunbar* Earl of *Murray*, was prefer'd before *Creichton*, who had married the el-

der,

der, by the power and interest that *William* Earl *Douglass* had with the King: which was so very great, that he did not only advance this brother to the Earldom of *Murray*, but another brother likewise to the Earldom of *Ormond*, and two of his Cousins to the Earldoms of *Angus* and *Morton* But this his greatness (a thing never to be trusted to when exorbitant) was his ruin soon after Under King James the fifth, his own brother, whom he had constituted Vicegerent of the Kingdom, enjoyed this honour And *James*, a natural Son of King James the fifth, had this honour conferred on him by his sister Queen *Mary*; who ill requited her, when, having got some few of the Nobility on his side, he deposed her; a most pernicious Precedent for crowned Heads. But the punishment of Heaven soon fell upon him, being quickly after shot through with a Musquet bullet His only daughter brought this title to her husband *James Steward of Down*, [(whose Father had been created Lord Down by King James the sixth,)] descended of the Blood Royal, to wit, of the Dukes of *Albany*; which *James* being slain by some who envied him, left behind him his son *James*, the successor in this honour; [and it still continues in the same Noble Family]

LOQHUABRE.

LL that tract of Land beyond the *Nesse*, which bends down to the western coast, and joins to the Lake *Aber*, is thence called *Loghuabre* (that is, in the ancient British, *The Mouth of the Lakes*,) as that which lies towards the northern coast, is call'd *Rosse*.

Loghuabre abounds in pastures and woods, and hath some veins of Iron, but little Corn. It is inferior to none for lakes and rivers, admirably well stock'd with fish Upon *Loghlothy*, stands *Innerlothy*, strengthen'd with a Fort, and formerly of much note for the great resort of Merchants; but having been ruined by the depredations and insults of the *Danes* and *Norwegians*, it hath been so abandoned and disused for many ages, that there scarce remain now any footsteps of what it has been, which is intimated in the Verses that I produced a little before. [In this Shire of *Invernesse*, *Æneas Macdonald* Laird of *Glengarie*, was by King Charles the second created Lord *Macdonald*, to him and the heirs-males of his body]

Innerlothy, or Innerlochy

I never yet read of any Earls of *Loghuabre*; but about the year 1050, we read of a most noted *Thane* thereof, one *Banqhuo*, who was made away by *Macbeth* the Bastard (when, by murder and blood-shed, he had seiz'd the Kingdom) out of jealousie that he might possibly disturb him. For he had found by a Prophecy of certain [a] Witches, that the time would come when *Macbeth's* line being extinct, *Banqhuo's* posterity should obtain the Kingdom, and thro' a long succession reign in Scotland Which fell out accordingly For *Fleanch*, son of Banqhuo, who, in the dark, escaped the snares that were laid for him, fled into Wales, where for some time he kept himself undiscovered and, having afterwards married *Nesta* the daughter of *Griffith ap Llewelin*, Prince of North-Wales, he had by her *Walter*, who returning into Scotland, suppress'd the Rebellion of the Islanders with the reputation of so great bravery, and managed the King's Revenues in these parts with so great prudence, that the King made him *Stewart* of the whole Kingdom of Scotland Whereupon, this name of Office gave the surname of *Stewart* to his posterity, who, spreading through all parts of Scotland in many noble branches, and being advanced to great honours, have long flourish'd there [b] Three hundred and thirty years ago, *Robert Stewart*, a descendant of this House, in right of *Marjory* his Mother, daughter of King *Robert Brus*, obtained the Kingdom of Scotland [c] And *James Stewart* the sixth of that name, King of Scotland, in right of *Margaret* his Great Grandmother, daughter of Henry the seventh, was by divine Wisdom, with the general applause of all Nations, advanced to the Monarchy of *Great-Britain*

Banqhuo Thane of Loghuabre

[a] *Magarum.*

The Original of the family of *Stewart*

[b] So said, ann 1607

[c] And now lately, C

ROSSE.

has his residence at *Tarbat*, is now Sheriff and Proprietor of that ancient Estate. Sir *George Mackenzie* of *Tarbat* Baronet, were created Viscount *Tarbat*, and Lord *Macleod* and *Castle-haven*, by King James the seventh; and was advanced by Queen Anne to the higher honour of Earl of *Cromartie*.

In this Country, resided the Lairds of *Kintail*, who, in the reign of King James the sixth, were advanced to the honour of Peerage, by the title of Lords *Mackenzie* of *Kintail*;Kintail. and after that to the higher honour of Earls of *Seaforth*.]

Above the Harbour, is *Littus Altum*,*Littus Altum*. mention'd by Ptolemy, and called now, as it should seem, *Tarbarth*: for there the shore rises to a great height;The River *Celnius* or *Killian*. enclosed on one side with *Cromer*, the secure Harbour we just now mentioned; and on the other, with the river *Celnius*, now *Killian*. And thus much of the places towards the Eastern Ocean.

Into the Western Sea runs the river *Longus*,Longus, riv. mentioned by Ptolemy, and now called *Logh-Longas*: Next, the *Cerones*Cerones. anciently dwelt where now *Assenshire* is; a Country, cut and divided by several Arms of the Sea. [*Andrew Keith* (one of the Commissioners sent to treat of a marriage between King James the sixth, and *Anna* then Princess of Denmark) was created Lord *Keith* of *Dingwall*; who dying without issue, the same King advanced to the same Honour Sir *Richard Preston*, who was in great favour with him, and had been made one of the Knights of the Bath, at his Majesty's Coronation.]

Earls of *Ross*. It would be a very difficult Work, to draw a perfect succession of the Earls of *Ross*, out of the several Historians. About † † Four, C.five hundred years ago, *Ferqhuard* flourish'd under this title; but upon the failure of issue-male, it came by a daughter to *Walter Lesley* (who, for his valiant atchievements under *Lewis* the Emperor, was deservedly stiled the *Noble* or *Generous Knight*;) by whom he had *Alexander* Earl of Ross, and a daughter married to *Donald* Lord of the Western Isles. This *Alexander* had issue one only daughter, who passed over all her right and title to *Robert* Duke of Albany; which so enrag'd *Donald of the Isles*, that in the reign of James the third, he proclaim'd himself *King of the Isles*, and *Earl of Ross*, and destroy'd the Country round with fire and sword. At length, King James the third did by Authority of Parliament, in the year 1476, annex the Earldom of *Ross* to the Crown; and in such manner, that it might not be lawful for his Successors to alienate from it

The *Cantæ*. *ROSSE*, so call'd from an old Scottish word, which some interpret a *Promontory*, others a *Peninsula*, was in *Ptolemy*'s time inhabited by a People called *Cantæ*; a word which imports something like it. This extends to such a wideness, that it hath a prospect of both Oceans. [It comprehends the Shires of *Tayn* and *Cromartie*. The first includes the greater part of *Rosse*, with the Isles of *Skye, Lewis*, and *Herris*; the second, a small part of *Rosse*, lying on the South-side of *Cromartie-Frith*. It is in length fifty, and in breadth thirty miles.] On that side, where it views the *Vergivian* or western Ocean, it rises up in swelling Mountains, with many Woods, full of Stags, Roe-bucks, fallow Deer, and wild Fowl. On the other side, next the German sea, it is more fruitful, having much Corn and Pasture-grounds, and is much better cultivated. [The Straths or Valleys upon the water-sides, are full of Wood; particularly, upon *Charron*, and upon the water of *Braan*, and near *Alfarig*, there are great Woods of Firr.]

In the very enterance into it, *Ardmanoch*,The Barony of *Ardmanoch*. no small territory (which is one of the titles of the second Sons of the Kings of Scotland) shoots up in very high Mountains †† *Nivi sidissimis*. generally covered with Snow. I have been told by some persons very strange Stories of their height;The height of Hills, and the depth of the Sea: *Plutarch. in P. Æmil.* concerning *Olympus*. and yet the ancient Geometricians have written, that neither the depth of the Sea, nor the height of the Mountains, exceed by line and level, ten Stadia, that is a mile and a quarter. Which, however, they who have beheld *Tenariff* among the Canary Islands (fifteen leagues high) and have sailed the neighbouring Sea, will by no means admit. In these parts stands *Lovet*,Lovet. a Castle and Barony of the noble family of the *Frasers*, who were made Barons, as it is said, by King James the second, for the singular Services they had done the Crown of Scotland. This Family had been entirely extinguished, in a Quarrel, by the *Clan-Ranalds*, a most bloody People, had not four-score of the principal of them, by good Providence, left their Wives big with child at home; who being delivered of so many Sons, renewed and restored the Family.

Tain. [*Tain*, a good trading Town, is a Royal Burgh, and gives name to the Shire. Its Firth is about twenty miles long, but admitteth not Ships. *Loughbruin-Bay*,Loughbruin-Bay. which is ten miles long, is famous for the vast number of Herrings taken in it. *Dingwall*,Dingwall. another Burgh-Royal, is situate in the utmost part of the Firth; to the North of which lies the great Mountain *Weeves*.]

At *Nesse-mouth* stood *Chanonry*,Chanonry. formerly a noted place, and so called from a rich College of *Canons* in the flourishing times of the Church; in which was erected a See for the Bishop of *Rosse*. [It had a large Cathedral Church, part whereof still remains. At present, it shows a stately House of the Earl of *Seaforth*, who has considerable Revenues in this County.] Cromartie. Hard by, is *Cromartie*, where *Urqhuart*, a Gentleman of noble extraction, † † Administers, C.administer'd Justice as hereditary Sheriff of this District: and this is so commodious, and so safe a Harbour for any Fleet, though never so great, that Mariners and Geographers give it the name of *Portus Salutis*,*Portus Salutis*. or the Haven of Safety. [It is a Royal Burgh, the Firth whereof is about fifteen miles long, and in many places two miles broad: though the entrance of it be narrow, yet is it very safe and easie. Into this, runneth the water of *Connel*, famous for the Pearls found in it. The Viscount of *Tarbat*, who

ROSSE.

The Cantæ

ROSSE, so call'd from an old Scottish word, which some interpret a *Promontory*, others a *Peninsula*, was in *Ptolemy's* time inhabited by a People call'd *Cantæ*, a word which imports something like it. This extends to such a wideness, that it hath a prospect of both Oceans. [It comprehends the Shires of *Tayn* and *Cromartie*. The first includes the greater part of *Rosse*, with the Isles of *Skye*, *Lewis*, and *Herris*; the second, a small part of *Rosse*, lying on the South side of *Cromartie Frith*. It is in length fifty, and in breadth thirty miles.] On that side, where it views the *Vergivian* or western Ocean, it rises up in swelling Mountains, with many Woods, full of Stags, Roe-bucks, fallow Deer, and wild Fowl. On the other side, next the German Sea, it is more fruitful, having much Corn and Pasture grounds, and is much better cultivated. [The Straths or Valleys upon the water-sides, are full of Wood, particularly, upon *Charron*, and upon the water of *Braan*, and near *Alfarig*, there are great Woods of Firr.]

The Barony of [illegible]

In the very entrance into it, *Ardmanoch*, no small Territory (which is one of the titles of the second Sons of the Kings of Scotland) shoots up in very high Mountains [a] generally covered with Snow. I have been told by some persons very strange Stories of their height, and yet the ancient Geometricians have written, that neither the depth of the Sea, nor the height of the Mountains, exceed by line and level, ten Stadia, that is a mile and a quarter. Which, however, they who have beheld *Tenariff* among the Canary Islands (fifteen leagues high) and have sailed the neighbouring Sea, will by no means admit. In these parts stands *Lovat*, a Castle and Barony of the noble family of the *Frasers*, who were made Barons, as it is said, by King James the second, for the singular Services they had done the Crown of Scotland. This family had been entirely extinguished, in a Quarrel, by the *Clan-Ronalds*, a most bloody People, had not four score of the principal of them, by good Providence, left their Wives big with child at home, who being delivered of so many Sons, renewed and restored the Family.

[a] [illegible] The height of Hills, and the depth of the Sea. Plutarch. in P. Æmil. concerning Olympus.

Lovat

[*Tain*, a good trading Town, is a Royal Burgh, and gives name to the Shire. Its Frith is about twenty miles long, but admitteth not Ships. *Innerlothan Bay*, which is ten miles long, is famous for the vast number of Herrings taken in it. *Dingwall*, another Burgh Royal, is situate in the utmost part of the Frith, to the North of which lies the great Mountain *Weves*.]

Tain · *Loxa flumen / Bay* · *Dingwall*

At [illegible] stood *Chanonry*, formerly a noted place, and so called from the Colledge of Canons in the flourishing times of the Church, in which was erected a See for the Bishop of *Rosse*. [It had a large Cathedral Church, part whereof still remains. At present, it shows a stately House of the Earl of *Seaforth*, who has considerable Revenues in this County.] Hard by, is *Cromarty*, which [illegible], a Gentleman of noble extraction, [b] administer'd Justice as hereditary Sheriff of this District: and this is so commodious, and so safe a Harbour for any Fleet, though never so great, that Mariners and Geographers give it the name of *Portus Salutis*, or the Haven of Safety. [It is a Royal Burgh, the Firth whereof is about fifteen miles long, and in many places two miles broad: though the entrance of it be narrow, yet is it very safe and easie. Into this, runneth the water of *Connel*, famous for the Pearls found in it. The Viscount of *Tarbat*, who has his residence at *Tarbat*, is now Sheriff and Proprietor of that ancient Estate. Sir *George Mackenzie* of *Tarbat* Baronet, were created Viscount *Tarbat*, and Lord *Macleod* and *Castle-haven*, by King James the seventh, and was advanced by Queen Anne to the higher honour of Earl of *Cromartie*.

Chanonry · *Cromarty* · *[b] Administers, C* · *Portus Salutis*

In this Country, resided the Lairds of *Kintail*, who, in the reign of King James the sixth, were advanced to the honour of Peerage, by the title of Lords *Mackenzie* of *Kintail*, and after that to the higher honour of Earls of *Seaforth*.]

Kintail

Above the Harbour, is *Littus Altum*, mentioned by Ptolemy, and called now, as it should seem, *Tarbarth*, for there the shore rises to a great height, enclosed on one side with *Cromer*, the secure Harbour we just now mentioned, and on the other, with the river *Celnius*, now *Killian*. And thus much of the places towards the Eastern Ocean.

Littus Altum · *The River Celnius, or [illegible]*

Into the Western Sea runs the river *Longus*, mentioned by Ptolemy, and now called *Logh Longas*. Next, the *Cerones* anciently dwelt where now *Assenshire* is, a Country, cut and divided by several Arms of the Sea. [*Andrew Keith* (one of the Commissioners sent to treat of a marriage between King James the sixth, and *Anna* then Princess of Denmark) was created Lord *Keith* of *Dingwall*, who dying without issue, the same King advanced to the same Honour Sir *Richard Preston*, who was in great favour with him, and had been made one of the Knights of the Bath, at his Majesty's Coronation.]

Longus, river · *Cerones*

It would be a very difficult work, to draw a perfect succession of the Earls of *Rosse*, out of the several Historians. About [c] five hundred years ago, *Farquhard* flourish'd under this title, but upon the failure of issue male, it came by a daughter to *Walter Lesly* (who, for his valiant Achievements under *Lewis* the Emperor was deservedly stiled the *Noble* or *Generous Knight*,) by whom he had *Alexander* Earl of Ross, and a daughter married to *Donald* Lord of the Western Isles. This *Alexander* had issue one only daughter, who passed over all her right and title to *Robert* Duke of Albany, which so enrag'd *Donald of the Isles*, that in the reign of James the third, he [illegible] himself *King of the Isles*, and *Earl of Ross*, and destroy'd the Country round with fire and sword. At length, King James the third did by Authority of Parliament in the year 1476, annex the Earldom of *Ross* to the Crown, [illegible], that it might not be lawful for his Successors to alienate from

Earls of Rosse · *[c] [illegible], C*

it either the Earldom it self, or any part thereof, or to grant the same to any person, but only to the King's second Sons lawfully begotten Whereupon *Charles* second Son of King [James the sixth,] and Duke of York, [d] enjoy'd that Title

[d] Now enjoys C

SUTHERLAND.

Cattey

ALL that tract of Land lying between *Portnacour* and *Dungeby*, was of old called *CATTEY* So much of it as lies Eastward from the hill *Orde*, was called *Catey nesse*, and afterwards *Cath-nesse*, but so much as lies on this side of *Orde*, was called *South-Catley*, and *Sutherland*]

Sutherland

Beyond *Ross*, lies *Sutherland* [as aforesaid] to the *German Ocean* [It contains the Country that pass'd under that name, with *Strathnaver Edernchiles*, and *Durinesse*, having *Cathnesse* to the East and North east, the main Ocean to the North, the country of *Assint* to the West, *Rosse* to the South, and the German Sea to the East and South-east From West to East, it is in length about fifty five miles, and in breadth from South to North twenty two miles, but, taking in *Strathnaver*, thirty three The Inhabitants of these parts are much given to hunting, and will endure a great deal of labour and toil The Shire affords plenty of Iron ore and some Pearls They have Coal, Free stone, Lime stone, and good Sclate, in abundance it is said also that they find some *Silver*, and it is supposed that there is *Gold* in *Durinesse* In several parts of the Country, they have much Salmon-fishing, and are also well provided with other Fish; and of the river *Schin*, it is reported, that it never freezes]

The Country is more fit for breeding of Cattle, than bearing of Corn Here are also Hills of white Marble, a thing very unusual in so cold a climate, but it is almost of no use, because Extravagance in buildings, and that vain ostentation of riches, has not yet reached these remote Countries Here, [in a Mote hard by the Sea,] stands *Dunrobin-Castle*, a place of the greatest note in these parts, [and especially remarkable for its fine Gardens,] the principal Seat of the ancient Earls of *Sutherland*, of the Family (if I mistake not) of *Murray* Of whom, *William* in the reign of King *Robert Brus*, was very famous, marrying King David's own sister, and having by her a son, whom King *David* declared his Successor in the Kingdom, and to whom he made his Nobles swear Allegiance But he died a little after without issue, and the Earldom in the end came hereditarily by a daughter and heir to *A Gordon*, of the Family of the Earls of *Huntley*, [from whom is descended *John*, the present Earl of *Sutherland*, who by his Valour and Conduct hath done signal Service in these parts, to his Prince and Country]

Hills of white Marble

Dunrobin Castle

Earls of Sutherland

CATH-

CATHNES.

SOmewhat higher, lies *Cathnes*, [called also the Shire of *Wike*,] which butts upon the German Ocean, and is indented (as it were) by the many windings and breakings of the shore [To the South and South west it is divided from *Sutherland* by the *Ord*, and a continued ridge of Hills, as far as the hill of *Knockfinn* Then, along the course of the river of *Hollowdail* from the rise to the mouth of it, and the Mountains *Drumna Hollowdale* The same river is the bound between it and *Strathnaver* To the East it is wash'd with the Ocean, to the North it hath *Pentland Frith*, which divideth it from *Orkney* Its length from South to North is thirty five miles, its breadth, about twenty The Woods here are but few and small, being rather Copices of birch In the Forest of *Mor.. ..ns* and *Berridale*, is great plenty of Red deer, and Roe-bucks They have good store of Cows, Sheep, Goats, and Wild-fowl At *Dennet*, there is Lead, at *Old wike*, Copper, and Iron ore in several places

Dennet. Old wike.

The whole Coast, except the Bays, is high rocks, so that they have a great number of Promontories, viz *Sandsidehead*, at the West-end of *Cathnesse*, pointing North to the opening of *Pentland-Frith* *Holborn-Head*, and *Dunnet head*, both pointing North to the Firth *Duncans bay head*, which is the North-east point of *Cathnesse*, where the Firth is but twelve miles over, and near it is the ordinary ferry to Orkney, called *Duncan's bay* *Noshead* pointing North east *Clythness*, pointing East]

Promontories

Here, in Ptolemy's time, dwelt the *Catini*, falsly written in some Copies *Carini*, amongst whom the same Ptolemy places the river *Ila*, which may seem to be the present *Wiske* Grazing and fishing are the main income of the Inhabitants of this Country The chief Castle therein is called *Girnego*, the usual residence of the Earls of Cathnes The Episcopal See is at *Dornok* [(standing between the rivers of *Portnecouter* and *Unes*,)] a Village otherwise obscure [heretofore, but now a Burrough Royal,] where King James the fourth appointed the Sheriff of *Cathnes* to reside, or else at *Wik*, as occasion should require

The Catini. The River Ila. Girnego

[A little East of *Dornok*, is a Monument like a Cross, called the *Thane* or *Earls Cross*; and another near *Eubo*, call'd the *King's Cross*, where one of the Kings, or chief Commanders of the Danes, is said to have been slain and buried

Though *Wick* be a Royal Burgh, and the head Courts kept there, yet *Thurso* (only a Burgh of Barony) is more populous, where also the Judges reside It is a secure place for Ships of any burthen to ride in, being defended by *Holbourn head*

Wick Thurso.

In these parts, are many foundations of antient Houses now ruinous, supposed to have formerly belonged to the *Picts* Many Obelisks also are erected here and there, and in some places several of them together]

The Earls of *Cathnes* were anciently the same with the Earls of the *Orcades*, but afterwards became distinct, and by the eldest daughter of one *Malise*, who was given in marriage to *William Sincler* the King's [a] Pantler, his Posterity came to the honour of Earls of *Cathnes*, which they still enjoy

Earls of Cathnes

[a] *Pantario.*

STRATH-NAVERN.

HE utmost Coast of all Britain, which with the front of the shore looks full against the North-pole, and hath directly over its head the middle of the tail of *Ursa Major*, that, as *Cardan* thought, causes Translations of Empires, was inhabited, as we may see in Ptolemy, by the *Cornabii* Among them, he places the river *Nabeus*, and these two names are so nearly related in sound, that the People seem to have taken their name from the river upon which they dwelt Neither is the modern name *Strath Navern*, that is, the *Valley by the Navern*, altogether unlike them in sound [The Earl of *Sutherland* is superiour of this Country, and his eldest Son is stiled from it Lord *Strathnavern* The chief Inhabitants are the *Mackays*, of whom Sir *Donald* was by King Charles the first created Lord *Rae*, from a place belonging to him in the County of *Cathnes*]

Cornabii. Nabeus a River

The Country hath little cause to brag of its fertility By reason of the sharpness of the air it is [a] very thinly inhabited, and thereupon extreamly infested with the fiercest of [b] Wolves, which, to the great damage of the Country, not only furiously set upon the Cattle, but even upon the Inhabitants themselves, to the manifest danger of their Lives Insomuch, that not only in this, but in many other parts of Scotland, the Sheriffs and respective Inhabitants are bound by Act of Parliament, in their several Sheriffdoms, to go a hunting thrice every year, to destroy the *Wolves* and their *Whelps* Yet all in this northern Climate it [illegible]

[a] [illegible] [b] No Wolves now in [illegible]

twenty five minutes, and the shortest night five hours and forty five minutes So that the ancient Panegyrist was in the wrong, when he said that the *Sun* did not set at all here, but slip'd aside, and glanced upon the Horizon, relying upon the authority of Tacitus, who says, *That the extreme points and plain levels of the earth, having low shades, rais'd no darkness at all* But Pliny speaks more truth and reason, where he treats of the longest days, according to the inclination of the Solar Circle to the Horizon *The longest days*, says he, *in Italy, are fifteen hours, in Britain seventeen, where the light nights in Summer prove that by* experience, which reason *obliges one to believe, That at the Solstice, when the Sun approaches nearer to the Pole of the World, the places of the earth under* [the Pole] *have day six months*, '*through the light's having but a narrow compass*, *and night for so long, when it is far remote in Winter*

In this utmost tract (that is carried further to the East by Ptolemy, whereas indeed it bears full North, for which *Roger Bacon*, in his Geography, taxed him long ago,) Tacitus says, *That a prodigious vast space of Land runs out in length, and grows narrow like a wedge* Here, three Promontories shoot out into the Sea, which are mentioned by ancient Writers *Berubium*, now *Urdehead*, near the Village *Berrifwale*, [illegible]*drum*, now *Dunsby*, otherwise *Duncans bay* which is look'd upon as the remotest Promontory of Britain, and *Orcas*, now *Howburn*, which is placed by Ptolemy over-against the *Orcades*, the utmost of all the Islands This is likewise called by Ptolemy *Tar*[illegible] and *Ta*[illegible], for this reason (if I guess aright) because it [illegible] Britain, [illegible] in the British tongue, [illegible] with which [illegible] to make an end of this Book [illegible] of the *Orcades*, [illegible] places

THE utmost Coast of all Britain, which with the front of the shore looks full against the North-pole, and hath directly over its head the middle of the tail of *Ursa Major*, that, as *Cardan* thought, causes Translations of Empires; was inhabited, as we may see in Ptolemy, by the *Cornabii.Cornabii.* Among them, he places the river *Nabeus;Nabeus* a River. and these two names are so nearly related in sound, that the People seem to have taken their name from the river upon which they dwelt. Neither is the modern name *Strath-Navern*, that is, the *Valley by the Navern*, altogether unlike them in sound. [The Earl of *Sutherland* is superiour of this Country, and his eldest Son is stiled from it Lord *Strathnavern*. The chief Inhabitants are the *Mackays*; of whom Sir *Donald* was by King Charles the first created Lord *Rae*, from a place belonging to him in the Country of *Cathnes*.]

The Country hath little cause to brag of its fertility. By reason of the sharpness of the air it is * * *Minus culta.*very thinly inhabited, and thereupon extreamly infested with the fiercest of † † No Wolves now in *Scotland.*Wolves; which, to the great damage of the Countrey, not only furiously set upon the Cattle, but even upon the Inhabitants themselves, to the manifest danger of their Lives. Insomuch, that not only in this, but in many other parts of Scotland, the Sheriffs and respective Inhabitants are bound by Act of Parliament, in their several Sheriffdoms, to go a hunting thrice every year, to destroy the *Wolves* and their *Whelps*. But (if in this northern Climate, it may be any comfort to them) these People, of all Britain, have the shortest nights, and longest days.The longest Day. For by its being distant fifty nine degrees and forty minutes from the Equator, the longest day is eighteen hours and twenty five minutes, and the shortest night five hours and forty five minutes. So that the ancient Panegyrist was in the wrong, when he said that the *Sun* did not set at all here, but slip'd aside, and glanced upon the Horizon; relying upon the authority of Tacitus, who says, *That the extreme points and plain levels of the earth having low shades, rais'd no darkness at all*. But Pliny speaks more truth and reason, where he treats of the longest days, according to the inclination of the solar Circle to the Horizon: *The longest days*, says he, *in Italy, are fifteen hours, in Britain seventeen; where the light nights in Summer prove that by* experience, *which* reason *obliges one to believe, That at the Solstice, when the Sun approaches nearer to the Pole of the World, the places of the earth under [the Pole] have day six months,* * * *Angusto Lucis ambitu.through the light's having but a narrow compass; and night for so long, when it is far remote in Winter*.

In this utmost tract (that is carried further to the East by Ptolemy, whereas indeed it bears full North; for which *Roger Bacon*, in his Geography, taxed him long ago,) Tacitus says, *That a prodigious vast space of Land runs out in length, and grows narrow like a wedge*. Here, three Promontories shoot out into the Sea, which are mentioned by ancient Writers. *Berubium. Berubium*, now *Urdehead*, near the Village *Bernswale*; *Virvedrum,Virvedrum.* now *Dunsby*, otherwise *Duncans-bay*, which is look'd upon as the remotest Promontory of Britain; and *Orcas*, now *Howburn*, which is placed by Ptolemy over-against the *Orcades*, the utmost of all the Islands. This is likewise called by Ptolemy *Tarvedrum* and *Tarvisium,Tarvisium Tarvodunum*
Martiano. for this reason (if I guess aright) because it *determines* Britain. For *Tarvus*,What *Tarvus* signifies. in the British tongue, signifies an *ending*; with which give me leave to make an *End* of this Book. I shall treat of the *Orcades, Ebudes*, and *Shetland*, in their proper places.

THUS *have I run over* SCOTLAND, *more Hastily than the Dignity of so great and noble a Kingdom Deserves; nor do I at all doubt, but that some Person hereafter will give a larger Draught of it, with a more exquisite Pen, and more certainty and exactness; since (as I said before)* * *the greatest of Princes hath now laid open to us these remote Countries, which have been hitherto shut up. In the mean time, if I have not been so vigilant as I ought (for the most watchful may sometimes nod;) or if my wandring in an unknown Country hath led me into a wrong way (as nothing is so easy as Error;) I hope the courteous Reader, upon this my Confession, will grant me his pardon, and kindly direct me into the right way.*

* K. James the 6th of *Scotland*, and 1st of *England*.

[An Additional

DESCRIPTION

OF THE

ROMAN WALL,

IN

SCOTLAND.

THE first occasion of building the *Roman Wall* (which now goes by the name of *Graham's Dike*) was given by *Julius Agricola*, of whom Tacitus has left us this character, *Non alium Ducem opportunitates locorum sapientius eligisse*, That never did any General use greater discretion, in the choice of places And here, particularly, he made good his claim to that Character, for, the Isthmus or neck of land upon which it was built, is not above sixteen miles over, betwixt the rivers of *Forth* and *Clyde* So that, having fortified that slip of ground with Garrisons, the Enemies were, as Tacitus has observed, *summoti velut in aliam Insulam*, removed in a manner into another Island

Agricola did not build a *Wall*.

But here, we must not imagine, that *Agricola* built a *Wall* along this tract, since neither Historians nor Inscriptions give us any reason to believe it Tacitus only observes, that this narrow slip of ground *Præsidiis firmabatur*, was secur'd by *Forts* and *Garrisons*, and we may be sure, if there had been any thing of a *Wall* he would not have omitted the mention of it So that it is probable that *Agricola* contented himself with placing Garrisons at such convenient distances, as that the Forces might easily draw together upon the first apprehension of danger Whether some of the Forts that are plac'd upon the Wall, were built by him at that time, or by others afterwards, is not certain, however, it seems probable that he built the following Garrisons

Garrisons

1. That which is call'd *Coria Damniorum*, from the Water of *Caron* that runs near it The neighbours thereabouts call it at this day *Camelon*. not that it is to be imagin'd, that this is the *Cumulodunum* mentioned by Tacitus, (which is some hundreds of miles distant from hence) but rather the *Camunlodunum*, which Ptolemy makes a Town of the *Brigantes*, whom he places *sub Elgovis & Ottadinis, ad utraque maria*, below the *Elgovæ* and *Ottadini*, adjoyning to the two Seas, and sets the Town in the 57th Degree of Latitude And indeed, the *Gadeni* which were placed here, were a tribe of the *Brigantes*, that possess'd the Country betwixt the Irish Sea and the *Firth* of *Forth* *Camalodunum* likewise is thought to import the *Palace of the Prince*; and it may be gathered from History, that this was the Palace of the Picts But by whomsoever it was built, the remains of the fortification, and the tracks of the Streets, are yet to be seen; and there is a Roman Military way which begins here, and runs South In antient times, it was wash'd by the Sea; which hath been confirm'd by an Anchor discover'd near it, within these hundred years, or thereabouts As a further confirmation of its Antiquity, they discover old Vaults, and meet with several Roman Coins about it, one particularly of brass, much of the bigness of a Half crown, with a *Shield* on one side, and above it a *Lion*; but the Impression on the other side is not legible Here it is, that Ptolemy places the *Legio Sexta Victrix*, and

and it seems to have been their head-quarters The *Dum Pacis* are very near it, and just over against it, on the North-side of *Carran Water*, is the *Ædes Termini*.

2 The second Fort, built by *Agricola*, seems to have been some six miles distant to the North-west, where the Town of *Sterling* is now For, besides that the narrowness of the river of *Forth* (which hath now a bridge over it in this place) required a Garrison; there is, upon a rock, this Inscription,

which sheweth that a Legion kept garrison here It is most probable, that this is the *Alauna* of Ptolemy

3 The third Garrison (for the out-guard of this, and for securing the tract where the river is but narrow) was plac'd about eight miles to the North-east from the second, [a] and is more fully described in the Account of *Thule*, written by Sir *Robert Sibbalds* It bids fairest for Ptolemy's *Victoria*, which name it might possibly get from the *Victory* obtained near it, by Agricola, over the Caledonians Roman Medals have been found at it and not far from it, there runs a Roman military way

[a] See after *The British Islands*

4 The fourth seems to be that which Bede calls *Guidi*, and which he placeth about the middle of the Wall, call'd at present *Kirkintilloch*, and antiently *Kaerpentalloch*, and situate upon the tract of the Wall Here are still to be seen the ruins of great fortifications, and near it several Inscriptions have been found, some whereof were deposited at the house of *Cadir* It is most probable, that this is the [b] *Coria* mentioned by Ptolemy

[b] See *Sterling*

5. The fifth was, where the Town of *Paisly* now is, which one would imagin from the situation to be the [c] *Bremenium* of Ptolemy

[c] See *Northumberland*

6 The sixth was the most remote to the West, call'd at this day *Dumbarton*, and conveniently situate in a point where the water of *Leven* runneth into *Clyde* But if this convenience were not testimony enough, the Inscriptions that are found in the neighbourhood, would put it beyond dispute

The Wall

The placing of these Garrisons was probably the occasion of building the Wall afterwards along this tract But in building, they took the directest line, which must be the cause why some of the Garrisons are at a distance from it It seems also to have been built at different times, and by different men, as the situation of the ground required, for repelling the Enemy, and covering the Provincials against their Invasions Bede tells us, *That they made it between the two Friths of the Sea, that where the water did not secure them, there the* Wall *might defend them against the Incursions of the Enemy* From which we may probably infer, that first they began it where the river of *Forth* is narrow, and so carried it along the neck of land, betwixt the Firth of *Clyde* and *Forth* But afterwards they found it convenient, that it should be carried farther East The *Penvahel* or *Penueltum* (where Bede says it begun) is call'd *Walltoun* at this day, where there is an artificial Mount dyk'd about The manner of the Wall will be more easily apprehended by this Draught of it, taken from the Papers of Mr *Timothy Pont* (who had exactly traced it) and from the Observations of some others, who after him had been at the pains to describe it.

Waltoun

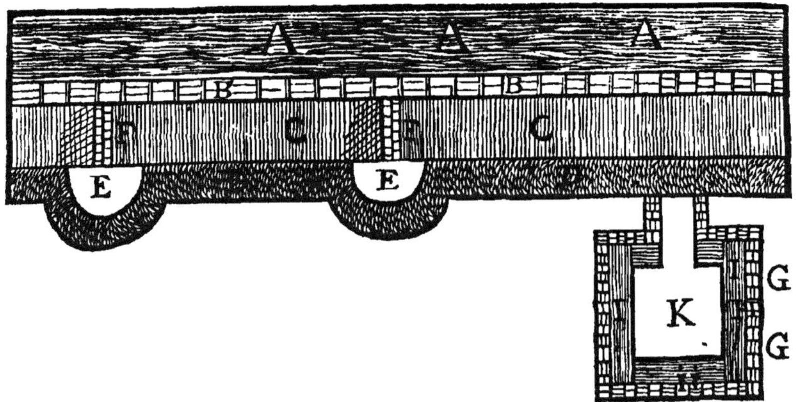

A A A. *A ditch of twelve foot wide before the Wall, towards the Enemies Country*

B B *A wall of squared and cut stone, two foot broad; probably higher than the Wall, to cover the Defendants, and to keep the Earth of the wall from falling into the Ditch*

C C. *The Wall it self, of ten foot thickness, but how high, not known*

D D *A paved way close at the foot of the Wall, five foot broad*

E E. *Watch towers within call one of another, where Centinels kept watch day and night*

F F *The wall of square stone, going through the breadth of the Wall, just against the Towers.*

G G *A Court of guard, to lodge a sufficient number of Soldiers against all sudden Alarms*

I I *The body of the Rampire, with an outer wall of cut stone, higher than the Rampire, to cover Soldiers*

K *The Void within, for the Soldiers Lodgings.*

Forts. Besides these, there were along the *Wall* great and Royal Forts strongly entrench'd (though within the Wall) able to receive a whole Army together For the Wall being long, and they not knowing where the Enemy would make their attacks, it was necessary that lodgings should be provided against all occasions In the fixing whereof, it is observable, that they did not so much look after high grounds, as places that were well-watered, but where these two concurr'd, they were sure to have a Fort

The Forts which remain'd in Mr *Pont's* time (who trac'd them all) were these One at *Lang town*, a mile east of Falkirk, one just at the *Rountree burnhead*; one at *Wester Cowdon* above Helen's Chapel, one at the *Croy-hill*, a very great one upon the top of the *Bar hill* (which hath had large Entrenchings, a fresh Spring, and a Well within it,) one at *Achindavy*, one at *Kirkin tilloch* or *Kaerpentalloch*, one at *East Calder*, one at *Hiltoun of Calder*; one at *Balmudy*; one at *Simerstone*; and over Kilvin river and *Ca[illegible]*, one at *Atermynie*; one at *Bal castle* over against Barhill; one at *Kaellibe* over against Cry hill, one at the *Roch hill* over against the Wester-wood, a large one at *Bankyir*, over against Castle Cary, one at *Dumbass*, &c

In the ruins of that at *Bankyir*, there was found a large Iron shovel, or some Instrument resembling it, so weighty that it could hardly be lifted by any man of this age At the same Fort also were discovered several Sepulchres, covered with large rough Stones, and at *Dunchroc chyr* near Mony-abroch, there have been large buildings

The length of the Wall is thirty six Scotch miles Beginning between the Queens ferry and Abercorn, it goes along west by the Grange and Kinnel to Inneravin; So on, to Falkirk (two miles west of which are the tracks of Camelon,) from whence it goeth directly to the forest of Cumernald (where hath been a great Fort call'd *Castle Cary*) Next, it runs to the great Fort at the *Bankhill*, where have been found several Stones, some with Inscriptions From thence, it goeth to the Peel of *Kirkintillo*, the greatest Fort of all, and so Westward to *Dunglastoun*, with a great Inch upon the Length and Course of the Wall

the North side of the Wall all along It had also along it many square Fortifications, in form of Roman Camps

As to the Inscriptions on or near the Wall, amongst those, one is said to have upon it these words,

COHORTIS HISPANORUM TIBICEN
HIC JACET

Others have been likewise found in these parts, pointing out some of the Forces that quartered hereabouts

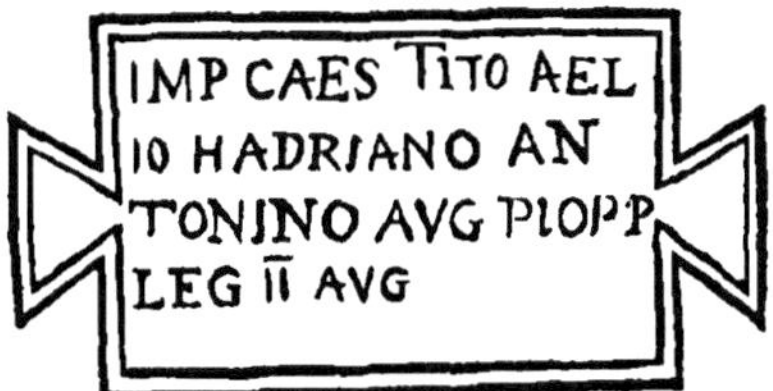

Philosoph Transact N 269 To these we will add the following Inscription, found at *Castlehill*, near *Kilpatrick*.

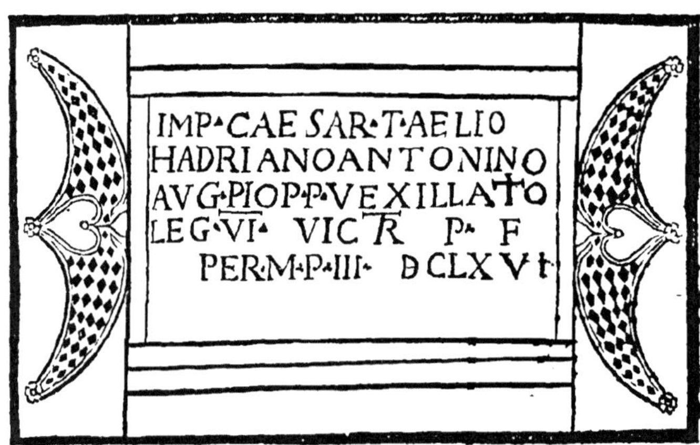

IRELAND.

IRELAND.

THE

GENERAL HEADS

IN

IRELAND.

IRELAND.

IRELAND.

The BRITISH OCEAN.

The British Sea. 

Have at last survey'd, or rather run over, the whole Island of BRITAIN, *namely those two flourishing Kingdoms,* ENGLAND *and* SCOTLAND, [*now united into one Kingdom of* GREAT BRITAIN] *And since I must necessarily cross the* Sea, *to come to* Ireland *and the other Islands, I hope it will not be thought a Digression, if I premise something concerning the* British Ocean.

That vast and wide Ocean, which surrounds Britain *on all sides but the South, ebbs and flows with so strong a tide, that* Pithœus Massiliensis *reports it to swell eighty cubits higher than*
Lib Hexamer c 3 *the* Island. *St. Basil calls it* the great Sea, to be dreaded by Mariners; *and St. Ambrose speaks thus of it,* The great Sea, unattempted by Mariners, is that roaring Ocean which
British Sea formerly unknown encompasses Britain, and extends into the most remote parts; of which we have not so much as a fabulous Account *Sometimes it overflows the Fields adjoining, and then retreats and leaves them. To speak with* Pliny, *it lies so wide and open, that*
a Vis Lunæ late grassantis [a] *the force and pressure of the Moon does considerably affect it, and it flows with such Force, that it not only drives back the rivers that run into it; but either surprizes the beasts upon the shore, it advances so fast; or leaves Sea-monsters upon the banks, it returns so quick. Every Age has seen so many Sea-monsters left behind upon the dry land, to the great amazement of the beholders, that Horace had good grounds for what he said,*

Belluo-

Belluosus qui remotis
Obstrepit Oceanus Britannis.

And Seas (where shapeless Monsters roar)
That wash Great Britain's *farthest shore.*

And Juvenal,

Quanto Delphino Balæna Britannica major.
As much as Dolphins yield to British *Whales.*

Nay, a voyage over our Sea *was thought such a notable Enterprise, that* Libanus, *the Greek Sophist, in his Panegyrick to Constantius Chlorus, exclaims,* This Voyage to Britain, seems equal to the noblest triumph! *And Julius Firmicus, not the Astrologer, but another who was a Christian, in a Treatise upon the Errors of prophane Religion, dedicated to Constans and Constantius, Emperours, says,* You have row'd over the swelling and raging billows of the British Ocean in the very Winter; a thing never yet done, nor ever to be done again. A Sea, almost unknown to us, hath submitted to you; and the *Britains* are terrified at the unexpected arrival of a Roman Emperor. What would you atchieve farther? The very Elements have yielded themselves Captives to your Valour.

Julius Firmicus

The learned Julius Scaliger, *in his Poems, would make the* Caurus *or north-west wind, the product of the British Sea; in opposition to* Lucan, *who writes thus,*

Caurus

Primus ab Oceano caput exeris Atlantæo,
Caure, movens æstus.

You fierce North-west, *that swell the raging tide,*
Raise from Atlantick *waves your low'ring head.*

For certain, this wind exceedingly annoys Ireland; *and for a great part of the year, as* Cæsar *says, it blows in this Island.*

Wicker-Ships of the Britains

That Ships first *ply'd upon this Sea, as some write, seems incredible to me. But that the Britains used small wicker Vessels, cover'd with leather, such as they call* Corraghs *at this day, is evident from Pliny; with whom* Lucan *agrees,*

Primum cana salix madefacto vimine parvam
Texitur in puppim, cæsoque induta juvenco,
Vectoris patiens tumidum super emicat amnem;
Sic Venetus stagnante Pado, fusoque Britannus
Navigat Oceano.

First little Boats of well soak'd twigs were made,
A reeking hide above the twigs was laid:
Thus rudely fitted, o're the waves they rode,
And stock'd with Passengers, outbrav'd the flood.
Thus rough Venetians *pass the lazie* Po,
And British *Keels the boundless Ocean plow.*

Thus likewise Polyhistor; In that Sea, which is between *Britain* and *Ireland*, they sail in wicker bottoms, cover'd with Ox-hides. During their Voyages (how long soever,) they do not eat.

As for the Commodities *and* Advantages *of this Sea; it's warmth, which cherishes the Earth; it's steam and vapour, which feeds the Air and bedews the Fields; the many Fish of all kinds bred in it,* viz *Salmon (which Bede calls* Isicii, *and Pliny* Esox,) *Plaice, Punger, Cod, Haddock, Whiting, Herring, Basse, Maccarel, Mullet, Turbet, Seal, Rochet, Sole, Pilchard, Scate, Oyster, Lobster, Crab, and innumerable others which swarm in great shoals on this Coast; these, I say, are not to my present purpose. Yet I must not forget to take notice of those* Jewels, *which* Jubas *tells us are roundish, and like Bees swim in clusters, with one like a Captain at the head of them.* Pearls *Thus also* Marcellinus, *after he has spoken of the* Persian *and* Indian *Pearls*; Which kind of Jewels, we know very well, are found in the creeks of the *British Sea*, tho' not so fine. *But although* Pliny *gives them the character of small and ill-colour'd, yet* Suetonius *makes them the great motive of* Cæsar's *coming hither, and says, they were so large, that he us'd to poize them in his hand, and dedicated a Breast-plate made of them to* Venus Genitrix; *which appears by the Inscription.* Origen *also to the same purpose:* The best Sort of Sea-pearl is found among the *Indians*, or rather in the *Red-Sea*. The next, are those pick'd up in the *British Ocean* In the third place are to be reckon'd those that are found near *Scythia* in the *Bosphorus*, being not so good as either of the other. *And a little after:* As for that Pearl which they say is found in *Britain*, it looks like gold, but is somewhat speck'd and cloudy, [b] and without the proper Lustre. *Thus also our Venerable Bede, concerning the* Shell-fish *of this Sea:* Among others, there are *Muscles*, in which they find the best *Pearl* of all colours, purple, violet, green, and especially white. There are [c] Cockles also in great abundance, with which they dye the

[b] *Luce obtusius*

[c] *Cochlea*

the Scarlet colour ſo ſtrong, that neither Sun nor Rain will change it: nay, the older it is, the better it looks. *Tertullian, reprehending the diſſolute luxury of his time, ſays,* If ambitious Luxury would feed it ſelf from the *Britiſh* or the *Indian* Seas, there is a kind of Shell-fiſh ſo agreeable to the palate, that it not only exceeds the Purple-fiſh, or the Oyſter, but even the *Scallop* it ſelf.

This Sea in general is call'd the Britiſh, *and* Caledonian Sea, *but yet has ſeveral names, according as it touches upon the ſeveral Coaſts*

On the Eaſt, towards Germany, they call it the German Ocean. *On the North it is called* Oceanus Hyperboreus, *which the Antients untruly deſcribed,* to be ſtill, and heavy to the oar, and for that reaſon not eaſily rais'd to a ſtorm. *This, Tacitus thought, was* becauſe Land and Hills, which are a great cauſe of Tempeſts, are rare here; and alſo the Sea itſelf is ſo wide and deep, that this weighty maſs of waters is not eaſily to be mov'd and driven. *To the Weſt, it is call'd* Oceanus Deucalidonius, *and* Vergivius; *and between England and Ireland, it goes by the name of the* Iriſh Sea, *or* St George's Chanel. *This the Antients deſcribe to be ſo* high and raging, that it was not navigable all the year round, except only ſome few days in Summer. *On the South, towards France, it is properly call'd the* Britiſh Sea: *but at this day, the Dutch, call it the* Chanel: *the Engliſh, the* Sleeve; *and the French in the ſame ſenſe,* Le Manche; *becauſe it grows narrow, by little and little, like a ſleeve. That the Sea as far as Spain, went under the name of the* Britiſh Sea, *we are aſſured by* Pomponius Mela, *who was himſelf a Spaniard; where he tells us, that the* Pyrenæan Hills *run out as far as the* Britiſh Sea.

Julius Solinus

See in K[illegible]

Nature has ſcatter'd certain Iſlands up and down this Sea, for ſhow and ornament; ſome few to the Eaſt and South; but on the Weſt and North-ſides, very many. For there, they ſtand ſo thick, that they do as it were, parcel and embroider the Sea But ſince Ireland *ſo far exceeds the reſt; both its* Largeneſs *and* Renown *may juſtly entitle it to the firſt place.*

IRELAND,

Minutes of Time
THE KINGDOM of IRELAND
by Robt Morden
Tory Island
DUNNAGALL
OR TYRCONNEL
County
Dunnagall
Prom Boreum
Dunnagall Bay
LETRIM
County
The Mullett
Templemor
Killala
MAYO
SLIGO
County
Templemore
Boyle
Elphin
CONNOUGHT
ROSCOMMON
County
COUNTY
PROVINCE
GALLOWAY
County
Tuam
Athlone

P. Moulin
Port Patrick
the Mulle of Galloway
Copland Isle
Bangor
Donaghadee
Glanarm Bay
Old Fleet Harbour
COUNTY
ANTRIM
LONDONDERRY
County
TYRONE County
Strabane
Belfast
Lisborn
Dromore
Down Patrick
Portaferry
Strangford Bay
Dundrum Bay
County of ARDMAGH
Monoghan
MONOGHAN
County
Newry
Carlingford Bay
Dundalk
Dundalk Bay
Cavan
Kilmore
CAVAN County
Longford
Louth
Atherdee
LOUTH
Slane
MEATH County
DUBLIN
Dublin
Lambay
Irelands Eye
Hooth Head
THE
IRISH
55
54
30
45
15

15
53
45
30
52
Galloway
Kilmore
RICHARDS
Clonefert
GAN
The Islands of Arran
MOND
or
CLARE
County
Laona
Killalow
Limrick
LIMRICK
County
New Castle
Charleville
Killmallock
County of
TIPPERA
Fort del Ore
Dingle
Dingle or Smerwick Sound
Trallee Island
VNSTER
CORKE
County
PROVINCE
KERRY County
Dunkeran
Old Head
Timoleague
Cork Haven
Rathbarry
Baltimore
4
20
40

SEA
KINGS COVNTY
QUEENS COVNTY
KILDARE
Kildare
WICKLOW County
Wicklow
North Ground
Black Castle
Midle Ground
Arklow
South Ground
OSSERY
CATHER LAGHS County
Kilkenny
KILLKEN County
WEXFORD County
Wexford
Ferns
Rusk
Ramme
Rosslare
Menapia
Tuskard
Barrells
Black Rock
WATERFORD County
Waterford
Dungarvan
Dungarvan Bay
Ardmore
Youghall Bay
S Davids
Byshop and Clerks
S Brides Bay
English Miles 60 to a Degree
Sold by Abel Swale Awnsham and John Churchill
53
52
7
6

IRELAND, in General.

The Vergivian Ocean.

IN the *Vergivian* Sea (so call'd, not as some think, *a vergendo*, from *bending*, but from *Mor Weridh*, which is the British name, or else from *Farigi*, which is the Irish name of it,) lies the most famous Isle of *IRELAND*, on the West side of Britain. Formerly, it was thought the most eminent Island in the World, but two. For thus the ancient Geographer writes of them. Τῶν νήσων πρωτεύει ἡ Ἰνδικὴ Ταπροβάνη μεγέθει καὶ δόξῃ μεθ' ἣν ἡ Βρεταννική, τρίτη ἑτέρα Βρετανῶν ἡ Ουερνία. i. e. *Among the Islands, Taprobane in India must take place first for renown and greatness, next to it,* Britain, *and in the third place,* Ireland, *another Island of the Britons.* And therefore Ptolemy calls it *Britannia Parva*, or *Little Britain*.

Idem. mag. Constructio nis.

Of the several names, see [illegible] Antiq. Hibern. p. 1.

^a By Orpheus it is called Ἰερνίς, by Aristotle and Claudian *Ierna*, by Juvenal and Mela, *Juverna*, by Diodorus Siculus, *Iris*, by Martianus Heracleota, Ἰουερνία, by Eustathius Οὐερνία, and Βερνία, by the Inhabitants, *Erin*, by the Britains, *Iwerdon*, and by the English, *Ireland*.

Concerning the original of these Names [illegible] upon a point so obscure and difficult, there have been many, and very different, Opinions. Some will have Ireland to be derived *ab [illegible] tempore*, others from *Iberus* a Spaniard, others from the River *Iberus* and the [illegible] of the *Eulogium*, from a Captain call'd *[illegible]*. Postellus, in his publick Lectures at Paris upon *Pomponius Mela* (to shew something exquisite and singular) derives it from the [illegible], to [illegible] with him, is [illegible] *Jarim*, that is, *a Land of the Jews*. For he says, *that the Jews, forsooth, being most [illegible] Southly [illegible], and [illegible] that the Empire of the World would at last settle in that strong angle towards the West, took possession of these parts, and of Ireland, very early, and that the Syrians, and the Tyrians also, endeavour'd to settle themselves there, as the Foundation of their future Empire.* I must beg the Reader's pardon, if I cannot subscribe to these Opinions, no, not to that which is generally received, *viz.* its being so called *ab hiberno tempore*, though I must own, I have heard that the [illegible] from whatever quarter it blows here, is cold and piercing as in winter. *Hibernia*, *Juverna* and Ουερνία, are without all question derived from *Ierna* (the name that we find in Orpheus and Aristotle,) and so likewise is *Ierna*, *Iris*, *Iwerdhon*, and *Ireland*, from *Erin*, the name by which the Inhabitants themselves call it.

^b *Winter.*

^c *Hiberniam.*

And therefore the original is to be traced by this Irish name *Erin* only. And here I am puzzled and must, like the Philosophers of old ^d suspend. For I am at a loss, nor can I tell what to think in this matter, unless it might perhaps come from *Hiere*, an Irish word signifying the *West* or a *Tract Westward*, and so *Erin* may import as much as a *West-country*, and be deriv'd from thence. This I have long thought a plausible Conjecture, both, because it is the most *Westward* Country in Europe, being but twelve degrees distant from the utmost point in that quarter, and also, because the [illegible] Westerly [illegible] in the [illegible] [*Kerna*], is [illegible] *Ierne* by [illegible], and the [illegible] Westerly Promontory in Spain, from whence our Irish were [illegible], is called *[illegible]* by Strabo, and the river next it, which [illegible] into more [illegible] than any other in Spain, is named *Ierna* by Mela. From this *Westerly* situation likewise, Spain [illegible] was termed *Hesperia*, the Western Coast in [illegible], *Hesperium cornu*, and in Germany *Westerreich*, *Westphalen*, &c. are so call'd from the same position. So that it is not at all strange, that this Country should derive its name from the *Western* situation.

^d Ἐπέχω.

Besides the names of *Ireland* already mention'd, the Irish Bards, in their Ballads, call it ^e *Innis-[illegible]*, ^f *Tuath de Danan*, and ^g *Bannagh*, as by far the most ancient names of this Island. [The first (which signifies *People of Belgia*,) and the second (which signifies *Damnonian People*,) were names of certain Septs of Inhabitants, such as *Scots*, *Picts*, *Saxons*, in Britain. It is possible, they might be Colonies of the *Belgæ* and of the *Damnonii* or *Danmonii* of Britain.] But as to *Bannagh* [(Blessed)] I know not how to account for it, unless it be the *Bannomanna*, which Pliny mentions out

^e *Tirvolia*, C.

^f *Totalanan*, C.

^g *Bann*, C.

out of Timæus, where he describes the utmost Parts of Europe, and the shore of the Northern Ocean on the left, from Scythia, as far as *Cadiz* For it does not yet appear to Geographers, what this *Bannomanna* was *Biaun* in Irish signifies *holy*, and the Island it self is call'd [h] *Sacred* or the *Insula Sacra*, by Festus Avienus, in his little Book, entitled *Oræ Maritimæ*, which he collected out of the most ancient Geographers, *Hecateus Milesius*, *Hellanicus Lesbius*, *Philæas Athenensis*, *Caryandæus*, *Pausymachus Samius*, *Damastus*, *Euctemon*, and others But I will subjoin his Verses, for when he speaks of the *Ostrymide-Islands*, he says,

Bannomanna

[h] V *Pindar Pyth* 4 & *Scholiast Sacra Insula Oræ Maritimæ*

Ast hinc duobus in Sacram, *sic insulam*
Dixêre prisci, solibus cursus rati est
Hæc inter undas multum cespitem jacit,
Eamque latè gens Hibernorum colit
Propinqua rursus insula Albionum patet

Hence to the *Holy Isle* (the ancient name)
Two Suns will bring you through the pathless stream
Where falling turf advanceth every tide,
O're spacious tracts the roving Irish spread,
And neighb'ring *Albion* shows her lofty head.

[Mr *Selden* thinks, that *Isacius Tzetzes*, in his [i] Commentary upon Lycophron, may intend *Ireland* by that expression, Γῆς ἐν ἄμφῳ Βρίτα νίας]

Pag 135

If that *Ogygia*, which Plutarch places on the West of Britain, was a matter of real truth, and not a mere dream, one would take *Ireland* to be signify'd by that name, though the stories which are told of it, are all Romantick and idle Nor is it easie to find a reason, why they should call it *Ogygia*, unless from the Antiquity of it for the Greeks never attributed that name to any thing that was not particularly antient *Robertus Constantinus* seems to be quite wrong, in affirming our *Ireland* to be the *Cerne* in Lycophron For *Lycophron* himself, and his Commentator *Tzetzes*, make *Cerne* to be situated in the East, and the learned are all of opinion, that *Madagascar* must be the place, which lies, as it were in another World, under the Tropick of Capricorn, over against Egypt

Ogygia In Lib de Macula in Luna

The Isle Cerne

Thus much of the *Names* of *Ireland*, not forgetting in the mean time, that in later ages it was call'd *Scotia* by *Isidore* and *Bede*, from the Scotch Inhabitants; and that from thence the name of *Scotland*, together with the Scots themselves, came into Britain But this has been already observ'd, and need not be repeated

Ireland call'd Scotland

This Island is stretch'd out from south to north, not broad nor long, as Strabo says, but of a lentel or oval form; nor yet of twenty days sail, as Philæmon in Ptolemy has related but according to modern computation, it is reckoned three hundred [English] miles in length, and scarce one hundred and twenty in breadth [From North to South, saith Sir *James Ware*, it contains upwards of two hundred miles, and from East to West, one hundred and twenty] On the east of it, lies *England*, sever'd by that boisterous Sea, call'd the *Irish Sea* On the west, it is bounded by the vast *Western Ocean*, on the north, by the *Deucaledonian*, and on the south, by the *Vergivian Sea*

Antiq Hibern c 3 § 2

The situation of IRELAND

A Country (says Giraldus) *uneven, mountainous, soft, washy, woody, windy, and so boggy that you may see standing waters upon the very Mountains* [But as it hath grown more populous, it is become less waterish and boggy, the Low-lands and Marshes being drained by the industry of the Inhabitants The Woods too are in good measure destroy'd, and as for corn, they have that in great abundance] *The Climate* (according to Mela) *is so unkind, that it does not ripen Corn, yet the Country produces Grass in such plenty (and that not only very rank but very sweet) that the Cattle fill themselves in a very little time, and will even burst, if they are not hinder'd from eating longer* [k] Upon this account, their Breed of Cattle is infinite, and are indeed the greatest wealth and support of the Inhabitants, as also Sheep, which they shear twice a year, and of the coarse Wooll make Irish rugs and mantles, which are carry'd into foreign parts Their *Horses* likewise (we call them *Hobbies*) are very excellent they go not as other Horses do, but [l] pace very soft and easie The *Hawks* also are not without their Excellencies, but these, as all other animals (besides men and greyhounds,) are of a less size here, than in England The air and ground are of too moist a nature, and this makes fluxes and rheums so usual in the country, especially among strangers, yet their [m] *Uskebah*, which is less enflaming and yet more drying than our's, is an excellent remedy for this distemper Giraldus says, that none of the three kinds of *Fevers* touch the Natives of this Country, which is daily refuted by experience Yet to cite the same Author as evidence in another matter, *The Country it self is of all others the most temperate, here are neither the scorching heats of* Cancer *to drive men into shades, nor the piercing colds of* Capricorn *to drive them to the fire The air is so mild and pleasant, that all seasons are in some degree warm* [Upon the whole, though there is not all the difference here imply'd, between the Climates of *England* and *Ireland*, yet of the two, *Ireland* seems to be the more temperate, that is, not so hot in Summer, nor so cold in Winter]

Giraldus Cambrensis in Topographia Hiberniæ

[k] Concerning the Excellencies of *Ireland*, see *Ware* p 34

Irish Mantles and Rugs

Horses

[l] *Mollis ac lenta crurum explicatio gratiosa*

Hawk

Diseases

[m] *Aqua vitæ* Usqueba.

Bees are so swarming and plentiful in this Country, that we find them not only in hives, but in the trunks of trees, and caverns of the earth Vines also grow here, but yield not so much benefit, by their fruit, as by their shade For as soon as the Sun has pass'd *Leo*, we have cold blasts in these parts, and the afternoon-heat in Autumn is too little, in strength and continuance, both here and in Britain, to ripen and concoct Grapes to perfection Moreover, *Ireland* has no Snakes, nor other venomous Creatures, [nor has it Frogs, or Moles;] yet it is [still] infested with Wolves [[n] on the wild and solitary Mountains, where there are few or no Inhabitants]

Bees

No C[ra]pes [i]n [Ireland] why

[n] All over ...

To wind up all Whether we regard the fruitfulness of the Soil, the advantages of a Sea with so many commodious Harbours, or the Natives themselves, who are warlike, ingenious, proper, and well complexion'd, soft skin'd, and exceeding nimble thro' a peculiar pliantness of the Muscles, this Island is in many respects so happy, that Giraldus might very well say, *Nature had been more favourable than ordinary, to this Kingdom of* Zephyrus And the reason why it is now and then reflected on, is, because of the Inhabitants, who are uncivilız'd in some places, and, which is strangely inconsistent, love Idleness and hate Ease They begin very early with their Amours; for among the wilder sort, when their daughters arrive at the age of ten or twelve, they marry them, as ripe and capable, without expecting that age and maturity which is requir'd in other Nations But in the end of this Book we shall treat more largely of their Customs, and in this place, if the Reader pleases, he shall hear *Ireland* speaking of it self and its Commodities, in the Verses of the most learned *Hadrianus Junius*

Illa ego sum Graiis olim glacialis Ierne
Dicta, & Jasoniæ puppis bene cognita nautis
Quæ Tartheßiaco propior se tingere soles
Flumine conspicio, Cauro subjecta procaci
Cui Deus, & melior rerum nascentium origo
Jus commune dedit cum Creta altrice tonantis,
Noxia ne nostris diffundant sibila in oris
Terrificæ creti tabo Phorcynidos angues
Et forte illati compressis faucibus atris
Viroso pariter vitam cum sanguine ponant
En ego cum regni sceptro, Mavortia bello
Pectora, & horriferas hominum, nil fingo, figuras,
Qui cursu alipedes norint prævertere cervos,
Dedico, piscososque lacus, volucrumque paludes
Omnigenûm lustris fœtas, stannique fodinas,
Et puri argenti venas, quas terra recessis
Visceribus manes imos visura recludit

I'm cold *Ierne*, me the *Grecians* knew,
Me *Jason*, and his *Pegasean* crew
Fix'd in the Ocean near the sportive West,
I see great *Phœbus* posting down to rest
And when his fiery Car the flood receives,
Hear the Wheels hissing in *Tartessian* Waves
On me kind Mother Nature hath bestow'd
The wondrous Gift, which grateful Heaven allow'd
To *Crete's* fair Isle that nurs'd the thund'ring God
That no vile Snake, sprung from *Medusa's* gore,
Should vent an hiss upon my peaceful shore
If hither brought, their feeble jaws they close,
And dearer life do with their Poyson lose
A Crown I bring, and Sons renown'd in fight,
And roving Savages, an hideous sight
On barren Cliffs their horned Troops appear,
And with unequal steps pursue the trembling Deer
These I present · and Lakes, the first in fame
For choicest Fish, and Fenns of flying game
And Mines of Tin, and Veins of Silver Ore,
Which mother Earth, unlocking all her store,
From her deep bosom yields as if she'd shew
A nearer passage to the shades below,
And wond'ring ghosts expose to mortal view

If what the Irish Authors relate, may be credited, this Island was not without good reason call'd *Ogygia* (or *very ancient*) by Plutarch For they begin their Histories from the highest Antiquity, so that other Nations are but modern, and as it were in their Infancy, in respect of their's They tell us, that one *Cæsarea*, a grand daughter of Noah, inhabited this Island before the deluge, and that three hundred years after the flood, *Bartholanus* a Scythian arrived here, and had great wars and conflicts with the Giants That, long after this, *Nemetha* the Scythian came hither, and that he was presently driven out by the Giants That afterwards *Dela*, with certain Greeks, possess'd himself of the Island, and that then *Gaothelus* with his wife *Scota*, the daughter of Pharaoh King of Egypt, came hither [and made the Tongue which is called Gaithelaf, as being a Collection out of all Tongues,] and that the Country took the name of *Scotia* from her, and the language the name of *Gaothela* from him, and that this was about the time when the Israelites departed out of Egypt Some few ages after, *Hiberus* and *Hermion* (call'd *Ever* and *Erimon* by the Irish writers) the Sons of Milesius King of Spain, planted Colonies in this Country (unpeopled by a Pestilence at that time,) with the permission of Gerguntius, King of the Britains, as the British History informs us I shall not meddle either with the *Truth* or *Falsity* of these relations Antiquity must be allow'd some liberty in his way

Why call'd Ogygia

Vid Polychron l 1 c 33 Girald Topogr dist 3 c 7

However, as I doubt not but this Island was inhabited, as soon as mankind began to multiply and disperse in the World, so it is very plain, that its first Inhabitants came from Britain * For, not to mention the vast numbers of British words which are to be met with in the Irish tongue, and the ancient names which savour of a British extraction; *The Nature and manners of the People* (as Tacitus says) *differ not much from the Britains* It is call'd by all the ancient writers, the *British Island*, Diodorus Siculus makes *Irin* a part of Britain, Ptolemy calls it *Britannia Parva*, as you may see by comparing his Geography with his *Magna Constructio*, and Strabo in his *Epitome* calls the Inhabitants expresly, *Britanns* Thus likewise the Island it self is call'd in *Island of the Britains*, by an ancient Geographer Festus Avienus shows the same thing from Dionysius, where he treats of the British Islands

Ireland first inhabited by the Britains.

* Of their original, and language whether the same with the British, see Ware, p 6

Britannia Parva

Eminus hic aliæ gelidi prope flabra Aquilonis
Exuperant undas, & vasta cacumina tollunt,
Hæ numero geminæ, pinguis sola, cespitis ampli,
Conditur occidua qua Rheni gurgitis unda,
Dura Britannorum sustentant agmina terris

Two others, that the North's cold streams divide,
Lift their proud cliffs above th' unequal tide
Wide are their Fields; their Corn and Pasture good
Where Western *Rhine* rouls on his hasty flood,
And furious *Britains* make their wild abode.

Nor is there any Country, from which, by reason of vicinity, it was more easy to transplant People into Ireland, that from our Britain; for from hence the passage is as short and easie, as from France to Britain But afterwards, when the Romans had establish'd an universal Empire, it is not to be question'd, but that abundance of people out of Spain, Gaul and Britain, retir'd hither, to be eas'd of the plagues and grievances of the Roman Tyranny; and I understand those words of Tacitus, to be with an eye to this *Ireland, situated exactly between Spain and Britain, lies very convenient for the French-Sea, and would unite the strong members of the Empire, with great advantage, its ports and havens are better known than those of Britain, by reason of the* resort *and* traffick *there* For, though *Julius Agricola* entertain'd a petty Prince of Ireland (who was forced from thence by his rebel-subjects,) that he might have a Pretence to invade that Island, which he thought could be conquer'd and kept in subjection with one Legion and some few Auxiliaries, and says moreover, that it would prove a mighty advantage to the Roman-Interest in Britain, if the Roman Arms were on all sides of it, and liberty banish'd as it were out of sight Yet we do not find that the Romans made any attempts upon it Some, indeed, think they did, and endeavour to strain this inference from that of Juvenal; *Romans did not conquer Ireland*

——*Arma quid ultra*
Littora Juvernæ promovimus, & modo captas
Orcadas, & minima contentos nocte Britannos?

What though the *Orcades* have own'd our power?
What though *Juverna's* tam'd, and *Britain's* shore,
That boasts the shortest night?——

The Panegyrick spoken to Constantine the Emperor, seems also to intimate, that Ireland was subject to him The words are, *Britain is so far recovered; that even those Nations which lie along the* coasts *of the same Island, are become obedient to your command* We are likewise informed by later Chronicles, that Ireland together with *Britain* and *Thule*, fell to the share of Constantine, son of Constantine the Great, in the division of the Empire And that silly story of *Cæsarea*, Noah's Grandchild, has at least so much of Cæsar in it, that it seems to intimate the arrival of some *Cæsar* or other in Ireland However, I cannot be perswaded, that this Island was conquer'd by the Romans. Without question, it had been well for it, if it had, as it would have been a means to civilize the Nation For wherever the Romans were Conquerors, they introduc'd humanity among the Conquer'd, and, except where *they* rul'd, there was no such a thing as humanity, learning, or politeness, in any part of Europe Their neglect of this Island may be charg'd upon them, as very inconsiderate For, from this quarter, Britain was spoil'd and infested with most cruel Enemies; which seems to have been foreseen by Augustus, when he neglected Britain for fear of the dangers that threatened from the adjacent Countries Towards the decline of the Roman Empire, a Nation of the Scots or Scythians (for *formerly*, as Strabo writes, *all the people westward were term'd Celto-Scythæ*,) grew potent in Ireland, and begun to make a great figure in the world In the reign of *Honorius* and *Arcadius* the Emperors, it was inhabited by Nations of the *Scots*, as Orosius writes Hence Claudian his Contemporary, *Cæsarea* *Scots, in Ireland*

Scotorum cumulos flevit glacialis Ierne

O're heaps of *Scots* when icy *Ireland* mourn'd

And in another place,

—— *Totam cum Scotus Hiberniam*
Movit

When *Scots* all *Ireland* mov'd to sudden war

For from hence the Scots made their Descents into Britain, and are often repuls'd with great loss *Irish from Spain*

But from whence they came into *Ireland*, Ninnius a very ancient Author and Disciple of Elvodugus (who by his own testimony liv'd in the year 830, under *Anaraugh*, King of Anglesey and Guineth,) will inform you For, when he has told us, that in the third age of the World the Britains came into Britain, and that the Scythians came into Ireland in the fourth, he proceeds to tell us, *That last of all the* Scots *came from Spain into Ireland. The first that arriv'd, was* Partholanus *with one thousand men and women, who multiply'd to the number of four thousand, and then a great mortality befel them, so that all dy'd in a week, without so much as one surviving The second that landed in Ireland was* Nemethus, *the Son of* Aguomine, *who by report was a year and half together upon the Sea, and at last got to a harbour in Ireland with his shatter'd Vessels From hence he return'd into Spain; and after that, the three Sons of a Spanish* † *Knight came hither in thirty* Cules, *with thirty wives in each* Cule, *and continued here a year The last that arriv'd, was Elam-ho'tor, whose posterity continues here to this day* With this, agrees Henry of Huntington *The Britains in the third age of the world came into Britain; and the* Scots *in the fourth age into Ireland And though these things are not very certain, yet that they came from Spain into Ireland is manifest, and, that some part of them set sail again, and made a third Nation among the* Britains *and* Picts *in Britain* The receiv'd Opinion among the Irish doth likewise confirm this; who value themselves upon being the offspring of the Spaniards Neither is it strange, that so many should come into Ireland from the north of Spain; which (as Strabo writes) is *Bartholanus in another place* *† Miles Or perhaps of one Milesius* *Otherwise call'd Clan Hector*

ery

very barren, and scarce habitable From that passage of Ninnius, we may infer that the coming over of Bartholanus and Nimetheus, is to be dated much *later*, than they have fix'd it I need not put the reader in mind again, that this Country was call'd *Scotia* from the *Scots*

Christianity in Ireland

* These Scots, not many years after, were converted to Christianity in Ireland (though they would have that Story in *Rufinus* concerning the conversion of the *Hibers* in Asia, to be meant of them) Then also Palladius the Bishop was sent to them by Pope Celestin Whereupon Prosper Aquitanus writes against *Collator*, *Celestin delivered the Britains from the* Pelagian *heresy, by banishing certain enemies to God's grace (who were then in their own native country) even from that unknown part of the Ocean, and, having Ordain'd a Bishop among the* Scots, *while he endeavour'd to preserve the Catholick Religion in an Island belonging to the Romans, he also induc'd a barbarous Nation to turn Christian* Yet Ninnius says that nothing was effected by Palladius (he being taken away by an untimely death,) and adds, upon the authority of the Irish writers, that the Christian Religion was planted in Ireland by *Patrick* This *Patrick* was a Britain, born in *Cluydsdal*, and related to *Martin* * of Tours, and was a disciple of St German, and appointed to succeed Palladius, by Pope Celestin He planted the Christian Religion in Ireland with such success, that the greatest part of that Country was converted, upon which, he was called the *Irish Apostle* Henricus Antisiodorensis or of Auxerres, an ancient writer, has this passage concerning him in his Book about the Miracles of St German *Forasmuch as the glory of a Father becomes most conspicuous in the government of his Sons, among the many Sons of Christ which are believed to be his Disciples, it shall suffice in short to mention one, the most famous of all others, as the course of his actions shew, and this is* Patrick, *the Apostle of the Irish Nation, who being eighteen years under his most holy Discipline, drew from that Fountain no small knowledge in the Holy Scriptures The godly Bishop, observing him to be stedfast in Religion, eminent for Virtue, and accomplish'd in Learning; and deeming it unfit, that a husbandman of such strength and skill should lie idle in the Lord's Vineyard, recommended him to the holy Pope Celestin, by Segetius one of his Presbyters, who was directed to inform the Apostolical See of the worth of this holy man Being therefore approved of, and enabled by the authority and blessing of his* Holiness, *he took a voyage into Ireland, and, being made the peculiar Apostle of that Nation, as he then instructed them by his preaching and miracles, so he does now, and will for ever, adorn them with the wonderful Power and Privileges of his Apostleship*

In the year 431
Palladius
Vincent lib 9 c 7
St *Patrick*
* *Turonensi*

St. *Patrick's* disciples were so great proficients in the Christian Religion, that in the age following Ireland was term'd *Sanctorum Patria*, *i e* the Country of Saints, and the Scotch Monks in Ireland and Britain were very eminent for their sanctity and learning, and sent many holy men into all parts of Europe, who were the first founders of *Luxeul Abby* in Burgundy, of *Bolby-Abby* in Italy, of *Wirtzburgh Abby* in France, of S *Gallus* in Switzerland, of *Malmesbury*, *Lindesfern*, and many other Monasteries, in Britain For, out of Ireland came *Celius Sedulius* the Presbyter, *Columba*, *Columbanus*, *Colman*, *Aidan*, *Gallus*, *Kilian*, *Maidulph*, *Brendan*, and many others, celebrated for their holy lives, and for their learning The forementon'd Henry of *Auxerre* is to be understood of these Monks, in this address of his to the Emperor *Carolus Calvus* *What should I speak of* Ireland, *which slighting the dangers of the sea, comes with great numbers of Philosophers into our Country, and the most eminent among them do voluntarily banish themselves, to attend the most wise Solomon*

The Monks of Ireland holy and learned

The *Monastick Profession*, then in its infancy, was very different from this of our age. They endeavour'd to be what they profess'd, and were above dissimulation and hypocrisy If they err'd, it was through simplicity, and not out of wickedness, or obstinacy As for wealth and the things of this world, they contemn'd them to such a degree, that they did not only not covet, but even reject them, when either offer'd to them, or descended by inheritance For *Columbanus*, who was himself a Monk of Ireland, being press'd (as Abbot *Walafrid* writes) by Sigebert King of the Franks, with many large promises, not to leave his Kingdom, made this noble reply (the same that Eusebius tells us of Thadæus) *That it became not them to gape after other men's riches, who had left and forsaken their own for the sake of Christ* The British *Bishops* seem no less to have despis'd riches, since they had no subsistence of their own Thus, as we find in Sulpitius Severus, *The Bishops of Britain in the Council holden at Rhimini were maintain'd by the publick, having nothing of their own to live upon* The Saxons in that age flock'd hither, as to the great mart of learning, and this is the reason why we find it so often in our Writers of the Lives of Saints, *Such an one was sent over into Ireland to be educated* *, and the reason also of this passage in the life of *Sulgenus*, who flourish'd † 700 years ago

Monks
Walafrid
Contempt of riches
The British Bishops
* V *Bed l* 3 *c* 7 & 27
† 600, C

> *Exemplo patrum commotus amore legendi,*
> *Ivit ad Hibernos, Sophia, mirabile, claros*

> With love of learning, and examples fir'd,
> To *Ireland*, fam'd for wisdom, he repair'd

And perhaps our fore fathers, the Saxons took the draught and form of their letters from them, their character being the same with that, which is at this day used in Ireland

The Saxons seem to have borrowed their letters from the Irish

Nor is there any reason to wonder, that Ireland, which for the most part is * now rude and barbarous, without any parts of polite Learning, did abound with persons of so great Piety and Abilities, in an age when learning was little heeded in any other part of Christendom, since the wisdom of Providence sows the seeds of Religion and Learning, now in one Nation, and then in another, as in so many *Beds*, to the end, that by every transplantation, a new growth may shoot up and flourish, to his glory and the good of mankind

* So said, ann 1607; but it is since much improved and civilized
Religion and Learning flourish sometimes in one Country, and sometimes in another

However, War by little and little put a stop to the study of Religion and Learning in this Kingdom For in the year 644, *Egfrid* King of Northumberland spoil'd Ireland with fire and sword, which was then a very kind ally to England, and for this he is heavily complain'd of and condemn'd by Bede Afterwards, the Norwegians, under the conduct of *Turgesius*, wasted this Country in a most dismal manner for the space of 30 years together, but he being cut off by ambush, the inhabitants fell upon the Norwegians, and made such an entire defeat and slaughter of them, that hardly one escaped These Norwegians were without doubt the Normans who (as Rheginus tells us) in Charles the Great's time *invaded Ireland, an Island of the Scots, and were put*

Ireland wasted by the *Northumbrians*
— by the *Norwegians*
Normanni

to

Ireland wasted by the Oustmanni Those perhaps, whom Tacitus calls Æstiones Eginardus, Aistij — and conquered by the Saxons

to fight by them Afterwards, the *Oustmanni*, i e the East men, came from the sea coast of Germany into Ireland, where, under colour of trade and merchandise, being admitted into some of their Cities, in a short time they began a very terrible war. Much about this time, *Edgar* the most potent King of the *English*, conquer'd a great part of Ireland For thus we find it in a certain Charter of his *Unto whom God has graciously granted, together with the Empire of England, the dominion over all the Kingdoms of the Islands, with their fierce Kings, as far as Norway; and the conquest of the greatest part of* Ireland, *with her most noble city* Dublin

Conquest by K Henry II

These storms from foreign parts, were soon succeeded by a much worse storm at home, namely *Civil* Dissentions, which made way for the English Conquest of that Country For Henry II King of England, seeing the differences and emulations among the petty Princes of Ireland, took the Opportunity, and in the year 1155 mov'd the Conquering of Ireland to his Barons, for the use of his brother William of Anjou However, by advice of his Mother *Maud* the Empress, this design was deferr'd to another time

Robert de Monte ad annum 1185

Dermic the son of Murchard

* Dermond Mac Morough

1167

Not many years after, *Dermicius* son of Murchard (* *Dermot Mac Morrog*, as they call him) who govern'd the east part of Ireland, called in Latin *Lagenia*, and commonly *Leinster*, was, for his tyranny and extravagant lusts (for he had ravish'd the wife of *O-Rorke*, daughter of a petty King of *Meath*) driven from his Country, and obtain'd forces of King Henry the second, to restore him He made this contract also with Richard Earl of Pembroke, surnamed *Strongbow*, of the family of Clare, that if he would assist him, he would insure the succession of his Kingdom to the Earl, and give him his daughter *Eva* to wife Upon, this the Earl forthwith raised a brave Army, consisting of Welsh and English, and drew over the *Fitz-Geralds*, *Fitz-Stephens*, and other of the English Nobility, to assist him and not only restor'd *Dermic* his Father-in law, but in a few years made such progress in the conquest of Ireland, that the King of England began to grow jealous of his power So that he set forth a Proclamation, requiring the said Earl and his adherents, upon great penalties, to return out of Ireland; declaring, that if they did not forthwith obey, they should be banish'd, and their goods confiscate Hereupon, the Earl did by deed and covenant make over to the King all that he had in Ireland whether in right of his wife or of his sword, and had the Earldoms of *Weisford*, *Offory*, *Carterlogh*, and *Kildare*, with some castles, bestow'd on him by the King, to hold of him

Richard Strongbow.

Henry II enters *Ireland*

Ware, Ant Hib p 270

Gerald Cambrens & MS in the hands of Baron Howth

* O Brian

† Meath, C

After this, King Henry the second raised an army, and sailed over into Ireland in the year 1172, and obtain'd the soveraignty of the Island, [(upon which a Colonie was sent thither from England and Wales, and had Lands granted and assigned them there)] For the States of Ireland transfer'd to him their whole power and authority (namely, *Rotheric O Conor Dun*, that is, *the brown Monarch of Ireland*, *Dermot Mac Carty*, King of Cork, *Donald* * *O Bren*, King of Limerick; *O Carel*, King of Uriel, *Mac Shaghlin*, King of Ophaly, *O Rorke*, King of † Brefny or Letrim, [who married the daughter of *O Maghlin* King of Meath,] *O Neale*, King of Ulster; with all the rest of the Nobility, and People, by Charters, sign'd, deliver'd, and sent to Rome; from whence it was confirmed by a * Bull of Pope Hadrian, and by a Ring, sent to him as a token of his Investiture, and also by the authority of certain Provincial Synods Afterwards, King Henry the second bestow'd the *Sovereignty of Ireland* upon his son *John*, which was confirm'd by a Bull from Pope Urban, *who in testimony thereof sent him a Crown of Peacocks Feathers embroider'd with Gold* 1186

* [illegible] and [illegible]

King John grants to the Pope Hoveden

Some Authors affirm, that when this Prince came to the Crown, he granted by his Charter, that both Ireland and England should be held of the Church of Rome, and that he received it from the Church, as a Feudatory and Vicegerent, and obliged his Successors to pay three hundred Marks to the Bishop of that See Yet the eminent [Sir] *Thomas Moor*, who sacrific'd his life to the Authority of the Pope, denies this to be true For he says, the Romanists can shew no such Grant, and that they have never demanded the said Money, nor have the Kings of England acknowledg'd it to be due However, with submission to this great man, the thing is really otherwise; as most clearly appears from the Parliament-Rolls, which are an Evidence incontestable For in a Parliament, in Edward the third's Reign, the Chancellor of England informs them, That the Pope intended to cite the King of England to Rome, as well for homage, as for the tribute due and payable from England and Ireland, to which King John had bound himself and his Successors, and desir'd their opinion in it The Bishops requir'd a day to consider of this matter apart, as likewise did the Nobles, and Commons The next day they met again, and unanimously voted and declared, That forasmuch as neither King *John*, nor any other King whatsoever, could put the Kingdom under such servitude, but by consent of Parliament (which was never had,) and further, seeing that whatever he had done in that way, was directly contrary to the Oath which he solemnly took before God at his Coronation, If the Pope would insist upon it, they were resolved to oppose him to the utmost, with their lives and fortunes Such also as are learned in the law, make the Charter of King *John* to be void, by the clause of reservation in the end, *Saving to us and our heirs, all our Rights, Liberties, and Royalties* But this is out of my road

Lords of Ireland

* So said ann 1607

From King John's time, the Kings of England were stiled *Lords of Ireland*, till, within memory of * our Fathers, Henry the eighth was declared *King of Ireland* by the States of that Realm assembled in Parliament, the title of *Lord* seeming not so sacred and awful to certain seditious persons, as that of *King* In the year 1555, when Queen Mary, by her Ambassadors, offer'd her obedience in the name of the Kingdom of England, to Pope Paul the fourth, this name and title of *Kingdom* of Ireland was confirm'd by the Pope in these words *To the praise and glory of Almighty God, and his most glorious mother the Virgin Mary, to the honour of the whole heavenly Choir, and the exaltation of the Catholick Faith We, at the humble Request of King Philip and Queen Mary, made unto us, do, by the advice of our brethren and the plenitude of our Apostolical authority erect Ireland into a* Kingdom, *and do for ever dignifie it with the title, dignity, honour, powers, rights, distinctions, prerogatives, precedence, Royal preeminences, and all other Privileges, which any Christian Realms have, use, and enjoy, or may have, use, and enjoy, in time to come*

Catalogue of those who conquer'd Ireland

Having met with a Catalogue of those English Noblemen, who went in the first invasion of Ireland, and with great valour subdu'd it to the Crown of England, lest I should seem to envy them and their posterity the glory of this atchievement, I will here give you your Names out of the Record in the *Chancery* of Ireland, with this title;

The

The Persons who came with Dermic Mac Morrog *into* IRELAND.

Richard Strongbow, Earl of Pembroke, who by *Eve* the daughter of *Morrog*, a petty King of *Ireland*, had one only daughter, who brought to *William Mareschall* the title of Earl of Pembroke with a fair Estate in Ireland, and had issue five Sons, who succeded one another, but all without issue; and as many Daughters, who enrich'd their Husbands (*Hugh Bigod*, Earl of Norfolk, *Guarin Montchensey*, *Gilbert Clare*, Earl of Glocester, *William Ferrars*, Earl of Derby, and *William Breose*,) with Children, Honours, and Possessions

Robert Fitz-Stephens
Harvey de Mont Marish
Maurice Prendergest
Robert Barr
Meiler Meilerine
Maurice Fitz-Girald
Redmund, nephew to *Stephen*
William Ferrand
Miles de Cogan
Richard de Cogan
Gualter de Ridensford
Gualter, *Alexander* } Sons of *Maurice Girald*.
William Notte
Robert Fitz-Bernard
Hugh de Lacy
William Fitz Aldelm
William Macarell
Hunfrey Bohun
Hugh de Gundevill
Philip de Hasting
Hugh Tirell
David Walsh
Robert Poer
Osbert de Harloter
William de Bendenges
Adam de Gernez
Philip de Breos
Griffin Nephew of *Stephen*.
Ralph Fitz-Stephen
Walter Barr
Philip Walsh
Adam de Hereford.

To whom, out of Giraldus Cambrensis, may be added,

John de Curcy
Hugh Contilon
Redmond Cantimore
Redmund Fitz-Hugh
Miles of St. Davids, and others.

THE GOVERNMENT OF THE KINGDOM OF IRELAND.

SINCE *Ireland* hath been subject to the Crown of England, the Kings of this Realm have sent their *Vice-Roys* to administer the publick affairs there; who at first, in their Letters Patents or Commissions, were stil'd *Keepers of Ireland*, after that, at pleasure, *Justices*, *Lieutenants*, and *Deputies* of *Ireland*. Their Jurisdiction and authority is ample and Royal, they make war and peace, [with Rebels, or Invaders, upon sudden Emergencies,] have power to fill all Places and Offices, except some very few, to pardon all Crimes, but that of High treason, to confer Knighthood, *&c.* These Letters Patents, when any one enters upon this honourable office, are publickly read, and after the new Deputy has taken the usual Oath before the Chancellor, the sword, which is to be carried before him, is delivered into his hands, and he is seated in a Throne, attended by the Chancellor of the Kingdom, the Members of the Privy Council, the Peers and Nobles, the King at Arms, a Serjeant at Arms, and other Officers of State. So that, whether we consider his jurisdiction and authority, or his train, attendance, and splendour, there is certainly no Vice Roy in Christendom that comes nearer the grandeur and majesty of a King.

Lords Deputies of *Ireland*.

His Council are, the Chancellor, the Treasurer, and such others of the Earls, Bishops, Barons, and Judges, as are of the Privy Council. For Ireland has the same Orders and Degrees of Honour that England has, namely, Dukes, Marquisses, Earls, Barons, Esquires, *&c.*

Orders or Degrees in *Ireland*.

THE

THE Courts or Tribunals OF IRELAND.

HE Supream Court in *Ireland*, is the *Parliament*, which, at the pleasure of the King of *England*, is called and dissolved by his Deputy, and yet in Edward the second's time it was enacted, *That Parliaments shou'd be held in Ireland every year* Here are like wise four Law Terms in the year, as in England, and [a] four Courts of Justice, the *Chancery*, *King's Bench*, *Common Pleas*, and the *Exchequer* [There was also the Court of *Star Chamber*, called *The Court of Castle-Chamber*, because it was usually kept in the Castle of Dublin, but it hath never been held since the Court of Star-Chamber was suppressed in England] Here are also *Justices of Assize*, *Nisi prius*, and *Oyer and Terminer*, as in England, and *Justices of Peace* in every County and the King has his *Serjeant at Law*, his *Attorney*, and *Solicitor General*

Clauf an An 12

Courts.

[a] Five—the Star Chamber, C

There [b] were also other Governors to administer justice in the remoter Provinces, (he in Conaught [c] was stiled *chief Commissioner*, and he in Munster, *President* who [d] had certain of the Gentry and Lawyers to assist them, and [e] were all directed by the Lord Deputy [But since the Country came to be well inhabited with English, and far more civilized than heretofore, these Presidencies of Munster and *Conaught* have been superseded, *viz* by King Charles the second, about the year 1671]

[b] Are, C

[c] Is, C

[d] Have, C

[e] Are, C

As for their Laws, the Common law us'd there, is the same with this of our's in England For thus it is in the Records of the Kingdom *King Henry the third, in the twelfth year of his reign, sent an order to his Justiciary in Ireland, that he should assemble the Archbishops, Bishops, Barons, and Knights, and* [illegible] *John to be read to them, which he did accordingly, and oblig'd them to take an oath to observe the Laws and Customs of England, and that they would be govern'd by the same.* And even the Parliamentary Laws, or Statutes, of England, were in use in Ireland, till King Henry the seventh's time For in the tenth year of his reign, they were establish'd and confirm'd by Authority of Parliament in Ireland But since that time, they have had Parliamentary Statutes of their own making

Law

Besides the civil Magistrates aforesaid, [f] they had also one Military Officer, named the *Marshal*, who [g] was very serviceable to the State, not only in restraining the insolence of the soldiers, but also in checking the rebels, who [h] were apt to be troublesom now and then [But there being now no War in the Kingdom, neither is there any Marshal] This office in old time belong'd hereditarily to the Lords *Morley* of England, as appears by the publick Records For King John gave it to be held in fee, in these very words *We have given and granted to John Marshal, for his homage and service, our Marshalship of Ireland, with all appurtenances We have given him likewise, for his homage and service, the* Cantred *wherein stands the town of Kilkenny, to have and to hold to him and his heirs, of us and our heirs* From him it descended, in a right line, to the Barons of *Morley* This Marshal [i] had under him one [k] *Provost Marshal*, and sometimes more, according to the difficulties and exigences of affairs, who exercised their authority by Commission and [illegible] under the Great Seal of Ireland But [illegible] other matters of this nature, I leave to the diligence of others Concerning the methods of [illegible] and *Government* among the *Wild Irish*, I shall insert somewhat in a more proper place, when I come to treat of their *Manners* and *Customs*

[f] They have, C

[g] Marshal of *Ireland* Is, C

[h] Are, C

[a] of King John

[i] Has, C

[k] Sometimes more, C [illegible]

THE

THE DIVISION OF IRELAND.*

* Vid Waræ's Ant Hib c 3 p 11

Division of *Ireland*

Reland, according to the *Manners* and *Customs* of the Inhabitants, is divided into two parts They who [would] reject all Laws, and live after a barbarous manner, are called *the Irishry*, or more commonly the *wild Irish*, but the civiliz'd part, who submit themselves [willingly] to the laws, are term'd the *English-Irish*, and their Country the *English Pale* for the first English that came hither, mark'd out their bounds in the more easterly and the richest part of the Island, Within which compass, even * at this day, some remain uncivilized, and pay little obedience to the laws, whereas some without, are as courteous and genteel as one would desire [However, the King's Writ runs now through the whole Kingdom, and every part thereof is amesnable to Law] But, if we consider the more early state of the Kingdom, it must, from its situation, or rather number of Governors, be divided into five parts (for it was anciently a *Pentarchy*, namely, *Munster* southward, *Leinster* eastward, *Connaught* westward, *Ulster* northward, and *Meath* almost in the middle Which, as to civil administration, are thus divided into Counties.

Ann 1607

In *Munster*, are the Counties of
- *Kerry*
- [d] *Desmond*
- *Cork*
- *Waterford*
- *Limerick*.
- *Tiperary*, [e] with the County of the *Holy Cross*

[d] Now, some such part of Kerry and part in Cork.

[e] Swallow'd up in Tipperary

In *Leinster*, are the Counties of
- *Kilkenny*
- *Caterlough*
- *Queen's County*
- *King's County*
- *Kildare*
- *Weishford*,
- *Dublin*

In * *Meath*, are the Counties of
- *East Meath*
- *West Meath*.
- *Longford*

* *Meath* is now swallowed up in *Leinster*

In *Connaught*, are the Counties of
- [f] *Twomund*
- *Galloway*.
- *Mato*.
- *Slego*.
- *Leitrim*
- *Roscommon*

[f] Or Clare formerly part of Munster but lately added to the Conaught Circuit

In

In *Ulster*, are the Counties of
- *Louth*
- *Caven*
- *Farmanagh*
- *Monaghan*
- *Armagh*
- *Doun*
- *Antrim*
- *Colran*
- *Tir Oen*
- *Tir-Conell*, or *Donegall*

Ecclesiastical Jurisdiction

The Ecclesiastical Government of Ireland hath been from ancient time by Bishops, consecrated either by the Archbishop of Canterbury, or by one another. But in the year 1152 (as we find it in Philip of Flattesbury) *Christianus Bishop of Lismore, Legat of all Ireland, held a famous Council at* [a] *Meath, where were present the Bishops, Abbots, Kings, Dukes and* [b] *Magistrates of Ireland, and there, by authority of the Pope, with advice of the Cardinals, and consent of the Bishops, Abbots, and others there met together, four Archbishopricks were establish'd in Ireland, Armagh, Dublin, Cassil,* and *Tuam*.

[a] Mell
[b] Majores natu

Ancient Ecclesiastical Division

The Bishopricks which were under these, formerly (for some have been abolish'd to feed the greedy humour of ill times, and others have been mix'd and united, and others again translated) I desire to subjoin in their ancient State, out of an old Roman Provincial copied from the Original, [adding only the changes that have been since made, to lead us, in some measure, to the *present* Ecclesiastical State or Division in Ireland.]

Under the Archbishop of *Armagh*, Primate of all Ireland, are the Bishops of
- *Meath*, or [c] *Cluanard*
- *Doun*, otherwise *Dundalethglass*
- *Clogh*, otherwise *Lugundun*, [now *Clogher*.]
- *Conner* [united to *Down*.]
- *Ardachad* [or *Ardagh*.]
- *Rathbot* [or *Rapho*.]
- *Rathluc*, [incorporated with *Derry*.]
- *Dalr-liguir*
- *Dearrib*, [now *Derry* or *London-derry*.]

[c] *Eluanirand*, C

Under the Archbishop of *Dublin*, are the Bishops of
- *Glendelac*, [united to *Dublin*.]
- *Fern*, [united to *Leighlin*.]
- *Offory*, otherwise *de Canic*, [and *Kilkenny*.]
- *Lechlin*, [or *Leighlin*.]
- *Kildare*, otherwise *Dare*

Under the Archbishop of *Cassil*, are the Bishops of
- *Laonie*, or *de Kendalnan*, [now *Killaloe*.]
- *Limrick*
- *Isle of Gathay*
- *Cellumabrath*, [*Kilfenora*, united to *Killaloe* or *Tuam*.]
- *Melice*, or *de Emileth*, [*Emly*, annex'd to *Cashel*.]
- *Rosse*, otherwise *Roscree*
- *Waterford*, otherwise *de Baltifordian*
- *Lismore*, [united to *Waterford*.]
- *Clon*, otherwise *de Cluanan* [now *Cloyne*.]
- *Corcage* [or *Cork*.]
- *De Rosalither* [united to *Cork*.]
- *Ardefert* [united to *Limerick*.]

Under the Archbishop of *Tuam*, are the Bishops of
- *Duac*, otherwise *Killmacduoc*, [*Kilmacough*, united to *Clonfert*.]
- *De Mageo*
- *Enachdun*
- *De Cellaiaro*
- *De Roscomon*
- *Clonfert*
- [d] *Achad* [united to *Killalla*.]
- *Lade* otherwise *Killaleth*, [now *Killalla*.]
- *De Conany*
- *De Killmunduach*
- *Elphin*

[Besides these Alterations already mention'd, the Bishopricks of *Dalnliquir*, *Isle of Galbay*, *Roscree*, *Mage*, *Enachdun*, *de Celaiar*, *Roscomon*, and *Conany*, are united to some of the rest, so that, at this day, there are no such in being; but in that ancient Catalogue, those of *Dromore* and *Killmore* are wholly omitted

Present Ecclesiastical Division. The present Ecclesiastical Division of the Church of Ireland, stands as follows.

Under the Archbishop of *Armagh*, are the Bishops of
- *Meath*
- *Kilmore* and *Ardagh*
- *Dromore*
- *Clogher*
- *Raphoe*
- *Down* and *Connor*
- *Derry*

Under the Archbishop of *Dublin*, are the Bishops of
- *Kildare*
- *Ferns* and *Laughlin*
- *Offory*

Under the Archbishop of *Cassil*, are the Bishops of
- *Waterford* and *Lismore*
- *Limerick*
- *Killaloe*
- *Corke* and *Rosse*
- *Cloyne*

Under the Archbishop of *Tuam*, are the Bishops of
- *Elphin*
- *Clonfert*
- *Killalla* and *Achonry*]

MOMO-

MOMONIA, *or* MOUNSTER.

OMONIA, *in Irish* Mown, [a] *in compounds* Wown, *and English* Mounster, *lies to the south, and is expos'd to the* Vergivian *sea, being separated from* Connaught *for some space by the river* Sheny *or* Shanon, *and from* Leinster *by the river* [b] Neor. *Formerly, it was divided into many parts, as* Towoun, *North Mounster*, Deswoun, *South Mounster*, Hierwoun, *West Mounster*, Mean-woun, *Middle Mounster, and* Urwoun, *the forepart of Mounster, but at this day it is divided into two,* West Mounster *and* South Mounster. West Mounster *was in old time the country of the* Luceni, *the* Velibri, *and the* Uterini, South Mounster *was that of the* Oudiæ *or* Vodiæ *and the* Coriondi, *but at present it is distinguish'd into* [c] *five Counties, viz.* Kerry, Cork, Limerick, Tiperary, *and* Waterford.

[a] In one ... context.

[b] Shure.

[c] Seven, C. by adding Desmond, and Holy Cross.

In the most westerly part of Ireland, and where it views the Cantabrian Ocean *fronting, at a great distance to the south-west,* Gallicia *in Spain, there formerly dwelt the* Velibri *and the* Luceni, *as* Orosius *tell's us. The* Luceni *(who seem to derive their name and original from the* Lucensi *of Gallicia on the opposite coast of Spain, of whose name some remains are to this day in the Barony of* Lyxnaw,*) were seated, as I suppose, in the County of Kerry, and in* Conoglogh *hard by, upon the River Shanon.*

The County of *KERRY*.

HE County of *Kerry*, near the mouth of the Shannon, shoots forth like a little tongue into the sea; the waves roaring on both sides of it. This County stands high, and has many wild and woody hills, between which lie many vallies, whereof some produce corn, others wood. This [a] was once reckon'd a County Palatine, and the Earls of *Desmond* had therein the dignity and prerogatives of Counts Palatine, by the gift of Edward the third, who granted them *all royalties, except four pleas, Fire, Rape, Forestall, and Treasure-trouve, with the profits arising* [b] *out of compositions for Manslaughter*, which were reserved to the Kings of England. But this Privilege, through the wickedness of such, who out of ignorance and perverseness abus'd it, became long since the sink of Mischief, and the refuge of Sedition, [and is now extinct.] In the very entrance into this County, there is a territory called *Clan moris*, from one *Moris*, of the family of *Raimund la Grosse*, whose heirs were call'd Barons of *Lixnaw*; and at this day, the Family of *Fitz Morris* are Barons, under the joint titles of *Kerry* and *Lixnaw*.] [c] Near it, runs a little river, now nameless; though perhaps, by its situation, the same which Ptolemy calls the *Dur*. It passes by *Trasley*, [[d] now a thriving Place; being the Shire-Town, and a Corporation;] where was once a House of the Earls of Desmund. Hard by, lies *Ardart*, the See of a poor Bishop, called of *Ardfert*. [In the Irish Histories and Records, the Bishops of this place are sometimes called Bishops of *Kerry*, (which is here observed, to prevent mistakes,) and now the Bishoprick it self is united to that of *Limerick*.] Almost at the end of this Promontory, there lies on one side *Dingle*, a commodious Harbour [is also a walled Town, and a Corporation,] and on the other side *Smerwick*, contracted from *St. Mary wic*, a road for Ships, where Girald Earl of Desmund, a person noted for treachery to his Prince and Country, wasting and spoiling *Mounster*, receiv'd some [e] confus'd Troops of Italians and Spaniards, sent to his assistance by Pope Gregory the thirteenth and the King of Spain, who fortifying themselves here, and calling it *Fort del Ore*, threaten'd the Country with ruin. But this danger was at an end by the coming and first attack of the Vice-roy, the most famous and warlike Baron, the Lord *Arthur Grey*. For they immediately surrender'd, and were most of them put to the Sword, which was thought, in policy, the wisest and safest course, considering the then present posture of Affair, and that the Rebels were ready to break out in all quarters. In conclusion, the Earl of Desmund was himself forc'd to fly into the Woods thereabouts, and soon after was set upon in a poor Cottage by one or two Soldiers, who wounded him, and being afterwards discovered, he was beheaded for his disloyalty, and for the vast mischief that he had done to this Country. 1583

[a] Is, C.

[b] De croc...

Clan Moris

[c] Cross the middle of it, C.

Dur, riv.

Trailey

[d] A small Town, now, almost desolate, C.

Bishoprick of Ardart

Dingle

Smerwick

[e] Tumultuaria.

Arthur Lord Grey.

[In

Killarny

Castlemaine

See *Essex*

Beerhaven

Castle Island

In *Kerry* also is a thriving Village called *Killarny*, and near it the famous Castle of *Rosse*; and a considerable Lead-Mine. From a place in this Shire, the *Palmers*, have taken their title of Earl of *Castlemaine*, which being extinct, as to that Family, the place hath since given the title of Viscount to Sir *Richard Child*, Baronet, of the Kingdom of *Great Britain*. In like manner, *Beerhaven* hath given the title of Viscount to the Family of *Berkley*, and now affords the same Title to the Family of *Chetwynd*. Also, the Families of *Petty*, and *Herbert*, have derived their respective titles from hence; the first (who was before Baron *Shelburn*) advanced lately to the honour of Viscount *Dunkieron*, and also of Earl of *Shelburn*; and the second, who are Barons under the style of *Castle Island*.]

A ridiculous persuasion of the wild Irish

[f] So said, ann. 160-

Perhaps some would impute it to want of gravity in me, should I barely mention an Opinion, or rather a Belief and Persuasion, of the [f] wild Irish, That he, who in the great clamour and outcry (which the Soldiers usually make before an Engagement) does not *huzza* as the rest do, is suddenly snatch'd from the ground, and carried through the air into these desolate Vallies, in what part of Ireland soever he be; that there he eats grass, laps water, has no sense of happiness or misery, has some remains of reason but none of speech, and that at long-run he is caught by the dogs in hunting, and brought back to his own home.

---

* Now annex'd part of it to *Kerry* and part to *Cork*

* DESMONIA or DESMOND.

Desmond

Beneath the Country of the old *Luceni*, lies *Desmond*, stretch'd out along way to the South. It is call'd in Irish *Deswown*, and in English *Desmond*, and was formerly peopled by the *Velabri*, and the *Iberni*, who in some Copies are call'd *Uterini*.

Velabri

The *Velabri* seem to derive their name from *Aber*, i. e. *Æstuaries*, for they dwelt among Friths, on parcels of Land divided from one another by great incursions of the Sea, from which the *Artabri* and *Cantabri* in Spain did also take their names. Among these Arms of the Sea, are three several Promontories (besides *Kerry* above mentioned,) shooting out with their crooked shores to the South-west, which the Inhabitants formerly called *Hierwoun*, i. e. *West moun ster*. The first of them, which lies between *Dingle-Icy* and the river *Mair* [otherwise *Kilmaire* or *Kinmaire*,] is called *Clan car* [or rather *Glancar*, from the river *Carah* and the *Glin* through which it runs, and is divided into the Baronies of *Iveragh* and *Dunkerran*,] and has a Castle at *Dunkeran*, built by the *Carews* of England, [but is now the possession of *Hayes*, an English Family.] In this Castle dwelt *Donald* * *Sullevan More*, a petty King of Irish descent, who in the year 1566 surrender'd his Territory to Queen Elizabeth, and had it restor'd to him, to hold of her after the English manner, by fealty and homage. At the same time, he was created Baron of *Valentia* (an Island adjoining) and Earl of *Clan-car*; being a person of great power and eminence in these parts, and formerly a bitter enemy to the *Fitz Giralds*, who dispossess'd his Ancestors (Kings, as he pretended, of *Desmond*) of this their ancient seat and inheritance. He enjoy'd not the honour very long, having but one daughter legitimate, whom he marry'd to *Florence Mac Carty*, and liv'd to be very old. [*Valentia*, the Island before mention'd, doth at this day give the title of Viscount to the Family of *Annesley*.]

* *Mac Carty*, C. 1565

Baron of *Valence*

Earl of *Glencar*

The second Promontory, lying between two Bays, *viz.* the *Maire* and the *Bantre*, is called *Bear*, the Soil of which is a hungry gravel mix'd with stones, where [b] liv'd *O Swillivant Bere* and *O Swilivant Bantre*, both of the same family, and men very eminent in these parts,

[b] Lives ... O Suilivant Bere

[but now the names are of no great note. A ridge of Hills running through this Promontory, makes the boundary between the Counties of *Cork* and *Kerry*. That part on the north-side, is the Barony of *Glanerough* in the County of *Kerry*; that on the South, is the half Barony of *Bear* in the County of *Cork*, to which the half Barony of *Bantry* joins.]

Iverah

The third Promontory, named *Eraugh* [or *Iveragh*, (at this day part of the Barony of *West Corbry* in the County of *Cork*,)] lies between *Bantre* and *Balatimore* or *Baltimore*, a Bay famous for plenty of Herrings, and yearly visited by a Fleet of Spaniards and Portuguese, in the very middle of winter, to fish for Codd. In this, the *O Mahons* had great possessions bestow'd upon them by *M. Carew*. This is that Promontory which Ptolemy calls *Notium*, or the South Promontory, and is at this day call'd *Missen head*. Under this Promontory (as we may see in that Author) the river *Iernus* falls into the Sea. As for the present name of that river, I dare hardly pretend to guess at it, unless it be that which is now call'd *Maire* [or *Kilmaire*,] and runs under *Drunkeran* aforesaid. I am as much at a loss for the People which Ptolemy places upon these Promontories, seeing their name differs in several Copies, *Iberni*, *Outerini*, *Iberi*, *Iverni*, unless perhaps they are a Colony of the *Iberi* in Spain, as well as their neighbours the *Luceni* and *Concani*.

O *Mahons*

The Promontory *Notium*

Iernus, riv.

Desmonia was formerly of great extent, even from the Sea to the river *Shanon*; and it was also call'd *South Mounster*. The *Fitz Giralds*, of the family of Kildare, having conquer'd the Irish, became Lords of very great possessions in these parts. Of these, *Maurice Fitz Thomas* (to whom *Thomas Carew*, heir to the Seigniory of *Desmond*, had made over his title) was in the third year of Edward the third created the first Earl of *Desmond*. Of the posterity of this Earl, many have been very rich and valiant, and Men of great Renown. But this glory was sully'd by *James*, who excluding his nephew, forcibly seiz'd the Estate, and impos'd upon the People those grievous tributes of *Coyne*, *Livery*, *Cocherings*, *Bonnughty*, &c. for the maintenance of his stout but ravenous Soldiers. His Son Thomas, as he was exceeding the same of

Earls of Desmond

the poor People, was apprehended by an Order from *John Tiptoft* Lord Deputy, and beheaded in the year 1467 for his own and his father's wickedness However, his Children were restor'd, and this honour was successively enjoy'd by his Posterity, till *Girald's* time, the rebel before mention'd; who being banish'd by Act of Parliament, *Desmond* was annex'd to the Crown, and reduc'd into a County, with a Sheriff to govern it from year to year; [and it is also an Earldom at this day, in the person of the Earl of *Denbigh* in England]

The most noted and considerable Families here, for Interest and Wealth, are those descended from the *Fitz Giralds*, who are known by several names, that have been assum'd by them upon several accounts

VODIÆ or *CORIONDI*.

EYOND the Iberi, *dwelt the* Odiæ *in a large Tract, who are call'd also* Vodiæ, *and* Udiæ, *a resemblance of which name remains very clear in the Territories of* Idou *and* Idouth, *as there doth of the* Coriondi *in the County of* Cork, *which borders upon them These People inhabited the Counties of* Cork, Tipperary, Limerick, *and* Waterford

The *Vodiæ*

The *Coriondi*

Comitatus Corcagiensis; commonly, *The County of* CORK

HE County of *Cork* (which was formerly a Kingdom, and contain'd all that Country upon the shore between *Lismore*, and St *Brend*, [[a] or Brandon-hills in *Kerry*,)] where it faces *Desmond* to the west, has in the midst of it *Muskeray*, a wild and woody Country, where *Cormac Mac Teg* [b] was very famous, and, towards the Sea, *Carbray*, where the *Mac Carties* were most considerable The first place that we come to upon the Coast, is *Ross* [a Bishop's See, now united to *Cork*] It is a road for Ships, and was formerly much frequented, but, now, by reason of a ridge of Sand, is disus'd From hence there shoots out a narrow neck of Land into a Peninsula, called, *The old head of Kinsale*, near which, the *Curcies* heretofore flourish'd in great state, descended from a brother of *John Curcy*, an Englishman, who subdu'd *Ulster* Of which Family, there still remains *Curcy* Baron of [c] *Kinsale*, but (such is the uncertainty of human Affairs) not considerable in point of Fortune [The ancient Seat here is now turn'd into a Light House]

[a] Perhaps *Mussinhead*, C

Muskeray

[b] Is, C

Carbray

Ross

Curcy, Baron of *Kinsale*

[c] *Ringrom*, C for *Ringroane*

Next, in a fertile Soil, upon the mouth of the river [d] *Bandon*, and well wooded, stands *Kinsale*, a very commodious Harbour, and a Town fortify'd with old Walls, under which, in the year 1601 the Kingdom of Ireland was at stake, and put to a fair trial whether it should belong to Spain or England For at that time, the Island was embroil'd by Enemies, foreign and domestick, and *Don John D' Aquila*, with an Army of eight thousand Veterans, had surpriz'd this place; relying upon the Censures which the Popes, Pius V, Gregory XIII, and Clement VIII, had thunder'd out against Queen Elizabeth, and upon the assistance of those Rebels, who had sent for them under pretence of establishing their Religion (the mask and disguise for all Villanies, in this degenerate age, wherein it occasions such warm Disputes!) In opposition to these, *Charles Blunt* Baron Montjoy Lord Deputy, though his Army was harrassed, and it was now winter, besieged the Town by Sea and Land, and at the same time took the Field against the Rebels, who were headed by the Earl of *Tir-Oen*, *O Donell Mac Gwyre*, and *Mac Mahound* and by his Valour and Conduct he so effectually suppress'd them, that, by the self-same Victory, he both recover'd the Town (which was surrender'd to him with the Spaniards in it,) and disarm'd the whole Kingdom of Ireland, when they had resolv'd to rebel, or rather were actually revolting Over against *Kinsale*, on the other side of the river, lies *Kerry wherry* [(called at this day *Kyrycurry*,)] a small territory [e] lately belonging to the Earls of *Desmond* Just before it, runs the River which Ptolemy calls [f] *Dourona*, and Giraldus Cambrensis, by the change of one letter, *Sauranus* and *Saveranus*, which, [(being at present called *Lee*, and,)] springing from the Mountains of *Muskery*, passes by the principal City of the County, adorn'd with an Episcopal See, to which the Bishoprick of *Clon* [g] was formerly annex'd Giraldus calls this *Corcagia*; the English, *Cork*, and the natives [h] *Corkig* It is of an oval form, enclos'd with Walls, and encompass'd with the Chanel of the River, which also crosses it, and is not accessible but by Bridges, lying along in one direct Street, that is continu'd by a bridge It is a populous [i] trading Town, and much resorted to, but so beset with [k] Rebels on all sides, that they are oblig'd to keep constant watch, as if the Town was continually besieged, and dare not marry out their Daughters into

[d] Bany C, Kinsale

The Spaniards driven out of *Ireland*

Kerry wherry

[e] So said, ann 1607

[f] *Avon more* near *Yoghal Ware*, p 2, Dauron, riv

[g] I, C

Cork

[h] *Corcach*, C

[i] Little trading Town, C

[k] Ann 1607, not so now

into the Country, but marry among themselves, whereby all the Citizens are related in some degree or other [At this day, it is mostly inhabited with English, who by their industry have so improved their Estates, Trade, and City, that it far exceeds any City in *Ireland*, *Dublin* only excepted In the Cemetery here, is a Steeple, which some think to have been a work of the Danes, and to have been used by them at first for a Watch Tower] They report, that *Brioc*, a very Religious Person (who in that fruitful age of Saints was so famous among the Gauls, and from whom the Diocese of *Sanbrioch* in Armorica, commonly call'd St *Brieu*, takes its name,) was born in this Town

St Brieu

Beneath *Cork*, the Chanel of the River is divided into two branches, which make a large and very pleasant Island [(called the *Great Island*)] over-against the chief Seat of the *Barrys*, an antient and eminent family, and thereupon it is called *Barry Court* For they are descended from Robert de Barry, an Englishman of great worth, *one who was ambitious rather to be really great, than to seem so, the first, that was wounded in the Conquest of Ireland and that ever* [l] *mann'd a Hawk in that Island* His Posterity also, for their great Loyalty and Valour, have been honour'd by the Kings of England, first with the title of Baron *Barry*, and afterwards with that of Viscount *Buttphant*, [and are now Earls of *Barrimore*, and, from their vast Estate, are call'd by the People, *Barry More*, or *Barry the Great* A little below this, the river *Saveren* (near *Imokelly*, formerly a large Estate of the Earls of Desmond,) falls from a creeky mouth into the Sea

Barry Court
Barons *Barry*
G Cambr
[l] *Nisum mansuefecit*
Viscount *Buttiphant* and Earl of *Barrimore*
Saveren, riv

As the *Saveren* waters the lower part of this County, so *Broodwater* [(now commonly call'd *Blackwater*,)] and formerly *Aven more*, that is, *a great water*, supplies the upper part [This by some is supposed to be the river *Daurona*, mentioned by Ptolemy] Upon it [m] was the Seat of the noble family *de Rupe*, or *Roch*, transplanted out of England to this place; where it exceedingly [n] flourish'd, and [o] enjoy'd the title of Viscount *Fermoy* In Edward the second's time, they were certainly Barons of Parliament, for *George Roche* was fined two hundred Marks, for not being present at the Parliament of Dublin, according to the Summons [The chief Seat of this Family was at *Castle-town Roche* in *Roche's Country*, on the river *Owbeg*]

Brood water
Ware, Ant p 25
[m] Is C
Baron *Roch*
[n] Flourishes, C
[o] Enjoys, C
Viscount *Fermoy*
Pat) *Pat an* 8 *Ed* III

Where the river *Broodwater* (for some time the boundary between this County and *Waterford*) runs into the Sea and makes a harbour; stands *Yoghall*, not very large, but walled round, of an oblong form, and divided into two parts the upper, which is the greater part, is stretch'd Northward having a Church in it, and a little Abbey without the Wall, called *North Abbey*, the lower part to the South, is called the *Base-town*, and has also an Abbey, called *South-Abbey* The convenience of the harbour, which hath a good *Kay*, as also the fruitfulness of the Country hereabouts, draws so many Merchants hither, that the Town is pretty populous, and has a Mayor for its chief Magistrate

Yoghall
North Abbey
Base town
South Abbey

[Besides the forementioned places, there are several good Towns, in the County of Cork, as, *Charleville*, *Mallow*, *Castlelyons*, *Macroome*, *Bantry*, *Skibereen*, and *Cloghnikilty*; but especially *Bandon*, in which are supposed to be no less than three thousand Inhabitants; all *Protestants* British or Irish The Town was walled by the industry and at the expence of the first Earl of Cork, and adorn'd with three very fine Castles for Gate houses, which, together with the Walls, were demolished by the French and Irish, in the year 1690, in revenge for their never suffering any Popish House-keeper to live among them]

Bandon

At present, the County of *Cork* is only of this extent; which (as I observed) was heretofore counted a Kingdom, and was of greater extent, containing [p] *Desmond* also within its bounds King Henry the second gave this Kingdom to *Robert Fitz Stephens* and *Miles de Cogan*, in these words *Know ye, that I have granted the whole Kingdom of* Cork, *except the City, and Cantred of* Oustmans, *to hold to them and their heirs, of me and my son John, by the service of sixty Knights* From the heir of this Fitz-Stephen, *George Carew*, [q] Baron Carew of Clopton, did descend in a right line; who [r] was President of Mounster, and, as I gratefully acknowledge, did readily give me light into some of the Affairs of *Ireland*

Kingdom of *Cork*
[p] it now contains part of it
[q] Now, C
[r] Not long since, C

[In the reign of King James the first, *Cork* was erected into an Earldom, in the Person of *Richard Boyle*, which honourable Family doth still enjoy it, and in the same County the Earldom of *Orrery* is enjoy'd by another branch of the same noble Family, and a third hath the honour of Viscount *Shanon* Besides which *Donerayle* affords the title of Earl to the family of *Saint leger*, and *Middleton* the title of Viscount to the right Honourable *Alan Broderick*, Lord Chancellour of *Ireland*, as doth *Baltimore* the title of Baron to the Family of *Calvert*; *Dunamore*, to the Family of *Hawley*, *Kingston*, to the Family of *King*, *Altham*, to a branch of the Family of *Annesley*, *Carbery*, to the Family of *Evans*; and *Burton* the same title to the Family of *Percival*]

Earldom of *Cork*
Orrery
Shanon
See *Longford*
Donerayle
Middleton
Baltimore
Dunamore
Kingston
Altham
Carbery
Burton

The

The County of *WATERFORD.*

TO the East, between the river *Broodwater* on the West, and the *Suire* on the East, the Ocean on the South, and the County of *Tipperary* on the North, lies the County of *Waterford* a County [for the most part mountainous and barren, but in some places] very agreeable, both in respect of pleasure and fertility. Upon Broodwater, at its leaving the County of Cork, stands *Lismor*, [i. e. a great Fort, the chief Seat of the Earl of Cork and Burlington, and adorn'd with a noble Park. It hath an Alms house and a Free-School, and is a Borough, sending two members to Parliament. It is also] remarkable for being a Bishop's See, where presided *Christian* the Bishop and Legat of Ireland, about the year 1148, a person highly deserving of the Church of Ireland, and educated at *Clarevall*, in the same Cloister with St Bernard and Pope Eugenius. [Here is a handsom Cathedral, but] by reason the possessions belonging to it were almost all alienated, it is annex'd to the See of *Waterford* [which union was made by Pope Innocent the sixth, in the year 1363. This place was also famous heretofore for a Publick School or Academy, which was govern'd for a time by St *Catald*, afterwards Bishop of Tarentum in Italy, whither men flock'd in great numbers for the advantages of a Religous and Liberal Education.

Lismor

Bishop Christian

Ware, Ant. p. 141

Near this, is *Tallow*, a flourishing Town, erected by the noble Earl of Cork, and situate in a beautiful and fertile Vale, near the river *Bride*, which, being navigable from hence to Youghall, renders this a place of good Trade, and it was also made a Corporation by King James the first.] Near the mouth of Broodwater, lies *Ardmor*, a small village, of which, and this river, *Necham* has this Distich.

Tallow

Ardmor

Urbem Lismor pertransiit flumen Avenmor,
Ardmor cernit ubi concitus æquor adit.

Avenmor guides his stream through *Lismor* town,
Small *Ardmor* to the Ocean sees him run.

[This *Ardmor* was also a Bishop's See in the infancy of the Irish Church, but was united to the See of *Lismore* after the coming-in of the English.]

The [a] large adjoyning territory is called [b] *Decies*, [and is the biggest Barony in this County, containing near half of it,] the Lord whereof descended from the Earls of *Desmond*, had, [c] in the last age, the honourable title of Viscount *Decies* conferred upon him, which died with him soon after, for want of issue male. Not far from hence, upon the Sea, stands *Dungarvan* a town well fortified with a Castle, and advantageously situated for a harbour. King Henry the sixth gave this, with the Barony of *Dungarvan*, to *John Talbot*, Earl of Shrewsbury, but afterwards, by reason it stood convenient to command that part of Mounster which was to be reduc'd, the Earldom was annex'd to the Crown of England for ever. [The greatest part

[a] Little C.
[b] *Desies*, C.
[c] In our time, C.

Dungarvan

of it belongs to Sir *John Osburn*, Baronet, whose Ancestors for several Generations have been of good note in this County.] Near *Dungarvan*, the *Poers*, an ancient and noble family, flourished from the first conquest of this country by the English, and were advanc'd to the honour of Barons *Curraghmore*, [and after that to the title of Earls of *Tyrone*, the sole daughter and heir of the last of whom married Sir [d] *Marcus Beresford*, Baronet, but the title of Baron of *Curraghmore*, the ancient Seat of the Family, descended to the Family of *Poer*.]

Poers, Barons of Curraghmore

[d] Now Viscount *Tyrone*. See *Tyrone*.

Upon the bank of the river *Suire*, stands *Waterford*, the chief City of the County, Of which, thus *Necham*:

Waterford

Surius insignem gaudet ditare Waterford,
Æquoreis undis associatur ibi.

Thee, *Waterford*, *Suir's* streams with wealth supply,
Hasting to pay their tribute to the sea.

This City, which the Irish and Britains call [e] *Portlarig*, and the English *Waterford*, was first built by certain Pirates of Norway; [who having embraced Christianity, and desiring a Bishop in their City, sent *Malchus* a Benedictine Monk of Winchester in England, to receive his Consecration from Anselm Archbishop of Canterbury, in the year 1096.] Though it is situated in a thick air, and on a barren soil, and is close built, yet by reason of the convenience of the harbour, [f] it is the second City in Ireland for wealth and populousness, and did ever continue particularly loyal to the Crown of England. For from the time that it was first taken by Richard Earl of Pembroke, it was so faithful and quiet, that in our Conquest of Ireland it always secur'd us from an Enemy on our backs. Upon this account, the Kings of England have granted it many, and those considerable, privileges, which were enlarg'd and confirmed by Henry the seventh, for their having behav'd themselves with great valour and conduct against *Perkin Warbeck*, a sham Prince, who being a young boy of mean extraction, had the impudence to aim at the Imperial Crown, by pretending to be Richard Duke of York, second son of King Edward the fourth. [With regard to these testimonies of their bravery, the Motto of this City was, *Intacta manet Waterfordia*, but in the course of the Irish Rebellion, begun *Ann.* 1641, by means of the Popish Clergy, it became exceedingly faulty. Now, that the English Inhabitants duly cherish it, we are not to doubt, but that it will [illegible] from the [illegible], *Richard [illegible]*, Earl of Scarborough in England, enjoys the honourable Title of Viscount *Waterford*.]

[e] Porthlargy, C.

[f] Not so since the growth of Cork.

King Henry the sixth gave the County of *Waterford*, together with the City, to the [illegible] of *John Talbot* Earl of Shrewsbury, in words which so clearly set forth the bravery of that [illegible], that I cannot but think it [illegible] perhaps some others may [illegible] to [illegible] from the Records, [illegible] I have

Earl of Waterford

brave Actions, *We therefore* (says the King, after a great deal more, wherein one sees the defects both of the *Latin* and *Eloquence* of the Secretaries of that age) *in consideration of the fidelity and valour of our most dear and faithful Cousin* John Earl of Shrewsbury and Weysford, Lord Talbot of Furnival and Lestrange, *sufficiently prov'd in the wars aforesaid, even to his old age, not only by the sweat of his body, but many times by the loss of his blood, and considering how our County and City of* Waterford, *in our Kingdom of Ireland, with the Castle, Seignory, Honour, Lands, and Barony of* Dungarvan, *and all the Lordships, Lands, Honours, and Baronies, and their appurtenances within the same County, which, by forfeiture of rebels, by reversion, or decease of any person or persons, by escheat, or any other title of law, have come to Us or our Progenitors, are, by reason of invasions or insurrections in these parts, become so desolate, and (as they lye exposed to the spoils of war) so entirely wasted, that they are of no profit to us, but have redounded, and now do, many times, redound, to our loss and also, that the said lands may hereafter be better defended by our said Cousin, against the attempts and incursions of enemies or rebels, We do create him Earl of* Waterford, *with the stile, title, name, and honour thereunto belonging And that all things may correspond with this state and dignity, we hereby, of our special grace, certain knowledge, and mere motion, that the Grandeur of the Earl our Cousin may be more honourably supported, have given, granted, and by these presents confirm'd unto the said Earl the County aforesaid, together with the aforesaid title, stile, name, and honour of Earl of* Waterford, *and the city of* Waterford *aforesaid, with the fee farms, castles, lordships, honours, lands, and baronies, and their appurtenances, within the County, as also all mannors, hundreds, wapentakes,* &c. *along the sea coast, from the town of* Yoghall *to the city of Waterford aforesaid To have and to hold the said County of* Waterford, *and the stile, title, name, and honour of Earl of* Waterford; *and likewise the city of* Waterford *aforesaid with the castle, seigniory, honour, land, and barony of* Dungarvan, *and all other lordships, honours, lands and baronies, within the said County, and also all the aforesaid mannors, hundreds,* &c *to the abovesaid Earl, and to the heirs-male of his body begotten, to be held of us and our heirs, by homage, fealty, and the service of being our Seneschal; and that he and his heirs be* Seneschals *of Ireland to us and our heirs, through out our whole land of Ireland, to do, and that he do in the said Office, that which his predecessors, Seneschals of England, were wont formerly to do for us in the said Office In witness whereof,* &c (Seneschal of Ireland)

While the Kings of England and their Nobility, who had large possessions in Ireland, were either taken up with foreign wars in France, or civil dissensions at home, Ireland was quite neglected, so that the English interest decay'd apace [g], and by reason of their absence, the power of the Irish grew formidable And then, to recover their interest, and to suppress this growing Power of the Irish, it was enacted, that the Earl of *Shrewsbury* should surrender the Town and County of *Waterford*, and that the Duke of *Norfolk*, the Baron *Barkley*, the Heirs Female of the Earl of *Ormond*, and all the Abbots, Priors, &c of England, who held any lands there, should surrender them to the King and his successors, for their absence and negligence in defending them (Ann 8 H VIII)

g Vid St of *Absence* the County of Carlogge

[At present the honourable family of *Talbot*, as abovesaid, enjoys the joint Titles of Earl of *Waterford* and *Wexford*; and the honourable family of Villers, the title of Viscount Grandison, in these parts]

The

The County of *LIMERICK.*

THUS far we have survey'd the maritime Counties of *Mounster* two remain, that are inland, namely, *Limerick* and *Tipperary*, which we now come to The County of *Limerick* lies behind that of *Cork* to the North, between Kerry, the river Shanon, and the county of Tipperary It is fruitful and well inhabited, but has few remarkable Towns The West part is called *Conilagh*, where, among the hills, *Knock Patrick*, i e *St Patrick's hill*, is the highest, from the top whereof, one has a pleasant prospect into the sea and along the river Shanon, which at a great distance falls from a vast wide mouth into the *Vergivian Ocean* At the bottom of this hill, the *Fitz Giralds* liv'd for a long time in great splendor; till *Thomas*, call'd the *Knight of the Valley*, or *de Glin* (when his graceless son was put to death for *Arson*, for it is treason, by the Laws of Ireland, to set Villages and houses a fire,) was found an accessary, as advising, and had his estate confiscated by Act of Parliament The head city of this County is *Limerick*, encompass'd by the *Shanon* a famous river, which divides its stream, and embraces it The Irish call it [a] *Loumnagh*, and the English, *Limerick* It is a Bishop's See, [built and endow'd by *Donald O Brian*, King of Limerick, about the time of the coming of the English into Ireland, and greatly augmented by *Donagh O Brian*, Bishop of the place, about the beginning of the thirteenth Century] This City is the great Mart of the Province of Munster, and was first taken by *Reimund le Gros*, an Englishman, the son of *William* [b] *Fitz Girald*, and afterwards, burnt by *Duvenald*, a petty King of *Twomund* At last, it was given *in fee* to *Philip Breos*, an Englishman; and fortify'd by King John with a castle At present, it is two towns, the *Upper* (for so they call that where stands the Cathedral and the Castle,) has two gates, and each a fair stone bridge leading to it, fortify'd with bulwarks and little draw bridges, one of which leads you to the West, the other to the East The *Lower* town which joins to this, is fortify'd with a Wall and Castle, and a fore-gate at the entrance More to the East, stands *Clan-William*, so call'd [c] from a family of that name, descended from the House *de Burgo* (the Irish call them *Bourk*,) who inhabit it Of this family, was that *William* (who slew *James Fitz Moris*, the plague and firebrand of his country,) upon whom Queen Elizabeth conferr'd the honour of Baron of *Castle-Conel* (where *Richard Rufus* Earl of Ulster, had fortify'd the Castle,) together with a yearly pension, in recompence of his own bravery, and the loss of his sons, who were slain in that Battle [Several good Families of the sirname of *Bourk* do still remain in these Parts]

In the South part of this county, stands [d] *Killmallock*, which is next in dignity to Limerick, both in respect of plenty, and populousness, and is wall'd round Likewise *Adare*, a little town, fortified heretofore, and situate upon [e] the river *Mage*, which presently runs into the *Shanon* Near this stands *Clan Gibbon*, the Lord whereof *John Fitz-Girald*, called *John Oge Fitz John Fitz Gibbon*, and, from his grey hairs, *the white Knight*, was attainted for certain Crimes by Act of Parliament, but by the Clemency of Queen Elizabeth, his son was restor'd, [and the name of *Fitz Girald* is at this day more numerous than any other in this Kingdom At present this Territory of *Clan Gibbon* stands in the County of Cork] The most noted and eminent Families in this tract (besides the *Bourks* and *Fitz Giralds*) [f] were the *Lacies*, the *Browns*, the *Hurleys*, the *Chacys*, the *Sapells*, the *Pourcells*, all of English extraction, and the *Mac-Shees*, the *Mac briens*, *O Brians*, &c of Irish extraction [Some of whom are now extinct and some others of no great note at present, but from the *O Brians* are the Earls of Thomond and Inchiquin, besides others of considerable Fortune and Character Divers noble Families derive their Titles of Honour from this County, namely, a Family of Hamilton, the title of Viscount *Limerick*, a Family of the Southwells, the title of Viscount Castle-Maltress, and a Family of the Lanes, the title of Baron Loughyre, and Viscount Lanes]

Conilagh

Knock Patrick

Knight of the Valley

Q Eliz An 11

Limerick

[a] Loumeagh, C

Ware, Ant p 140

[b] Girald, C

Clan William

[c] From a *Bourk*, whose Name was *William*

Baron of Castle Conel

[d] *Kil mallo*, C

Killmallock

Adare

[e] The same river, C

Clan Gibbon

[f] Are, C

Visc Limerick

The

The County of *TIPPERARY.*

HE County of *Tipperary* is bounded on the west with that of Limerick and the river Shanon, on the east, with the County of Kilkenny; on the south, with the Counties of Cork and Waterford, and on the north, with the territory of the O Carolls The south part is a fruitful soil, and produces much corn, and is well built and inhabited The west part of it is water'd by the long course of the river *Glason*, not far from the bank whereof, stands *Emely*, or *Awn*, a Bishop's See, [(now annex'd to Cashel,)] and, by report, a very populous city heretofore [At present, a branch of the honourable Family of *Fairfax*, take the title of Viscount from this place.]

Emely

The *Sewer* or *Swire*, a noble river which rises out of *Bladin-hill*, runs through the middle of it and so through the *Lower Ossory*, which by the Favour of King Henry VIII, gave the title of Earl to the *Butlers*, [(as *Upper Ossory* hath given the title of Baron to the *Fitz-Patricks*,)] and then through *Thurles*, which gave the *Butlers* the title of *Viscounts* From whence it passes by *Holy-Cross*, a famous Abby heretofore, which makes the Country about it to be commonly called the *County of the Holy-Cross of* Tipperary, and hath derived to this Tract certain special privileges, anciently bestowed on the Abbey, in honour to a piece of Christ's Cross preserv'd there *The whole world*, says St Cyril, *is fill'd with pieces of this Cross, and yet*, as St Paulinus says, *by a constant miracle it is never diminished* This was the belief and opinion of Christians, in ancient times And it is incredible what a concourse of people do still throng hither out of devotion For this nation obstinately adheres to the religion [or rather superstition] of their fore-fathers, which [heretofore] gain'd ground exceedingly by the neglect and ignorance of the Bishops, ᵃ while there were none here to instruct them better

Lower Ossory

The County of the Holy Cross of Tipperary

The wood of the Cross

ᵃ For there are, C

From hence the Swire passes by *Cassil*, adorn'd with an Archbishop's See by Pope Eugenius the third, which had many Suffragan Bishops under it in old time [At first, the people of *Cassil* are supposed to have been subject to the See of *Emly*, twelve miles distant Who was the founder of this Church, is not certain, but thus much is clear, that about the time of the coming of the English, *Donald O Brian* King of Limerick, built a new Church from the ground, and endowed it, converting the old one into a Chapel or Chapter house on the south side of the Choir It is situate without the City, and fortified with a rocky and steep hill, but is, by reason of the height of its situation, too much exposed to the Winds In the ascent to it, is a great stone, at which (as is the tradition of the Inhabitants) every new King of Munster was publickly proclaim'd From this City, the family of *Bulkley* derived their title of Viscount *Cassil*, and from two other places in these parts, the family of *Davys* derive their title of Viscount Mountcashel, and the family of *Cockain* their title of Viscount Cullen]

Cassil

Ware, Ant p 139

Mountcashel Cullen

From *Cassil* the Swire runs forward, making many Islands as it goes, till it encompasses *Cahir Castle*, which has its Baron, one of the Family of the *Butlers*, who was raised to that honour by Queen Elizabeth But his Son proving disloyal, suffered accordingly for it, the castle being taken by the Earl of Essex in the year 1599, and he himself committed to prison From thence, it runs by *Clonmell*, a market town of good resort, and well fortified, and also by *Carick Mac-Griffin*, situate upon a rock, from which it takes its name, a Seat of the Earls of Ormond, which) with the honour of Earl of *Carrick*) was granted by King Edward the second, to *Edmund Boteler* or *Butler* Here the Swire leaves *Tipperary*, and becomes a boundary to the Counties of *Waterford* and *Kilkenny*

Clonmell

Earl of Carrick Anno 9 Edw II

Thus much concerning the south part of this County The north part is barren and full of mountains, twelve of which are heap'd together above the rest, and these they call *Phelemge-Modona* This part is call'd in Latin *Ormondia*, in Irish *Orwowon*, that is, *The front of* Mounster, in English, *Ormond*, and by many very corruptly *Wormewood* All its glory is from the Earls, who have been many, since *James Butler*, to whom and his heirs King Edward the third gave this title ᵇ for term of life, *together with the royalties and other liberties, as also the Knights-fees in the County of* Tipperary, which by the favour of the Kings of England, his posterity ᶜ enjoy'd, [until, by the Grant of King Charles the second, the Title was changed from that of Earl to the more honourable ones, first of *Marquis*, and then *Duke*, of Ormond] On account of the forementioned Royalties, this County is reputed *Palatine*, and he has been call'd by some the Earl of Tipperary

Ormondia

Butler Earls of Ormond

An 2 Ed III ᵇ [illegible]

ᶜ Still enjoys, C

Earl of Tipperary

The ancestors of this *James* were honorary *Butlers* of Ireland, from which they derive the name of *Le Boteler* or *Butler* It is certain, that this family was nearly related to *Thomas Becket*, Archbishop of Canterbury, being descended from his sister, and that after his murder, they were translated into Ireland by King Henry the second, who hop'd to wipe off the scandal of that fact, by preferring his relations to wealth and honours [Of these, one branch doth enjoy the honourable title of Viscount *Ikerin*, in this County]

Ikerin

The first Earl of Ormond of this family, was *James* son of Edmund Earl of *Carrick*, who married the daughter of Humphry *Bohun*, Earl of Hereford, by a daughter of King Edward the first, and this relation was the means of their advancement Hereupon, his son *James* was commonly called by the people, *The Noble Earl* The fifth Earl of this family (not to be particular in the account of every one of them) had the title of Earl of Wiltshire given him by King Henry the sixth, *To him and the heirs of his body* but being Lord Deputy of Ireland, and some others of this family have been, and Treasurer of England, he was attainted by Edward the fourth, and soon after taken and beheaded His brothers were attainted likewise, and [illegible] *John* died at Jerusalem without children; *Thomas*, by the favour of Henry the seventh, had his attainder revers'd, and died in the year 1515, leaving two daughters, [illegible] marry'd to James de St Leger and *Margaret* the wife of William Bullein, who had [illegible]

Thomas

Thomas Bullein, who was made first Viscount Rochfort, and after that Earl of Wiltshire and Ormond, by King Henry the eighth, upon his marriage with *Ann Bullein*, the Earl's daughter By her he had *Elizabeth* Queen of England, whose memory will be ever precious to the English Nation After the death of *Thomas Bullein*, *Peter* or *Pierce Butler*, a person of great power in Ireland, and of the Earl's family, (who had been before created *Earl of Ossery* by King Henry the eighth), was now also advanc'd to the Earldom of *Ormond* He dying, left it to his son, *James*, who by the daughter and heir of James Earl of Desmond, had a son, *Thomas* Earl of Ormond, [d] whose fidelity and loyalty [e] shone forth in the most difficult and dangerous times He married his only daughter to *Theobald Butler* his brother's son, upon whom K James [the 1st] [f] conferr'd the title of Viscount *Tullo* [As to the *Earldom*, after a continuance of many ages, it was raised, first to a *Marquisate*, and then to the higher honour of a *Dukedom*, by King Charles the second, in the person of *James*, Marquis of Ormond and Earl of Ossery, in consideration of his eminent Loyalty, and Sufferings in the cause of the Royal Family Which James was also afterwards created by the same King, Duke of Ormond in England, (to enjoy the dignity of an English Duke, under that title,) and was father of Thomas Earl of Ossery, a person of great Valour, who dy'd in the life-time of the said Duke, and left a Son, *James*, who succeeded his Grandfather in all his Honours, and gave many Proofs of Valour, during the French wars in the reign of King William the third; but being, in the next Reign, unhappily drawn into such Measures and Practices, as were thought highly dishonourable and injurious to his Country, and being impeached in Parliament for the same, he thereupon fled out of the Nation, and stands attainted of High Treason]

[d] Now living, C

[e] Hath shone, C

[f] Hath lately confer'd, C

Men turn'd into Wolves.

As to what is said by some of the Irish (and those too, such as would be thought very credible witnesses,) that certain men in these parts are every year converted into wolves, it is without doubt fabulous unless, perhaps, through excess of melancholy, they may be affected with the distemper that the Physicians call Λυκανθρωπία, which makes them fansy and imagin themselves to be so transform'd And as for those metamorphos'd *Lycaones* in Livonia, so much talked of, I cannot but have the same opinion of them also

President of Munster.

Thus far we have continu'd in the Province of Mounster, which Queen Elizabeth, with great wisdom, and to advance the wealth and happiness of this Kingdom, committed to the government of a Lord President, who (with one Assistant, two Lawyers, and a Secretary,) might correct the insolencies of this Province, and keep all men to their duty The first President was *Warham St Leger* Kt who was constituted in the year 1565, being a person of great experience in the affairs of Ireland [But this Office (as hath been said) was superseded by King Charles the second, (the last being the ingenious and noble Earl of Orrery,) and no more remains to be said concerning this Province, but that the honour of Dutchess of Munster was conferr'd upon *Erengart Melusina Schulenburg*, who hath since been also advanc'd to the honour of Dutchess of *Kendal* in England, as we have already mentioned]

LAGENIA, or LEINSTER.

NOTHER part of Ireland, *call'd by the Inhabitants* Laghinigh, *by the British* Lein, *by the English* Leinster, *by the Irish* Lagenia, *and by the old Legends* Lagen, *lies to the east entirely upon the Sea. It is bounded* [a] *towards* Conaught, *for a good way, by the* Shannon, *and towards* Meath, *by its own limits. The Soil is rich and fruitful, the Air very warm and temperate, and the Inhabitants near as civil and gentle in their Modes of living, as their neighbours in England, from whom, generally speaking, they are descended. In Ptolemy's time it was peopled by the* Brigantes, Menapii, Cauci *and* Blani. *From these* Blani, *perhaps, are derived and contracted the modern names,* Lein, Leinigh, *and* Leinster. *It* [b] *was subdivided into the Counties of* Kilkennigh, Caterlogh, Queens County, Kings County, Kildare, Weisford *and* Dublin: *not to mention* Wicklo *and* Fernes, *which either* [c] *are already, or will be, added to it.* [*At this day,* Leinster *contains the Counties of* Dublin, Wicklow, Wexford, Caterlogh, Kilkenny, Kings County, Queens County, Kildare, Meath, West Meath, *and* Longford.]

[illegible marginal notes]

BRIGANTES, or *BIRGANTES*.

HE Brigantes *seem to have been seated between the mouth of the river* Swire, *and the confluence of the* Neor *and* Barrow, *which last is call'd by Ptolemy* Brigus [illegible] *because there was an ancient City of the* Brigantes *in* Spain, *call'd* Brigantium, Florianus del Campo *takes a great deal of pains to derive these* Brigantes *from his own country of* Spain. *But if conjectures are to be allow'd, others may as probably derive them from the* Brigantes *of Britain, a Nation both near and populous. However, if what I find in some Copies be true, that these People were call'd* Birgantes, *both he and others* [illegible] *mistake; for then they take their name from the river* Birgus [*now* Barrow,] [illegible] *inhabit, as appears from the affinity of the names. These* Brigantes (*or* Birgantes, *which you please*) *peopled the Counties of* Kilkenny, Offery, *and* Caterlogh, *all water'd by the river* Birgus.

The

The County of *KILKENNY*.

THE County of *Kilkenny* is bounded on the west with the County of *Tipperary*, on the east with the Counties of Weisford and Caterlogh, on the south with the County of Waterford, on the north with the Queens-County, and on the north west with the upper-Offery, and is adorn'd on all sides with Towns and Castles, and more plentiful in every thing, than any of the rest Near *Offery* are those huge copling Mountains, named *Slaew Bloemy* (which Giraldus calls *Bladinæ Montes*,) of a vast height, out of the bowels whereof, springs the river *Swire* aforesaid, as also the *Neor* and *Barrow* These descend in three several Chanels, but join in one before they fall into the Sea, which made the Ancients call them *The three Sisters*

Bladin hills

Neor, riv

The *Neor*, commonly called the *Neure*, does in a manner divide this County in two, and when, with a swift stream, it has pass'd the *Upper-Offery* (the first Baron whereof was *Barnabas Fitz Patrick*, advanc'd to that honour by King Edward the sixth,) and many Forts on both sides, it arrives at *Kilkenny*, i e the *Cell* or *Church of Canic*, who was an eminent Hermit in this Country It is a Town Corporate, [now a City,] neat, fair-built, and plentiful, and by much the best midland town in the Island It is divided into the *English*, and the *Irish town* The *Irish town* is, as it were, the Suburbs, where stands the Church of St *Canic*, which has both given name to the Town, and a See to the Bishops of Offery [Their See was at first at *Saiger*, which we now call *Seirkeran*, in *Ely O Carol*, and was translated from thence to *Agabo* in Offory, in the year 1052, as is supposed, and at last, to *Kilkenny*, by *Felix O Dullany* Bishop of Offory, about the end of Henry the second's reign The situation of the Cathedral is render'd exceeding pleasant, by it's standing on a hill gently raised, from which is a delightful prospect over the City and the fertile Country thereabouts]

Upper Offery

Barons of the Upper Offery

Kilkenny

Ware Ant p 127

The English town is much newer; being built (as I have read) by *Ranulph* the third Earl of Chester, and wall'd on the west-side by *Robert Talbot*, a nobleman, and fortified with a Castle by the *Butlers*, when the daughters of William Mareschal, Earl of Pembroke, made a partition of their Lands; it is certain, that this fell to the share of the third Sister, who was married to *Gilbert de Clare*, Earl of Glocester Lower, upon the same River, stands a little fortify'd Town called in English *Thomas town*, in Irish *Bala mac Andan*, i e the Town of *Anthony's Son*, both deriv'd from the founder, *Thomas Fitz Anthony*, an Englishman, who flourished in Henry the third's time, and whose heirs [a] were long Lords of the place Below this, the river *Callan* runs into the *Neor*, upon which stands the third *Corporation* of this County, that takes the name *Kallan* from it, and also *Inis-Teag*, a fourth

Thomas-Town

[a] Are at this day, C

Collan, riv

Inis Teag

The family of the *Butlers* spreads its branches almost all over this Country, and has long flourish'd in great honour, having been, for their eminent Services and Merits, dignify'd with the title of Earls of *Ormond*, of *Wiltshire* in England, [of *Brecknock* in Wales,] and (as we said) of *Offery* Besides [b] the Earl of Ormond, Viscount *Thurles*, and Knight of the Garter, there are of this family the Viscount *Mont-Garret*, the Viscount *Tullo*, the Barons *de Dunboyn* and *Cahyr*, with many other noble branches The other Families of note in these parts, were also of English original, namely, the *Graces*, *Walshes*, *Lovels*, *Foresters*, *Shortels*, *Blanchfields* or *Blanchevelstons*, *Drilands*, *Comerfords*, &c [But at this day, the greatest part of these are only of private condition, and some are wholly extinct

[b] So said, ann 1607

See Ormond

From three several places in this County, the following Titles of Honour have been respectively taken the title of Viscount *Castlecomer*, by the family of *Wandesford*, the title of Baron of *Gowran*, by the *Fitz Patricks*, and the title of Baron of *Killaghy*, by General *George Carpenter*, in England]

Castle comer

Gowran

Killaghy

The County of *CATERLOGH.*

THE County of *Caterlogh*, by contraction *Carlogh*, borders upon Kilkenny to the east; lying mostly between the rivers, *Barrow* and *Slane* The Soil is fruitful, and well shaded with Woods It hath in it two towns of note, both situate upon the west bank of the *Barrow* · The one, *Caterlogh*, about which *Leonel* Duke of Clarence began to build a Wall; and Bellingham, the famous and excellent Lord Deputy, built a Castle for the defence of it The other is *Leighlin*, in Latin *Lechlinia*, where was formerly a Bishop's See, that is now annex'd to the Bishoprick of *Fernes* These Towns have both of them their Wards and Constables, [and at *Leighlin-bridge*, a mile south of *Old Leighlin*, was a Commandery of the Knights Templars, which is still of some use to guard that considerable Pass]

The Stat of Absentees

The greatest part of the County belonged by inheritance to the *Howards*, Dukes of Norfolk (descended, by the Earls of Warren, from the eldest daughter of William Marshal Earl of Pembroke,) but King Henry the eighth, by Act of Parliament, had all the Lands and Possessions granted him, which belong'd either to him and the other English Gentry, or to the Monasteries here in England [a], because, by their absence, and neglect of their own private Affairs there, they had endangered the publick interest of the Nation

[a] V County of Waterford, last Paragr

Baron Ydron

From hence the *Barrow* runs through the Barony of *Ydron*, which hath belong'd to the *Carews* of Devonshire, ever since Sir *N Carew*, an English Knight, married the daughter of *Digo* an Irish Baron, and which [b] in the memory of the last age, was recover'd, after a long usurpation, by *Peter Carew*

[b] In our memory, C

Tullo

Upon the river *Slane* stands *Tullo*, memorable for *Theobald Butler*, brother's son to the Earl of Ormond, who was honour'd by King James [the first] with the title of Viscount *Tullo*. The *Cavanaughs* are very numerous in these parts, (descended from *Duvenald*, a younger Son, or Bastard (as some say,) of *Dermot* the last King of *Leinster*,) warlike-men, and famous for good horsemanship; and though they are [generally] very poor at this day, yet are they of as much honour and bravery, as their forefathers, [and some of them of good note] Upon the account of some slaughters, which [c] many years ago they committed upon one another, they [d] lived in a state of war, plunder, and blood-shed Some of them, being entrusted by the English to manage their Estates in these parts about King Edward the second's time, usurp'd all to themselves, assuming the name of *O-More*, and taking the [e] *Tools* and *Birns* into their confederacy; by which means they dispossess'd the English, by degrees, of all that territory between *Caterlogh* and the *Irish* Sea [f] Below these, the river *Neor* joins the *Barrow*, and after they have travell'd some miles together in one stream, they quit their names, and give up that, with their waters, to their eldest sister the *Swire*; which empties it self soon after from a rocky mouth into the Sea where, on the left, there is a little narrow neck'd Promontory, upon which stands a [g] high tower, built by the Merchants of *Rosse* while they flourish'd, to direct Vessels into the mouth of the River

Cavanaughs

[c] So said, ann 1607

[d] Live, C

O More

[e] From a book of Patrick Fingla

Toles id

Bren C

[f] Among, C

[g] Th [illegible] *Rosse* in *Wexford* Hoc [illegible]

[The title of Marquiss of *Caterlogh* is enjoy'd by his Grace the Duke of *Wharton* in England]

QUEENS-COUNTY.

The Leise

O the north-west, above *Caterlogh*, lies a woody, boggy Tract, call'd in Irish *The Leise*, in English, *The Queen's County*; which Queen Mary, by *Thomas Ratcliff* Earl of Sussex and Lord Deputy at that time, first reduced into a County Hence the chief Town is call'd *Mary Burgh* [(from whence the Family of *Molineux* have the title of Viscounts), defended by a garrison under the command of a [h] Steward, [i] who with much ado kept off the *O Mores*, pretending to be the ancient Lords of it, as also the *Mac Gilpatricks*, the *O Dempsies*, and others (a mischievous and restless sort of people,) who are daily conspiring against the English, and endeavouring to free themselves from their Government At the first coming of the English into these parts, *Meilere* was sent to subdue this wild and stubborn part of the Country *Hugh Lacy*, Lord Deputy, built a Castle at *Tahmelio*, another at *Obowy*, a third upon the river *Barrow*, and a fourth at *Norrach* But the most famous was *Donemaws*, an ancient Castle, situate in a very fruitful part, which fell to the *Breoses* Lords of *Brecknock* by *Eva* the youngest daughter of William Marshall Earl of Pembroke Where also the *Barrow*, rising out of *Slew-Blomey hills* on the west, after a solitary course through the Woods, sees the old City *Rheba*, a name which it still preserves entire in its pre

Mary Burgh

[h] *Seneschallo*

[i] This was the State of it, ann 1607

Donemaws

Rheba

4 sent

sent one *Rheban*, though instead of a City, it is now but the shadow of a City, consisting of some few Cottages and a Fort However, it [c]gave the title of Baronet to an eminent Gentleman N of *S Michael*, commonly called *the Baronet of Rheban*, [but that Family is now wholly extinct. Their title, while they remain'd, was in some sense, that of Baron, but being created by the Lord of the Palatinate, and not by the King, they were not Lords of Parliament

c Gives, C Baronet of Rheban

This County is now well inhabited, and much improved, and contains, besides the Burrough of *Mary-burrough*, the Burrough of *Ballynakill*, and the considerable Towns of *Montrath*, *Mountmelick*, *Abbylease*, and *Durrow*, the first of which gives the title of Earl of *Montrath*, to the Honourable Family of *Coote*.]

The KINGS-COUNTY.

AS the *Queen's* County was so nam'd from Queen Mary, so the adjacent little County on the north (divided by the river *Barrow*, and called heretofore *Offalie*) was called, in honour of Philip of Spain her husband, *the King's County*, and the head town, *Philips-town* where [a] was a garrison, a *Seneschal*, and several noted families of the English, the *Warrens*, *Herberts*, *Colbies*, *Mores*, and the *Leicesters*, and of the Irish, the family of *O Conor*, to whom a great part of it formerly belong'd, as also of *Mac Coghlain*, and *O maily*, *Fox*, and others, who stoutly [b]defended the possessions left them here by their ancestors These native Irish [c]complain'd that the estates of their families [d]were taken from them, and no others in lieu thereof assigned them to live upon For this reason they [e]broke out into rebellion upon every occasion, and being thus wrought into a Spirit of Revenge, [f]annoy'd the English with great outrage and cruelty [But now all those Families, both English and Irish are extinct, except the *Leicesters*, who are in a low state, and the *Mores* who are in a flourishing condition, and have been lately advanced to the honour of Barons of Tullamore This County is now well improved and inhabited, and, besides the Borough of *Philips town* (which gives the title of Baron to the Lord Viscount Molesworth,) hath the Borough of *Bonager*, and *Edenderry*, a large Town, with several pretty Villages, and from *Geshill* herein, the honourable Family of Digby in England take their title of Baron]

Philips town
a Is C
b Defend C
c Complain, C
d Are, C
e Break, C
f Annoy C
Geshil

The County of KILDARE.

THE County of *Kildare* is stretch'd out like a fore land to the *King* and *Queen's* Counties on the east, and is very rich and fruitful Giraldus Cambrensis applies those verses of Virgil to the pastures here

Et quantum longis carpunt armenta diebus,
Exigua tantum gelidus ros nocte reponit

What in long days the browzing cattle crop,
In the short nights the fertil dew makes up

Kildare
S Brigid
Two C

The principal town of this County, is *Kildare*, eminent in the first ages of the Irish Church for *Brigid*, a Virgin much renown'd for her devotion and chastity, not she, who about [t]three hundred and forty years since instituted the Order of the Nuns of St *Brigid* (namely, That in one Monastery both Monks and Nuns should live together but in several apartments, without seeing one another, but one more ancient, who liv'd about a thousand years ago, and was a disciple of S Patrick, and very famous in Ireland, Scotland, and England Her Miracles, and the Fire never going out (being preserved and cherished in the [h]inner Sanctuary, like that of *Vesta*, by the Nuns,) and still burning without any increase of ashes, are related by Authors at large This Town has the honour of being a Bishop's See, who was formerly stil'd in the Pope's Letters, *Darensis* [It is said to have been founded by St *Conleth*, with the assistance of St *Bridget*, and among the Suffragan Bishops of Ireland, in Councils and elsewhere, as the Bishop of Meath had the first place, so the Bishop of Kildare had the next] This Town was, first, the habitation of *Richard* Earl of Pembroke, afterwards of *William Marshal* Earl of Pembroke his son in-law, by whose fourth daughter *Sibill*, it came to *William Ferras* Earl of Derby, and by a daughter of his (by her likewise) to *William Vesey*, whose son William Vesey, Chief Justice of Ireland, being out of favour with King Edward the first upon a quarrel between him and

h Antis penetralibus
Ware, Ant. p 136

and John the son of Thomas Girald, and having lost his only legitimate son, gave *Kildare*, and other Lands of his in Ireland, to the King, upon condition that he should infeoff his natural son sirnamed *de Kildare*, in his other Lands in England A little after that, the said *John*, son of Thomas Girald (whose Ancestors, descended from *Girald Windesor*, *Castellan*, of Pembrook, did great service in the conquest of Ireland,) had the castle and town of Kildare, together with *the style and title of Earl of* Kildare, bestow'd on him by King Edward the second These *Fitz Giralds*, or *Geraldins* as they now call them, were Men of great note, and particularly eminent for their brave actions, who of themselves (as one says) *preserv'd the Sea Coasts of Wales and conquer'd Ireland* And this family of *Kildare* flourish'd a long time with their honour and reputation unsully'd, having never had any hand in rebellions, till in Henry the eighth's time, *Thomas Fitz Girald* (son of Girald Fitz Girald Earl of Kildare and Lord Lieutenant of Ireland,) upon the news that his father (who had been sent for into England, and charg'd with male-administration in Ireland) was execu'ed, was so far transported by the heat of youth with this false rumour, that he unadvisedly took up arms against his King and Country, invited Charles the fifth to take possession of Ireland, wasted the Country with fire and sword, besieg'd [the Castle of] Dublin, and put the Archbishop thereof to death For which outrage, he was soon after hang'd, with five of his Uncles, his Father being dead of grief before However, this family was restor'd to its ancient grandeur by Queen Mary, who advanc'd Girald, brother of the said Thomas, to the Earldom of *Kildare*, and the Barony of *Offaly*, whose two sons, Henry and William, having both succeeded, and dying without issue-male, the title of Earl came to *Girald Fitz Girald* their Cousin german

Archiva Regia

Earls of Kildare

Ch 9 Edw 2 N 12

The other remarkable Towns in this County, are, *Naas*, a Market-town[e], *Athie*, situate upon the river Barrow, *Mainoth*, a Castle of the Earls of Kildare, and a Town, with the privilege of a Market and a Fair granted by King Edward the first, in favour of *Girald Fitz-Moris*, [but now the Castle is in rubbish] *Castle-Martin*, the chief seat of the family of *Fitz-Eustace*, descended from the *Poers* in the County of Waterford, of whom, *Rowland Fitz Eustace*, for his great merit and virtue, was made a Baron of Parliament by Edward the fourth, and had the Manour of *Portlester* bestow'd upon him, as also the title of Viscount *Baltinglas* by Henry the eighth, all which Honours *Rowland Fitz-Eustace* lost, being banish'd in Queen Elizabeth's time for his treachery

e *Vid infrà*

Barons F Eustace

Pat 2 Ed 4

Viscounts Baltinglas

[The first of the above mention'd Towns, namely *Naas*, is the Shire Town, near which, at *Siggingstowne*, Thomas Earl of Strafford, Lord Lieutenant of Ireland, erected a large and magnificent Pile, designing to make it the Seat of his Family Almost two miles from thence, are two Stones, of a remarkable Bigness, call'd from thence *Long Stones*, but when, or for what end, they were plac'd there, Historians give no account]

Sigginstowne

Usher, Primord p 242

The more considerable families here, besides the *Fitz Giralds*, are all likewise English, the *Ougans*, *De la Hides*, *Ailmers*, [d]*Walshes*, [d]*Boisels*, *Whites*, [d] *Suttons*, &c [Within this County, the two honourable Families of *Loftus* and *Allen*, have their respective Titles of Honour; the first of Viscount *Loftus* of *Ely*, and the second of Viscount *Allen*]

d These, extinct or obscure

As for the *Gyant's dance*, which Merlin by Art-magick transferr'd (as they say) out of this territory to *Salisbury*-Plain, as also the bloody battle to be fought hereafter between the English and the Irish at *Moleaghmast*, I leave them to those credulous heads, that doat upon the fabulous part of Antiquity, and are admirers of old Prophesies For my own part, I shall not regard such Stories These are the Midland Counties of *Leinster* Now, we proceed to those upon the Sea-coast

The County of *WEISFORD*.

ELOW that mouth, from which the three sister-rivers, the *Barrow*, the *Neore*, and the *Swire*, empty themselves into the Sea, upon a Promontory eastward, which makes a winding shore, lies the County of *Weisford* or *Wexford*, in Irish County *Reogh* [(i e coarse or rough ,)] where the *Menapii* are plac'd by Ptolemy That these *Menapii* were the offspring of the *Menapii* upon the Sea-coast of the Lower Germany, the name itself seems to intimate But whether that *Carausius* who set up for Emperor in Britain against Diocletian, is of this, or that Nation, I leave to the Enquiry of others For Aurelius Victor calls him a Citizen of *Menapia*; and the City *Menapia* is plac'd by Geographers in Ireland, and not in the Low Countries

Menapii

Carausius.

Published by Schottus

Upon the river *Barrow* in this County, formerly flourish'd *Ross* [*] a large City, [now a Burrough,] of good trade, and well-peopled fortified with a wall of great compass by Isabel daughter of Earl *Richard Strongbow*; which is the only remains of it at this day For the dissension between the Citizens and the Religious here, did long since ruin the Town, and reduc'd it almost to nothing [It had anciently a Cathedral and a Bishop, but the See was afterwards united to that of *Fernes* The Honourable Family of *Parsons* have been advanced to the dignity of Viscounts, and more lately, of Earls, of Ross]

More eastward, *Duncanon*, a garrison'd castle, is so seated upon the river, that no Ships can pass to Waterford or Ross, but by its leave, and therefore they took care to fortifie it in the year 1588, when the Spaniards made a defcent

Duncanon

descent into Ireland From hence, to the very mouth of the river, a narrow neck of land shoots out, upon which stands a high tower built by the Citizens of Ross in the time of their prosperity, for the direction of Sailors in to the river's mouth At a little distance from hence, upon a winding shore, stands *Tintern*, where William Marshall Earl of Pembrooke built a famous Monastery, and call'd it *De Voto*, because, in a dangerous storm, he had made a *Vow* to found one, and, being here cast upon the shore, perform'd it in this place

This very Promontory, Ptolemy calls *Hieron*, i e *Sacred*, and I question not but it was call'd by a name of the same import among the Inhabitants For the first town in it, where the English landed when they first invaded this Island, is call'd in Irish *Banna*, which signifies *holy*

From this *Holy Promontory* the shore turns eastward, and runs for a long way towards the north, over-against which, the Sea is full of flats and shallows that are very dangerous, and are call'd by the Seamen *the Grounds* Here, Ptolemy fixes the river *Modona*, and the city *Menapia* at the mouth of it, names, so utterly lost at this day, that I despair of giving light to a matter so very obscure Yet, seeing there is but one river which empties it self here, and, in a manner, parts the County in two, and is call'd *Slane*, and since upon the mouth, where it stagnates, there stands a City call'd by a German name, *Weisford*, the head Town of the County, methinks, it is very probable, that this *Slane* is the old *Modona*, and this *Weisford*, that *Menapia*, and the rather, because the present name is but novel, and of a German original, having been given it by those Germans whom the Irish call *Oustmen* This is [b] a large Town [and a Corporation, and is much frequented by Strangers in Summer, by reason of a good Chalybeat Spring that is near it] The Town is remarkable upon this account, that it was the first of the Island that submitted to the English, being reduc'd by *Fitz Stephens*, a valiant Commander, and made an English Colony So that this Shire is very full of English, who [c] dress after the old fashion of the English, and speak the English Language, but with a mixture of Irish *Dermot*, who invited the English hither, gave this City and the Territory about it to *Fitz Stephen* for ever, who began a [d] Burrough-town hardly at *Carrick*, and improv'd the natural strength of the place by great additions of Art But he having surrender'd his right to Henry the second, the King made it over to Richard Earl of Pembrook in fee, to hold of him and the Kings of England for ever From whom by the Earl's *Mareschals*, the [illegible] of [illegible] a Family in France, and the *Hastings*, it came to the *Greys* Lords of Ruthin, who are frequently call'd in old Charters *Lords of Weisford*, tho' in Henry the sixth's time *J Talbot* is once mention'd in the Publick Records, by the title of *Earl of Shrewsbury and Weisford* [The Island *Edri*, by Pliny call'd *Andros*, is seated by Ptolemy among the Islands in the west of Ireland and the learned [illegible] Author of the *Antiquities* of this Kingdom, believes it to be the same with *Beg-Eri*, i e Little Ireland, an Isle, in the mouth of the river *Slane*] Concerning which river, take this Distich of *Neckam*, such as it is

> *Ditat* Eniscotium *flumen* quod Slana *vocatum*,
> *Hunc cernit* Weisford *se* [illegible]
>
> Enrich'd by *Slane* does *Eniscort* appear,
> And *Weisford* sees him join his stream with her

For [e] *Eniscorthy*, a Burrough-town, stands upon this river, as also more inward upon the same, *Fernes* (only famous for its Bishop's See,) which the Fitz Geralds formerly fortified with a Castle Hard by, on the other side the *Slane*, live the *Cavenaghs*, the *Donels*, the [f] *Montaghs*, and [f] *O-Mores*, Irish Families of very turbulent and seditious spirits, as also, the *Sinotts*, the *Roches*, and the [g] *Peppards*, all English On this side the *Slane*, those of greatest note, [h] were the Viscounts Mont Garret (the first of whom was *Edmund Butler*, a younger son of Peter Earl of Ormond, dignify'd with that title by Edward the sixth,) and many more of the same name, with the *Devereux*, *Staffords*, *Cheevers*, *Whites*, *Fercongs*, *Fitz Harrys*, *Browns*, *Hores*, *Haies*, *Codles*, and *Masters*, of English Extraction (as are very many of the common people,) [all, or most of whom, are now in a low condition but the *Roches* and *Sinotts*, before-mentioned, remain in a good state

From Newborough, in this County, the title of Baron is enjoy'd by the Honourable *George Cholmondley*, on whom also hath been confer'd the honour of a Baron, in the Kingdom of Great Britain]

The Grounds. The river Modona.

The river Slane. Weisford.

[b] None of the greatest. C.

[e] *Enscort*, C

Ann. 1607.

[f] Extinct

[g] Extinct

[h] Are, C

Newborough

Vid. *Anglesey*, p. 811

CAUCI.

The County of WICKLOW.

The Cauci.

T HE *Cauci*, who were also a People upon the Sea coast of Germany, inhabited that part of the Country that is next the *Menapii*, but not at the same distance as those in Germany They lived in that Maritim Tract, which is now possess'd by the *O-Tools* and *Birns*, Irish families that [a] subsist by rapin and blood, being ever restless and unquiet; and, confiding in the strength of their Forts and Garrisons, they obstinately defy all Laws, and live in implacable enmity against the English To put a stop to their outrage, and to make them conformable to the Laws, it was debated by some knowing men in the year 1578, how those parts might be reduced into a County, and at last they were divided into six several Baronies, which should make the County of *Wicklo* or *Arcklo* For this is the chief place hereabouts, and [b] was a Castle of the Earls of Ormond, who, among other titles of honour, [c] stiled themselves Lords of *Arcklo*. [Besides this, it hath the Town of *Wicklow*, which is a Corporation, and the Shire-Town, and gives the title of Baron to the honourable Family of *Maynard*, and is famous for the best *Ale* in Ireland [d], and *Blessington* which gives the title of Baron to a branch of the honourable Family of *Boyle* Also, it hath several pretty Villages, with some Noblemen's Seats, and it is so well inhabited with English, and by them improved to that degree, as to make it inferior to few Counties in this Kingdom]

O-Tools, Birns · [a] So said, ann 1607 · *Wicklo, or Arcklo.* · [b] Is, C · [c] Stile, C · *Blessington.* · [d] See p 1364, 1366.

Below *Arcklo*, the river call'd *Ovoca* in Ptolemy, runs into the Sea, and (as Giraldus Cambrensis says) *is of that nature, that as well when the tide flows as ebbs, the water in this creek retains its natural taste and freshness, preserving it self unmix'd and free from any tincture of salt, to the very Sea*

[In this County, at *Windgate*, is a remarkable heap of Stones, concerning which, the learned Writer of the Antiquities of Ireland gives a threefold Conjecture, That it must be, either for the burial of persons slain in Battel, or a Mercurial Monument, laid there by Travellers, according to the custom of Antiquity, in honour of *Mercury*, the Protector of travellers, or one of those heaps of Stones, which were heretofore laid to mark out the Meas or Bounds of Land, and were called *Scorpions* Also, in this County, near *Glandelach*, certain Country people, in the year 1639, found a great quantity of ancient Irish Coins]

Ware, Ant. p 133 · *Ibid p 71, and 53*

The County of *DIVELIN* or *DUBLIN*

B Eyond the *Cauci*, liv'd the *Eblani*, in that tract which is now the County of *Dublin* or *Divelin*, bounded on the east by the Irish Sea, on the west by the County of Kildare, on the south by the little territories of the *O-Tools* and *O Birns*, and of those which they term the *Glinnes* [(now part of the County of Wicklow,)] and, on the north, by the County of *Meath* and the river *Nanny* The Soil produces good Corn, and Grass in great plenty, and the County is well stock'd with game, both for hunting and fowling, but so naked for the most part, that they generally burn a fat kind of turf, or else coal out of England, instead of wood In the south part, which is less improv'd and cultivated, there is here and there a hill pretty well wooded, under which lie the low vales call'd *Glynnes*, thick set with woods, and these [a] were heretofore sadly infested with those pernicious People, the *O Tooles* and *O Birnes*; [but are not so at this day, but on the contrary as safe and secure as any part of Ireland] Among these *Glynnes* is the Bishoprick of *Glandilaugh* which has lain desolate ever since it was annex'd to the Archbishoprick of *Dublin* In other parts, the County is very well town'd and peopled, and surpasses the other Provinces of Ireland in improvements of all sorts, and a peculiar neatness and elegance It is divided into [i] six Baronies, *Rathdown*, *Newcastle*, *Cast[illegible]*, *Knoc*, *Coulock*, *Lahodiy*, and *Nethercross* which

The Glinnes · [a] Are sadly, C · [i] Five C.

I cannot (as I could desire) give a *particular* account of, because I am not well enough acquainted with the several bounds First, therefore, I will survey the Sea coast, and then follow the Rivers, as their course leads me into the inner parts of this County, none of which are twenty miles distant from the shore

To begin in the South, the first place that we meet with upon the coast, is [g] *Bra[illegible]*, where is a narrow haven with a rock hanging over it, enclosed with good walls, instead of a Castle, which (as other Castles of this Kingdom) was by Act of Parliament, not to be commanded by any Governour, that [h] was not an Englishman by reason the Irish who had born that charge heretofore [illegible], to the great damage of the Government, made small resistance in case of assaults, and suffer'd Prisoners to escape by connivance But let us hear what Giraldus says of this Port, who calls it *Winchiligillo* *There is a Port at* Winchiligillo, *on the side of Ireland next to Wales, which, at every general* Ebb *of the Sea, receives the Waves, and at the general* Flow *of the Sea [illegible] them out again and after the Sea is gone back, [illegible] is quite left [illegible] the River, which runs into the Sea here, [illegible] every corner, [illegible]*

Next, upon the top of a hill by the Sea side, stands *New Castle*, where [illegible] may be seen those shelves of Sand call'd the *Grounds*, which lie along this coast, [illegible] the shore, the water is [illegible] seven fathoms deep A little higher, where the *Bra[illegible]* [illegible]

[g] [illegible] p 13[illegible] · [h] [illegible] C [illegible] · *New [illegible]*

river) runs into the Sea, stands *Old Court* [which anciently belong'd to the *Talbots*, and *Old Conaught*,] the estate of the *Wallenses* or *Walshes* of *Caryckmain*, a family, [which was] not only ancient and noble, but very numerous in these Parts. Next to this is *Powers Court*, formerly (as the name it self shews) belonging to the *Poers*, a very large Castle, till *Tirlaugh O Tool*, in a rebellion, demolished it. [This is a fine Seat, and from hence the *Wingfields* took their title of Viscounts, and tho' the title be lately extinct, the Estate still remains in the same name.

Powers Court

This river, *Bray*, is the present Bound between the Counties of Dublin and Wicklow, so that the part already described, south of that River, is properly in the County of *Wicklow*.]

From the mouth of the *Bray*, the shore draws in, and makes a Bay, where at the very turn of the [g] *elbow*, lies the little Island of S. *Benedict*, which belongs to the Archbishop of Dublin. This Bay is call'd *Dublin-haven*, into which runs the *Liffy*, the noblest river of this County, and though the spring of it is but fifteen miles from the mouth, the course is so winding and crooked, that first it goes south by St. *Patrick's land*, and then west, after that, northward, watering the County of *Kildare*, and at length eastward, by *Castle Knoc*, heretofore the Barony of the *Tyrrels* (whose estate by females was transferr'd to other families about the year 1370,) and by *Kilmainam*, formerly belonging to the Knights of the order of S. John of *Jerusalem*, and [h] heretofore a place of retirement for the Lord Deputy. [But now it belongs to the Earl of *Rosse*, and is the place of the County Sessions. And the Country Palace for the Government is at *Chapel-Izod*, on the north side of the river, where is a noble Park, call'd the *Phœnix park*.]

[g] Cubitus.

Dublin haven.

Liffi, by Giraldus, Aven Liff.

[h] Now, C.

This *Liffy* is certainly mentioned in Ptolemy, though the carelesness of Librarians has depriv'd it of its proper place. For the river *Libnius* is describ'd in the Copies of Ptolemy, to lie in the same latitude on the other side of the Island, where there is no such river [i]; and therefore now, with the Reader's leave, let it be re-call'd, and restor'd to its *Eblana*. Concerning this River, *Neckam* writes,

[i] The Bay of Sligo says H.

> *Visitera Castle Knock nonde'ignatur Aven Liff,*
> *Ipsum Dublinia jus [illegible]*
>
> Nor thee, poor *Castle Knock*, does *Liffy* scorn,
> Whose stream at *Dublin* to the Ocean's born.

For *Dublin* is but seven miles from the mouth of it, eminent, and memorable, above all the Cities of Ireland, the same which Ptolemy calls *Eblana*, we *Develin*, the Latins *Dublinium* and *Dublinia*, the Welsh *Dinas Dulin*, the Saxons *Duflin*, and the Irish *Balacleigh*, that is, a Town upon *Hurdles*, for so they think the foundation lies, the ground being soft and quaggy, like *Sevil* in Spain, that is said by Isidore to be so call'd, because it stood upon piles fasten'd in ground which was loose and fenny. As for the Antiquity of *Dublin*, I have met with nothing certain concerning it; but that the City must be very ancient, I am satisfy'd upon Ptolemy's authority. [illegible]

Canes Dub [illegible]

us, it was sadly shatter'd in the Danish wars; afterwards, it fell under the subjection of Edgar King of England, as his Charter, already mention'd, testifies. Next, the Norwegians got possession of it, and therefore in the life of *Gryffith ap Cynan*, Prince of Wales, we read, that Harald the Norwegian, after he had subdu'd the greatest part of Ireland, built Dublin. This Harald seems to be that [k] *Harfager* (or *Fair-hair*) the first King of Norway, whose pedigree stands thus in the life of *Gryffith*. To Harald was born [l] *Aulocd*, to Aulocd, another of the same name. This Aulocd had a Son, *Sitric*, King of Dublin. Sitric had a Son, *Aulocd*, whose daughter *Reeseb* was mother to Gryffith ap Cynan, born at Dublin, when [m] Tirlough reign'd in Ireland. This, by the by. At length, upon the first arrival of the English in Ireland, *Dublin* was soon taken, and gallantly defended by them, when *Aust* [illegible] Prince of Dublin, and afterwards *Gothred* King of the Isles, assaulted it vigorously on all sides. A little after, an English Colony was transplanted hither from Bristol, by King Henry the second, who gave them this City (being perhaps at that time drain'd of Inhabitants) in these words, *With all the liberties and free customs, which those of Bristol enjoyed*. From that time, it flourished more and more, and in times of the greatest difficulty has given many and ample proofs of its loyalty to the Kings of England.

[k] Pulchricomus.

[l] Otherwise call'd Ablaicus, Aulafus, and Olavus.

[m] T[illegible]

This is the Royal City of *Ireland*, and the most noble [n] *Mart*, wherein the Courts of Judicature are held. The City is well wall'd, neatly built, and very populous, [being exceedingly encreas'd, in this and the last age, not only in bigness (for it is as large again as it was before,) but also in People, Buildings, and Magnificence of all kinds.] An ancient writer describes it to be *nobly peopled, very pleasantly situated, and well supply'd with Fish from the river and the sea; famous for trade, and for those sweet plains, oaky woods, and fine parks, so entertaining, about it*. Thus also William of Newborow, *Dublin a Maritime City, is the Metropolis of Ireland, it enjoys the benefit of a famous* [illegible]. Its situation is particularly pleasant and wholsom, having hills on the south, plains on the west, the Sea hard by on the east, and the river *Liffy*, where Ships ride safely. [This river was heretofore the bound to the north, but the City is much enlarged, [illegible] on the north side, that now it [illegible] in the middle of it.] Upon the river, there are Keys (as we call them) or certain Banks set up to check the violence of the water. For [illegible] [illegible] is the most [illegible] [illegible] Here the City wall [illegible] [illegible] fortified on [illegible] with six gates, which [illegible]

[n] Emporium.

Johannes de Fordun, in the [illegible] of St. Patrick. [illegible] rerum Anglicarum, c. p. [illegible]

[o] On the north, C.

Ab Algon lib [illegible]

The Entrance on the East, is by *Dames Gate*, [illegible] the King's castle upon [illegible], well fortified with ditches and towers, [illegible] with a good Arsenal [illegible] [illegible] *Henry* [illegible] [illegible] *Henry the Second, King of England* [illegible] [illegible] *Ports of Ireland*, [illegible] On [illegible] a fine College on the [illegible] *Monastery* heretofore [illegible] [illegible]

[o] South, C.

All-hallows Monastery.

University begun and founded in 1591, May 3. Students admitted in the year 1593. ^s Lately, C. ^t So said, ann. 1607. 1320. L. MS. of Baron Howth.

stood) dedicated to the *Undivided and Holy Trinity*, and endow'd with the privileges of an University by Queen Elizabeth of blessed memory for the education of youth, and ^q furnish'd with an excellent Library, all which give no small hopes that Religion and Learning, will, ^r after a long exile, return to Ireland, to which foreigners once resorted, as to the great Mart of liberal Arts and Sciences. In the reign of Edward the second, *Alexander Bicknor*, Archbishop of Dublin, first began to recall them; having obtained of the Pope the Privileges of an University for this place, and instituted publick Lectures: but this laudable design was defeated by the turbulent times that followed.

The north-gate opens towards the bridge, which is arched, and was built of free stone by King John, who joined *Oustman town* to the City. For here, the *Oustmanni*, which Giraldus says came from Norway and those Northern Islands, settled (according to our Histories) about the year 1050. In this Suburbs, stood formerly the famous Church of St. Mary *de Oustmanby* (for so it is call'd in King John's Charter,) and also an House of *Black Friers*, whither the Courts of Judicature were ^s transfer'd. [This is now call'd *The King's-Inns*, and here the Judges and Lawyers meet in Commons one week in every Term. But as to the Courts of Judicature, they are now removed near Christ-Church, to a sumptuous Fabrick erected for that purpose.]

^s Lately, C. Kings Inns.

On the west part of Dublin, are two gates, *Ormonds-gate*, and *Newgate* (which is the common Gaol,) both leading to the longest Suburbs of this City, named St. *Thomas*, where stands also a noble Abbey of the same name, called *Thomas Court*, founded and endow'd with large revenues by King Henry the second, to atone for the death of Thomas Archbishop of Canterbury; [but now turn'd into Houses and Streets.]

Thomas Court.

On the South, we enter by St. *Paul's* gate, and that call'd St. *Nicholas*, which opens into St. *Patrick's Suburbs*, where stands the Palace of the Archbishop, known by the name of St. *Sepulcher*, with a stately Church dedicated to St. *Patrick*, and famous ^t for the curious workmanship within, and for its stone pavements, arch'd roof, and high steeple. It is uncertain when this Church was first built, but that Gregory King of Scots, about the year 890, ^u came in pilgrimage to it, is plain from the Scotch History. Afterwards it was much enlarged by King John, and made a Church of Prebendaries by John Comyn Archbishop of Dublin, which was confirmed by Pope Celestine the third, in the year 1191. After that, *Henry Loundres*, his successor in the See of Dublin, augmented it with *Dignities of* ^w *Parsonages*, as the words of the Founder are, and, in immunities, orders, and customs, made it conformable to the Church of Salisbury. At present, it consists of a Dean, a Chanter, a Chancellor, a Treasurer, two Archdeacons, and twenty two Prebendaries, *the only light and lamp* (not to conceal a very noble Character which a Parliament of this Kingdom gave it) *of all pious and Ecclesiastical discipline and order, in Ireland.*

^t Opere intestino. ^u Ad eam accessit. ^w Personatuum. Stat. Parl. 18 Hen. VIII c. 15.

Here is also another Cathedral Church in the very heart of the City, dedicated to the *Holy Trinity*, but commonly call'd *Christ's Church*. Concerning it's foundation, we have this passage in the Archives of that Church. *Sitric King of Dublin, son of Ableb Count of Dublin, gave a place of ground to the Holy Trinity, and to Donatus the first Bishop of Dublin, to build a Church in honour of the Holy Trinity; and not only that, but gold and silver sufficient for the design, and to finish the* ^x *Church-yard.* This was done about the year ^x [illegible] 1012, at which time *Lancarvanensis* affirms, that *Sitrick* son of *Abloic* (so he calls him) did flourish. The work was begun by Donatus, but finish'd by Laurence, Archbishop of Dublin, *Richard Strongbow* Earl of Pembroke (commonly call'd *Comes Strigulia*, whose tomb, repair'd by Henry Sidney Lord Deputy, is to be seen here,) *Robert Fitz Stephens*, and *Reimond Giraldi*.

On the south side of the Church, stands the Town-hall, built of square stone, and call'd *Tolestale*, where Causes are try'd before the Mayor, and where the publick meetings of the Citizens are held. The City enjoys many Privileges. Formerly, it was govern'd in chief by a Provost, but in the year 1409, King Henry the fourth gave them the privilege of choosing every year a Mayor, with two Bailiffs, and of carrying a gilt Sword before him. Afterwards, King Edward the sixth changed these Bailiffs into Sheriffs. There is nothing wanting to the grandeur and happiness of this City, but the removal of those heaps of Sand, that by the ebbing and flowing of the Sea, are wash'd into the mouth of the river *Liffi*, and hinder great Ships from coming up, except at high water. Thus much of *Dublin*, the account of which I confess to be mostly owing to the diligence and learning of *James Usher*, Chancellor of St. *Patrick's*, whose Knowledge and Judgment, are very far beyond his years.

Tolestale.

As for *Robert Vere* Earl of Oxford, whom Richard the second (who was very profuse in bestowing titles of honour) made Marquiss of Dublin, and afterwards Duke of Ireland, I have spoken of him before, and need not repeat it here.

Marquiss of Dublin.

[In the year 1646, while they were working the lines of Fortification in the East Suburbs of Dublin, they dug up an ancient Sepulchre built of eight Marble Stones, whereof two cover'd, and the rest supported it. Therein, was found a great quantity of Coals, Ashes, and Bones of men, some *burnt*, some half burnt; and, on that account, it is reckon'd to have belong'd to the Danes, and to have been built for some of their Nobility, before they became Christians.]

Ware, Ant. p. 152. [illegible] *Dan*[illegible] *Lib.* [illegible]

Where the river *Liffy* runs into the Sea, stands *Howth*, almost encompassed by the Salt water, which gives the title of Baron to the noble family of St. *Laurence*, who have liv'd there so happy, that in a long series of successors (for they carry their pedigree as high as Henry the second,) no one, as it is ^y said, has been ever attainted of treason, or left a Minor. At a little distance from hence is *Malahide*, eminent for its Lords the *Talbots*, an English family.

Baro[illegible] St. L[illegible] [illegible] Ma[illegible]

[Near the shore of Dublin, is the Island of *Lambay*, where the learned Antiquary of this Nation hath plac'd the *Limnum* of Ptolemy, as agreeing better, both in name and situation, than Ramsey Island, where it was plac'd before.]

[illegible] p. [illegible]

More inward, to the north, stands *Fingall*, which is an Irish word, and signifies a *nation of Foreigners* (for they call the English, *Gall*, i.e. *Strangers*, and *Saxons*, i.e. Saxons,) a small territory, well cultivated [illegible] is it were the granary of this Kingdom, it yields such plentiful crops every year [illegible], the earth [illegible] were, [illegible] and [illegible] the labour of the husbandman, [illegible] other parts of the [illegible], that it seems to com-

plain

plain of t e noth and rudeness of the Inhabitants There [a] are scatter'd up and down this County, many eminent families of the English as, besides those but now mention'd, the *Plunkets, Barnwells, Russels, Talbots, Dillons, Nettervills, Holywoods, Lutterels, Burnells, Fitz Williams, Goldings, Ushers, Cadleys, Finglases, Sarfelds, Blackneys, Cruces, Baths,* &c [Of whom, the *Plunkets, Barnwells, Lutterels, Fitz Williams, Talbots, Dillons, Nettervills,* and *Ushers,* are still in a flourishing condition. In this County, the Honourable title of Earl of Bellomont is vested in the Family of Coote, that of Viscount *Swords* in the Family of Molesworth, that of Viscount *Kingsland,* in the Family of Barnwall, that of Viscount *Fitz-Williams* of Merion, in the Family of Fitz-Williams, that of Viscount *Rathcoole,* in the family of Tracy, and that of Baron *Santry,* in the Family of Barry]

[a] Ann 1607

Swords

Kingsland

Merion

Rathcoole

Santry

Thus much, as briefly as I could, of *Leinster,* which formerly went no farther I know not whether I deserve to be thank'd or laugh'd at, if I tell you how *Thomas Stukely,* when he had lost his reputation and fortune, both in England and Ireland, and escap'd the justice of the Law, did by fair promises and big words insinuate himself so much into the favour of Pope Gregory the thirteenth, that he conferr'd upon him the titles of *Marquiss of Leinster, Earl of Wexsford* and *Caterlagh,* Viscount *Murrough,* and Baron of *Ross* and *Ydron* Thus, exalted with these pompous titles, and intending to invade Ireland, he turn'd into Africa, and together with three Kings was slain in one battel, and so ended a Romantick Life honourably enough

Thomas Stukely

METH.

HE remaining part of the Country of the *Eblani,* was formerly a Kingdom, and the fifth part of Ireland; call'd in Irish *Mjh,* in English *Methe,* and by Giraldus *Midia* and *Media,* possibly, because it lay in the very *middle* of the Island For they say that *Kil lair,* a Castle in these parts (which seems to be Ptolemy's *Laberus,* as the name it self intimates) is as it were the *Navel* of Ireland, and *Lair* in Irish signifies the middle This *Meth* [(comprehending also *West Meath* and *Longford,*)] extends from the Irish Sea to the river Shanon *The soil* (as Barthol Anglicus tells us) *yields plenty of corn, and good pasture, which is well stock'd with cattle* *The County is also well furnish'd with fish and flesh, and other victuals, as butter, cheeses and milk, and well water'd with rivers The situation is pleasant, and the air whol som By reason of woods and marshes in the borders of it, the entrance, or access, is difficult, so that, for the great number of inhabitants, and the strength of its towns and castles, it is commonly (on account of the Peace it enjoys) call'd the* Chamber of Ireland Within the memory of [a] our Fathers, when the Country was too large to be govern'd by one Sheriff, for the more easie administration of Justice, it was, by Act of Parliament, in the thirty eighth year of Henry the eighth, divided into two, viz the County of *Meth,* and the County of *West Meth*

Laberus.

[a] So said, Ann 1607.

The County of *METH.*

HE County of *Meth,* on the South, bounds upon the County of Kildare, on the East, upon the County of Dublin and the Sea; on the North, upon the County of Louth; and on the West, upon the County of West-Meth The whole is subdivided into eighteen Baronies, *Duelike, Scrine, Slane, Margal'an, Navan, Kenles,* the moiety of the Barony of *Fower* near *Kenles, Killalou, Demsfore, Clove, Moylagh, Logbern, Old castle, Luyn, Moyfenaragbe, Deese, Rathtouth* and *Dunboyn* The *Boyn,* call'd in Ptolemy *Buvinda,* and in Giraldus, *Boandus,* a noble river rising in the North side of the *King's County,* runs through the middle of it In the hither part, on this side the *Boyne,* the places most memorable are *Galtrim,* where the Family of the *Huseys* [a] did long dwell; *Killin Castle,* built by Hugh Lacy, Governor of Ireland in Henry the second's time; and *Dunsany,* which [b] had its Barons of Parliament, eminent for their antient Nobility, and descended from the *Plonkets* others derive them from the Danes; but their Arms are the same, only in different colours, with those of *Allan Plonket* of *Kilpeck* in England; who was also a Baron in Edward the first's time These [c] *Plonkets*

R. Boyn.

[a] Have long dwelt C

Galtrim

Killin

Dunsany

[b] Has, C.

[c] See Fingall.

kets in Ireland have been very eminent, ever since *Christopher Plonket* (a person of great valour and wisdom, who was *Deputy* to Richard Duke of York, Viceroy in Henry the sixth's time) was rais'd to the dignity of Baron of *Killin*, which came to him by his wife, as heir to the Family of the *Cusakes*; and his second son had the title of Baron of *Dunsany* confer'd upon him, for his great worth and valour

Baron Dunsany

Baron Trimletston

Barnwell

Beyond the *Boyn*, stands *Trimletstoun*, which is a Barony belonging to one of the Family of the *Barnwells* For John Barnwell was made a Baron of Parliament by King Edward the fourth Then *Gormanston*, which has its [d] honorary Viscounts, descended from the *Prestons* of Lancashire, as it is thought, and who have deserv'd exceeding well of their King and Country, and *Slane*, which has also its Barons, of the Family of the Flemings, among whom is [e] *Athboy*, a populous Market town The *Boyn*, after it has passed *Glan Iores*, i e the *land of the sons of George* (who was of the Family of the Birminghams, and whose heir by marriage brought a fair Estate, with the Castle of *Carbray*, to the *Prestons*,) it arrives at *Trim*, a noted little Market-town, where *William Pepard* built a Castle This was an ancient Barony of the *Laceyes*, which afterwards became one of the titles of the Dukes of York, who wrote themselves *Lords of Trim* After that, it runs by *Navan*, which has its Baron or Baronet, but not Parliamentary, and is honour'd with the ordinary residence of the Bishop of this Diocese, who has now no Cathedral Church, [nor Dean, nor Chapter,] but acts in all matters with the assent of the *Clergy of Meth* His See seems to have been at *Cluanarard*, call'd also *Clunart*, where Hugh Lacy formerly built a Castle for thus we find it in the [f] Apostolical Letters, *Episcopus Midensis sive Clunarardensis*, and corruptly, as it seems, in a Roman Provincial, *Elnamirand* [The truth of that matter, is thus In Meath, were heretofore many Episcopal Sees, as, *Clonard*, *Damleag*, *Kenlis*, *Trim*, *Ardbraccan*, *Donshaghlin*, and *Slane* with others of less note, all which (except two *Damleag* and *Kenlis*) were united, and their common Seat constituted at *Clonard*, as those two were also afterwards united The first Bishop of *Clonard*, was the famous St *Finian* or *Finan*, who, with his Episcopal See, instituted a School or Academy in this place, wherein many persons, afterwards eminent for Piety and Learning, received their Education The last of the Bishops of this Diocese, who sat at Clonard, was *Simon de Rochfort*, who, like his Predecessor Eugenius, changed his Style, and was called Bishop of Meath, as all his Successors have been to this day]

Viscounts Gormanstoun

[d] *Vicecomites honorarios*

Barons *Slane*

[e] Aboy, C

Carbray

Trim

Navan.

[f] *Apostolicis*

Ware, Ant p 128

The Boyn now grown larger, after a speedy course for some miles, falls into the sea near *Drogbeda*. And what if one should think that this river was so call'd from its rapid stream? for *Boan* not only in Irish, but in British also, signifies *swift*; and our Countryman Necham sings thus of it,

> *Ecce Boan qui Trim celer influit, istius undas*
> *Subdere se salsis Drogbeda cernit aquis.*

> See, how swift *Boyn* to *Trim* cuts out his way!
> See, how at *Drogbeda* he joins the Sea

[This is the river, famous in our modern Histories, for the Victory obtained on the banks of it, by King *William* the third, over King *James* the second and the Irish, on the first day of July 1690, and very lately the Right Honourable Gustavus, Baron Hamilton of Stackallan, hath been advanced to the honour of Viscount Boyne Visc Boyne

At a place called *Dardistoune*, about two miles from Drogheda, were found in digging, three heads, with horns *prodigiously large*, of the *Deer* kind, and many more of the like kind have been also found in other parts of Ireland, to which the horns of the fairest Buck, now a days, bear no more proportion, than those of the smallest young Fawn, do to the largest overgrown Buck They are commonly called by the People *Elcbe's-borns*, but these, upon the comparison, appear to be different in figure, and much inferior in size, and no description of the horns of such Animals in any other Country, is found to agree so well with these, as that of the *Moose*-Deer in the West-Indies, *with exceeding fair horns with broad Palms, some of them two fathom or twelve foot from the tip of one horn to the other*, i e only fourteen inches wider than some of these]

Phil Trans. N 227

Josselin's New England Rarities

The families of greatest note in this County (besides those already mention'd, *viz* the *Plonkets*, *Flemings*, *Barnwells*, and *Husseys*,) are the *Darceys*, *Cusakes*, [f] *Dillons*, *Bermingbams*, *De la Hides*, *Netervills*, *Garzies*, *Cadells*, [*Wellons*, *Cruses*, *Drakes*, *Lloyds*, *Jones*,] and others, who, I hope, will pardon me for omitting their names, as well as those I mention here and elsewhere, if I place them not exactly according to their several degrees and qualities

[f] Of Rathmon

[This County gives the title of Earl to the Honourable Family of *Brabazon*, and within it several other Noble Families have also their respective Titles of Honour, Cholmondley, that of Viscount Kells, Grimston, that of Baron of Dunboyne and Viscount Grimston, Bellew, that of Baron Bellew of Doleek, and Aylmer, that of Baron Balrath]

Kell. Dunboyne Doleek Balrath

The

The County of *WEST-METH.*

HE County of *West-Meth*, so call'd in respect of the former upon which it borders to the West, comes up to the *Shanon*, and lies between the *King's County* on the South, and the County of *Longford* on the North It is not inferior to either, in fruitfulness, number of inhabitants, or any other advantage, [a] except neatness and good breeding *Molingar*, by Act of Parliament, was made the head town of this County, lying about the middle of it The whole is divided into twelve Baronies, *Fertulogh*, where the *Tirells* live, *Ferbille*, the seat of the *Darcies*, *Delvin*, which gives the title of Baron to the *Nogents*, a famous English family, descended from *Gilbert Nogent*, whom *Hugh Lacy*, (who conquer'd *Meth*) in consideration of his great services in the wars of Ireland, rewarded with these Lands and those of *Furrey*, as that learned Gentleman *Richard Stanihurst* has observ'd Then, the *Furrey* aforesaid, as also *Corkery*, where the Nogents dwell, *Moyassel*, the territory of the Tuts and Nogents, *Magirtiernan*, of the Petits and Tuts (who are very numerous,) *Moygoisy*, of the Iuts and Nangles, *Rathcomire*, of the Daltons, *Magirquirke*, of the Dillons, all English families also *Clonlolan*, where the *O Malaghlins*, who are of the old Royal Line of Meth, and *Moycassel*, where the *Magobigans*, native Irish, do live; with many others, called by strange barbarous names But however, as *Martial* the Poet said, after he had reckon'd up certain barbarous Spanish names of places, being himself a Spaniard, That he liked them better than *British* names; so the Irish admire these more than the English names, and one of their great men was wont to say, he would not learn English, lest it should set his mouth awry Thus, all are partial to themselves, and being immoderately pleas'd with their own, despise the rest of the world.

[a] So said ann 1607 Molingar

Barons Delvin

Ann 1607

Ann 1607

Meth had its Kings in old time, or rather Petty Kings, and Slanius, the Monarch of Ireland, as it is said, appropriated the revenues of this County to supply provisions for his own table But when the English got footing in the Kingdom, Hugh Lacy conquer'd the greatest part of of this County, and King Henry the second gave it him in fee, with the title of *Lord of Meth*, who in the building of *Derwarth Castle*, had his head struck off by a Carpenter, as he was stooping down to give him directions.

Lords of Meth

This Hugh had two sons, *Hugh* Earl of Ulster, of whom more hereafter, and *Walter* Lord of *Trim*, who had a son *Gilbert*, that dy'd in the life time of his father By the daughters of this *Gilbert*, viz *Margaret* and *Maud*, one half of this estate, by the *Genevills* (who are said to be of the *Lorain* Family) and by the *Mortimers*, came to the Dukes of *York*, and so to the Crown For *Peter de Genevill*, Son of Maud, had a daughter nam'd *Joan*, who was married to Roger Mortimer, Earl of Merch the other half, by *Margaret* wife of John Verdon, and by his Heirs, who were Constables of Ireland, came at length to several families in *England* [This County hath afforded the title of Earl to the Honourable family of *Nugent*]

Genevills

Constables of Ireland

The County of *LONGFORD.*

TO *West-Meth*, on the North, joins the County of *Longford*, which was reduc'd into the form of a County by *H Sidney*, Lord Deputy, [a] some years ago It was formerly called *Anale* [or *Annaly*,] and inhabited by a numerous family of the *O Pharols* [called *O Ferrels*,] of which there [b] were two petty Princes, one in the South part, called *O Pharoll Boy*, or the *Yellow*; and the other in the North, call'd *O Pharoll Ban*, i e the *white* Very few Englishmen live among them, and those who do, are of a long standing

[a] So said ann 1607 Annaly O Pharoll

[b] Are [c] Doyle

Ann 1607

One side of this County is water'd by the *Shanon*, the noblest river in all Ireland, which (as we observed) runs between Meth and Connaught Ptolemy calls it *Senus*, Orosius *Sena*, and in some Copies *Sacana*, and Giraldus, *Flumen Senense* The Inhabitants thereabouts call it the [c] *Shannon*, that is (as some explain it) *the ancient river* It rises in the County of *Letrim* out of the mountains of *Thernie*, from whence, as it runs southward, it grows very broad in some places, like a Lake Then it contracts it self into a narrow stream, and after it has made a lake or two, it gathers in it self again, and runs to *Macolicum*, mention'd in Ptolemy, now call'd *Malc*, as the most learned Geographer G *Mercator* has observ'd [But Sir *James Ware* declares, that he could not find any place of that name, unless it may be *Malick* by the river *Shannon*; which is in the County of Galway]

Senus.

Shanon, and Shannon

[c] Shan awn

Macolicum Malc

Ant p 27

Soon after, the *Shannon* is received by another broad lake (called *Lough Regith*,) the name and situation whereof make it probable, that the

City

Rigia City *Rigia* (which Ptolemy places in this Country) stood not far off When it has pass'd this lake, it contracts it self again within its own banks, and runs by the town of *Athlon*, of which in its proper place From hence the

* Killaloe, C Shanon, having passed the Cataract at * *Killalo* (of which I shall take notice by and by,) carries ships of the greatest burthen; and, dividing its stream, encompasses the city of *Limerick*, of which I have spoken already From hence, in a direct course of threescore miles (wherein it makes an Island here and there, and is broad, and deep) it runs very swiftly to the West Where-ever it is fordable at low water, it has been guarded with little Forts by our provident forefathers, to secure the country against inroads and plunder Then, it falls from a huge mouth into the [f] Western Ocean, beyond *Knoc-Patrick*, i e *Patrick's hill*, for so Necham calls it in these Verses upon the Shanon,

[f] Called by others *Mare Bredanicum*

> *Fluminibus magnis lætatur Hibernia,* Sineus
> *Inter Connatiam, Momoniamque fluit*
> *Transit per muros Limerici,* Knoc Patrick *illum*
> *Oceani clausum sub ditione videt*
> Great streams do *Ireland's* happy tracts adorn,
> *Shanon* between *Conaught* and *Munster's* born.
> By *Limerick's* walls he cuts his boundless way,
> And at *Knoc-Patrick's* shore is lost i'th' sea.

[The right honourable family of *Aungier* did lately enjoy the title of Earls of *Longford*, and that of *Boyle*, the title of Viscounts *Shanon* Also *Granard* gives the title of Earl to the Family of *Forbes*; and *Lanesborough* the title of Viscount to the Family of *Lane*] Earl of Longford Visc Shanon Granard Lanesborough

CONAGHT.

CONAGHT.

HE fourth part of Ireland, which looks westward, and is enclosed with the river Shanon, and the [a] out-let of Lough Erne (by some called Trovis, by others Bana;) and with the Western Ocean; is called by Giraldus Cambrensis, Conaghtia and Conacia, by the English Conaght, and by the Irish Conaghty. Antiently, as appears from Ptolemy, the Gangani, otherwise called the Concani, Auteri, and Nagnatæ, dwelt here. These Concani or Gangani (descended, like the Luceni, their neighbours, from the Lucensii of Spain) are probably, from the affinity and nearness both of names and places, deriv'd from the Concani of Spain, who in different Copies of Strabo are writ Coniaci, and Conisci These were originally Scythians, and drank the blood of horses, as Silius tells us. a thing not unusual heretofore among the wild Irish.

[a] Emissarie.

Gangani Concani Auteri Nagnatæ

Et qui Messagetem monstrans feritate parentem,
Cornipedis fuso satiaris, Concane, vena

Concans that prove themselves of Scythian strain,
And horse's blood drink from the reeking vein

And Horace also,

Et lætum equino sanguine Concanum.

And Concans warm with horse's blood

Unless Conaughty, the Irish name, may be thought to be a compound of Concani and Nagnatæ The Country, as in some places it is pleasant and fruitful, so in others which are wet and marshy (called Boghs, from their softness, which are common also in other parts of this Island,) it is dangerous; but produces good grass, and very much wood The Sea coast has so many bays and navigable rivers in it, that it seems to invite the inhabitants to Navigation However, these advantages have not that effect upon a people so charm'd with sloth and idleness, that they had much rather go from door to door, than labour for their living in an honest way At present, it is divided into these Counties, Twomond or Clare, Gallway, Maio, Slego, Letrim, and Roscoman

So said, ann. 1607

The formentioned Concani peopl'd the South part of Conaght, where are now the Counties of Twomond or Clare, Gallway, the Territory of Clan-Richard, and the Barony of Atterith.

TWOMOND, or the County of CLARE.

Twomon or *Twomond*, call'd by Giraldus *Thuetmonia*, and by the Irish *Towown*, i. e. the *North-Mounster*; shoots out into the sea with a very great Promontory, which tapers by little and little Though it lye beyond the Shanon, it was [always] counted within *Mounster*, till *Henry Sidney*, Lord Deputy, laid it to Conaght On the East and South side, it is enclosed by the winding course of the Shanon, waxing bigger and bigger; on the West, it is so shut up by the Sea, and on the North by the County of Gallway, that there is no coming to it by land, but through the territory of *Clan-Richard* Neither the Sea nor the Soil would be wanting to the happiness of this County, if the Inhabitants would contribute their pains, which was formerly endeavour'd by *Robert de Muscegros*, an English Gentleman, and by *Richard Clare*, and *Thomas Clare*, younger sons of the family of the Earls of Glocester, to whom Edward the first gave this County They built many Towns and Castles, and exhorted the Natives to a more sociable kind of Life From their name, the head town of the County is call'd *Clare*, which is now the Seat of the Earl of *Twomond*, and gives name to the County of *Clare* The places of note, are, *Kilfennerag*, [in Latin *Fenaborensis*, heretofore a Bishop's See, and now united to *Tuam*,] and *Killaloe* (or *Laonensis*) [still] a Bishop's See This, in the Roman *Provincial*, is call'd *Ladensis*, [and, about the end of the 12th Century, the See of Roscree was united to it, which made it a large Diocese, containing about a hundred Parish-Churches, besides Chapels] Here, a Rock stands in the middle of the Shanon, from whence the water falls with great noise and violence, and this rock hinders Ships from sailing further; but if it could be [a] cut through, or removed, or if the chanel could be drawn round it, the river would bring up Ships much higher, to the great benefit of the Country Not far from the Shanon, stands *Bunraty*, for which *Robert Muscegros* obtained the privilege of a Market and Fair, from Henry the third; and after he had fortified it with a Castle, he gave it to King Edward, who granted this and the whole County to *Richard Clare*, already mention'd Seven miles from hence, stands *Clare* [(once] the chief town of the County) upon a Creek of the Shanon that is full of Islands; and these [b] were the only two Market-town in the County [But at this day, they are mean Villages, and *Ennis* is the Shire-Town, and by much the best in the County] Many of the English who were formerly transplanted hither, are either rooted out, [c] or turn'd Irish [From *Kilmurry*, the Family of *Needham* take the honourable title of Viscount; and *Killard* gives that of Baron to the Family of *Allington*]

Killaloe

A Cataract

[a] *Expandere-tur*

Bunraty

Clare.

[b] Are, C

[c] *Vel degenerârunt*

Kilmurry
Killard

This County [d] was under the Government of the Irish, the *Mac* [e] *Nemaras*, *Mac-Mahons*, [f] *O Loghtons*, and the most powerful of all, the *O-Briens*, descended from the ancient petty Kings of *Conaght*, or, as themselves say, from the Monarchs of Ireland Of these, *Morogh O-Brien* was the first Earl of *Twomond*; who had that honour given him by King Henry the eighth for term of life, and after, to his Nephew *Donagh*, who was made at the same time Baron of *Ibercan*. he succeeded him in the Earldom, and was slain by his brother *Donell*, *Connogher*, *O-Brien*, son of this *Donogh*, was the third Earl, and father of *Donogh*, the fourth Earl, who [g] gave his King and Country most ample proofs of his Loyalty and Valour.

[d] At present is, C

[e] *Nemars*, C

[f] None of this name, now, of any note

Earls of *Twomond*

[g] Hath given, C

[At present, the right Honourable *Henry O-Brien* is Earl of Twomond, and another honourable person, of the same name, enjoys the title of Earl of *Inchiquin*]

Earl of Inchiquin

The County of GALLWAY.

THE County of *Gallway* borders on the south side upon Clare, on the west upon the Ocean, on the north upon the County of Meath, and on the east upon the river Shanon The Soil very well requires the pains of the husband-man and the shepherd The western shore is much chop'd and dinted with little Bays, and border'd all along with a mixture of green Islands and rugged rocks. Among them, are the four Islands called *Arran*, which make a Barony; and are mention'd in Romances as the *Islands of the Living* [From these, the right Honourable *Charles Butler* hath the title of Earl of *Arran*]

Next, *Inis ceath*, formerly famous for a Monastery of Scots and English founded by *Colman*, a person of great sanctity and *Inis Bovind*, which signifies in Scotch (as Bede explains it) the *Isle of white heifers*; though the word is purely British This Monastery was soon abandoned by the English, who could not live peaceably and easie with the Scots More inward, lies *Lough Corbes* (where Ptolemy places the river *Ausoba*) about twenty miles in length, and three or four in breadth It is navigable, and adorn'd with three hundred Islands, which produce much grass, and Pine-trees To, wards the Sea it grows narrow, and runs by *Gallway*, in Irish *Gallive*, possibly, from the *Gallaci* in Spain This is by far the most emi-

Inis ceath.

Inis bovind

Bede, lib. iv c. 4. *Eccl. Hist.*

Lough Corbes

Gallway

nent City in the County, and at least the third in the Kingdom It is neat, and fair-built of solid Stone, of an oval form, and tower-like; and [was once] famous for a Bishop's See. By reason of its harbour and the forementioned road just under, it has abundance of Merchants, and is enrich'd by a great trade in many Commodities, by Sea and Land [Now, it is not the See of a Bishop, but is within the Archbishoprick of *Tuam*, though the Warden of *Galway* hath contested the Jurisdiction, pretending it a *Peculiar*] Scarce four miles from hence, stands *Knoc-toe*, i e *A hill of hatchets*; below which, the greatest body of Rebels that had been seen in Ireland, was drawn together by *William de Burgo*, *O Brien*, *Mac Nemare*, and *O Carrall*, and defeated, with great slaughter, by the famous *Girald* Earl of Kildare, who, [a] at several times, was thirty three years Lord Deputy of Ireland To the east, at no great distance from hence, stands *Aterith* (in which word the name of the *Auteri* is still preserv'd,) it is commonly call'd *Athenry*, and is enclos'd with walls of a great compass, but thinly inhabited. It has had the honour of giving the title of Baron to the valiant *John de Bermingham*, an Englishman; of which family was the Earl of *Louth* However, these *Berminghams* of *Aterith* [b] were so much degenerated into the [c] Irish barbarity, that they hardly [d] own'd themselves English [But the present Lord, the heir-male of that Family, is a Protestant, and a Person of great Probity and Honour In the Church of the Friers Predicants here, are several Monuments of the Bishops of *Kilmacough*, and others; but the most memorable is that of *William Bermingham*, fix'd in the Wall, on the north side of the Altar]

The battle of *Knoc-toe*, 1516

[a] *Per intervalla*

Aterith

Bermingham

[b] Are, C

[c] So said, ann 1607

[d] Own, C

The Irish families of note in these parts, [e] were the *O Kellies*, [f] *O Maddens*, [g] *O-Flagbertys*, *Mac-Dervis*, &c [who are much reduced]

[e] Are C

[f] *O Madins*, C

[g] *O Flairtis*, C

Clan Richard, i e *the Sons or Tribe of Richard*, or *the Land of the Sons of Richard*, borders upon these, and is reckon'd within this County. They take their name, after the Irish manner, from one *Richard*, of an English Family surnam'd *De Burgo*, which afterwards came to have great anthority and interest in these parts *Ulick de Burgo* of this Family was by Henry the eighth made Earl of *Clan-Richard*; whose eldest son enjoys the title of [h] *Dun-Kellin* He had a Son Richard, the second Earl, whose children (by several venters) involv'd their father, their country, and themselves, in great troubles and difficulties *Richard*, who died old, was succeeded by his son *Ulick*, the third Earl, and father of *Richard* the fourth Earl, whose untainted loyalty to the English, and great valour, were signaliz'd at a time when the English Interest was at it's lowest ebb The Archbishop of *Toam's* See lies in this County, which had formerly several Episcopal Sees under it, at present it hath those of [i] *Anagchony*, *Duac*, and *Maio* The Bishoprick of *Kilmacough* (which is not mention'd in the old *Provincial*, unless the [k] name there be corrupted) as also the Bishoprick of *Clonfert*, are both in these parts, and as I am inform'd, under the See of *Tuam*

Clan-Richard. Earl Clan-Richard.

[h] *Insikellin*, C

Archbishoprick of *Toam*

[i] *Enaghduen sis*, i e *Aghconry*; united to *Killalla*

[k] *Dua consis*—united to *Clonfert*

[As to *Tuam*, the first Bishop that fixed his See here, was St *Jarlath*, who flourished in the beginning of the sixth Century Some ages after, about the year 1152, the Cathedral was new-built by *Edan O Hoisin*, the first Archbishop of Tuam who had the use of the Pall. The Honourable Family of *Wenman* have taken the title of Viscount Tuam from this place; and as to the County, it hath given that of Earl of Gallway to *Henry de Massue*, a person of great wisdom and valour Also, the Honourable Family of *St George* enjoy the title of Barons St George of Hatley]

[l] No Bishop of *Maio*, by that title See *Maio*

[n] It is *Duac*

Viscount *Tuam*

Earl of Gallway

Hatley

The County of *MAIO*

THE County of *Maio* lies upon the Western Ocean; bounded on the South by the County of *Gallway*, on the East by *Roscommon*, and on the North by *Slego* It is fertile, pleasant, and well stock'd with Cattle, Deer, Hawks, and Honey It is so call'd from *Maio*, a little Episcopal City, which in the Roman *Provincial* is writ *Mageo* At present this See is annex'd to its Metropolis, the Archbishoprick of *Toam*, and the neighbours [a] live under the jurisdiction of the Bishop of *Killaley*, in the Barony of *Tir auley*, [from whence the Honourable Sir *Charles O Hara* hath been advanced to the dignity of Baron of Tyrawly]

Maio.

[a] *Respiciunt* Bishoprick of *Killaley*

Baron *Tyrawly*

In *Maio* (if I mistake not,) *Colman* Bishop of Ireland, founded a Monastery, as Bede says, for about thirty English who had been educated Monks, and brought over by him into Ireland But let him speak in his own words *Colman found a place in Ireland very proper for a Monastery, which was called* Magio *by the Scots, and so he purchas'd a small part of it of the Earl to whom it belong'd, that he might build a Monastery on it, with this condition annex'd, That the Monks residing there, should offer up Prayers for the Earl, who had granted them a Seat The Monastery, with the assistance of the Earl and the neighbours thereabouts, was soon finish'd, and (leaving the Scots in the Isle of* Bovind*) he placed the English there The Monastery is to this day possess'd by the English, being grown much greater, and the same which is usually call'd* In Mago *Here, the Institution and way of living have been very much reform'd; so that they are now a most regular Convent, being all transplanted thither out of England, and living, by the labour of their own hands, under certain Rules and a Canonical Abbot, after the example of the ancient Fathers, with great continence and simplicity* About the year 1115 this Monastery was at last repair'd and continu'd in a flourishing state in King John's time, who by his Letters Patent confirm'd their title to several of their Estates From hence, we meet with no other place

L 4 C iv

Logh Mesk place remarkable, but *Logh Mesk*, a large lough full of Fish, containing two small Islands well fortify'd and formerly belonging to the family *de Burgo*, or the *Burks*.

This County is not so [b] eminent for Towns, as for Inhabitants; who are either of Irish Original, as the *O-Males*, *Ioies*, [c] *Mac-vadufes*, or Scots transplanted from the *Hebrides* and the family of *Donell*, from thence called *Clan-Donells* (who are all *Galloglasses*, and a kind of mercenary [d] Soldiers, armed with two edg'd axes and [e] coats and mail; and who being formerly invited over by the Rebels, were rewarded with Lands among them;) or else English, as the *Burks* aforesaid, the *Jordans*, descended from *Jordan* of Exeter, the [f] *Nangles* of Castlough, and [g] *Prendergest* of Clan morris. But the most powerful, are the *Burks*, who owe their original and glory to *William*, younger Brother of *Walter de Burgo*, Earl of Ulster He was famous for his bravery in the wars, and carry'd Prisoner into Scotland; where leaving his wife a hostage, he was dismiss'd, and valiantly recover'd *Conaught*, out of which the English had been banish'd in his absence by *Phelim O Connor* He slew *Phelim O Conor*, *Mac-Dermond*, and *Tego O Kelly*, in battel, and himself was at last kill'd, in revenge, by *Cormac Mac-Dermond* His Grandson *Thomas* (by his son *Edmund*, who was surnam'd *Albanach*, from his birth in Scotland) seeing the fair Estate of this family devolved upon *Leonell* Duke of Clarence by a female, was much concern'd, and drawing together a desperate Body of men (who are ever to be had in Ireland, as well as other places) enter'd by force upon the estate of the Earls of Ulster in this County, and from his Grandfather, whose Authority and Interest among them were fresh in their minds, called himself *Mac William*, i e *The Son of William* His Posterity, under that title, did long tyrannize over these parts, breaking in upon one another with slaughters, and upon the poor people with rapine and plunder; so that hardly a Village [h] was left standing, or [i] unrifled by them

[b] There are now several good Towns in it, and many of the Families are decay'd

[c] None of this name, now, of note here *Galloglasses*

[d] *Triarii mercenarii*

[e] *Loricis annulatis*

[f] None, of these names, now, of note here.

Mac William, also call'd *Mac William Eughter*

[g] Is, C

[h] *Exteris*[illegible]

[i] *Dynastes*

Richard Bingham, Governour of Conaught, a sharp man, and fit to rule in such a fierce Province, thought this was not to be endured; wisely observing that these practices were the causes of rebellion, barbarity, and poverty in Ireland, and that they had so far alienated the affections of the Subjects from their Prince, that they hardly knew or acknowledged any other but their own Lords. Accordingly, he resolv'd to employ all his thoughts and abilities to re establish the regal Power, and overthrow the tyranny of this *Mac-William* and others, wherein he persevered, tho' often complain'd of both to the Queen and the Lord Deputy The *Burks* and their dependants, who denied the authority of all Laws, took up arms against him; drawing to their assistance the *Clan Donells*, *Ioies*, and others, who were also apprehensive of danger to themselves, and of the diminution of their authority. However, *Bingham* easily suppress'd them, and forc'd their Castles, and drove them to the woods and holes, till the Lord Deputy, upon their Petition, commanded him by Letters to desist, and to permit them to live quietly. But they who had first broken the peace, were so far from a sense of the miseries of war, that they were no sooner restored, and had their lives given them, but they took up arms again, made inroads into the Country for spoil, and put all in confusion, saying, they would either have their *Mac-William* to rule over them, or send for one out of Spain; that they would admit no *Sheriffs* for the future, nor be subject to Laws So, they privately invited the Scots from the *Hebrides* to their assistance, with a promise of large Estates The Lord Deputy sent orders to the Governor to suppress these insolences; who immediately thereupon offer'd them terms; which being rejected, he drew an Army together, and press'd them so closely in the woods and forests, that after six or seven weeks grievous famine, they were forced to submit At the same time, their reinforcement from Scotland was upon their march, seeking by-ways into the County of *Mayo*; but their motions were so well watched by the Governour (who was night and day upon his march) that at length at *Ardnary* he intercepted, engag'd and defeated them; there being kill'd or drown'd in the river *Moin* about three thousand This Victory was not only glorious for the present, but of great consequence to after-times, as having put an end to that rebellion, and the title of *Mac-William*, and cut off *Donell Gormy*, and *Alexander Carrogh*, the sons of *James Mac Conell*, with those Islanders, who above all others had infested Ireland These things I have briefly related, though beyond my Design; such noble Exploits being a more proper subject for an Historian

[The honourable Family of *Bourk*, enjoy the title of Viscount *Mayo*]

Viscount *Mayo*.

The

The County of *SLEGO*.

HIGHER up, the County of *Slego* (very proper for grazing,) lies full upon the Sea, bounded on the North by the River *Trobis*, which Ptolomy calls *Ravius*, and which springs from the Lough *Ern* in Ulster It is divided from *Letrim* and *Roscoman* by the rugged *Curlew mountains* and the river *Succus* Hereabouts, Ptolomy places the City of *Nagnata*, but I have not been able to discover it

Nagnata.

The same Author has likewise the River *Libnius* in these parts, but misplac'd by error of the transcribers, and a little above reduc'd to *Dublin*, [(altho', the Learned Antiquary of this kingdom, contends that the position is right)] The place which Ptolomy points at, is now call'd *the Bay of Slego*, a cricky road for Ships just under the town, which is the chief in this County, and is adorn'd with a Castle, now the seat of the *O Conners*, who are sirnamed, *de Slego* from this place, and descended, as they say, from that *Rotheric O-Conor Dun*, who was so potent, that when the English first invaded Ireland, he acted as Monarch of that Kingdom, and could hardly be brought to submit to King Henry the second, but, though he promis'd submission, was ever and anon raising a Rebellion And, as an anonymous writer of that age says, he was wont to exclaim against these words of Pope Adrian in his *Diploma* to the King of England, as very injurious to him, (*You may enter into that Island, and do any thing therein that will contribute to God's glory, and the Salvation of the Country, and let the people of that Island receive you and respect you as their Lord,*) till Pope Alexander the third, by another *Diploma*, confirm'd this right to the Kings of England For then, he grew more tame, and willing to hear of terms, as we shall observe hereafter The chief families in this County, besides the O Conors, [a] were, O Don, [b] O-Hara, [c] O-Gara, and Mac Donagh, [but now few of them are of any considerable Fortune

Libnus, riv

Slego Bay

F Dipl lib ii cap 6

Girald Cambren de Expugnatione, p 787

[a] Are, C [b] O Harra, C [c] O Ghar, C

A mile from Castle-Conner, in this County, is a round hill, an Entrance into which being discovered, and open'd in the year 1640, they found, within it, *quadrangular Chambers*, made of great Stones, and arched, the passages to which, are circular To this, we may add the Caves of the Hill (or rather *Rock*) of *Corren*, in the same County, where, within a steep and almost inaccessible Entrance, Antiquity hath formed out of the very Rock many strange Habitations and Recesses Before these Caves, is a path of about one hundred paces long, cut likewise out of the Rock, but whether this work (which they call the *Giant's house*,) was *Irish* or *Danish*, and for what use, either it or the forementioned Chambers, were made, is difficult to determine at this great distance of time

Ware, Ant p 152, 153.

We shall only observe further, that the Honourable Family of *Scudamore* hath from hence deriv'd the title of Viscount *Slegoe*]

Viscounts Slego

The County of *LETRIM*.

Breany

NEXT to Slego on the East, lies *Breany*, which was the Estate of the ancient family of *O Rorck*, descended from *Rothericus*, Monarch of Ireland, (whom they call *Rorik*, after their way of contracting,) and was enjoy'd by them, till *Brien O Rorck*, Lord of *Breany* and *Minterolise*, was inveigled by the Pope (*Sixtus Quintus*) and the King of Spain into a Rebellion against Queen Elizabeth Upon which, he was presently forc'd to seek refuge in Scotland, from whence he was sent into England, and hang'd there for his folly and rashness The Estate being forfeited to the Crown, this territory was reduc'd into a *County* by *John Perrott* the Lord Deputy, and, from the head Town in it, call'd *Letrim* This is a mountainous County, very rank in grass, but not so much as to verify that of Solinus, *Grass grows so plentifully in Ireland, that the Cattle are certainly infested, if they are not now and then hinder'd from feeding* So many herds of Cattel are kept in this narrow County, that it has had above a hundred and twenty thousand head at one time The Bishoprick of *Achonry*, (now united to the See of [a] *Killalla*) lies in this County, as also the head of the Shanon, the chief river in Ireland, which in a winding chanel, sometimes broad and sometimes narrow, passes through several Counties, as we have already observed The chief families, [b] were the *O Rorcks*, *O Murrens*, *Mac Lochlein*, *Mac Glanchies*, and [c] *Mac Granells*, all pure Irish, [but now these Families are of small figure and fortune]

[a] Elphin, C

[b] Are, C

[c] This name, now turn'd into English, and call'd Reynolds

John de Burgo, the son of Richard Earl of Clan Richard (who was created Baron of *Letrim* by Queen Elizabeth, and soon after murder'd by some envious hands) took his title (as some say) from another place, and not from this *Letrim*, and I have not learn'd the truth of that matter [But at present, the title of Baron of *Letrim*, is vested in the Right Honourable *Bennet Sherard*, now Earl of *Harborough* in England]

Baron Letrim

The County of ROSCOMAN.

FROM Letrim to the south, lies the County of *Roscoman*, first made so by *Henry Sidney* Lord Deputy. It is of a great length, but narrow, bounded on the west by the river *Suc*, on the east by the *Shanon*, and on the north by the *Curlew* mountains. This is for the most part a Champian country, and is fertile, and well-stock'd with Cattle, and ever plentiful in Corn by the help of a little good husbandry. Towards the north, are the *Curlew*-mountains, steep, and heretofore unpassable, till with much pains and difficulty a way was cut through them by *George Bingham*. They are famous for the slaughter of *Comers Clifford* Governour of Conaught and of other brave Veterans, who were cut off there by his negligence. There are [(besides the two half Baronies of *Ballymore* and *Moycarne*,)] four Baronies in this County. First, the *Barony of Boile*, under the Curlew mountains upon the Shanon, where formerly stood a famous Monastery, founded in the year 1152, together with the Abbey of *Beatitude*. This [a] was the Seigniory of *Mac-Dermot*, [but the lands of the Barony are now the possession of Sir *John King*.] Next, the Barony of *Balin Tobar* upon the *Suc* (where *O Conor Dun* [b] had the chief Power and Interest,) neighbouring upon the Bishoprick of *Elphin*. Lower down lies *Roscoman*, [heretofore] the Barony of *O Conor Roo*, that is, *O Conor the red*, wherein stands the chief Town of this County. It is fortify'd with a castle, built formerly by *Robert Ufford*, Chief Justice of Ireland, but the houses of the Town are all thatch'd. More to the south, lies *Athlone* [heretofore] the Barony of the *O-Kellies*, and so call'd from the principal Town in it, which has a Castle, a Garrison, and a fair stone-bridge, built within the memory of [c] this age by *Henry Sidney*, Lord Deputy (to the great terror of the Rebels) at the command of Queen Elizabeth, when she design'd to make this the Seat of the Lord Deputy, as most convenient for the suppressing of Insurrections. [From hence, General *Godart Ginkle* had the title of Earl confer'd upon him by King William the third, for his eminent Services in the Wars of Ireland.

Curlew mountains

Barony of *Boile*

[a] Is, C

Mac Dermot [illegible]

Balin Tobar [illegible] Has, C

Roscoman

1265

Athlone

[c] So said ann. 160,

Earl of [illegible]

In this County, at the Abby of *Cluinmacnos*, is the following Sepulchral Inscription,

Phil. Transf. p. 790. Vol. 22.

OR ANDIL
LA JIARAIN

From this County, the Family of *Dillon* hath derived the honourable title of Earl of *Roscommon*; and another Family, of the same name, enjoys the title of Viscount *Castellogallen*.]

Earl of *Roscommon*

Castellogallen

The Lords of CONAGHT.

IT appears by the Irish Histories, that *Turlogh O Mor O Conor* formerly reign'd over this Country, and divided it between his two sons *Cahel* and *Brien*. But when the English invaded Ireland, it was govern'd by *Rotheric*, under the title of *Monarch* of Ireland, who being apprehensive of the English Power, submitted himself to King Henry the second, without the hazard of a battle. Soon after he revolted, and thereupon *Conaght* was first invaded by *Milo Cogan* an Englishman, but without success. However the King of Conaght was reduced to such straits, that he was fain to acknowledge himself *a liege man of the King of England so as to serve him faithfully as his man, and pay him every year [illegible] head of cattle, one [illegible]* [illegible] by the grant of King John, he was to have and to hold the third part of Conaght *to him and his heirs by the payment of* [illegible] However, this County was still [illegible] civiliz'd by *William Fitz-Hugh*, [illegible] sterity are the *De Burgo's* in Latin, or, as the Irish call them, *the Burks* and [illegible] *Muscegros*, *Gilbert Clare* Earl of Glocester, and *William de Birmingham* [illegible] or *Bourks*, and his posterity, [illegible] Lords of *Conaght*, [illegible]

Pro

Province of Ulster, for a long time, in peace, and enjoy'd considerable Revenues therein, till it went out of the family by the only daughter of *William de Burgo*, sole heir to Conaught and Ulster, who was married to *Leonel* Duke of *Clarence*, son of King Edward the third But he generally residing in England, as well as his successors the *Mortimers*, this Estate in Ireland was neglected so that the *Bourks*, their relations and stewards here, finding their Lords absent, and England embroiled at that time, grew into a defiance of the Laws, confederated with the Irish by leagues and marriages, seiz'd almost all Conaght as their own, and by little and little degenerated into the Irish barbarity Those of them who are descended from Richard de Burgo, are called *Clan-Richard*; others *Mac William Oughter*, i e *Upper*, others *Mac William Eughter*, i e *Lower* So, those of greatest interest and authority in the County of *Maio*, chose to be call'd *Mac William* (as a title of very great honour,) being descended from *William de Burgo*, already mention'd [The Heir of the same ancient and noble Family hath been call'd to Parliament, by Writ, under the title of Baron of *Dunkellin*]

The *Bourks*

Baron Dunkellin

ULSTER.

ULSTER.

ALL that part of the Country to the north, beyond the mouth of the river Boyn, and the County of Meath and Longford, and the mouth of the river Ravie, makes the fifth part of Ireland, call'd in Latin Ultonia and Ulidia, in English Ulster, in Irish Cui Guilly, i.e. the Province of Guilly, and in Welsh Ultw. In Ptolemy's time, it was peopled by the Voluntii, Darni, Robogdii, and the Erdini. This is a large Province, and is water'd with many considerable loughs, and shelter'd with huge woods. It is fruitful in some places, and barren in others, yet very green and sightly in all parts, and well stock'd with Cattle. [a] But as a great part of it by nature is rough and barren, so the Inhabitants for want of Education and Learning, are very wild and barbarous. To keep them in subjection and order (for neither the bonds of right, modesty, nor duty could restrain them) this hither part was divided into three Counties, Louth, Down, and Antrimme; and since, the rest [b] was divided into these seven Counties, Cavon, Fermanagh, Monaghan, Armagh, Colran, Tir-Oen, and Donegall or Tirconell, by the wise contrivance of John Perrott Lord Deputy, a person truly great and famous, and throughly acquainted with the temper of this Province. For being sensible, that nothing would more effectually appease the tumults of Ireland, than the regulation and settlement of these parts of Ulster, he went thither in person in that troublesome and dangerous juncture, when a Spanish descent was daily expected there and in England; and by his gravity and authority, while he took care to punish Oppressions (the great causes of Rebellion) he gain'd so much upon the [c] petty Kings here, that they willingly suffer'd their Seigniories to be divided into Counties, and admitted Sheriffs to govern them. But he being quickly recall'd, and aspiring to greater honours, some envious persons, who were too powerful for him, together with the licentiousness of his own tongue (for he had thrown out some words against his Sovereign, whose Majesty may not be violated by word or thought,) brought him unawares to ruin.

a Ann. 1[illegible]

Now, the ... County of [illegible]

Jo. Perrot Lord Deputy 158[illegible]

c Dynastus

[But when we speak of the wildness and barbarity of the Inhabitants of Ulster, this is to be understood of the Irish Inhabitants only, who are now so routed out and destroyed by their many Rebellions, and by the accession of Scots, (who for the most part inhabit this Province,) that there are not supposed to be left ten thousand Irish, able and fit to bear Arms in all Ulster.]

The County of *LOUTH*.

THE County of *Louth*, call'd in ancient Books *Louth* and *Luda*, and in Irish *Lo* or *Lowd* (if that it is not rather a part of this County), lies beyond the County of *Meath* and the mouth of the river *Boine*, running northward upon a winding and uneven shore of the Irish Sea. It is so full of forage, and so fruitful, that the Husbandman finds plentiful Returns with moderate Labour.

Near the mouth of the *Boine*, stands *Drogheda* or *Droghda*, in English *Tredah*, a neat and populous Town, so call'd from the bridge [(and therefore by Sir *James Ware* named *Pontana*,)] and divided in the middle by the *Boine*. King Edward the second granted it the privilege of a Market and Fair, at the instance of *Theobald Verdon*, and several Immunities and Privileges have been also granted to it by the Kings of England, particularly that of a Mint. [By authority of a Parliament held here in the year 1365, an Academy was erected, and endowed with the Privileges of the University of Oxford, but for want of Maintenance, it soon expir'd. It is now an Earldom in the Honourable Family of the *Moores*.] Near this Town stands *Mellefont Abbey*, founded by Donald King of Uriel, and commended by S. Bernard. It was given by Queen Elizabeth to Sir *Edward Moor* Knight, a Kentish Gentleman, very deserving for his wise conduct both at home and abroad, the Monks having been turn'd out some time before. [His descendant is the Earl of Drogheda, just now mention'd, whose chief Seat is at this place.

Lo[illegible] Latin[illegible]

Sol[illegible] fal[illegible]

Drogheda [illegible]

Mellefont Monastery

At *Munster Bayes*, near *Droghedah*, is a stately Cross, with two Cats on it, and this odd Inscription,

Phil. Tr[illegible] Vol. [illegible] P. 79[illegible]

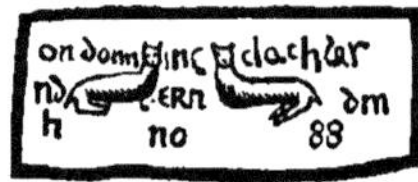

]

[b] *Ardtt* C Seven miles from *Drogheda*, stands [b] *Ardee*, a mid land town of some note; and higher in the Country,

Dundalk *Dundalk*, which has the benefit of a good harbour, and was formerly fortify'd with strong walls It was burnt by *Edward Brus*, brother of the King of Scots, who had proclaimed himself King of Ireland, but was soon after cut off near this place, with eight thousand and two hundred of his men Within the memory of this age, it was besieged by *Shan O Neal*, who was quickly obliged to raise the siege with dishonour, [and since, it hath been erected into a Barony, and enjoy'd by the Honourable Family of *Gorges*] Eight miles

Carlingford from hence stands *Carlingford*, a pretty famous harbour, [from whence the Family of *Taaf* hath derived the honourable title of Earl in like manner, as those of *Tichbourn*, and *Butler*, derive their respective titles from this County, the first, that of Baron *Farrard* of Beaulieu,

Farrard Newton and the second, that of Baron *Butler* of Newton Butler] And these are all the places that I know of, memorable in this County

Louth hath given the title of Earl to *John* *Bermingham*, an English man, which was conferr'd upon him by King Edward the second as a reward of his great valour (after he had engag'd, defeated, and slain *Edward Brus*, that *momentary* King of Ireland, who for some time had ravag'd the Country with great cruelty and slaughter,) and gave him the said Earldom *to have and to hold, to him and his heirs males*, as also the Barony of *Athenry, to him and his heirs* But as the honour begun in this Gentleman, so it expir'd with him, for after he had conquer'd his enemies, he was overcome and slain in a popular insurrection in these parts, with many others of the same name; leaving no issue behind him This County likewise, in the memory of the [c] last age, gave the title of Baron to *Oliver Plonket*, which was conferr'd upon him by King Henry the eighth, [and since, *Douth* in this County hath afforded the title of Viscount to the Honourable Family of *Netterville*]

Bermingham, who are also call'd *Barons* of *Athenry*. Earl of *Louth*

[c] So said ann 1607 Barons of *Douth*

Families still remaining in this County, are the *Verdons*, *Tates*, *Clintons*, *Bellews* or *de Bella Aqua*, *Dowdalls*, *Gernons*, *Hadsors*, *Wottons*, *Brondons*, *Mores*, *Warrens*, *Chamberlains* [who have changed their name into *Brownlow*,] and many other English Families, of Irish extraction, are the *Mac-Mahons*, &c

[*Athenry*, before mention'd, is suppos'd by the Learned Antiquary of this Nation, to be the *Rigia* or *Regia* of Ptolemy] *Ware*, Ant p 28

The County of *CAVON*.

East Breany NEXT to this on the west, lies the County of *Cavon*, formerly call'd *East Breany*, where [a] liv'd the Family of the *O-Reileys*, who [b] derived themselves from the *Ridleys* of England; though in their manners and methods of life, mere Irish [but they are now extinct] [c] Not long ago, this family was eminent for their Cavalry, which were weaken'd by the wise conduct of *Henry Sidney*, who divided this territory into seven Baronies The Lords, all of this family, [d] held immediately by Knights-service of the Crown of England The way of living [e] was not in Towns, but in Castles, [but now they have several good Towns, and pretty Villages] They have a Bishoprick among them [which was heretofore] but poor, the See whereof is at *Kilmore*, and yet this Bishop [f] was not so poor, as were those Irish Bishops, who had no other revenues or subsistance than three Milk cows, with this custom, that if they went dry, the Parish was to give others in exchange for them, as Adam Bremensis relates from the information of some of them, in their return out of Italy through Germany

[a] Lives, C
O Rely
[b] Derive, C
[c] So said, ann 1607
[d] Hold C
[e] Is, C
Bishoprick of *Kilmore*
Poor Bishops
[f] Is, C

[As to the Bishoprick, being joined with Ardagh, it may be reckon'd among the richest in the Kingdom, and as to the Bishops of Kilmore, they are in our Historians sometimes call'd *Brefinienses*, from the County of *Brefiny*, and sometimes *Triburnenses*, from an obscure little Village called *Triburna*, where they were formerly seated, till, in the year 1454, the See was settled at Kilmore *Ware*, Ant p 133

Cavon hath been erected into an Earldom, in the Honourable Family of *Lambert*] Earls of *Cavon*

The County of *FERMANAGH.*

Fermanagh. Lough Erne.

ON the weſt and north beyond *Cavon*, lies *Fermanagh*, formerly inhabited by the *Erdini*, a Country full of wood and bogs In the middle of it, lies the greateſt and moſt famous Lake in this Kingdom, call'd *Lough Erne*, forty miles in length, and ſhaded with thick Woods, and full of inhabited Iſlands, ſome of which contain two or three hundred acres a-piece And withal, it is ſo well ſtored with Pike, Trout, Salmon, and other Fiſh, that the Fiſhermen oftner complain of breaking their nets by the plenty, than of want of Fiſh This Lake does not lie from eaſt to weſt as the Maps deſcribe it, but (as I am inform'd by thoſe who have taken a full ſurvey of it,) it begins at *Baltarbet*, which is the utmoſt Village in the County of *Cavon* to the north, and reaches from ſouth to north; being fourteen miles in length, and four in breadth Afterwards, it contracts it ſelf, as narrow as the chanel of a good large river, and ſo continues for ſix miles together

Baltarbet.

Upon the Lough, in this narrow place, ſtands *Iniſkilling*, the beſt Fort of theſe parts, and defended in the year 1593 by the Rebels, and taken by *Dowdall*, a moſt gallant Captain [It is frequently mentioned in the Hiſtories of the preſent age, during the courſe of the great Rebellion in 1641, and of the late Wars there, and is now a Barony in the Family of *Macgwire*] From hence, turning to the weſt, it is at its full bigneſs, being as far as *Belek* (for twenty miles together) at leaſt ten miles broad, and near that place, it has a great fall or Cataract, which they call *the Salmons leap* Here is a current report among the people, that this Lough was formerly firm ground, well cultivated, and full of Inhabitants, and that it was ſuddenly drown'd and turn'd into a Lake, as a puniſhment for the abominable Sin of Buggery, then practis'd among them *God Almighty* (ſays Giraldus) *the author of Nature, condemn'd this ground as privy to thoſe filthy and unnatural Acts, which render'd it not only unfit for the firſt Inhabitants, but for any others in ſucceeding times* The Iriſh Annals lay this to the charge of certain Scotch Refugees, who were driven from the *Hebrides* and ſkulk'd in theſe parts The moſt conſiderable among the [a] petty Princes here, is *Mac* [b] *Guire* Thoſe of that family live on both ſides the Lake, ſo as they on the other ſide are reckon'd of *Ulſter*; and they on this, of *Conaght*

Iniſkiling. Barons of *Iniſkilling*. Belek.

[a] So ſaid ann 1607 [b] Guiri, C

[In the Pariſh of *Kilaſher* within this County, have been diſcover'd *Marble-Rocks*, whoſe perpendicular height is fifty or ſixty feet They ſhow'd themſelves, by the means of Subterraneous Rivers, which, by degrees, have waſh'd away the Earth and looſe ſtones, and diſcover'd theſe mighty Rocks Alſo, in this County, have been found Urns in ſtone Coffins, within a Circle of very large Stones ſtanding on end, and encompaſſing a great heap, but removed by degrees, for the paving of the ways

Kilaſher Marble Rocks. Urns.

From this County, the Honourable Family of *Varney*, have taken the title of Viſcount *Fermanagh*]

Viſcount *Fermanagh*.

The County of *MONAGHAN.*

ON the eaſt ſide of *Lough-Erne*, lies the County of *Monaghan*, very mountainous, and woody It has not one remarkable Town, beſides *Monaghan*, which gives name to the whole County, [and is a Barony, in the Honourable Family of *Blaney*] This Shire is divided into five [a] Baronies, and contains *Iriel*, *Dartre*, *Fernis*, and *Loghty*, which, for Rebellion, were taken from the *Mac Mahons*, by Act of Parliament, together with the territory of *Donemain*, which was given by Queen Elizabeth to *Walter D'evreux*, Earl of Eſſex Theſe *Mac Mahons* (a name ſignifying in Iriſh *the Sons of a Bear*) for a long time govern'd theſe parts, and are deſcended from *Walter Fitz Urſe*, who had a hand in the murder of *Thomas* Archbiſhop of Canterbury The moſt powerful man of the family, according to the cuſtom of this Nation, was wont to Lord it over the reſt, under the title of *Mac Mahon* And [b] while they were contending for this ſoveraignty, by ſlandering, fighting, bribing, and other foul Practices; they drew the Lord Deputy, *William Fitz Williams*, among them, and he cited *Hugh Roe Mac Mahon* (whom by his Authority he had advanc'd to this Seigniory,) and found him guilty of Treaſon, and order'd him to be hang'd, and that he might extinguiſh the name and ſovereignty of the *Mac Mahons* for ever, he divided the territory between the relations of the ſaid *Hugh*, and certain Engliſh men, to have and to hold to them and their heirs, by the Engliſh tenure

Barons of *Monaghan*.

[a] Now call'd *Trough Monaghan*, *Dartree*, and *Donaghmaine* *Mac Mahon*

Fitz Urſe.

[b] Camden, C 1590

[On the borders of this County and *Monaghan*, were diſcover'd, a few years ſince, about four yards deep, four Teeth of an extraordinary ſize, two of them, in weight, two pounds three quarters each; and two, ſix ounces each Upon comparing them with the like Teeth, which have been found in England, the Royal Society were clearly of opinion, that they could be no other, than the Teeth of an Elephant]

Phil Tranſ Vol xix p 365 Extraordinary Teeth.

The

The County of *ARMAGH*

ON the east side of this Lough, lies also the County of *Armagh*, bounded on the east by the river *Neury*, on the south by the County of *Louth*, and on the north by *Blackwater* This soil (as I have often heard the Earl of *Devonshire*, Lord Deputy, say) is the richest of any in Ireland, insomuch, that if manure be laid on to improve it, it grows barren, as if angry and affronted [Besides the City of Armagh, and the Borough of Charlemont, it hath now in it several pretty Towns]

Fewes.

The first tract that we meet with in this County, is *Fewes*, [heretofore] belonging to *Turlogh Mac Henry*, of the family of *O Neal*; and full of woods and unpassable fens [It is a long ridge of mountainous wast-ground, and belongs now to several Gentlemen whose Lands border upon it, and the name and nation of Turlogh Mac Henry are forgotten in these parts] Next, *Orry*, in which is very little wood here lives *O-Hanlon*, and here stands the fort *Mont-Norris*, built by Charles Baron Montjoy, Lord Deputy, and so call'd by him in honour of *John Norris*, under whom he first serv'd in the wars

Orry
Mont-Norris

Armagh

Eight miles from hence, near the river *Kalin*, stands *Armagh*, an Archbishop's See, and the Metropolis of the Island, [wherein also a publick *School* or *Academy* was very early instituted (as appears by the life of St Patrick,) and was the first in this Kingdom] The Irish tell you, it was so call'd from Queen *Armacha*; but in my opinion, this is the very same that Bede calls *Dearmach*, which, he says, signifies in the Scotch or Irish tongue, *a field of oaks* It was call'd *Drumsailick*, till St Patrick built a city here, *very fine in respect of situation, form, bulk, and compass, the Angels (as my Author says) having contriv'd and model'd it for him* This *Patrick* was a Britain, and S Martin's Sister's Son He was baptized by the name of *Sucat*, and sold into Ireland, where he was Shepherd to King *Miluc* Afterwards, he was called *Magonius* by St German, whose disciple he was, and then by Pope Celestine, *Patricius*, that is, *Father of the Citizens*, and was sent into Ireland to convert them to the Christian Faith Yet some are of opinion, that Christianity was in Ireland before his time, grounding upon an ancient Synodal, wherein St Patrick's own authority is urg'd against the *Tonsure*, which was usual at that time in Ireland; namely, on the fore part of the head only, and not in the shape of a crown A custom, which by way of contempt, they father upon a certain Swineherd of King *Lagerius*, the son of Nell, and the writers of that age cry'd out against it, as an Institution of Simon Magus, and not of St Peter About the year 610 *Columbanus* built a famous Monastery in this place, *from which many others were propagated and planted, both in Britain and Ireland, by his disciples* St Bernard speaks thus of it *In honour of St Patrick, the Irish Apostle, who in his life time presided in this Island, and dying, was bury'd in it; this is an* Archiepiscopal See, *and the metropolis of the Islands, and was formerly held in such veneration and esteem, that not only Bishops and Priests, but Kings and Princes, were subject to the Metropolitan, and he alone govern'd them all But, through the hellish ambition of some Potentates, it grew into a custom, that this holy See should be held by inheritance, and permitted to depend to none that were not of their tribe or family And this horrid method continu'd for no less than fifteen generations, or thereabouts*

S Patrick

Marianus Scotus

Tonsure in Ireland

Vid Bed, l v 22

Bede

S Bernard in vita Malachiæ

Thus, by degrees, Church discipline began to slacken in this Island (while in towns and cities, the numbers and the translations of the Bishops were just as the Metropolitan thought fit,) and *John Papyrio* a Cardinal, was sent over by Pope Eugenius the fourth, to reform these matters, as we learn from an Anonymous writer of that age *In the year of our Lord* 114[illegible], John Papyrio, *Cardinal* [illegible] *Eugenius the fourth*, P R *together with* Christian *Bishop of Lismore, and Legat of Ireland, came into this Island This* Christian *held a Council at* Mel[illegible], *where were present the Bishops,* [illegible], *Dukes, and the* [illegible] *States of Ireland, by* [illegible] *sent, there were four Archbishopricks* [illegible], Armagh, Dublin, Cashel [illegible], *which were fill'd at that time by* Gelasius, Gregorius, Donatus, *and* Edanus *After this, the Cardinal gave the Clergy his Benediction, and return'd to Rome* Before, the Bishops of Ireland were always consecrated by the Archbishops of Canterbury, by reason of their Primacy in that Kingdom This was acknowledg'd by the Citizens of Dublin, when they recommended Gregory, Bishop elect of Dublin, to Ralph Archbishop of Canterbury, for Consecration, in these words *We have always willingly subjected our* [Prelates] *to your Predecessors, from whom we consider that ours have received their spiritual dignity,* &c. This is likewise evident from the letters of *Murchertach* King of Ireland, of a more early date, to Anselm Archbishop of Canterbury, about the ordaining of the Bishops of *Dublin* and *Waterford*, as also from those of King *Gothrick* to Lanfrank his predecessor, in behalf of one Patrick a Bishop, and from those of Lanfrank to Therdeluac King of Ireland, complaining, *That the Irish leave their wives at pleasure, without any Canonical Cause, and match with others, either related to themselves, or to* [illegible] *they have put away, or such as le*[illegible] *forsaken wickedly by others in the* [illegible], *which is not to be look'd upon as marriage, but punish'd as fornication* And if these vices had not continu'd among them[a] till our times, the Successions had been more certain, and neither the Gentry nor Commonalty so much stain'd with the blood and murther of their own relations, about the right of inheritance, nor the Kingdom so infamous among foreign nations upon this account But this falls not within the compass of my design

Flatsbury says much the same

Major una[illegible]

[a] So find ann 1007

This Archiepiscopal See had not been long instituted, before it was again confirm'd by *Vivian* the Pope's Legat, so that the opinion of some, who prefer the See of Armagh, and make it more ancient than that of Canterbury, pleading, that in this respect it ought to take place in all General Councils, is very groundless, for *Armagh* is the younger sister, by [illegible] And besides, precedence in General Councils [illegible] never given according to the antiquity of Sees, *but all Prelates, of* [illegible] *among them* [illegible] *according to their* [illegible] *tion or Promotion*

[illegible] of holy Ceremonies Sect 14

During *Vivian's* abode in Ireland, *Armagh*

was reduc'd and subjected to the English by John de Curcy, who did no hurt to the Country, but is said to have been very favourable to the Religious there, and to have repaired the Church, which [c] in our time was burnt, together with the whole City, by *John O-Neal*, so that nothing remains [d] at this day but some few thatch'd cottages, and the ruinous walls of the Monastery, Priory, and Archbishop's Palace Among the Bishops of this See, the most eminent are, S *Malachy*, the first who restrain'd Clerks from marrying in Ireland, a person of great piety and learning for that age, and *who was no more tainted with the barbarity of the Country than Sea fish with the saltness of the sea-water*, as S Bernard has told us, who wrote his life at large Then, *Richard Fitz Rauls*, commonly call'd *Armachanus*, who wrote sharply against the Friers Mendicants about the year 1355, abhorring that voluntary way of begging, in a Christian

c So said ann 1607

d Ann 1607

Upon a hill near Armagh, are still visible the remains of an old Castle (call'd *Owen-Maugh*,) which is said to have been the Seat of the ancient Kings of *Ulster* More to the East is *Black water*, in Irish *More*, i e *great*, the boundary between this County and *Tr-Oen*, of which we shall speak in its proper place In and about this County, all the power and interest [e] was in the *Mac Gensses*, *O-Hanlons*, *O Hagans*, and many of the family of the *O Neals*, who have distinguish'd themselves by several surnames [But now the Lands of the *O-Hanlons*, are in the possession of the *St Johns*, an English Family, and the *O-Hagans* are not of any considerable figure,

O wen-Maugh

Black water

e Is, C

In this County, the honourable Family of *Caulfield* enjoy the title of Viscount Charlemont]

The County of *DOWN*

Ext, on the east, lies the County of *Down*, very large and fruitful, and reaching as far as the Irish sea [This is a populous, rich, and flourishing Country, containing in it six Boroughs, besides other considerable Towns] It is bounded on the north with Lough *Eaugh* (call'd by a later name, *Logh Sidney*,) and on the south with the County of *Louth*; from which it is separated by the river *Newry* Upon this river, at its very entrance into the County, a Town of the same name was built and fortify'd [a] in our memory, by *Nicholas Bagnal*, Marshal of Ireland, who, with excellent conduct, did many memorable exploits here, and by his diligence very much improv'd the County Not far from hence, lies the river *Ban the less*, which rising out of the solitary mountains of *Mourne*, runs through the territory of [b] *Evaugh*, belonging [in part] to the family of *Mac Gennis*, who had formerly a Controversy with the *O Neals* (the tyrants of Ulster) whether they should find provision, *&c*, for the Soldiers of *O Neal*; which kind of service they call'd *Bonoghty* It has also an Episcopal See at *Dromore*, [which place also hath given the Title of Viscount to the Honourable Family of Fanshaw] Above this, upon the bank of *Lough* [c] *Neagth*, [(the water of which is useful for the Cure of the King's Evil, and other running Sores, and Rheumatisms; but hath no petrifying Virtue, as hath been reported,)] do lie the territories of [d] *Kilulto* and *Kilwarny*, much incumber'd with woods and boggs [Near *Banbridge*, have been discover'd three Urns in three small stone Chests, under a great Kern, or heap of Stones] Thus much of the inner parts

a So said, ann 1607

b Evagh, C Mac Gennis

Viscount Dromore

c En h, C Phi Trans 1713 p 63

d Kilwulto, C

Banbridge Urns

Upon the coast, the sea winds in with so many chops and creeks, and the Lough spreads so much, near *Dufferin* (a woody vale, heretofore the Estate of the *Mandevills*, and since of the *Whites*, [and now of the *Hamiltons* and *Stevensons*;] that it makes two Peninsulas, viz *Lecal* on the south, and *Ardes* on the north *Lecal* is a rich soil, the remotest part of Ireland to the east The utmost promontory in it, is now call'd by the Seamen S *John's Foreland*, but by Ptolemy *Isamnium*, perhaps from *Isa*, a British word, signifying *lowest* In the very [f] neck stood *Dunum*, a flourishing town, mention'd by that name in Ptolemy, but not in its proper place [g] It is now call'd *Down*, and is very ancient, and a Bishop's See, [(erected about the end of the fifth Centu y,)] and remarkable for the tombs of S *Patrick*, S *Brigid*, and S *Columba*, who had this rhyming distich writ over them,

e Ards, Lecal

The Promontory Isamnium

f Isthmus Dunum

g Dunum ubi in Queen's County, Harris Down

S Patrick's Sepulchre

Hi tres in Duno tumulo tumulantur in uno,
Brigida, Patricius, atque Columba pius

One tomb three Saints contains, one vault below,
Does *Brigid*, *Patrick* and *Columba* show

This monument is said to have been demolish'd by *Leonard Gray*, Lord Deputy, in Henry the eighth's time and thus much is certain, that upon his being accused of male-administration in Ireland, and found guilty, the prophanation of St *Patrick's* Church, was, among other things, objected against him The Religious have contended as much about the burial place of S *Patrick*, as the Cities of Greece did about the birth-place of *Homer* Those of *Down* will have it there, upon the authority of the foresaid verses Those of *Armagh* claim it, upon that passage cited but now from S Bernard The Monks of *Glastenbury* in England have challeng'd it, offering the ancient Records of their Abbey, in evidence of their title And lastly, some of the Scots affirm him not only to have been born near *Glasgow*, among them, but bury'd there too

In this *Down* it was, that *John Curcy* (a warlike Englishman, and more devout than Soldiers generally are,) first settled the Benedictine Monks, after he had reduc'd these parts; and he also translated the Monastery of *Carrick* (which Mac *Dunlef*, King of Ulster had built in *Ermagh* ... *Finan Mac Nell's* Well) into the Isle of *Inis Curcy* (so called from him,) and endow'd it plentifully Before that, the Monks of ...

(like those anciently in Egypt, whose Order the pious *Congellus*, that is, as they interpreet it, *A fair pledge*, brought into Ireland) were wholly devoted to prayer, and supply'd their own and others wants, by the labour of their hands. But this, like all human Institutions, was but short liv'd, their manners grew corrupt, and riches by degrees stifled that Piety which first gave them being in the world *Robert*, Abbot of *Molism* in Burgundy, took a great deal of pains to recover the ancient discipline, *persuading his disciples to live by the labour of their hands, and to quit tithes and oblations, leaving them to the Clergy of the Diocese, and to wear woven or leathern breeches no longer But they flatly refused to depart from the Customs observ'd in the Monasteries of the west, which were clearly instituted by* S Maurus, *a disciple of* S Benedict, *and by* S Columbin But this is too great a digression, [and we will only add, that the title of Viscount *Down*, is now vested in the Honourable Family of *Dawney* in England]

Robert de Monte de Immutatione Ordinis Monachorum

Viscount Down

Upon the Sea coast, stands *Arglas*, where S Patrick is reported to have built a Church, [and lately, the honourable *John Barrington* in England, hath been advanc'd to the dignity of Baron Barington of Newcastle near Dublin, and Viscount Barington of Ardglass] Then *Strangeford*, formerly *Stranford*, a safe harbour, where the river *Coyn* runs into the sea, with great noise and violence, [and from which place, a family of the name of *Smith* take the honourable title of Viscount] In the Peninsula hard by, Queen Mary (always bountiful to the Nobility) gave much lands to the Earl of *Kildare* The *Russels*, *Audleys*, *Whites*, and they who setled last here, the *Bagnalls*, all of English descent, [i] liv'd up and down amongst the wild Irish in these parts, against whose Incursions they stoutly [k] defended the Estates left them by their Ancestors; but three of these, *viz* the Audleys, the Whites, and the Bagnalls, are now extinct]

Viscount Barrington

Viscount Strangford

i Live, C

k Defend, C

Ardes, the other Peninsula, lies over-against this, and is separated by a small chanel from Lough *Coyn*, with which it is enclos'd on the west, as it is on the east, by the sea, and on the north, by the bay of *Knoc Fergus* You may resemble it to a bended arm; for, by a very narrow *Isthmus*, it grows to the main land, as the arm grows to the shoulder The soil is very good in every part, unless it be in a flat boggy plain in the middle, about twelve miles long The shore is well stock'd with Villages, and had formerly a famous monastery, situate upon the bay of *Knoc Fergus*, of the same order and name with that eminent and very ancient Monastery in England near Chester, call'd *Banchor* Which of them produc'd the Arch-heretick *Pelagius*, is uncertain, some will have him from this, others from that of Britain, but neither upon any good authority That he was a Britain, is most certain, as from other testimonies, so particularly from that Distich of *Prosper Aquitanus*, inveighing against his impiety,

Ardes

Banchor Monastery Pelagius

I procul insana impietas, artesque malignas
Aufer, & authorem comitare exclusa Britannum

Far hence with wicked arts profaneness fly,
And bear thy British patron company

But let us hear what S Bernard says of this place *A man of great power and riches gave Banchor to Malachy, to build, or rather re build, a monastery there For it had been a noble monastery before, under* Congell *the first father, and had bred many thousand Monks, and been the mother of many Monasteries A place truly pious, abounding with Saints, and zealously promoting Godliness, insomuch that one of the sons of that holy Society, called* Luan, *is said to be the founder of a hundred Monasteries which I mention, that by this instance the Reader may guess, how numerous they were in all By this means, it fill'd both Ireland and Scotland with its off-springing. One of which,* S Columban, *came into these parts of* France, *and built the Monastery of* Luxovium, *which grew up to a very great society It is said to have been so large, that divine service continued both night and day without ceasing one moment, by the many Quires they could make, to succeed one another And thus much in praise of the ancient monastery of* Banchor *Being destroyed by Pirates, it was repair'd by* Malachy, *who undertook it in regard to its ancient dignity, and with a design to replant a sort of Paradise, on account of the many Saints that lay bury'd in it For, not to mention those who had departed in peace, nine hundred are said to have been put to death in one day, by the Pirates The lands belonging to it, were very large and numerous, but* Malachy *contenting himself with the holy place only, gave them all to another For, from the time it was destroyed it continued to be held with all its possessions For Abbots were still elected, and enjoyed it under that name, keeping it nominally, though not really, the same as heretofore Although many dissuaded him from alienating these Lands and Possessions, and advised him to keep them; he was so much in love with Poverty, that he made one to be chosen as formerly to hold them, reserving only, (as we have already said) the* Place, *to himself and his Within a few days, the Church was finish'd, which was made of wood plain'd and firmly jointed, after the Scotch manner; and pretty beautiful* Malachy *thought it proper, afterwards, to have a stone Church in* Banchor, *like those he had seen in other Countries When he began to lay the foundation, the natives were struck with admiration at it, having never seen any building of that nature in all the Country So that one of them cry'd out, Good Sir! Why these new fashions from other Countries? We are Scots, and not Frenchmen What means this levity? what needs this superfluous and stately fabrick?*

In the life of Malachy

More inward, upon the lake, is the Bishoprick of *Coner*, of which S Malachy was Bishop, but how far his flock was short of him in point of piety, we may learn from S Bernard *Malachy was made Bishop of Conereth (for that is the name of the city,) near the thirtieth year of his age When he began to do his duty among them, this man of God soon saw that he was not sent to men but to beasts, such as he had never before met with, in all kinds of barbarity, in manners so froward, in customs so devilish, in Faith so corrupt, in laws so barbarous, to discipline so averse, and in life so filthy They were nominally Christians, but really Pagans No tithes nor first fruits, no lawful marriages, nor Confessions, among them No one either to ask or give penance, and very few Ministers of the Altar But what need I enlarge, when those very few had scarce any work among the Laity No fruit could be expected of their Endeavours, among so lewd a people For there was neither preaching nor singing to be heard in the Churches And what could the Lord's Champion do in such a case? He must either retire with dishonour, or fight on with danger But he knowing himself a Shepherd, and not a Hireling, chose to stand rather than fly, being ready to lay down his life for his flock And, notwithstanding they were all wolves and no sheep,*

Bishoprick of Coner

 he

be stood in the midst of them like an undaunted Shepherd, considering all possible ways how to convert his wolves into sheep. Thus St Bernard [a] and, as I am inform'd, the Bishop [b] at this day is not able to give them a much better Character [The two Sees of *Down* and *Coner*, were united into one, in the year 1441, by Pope Eugenius the fourth, at the request of *John* Bishop of *Coner*]

[a] So said, ann 160-

This *Ardes*, before mention'd, was formerly the estate of the *Savages*, an English family, one of which is famous for that stout and witty saying *That he would not rely upon a Castle of stones, but a Castle of* bones, meaning his own body. Afterwards, the *O Neals* took it out of their hands; but they being attainted of treason, Sir *Thomas Smith*, Knight, and of the Privy Council to Queen Elizabeth, by her permission, planted a Colony there, an excellent design, but very unsuccessful. For after great expence, his natural son, whom he had set over it, was taken by an Ambuscade of the Irish, and thrown alive to the dogs; a piece of cruelty, for which those Wretches severely suffer'd, being themselves but to death, and expos'd to the wolves. Above *Ardes* to the west, lies the southern *Clanboy*, i e a *Yellow Clan*, or the family of *Hugh the Yellow*, (as they interpret it,) a Country well wooded, which extends to the bay of *Knoc Fergus*. It is inhabited by the *O Neals*, and is the very utmost Tract of this County of *Down*.

Savages

Clan boy the Upper

[In this County, the Honourable title of Earl of Mount Alexander is enjoy'd by the family of *Montgomery*; that of Baron Coningsby of *Clan-Brazil*, by Thomas Earl of Coningsby in England, and that of Viscount Hillsborough by the family of *Hill*.]

Mount Alexander

Clan Brazil, Vide Herefordshire

Hillsborough

The County of *ANTRIM*.

THE next County to [a] Down northward, is the County of *Antrim*, so call'd from *Antrim*, [heretofore] a small town, and only remarkable for giving name to the shire (which is bounded by the bay of *Knock-Fergus*, the Lough *Eaugh*, and the river *Ban*) [But now Antrim is a considerable thriving Corporation, pleasantly situated on both sides of Six mile water, and united by a handsom Bridge, and adorn'd with a fine Park, and a stately Mansion-house belonging to the Lord Viscount Massareen. And the County also is populous and flourishing, being mostly inhabited by British Protestants.] The [fore mentioned] Bay of *Knock-Fergus*, that is call'd *Vindersius* in Ptolemy, took it's name from a town situate upon it, which the English call *Knock-Fergus*, and the Irish *Carig-Fergus*, that is, *the rock of Fergus*, both from the famous *Fergus* drown'd there, who first brought the *Scots* out of Ireland into Britain. This town is more famous than any other upon the coast, by reason of a commodious harbour, and for its fortification (though [b] unfinish'd,) as also for its castle standing upon a high rock, which a garrison to keep the country in subjection, and an ancient Palace, now converted into a magazine. [But now, *Belfast* at the bottom of the bay, is much more rich and populous, of greater Trade, and more frequented.] Near Carrigfergus, lies *Clane boy* the lower, inhabited likewise by the *O Neals*, and memorable for the death of that wicked rebel *Shan* or *John O Neal*, who, after a long course of Plunder and Rapine, was defeated in one or two Battles by *Henry Sidney* Lord Deputy, and reduc'd to such streights, that he was resolved to go and address himself to the Lord Deputy with a halter about his neck, but his Secretary perswaded him rather to seek assistance from those Islands Scots, who under the conduct of Alexander *Oge* were now encamped here, and ravaged the country. Accordingly, he went to them, and was kindly received, but was put to death soon after, with his whole party, for the slaughter which he had formerly made among their relations. The war being ended by his death, and he and all his men attainted; Queen Elizabeth bestow'd this *Claneboy* upon *Walter D'Evereux* Earl of Essex, who came over hither, being sent, perhaps by means of some Courtiers, under a pretence of doing him honour (for he was made Governor of *Ulster* and *Mareshall* of Ireland,) into a Country ever rebellious and ungovernable. The Earl endeavouring with great expence to compose affairs in these parts, and to reduce them to some order, he was at last, after many and great difficulties both at home and abroad, taken away in the flower of his Age, to the grief of all good men, and to the benefit of the *O Neals*, and of *Brian Carragh* of the family of the *Mac-Conells*, who thereupon got possession of this territory, and have [c] since been perpetually at war with one another about it. Near *Knock Fergus*, lies a *Peninsula* join'd by a small neck of land to the continent, which is call'd the *Isle of Magie*, four miles in length, and one in breadth. Some suppose that the Monastery of *Magio* (so much commended by Bede, and which I have already mention'd in the County of *Maio*,) stood in this place.

[a] Louth, C

Knock Fergus.

[b] So said ann 160-

Clan boy the Lower

[c] So said, ann 1607

Isle of Magie

Then, the *Glinnes*, that is, *the Valleys*, begin at *Older fleet*, a dangerous road for ships, and run a great way by the sea-side. This territory belong'd formerly to the *Bissets*, Noblemen of Scotland, who making away *Patrick* Earl of *Athol* upon a private grudge, were banished hither, and (by the favour of Henry the third King of England) settled in an estate in this tract. For *John Bisset*, who died in the beginning of Edward the first, had a great estate here, and in Edward the second's reign, *Hugh Bisset* forfeited part of it by his rebellion. In [d] the last age, this was invaded by the [e] Irish Scotch Rapparees, from *Cantire* and the *Hebrides*, under the conduct of *James Mac Conell*, Lord of Cantire in Scotland, who claimed it as descended from the *Bissets*. But *Shan O Neal* having slain their Captain, easily repell'd them. Yet they returned, and made cruel ravages in these parts, foment ng

Glinnes

Bissets

[d] So said, ann 1[illegible]

[e] Scots [illegible]

fomenting rebellions in the Kingdom, till *John Perrot*, Lord Deputy, ^r^ reduc'd, first *Donall Gorran* (who was slain, together with his brother Alexander, in Conaught by Richard Bingham) and afterwards, *Agnus Mac Conell*, the sons of *James Mac Conell*, to such straits, that they submitted themselves to the Queen of England, and retriev'd this Country to hold of her by Knight's service, on condition that they should bear arms in Ireland for none but the Kings of England, and should pay a certain number of Cows and Hawks yearly, *&c*

r Very lately, C.

Above these, as far as the river *Bann*, the Country is call'd *Rowte*, and ^s^ was inhabited by the *Mac Guillies*, a family of no small note among the Irish, but pent up in this narrow corner by the continual depredations of the *Island-Scots* For *Surley Boy*, that is, *Charles the yellow*, brother to *James Mac-Conell* who possess'd the *Glinnes*, did in a manner make himself master of all this tract, till *John Perrot*, the aforesaid Lord Deputy, having taken the castle of *Donluse* (strongly situate upon a rock hanging out into the Sea, and severed from the land by a deep ditch,) drove out him and his party However, the year following, he recover'd it by treachery, after he had slain *Carie* the Governour, who made a stout defence Upon this, the Lord Deputy sent *Merimon* (an experienc'd Captain) against him, who cut off the two sons of *James Mac Conell*, with *Alexander* the son of *Surley-Boy*, and pressed him so close (driving away his Cattle, the only riches he had, for he had fifty thousand Cows of his own stock,) that he surrender'd *Donluse*, and came to Dublin, and made a publick Submission in the Cathedral, petitioning for mercy When he was, after this, admitted into the Governour's Lodgings, as soon as he saw the Picture of Queen Elizabeth, he threw away his sword, and fell down before it twice, thereby devoting himself entirely to Her Majesty's Service And, being received into favour and protection, among the other Subjects of Ireland, he abjur'd, both in the Chancery and Kings-Bench, all allegiance to any foreign Prince whatsoever, and by the bounty of Queen Elizabeth, had four territories or *Toughs* (as they call them) from the river *Boys* to the *Ban*, bestow'd on him, namely, *Donseverig*, *Loghill*, and *Ballamonyn*, together with the government of *Donluse* castle, *to him and the heirs male of his body*, to hold of the Kings of England upon this condition, that neither he nor his Dependants, nor any of his Posterity, should take up arms in behalf of any foreign Prince, without special Licence, and that they should restrain their Dependants from depredations, and find twelve horse and forty foot at their own charge for forty days together in time of War, and pay every year a certain number of oxen and hawks to the Kings of England, *&c*

The Rowte
s Is, C.
Mac Guilly.
Surley Boy
also Chairly-boy.
Donluse

[The *Rowte* beforementioned is now the Estate of the *Macdonell's*, who drove out the *Macguillins*, and who enjoy the honourable title of Earls of *Antrim*, in which County also the family of *Vaughan*, have the title of Viscount *Lisburn*, and the family of *Conway* are Barons of *Killultagh*

Earl of *Antrim*
Viscount *Lisburn*
Killultagh

About eight miles north-east from *Colrain*, is a place called the *Giants Causway*, consisting of many thousand Pillars, which stand most of them perpendicular to the Plain of the Horizon, and so close to one another that a knife can hardly be thrust in between them They are, for the greatest part, *Pentagonal* or *Hexagonal*, and yet almost all irregular, none of their sides being of equal breadth With regard to *composition* and *figure*, the Stones have been observ'd by persons of great skill and curiosity who have viewed them, to come near the *Entrochos*, and the *Astroites*, or *Lapis Stellaris*, and the nearest to the *Lapis Basanus* or *Basaltes* The Causway is plainly the work of nature, and runs from the bottom of a high hill into the Sea, no one knows how far At low water, the length is about six hundred foot, if not more, the breadth, in the broadest place, two hundred and forty foot, and in the narrowest one hundred and twenty, the height, in some places, thirty six, and in others about fifteen foot]

Phil Transf N. 212, and 241 at large
Giants-Causway

The County of *COLRAN*, [or LONDON-DERRY.]

BEyond the *Glinnes*, westward, lies *Krine*, call'd [heretofore] the County of *Colran* from the chief town in it, [but now the County of *London derry*, from the City of *London derry*, which was built and planted by the *Londoners*] It is bounded by the river *Bann* on one side, by the *Lough Foile* on another, and by the County of *Tir-Oen* to the south This *Bann* (as Giraldus says) is a very beautiful river, which its name intimates It rises out of the *Mourne hills* in the County of *Downe*, and being empty'd into the large Lough of *Laugh* or *Sidney*, where it loses both it self and its name, after some thirty miles (for so long this *Lough* is counted) it receives the name again at *Tome* castle From whence, crown'd with wood on both sides, it runs in a full chanel by *Glancolkein*, (which, by the benefit of thick woods and unpassable bogs, is a safe refuge for the Scotch Islanders and rebels as the English were sensible by their pursuit of *Surley-boy*, who absconded here) and so, into the Sea It is the best stock'd with Salmon, of any river in Europe, by reason (as some imagin) of its Clearness above all other rivers; a quality with which that kind of Fish are particularly delighted, The *Cahans* ^a^ were of greatest authority in these parts, the chief of which Family ^t^ was *O Cahan*, the first of those Potentates or *Uraights* (as they term them) who held of *O Neal* the tyrant of *Ulster*, being the person, who, in the election of an *O Neal* (perform'd with barbarous

Bann, riv
Glancolkein
Salmons
a Are, C.
t Is, C.
O-Cahan
Uraights
The election of O Neal

c Has, C
d Is, C
The Island Scots
e Leave, C Ann 1607
f Come, C
g Take, C

rous ceremonies upon a high hill, in the open air) c had the honourable Office of throwing a Shoe over the head of the *O Neal*, then chosen Yet his power d was not so great, as to restrain the Island-Scots, who to spare their own at home, in the Summer e left those barbarous and fruitless Islands, where there is nothing but want and beggary, and f came hither for Provisions; where they g took all opportunities to raise and cherish Rebellions; so that it was by an express Law declar'd High treason, either to call them into Ireland, or to receive them in it [But now there is no Cahan of any note in this County; and the Lands are chiefly holden of the *London*-Society, and of the Bishop of Derry

Baron Colrain

The title of Baron of *Colrain* is enjoy'd by the honourable Family of *Hare* in England]

The County of TIR-OEN.

BELOW *Colran* southward, lies the County of *Tir Oen*, that is, *the Land of Eugenius* This is a midland County; divided from *Tir Conell* on the west by the river *Liffer*, from the County of Antrim on the east by the *Lough Eaugh*, and from the County of Armagh on the south by *Blackwater* (which is call'd in Irish *More*, *i e a great water)* Though it is somewhat rough and uneven, yet it is fruitful and very large (being sixty miles in length, and thirty in breadth,) and divided into the *Upper Tir-Oen* on the north, and the *Nether Tir-Oen* on the south, by the mountains of *Slew Gallen* In this, lies *Cloghar*, a a small Bishoprick, [but well endow'd It was founded by St *Patrick*, who gave it to his beloved disciple and indefatigable Assistant, St *Macartin* The name is said, in the Register of *Clogher*, to be taken from a golden Stone; by which, as from an Oracle, Answers were given in the times of Gentilism] Then *Dunganon*, [heretofore] the chief Seat of the Earls, which by the favour of Henry the eighth, gave the title of Baron to *Matthew*, son to the first Earl of *Tir-Oen* The house is more neat and elegant, than is generally to be met with in this County, but hath been often burnt by the Lord of it, to save the enemy that trouble [From hence, the honourable Family of *Trevor* took the title of Viscount Dungannon; aud lately, *William Vane* Esq, hath been created Baron Vane of Dungannon, and Viscount Vane] Next, *Ublo ganell*, where *O-Neal*, who b will have himself solemnly Inaugurated King of *Ulster*, has that Ceremony perform'd after the barbarous custom of the Country Then the Fort upon *Blackwater* or the river *More*, which hath suffer'd exceedingly from the Wars, being the only passage into this Country, c which is the constant harbour of Rebels But it has been neglected, ever since the discovery of another Ford below, which is defended by Forts on both sides, and was built by *Charles Montjoy* Lord Deputy when he pursu'd the rebels into these parts At the same time, he made another Fort, called from himself *Montjoy*, and situate upon the *Lough Eaugh*, or *Sidney* (as the Soldiers, in honour of *Henry Sidney*, call it d at this day) which encloses the west side of the Shire, and is either wholly made or much enlarg'd by the river *Bann*, as I have already observ'd [At this day, the Honourable Family of *Stewart* enjoy the title of Viscount Mountjoy]

Cloghar
a *Satis exilis* C
Ware, p 130
Bishoprick of Cloghar
Dunganon
Barons of Dunganon
Ubloganell
b So said, ann 1607
Fort upon Blackwater
c So said ann 1607
Lough Sidney
d Ann 1607
Viscount *Montjoy*

The *Lough Eagh* is very beautiful and full of Fish, and very large, being about thirty miles in extent, so that this, as the Poet says,

Dulci mentitur Nerea fluctu

With his sweet water counterfeits the Sea

Ann 1607

And considering the Varieties upon the banks, the shady Groves and Meadows always green, and rich Corn fields, where they meet with husbandry; as also the gentle hills and pleasant brooks (all contriv'd for pleasure and profit,) Nature seems to upbraid the Inhabitants, for suffering them to be so wild and barbarous, for want of care.

Tir Oen the upper
Straban
e Ann 1607

In the *Upper Tir Oen*, stands *Straban*, a noted castle, inhabited e in our time by *Turlogh Leneagh* of the family of *O Neal*, who, after the death of *Shan O-Neal* (as I shall tell you by and by) was elected by the people to the dignity of *O-Neal* [This is now a large Town, and a flourishing Corporation, and from hence, an honourable Person of the name of *Hamilton* (to whom it belongs) enjoys the title of Viscount]

Viscount *Straban*

The Castles of Ireland
f *Foramibus*

Here are also some others Castles of less note, which, like those in other parts of the Island, are no more than towers, with narrow f *loop holes*, rather than windows; to which adjoins a Hall of turf roof'd with thatch, and a large yard fenc'd round with a ditch and hedge, to preserve their Cattle from thieves.

Phil Trans an 1713 p 254
Urns

[Several remains of Antiquity have been discovered in this County As near *Omach* (the Shire-Town) Urns in Chests, under two heaps of Stones Near *Cookston*, an Urn, in a hole encompass'd with six Stones of great Bigness, which made a Hexagon, wherein the Urn stood At *Dungannon*, another Urn, of an uncommon bigness, being large enough to hold about three quarts and at *Killmeile*, near *Dungannon*, within a circle of Stones on the top of a Hill, have been found other Urns.

Altar

All these were Repositories for the Bodies, when burnt; and on the last mentioned hill, at about thirty yards distance to the Eastward of that Circle of Stones, was discover'd the *Altar*, on which they used to burn their dead, in the times of Heathenism, with Coals and Bones, fresh, among the Stones, and the stones burn'd with the fire At the east end of the Altar, was found a Pit, that was the Receiver into which they swept whatever remain'd on the Altar, after burning Upon digging deeper, the substance of the Earth appear'd all alike, *viz* black and greasy and it had tinged the Hill in a streight line, from the Pit to the bottom of the Hill

Phil Trans ann 1713 p 250 Trumpets

In the lower Barony of *Dungannon*, have been discover'd several *Trumpets* of an uncommon make; which are supposed by some to have been used by the Priests in the Pagan times, at their funeral Rites, in consort with those who made a noise on such occasions perhaps, the same Howling Noise which is us'd at Funerals, among the Natives to this day]

If this County is famous or eminent for any thing, [except the Antiquities before mention'd,] it is for its Lords, who have rul'd as Kings, or rather Tyrants over it, of whom, two have been Earls of *Tir-Oen*; namely *Conus O-Neale*, and *Hugh* his Grandchild by a son Earls of *Tir-Oen* But when I treat of the Earls and Lords of *Ulster*, I will speak more at large of these, [and only observe here, that Sir *Marcus Beresford*, Baronet, hath been lately created a Baron and Viscount of this kingdom, by the title of Baron *Beresford* of *Beresford* in the County of *Cavan*, and Viscount *Tyrone*]

The County of *DONEGALL* or *TIR-CONEL*.

ALL that remains in Ulster, towards the north and south was inhabited by the *Robogdii* and *Vennicnii* At present, it is call'd the County of *Donegall* or *Tir-Conell*, that is, as some interpret it, *the land of Cornelius*, and as others, *the Land of Conall*, and accordingly Marianus calls it *Conallea* The County is in a manner all champain, and full of Harbours, [and is well stock'd with British Inhabitants] It is bounded on the north and west sides by the Sea, and on the east by the

Liffer riv Phil Trans N 314

river *Liffer*, and is divided from *Conaght* by the Lake *Erne* [The *boggy* and heathy Ground, in this County and *London derry*, hath been much improv'd by *Shells*, which the Country people carry away in Boats at Low-water, and leaving them in heaps on the shore till they drain and dry, do then lay them upon their ground (with great effect and advantage,) instead of *Manure*]

The *Liffer*, not far from its rise, spreads into a broad Lake, which contains an Island, and therein stands a little Monastery, near which is a narrow Vault, famous for I know not what terrible Apparitions, or rather *Religious Dreams*, and (as some foolishly imagin) dug by Ulysses, when he made his descent into Hell, the natives at this day call it *Ellan u' frugadory*, that is, *the Isle of Purgatory*, and *Patrick's Purgatory* For some are so piously credulous, as to believe that *Patrick* the Irish Apostle, or some other Abbot of the same name, obtain'd of God by his fervent Prayers to make the People eye-witnesses of those punishments and tortures, which the wicked endure after this life; to the end he might recover the Irish from their sinful state, and the errors they then lay under Seeing this place is call'd

Patrick's Purgatory

Regli, Regia a Athenry, or Louth H

Reglis in the life of St *Patrick*, I am apt to think it the other a *Regia* in Ptolemy; for the situation is agreeable to the account which he gives of it [But to be somewhat more particular in the description of this place; The Vault or Cave was built of freestone, and cover'd with broad flags, and green turf laid over them It is in length, within the Walls, sixteen foot and an half; in breadth, two and an inch; and, the door being shut, there is no light, but what enters in at a little Window in the corner In the Island also, are divers *Circles*,

Ware, Ant p 99

commonly called *Beds*, and denominated from several Saints, they are enclos'd with stone-walls, scarce three foot high, and are the Places where Pilgrims performed their Penance The Cave was demolish'd as a fictitious thing, on St. *Patrick's* day, in the year 1497, by Authority of Pope Alexander the sixth; but it was afterwards restored, and visited frequently by Pilgrims]

Besides this of St *Patrick*, there is another Purgatory of *Brendan* in this Island I cannot tell you the very place, and therefore take all that I could learn of it, in this tetrastick of Necham,

Asserit esse locum solennis fama dicatum
Brendano, qua lux lucida sæpe micat
Purgandas animas datur hic transire per ignes,
Ut dignæ faciet judicis esse queant

From Brendan nam'd a wondrous Lake is shown,
Where trembling lights along dark caverns run
Here mortal dregs the purging flames consume,
And cleanse foul Souls against their final doom

As the *Liffer*, enlarg'd by other rivers, draws near the Sea, it spreads into another Lake, which Ptolemy calls b *Logia*, now *Logh Foyle*, and *Logh Der* Hence Necham, b Logh eagh Ware See Tir Oen

Lough Der aquis dives lacus est, Ultonia novit
Commodus indigenis utilitate placet

Of thee, great *Logh Der*, spacious *Ulster's* proud,
And neighb'ring Lands commend thy useful flood.

Upon this, formerly, stood *Derry*, a Monastery, and a Bishop's See; [which had been first constituted at *Ardsrath*, and was from thence remov'd to *Magher*; and at length, about the year 1150, to this place] Here, in the year 1566, *Edward Randolf* (eminent for his long Services in the Wars) lost his life in defence of his Country, and did so entirely de- Derry feat *Shan O Neal*, that he was never after able to make head.

Lately, C

But [c] Sir *Henry Docwra* Knight, whose Valour and Conduct shone forth, to his immortal honour, in the Wars of Ireland, planted there a garrison, and afterwards a colony, to bridle the insolence of the Earl of *Tir Oen*; which he settled in such order and method, that it [d] proved an excellent defence against the Rebels, and a means to inure those barbarous People to their duty. [It is now call'd *London derry*, and annexed to the County of that name, and is famous in our Histories, for resisting two memorable Sieges, one in the year 1649, and the other in 1689, and it gives the title of Baron to the Family of *Pitt*.]

[d] Proves, C

Baron *London derry*

The *Robogdii*, seated above *Logia*, possess'd all this northern coast, where *O-Dogherty*, a petty King of no great note, has the chief interest. Here, in *Robogh*, a small episcopal Town, are the remains of the old name *Robogdii*. As for the Promontory *Robogdium*, I cannot tell where to fix it, unless it be *Faire Forland*. From this rocky place, the shore winds back by the mouth of the Lake *Swilly*, which Ptolemy seems to call *Argita*.

Robogh

The Promontory Robogdium

Beyond this to the west, liv'd the *Vennicnii*, which tract [e] was enjoy'd by [f] *Mac-Swiny Fanid*, *Mac Swiny Na doe*, and *Mac-Swiny Bane*, [and here are still several Families of the same name (but now inconsiderable) who farm small Portions of Land, which were heretofore *held in fee* by the *Mac Swinnies*.] In these parts, Ptolemy places the river *Vidua*, now call'd *Crodagh*, and the Promontory *Vennicnium*, now *Ram's head*; and *Boreum*, now S *Helen's head*.

[e] Is, C

[f] Mac Swiny Faid, Mac Swiny Nato ith and Mac Swyny Banagh, C

As the shore winds back from hence, we come to a commodious harbour and road for Ships, at *Calebeg*, from whence the remains of *Sligib* castle are still visible. It was built in the year 1242, by Maurice Fitz Girald Chief Justice of Ireland, after he had reduc'd this part of the Country. But John Fitz Girald, the first Earl of Kildare, was depriv'd of this castle, and of a great estate in these parts, and was also deeply fin'd, for raising a dangerous rebellion against the Earl of *Ulster*.

Calebeg

Sligah

Lower down, not far from the mouth of the lake *Earne*, stands *Donegall*, a Monastery and Town, which gave name to this County, when it was first made one. This territory [g] was govern'd for many ages by those of the family of *O Donell*, who are of the same extraction with the *O-Neals*, without any other title than O Donell, and *Lords of Tir Conell*. For the obtaining of which, and of their popular election and inauguration with the accustom'd ceremonies, at a certain Stone near *Kilmacrenar*, they us'd to contend with great heat and blood shed, till King James [the first] [h] by his Letters Patents confer'd the *honour*, *title*, and *stile* of Earl of *Tir Conell*, upon *Roderick O-Donell* brother to *Hugh* the Rebel, who being banish'd, fled into Spain and there died. The title of Earl of *Tyrconell* was confer'd by King James the Second, on Colonel *Richard Talbot*, a most zealous Papist, and since the Accession of King George to the Throne, the title of Viscount *Tyrconnel* hath been conferred on a noted Family in *England*, of the name of *Brownlow*, but that of Earl of *Donegall* is vested in the honourable Family of *Chichester*, and as to the Territories hereabouts (formerly part of the Inheritance of *O Donnel*,) they are now enjoy'd by the Families of *Gore*, *Hamilton*, *Conolly*, &c.

Donegall

[g] Hath been, C

O Donell

[h] Honorarius titulus

Earl of Tyrconell

South from *Donegall*, is *Belishannon*, near which, not many years ago, were dug up two pieces of Gold, discover'd by a method very remarkable. The Lord Bishop of *Derry*, happening to be at dinner, there came in an Irish Harper, and sung an old Song to his Harp. His Lordship not understanding Irish, was at a loss to know what the Song meant. But the Herdsman being called in, they found by him the substance of it to be this, That in such a place (naming the very spot) a man of a gigantick stature lay buried, and that over his breast and back there were plates of pure gold, and on his fingers rings of gold, so large that an ordinary man might creep through them. The place was so exactly described, that two persons there present were tempted to go in quest of the golden Prize, which the Harper's Song had pointed out to them. After they had dug for some time, they found two thin pieces of gold, exactly of the form and bigness of this Cut.

Belanonsh

This discovery encourag'd them, next morning, to seek for the remainder, but they could meet with nothing more. The passage is the more remarkable, because it comes pretty near the manner of discovering King Arthur's body, by the directions of a British Bard. The two holes in the middle of this, seem to have been for the more convenient tying of it to the arm, or some part of the body.

The Family of *Folliot* now enjoys the honourable title of Baron of *Belishannon*, and the Family of *Fitz Williams* hath been honoured with the Title of Baron of *Lifford*.]

Baron of Belishannon

Baron of Lifford

The ancient Inhabitants of Ulster, as of all the other parts of the Kingdom, were call'd formerly by one common name of *Scots*, and from hence they brought the name into the Northern parts of Britain. *For* (as Giraldus says) *the six Sons of* Mured, *King of Ulster*, *possess'd themselves of the North of Britain about four hundred years after Christ*, *from which time it has been call'd by the name of* Scotland. Yet the Annals of that Kingdom shew us, that this happen'd much more early. Also, *Fergus* the second, who establish'd the Kingdom of the Scots in Britain, came from hence, Patrick having foretold this of him. *Tho' you seem now mean and contemptible to your Brethren at this day*, *it will shortly come to pass*, *that you shall be a Prince*, *and Lord of them all*. To make good this, the same Writer adds; *That not long after*, Fergus, *according to the Prediction of this holy man obtain'd the Sovereignty in these parts, and that his posterity continu'd in the throne for many generations. From him was descended the most valiant King* Edan, *son of* Gabrian, *who conquer'd Scotland* (*call'ed* Albania,) *where his posterity in a continu'd succession reigns to this day.*

The Scots

The [illegible] of

John Curcy, in the reign of Henry the second, was the first Englishman who attempted the

 redu-

reduction of this County, and, having taken *Down* and *Armagh*, made himself master of the whole, either by force or surrender, and was the first who had the title of Earl of *Ulster* But his success made him so much envy'd, that, for his own worth and the unworthiness of others, he was banish'd, and, by King John's appointment, was succeeded by *Hugh de Lacy*, second son of *Hugh Lacy* Lord of Meth, who was made Earl of Ulster *by the delivery of a Sword*, with orders to [i] pursue the War Yet he was depriv'd of this honour by the same King, upon his insolence, and popular practices, but was receiv'd again into favour

Earls of Ulster

[i] Illum bello prosequi jussus An 7 Jo

In confirmation of this, I will give you, word for word, what I find in the Records of Ireland *Hugh de* Lacy, *formerly Earl of Ulster, held all Ulster (exempt and separate from any other County)* in capite *of the Kings of England, by the service of three Knights, whenever a Proclamation issu'd for War And he might try in his own Court all Pleas whatsoever belonging to the Chief Justice and the Sheriff, and he also held a Court of Chancery*, &c *After this, all Ulster was forfeited to our Lord King John, by the said Hugh; who had it afterwards granted him for term of life by King Henry the third After Hugh's decease, Walter de Burgo did those Services to our Lord Edward, King Henry's son, and Lord of Ireland, before he was King The same Lord Edward infeoff'd the foresaid Walter in the foresaid Lands of Ulster, to have and to hold, to him and his heirs, by the service aforesaid, as amply and freely as the said Hugh de Lacy did, except the advowsons of Cathedral Churches, and the [k] Jurisdiction over the same, as also the Pleas of the Crown, viz Rapes, Forstalls, Arsoneys, and Treasure trouves, which our soveraign Lord King Edward reserv'd to himself and his heirs*

[k] Dominio co-rundem

This Walter *de Burgo* (who was Lord of Conaught and Earl of Ulster) had by the only daughter of Hugh de Lacy, Richard Earl of Ulster; who died, after a perplex'd and uneasie life, in the year 1326 Richard had a son *John de Burgo*, who died in his Father's life-time, after he had had a son *William* (by his wife Elizabeth, sister and co-heir of *Gilbert Clare* Earl of Glocester,) who succeeded his Grandfather William was murder'd by his own People in his youth; leaving a little daughter, *Elizabeth*, afterwards marry'd to *Leonel* Duke of Clarence; by whom she had likewise one only Daughter, marry'd to Edmund Mortimer Earl of March; and by her the Earldom of *Ulster*, with the Province of *Conaught*, came to the Mortimers; from whom, together with the Kingdom of England, it came to the house of York; and then, by King Edward the fourth was annex'd to the Crown A civil War breaking out at that time in England, and the Nation falling into factions and parties, and the English in Ulster returning into England to support their several sides, these Countries were seiz'd by O-*Neal* and others of the Irish so that the Province grew wild and barbarous to a very great degree, and whereas it formerly yielded a considerable revenue to the Earls, it has hardly, [l] since that time, paid any to the Kings of England

See Radn , and Yorkshire north riding.

[l] So said, ann 1607

And if I may be allow'd to speak freely, the piety and wisdom of the Kings of England [m] has not been more defective in any one thing than in a due administration of this Province, and I may add, of all Ireland, as to the propagating Religion, and modelling the State, and civilizing the Inhabitants, which things, for many ages, have been very little regarded Whether this neglect is to be imputed to Carelesness or Parsimony, I know not But one would think, an Island so great, and so near, where the Soil is so good and the Pastures so rich, which has so many Woods, and Mines, so many Rivers and commodious Harbours on all sides, convenient for trading to the richest parts of the World, with the Customs and Revenues arising from thence, and lastly, an Island so full of Inhabitants, and a People who, in respect of minds and bodies, are capable of the highest Employments in Peace or War All these together (one would think) should deserve and challenge our future Care

[m] So said, ann 1607

THE

THE ANTIENT AND Modern Customs OF THE IRISH.

T is requisite, that I say something in this place, of the *Manners* and *Customs* of the Irish As for the more antient ones, the account which I give of them is borrow'd from ancient writers, but their modern customs are recited from the observations of a modern Author, both learned and industrious

The Irish of old time, while rude and barbarous like all other nations in this part of the world, are thus describ'd by the Antients

Strabo, l iv *I can say nothing of Ireland upon good authority, but that the people are more barbarous than the Britains They feed upon man's flesh, and* [a] *eat to great excess They look upon it as very innocent, to eat the bodies of their dead Parents, and to lie in publick, not only with strange women, but with their own mothers and sisters However, I must caution the Reader, that I pretend not to warrant the truth of this relation It is said indeed, that man's flesh was eat among the Scythians, and that, in the extremities of a siege, the Gauls, Spaniards, and many others, have frequently done it*

[a] Πολυφάγοι, but in the Epitome ποηφάγοι, upon herbs and roots

Pomponius Mela, lib iii *The Inhabitants are barbarous, and have no sense, either of Virtue or Religion*

Solinus, cap xxiv *Those who conquer, first drink of the blood of the Slain, and then besmear their faces with it, and know no distinction between right and wrong When a man-child is born, the mother feeds it first upon the point of her husband's sword, which she carries gently into the mouth of her little one; thinking this to be ominous, and wishing, after their heathenish way, that it may never refuse death in the midst of war Such as affect gaiety, adorn the hilts of their swords with the teeth of Sea monsters, which are as white as Ivory For here the great glory of the Men, is* [b] *in the fineness and well keeping of their arms*

[b] In armis nitor

These are their *antient* customs As for the usages of the middle age, we have them in *Giraldus Cambrensis*, and in others from him But, for their later customs, they are describ'd by an industrious modern Author, whom I take to be *J Good*, a Priest, educated at *Oxford*, and School master of *Limerick*, about the year 1566, from whom I shall relate them word for word Yet since I promis'd some account of the administration of Justice among them, I will first discharge that

The great men, who have the fourth vowel prefix'd to their names, to denote their quality and eminence, as *O Neal*, *O Rork*, *O-Donell*, &c and others who have *Mac* before their names, [c] enjoy a large Prerogative In virtue of which, they Lord it at a mighty rate; and by the tributes,

[c] O prefix'd the name the Noblemen of Ireland by way of excellence This was ... Description

taxes,

is according to the state of them, ann. 1597 taxes, and other impositions which they exact for maintaining of their Soldiers, namely their Galloglasses, Kernes, and Horsemen, they make their poor Vassals very miserable; especially, in times of civil war, they drain their very blood and spirits

Breahan. These Great men have their Lawyers, whom they call *Breahans*, as the Goths did their's, *Bellagines*, a mean ignorant sort of people, who at certain times try the causes of the neighbourhood upon the top of some high hill The Plaintiff opens his cause before them with great complaints of the injuries he has suffer'd, to which the Defendant pleads *Not guilty* If the Defendant is convicted of theft, they award Restitution, either of the thing or the value These great men have likewise their particular Historians, to chronicle the famous actions of their lives, their Physicians and Poets (whom they call *Bards*,) and Harpers, who all have their several estates and possessions assign'd them And in each territory there are certain particular families for the several employments, for instance one for *Breahans*, another for *Historians*, and so of the rest, who take care to instruct their children and relations in their respective professions, and have always one of the same race to succeed them

Professions hereditary Among the Grandees, the rules of succession and inheritance are little regarded who ever is descended of a good family, and has the greatest power, retinue, and courage, assumes the Sovereignty, either by election of the People, or usurpation, and excludes the sons, nephews, and nearest relations of the person deceased, being, after their barbarous way, enthron'd in a stone seat, plac'd in the open air upon a certain hillock At the same time a successor is sometimes declared, according to the Law of *Tanistry* and they call him *Tanist*, but whether from the Danes, among whom as among the Northern Inhabitants of Britain, *Thane* was us'd for many ages to signify a person of honour and the King's Officer, I cannot positively say

But now take the observations of Mr *Good* in whose behalf I observe once for all, that there is nothing in them malicious or partial, but all are exactly true, and that they are only to be

And as these were, ann 1560 understood of the wild and native Irish, who are as yet uncivilized as living in the remote parts of the Kingdom

These people are generally strong, bodied nimble, bold, haughty, quick witted, [illegible] venturous, inur'd to cold and hunger, [illegible] hospitable, constant in their love, [illegible] malicious, credulous, [illegible] and, according [illegible] *al [illegible] good [illegible]*

Name *They [illegible] plaine nam[illegible] cr [illegible] colours, [illegible] as scar'd, [illegible] Rob [illegible] the [illegible] upon [illegible] family [illegible] to any [illegible] es unlawful When [illegible] takes his name, lest [illegible] should be forgotten, and if any of the Ancestors [illegible] ments, [illegible] the rather, [illegible] the Poets celebrating the [illegible] great*

additions of their own, and growing very rich by the rewards they have For Brides, and women big with child, think it scandalous, if they present not even their best cloaths to a person so instrumental in Glory

Nursing the Children *Women, within six days after their delivery, return to their husband's bed, and put out their children to nurse Great application is made from all parts, to be nurses to the children of these Grandees, who are more tender to the foster-children than their own And notwithstanding a very ill temper of body, by reason of bad air, a moist soil and diet, and licentiousness, for want of laws, nay, tho' they think it a disgrace to suckle their own children, yet for the sake of nursing these, man and wife will abstain from each other, and in case they do not, they find another nurse at their own charge The nurses here are almost as numerous as the menial servants and they think it a good reason to be lov'd, to have the suckling of an infant If the infant is sick, they sprinkle it with the stalest urine they can get, and for a preservative against mischance, they hang not only the beginning of St* John's *Gospel about the child's neck, but a crooked nail out of a horse's foot, or a piece of wolf's skin For this very purpose also, both [illegible] and sucklings wear always a girdle of [illegible] about them It is moreover observ'd, that [illegible] present their Lovers with bracelets of such [illegible], whether in imitation of the Girdle of Venus call'd Cestos, I cannot tell The Foster fathers take much more pains, spend much more money, and bestow more affection and kindness upon these children, than their own From these, they take, or rather unnaturally extort, cloaths, money, and portions, to carry on the designs, buy the arms, and gratify the lusts of the others, even driving away [illegible] their Cattle for them All who have suck'd the same breast, are very kind and loving, and confide more in each other than if they were natural brothers, so that they will have an aversion even to their own brothers for the sake of these If their parents chide them, they fly to their foster fathers [illegible] by whom they are often excited to open [illegible] them, and being train'd up in the [illegible] they [illegible] the [illegible] the sons but the daughters, are brought up by these nurses, [illegible] one of these [illegible] is [illegible] incredible how [illegible] eat a very [illegible] attend [illegible] Nay, [illegible] to be imparted to [illegible] other [illegible] Nurse*

Bod[illegible] [illegible] the flesh of [illegible] they [illegible] prayers, [illegible] so that the [illegible] of their Monks [illegible] The very [illegible] fast every [illegible] day and Sat[illegible] Some [illegible] St Cather[illegible] on a [illegible] to the [illegible] Virgins may get good husbands, [illegible] may become happier

O prefix'd to the names of the Noblemen of Ireland, by way of excellency. The great men, who have the fourth vowel prefix'd to their names, to denote their quality and eminence, as *O-Neal, O-Rork, O-Donell*, &c, and others who have *Mac* before their names; * * This whole Descriptionenjoy a large Prerogative. In virtue of which, they Lord it at a mighty rate; and by the tributes, is according to the state of them, ann. 1607. taxes, and other Impositions which they exact for maintaining of their Soldiers, namely their Galloglasses, Kernes, and Horsemen, they make their poor Vassals very miserable; especially, in times of civil war, they drain their very blood and spirits.

These Great men have their Lawyers; whom they call *Breahans*,Breahans. as the Goths did their's, *Bellagines*; a mean ignorant sort of people, who at certain times try the causes of the neighbourhood upon the top of some high hill. The Plaintiff opens his cause before them with great complaints of the injuries he has suffer'd, to which the Defendant pleads *Not guilty*. If the Defendant is convicted of theft, they award Restitution, either of the thing or the value. These great men have likewise their particular Historians, to chronicle the famous actions of their lives; their Physicians and Poets (whom they call *Bards*;) and Harpers, who all have their several estates and possessions assign'd them. Professions hereditary. And in each territory there are certain particular families for the several employments; for instance, one for *Breahans*, another for *Historians*, and so of the rest; who take care to instruct their children and relations in their respective professions, and leave always one of the same race to succeed them. Among the Grandees, the rules of succession and inheritance are little regarded: whoever is descended of a good family, and has the greatest power, retinue, and courage, assumes the Sovereignty, either by election of the People, or usurpation; and excludes the sons, Nephews, and nearest relations of the person deceased; being, after their barbarous way, enthron'd in a stone seat, plac'd in the open air upon a certain hillock. At the same time a successor is sometimes declared, according to the Law of *Tanistry*; and they call him *Tanist*; but whether from the Danes, among whom (as among the Northern Inhabitants of Britain) *Thane* was us'd for many ages to signify a person of honour and the King's Officer; I cannot positively say.

But now take the observations of Mr. *Good*; in whose behalf I observe once for all, that there is nothing in them malicious or partial, but all are exactly true; and that they are only to be understood of the * * And as these were, ann. 1607.wild and native Irish, who are as yet unciviliz'd, as living in the remoter parts of the Kingdom.

These people are generally strong bodied, nimble, bold, haughty, quick-witted, warlike, venturous, inur'd to cold and hunger, lustful, hospitable, constant in their love, implacably malicious, credulous, vain-glorious, resenting; and, according to their old character, *violent in all their affections: the bad not to be match'd, the good not to be excell'd.*

Names. *They commonly baptize their children by prophane names, adding somewhat from one accident or another: from some old wive's tale; or from colours, as red, white, black*, &c. *from distempers, as scab'd, bald*, &c. *or else from some vice, as* Robber *or* Proud; *and, though they cannot bear reproach, yet the greatest among them, such as have the letter O prefix'd to their names, are not asham'd of these appellations. It is look'd upon as foreboding a speedy death to the parent or other of the Family then living, to give his or their names to any of the children; and therefore they avoid it as unlawful. When the father dies, the son takes his name, lest it should be forgotten; and if any of the Ancestors have been famous for their atchievements, the like bravery is expected from him. And the rather, upon account of the Poets celebrating their actions; yet magnifying them with great additions of their own,*

Ireland Customs 1617-18

and growing very rich by the rewards they have. For Brides, and women big with child, think it scandalous, if they present not even their best cloaths to a person so instrumental in Glory.

Nursing the Children. *Women, within six days after their delivery, return to their husband's bed, and put out their children to nurse. Great application is made from all parts, to be nurses to the children of these Grandees; who are more tender to the foster-children than their own. And notwithstanding a very ill temper of body, by reason of bad air, a moist soil and diet, * * Juris exilium.and licentiousness, for want of laws; nay, tho' they think it a disgrace to suckle their own children; yet for the sake of nursing these, man and wife will abstain from each other, and in case they do not, they find another nurse at their own charge. The nurses here are almost as numerous as the maid-servants: and they think it a good reason to be lewd, to have the suckling of an infant. If the infant is sick, they sprinkle it with the stalest urine they can get; and for a preservative against mischances, they hang not only the beginning of St.* John's *Gospel about the child's neck, but also a crooked nail out of a horse's foot, or a piece of a wolf's skin. For this very purpose also, both nurses and sucklings wear always a girdle of womens hair about them. It is moreover observ'd, that they present their Lovers with bracelets of such hair; whether in imitation of the Girdle of* Venus *call'd* Cestos, *I cannot tell. The Foster-fathers take much more pains, spend much more money, and bestow more affection and kindness, upon these children, than their own. From these, they take, or rather unnaturally extort, cloaths, money, and portions, to carry on the designs, buy the arms, and gratifie the lusts of the others; † † Etiam prædis abactis.even driving away their Cattle for them. All who have suck'd the same breasts, are very kind and loving, and confide more in each other than if they were ¦ ¦ Germani.natural brothers; so that they will have an aversion even to their own brothers for the sake of these. If their parents chide them, they fly to the Foster-fathers for protection, by whom they are often excited to open war against them; and being train'd up in this manner, they grow the vilest profligates in nature. And not only the sons, but the daughters, are brought up by these nurses, to all manner of lewdness. If one of these foster-children happen to be sick, it is incredible how soon the nurses hear it, though they live at a very great distance; and with what concern they attend the child day and night upon this occasion. Nay, the greatest corruptions and debaucheries of Ireland, it is believed, are to be imputed to no other cause, than this method of Nursing.*

Bodies. *It is probable, that this country is more hot and moist than others, by reason that the flesh of the natives is particularly soft; proceeding as well from the nature of the climate, as their use of certain washes. This softness of the muscles makes them also extraordinary nimble, and pliant in all parts of their body. The people are strangely given to idleness, think it the greatest wealth to want business, and the greatest happiness to have liberty. They love musick mightily, and above all instruments, are particularly taken with the harp, strung with brass wire, and play'd on with their crooked * * Unguibus.nails. They that are religious, mortifie with wonderful austerity, by watching, praying, and fasting; so that the Relations which we find of their Monks heretofore, are not to be look'd on as incredible. The very women and maidens fast every Wednesday and Saturday the year round. Some also upon St.* Catherine'*s day; and never omit, though it fall on a Birth-day, or though themselves be ever so sick; to the end, some say, that the Virgins may get good husbands, and that the Wives may become happier in a married state, either by the death or desertion of their husbands, or else by*

their reformation and amendment.

in a married state, either by the death or desertion of their husbands, or else by their reformation and amendment But such among them as once give themselves over to a vicious course, are the vilest creatures in the world.

Dying of Cloaths *With the bark of Alders, they die their cloaths black, in dying yellow, they make use of Elder-berries With the boughs, bark, and leaves of poplar-trees, beaten together, they die* [i] *their loose shirts of a saffron colour (which are now much out of use) mixing the bark of the wild Arbut tree, and salt and saffron In dying, their way is, not to boil the thing long, but to let it soak for some days together in cold urine, that the yellow may be deeper and more durable*

[i] *Laxa indusia.*

Robberies *Robberries here are not look'd on as infamous, but are committed with great barbarity in all parts of the Country When they are upon such a design, they pray to God to bring booty in their way, and look upon a prize as the effect of his bounty to them They are of opinion, that neither violence, robbery, nor murther is displeasing to God If it were, they say God would not tempt them with an opportunity, nay, they say it would be a sin, not to lay hold of it One shall bear the very Rogues and Cut throats, say,* The Lord is merciful, and will not suffer the price of his own blood to be lost on me *Moreover, they say they do but follow the example of their Fore-fathers, that this is the only method of livelihood they have, and that it would sully the honour of their family, to work for their bread, and give over their desperate adventures When they are upon the road, for robbing, or any other design, they take particular notice who they first meet in a morning, that they may avoid or meet him again, as their luck answers that day They reckon it want of spirit and courage to be in bed in a stormy night, and not on an Adventure, at what distance soever, for the sake of a good prize Of la e, they spare neither Temples nor Sanctuaries, but rob them, burn them, and murder such as have hid themselves there*

Viciousness of their Clergy *The vileness of the lives of their priests is the great cause of all this, who have converted the Temples into Stews their whores follow them wherever they go, and in case they find themselves cast off, they endeavour to revenge the injury by poison The Church is the habitation of the Priest's whores and Bastards, there they drink, whore, murder, and keep their Cattle Among these wild Irish, there is nothing sacred, nor signs of Church or Chapel, save outwardly, no Altars, or at most such only as are polluted, and if there be a Crucifix thereon, it is defaced and broken the sacred Vestments are so nasty, that they turn one's stomach, their moveable Altar without a cross is broken and deform'd, the Mass book torn, and without the Canon, and is us'd also in all oaths and perjuries, their Chalice is of lead without a cover, and their Communion cup of horn The Priests think of nothing but providing for their Families and getting Children The Rectors turn Vicars, and hold many Parishes together, being great pretenders to the Canon law, but absolute strangers to all parts of learning The sons succeed their fathers in their Churches, having dispensations for their Bastardy These will not go into Priest's orders, but commit the charge to* [k] *Curates, without any allowance, leaving them to live by the Book, i e by the small oblations at baptism, unctions, or burials, which proves but a very poor maintenance*

[k] *Presbyteri*

The sons of these Priests, who follow not their studies, grow generally notorious Robbers For those who are called Mac Decan, Mac-Pherson, Mac Ospac, *i e the son of the Dean, Parson, and Bishop, are the greatest Robbers, being enabled by the bounty of their Parents to raise a greater gang of accomplices; and the more, because, in imitation of their Fathers, they keep no hospitality The daughters of these, if married in their fathers life time, have good portions, but if not, they either turn whores or beggars*

Swearing *They hardly speak three words without a solemn oath, by the* Trinity, God, *the* Saints, St Patrick, St Brigid, *their* Baptism, *their* Faith, *the* Church, *their* Godfather's hand, *and,* by thy hand *Though they take these oaths upon the Bible or Mass book laid on their bare heads, yet if any one put them in mind of the danger of damnation for perjury, they presently tell him,* That God is merciful, and will not suffer the price of his own blood to be lost Whether I repent or not, I shall never be thrown into Hell *For performance of promises these three things are looked on as the strongest obligations 1 To swear at the Altar with his hand upon the book, as it lies open on his bare head 2 To invoke some Saint or other, by touching or kissing his bell, or crooked staff 3 To swear by the hand of an Earl, or by the hand of his Lord, or any other Great man For perjury in the two first cases makes him infamous, but in this last oath, the Grandee, by whose name he swore, fines him in a great sum of Money and number of Cows, for the injury he has done his name*

Cows *For Cows are the most valuable treasure here Of which this is remarkable* (as the same writer tells us) *that cows are certain to give no milk in Ireland, unless either their own calves be set by them alive, or the skin of it stuff'd with straw, to represent the live one, in which they meet with the scent of their own Matrix If the cow happens to be dry, a witch is sent for, who settles the cow's affections upon another calf by certain herbs, and makes her yield her milk*

Marriages *They seldom marry out of their own town, and contract with one another, not* de præsenti, *but* de futuro, *or else agree without deliberation Upon this account, the least difference generally parts them, the husband taking another wife, and the wife another husband, nor is it certain whether the Contract be true or false, till their dying day Hence arise wars, rapines, murders, and deadly feuds, about successions and inheritances The cast-off-wives have recourse to the witches, these being looked on as able to afflict either the former husband, or the new wife, with barrenness or impotency, or some dangerous distemper All of them are very prone to incest, and divorces under pretence of conscience are common Both men and women set a value upon their hair, especially if it is of a golden colour, and long, for they plat it at full length for show, and suffer it to hang down finely wreath'd, winding about their heads many ells of fine linnen Which sort of round dress is used by all who can compass it (be they wives or strumpets) after child bed*

Superstition *To these may be added, abundance of superstitious customs Whether or no they worship the Moon, I know not; but when they first see her after the change, they commonly bow the knee, and say the Lord's Prayer, and, near the wane, address themselves to her with a loud voice after this manner,* Leave us as well as thou found'st us *They honour Wolves* [l] *as Parents, calling them* Chari Christi, *praying for them, and wishing them happy; and then they think they will not hurt them They look through the blade-bone of a shoulder of mutton, when the meat is pick'd clean off, and if they find a spot in any part, they think it portends a Funeral out of that family They take any one for a witch that comes to fetch fire on May day, and therefore refuse to give any, unless the party asking it be sick, and then it is with an Imprecation, believing, that all their butter*

[l] In pace

will

will be stole the following summer by this woman On May-day, likewise, if they can find a hare among their herd, they endeavour to kill her, out of a notion, that it is some old witch that has a design upon their butter If their butter be stolen, they fancy they shall recover it, if they take some of the thatch that hangs over the door, and throw it into the fire But they think it foretells a plentiful dairy, if they set boughs of trees before their houses on May day In Towns, when any Magistrate enters upon his Office, the wives in the streets, and the maidens out of the windows, strew him and his retinue with wheat and salt Before they sow their field, the wife sends salt to it To prevent the Kite's stealing their chickens, they hang up the egg shells in which the chickens where hatch'd, somewhere in the roof of the House It is thought unlawful to clean their horses feet or curry them, or gather grass for them, on a Saturday, though all this may be done upon their highest Festivals

Horses

If they never lend fire to their neighbours, they imagin it adds to their horses length of life and health When the owner of a horse eats eggs, he must be very careful to eat an even number, otherwise they endanger the horses Jockeys are not allow'd to eat eggs, and whatever horseman does it, he must wash his hands immediately after When a horse dies, the master hangs up the feet and legs in the house, and looks upon the very hoofs as sacred If one praise a horse, or any other creature, he must cry, God save him, or spit upon him, and if any mischief befalls the horse within three days, they find out the person who commended him, who is to whisper the Lord's Prayer at his right ear They believe, that the eyes of some people bewitch their horses, and in such cases, they repair to certain old women, who by muttering a few prayers, set them right again The horses feet are very much subject to a worm, which, creeping upwards, multiplies exceedingly, and at last corrupts the body The remedy in this case, is thus They send for a witch, who must be brought to the horse on two Mondays and one Thursday, at which times, breathing upon the part affected, and repeating her charm, the horse recovers Many give a good price for the knowledge of this charm, and are sworn, not to divulge it

Charms

They think, the women have peculiar charms for all evils, shar'd and distributed among them, and therefore they apply to them according to their several Ailings They begin and conclude their Inchantments with a Pater-noster and Ave Maria When any one gets a fall, he springs up, and turning about three times to the right, digs a hole in the ground with his knife or sword, and cuts out a turf, for they imagin [m] there is a spirit in the earth In case he grow sick in two or three days after, they send one of their Women skill'd in that way, to the place, where she says, I call thee P from the east, west, south and north, from the groves, the woods, the rivers, the fens, from the fairies, red, black, white, &c And after some short ejaculations, she returns home to the sick person, to see whether it be the disease Esane (which they imagin is inflicted by the Fairies) and whispers in his ear another short prayer, and a Pater noster, after which she puts coals into a pot of clear water, and then passes a better judgment upon the distemper, than all the Physicians

[m] Terram umbram reddere

Armies

Their armies consist of horsemen, and of [n] veterane soldiers reserved for the rear (whom they call Galliglasses, and who fight with sharp hatchets,) and of light arm'd foot (they call them Kernes,) armed with [o] darts and daggers When horse or foot march out of the gate, they think it a good omen to be huzza'd, and if not, they think it forebodes ill They use the bag pipe in their wars instead of a trumpet, they carry Amulets about them, and repeat short prayers, and when they engage, they cry out as loud as they can, Pharogh (which, I suppose, is that military Barritus, of which Ammianus speaks,) believing, that he who joins not in the general shout, will be snatch'd from the ground, and hurried as it were upon the wing through the air (avoiding ever after the sight of men) into a certain valley in Kerry, as I have already said

[n] Triarii

[o] Jaculis armentatis

See that County

Sick persons.

Those who are about the sick, never mention a word of God, or the salvation of the soul, or making their wills, but flatter them with the hopes of recovery They give them over, if they once desire the Sacrament The wives are not sollicitous that their husbands should make wills, because it is a custom, for them to have a third of his goods, and the rest is to be distributed by equal portions among the children, unless the Estate be seiz'd by violence, when he that is mightiest, gets the best share; for he who has most power, whether Uncle or Nephew, oft times seizes the Estate, excluding the sons When a sick person is departing, before he dies, certain women being hired mourners, and standing where four streets meet, and spreading out their hands, make a hideous outcry suited to the occasion, and endeavour to stay the departing soul, by recounting what blessings he enjoys in goods, wives, beauty, fame, kindred, friends, and horses, asking him, why he will depart, to what place and to whom he would go? and, expostulating with the Soul, they accuse it of ingratitude, and at last complain that the expiring soul transmigrates into Night-haggs (a sort of women that appear at night, and in the dark,) but when the soul is once departed, they fall into mournings, clapping of hands, and hideous howlings They attend the funeral with so much noise, that a man would think the living, as well as the dead, past recovery At these mournings, the nurses, daughters, and strumpets, are most passionately sorrowful, nor do they less bemoan those who are slain in the field, than others that die in their beds, though they say, it is the easier death of the two, to die fighting or robbing They rail at their adversary with the utmost spite, and bear an immortal hatred against all his kindred They think the souls of the deceased are in company with the famous men of those places; concerning whom they retain many stories and sonnets, as of the gyants, Fin-Mac Huyle, Osshin Mac Osshin, and are so far deluded as to think they often see them

Diet

As to their diet, they delight in herbs, especially cresses, mushrooms, and roots, so that Strabo had reason to call them ποηφαγοι, i e Eaters of herbs; for which, in some copies, it is falsly read πολυφαγοι, i e Gluttons They love butter mixed with oatmeal, milk, whey, beef broth, and flesh, oft-times without bread What corn they have, they lay up for their horses, which they take great care of When they are sharp set, they make no scruple to eat raw flesh, after they have squeezed out the blood, to digest which, they drink Usquebagh in great quantities They let their Cows blood, which, after it is curdled and spread with butter, they eat very greedily

Garments

They generally go bare headed, save when they wear a head-piece, having a long head of hair, with curled Glibbes, which they highly value, and take it heinously if one twitch or pull them They wear linnen shirts, very large, with wide sleeves hanging down to their knees, which they generally dye with saffron They have woollen jackets, but very short; plain breeches, close to their thighs, and over these they cast their mantles or shag rugs, which

Glibbes

Indusia

Mantles

Heteromallæ *which Isidore seems to call* Heteromallæ, *fring'd with an agreeable mixture of colours, in which they wrap themselves up, and sleep upon the bare ground Such also do the women cast over the garment which comes down to their ankles, and they* load *their heads (as I said) rather than* adorn *them with several ells of fine linnen roll'd up in wreaths, as they do their necks with neck laces, and their arms with bracelets*

These are the Manners and Customs of the Wild Irish, describ'd out of the aforesaid Author. As for the rest, who inhabit the English Pale (as they call it,) they are not defective in any point of civility or good breeding, which they owe to the English Conquest and much happier would it have been for the whole Island, had they not been blinded with a stubborn conceit of their own Customs, in opposition to much better But the Irish are so wedded to those, that they not only retain 'em themselves, but corrupt the English among them; and it is scarce credible how soon these will degenerate Such a proneness there is in human nature, to grow worse The English Pale

[p] See the County of Tir Oen, p 1410

I Just now [p] *intimated, That I would give some account of the* O Neals, *who pretend to be Lords of* Ulster, *and I promis'd an excellent Friend of mine a History of the Rebellions which they have rais'd* [q] *in our age Tho' that Gentleman is now happy in a better world, yet I had so high an esteem of him, that I cannot but perform my Promise to his very Memory This only I think necessary to be premised, that my Materials are not drawn from uncertain Reports, or other weak Authorities, but from the Original Papers which came from the Generals, and from such as were Eye witnesses, and had a share in the Transactions, and that I have handed them so sincerely, that I doubt not of the thanks of all such Readers who seek for Truth in earnest, and desire to be let into the Affairs of* Ireland, *which are so much a secret to most men, hoping to escape the Censure of all, except those who shall be galled at a true Representation of their own wicked Actions* [r].

[q] So said ann 160

[r] This Account of the *O Neals*, being merely Historical, is placed in the Appendix

THE

The Smaller

ISLANDS

IN THE

BRITISH OCEAN.

GENERAL HEADS IN THE BRITISH ISLANDS.

THE

The Smaller ISLANDS IN THE BRITISH OCEAN.

I WILL now set sail from IRELAND, *and take a Survey of the Islands scatter'd upon the Coast of* Britain. *If I could depend upon my own sufficiency for the Work, I would visit every one of them: but since my Design is only Antiquities; such of them as are of little note, I shall pass by, but such as are more eminent, I will land at, and make some short stay in; that now at last, I may be so happy as to restore them to the honour of their respective Antiquities.*

That this Voyage may be regular and orderly, I will steer my course, from Ireland *to the Severn-Sea; and from the Irish-Sea (after I have doubled the utmost Point of* Scotland) *to the German Ocean; from hence, I will sail as successfully as I may, through the British Sea, which reach'd as far as* Spain. *But not without apprehension, that this Ship of Antiquity, having so unskilful a Pilot, will now and then touch upon the rocks of Error, or sink in the depths of Ignorance. However, I am embark'd, and must go through,* Τόλμα [illegible] ἀρχηγὸς, *i. e* Courage is the best Pilot, *says Antiphilus; and whoever shall* follow *me, may perhaps make a more successful Voyage.*

But first, it will not be foreign to my Business, to set down what Plutarch reports of these Islands in general, from a fabulous relation of Demetrius, who seems to have liv'd in the time of Hadrian: That of the Islands about *Britain*, a great part are Desolate and Solitary; some of which are consecrated to Dæmons, or Demi Gods: and, That himself, at the command of the Emperor, sail'd out of curiosity to one that was nearest these, where he found few Inhabitants, but those look'd upon by the *Britains*, as sacred and inviolable. Not long after he arriv'd there the weather grew foul and very tempestuous, and there followed a terrible storm of wind and thunder, which at length ceasing, the Inhabitants told him, that one of the [a] Heroes was deceased. *A little after he says,* That in one of those Islands, Saturn is detained prisoner, and fast a-sleep, in the custody of Briareus; That sleep is instead of chains and fetters; and, That he has several of those Dæmons about him for attendants. *Thus our forefathers, as we at this day, took the liberty of telling monstrous things of Places far off; which it must be own'd, is a* safe *way of Romancing.*

[a] *E præstantioribus*

The Wamses
Noddam
Bransman I
Oakscar
Staple I
Megstone
Pinnacle
Lighthouse
Wido pens at Crumeston
Part
FARNE I
Bamborough Cas
of Northumberland
2 Miles
S
Golwick
PART OF
NORTHUMBERLAND
Sandhills
HOLY: I.
Town
Castle
Plough
Kyley
the Abby
Shingles
2 Miles
Buckton
MAN: I.
MONA Cæsar
MONOEDA Ptol
MONABIA Plin.
MENAVIA Orosius et Bede
MENAW
Nennius
et EUBONIA
MENOW Britans
Point of Ayre
Kirk Patrick
Ramsey
S Michell
Peel Castle

PART OF
HAMPSHIRE
Fareham
Tichfield
Calshot Castle
Bramble
Middle
Spit
Bewley
Limington
Salt Pitts
Hurst Castle
Newton Haven
W Cows
E Cows
Ryde
EAST
WIGHT
WEST
MEDINE
Newport
Carisbrook Castle
Yarmouth
Freshwater Isle
Fresh Water Bay
Kingston
Brixton
Shorwell
Arreton
Newchurch
Sandham Bay
Shankling
Dunnose
Rocken end
Chale Bay

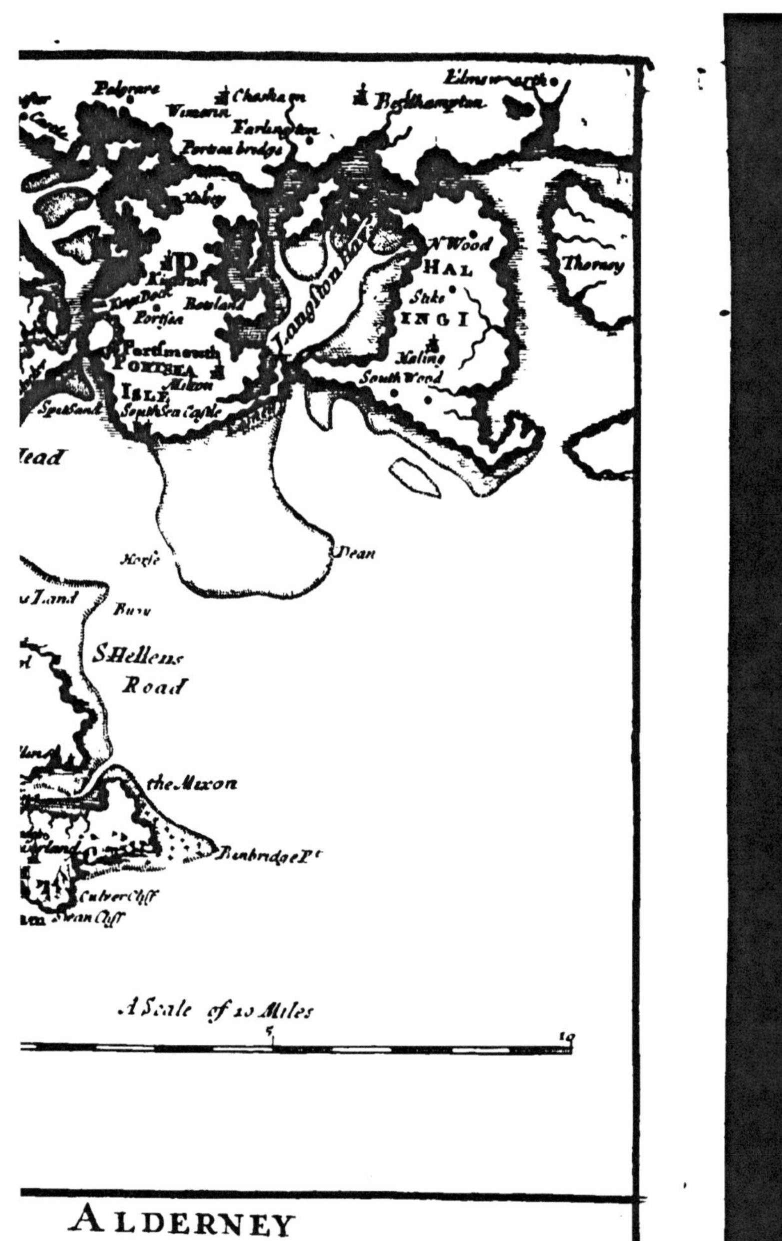
Chasham
Farlington
Bedhampton
N Wood
HAL
INGI
South Wood
Thorney
Langston Har
Portsmouth
PORTSEA
ISLE
South Sea Castle
Dean
S.Hellens
Road
the Mixon
Culver Cliff
A Scale of 10 Miles
5
10

ALDERNEY

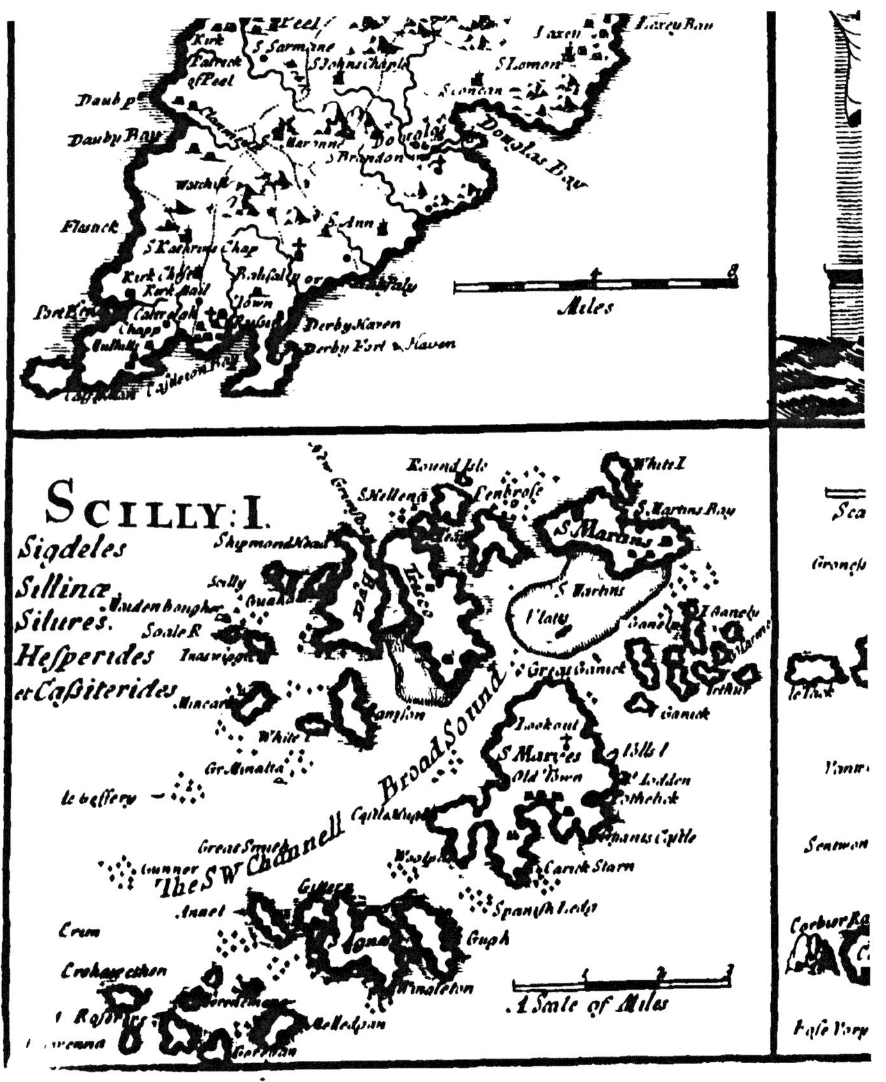

SCILLY: I.
Sigdeles
Sillinæ
Silures.
Hesperides
et Caßiterides
Round Isle
White I
S. Martins
S. Martins Bay
S. Martins Flats
Great Ganick
S. Maries
Old Town
Carick Starn
Spanish Ledg
Great Smith
Gunner
Annet
Broad Sound
The S W Channell
A Scale of Miles
Laxey Bay
Douglas Bay
S. Ann
Derby Haven
Derby Fort & Haven
Miles

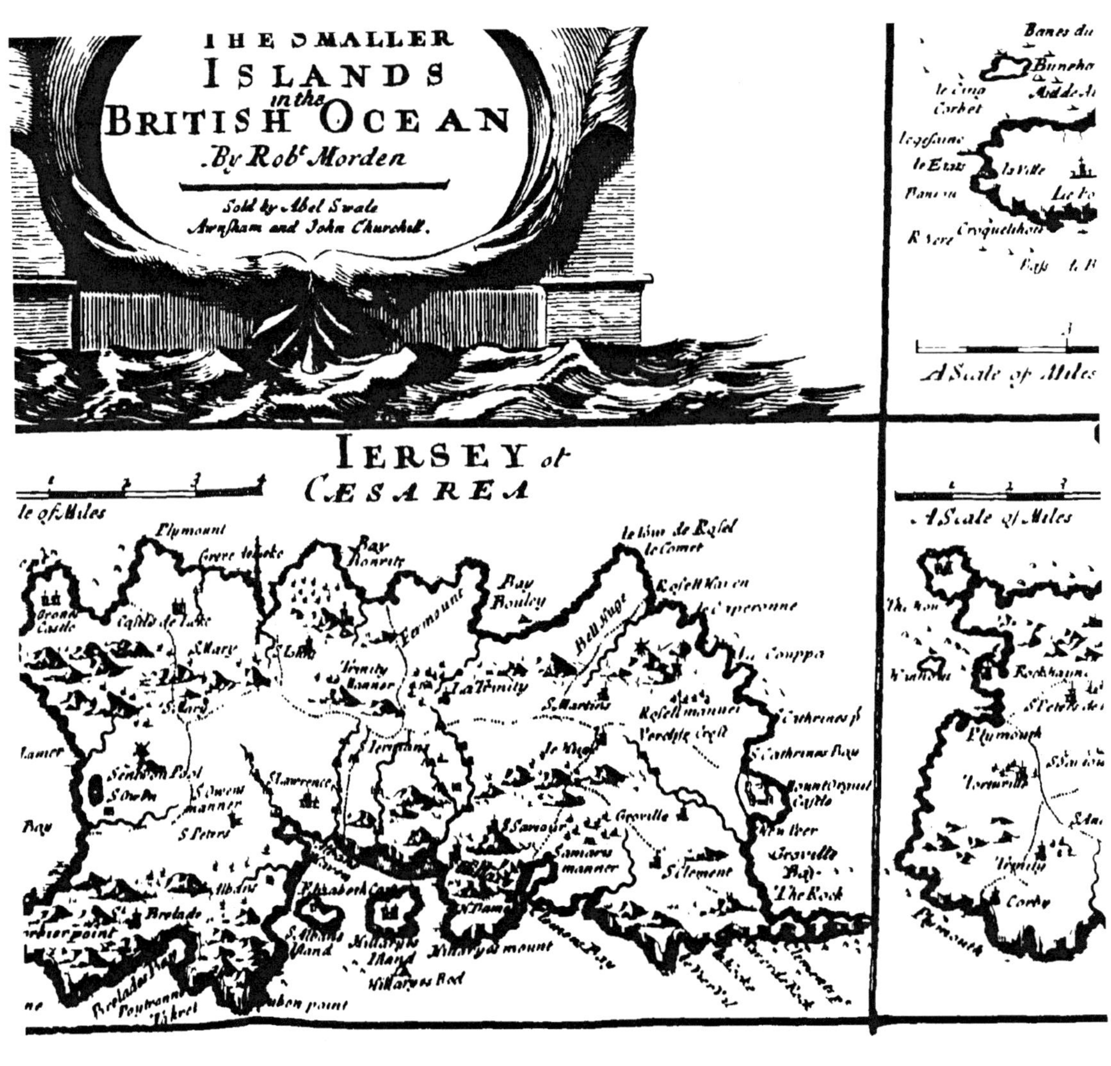
THE SMALLER
ISLANDS
in the
BRITISH OCEAN
By Robt Morden
Sold by Abel Swale
Awnsham and John Churchill.
IERSEY or
CÆSAREA
A Scale of Miles
Plymount
Bay
Bay Bouley
le Comet
Rosell manner
S. Martins
S. Catherines Bay
S. Lawrence
S. Peters
S. Saviour
Grovelle
Samarez manner
S. Clement
The Rock
Elizabeth Castle
S. Albans Iland
Hillaryes Iland
Hillaryes Bed
Hillaryes mount
Trinity manner
La Trinity
Bell Ruge
Plymouth
Trinity
Corby
Banes du
Croquelihou
le Etats
la Ville

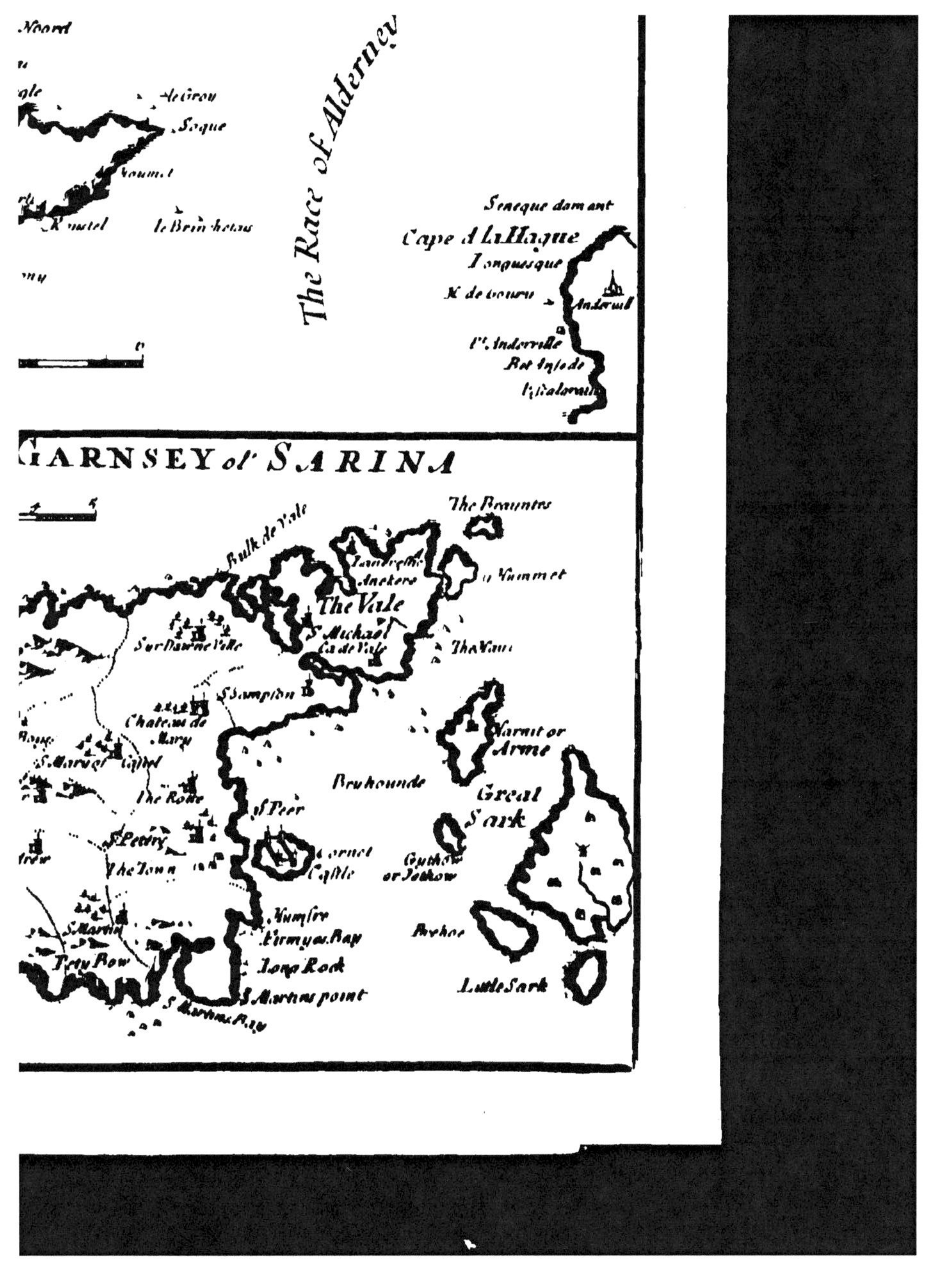

The Race of Alderney
Cape d La Hague
GARNSEY or SARINA
The Vale
The Beauntes
Great Sark
Little Sark
Long Rock
Cornet Castle

[ISLANDS TO THE WEST of BRITAIN.]

Flatholme IN the Severn-Sea, there first appear two small Islands The one, being flat and level, is called *Flatholme*, and in the same sense with *Planarie* in Italy; the other Stepholme being steep, is call'd *Stepholme*, and in British *Reoric*; but the Britains call'd both *Echni*, and Holmes we call both *Holmes*, for so the Saxons nam'd a grassy plot of ground enclosed with water They are not famous for any thing in Antiquity, but for the Danes harbouring there and for the burial of *Gualch*, a Britain of great piety, whose Disciple *Barruch* has given name to the Barry Isle of *Barry* in Wales, as we learn from an an-Giraldus, ᵛ P 739 cient Monument of the Church of Landaff, and the Island itself has done the same to the *Barries*, a noted family in Ireland Hard by Silly this lies *Silly*, a small Island upon the coast of the ancient *Silures*, of which word the present name has very plain foot steps, as has also a small Town over-against it, in Glamorganshire Yet I dare not affirm this to be the *Silura*, or *Insula Silurum*, which Solinus speaks of, because there are other Islands of the same name, at a great distance from the *Silures*

Caldey. From hence we arrive at *Caldey*, in British *Inispir*, pretty near the shore, and over-against Londey it, more into the Sea, is *Londey*, which [a] faces ᵃ *Spectans ad* Devonshire, being fourteen miles from the Promontory *Hertness* in that County This is reckon'd the larger of the two, and yet not much above two miles broad, and a mile long, and is so pent in with rocks, that there is no coming to it, but by one or two Entrances Here has formerly been a Fort, the ruins of which, as also the remains of St Helen's Chapel, are still visible Heretofore, it has been plow'd, as is manifest from the furrows, but now all their gain and profit arises from the Sea fowl, with which it abounds No trees grow in it, except stinking elders, to which the Starlings flock in such numbers, that one can hardly come at them for dung But why do I enlarge upon this, when Sir *Thomas D[illegible]mere*, Knight, has [illegible] describ'd it, where he tells us, how poor King Edward the second endeavour'd to shelter himself here from his troublesome Wife and rebellious Barons *Londay* (says he) *is an Island situate in the mouth of the Severn, about two miles over, every way, full of good pasture, and well stock'd with Rabbets, Pigeons, and Starlings* (Alexander Necham *calls them* Ganimede's *Birds*,) *which are breeding continually Though it is encompass'd with the Sea, yet it affords the Inhabitants fresh Spring water It has only one way to it, which is so strait that two men can hardly walk a-breast On all sides else, the horrible steep Rocks make it inaccessible* Our Historians scarce mention it, but on the account of *William de Marisco*, a mischievous Pirate, who from hence infested these coasts in the reign of Henry the third In Edward the third's time, it was part of the estate of the Luttrels

I rom hence we arrive at *Gresholm*, *Stockholme*, Gresholme, Stockholme and *Scalemy*, lying at the very bend or turning Scalemy of Pembrokeshire In these there is good store of grass and plenty of wild thyme I was heretofore of Opinion, that this *Scalemy* was the *Silimnus* of Pliny, but since, I have had reason to be of another mind For the *Silimnus* in Pliny may Silimnus probably, from the resemblance of the two names, be the [b] *Limnu* in Ptolemy That this *Limnu* is ᵇ *Lamb ey* in Ireland [illegible] the same which the Britains call'd *Lymen*, is clear from the name it self, tho' the English have given it another, *viz* that of *Ramsey* It lies over Ramsey against the Episcopal See of St *David*, to which it belongs, and was famous in the [c] last age for ᶜ So said ann 1607 the death of *Justinian* a holy man, who in that fruitful age of Saints retir'd hither out of Bretagne in France, and, having for a long time devoted himself wholly to God, as a Hermit, here, he was at last slain by [d] a servant, and canonized for a Martyr ᵈ *Servulo* In the history of his life, this Island is often call'd *Insula Lemeneia*, which name, compar'd with that of *Limen* (as the Britains call it) shews the supineness of that Writer, who would have the Island next above it to be Ptolemy's *Limnos*, call'd at present by the Welch *Enhly*, and by the English *Berdsey*, that is, *an Island of Birds* One may [e] infer from the signification of the word that [f] this is it, which Ptolemy call *Edri*, and Pliny *Andros*, or [g] *Adros*, as some Copies have it For *Ader*, among the Britains signifies a Bird, and so the English in the same sense call'd it ᵉ Perhaps, [illegible] ᶠ Or, *Bardsey*, in *Hereford*; who like

after

afterwards *Berdsey* The name *Enbly* is modern, and deriv'd from a certain Religious person, who liv'd a Hermit here For this Isle (which on the east shoots out in a high Promontory, but on the west is level and fruitful) has been formerly inhabited by so many Saints, that, without reckoning *Dubritius* and *Merlin* the Caledonian, no fewer than twenty thousand are said in ancient Histories to lie buried in it Next to this, is *Mona*, or the Isle of *Anglesey*; call'd by the Britains *Mon*, *Tir-Mon*, and *Inis Dowyll*, that is, the Dark Island, and by the Saxons Monege of which I have already [a] spoken

Mona Anglesey.

[a] In *Wales*.

Near *Anglesey*, lie three lesser Islands To the northwest, *Moyl Rhonad*, that is, the Isle of Seals (This was unjustly detain'd by certain Invaders, from the Bishops of *Bangor*, to whom it belong'd; till *Henry Deney* Bishop of *Bangor*, as we read in the Canterbury History, recover'd it by the assistance of a Fleet and Army, in Henry the seventh's time) To the east, below it, *Ynis Ligod*, that is, the *Isle of Mice*, and *Prestholme*, i e *the Isle of Priests*; where I saw nothing, but the [b] Steeple of St *Cyriac's* Chapel, visible at a great distance The neighbours report incredible things of the number of Sea-fowls breeding here; and, what is no less strange, of a Causey that went out from hence through the Sea, to the foot of that huge Mountain call'd *Pen-Maen-Maur*, for the convenience of such as came in Pilgrimage hither I take no notice of *Lambey*, a small Island over-against this upon the Irish shore, though *Alum* has been [c] sought there, at the great expence of the Undertakers

MoylRhonad. Ynis Ligod. Prestholme. [b] Sa ram tur rim. Lambey. [c] Lately, C

[The *ISLE* of *MAN*.]

The Isle of Man

MORE northward, lies the *Mona* which Cæsar mentions, situate, as he says, in the middle between Britain and Ireland Ptolemy calls it *Monoeda*, *Mon-eitha*, that is (if I may be allow'd a conjecture) *the more remote Mona*, to distinguish it from the other *Mona* or *Anglesey* Pliny calls it *Monabia*; *Orosius*, *Menavia*; and Bede, *Menavia secunda*, by whom Mona or Anglesey is call'd *Menavia prior*, and both, *British Islands*, yet I must note, that it is falsly read *Mevania*, in these Writers Ninius, who goes also by the name of *Gildas*, calls it *Eubonia* and *Manaw*, the Britains call it *Menaw*, the Inhabitants *Maning*, and the English, the *Isle of Man* *It lies in the middle between the north parts of Ireland and Britain* (says Giraldus Cambrensis,) *and this rais'd no small dispute among the Ancients, to which Country it belong'd At last, the difference was thus adjusted Since it appear'd, that venomous Creatures (brought over or the experiment) would live here, it was unanimously adjudg'd to Britain* Yet the inhabitants are very like the Irish, both in Speech and Manners, but not without some thing of the *Norwegians* too

Mona or Menavia

Lib ii c 9 In a certain copy of Ninius, it is call'd *Manau Gaotodin*

It is from north to south about thirty Italian Miles in length; but, in the widest part, not above fifteen broad, nor above eight, in the narrowest In Bede's time it contain'd three hundred families, and *Mona* nine hundred and sixty at present it has seventeen Parish Churches It produces Flax and Hemp in great plenty; and here are good Pastures and Cornfields It has good store of Barley and Wheat, but especially of Oats, and for this reason the People generally feed upon oat bread All over the Island, are great herds of Cattle, and flocks of Sheep, but both Sheep and Cattle, are (like those in their neighbouring Country of Ireland) much less than in England, and not so well headed The want of wood for fuel, is supply'd by a bituminous turf, in digging for which they often find trees bury'd underground In the middle, the Isle is mountainous; the highest Hill is *Scenfell*, from which in a clear day they can see *Scotland*, *England*, and *Ireland* The chief Town is *Russin*, situate on the south side of the Island, which, from a Castle with a garrison therein, is commonly call'd *Castle town* Here, at *Castle-town*, within a little Isle, Pope Gregory the fourth, [is said to have] erected an Episcopal See, the Bishop of which (nam'd *Sodorensis*, from the Island as is believ'd,) had formerly jurisdiction over all the Islands of the *Hebrides* But it is now limited to this Island, and his Metropolitan is the Archbishop of York This Bishop has neither Seat nor Vote, among the Lords of Parliament in England The most populous Town is *Duglas*, for it has the best harbour, and the most easie entrance, and is frequented by the French and other foreigners, who bring hither their Baysalt, and buy up the Commodities of the Island, viz Leather, coarse Wooll, and salt Beef On the south side of the Island, stands *Bala Curi*, where the Bishop generally resides, and the *Pile*, and a Fort erected in a small Island, and defended by a pretty good garrison Before the south Promontory, lies a little Island which they call the *Calf of Man*, where are great store of *Puffins*, and of those *Ducks* and *Drakes* said to breed in rotten wood, which the English call *Bernacles*, and the Scots [a] *Clakes and Soland Geese*

Scenfell. Russin, or Castle town. Episcopus Sodorensis. See below. Duglas. Bala Curi. Pile.

[a] Those of *Scotland* are quite of another kind

What remains concerning this Island, is added out of a Letter which I receiv'd from the most learned and Right reverend Father in God, *John Meryk*, Bishop of this See *This Island not only supplies its own wants with its own cattle, fish, and corn, but, by the industry of the Inhabitants more than the goodness of the Soil, it exports great quantities of Corn every year The happiness which the Isle enjoys, is owing to nothing more, than the government of the Earl of* Derby, *who at his own proper charges defends it with a standing guard against its neighbouring enemies, and lays out the greatest part of the revenue upon it All causes are decided here without writing or expence, by certain judges whom they choose among themselves, and call* Deemsters *For the Magistrate takes up a Stone, and after he has mark'd it, he gives it to the Plaintiff, by virtue whereof he summons his witnesses and the Defendant If the case is difficult, and of consequence, it is referred to the hearing of* [b] *twelve men, whom they call*

Deemsters. [b] Now 24

Keys of the Island

Annos

call the Keys of the Island *They have also Coroners, call'd Annos, who execute the office of Sheriffs As for the Ecclesiastical Judge, he cites the Parties, and determines the Cause, and in eight days they must either obey his Sentence, or go to Gaol As their* Language *is peculiar, so likewise were their* Laws *and* Money, *as I have been told, which are signs of a distinct soveraignty The Ecclesiastical Laws in force here, come nearer the Civil than Canon Law Neither Judges nor* ' *Clerks have any Fees As for those Witchcrafts spoken of by English writers, there is no such thing here The richer sort imitate the Gentry of Lancashire, in splendid living and a frankness of temper The women never stir abroad but with their winding sheets about them, to put them in mind of mortality If a woman be* [illegible] *and receive sentence of death, she is* [d] *sew'd up in a sack, and thrown from a Rock into the Sea Stealing and begging from door to door, is universally detested The people are wonderfully religious, and, to a man, zealously conformable to the Church of* [illegible] *great enemies to the Disorders* [illegible] *and Ecclesiastical, of the neigh*[illegible]*, And as the whole Isle is divided* [illegible] *south and north; the Language of th*[illegible] *is* Scotch, *and of the other, near the* Irish

' Formular

[d] Now hanged as Men except Witches, who are burn

[Thus far, is a *general* Account of the Isle of Man, and of the Laws and Usages thereof, as they stood in the reign of King James the first Which being much too short, and the *state* and *manner* of Places, Persons, and Things, having also been much alter'd since that time, I will here subjoin a very exact and particular Account of this Island, as it was drawn, at my request, by the present pious and learned Bishop thereof, Dr *Thomas Wilson*, and courteously communicated to me by his Lordship, to be inserted in this Work, in order to supply the Defects of all former Accounts

---

A new Survey and Description of the ISLE *of* MAN.

Name

THE Isle of Man, very probably had the Name it goes by *now*, from the Saxon word Mang, *Among*, as lying, almost at an equal distance, between the Kingdoms of England, Scotland, Ireland, and Wales Hence it is, that the neighbouring nations use the expressions *Mancks-men*, *Mancks-Language*, &c

Extent and Situation

The extent and situation of this Island is exact enough according to Mr Camden, and need not here be repeated Let this only be added, That Bishop's Court, which is near the middle of the Island lieth in the fifty fourth degree, sixteen minutes, of Northern Latitude It lies so directly in the chops of the Chanel that runs betwixt Scotland and Ireland, that if this Island did not very much break the force of the Tides and westerly winds, it might be much worse for that part of England which lies opposite to it

The Soil

The Soil in this, as in most other Places, is very different The Lime stone ground to the South, is as good as can be desir'd The Mountains are cold, and consequently less fruitful, here as well as elsewhere The Valleys betwixt them afford as good Pasture, Hay, and Corn, as in most other places Towards the North indeed there is a dry, barren, sandy earth, but then this might, and no doubt in time will be help'd, when once the Husbandman comes to know the value of Marle (of which there is good store in the Northern Parishes) and can be perswaded to make use of it, which yet he is not willing to do, finding the Improvements made by liming the ground to yield a present great advantage, with less charge than that of Marling

Curragh

A large tract of Land call'd the *Curragh*, runs the breadth of the Isle betwixt Ballaugh and Ramsea It was formerly a Bog, but since it has been drain'd, it is one of the richest parts of the Island, and though the Peat is six, eight, ten, foot deep, yet by husbandry and burning they have got a Surface which will bear the Plow And the same place supplies the neighbourhood both with Bread and Fuel In this place, have been found very large Trees of Oak and Fir, some two foot and a half Diameter and forty foot long, suppos'd by the Inhabitants to have lain here since the Deluge The Oaks and Firs do not lie promiscuously, but where there are plenty of one sort, there are generally few or none of the other In some places of this Tract, there is a remarkable Layer of Peat for some miles together, of two or three foot thick under a Layer of Gravel, Clay, or Earth, two, three, and even four foot thick

A high Ridge of Mountains runs almost the length of the Island, which supply the Inhabitants quite round with Water and Fire Abundance of little Rivulets and Springs of excellent Water (by the sides of which the Inhabitants have for the most part built their Houses) run hence to the Sea, and the sides of the Mountains are stored with Heath, and an excellent Peat for Fuel The highest of these Mountains is call'd *Snafield*, its heigth, as taken by an exact Barometer, being about five hundred and eighty yards, the Mercury subsiding two inches and one tenth From the Top of this Mountain they have a fair Prospect of *England*, *Scotland*, *Ireland*, and *Wales* Mountains

Snafield

The Air

The Air is sharp and cold in Winter, but then this must be understood of such Places only as are expos'd to the Winds which, considering the Situation, must needs be very boisterous But in all such Places as [illegible] natural shelter, or [illegible] from [illegible] the Air is as mild as in *Lancashire*, the Frosts being short, and the Snow not lying long on the ground, especially near the Sea

This is plain from the [illegible] have been made [illegible] Orchards and Gardens [illegible] and Necessar[illegible]

the neighbouring Countries. But if the winds be frequent and ſometimes troubleſome, they are alſo wholeſome and drive away noxious Vapours; ſo that it has been truly obſerv'd, that the Plague was never remember'd to be here, and the Inhabitants, for the moſt part, live to a good old age

Cattle

The Black Cattle and Horſes are generally leſs than thoſe of England, but as the Land improves, ſo do theſe, and of late there have been ſome bred here as large as in other places They have indeed a ſmall hardy breed of Horſes in the Mountains, very much coveted by Gentlemen abroad for their Children, but beſides thoſe, they breed Horſes of a ſize fit either for the Plow or the Saddle

In the Mountains they have alſo a ſmall breed of Swine call'd Purrs, or wild Swine not that they are *Feræ Naturâ* or wild (for every Man knows his own) but becauſe they are bred and live continually in the Mountains without coming to their Houſes, and both theſe and the wild Sheep are counted incomparable meat Among the Sheep they have ſome call'd *Loughtan* of a Buff colour the Wool is fine, and makes a pretty Cloth without any dye

Noxious Animals

There are ſeveral noxious Animals, ſuch as Badgers, Foxes, Otters, Filmerts, Moles, Hedge-hogs, Snakes, Toads, *&c* which the Inhabitants know no more of, than their names, as alſo ſeveral Birds, ſuch as the Woodpecker, the Jay, the Maup, *&c* And it is not long, ſince a perſon more fanciful, than prudent or kind to his Country, brought in a breed of Magpies, which have increas'd incredibly, ſo as to become a nuſance And it is not two years, ſince ſome body brought in Frogs, which they ſay increaſe very faſt

Eagles and Hawks

There is one Airy of Eagles, and at leaſt two of Hawks of a mettled kind for which reaſon it was that Henry the fourth of *England*, in his Letters Patents of the Grant of this Iſle to Sir *John Stanley*, firſt King and Lord of Man of that name and Family, did oblige him, in lieu of all other Services, to preſent him and his Succeſſors, upon the day of their Coronation, with a caſt of Faulcons

Quarries of Stone

There are not many Quarries of good Stone One there is near *Caſtle town*, which yields a tolerable good black Marble, fit for Tomb-ſtones and for Flagging of Churches, of which ſome Quantities have of late been ſent to *London* for thoſe Uſes

Here are alſo good Rocks of Lime Stone, which, being burnt with Peat or Coal, is become a great Improvement of barren Lands Theſe Stones, eſpecially about *Bal'y lool*, are full of petrefy'd Shells of different kinds, and ſuch as are not now to be found on theſe Coaſts

There are ſome few Rocks about *Peel* of a red Free-ſtone, capable of being form'd into regular ſhapes, but the greateſt part of the Quarries are a broken Rag-Stone, ſometime riſing in courſe uneven Flags, or in irregular Lumps, fit only for courſe Walls, with which nevertheleſs they make a ſhift to build good ſubſtantial Houſes, tho' an Engliſh Maſon would not know how to handle them, or would call their Walls, as one merrily did, a *Cauſeway rear'd up upon an edge*

Here are alſo a good many Quarries of a blew, thin, light Slate, one of the beſt coverings for Houſes; of which good Quantities are exported And at a place call'd the *Spaniſh Head*, there is a Rock, out which are wrought long Beams (if one may uſe that expreſſion) of tough Stone, fit for Mantle trees of twelve or fifteen foot long, and ſtrong enough to bear the weight of the higheſt Stack of Chimneys

Mines

Mines of *Coal* there are none, tho' ſeveral attempts have been made to find them But of *Lead*, *Copper*, and *Iron* there are ſeveral, and ſome of them have been wrought to good advantage, particularly the Lead, of which Ore many hundred Tuns have of late been ſmelted, and exported As for the Copper and Iron Ores, they are certainly better than at preſent they are thought to be, having been often try'd and approv'd of by Men ſkill'd in thoſe matters However, either thro' the ignorance of the Undertakers, or by the unfaithfulneſs of the workmen, or for ſome other cauſe, no great matter has yet been made of them

Kings and Lords of Man

This Iſland has had many Maſters They have an old Tradition, and it has got a Place in the Records, that one *Mananan Mac-Lir* a Necromancer was the firſt Proprietor, and that for a long time he kept the Iſland under Miſts that no ſtranger cou'd find it, till St *Patrick* broke his charms But a late Iriſh [a] Antiquary gives a particular account of this *Mananan*, viz That his true name was *Orbſanius*, the Son of *Alladius* a Prince in Ireland, That he was a famous Merchant, and, from his trading betwixt Ireland and the Iſle of Man, had the name of *Mananan*, and *Mac-Lir*, i e the Son of the Sea, from his great ſkill in Navigation, and, that he was at laſt ſlain at *Moycullin* in the County of *Gallway* in *Ireland* And it is not improbable, that the Story of his keeping the Iſland under a Miſt, might riſe from this, that he was the only perſon, in thoſe days, that had a Commerce with them

[a] *Flaharti*, p 172

The *Norwegians* conquer'd *this*, when they made themſelves Maſters of the Weſtern Iſles, which they ſent Kings to govern, who generally choſe the Iſle of Man for their place of Reſidence This continued till 1266, when there was a very ſolemn Agreement made betwixt *Magnus* the fourth of *Norway*, and *Alexander* the third of *Scotland*, by which, this Iſle, amongſt the reſt, was ſurrender'd to the *Scots* for four thouſand Marks to be paid in four years, and one hundred Marks yearly Purſuant to which, *Alexander* drives out the King of Man, *A D* 1270, and unites it to *Scotland*

In 1312 there is a ſecond Agreement, betwixt *Hacquin* the fifth and *Robert* the firſt of *Scotland*, and in 1426 a third Agreement (all which are ſet down at large in *Torfeus* his Hiſtory of the [b] *Orcades*) But before this laſt Agreement, the Iſland was in poſſeſſion of *John* Lord *Stanley* and of *Man*, who had it given him by Henry the fourth, *A D* 1405 However, for as much as by the laſt Agreement betwixt the Kings of *Norway* and *Scotland*, the latter claimed a right to this Iſland, the Lords of *Man* were obliged to keep a conſtant ſtanding Army and Garriſons for the Defence of it, till the Reign of King *James* the firſt of *England* And in this Honourable Houſe it has continued ever ſince, except for twelve years during the Civil Wars, when it was given by the Parliament to the Lord *Fairfax*; but return'd to its ancient Lords at the Reſtoration

[b] *Pag.* 169

Tho' this Iſland (as the Lord *Cook* ſays) be no parcel of the Realm of *England*, yet it is

pare

part of the Dominions of the King of *England* to whom therefore Allegiance is reserv'd in all publick Oaths administer'd here

The Lords of it have for a long time wav'd the title of *Kings*, and now are only stil'd *Lords of Man and the Isles*, though they still have most of the *Regalia*, as the giving the final Assent to all new Laws, and the power of pardoning offenders, of changing the sentence of Death into Banishment, of appointing and displacing the Governour and Officers, with a Right to all Forfeitures for Treason, Felony, *Felo de se*, *&c*

The manner of holding a Tinwald

The manner of the Lord of Man's investiture, and receiving the homage of his people at his first accession, was this, He was to sit on the Tinwald Hill, in the open air, in a chair of state, with a royal cloth or canopy over his head, his face to the east (towards a Chapel eastward of the hill, where there are publick Prayers and a Sermon on these occasions) and his Sword before him, holden with the point upward His Barons, *viz* the Bishop and Abbot, with the rest in their degrees, sat beside him, his Beneficed men, Council, and Deemsters sat before him His Gentry and Yeomanry in the third degree, and the twenty four Keys in their order, and the Commons, stood without the circle, with three Clerks in their surplices

Governour

The Lord sends a Governour, Lieutenant or Captain, who constantly resides at *Castle-town*, where he has a handsome house, salary, and other conveniences befitting his station He is to take care that all Officers, Civil and Military, discharge their trusts and duty He is Chancellor, and to him there is an Appeal in matters of Right and Wrong, and from him to the Lord, and finally (if occasion be) to the King of England in Council

The Governour's Oath is something peculiar He is sworn to do right betwixt the Lord and his people, as uprightly *as the Staff* (the Ensign of his authority, then in his hand) *now standeth*, that it may be a constant Monitor to him of the obligations he lies under

Inhabitants

The Inhabitants are an orderly, civiliz'd people, and courteous enough to strangers, and if they have been otherwise represented, it has been by those that knew them not, or perhaps it is because they have sense enough to see when strangers (who are too apt to have a mean opinion of them) would go about to impose upon them, which they are not willing to suffer, if they can help it

They have ever had a profound respect for their Lords, especially for those of the House of Derby, who have always treated them with great regard and tenderness At the same time they are jealous of their ancient Laws, Tenures, and Liberties They have a great many good Qualities They are generally very charitable to the poor, and hospitable to strangers, especially in the country, where the people, if a stranger come to their houses, would think it an unpardonable Crime not to give him a share of the best they have themselves to eat or drink They have a significant proverb (which generally shews the Genius of a people) to this purpose, *Tra ta yn derry Vought cooney lesh bought elley, ta yee beaegai aghtee*, *i e* when one poor man relieves another, God himself rejoices at it; or, as it is in Mancks, laughs outright

They have generally hated Sacrilege to such a degree, that they do not think a Man can wish a greater curse to a Family, than in these words, *Clogh ny Killagh ayns Corneil dty Hie Moar*, *i e* May a stone of the Church be found in the corner of thy Dwelling house And though the Covetousness of some have taken advantage of the former great Poverty of the Clergy, and of the little power they had to defend themselves in the Bishop's absence from his Diocese, to introduce Prescriptions (which yet, if the observations of the people are just, they have no great reason to boast of,) yet the piety of some others has led them to fling up such Prescriptions, which are so very injurious to the Rights of the Church, and of so evil an example, and an handle for others to attempt the same injustice

The Inhabitants are laborious enough, and those who think them otherwise, because Improvements go so slowly on, do not see the difficulties that too many of them have to struggle with Indeed, the present Lord of Man has, to his great honour, remov'd one of the heaviest discouragements to Industry and future Improvements His Lordship, at his accession, found his people complaining, as their Ancestors had been for more than one hundred years, of the uncertainty of their Holdings, they claiming an ancient Tenure which they call'd, *The Tenure of the Straw*, by which they might leave their Estates to Posterity under certain Rents, Fines, and Services, which his Officers could not allow of, because of the many breaks that had been made by Leases, *&c* in that manner of Holding He therefore appointed Commissioners to treat with his people in his presence, and at last came to a Resolution to restore them by a publick Act of Tinwald to a Tenure of Inheritance, under certain Fines, *&c.* And the very great improvements which have since been made, shew plainly, that there wanted such a Settlement to encourage Industry, and the present and future Ages will have reason to remember it with the greatest sense of Gratitude

Act of Settlement

Language

But to return to the Inhabitants, whose Language is the *Ers*, or a Dialect of that spoken in the Highlands of Scotland, with a mixture of some words of Greek, Latin, and Welsh, and many of English Original, to express the names of things which were not formerly known to the people of this Island, whose ancient simplicity of living and speaking appears in many Instances Thus, for example, they do not generally reckon the *Time* in Mancks, by the hours of the day, but by the *Tra Shirveish*, *i e* the Service-time, *viz* nine in the morning or three in the evening, an hour, or two hours, before or after, Service time, *&c*

In this Language, the Substantive is generally put before the Adjective, and many things which in the English Tongue, are deriv'd from the Latin or Greek, and little understood by those that know nothing of those Languages, in Mancks are express'd by a Periphrasis easily understood by the common people

It has been often said, that the Holy Bible was by Bishop *Phillips's* care translated into the Mancks Language, but, upon the best enquiry that can be made, there was no more attempted by him than a translation of the Common Prayer, which is still extant, but of no use to the present Generation The New Testament is at present in the hands of one who is master of the Mancks Language, and very well qualified to translate it from the Original, which, it is hop'd, will one day, be a blessing to this country

In their *Habit* and *manner of Living*, they imitate the Engliſh; only the middle and poorer ſort amongſt the Men, uſually wear a kind of Sandal, which they call *Kerranes*, made of untann'd Leather; and which, being croſs laced from the Toe to the upper part of the Inſtep, and gather'd about the Ankle, makes a very cheap, convenient, and not unhandſome ſhoe

The Iſland is certainly more populous now than ever it was there being at preſent about twenty thouſand Natives, beſides Strangers, which obliges them every where to enlarge their Churches, ſo that they are ten times as many as in Bede's time, when they were but about three or four hundred families

Diviſion of the Iſland — The *Diviſion* of the Iſland as to its *Civil* concerns, is, into ſix *Sheadings*; every Sheading has its proper Coroner, who, in the nature of a Sheriff, is entruſted with the peace of his Diſtrict, ſecures Criminals, brings them to juſtice, *&c*

Beſides this, there are in every Sheading as many Moars and Captains, as there are Pariſhes These Moars are the Lord's Baylifs for one year, and are anſwerable for all the Rents in their reſpective Diviſions, and the Captains are entruſted with the care of the Militia or Train bands

The Iſland as to *Eccleſiaſtical* concerns is divided into ſeventeen Pariſhes, every Church bearing the name of the Saint to which it is dedicated, as Malew to St Lupus, *&c*

Towns — The principal Towns are only four, which are all ſituate near the Sea, each of them has its Harbour, and a Caſtle or Fort to defend it

Caſtle town — *Caſtle-town*, to the ſouth, (call'd alſo *Caſtle-Ruſhin*, from a very ancient, but yet entire beautiful Caſtle, built of a coarſe, but for ever durable marble,) is the firſt town of the Iſland Here, the Governour reſides, as do moſt of the Lord's Officers Here, the Chancery Court is kept every firſt Thurſday of the month, and here alſo is held the Head-Court or Gaol delivery, twice a year This Caſtle is ſaid to have been built by *Guttred* King of Man about the year 960, and it is very probable, for about that time the Norwegians began to be troubleſome to all places, by their Piracies

Peel — *Peel*, to the weſt, call'd by the Norwegians *Holm Town*, from a ſmall Iſland cloſe by it, in which ſtands the Cathedral dedicated to St German, the firſt biſhop of this Iſle This little Iſle, naturally very ſtrong, was made much more ſo by art; *Thomas*, Earl of Derby encompaſſing it with a Wall, Towers, and other Fortifications, and making it in thoſe days impregnable At preſent there is a ſmall garriſon kept there, and it is the Priſon for all Offenders againſt the Eccleſiaſtical Laws, whether for Inceſt, Adultery, *&c* or Diſobedience, and is call'd St Germain's priſon

Douglaſs — *Douglaſs*, to the eaſt, is much the richeſt town, the beſt market and the moſt populous, of any in the whole Iſland As it has of late years increas'd its trade, it has done ſo in Buildings There is a neat chapel, a publick School, and ſeveral good houſes, and excellent Vaults and Cellars for Merchants goods; but any body that ſees it, would wiſh that Authority had interpos'd to have made the Buildings and Streets more regular The harbour, for Veſſels of a tolerable burthen, is the ſafeſt in the Iſland; the Ships lying in it, as quiet as in a Dock or Baſin

Near to Douglaſs, ſtood formerly a Nunnery, now a good houſe pleaſantly ſeated and ſhelter'd with Trees

Ramſea to the north, is moſt noted for a ſpacious Bay, in which the greateſt Fleet may ride at anchor with ſafety enough from all winds but the north eaſt, and in that caſe they need not be embay'd This town ſtanding upon a Beach of looſe ſand or ſhingle, is in danger, if not timely prevented, of being waſh'd away with the ſea — Ramſea

Bally Salley, though not uſually reckon'd amongſt the towns, is yet a conſiderable inland village Here formerly ſtood the Abbey of Ryſhen, founded *Ann Dom* 1134 upon Lands given by Olavus King of Man, the ruins of which do ſtill remain This was the lateſt diſſolv'd Monaſtery in theſe Kingdoms — Bally Salley; Ex MS antiq

The reſt of the Inhabitants have their houſes built in the moſt convenient part of their Eſtates, for water, and ſhelter The better ſort have good ſubſtantial houſes of ſtone, and cover'd with ſlate, others with thatch, which they have found a way to ſecure againſt the winds (that in Winter are boiſterous enough) by ropes of ſtraw, very readily made, and neatly croſs'd like a net one over another, which no ſtorms can injure

The way of improving their Lands, is either by Lime, by ſea wreck, or by folding their ſheep and cattle in the night, and during the heat of the day, in little incloſures rais'd every year to keep them within a certain compaſs; which in about fourteen days time is ſo enrich'd with the urine and dung of the cattle, as to yield a plentiful crop Theſe little hedges are very eaſily rais'd by a ſpade peculiar to the country, and being burn'd by the heat of the ſun, and flung down before ſeed-time, yield very good corn, either wheat, barley, rye, or oats — Improvement of Land

Oats is the common Bread of the Country made into thin cakes, as in the Fell country in *Lancaſhire*

Many of the rivers (or rather Rivulets) not having water ſufficient to drive a mill, the greateſt part of the year, neceſſity has put them upon an invention of a cheap ſort of mill, which, as it coſts very little, is no great loſs though it ſtands ſix months in the year The Water wheel, about ſix foot Diameter, lies Horizontal, conſiſting of a great many hollow ladles, againſt which the water, brought down in a trough, ſtrikes forcibly, and gives motion to the upper ſtone, which by a Beam and Iron is join'd to the center of the water wheel. Not but that they have other Mills both for corn and fulling of cloth, where they have water in ſummer more plentiful — Horizontal Mills.

The Commodities of this Iſland are Black cattle (of which ſix hundred, by the Act of Navigation, may be imported yearly into England) Lambs wool, fine and coarſe Linen, and coarſe woollen cloth, hides, ſkins, honey and tallow, and heretofore ſome corn and beer, which now, ſince the great reſort of ſtrangers, are little enough for their own uſe — Commodities

But formerly Herrings were the great and ſtaple commodity of this Iſle, of which (within the memory of ſome now living) near twenty thouſand Barrels have been exported in one year to France and other places — Herring

The time of Herring fiſhing is betwixt July and All hallow-tide

The whole fleet of boats (every boat being about the burthen of two tons) are under the Government of the Water bayliff on ſhore, and under one call'd a Vice Admiral at ſea, who, by the ſignal of a Flag, directs them when to ſhoot their nets, *&c* There is due to the

Lord

Lord of the Isle, as Royalty, ten shillings out of every boat that takes above ten Mease (every Mease being five hundred herrings,) and one shilling to the Water-baylisf

In acknowledgement of this great blessing, and that God may be prevail'd with to continue it (this being the great support of the place) the whole Fleet do duly attend Divine Service on the shore, at the several Ports, every evening before they go to sea, the respective Incumbents, on that occasion, making use of a Form of Prayer, Lessons, &c lately composed for that purpose. Besides this, there is a Petition inserted in the Litany, and used in the publick Service throughout the year, for the blessings of the Sea, on which the comfortable subsistence of so many depends And the Law provideth, that every boat pay *Tythe-Fish*, without any pretence to Prescription

Trade

The Trade of this Island is very much improv'd of late years, foreign Merchants having found it their interest to touch here, and leave part of their Cargoes, either to bring the remainder uuder the custom of Buttleridge, or because the Duties of the whole would be too great a sum to be paid at once in England; or, lastly, to lie here for a market, the Duties and Cellarage being so small

The ancient method of Commerce, which was, to have four sworn Merchants, who were to agree with the foreign Merchant for the price of the Goods imported, as also for the price of the Commodities the Island had to spare, which both sides were bound to stand to, is entirely laid aside

Religion

The Religion and Worship is exactly the same with that of the Church of England The Isle of Man was converted to the Christian Faith by St Patrick about the year 440, at which time the Bishoprick of Man was erected, St Germain, to whose name and memory the Cathedral is dedicated, being the first Bishop of Man, who, with his Successors, had this Island only for their Diocese, till the Norwegians had conquer'd the Western Isles, and soon after Man, which was about the beginning of the eleventh Century It was about that time, that the *Insulæ Sodorenses*, being thirty two (so call'd from the Bishoprick of Sodor erected in one of them, *viz* the Isle of *Hy*) were united to Man, and from that time, the Bishops of the United Sees were stil'd *Sodor & Man*, and sometimes *Man & Insularum*, and had the Archbishop of Drontheim (stil'd *Nidorensis*) for their Metropolitan And this continued, till the Island was finally annex'd to the Crown of England, when Man had its own Bishops again, who stil'd themselves variously, sometimes Bishops of Man only, sometimes *Sodor & Man*, and sometimes *Sodor de Man*, giving the name of *Sodor*, to a little Isle before mention'd, lying within a musket-shot of the main land, call'd by the Norwegians *Holm*, and by the Inhabitants *Peel*, in which stands the Cathedral For, in these express words, in an instrument yet extant, Thomas Earl of Derby and Lord of Man, *A D* 1505 confirms to *Huan Hisketh* Bishop of Sodor, all the Islands, &c anciently belonging to the Bishops of Man, *viz Ecclesiam Cathedralem Sancti Germani in Holm, Sodor vel Pele vocatum, Ecclesiamque Sancti Patricii ibidem, & Locum præfatum in quo præfatæ Ecclesiæ sitæ sunt* This Cathedral was built by *Simon* Bishop of Sodor, who dy'd *A D* 1245, and was there buried

When converted to Christianity

The Reformation was begun something later here than in England, but so happily carried on, that there has not for many years been one Papist a native, in the Island; nor indeed are there Dissenters of any denomination, except a family or two of Quakers, unhappily perverted during the late Civil Wars; and even some of these have of late been baptized into the Church

Bishop's Palace

The Bishop has his residence in the Parish of Kirk Michael, where he has a good House and Chapel (if not stately, yet convenient enough,) large gardens and pleasant walks, shelter'd with groves of Fruit and Forest-trees (which shews what may be done in that sort of improvement,) and so well situated, that from thence it is easy to Visit any part of his Diocese, and to return the same day

Bishop

The Bishops of Man are Barons of the Isle They have their own Courts for their Temporalties, where one of the Deemsters of the Isle sits as Judge

This peculiar privilege the Bishop has at this day, that if any of his Tenants be guilty of a capital crime, and is to be try'd for his life, the Bishop's Steward may demand him from the Lord's Bar, and try him in the Bishop's Court by a Jury of his own Tenants, and, in case of conviction, his Lands are forfeited to the Bishop, but his Goods and person are at the Lord's dispofal

The Abbot of Rushen had the same privilege, and so has the Steward of those Lands to this day

By whom nam'd

When the Bishoprick falls void, the Lord of the Isle names a person, and presents him to the King of England for his Royal Assent, and then to the Archbishop of York to be Consecrated After which, he becomes subject to him as his Metropolitan, and both he and the Proctors for the Clergy are constantly summon'd with the rest of the Bishops and Clergy of that Province to Convocation, the Diocese of Man, together with the Diocese of Chester, being by an Act of Parliament of the 33d of *Hen* VIII (confirm'd by another of the 8th of *James* I) annex'd unto the Metropolitical See of York

Ex Chart MS Man Furnes in Offic Cam Duc Lanc

How the Bishops of Man were *chosen* before, we find in a Bull of Pope *Celestine* to *Furnes-Abbey*, *In eligendo Episcopum Insularum, Libertatem quam Reges earum bonæ memoriæ Olauos & Godredus filius ejus Monasterio vestro contulerunt, sicut in Autenticis eorum continetur, Autoritate vobis Apostolica confirmamus Dat Romæ*, 10 *Kal Julii, Pontificatus nostri* 4 i e In chusing a Bishop of the Isles, we do, by our Apostolical Authority, confirm the liberty, which the Kings of the Isles *Olavus* and *Godred* his son vested in your Monastery, as it is express'd in their original Grants, Dated at Rome, on the 10th of the Kalends of July, and the 4th year of our Pontificate

Archdeacon

The Archdeacon, in all inferiour causes, has alternate Jurisdiction with the Bishop He holds his Courts either in person or by his Official, as the Bishop does by himself and Vicars general, which are two, for the North and South division of the Isle

Clergy

The Clergy are generally Natives, and indeed it cannot well be otherwise, none else being qualify'd to preach and administer the Sacraments in the Manks Language, for the English is not understood by two thirds at least of the Island, although there is an English School in every Parish, so hard it is to change the Language of a whole country

Livings

The Livings are generally small The two Parsonages are indeed worth near sixty pounds a year, but the *Vicarages*, the Royal Bounty included,

cluded, are not worth above twenty five Pounds, with which notwithstanding the frugal Clergy have maintain'd themselves, and sometimes pretty numerous Families, very decently Of late, indeed, the great Resort of Strangers has made Provisions of all sorts as dear again as formerly

Royal Bounty

That through the Poverty of the place the Church might never want fit persons to perform Divine Offices, and to instruct the People in necessary Truths and Duties, the pious and worthy Doctor *Isaac Barrow*, soon after the Restoration, being then Bishop of *Man*, did so effectually make use of his Interest with His Majesty King *Charles* the second, and other noble Benefactors, that he obtain'd a Grant of one hundred pounds a year, payable out of the Excise for ever, for the better maintenance of the poor Vicars and Schoolmasters of his Diocese And the Right Honourable *Charles* Earl of *Derby*, being pleas'd to make a long Lease of the Impropriations of the Isle in his hands, which either as Lord or Abbot, were one third of the whole Tythes, the good Bishop found means to pay for the said Lease, which (besides an old Rent and Fine, still payable to the Lord of the Isle) may be worth to the Clergy and Schools about one hundred Pounds more

Besides this, he collected amongst the English Nobility and Gentry (whose Names and Benefactions are Register'd and preserv'd in Publick Tables in every Parish) six hundred Pounds, the Interest of which maintains an Academic Master, and, by his own private Charity, he purchas'd two Estates in Land worth twenty Pounds a year, for the support of such young Persons as shou'd be design'd for the Ministry So that the name and good Deeds of that excellent Prelate, will be remember'd with gratitude, as long as any sense of Piety remains amongst them

Ecclesiastical Discipline

There is nothing more commendable than the Discipline of this Church

Publick Baptism is never administer'd but in the Church, and Private as the Rubrick directs

Good care is taken to fit young Persons for *Confirmation*, which all are pretty careful to prepare themselves for, lest the want of being Confirm'd shou'd hinder their future marriage, Confirmation, Receiving the Lord's Supper, *&c* being a necessary Qualification for that State

Offenders of all Conditions, without distinction, are oblig'd to submit to the Censures appointed by the Church, whether for Correction or Example (commutation of Penances being abolish'd by a late Law, and they generally do it patiently) Such as do not submit (which hither to have been but few) are either imprison'd or excommunicated; under which Sentence if they continue more than forty days, they are deliver'd over to the Lord of the Isle, both Body and Goods In the mean time, all Christians are frequently warn'd not to have any unnecessary Conversation with them, which the more thoughtful People are careful to observe

The Bishop and his Vicar General, having a Power to commit such to Prison as refuse to appear before them, there is seldom occasion of passing this Sentence for Contumacy only, so that People are never Excommunicated, but for Crimes that will shut them out of Heaven; which makes this Sentence more dreaded

Before the beginning of Lent (which is here observ'd with great strictness) there is held a Court of Correction, where Offenders, and such as have neglected to perform their Censures; are presented, and if there are many, or their Crimes of a heinous nature, they are called together on *Ash Wednesday*, and after a Sermon explaining the Design of Church Censures, and the Duty of such as are so unhappy as to fall under them, their several Censures are appointed, which they are to perform during Lent, that they may be receiv'd into the Church before *Easter*

Penance.

The manner of doing penance is Primitive and Edifying The Penitent clothed in a Sheet, *&c* is brought into the Church immediately before the Litany, and there continues till the Sermon be ended, after which, and a proper Exhortation, the Congregation is desired to pray for him *in a Form* provided for that purpose And thus he is dealt with, till by his Behaviour he has given some Satisfaction that all this is not feign'd, which being certify'd to the Bishop, he orders him to be receiv'd, by a *very Solemn Form for Receiving Penitents, into the Peace of the Church*

But if Offenders, after having once done Publick Penance, do relapse into the same or other scandalous Vices, they are not presently permitted to do Penance again, though they shou'd desire it ever so earnestly, till they shall have given better Proofs of their resolution to amend their Lives During which time, they are not permitted to go into any Church in time of Divine Service, but stand at the Church Door, until their Pastor, and other grave Persons are convinced by their Conversation, that there are hopes of a lasting Reformation, and certify the same to the Bishop

There is here one very wholsom Branch of Church-Discipline, the want of which in many other places, is the occasion that infinite Disorders go unpunish'd, namely, the enjoyning Offenders *Purgation* by their own Oaths, and the Oaths of Compurgators (if need be) of known Reputation, where the Fame is common, the Crime scandalous, and yet not Proof enough to convict them and this is far from being complain'd of as a grievance For if common Fame has injur'd any person, he has an opportunity of being restor'd to his good name (unless upon Trial the Court finds just cause to refuse it,) and a severe Penalty is laid upon any that shall after this revive the Scandal On the other hand, if a man will not swear to his own Innocency, or cannot prevail with others to believe him, 'tis fit he shou'd be treated as guilty, and the Scandal remov'd by a proper Censure

Convocation.

In order to secure the Discipline of the Church, the Bishop is to call a Convocation of his Clergy, at least once a year The day appointed by Law is *Tuesday* in Whitson week, (if the Bishop is in the Isle,) where he has an opportunity of enquiring how the Discipline of the Church has been observ'd, and, by the advice of his Clergy, of making such Constitutions as are necessary for its better Government

Law

The Laws of the Island are excellently well suited to the Circumstances of the Place, and the condition of the People Anciently, the Deemsters (*i e* the Temporal Judges, determin'd most causes which were then of no great moment, the Inhabitants being mostly Fishermen,) either as they could remember the like to have been judg'd before, or according as they *deem'd* most just in their own Conscien-ces,

ces; from whence came the name of *Breast Laws*.

But as the Island every day improv'd, under Sir *John Stanley* and his Successors, so they, from time to time observing the many Inconveniences of giving Judgment from Breast Laws, order'd, That all Cases of Moment or Intricacy decided in their Courts, should be written down for Precedents to be a Guide when the same or the like cases should happen for the future.

And that these Precedents might be made with greater caution and Justice, the Law has expresly provided, that in all great matters and high Points that shall be in Doubt, the Lieutenant or *any of the Council for the time being*, shall take the Deemsters to them, with the Advice of the Elders of the Land, *viz.* the 24 Keys, as is elsewhere more fully explain'd, to *Deem* the Law truly, as they shall answer it.

Now if to this we add, that once every year, *viz* on St *John Baptist's* day, there is a meeting of the Governour, Officers Spiritual and Temporal, Deemsters, and 24 Keys, where any person has a right to Present any uncommon Grievance, and to have his Complaint heard in the face of the whole Country, there cannot be imagin'd a better Constitution, Where the Injur'd may have a Relief, and those that are in Authority, may, if they please, have their Sentence and Actions, if righteous, justify'd to all the World.

Tinwald. This Court is call'd the *Tinwald*, from the Danish word *Ting*, i.e. *Forum Judiciale*, a Court of Justice, and *Wald*, i.e. fenc'd. It is held on a Hill near the middle of the Island, and in the open air. At this great Meeting where all persons are suppos'd to be present, all new Laws are to be publish'd, after they have been agreed to by the Governour, Council, Deemsters, and 24 Keys, and have receiv'd the Approbation of the Lord of the Isle.

Council. The Council consists of the Governour, Bishop, Archdeacon, two Vicars General, the Receiver General, the Comptroller, the Water-bailiff, and the Attorney General.

Keys. The twenty four *Keys*, so call'd (it is said) from unlocking, as it were, or solving the Difficulties of the Law, do represent the Commons of the Land, and do join with the Council in making all new Laws, and with the Deemsters in setting and determining the meaning of the ancient Laws and Customs in all difficult Cases.

The manner of chusing them at present is this. When any Member dies or is discharg'd, either on account of Age, or for any great Crime, which upon tryal by his Brethren, he is found guilty of, the rest of the Body present two persons to the Governour, out of whom he makes choice of one, who is immediately sworn to fill up the Body. And this Body determines any Case of Common Law that comes before them, for, besides that they are a part of the Legislature, they do frequently determine Causes touching titles of Inheritance, where inferior Juries have given their Verdicts before.

The Deemsters. The two *Deemsters* are the Temporal Judges, both in cases of common Law, and of Life and Death. But most of the Controversies, especially such as are too trivial to be brought before a Court, are determined at their Houses.

Deemster's Oath. The *Deemster's* Oath which he takes when he enters upon his Office, is pretty singular, *viz* 'You shall do Justice between Man and Man,

"as equally *as the Herring Bone lies betwixt the* "*two sides*;" that his daily Food (for, in former days, no doubt, it was so) might put him in mind of the Obligation he lay under to give Impartial Judgment.

Ecclesiastical Courts. The Ecclesiastical Courts are either held by the Bishop in person, or his Archdeacon, (especially, where the Cause is purely Spiritual) or by his Vicars General, and the Archdeacon's Official, who are the proper Judges of all Controversies which happen betwixt Executors, &c. within a year and a day after Probate of the Will, or Administration granted.

In matters Spiritual, it is easy to observe very many footsteps of Primitive Discipline and Integrity. Offenders are neither overlook'd, nor treated with Importunateness. If they suffer for their Crimes, it is rarely in their Purses, unless where they are very obstinate, and relapse into their former, or other great Offences.

As for Civil Causes that come before these Courts, they are soon dispatch'd, and almost without any charge (Attorneys and Proctors being generally discountenanc'd,) unless where litigious Persons are concern'd, who can find ways to prolong Law Suits even against the will of the Judge, whose Interest it is to shorten them, as much as may be, as getting nothing by their length, but more trouble. But besides what is transacted in open Court, the Vicars General compose an infinite number of Differences at their own Houses, which makes that Office very laborious and troublesome.

Attorneys. In all the Courts of this Island Ecclesiastical and Civil, both Men and Women do usually plead their own Causes, except where Strangers are concern'd, who being unacquainted with the Laws and Language, are forc'd to employ others to speak for them. It is but of late years, that Attorneys, and such as gain by Strife, have even forc'd themselves into Business, and except what these get out of the People, Law-Suits are determin'd without such Charges.

There are a great many Laws and Customs, which are peculiar to this Island, [illegible]

The eldest Daughter [illegible] Inherits, tho' there be more Children.

The Wives, thro' the [illegible] Power to make their Will [illegible] a living, of one half of all the [illegible] able and unmoveable [illegible] Parishes, where the wife [illegible] den [illegible] Goods. And this [illegible] South [illegible] North [illegible] Bed.

A Wo[illegible] Estate, [illegible]

When any of [illegible]

A C[illegible]

Executors of Spiritual Men have a right to the year's Profits, if they live till after 12 of the Clock on *Easter* day

They still retain an Usage (observ'd by the Saxons before the Conquest) that the Bishop, or some Priest appointed by him, do always sit in their Great Court along with the Governour, till Sentence of death (if any) be to be pronounc'd The Deemster asking the Jury (instead of Guilty or not Guilty) *Vod Fir charree sote?* which, literally translated, is, *May the Man of the Chancel, or he that Ministers at the Altar, continue to sit?*

When any Laws which concern the Church are to be Enacted, the Bishop and whole Clergy shall be made privy thereunto, and join with the Temporal Officers, and have their Consents with them, till the same shall be established

If a single Woman prosecutes a single Man for a Rape, the Ecclesiastical Judges impannel a Jury; and if this Jury finds him guilty, he is so return'd to the Temporal Courts, where, if he is found guilty, the Deemster delivers to the Woman a Rope, a Sword and a Ring, and she has it in her choice to have him hang'd, or beheaded, or to marry him

If any Man get a Farmer's daughter with child, he shall be compell'd to marry, or endow her with such a Portion as her Father wou'd have given her

No Man heretofore cou'd dispose of his Estate, unless he fell into Poverty And at this day, a man must have the Approbation of the Governour and Officers, before he can alienate

Tokens

The manner of calling any Person before a Magistrate Spiritual or Temporal, is pretty singular The Magistrate, upon a piece of thin slate or stone, makes a Mark, generally, the first letters of his Christian and Sirname This is given to a proper Officer, the Summoner, if it be before an Ecclesiastical Magistrate; or the Lock man, if before a Temporal, with two pence, who shews it to the Person to be charg'd, with the time when he is to appear, and at whose Suit; which if he refuses to obey, he is fined or committed to Prison, until he gives Bonds to obey and pay costs

Curiosities

Here are more *Runick Inscriptions* to be met with in this Island, than perhaps in any other Nation, most of them upon Funeral Monuments They are generally, on a long flat, ragg Stone, with crosses on one or both sides, and little embellishments of Men on horseback, or in Arms, Stags, Dogs, Birds, or other Devices; probably the Atchievements of some notable person The Inscriptions are generally on one edge, to be read from the Bottom upwards Most of them, after so many ages, are very entire, and writ in the old Norwegian Language, now understood in the Isle of *Tero* only One of the largest of these stands in the High-way, near the Church of St *Michael*, erected in memory of *Thurulf*, or *Thrulf*, as the name is now pronounc'd in *Norway*

Runick Inscriptions

Very many Sepulchral *Tumuli*, or Burying Places, are yet remaining in several parts of the Island, especially in the neighbourhood of the Bishop's Seat The Urns which have been taken out of them, are so ill burnt, and of so bad a clay, that it is scarce possible to take them out without breaking them They are full of burnt Bones, white and fresh as when first interr'd

As for Medals, Coins, or Weapons, none have hitherto been found in these Places; tho' it is probable that such *Tumuli* were cast up after some great Engagement, being for the most part in a champain Country, and within the compass of a pitch'd Battle

There are some few large heaps of small Stones (one, especially, in the Parish of Kirk *Michael*, call'd *Karn Viael*,) as also some very large white Stones brought together, but on what occasion, no body pretends to guess.

Some few Brass-Daggers, and other Instruments of Brass, were found not many years ago, buried under-ground they were well made and pois'd, and as fit for doing execution, as any that are made of Steel And very lately, were found some Nails of Gold without Allay, with Rivets of the same Metal on the small end their Make shews plainly that they were the Nails of a Royal Target, such as are at this day to be found amongst the Highlanders of *Scotland*

There is a small Island call'd the *Calf*, about three miles in Circumference, and separated from the South end of *Man* by a Channel of about two Furlongs — The Calf of Man

This little Island is well stor'd with Rabbets, and at one time of the year with *Puffins*, which breed in the Rabbet-holes, the Rabbets leaving their Holes for that time to these Strangers About the 15th of *August*, the young Puffins are ready to flie, and it is then they hunt them, as they call it, and take great numbers of them, few years less than four or five thousand The old ones leave their young all the day, and flie out to the main Sea, where having got their Prey, and digested it in their own Stomachs, they return late at night, and disgorge it into those of their young, for at no time is there any thing found in the Stomachs of the young, but a digested Oil and leaves of Sorrel This makes them one lump, almost, of Fat They who will be at the expence of Wine, Spice, and other Ingredients to pickle them, make them very grateful to many Palates, and send them abroad, but the greatest part are consum'd at home, coming at a very proper time for the Husbandman, who is now throng in his Harvest

About the Rocks of this little Island, an incredible number of all sorts of Sea Fowl breed, shelter, and bask themselves in Summer, and make a Sight so agreeable, that Governour *Chaloner* was at the pains to have a Sketch of one of these shelving Rocks, with the vast variety of Birds sitting upon it, taken, and printed along with his Account of the Isle

Thus far is the Account of the said Right Reverend and worthy Prelate, the present Bishop of this Place]

IF I here subjoin a short History of this [illegible] Island, it may perhaps be worth the while, and [illegible] truth it self seems to challenge it, to preserve the memory of such Actions, as are, if not already bury'd in oblivion, yet very near it

That this Island, as well as Britain, was possess'd by the Britains, is granted on all hands But when the northern Nations broke in, like a torrent, upon these southern parts, it became subject to the Scots In the time of Honorius and Arcadius, Orosius says it was inhabited by the Scots, as Ireland was, and Ninnius tells us of one *Binle* a Scot who possess'd it The same Author observes, that they were driven out of Britain and the Isles belonging to it, by *Cuneda* the Grand-father of

Ma

Maglocunus, who from the devastations he made in these Islands, is call'd by Gildas the *Dragon of the Isles* Afterwards, this Island, and likewise *Anglesey*, was subjected to the English Monarchy by Edwin King of the Northumbrians, if we suppose both to be included in the name *Menavæ*, as Writers tell us they are At that time it was reputed a *British* Island But when the North sent out a second Brood (viz Normans, Danes, and Norwegians,) to seek their fortune in the world, the Norwegians, who particularly infested the northern Sea by their piracies, possess'd themselves of this Island and the *Hebrides*, and set petty Princes over them, of whom I will here add a short History, as it is word for word in an ancient Manuscript, lest it should perish by any unlucky accident The title it bears, is *Chronicon Manniæ*, i e *A Chronicle of Man*, and it seems to have been written by the Monks of *Russin*, the most eminent Monastery in this Island

This Chronicle is now printed in the *Appendix* at the end of the Book.

Four RUNICK Inscriptions in the ISLE of MAN.

I Upon a Stone-Cross laid for a Lintel over a Window in *Kirk Michael* Church

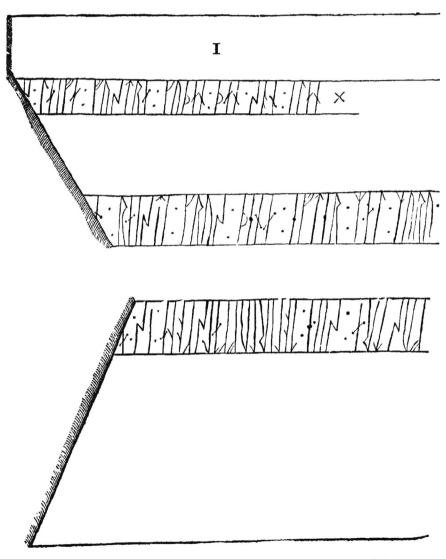

I

II Upon a Stone Crofs at *Kirk Michael*

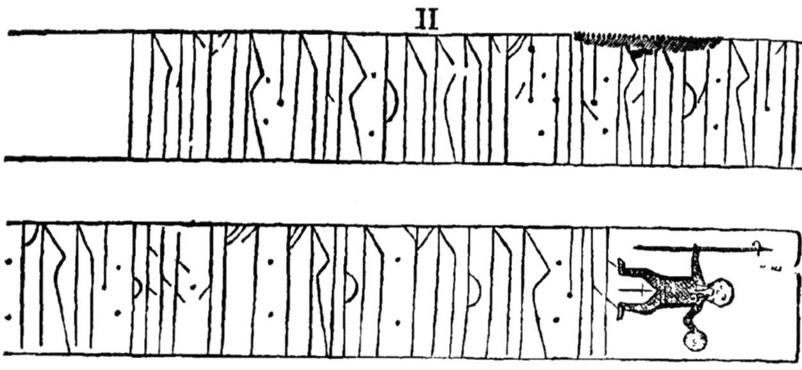

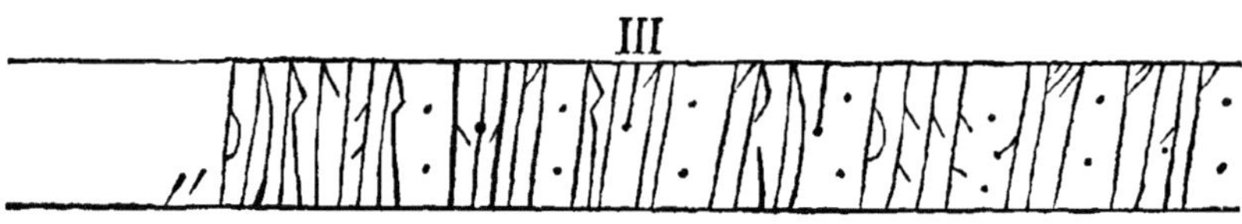

III Upon a Stone Crofs at *Kirk Braddan*

IV Upon a Stone Crofs in *Kirk Andrew's* Church-yard

(*Note, That the Infcriptions on the feveral* Stones *are in one fingle Line* [illegible] *too* [illegible] *for the Page, there was a neceffity of* dividing *the Lines, in thefe Draughts.*)

The

The *HEBRIDES*, or *WESTERN ISLES*]

ROM the *Isle of Man*, as far as the *Mull of Galloway*, or the Promontory of the *Novantes*, we meet only with small and inconsiderable Islands, but after we are past that, in the Frith of *Glotta* or *Dunbritton Frith*, we come to the Isle *Glotta*, mention'd in Antoninus, and call'd by the Scots at this day *Arran*; whence the Earls of Arran in that Kingdom take their title. And then, to a neighbouring Island, formerly call'd *Rothesia*, now *Bute*, from a little *Cell* which *Brendan* built in it, for so the word signifies in Scotch. After these, we arrive at *Hellan*, heretofore *Hellan Lenow*, that is (as *Fordon* explains the word) *the Isle of Saints*, and *Hellan Tinoc*, *the Isle of Swine*, both in the same Frith. But of these we have spoken already.

The Isle Glotta

Arran

Beyond this æstuary, lie a cluster of Isles, which the Scotch Inhabitants call *Inch Gall* (signifying perhaps *the Isles of the Gallæcians*,) the English and the rest of the Scots, the *Western-Isles*, the writers of the last age, *Hebrides*, but *Ethicus*, an antient Author, *Beteoricæ* Giraldus calls them sometimes *Inchades*, and sometimes *Leucades*, Pliny, Solinus, and Ptolemy, *Ebudes*, *Hebudes*, and [illegible]. Unless it had this name from the barrenness of the Soil, which yeilds no Corn; I must confess I can give no reason of it. For Solinus writes, that the Inhabitants thereof know nothing of Corn, but live wholly upon Fish and Milk, and the word *Eb [illegible]* signifies in British *fruitless*, or *without Corn*. *The Inhabitants* (take the words of Solinus) *know not what Corn is, but live upon fish and milk. They are all govern'd by one King, and are sever'd from one another by very narrow arms of the Sea. The King himself has nothing that he can call his own; all things are in common; but he is bound by certain Laws to be equitable, and, lest he should break them out of covetousness, his Poverty teaches him Justice, having no property, but being wholly maintain'd by the Publick. He is not allow'd one woman to himself, but takes by turns whichsoever he fansies for the present, by which means he lives without desire, or hope, of children of his own.*

Inch Gall

Hebrides

Scottish or Western Isles

[The western Isles lie upon the *west side* of Scotland, to which Crown (when distinct and separate from that of England) they belong'd. The Inhabitants speak the Irish Language, and retain the manners, customs, and habits of the ancient Scots, as the Highlanders on the Continent do.]

These Islands are commonly thought to be forty four in number, but they are many more. Pliny says there are thirty, Ptolemy five, [and those who have travel'd them, reckon them above three hundred.] The first is *Ricina*, in Pliny *Ricnea*, and in Antoninus *Riduna*, but call'd at this day, *Racline*, and I am of opinion, that *Riduna* in Antoninus should be read *Riclina*, c [illegible] being easily turned into *d*, by a connexion of the strokes. This small Isle lies over-against Ireland, and was known to the ancients upon account of its situation in this narrow sea between that and Scotland. At this day, it is only remarkable for the slaughter of the Irish Scots, who were often masters of it, but were at last entirely driven out by the English. The next is *[illegible]*, which from the name seems to me (as well as to that excellent Geographer *G. [illegible]*) to have lain near the promontory and shore of the *Epidii*. And seeing *[illegible]*, a pretty large Island, [illegible] level and fertil, lies in this manner, I take it to be the *Epidium*, and *the Isle of the Epidii*, for sometimes it is read, [illegible]. Its length is [a] twenty miles, [from north to south,] and its [illegible] breadth sixteen. It is so well stock'd with cattle, corn, and stags, that, next to *Man*, it was always the chief seat of the Kings of the Isles, as it [b] was afterwards of the *Mac Conels*, who [c] had their castle here at *Dunyweg*, [but] now it belongs to the Earl of [illegible]. In this Island, is found [illegible], and it hath several Woods, Bays, and Loughs. In the year 1706 *Archibald Campbell* (second son of *Archibald*, first Duke of Argyle,) having distinguished himself very early by his eloquence and knowledge in the Laws, and by other Accomplishments, was advanc'd by her Majesty Queen Anne to the title and honour of Earl of Ila.]

Rachlin

Epidium

Ila

[a] 24 C.

[b] [illegible] at this day [c] Have, C.

Between *Ila* and *Scotland*, lies *Jona*, which [illegible] Bede calls *Hy* and *Hu*, and which was [illegible] to the Scotch Monks by the Picts, for [illegible] the Gospel among them. In [illegible] stery famous for the burial of the Kings of Scotland, and for the residence of many holy men. One of the most eminent, was *[illegible]* the Apostle of the Picts, from whose Cell this Isle, as also the man himself, was call'd [illegible] compound name *Columbkill*, as Bede tells [illegible]. Here, at last, as some say, a Bishop's See [illegible] erected in Sodor a little village, from which [illegible] the Isles took the name of *[illegible]* within his Diocese. [*Jona* is two miles in length, almost from east to west, and [illegible] in breadth. There is found in it *Marble* of several colours, with very beautiful veins. The [illegible] is exceeding bad, and full of rocks, and the tides very violent. It has a Church of considerable largeness dedicated to St *Columbanus*, which is the Cathedral of the Bishop of the Isles. Here, at *Columbkill*, are still remaining the [illegible] two Irish Sepulchral Inscriptions, belonging to [illegible] Scottish Princes.

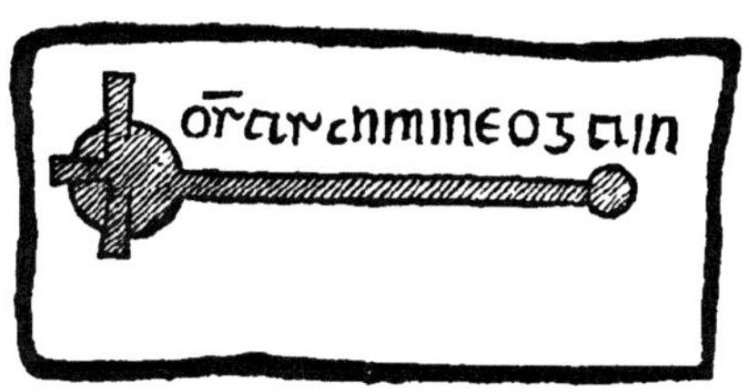

Maleos
Mula
Vide de his G. Buchan

After this, we arrive at the Iſle *Maleos*, as Ptolemy calls it, now *Mula*, which Pliny ſeems to mention in this paſſage, *Reliquarum Mella xxv mill paſs amplior proditur*, i e *Mella* is reported to be twenty five miles larger, than the reſt For ſo the old Venice Edition has it, whereas the common books read it *Reliquarum nulla* [This Iſle, upon the north-eaſt, is ſcarce four miles diſtant from the *Morvein*, a part of the Continent It is in length above twenty four miles, and in breadth almoſt as many It abounds with wood and deer, and hath a good road called *Polcarf*, and ſeveral freſh-water loghs, and bays, where abundance of herrings are taken The chief houſes, are, the caſtle of *Dowart*, a ſtrong hold upon a crag on the ſea-ſide, the caſtle of *Lochburg*, and the caſtle of *Aroſſe* In this Iſle are ſeven Pariſh Churches]

Polcarf

Dowart

Hebuda

Then we come to *Eaſt Hebuda*, now *Skie*, which is ſtretch'd out for a long way, facing the coaſt of Scotland [It is about forty two miles in length, and in breadth twelve, though in ſome places but eight The ſouth part of it is called *Slate*, and is divided from the Continent by a narrow Firth The air is temperate, and the whole Iſle very fertile in corn it abounds alſo with cows, goats, ſwine, deer, and wild fowl, and has about ten Pariſh Churches]

Slate

Lewes

Then *Weſt Hebuda*, ſo call'd becauſe it lies more to the weſt, but now *Lewes*, the Lordſhip of *Mac Cloyd*, which in an old book of *Man* is call'd *Lodhus* It is craggy and mountainous, and very thinly inhabited, but of greater extent than any of the reſt, and is divided from *Laſt*, by a ſmall arm of the Sea [*Lewes* hath its name from a part of it, properly ſo called; but by ſtrangers it is called the *Long Iſland*, being (with the *Harris*, join'd to it by a ſmall neck of land) ſome threeſcore miles in length, and in ſeveral places ſixteen broad By arms of the ſea, and Sounds, it is divided into five ſeveral Counties, belonging to five ſeveral Heretors *Barray*, to the Laird of Barray, *South-Wiſt* to the Captain of Clan Rald, *North Wiſt* to Mack Donald of Slate, the *Harris* to Mackland of Dunvegan, and that which is properly called the *Lewes*, to Seaforth Upon the eaſt-ſide of the Country, are four Loghs, wherein ſhips of great burthen may ride]

Laſt

Long iſland

Hirth

The reſt are all inconſiderable, beſides *Hirth*, being either rough and ſtony, or inacceſſible by reaſon of craggy cliffs, and ſcarce a green turf to be ſeen in them [Of all the Iſles about Scotland, this of *Hirta* lieth fartheſt into the ſea, being about fifty miles from the neareſt land It is two miles in length, and about one in breadth, and has in it ſome ten families It is very mountainous, and not acceſſible, but by climbing One can hardly imagin, what prodigious numbers of Fowl frequent the rocks, of which as there are many ſorts, ſo ſome are of ſtrange ſhapes Amongſt theſe, there is one they call the *Gare Fowl*, which is bigger than a Gooſe, and lays great eggs, and is diſtinguiſh'd by a great white ſpot upon the Breaſt They ſtuff the ſtomach of it with the fat of other fowl in the Iſle, and having dried it in the chimney, ſell it to their neighbours on the continent, as a remedy againſt aches and pains Their ſheep are different from all others, having long legs, and long horns, and inſtead of wool, a bluiſh hair upon them Of the milk of their ſheep they make butter, and a ſort of cheeſe very pleaſant to the taſt They have no ſalt, but what they make of ſea-tangle by burning it Their greateſt trade is in feathers, which they ſell, and the exerciſe they affect moſt is climbing of ſteep rocks Some corn they have, though but little their food is eggs and young ſea fowls, and their drink, whey

Gare Fowl

whey and water They keep their holidays very strictly in their little Chapels The women cultivate the land, and the men climb the rocks for fowl The duty they pay their Master, is reasted mutton, reasted wild fowl, and selch-skins.

Jura

Others of these Islands, that are less considerable than those already mentioned, are, *Jura*, lying over against Knapdail; some twenty four miles in length, and in breadth, where broadest, about six miles The sea-coast is fertil in corn, and the middle parts are fit for pasture (Betwixt this and *Ila*, runneth that most dangerous channel called the *Sound of Ila*, near ten miles long and two broad) *Scarba*, about two miles distant from *Jura*, some four miles long, and one broad It is a high rough Isle, and hath some wood in it Betwixt this and *Jura*, runs a stream called *Arey-Brescen*, eight miles long, which is not to be ventured on, but at certain tides, for there is no sailing or rowing against it *Terie*, lying off the Isle of Mull towards the west, about eight miles in length, and three in breadth, where broadest The coast of it is dangerous for rocks, banks, and violent tides, and the entries are very bad *Colle*, north of *Terie*, about twelve miles in length, and two in breadth It is fertile enough, and affords plenty of Iron ore *Wyst*, about thirty four miles long and six broad *Barray*, seven miles long, and four broad *Rona*, a little Isle, low and well manured, which hath for many generations been possessed by five Families, who seldom exceed the number of thirty persons They have a kind of Common wealth among themselves; and if any one has more children than another, he that has fewer takes from his neighbour so many as will make his number equal Those that are above thirty, are sent with the sea boat to *Lewes*, to *Seaforth* their Master, to whom they pay yearly a quantity of meal stitched up in sheep skins, and some feathers of sea fowls All things are common amongst them They have no fuel for fire; but the sea yearly casts in as much timber, as serves them for that use]

Sound of Ila; Scarba; Arey Brescen; Terie; Colle; Wyst; Barray; Rona

These, as we have observ'd before, were all purchased of the King of Norway by the Scots, as a security to their kingdom; though they turn to little or no advantage, by reason of the temper of the inhabitants, who are of the ancient Scots or Irish, men of great spirit and boldness, that will not subject themselves to the penalties of Laws, nor the Sentences of Courts As for their manners, dress, and language, they differ little, or nothing, from the wild Irish, of whom we have already treated, so that you may easily know them to be one and the same nation The persons of interest and authority here, are *Mac-Conell*, *Mac Alen*, or (as others call him) *Maclen*, *Mac Cloyd de Lewes*, and *Mac Cloyd de Harich* But the most potent of these families, is that of the *Mac Conells* deriving themselves from *Donald*, who in the reign of James the third, took the title of *King of the Isles*, and ravaged Scotland with all the outrage and cruelty imaginable, for which his son *John* was attainted, and forc'd to submit himself, and all he had, to the mercy of the King, who gave him certain lands in *Cantir* In the [a] last age, flourish'd *Donel Gormy Mac Conell* of this family, that is, the *blue*, perhaps so call'd from his cloaths who had issue *Agnus Mac Conell*, and *Alexander*, who leaving the poor and barren soil of *Cantir*, invaded the *Glinnes* in Ireland This *Agnus Mac-Conell* was father of *James Mac-Conell*, who was slain by *Shan O Neal*, and of *Surley Boy*, who had lands given him in *Rowt* in Ireland by the bounty of Queen Elizabeth *James Mac Conell* had issue *Agnus Mac Conell*, (but of him we have spoken already) between whom and *Mac Clen* there was such an inveterate enmity, as the relation between the two families could not extinguish nor restrain them from seeking the blood and ruin of each other

So ann 1607; [a] So said ann 1607; See Ann in 1586, and 1598

[The ORCADES, or Isles of ORKNEY.]

AS we coast from the *Hebudes*, to the north east, we come in sight of the *Orcades*, now *Orkney*, being a cluster of [a] thirty Isles, separated from one another by little arms of the Sea they are said in a certain old manuscript to be so call'd from *Argat*, that is (as it is there explain'd) *Above the Getes* But I had rather interpret it, *Above the Cat*; for it lies over against *Cath*, a Country of Scotland, which, from the promontory, is now called *Catness*; the Inhabitants whereof seem to be falsly called, in Ptolemy, *Carini* instead of *Catini* These Islands, in Solinus's time, were without Inhabitants, and overgrown with rushes; but now they are cultivated, and [b] produce much barley; but no wheat, nor woods, nor trees

Orcades; Orkney; [a] Only 26 inhabited See below; [b] See below

[But to be more particular, concerning the *Situation*, *Air*, *Seasons*, and *Tides*, we will follow the account, which Mr *James Wallace* (a person well vers'd in Antiquities, and Minister of *Kirkwall*,) hath given, in his Description of these Isles

Orkney lies in the Northern temperate *Zone* in longitude 22 degrees 11 minutes, in latitude 59 degrees 2 minutes The length of the longest day is eighteen hours and some odd minutes For a great part of *June* it will be so clear at midnight, that one may read in their chamber yet what a late writer tells us cannot be true, that from the hill of *Hoy* a man may see the sun at midnight It cannot be the true body of the sun, but only the image of it refracted through the sea, or some watery cloud about the Horizon; seeing it must be as far depressed under our Horizon in *June*, as it is elevated above it in *December*, and from that hill, the sun is to be seen in the shortest day of *December* above five hours and a half

The air and clouds here, by the operation of the sun, do sometime generate strange things For instance; Not many years since, while some fishermen were fishing half a league from land over against

against *Copinsha*, on a fair day, there fell down from the Air a Stone about the bigness of a foot ball: it fell in the midst of the Boat, and sprung a leak in it, to the great hazard of the lives of the men who were in it which could be no other but some substance generated in the clouds The Stone was like condensed or petrified Clay, and was a long time in the custody of Captain *Andrew Dick*, at that time Stewart of the Country

Seasons Here our Winters are generally more subject to rain than snow nor does the frost and snow continue so long here as in other parts of *Scotland*; but the winds, in the mean time, will often blow very boisterously Sometimes the rain descends not by drops, but by spouts of water, as if whole clouds fell down at once About four years ago, after a thunder, in the month of *June*, there fell a great flake of Ice more than a foot thick

Situation This Country is wholly surrounded with the Sea, having *Pightland-Firth* on the south, the *Deucalidonean* Ocean on the west, the Sea that divides it from *Zetland* on the north, and the *German* Sea on the east *Zetland* stands north east and by east from *Orkney*, and, from the Start in *Sanda* to *Swinburgh head*, the most southerly point in *Zetland*, is about eighteen leagues, where there is nothing but Sea all the way, save *Fair Isle*, which lies within eight leagues of *Swinburgh-head*

Pightland-Firth. *Pightland-Firth*, which divides this Country from *Caithness*, is in breadth from *Duncans-bay*, to the nearest point of *South Ronaldsha* in *Orkney*, about twelve miles in it are many tides (to the number of twenty four) which run with such an impetuous current, that a Ship under sail is no more able to make way against the tide, than if it were hinder'd by a *Remora*; which I conceive is the cause, why some have said, that they have found the *Remora* in these seas.

Stroma In this Firth, about two miles from the coast of *Caithness*, lies *Stroma*, a little Isle, but pleasant and fruitful and because of its vicinity to *Caithness*, and its being still under the jurisdiction of the Lords of that Country, it is not counted as one of the Isles, of *Orkney* On the north side of this Isle, is a part of the Firth called the *Swelchee* of *Stroma*; and at the west-end of it, betwixt it and *Mey* or *Caithness*, there is another part of it, called the *Merrie Men of Mey*; both which are very dangerous

Tides The Sea ebbs and flows here as in other places; yet there are some *Phænomena*, the reason of which cannot easily be found out as, in the Isle of *Sanda*, it flows two hours sooner on the west side, than on the east; and in *North Faira* (which lies between *Eda* and *Westra*) the sea ebbs nine hours, and flows but three And at *Hammoness* in *Sanda*, both ebb and flood runs one way, except at the beginning of a quick stream, when for two or three hours, the flood runs south

The Sea here is very turbulent in a storm, and as pleasant in a calm The Tides are very swift and violent by reason of the multitude of the Isles, and narrowness of the passages, for when all the rest of the Sea is smooth, these tides carry their waves and billows high.

The Tides run with such violence, that they cause a contrary motion in the Sea adjoining to the land, which they call *Easter birth*, or *Wester-birth*, according to its course Yet notwithstanding all this rapidity of the tides and births, the Inhabitants do almost daily travel from Isle to Isle, about their several business, in their little Cock-boats.

The first Planters and Possessors of this Country, are said by the Inhabitants, and the generality of Historians, to have been the Picts, and the same Historians, call *Orkney*, *Antiquum Pictorum regnum*, the ancient Kingdom of the Picts: there being in this Country several strange antick Houses (many of which are overgrown with Earth,) that are still call'd Picts Houses; and the Firth that runs between this and *Caithness*, is from them call'd *Pictland Firth* i e the Firth that runs by the Land of the Picts Though *Buchanan* (to establish his Opinion) would rather have it called *Fretum Penthlandicum*, from *Penthus*, a man of his own making. These Verses of the Poet *Claudian*, Picts

——— Maduerunt Saxone fuso,
Orcades, incaluit Pictorum sanguine Thule.

The *Orkney* Isles with *Saxon* Blood were wet,
And *Thule* with the *Pictish* gore did sweat,

do evidently prove, that the *Picts*, with some other Colony of the *German Nation* (particularly the *Saxons*) were at that time the Possessors and Inhabitants of these Northern Isles Moreover, to this day many of the Inhabitants use the *Norse*, or old *Gothick Language*, which is not much different from the Old *Teutonick*, or the Language which the Picts used. Besides, the Sirnames of the ancient Inhabitants are of a *German* Original; for the *Seaters* are so called from *Seater*, one of the old *German* Idols which they worshipped for *Saturn*: The *Taits* from *Twisk*, i e the *Dutch*, who had that name from *Twisco* the son of *Noe* and *Tythea*, the famous progenitors of the *Germans*, The *Keldas*, from the ancient *Culdees* or *Keldees* (as *Spotswood* thinks) who were the ancient Priests or Ministers of the Christian Religion among the *Picts*, so call'd because they liv'd in *Cells* The *Baikies*, from some small running water, which in the *Teutonick* is called a *Baikie*. So, the names that end in *Stane*; as *Hourstane*, *Corstane*, *Yorstane*, *Beistane*, &c which is a *Pictish*, or *Teutonick* termination of Sirnames, signifying the superlative degree or comparison And many more might be added, if it were needful, to shew that the *Pictish* Blood is as yet in this Countrey, and that that People were the first Possessors of it.

But at what time the *Picts* first planted these Isles, is controverted by our writers: some say, that in the year of the World 4867, the Picts having left their native Country, to seek out some new habitation, came first to *Orkney*; where they left a Colony to plant the Country, and then, with their main body, ferrying over *Pictland firth*, and passing through *Caithness*, *Ross*, *Murray*, *Marr*, and *Angus*, at last settled themselves in *Fife* and *Lothian*, which, from them, is by our Writers called *Pictlandia* Others more probably think, that the Picts did not settle here till the time of *Reuther* King of *Scots*; when the *Scots*, by an intestine division, warring upon one another, each Party being afflicted sisted by a considerable number of the Picts, they fought so desperately, that, besides *Gethus* King of the Picts, the greatest number both of *Scots* and *Pictish* Nobility were killed, with many thousands of the Commons of both Nations Which great slaughter, with the invasions of the *Britons* at the same time, constrain'd the Picts (who perceived themselves unable to resist) to fly, some by land and others by sea, to *Orkney*, where they abode for a time, and made *Gethus*, brother of the foresaid *Gethus*, their King. And after a few years, having left some of their number to people and plant the Countrey, they return'd to *Louthian*; and having expelled the *Britons*, settled themselves again in their ancient possessions.

The Country being thus planted, the People grew and multiplied, and for a long time were govern'd by Kings of their own, after the manner of the Picts and other Nations. There is still a place in this Country, that by reason of its name and antick form, should seem to have been the Residence of some of those Kings, for it is call'd *Cuningsgar*, though now a dwelling house of the Minister of *Sandwick* But the memory of the Names and Actions of these Kings are, by iniquity of time, and carelesness of Writers, buried in silence, except a Memorial of one of them (viz *Belus*) which is at this time on a Stone in the Kirk of *Birsa* (where probably the King had his principal Residence, and at this hour, one of our King's chiefest Palaces remains,) having the name, *Belus*, engraven on it, in ancient Characters The knowledge which the Romans had in these parts appears among other Testimonies, from the Names which they gave to some of the Islands] The chiefest, and most remarkable of which, is *Pomona* [since] a Bishop's See, call'd by *Solinus Pomona Diutina*, from the length of the days there, but by the present Inhabitants [c] *Mainland*, as if it were a *Continent* It is adorn'd with a Bishop's Seat, at *Kirkwall* a little Town, and with two Castles, and abounds in Tin and Lead *Ocetis* is also reckon'd among these Isles by Ptolemy; I suppose it may be that, which we now call *Hethy* But whether *Hey*, which is one of these, be Pliny's *Dumna*, is a question that I cannot yet resolve If it is not, I should be more apt to think *Fair Isle*, to be *Dumna*, (in which the only town is call'd *Dum*,) than *Wardhuys* in Lapland, as Becanus does

Romans. Pomona. See below. Kirkwall. Ocetis. Hethy. Hey. Dumna.

Julius Agricola, the first who sail'd round Britain, discover'd the *Orcades* in that Voyage, (unknown to the World till that time,) and conquer'd them So little right has *Claudius* to this conquest, as St. Hierom, in his Chronicle, would have it, that Juvenal, in Hadrian's time, writes thus of them,

Tacitus.

——— Arma quid ultra?
Littora Juvernæ promovimus & modo captas
Orcades, & minima contentos nocte Britannos

What tho' the *Orcades* have lately own'd
our power?
What tho' *Juverna*'s tam'd, and *Britain*'s
shore
That boasts the shortest night? ———

Afterwards, when the Roman Empire was extinct in Britain, [d] the Picts planted themselves in these Islands, and Claudian says in his poetical way,

[d] See before.

Maduerunt Saxone fuso
Orcades

The *Orcades* with *Saxon* gore o'erflow'd

Ninnius also tells us that *Octha* and *Ebissus*, both Saxons, who serv'd under the Britains, sail'd round the Picts in vi Kyules, and wasted *Orkney*

[e] After that they came under the dominion of the Norwegians (by which means the Inhabitants speak *Gothick*) upon the grant made by Donald Ban, who after the death of his brother *Malcolm Can Mor* King of Scots, had excluded his nephews and usurp'd the Kingdom; and hop'd to be supported by the Norwegians in these wicked Usurpations The Norwegians continu'd in possession of them till the year 1266 [f] Then, Magnus the fourth of that name, King of Norway, being exhausted by a war with Scotland, surrender'd them to Alexander the third King of Scots by treaty, and they were afterwards confirm'd to King Robert Brus in the year 1312, by Haquin King of Norway [g] At last, in the year 1468, *Christian*, the first King of Norway and Denmark, renounc'd all right and title for himself and his Successors, to *James* the third, King of Scotland, upon a marriage between him and his daughter; and so transferr'd his right to his son-in-law, and his successors for ever, and to corroborate it further, it was also confirm'd by the Pope.

[e] See below. [f] See below. [g] See below.

[But to give a larger (tho' somewhat different) View of those Revolutions in Government here; let us betake our selves to our former Guide

Mr Wallace.

This Country, it is like, continu'd under the Government of their own Princes, till the fatal ruin and subversion of the Pictish Kingdom in *Scotland*, in the year of our Lord 839 At which time, *Kenneth* the second, that martial King of Scots, having in many battles overthrown the Pights, at last expell'd them out of *Scotland*, and seizing on *Fife* and *Louthian*, and the other large territories they had therein, pursued them to *Orkney*; vanquishing these Isles, and adding them to his other Dominions.

Scots.

Orkney being thus annexed to the Crown of *Scotland*, continued many years under the Government of Scottish Kings and their Lieutenants, till about the year 1099 At which time, *Donald Bain*, Lord of the Isles (having usurped the Crown, and caused himself to be proclaimed King of *Scotland*, and being thereupon put hard to it by the injur'd Heir, and discontented Nobility;) that he might not lose what he had unjustly usurp'd, invited *Magnus* King of *Norway*, to come to his assistance, with an offer of the Isles for his pains Who coming with his Navy, invaded *Orkney* and the Western Isles; putting Garrisons in all convenient places

By this means, the Norwegians got possession of this Country, and held it for the space of 164 years; when they came to lose all again upon this occasion *Anno* 1263, *Alexander* the third being then King of *Scotland*, Acho (by some called *Hagin*) King of *Norway*, hoping (from the divisions that were then in the Kingdom

Norwegians.

dom, and the famine that then press'd the land) to make some further conquest in *Scotland*, comes with a great Navy and Army of *Danes* and *Norwegians* to the West Isles, and conquers *Arran* and *Bute* (which were the only Isles at that time, under the Dominion of the Scots) and from this success, hoping for greater, he lands on the Continent, and takes-in the Town and Castle of *Air* But King *Alexander* having assembled a great Army, assaults him in battle at *Largis*, kills his Nephew, a person of high renown, and after a great slaughter of his Soldiers (to the number of twenty four thousand) puts the remainder to flight. Immediately upon this defeat, King *Acho*, hears of another sad loss, namely, that his Fleet, consisting of an hundred and fifty Ships, were, by the force of an outragious tempest, all cast away, and broken against the rocks, except four, in which he presently embarked, and fled to *Orkney* Being come thither, he sent to *Norway* and *Denmark* for a new Army and Fleet, with an intention to invade *Scotland* the next Summer; but he died in the beginning of the following year, and was buried in that place, where the Cathedral now stands, under a marble Stone, which is seen to this day *Jan 22, 1264*

After his death, King *Alexander* invaded the Isle of *Man* and the Western Isles; which, after some opposition, he recovered; and intending to make the like attempt for the recovery of *Orkney* and *Zetland*, there came Ambassadors to him from *Magnus* King of *Norway* and *Denmark* (who succeeded his father *Acho* in these Kingdoms) a person well inclin'd, and one that feared God After several Treaties, it was at last agreed on, that King *Alexander* should pay to the King of *Norway* the Sum of four thousand Marks Sterling, with the Sum of an hundred Marks by year and that for this, *Magnus* King of *Norway*, should quit all right that he might pretend to in the Isles of *Orkney* and *Zetland*, and the other Isles of *Scotland* which accordingly he did by Letters under his great Seal; renouncing and giving over all right or claim that he had, or might have, both for him and his Successors, to these and all the other Isles of *Scotland* And for the better confirmation hereof, a marriage was agreed on between the Lady *Margaret*, daughter of *Alexander*, and *Hangonanus* (or *Hannigo*, or *Aquine*, as others call him) son to King *Magnus*, both children, to be compleated when they came to a marrigeable estate

This *Magnus* King of *Norway* was a Prince of great piety and devotion; for which he was reputed a Saint, and commonly called Saint *Magnus* He greatly advanced the Christian Religion in this Country, whose Patron he is held to be; and is thought to have founded that stately edifice in *Kirkwall*, which is now the Cathedral, call'd from him St *Magnus's Kirk*

The opinion of his Sanctity and Miracles, made him so famous, that the day wherein King *Robert Bruce* gave that great and memorable defeat to the English at *Banockburn*, there was seen riding through *Aberdeen* (as the tradition hath gone) a horse-man in shining armor, who told them of the Victory and afterwards was seen riding over *Pightland Firth*. Whereupon, it was concluded (saith *Boethius*, who tells this story) that it was St *Magnus*. And upon that account, the King, after the Victory, order'd, that five Pounds Sterling should be paid for ever to St. *Magnus's* Kirk in *Kirkwall*, out of the Customs payable by the Town of *Aberdeen*

Having thus far treated of the Isles of *Orkney*, in general; we will now proceed to a more particular Enumeration of them. And whatever the Ancients have written of the number of the Isles of *Orkney*, it is certain, there are but twenty six at present inhabited, viz *South Ronaldsha*, *Swinna*, *Hoy*, *Burra*, *Lambholm*, *Flotta*, *Faira*, *Cava*, *Gramsey*, *Mainland*, *Copinsha*, *Shapinsha*, *Damsey*, *Inhallo*, *Stronsa*, *Papa-Stronsa*, *Sanda*, *North Ronaldsha*, *Eda*, *Rousa Wyre*, *Gaersa*, *Eglesha*, *North-Faira*, *Westra*, *Papa Westra* The rest of the Isles are called *Holms*, and are only used for Pasturage, all of them being separated from one another, by some narrow streights here You may remark that most of the names end in *A*, or *Ey*, which in the *Teutonick Tongue* signifieth *water*; to shew that these Isles are peices of land surrounded with water *Number and Nature of the Isles of Orkney*

They are of different natures; some sandy, some marsh, some abound in moss, and some have none, some are mountainous, and some plain Of these, some are called the *south*-Isles, and others the *north*-Isles, and this, as they stand to the south or north of the greatest Isle, called the *Mainland* *South Isles*

South Ronalsha, is the Southermost of these Isles, being five miles long, and fertile in Corn, and abounding with People To the South east, lie the *Pightland Skerries*, dangerous to Seamen but to the North, is St *Margaret's Hope*, a very safe Harbour for Ships, which has no difficulty in coming to it, save a Rock in the midst of the Sound, betwixt this Isle and *Burra*, called *Lippa* From *Burwick* in this Isle, is the usual Ferry to *Duncans-bay* in *Caithness* *South Ronalsha*

A little separated from this, to the South west, lies *Swinna*, a small Isle, and only considerable for a part of *Pightland* Firth, lying a little to the west of it, and called the Wells of *Swinna*, which are two whirlpools in the Sea (occasioned, as it is thought, through some *hiatus* that is in the earth below;) and these turn round with such violence, that if any boat or ship come within their reach, they will whirl it about, till it be swallowed up and drown'd They are only dangerous in a dead calm, for if there be any wind, and the boat under sail, there is no danger in going over them If a boat happen to come near them in a calm, through the force of the tide, the Boats men take this way for their preservation, they throw a barrel, or oar, or any thing that comes next to hand, into the Wells, and when it is swallowed up, the Sea remains smooth, for a time, for any boat to pass over *Swinna*

Beyond this, and to the west of the *South Ronaldsha*, lies *Waes* and *Hoy*; which are but one Isle, about twelve miles long, full of high Mountains, and but thinly inhabited, unless in *Waes*, where the ground is more pleasant and fertile From *Snel-setter*, is the other Ferry out of this Country, to *Ham* in *Caithness* Here are several good Harbours, *Kirk hope*, *North hope*, *Ore hope*, and others; but not much frequented *Waes and Hoy*

To the north of *South Ronaldsha*, about a mile, lies *Burra*, a pleasant little Isle, fruitful in Corn, and abounding with Rabbets *Burra*

Betwixt it and the *Main land*, is *Lambho'm*; and to the west, towards *Hoy mouth*, lie *Flotta*, *Faira*, *Cava*, and *Gramsey*, all of them fruitful and pleasant Isles, though not large *Lambholm*

Next

Main-land

Next to theſe, is the *Main-land* before mention'd, ſome twenty four miles long, and well inhabited About the middle of this Iſle, looking to the North, ſtands *Kirkwall*, the only good Town in all this Country There are in it four remarkable and excellent Harbours for Ships One is at *Kirkwall*, both large and ſafe, without danger of ſhoals or blind rocks as they come to it, unleſs they come from the Weſt by *Inhallo* and *Gairſa* Another is at *Deirſound*, which is a great Bay, and a very ſafe road for Ships, having good anchoring-ground, and capable to give ſhelter to the greateſt Navies The third is at *Grahamſhall*, toward the Eaſt-ſide of this Iſle, where is a convenient road; but the Ships that ſail to it from the eaſt, keep betwixt *Lambholm* and the *Main land*, for the other way, betwixt *Lambholm* and *Burra* (which appears to be the only open way,) is found very ſhallow and dangerous, even for ſmall Ships The fourth is at *Kairſton*, a ſmall Village at the weſt end of the *Main-land*, where is a very ſafe and commodious Harbour, well fenced againſt all winds and weathers by two ſmall Holms that ſtand at the entry

Copinſha

To the eaſt of *Main land*, lies *Copinſha*, a little Iſle, but very conſpicuous to Sea-men; in which, and in ſeveral other places of this Country, are to be found in great plenty excellent Stones for the game called Curling To the North eaſt of this Iſle, is a Holm called *The Horſe of Copinſha*

North Iſles Shapinſha

To the North of *Main-land*, lie the North Iſles, the firſt of which is *Shapinſha*, betwixt five and ſix miles long, with a ſafe Harbour for Ships at *Elwick*

Stronſa

Of an equal bigneſs to that, toward the South-eaſt, lies *Stronſa*, which hath two convenient Harbours, one at *Lingaſound*, fenced with *Linga holm*, the other at *Strynie*, fenced with a little pleaſant Iſle to the North of it called *Papa-Stronſa*

Sanda

Beyond theſe to the North, at a pretty diſtance, lies *Sanda*, about eleven or twelve miles in length, but very narrow; well ſtored with Corn and Rabbets It hath two roads for Ships, one at *Kitle-toft*, guarded by a little Holm, called *The Holm of Elneſs*, the other at *Otterſwick*, guarded by the moſt Northern Iſle in all this Country, called *North Ronalſha*, which is a little fruitful Iſle, but both it and *Sanda* are deſtitute of moſs ground, and are forced to bring their peits or turfs a great way off, from the adjacent Iſle *Eda*

North Ronalſha

Eda

This *Eda* lieth to the South eaſt of *Sanda*, and is near five miles in length, and full of moſs and hills; but thinly inhabited, unleſs it be about the ſkirts of it It hath a ſafe road to the North, call'd *Calf-ſound*, guarded by a large Holm call'd *The Calf of Eda*, in which is a good Salt-Pan

Damſey

Three miles to the Weſt of *Kirkwall*, at the bottom of a large Bay, lies a little Iſle, called *Damſey*, with a Holm beſide it, as big as it ſelf

Rouſa

To the North weſt lies *Rouſa*, a large Iſle, about ſix miles long, full of heatherly hills, and well ſtored with Plover and Moor fowl it is but thinly inhabited

Inhallo

Betwixt it and the main land, lies *Inhallo*; and toward *Kirkwall* lies *Wyre* and *Gairſa*, ſmall but profitable, Iſles

Egleſha

North from *Kirkwall*, at eight miles diſtance, ſtands *Egleſha*, ſomething more than two miles long, but pleaſant and fertile, having a convenient road for Ships betwixt it and *Wyre* There is in it a little handſome Church, where it is ſaid that St *Magnus*, the Patron of this Country, lies buried

Weſtra

To the North of *Egliſha* is *Weſtra*, ſeven miles long it is pleaſant, fertile, and well-inhabited, and hath a convenient Harbour for Ships at *Pirriwa*. At the Eaſt end of it lies *Faira*, called for diſtinction *Faira be North*; and to the North-and-by-eaſt is *Papa-Weſtra*, a pleaſant Iſle, three miles in length, and famous for St *Tredwel's* Chapel and Loch, of which many things are reported by the vulgar

Product of the Iſles

All theſe Iſles are indifferently fruitful, well ſtored with fields of Corn and herds of Cattle; and abound with Rabbets, but are deſtitute of Wheat, Rye, and Peaſe

The chief Products of this Country, and which are exported yearly by the Merchant, are Beer, Malt, Meal, Fiſh, Tallow, Hides, Stockings, Butter, Selch ſkins, Otter ſkins, Rabbet-ſkins, Lamb-ſkins, white Salt, Stuffs, Writing Pens, Downs, Feathers, Hams, Wool, &c

They have good ſtore of field and garden-plants; and make great quantities of Butter Their Ewes are ſo fertile, that moſt of them have two at a birth, and ſome three; nay [k] my Author affirms, that he has ſeen four at a birth all living, and following the Dam Their Horſes are but little, yet ſtrong and lively. they have great herds of Swine, and Warrens (almoſt in every Iſle) well ſtor'd with Rabbets That they can want either Fiſh or Fowl, conſidering the ſituation of the Country, we cannot well imagine The Eagles and Kites are there in great plenty, and are very troubleſome, ſeizing ſometimes upon young Children, and carrying them a good way, ſo that if any one kills an Eagle, he may by law claim a hen out of every houſe in the Pariſh where it is killed. Hawks and Falcons have their neſts in ſeveral parts of the Iſlands; and the King's Falconer comes every year and takes the young, who has twenty pounds Sterling in Salary, and a Hen or a Dog out of every Houſe in the Country, except ſome Houſes that are privileged

[k] Mr Wallace

They have ſeveral Mines of *Silver*, *Tin*, and *Lead*, and perhaps of other Metals; but none are improved They find abundance of *Marle*, which turns to good account to the Huſbandman Free-ſtone quarries, with grey and red Slate, are in many places, and in ſome, Marble and Alabaſter

When the Winds are violent, the Sea caſts in pieces of trees, Ambergreeſe, exotick Fowls, and other things

Foreſt or Wood they have none, nor any Trees, except in the Biſhop's gardens at *Kirkwall*, where are ſome *Aſhes*, *Thorn*, and *Plum trees* Here and there, in a Gentleman's garden, there are Apples and Cherry trees, but the Fruit ſeldom comes to any degree of maturity Yet it ſhould ſeem, that there have been Woods formerly; for they find Trees in the Moſſes, of twenty or thirty foot in length with their branches entire.

Where the Country is divided into ſo many ſmall Iſlands, it cannot be expected there ſhould be any large Rivers yet bourns and torrents they have, well repleniſhed with Trouts There are many *Lochs*; but they ſerve for no other uſe, than affording water to their Mills or Cattle The many excellent roads, bays, and ports, make it exceeding commodious for navigation

Mr *Wallace's* Account of *Kirkwall*

Thus much of the several Isles, and the Products of them. As to particular places, The only remarkable Town in this Country, is *Kirkwall*, and being the only one of note, in which also is the *Cathedral Church*, and *Bishop's Palace*, and both the Civil and Ecclesiastical Administration of the Isles; we connot pass it over, without a particular description of the state of it. This then is an ancient Borough, long possess'd by the Danes, by whom it was called *Cracoviaca*, and built upon a pleasant Oyse or inlet of the Sea, near the middle of the Main land. It is near a mile in length, with narrow Streets, and has a very safe harbour and road for Ships. Here is the Seat of Justice. the Stewart, and Sheriff, keeping their several Courts in this place, where all publick business is done. Almost all the Houses in it are slated, but the most remarkable Edifices, are St *Magnus's* Church, and the Bishop's Palace. As for the King's Castle, it is now demolished, but by the ruins, it appears to have been a strong and stately Fort, and was probably built by some of the Bishops of *Orkney*, as appears from a remarkable Stone set in the midst of the wall that looks towards the Street, which has a Bishop's Mitre and Arms engraven on it. There is in it a publick School for the teaching of Grammar, endow'd with a competent Salary, and at the north end of the Town, is a place built by the English, ditch'd about, on which, in time of war, they plant Cannons for the defence of the Harbour against the Ships of the Enemy. As it fell out *anno* 1666, when there was war between our King and the Hollanders, and a *Dutch man of war* coming to the road (who shot many guns at the Town, with a design to take away some of the Ships that were in the harbour) was by some Cannon from the Mount so bruised, that he was forced to flee with the loss of many of his men.

Dat. *Edinb. Mar. ult.* 1486

This Town had been erected into a royal Borough in the time of the Danes. and *Anno* 1480, King *James* the third gave them a Charter, confirming their old erection and privileges, and specifying their Antiquity, and giving them power to hold Borough-Courts, to arrest and imprison, to make Laws and Ordinances, and to elect their own Magistrates yearly, for the good government of the Town. to have a weekly Market on Tuesday and Friday, and three Fairs in the year, one about *Palm Sunday*, another at *Lammas*, and the third at *Martinmas*, each to continue three days. He moreover bestowed on them some Lands about the Town, with the customs and shore-dues, and the power of a Pit and Gallows, and all other privileges granted to any Royal Borough within the Kingdom, exempting them at the same time from sending any Commissioners to Parliament, unless their own necessities requir'd it. And in the year 1536, King *James* the fifth ratified the former Charter, by a new Charter of Confirmation. And in the year 1661, King *Charles* the second, after his Restoration, ratified the former Charters by a Signature under his Royal hand. Whereupon the Parliament at *Edinburgh* confirmed all by their Act; yet with this special provision, *That what was granted to them by that Act, might not prejudice the interest of the Bishop of* Orkney.

Febr. 8

Dated, *White hall, May* 25. *Aug.* 22. 1670.

The Town is govern'd by a Provost, four Bailiffs, and a Common Council, as in other Boroughs.

Church Government. Bishop

The Church of this Country, as also that of *Zetland*, was under the government of one Bishop, stiled the Bishop of *Orkney* and *Zetland*. The Bishop's Revenue was great heretofore, but afterwards did not amount to much more than eight thousand Marks, Chamberlains, and other Officers Fees being paid.

St *Magnu*

The Cathedral Church is St *Magnus's* Church in *Kirkwall*. It was founded (as is thought) by St *Magnus*, King of *Norway*, but afterwards greatly enlarged by some of the pious Bishops of that See. Bishop *Stewart* enlarged it to the east, all above the Grees; and Bishop *Reid*, with three Pillars to the west. It is a very beautiful and stately Structure, built cross-ways, and for the most part free-stone, standing on Pillars, all most curiously vaulted. The three Gates by which they enter into it, are chequer'd with red and white polish'd Stones, embossed and flower'd in an elegant way, and the Steeple is raised to a great height (standing on four stately Pillars) in which is a set of excellent and harmonious Bells. In the year 1670, the Pyramid of the Steeple, being covered with wood, was burnt by Thunder; but, by the industry of Bishop *Mackenzie*, and liberality of some charitable persons, it was again repair'd, and the largest Bell (which had been damaged by the fall it had at the burning of the Steeple) hath been re-founded, and cast again, in *Holland*.

Besides the Cathedral, there are thirty one Churches more in this Country, wherein Divine Service is celebrated, as also a great many ancient Chapels, above an hundred in number, which shews, that the Country was no less anciently, than it is at present, serious in Devotion.

Cathedral

This Diocese had its several ancient Dignities and Privileges for a long time. but these, by the constant trouble that this Country was in by the change of Masters, being lessen'd; Bishop *Robert Reid* made a new erection and foundation, consisting of seven *(a)* Dignities, seven Prebends, thirteen Chaplains or Vicars Choral, one Sacrist, and six Choristers, a particular Account of which we insert, by way of Note.

Mr *Wallace's* Account of the ancient Constitution of the Cathedral of St *Magnus*

(*a*) The chief was a *Provost*, to whom, under the Bishop, the correction and amendment of the Canon, Prebends, and Chaplains was to belong, he had allotted to him the Prebendary of the Holy Trinity, and the Vicaridge of *South Ronaldsha*, with the maintenance of the Kirk of *Bura*. 2. An Arch-Deacon, who was to govern the People according to the disposition of the Canon-law, and to him was allotted the Arch-Deacon's ancient rights, the Vicaridge of *Birsa*, and Chaplainry of St *Ola*, within the Cathedral Kirk of *Kirkwall*, together with the maintenance of the Kirk of *Hare*. 3. A Precentor, who was to rule the Singers in the Quire, and to him were allotted the Prebendary of *Orphir*, and Vicaridge of *Stennis*. 4. A Chancellor, who was to be learned in both Laws, and was bound to read in the Pontifical Law publickly in the Chapter, to all who ought to be present, and to look to the preserving and mending the Books of the Quire and Register, and to keep the common Seal and Key of the Library. to him was allotted the Prebendary of St *Mary* in *Sanda*, and Vicaridge of *Sanda*. 5. A Treasurer, who was to keep the Treasure of the Church, and sacred Vestments; and to have care of the Bread, Wine, Wax, Oyl, and nourishment for the Lights of the Kirk; to him was allotted the Rectory of St *Nicholas* in *Stronsa*, and Vicaridge of *Stronsa*. 6. A Sub dean, who was to supply

Note, to gratify the Curiosity of the Reader

In which condition the Church continued, as long as Popery stood, but the Reformation coming in, and *Robert Stewart*, Earl of *Orkney*, having obtained the Bishoprick from Bishop *Bothwel* (by the exchange of the Abbey of *Holy-Rood House*,) became sole Lord of the Country whereupon, he, and his son Earl *Patrick*, who succeeded him, did in the Church as they pleased

At last, *James Law* being made Bishop of *Orkney*, and the Earldom being united to the Crown (by the death and forfeiture of the aforesaid *Patrick Stewart*,) He, with the consent of his Chapter, made the following Contract with King James the sixth They resign'd to the King and his successors, all their Ecclesiastical Lands and Possessions, with all rights and securities belonging thereto, to be incorporated and united to the Crown, especially, such as should be thought necessary to be united to it And the King gave back, and disponed to the Bishop, several Lands in the Parishes of *Ham*, *Orphir*, *Stromness*, *Sandwick*, *Shapensha*, *Waes*, *Hoy*, St *Ola*, and of *Evie*, *Burra* and *Flotta*, to be a Patrimony to the Bishop and his Successors for ever, together with (*b*) many other Powers, Privileges, and Jurisdictions

This Contract was made *Anno* 1614, And in the year following by an Act dated at *Edinburgh* the 22[d] of *November*, the several Dignities and Ministers, both in the Bishoprick and Earldom, were provided to particular maintenances (besides what they were in possession of before,) payable, by the King and Bishop, to the Ministers in their several bounds respectively

---

supply the place of the Provost in his absence, for the amending of the defects of the Chapter, to him was allotted the Parsonage of *Hoy* and the Vicaridge of *Waes* 7 A Sub-Chantor, who was bound to play upon the Organs each Lord's day, and Festivals, and to supply the place of the Chantor in his absence to him was allotted the Prebendary of St *Colme*

Likewise, he erected seven other Canons and Prebendaries, to wit, 1 The Prebend of *Holy Cross*, to him was given the Parsonage of *Cross-kirk* in *Sanda* he was to be a special Keeper of Holy Things, under the Treasurer, and was to take care of the Clock, and ringing of the Bells at hours appointed, and to take care that the floor of the Kirk was cleanly swept 2 The Prebend of St *Mary*, to whom was given the Chaplainry of St *Mary*, and Vicaridge of *Evie* he was to have the care of the roof and windows of the Cathedral, and to see them amended if need were 3 The Prebend of St *Magnus*, to whom was allotted the Prebendary of St *Magnus* he was to be Confessor of the houshoulds of the Bishop, Provost, Canons and Chaplains, and the Servants in the time of *Easter*, and to administer the Eucharist to them The fourth Prebend was to have the Chaplainry of St *John* the Evangelist, in the said Cathedral Kirk The fifth Prebend was to have the Chaplainry of St *Lawrence* The sixth was to have the Prebendary of St *Catharine* and the seventh Prebend was to have the Prebendary of St *Duthas* To which seven Dignities, and seven Prebendaries, he moreover assigned and allotted (besides the former Kirks, and Titles) the Rents and Revenues of the Parsonages of St *Colme* in *Waes*, and *Holy Cross*, in *Westra*, as also the Vicaridges of the Parish-Churches of *Sandwick* and *Stromness*, with their appurtenances, for their daily distributions

Besides these, he erected thirteen Chaplains to the first was allotted the Chaplainry of St *Peter*, and he was to be Master of the Grammar School To the second was allotted the Chaplainry of St *Augustin*, and he was to be Master of the Singing School The third was to be Stallarius, or the Bishop's Chorister The fourth, the Provost's Chorister The fifth, the Arch Deacon's The sixth, the Precentor's The seventh, the Chancellor's The eighth, the Treasurer's The ninth, the Sub Dean's The tenth, the Prebendary's of *Holy-Cross* The eleventh, the Prebendary's of St *Mary* The twelfth, the Prebendary's of St *Catharine* The thirteenth, the Chaplain's of *Holy Cross* Every one of these Choristers were to have twenty four Meils of Corn, and ten Marks of Money for their Stipend yearly, besides their daily distributions, which were to be raised from the Rents of the Vicaridge of the Cathedral Kirk, and from the foundation of *Thomas*, Bishop of *Orkney*, and of the twelve pounds amortised by King *James* the third, and King *James* the fourth, Kings of *Scotland* The office of which Choristers, was to sing Mass, evening and morning, by turns

To these he added a Sacrist, who was to ring the Bells, and light the Lamps, and carry water and fire into the Church, and to go before the Procession with a white rod, after the manner of a Beadle, and for this, he was to have the accustomed Revenue, together with forty Shillings from the Bishop yearly

Moreover, he ordained six Boys, who were to be Taper bearers, and to sing the responsories and verses in the Quire, as they were to be ordered by the Chantor Of which six Boys, one was to be nominated and maintained by the Bishop The second, by the Prebend of St *Magnus* The third, by the Prebend of St *John* The fourth, by the Prebend of St *Lawrence* The fifth, by the Prebend of St *Catharine* The sixth, by the Prebend of St *Duthas* And every one of them, besides their maintenance, was to have twenty Shillings Scotch, a year

Moreover, to every one of the aforesaid Dignities, Canons, and Prebends, he assigned certain Lands in *Kirkwall* for their Mansions

The Charter of this Erection, is dated at *Kirkwall*, *October* the 28th, *Anno* 1544 And, in the following year, it was confirmed by another Charter, granted by *David Beaton*, Cardinal of St *Stephen* in *Monte Celio*, Presbyter of the Church of *Rome*, and Archbishop of St *Andrews*, having authority so to do It is dated at *Sterling*, the last of *June*, and the eleventh year of Pope *Paul* the third, and was confirmed by Queen *Mary* at *Edinburgh*, the last of *April*, *Anno Regni* 13

(*b*) Disponing to him and his Successors, the right of patronage to all the Vicaridges of *Orkney* and *Zetland*, with power to Present qualified Ministers as oft as any Kirk shall be vacant Disponing also to them the heritable and perpetual right and jurisdiction of Sheriffship and Bailiffry within the Bishoprick and Patrimony thereof, and exempting the Inhabitants and Vassals of the Bishoprick, in all causes, civil and criminal, from the jurisdiction of the Sheriffs and Stewards of the Earldom As also, he disponed to the Bishop and his Successors, the Commissariot of *Orkney* and *Zetland*, with power to constitute and ordain Commissaries, Clerks, and other members of Court In which contract, it was moreover agreed, that the Minister of *South Ronalsha*, Dean, the Minister of *Birsa*, Arch Deacon, the Minister of *Lady-Kirk* in *Sanda*, Chancellor, the Minister of *Stronsa*, Treasurer, and the Parson of *Westra*, should be a sufficient Chapter And that their consents should be as available for any deed to be done by the Bishops of *Orkney*, as the fullest Chapter of any Cathedral Kirk within the Kingdom

Thus

Thus far of the *present* State of the Isles of *Orkney*; the *Antiquities* which have been observ'd in them, are as follow

Their Antiquities; from the same Author. Dwarfie-Stone

There is in *Hoy*, lying between two Hills, a Stone called the *Dwarfie Stone*, thirty six foot long, eighteen foot broad, and nine foot thick; hollowed within by the hand of some Mason, (for the prints of the Mason's Irons are to be seen on it to this hour) with a square hole of about two foot high for the entry; and a stone proportionable, standing before it for the door. Within it, at one end, is a Bed excellently hewen out of the stone, with a Pillow, wherein two men may conveniently lie at their full length; at the other end is a Couch, and in the middle a hearth for a fire, with a round hole cut out above, for the chimney. It is thought to be the residence of some melancholy Hermit but the vulgar Legend says, there was once a famous Giant residing in that Island, who, with his wife, lived in that same Stone, as their Castle.

Wart hill

At the west-end of that Stone stands an exceeding high Mountain of a steep ascent, call'd *The Wart hill of Hoy*. Near the top of which, in the Months of *May*, *June*, and *July*, about mid-day, is seen something that shines and sparkles in a suprizing manner, and which may be discerned a great way off. It hath formerly shined more brightly than it does now but what that is (though many have climbed up the hill, and attempted to search for it) none could ever find. The vulgar talk of it as some inchanted Carbuncle, but I rather take it to be some water, sliding down the face of a smooth rock, and when the Sun, at such a time, shines upon it, the reflection causeth that wonderful shining.

Stennis Rounds, probably Heathen Temples

At *Stenms*, where the Loch is narrowest, in the middle, having a Causey of Stones over it for a bridge, there is, at the south-end of the bridge, a Round, set about with high smooth stones or flags (without any engraving) about twenty foot high above-ground, six foot broad, and a foot or two thick. Between that Round and the Bridge, are two Stones standing, of the same largeness with the rest; whereof one hath a round hole in the midst. And at the other end of the Bridge, about half a mile removed from it, is a larger Round, about an hundred and ten paces diameter, set about, with such Stones as the former, only some of them are fallen down. And both to the East and West of this bigger round, are two green Mounts, artificial as is thought. Both these Rounds are ditched about. Some conceive, that these Rounds have been places wherein two opposite Armies encamped; but others more probably think, that they were the High places in the Pagan times, whereon Sacrifices were offered; and that these two Mounts were the places where the Ashes of the Sacrifices were flung. And this is the more probable, because *Boethius*, in the life of *Mainus*, King of Scots, makes mention of that kind of high Stones; calling them the Temples of the Gods. His words are these, *In memory of what King* Mainus *ordained concerning the worship of the Gods, there remain yet in our days many huge Stones, drawn together in form of a Circle, and named by the people*, The ancient Temples of the Gods; *and it raises no small admiration, to consider, by what art or strength such huge Stones have been brought together.*

Obelisks

You will find besides, in many other places of this Country, *Obelisks*, or hugh high Stones, set in the ground like the former, and standing apart, and indeed they are so large, that whoever sees them, must wonder by what Engines they have been erected. These are thought to have been set up either as a Memorial of some famous battle, or as a Monument of some remarkable person who has been buried there, that way of honouring deserving and valiant men, being the invention of King *Routha*, as *Boethius* says.

Camps of Jupiter Fring

There is in *Rousay*, amidst high mountains, a place called *The Camps of Jupiter Fring*: the name is strange, and should import some notable accident, but what it was I have not been able to learn.

Street, with figured Stones

At the West end of the *Main-land*, near *Skeall*, on the top of high rocks, above a quarter of a mile in length, there is something like a Street, all set in red clay, with a sort of reddish Stones of several figures and magnitudes; having the images and representations of several things, as it were engraven upon them. *And which is very strange, most of* these Stones, when they are raised up, have that same image engraven under, which they had above. That they are so figured by art, is not probable; nor can the reason of nature's way, in their engraving, be readily given.

Burying Places

In the Links of *Skeall*, where Sand is blown away with the wind, are found several places built quadrangularly, about a foot square, surrounded with Stones well-cemented together, and a Stone lying in the mouth; having some black earth in them. The like of which are found in the Links of *Roussum* in *Stronsa*, where also is a very remarkable Monument. It is a whole round stone like a barrel, hollow within, and sharp edged at the top, having the bottom joyn'd like the bottom of a barrel. On the mouth, was a round stone, answerable to the mouth of the Monument, and above that, a large stone for the preservation of the whole. within was nothing but red clay and burnt bones; which was sent to Sir *Robert Sibbald*, but the Monument it self was broken in pieces, as they were taking it from its seat. It is like, that this, as also the other four square Monuments, have been some of those antient Urns, wherein the Romans, when they were in this country, laid up the ashes of their dead.

Likewise in the Links of *Tranabie* in *Westra*, have been found graves in the sand (after the sand hath been blown away by the wind,) in one of which was seen a man lying with his sword on the one hand, and a Danish ax on the other. and some; who have had dogs, and combs, and knives, buried with them. This seems to be an instance of the way, in which the *Danes* (when they were in this country) buried their dead; as the former was of the Roman manner. Beside, in many places of the country, are found little hillocks, which may be supposed to be the Sepulchres of the antient *Peights*. For *Tacitus* tells us, that it was the way of the antient Romans, and *Verstegan*, that it was the way of the ancient Germans and Saxons, to lay dead bodies on the ground, and cover them over with turfs and clods of earth, in the fashion of a little hillock. Hence it seems, that the many houses and villages in this country which are called by the name of *Brogh*, and which are all built upon or beside some such hillock, have been cemeteries for the burying of the dead in the time of the Pights and Saxons. for the word *Brogh* in the Teutonick Language, signifies a *burying-place*

In one of these Hillocks, near the circle of high Stones, at the North end of the bridge of *Stennis*, there were found nine *Fibulæ* of Silver, of the shape of a Horse-shoe; but round.

Ruins of ancient Buildings. Pight houses Moreover, in many places, are to be seen the ruins and vestigia of great, but antique, buildings, most of them now covered with earth, and called *Pight-houses*; some of which, it is like, have been the forts and residences of the *Pights* or *Danes*, when they possess'd this country

Copprow-Castle Among the rest, there is one in the Isle of *Wyre*, called *The Castle of Cubberow* (or rather *Copptrow*, which, in the Teutonick Language, signifies *a tower of security from outward violence*) It is trenched about but nothing now remains, besides the first story. It is a perfect square, and the wall is eight foot thick, and strongly built, and cemented with lime The breadth or length within the walls is not above ten foot, having a large door and a small slit for the window Of this *Cubbirow*, the common people report many idle fables, not fit to be inserted here

Unusual Fires and Lights Evie In the Parish of *Evie*, near the Sea, are some small hillocks, which frequently, in the night time, appear all in a fire Likewise, the Kirk St *Nicholas* of *Evie*, called St *Nicholas*, is seen full of lights, as if torches or candles were burning in it all night. This amazes the people greatly, but possibly it is nothing but some thick glutinous meteor, that receives that light in the Night-time

Superstition about Iron Less At the *Noup-head*, in *Westra*, is a rock surrounded with the Sea, called *Less*; which, the Inhabitants of that Isle tell you, has this strange property, that if a man go upon it, having any Iron about him (if it were but an Iron nail in his shoe) the Sea will instantly swell in such a tempestuous way, that no boat can come near to take him off; and that the Sea will not be settled, till the piece of Iron be flung into it A [b] person, being there to make an experiment of it, offered a Reward to a poor man to go upon the rock with a peice of Iron, but he would not do it on any terms

[b] Mr *Wallace*

Sometimes, about this country; are seen those men, which are called *Finnmen* In the year 1682, one was seen, sometime sailing, sometime rowing in his little boat, at the South-end of the Isles of *Eda* most of the people of the Isle flocked to see him, and when they adventured to put out a boat with men, to try if they could apprehend him, he presently fled away, with great speed And in the year 1684, another was seen from *Westra*, and, for a while after they caught few or no fish for they have this remark here, that the *Finnmen* drive away the fish from the place to which they come These *Finnmen* seem to be some of the People that dwell about the *Fretum Davis*, a full account of whom may be seen in *The natural and moral History of the Antilles* One of their boats, sent from *Orkney* to *Edinburgh*, is to be seen in the Physicians hall, with the oar, and the dart that he makes use of for killing of fish] Finn-men Chap 18

As for the Earls of *Orkney*, not to mention the more ancient ones, who also held the Earldom of Cathness and Strathern by inheritance; this title did at last by an heir female descend to *William de Sentcler*, and *William*, the fourth Earl of that Family, sirnam'd *the Prodigal*, who run out his estate, and was the last Earl of the family Yet his posterity have enjoy'd the honour of Barons *Sentcler*, till [i] this time, and [i] the title of *Cathness* also remains at this day, in the posterity of his brother But as for the honourable title of Earl of *Orkney*, it was [k], together with the title of Lord of *Shetland*, conferr'd upon *Robert*, a natural son of King James the fifth, which his son *Patrick Steward* [l] forfeited for Treason Earls of Orkney

[i] Anno 1607 [k] In our time, C [l] Enjoys at this day, C.

[In our time, the title of Earl of *Orkney* hath been conferr'd upon Lord *George Hamilton*, Son of *William* Duke of *Hamilton*, on account, as well of his high Birth, as his signal Services to the Crown in the Wars of *Ireland* and *Flanders*]

[The *THULE* of the ANCIENTS.]

The Fortunate Islands

EYOND the *Orcades*, and above Britain, the old Scholiast upon Horace places the *Fortunate Isles*, which none but pious and just men are said to inhabit; a Place, celebrated by the Greek Poets for its pleasantness and fertility, and call'd by them the *Elysian Fields* But take another account of these Isles from Isacius Tzetzes, a fabulous Greek, in his Notes upon Lycophron *In the Ocean, is a British Island, between the west of Britain, and Thule towards the east Thither (they say) the souls of the dead are transported For on the shore of that Sea within which Britain lieth, there dwell certain fishermen, who are subject to the French, but accountable for no tribute, because (as they say) they ferry over the souls of the deceas'd These fishermen return home, and sleep in the evenings; but a little after, hear a rapping at their doors, and a voice calling them to their work Upon that they presently rise and go to the shore, without any other business, and find boats ready for them, but none of their own, and no body in them, yet when they come on board and fall to their oars, they find the boats as heavy as if they were laden with men, though they see none After one pull, they presently arrive at that* British Island; *which at other times, in Ships of their own, they hardly reach in a day and a night When they come to land in the Island, they see no body, but hear the voice of those who receive their passengers, counting them by the stock of Father and Mother, and calling them singly according to the title of their Dignity, Employment, and Name After they have unladed, they return back with one stroke From hence, many take these to be the* Islands of the Blessed That of the poetical Geographer, mention'd by Muretus in his Various readings, is much of the same stamp, *viz* that *C Julius Cæsar* sail'd thither in a [a] great Gally with a hundred men on board, and was so much taken with the pleasantness of the place, that he would have settled there, but was thrust out by certain invisible Inhabitants, much against his will

[a] Trir. mi

Thule

Solinus places *Thule* at five days sail from Orkney An Island, very much celebrated by the Poets, who (as if it were the remotest part of the world) always use it to express a very great distance Hence Virgil,

—— *Tibi serviat ultima Thule*

Let utmost *Thule* own your boundless pow'r

Seneca,

—— *Terrarum ultima Thule*.

Thule, thou utmost of the spacious earth.

Juvenal,

—*De conducendo loquitur jam Rhetore Thule*

Nay, *Thule's* self now courts her Orator

Claudian,

—*Thulem procul axe remotam*

Thule far distant from the Pole ——

And in another place,

——— *Ratibusque impervia Thule*

And *Thule* where no Ship durst ever steer

Statius,

—— *Ignotam vincere Thulen*

To conquer *Thule* scarce yet known to Fame.

And Ammianus Marcellinus uses this Adage, *Etiamsi apud Thulem moraretur*, i e *Tho' his stay were at Thule*, not to mention many others But one thing I must observe, that Statius in these Verses, uses *Thule* for Britain

Thule used for Britain

Cærulus haud aliter cum dimicat incola Thules,
Agmina falcifero circumvenit arta covino

Thus purple *Thulians* when to war they go,
In Chariots arm'd with Scythes surround the foe

Also in his *Sylvæ*,

——— *Refluo circumsona gurgite Thule*

And *Thule* sounding with the neighbouring tide

Suidas says, it took the name from *Thule*, a King of Egypt; Isidore, from the *Sun*; Reynerus Reineccius, from the Saxon word *Tell*, *a limit*, as if it were the *bound* or *limit* of the north and west But Sinesius makes it a question, whether there is any such place as *Thule*; and our Giraldus says, that if there be such a place, it is not yet discover'd; and as for the learned, they vary in their Opinions about it Many have thought *Iseland* (condemn'd to a cold Climate, and continual Winter) to be the *Thule* of the ancients. But Saxo Grammaticus, Crantzius, Milius, Jovius, and Peucerus, are of a contrary opinion I know, Procopius has describ'd that vast Country of *Scandia*, under the name of *Thule* But if that of the learned *Gaspar Peucerus*, in his Book *De Terra Dimensione*, be true, that Schetland is by the Seamen call'd *Thilensell* (and I know no reason to except against his testimony) *Thule* is undoubtedly discover'd, and the Controversie at an end For this *Schetland* is an Island belonging to the Scots, encompass'd with others of less note; extremely cold, and expos'd on all hands to storms; where the Inhabitants like those of *Iseland* use fish dried and pounded, for Bread. And though the north-Pole is not so elevated here, that it has Day continually for six Months together, as Pithæas of Marseilles has falsly said of *Thule* (for which he is justly reprehended by Strabo, for this is not the case of *Iseland* it self, where cold and winter are perpetual, and the cold scarce to be endur'd,) yet, that *Schetland* is the same with *Thule*, we may believe, First, from the situation of it in Ptolemy for *Thule* is plac'd in the sixty third degree from the Æquinoctial by Ptolemy, and so is Schetland Again, it lies between *Scotland* and *Norway*, where Saxo Grammaticus places *Thule*, as but two days sail from the point of *Cathness*, in which Distance Solinus also places it And Tacitus says that the Romans spy'd it afar off, as they sail'd by the *Orcades* in their voyage round Britain Lastly, it faces the coast of *Bergæ* in Norway, and so lay *Thule*, according to Pomponius Mela, in which author the text is corruptly *Belgarum littori*, instead of *Bergarum littori* For *Bergæ*, a City in Norway, lies over against *Shetland*, and Pliny makes *Bergos* to be in this tract, which I take to be the small Country wherein *Bergæ* is seated, as none will deny that Norway is Pliny's *Nerigon*

Lib ii Bell. Gothici

Schetland

call'd by some Hethland

Thus much may suffice concerning *Thule*, which is hid from us, as well as it was from the ancients, *by Snow and Winter*, as a certain Author expresses it Neither was any of them able to say, which of the Northern Isles they meant, when they talk'd of *Thule* As for the length of the Days in that unknown Island, *Festus Avienus*, where he treats of Britain, translates these Verses out of *Dionysius* concerning it

Longa dehinc celeri si quis rate marmora currat,
Inveniet vasto surgentem gurgite Thulen,
Hic cum plaustra poli tang . Phœbeius ignis,
Nocte sub inlustri [illegible] flagrat
Continuo, clarumque diem nox æmula ducit

Hence urge your course along the watry road,
You'll come where *Thule* swells above the flood
Here *Sol's* bright wheels, when near the Northern Pole,
They cut their way, still [illegible] as they rowl
Not here vain men expect the Light's return
But every Night's a rival of the Morn

Pompo

Pomponius Mela hath made the same remark. *Over-against the coast of the* ᵃ Belgæ, *lies* Thule, *an Island much celebrated both by the Greek Poets and by ours, by reason the days are very long there, and the nights very short Though in winter the nights are dark as in other places, they are light in summer, for though the face of the Sun be not seen, the Sun is so much above the horizon, that his light is clearly visible During the* Solstice, *there is no night at all, for the Sun being then higher, not only it's light but the greatest part of it's body is visible*

Bergæ.

[As for *Shetland*, (suppos'd before to be the ancient *Thule*) the nearest part of it is some fourscore miles from *Orkney*, and the Sea between them is very turbulent and stormy Of those that are properly called Isles, there are about forty six, with forty Holms, and thirty Rocks, all which go under the general name of *Shetland*, though each of them has also its particular name About twenty six are inhabited, others (though large enough) are only made use of for feeding of Cattle Many of the Gentry came from Scotland, and settled here but the common people that are natives, are descended from the *Norvegians*, and commonly speak a corrupt Norse tongue, called *Norn* They are generally healthful, living commonly to five, six, or sevenscore years of age There are several *Obelisks* still standing, and many old Fabricks, which are said to have been built by the Picts They are in the fashion of Pyramids, with a winding pair of stairs within, to the top Under them, they had Cells all vaulted over, and from the top of them they made a sign by fire, when there was any imminent danger The ground is clean, and the Soil naturally inclines to a sandy clay The Product of the Country, is mainly *fish, butter, oyl, wool, feathers, beef, tallow, hides, stuff, stockings*, with *woollen gloves*, and *garters* There have been seen at one time in *Brassay*-sound, fifteen hundred sail of Hollanders After *Fara* (an Island lying in the mid-way between *Orkney* and *Shetland*,) the first that appears is called *Main land*, of which we have treated before

Fara

The Country belongs to the Crown of Scotland, being part of the Stewartry of Orknay, and govern'd either by the Stewart or his Deputy They have one Presbytery, which meets at *Scalloway*]

The Sea above these Islands, is term'd the *slow, frozen*, and *icy* Sea, and is rough and almost unnavigable by reason of great flakes of Ice It was also call'd *Cronium*, from Saturn, for the Ancients had a notion (as Plutarch writes) that Saturn was kept sleeping in a deep cave of Pumice stone in some Brittish Island hereabouts, that *Jupiter* had thrown him into a deep sleep, which serv'd instead of fetters, that the Birds brought him Ambrosia, which was so fragrant that all the place was perfum'd with it, and that many Spirits were here in attendance on him, by whom he was serv'd with great diligence and respect This Fable, if I mistake not, points at the veins of metal (over which Saturn presided,) that lie in these Islands, and are useless only for want of wood to supply Furnaces

The Icy Sea, or Cronium

Saturn a Prisoner hereabouts

[A

DISCOURSE

Concerning the

THULE of the ANCIENTS.

By Sir *Robert Sibbald*

THERE is no place oftner mention'd by the Ancients, than *Thule*, and yet it is much controverted what place it was some have attempted the discovery of it, but have gone wide of the marks which the Ancients left concerning it, yet they seem all to agree that is was some place towards the North, and very many make it to be one of the *British* Isles and since *Conradus Celtes* says, it is encompass'd with the *Orkney Isles*, it will not be amiss to subjoyn to the foregoing description of *Orkney*, this Essay concerning it

Some derive the name *Thule*, from the Arabick word *Tule*, which signifies *Far off*, and, as it were with allusion to this the Poets usually call it *ultima Thule*, but I rather prefer the reason of the name given by the learned Bochartus, who makes it to be *Phœnician*, and affirms, that it signifies, *darkness* in that language, Thule *in the Tyrian language, was a Shadow; whence it is commonly used to signifie* Darkness, *and the* Island Thule, *is as much as an Island of* Darkness, *which name how exactly it agrees to the Island so called at the utmost point of the north, is known to every body* Hence Tibullus, speaking [illegible] of the Frigid Zone, hath this,

Thule in the North

[illegible] 40

Illic & densa tellus absconditur umbra,

And there the Earth is hid in a dark shade

And these places of *Homer* [illegible] *Darkness*, and [illegible] *Neque enim scimus ubi sit caligo, Darkness*, [illegible] Strabo interpreted, *Nescimus ubi sit* [illegible] of the *North*, We know not where the [illegible] And consonant to this, Statius,

Vel super Hesperiæ vada caligantia Thules,

Or the dark Fords of the Hesperian Thule

And,

[illegible]

——*aut Nigræ Littora Thules*

——Or shores of the black Thule

And indeed, this derivation of the word carries more reason than any other they give, and is an evident proof, that the Ancients agreed in placing their *Thule* towards the *North* We shall see next what Northern Country they pitched on for it

Thule, one of the British Isles

The Ancients seem most to agree, that *Thule* was one of those Isles that are called *British* Strabo one of the most ancient, and best Geographers extant, speaks thus, *Pytheas Massiliensis says, it is about Thule, the furthest north of all the British Isles* Yet he himself maketh it nearer than *Pytheas* did; *But I think* (says he) *that northern bound to be much nearer to the South for they who survey that part of the Globe, can give no account beyond* Ireland, *an Isle which lies not far towards the North, before Britain, inhabited by wild People, almost starved with cold there, therefore, I am of opinion, the* utmost bound *is to be plac'd* So that in his opinion, that which he calls *Ireland*, must be *Thule*

Ad Furium

Catullus seems to be of the same mind, in these Verses,

Sive trans altas
Gradietur Alpes,
Cæsaris visens
Monumenta Magni,
Gallicum Rhenum,
Horribilesque &
Ultimos Britannos

Whether he o'er the *Alps* his way pursue,
The mighty *Cæsar's* Monuments to view,
As *Gallique Rhine* and *Britons* that excel
In fierceness, who on the *Earth's limits* dwell

Carm lib i Ode 35

And *Horace*,

Serves iturum Cæsarem
In ultimos orbis Britannos

Preserve thou *Cæsar* safe, we thee implore,
Bound to the World's remotest *Briton's* shore

Lib i

And *Silius Italicus*, in these Verses,

Cærulus haud aliter cum dimicat Incola Thules,
Agmina falcifero circumvenit acta covino

As *Thule's* blue inhabitants surround
Their Foes with Chariots hook'd, and them confound.

For it appears from Cæsar's Commentaries, that the *bluish* colour, and the fighting out of the hooked *Chariots*, were in use among the Inhabitants of *Britain* *Pliny* likewise seems to be of this Opinion; for he treats of *Thule* in the same Chapter where he treats of the British Isles and *Tacitus* says when the Roman Navy sail'd about Britain, *despecta est & Thule*, They saw *Thule* also

In Vit Agric

Ireland

Ireland, properly so called, was the first of the British Isles which got the name *Thule*, as being the first that the *Carthaginians* met with, as they steer'd their course from *Cadiz* to the West And hence it is that *Statius* calls *Thule*, *Hesperia*.

Ad Claud Uxorem.

——*Et si gelidas irem mansurus ad Arctos,*
Vel super Hesperia vada caligantia Thules.

I

If I in the cold North go to abide,
Or on dark Seas which Western *Thule* hide

And it seems to be the same, that is said by *Aristotle* to have been discovered by the *Carthaginians*, where he speaks thus, *Beyond Hercules's Pillars, they say the Carthaginians found a fertil island uninhabited, abounding with wood, and navigable Rivers, and stored with very great plenty of* [t] *Fruits of all sorts, distant several days voyage from the Continent* And *Bochartus* confirms this by what he observes, that an ancient Author, *Antonius Diogenes*, who wrote twenty four Books of the strange things related of *Thule* not long after the time of *Alexander* the Great, had his History from the *Cipars* Tables, dug at *Tyrus* out of the Tombs of *Mantinia* and *Dercilis*, who had gone from *Tyrus* to *Thule*, and had staid some time there

De mirab. Auscult

[t] Fructibus

But though this be the first *Thule* discover'd by the *Carthaginians*, yet it is not that mention'd by the Roman writers, for they speak of the *Thule* which the Romans were in, and made conquest of but it is certain they never were in *Ireland*, properly so call'd That they were in *Thule*, appears from these Verses of *Statius*,

The Romans were in Thule

Lib v Protrept ad Crisp

——*Tu disce patrem, quantusque nigrantem*
Fluctibus occiduis, fessoque Hyperione Thulen
Intrârit, mandata gerens

Learn from thy sight, how glorious he was,
When he did with the Senate's order pass
O're to dark *Thule*, in that Ocean, west,
Where *Phœbus* gives his weary horses rest

Now the Father of *Crispinus*, to whom he writes, was *Bolanus*; the same *Vectius Bolanus*, who was governour of *Britain* under *Vitellius*, (as *Tacitus* informs us,) which is yet more clearly proved by the following Verses of the same Poet

Vit Agric

Quod si te Magno, tellus frenata parente
Accipiat ———
Quanta Caledonios *attollet gloria campos,*
Cum tibi Longævus referet trucis incola terræ,
Hic suetus dare jura parens, hoc cespite turmas
Affari nitidas speculas, castellaque longe
Aspicis ille dedit, cinxitque hæc mœnia fossa
Belligeris, hæc dona Deis, hæc tela dicavit,
Cernis adhuc titulos Hunc ipse vacantibus armis
Induit, hunc Regi rapuit thoraca Britanno

If thou received be by that far land,
Subdued by thy conquering Father's hand;
What glory will it be, when thou hear'st tell,
By old fierce *Scots*, in *Caledon* that dwell,
How in this place, thy Sire us'd to give law,
How there the Troops they him haranguing saw,

And

And point out Towers and Castles through the Land,
Which all erected were by his command
These walls he with a ditch did round enclose,
And to the Gods he consecrated those;
These weapons, he did also dedicate,
As the Inscriptions, to be seen, relate
This Corslet, he, in time of peace put on;
And this, he from the *British King* had won.

The words *Caledonios*, and *Trucis incola Terræ*, do clearly shew, that by *Thule*, is meant the North part of *Britain*; which was then possess'd by the *Pights*, design'd by the name *Caledonios*, and by the *Scots* design'd by *Trucis Incola Terræ* The same epithet, that *Claudian* gives to the *Scots*, in these Verses,

Thule, in the *North*-part of Britain

Venit & extremis legio prætenta Britannis,
Quæ Scoto *dat fræna truci*

That Legion also, sent fierce *Scots* to tame

And of this North part of *Britain*, that Verse of *Juvenal* is likewise to be understood,

De conducendo loquitur jam Rhetore Thule.

The best exposition of which, is taken from *Tacitus*, "*Jam vero principum filios, liberalibus* "*artibus erudire, & ingenia* Britannorum *studiis* "Gallorum *anteferre, ut qui modo linguam* Ro-"manam *abnuebant, eloquentiam concupiscerent*," &c Thus render'd by Sir *Henry Savil*. "Moreover, the nobleman's sons he took and instructed in the liberal Sciences, preferring the wits of the *Britons* before the Students of *France*, as being now curious to attain the *Eloquence* of the Roman Language, whereas they lately rejected the *Speech*" After that, Our attire grew to be in account, and the *Gown* much used among them

Vit Agric

Claudian does yet more particularly give the name of *Thule* to the North part of Britain, while he speaks of the great exploits done there by *Theodosius*, the father of *Theodosius* the Emperor, and Grand father of *Arcadius* and *Honorius*

De 3 Consul Honor

Facta tui numeravit avi quem littus adustæ
Horrescit Libyæ, ratibusque impervia Thule;
Ille leves Mauros, nec falso nomine Pictos
Edomuit, Scotumque *vago mucrone secutus*,
Fregit Hyperboreas remis audacibus undas,
Et geminis fulgens utroque sub axe tropheis,
Tithyos alterna refluas calcavit arenas.

He did the deeds of thy Grand father tell,
Before whose face the Tawny-Moor grew pale
And *Thule*, where no Ships could ever sail,
He tam'd the nimble Moors, and painted Pights,
With brandish'd Swords the *Scots* close he pursu'd,
And with bold Oars their Northern Seas he broke
His Trophies thus under both Poles he plac'd,
Where e're the Ocean either ebb'd or flow'd

And in these Lines.

Ille Caledoniis posuit qui castra pruinis,
Qui medio Libyæ sub Casside pertulit æstus
Terribilis Mauro, debellatorque Britanni
Littoris, ac pariter Boreæ vastator & Austri,
Quid riger æternus Cœli? quid sidera prosunt?
Ignotumque fretum? Maduerunt Saxone fuso
Orcades; incaluit Pictorum sanguine Thule,
Scotorum cumulos flevit glacialis Ierne.

In *Caledonian* frosts his tents he pitch'd,
And *Libya's* scorching heat endur'd in field,
The coal-black Moors, and British shore he tam'd,
Thus forcing both the South and North to yield,
What then avail'd, cold clime, strange Seas and Stars?
When *Orkney* Isles he dy'd with Saxon gore,
Then *Thule* with the Pictish blood grew hot,
Icy *Stratbern* bemoan'd huge heaps of Scots.

Where, by placing the Moors and Britains as the *remotest* People then known, and mentioning the Scots and Pights as the Inhabitants of *Thule* and *Ierne*, he demonstrates clearly, that *Thule* is the North part of the Isle of *Britain*, inhabited by the Scots and Pights. For this *Ierne*, or as some read it *Hyberne*, can no way be understood of *Ireland*, properly so call'd; First, because *Ireland* can never deserve the Epithet *Glacialis*, since by the testimony of the Irish writers, the Snow and Ice continue not any time there: Secondly, the Romans were never in *Ireland*; whereas, according to the forementioned Verses, *Theodosius* past our Firths of *Forth* and *Clide*, call'd by him *Hyperboreæ undæ*, and entered *Stratbern*, which to this day bears the name *Ierne*, in which Roman *Medals* are found, and the Roman *Camps* and *Military ways* are to be seen, the undoubted testimonies of their being there; and therefore is so to be understood in the same Poet's lines upon *Stilico*, who was employ'd in the British wars.

Ierne, not *Ireland*, properly so called

Me quoque vicinis pereuntem gentibus inquit,
Munivit Stilico, totam cum Scotus Iernem
Movit, & infesto spumavit remige Thetis,
Illius effectum curis, ne bella timerem
Scotica, nec Pictum tremerem

Me

Me to ill neighbours long a prey expos'd
With safety now hath *Stilico* enclos'd,
While that the Scots did all *Ierne* raise,
And *Forth* and *Clide* with hostile rowers foam'd,
By his great care it came to pass, that I
Fear'd neither Scot nor Pight. ———

Now *Thetis* in these Verses, and the *Undæ Hyperboreæ* in the Verses before mention'd, cannot be understood of the Sea between *Scotland* and *Ireland* for *Ireland* lies to the *South* of the Roman Province; and the situation of the Scots and Pights Country is to the *North* of it For it was separated by the two Firths of *Forth* and *Clide*, from the Roman province; which clearly shows, it was to be understood of them the same thing that is also imported by the words *Hyperboreas Undas*, and *Remis*; for these cannot be understood of the Irish Sea, which is to the south of the Roman Province, and is very tempestuous, and cannot so well be past by Oars as the Firths of *Forth* and *Clide* But the same Poet has put this beyond all doubt, in these Verses,

Venit & extremis legio prætenta Britannis,
Quæ Scoto dat fræna truci, ferroque notatas
Perlegit exanimes Picto moriente figuras

Hither the Legion came, in garrison oppos'd
To utmost *Britons*, bridling the fierce *Scot*,
And saw the *Pighs*, whose bodies are mark'd o'er
With various figures, dying in their gore

For were it to be understood of the *Irish* Sea, then the Wall and the *Prætenturæ* should have been plac'd upon the *Scottish* shore, that was over against *Ireland*; whereas they were placed over against that Country which is call'd *Strathern* now, and is the true *Ierne*, not only mention'd by *Claudian*, but likewise by *Juvenal*, in these Verses,

——— *Arma quid ultra*
Littora Juverna promovimus, & modo captas
Orcadas, & minima contentos nocte Britannos?

What though the *Orcades* have own'd our Power,
What tho' *Juverna*'s tam'd, and Britain's shore,
That boasts the shortest night? ———

Where he directs us to the situation of the Country of the *Scots* and *Pighs*. *Juverna* was the Country of the *Scots*, which had been over run in part by *Julius Agricola*, Governour of *Britain* under *Domitian* the Emperor, who first enter'd the *Orcades*; and, as *Tacitus* observes, (*Despecta Thule*,) he saw the North part of the Country beyond *Ierne*, which is the Country of the *Pighs*, lies to the North of the Firth of *Forth*, and upon the German Sea, and is design'd in these words, *minima contentos nocte Britannos*, which particularly relate to *Ross* and *Caithness* And the Inhabitants of *Juverna* and *Thule*, are the very same that the Panegyrist *Eumenius* speaks of, in his Oration to *Constantine* the Great; where he saith, that the Nation of *Britain*, in the time of *Cæsar*, was *rudis & soli Britanni Pictis modo & Hibernis assueta hostibus seminudis*; Had not been us'd to war, but only with the People of the British Soil, the *Pighs* and the Irish who (for their loose and short garments) may be called *half naked*

These were called *Hiberni*, as being at first a Colony from *Ireland*; and as possessing that tract of the Isle of *Britain*, which is called by the ancient writers *Ierne glacialis*, and *Ierne* simply, and by the writers of the middle age *Hibernia*; as you may see in the Roman Martyrology, at *S Becanus*, Bishop of *Aberdeen*, in *Ireland* Now never any Irish writer could yet say, that in *Ireland*, properly so call'd, there was a town called *Aberdeen*, or a river call'd *Don*

Why the West part of *Scotland* call'd *Hibernia*

And that this part of *Britain*, then possess'd by the *Scots*, was called *Hibernia*, is clear from the testimony of Venerable *Bede*, who calls it *Hibernia*, in the beginning of the Chapter, and in the next page, calls the same Country *Scotia*

Eccl Hist L iv c 6

It is certain, that as the wall betwixt *Tine* and *Solway* Firth called *Murus Picticus*, was built to exclude the *Pighs*, so was that betwixt *Edinburgh* and *Dumbarton* Firth, to exclude the *Scots Highlanders*, and was design'd first by *Agricola*, as appears by *Tacitus*, where he saith, "*Nam Glotta & Bodot ia diversi maris æstu per*-" *immensum revecti, angusto terrarum spatio diri*-" *muntur, quod tum præsidiis firmabatur, summo*-" *tis velut in aliam insulam hostibus* That is, "For *Clide* and *Forth*, two arms of two contrary Seas, shooting mightly into the land, were only divided by a narrow partition of ground, which passage was then guarded and fortified with garrisons and castles, so that the Romans were absolute Lords of all on this side, having cast out the enemy, as it were, into *another* Island" And indeed, as *Tacitus* remarks, *Inventus in ipsa* Britannia *terminus*, i e a boundary was found in Britain it self, for the Romans made this the utmost limit of their Province, and gave the name *Britain* to that part of the Island within the Roman wall, which wall was built on this narrow neck of ground, between the two Firths, where the Legion, mention'd above, lay

Agric

Pag 1250

And hence it is, that Venerable *Bede* calls these People who dwelt beyond the wall, *Transmarinæ Gentes*, but explains himself thus, *Now, we call them* Transmarine Nations, *not because they are out of Britain*; *but because they are in some sense divided from it*; *two Arms of the Sea, one from the East, and the other from the West, breaking in a long way into the Land, on each side* And a little before this, he tells us, who these *Transmarinæ Gentes* were; *viz. Scotorum à Circio*, that is, the *Scots* from the *North-west*, and *Pictorum ab Aquilone*, the *Pighs* from the *North*, which relates to that part of the Isle without the *Roman* Province · for *Ireland*, properly so called, cannot be said to lie to the *North-west* of the *Roman* Province

Lib 1 c 12

Now we will endeavour to shew, that what *Juvenal* saith in these Verses before mentioned,

——— *Arma*

——— *Arma quid ultra*
Littora Juvernæ promovimus, &c

is to be meant of that part which is now call'd *Stratbern*, and the rest of *Pearthshire*, and the *West Highlands*; the Country of the *Scots*, design'd by *Bede*, *à Circio*, which are truly so situate in respect of the *Roman* Province And this we will make out from what we meet with in *Tacitus* For first, he saith, *The third year's expedition discover'd People they were not before acquainted with, having over-run all them that were on this side* Tay, which he describes to be a *Firth* It appears by this, that they were other People than those he had to do with before, because they are call'd *Novæ Gentes* In the next place, he says, The fourth Summer was spent in taking possession of what they had over run And he observes in that Expedition, that the small *Isthmus*, or neck of land, that kept *Clyde* and *Forth* from meeting, was secured by garrisons, *summotis velut in aliam insulam hostibus*, by this means the enemy were removed, as it were, into another Isle

Vit Agric

Now, whoever will compare what we observed out of *Bede*, of the *Gentes Transmarinæ* beyond these two Firths, will see clearly, that these *Novæ Gentes* were the *Scots* and the *Pights*; the *Scots*, in the Country towards the North west, and the *Pights*, in the Country North-east. But this is yet more confirm'd by the account that is given by *Tacitus*, of the action in the sixth Summer of *Agricola's* Government, (*Ampla civitate trans Bodotrium sita*, Being inform'd of a great People that dwelt beyond *Forth*) now, *Civitate* being in the singular, makes it understood of the People that lie nearest, that is, the *Scots* And *Quia motus universarum ultra gentium & infesta hostilis exercitu itinera timebantur*, *Because he apprehended that all the People beyond* Forth *would rise against him*, and feared that in his passage he might be attack'd by the Enemy's Army, he try'd their Harbours with his Fleet Where, by the by, there is a pretty Description of the nature and quality of the Country, in these words, "*Ac modo sylvarum & montium profunda, modo tempestatum ac fluctuum adversa, hinc terra & hostis, hinc victus Oceanus militari jactantia compararentur*, i e *One while the depths of Woods and Mountains; another while the terrible force of tempests and waves, on one hand, the land and the enemy, on the other hand the Ocean swell'd by the Tides; were compared, and the difficulties boasted of by the Soldiery* Which very well agrees to the woody and mountainous Country, mixed with Valleys, that lyeth North of these Firths; and to the roughness of the Firths, when agitated with winds and a little below this he saith, *that the People inhabiting* Caledonia, *betook them to their Arms*, where he gives an account of a sore battel they had with the *Romans*, when *Agricola* was so hard put to it, as to make use of all his force, and art

Caledonia

What is meant by *Caledonia*, he has told us, where he speaks of the figure of *Britain*, that what the ancients said of it, agreed to that part on this side of *Caledonia*; *sed immensum & enorme spatium procurrentium extremo jam littore terrarum, velut in cuneum tenuatur*, i. e a vast and almost boundless space of Land running into the Sea, towards the end, lessens into the form of a Wedge; by which he makes *Caledonia* to contain all the rest of *Britain*, to the North of these two Firths and that they were different People, who were possess'd of it, is clear by the words, *Caledoniam incolentes populi* By the *Caledonii*, simply, the *Romans* understood the *Pights* who inhabited the Country that lay upon the *German* Sea; but as he mentions several People here, so he gives you afterwards the *Horesti*, that is, the *Highlanders* the name given of old to the ancient *Scots*, and kept by their Descendents to this day. And after he has given an account of the great preparations, he relates the great battle that he fought with these people, the last Summer of his government: He tells us, that he marched up to the *Grampion Hills*, where the Enemy were encamp'd Here, any who will but consider the ground they were encamp'd on, and the way of their fighting, and the description he makes *Galgacus* their Commander in chief to give of them, may clearly see that they were different people, and no other than those whom *Claudian* and other authors call *Scots* and *Pights*

But, because it is controverted by some late writers, whether they were Natives of *Britain*, or *Irish*, who from *Ireland*, properly so called, invaded *Britain*; we shall bring some arguments that *Tacitus* furnishes us withal, to prove that they were Natives of the *British* Soil For in the account even of this last expedition, he says, "*Nam Britanni nihil fracti pugnæ prioris eventu, & [illegible]nem aut servitium expectantes, tandemque docti commune periculum concordia propulsandum, legationibus & fœderibus omnium civitatum vires exciverant, jamque supra triginta millia armatorum aspiciebantur, & adhuc affluebat omnis juventus, & quibus cruda & viridis senectus*, &c i e *For the* Britains, *not at all discouraged by their former misfortune, and thinking of nothing but either Revenge or Servitude, and having learnt withal the necessity of a Confederacy among themselves, to fence against a danger common to all; had by embassies and leagues engaged the strength of all their Cities, and got together above thirty thousand men in arms, besides others, not only of their Youth, but also of the more lusty and vigorous among the old Men, who were continually flocking in*, &c Where it is observable, that although he called them before *Novæ Gentes*, yet here he calls them *Britanni*; which was the name the *Romans* gave to all that inhabited this Island, but it was never given by any of the Roman Authors to the Inhabitants of *Ireland* The words *Legationibus & fœderibus omnium civitatum vires exciverant*, show, that both *Scots* and *Pights* were united, and composed their Army For the *Britains* spoken of here, are the Inhabitants of *Caledonia*; and so it is, that *Tacitus* says, *Galgacus* design'd them in these words, *Ostendamus quos sibi Caledonia viros seposuerit*, i e *Let us show what glorious Men* Caledonia *has in reserve*.

We find likewise in our Author, several marks of distinction First, they are *Gentes* now, the Criticks have observ'd that *Gens* is a more general name, and so *all the Britains are called* Gens Britannorum, *Natio* is a particular People, a part comprehended under the general name *Gens*: So, the *Caledonii*, the *Silures*, and the rest mention'd by *Ptolemy* in his Map of *Britain*, are *nationes Britannicæ*, British Nations Our *Author* also speaks of *Civitates*, which are not Towns but *Gentes*, People, and the Clans that composed them, which lived under the command of their Chiefs: So *Galgacus* is described here, *inter plures duces virtute & genere præstans*, i e *Of their many Leaders, the most considerable for Valour and Birth* And these same names which we find in *Ptolemy*, are certainly the

the ancient names of the Clans, but *Ptolemy* has been deficient, in that he has not set down the general names that the People call'd *themselves* by, which in this part of the Island, was *Albanich* and *Peaghts*, that is, *Albanenses* and *Picti* These two names prove them to be the ancient and first Inhabitants of *Britain*, whom *Cæsar* designs in these words, *Interior pars ab iis incolitur, qui se natos in insula dicunt*; i e *the inner part is inhabited by those who call them selves* Aborigines, which *Galgacus* owns here, speaking to his Army he calls them *nobilissimi totius Britanniæ eoque ipsis penetralibus siti*, i e *the most noble of all the* Britains, *and so placed in the most inward parts.* The reason of the names *Albanich* and *Peaghts* is given in the *Scotia Antiqua*; it is enough here to remember, that that part of the Island which lay to the North of *Humber*, was by the confession of the most learned of the *British* Historians (as *Priscus Defen Hist Britan. Pag* 60 *Ranulph Higden Polychronic Lib* 1 *Luddus fragment*) called *Albania*, and a part of the Country still carries the name of *Broad-Albine*

Likewise, that those whom he calls *Caledoniam incolentes populi*, are the same that were called *Novæ gentes*, appears from this which follows; that when (because of the Summer's being far spent) *the War could not be suppressed, he led his Army into the bounds of the* Horesti, and, a little after, *himself carrying the foot and horse by slow marches (for a greater terror to the* New Nations) *into winter-quarters*, where they are call'd by the same name *Novæ Gentes* For *Tacitus* here relates, that because the Summer was spent, and the War could not be extended against the *Pights* and *Scots* both, he marched with his Army to the borders of the *Scots* whom he calls *Horesti*, that is, Ὀρεινοί, *Montani*, *Highlanders* And indeed I have seen Roman Medals which were found in *Argileshire*, and many have been found in several parts of *Perthshire* Besides, a great many Roman Camps are there and you may see by *Tacitus*, that in the sixth year of *Agricola's* Government, some of these Camps had been attack'd by those People who dwelt in *Caledonia*; for he saith, *that having attack'd their* [h] Castles or Camps, *they had made themselves more formidable, as Aggressors*, and, a little after, it is said of the same People concerning the Attack of the ninth Legion, that *they fought in the very* [i] *Camps* This Camp seems to be the same which is yet to be seen near *Airdoch*, the figure of which is here given.

[h] Castella

[i] Castris

Camp at Airdoch Pag 1240

See pag. 1240

DIS MANIBVS
AMMONIVS DA
MIONIS 7 COH
I HISPANORVM
STIPENDIORV
M XXVII HERE
DES F C

100 pas

24 pas

Velt

Roman Camp at Airdoch

And the reason why I take this to have been one of *Agricola's* Camps, is, for that *Tacitus* hath observed before, *That no General was more dextrous in the choice of Places than* Agricola, *nor was any Camp that he had form'd, ever taken or deserted* For if we consider this Camp, we shall find it has all the Advantages that *Vegetius* saith a Camp should have *Camps ought to be made in a safe place, where is plenty of wood, forrage, and water; and if the continuance there is to be long, the Air is also to be regarded But great care is to be taken, that there be not in the neighbourhood a higher hill, where the Enemy may post themselves, and from thence annoy the Camp; and that the Field be not subject to Inundations by reason of any Torrents* This is, indeed, upon a Heath in a sloping ground it hath the Water of *Kneck* running close by it, whose banks are so high, that it could not overflow; and there is wood near it, and more has been about it; there is no Mountain nor considerable Height so near, as that they could from thence annoy it The same *Vegetius* adds, *These Camps, like Towns, are often built, both on the borders of the Empire, and where are perpetual Stations* [k] *and Guards against the Enemy* And the largeness of this Camp, and its situation upon the frontier makes this to be a *Prætentura*

l i c 21

[k] P r

The *Prætorium*, or the General's Quarter, is a large Square, about a hundred paces every

way

way. round it, are five or six *Aggeres* or Dykes, and as many *Valla* or Ditches, the deepness of a man's height There are Ports to the four Quarters of the World, and to the East, are several larger Squares, with their Circumvallations continued for a good way To the West is the Bank of the water of *Kneck*, and five or six miles to the North-east of this, hard by the Water of *Earn* near *Inch Paferay*, is a lesser Camp, the *castrum exploratorum*, or Camp for the Advance-Guard and a little to the East ward of this, beginneth the *Roman Via militaris*, call'd by the common People, the *Street way* This, in some places, is raised from the ground almost a Man's height, and is so broad, that one Coach may pass by another with ease upon it It runs towards the River *Tay*, the whole length of which *Agricola's* devastations reached, as *Tacitus* tells us, *The devastations were carried as far as the River* Taus And the *Grampian hills* (towards which he marched when he fought the last Battle in the last year of his Govern ment) are but a few miles distant from these Camps

Street way

The Inscription, of which we have given the Figure above, was taken up out of the *Pretori um* of the *Pretentura* below which, are Caves, and out of them some pieces of a shield were also taken up, and several Medals have been found thereabouts I saw a Medal of Silver of *Antoninus Pius*, found there The People, who live in the neighbourhood, report, that a large Roman Medal of Gold was also found, as great quantities of Silver ones have been found near the water of *Earn*, amongst which I have seen some of *Domitian*, some of *Trajan*, some of *Marcus Aurelius* the Philosopher Besides, whereas it is said that the man, for whom this Sepulchral Inscription was made, was *Cohortis primæ Hispanorum*; i e of the first Cohort of the Spaniards; if you will look into the *Notitia Imperii Romani*, you will find that amongst the Troops placed *secundum lineam valli*, i e along the Wall, this *Cohors prima Hispanorum* was one. And it should seem that the Poet *Claudian* had this very same *Pretentura* in his eye, in these Verses,

Venit & extremis legio pretenta Britannis,
Quæ Scoto *dat fræna truci*, &c.

Hither the Legion came, in garrison oppos'd
To utmost *Britons*, bridling the fierce *Scot*.

And so, without all question, the *Glacialis Ierne* is meant of this very Country, which carries now the name *Strathern*; where all these footsteps of the Roman Exploits are found And these who are called *Scots* by *Claudian*, are the very same People that *Eumenius* calls *Hiberni soli Britanni*, the Irish of the British Soil, and *Tacitus*, *Horesti*, *Highlandmen*, or *Braemen*; which name some of their Descendants yet bear While, on the contrary, all Authors, both ancient and modern, agree, that the Romans were never in *Ireland* properly so call'd; and there are no Roman Camps, Military Ways, nor Coins, to be seen there.

Pights

It remains now, that we show where the Country of the *Pights* was, who, in the Verse last cited, are joined with the *Scots*, and were not very far from this same *Pretentura*, since the Poet immediately subjoyns to,

Quæ Scoto *dat fræna truci*,—— these words,

——— *Ferroque notatas,*
Perlegit exanimes Picto moriente figuras

And saw the *Pights*, whose Bodies are mark'd o're
With various figures, dying in their gore

That this *Thule* was a part of *Britain*, the Roman writers seem to be very clear, especially *Silius Italicus*, in these Verses, Lib xvii

Cærulus haud aliter cum dimicat incola Thules,
Agmina falcifero circumvenit acta covino

As *Thule's* blue Inhabitants surround
Their Foes with Chariots hook'd, and them confound

For *Silius* here seems to have in his eye, what *Cæsar* in his Commentaries hath deliver'd, of the *Britons* fighting in *Essedis*, and *Pomponius Mela*, where he speaks of the *Britons*, says, *That they fight not only with Horse and Foot, but with* [1] *Carts and Chariots*, the axle trees of which he observes, were *armed with hooks* And *Tacitus* tells us, that in the Battle fought with our Countrymen at the *Grampion-hill*, *media covinarius & eques strepitu ac discursa complebat*, The middle of the Field was filled with the clattering and running of *Chariots* and *Horsemen*. And a little below that, *Covinarii peditum se prælio miscuere, & quanquam recentem terrorem intulerant, densis tamen hostium agminibus & inæqualibus locis hærebant*, In the mean time the *Chariots* mix'd themselves with the Foot, which, although they had lately caused great terror, were now entangled in the thick ranks of the Enemies, and in uneven ground These *Covinarii* are call'd by Cæsar *Essedarii*; and so, I think no body will doubt, but that *Silius* the Poet, by *Cærulus Incola Thules*, meant the *Britains* We also find an appellation of the same nature given to one of the tribes of the Scots, by *Seneca*, in these Verses, In Ludo

L iii c 6.

[1] Bigis

Ille Britannos,
Ultra noti
Littora ponti
Et Cæruleos
Scoto-*Brigantes*
Dare Romuleis
Colla catenis
Jussit.

He to submission *Britains* did compel,
Beyond the utmost Ocean's bounds who dwell
The *Irish Scots* who painted are with blew,
He forc'd unto the Roman yoke to bow

Exercit Plin p 189 For so it is read by *Joseph Scaliger*, and by *Salmasius*, who came next in learning to him And it should seem by those Verses,

> *Et caruleos*
> Scoto *Brigantas,*
> *Dare Romuleis*
> *Colla catenis*
> *Jussit.*

that *Seneca*, who was contempory with *Claudius*, had in his eye the Victory which *Ostorius* Governour of Britain, under *Claudius* the Emperor, obtain'd over *Caratacus* His History may be seen elegantly written by *Tacitus* in the twelfth Book of his Annals, where he shows us, that *Caratacus*, being brought before *Claudius* in Chains, made a brave Speech to him; and, amongst other things, spoke of the *several Nations* which he had govern'd And without doubt, besides the *Silures* mention'd there by *Tacitus*, these *Scoto brigantes* were of the number of the *Gentes* which he commanded

- which t of Bri 1 *Thule* ..s But to make it appear which part of Britain the *Thule* was which is mention'd by the Romans, it will be fit to see, to which part of Britain the Epithets attributed by writers to *Thule*, do best agree First then, it was a remote part, *Ultima Thule*, as if this were the *remotest* part of Britain so *Tacitus* brings in *Galgacus* expressing it, *We, the utmost Bounds of Land and Liberty*, &c Then, *Thule* was towards the North, and so was this Country, with respect to the Roman Province And, thirdly, it might deserve the name *Thule*, because of its *obscure* and *dark* aspect; it being in those days all over-grown with Woods Fourthly, the *length* of the day annex'd to *Thule*, and upon this account it must be the Country to the North, and to the East of *Ierne*, by the Verses of *Juvenal*, before-mention'd,

> ———— *Arma quid ultra*
> *Littora Juvernæ promovimus & modo captas*
> *Orcadas, & minimè contentos nocte Britannos?*

For it is of the North and East parts of Britain, that the Panegyrist saith, *O Britain, happy and fortunate beyond all Lands*; and a little below, he speaks of their *long days* and *light nights*, and the Sun's rather *passing by* than *setting* This is applied to the Northmost part of Britain by *Tacitus*, where he says of it, *The length of the Day is much above the measure of our Climate; the Nights are light, and in the furthermost part of the Island so short, that between the going out and coming in of the day, the space is barely perceiv'd; and when Clouds do not hinder, they affirm that the Sun shine is seen in the night, and that it neither sets nor rises, but passes along*

The ancient Scholiast, upon the word *Juverna*, says, *It is an Island of* Britain *placed in the Ocean, not far from the thirty Isles of the* Orcades; and adds, that in *Hibernia, which is a part of Britain, at the Summer Solstice, there is no Night, or next to none* The Day here is eighteen hours and twenty five minutes; and as *Lesly* in his History of Scots, in *Ross*, *Caithness*, and the Isles of *Orkney*, the Nights for two months are so clear, that one may read and write in them; which is confirm'd by those who live there

Another property of *Thule*, given by *Tacitus*, is, that about it, is *mare pigrum & grave remigantibus*, a slow Sea, and difficult to Sailors Which agrees indeed to the Sea upon the North-east part of Scotland, but not for the reason that *Tacitus* gives, i e for want of winds; but because of the contrary tides which drive several ways, and stop not only Boats with oars, but Ships under sail, so that there, if any where, it may be said of the Sea,

> —— *Nunc spumis candentibus astra lacessit,*
> *Et nunc Tartareis subsidit in ima Barathris*

> Sometimes the foaming Billows swell amain,
> Then suddenly sink down as low again.

But *Thule* is most expresly described to be this very same Country that we treat of, by *Conradus Celtes*, *Itin Balt*

> *Orcadibus qua cincta suis Tyle & glacialis Insula* ——————

> Where *Tyle*, and the Icy Island's found,
> With their own *Orkney* Isles encompass'd round.

This same Epithet *Claudian* gives to *Ierne*, where he calls it *Glacialis Ierne*, and this *Thule* he makes to be encompass'd *suis Orcadibus*, with it's *Orcades*, which Isles lie over-against it and a little after, he gives it the like Epithet with *mare pigrum*, the slow Sea

> *Et jam sub septem spectant vaga rostra Triones,*
> *Qua Tyle est rigidis insula cincta vadis.*

> Now from their Ships they *Charles's wain* espy,
> Where *Tyle* in the *rigid Seas* doth lie

And afterwards, he makes the *Orcades* to lie over-against this *Thule*, and seems to have in in his eye the Skerries and Wheels in *Pightland Firth*, in these lines;

> *Est locus Arctoo qua se Germania tractu*
> *Claudit, & in rigidis Tyle ubi surgit aquis*
> *Quam juxta infames scopuli, & petrosa vorago,*
> *Asperat undisonis saxa pudenda vadis*
> *Orcadas has memorant dictas a nomine Græco*

> Near th' utmost Northern point of German shore,
> And where in frozen Waters *Tyle* stands,
> Are monstrous Rocks; and there, amidst the Rocks,
> A Weel fills Shore and Rocks with dismal Roar
> These, *Orcades*, by a Greek name are call'd

But the clearest Testimony of all, we owe to *Arngrimus Jonas* (*Specimen Island historic part* II *pag* 120) where he brings in the Verses of *Fortunatus*;

> ——— *Penetravit ad Indos,*
> *Ingeniumque potens ultima Thule colit.*

> His Eloquence did reach the utmost Indies,
> And powerful Wit enlighten'd *farthest Thule*

And

And then, reckoning up the several Nations enlighten'd by him, he mentions *Britain* among the rest.

Thrax, Italus, Scytha, Persa, Indus, Geta, Daca, Britannus

To which he adds, *From whence it may fairly enough be inferr'd, that either Britain*, or (as Pliny will have it) *some Island of Britain, was the* Ultima Thule And afterwards, *To confirm the Opinion of* Pliny *and his followers, who will have some of the British Isles or particularly that furthest in the Scottish Dominions, to be* Thule; *I must acknowledge, that the History of the Kings of Norway says the same thing*, in the life of King *Magnus, who in an Expedition to the Orcades, and Hebrides, and into Scotland and Britain, touched also at the Island of* Thule, *and subdued it*

By all which, I think, it appears sufficently, that the North-east part of Scotland, which *Severus* the Emperor and *Theodosius* the Great invested with their Armies, and in which, as *Boethius* shews us, Roman Medals were found; is undoubtedly the *Thule* mention'd by the Roman Writers And this also, if we will believe the learned *Arngrimus Jonas*, was meant by *Ptolemy*, where he saith, that to the 21st Parallel drawn through *Thule* by Ptolemy, the Latitude answers fifty five degrees, and thirty six minutes So that our Country in those antient times pass'd under the name of *Thule* and *Hiberma* and the *Hiberni*, and *Picts incola Thules*, are the same People who were afterwards call'd *Scots*.

It looks indeed, as if the name *Scot* at first was only proper to some Tribes of those People who call'd themselves *Albinich* such as the *Scoto-Brigantes* mention'd by *Seneca*, and the *Scottedeni* in *Ptolemy*, which by the corruption of Copies is now read *Ottedeni* But they, it seems, were never called *Scots* generally, nor their Country *Scotia*, till after the time of *Keneth* the second, who subdued the *Pights*, and incorporated them into one Nation with our Ancestors Yet *Wernerus Rolwingius* saith, *In the time of Pope* Linus, *arose the Scottish Nation, of Picts and Hibernians, in Albania, which is a part of England*; which confirms very much what we have been proving all along, but makes the name to have been used generally, sooner than appears to us from our Historians — *Fasic. Temp*

I shall only add one remark more, and that is, that we need not have recourse, for the rise of the name *Scot*, to the fabulous account of the Monks, who bring it from *Scota, Pharaoh's* daughter, married to *Gathelus*; since, without that strain, if it be granted that the Country was once call'd *Thule*, which in the Phœnician Language signifies *Darkness*, we have a very clear Reason for the name *Scotia*, which signifies the same in the Greek Tongue And it is very well known, that it was usual with the Greeks (who next to the Phœnicians were the best Navigators,) not only to retain the Phœnician name of the place, but likewise to give one in their own language of the same import And since the learned *Bochartus* has very ingeniously deduced the Greek name of the whole Island, Βρεταννική, from *Bratanack* and *Barat anac*, in the Phœnician tongue signifying a *Land of Tinn*, (which the Greeks not only reduced to their own termination, but likewise call'd the British Isles Κασσιτερίδες, that is, *Lands of Tin*, as is the signification of the Phœnician and Greek names,) we may take the same liberty to derive the Greek name *Scotia*, from the Phœnician *Thule* This is so fully treated of in the *Scotia Antiqua*, that I need say no more

ISLANDS *in the GERMAN OCEAN.*]

BELOW *Thule* to the South, lies the *German* Ocean, wherein Pliny will have the seven *Acmodæ*, or *Hæmodes* (as Mela calls them) to be situate. But because it is certain that these belong to Denmark, and are the Isles of *Lelant, Funen, Lagland, Muen, Falstor, Leyland*, and *Femerem* in the *Sinus Codanus*, or the Baltick, they fall not within the compass of my design any more than *Glessaria*, or *Electrida*, so call'd from the Electer or Amber which the Sea casts up, and which *Sotacus* believ'd to drop originally from the trees in Britain And by the way, since the old Germans call'd Amber *Glessa*; I readily concur with the learned *Erasmus Michael Lætus*, that the Isle of *Lesse* near Scagen, a Promontory of Denmark, was the old *Glessaria* — *Acmodæ* — *Glessaria*

In the German Ocean, upon the coast of Britain there are very few Islands besides those in the Frith of Edinburgh, namely *May, Bassa, Keth*, and *Inche Colme*, or the *Isle of Columba* On the coast of Northumberland over-against the river *Lindi*, we see *Lindisferne*, call'd by the Britains *Inis Medicante, which* (as Bede says) *is twice Isle, and twice Continent, in one day, being incompassed with water at every flow, and dry at every ebb*, whereupon, he calls it very aptly a *semi-Isle* Towards the west, it is narrow, and left wholly to the rabbets, which is joyn'd to the east part (where it is much broader) by a very small slip of land; towards the south, it has a small Town, with a Church and Castle; which was formerly a Bishop's See, erected by *Aidan* the Scot He was call'd hither to preach the Gospel to the *Northumbrians*, and was much taken with the solitude and retiredness of the place Eleven Bishops presided in this See Afterwards, upon the Danish Invasion, it was translated to *Durham* Under the Town, lies a good commodious Harbour, defended by a Fort upon a Hill to the South-east — *Lindisfarne* — *In the life of St Cuthbert*

This Island, from the Monks who liv'd in it is call'd by the English *Holy Island* Of which, *Alcuin*, in a Letter to *Egelred* King of Northumberland, writes thus *The most venerable place in Britain left to the mercy of Pagans and where the Christian Religion was first preach'd in this Country, after St* Paulinus *left* York, *there* — Holy Island *we have suffer'd it's destruction to begin.* Seven miles from hence, to the South-east, lies *Farn-Island*, distant about two miles from *Banborrow-castle*; it is surrounded by the main Ocean, and edg'd round with a ridge of rocks Almost in the middle of it there is a Fort, in the very place, as some say, where *Cuthbert* Bishop of *Lindesfarn*, the tutelar Saint of the North, built *a City* for Religious Retirement, *fit for his own Government* (as Bede expresses it,) *with Houses therein, suitable to that end For the building was almost round, and four or five perches wide between wall and wall The wall on the out-side was more than a man's height; but he made it much higher within by sinking a huge rock, to restrain the eyes and thoughts from rambling, and to fix the mind upon Heaven, by hindering the devout Inhabitants from any other prospect The wall was not made of square-stone or brick, nor cemented with mortar, but of rough unpolish'd stone, and turf dug-up in the middle of the place Some of them were so big, that it hardly seem'd possible for four men to lift them In this Mansion, he had two Houses, a Chapel, and a Room for common use The walls were the natural earth, made* * *by digging or paring off within and without The roof was timber unhewn, and thatch'd Moreover, at the Harbour of this Island, was a larger House, wherein the Brethren who came to visit him, might be receiv'd and lodg'd; not far from which, there was a Fountain convenient for them* Near this, lie some lesser Islands to the North, namely, *Widopens*, and *Staple-Island*, which is two miles off, with *Brousman*; and two less than these, call'd the *The Wambes* After these, over against the mouth of the River *Coquet*, lies an Island call'd *Coquet*, where is great store of Sea-coal

Farn Island. *Bede*, in the life of *Cuthbert*. * *Circumfodiendo sive caedendo*. Widopens. Staple Island. The *Wambes*. Coquet riv.

These are the remarkable Islands on this Coast; but over against it are the *Saxon Isles*, (now *Heilichlant*, that is, the *Holy Island*,) which lie in a continu'd range, along the Coast of *East* and *West Friesland*. Of these, that which *Strabo* calls *Birchanis*, was best known to the Romans Pliny calls it *Birchana*, and the Romans *Fabaria*, fro ma grain like a *bean* naturally growing there, which (that I may restore it to its proper place, tho' not within the compass of my design) is undoubtedly that *Burkun* which is over against the mouth of the *Ems*, as the name itself demonstrates

The Saxon Isles. Holy-Island. *Birchanis* *Lib* vii. Burkun.

Lower down upon the Coast of Holland, and near the old mouth of the *Rhine*, the foundation of a very ancient Arsenal appears sometimes at low water; which is indeed an admirable piece of Antiquity, and shows how noble the building itself has been; as *Abraham Ortelius* (the great restorer of antient Geography, and my very intimate friend) has elegantly describ'd it, and as it were *fish'd* it out of the Sea I was the more willing to take notice of it in this Work, because the Hollanders call it by the name of *Huis te Britten*, that is a *British house*; so that the name at least is our's For as it is granted, that *Caligula* in that mock-expedition against Britain built this for a Watch-tower; so it is manifest from an old Inscription dug up here, that *Septimius Severus* repair'd it As for the original of this name *Britten*, it is uncertain but it is most likely from the *Britains*; from whom also *Bretta* the birth place of *Philip Melancthon*, had its name, as himself thinks; and we read that the Mountains in *Henault*, call'd *Breten*, took their name from the Britains And therefore, as Pliny thinks it very unaccountable, that an herb peculiar to Holland should be call'd *Britannica*, unless the People bordering upon the Ocean may be suppos'd to have call'd it so, because of the vicinity to Britain, so I cannot but wonder, why this tower should be call'd *British*, unless the Dutch gave it the name, as being over against *Britain* Pliny calls a place in Picardy the *Portus Morinorum Britannicus*, i e. the British Harbour of the *Morini*, either because they took Ship there for Britain, or because it lay opposite to Britain Why therefore might not this tower be call'd *Britten* for the same reason? For it cannot be deny'd, that the Britains came often hither, and that this was a common passage from Germany into Britain; since *Zosimus* particularly computes the breadth of the Ocean between Britain and the mouth of the *Rhine* (as a *common passage*) at nine hundred *Stadia*; and writes, that supplies of Corn were brought hither out of Britain, and convey'd in boats up the *Rhine*, to the Roman Camps and since also Julian the Emperor, as Marcellinus tells us, *built Granaries for the reception of the Corn usually transported from Britain* About that time this tower seems to have been converted into a Granary, and call'd from the *British* Corn, *Britten*, which is the more probable, because it is written *Britenburgh*, in the Records of Holland For in that age, they call'd such Castles as stood conveniently for that purpose, and were stor'd with Corn, *Burgs*, as appears by the History of the Burgundians But what if we should say (for this is only multiplying conjectures upon a point that has already puzzled many an Enquirer) that the Britains took this tower, and left it the name, when they set up *Magnus Maximus*, or *Clemens Maximus* as others call him, against *Gratian* for he certainly landed at the mouth of the Rhine Or, if the name be of later date, what if we say, that it was called *Huis de Britten* by the Saxons? since they set sail from hence, when they infested our Coast with their Pinaces, or *Ciules* as they call them For Zosimus tells us, that the Saxons drove out the * *Salian* Franks, and possess'd themselves of *Batavia*, and, that thence they made their descent into Britain, is manifest This seems also to be intimated by the noble and learned *Janus Dousa*, in an Ode of his upon *Leyden*; as I observ'd before. But lest I seem partial to my own Country, I must add, that seeing the learned *Hadrianus Junius*, a Dutchman born, deduces the herb *Britannica* from *Britten* (a word of his own country) as growing plentifully upon those turfs which they call *Britten*, and of which they make dikes to keep the Ocean from breaking in; there seems to be no absurdity, if we give this *Huis de Britten* the same Original, and suppose it to be so call'd, because it was fenc'd with banks of turf or *Britten*, against the incursions of the Sea, and that it might be overflow'd by the Sea, upon some breach made in these banks But I leave the determination of this Controversie to them who are better acquainted with the nature of the word, and the situation of the place; after I have ask'd their pardon for trespassing thus far, where I had no right.

Britten Huis. *Portus Morinorum Britannicus*. *Burg*, what. Zosimus, l. iv. Saxons in Holland. * *Salii Franci*. Janus Douza. In his *Vocabulary* the herb *Britica*.

On this Coast, lie also the Isles of *Zealand*, surrounded by the rivers *Scald*, *Maese*, and the Ocean I have only this to say of them, that the name *Valachria* (this is the chief of them,) is guess'd by *Lemnius Levinus* to come from *Wallia* or *Wales* Over-against Zealand, lies the mouth of the *Thames*, the noblest river in Britain; where Ptolemy places *Toliapis*, and

Zealand. Toliapis.

Caunu

Canvey Shepey *Cauna* or *Convennos* I have treated of Toliapis, which I take to be Shepey, in Kent; [and, of *Convennos*, in Essex]

Beyond the mouth of the Thames eastward, before the Isle of Tanet, lies a long shelf of Goodwin Sands Sand very dangerous to Sailors, call'd the *Goodwin-Sands*, where, in the year 1097, our Annals tell us, that an Island which belong'd to Earl *Goodwin*, was swallow'd up John Twine writes thus of it, *This Isle was very fruitful, and had good Pastures, and was situated lower than Tanet, from which there was a passage of about three or four miles by boat The said Isle, in an unusual storm of wind and rain, and a very tempestuous Sea, sunk down, and was cover'd with heaps of Sand, and so, was irrecoverably chang'd into an amphibious nature between Land and Sea I know very well what I say, for sometimes* † *it floats, and sometimes at low water one may walk upon it* ** This is perhaps the old *Toliapis*, unless you had rather read *Thanatus* for *Toliapis*, which is written *Toliatis* in some Copies But of this we have already spoken in Kent

† *Tota fluitat*

** How these Sands happen'd and why so call'd, See Somn *Ports and Ports*

[ISLANDS *in the BRITISH OCEAN.*

The BRITISH SEA]

The British Sea  HERE, this vast body of Waters is pent within so small a Chanel, that between Britain and the Continent of Europe, the Ocean is not above thirty miles broad This narrow Sea is call'd by some the *Streight of Britain*, and by others the *Streight of France*, and is the Bound of the *British Ocean*, which by little and little inlarges the distance between the two shores, that were in a manner united, and by an equal retirement of the Land on both sides, divides *Britain* and *France* from East to West Here, the British Ocean begins, in which the first Island (or rather Peninsula) that we meet with, is *Selsy*, in Saxon Seolres-ea, that is, according to Seals In Sussex Bede, *an Isle of Seals or Sea-Calves* But this has been already treated of

Vecta Above this, lies the Isle *Vecta*, call'd in Welch *Guith*, in Saxon Ƿiht-land and Ƿiht ea (for Ea, signifies an Island,) and by us, the Isle of The Isle of Wight, v Southam *Wight* and *Whight*, which we have described already

Portland, v Dorset As for *Portland*, which is not now an Isle, but join'd to the Continent, it has likewise been describ'd in *Dorsetshire*

From hence, I will cross over to the opposite Coast of France, which, from *Beerfleet* in Normandy, the Seamen think to be lin'd with rocks and craggs, as far as the very middle of the Chanel Among these, *William* the Son of *Henry* the first, and heir apparent to the Crowns of England and Normandy, was cast away (together with his Sister and a Bastard-brother, and others of the greatest of the Nobility who accompany'd him) in the year 1120, as he was sailing from Normandy to England Hence a Poet of that age,

Abstulit hunc terræ matri maris unda noverca,
Proh dolor! occubuit Sol Anglicus, Anglia plora!
Quæque prius fueras gemino radiata nitore,
Extincto nato vivas contenta parente

He from's dear mother Earth was snatch'd away
By's cruel Step-mother the barbarous Sea
Weep, weep, the Light that is for ever gone,
Weep *England*, that could'st boast a double Sun,
But sadly now must be content with one

Unus plangendum! privat lapis æquoris unus,
Et ratis una suo principe regna duo

Sad Fate! one Rock beneath deceitful Waves
Two helpless Kingdoms of their Prince bereaves.

Another of the same Age writes thus upon the same Occasion,

Dum Normannigenæ Gallis claris superatis,
Angliaca regna petunt, obstitit ipse Deus
Aspera nam fragili dum sulcant æquora cymba,
Induit excito nubila densa mari
Dumque vagi cæco rapiuntur tramite nautæ,
Ruperunt imas abdita saxa rates
Sic mare dum superans tabulata per ultima serpit,
Mersit rege satos, occidit orbis honos

While *Norman* Victors o're the Waves were born,
A fiercer Foe oppos'd their wish'd return
Now homeward the triumphant Vessel stood,
When sudden tempests rouz'd the sudden flood
The trembling Pilots fearful of delay,
Thro' unknown shallows cut their fatal way,
And fell on secret Rocks, an heedless prey
And conqu'ring Billows now by sad degrees
Above the Prince's Cabbin proudly rise
Ne'er could the Ocean boast a nobler prize

[BRITISH ISLANDS *on the Coast of FRANCE.*]

MORE Westward, some Islands shew themselves in the Sea near *France*, yet belonging to the Crown of *England* The first that appears hard by *Normandy*, otherwise the Coast of the *Lexobii* (whom our *Welch* call *Lettaw*, as much as to say *Coasters*) is *Alderney*, termed in the Records of the Tower *Aurney*, *Aureney*, and *Aurigney*, so that one would take it for the *Arica* which *Antoninus* (according to a Manuscript in the King of *Spain*'s possession) reckons among the Islands of the British Sea Others suppose it to be that *Ebodia* or *Evodia*, of which *P Diaconus*, who was but little acquainted with these Parts, makes mention, and none else but he, placing it thirty Miles distant from the mouth of the River *Seine*, and tells us *of a continual noise of Waters, as it were from a* Charybdis or Whirlpool, heard to a great distance hereabouts [This is Poetical and exaggerated But thus much is true, that the many rocks and foul grounds along this Coast, make a very terrible and roaring Sea in bad weather]

Alderney

Arica

Evodia

This *Alderney* is about one good League and a half from Cape *La Hague* in *Normandy*, in circuit about eight Miles, enjoys a fruitful Soil, either for Corn or Pasture, and has in it one Church, and * fourscore Houses. I am in doubt whether I ought to take notice of a Giant's Tooth found here, of the bigness of a man's Fist, seeing St. *Augustin* writes he had seen one so large that it might be cut into a hundred others as big as any ordinary man's [*Alderney* is a high Land (as are all the Isles in this Tract) and much the nearest to *France* That narrow Sea which runs betwixt the two Shores, is by them called *Le Ras de Blanchart*, and by us, *the Race of Alderney*, and is reputed a dangerous Passage, when the Currents, which are very strong, encounter with tempestuous Winds, and both meet in contrary Motion Otherwise, it is safe enough, and has a depth of Water sufficient for the biggest Ships Through this Race part of the French Fleet made their escape, after their defeat at *La Hougue*, in the year 1692 The Habitations lie not here dispers'd as in the other Islands, but are brought together for greater safety into one Town of about two hundred Houses, and a thousand Inhabitants Nor is this Island so much inclosed as the others They boast of a common Field of about five hundred Acres, that bears excellent Corn, and has not lain fallow once this hundred years It is kept thus always in heart by manuring it with *Vraic*, that Sea-weed, of which mention is made below. The Harbour is to the South, capable only of small Vessels, and the Island is a dependance of the Government and Jurisdiction of *Guernsey*]

* So, ann 1607 but now more See below

Giant's tooth

De Civ Dei, Lib xv c 9

Race of *Alderney*

From hence Westward there stretches out a range of high Rocks dreadful to Mariners, who call them *Casquets* [By *Casquet*, in the singular Number, is meant that principal Rock which advances at the head of all the rest, and looks into the Chanel; and by *Casquets* in the plural, is meant the whole Range, lying for three Leagues together betwixt that main Rock and *Alderney* A Light upon *Casquet* would be a great Security to the Navigation of the Chanel, from the middle whereof one may at once, in a clear Day, descry this Rock and the Head of *Portland* in *England* Sure it is, that for want of such a Light, many good Ships have been lost here and on the back of *Guernsey* This was the fatal Place, where *William* Son of *Henry* the first, so miserably perished, in his Passage from *Normandy* to *England*, as the Norman writers testify, and as hath been mention'd above]

Casquets

Southward of these [*viz* of *Alderney* and the *Casquets*,] and * about nine Leagues distant, lies *Cæsarea*, mention'd by *Antoninus* The French have now contracted this name of *Cæsarea* into that of *Gearzey*, as they have done *Cæsaris-burgum*, which is a Town of *Normandy*, into *Cherbourg*, and the Spaniards their *Cæsar-Augusta* into *Saragosa*. *Gregorius Turonensis* calls it *the Island of that Sea which is nearest to the City of Coutance*; where he relates how *Prætextatus* Bishop of *Rouen* was banished hither In like manner *Papirius Massonius* calls it *the Island of the Coast of* Coutance, because it lies over-against the ancient City of that name [*Aymonius Monachus* describes it also by this Character of its nearness to *Coutance*] Which *Coutance* seems to be the *Castra Constantia* in *Ammianus*, and the *Moritonum* of former times. For *Robertus Montensis* writes thus, *Comes Moritonii*, i e *Constantiarum*, unless here be an interpolation of the Transcriber [as it must be, if *Mortaigne* be there meant,] because *Moritonium* (or *Mortaigne* as it is now called) is more remote from the Sea [But in truth, *Moritonium* is not *Mortaigne*; but *Mortain*, lying within the *Coûtentin*, which is a large Tract of *Normandy* so denominated from the City of *Coutance* It is this *Mortain*, that gave the Title of Earl to our King *John*, while he was a Subject Its being within the *Coutentin*, the *Ager Constantiensis*, might cause *Robert du Mont* to express himself so loosely But the City of *Coutance* was never call'd *Moritonium* As for *Mortagne*, there are two or three of that name, but a great way off, and the Latin of them is *Moritania*, *Moritania*, &c]

* Scarce 12 miles C

Cæsarea.

JERSEY

Coutance

De Gest Franc Lib 3 *cap* 26

Castra Constantia

Moritonium

The Island [of *Jersey*] is † above thirty Miles in compass, and is defended by Rocks and Shelves, which are dangerous to such as sail that way [being Strangers]

† About, C.

It is twelve Miles long, and about six wide at each of the two extremities, for in the middle it is narrower It is in the Latitude of forty-nine Degrees, twenty-five Minutes, four Leagues from the nearest Coast of *Normandy*, and twenty-five, or more, from the nearest Point of Land in *England* The Winters are generally milder, but more windy than in *England* It abounds with Springs of pure and clear Water, perhaps above any Country under Heaven The populousness of the Place, the solidity of the Buildings, all of Stone, (for here is no such thing as Mud or wooden Cottages) the many Quicksets and Inclosures, Gardens and Orchards, the double rows of Trees set in the Avenues leading to the Houses, and often along the Highways, all these give a beauty to the Country When the People shall please to reduce some of their too numerous Plantations for Cider, back unto Arable, they may be said to want nothing necessary to Life, though they may be still beholden to their Neighbours for Superfluities and some Conveniencies Of Flesh, Fish, and Fowl, they have plenty; each good in its kind. Their Honey and

and Butter peculiarly excell Their Bread cannot be so much commended, especially that which the ordinary People eat, because made of Barley, like the Rye or Oaten Bread in many Parts of *England* They know not else what to do with that Grain, having little occasion for Malt in such a plenty of Cider, [which they prefer to Beer]

The Soil is sufficiently fruitful, bearing various sorts of Grain, and well stock'd with Cattle Of Sheep it feeds good store; among which many * were remarkable for having four, [and six,] horns. [But these are now very rare, if any at all be remaining in the Island Of the six Horns, two were bending forwards towards the nose, two bending back towards the neck, and two erect in the midst.] It enjoys a very wholsome Air, and † was heretofore subject to no other Distemper but certain Fevers, which come in the Month of *September*, and are for that reason called *Septembrieres*, so that there ‖ was no occasion here for Physicians [And it is still true, that naturally no Place is healthier; but a way of Living, fallen into, very different from that of the more sober ancient Inhabitants, has brought in Gouts, and other Distempers, either wholly unknown, or not so common, a hundred years ago]

* Are, C Sheep with six horns
† Is, C
‖ Is, C

The Place * not affording Fuel sufficient, they use [especially in Country houses] instead of Wood, a Sea weed by them called *Vraic*, thought to be the *Fucus Marinus* of *Pliny*, which the little ragged Isles and Rocks round the Coast produce in great plenty Being dry'd in the Sun, it serves for firing, and afterwards with the Ashes as with so much Marl and Dung, they manure and greatly enrich their Land Nor is it permitted to be gather'd, unless in the Spring and Summer, and then only on certain Days appointed by the Magistrate At which times the People, in a rejoycing sort of manner, repair on all sides to the Sea-shore with their Carts, and in Boats get over to the neighbouring Rocks, striving who shall be foremost But what of this Weed is driven ashore by the Sea, the poorer sort are allow'd to carry off for their use [However, it is certain, that the Island is now pretty well planted with Wood, but yet the *Vraic* affords still considerable help, and (as hath been said) in Country-houses is generally used for the Kitchin, where it makes a hot glowing fire But a great deal of this Weed is burnt upon the Sea-shore, merely for the sake of the Ashes, which are laid up afterwards in heaps for Sale, and not only the Ashes, but the *Vraic* it self, green, and as comes from the Sea, being spread on the Land, and buried in by the Plough, fertilizes like Dung, of which an Example has been given above, speaking of *Alderney* And it is well known, that in many Countries where they have the advantage of the Neighbourhood of the Sea, almost every thing that it casts up, dead Fish, Shells, Mud and Slime, nay Sand and the Sea water it self, are thus employ'd to very good purpose]

* Affording but little Fuel, C
* Vraic a Sea weed

The Island in the middle swells up gently into Hills, under which lie pleasant Valleys water'd with Brooks, and set with Fruit-trees, and † Apple trees; of the Fruits of which the Drink of the Country is made [But to be more particular The Island is as it were one great continued Hill, stretching it self from East to West in the figure of an oblong Square The North side is exceedingly raised, and looks down on the Sea below, from Cliffs of forty Fathoms perpendicular height; and the South-side is declining, and indented or cut into many pleasant Hollownesses or Valleys Nor is it only in these Valleys that one sees Fruit-trees, (whatever might be formerly,) the upper Level of the Island abounding no less with them For within these fifty or sixty years last past, the Humour of the People has so run upon Planting, that much of the best Arable Land has been converted into Orchards Whereby these two inconveniencies have happen'd; first, a deficiency of Bread-Corn in proportion to the number of the People, whereas there used to be an Overplus, bought up by the Spanish and other Merchants, and secondly, an Inundation of a Liquor, which has occasion'd much excess For whether it be from the nature of the Soil, or the Qualities of the Fruit, or the Liquor it self being kept unrack'd and undrawn from the Lees for years together, in large Vessels containing three, four, or more Hogsheads; it is certain, that the *Jersey-Cider*, made pure, and drunk upon the place, is stronger and more inebriating than English Cider *Tertullian*, I remember, speaks of Apples from which he and other *Montanists* refrained in their *Xerophagias*, because of their too generous and *vinous* Juice; *Ne quid vinositatis*, says he, *vel edamus, vel potemus* It has been computed, that twenty four thousand Hogsheads of Cider have been made here in one year]

† Plus Cider
Fruit trees
De Jejun adv Psych cap 1

The Island is thick-set with Villages and Houses, and divided into twelve Parishes, and has on all sides commodious Bays and Creeks made by the winding in of the Shore, the safest of which is on the South-side of the Island, betwixt the ‖ Towns call'd St *Hilary* and St *Alban* This Bay has within it a small Isle of it own, kept by a Garrison, and cut off from all access, where it is said, that St *Hilary* Bishop of *Poictiers*, sent hither into Banishment, lies buried For just opposite to it, stands the Town dedicated [(as hath been suppos'd)] to his name, and reckon'd the chief of the Country, both because it is the Market, and because it is likewise the Seat of Justice [But the true names of the two forementioned Towns, are St *Helier*, and St *Aubin*, and what is commonly said concerning St *Hilary* Bishop of *Poictiers* (as before) is a mistake He was indeed, driven for a time from his See, by the violence of the *Arians*, for opposing their measures in the Council of *Beziers*, *Ann* 356 They complain'd of him to the Emperor *Constantius* who favoured them, and he at their Sollicitation order'd the good Bishop into Banishment But the place of his Confinement was not *Jersey*, but *Phrygia*, on the other side of the *Hellespont* For so St *Jerom* tells us expressly, adding that he died at *Poictiers* And *Sulpitius Severus* confirms his dying at *Poictiers*, the place of his Birth, six years after his return from Banishment His death falls in the year 367, and we have nothing in ancient writers so high as that Time concerning *Jersey*, except its bare name of *Cæsarea* in *Antoninus* He then of whom the chief Town in *Jersey* is named, is not St *Hilary* of *Poictiers*, but St *Helier*, in Latin *Helerius*, or without the aspiration, *Elerius*; a holy man, who liv'd some Centuries after in this Island, and was slain by the *Normans* (as yet Pagans and Heathens,) at their first coming into these Parts As a sufferer for the Faith of Christ, he has a Place in the Martyrology of *Coutance*, and in memory of him, a noble Abbey of Canons Regular

‖ Little Towns C St Hil. St Aubin
St Hilarius
Catal Script Eccl Num Hist Sac lib 2 Prope finem

Was

was in after-time founded on that ſmall Iſle of the Bay, before-mention'd The little ſolitary Hermitage, which the holy man had choſen for his retreat from the World, according to the Piety of thoſe times, with a Bed cut into the hard Stone, remains yet ſtanding on one of the out-lying Rocks, and is viſited by the curious As for the Abbey, it's fate was to be annex'd to that of *Cherbourg* in *Normandy*, in the Reign of *Henry* the ſecond, ſo that, at it's ſuppreſſion, it was no more than a Priory

Vid du Monſtier Neuſtria Pia in S Helerio p 712

The two Towns, of St *Helier*, and St *Aubin*, beforemention'd, are ſeated in one and the ſame Bay, call'd from the latter St *Aubin*'s Bay, and are about three miles aſunder; but the whole compaſs of the Bay is a great deal more This Bay opens to the South, and at the Eaſt-end is St *Helier*, a well built and well inhabited Town, which hath been improv'd very greatly (within theſe hundred years) by accommodating it with publick Conveniencies, and enlarging it with new Streets The Market-Place in the midſt of the Town, is ſpacious, faced round with handſome Houſes, and among them with the *Cohur Royale*, which is the Court of Judicature Hither doth the whole Iſland (in a manner) rendezvous upon a *Saturday* (which is the Market day,) for Buſineſs, or Converſation To the Weſt end is St *Aubin*, a Town properly of Merchants and Maſters of Ships, who have been invited by the neighbourhood of the Port to build and ſettle there It is leſs than St *Helier* by more than one half, tho' greatly increas'd within theſe hundred years The Port is made by a ſtrong Stone work, or Mole, carried a good way into the Sea, where Ships of good burthen lie ſafe under the Guns of a Fort contiguous to it.

St *Aubin's* Bay

In this ſame Bay, but more to the Eaſt, is the ſmall Iſle of St *Helier*, ſhut in by the Sea, at, or about, every half-Flood, and having in Circuit near a mile. Here ſtood the Abbey of St *Helier*, and now in it's place, *Elizabeth-Caſtle*, which is one of the largeſt and ſtouteſt Fortreſſes in the King's Dominions. Queen *Elizabeth* began it, and gave it her name, King *Charles* the firſt enlarg'd it, and King *Charles* the ſecond perfected it It takes up the whole ground of the ſmall Iſle on which it ſtands, and is the Reſidence of the Governor, with a Garriſon in time of Peace no leſs than War In all other Openings and Creeks round the Iſland, where an Enemy might land, there are Lines and Batteries caſt up, mounted with Canon, and ſeventeen or eighteen Watch-Houſes on the moſt prominent Points, to diſcover Ships afar off The whole number of Inhabitants is computed ſomething under twenty thouſand, and of them three thouſand are able to bear Arms, and are formed into Regiments, and better diſciplin'd than a Country-Militia uſually is [When at a general Review, this Militia is drawn up in the Sandy Bay, betwixt St *Helier* and St *Aubin*, with a Train of twenty or more Braſs-Field-Pieces belonging to the Pariſhes in their Center, two ſmall Bodies of Horſe upon the Wings, their Officers at their head, and the Governor giving Orders to the whole; they make a handſome appearance and, being unanimous in their Affection to *England*, would doubtleſs behave well upon occaſion]

Iſle of St *Helier*

On the Eaſt ſide, where the Iſland faces the oppoſite City of *Coutance*, there ſtands upon a high craggy Rock, a Caſtle, [heretofore] very ſtrong, called by the lofty name of *Mont-Orgueil*, and owing much to *Henry* the fifth as its reſto-

Mon Orgueil

rer, and he who † was appointed over the whole Iſland, * did command therein with a Garriſon, whoſe Stile and Title formerly was that of *Cuſtos Inſulæ*, i e *Warden of the Iſland*, and his Salary in the Reign of *Henry* the third, two hundred Pounds yearly [But this Caſtle was a Place of note and ſtrength, before *Henry* the fifth did any thing to it. It had, in the declining years and Fortune of *Edward* the third, ſuſtained a Siege from the *French*, with the famous Conſtable *Du Gueſclin* in Perſon at their head, and could not be taken, although every where elſe, at that fatal juncture, all reſiſtance fell before that too ſucceſsful Enemy of the *Engliſh* It is now ſlighted, and the Reſidence of the Governor transferr'd to *Elizabeth-Caſtle*, yet even in it's neglected State, it retains an appearance and air of Greatneſs, very well anſwering it's name]

† i e C * Command, C

Elizabeth Caſtle

From the South ſide of the Iſland, but at a greater diſtance [than from the Eaſt-ſide to *Coutance*,] one † ſees St *Malo*, which takes its preſent name from *Maclovius*, a man renown'd for Piety It was before, call'd the City of the *Diablintes*, and *Aletum* in the old *Notitia* For ſo in a Manuſcript of *Iſidorus Mercator*, we expreſly read, *Civitas Diablintum*, *quæ alio nomine Aletum*, i e the City of the *Diablintes*, otherwiſe called *Aletum* [Theſe *Diablintes* were one of the *Armorican* Nations, mentioned by *Cæſar* In ſucceeding Ages (as hath been ſaid) we find their City call'd *Aletum*, of which *Maclovius*, vulgarly St *Malo*, was Biſhop, in the year 540 *Aletum* falling afterwards to decay, a new City roſe up two miles from it, which from the Biſhop, tho' dead many years before, was named St *Malo* Where *Aletum* ſtood, is now a ſmall Village call'd *Quidalet*]

† St *Malo* lies low and cannot be ſeen from hence

St *Malo*

Aletum

De B G l 3

D Argentré Hiſt de Bretagne l 1

The Inhabitants [of *Jerſey*] uſe the Fiſhing Trade, but are more bent upon Tillage and Husbandry Their Women gain conſiderably by knitting of Stockings, which we therefore call *Jerſey-Stockings* [And this Manufacture is alſo carried on in all the Iſlands, but is much ſunk from what it was heretofore]

Employment

Jerſey Stockings

As to what concerns their Polity, the Governor ſent by the King of *England* is the Supreme Magiſtrate [Heretofore] he * appointed a *Bailly*, who with twelve Jurats his Aſſeſſors, choſen out of each of the twelve Pariſhes by the Votes of the Pariſhioners, † held the Pleas in Civil Matters In Criminal Cauſes, with ſeven of the Jurats, in Cauſes of mere Right and Property, with three [His Power was once much larger, but that wiſe King, *Henry* the ſeventh, who had been in *Jerſey*, thought it too great, and accordingly qualified it However, the Governor is ſtill the firſt in Dignity, and more immediately repreſents the Sovereign But the Bailly now, is neither of his nomination, nor dependant on him The one has the Military Command, with ſome Special Powers reſerved to him for the preſervation of the Peace The other is at the head of the Civil Juriſdiction The twelve Jurats are Gentlemen of the beſt Families and Intereſt in the Iſland Nor is it required, that they ſhould be one out of each Pariſh, but they are choſen with a Latitude, ſo that two, three, or more, may be, and frequently are, of the ſame Pariſh And becauſe the word *Bailly*, ſounds ſomewhat low and mean in Engliſh, it is not amiſs to obſerve, that it has quite another ſignification in this Iſland, as well as in *France* and other Countries It is an Office here of great Honour, of which let this be an

Civil Government

* Appoints, C

† Holds, C

Argument, that a Peer of *England*, the Lord *Carteret*, one of his Majesty's Principal Secretaries of State, disdains not to hold it at this Day.

And thus much of the Island of *Jersey*; to which we shall only add, that in the ninth year of King *William* the third, it was erected into an Earldom in the person of *Edward* Viscount *Villiers*; upon whose Death, the titles descended to his Son and heir, the present Earl.]

Sarnia. Garnsey. Perhaps *Grunona* (by a transposal of Letters) which *Antoninus* mentions in the *Route*.

Twenty miles North-west of this, is another Island, call'd *Sarnia* by *Antoninus*, and by us at this day *Garnsey*; laid out from East to West in fashion of a Harp. It is not to be compared to the *Cæsarea* before described, for extent or fruitfulness; for it has in it no more than ten Parishes, yet to be preferr'd in this respect, that it breeds no venomous Creatures, like the other. It is also more safe and secure by Nature, as being surrounded with steep and craggy Rocks, and among these is found the *Smyrі*, which is a very hard sharp Stone, used by Lapidaries for polishing Jewels, and by Glaziers for cutting their Glass. We call it *Emeril*. Its having likewise a more commodious Port, and in consequence a larger concourse of Merchants, gives it a greater reputation for Trade. For at almost the extremity of the Island Eastward, * where it joins to the South-side, the Shore bends it self in, like a Half-moon, and makes a Port capable of receiving large Ships: And hereon stands the little Town of St *Peter*, stretching it self in one long and narrow Street. [The Port consists of a good Road, from whence Ships may go out to Sea with any Wind, in which it is confessedly better than St *Aubin*'s Bay in *Jersey*. From this Road, Ships pass under the Guns of the Castle into the Peer, close up to the Town, which Peer is indeed a noble Work, and the Glory of this Island. It is all of vast Stones, piled up one upon another to a great height, and laid close together with much Regularity and Art. It has stood firm against all the violence of the Sea upwards of four hundred Years, its Foundation being laid in the beginning of the reign of *Edward* the first, and it may so stand to the end of the World. It is not only a security to the Shipping within it, but being contiguous to the Town, is handsomely laid at top with large smooth Flags, and guarded with Parapets, and also being of great length and proportionable breadth, it serves for a Place of Pleasure, and is the ordinary Walk of the Gentlemen and Ladies of the Town, and from thence is a fine Prospect to the Sea and the neighbouring Islands. The Town, call'd St *Peter's Port*, is the only one in the Island, a good Town, but so straitened betwixt the Sea and the overhanging Hills, that it cannot easily be extended. It is the Market, and admirably supply'd with Fish at all Times.]

* On the South-side, C.

St *Peters*.

This Town is well replenish'd with Military Stores, and [was] very much frequented by Merchants upon the breaking out of any War. For by an ancient Privilege of the Kings of *England*, there is here a kind of perpetual Truce, and how hot soever the War be, the *French* and others have liberty to come hither to Trade, and depart again without molestation. [Which notable Privilege belong'd equally to all these Islands, and not singly to *Guernsey*; and was not owing to the Favour of the Kings of *England* only, but to the joint concurrence of neighbouring Princes also, and was strengthen'd moreover by a Bull of Pope *Sixtus* the fourth, denouncing the highest Censures of the Church against the infringers of it, which Bull is recited at length in an *Inspeximus* of *Henry* the eighth. Every one readily understands the benefit of free and neutral Ports. But though this Privilege be declared and confirm'd in all the Charters of these Islands ever since, it is now as good as given up and forgotten; the Islanders themselves having in truth render'd it impracticable by their Privateering in time of War.]

Free Trade.

The entrance of the Port, pretty well set off with Rocks, is on both sides guarded by Castles. On the left, by an old Castle [of no account.] On the right, by another call'd *Cornet*, lifted up indifferent high on a solid rocky Mass, with the Sea quite round it when the Tide is in. In Queen *Mary*'s Time, new Fortifications were added to it by Sir *Leonard Chamberlan*, Governor of the Island, and * since that, by [Sir] *Thomas Leighton*, who succeeded him. For therein resides for the most part the Governor of the Island, with a Garrison, who on no account will suffer either *French*, or Women, to come into it. [This *Castle* is indeed of great Importance, as it commands the Town and Harbour, and is separated from the Land by an arm of the Sea, which is not less than six hundred yards wide, and not fordable but at low Water, in great Spring-Tides. It made a better figure, before its upper Walls and Buildings, which were very high and noble, with a lofty Tower seen above all the rest, and carrying the Standard, were blown up by Lightning. As to its strength, it remains the same in the main, the Powder having had little or no effect on the Ramparts and Batteries which lay lower. That terrible Accident happen'd in the year 1672, under the Lord Viscount *Hatton*'s Government, who himself was wonderfully preserved, but his Lady was kill'd.

Cornet Castle.

* Lately, C.

To return once more to the Port. Upon a Survey of this Island by the Lord *Dartmouth*, in the Reign of King *Charles* the second, a Place was found and pitch'd upon to the North-west, and more in the Chanel, for making another. It was to be a Mole, which would have admitted of very large men of War, and was for it's defence and security to have a Citadel added to it. But the Estimate of the Charge ran too high, for the condition that the Exchequer was in at that Time. How glad would the *French* be to have but one such Place any where betwixt *Dunkirk* and *Brest*, and how little would they value any cost to render it fit for their purpose!]

To the North of the Island, adjoins a Peninsula, call'd *Le Val*; which once had a House of Religious on it, by the name of a Priory. To the West, near the Sea, is a Lake of a mile and a half compass, well stored with Fish, Carps especially, which are much commended for their largeness and exquisite Taste. The Inhabitants do not use the like Industry, in cultivating their Land, as they of *Jersey*; but very busily apply themselves to Navigation and Merchandize, for a more uncertain gain. Every man's humour being here to have his own ground to manage apart, the whole Island is thereby broken into small Parcels by Hedges and Inclosures, which they reckon not only an Improvement, but a Security to the Country against an Invader.

Le Val.

[In the second year of Her Majesty Queen *Anne*, *Heneage Finch*, second Son of *Heneage* late Earl of *Nottingham* and Lord High Chan-

See *Ailesford*, in Kent.

Chancellor of *England*, was advanced to the Honour of Baron *Guernsey*

Comparison of *Jersey* and *Guernsey*

These two Islands, having been described separately, are now, in some particulars, to be compared, and then to be jointly considered Of late years, particularly before the two last Wars with *France*, *Jersey* hath been thought to equal, if not surpass, *Guernzey*, in Commerce and number of Shipping And as to *Inclosures*, (which are mention'd above,) *Jersey* is far more inclosed, thicker planted, and better wooded *Guernsey* lies naked enough, and bare of Forest-Trees. Neither is it so well peopl'd. Their Train-bands muster but about twelve hundred Men, therefore not regimented as in *Jersey* The Land is high on the South, and declines to the North, quite contrary to *Jersey*]

Things common to *Jersey* and *Guernsey*

Both Islands are adorn'd with many Gardens and Orchards, which supply them with an artificial sort of Wine, made of Apples Some call it *Sisera*, we *Sydre*. The Inhabitants of both are originally either *Normans* or *Britons*, and their Language is French, yet they cannot endure to be thought or call'd *French*, but are pleas'd when you call them *English*. In both, *Vraic* is the Fuel for firing, or Sea coal brought to them from *England* Both abound with Fish, and both have the same form of Government, [varying a little, in some Particulars]

Both belong'd to *Normandy*

These two Islands, with the others in the neighbourhood, belong'd once to *Normandy* But after that *Henry* the first King of *England*, had in the year 1108 defeated his Brother *Robert*, he annex'd both *Normandy* and these Islands to the Crown of *England*; and ever since they have stedfastly adher'd to *England*; even at that juncture when King *John* of *England*, being convicted of the murther of his Nephew, was by formal Sentence adjudged to have forfeited his right to *Normandy*, which he held as Vassal of the French King, and the whole Province fell off from him, and also when afterwards *Henry* the third King of *England* quitted all claim to *Normandy* for a Sum of Money. From thence-forward they have with great constancy, and much honour to themselves, stood ever true to their Faith and Allegiance plighted to the *English*; and are all that now remains to the Kings of *England*, of their Ancestor *William the Conqueror*'s Inheritance, and of the Dutchy of *Normandy*; and that in despight of all attempts made upon them by the *French*, to whom it has long been a great eye-sore to have these Islands in view of their Coast, and see them not in their's, but in the English possession. [Nor is it merely out of a Punctilio of Honour, that the *French* see with uneasiness these Islands so near them under the English Power. Their want of Harbours upon the Chanel, with which these Islands would furnish them, and the annoyance they receive from them in time of War by Privateering, are Reasons of great weight and force, to make them wish themselves Masters of them But the same reasons must ever oblige *England*, so long as it understands its Interest, to hold them fast, and to have a vigilant Eye on their Preservation: not to say, that the Fidelity of the Inhabitants well deserves protection and defence]

Attempts of the *French* to recover them

It appears from the Records of the Kingdom, that in the Reign of *Edward* the fourth, the French seiz'd * *Jersey*, but through the Valour of *Richard Harleston*, *Valett of the Crown*, (as the Style ran in those Days) they were † driven out again; for which brave Action the King rewarded him with the Government of both the Island and the Castle Likewise in the Year 1549, when *England* under an Infant-King was embroiled with Rebellions at Home, *Leo Strozzi*, Commander of the French Galleys, invaded the same Island, but having lost many of his Men in the repulse given him, was forced to desist from that Enterprize. [The first of these happen'd during the Contest betwixt *Henry* the sixth and *Edward* the fourth for the Crown; when the *French* had found means to surprize *Mont-Orgueil* Castle in *Jersey* by Treachery, and to get possession of about half the Island; while *Philip de Carteret*, Seigneur of St *Ouen*, secured the other half for *England*. *Henry* the sixth being dead, and Sir *Richard Harlinston* Vice-Admiral of *England* coming to *Guernsey* with a Squadron of Ships, his Assistance was crav'd, and the Castle (hardly otherwise to be recover'd) surrender'd for want of Provision But as to *Strozzi*'s Galleys, their main design seems to have been against some English Ships at Anchor in the Road of that Island. Not succeeding therein, they sailed to *Jersey*, and there it was that the Descent was made, and that they were repuls'd]

* *Guernsey*, C

† Soon driven out, C

Francica, 16 Edw 4

Ecclesiastical Government

As to Ecclesiastical Affairs, they were subject to the Bishop of *Coutance* in *Normandy*, until he, * within our memory, refus'd to renounce the Authority which the Pope claims in *England*, as our Bishops do Upon that, follow'd a separation and dismembring of them from the Diocese of *Coutance* by Queen *Elizabeth*, and they were annex'd to the Diocese of *Winchester* for ever; so that the Bishop of *Winchester* and his Successors are to perform and execute all things here, which pertain to the Episcopal Jurisdiction. Nevertheless, the Discipline of the Church of *Geneva* having been introduc'd by French Ministers, it * continu'd a good while to be the Rule by which Church Matters || were directed [But to be somewhat more particular upon these heads While these Islands were along with *Normandy*, they could not be more conveniently laid, than to the See of *Coutance*, which is nearest to them After they became English, that Bishop held his Jurisdiction over them very precariously, notwithstanding the sameness of Religion King *John* threaten'd to substract them, and annex them to *Exeter* *Henry* the seventh actually procur'd a Bull from Pope *Alexander* the sixth to unite them to *Salisbury*; and then, changing his mind as to the Diocese, he got another from the same Pope to transfer them to *Winchester*. And the reason recited in the Bull for obtaining it, is the danger which might accrue to the Islands, by the *French* having access to them, and visiting them at pleasure, under pretence of a subjection to them in Spirituals It is added in the Bull, that for a like reason, *Calais*, then in the hands of the *English*, had been exempted from its Metropolitan the Archbishop of *Tours*, and laid to *Canterbury* But however this Bull is in Bishop *Lanton*'s Register, it remain'd without execution But when Religion came to be concern'd, the Substraction was effectually made by an Order of Council, in the year 1568, the 10th of Queen *Elizabeth*. As to the *Discipline* before-mention'd, how undesignedly soever it might be brought in at the first, the means afterwards us'd to establish it were not so warrantable; of which a good account is given by Dr *Heylin*, and to him the Reader must be referr'd. It prevailed in *Jersey* until the twenty first year of King *James* the first; and in *Guernsey*, *Alderney*, and *Sark*, until the Restoration of King *Charles* the second At this day,

* So said, ann 1607

* Continues, C

|| Are still, C

Survey of *Guernsey* and *Jersey*, Pas sim

day, the Liturgy of the Church of *England*, translated into French, is received in all the Islands; nor is there one Publick Congregation professing a dissent from it The twelve Parishes in *Jersey* have each their Minister, call'd Rector, no Pluralities being there allow'd Four of the ten Parishes in *Guernsey* being united, that Island has but eight Ministers; and *Alderney* has one, and *Sark* another This is meant only of such as have *Institution*; for, besides them, Assistants are sometimes taken in, in the nature of Lecturers In the two former Islands, one of the Ministers is Commissary to the Bishop of *Winchester*, and is call'd the *Dean* He has a Jurisdiction, and keeps his Court; but the other Ministers sit with him in Judgment, and he takes their Opinion before he gives Sentence The Churches generally are large and strongly built, with lofty Towers or Spires of Stone, but somewhat too naked of Ornaments within; which in great measure is owing to the Discipline that once obtain'd here]

Parishes.

Dean.

Civil Government

As to the Civil Customs and Constitutions of these Islands, I might, by the help of our public Records, mention some of them here, as namely, That King *John* instituted *Twelve sworn* Coroners, [now better known by the name of *Jurats*, and *Justices*, of whom mention was made before, in *Jersey*,] *to hold the Pleas, and preserve the rights belonging to the Crown, and granted, for the Security of the Islanders, That the Bailly might thenceforward, with the* * *View and Concurrence of the Coroners, Try Causes, without Writ of* Novel Disseisin *within the year, of* Mortdancester *within the year, and of* Dowry *within the year*, &c That *the* Jurats *shall not delay Judgment beyond the year; That in Customs* [or Duties upon Merchandize] *and in all other Affairs, the People of these Islands shall be treated as* Englishmen *born*, and not as foreigners But I think it best to leave these Matters to the more curious enquiry of others In general this may be said, that the Norman *Customs*, [or Laws] prevail here in most things [For the Body of the Norman Laws is call'd *La Coûtume de Normandie* And this *Custom of Normandy*, as it stood pure and unalter'd, before that Dutchy was wrested from *England*, is still the Law of these Islands King *John*'s Constitutions, mention'd (in part) above, and the Ordinances of *Henry* the seventh, and of other English Kings, have been superadded since By means of all which, these Islands enjoy many valuable Privileges and Immunities For instance, That for any Matter or Cause arising within the Islands, the Inhabitants shall not be drawn into the Courts of *Westminster*, nor shall be obliged to obey any Writ or Process issued out from thence; That when the King shall please to send over Commissioners (as in some extraordinary Cases has been done) such Commissioners shall come with no less Authority than of his Broad Seal, shall proceed according to the Laws and Customs of the Islands, and shall have the Bailly and Jurats of the Place sitting and making conjunctive Records with them; with other Privileges of the same nature, of which it were too long to speak here

* *Visum*

If ought occurs, which concerns the whole Community, the *States* are call'd to deliberate about it When Sir *Edward Hyde*, afterwards the great and noble Earl of *Clarendon*, was in *Jersey*, attending on the Prince in that Tragical year 1648, he was surpriz'd to hear them talk of *calling the States*, but found no impropriety in the Word, when he understood, that, bating the vast disproportion betwixt them and the States of great Kingdoms, they truly had what is most essential to such Assemblies. Nor did the Crown ever deny them the honour of receiving Addresses and Deputations from them under that name These *States* consist of the Bailly and Jurats, as the first Body; of the Beneficed Clergy, that are Natives or naturaliz'd, as the second, and of the Representatives of the Parishes, as the third; with the Governor, or his Lieutenant, inspecting their Debates, that nothing pass in prejudice of the King's Service; in which Case he has a Negative upon them, till his Majesty's Pleasure be known, otherwise not Briefly, the whole Civil Polity of these Islands is well framed, and wisely constituted, and bears withal signal Marks of the indulgence and gentleness of the English Government]

Sark

I need say but little of *Sark*, *Jethow*, and *Arne*; because not mention'd in ancient Writers. The first a small Island, seated in the midst of all the rest, and moated round with Rocks and Precipices, and by Queen *Elizabeth* granted to *J* [*Philip de Carteret, Seigneur*] *de St. Ouen* in *Jersey*, who made a Settlement on it (to the bettering, they say, of his Estate,) when before the Island lay waste, the * Antiquity of which Gentleman's Family, some, upon what ground I know not, carry up even beyond St. *Ouen*'s time The *second*, serving the Governor of *Garnsey* for a Park to fatten Cattle, and keep Deer, Rabbits, and Pheasants in The *third*, bigger than this, having *once* a House of *Franciscans* on it [*Sark* indeed, was not without a name pretty early, on account of the Convent of St *Maglorius*, a very antient foundation here. This was a holy man, a Christian *Briton*, who, with many others, flying from before the prevailing Heathen *Saxons* into *Armorica*, was made Bishop of *Dol*, and became the happy instrument of planting Christianity in these Islands, about the year 565 The Convent bearing his name, and in which he himself is said to have sometime resided, was standing in the Reign of *Edward* the third, and had a Pension paid to it yearly out of the Exchequer As for the Island, the *French* have laid hands on it, and kept it a while, it was recover'd in Queen *Mary*'s Reign; yet so, that after they were gone, it remain'd uninhabited Lest they should return, and by their neighbourhood create perpetual trouble to the other Islands, *Philip de Carteret*, mention'd above, a worthy Gentleman, and of a publick Spirit, undertook to place such a Colony in it as should keep out the *French* He got a grant from Queen *Elizabeth*, and the Island was made over to him and his heirs, to hold it of the Crown under a small acknowledgment And now, in short, it is a very pretty Island, tho' but two miles long; being well supplied with good Water, and bearing excellent Corn, even more than the Inhabitants need for their use, who are in number about three hundred; all, Tenants to the Seigneur of St *Ouen*, and living happily and easily under him It is by it's situation one of the strongest places in the World, the Land being vastly high, and wholly inaccessible, except in two or three places, where yet the Ascent is very steep and difficult There was no way for Draughts and Carriages from the Sea Therefore *Philip de Carteret* caused one to be cut, with hands, through the overhanging Cliff, going a while under ground and in the dark, and then rising up within the Island;

See below

Jethow.

Arne

Island; much like the famous Passage through Mount *Pausilyppus* near *Naples*; and this moreover is secured by a Gate, and defended with Canon. As *Alderney*, so is this Island also a Dependance of *Guernsey* For tho' here have been four Islands accounted for, yet are there no more than two Governments and Jurisdictions *Jersey* of it self, is one; *Guernsey*, *Alderney*, and *Sark* together, are the other *Jethe* and *Arm* are not reckon'd, as being inconsiderable; they are nevertheless of great use, as plac'd by nature, where they are, for giving shelter to the Road of *Guernsey* As to the Antiquity ascribed to the Family of *Philip de Carteret*, as intimated above, it is certainly very great For, to go back from the Year 1564, when *Philip de Carteret* began his settlement on *Sark*, to the year 677, when St. *Ouen* Archbishop of *Rouen* died, it is no less than 887 years And yet there is extant an old Manuscript-History of *Jersey*, brought down to the year 1585, written with as much appearance of Truth and Sincerity as any History ever was, which tells us of such a Succession of Seigneurs of St. *Ouen*, of the name of *Carteret*, following one another from Father to Son in a direct Line, as will more than fill up that space Be that as it will, it is unquestionably a Family of great Antiquity, and mention'd with honour in the History of *Normandy* For there the name of *Renaud de Carteret* stands upon the List with those of the Count *d' Eu*, and other distinguished Noblemen and *Chevaliers*, who accompanied Duke *Robert* to the Conquest of the Holy Land The name of *Carteret* is from a *Seigneurie* and Tract of Land in *Normandy*, so call'd to this day, once possess'd by this Family, till lost for their adherence to *England* at the Revolution of that Dutchy under King *John*, as on the other hand, divers Norman Gentlemen who had Estates in these Islands, forfeited them for transferring their Allegiance to *France* Of later years, this Family hath been deservedly raised to the Dignity of * Peers of *England*, and now of *Great Britain*.]

Philip de Carteret

Du Moulin Hist. de Normandie vers la fin

* See p 340

After these, upon the same Coast, appears an Island, which Antoninus calls *Liga*, and which it still retains in the present name *Ligon* Next to this, lie seven Islands which Antoninus calls *Siadæ* from the number (for *Saith* in British signifies seven) and the French at this day, *Le jet Isles* These I take to be corruptly call'd *Hiadatæ* by Strabo, from which he tells us it is not a day's-sail to Britain Seven furlongs from these *Siadæ*, lies *Barsa*, mention'd also by Antoninus; the French call it the *Isle de Bas*, the English *Basepole* for *bas* in British signifies *shallow*, and so the Sailors find the Sea here, when they found it. For it is hardly above seven or eight fathom deep, whereas in other parts of the Coast, they find twelve, eighteen, or twenty fathom water, as we may see by their Hydrographical Charts Between these *Islands* and *Foy* in *Cornwall*, they find the British Sea very deep, namely, fifty eight fathom or thereabouts in the Chanel

Liga

Barsa.

Spec. Britan.

Where the British Seas is deepest.

[*The* CASSITERIDES, *or* SILLY ISLANDS.]

FROM hence I will set sail for our own Coast of Britain As we steer along the Shore, after we have pass'd *Ideston*, *Mousehole*, and *Long ships* (which are rather infamous Rocks, than Islands,) we come within sight of Antoninus's *Lisia*, at the very utmost point of Cornwall; which is call'd by the People thereabouts *Lethowsow*, and by others *the Gulfe*; and is only visible at low water This I take to be that which the Antients call'd *Lisia*; because *Lis* (as I have heard) signifies the very same in British For *Liso* implies a great sound and roaring, like that which is made by Whirlpools; and from this place the tide presses both to north and east with great noise and violence, being streighten'd between Cornwall and those Islands which Antoninus calls *Sigdeles*, Sulpitius *Sillina*, Solinus *Silures*, the English *Silly*, the Dutch Seamen *Sorlings*, and the ancient Greeks *Hesperides* and *Cassiterides*. For Dionysius Alexandrinus calls them *Hesperides* (from their western situation) in those Verses

Lisia

Scilly

The Gulf *Lisia*, by transposal makes *Silia*

——Αὐτὰρ ὑπ' ἄκρην
Ἱερὴν ἣν ἐνέπουσι κάρηνον ἔμμεν Εὐρωπείης

Νήσους δ' Ἑσπερίδας, τόθι κασσιτέροιο γενέθλη,
Ἀφνειοὶ ναίουσιν ἀγαυῶν παῖδες Ἰβήρων.

Which Priscian translates thus

*Sed * summam contra Sacram, cognomine dicunt*
Quam caput Europæ, sunt stanni pondere plenæ
Hesperides, *populus tenuit quas fortis Iberi*

* Sacrum promontorium

Th' *Hesperides* along the Ocean spread
With Mines of Tin and wealthy Hills abound;
And stout *Iberians* till the fertile ground

Festus Avienus calls them the *Ostrymnides*, in his Poem *De oris Maritimis*, or the Sea coasts; wherein he has these Verses, according to the Paris edition, and the Notes on them

In quo insulæ sese exerunt Oestrymnides,
Laxe jacentes, & metallo divites
Stanni atque plumbi multa vis hic gentis est,
Superbus animus, efficax solertia,

Nego-

Negotiandi cura jugis omnibus
* *Notisque cumbis turbidum latè fretum*
Et belluosi gurgitem Oceani secant ;
Non hi carinas quippe pinu texere
Facere morem non abiete, ut usus est,
Curvant phasello · sed rei ad miraculum
Navigia junctis semper aptant pellibus,
Corioque vastum sæpe percurrunt salem.

* *Non usque navibus*, we read in the notes of Paris.

Where the wide Isles *Oestrymnides* are seen,
Enrich'd with deepest veins of Lead and Tin
Stout are the Natives, and untam'd in war,
Gain is their study, Trade their only care.
Yet not in Ships they try the watry road,
And rouze the shapeless Monsters of the flood
For neither Gallies of the lofty pine
They know to frame, nor weaker maple join
In shallow barks but skins to skins they sew ;
Secure in these to farthest parts they go,
And pathless Seas with keels of leather plow

Such also were us'd in this Sea in the year 914 For we read of certain pious men transported from Ireland into Cornwal, in a *Carab* or *Caroch*, which was made of two hides and an half Thus also the same Avienus speaks of these Islands, afterwards

Tartesiisque in terminos Oestrymnidum
Negotiandi mos erat, Carthaginis
Etiam colonis ——

Oft the *Tartessians*, thro' the well known Seas,
Would sail for traffick to th' *Oestrymnides*,
And *Carthaginians* too ——

Other Greek writers call'd these the *Cassiterides*, from their *Tinne* as Strabo calls a certain place among the *Drangi* in Asia, *Cassiteron*, for the same reason ; and Stephanus in his Book *de Urbibus* observes from Dionysius, that a certain Island in the Indian Sea was call'd *Cassitera*, from Tinne ; As for *Mictis*, which Pliny (upon the authority of Timæus) says is six days sail, * inward, from Britain, and produces white Lead, I dare not say it was one of these Yet I am aware, that the learned *Hermolaus Barbarus* found some Manuscripts that have it *Mitteris* for *Mictis*, and thereupon would read it *Cartiteris* However, I may (from the authority of the Ancients, from the situation, and from their veins of Tinn) warrant these to be the very *Cassiterides*, so much sought for *Over-against the* Artabri, *who are opposite to the west parts of Britain*, says Strabo, *and north of them, lie those Islands which they call* Cassiterides, *situate in effect in the same Climate with Britain* Thus also in another place *The Sea is much wider between Spain and the* Cassiterides, *than between the Cassiterides and Britain* *The* Cassiterides *face the coast of Celtiberia*, saith Solinus Diodorus Siculus, *In those Islands next the Iberian Sea, call'd from the Tinn,* Cassiterides Eustathius, *The* Cassiterides *are Ten Islands lying close to one another, in the north*

* *Introrsum a Britannia*

Now, considering that these Isles of *Silly* are opposite to the *Artabri*, i. e *Galitia*, in Spain ; that they stand directly north of them ; that they lie in the same Climate with Britain ; that they face *Celtiberia* ; that the Sea is much broader between them and Spain than between them and Britain ; that they lie just upon the *Iberian* Sea, and close to one another, northward ; that there are only ten of any note, *viz.* St. *Maries*, *Annoth*, *Agnes*, *Sampson*, *Silly*, *Bresar*, *Rusco* or *Trescaw*, St. *Helens*, St. *Martins*, and *Arthur* ; again, considering, what is far more material, that they have veins of Tinn as no other Isle in these parts has ; and lastly, that two of the lesser sort, *Minan-Withan* and *Minuisisand*, seem to derive their names from *Mines* From so many concurring testimonies, I should rather conclude these to be the *Cassiterides*, than either the *Azores* which lie too far westward, or *Cisarga* (with Olivarius) which in a manner joins to Spain, or even Britain it self, with Ortelius ; since there were *many* of the *Cassiterides*, and Dionysius Alexandrinus, after he has treated of the *Cassiterides*, gives a *separate* account of Britain

If any deny these to be the *Cassiterides*, because there are more than *ten* ; let him also reckon the *Hæbudes*, and the *Orcades* and if at the foot of his account he find the number of the *Hæbudes* * more or less than five, and of the *Orcades*, than thirty, as Ptolemy reckons them, let him inquire for them in some other place, than where they are generally suppos'd to be, and I am pretty sure he will never find them by going this way to work For the truth is, the ancient writers had no more certainty concerning these remote Parts and Islands, than we have of the Islands in the Streights of *Magellan*, and the Country of *New Guiney*

* Neither more, J. C

It is not to be thought strange, that Herodotus thought nothing of them, for he freely confesses, that he had no certain knowledge of the more remote parts of Europe Yet Lead was first transported from this Island into Greece *Lead* (says Pliny,) *was first brought hither from the Isle of* Cassiteris, *by Midacritus* But concerning this matter, let us hear Strabo, towards the end of the third Book of his Geography *The Isles of* Cassiterides *are ten in number, close to one another, and situate in the main* Ocean *to the north of the Port of the* Artabri *One of them is desert and unpeopl'd, the rest are inhabited The People wear black cloaths and coats reaching down to their ancles, and girt about the breast, with a staff in their hand, like the* Furies *in Tragedies They live by Cattle, and straggle up and down without any certain dwelling They have Mines both of Tin and* Lead, *which Commodities, as also Skins, they exchange to the Merchants for earthen Vessels, Salt, and † Instruments of Brass At first, the* Phœnicians *only traded hither from* Gades, *concealing these Voyages from others The* Romans, *to find the place where they drove this trade, employ'd one to watch the master of a Vessel, but he run his Ship upon a shallow out of spight, and after he had brought them into the same danger, escap'd himself, and receiv'd the value of his Cargo out of the* common *treasury, by way of recompence However, the Romans by many attempts, did at last find out this Trade Afterwards,* Publius Crassus *having sail'd thither, and seen them work these Mines which were not very deep ; and that the people lov'd Peace, and at their leisure Navigation also instructed them how to carry it on, tho' the Sea they had to cross, was wider than that between it and Britain*

Plumbum, R. D. Rer' ...

† *Χαλκώματα*

Silly

But now concerning *Silly* About a hundred and forty five Islands go by the name of *Silly*, all clad with grass, and cover'd with greenish moss, besides many hideous rocks and huge Stones above water, plac'd in a kind of circle, eight leagues from the utmost Promontory of Cornwal Some of them afford good plenty of Corn; and are all stock'd with Rabbits, Cranes, Swans, Herons, and Sea-fowl The largest is that which takes its name from St *Mary*, where is a Castle and a Garrison *These are the Islands, which* (as Solinus says) *are sever'd from the coast of the* Danmonii *by a rough narrow Sea of two or three hours sail; the Inhabitants whereof live according to the old methods They have no Markets, nor does money pass among them; they give and take one thing for another, and provide necessaries rather by exchange than price They are very Religious All, both men and women, pretend to the art of Divination* Eustathius, out of Strabo, calls the People *Melanchlani*, because they wore long black Coats as low as their ankle Sardus was persuaded, that they liv'd till they were weary of life for they threw themselves from a rock into the Sea, in hopes of a better life, which was certainly the Opinion of the British *Druids* Hither the Roman Emperors us'd to send such as were condemn'd to the Mines For Maximus the Emperor, having pass'd Sentence of death upon *Priscillanus* for Heresie, commanded Instantius, a Bishop of Spain, and Tiberianus, to be transported into the Silly-Islands, their goods being first confiscate So also Marcus the Emperor banish'd one (for pretending to prophesie at the time of the insurrection of Cassius, and foretel things to come, as if he were inspir'd,) into this Island, as some imagin, who would read *Sylia Insula* for *Syria Insula*, since Geographers know no such Island as *Syria*. This Relegation, or Transportation to foreign Islands, was one kind of banishment in those days, and the Governors of Provinces could banish in this manner, in case their Province had any Islands appertaining to it, if not, they wrote to the Emperor to assign some Island for the *Relegation* of the condemn'd Party Neither was it lawful to remove the body of the party thus exil'd, to any other place for burial, without special Licence from the Emperor

Sulpitius Se verus

Ulp lib 7 de Mathematicis

Relegation

We meet with nothing of these Islands, not so much as the name, in the writers of the middle age, but only that King *Athelstan* conquer'd them, and after his return built the Church of St *Beriena* or *Buriena*, in the utmost Promontory of Britain westward, where he landed

I Cornwall, p 11, 12

Over-against these on the Coast of France, just before the *Osissimi* or *Britannia Armorica*, lies the Island which Pliny calls *Axantos*, and which retains the same name, being now call'd *Usbant* Antoninus calls it *Uxantissena*, which is a compound of the two names *Uxantis*, and *Sena* For this last is an Island somewhat lower, which is now call'd *Sayn*, over-against Brest; in some Copies it is call'd *Siambis*, and corruptly by Pliny *Sounos*, which, from east to west, for seven miles together, is encompass'd with Rocks rather than Islands, very close to one another As for this *Sayn*, take what Pomponius Mela has said of it *Sena, situate in the British Sea, over-against the Coast of the* Osissimi, *is famous for the Oracle of a French God, whose Priests are said to be nine in number, all under a Vow of perpetual Virginity The French call them* Zenæ *or* Lenæ (for so I rather read it, with Turnebus, than *Gallicenæ*;) *and they think them so strongly inspir'd, that they can raise the Sea or the Winds with their Songs, can transform themselves into what Creatures they please, cure Distempers that are beyond the skill of others, and know and foretel what is to come*, &c. Beneath these, there lie other Islands, viz *Isles aux Muttons*, near *Pen-Marc*, that is, the *Horse-head*, *Gleran*, over-against old *Blavia* (now *Blavet*) *Grois* and *Belle-Isle*, which Pliny calls *Veneticæ* For they lie over-against the *Veneti* in little *Bretagne*, and might perhaps take that name from their being *Fishermen*: for so *Venna* seems to signifie in the language of the old Gauls Strabo takes these to have been the Ancestors of the *Venetians* in Italy, and says also, that they design'd to engage Cæsar by Sea, when he was about to make his expedition into Britain Some, from *Dionysius Afer*, call these *Insulæ Veneticæ*, *Nesides*; whereas in the Greek Copy we find it Νησσιάδων πόρος, that is, *a Tract of Islands* Of which, Priscian from him writes thus

Axantos

Usbant

Siambis

The Mariners call it the Saim

Veneti Insulæ Veneticæ

Nesides

Vannes Venna Caroli i ejus catio Caroli, as Helgarius says

Nec spatio distant Nessidum littora longè,
In quibus uxores * *Amnitum Bacchica sacra*
Concelebrant hederæ foliis, tectæque corymbis
Non sic Bistonides Absinthi ad flumina Thraces,
Exertis celebrant clamoribus εἰραφιώτῃ

* *Samnitium*

Here the *Nessides* shew their neighbouring shore,
Where *Samnite* Wives at sacred *Orgies* roar,
With Ivy leaves and berries cover'd o'er
Not with such cries the wild *Bistonian* dames,
Near fair *Absinthus* fill the *Thracian* streams.

This is also express'd in Festus Avienus,

Hinc spumosus item ponti liquor explicat æstum,
Et brevis e pelago vortex subit hic chorus ingens
Fœminei cœtus pulchri colit Orgia Bacchi,
Producit noctem ludus sacer aera pulsant
Vocibus, & crebris late sola calcibus urgent
Non sic Absynthi propè flumina Thraces, & almæ
Bistonides, non qua celeri ruit agmine Ganges,
Indorum populi stata curant festa Lyæo

Hence constant tides the foaming deep supplies,
And noisy Whirlpools on the Surface rise
Here a great quire of Dames by custom meet,
And *Bacchus Orgies* every year repeat
And spend in sacred Rites the joyful night.
Through all the air their tuneful voices sound,
Their nimble feet salute the trembling ground
Not in such troops *Bistonian* Matrons croud
To the great Feast at fam'd *Absinthus* flood
Nor so the *Indians* praise their drunken God

Now, that *Belle-Isle* is one of these *Nessidæ*, Strabo's authority, grounded upon the relations of others, is a sufficient proof For it lies before the mouth of the river *Loire*, and Ptolemy places the *Samnites* on the Coast of France, over against it. For thus Strabo. *They say there is a small Island in the Ocean but not very far in, over against the mouth of the Loir It is inhabited by the Wives of the* Samnites, *who are inspir'd by Bacchus, and worship him with Ceremonies and Sacrifices No men are suffer'd to come hither, but the Women take boat, and after they have lain with their husbands, return into the Island It is also a custom here, to take off the roof of their Temple every year, and to cover it again the same day before Sun-set; every one of the women being oblig'd to bring in a burden to it; and whoever lets her burden fall, is torn in pieces by the rest They never give over gathering the pieces drept in carrying till their fit of Frenzy is over It always happens that one or other is thus torn in pieces, for letting her burden fall* Thus did the Ancients, in treating of the more remote parts of the World, give themselves over to Lies and Fables But he tells us, *That as for those things which are said of* Ceres *and* Proserpine, *they are more probable For the report is, that in an Island near Britain, they sacrifice to these Goddesses after the same manner as they do in Samothracia*

Since Mela (who was himself a Spaniard) Lib. 2.
makes the British Sea to reach as far as the Coast of Spain and the Pyrenees, it would fall within the compass of my design to treat of *Normonstier, L'isle de Dieu*, and *L'isle de Rey* likewise; which are famous for their store of Bay Salt, but the bare mention of them is sufficient, since they are not taken notice of by the ancient Geographers

The next Island to this, now known by the name of *Oleron* (but call'd *Uliarus* in Pliny) lies, *Oleron*
as he says, in the Bay of Aquitain, at the mouth *Uliarus*
of the river *Charonton*, now *Charente*, and was endow'd with many Privileges by the Kings of England, when Dukes of Aquitain In those days, it was so eminent for Shipping and naval Strength, that Laws were made in it for the regulation of these Seas in the year 1266, as there were in *Rhodes* heretofore for the government of the Mediterranean

[The CONCLUSION.]

HAVING now brought this Work (through so many Shelves of the Ocean and rugged Rocks of Antiquity,) safe into the Harbour Nothing now remains, but that, like the Mariners of old, who us'd to dedicate their tatter'd *Sails*, or a votive *Plank*, to Neptune, I also consecrate something to the *Almighty*, and to Venerable *Antiquity* * A Vow, which I most willingly make, and which, by the blessing of God, I hope to discharge in due time In the mean while, let me desire the Reader to consider, that through this whole Work I have been struggling with that malicious and devouring Enemy, *Time*, of which the Greek Poet has this admirable passage,

* He seems to mean the *History Lecture*, which he settled in *Oxford*

> Ἀργαλέως φέρεται παλιὸς χρόνος, ἀλλὰ παρέρπων,
> Καὶ φωνὰς κλέπτει φθεγγομένων μερόπων
> Καὶ μὴ φαινόμενος τοὺς φαινομένους φανίζει
> Καὶ μὴ φαινομένους, εἰς φανερὸν προφέρει

> Old Time moves slowly, though he knows no stay,
> And steals our Voices as he creeps away
> Unseen himself, he hides from mortal view
> Things that are seen, and Things unseen does shew

However, I comfort my self with that Distich of *Mimnermus*, which I know by experience to be true

> Τὴν σ' αὐτοῦ φρένα τέρπε, δυσηλεγέων δὲ πολιτῶν
> Ἄλλος τίς σε κακῶς, ἄλλος ἄμεινον ἐρεῖ.

> *Oblectes animum, plebs est morosa legendo,*
> *Ille bene de te dicet, at ille malè*

> [illegible] contented, for thou'lt ever find,
> Thy Labours some will blame, and some commend

THE

APPENDIX.

I. Annals of *IRELAND.*

II. Hiſtory of the *O-NEALS*, and their Rebellions in *Ireland.*

III. Chronicle of the Kings of *MAN.*

THE

PREFACE

TO THE

Annals of Ireland.

HEN the Press had got * *thus far, the Right Honourable* William *Lord* Howard *of Naworth, out of his great Zeal for promoting the Knowledge of Antiquity, communicated to me the* Annals of Ireland *in Manuscript, from the Year* 1152 *to the Year* 1370 *And seeing there is nothing extant, that I know of, that is more perfect in the kind, since* Giraldus Cambrensis ; *seeing also that the excellent Owner has given me leave*; *I think it very proper to publish them The World is, without doubt, as much indebted to the noble Owner for preserving them, as to the Author for writing them The Stile is rough and barren, according to the Age it was written in*; *yet the Contents give great Light into the Irish History, and would have been helpful to me, if they had come to my Hands sooner As they are, I here present them to the Reader, faithfully copy'd from the Original, even with the Errors If he has any thing of this nature more perfect, he will be so kind to communicate it, if not, he must be content with this, till some one or other will give us a more compleat account of these Affairs, and continue it to the present Time with greater Elegance, a Work that would not cost very much pains*

* To the end of the Description of Ireland

[*Note*, In this Edition, the word † *Dominus*, which in the former was for the most part translated *Sir*, is now translated *Lord*; most of the persons to whom that title is given, having been probably either of the greater Nobility, or of the lesser sort of *Barons* or *Lords*, and not *Knights* Therefore the word *Sir* is not prefix'd to any name as the translation of the Latin *Dominus*, but only where the person is expresly said to have been a *Knight*]

† See the Degrees of England p. ccxlvii

THE

ANNALS of IRELAND.

N the Year of our Lord MCLXII died Gregory, the first Archbishop of Dublin, a worthy Person in all respects, and was succeeded by S *Laurence O Thothil*, Abbot of S Kemnus de Glindelagh, Thomas is made Archbishop of Canterbury

MCLXVI. Rothericke O Conghir, Prince of Conaught, was made King and Monarch of Ireland

MCLXVII. died Maud the Empress This Year Almarick King of Jerusalem took Babylon, and Dermic Mac Morrogh Prince of Leinster, while O Rork King of Meth was employed in a foreign expedition, carry'd away his Wife, who suffer'd herself to be ravish'd with no great difficulty; for she herself contriv'd it, as we find in *Cambrensis*

MCLXVIII Donate King of Uriel, founder of Mellifont Abby, departed this Life This Year, Robert Fitz Stephens, neither unmindful of his promise, nor regardless of his faith, came into Ireland with thirty * Knights

* *Militibus*

MCLXIX Richard Earl of Strogul sent before him into Ireland, a certain young Gentleman of his own Family, nam'd Remund, with ten Knights, about the Kalends of May. The same Earl Richard, this Year, attended with about

200 Knights, and others to the number of a thousand or thereabouts, arriv'd here on S. Bartholomew's eve. This Richard was the son of Gilbert Earl of Strogul (that is *Chippestow*, formerly Strogul) and of Isabel, † Aunt by the Mother's side to King Malcolm and William King of Scotland, and Earl David a hopeful [illegible] man; and, the morrow after the same Apostle, they took the said City, where Eva, Daughter of Dermick, was lawfully marry'd to Earl Richard, and her Father gave her

† *Matertera*

MCLXX S Thomas Becket, Archbishop of Canterbury, suffer'd martyrdom. This same year, the City of Dublin was taken by Earl Richard, and his party; and the Abby de *Castro Dei*, i. e of God's Castle, was founded.

MCLXXI. died Dermick Mac Morrah, of a great age, at Fernys, about the Kalends of May

MCLXXII The Valiant King Henry arriv'd at Waterford with 500 Knights; and, among other things, bestow'd Meth upon * Sir Hugh Lacy. The Abby *de Fonte vivo* was founded this year

* *Domino*

MCLXXIV Gelasius Archbishop of Armagh, the first Primate of Ireland, a pious man, died at a great age. He is said to have been the first Archbishop that wore the Pall · His Predecessors were only titular Archbishops and Primates, in reverence and honour to S Patrick, the Apostle of this Nation, whose See was had in so much Veneration by all, that not only Bishops and Priests, and those of the Clergy, submitted themselves to this Bishop, but all the Kings and Princes Gilbert, a Prelate of great worth, succeeded him in the Archbishoprick.

MCLXXV William King of Scots was taken Prisoner at Alnwick

MCLXXVI Bertram de Verdon founded the Abby of Crokisdenne

MCLXXVII Earl Richard dy'd at Dublin about the Kalends of May, and was buried in Trinity-Church there This year, Vivian Presbyter Cardinal of S Stephen in *monte Callio*, was sent Legat of the apostolick See into Ireland, by Pope Alexander.

MCLXXVIII On the ninth of the Kalends of December, the Abby of Samaria was founded This same year Rose-Vale, that is, *Rossglass*, was founded

MCLXXIX. Miles Cogan, and Ralph the son of Fitz-Stephen, his Son-in-law, was slain between Waterford, and Lismore, &c as we read in *Cambrensis* The same year, Harvie Mont-Marish enter'd into the Monastery of S Trinity in Canterbury; who founded the Monastery of S Mary de Portu, i. e. of *Don Broth*.

MCLXXX. was founded the Abby of the Quire of St Benedict; and also the Abby of Geripount. This year, Laurence Archbishop of Dublin, on the eighteenth of the Kalends of December, was bury'd in Normandy in the Church of S Mary of Aux To him succeeded John Cumin, an Englishman, born at Evesham, and elected unanimously by the Clergy of Dublin (the King himself soliciting for him) and was confirm'd by the Pope This John, afterwards, built S Patrick's Church at Dublin.

MCLXXXIII was confirm'd the Order of the Templers and Hospitallers; and the Abby *De Lege Dei* was founded.

MCLXXXV John, the King's Son, made *Lord* of Ireland by his father, came into Ireland, in the twelfth year of his age; which was the thirteenth since his father's first coming, the fifteenth since the arrival of Fitz-Stephens, and the fourteenth since the coming of Earl Richard; and return'd again in the same fifteenth year

MCLXXXVI. was confirm'd the Order of the Carthusians, and the Grandians This year, Hugh Lacy was kill'd treacherously by an Irishman at Dervath, because the said Hugh intended to build a Castle there; and as he was shewing the Irishman how to work with a Pick-axe, and bow'd his head [illegible], resting on both his hands, the Irishman struck off his head with an Axe; and there the Conquest ended. The same year Christian Bishop of Lismore (formerly Legat of Ireland, who enjoy'd those virtues which he had seen in, and heard from, his holy father St. Bernard, and Pope Eugenius, a venerable person, with whom he liv'd in the Probatory of Clareval, and by whom he was made Legat of Ireland,) after his Obedience perform'd in the Monastery of Kyneleyson, departed this Life Jerusalem, and our Lord's Cross, was taken by the Sultan and the Saracens; and many Christians slain

MCLXXXVII. On the Kalends of July, the Abby of Ynes in Ulster was founded

MCLXXXIX. K Henry, Son of the Empress, departed this Life, and was succeeded by his Son Richard, and buried in Font Evrard This same year was founded the Abby de Colle Victoriæ, i e *Cnokmoy*

MCXC King Richard and King Philip made a Voyage to the Holy Land

MCXCI In the Monastery of Clareval, the Translation of Malachy, Bishop of Armagh, was celebrated with great solemnity

MCXCII. The City of Dublin was burnt

MCXCIII Richard, King of England, in his return from the Holy Land, was taken Prisoner by the Duke of Austria, and paid the Emperor 100000 Marks for his Ransom, besides 30000 to the Empress, and 20000 to the Duke, † upon an Obligation, made to them, in behalf of Henry Duke of Saxony He was detain'd in Prison by the Emperor, a year, six months, and three days; almost all the Chalices throughout England were sold for his ransom This year was founded the Abby *De Jugo Dei*

† *Pro obligatione quam fecerunt ei, pro Henrico*

MCXCIV The Reliques of S Malachy, Bishop of Clareval, were brought into Ireland, and receiv'd with great honour, in the Monastery of Mellifont, and the other Monasteries of the Cistercians

MCXCV Matthew Archbishop of Cassil Legat of Ireland, and John Archbishop of Dublin, took the Corps of Hugh Lacy who conquer'd Meth, from the Irish; and inter'd it with great solemnity in the Monastery of *Betty*, or *Blessedness* but the Head of the said Hugh was laid in S Thomas's Monastery in Dublin.

MCXCVIII The Order of the Friers Predicants was begun about Tolouse, being founded by Dominick II

MCXCIX. died Richard King of England, and was succeeded by his Brother John, who was Lord of Ireland and Earl of Moriton which John slew Arthur the lawful Heir, Son of Geffrey, his Brother

The death of Richard was after this manner. When King Richard besieg'd the Castle of Chaluz in Little Bretagn, he receiv'd his mortal Wound by an Arrow, that was shot by one of those in the Castle, nam'd Bertram de Gourdon As soon as the King found there was no hope of Life, he committed his Kingdom of England and all his other Possessions, to the Custody of his Brother All his Jewels and the fourth part of his Treasure he bequeath'd to his Nephew *Otho* Another fourth part of his Treasure he left to be distributed among his Servants and the poor People When Bertram was taken and brought

brought before the King, he ask'd him for what injury he had kill'd him? Bertram, not at all dismay'd, told him, Thou hast kill'd my Father and two of my Brothers with thy own Hand, and didst intend to do the same with me: take therefore what Revenge thou pleasest, I care not, since thou art kill'd who hast done so much mischief in the World. The King pardon'd him, and order'd him to be set at liberty, and to have 100 Shillings Sterling given him. Yet after the King's death, some of the King's Officers flea'd and hang'd him. The King died on the eighteenth of the Ides of *April*, which happen'd to be the fourth day before Palm-sunday, and the eleventh day after he was wounded. He was buried at Font Eberard, at the feet of his Father. A certain Versificator writ this Distich upon his death,

Istius in morte perimit Formica Leonem,
Proh dolor! in tanto funere mundus obit.

An Ant a Lyon slew, when Richard fell,
And his must be the World's great Funeral.

His Corps was divided into three Parts, Whence this of another Poet,

Viscera Carceolum, Corpus Fons servat Ebrardi,
Et cor Rothomagum, magne Richarde, tuum.

Great Richard's Body's at Fontevrault shown,
His Bowels at Chalons, his Head at Roan.

After the death of King Richard, his Brother John was girt by the Archbishop of Roan with the Sword of the Dukedom of Normandy, on the seventh of the Kalends of May next following. The Archbishop put a Ducal Coronet set round with golden Roses upon his Head. Afterwards, on the sixth of the Kalends of June, he was anointed and crown'd King of England, in St Peter's Church Westminster, upon Ascension-day, being attended with all the Nobility of England. Afterwards, he was summon'd to a Parliament in *France* to answer for the death of his Nephew Arthur, and was depriv'd of Normandy, because he came not accordingly. The same Year was founded the Abby of Commerer.

MCC. Cathol Cronerg, King of Conaught, founder of the Abby *De Colle Victoriæ*, is expell'd Conaught. This Year the Monastery *De Voto* was founded (that is, Tyntern Monastery) by William Marshall Earl Marshal, and of Pembroch, who was Lord of Leinster, *viz.* of four Counties, Weisford, Offory, Caterlagh and Kildare, in right of his Wife. he marry'd the daughter of Richard Earl of Stroghul and of Eve the daughter of Dermic Murcard. This William Earl Marshal being in great danger of Shipwreck a † night and a day, made a Vow, That if he escap'd and came to Land, he would found a Monastery, and dedicate it to Christ and the Virgin *Mary*. So, as soon as he arriv'd at Weysford, he founded this Monastery of Tynterne according to his Vow, and it is nam'd *De Voto*. This year also was founded the Monastery *de Flumine Dei*.

† *Die noctuq.*

MCCII. Cathol Cronerg, or Crorobdyr King of Conaught, was restor'd to his Kingdom. The same year was founded the house of Canons of S. Marie of Connal, by the Lord Meiler Fitz-Henry.

MCCIII. The Abby of S Saviour, *i. e.* Dowisky, which was founded before, was finished in this Year and the next.

MCCIV. A Battle was fought between John Courcy first Earl of Ulster and Hugh Lacy, at Doune, with great slaughter on both sides. Yet John Courcy had the Victory. Afterwards, on the sixth day of the Week, being Good-Friday, as the said John was unarm'd and going in Pilgrimage barefoot and in a linnen Vestment, to the Churches, according to custom, he was treacherously taken Prisoner by his own People, for a sum of Money, part in hand, and part promis'd to be paid afterwards, and was deliver'd to Hugh Lacy, who brought him to the King of England, and receiv'd the Earldom of Ulster, and the Seignory of Conaught upon that account, both belonging to John Courcy. Hugh Lacy being made Earl, rewarded the said treacherous Persons with Gold and Silver, tho' much less, but hang'd them as soon as he had done, and seis'd all their Goods. by this means, Hugh Lacy rules in Ulster, and John Courcy is condemn'd to perpetual Imprisonment, for his former Rebellion against King John, refusing to do him homage, and accusing him of the death of Arthur, the lawful and right Heir to the Crown. While the Earl was in Prison and in great Poverty, having but a small allowance of Provisions, and the same mean and coarse, he said, O God, why dost thou deal thus with me, who have built and repair'd so many Monasteries for thee and thy Saints? After many sorrowful Expostulations of this kind, he fell asleep, and the Holy Trinity appear'd to him, saying, Why hast thou cast me out of my own Seat, and out of the Church of Doun, and plac'd there my S Patrick the Patron of Ireland? For John Courcy had expell'd the Secular Canons out of the Cathedral Church of Doun, and introduc'd the black Monks of Chester in their room. And the Holy Trinity stood there ‖ upon a stately Shrine, and John himself took it down out of the Church, and order'd a Chapel to be built for it, setting up the Image of S Patrick in the great Church, which displeas'd the most-high God. Wherefore he told him, Assure thy self, thou shalt never set foot in thy Seignory again, but in regard of other good Deeds thou hast done, thou shalt be delivered out of Prison with Honour, which happen'd accordingly. For a Controversy arising between John King of England and the King of France about a Lordship and certain Castles, the King of France offer'd to try his right by a Champion. Upon this, the King call'd to mind his valiant Knight John Courcy, whom he cast in Prison upon the information of others, so he sent for him, and ask'd him if he were able to serve him in this Combat? John answer'd, He would not fight for him, but for the Right of the Kingdom he would, which he undertook to do afterwards. And so, refresh'd himself with Meat, Drink and Bathing in the mean while, and recovered his Strength. Whereupon, a day was appointed for the Engagement of those Champions, namely, John Courcy, and the other. But as soon as the Champion of France heard of his mighty † Stomach, and Valour, he refus'd the Combat, and the said Seignory was given to the King of England. The King of France then desir'd to see a Blow of the said Courcy. Whereupon, he set a strong Helmet * full of Mails upon a large Block; and the said John took his sword, and after he had look'd about him in a grim manner, struck the Helmet through from the very Crest, and the sword stuck so fast in the Block, that no one there was able to pull it out, till he himself

‖ *In sede magnitudinis*

† *Comestione*

* *Plenam loricis*

himself, at the request of the two Kings, did it with ease Then they ask'd him, Why he look'd so grim behind him, before he struck? So he told them, If he had fail'd in giving it, he would have certainly cut them all off, as well Kings as others. The Kings made him large Presents, and the King of England restor'd him to his Seignory, viz Ulster John Courcy attempted fifteen several times to sail over into Ireland, but was always in danger, and the Winds cross; so he waited a-while among the Monks of Chester At last he return'd into France, and there dy'd

MCCV The Abby of Wetheny in the County of Limerick was founded by Theobald the Son of Walter Butler, Lord of Carryk

MCCVI The Order of Friars Minors was begun near the City Assisa, by S. Francis

MCCVIII William de Brewes was banish'd out of England, and came into Ireland England was put under an Interdict for the Tyranny of King John A great defeat and slaughter was given at Thurles in Munster by the Lord Geffery Mareys, to the Chief Justice of Ireland's Men

MCCX John King of England came to Ireland with a great Fleet and a strong Army, and the Sons of Hugh Lacy, viz Walter Lord of Meth, and Hugh his Brother, for their Tyranny, and particularly for the Murder of Sir John Courson, Lord of Rathenny and Kilbarrock (for they had heard, that the said John had accus'd them to the King) were driven out of the Nation by the King So they fled into France, and serv'd in the Monasteries of S Taurin unknown, being employ'd in Clay and Brick-work, and sometimes in Gardens, as Gardeners But at length they were discover'd by the Abbot, who intreated the King on their behalf; for he had baptiz'd their Sons, and had been as a Father to them in many things. So, Walter Lacy paid two thousand five hundred Marks, and Hugh Lacy a great Sum of Money, to the King, for their Ransom; and they were restor'd to their former Degree and Lordship, by the Abbot's Intercession Walter Lacy brought with him John the son of Alured, i e Fitz-Acory, Son to the aforesaid Abbot's Brother, and knighted him, giving him the Seignory of Dengle, and many others. Moreover, he brought Monks with him out of the said Monastery, and bestow'd many Lands upon them, with the Cell called Foury; for their Charity, Gratitude, and good Counsel Hugh Lacy Earl of Ulster built a Cell for the Monks, in Ulster, and endow'd it, in a place call'd—. John King of England having taken many Hostages, as well of the English as the Irish, and hang'd a number of Malefactors upon Gibbets, and settled Affairs; return'd into England the same Year he came

MCCXI. The Lord Richard Tuyt was crush'd to death by the fall of a Tower at Alone. He founded the Monastery de Grenard.

MCCXII The Abby of Grenard was founded The same year dy'd John Comyn Archbishop of Dublin, and was buried in the Quire of Trinity-Church; he built S Patrick's Church at Dublin. Henry Londres succeeded him, surnam'd *Scorche-Villeyn*, from a certain Action of his For having call'd in his Tenants one day, to know by what Tenure they held of him, they show'd him their Deeds and Charters to satisfie him; whereupon he order'd them to be burnt, and hence had the name of *Scorche-Villeyn* given him by his Tenants This Henry Archbishop of Dublin was Justiciary of Ireland, and built Dublin-castle

MCCXIII. William Petit and Peter Messet departed this life Peter Messet was Baron of Luyn, hard by Trim; but dying without Heir-male, the Inheritance fell to three Daughters, of whom the Lord Vernail marry'd the eldest, Talbot the second, and Londres the third; who shar'd the Inheritance among them.

MCCXIX The City of Damieta was miraculously won on the Nones of September about Midnight, without the loss of one Christian

The same year dy'd William Marshall the Elder, Earl Marshal and Earl of Pembroch, * who by his Wife, the Daughter of Richard Strongbow Earl of Strogul, had five Sons The eldest was call'd William, the second Walter, the third Gilbert, the fourth Anselm, and the fifth Richard, who lost his life in the War of Kildare; every one successively enjoy'd the Earldom of their Father, and all died without Issue So the Inheritance devolv'd to the Sisters, namely, the Daughters of their Father, who were, Maud Marshall the eldest, Isabel de Clare the second, Eva de Breous the third, Joan de Mount Chensey the fourth, and Sibill Countess of Firrars the fifth. Maud Marshall was marry'd to Hugh Bigod Earl of Norfolk, who was Earl Marshal of England in right of his Wife By whom he had Ralph Bigod, Father of John Bigod, the Son of the Lady Bertha Furnival, and ‖ Isabel de Lacy Wife to the Lord John Fitz-Geffery, by whom, after the death of Hugh Bigod Earl of Norfolk, she had John de Guaren, Earl of Surrey, and his Sister Isabel de Albeny Countess of Arundel. Isabel the second Sister was marry'd to Gilbert Clare Earl of Glocester, she had Richard de Clare Earl of Glocester, and the Lady Anise Countess of * *Averna*, who was Mother of Isabel the † Mother of the Lord Robert Brus, Earl of Carrick in Scotland, afterwards King of that Nation. From Eva de Breous the third Sister, descended Maud, the Mother of the Lord Edmund Mortimer, Mother of the Lady Eva de Cauntelow, Mother of the Lady Missoud de Mohun, who was Mother to Dame Eleanor, Mother to the Earl of Hereford. Joan Marshal the fourth Sister was marry'd to the Lord Guarin of Mount Chensey, and had Issue Joan de Valens Sybil Countess of Ferrers, the fifth Sister, had Issue seven Daughters; the eldest call'd Agnes Vescie, Mother of the Lord John and the Lord William Vescie; the second Isabel Basset, the third Joan Bohun, Wife to the Lord John Mohun, Son of the Lord Reginald; the fourth, Sibyl de Mohun, Wife to the Lord Francis de Bohun Lord of Midhurst; the fifth Eleanor Vaus, Wife to the Earl of Winchester; the sixth * Agas Mortimer, Wife to the Lord Hugh Mortimer; the seventh Maud Kyme, Lady of Karbry. All these, both Males and Females, are the Posterity of the said William Earl Marshal

* The Genealogy of the Earl Marshal.

‖ The Widow of *Gilbert Lacy*

* Perhaps *Devonia*

† Perhaps *Uxoris* This place is corrupted

* *Agatha*

MCCXX. The Translation of S Thomas of Canterbury. The same year died the Lord Meiler Fitz-Henry, founder of Connal, and was bury'd in the Chapter-House of the said Foundation

MCCXXIV The Castle of Bedford was besieg'd, and the Castle of Trim in Ireland

MCCXXV Dy'd Roger Pippard; and in the year MCCXXVIII dy'd William Pippard, formerly Lord of the Salmon leap This year dy'd likewise Henry Londres, *alias* Scorche-Villeyn, Archbishop of Dublin, and was bury'd in Trinity-church there

MCCXXX Hen-

MCCXXX Henry K of England gave Hubert Burk the Justiceship, and the Third-Penny of Kent; and made him Earl of Kent. Afterward, the same Hubert was imprison'd, and great Troubles arose between the King and his Subjects, because he favour'd Strangers more than his own natural Subjects

MCCXXXI William Mareschall the younger, Earl Marshal and Earl of Pembroch, departed this life, and was bury'd in the Quire of the Friers Predicants in Kilkenny

MCCXXXIV Richard Earl Mareschall Earl of Pembroch and Strogul, was wounded in a Battel on the Plain of Kildare on the first of the Ides of April, and some few days after dy'd in Kilkenny, and was there buried, hard by his * Brother, *viz William*, in the Quire of the Friers Predicants Of whom this is written,

* *Germanum*

Cujus sub fossa Kilkenna continet ossa

MCCXL Walter de Lacy Lord of Meth dy'd this year in England, leaving two Daughters to inherit, of whom, the first was married to the Lord Theobald de Verdon, and the second to Geffery de Genevile

MCCXLIII This year dy'd Hugh Lacy Earl of Ulster, and was buried at Cragfergous, in the Convent of the Friers Minors; leaving a Daughter and heir, who was married to Walter Burk Earl of Ulster The same year dy'd the Lord Gerald Fitz-Maurice, and Lord Richard de Burgo.

MCCXLVI An Earthquake about nine of the Clock over all the West

MCCXLVIII Sir John Fitz-Geffery Knight came Lord Justiciary into Ireland

MCCL Lewis King of France and William Long-Espee were taken Prisoners, with many others, by the Saracens. In Ireland Maccanewey, a Son of Belial, was slain in Leys, as he had well deserv'd

In the year MCCLI The Lord Henry Lacy was born Upon Christmas-day likewise, Alexander King of Scots, in the 11th year of his Age, was contracted to Margaret, the Daughter of the King of England, at York

MCCLV Alan de la Zouch was made and came Justiciary into Ireland

MCCLVII. This year dy'd the Lord Maurice Fitz-Gerald

MCCLIX Stephen Long-Espee came Justiciary into Ireland The green Castle in Ulster was demolish'd William Dene was made Justiciary of Ireland

MCCLXI The Lord John Fitz-Thomas, and the Lord Maurice his Son were slain in Desmond by Mac Karthy Also, William Dene Justiciary of Ireland dy'd, and the Lord Richard Capel was put in his room the same year

MCCLXII. Richard Clare Earl of Glocester died this year; as also, Martin de Maundevile on the morrow of S Bennet

MCCLXIV Maurice Fitz-Gerald and Maurice Fitz-Maurice took Prisoners Richard Capel, the Lord Theobald Botiller, and the Lord John Cogan, at Tristil-Dermot

MCCLXVII. David de Barry was made Justiciary of Ireland

MCCLXVIII Comin Maurice Fitz-Maurice was drown'd Also, the Lord Robert Ufford was made Justiciary of Ireland

MCCLXIX The Castle of Roscomon was begun this year Richard of Exeter was made Justiciary

MCCLXX The Lord James de Audley came Justiciary into Ireland

MCCLXXI Henry the son of the King of Almain was slain in the Court of Rome. Plague, Famine, and Sword rag'd this year, particularly in Meth Nicholas de Verdon and his Brother John were slain. Walter de Burgo Earl of Ulster dy'd.

MCCLXXII The Lord James de Audley, Justiciary of Ireland, was kill'd by a fall from his Horse in Tothomon, and was succeeded in the Office of Chief Justice by the Lord Maurice Fitz-Maurice

MCCLXXIII The Lord Geffery de Genevile return'd from the Holy Land, and was made Justiciary of Ireland

MCCLXXIV *Edward, son of King Henry, * was anointed and crown'd King of England by Robert Kilwarby, of the Order of Friers-Predicants, and Archbishop of Canterbury, upon S Magnus the Martyr's day, in the Church of Westminster, in the presence of all the Nobility of England. His Profession or Oath was in this form I Edward, son and heir of King Henry, do profess, protest and promise before God and his Angels, from this time forward, to maintain without favour or affection, the Law, Justice and Peace of the Church of God, and the People subject unto me, so far as we can devise by the counsel of our faithful Ministers; as also, to exhibit due and canonical Honour to the Bishops of God's Church, and to preserve unto them inviolably whatsoever has been granted by former Emperors and Kings to the Church of God; and to pay due Honour to the Abbots and the Lord's Ministers; according to the advice of our Council, *&c* So help me God, and the Holy Gospels of the Lord. This year dy'd the Lord John Verdon, and the Lord Thomas de Clare came into Ireland And William Fitz-Roger Prior of the Hospitallers was taken Prisoner at Glyndelory, with many others; and more were slain

* King Edward I

MCCLXXV The Castle of Roscomon was built again. The same year Moydagh was taken Prisoner at Norragh by the Lord Walter le Faunte

MCCLXXVI Robert de Ufford was made Justiciary of Ireland, upon the surrender of Geffery de Genevill

MCCLXXVII O Brene slain

MCCLXXVIII The Lord David de Barry died this year, as also the Lord John de Cogan

MCCLXXIX The Lord Robert d'Ufford went into England; and appointed Frier Robert de Fulborne, Bishop of Waterford, to supply his place In whose time the Money was chang'd. A Round Table was also held at Kenylworth by the Lord Roger Mortimer

MCCLXXX Robert d'Ufford return'd from England, being still Justiciary, as before His Wife dy'd this year

MCCLXXXI Adam Cusak the younger kill'd William Barret and many others in Conaught. Frier Stephen Fulborne was made Justiciary of Ireland The Lord Robert d'Ufford return'd into England

MCCLXXXII This year Moritagh and Arte Mac-Murgh his Brother were slain at Arclowe on S Mary Magdalen-Eve And the Lord Roger Mortimer dy'd

MCCLXXXIII The City of Dublin was in part burnt; and the Belfrey of Trinity-Church, on the third of the Nones of January

MCCLXXXIV. The Castle of Ley was taken by the petty Kings of Offaly, and burnt, the morrow after S Barnaby's Day Alphonsus the King's son, being twelve years old, departed this Life

MCCLXXXV The Lord Theobald le Botiller dy'd on the 6th of the Kalends of October, in the Castle of Arclowe, and was buried there in the Convent of the Friers Predicants Gerald Fitz-Maurice was taken Prisoner by his own Irish Subjects in Offaly, with Richard Petit and S. Doget, and many others; and at Rathode there was a great slaughter

MCCLXXXVI Le Norragh and Arfsol, with other Villages, were successively burnt by Wm Stanton, on the 16th of the Kalends of Decem About this time Eleanor Q. of England, mother of K Edward, took the religious habit at Ambresbury on the day of S Thomas's translation, having her dower confirmed by the Pope, and assur'd to her Also, Calwagh was taken Prisoner at Kildare The Lord Thomas Clare departed this Life.

MCCLXXXVII This year dy'd Stephen Fulborne, Archbp of Tuam, and was succeeded in the Office of Justiciary, for a time, by John Sampford Archbp of Dublin This year the K of Hungary renounc'd Christianity, and turn'd Apostate, and having fraudulently assembl'd his Nobility under pretence of a Parliament, Miramomelius, a potent Saracen came upon them with an Army of 20000 men, and carry'd away the King and all the Christians there, prisoners, on S John Baptist's eve As the Christians were carried along, the weather turn'd from fair to cloudy, and a sudden tempest of Hail kill'd many thousands of the Infidels The Christians return'd to their own homes, but the Apostate K went alone with the Saracens The Hungarians crown'd his Son King, and continued in the Catholick Faith

MCCLXXXIX Tripoly, a famous City, was demolish'd, after great effusion of Christian blood, by the Sultan of Babylon Who commanded the Images of the Saints to be dragg'd at the horses tails thro' the ruinous City, in contempt of Christ

MCCXC

Inclyta stirps Regis sponsis datur ordine legis.

The Issue of the King becomes a Spouse

The Lord Gilbert de Clare took to Wife the Lady Joan de Acan, daughter of our Lord K Edward, in the Abby of Westminster; and the marriage was celebrated in May And John son of the Duke of Brabant, marry'd Margaret the said King's daughter, in the Church aforesaid, in July This year the Lord William Vescie was made Justiciary of Ireland, and enter'd upon the Office on S Martin's day Also, O Molaghelyn King of Meth was slain

MCCXCI Gilbert de Clare, son of Gilbert and the Lady Joan de Acon, was born on the 11th of May, betimes in the morning Also, there was an army led into Ulster, against O Hanlan and other petty Princes who had broken the Peace, by Richard Earl of Ulster and William de Vescie Justiciary of Ireland Also, the Lady Eleanor, formerly Queen of England and mother of King Edward, dy'd on S John's day, after a laudable life spent for four years eleven months and six days in a religious habit, in the Abby of Ambresby, where she was a Nun. Also, the news came to our Lord Pope Martin, on the eve of S. Mary Magdalen, concerning the city of Acon in the Holy Land, (which was the only place of refuge for the Christians,) that it was besieg'd by Milkadar the Sultan of Babylon, with a numerous army He besieg'd it hotly for about forty days, viz from the 8th of the Ides of April till the 15th of the Kalends of July At last, the wall was pull'd down by the Saracens, and they enter'd the city in great numbers, many Christians being slain, and some drown'd in the sea through fear. Among whom was the Patriarch and his Train. The King of Cyprus and Oto de Grandison escap'd in a ship, with their followers Also, the Lord Pope Martin granted our Lord King Edward the tenth of all Ecclesiastical Benefices in Ireland, for seven years, towards the relief of the Holy Land Also, the eldest son of the Earl of Clare was born

MCCXCII. Edward King of England enter'd Scotland again, and was chosen King The Lord John de Balliol of Gallweya obtain'd the whole Kingdom of Scotland by right of Inheritance, and did homage to our Lord Edward King of England at Newcastle upon Tyne on S Stephen's day Florentius Earl of Holland, Robert Brus Earl of Carrick, John Hastings, John Comin, Patrick de Dunbar, John Vescie, Nicholas Soul, and William Roos (who had Estates in the said Kingdom) submitted themselves to the Judgment of King Edward

Also, a fifteenth of all the Goods of the Laity in Ireland was granted to our Lord the King of England, to be collected on the Feast of S Michael Also, Sir Peter de Genevile Knight dy'd this year Also, Rice ap Meredyke was brought to York, and there * pull'd to pieces at horses tails, &c

* A c[illegible] equ[illegible] [illegible]

MCCXCIII A general and open war was this year wag'd at sea with the Normans Also, no small number of the Normans was cut off in the sea-fight, by the Barons of the Ports of England, and others then assistants, between Easter and Whitsuntide Upon this, a war broke out between England and France, and Philip King of France directed his letters of citation to the King of England to appear in person at his Parliament, to answer what the King had to object to him, but finding no compliance with this order, he forthwith, by the counsel of his Parliament, declar'd him outlaw'd, and condemn'd him Also, Gilbert de Clare Earl of Glocester and his wife came into Ireland, about the Feast of S Luke

MCCXCIV William Montfort dy'd suddenly, in the King's Council at Westminster before the King He was Dean of S Paul's in London The Bishops and Clergy, who doubted how much the King would expect from every one of them, and were willing to be satisfied, had instructed him as a person whom the King would confide in, what to signify from them to his Majesty, and as soon as he return'd to the King and was addressing himself to speak as he had design'd, he was speechless, and fell down, and was carry'd out by the King's servants in a miserable condition Upon this sight people grew fearful, and began to recollect how he was the great procurer of the Tenths of ecclesiastical benefices to the King, and of the Inquisition upon the fold of Christ, as also of the contributions granted to the King afterward Also, the city of Bordeaux with the adjacent country of Gascoign was taken into possession by the servants of the King of France upon certain conditions, but was detain'd unjustly and treacherously by the said King John Archbishop of Dublin, and some other great men, were sent to the King in Almain upon this account: After they had receiv'd their answer in Lordran, the Archbishop return'd into England, and dy'd on S Leodegary's day The bones of which John Sampford were interr'd in S Patrick's trick's Church in Dublin, on the 10th day of the Kalends of March

The same year there arose a debate between the Lord William de Vescy, then Justiciary of Ireland, and the Lord John Fitz-Thomas, and the said Lord William de Vescy went into England, and left the Lord William de la Hay to officiate as Justiciary But when both were before the King for combat, upon an appeal, for treason, William Vescy fled into France, and would not fight Whereupon, the King of England gave all the Seignories, that belong'd to him, to the Lord John Fitz Thomas, *viz* Kildare, Rathemgan, and many others

The same year, Gilbert de Clare, Earl of Glocester, return'd out of Ireland into England Likewise Richard Earl of Ulster, soon after S Nicholas's day, was taken prisoner by the Lord John Fitz-Thomas, and kept in the castle of Ley, till the feast of S Gregory, Pope, but was then set at liberty by the Council of our Lord the King in a Parliament at Kilkenny The said Lord John Fitz Thomas gave all his lands, which he had in Conaught, *viz* Slygo, with other Possessions, for taking him

Also, this year, the Castle of Kildare was taken, Kildare and the Country round it was wasted by the English and the Irish Calvagh burnt all the Rolls and Tallies of the Earl This year, and the two following, there was a great Dearth and Pestilence throughout Ireland

Also, the Lord William Dooddyngzele was made Justiciary of Ireland

MCCXCV Edward King of England built the Castle *de Bello Marisco*, i e Beaumaris in *Venedocia*, which is call'd the mother of Cambria, but commonly *Anglesey*, and enter'd it immediately after Easter, making the *Venedotes*, i e the able men of Anglesey, subject to him Soon after this, *viz* about the Feast of S Margaret, Madock (at that time Elect of Wales) submitted himself to the King's mercy, and was brought to London by the Lord John de Haverings, where he was put in the Tower, to wait the King's grace and favour This year dy'd the Lord William Dooddyngzele Justiciary of Ireland, the day after S Mary of Egypt The Lord Thomas Fitz Maurice succeeded him Also, about the same time, the Irish in Leinster destroy'd that Province, burning the new Castle, with other Villages Also, Thomas de Torbevile, a seducer of the King and betrayer of his Country, was drawn through the middle of London, naked and prostrate, and encompass'd with four Executioners in Vizards, who revil'd him as he went along At last, he was gibbeted, and deny'd the privilege of Burial; having none to attend his Funeral, but Kites and Crows This Thomas was one of those, who in the Siege of the Castle of Rions were taken, and carry'd to Paris Whereupon, he promis'd the Nobility of France, that he would deliver to them the King of England, and leaving his two Sons as hostages, he came over, and told the King of England and his Council, how narrowly he escap'd out of Prison When he had inform'd himself of the designs of the King, and state of the Kingdom, he sent the whole in writing, to the Provost of Paris Of which being convicted, he was executed in the manner aforesaid About the same time, the Scots having broken the Peace, which they had enter'd into with our Lord the King of England, made a new league with the King of France, and conspiring together, rose up in Arms against their own Sovereign Lord and King John Balliol, and shut him up, in the inner parts of Scotland, in a Castle encompass'd with high Mountains They chose, after the custom of France, twelve Peers, namely four Bishops, four Earls, and four other Noblemen, to administer the Government This was done in pure spight to the King of England, because he had set the said John over them, against their will and consent The King of England carry'd another Army into Scotland the Lent following, to chastise the Scots for their presumption and arrogance against their own Father and King Also, the Lord John Wogan was made Justiciary of Ireland, and the Lord Thomas Fitz-Maurice surrender'd This John Wogan, Justiciary of Ireland, made a Truce for two years, between the Earl of Ulster, and John Fitz Thomas, and the Geraldines About Christmas-day this year the Lord Gilbert de Clare Earl of Glocester departed this life Also, the King of England sent his Brother Edward with an Army into Gascoign

MCCXCVI The Lord Edward King of England, on the third of the Kalends of April, *viz* on Friday (then Easter-week) took Berwick, with the slaughter of about seven thousand Scots, and not of above one of the English Knights, *viz* the Lord Richard of Cornwall, and seven more of the Foot Shortly after, on the fourth of May, he enter'd the Castle of Dunbar, and took about forty of the Enemy Prisoners (who submitted themselves to the King's mercy) having before defeated the whole Army of the Scots, that is to say, slain seven hundred Horse, with the loss of Foot only on the English side

Also, on S John Port-latin-day, about 15000 Welch were sent to invade Scotland by the King's Order At the same time, the Nobility of Ireland, *viz* John Wogan Justiciary, Richard Bourk Earl of Ulster, Theobald Butler and John Fitz-Thomas, with others, came to assist in this Expedition, and sail'd to Scotland The King of England entertain'd them, with others of the English Nobility (on the third of the Ides of May, *viz.* Whitsunday) at a noble Feast, in the castle of Rokesburgh Also, on the Wednesday next, before S Barnabas, he enter'd the Town of Edinburgh, and won the castle before the Feast of S John Baptist shortly after, the same Summer, all the castles in Scotland were surrender'd to him Also, John Balliol King of Scotland came (tho' much against his will) to the King of England, on the Sunday next after the Translation of S Thomas the Archbishop, attended with many Earls, Bishops and Knights, and they surrender'd all to the King's mercy, saving life and limb, and their Lord John Balliol gave up all his Right and Title in Scotland to the King of England, who sent him under a safe guard towards London

Also, Edmund, Brother of the King of England, dy'd in Gascoign

MCCXCVII Our Lord Edward, King of England, sail'd into Flanders with an Army against the King of France, because of the war begun between them; where, after much expence and altercation, it was concluded between them, that they should stand to the award and judgment of the Pope Messengers were sent to the Court of Rome by both sides; but while the King was in Flanders, William Walleis (according to a general Resolution of the Scots) came with a great Army to Strivelinbridge and engag'd the Lord John Warren; in which Battel many were slain on both sides, and many drown'd, but the English were defeated This occasion'd a general Insurrection in in Scotland, of Earls as well as Barons, against the King of England There was also at this time a Quarrel between the King of England and Roger Bigod Earl Marshal, but this was soon made up S Lewis, Son of the King of Sicily (a Frier minor and Archbishop of Cologn) dy'd Also, the son and heir of the King of Maliager, i e of the Islands of Majorca, instituted the Order of the Friers minors, at the direction of S Lewis, who bid him go and do it Also, Lechlin in Ireland, with other Towns, were burnt by the Irish of Slemergi

Also, Calwagh O Hamlen, and Yneg Mac-Mahon, were slain in Urgale.

MCCXCVIII Pope Boniface IV on the morrow of the Feast of S Peter and S Paul, all things being then quiet, made Peace between England and France, upon certain Terms Also, Edward King of England led an Army again into Scotland, to conquer it There were slain in this Expedition (about the Feast of S Mary Magdalen) many thousands of the Scots, at Fawkirk The Sun appear'd that day as red as Blood, in Ireland, while the Battel at Fawkirk continu'd Also, about the same time the King of England gave to his Knights the Earldoms and Baronies of those Scots that were slain In Ireland, Peace was concluded between the Earl of Ulster and the Lord John Fitz-Thomas, about the Feast of Simon and Jude Also, the morrow after the Feast of the seven Sleepers, the Sun-beams were chang'd into a bloodish colour, from morning, to the great admiration of every one Also, this year dy'd the Lord Thomas Fitz-Maurice Knight, and the Lord Robert Bigod, sometime Justiciary in the Bench Also, in the City Artha, and in Reath in Italy, during the stay of Pope Boniface in those parts, there happen'd so great an Earthquake, that Towers and Palaces fell down; and the Pope and his Cardinals fled out of the City in great consternation

Also, on the Feast of Epiphany, there was an Earthquake in England, from Canterbury to Hampton, but not very violent

MCCXCIX The Lord Theobald le Botiller the younger, dy'd in the Manour of Turby, on the second of the Ides of May His Corps was convey'd towards Weydeneyam, i e Weney, in the County of Limerick, on the sixth of the Kalends of June

Also, Edward King of England marry'd the Lady Margaret, Sister to the illustrious King of France, in Trinity church at Canterbury, about the Feast of the Holy Trinity Also, the Sultan of Babylon with an Army of Saracens, was defeated by Cassan King of Tartary

MCCXCIX On the day after the Purification, there was an infinite number of Saracen-horse slain, and besides, an infinite number of Foot Also, there was this year a Fight of Dogs at Genelon-Castle in Burgundy; the number of the Dogs was 3000, and they were all kill'd but one Also, this year many Irish came to the Castle of Roch, before the Annunciation, to annoy the Lord Theobald de Verdon

MCCC The * Pollard-money was prohibited in England and Ireland Also, Edward King of England enter'd Scotland with an Army in Autumn, but was forbid by an order from Pope Boniface; and, to excuse himself, he sent special messengers to the Court of Rome. Also, Thomas, son of the King of England, was born at Brotherton, by Margaret the King of France's Sister, on the last of May Also, Edward Earl of Cornwall dy'd without Issue, and was bury'd in the Abby of Hailes

* Numisma Pollardorum

MCCCI Edward King of England enter'd Scotland with an Army, and the Lord John Wogan Justiciary of Ireland, and the Lord John Fitz-Thomas, and Peter Bermingham, and many others, set sail from Ireland to assist him Also, a great part of the city of Dublin was burnt down, together with the Church of S Warburga, on S Columb's night Also, the Lord of Genevil marry'd the Daughter of the Lord John de Montefort, and the Lord John Mortimer marry'd the daughter and heir of the Lord Peter de Genevil; and the Lord Theobald de Verdon marry'd the daughter of the Lord Roger Mortimer The People of Leinster took up Arms in Winter, and burnt the Towns of Wykynlo and Rathdon, &c but they suffer'd for it, for the greatest part of their Provisions at home was burnt, and their Cattel made plunder, so that they had certainly been undone for ever, if a sedition had not happen'd among the English at that juncture Also, a small company of the Brenies were defeated by the Tolans, and 300 of those Robbers were cut off Also, a great part of Mounster was wasted by Walter Power, and many houses burnt

MCCCII This year, dy'd the Lady Margaret, Wife of the Lord John Wogan, Justiciary of Ireland, on the third of the Ides of April and the Week following, Maud Lacy, the Wife of the Lord Geffery de Genevil, dy'd likewise Also, Edmund le Botiller recover'd the Manour de † S Bosco, with the Appurtenances thereunto belonging, from the Lord R de Feringes Archbishop of Dublin, upon an Accommodation made between them in the King's Bench, after the Feast of S. Hilary

† Holywood forte

Also, the Flemings defeated the French in Flanders at Courtenay, the Wednesday after the Feast of the Translation of S Thomas In this Engagement, were slain the Earl of Artois, the Earl of Albemarle, the Earl of Huc, Ralph de Neel Constable of France, Guy de Nevil, Marshal of France, the Earl of Hennand's son, Godfrey de Brabant and his Son, William de Fenlys and his son James de S Paul lost his hand, and forty Baronets were slain that day, with Knights, Squires, &c without number

Also, The Tenths of all Ecclesiastical Benefices in England and Ireland were exacted by Pope Boniface for three Years, for the support of the Church of Rome against the King of Arragon Also, on the day of the Circumcision, the Lord Hugh de Lacy plunder'd Hugh Vernail This Year, Robert le Brus Earl of Carrick, marry'd Elizabeth, daughter of the Lord Richard Bourk, Earl of Ulster Also, Edward Botiller marry'd the daughter of the Lord John Fitz-Thomas Also, the City of Bourdeaux, with others thereabouts (which Edward King of England had formerly lost by the sedition of the French) were restor'd upon S Andrew's-eve, by the means of the Lord John Hastings

MCCCIII Richard Bourk Earl of Ulster, and the Lord Eustace de Power, invaded Scotland with a strong Army But after the Earl himself had made 33 Knights in the Castle of Dublin, he passed over into Scotland to assist the King of England Also, Gerald son and heir of the Lord John Fitz-Thomas departed this life This year the King and Queen of France were excommunicated, with all their Children, by Pope Boniface; who also confirm'd all the privileges of the University of Paris Soon af-

ter,

ter, the Pope was taken, and kept, as it were in Prison, three whole days Soon after, the Pope dy'd The Countess of Ulster dy'd likewise about this time Also, Walran de Wellesly and Lord Robert de Percivall were slain this year, on the eleventh of the Kalends of November

MCCCIV A great part of Dublin was burnt down, *viz* the Bridge street, a good part of the Key, the Church of the Friers Predicants, the Church of the Monks, and a great part of the Monastery, on the Ides of June, namely, on the Feast of S Medard Also, this year was laid the foundation of the Quire of the Friers Predicants, in Dublin, by the Lord Eustace le Power, on the feast of S *Agatha* the Virgin

Also, after the Purification, the K of France invaded Flanders in person, with a brave Army He behav'd himself gallantly in this War, and in one Battel had two or three Horses kill'd under him But at last he lost the Cap under his Helmet, which the Flemings carry'd off as a * Standard upon a Spear, in derision, and in all the Fairs in Flanders it was hung out at the high Window of some great House, like the Sign of an Inn, as a token of their Victory

* *Vexillum.*

MCCCV Jordan Comyn and his Accomplices, kill'd Moritagh O Conghir, King of Offaley, and Calwagh his † whole Brother, and certain others, in the court of the Lord Peter de Brymegham, at Carryck in Carbery Likewise the Lord Gilbert de Sutton Seneschal of Weisford was slain by the Irish, near the Village of Haymond de Grace, which Haymond fought stoutly in this skirmish, and escap'd by his great Valour

† *Germanum.*

Also, in Scotland, the Lord Robert de Brus Earl of Carrick, not regarding his Oath of Allegiance to the King of England, slew the Lord John Rede Comyn within the Cloister of the Friers-minors of Duntrese, and soon after got himself crown'd King of Scotland by the hands of two Bishops, of S Andrews and Glasco, in the Town of Scone, to the ruin of himself and many others

MCCCVI In Offaly near Greshil-castle, a great defeat was given to O Conghor by the O Dympcies, on the Ides of April, in which O Dympcy † Commander of the Regani, with a Retinue, was slain Also, O Brene K of * Towmond dy'd this year Also, Donald Oge Maccarthy slew Donald Rusi, King of Desmond Also, a sad overthrow was given to a party of the Lord Piers Brymegham, in the marches of Meth, on the fourth of the Kalends of May Also, Balimore in Leinster was burnt by the Irish, and Henry Calle was slain there at the same time, and a war broke out between the English and the Irish in Leinster, and a great Army was drawn together from all parts to keep the Irish of Leinster within bounds Sir Thomas Mandevil, a gallant Knight, had in this Expedition a sharp conflict with the Irish near Glenfell, wherein he fought bravely till his Horse was slain, and won great honour, for the saving the lives of several others as well as his own

† *Dux*

* *Thomonia*

Allo, Master Thomas Cantok Chancellor of Ireland, was consecrated Bishop of Ymelacen, in Trinity-Church in Dublin, with great honour the || Elders of Ireland were all present at this Consecration; and there was such great feasting both for rich and poor, as had never been known before in Ireland Allo, Richard de Feringes Archbishop of Dublin dy'd on S Luke's eve, and was succeeded by Master Richard Haverings, who held that Sec almost five years by the Pope's dispensation. At last he resign'd his Archbishoprick, and was succeeded by John Lech

|| *Majores natu.*

The cause of this resignation (as the Archdeacon of Dublin, his nephew, and a very good man, related it) was a dream which he had one night, That a certain monster, heavier than the whole World, stood upright upon his breast, and that he would have renounced all he had in this world, to be rid of it When he awak'd, he began to reflect, that this was certainly the Church of Dublin, the profits whereof he had receiv'd, without taking pains to deserve them. Upon this, he went to the Pope, with whom he was much in favour, as soon as he possibly could, and relinquish'd his Archbishoprick For he had (as the same Archdeacon aver'd) other benefices of greater value, than the Archbishoprick itself

Also, on the feast of Pentecost, at London, King Edward confer'd Knighthood upon his son Edward, and about 400 Knights * were created at the same feast; sixty of whom were made by the said Edward of Carnarvan, as soon as himself had been knighted He held the feast in London, at the new Temple, and his father gave him the Dutchy of Aquitain

* *Novi milites*

Also, on the feast of S Potentiana, the Bishops of Winchester and Worcester, by order from the Pope, excommunicated Robert Brus, the pretended King of Scotland and his party, for the death of John Rede Comyn This year on S Boniface's day, Aumar de Valence Earl of Pembroch, and Lord Guy Earl cut off many of the Scots, and the Lord Robert Brus was defeated near the town of S Johns This year at the nativity of S John Baptist, King Edward went † by water from Newark to Lincoln, toward Scotland

† *Per aquam de Newark usque Lincolniam*

Also, this year the Earl of Asceles, the Lord Simon Freysell, and the Countess of Carrick, the pretended Queen of Scotland, daughter to the Earl of Ulster, were taken prisoners The Earl of Asceles, and the Lord Simon Freysell, were * torn in pieces The Countess remain'd with the King in great honour, but the rest dy'd miserably in Scotland

* *Dilaniatur*

Also, about the feast of the Purification, two brothers of Robert Brus who were both Pyrates, going out of their Gallies ashore for plunder, were taken prisoners, with sixteen Scots besides, the two brothers were torn in pieces at Carlisle, and the rest hang'd

Also, upon S Patrick's day, Mac Noch and his two Sons were taken prisoners near the new Castle, in Ireland, by Thomas Sutterby, and there, Lorran Oboni, a stout robber, was beheaded

MCCCVII On the third of the Kalends of April Murcord Ballagh was beheaded by Sir David Caunton, a valiant Knight, near Maston, and soon after, Adam Dan was slain

Also, on S Philip and S Jacob's day, Ofchels gave the English a bloody defeat in Conaught

Also, the Castle of Cashill was pull'd down by the rapparees of Offaly; and on the eve of the translation of S Thomas they burnt the town of Lye, and besieg'd the Castle, but the siege was soon rais'd by John Fitz Thomas and Edward Botiller

Also, this year dy'd King Edward [the first,] and his son Edward succeeded him; who buried his father in great state at Westminster, with honour and reverence

Allo, the Lord Edward the younger marry'd the Lady Isabella, daughter of the King of France,

France, in S Mary's church at Bologn, and shortly after, they were both crown'd in Westminster Abby

Also, the Templars in foreign parts being condemn'd for a certain heresy, as was reported, were apprehended and put in prison by the Pope's mandate In England likewise, they were all taken the very next day after Epiphany In Ireland also, they were taken and imprison'd the day after the Purification

MCCCVIII On the second of the Ides of April dy'd the Lord Peter de Bermingham, a noble champion against the Irish

Also, on the fourth of the Ides of May the castle of Kenin was burnt down, and some of the Garrison slain, by William Mac Balthor, Cnygnitmy Othothiles, and his partisans

Also, on the sixth of the Ides of June, the Lord John Wogan, Justiciary of Ireland, was defeated with his Army, near Glyndelory In this encounter were slain, John call'd Hogelin, John de Northon, John de Breton, and many others

Also, on the sixteenth of the Kalends of July Dolovan, Tobyr, and other towns and villages bordering upon them, were burnt down by the said malefactors

Also, soon after this, a great Parliament was held at London wherein a terrible difference arose between the King and Barons, upon the account of Piers Gaveston, who was banish'd out of the Kingdom of England the day after the feast of S John Baptist's nativity, and went over into Ireland about the feast of the Saints Quirita and Julita, together with his wife and sister, the Countess of Glocester, and came to Dublin in great state, and there continu'd

Also, William Mac Baltor, a stout robber and incendiary, was condemn'd in the court of our Lord the King at Dublin, by the Chief Justice the Lord John Wogan, on the twelfth of the Kalends of September, and was drawn at a horse's tail to the gallows, and there hang'd, as he deserv'd

Also, this year, a marble cistern was made, to receive the Water from the conduit in Dublin (such as was never before seen here) by the Mayor of the City, Master John Decer, and all at his own proper charge This same John, a little before, made a bridge to be built over the river Aven-Liffie, near the priory of S Wolstan He also built the Chapel of S Mary of the Friers minors, wherein he was buried, and the Chapel of S Mary of the Hospital of S John in Dublin

Also, this John Decer was bountiful to the convent of Friers Predicants in Dublin he made one stone-pillar in the Church, and laid the great stone upon the high altar, with its ornaments

Also, he entertain'd the Friers at his own table on the sixth day of the Week, out of pure charity; as the seniors have reported to their juniors

Also, the Lord John Wogan went over in Autumn, to be at the Parliament of England, and the Lord William Bourk was appointed Keeper of Ireland in his room

Also, this year on the eve of S Simon and Jude, the Lord Roger de Mortimer and his Lady, the right heir of Meth, the daughter of the Lord Peter son of the Lord Geffery Genevil, arriv'd in Ireland As soon as they landed, they took possession of Meth; the Lord Geffery Genevil giving it to them, and entring himself in the Order of the Friers Predicants at Trym, the morrow after S Edward the Archbishop's day

Also, Dermot Odympsy was slain at Tully, by the servants of the Lord Piers Gaveston

Also, Richard Bourk Earl of Ulster, at Whitsontide, made a great feast at Trym, and confer'd Knighthood upon Walter Lacy and Hugh Lacy In the vigil of the Assumption, the Earl of Ulster came against Piers Gaveston, Earl of Cornwal, at Drogheda, and at the same time turn'd back towards Scotland

Also, this year Maud the Earl of Ulster's daughter imbark'd for England, in order to a marriage with the Earl of Glocester, which within a month was perform'd

Also, Maurice de Caunton kill'd Richard Talon, and the Roches afterwards kill'd him

Also, the Lord David de Caunton was hang'd at Dublin

Also, Odo, son of Cathol O Conghir, kill'd Odo O Conghir King of Conaught

Also, Athi was burnt by the Irish

MCCCIX Piers Gaveston subdu'd the O-Brynnes in Ireland, and rebuilt the castle of Mackingham, and the castle of Kemny, he also cut down and scour'd the pass between Kemny castle and Glyndelagh, in spite of all the opposition the Irish could make, and so went and offer'd in the Church of S Kimny

The same year the Lord Piers Gaveston went over into England on the eve of S John Baptist's Nativity

Also, the Earl of Ulster's son's wife, daughter to the Earl of Glocester, came into Ireland, on the fifteenth of October

Also, on Christmas-eve, the Earl of Ulster return'd out of England, and landed at Drogheda

Also, on the Purification of the Blessed Virgin, the Lord John Bonevil was slain near the town of Arstol by the Lord Arnold Pover and his accomplices, and bury'd at Athy, in the Church of the Friers Predicants

Also, a Parliament was held at Kilkenny, in the octaves of the Purification of the blessed Mary, by the Earl of Ulster, John Wogan Justiciary of Ireland, and others of the nobility, wherein a difference among certain of the great men of Ireland was adjusted, and many proviso's made in the nature of statutes, which might have been a great advantage to the Kingdom, if they had been observ'd

Also, shortly after, the Lord Edward Botiller return'd out of England, where he had been knighted, at London

Also, the Earl of Ulster, Roger Mortimer, and the Lord John Fitz-Thomas, went over into England

Also, this year dy'd the Lord Theobald de Verdon

MCCCX K Edward and the Lord Piers Gaveston march'd for Scotland against Robert Brus

Also, there was this year a great scarcity of corn in Ireland an * Eranc of corn was sold for twenty shillings and upwards

* E anca

Also, the Bakers of Dublin were punish'd after a new way for false weights For on S Sampson the Bishop's day, they were drawn upon hurdles at horses tails along the streets of the City

Also, in the Abby of S Thomas the Martyr at Dublin, the Lord Nigel de Bruin Knight, Escheator to our Lord the King in Ireland, departed this life; and his body was bury'd at the Friers-minors in Dublin, with such a number of tapers and wax-lights, as had never been seen in this Kingdom

Thus

This year a Parliament was held at Kildare, wherein the Lord Arnold Pover was acquitted of the death of the Lord John Bonevil; for it was found *se defendendo*

Also, on S Patrick's day, Alexander Bickenor, was (with the unanimous consent of the Chapter) chosen Archbishop of Dublin.

Also, the Lord Roger Mortimer, in the octaves of the nativity of the blessed Virgin, return'd into Ireland.

Also, this year dy'd the Lord Henry Lacy, Earl of Lincoln

MCCCXI In Thomond at Bonnorathie, the Lord Richard Clare gave the Earl of Ulster's party a very wonderful defeat The Lord William Bourk, and John son of the Lord Walter Lacy, were taken prisoners, with many others This battle was fought on the 13th of the kalends of June, and great numbers, both of the English and the Irish, were slain in it

Also, Tassagard and Rathcante were invaded by the rapparees, namely the O Brinnes, and O Tothiles, the day after S John Baptist's nativity Whereupon, in Autumn, soon after, a great Army was rais'd in Leinster, to attack them, where they skulk'd in Glindelory and in other woody places

Also, in August, a Parliament was holden at London, between the King and the Barons, to consider the state of the Kingdom and the King's houshold, to be administer'd by six Bishops, six Earls, and six Barons, for the good of the Realm.

Also, on the second of the Ides of November, the Lord Richard de Clare cut off six hundred Galegolaghes

Also, on All-saints day last, Piers Gaveston was banish'd England by the Earls and Barons, and many good statutes were made by them for the benefit of the Kingdom Gaveston was banish'd the Realm about the feast of All-saints, and went into Flanders; from whence in four months he return'd, soon after Epiphany, privately into England, keeping so close to the King, that the Barons could not easily come near him He went with the King to York, making his abode there in Lent, whereupon, the Bishops, Earls and Barons of England came to London, to consider the state of the Kingdom, lest the return of Gaveston might breed disturbance therein

Also, Sir *John Cogan*, Sir *Walter Faunt*, and Sir *John Fitz-Rery*, Knights, dy'd this year, and were bury'd in the Church of the Friers Predicants in Dublin

Also, John Macgoghedan was kill'd by Omolmoy

Also, this year dy'd William Roch, being kill'd at Dublin, by an arrow, which an Irish-highlander shot at him.

Also, Sir Eustace le Pover Knight, dy'd

Also, on the eve of S Peter's *Chair*, a riot was occasion'd in Urgaly by Robert Verdon

Also, Donat Obrene was traiterously kill'd by his own men, in Tothomond

MCCCXII. The Lord Piers Gaveston went into the castle of Scardeburg, to defend himself against the Barons. But soon after the kalends of June, he surrender'd himself to the Lord Aumare de Valence (who besieg'd him) upon certain conditions Valence was carrying him to London, but the Earl of Warwick intercepted him at Dedington, and brought him to Warwick; where, on the 13th of the kalends of July, after a Consultation among the Earls and Barons, he was beheaded, and bury'd in the Church of the Friers Predicants, at Langley.

Also, the Justiciary of Ireland, John Wogan, set out at the head of an army against Robert Verdon, and his accomplices; and on the 6th of the ides of July, had a terrible defeat. In this battle, Nicholas Avenel, Patrick Roch, and many others were cut off Upon this, the said Robert de Verdon and many of his followers, surrender'd themselves to the King's mercy, in his prison at Dublin

Also, on Thursday, the day after S *Lucy* the Virgin, in the 6th year of King Edward, the Moon seem'd to be of several colours; and that day, it was resolv'd, that the Order of the Templars should be abolish'd

Also, the Lord Edmund le Botiller was made Lieutenant to the Lord John Wogan, Justiciary of Ireland, which Edmund, the Lent following, besieg'd the O Brinnes in *Glyndelory*, and forc'd them to surrender, nay, had utterly destroy'd them, if they had not submitted in time

Also, the day after the feast of S Dominick, the Lord Maurice Fitz-Thomas marry'd Catharin the Earl of Ulster's daughter, at Green-Castle, and Thomas Fitz-John marry'd another daughter of the Earl, the day after the Assumption, in the same place

Also, the Sunday after the feast of the Exaltation of the Holy Cross, the daughter of the Earl of Glocester, wife to the Lord John Burk, was deliver'd of a son

MCCCXIII Frier Roland Joce, Primat of Armagh, arriv'd in the Isle of Houth, the day after the Annunciation of the blessed Mary, and, in the night, got privately out of his bed, and took his Cross, and carry'd it as far as the Priory of Grace-dieu; where he was encounter'd by some of the Archbp of Dublin's servants, who made him leave his Cross, and drove the Primat himself out of Leinster, in confusion

Also, a Parliament was held at London, but little or nothing done towards a peace The K left them, and went into France, in compliance with an order from that Court, taking the Cross upon him, with many of his Nobles

Also, Nicholas Fitz-Maurice and Robert Clonhul were knighted by the Lord John Fitz-Thomas, at Adare in Munster.

Also, on the last of May, Robt de Brus sent out some Gallies with Pirates in them, to pillage Ulster; but the people made a stout defence, and drove them off It is reported, that Robert himself landed with them, by the Earl's permission, in order to a Truce

Also, this Summer, Master John Decer, a Citizen of Dublin, caus'd a bridge to be built (as was very necessary) reaching from the Town of Balybought to the Causey of the Mill-pool of Clontarf, which before was a very dangerous passage But after great charge, the whole bridge, arches and all, was thrown down by an inundation

Also, on the feast of S Laurence, dy'd John de Leeks, Archbishop of Dublin Two were elected to succeed; the Lord Walter Thornbury the King's Chancellor in Ireland, and the Lord Alexander Bicknore, Treasurer of Ireland But the Lord Walter Thornbury, with about an hundred and fifty-six more, were cast away at Sea the night following And, when he dy'd, Bicknor was expecting the Pope's favour, and was afterwards made Archbishop of Dublin

Also, the Lord Miles de Verdon marry'd the daughter of the Lord Richard de Exeter

Also, this year the Lord Robert de Brus demolish'd the Castle of Manne, and on S Barnaby's by's day overcame the Lord Donegan Odowill On the feast of Marcellus and Marcellianus, the Lord John Burk, heir of Richard Earl of Ulster, dy'd at Gallway

Also, the Lord Edmund le Botiller, on Sunday, being the feast of S Michael, made thirty Knights in Dublin-Castle

MCCCXIV The Hospitallers had the lands of the Templars in Ireland bestow'd on them

Also, the Lord John Parice was slain at Pount

Also, on S Silvester's day, the Lord Theobald de Verdon came Justiciary in Ireland

Also, the Lord Geffery de Genevile, a Frier, dy'd the 12th of the kalends of November, and was bury'd with his own order of Friers Predicants of Trym he was also Lord of the Liberty of Meth

Also, on S Matthew's day, this year, Loghseudy was burnt, and the Friday following, the Lord Edmund le Botiller receiv'd his Commission to be Justiciary of Ireland

MCCCXV On S John Baptist's day, the Earl of Glocester was kill'd in an engagement with the Scots, and others without number were kill'd and taken prisoners by them The Scots grew insolent upon this success, and possess'd themselves of much land and tribute in Northumberland

Also, shortly after they invested Carlisle, where James Douglas was crush'd to death by a wall that fell upon him

This year the Scots, not content with their own Territories, arriv'd in the north part of Ireland at Clondonne, to the number of 6000 fighting men and expert soldiers, namely, Edward le Brus, whole brother to Robert, King of Scots, with the Earl of Morreth, John de Meneteth, John Steward, the Lord John Cambel, Thomas Randolfe, Fergus de Andressan, John de Bosco, and John Busset, who possess'd themselves of Ulster, and drove the Lord Thomas Mandevile, and other subjects, out of their estates

The Scots enter'd Ireland on the Feast of S Augustin the English Apostle, in the month of May, near Cragfergus in Ulster The first Encounter between the English and them, was near Banne, wherein the Earl of Ulster was put to flight, and William Burk, John de Stanton, and many others, were taken Prisoners many of the English were kill'd, and the Scots got the day

The second Encounter was at Kenlys in Meth, where Roger Mortimer and his soldiers were put to flight

The third was at Sketheris, hard by Arstol, the day after S Paul's Conversion, the English fled, and were routed by the Scots Whereupon, the said Edward le Brus, after the feast of S Philip and S James, got himself crown'd King of Ireland Having taken Green-Castle, they posted themselves in it, but the citizens of Dublin soon remov'd them, and recover'd it for the King; and finding there the Lord Robert de Coulragh, the Governor of the Castle, they brought him to Dublin, where he was imprison'd, and, being kept to hard diet, dy'd

Also, on S Peter and S Paul's day, the Scots came to Dondalk, took it, plunder'd it, and then burnt it, after they had kill'd all who oppos'd them A great part of Urgale was likewise burnt by them as was also the Church of the blessed Virgin Mary * in Atterith (full of men, women, and children) by them and the Irish

* Dr ... Dr.

The same year, the Lord Edmund le Botiller, Justiciary of Ireland, about the feast of S Mary Magdalen, drew considerable forces out of Munster, Leinster, and other parts, and joyn'd the Earl of Ulster at Dondalk, who had drawn a mighty army out of Connaght and those parts, and march'd thither to meet him. There they concerted what measures they should take to destroy the Scots What their resolutions were, is not known, but the Scots fled; and if they had not, they had (as was hop'd) been taken Prisoners

After this, the Earl of Ulster and the said Justiciary, with the rest of the Nobility, resolv'd, as soon as they had cut off the Scots, to bring the Lord Edmund Brus dead or alive to Dublin Accordingly, the Earl pursu'd them as far as the river Branne, and then retir'd towards Coyners. Brus perceiving this, pass'd the river privately, and follow'd him, and put him to flight, with some others of the Earl's side, having wounded George Roch, and slain the Lord John Stanton, Roger Holiwood, and others Many were likewise kill'd on Brus's side, and on the 10th of September, the Lord William Burk was taken Prisoner, and the Earl was defeated near Coyners; whereupon an Insurrection of the Irish against the King and the Earl of Ulster, follow'd in Conaught and Meth, and they burnt the Castles of Atholon, Raudon, and others In the said battle of Coyners, the Baron of Donull signaliz'd his valour, but he suffer'd very much in his goods, and the Scots drove them as far as Cragfergus, where some of the Earl's party fled, but others enter'd the Castle, and defended it with great valour Afterwards, certain Seamen came suddenly from the Port-Towns of England, and surpris'd the Scots, and kill'd forty of them, carrying their Tents, &c away The day after the Exaltation of the Holy Cross, the Earl of Morreff went over with four Pirate-ships laden with Irish Commodities, into Scotland, and carry'd with them the Lord William Burk; intending there to pick up a Reinforcement of his Army One of the Ships was cast away All this while, the said Brus was carrying on the siege of Cragfergus-castle At the same time, Cathil Roge demolish'd three Castles of the Earl of Ulster's in Connaught, where he likewise burnt and plunder'd many Towns And then also the English Seamen above-mention'd went to the said Castle, and the Lords skirmish'd with one another, and kill'd many of the Scots Richard de lan de O-Fervil was slain also about this time by an Irishman

Also, afterwards, upon S Nicholas day, le Brus left Cragfergus, and was joyn'd by the Earl of Morreff with 500 Men, so, they march'd together towards Dundalk Many flock'd in to them, and gave them their assistance From thence they pass'd on to Nober, where they left many of their Men, about the feast of S Andrew Brus himself burnt Kenleys in Meth and Grenard, and rifled and spoil'd the said Monastry He also burnt Finnagh and Newcastle, and all that Country, and after they had kept their Christmas at Loghsudy, they burnt that likewise After this, they march'd forward by Totmoy to Rathymegan and Kildare, and the Country about Tristeldermot, Athy, and Reban, in which Expedition they lost several Men After that, le Brus advanc'd to Skethy near Arlcoll in Leinster where he was engag'd by the Lord Edmund Botiller Justiciary of Ireland, the Lord John Fitz-Thomas, Thomas Arnald Power, and other

Noble

Noblemen of Leinster and Munster; so strong, that any single Lord of them might have been an over-match for Brus and his whole Party But a difference arising, they left the Field, in great disorder and confusion, to him, according to that which is written, *Every Kingdom divided against it self is brought to desolation* Haymund le Grace, a noble 'Squire, and particularly loyal to his King and Country, and Sir William Prendregrest, Knight, were both slain The Scots lost the Lord Fergus Andrissan, the Lord Walter Morrey, and many others, who were buried at Athy, in the Convent of the Friers Predicants

Afterwards, Brus, in his return towards Meth, burnt the castle of Loy, and so the Scots march'd to Kenlis in Meth, where the Lord Roger Mortimer took the field against them with a numerous Army, amounting to 1.000, but not unanimous and true to one another, as was believ'd For tho' this Body was all under the Command of the said Roger, yet they ran away about three a clock, and deserted him, particularly, the Lacies, so that the Lord Mortimer was oblig'd to retreat to Dublin with a small Party, and the Lord Walter Cusake to the Castle of Trym, leaving the Country and the Town of Kenlis, to the Scots

Also, At the same time, all the South-part of the Country was burnt by the Irish of those parts, *viz* Arclo, Newcastle, Bree, and all the adjacent Villages, under the conduct of the Otothiles and the O Brynnes The Omorghes also burnt and wasted part of Leys in Leinster, but most of them were cut off by the Lord Edmund Botiller, Justiciary of Ireland, and about eight hundred of their Heads carry'd to Dublin-castle

Also, This year, about the feast of the Purification of the blessed Virgin, some of the Irish Nobility, and the Lord Fitz-Thomas, Richard Lord Clare, the Lord John le Pover and the Lord Arnold Pover, came to the Lord John de Hotham (who was appointed on the part of the King) to establish a Peace for their future quiet and safety, so, they took their Oaths to stand by the King of England with their lives, and to do their best to preserve the peace, and to destroy the Scots For performance whereof, they gave Pledges, before God, and so return'd All the rest of the Irish Nobility who should refuse to follow the same course, were to be look'd upon as Enemies to the King

Also, The Lord John Byssett departed this life, and the Church of the new Village of Leys, with the Belfrey, was burnt by the Scots The Castle of Northburg in Ulster was also taken by them

Also, Fidelmicus O Conghyr, King of Conaught, kill'd Rorick the son of Cathol O Conghyr

Also, This year dy'd the Lord William Maundevil, and the Bishop of Coner fled to the Castle of Cragfergus, and the Bishoprick was laid under an Interdict Lord Hugh of Antony was slain in Conaught

Also, This year, on Valentin's-day, the Scots made a halt near Gesshil and Offaley, and the English Army near Kildare, and the Scots, were so pinch'd for Provision, that many of them were starved; so, they broke up secretly, and march'd towards Fowier in Meth The Sunday following, they were so much weaken'd with hunger and hard Service, that many of them dy'd

Afterwards, a Parliament of the Nobility was held, but they came to no Resolutions, and in their return they laid waste the Country The Lord Walter de Lacy came to Dublin, to clear his reputation, and give security to the King, as others of the Nobility did At this time, Edward de Brus was in Ulster, but did no mischief

Also, The Otothiles, the O Brynnes, Archibaulds and Harolds, combined, and wasted the Village of Wikelowe, and the Country thereabouts The first Week in Lent, the Earl of Morreff sail'd into Scotland, and le Brus took cognizance of all Pleas in Ulster, and condemn'd many to the Gallows

Also, In the middle of Lent he try'd Causes, and executed the Logans, and took the Lord Alan Fitz-Warin and carry'd him into Scotland

Also, This year Bennynger O Conghyr slew Cale-Rothe, together with the Galloglaphes, and about three hundred more This Lent Corn sold after the rate of eighteen Shillings, and the Easter following for eleven

MCCCXVI The Lord Thomas Maundevile march'd out of Drogheda with a strong party to Cragfergus, * on Maundy-thurday, and engag'd the Scots, and put them to flight, and kill'd about thirty of them Afterwards, on Easter-eve, he attack'd them again, and, about the Kalends, kill'd many of them In this Encounter, the Lord Thomas Maundevile was slain in his own Country, † in defence of his own rights

* De Jeju-n Cana Domini

† Pro jure suo

Also, Many Irish were slain in Conaught and thereabouts, by the Lord Richard de Clare and the Lord Richard Bermyngham

Also, on the Sabbath next after the Ascension, Donnyger O Brynn, a stout Rapparee, with twelve of his Accomplices, were all cut off by the Lord William Comyn and his Party, who kept the Peace, and their Heads were brought to Dublin

Also, The People of Dundalk sally'd out upon O Hanlan, and kill'd about two hundred of the Irish, and here, Robert de Verdon, a warlike 'Squire, was cut off

Also, At the feast of Pentecost this year, Richard de Bermyngham slew three hundred Irish, or more, in Munster, and after, about the Nativity of S John Baptist, le Brus came to Cragfergus-castle, and commanded the Keepers to surrender it, according to an agreement between them, as he alledg'd They answer'd, That they were oblig'd to do so, and order'd that thirty might be sent to them, and that they might have their lives spar'd All this was agreed to But as soon as the thirty Scots were within the Castle, they shut them up and imprison'd them

About this time, the Irish of O Myll march'd towards Tullagh, and there fought in this Battle about four hundred of the Irish were slain, and their Heads sent to Dublin Many strange things were seen there afterwards, dead men seeming to rise and fight with one another, crying out, Fennokabo, as the signal

About the feast of S Thomas's Translation, eight Ships were set out at Drogheda, with Provisions for Cragfergus But these were disturb'd in their Voyage by the Earl of Ulster, for the redemption of William de Burgo, who was taken with the Scots On the Sabbath day following, the Earl of Ulster, the Lord John Fitz-Thomas, and many others of the Nobility, enter'd into an union at Dublin, and agreed to maintain the peace of Ireland, with their lives and fortunes

This

This same year we had News from Conaught, That many of the English, viz. the Lord Stephen of Exeter, Miles Cogan, many of the Barnes, and about eighty of the Lawles, were kill'd by O Conghyr.

Also, The Week after S Laurence's day, four of the Irish Kings in Conaught broke out into open War against the English; whereupon, the Lord William Bourk, the Lord Richard Bermyngham, the Lord of Anry, and their Followers, took the Field against them, and cut off about 11000 of them near Anry, which Village was afterwards wall'd round with the Arms and Spoil of the Enemy; for every Englishman who had taken two Weapons from the Irish, contributed one towards that Work. In this Engagement, Fedelmic O Conghyr, King of Conaught, with O Kelly, and several other petty Kings, were slain. John Husee, the * Executioner of *Anry*, was in this Battle; and the same night stood among the dead, according to his Lord of Anry's order, to find out O Kelly, who unkennell'd at last; and, as he and his 'Squire came forth, call'd to the said Husee with a loud Voice, Go with me, and I will make thee a great Lord in my Dominions. But Husee answer'd him, I will not go with thee; but thou shalt go to my master Richard Bermyngham. O Kelly told him, Thou hast but one Servant, and I have a trusty 'Squire; therefore come with me, and save thy Life. Husee's Servant press'd him, saying, Comply and go to O Kelly, that we may be sav'd and enrich'd, for they are stronger than we. But Husee first kill'd his own Servant, and then kill'd O Kelly and his 'Squire, and cut off the three Heads, and brought them to Richard Bermyngham his Master, who gave him much Land for his Service, and confer'd Knighthood upon him as he well deserv'd.

* *Carnifex*

The same year, about S Laurence's-day, O Hanlan came to Dundalk, in order to distrain; but the People of Dundalk fell upon him, and kill'd many of his men.

Also, On the Monday before the feast of the Nativity of S Mary, David O Totothil with four more, came and hid themselves all night in the Wood of Coleyn; but being discover'd by the Dublinians and the Lord William Comyn, they issu'd out and drove them back six Leagues, killing about seventeen, and wounding many of them mortally.

Also, A Report came to Dublin, That the Lord Robert de Brus King of Scotland, was landed in Ireland to assist his Brother Edward; and that the Scots had besieg'd Cragfergus-castle in Ulster. The Monasteries of S Patrick, de Duno, and de Seballo, and several others, both Monks, and preaching Canons and Minors, were destroy'd by them in Ulster.

Also, the Lord William Bourk gave his son for an Hostage, and was set at liberty in Scotland. The Church of Bright in Ulster was burnt by the Scots and Irish of that Province, almost full of Men and Women.

At the same time came News from Cragfergus, That the Garrison liv'd upon Hides for want of Victuals, and had eat up eight Scots who were taken; so that it was much lamented that no body reliev'd such brave men.

On the Friday following, came News, That Thomas son of the Earl of Ulster was dead.

And on Sunday following, being the next after the Nativity of the blessed Virgin, the Lord John Fitz Thomas dy'd at Laraghbrine near Maynoth, and was buried among the Friers-minors at Kildare. He is said to have been made Earl of Kildare a little before his death. His son and heir the Lord Thomas Fitz-John, a very wise Man, succeeded him.

After this, we had News that the Castle of Cragfergus was surrender'd to the Scots, upon condition that the lives of the Garrison should be saved.

On the day of the Exaltation of the holy Cross, Conghor was slain, together with Mackeley and fifty Irish, by the Lord William Burk and Richard Bermyngham, in Conaught.

Also, on the Monday before All-Saints-day, many of the Scots were slain in Ulster by John Loggan, and the Lord Hugh Bisset, namely, about 100 with double Arms, and 200 with single Arms. The slain in all, amounted to 300, besides foot. Afterward, on the Eve of S Edmund the King, there was such a Storm of Wind and Rain, as threw down many Houses, and beat down the Bell of Trinity-church in Dublin, and did much mischief both by Sea and Land.

Also, on the Eve of S Nicholas, the Lord Alan Stewart, who was taken Prisoner in Ulster by John Loggan and the Lord John Sandale, was carry'd to Dublin-castle.

This same year, there came News from England, of a dissension between the King and the Earl of Lancaster, that they were for taking one another Prisoners, and that the whole Kingdom was embroil'd about it.

This year also, about the feast of Andrew the Apostle, the Lord Hugh le Despencer, and the Lord Bartholomew de Baldesmere, the Bishop of Worcester, and the Bishop of Ely, were sent to Rome, to negotiate some important Business of the King's, concerning Scotland, who return'd again into England about the feast of the Purification.

Also, the Lacies came to Dublin after the same feast, and shew'd by Inquisition, that the Scots were not brought into Ireland by their means, whereupon they were acquitted, and had the King's Charter for protection and safety, upon taking their Oaths to keep the Peace, and do their utmost to destroy the Scots.

Also, This year, after the feast of the Circumcision, the Scots march'd privately as far as Slain with 20000 arm'd Men, and ravag'd the Country; the Army of Ulster flying before them.

Afterwards, on the Monday before the feast of S Matthias the Apostle, the Earl of Ulster was apprehended in S Mary's Abby by the Mayor of Dublin, *viz* Robert Notyngham, and carry'd to Dublin-castle, where he was long imprison'd, and the Chamber wherein he was kept, was burnt, and seven of the Earl's Attendants slain.

The same Week, on the Eve of S Matthias, Le Brus march'd towards Dublin at the Head of his Army; and, hearing of the Earl's Imprisonment, turn'd off towards Cnok-castle, which he enter'd, and therein took the Lord Hugh Tirell with his Wife, who was Baron of it; and they were afterwards ransom'd for Money.

That Night it was agreed, by common consent, among the Citizens of Dublin, That S Thomas's-street should be burnt down for fear of the Scots, the flames whereof unfortunately got hold of S John's church, and burnt it down likewise, with Magdalen chapel, and all the Suburbs of the City, and S Mary's Monastery. The Church of S Patrick was spoil'd by the said Villains.

Also, the Church of S Saviour, which belongs to the Friers-Predicants, was destroy'd by the Mayor and the Citizens, and the Stone converted to the building of the City walls, which

which were enlarg'd on the north part above the Key; for formerly the Walls ran by the Church of S Owen, where we still see a Tower beyond the Gate, with another Gate in the Street where the Taverns are However, the Mayor and Citizens were afterwards commanded by the King of England to make another Convent as formerly After the feast of St Matthias, Le Brus understanding that the City was fortify'd, he march'd towards Salmon's-leap, where Robert le Brus, King of Scotland, with Edward le Brus, the Earl of Morrey, John de Meneteth, the Lord John Steward, and the Lord Philip Mountbray, encamp'd themselves, and continu'd four days, during which they burnt part of the Village, and broke open the Church and rifled it, and then march'd towards Le Naas The Lacies, contrary to their Oaths, conducted and advis'd them, and the Lord Hugh Canon made Wadin White, his Wife's Brother, be their guide through the Country So they came to Le Naas, plunder'd the Village, enter'd the Churches, and open'd the Graves in the Church-yard for hidden Treasure, and did many other Mischiefs during the two days they stay'd there After this, they took their march towards Trestildermote, in the second week in Lent, and destroy'd the Friers-minors, taking away their Books, Vestments, and other Ornaments From hence they retir'd to Baligaveran, and so to Callan, about the feast of S Gregory, Pope, leaving the Village of Kilkenny

At the same time, Letters were brought by the Lord Edmund Botiller Justiciary of Ireland, and by the Lord Thomas Fitz-John Earl of Kildare, the Lord Richard de Clare, the Lord Arnold le Pover and the Lord Maurice Fitz-Thomas, to suffer the Earl of Ulster to be bail'd and set at liberty by the King's Writ, but nothing was done in it at that time

The People of Ulster came afterwards in a great Body amounting to IIM and desir'd assistance from the King against the Scots Upon which, the King's Banner was deliver'd to them, but as soon as they got it, they did more mischief than the Scots themselves, they eat Flesh all the Lent, and almost destroy'd the whole Country, for which they were accurs'd both by God and Man

Edmund * Butler gave the Irish a great defeat near the desert of Dermic, i e Trestildermot

* Pincerna

Also, The said Edmund being now Justiciary of Ireland, defeated O Morghe at Balilethan with great slaughter The Scots under le Brus were got as far as Limerick But the English in Ireland, being drawn together in great Bodies to Ledyn, they retreated privately in the night from Conninger-Castle

About Palm-sunday News came to Dublin, That the Scots were at Kenlys in Ossory, and that the Irish Nobility were at Kilkenny, and had drawn a great Army together there, to engage le Brus On the Monday following, the King sent an Order to the People of Ulster to advance against the Scots with all speed, under the command of Thomas Fitz-John Earl of Kildare Whereupon they march'd, Le Brus being then at Cashell, from whence he mov'd to Nanath, where he stay'd some time, and burnt and destroy'd all the Possessions of the Lord Butler

MCCCXVII On Maundy-Thursday, the Lord Edmund le Botiller Justiciary of Ireland, the Lord Thomas Fitz-John Earl of Kildare (for the King had conferr'd upon him the jurisdiction and liberty of the Earldom of Kildare) Richard de Clare with the Ulster-Army, the Lord Arnold Pover Baron of Donnoyll, Maurice Rochford, Thomas Fitz-Maurice, and the Cauntons with their Followers, met together to concert measures against the Scots; this Debate continu'd a whole Week, and at last they came to no Resolution, tho' their Army amounted to 30000 Men, or thereabouts, well arm'd On Thursday in Easter-week, Roger Mortimer arriv'd at Yoghall with the King's Commission, for he was Justiciary at that time; and the Monday following went in great haste to the Army, having sent a Letter to Edmund Botiller, who, as has been said, was formerly Justiciary, to enterprise nothing against the Scots till his Arrival, but before Mortimer got to the Camp, le Brus had secret Advice to retreat, so, the Night following, he march'd towards Kildare, and the Week after, the English return'd to their several Countries, and the Ulster-Army came to Naas

At the same time, two Messengers were sent from Dublin to the King of England, to give him an account of the state of Ireland, and to pray his Majesty's Instructions, and also of the letting at Liberty of the Earl of Ulster

At the same time likewise, the Lord Roger Mortimer, Justiciary of Ireland, and the Irish Nobility, met together at Kilkenny, to consider how they might oppose Le Brus, but came to no Resolution

About a month after Easter, Le Brus came with an Army within four Leagues, or thereabouts, of Trym, under the cover of a certain Wood, and there continued a Week or more, to refresh his Men, who were ready to die with fatigue and hunger, which occasion'd a great mortality among them

Afterwards, on S Philip and S James's day, the said Brus began his march towards Ulster, and after the said feast, the Lord Roger Mortimer Justiciary of Ireland, came to Dublin, with the Lord John Wogan, the Lord Fulk Warin, and thirty Knights, with their Retinue, who held a Parliament with all the Nobility of the Kingdom at Kylmaynan, but did nothing, except only what passed concerning the letting at Liberty of the Earl of Ulster

On the Sunday before Ascension they held another Parliament at Dublin, and there the Earl of Ulster was deliver'd upon Mainprise, Hostages, and Oaths, which were, That he should never by himself nor any of his Friends and Followers, do or procure any mischief to the Citizens of Dublin for apprehending him, save only what the Law allow'd in those Cases against Offenders, to which end, he had till the Nativity of S John allow'd him, but he came not at the day

Also, This year, Corn and other Provisions were exceeding dear Wheat was sold at three and twenty Shillings the Cranock, and Wine for eight pence, and the whole Country was in a manner laid waste by the Scots and those of Ulster Many House keepers, and such as were formerly able to relieve others, went a begging; and great numbers dy'd of hunger The Pestilence and Famine were so severe, that many of the Poor dy'd

At the same time, Messengers arriv'd at Dublin from England, with Pardons to make use of as they should see fit, but the Earl was deliver'd before they came At the feast of Pentecost, Mortimer the Justiciary set out for Drogheda, from whence he went to Trym, sending his Letter to the Lacies to repair to him, but they rejected the Summons with contempt

 5 S Afterwards,

Afterwards, the Lord Hugh de Croftes, Knt was sent to treat of a Peace with the Lacies, but was slain by them, (a fact much to be lamented!) After that, Mortimer the Justiciary drew an Army together against the Lacies; by which their Goods, Cattle, and Treasures, were all seiz'd, many of their Followers cut off, and themselves driven into Conaught, and ruin'd

It was reported, That the Lord Walter Lacy went out as far as Ulster, to seek Brus

Also, about the feast of Pentecost, the Lord Aumar de Valencia and his son were taken Prisoners in S Cinere, a Town in Flanders, and convey'd into Almain The same year, on the Monday after the Nativity of S John Baptist, a Parliament of the Nobility was held at Dublin, where the Earl of Ulster was set at liberty; who took his Oath, and found Security, to answer the King's Writs, and to fight against the King's Enemies, both Scots and Irish

Also, On the day of S Process and Martinian, Thomas Dover, a resolute Pyrate, was taken in a Sea-fight by the Lord John de Athy, and forty of his Men, or thereabouts, cut off; and his Head was brought by him to Dublin

Also, On the day of S Thomas's Translation, the Lord Nicholas de Balscot brought News from England, That two Cardinals were come from the Court of Rome to treat of a Peace, and that they had a Bull for excommunicating all such as should break the King's Peace

Also, On the Thursday next before the feast of S Margaret, Hugh and Walter Lacy were proclaim'd Felons and Traytors to their King, for breaking out into war against their Sovereign

Also, On the Sunday following, the Lord Roger Mortimer Justiciary of Ireland, march'd with his whole Army towards Drogheda

At the same time, the Ulster-men took a good Booty near Drogheda, but the Inhabitants sallied out and retook it In this Action Miles Cogan and his Brother were both slain, and six other Lords of Ulster were taken Prisoners, and brought to the Castle of Dublin

Afterwards, Mortimer the Justiciary led his Army against O Fervill, and commanded * Malpais to be cut down, and all his Houses to be destroy'd After this, O Fervill submitted, and gave Hostages

* Passum malum

Also, The Lord Roger Mortimer Justiciary march'd towards Clony, and † empannell'd a Jury upon the Lord John Blound, viz White of Rathregan. by this, he was found guilty, and fin'd two hundred marks On Sunday after the feast of the Nativity of the blessed Virgin, Mortimer march'd with a great Army against the Irish of O-Mayl, and came to Glinsely, where many were slain both English and Irish, but the Irish had the worst Soon after, O Brynne came and submitted Whereupon, Roger Mortimer return'd with his Men to Dublin-castle.

† Cepit Inquisitionem

On S Simon and S Jude's-day the Archeboldes had the King's Peace, upon the Engagement of the Earl of Kildare

At the feast of S. Hilary following, a Parliament was held at Lincoln, to treat of a Peace between the King and the Earl of Lancaster, and the Scots The Scots continu'd peaceable and quiet and the Lord Archbishop of Dublin and the Earl of Ulster stay'd in England by the King's Order to attend that Parliament About the feast of Epiphany, News came to Dublin, That the Lord Hugh Canon, Justice of the King's-bench, was slain between Naas and Castle-Martin, by Andrew Bermyngham

Also, At the feast of the Purification of the blessed Virgin Mary, came the Pope's Bulls; whereupon Alexander Bicknor was confirm'd and consecrated Archbishop of Dublin, and the Bulls were read and publish'd in Trinity-church Another Bull was read at the same time, for a Peace for two years between the King of England, and Robert Brus King of Scotland But Brus refus'd to comply with it. These things were transacted about the feast of S. Valentine

Also, the Sunday following, the Lord Roger Mortimer came to Dublin, and knighted the Lord John Mortimer and four of his Followers The same day, he kept a great feast in the castle of Dublin

Also, There was a great slaughter of the Irish in Conaught at this time, by reason of a Quarrel between two of their Kings The number of the slain amounted to about 4000 men on both sides After this, a severe Judgment fell upon the Ulster-men, who had done great mischief during the depredations of the Scots here, and eat Flesh in Lent without any manner of necessity, for which sins, they were at last reduc'd to such want, that they eat one another, so that of 10000, there remain'd but about 300, who hardly escap'd By which appears the divine Vengeance Also, It was reported, and that truly, That some of the said Profligates were so pinch'd with Famine, that they dug up dead Bodies in Church-yards, and after they had boil'd the Flesh in the Skull of the dead Body, eat it, nay, that some Women eat their own Children.

MCCCXVIII On the Quindene of Easter, there came News from England into Ireland, That the Town of Berwick was betray''d, and taken by the Scots Afterwards, the same year, Master Walter de Islep, the King's Treasurer in Ireland, arriv'd here, and brought a Letter to the Lord Roger Mortimer, to attend the King Accordingly, he did so, substituting the Lord William Archbishop of Cashil, Keeper of Ireland; so that at one and the same time, he was Justiciary of Ireland, Chancellor, and Archbishop.

Three weeks after Easter, News came to Dublin, That the Lord Richard de Clare and four Knights, viz Sir Henry Capell, Sir Thomas de Naas, Sir James de Caunton, and Sir John de Caunton, as also, Adam Apilgard, with eighty Men more, were all slain by O Brene and Mac-Carthy, on the feast of S Gordian and Epimachus The Lord Clare's Body was reported to be torn in pieces out of pure spite But the Remains were interr'd among the Friers-minors in Limerick

Also, On Sunday, in Easter-month, John Lacy was remov'd from Dublin-castle to Trym, for his Trial, and to hear his Sentence, which was, to be stinted to a Diet; and so he dy'd in Prison

Also, On the Sunday before Ascension, the Lord Roger Mortimer set sail for England, but paid nothing for his Provisions; which he had taken in the City of Dublin, and no where else; as much as amounted to 1000 *l*

Also, This year, about the feast of S John Baptist, the Wheat which before was sold for sixteeen Shillings, by the great mercy of God went now for seven Oats sold for five Shillings, and there was also great plenty of Wine, Salt, and Fish Nay, about the Feast of S James, there was Bread of new Corn; a thing seldom or never before known in Ireland This was an Instance of God's mercy, and was

owing

owing to the prayers of the Poor, and other faithful People

Alſo, on the Sunday after the feaſt of S Michael, news came to Dublin, that the Lord Alexander de Bykenore King's Juſtice in Ireland and Archbiſhop of Dublin, was arriv'd at Yoghill. On S Dennis's day he came to Dublin, and was honourably receiv'd by the Religious and Clergy, as well as the Laity, who went out in Proceſſion to meet him

Alſo, on Saturday, which was the feaſt of Pope Calixtus, a battle was fought between the Scots, and Engliſh of Ireland, two leagues from Dundalk. on the Scotch ſide, there were the Lord Edward de Brus, who call'd himſelf King of Ireland, the Lord Philip de Mountbray, the Lord Walter Sules, the Ld Alan Stewart, with his three brothers, as alſo, the Ld Walter de Lacy, and the Lords Robert and Aumar Lacy, John Kermerdyne, and Walter White, with about 3000 more Againſt whom on the Engliſh ſide, were the Ld. John de Bermingham, the Ld Richard Tuit, the Ld Miles Verdon, the Ld Hugh Tripton, the Ld Herbert de Sutton, the Ld John de Cuſak, the Ld Edward and the Ld William Bermingham, and the Primate of Armagh, who gave them all Abſolution, beſides the Ld Walter de Larpulk, and John Maupas, with about twenty more choice Soldiers and well arm'd, who came from Drogheda. The Engliſh gave the onſet, and broke in upon the Van of the enemy with great vigour And in this encounter the ſaid John Maupas kill'd the Lord Edward de Brus valiantly and honourably, and was afterwards found ſlain upon the Body of the ſaid Edward The ſlain, on the Scots ſide, amounted to 2000 or thereabouts, ſo that few of them eſcap'd, beſides the Ld Philip de Mountbray, who was alſo mortally wounded, and the Ld. Hugh de Lacy, the Ld Walter de Lacy, and ſome few more, who with much ado got off This battle was fought between Dundalk and Faghird Brus's head was brought, by the Ld John Bermingham, to the K of England, who conferr'd the Earldom of Louth upon him and his heirs male, and gave him the Barony of Atenth One of his Quarters, together with the Hands and Heart, were carry'd to Dublin, and the other Quarters ſent to other Places.

MCCCXIX The Ld Roger Mortimer return'd out of England, and was made Juſticiary of Ireland The ſame year at the feaſt of All-ſaints, came the Pope's Bull for excommunicating Robert de Brus K of Scotland at every Maſſe The Town of Athiſell, and a conſiderable part of the Country was burnt by the Ld John Fitz-Thomas, whole-brother to the Ld Moris Fitz-Thomas John Bermingham aforeſaid, was this year created Earl of Louth Alſo, the Stone-bridge of Kil-colyn was built by Maſter Moris Jak, Canon of the Cathedral Church of Kildare

MCCCXX In the time of John XXII Pope, and of Edward ſon to King Edward, who was the 25th King from the coming of S Auſtin into England (Alexander Bicknore being then Archbiſhop of Dublin) was founded the Univerſity of Dublin William de Hardite, a Frier-predicant, was the firſt Maſter in the ſaid Univerſity, who alſo proceeded in Divinity under the ſame Archbiſhop Henry Cogry of the Order of Friers minors was the ſecond Maſter in the ſame Faculty the third was William de Rodyard, Dean of S Patrick's Cathedral in Dublin, who afterwards commenc'd Doctor of the Canon-law, and was made the firſt Chancellor of this Univerſity The fourth Maſter in Divinity, was Frier Edmund de Kermerdyn Alſo, Roger Mortimer Juſticiary of Ireland, return'd into England, leaving the Lord Thomas Fitz-John, then Earl of Kildare, his Deputy

Alſo, the Lord Edmund Botiller went into England, * and then came to St James's

Alſo, Leghelyn bridge was built by Maſter Moris Jak, Canon of the Cathedral Church of Kildare

* Et inde ad S Jacobum ivit

MCCCXXI The O Conghors were put to great ſlaughter at Balibogan on the ninth of May, by the People of Leinſter and Meth

Alſo, the Lord Edmund Botiller dy'd in London, and was buried at Balygaveran in Ireland John Bermingham Earl of Lowth, was made Juſticiary of Ireland John Wogan dy'd alſo this year

MCCCXXII Andrew Bermingham and Nicholas de la Lond Knight, were ſlain, with many others, by O Nalan, on Michaelmas-day

MCCCXXIII A Truce was made between the King of England and Robert Brus King of Scots, for fourteen years Alſo, John Darcy came Chief Juſtice into Ireland Alſo, John eldeſt ſon of the Lord Thomas Fitz John Earl of Kildare, dy'd in the ninth year of his Age

MCCCXXIV Nicholas de Genevile, ſon and heir to the Lord Simon de Genevile, dy'd this year, and was bury'd in the Church of the Friers-predicants, at Trym Alſo, there happen'd a very high Wind on the Epiphany at night

Alſo, there was a general murrain of Oxen and Kine, in Ireland

MCCCXXV Richard Lederede, Biſhop of Offory, cited Dame Alice Ketyll, to anſwer for her heretical Opinions, and forc'd her to appear in Perſon before him And being examined for Sorcery, it was found that ſhe had us'd it Among other inſtances, this was diſcover'd, that a certain † Spirit, call'd Robin Artyſſon, lay with her; and that ſhe offer'd nine red Cocks at a certain Stone-bridge, where four Highways met

† Dæmon Incubus

Alſo, that ſhe ſwept the ſtreets of Kilkenny with Beeſoms, between Complin and Courfew, and in ſweeping the Filth towards the houſe of William Utlaw her ſon, was heard to wiſh, by way of conjuring, Let all the wealth of Kilkenny flow to this houſe The accomplices of this Alice in theſe wretched practices, were Pernil of Meth, and Baſilia the daughter of this Pernil Alice being found guilty, was fin'd by the Biſhop, and forc'd to abjure her ſorcery and witchcraft But being again convicted of the ſame practice, ſhe made her eſcape with the ſaid Baſilia, and was never found after But Pernil was burnt at Kilkenny, and at her death declar'd, That William above-ſaid deſerv'd death as well as ſhe, and that for a year and a day he wore the Devil's girdle about his bare body Hereupon, the Biſhop order'd the ſaid William to be apprehended and impriſon'd in the Caſtle of Kilkenny for eight or nine weeks, and gave orders that two men ſhould attend him, but that they ſhould not eat or drink with him, and that they ſhould not ſpeak to him above once a day At length, he was ſet at liberty by the help of the Lord Arnold Poer, Seneſchal of the County of Kilkenny, and he gave a great ſum of money to the ſaid Arnold, to impriſon the Biſhop. Accordingly, he kept the Biſhop in Priſon about three months Among the goods of Alice, they found ‡ a wafer with the Devil's name upon it; and a Box of Ointment,

‡ Hoſtia.

i

ment,

ment, with which she us'd to daub a certain piece of wood, call'd a Cowltre, after which she and her accomplices could ride upon it round the world, without hurt or hindrance. These things being notorious, Alice was cited again to appear at Dublin, before the Dean of S Patrick's Having some hopes of favour given her, she made her appearance, and demanded a day to answer, having given sufficient bail, as was thought But she appear'd not, for by the advice of her son and others unknown, she hid herself in a certain village till the wind would serve for England, and then she fail'd over, but it is not known whither she went William Utlaw being found by the trial and confession of Pernil (who was condemn'd to be burnt) to have been consenting to his mother, in her sorcery and witchcraft, the Bishop caus'd him to be arrested by the King's writ and put in prison, yet he was set at liberty again by the intercession of the Lords, upon condition that he should cover S Mary's Church in Kilkenny with lead, and do other acts of charity, within a certain day, and that if he did not perform them punctually, he should be in the same state, as when first taken by the King's writ

MCCCXXVI At Whitsontide a Parliament was held in Kilkenny, where was present the Lord Richard Burk, Earl of Ulster, though somewhat infirm, and all the Lords and great men of Ireland, who, with the people, were nobly feasted by the Earl Afterwards, the Earl, taking leave of the Lords and Nobles, went to Athisel, and there dy'd A little before the feast of John the Baptist, he was there interr'd The Lord William Burk was his heir

MCCCXXVII There happen'd an out-fall between the Lord Moris Fitz-Thomas and the Lord Arnald Pover The Lord Moris was seconded by the Lord le Botiller, and the Lord William Bermingham; and the Lord Arnald by the Bourkeyns; many of whom were slain in this fray by the Lord Moris Fitz Thomas, and some driven into Conaught

The same year, after Michaelmas, the Lord Arnald came to assist the Bourkeins, and, upon the Lord Arnald's giving ill Language, and calling him *Rymour*, Lord Moris raised a great Army again, and together with le Botiller, and the said William Bermingham, burnt and wasted the lands and territories of the Lord Arnald, in Ofath Bermingham burnt also the lands and mannor-houses, which belong'd to him in Mounster, and burnt Kenlys in Ossory So that the Lord Arnald was forc'd to fly with the Baron of Donnoyl to Waterford, where they remain'd a month, till the Earl of Kildare, Justiciary of Ireland, and others of the King's Council, order'd them a day of parley The Lord Arnald did not observe it, but came to Dublin, and about the feast of the Purification embark'd for England Upon this, Moris, Botiller, and the Lord William Bermingham, came with a great Army and burnt and wasted his land The King's Council began to dread this powerful Army, and the mischiefs they had done; so much, that they strengthen'd their Cities with Guards and Watches, lest they should be surpriz'd The Lord Moris, Botiller, and Bermingham, hearing of this provision against them, sent to the King's Council, that they would come to Kilkenny and there clear themselves, to satisfy them they had no design upon the lands of their Lord the King, but only intended to be reveng'd of their enemies The Earl of Kildare, Justiciary of Ireland, the Prior of Kilmaynon, namely Roger Outlaw Chancellor of Ireland, Nicholas Fastal Justiciary of Bench, and others of the King's Council, came accordingly to this Parliament. The Lord Moris, Botiller, and Bermingham demanded the King's Charter of peace. But they of the King's Council warily took time, till a month after Easter, to consider of it with their Brethren

Before Lent this year, the Irish of Leinster assembled, and set up Donald the son of Arte Mac Murgh for their King Whereupon, he commanded to set up his Banner within two miles of Dublin, and to march from thence into all parts of Ireland But God seeing his pride and malicious designs, suffer'd him to fall into the hands of the Lord Traharn, who brought him to the Salmon leap, and had two hundred pounds ransom for him, from thence he carry'd him to Dublin, to remain in the castle till the King's Council should give farther Orders After he was taken, the Irish in Leinster underwent many misfortunes, David O Tothil was taken prisoner by the Lord John de Wellesley, and many of them were cut off

The same year Adam Duff, son of Walter Duff of Leinster, who was related to the O Tothiles, was convicted of denying (contrary to the catholick Faith) the incarnation of Christ, and holding that there could not be three persons and one God and he affirm'd, that the blessed Virgin our Saviour's mother was an harlot, that there was no resurrection; that the holy Scripture was a meer fable, and that the apostolical See was an imposture and usurpation Upon these Articles, and every of them, Duff was adjudg'd a Heretick and Blasphemer, and was thereupon burnt, pursuant to the decree of the Church, at Hoggis near Dublin, on the Monday after the octaves of Easter in the year 1328

MCCCXXVIII On Tuesday in Easter-week, Thomas Fitz-John Earl of Kildare and Justiciary of Ireland, departed this life and was succeeded in the office of Justiciary by Frier Roger Outlaw, Prior of Kilmaynan. The same year David O Tothil, a stout rapparee, and an enemy to the King, who had burnt Churches and destroy'd much People, was brought out of the Castle of Dublin to the Toll of the City, before Nicholas Fastol and Elias Ashburne Justices of the King's-Bench, who sentenc'd him to be dragg'd at a horse's tail through the City to the Gallows, and to be hang'd upon a Gibbet, which was excuted accordingly Also, the same year, the Lord Moris Fitz-Thomas rais'd a great army to destroy the Bourkeyns and the Poers

The same year the Lord William Bourk Earl of Ulster was knighted at London on Whitsunday, and the King gave him his Seignory Also, this year, James Botiller marry'd the daughter of the Earl of Hereford in England, and was made Earl of Ormond, being before call'd Earl of Tiperary

The same year a Parliament was held at Northampton, where many of the English Nobility met, and a peace was renew'd between the Kingdoms of England, Scotland, and Ireland, and confirm'd by * marriages It was resolv'd also, that the Earl of Ulster, with several of the English Nobility, should go to Berwick upon Tweed, to see the Espousals

The same year, after the solemnity of this marriage at Berwick, Robert Brus King of Scots, the Lord William Burk Earl of Ulster, the Earl of Meneteth, and many other of the Scotch Nobility, came peaceably to Cragfergus; whence

whence they sent to the Justiciaries of Ireland and the Council, that they would meet them at Green Castle, to treat of a Peace between Scotland and Ireland; but the Justiciary and Council coming not according to the King's desire, he took leave of the Earl of Ulster, and return'd into his own Country after the Assumption of the Blessed Virgin, and the Earl of Ulster came to the Parliament of Dublin, where he staid six days, and made a great Feast, after which he went into Conaught

The same year, about the feast of S Catharin the Virgin, the Bishop of Ossory certify'd the King's Council, that the Lord Arnald Pover was, upon divers Articles, convicted before him of heresie Whereupon, at the Bishop's suit, the said Lord Arnald, by virtue of the King's Writ, was arrested, and put in the Castle of Dublin, and a day was appointed the Bishop, to come to Dublin, in order to prosecute him, but he excused himself from coming at that time, because his Enemies had way laid him So that the King's Council could not put an end to this business wherefore the Lord Arnald was kept prisoner in the Castle of Dublin, till the following Parliament, which was in Midlent, where all the Irish Nobility were present Also, the same year, Frier Roger Outlaw, Prior of the Hospital of S John of Jerusalem in Ireland, Lord Justiciary and Chancellor of Ireland, was charg'd by the said Bishop with favouring of heresy, and for advising and abetting the said Lord Arnald in his heretical opinions Wherefore, the Frier finding himself so unworthily defam'd, petition'd the King's Council, that he might have leave to clear himself; which upon consultation they granted, and caused Proclamation to be made for three days together, That if there was any person who could inform against the said Frier, he should come in and prosecute him, but no body came Upon which, Roger the Frier procur'd the King's Writ to summon the Great men of Ireland, *viz.* the Bishops, Abbots, Priors, and the Mayors of the four Cities, Dublin, Cork, Limerick, and Waterford, and of Drogheda, also the Sheriffs and Seneschals, together with the Knights of the Shires, and the Free-holders, to repair to Dublin; out of which six were chosen to examine the cause, *viz* M William Rodyard Dean of the Cathedral-Church of S Patrick in Dublin, the Abbot of S Thomas, the Abbot of S Mary's, the Prior of the Church of the holy Trinity in Dublin, M Elias Lawles, and Mr Peter Willebey They convened those who were cited, and examin'd them a-part; who depos'd upon Oath that he was an honest, faithful and zealous embracer of the Christian Faith, and would, if occasion serv'd, lay down his Life for it For the greater Solemnity of his Purgation, he made a noble Feast for all that would come

Also, The same year, in Lent, dy'd the Lord Arnald Pover in the Castle of Dublin, and lay a long time unbury'd in the house of the Friers Predicants

MCCCXXIX After the feast of the Annunciation of the blessed Virgin Mary, the Irish Nobility came to the Parliament at Dublin, to wit, the Earl of Ulster, the Lord Moris Fitz-Thomas, the Earl of Louth, William Bermingham, and the rest of the Lords; where was a new peace made between the Earl of Ulster, and the Lord Moris Fitz Thomas; and the Lords with the King's Council made a strict Order against breaches of the King's peace; so that every Nobleman should govern within his own Seignory

The Earl of Ulster made a great feast in the Castle of Dublin; and the day after, the Lord Moris Fitz-Thomas made another in S Patrick's Church in Dublin; as did also Frier Roger Outlaw, Justiciary of Ireland, on the third day, at Kylmaynan; and so they departed.

The same year on S Barnaby's-eve, the Lord John de Bermingham, Earl of Louth, was kill'd at Balybragan in Urgale by the inhabitants of Urgale, and with him his own lawful brother Peter Bermingham, besides Robert Bermingham his putative brother, and the Lord John Bermingham, son to his brother Richard Lord of Anry, William Finne Bermingham, the Lord Anry's Uncle's son, Simon de Bermingham son of the aforesaid William, Thomas Bermingham son of Robert of Conaught, Peter Bermingham son of James of Conaught, Henry Bermingham of Conaught, and Richard Talbot of Malaghide a man of great Valour, besides 200 more, whose names are not known.

Also, After this slaughter, the Lord Simon Genevil's men invaded the Country of Carbry, to plunder the inhabitants, for the thefts and murders they had so often committed in Meth; but they of Carbry, by rising, prevented the invasion, and slew seventy-six of the Lord Simon's men Also, The same year on the day after Trinity-sunday, John Gernon and his Brother Roger Gernon, came to Dublin in the behalf of those of Urgale, and pray'd that they might be try'd by the Common-law And on the Tuesday, next day after S John's feast, John and Roger hearing that the Lord William Bermingham was coming to Dublin, left it The same year, on S Laurence's-eve, the Lord Thomas Botiller march'd with a great army into the Country of Ardnorwith; where he fought with the Lord Thomas Williams Macgoghgan; and was there kill'd, to the great loss of Ireland, and with him the Lord John de Ledewich, Roger and Thomas Ledewich, John Nangle, Meiler and Simon Petitt, David Nangle, the Lord John Waringer, James Terel, Nicholas White, William Freynes, Peter Kent, and John White; besides 140 others, whose names we know not The Tuesday before the feast of S. Bartholomew, the said Lord Thomas le Botiller's body was convey'd to Dublin, and lay in the house of the Friers predicant unburied, till the sunday after the Decollation of S John Baptist, when he was very honourably carried through the City, and interr'd in the Church of the Friers predicant, on which day, his wife had a great Feast

The same year the Lord John Darcy came a second time Justiciary of Ireland, who at Maynoth on the third of July marry'd the Lady Joan Burg Countess of Kildare

Also, Philip Staunton was slain, and the Lord Henry Traharn was treacherously surpris'd in his own house at Kilbego by Richard son of Philip Onolan Also, the Lord James Botiller Earl of Ormond burnt Foghird, in revenge to Onolan, for his said brother Henry.

The same year, the Wednesday after the feast of the Ascension of the blessed Virgin, the Lord John Darcy, Justiciary of Ireland, went towards the new castle of Mackingham, and Wikelow, against the O Brynnes; and the Monday following, some of the Lawles were kill'd, and more wounded; and Robert Locam was wounded; and of the Irish, the better sort was slain, and many wounded, and the rest ran away. But Murkad O Brynne, with his son, and uncle, and uncle's son, yielded themselves hostages, and were carry'd to the Castle of Dublin, but were

 afterwards,

afterwards, in exchange for other Hostages of the best of their Kindred, set at liberty

The same year the Lord John Darcy Justiciary, and the King's Council in Ireland, about the feast of the Circumcision, commanded the Lord Moris Fitz-Thomas of Desmond to march with his Army against his Majesty's enemies to subdue them; adding, that the King would take care to defray the Charge he should be at, for himself and his Army So the said Lord Moris, accompany'd by Briene-O-Brene, came with an Army of ten thousand Men, with which he march'd against the O-nolanes, and conquer'd them, having got a considerable Booty, and destroy'd their Country with fire · the O-nolanes fled, but afterwards deliver'd Hostages, who were sent to the Castle of Dublin Hence he march'd against the O-Morches, who gave Hostages, with a promise to keep the Peace

At the same time, the Castle of Ley, which O-Dympcy had taken and held, was surrender'd to the said Moris This year, after the Epiphany, Donald Arte Mac-Murgh made his escape out of the Castle of Dublin, by a Cord which one Adam Nangle had brought him, who, for his pains, was afterwards drawn and hang'd

MCCCXXX About the feasts of S Catherine, S Nicholas, and the Nativity of our Lord, the winds were in several places very high, so that, on S Nicholas-eve, they blew down part of the wall of a House, which in the fall kill'd the Lord Miles de Verdon's wife and daughter there was never known such a wind in Ireland

Also, there was such an overflow of the River Boyn this year, as was never seen before, which flung down all the Bridges upon this River, both Wood and Stone, except Babe-bridge The water also carry'd away several Mills, and did much damage to the Friers minors of Trym and Drogheda, by breaking down their Houses

The same year about the feast of S John Baptist, there began to be a great dearth of Corn in Ireland, which lasted till Michaelmas A cranoc of Wheat was sold for twenty Shillings, and a cranoc of Oats, Pease, Beans and Barly, for eight Shillings This dearth was occasion'd by the immoderate Rains, so that a great deal of Corn could not be cut before Michaelmas

The same year about Lent, the English in Meth killed some of the Irish, viz the Macgoghiganes near Loghynerthy This did so incense Mac-goghigan, that he burnt and plunder'd in those Parts fifteen small Villages which the English seeing, gathered together in a Body against him, and kill'd 110 of his men; among whom were three sons of petty Kings of Ireland

Also, the Lord William Burgh, Earl of Ulster, march'd with his Army out of Ulster, against Briene O-Brene in Munster

Also, the Lady Joan, Countess of Kildare, was, at Maynoth, brought to Bed of William her first Son which the Lord John Darcy had by her, who was then in England

Also, Reymund Lawles was treacherously kill'd at Wickelow

Also, this year, Frier Roger Utlaw Prior of Kylmainan, then * Deputy to the Justiciary of Ireland, held a Parliament at Kilkenny, where were present Alexander Archbishop of Dublin, William Earl of Ulster, James Earl of Ormond, the Lord William Bermingham, and Walter Burg of Conaught; who all went with a great army, to drive Briene O-Brene out of Urkyff near Cashill

* *Locum tenens Justiciarii*

Also, Walter Burg, with the Forces he rais'd in Conaught, plunder'd the Lord Moris Fitz-Thomas's lands, and brought away the Booty to Urkyff.

Also, the Earl of Ulster, and the Earl of Desmond, viz the Lord Moris Fitz-Thomas (this is the first time that I call him *Earl*) were, by Frier Roger Utlaw, then Justiciary of Ireland, committed to the custody of the Marshal at Limerick But the Earl of Desmond cunningly made his escape

MCCCXXXI The Lord Hugh Lacy, having got the King's Pardon, came into Ireland Also, the Earl of Ulster came into England Also, the 19th of April, the English beat the Irish in O Kenseley Also, on the one and twentieth of April, the Irish took the Castle of Arclo, by treachery

Also, the same day, on S Mark the Evangelist's-eve, the O-Totheles came to Tanelagh, and took from Alexander Archbishop of Dublin 300 Sheep, and kill'd Richard White, with other Gentlemen of his Retinue The news of this Plunder and Slaughter came to Dublin, and Sir Philip Bryt, Knight, Frier Moris Fitz-Gerald, Knt of the Order of the Hospitalers, Hammund Archdekyn, John Chamberlaine, Robert Tyrell, and two sons of Reginal Bernewall, besides many others, especially of the Archbishop of Dublin's Family, were kill'd by David O-Tothill, in an Ambuscade in Culiagh

Also, the Lord William Bermingham march'd with a great Army against the foresaid Irish, to whom he did much harm, and, had not the Irish made some false Promises would have done them much more

Also, the third of June, the Lord Anthony Lucy came over Chief Justiciary of Ireland

Also, this year, the English who dwell about Thurles, did in the month of May give the Irish under the command of Briene O Brene, a great overthrow. Also, upon the 11th of June, another was given at Finnagh in Meth, by the English of those parts

Also, the 27th of June, when there was a great Famine in Ireland, through God's mercy there came a-shoar such a vast number of Sea-fish, called Thurlhedis, as had not been seen in many Ages, for, according to the common estimate, there were above 500 This happen'd about the evening, near Connyng, and the water call'd Dodyz in Dublin haven The Lord Anthony Lucy then Justiciary of Ireland, with his own Servants, and some of the Citizens of Dublin, among whom was Philip Cradok, kill'd above 200 of them, and gave leave to every body to fetch away what they would

The Lord Anthony Lucy, Justiciary of Ireland, appointed a Parliament to be held at Dublin in the Octaves of S John Baptist, whither some of the Irish Nobility came not Then he remov'd to Kilkenny, and prorogued the Parliament to the Feast of S Peter ad vincula Hither came the Lord Moris Fitz Thomas, and many more Noblemen, who were not there before, and submitted to the King's mercy And the King, for his part, graciously forgave them whatever mischief they had done, under a certain form

Also, in August, the Irish, by treachery, took the Castle of Firnis, which they burnt

Also, the said Lord Moris Fitz Thomas of Desmond, by an order of Council, was taken the day after the Assumption of the blessed Virgin, at Limerick, by the said Justiciary, and by him brought to the Castle of Dublin the 7th of October.

Also,

Alſo, in September, Henry Mandevill, by virtue of a Warrant from Simon Fitz-Richard Juſticiary of the Bench, was taken, and brought to the Caſtle of Dublin

Alſo, in November, Walter Burck and his two whole-Brothers were taken in Conaught, by the Earl of Ulſter, and in February were by him brought to the Caſtle of Northburg

Alſo, in February, the Lord William Bermingham, and his Son Lord of Bermingham, were taken at Clomel by the ſaid Juſticiary, notwithſtanding he had before granted them his Majeſty's Pardon; and on the nineteenth of April were carry'd to Dublin-caſtle.

Alſo, the Iriſh of Leinſter plunder'd the Engliſh, and burnt their Churches, and, in the Church of Freineſton, burnt about eighty Men and Women, and a certain Chaplain of that Church, whom they hinder'd with their Javelins from coming out, tho' in his holy Veſtments, and with the Lord's Body in his hand, burning him with the reſt in the Church The news of it came to the Pope, who ſent his Bull to the Archbiſhop of Dublin, commanding him to excommunicate thoſe Iriſh, and all their adherents, and to interdict their Lands The Archbiſhop fulfill'd the Pope's commands, but the Iriſh deſpiſed the Bull, Excommunication, and Interdict, and the Authority of the Church, and, continuing in their wickedneſs, got together again and made an inrode into the County of Weisford, as far as Carcarn, and plunder'd the whole Country Richard White, and Richard Fitz-Henry, with the Burghers of Weisford, and other Engliſh, made head againſt them, and kill'd about 400 of the Iriſh, beſides a great many more who, in the purſuit, were drown'd in the river Slane.

MCCCXXXII The eleventh of July, William Bermingham, by the ſaid Juſticiary's Order, was put to death, and hang'd at Dublin, but his ſon Walter was ſet at Liberty The ſaid Ld William was a noble Knight and one of a thouſand in warlike exploits Alas! what pity it was! for who can think of his death without Tears? He was afterwards bury'd at Dublin among the Friers Predicant Alſo, the Caſtle of Bonraty was taken, and, in July was ras'd to the ground by the Iriſh of Totomon Alſo, the Caſtle of Arclo was taken from the Iriſh by the ſaid Juſticiary and the Citizens of Dublin, with the help of the Engliſh of that Country, and on the eighth of Auguſt, was in the King's Hands; being in part rebuilt The Ld Anthony Lucy Juſticiary of Ireland, was put out of his place, and in November return'd into England with his wife and children. The Lord John Darcy ſucceeded him, and came into Ireland the thirteenth of February There was, about this time, a great ſlaughter of the Iriſh in Munſter, made by the Engliſh Inhabitants of that Country upon Briene O-Brene and Mac Karthy

Alſo, John Decer a citizen of Dublin dy'd, and was bury'd in the Church of the Friers-minors, he was a man who did a great deal of good Alſo, a diſeaſe called Mauſes ſpread over Ireland, and infected all ſorts of People, old and young, men and women

Alſo, the Hoſtages who were kept in the Caſtle of Lymerick, kill'd the Conſtable and took the Caſtle, but upon the citizens regaining it by force, they were put to the ſword Alſo, the Hoſtages took the Caſtle of Nenagh; but part of it being burnt, it was again recover'd, and the Hoſtages kept Alſo, one of * wheat about Chriſtmas was ſold for twenty-two Shillings; and ſoon after J aſter, and ſo on, very commonly for twelve pence The Town of the New-caſtle of Lions was burnt and plunder'd by the O Toohiles

* Frumenti

MCCCXXXIII The Lord John Darcy, Juſticiary of Ireland, arriv'd at Dublin

Alſo, the Berminghams of Carbery got a great booty of above 2000 Cows from the O-Conghirs The Lord John Darcy Juſticiary of Ireland, order'd the paſs at Ethrgovil in Offaley to be cut down againſt O-Conghir

The Lord Moris Fitz-Thomas Earl of Deſmond, after he had been impriſon'd a year and half in Dublin, was let out, having got many of the Iriſh Nobility, as mainprizes, to be bound for him under penalty of their lives and all they had, if he ſhould attempt any thing againſt the King, and the ſaid Lords not produce him to be try'd

Alſo, William Burk Earl of Ulſter on the 6th of June, between New-Town and Cragfergus in Ulſter, was (alas) treacherouſly murder'd by his own Company in the twentieth year of his age Robert ſon of Maunton Maundevile gave him the firſt blow As ſoon as his wife heard of it, who was then in Ulſter, ſhe imbark'd with her daughter and heir, and went for England The Lord John Darcy Chief Juſticiary of Ireland, to revenge this murder, did, by the advice of the Parliament then aſſembled, ſhip off his army, with which, the firſt of July, he arriv'd at Cragfergus The people of that country, glad at his arrival took courage, and unanimouſly reſolv'd to revenge the Earl's death, and in a pitch'd battle got a victory over the murderers ſome they took, others they put to the ſword When this was over, the ſaid Juſticiary went with his army into Scotland, leaving M Thomas Burgh then Treaſurer of Ireland, to ſupply his place

Alſo, many of the Iriſh nobility, and the Earl of Ormond, with their retinue, aſſembled on the eleventh of June at the houſe of the Carmelite Friers in Dublin During this Parliament, as they were going out of the court yard of the Friers houſe, Murcardus or Moris ſon of Nicholas O-Tothil was ſuddenly murder'd in the croud, upon which, the nobility, ſuppoſing there was treaſon, were very much affrighted, but the murderer got off, reſolutely, without being known ſo much as by name

Alſo, the Lord John Darcy return'd Juſticiary of Ireland

Alſo, in February the Lord Walter de Bermingham, ſon of Lord William de Bermingham, was let out of Dublin caſtle

Alſo, the Lord Moris Fitz-Thomas, Earl of Deſmond, by a fall of his horſe, broke his leg

Alſo, it happen'd to be ſo dry a ſummer, that at the feaſt of S *Peter ad vincula*, there was bread made of new wheat; and wheat was ſold in Dublin for ſix-pence a peck

Alſo, Sir Reimund Archedekin, Knight, with many others of his family, were kill'd in Leinſter

MCCCXXXVII On the eve of S Kalixtus the Pope, ſeven partridges leaving the fields, God knows why, came directly to Dublin; where flying ſwiftly over the Market-place, they ſettled on the top of * an Inn which belonged to the Canons of S Trinity in Dublin Some of the citizens came running to this ſight, wondering very much at ſo ſtrange a thing, the Town-boys caught two of them alive, and a third they kill'd, at which the reſt being frighten'd, took a ſwift flight, and eſcap'd into the oppoſite fields

* Pandoxatorium

But

But what this should portend (a thing unheard of before) I shall leave to better judgments

Also, the Lord John Charleton, Knight and Baron, came with his wife, sons, daughters, and family, chief Justiciary of Ireland, on the feast of S. Kalixtus the Pope; and some of his sons and family dy'd

Also, the same day, came into Dublin harbour D Thomas Charleton Bishop of Hereford, as Chancellor of Ireland, with the chief Justiciary his brother; and with them M John Rees Treasurer of Ireland and Master in the Decretals, besides 200 Welchmen.

Also, whilst the Lord John Charleton was Justiciary, and held a Parliament at Dublin, Mr. David O Hirraghcy Archbishop of Armagh being call'd to the Parliament, laid in his provisions in the Monastery of S Mary near Dublin; but the Archbishop and his Clerks would not let him be there, because he would have his Cross carry'd before him

Also, the same year dy'd David Archbishop of Armagh, to whom succeeded a person of great parts, M Richard Fitz-Ralph Dean of Litchfield, who was born in Dundalk.

Also, James Botiller the first Earl of Ormond, dy'd the sixth of January, and was bury'd at Balygaveran

MCCCXXXVIII The Lord John Charleton, at the instigation of his brother Thomas Bishop of Hereford, was by the King turn'd out of his place, upon which he came back with his whole family into England, and Thomas Bishop of Hereford was made Keeper and Justiciary of Ireland

Also, the Ld Eustace Pover and the Ld. John Pover his Uncle, were by the said Justiciary brought from Munster to Dublin, where, the 3d of Feb they were imprison'd in the Castle

Also, in Ireland, they had so great a frost that the river Aven-liffie on which the City of Dublin stands, was frozen hard enough to dance, run, or play at ball on, and they made wood and turfe fires upon it, to broil Herrings The Ice lasted a great while I shall say nothing of the great Snow which fell during this frost, since the depth thereof is almost incredible. This Frost continu'd from the second of December to the tenth of February; such a season was never known in Ireland

MCCCXXXIX All Ireland was in Arms The Lord Moris Fitz-Thomas Earl of Desmond, with the Geraldines who live about Kernige, made a great destruction of the Irish; killing and drowning, to the number at least of 1200 Men

Also, the Lord Moris Fitz-Nicholas, Lord of Kernigy, was by the Lord Moris Fitz-Thomas Earl of Desmond apprehended and put in prison, where he dy'd of hunger, being stinted to a diet; because he had openly rebell'd with the Irish against the King and the Earl.

Also, a great number of the O Dympcies and other Irish were by the English and the vigorous pursuit of the Earl of Kildare, kill'd and drown'd in the Barrow

Also, the latter end of February, Thomas Bishop of Hereford, Justiciary of Ireland, with the help of the English of that Country, took from the Irish about Odrone such a great booty of all sorts of cattle, as had not been seen in Leinster

MCCCXL the said Bishop of Hereford Justiciary of Ireland, being commanded home by his Majesty, return'd into England the tenth of April; leaving Frier Roger Outlaw Prior of Kilmainan in his place Also, the Lord Roger Outlaw Prior of Kilmainan, and Justiciary and Chancellor of the said Kingdom, dy'd the thirteenth of February

Also, the King of England made John Darcy Justiciary of Ireland, for life.

MCCCXLI In May the Lord John Moris came Justiciary of Ireland, as Deputy to John Darcy.

Also, in the County of * Leicester, there happen'd such a strange prodigy, as has not been heard of A person travelling along the road found a pair of Gloves, fit for his use as he thought, but when he put them on, he lost his speech immediately, and began to bark like a dog, nay, from that moment, the men and women throughout the whole County bark'd like great dogs, and the Children like whelps. This plague continu'd with some, eighteen days; with others, a month, and with some, two months; and also infected the neighbouring Counties, and set them a barking too

* Louthe

Also, the King of England revok'd all Grants, that either he or his Father had made to any in Ireland in what manner soever, whether of liberties, lands, or goods. which occasion'd a general murmur and discontent; insomuch that the whole Kingdom was upon the point of revolting.

Also, a Parliament was call'd by the King's Council to sit in October Mons Fitz-Thomas Earl of Desmond absented Never before was there seen so great and open a division between the English born in England, and the English born in Ireland At last, without asking Counsel of the Justiciary or any of the King's Ministers, the Mayors of the King's Cities, together with the Nobility and Gentry of the Kingdom, resolv'd among other things to hold another Parliament at Kilkenny in November, in order to treat of such matters as might be for the benefit of the King and Kingdom.

Neither the Justiciary nor any other of the King's Ministers durst repair thither It was therefore concluded in this Parliament, by the Nobility and the Mayors aforesaid, immediately to dispatch messengers to the King of England to intercede for relief, and represent the wicked and unjust administration of the great Officers in Ireland, and to declare that they would no longer endure their oppressions; and to desire that Ireland might be govern'd by Ministers of its own, as usual They were instructed, in their complaints of the said Ministers to ask, how a Land so full of wars, could be govern'd by a Person who was a Stranger to warlike Affairs? how a Minister of the King's could grow so rich in so short a time? what was the reason that the King of England was never the richer for Ireland?

MCCCXLII On the eleventh day of October, and the elventh of the Moon, two several Moons were seen by many about Dublin, in the morning, before day The one was bright, and according to its natural course, in the West; the other, of the bigness of a round loaf, stood in the East, with very little light

MCCCXLIII St Thomas's-street in Dublin was set on fire, on S Valentine the Martyr's-day

Also, the thirteenth of July, the Lord Ralph Ufford, with his wife the Countess of Ulster, came chief Justiciary of Ireland; upon whose coming the fair Weather suddenly turn'd foul, and here was nothing but rainy and tempestuous Weather, while he liv'd None of his Predecessors were near so bad; for (alas!) instead of doing Justice, he oppress'd the Irish, and robb'd

both

both Clergy and Laity of their Goods; neither did he ſpare Poor, any more than Rich. under colour of doing Good, he defrauded many He obſerv'd neither the Laws of the Church nor of the Land. He was injurious to the natural Iriſh, and did Juſtice to few, if any; wholly diſtruſting all the Natives, except ſome few And being miſled by his wife's Counſel, theſe things were his daily practice

Alſo, the ſaid Juſticiary, as he was going into Ulſter in March, through a paſs call'd Emerdullan, was ſet upon by one Maccartan, who robb'd him of his cloaths, money, goods, plate and horſes, and kill'd ſome of his men But at laſt the Juſticiary, with the help of the Ergalians got the Victory, and made his way into Ulſter

MCCCXLV The ſeventh of June, there was a Parliament held at Dublin, whither the Lord Moris Fitz Thomas Earl of Deſmond did not come

Alſo, the Lord Ralph Ufford, Juſticiary of Ireland, after S John Baptiſt's day, did without conſent of the Iriſh Nobility ſet up the King's Standard againſt the Lord Moris Fitz-Thomas Earl of Deſmond, and march'd into Munſter, where he ſeiz'd the Earl's Eſtate into the King's hands, and farm'd it out to others for a certain yearly rent to be paid the King

Alſo, whilſt the ſaid Juſticiary was in Munſter, he gave Sir William Burton, Knight, two writs, who was to give one of them to the Ld Moris Fitz-Thomas Earl of Kildare: The contents of this, were, That upon pain of forfeiting his whole Eſtate, he ſhould forthwith repair unto him with a good force, to aſſiſt the King and him The other, was an Order to the ſaid Sir William to apprehend the Earl of Kildare, and impriſon him, but he finding it impracticable, perſuaded the Earl, who was preparing his Army, and levying forces to aſſiſt the Juſticiary, that before he march'd he ſhould go to the King's Council in Dublin, and act by their Advice, that in his Abſence his Lands might be ſafe, and if any harm ſhould come to them, it might be through the fault of the King's Council, and not his own Upon this, the Earl not diſtruſting the Knight, nor ſuſpecting any Plot againſt him, prepar'd to go for Dublin; where, when he came (altogether ignorant of the Treachery) as he was conſulting with the King's Council in the Exchequer, on a ſudden the ſaid Sir William arreſted him, and he was taken, and carried to the Caſtle of Dublin

Alſo, the ſaid Juſticiary march'd with his Army into the Country of O-Comill in Munſter, and Kering, and by treachery took two caſtles of the Earl of Deſmond, viz the caſtle of Ynyſkyſty and the caſtle of the Iſle, in which were the Lord Euſtace Pover, the Lord William Graunt, and the Lord John Cottrell, who were firſt drawn, and then hang'd, in October

Alſo, the ſaid Juſticiary baniſh'd the ſaid Earl of Deſmond, with ſome others of his Men After that, in November, he return'd with his forces out of Munſter, to his wife then big with child at Kylmainan near Dublin Beſides what he had done to the Laity, in indicting, impriſoning, and robbing them of their Goods; he had alſo plagued the Eccleſiaſticks, as well Prieſts as Clerks, by Arreſts and Impriſonments; and extorted great ſums of Money from them.

Alſo, having taken away the Lands, he revok'd the Grants and Demiſes of them, beſtowing them upon other Tenants, as has been ſaid; and alſo the writings concerning thoſe Grants, which were ſign'd by him, and ſeal'd with the King's Seal, he took and cancell'd

Alſo, the Earl of Deſmond's 26 Mainpriſers, as well Earls, as Barons, Knights, and others, viz the Lords William Burke Earl of Ulſter, James Botiller Earl of Ormond, Richard Tuit, Euſtace le Pover, Gerald de Rochfort, John ſon of Robert Pover, Robert de Barry, Mons Fitz-Gerald, John de Wellesly, Walter Lenfaunt, Roger de la Rokell, Henry Traharn, Roger le Pover, John Lenfaunt, Roger le Pover, Matthew Fitz-Henry, Richard le Wallis, Edward Burk ſon of the Earl of Ulſter, Knights; David de Barry, William Fitz-Gerald, Fulk Aſh, Robert Fitz-Moris, Henry de Barkley, John ſon of George Roch, and Thomas de Lees de Burgh (notwithſtanding ſome of them had been at great Pains and Charge, with the Juſticiary, in his wars, and in purſuing of the Earl of Deſmond were judicially depriv'd by him of their Eſtates, and diſinherited, and ſent to Priſon till the King's pleaſure ſhould be known, except four, viz William Burk Earl of Ulſter, James le Botiler Earl of Ormond, &c

MCCXLVI On Palm-ſunday, which was on the ninth of April, D Ralph Ufford Juſticiary of Ireland dy'd, whoſe death was very much lamented by his Wife and Family, but the loyal Subjects of Ireland rejoyc'd at it, and both Clergy and Laity, for Joy, had a ſolemn feaſt with dancing, at Eaſter Upon his death, the Floods ceaſed, and the Air grew wholeſome, and the common People bleſs'd God for it Being laid in a ſtrong ſheet of lead, his very ſorrowful Counteſs convey'd his bowels (with his Treaſure not worthy to be plac'd among ſuch holy relicks) into England, where he was interr'd And at laſt, on the ſecond of May (a Prodigy! which without doubt was the effect of divine Providence,) this Lady who came ſo glorious into Dublin with the enſign of Royalty, and a great number of ſoldiers attending her through the ſtreets, where ſhe liv'd a ſhort time like a Queen of Ireland, went out privily at a back gate in the caſtle, to avoid the people's clamours for their debts, and, at her diſgraceful return home, was attended with the ſymptoms of death, ſorrow, and heavineſs.

Alſo, after the death of the ſaid Juſticiary, the Lord Roger Darcy, by the conſent of the King's Miniſters and others, was choſen to ſupply the office of Juſticiary for the time being

Alſo, the caſtles of Ley and Kylmehede were taken and burnt by the Iriſh, in April

Alſo, the Lord John Moris being made chief Juſticiary of Ireland, arriv'd here the fifteenth of May

Alſo, the Iriſh of Ulſter gave a great ſlaughter to the Engliſh of Urgale in June, and at leaſt three hundred were cut off

Alſo the ſaid Lord John Moris Juſticiary of Ireland was turn'd out of that office by the King, and the Lord Walter de Permingham put in; who came into Ireland with his commiſſion in June, ſome time after the great ſlaughter juſt now mention'd

Alſo, the preſervation of the peace was committed by the King for ſome time, to the Lord Moris Fitz-Thomas Earl of Deſmond Having receiv'd this order, on the eve of the Exaltation of the holy Croſs, he embark'd with his wife and two ſons at Yoghil, and arriv'd in England, where he vigorouſly proſecuted the Ld Ralph de Ufford, late Juſticiary of Ireland, for the wrongs he had done him

Also, by the King's order, the said Earl was to be allow'd twenty shillings a day from the time of his first arrival, during his abode there

Also, in Nov the Ld Walter de Bermingham, Justiciary of Ireland, and the Ld Moris Fitz-Thomas Earl of Kildare, took up arms against O Morda and his Accomplices, who burnt the castle of Ley and Kilmehede, and attack'd them so vigorously with fire, sword, and rapin, that altho' their number amounted to many thousands of Irish, and they made a resolute defence, yet at last, after many wounds and great slaughter they were forc'd to yield, and so submitted to the King's mercy and the discretion of the Earl

MCCCXLVII The Earl of Kildare, with his Barons and Knights, set out in May to join the King of England, who was then at the siege of Caleys Also, the inhabitants surrender'd Caleys to the King of England, on the fourth of June

Also, Walter Bonevile, William Calfe, William Weleſly, and many other brave English, Welch, and Irish Gentlemen, dy'd of the Distemper which then rag'd at Caleys

Also, Mac Murgh, *viz.* Donald Mac-Murgh son of Donald Arte Mac-Murgh, King of Leinster, was perfidiously kill'd by his own Men, on the fifth of June

Also, the King knighted Moris Fitz Thomas Earl of Kildare Also, the said Earl marry'd the daughter of Barth de Burwashe

Also, on St Stephen the Martyr's-day, the Irish burnt the Town of Monaghan, and destroy'd the Country about it

Also, the Lady Joan Fitz-Leones, formerly wife to the Lord Simon Genevile, dy'd, and on the second of April was bury'd in the Convent of the Friers-Predicants at Trym

MCCCXLVIII The twenty second year of Edward the third, the first Pestilence, which had been before in other Countries, got into Ireland, and rag'd exceedingly

Also, this year the Lord Walter Bermingham, Justiciary of Ireland, went into England, and left John Archer Prior of Kylmainan to supply his Place The same year, he return'd, and had the Barony of Kenlys, which lies in Offory, conferr'd on him by the King, to requite his great service in leading an Army against the Earl of Desmond, with Raulf Ufford, as before was said This Barony belong'd formerly to the Lord Eustace le Pover, who was drawn and hang'd at the castle of the Isle

MCCCXLIX The Ld Walter Bermingham, the best Justiciary that ever was in Ireland, surrender'd his office, and was succeeded in the same by the Lord de Carew Knight and Baron

MCCCL In the twenty fifth year of the Reign of King Edward, Sir Thomas Rokesby, Knight, was made Justiciary of Ireland

Also, this year on the eve of S Margaret the Virgin, the Lord Walter Bermingham, Knight, some time the most worthy Justiciary of this Kingdom, dy'd in England.

MCCCLI dy'd Kenwrick Sherman, sometimes Mayor of the City of Dublin, and was bury'd under the Belfrey of the Friers-Predicants there, which he himself had built; as he had likewise glaz'd the great Window at the upper end of the Quire, and roof'd the Church with many other pious Works He dy'd in the same Convent on the sixth of March; and, leaving an Estate to the value of three thousand marks, he bequeath'd great Legacies to the Clergy, both regular and secular, within twenty miles of the City

MCCCLII Sir Robert Savage, Knight, began to build new Castles in many places of Ulster, and particularly in his own Manors, saying to his son and heir apparent Henry Savage, Let us thus fortify ourselves, lest the Irish hereafter break in upon us, and take away our place and nation, and make us a reproach to all Nations. His son answer'd, Wherever there are valiant Men, there are forts and castles, according to that saying, *Filii castrametati sunt*, the sons are encamp'd, i e brave Men are design'd for War; and for this reason I will take care to be among such, and so I shall live in a castle, adding the common saying, a castle of *Bones* is better than a castle of *Stones* Upon this reply, his Father gave over in great anger, and swore he would never more build with stone and mortar, but keep a good house and great retinue about him, foretelling however, that his Posterity would repent it, as indeed they did, for the Irish destroy'd the whole Country for want of castles to defend it

MCCCLV In the thirtieth of the same Reign, Sir Thomas Rokesby, Knight, surrender'd his office of Justiciary on the twenty sixth of July; which was given to Mons Fitz-Thomas Earl of Desmond, and he continu'd in it till his death

Also, on the conversion of S Paul, the said Lord Moris Fitz-Thomas dy'd Justiciary of Ireland, in the Castle of Dublin, to the great grief of his friends and kindred, and the fear of all who lov'd the peace of Ireland First, he was bury'd in the Quire of the Friers Predicants of Dublin, and afterward in the Convent of the Friers-Predicants of Traly He was just in his office, and stuck not to condemn those of his own blood for theft, rapin, and other misdemeanors, as if they had been strangers. The Irish stood in great awe of him

MCCCLVI In the thirty first year of this Reign, Sir Thomas Rokesby was the second time made Justiciary of Ireland, who kept the Irish in good order, and paid well for the provisions of his House, saying, I will eat and drink out of wooden vessels, and pay gold and silver for my food, cloths, and servants

The same year the said Sir Thomas, Justiciary of Ireland, dy'd in the castle of Kylka

MCCCLVII In the thirty second of this King's reign, the Lord Almarick de Saint Armund was made Justiciary of Ireland, and enter'd upon his office

About this time arose a great dispute between the Lord Archbishop of Armagh, Richard Fitz-Ralfe, and the four orders of Friers-mendicants in conclusion, the Archbishop was worsted, and silenc'd by the Pope's Authority

MCCCLVIII In the 33d of the same reign, the Lord Almarick de Saint Armund, Justiciary of the Kingdom, went over into England

MCCCLIX In the 34th of this King's reign, James le Botiller Earl of Ormond, was made chief Justiciary of Ireland

Also, on S Gregory's day, this year, dy'd the Lady Joan Burk Countess of Kildare, and was bury'd in the Church of the Friers minors of Kildare, with her Husband the Lord Thomas Fitz-John, Earl of Kildare

MCCCLX In the 35th of this same reign, dy'd Richard Fitz Rault Archbishop of Armagh, in Hanault, on the 16th of December His bones were convey'd into Ireland, by the reverend Father Stephen Bishop of Meth, and bury'd in S. Nicholas Church at Dundalk, where he was born; yet it is a question, whether these were his bones, or some other man's

Also,

Alſo, this year dy'd Sir Robert Savage in Ulſter, a valiant Knight, who near Antrim ſlew in one day 3000 Iriſh with a ſmall Party of Engliſh, but before the Engagement, he took care to give every Engliſh man a good doſe of Wine or Ale, of which he had great ſtore, and reſerv'd ſome for them at their return Beſides this, he order'd, that Sheep, Oxen, Veniſon, and Fowl, both wild and tame, ſhould be kill'd, and made ready to entertain the Conquerors, whoſoever they ſhould be, ſaying, it would be a ſhame that Gueſts ſhould come, and find him unprovided It pleaſing God to bleſs the Engliſh with Victory, he invited them all to Supper to rejoice with him, giving God thanks for his ſucceſs He ſaid, I thank God, becauſe thus it is better to ſave, than to pour on the ground, as ſome adviſed He was bury'd in the Convent of the Friers-predicants of Coulrath, near the river Banne

Alſo, the Earl of Ormond, Juſticiary of Ireland, went into England, and Moris Fitz-Thomas Earl of Kildare, was made Juſticiary of Ireland by charter or commiſſion, in this form *Omnibus*, &c *To all, to whom theſe Preſents ſhall come, greeting Know ye, that we have committed to our faithful and loving Subject* Moris Earl of Kildare, *the office of Juſticiary of our Kingdom of Ireland, together with the Nation, and the Caſtles, and all Apartenances thereunto belonging, to keep and govern them, during our will and pleaſure Commanding, that while he remains in the ſaid office, he receive the ſum of five hundred pounds yearly out of our Exchequer at Dublin Upon which conſideration, he ſhall perform the ſaid office, and take care of the Kingdom, and maintain twenty Men and Horſe, in arms conſtantly, whereof himſelf ſhall be one, during the ſaid commiſſion* In witneſs whereof, &c Given at Dublin, by the hands of our beloved Brother in Chriſt, Thomas Burgey, Prior of the Hoſpital of S John of Jeruſalem in Ireland, our Chancellor of that Kingdom, on the 30th of March, in the 35th year of our reign Alſo, James le Botiller, Earl of Ormond, return'd to Ireland, being made Juſticiary, whereupon the Earl of Kildare reſign'd to him

MCCCLXI Leonel, ſon of the King of England, and Earl of Ulſter in right of his Wife, came to the King's Lieutenant into Ireland; and on the 8th of September, being the Nativity of the bleſſed Virgin, arriv'd at Dublin with his Wife Elizabeth, Daughter and Heir of the Lord William Burk, Earl of Ulſter

Another Peſtilence happen'd this year There dy'd in England, Henry Duke of Lancaſter, the Earl of March, and the Earl of Northampton

Alſo, on the 6th of January, Moris Doncref a Citizen of Dublin, was buried in the Church yard of the Friers-predicants of the ſame City; having given forty Pounds to glaze the Church of that Convent

Alſo, there dy'd this year the Lady Joan Fleming, wife to the Lord Geffery Trevers, and the Lady Margaret Bermingham wife to the Lord Robert Preſton, on S Margaret's eve they were bury'd in the Church of the Friers-predicants of Tredagh

Alſo, the Lord Walter Bermingham the younger, dy'd on S Laurence's day, who divided his Eſtate among Siſters; one of whoſe Shares came to the aforeſaid Preſton

Alſo, the foreſaid Leonel being arriv'd in Ireland, and having refreſh'd himſelf for ſome few days, made War upon O Brynne, and made Proclamation in his Army, That no native Iriſh man ſhould be ſuffer'd to come near it; and a hundred of his Stipendiaries were ſlain Leonel, thereupon, drew both Engliſh and Iriſh into one body, and went on ſucceſsfully, and by God's mercy and the help of the people of Ireland, grew victorious in all places againſt the Iriſh Among many, both Engliſh and Iriſh, whom he knighted, were theſe, Robert Preſton, Robert Holiwood, Thomas Talbot, Walter Cuſacke, James de la Hide, John Aſh, and Patrick and Robert Aſh

Alſo, he remov'd the Exchequer from Dublin to Carlagh, and gave 500 *l* to wall the Town

Alſo, on the feaſt of S Maur the Abbot, there happen'd a violent Wind that ſhook and blew down Pinnacles, Chimnies, and other high Buildings, with very many Trees and ſeveral Steeples, particularly the Steeple of the Friers predicants.

MCCCLXII In the 36th year of this King's reign, and on the 8th of April, S Patrick's Church in Dublin was burnt down, through negligence

MCCCLXIV In the 38th year of this reign, Leonel Earl of Ulſter arriv'd on the 22d of April in England, leaving the Earl of Ormond to adminiſter as his Deputy On the 8th of December following, he return'd

MCCCLXV In the 39th year of this reign, the ſame Leonel Duke of Clarence went again into England, leaving Sir Thomas Dale Knight, Keeper and Juſticiary in his abſence

MCCCLXVII A great feud aroſe between the Berminghams of Carbry and the People of Meth, occaſion'd by the depredations they had made in that Country Sir Robert de Preſton Knight, Chief Baron of the Exchequer, put a good Garriſon into Carbry-caſtle, and laid out a great deal of money againſt the King's Enemies, to defend what he held in right of his wife.

Alſo, Gerald Fitz-Mons, Earl of Deſmond, was made Juſticiary of Ireland

MCCCLXVIII In the 42d year of the ſame reign, after the holding of a Conference between the Engliſh and Iriſh, Frier Thomas Burky Prior of Kylmanon, the King's Chancellor in Ireland, John Fitz-Reicher Sheriff of Meth, Robert Tirill Baron of Caſtle knoke, and many more, were taken Priſoners in Carbry by the Berminghams and others of that Town Then, James de Bermingham, who was kept in Irons as a Traytor in the Caſtle of Trim, was ſet at liberty in exchange for the ſaid Chancellor; the reſt were forc'd to ranſom themſelves

Alſo, the Church of S Maries in Trim, was burnt down by the fire in the monaſtery

Alſo, on the Eve of S Luke the Evangeliſt, Leonel Duke of Clarence dy'd at Albe in Pycmont He was firſt bury'd in the city of Pavia near S Auguſtin, the great Doctor, and afterwards in the Convent of the Auſtin Friers at Clare in England

MCCCLXIX In the 43d year of this reign, the Lord William de Windſore, a Perſon of great valour and courage, being made the King's Lieutenant, came into Ireland on the 12th of July, to whom Gerald Fitz-Moris, Earl of Deſmond, reſign'd the Office of Juſticiary

MCCCLXX In the 44th year of this reign, the third Peſtilence rag'd in Ireland, and was more violent than either of the former two many of the Nobility and Gentry, as alſo Citizens, and Children without number, dy'd of it

The ſame year, Gerald Fitz-Maurice Earl of Deſmond, the Lord John Nicholas, the Lord Thomas Fitz John, and many others of the Nobility, were taken Priſoners on the [illegible] of July, near

near the Monastery of Magio in the County of Limerick, by O-Breen and Mac Comar of Thomond many were slain in the Fray Whereupon, the Lieutenant went over to Limerick, in order to defend Mounster, leaving the War against the O-Tothiles and the other Irish in Leinster

This year dy'd the Lord Robert Terell Baron of Castle Knock, with his Wife Scolastica Houth, and their son and heir; so that the Inheritance was shar'd between Joan and Maud, sisters of the said Robert

Also, the Lord Simon Fleming, Baron of Slane, the Lord John Cusak Baron of Colmolyn, and John Taylor sometimes Mayor of Dublin, a very rich man, dy'd this year.

The Continuation is taken from the Manuscript Chronicle of HENRY MARLEBURGH

MCCCLXXII The Lord Robert de Asheton came Justiciary into Ireland

MCCCLXXIII A great war between the English of Meth, and O-Feroll, with much slaughter on both sides

Also, the Lord John Husse Baron of Galtrim, John Fitz-Richard Sheriff of Meth, and William Dalton, were kill'd by the Irish in Kynaleagh, in May

MCCCLXXV dy'd Thomas Archbishop of Dublin the same year Robert of Wickford was consecrated Archbishop of Dublin

MCCCLXXXI Edmund Mortimer the King's Lieutenant in Ireland, and Earl of March and Ulster, dy'd at Cork

MCCCLXXXIII A raging pestilence in Ireland

MCCCLXXXV Dublin-bridge fell down

MCCCXC dy'd Robert Wikford Archbishop of Dublin

This year was the Translation of Robert Waldeby Archbishop of Dublin, of the Order of the Austin Friers

MCCCXCVII The Translation and death of Frier Richard de Northalis, Archbishop of Dublin, of the Order of the Carmelites

This year Thomas Crauley was consecrated Archbishop of Dublin

This year the Lord Thomas Burk and the Lord Walter Bermingham cut off 600 of the Irish, and Mac Con their Captain

* Read Roger

* Edmund Earl of March, Lieutenant of Ireland, with the assistance of the Earl of Ormond, wasted the Country of O Bryn, and made seven Knights, Christopher Preston, John Bedeleu, Edmund Loundris, John Loundris, William Nugent, Walter de la Hide, and Robert Cadel, at the storming of a strong mannor-house of the said O Bryn

MCCCXCVIII Forty English, among whom were John Fitz-Williams, Thomas Talbot, and Thomas Comyn, were unfortunately cut-off on Ascension-day by the Lords Lez Tothils

On S Margaret's day, this year, Roger Earl of March, the King's Lieutenant was slain, with many others, by O Bryn and other Irish of Leinster, at Kenlys in that province Roger Grey was appointed to succeed him in the office of Justiciary

On the Feast of S Mark, Pope and Confessor, the noble Duke of Sutherey came to Dublin, being ma[illegible] the King's Leutenant in Ireland; accompany'd with Thomas Crawley, Archbishop of Dublin.

MCCCXIX In the 23d of King Richard, being Sunday, the morrow after S Petronil or Pernil the Virgin, King Richard arriv'd at Waterford with 200 sail

At Ford in Kenlys in the County of Kildare, on the 6th day of that week, two hundred of the Irish were slain by Jericho and others of the English, and the next day, the People of Dublin made an Inroad into the Country of O Bryn, and cut off thirty-three of the Irish, and took prisoners to the number of eighty, men, women, and children The King came to Dublin this year on the fourth of the Kalends of July, and embark'd in great haste for England, upon the news that Henry duke of Lancaster was arriv'd there

MCCCC At Whitsontide, the first year of King Henry IV the Constable of Dublin-castle and several others engag'd the Scots at Stranford in Ulster, which prov'd unfortunate to the English, many of them being cut off and drown'd in that encounter

MCCCCI The second year of this reign, the Lord John Stanley the King's Lieutenant, went over into England in May, leaving the Lord William Stanley to supply his place.

On Bartholomew eve this year, Stephen Scrope came into Ireland, as Deputy to the Lord Thomas of Lancaster, the King's Lieutenant

The same year, on the feast of S Brice, Bishop and Confessor, the Lord Thomas of Lancaster, the King's son, being Lieutenant of Ireland, arriv'd at Dublin

MCCCCII The Church of the Friers Predicants in Dublin was consecrated on the 5th of July, by the Archbishop of Dublin The same day 493 Irish were slain by John Drake Mayor of Dublin, assisted with the Citizens and the Country people, near Bree, where they gain'd a considerable victory

In September this year, a Parliament was held at Dublin Sir Bartholomew Verdon, Knight, James White, Stephen Gernon and their accomplices, kill'd John Dowdal Sheriff of Louth, in Urgal, during this session

MCCCCIII In the fourth of King Henry the fourth, Sir Walter Beterley, a valiant Knight, with thirty more, was kill'd in Ulster in May, being Steward there

About the feast of S. Martin this year, the King's Son, Thomas, went over into England, leaving Stephen Scroup his Deputy, who return'd also about the beginning of Lent into England; after which the Lords of the Kingdom chose the Earl of Ormond Justiciary of Ireland

MCCCCIV The fifth year of King Henry the fifth dy'd John Coulton Archbishop of Armagh on the fifth of May, and was succeeded by Nicholas Fleming The same year on S Vitali's day, a Parliament was held at Dublin by the Earl of Ormond, at that time Justiciary of the Kingdom, where the Statutes of Kilkenny and Dublin, and the Charter of Ireland, were confirm'd

Patrick Savage was, this year, treacherously slain in Ulster by Mac Kilmori his brother Richard also, being given as a hostage, was murder'd in prison after he had paid a ransom of 200 marks

MCCCCV The sixth of King Henry, three Scotch Galleys, two at Green-Castle and one at Dalkay, were taken in May, with the Captain Thomas Mac Golagh

The merchants of Tredagh enter'd Scotland this year, and took hostages and booty

The

The same year Stephen Scroop went into England, leaving the Earl of Ormond Justiciary of Ireland.

In June this year, the people of Dublin enter'd Scotland at S Ninian's, where they behav'd themselves gallantly, after which they made a descent into Wales, and did great hurt among the Welch in this expedition they carry'd away the shrine of S. Cubie, to the Church of the holy Trinity in Dublin

The same year on the eve of the blessed Virgin, dy'd James Boteler Earl of Ormond at Baligaurin, during his office of Justiciary; he was much lamented, and succeeded in the office by Gerald Earl of Kildare

MCCCCVI In the seventh of King Richard, the Dublinians, on *Corpus Christi* day, with the assistance of the country people, overcame the Irish and kill'd some of them, they took two Standards, and carry'd several heads to Dublin

The same year, the Prior of Conal, in a battle with 200 Irish well-arm'd did vanquish them by his great valour, on the plain of Kildare; killing some, and putting the rest to flight The Prior and his party were not above twenty; such is the regard of Providence to those who trust in it

The same year, after the feast of S Michael, Scroop, Deputy Justice to the Lord Thomas the King's son Viceroy of Ireland, arriv'd here

The same year dy'd Pope Innocent VII and was succeeded by Gregory

The same year on S Hilaries day, a Parliament was held at Dublin, which broke up in Lent, at Trym Meiler Bermingham slew Cathol O Conghir in the latter end of February and Sir Geffery Vaux, a valiant Knight of the County of Carlagh, dy'd

MCCCCVII A perfidious Irishman call'd Mac Adam Mac Gilmori, who had been the occasion of destroying forty Churches, and was never christen'd, and therefore called *Corbi*; took Patrick Savage prisoner, and forc'd him to pay 2000 marks for his ransom, and after all, kill'd both him and his brother Richard

The same year on the feast of the Exaltation of the Holy Cross, Stephen Scroop deputy Lieutenant to the King's son Thomas, accompany'd with the Earls of Ormond and Desmond, the Prior of Kilmainan, and many others from Meth, march'd out of Dublin, and invaded the territories of Mac Murgh Upon engaging, the Irish at first had the better, but they were at last beat back by the bravery of these commanders O Nolam, with his son, and others, were taken prisoners But upon the news that the Bourkeins and O Kerol had continued two days together over-running the County of Kilkenny, they march'd in all haste to the village of Callan, and surpriz'd them, and put them to flight O Kerol, and 800 more, were cut off in this action

Stephen Scroop went over into England this year, and James le Botler Earl of Ormond was * by the Country elected Justiciary

* *Per eriam.*

MCCCCVIII The said Justiciary held a Parliament at Dublin, which confirm'd the Statutes of Kilkenny and Dublin, and a Charter was granted under the great seal of England against Purveyours

The very day after the feast of S Peter *ad vincula* this year, the Lord Thomas of Lancaster the King's son and Lieutenant, arriv'd at Carlingford in Ireland, from whence he came the week after to Dublin As the Earl of Kildare came to him, he arrested the Earl with three more of his retinue His Goods were all convey'd away by the Lord Lieutenant's servants, and himself imprison'd in the castle of Dublin, till he paid 300 marks

On S Marcellus's day, the same year, dy'd Stephen Lord Scroop at Tristeldermot

The said Thomas of Lancaster was this year wounded at Kilmainan, and almost mortally. Afterwards, he made Proclamation, That all who were indebted to the King upon the account of Tenure, should make their appearance at Rosse After S Hilary, he held a Parliament at Kilkenny to have *Tallage* granted him On the third of the Ides of March, he went into England, leaving the Prior of Kilmaynan his deputy

This year Hugh Mac-Gilmory was slain at Cragfergus in the Church of the Friers minors, which he had formerly destroy'd, and broke the Windows thereof (for the sake of the Iron bars) which thereby gave his Enemies, *viz* the Savages, admittance

MCCCCIX In the 10th of King Henry, in June, eighty of the Irish were cut off by the English, under the conduct of Janico of Artoys in Ulster

MCCCCX. On the 13th of June, a Parliament was held at Dublin, which continued sitting three weeks, the Prior of Kilmainan being deputy for the Justiciary

The same year on the 10th of July, the said Justiciary took the castle of Mibrackly de O Feroll, and built De la Mare: There was great scarcity of corn this year

The same year, the said Justiciary invaded the Territory of O Brin at the head of fifteen hundred Kerns, of whom eight hundred deserted and went over to the Irish, so that if the People of Dublin had not been at hand, there would have been much woe and shame however, John Derpatrick lost his life

MCCCCXII About the feast of Tiburce and Valerian, O-Conghir did much harm to the English in Meth, and took 160 prisoners

The same year, O-Doles a Knight, and Thomas son of Moris Sheriff of Limerick, kill'd each other

On the 9th of June this year, dy'd Robert Monteyn, Bishop of Meth, and was succeeded by Edward Dandisey, formerly Archdeacon of Cornwall

MCCCCXIII On the 7th of October, John Stanley the King's Lieutenant in Ireland, arriv'd at Cloucarse; and on the 6th of January, dy'd at Aterith

The same year, after the death of John Stanley Lieutenant, Thomas Cranley Archbishop of Dublin was elected Justiciary of Ireland on the 11th of February Another Parliament was held at Dublin on the morrow of S Matthias the Apostle, which continu'd fifteen days, and during that term, the Irish set many Towns on fire, as they us'd to do in Parliament times; upon which a Tallage was demanded, but not granted.

MCCCCXIV The O-Mordnes and O-Dempsies, Irish, were cut off by the English, near Kilka, as the Justiciary Thomas Cranley Archbishop of Dublin, went in Procession in Tristeldermot, praying with his Clerks; and 100 Irish were likewise routed by his Servants and others, their countrymen

Upon the feast of S Gordian and Epimachus, the English of Meth were defeated; Thomas Maureuard Baron of Scrin, and many others were slain, and Christopher Fleming, and John Dardis taken prisoners, by O-Conghir and the Irish.

On S. Martin's-eve, John Talbot Lord of Furnival, being made Lieutenant of Ireland, arriv'd at Dalkay

MCCCCXV Robert Talbot, a Nobleman, who wall'd the Suburbs of Kilkenny, dy'd in November this year

Also, after All-Saints, dy'd Frier Patrick Baret, Bishop of Ferne and Canon of Kenlis, where he was bury'd

MCCCCXVI On the Feast of S Gervasius and Prothasius, the L. Furnival had a son born at Finglasser About this time, the reverend Stephen Fleming Archbishop of Armagh departed this life, and was succeeded by John Suang At the same time, the Bishop of Ardachad dy'd likewise, *viz* Frier Adam Lyns, of the order of the Friers-Predicants

Also, on S Laurence's-day, dy'd Thomas Talbot, son of the Lord Furnival, lately born at Finglas, and was bury'd in the Quire of the Friers-Predicants at Dublin, within the Convent. [A Parliament was held at Dublin,] during which the Irish fell upon the English and slew many of them; and among the rest, Thomas Ballmore of Baliquelan

This Parliament continu'd here for six Weeks, and then adjourn'd till the eleventh of May at Trym; where it sat eleven days, and granted four hundred Marks to the Lieutenant.

MCCCCXVII On the eve of S Philip and Jacob, Thomas Cranley Archbishop of Dublin, went over into England, and dy'd at Farindon, and was bury'd in New-college in Oxford; a Person very liberal and charitable, a great Clerk, a Doctor in Divinity, an excellent Preacher, a great Builder, beautiful and gay, sanguine and tall, so that it might be well said of him, *Thou art fairer than the children of men, full of Grace are thy Lips, by reason of thy Eloquence* He was eighty years old, and govern'd the See of Dublin peaceably almost twenty years

MCCCCXVIII The feast of the Annunciation happen'd this year on Good Friday, immediately after Easter, the Tenants of Henry Crus and Henry Bethat were plunder'd by the Lord Deputy

Also, on S John and S Paul's day, the Earl of Kildare, the Lord Christopher Preston, and the Lord John Bedleu, were arrested at Slane, and committed to Trym-castle; who desir'd to speak with the Prior of Kilmainan On the fourth of August, dy'd the Lord Matthew Husee Baron of Galtrim, and was bury'd in the Convent of the Friers-Predicants of Trym

MCCCCXIX On the eleventh of May, dy'd Edmund Brel, sometimes Mayor of Dublin, and was bury'd in the Convent of the Friers-Predicants in the same City. A * Parliament was held at Naas, and three hundred Marks granted to the Lieutenant [* *Concilium Regale*]

At the same time, dy'd Sir John Loundres, Knight. On the fifth day in Passion-week, O-Thoil took four hundred Head of Cattle that belong'd to Balimor, by which he broke his own Oath and the publick Peace

On the fourth of May, Mac Morthe the chief Captain of that Sept, and of all the Irish in Leinster, was taken Prisoner Hugh Cokesey was knighted the same day

On the last of May, the Lieutenant, and the Archbishop of Dublin, and the Mayor, made the Castle of Kenini to be demolish'd

The day after S Processus and Martinian, the Lord William Burgh, with others of the English, slew five hundred Irish, and took O Kelly prisoner.

On the feast of S. Mary Magdalen, the Lieutenant, John Talbot, went into England, leaving the Archbishop of Dublin to administer in his absence; carrying many Curses along with him, for he paid little or nothing for his Provisions, and was indebted to many

About the feast of S. Laurence, several dy'd in Normandy, *viz.* the Brother of Thomas Botiller, Prior of Kilmainan, with many others.

Frier John Fitz-Henry succeeded him in the Priory. The Archbishop being left Deputy, fell upon the *Scobies*, and cut off thirty Irish, near Rodiston

Also, on the Ides of February, dy'd Frier John Fitz-Henry, Prior of Kilmainan, and was succeeded by Frier William Fitz-Thomas, who was elected and confirm'd the morrow after S. Valentine's-day

Also, † the morrow after the feast of S Peter [† *In crastino Cathedræ*] *in Cathedra*, John Talbot Lord of Furnival surrender'd his place to Richard Talbot Archbishop of Dublin, who was after chosen Justiciary of Ireland

MCCCCXX On the fourth of April, the Lord James Botiller, Earl, arriv'd at Waterford, being Lieutenant of Ireland; and soon after permitted a Combat between two of his Cousins; of whom, one dy'd in the Field, and the other was carry'd off wounded to Kilkenny. On St George's-day, the said Lieutenant held a Council at Dublin, and gave order for a Parliament In the mean time, he took a large Booty from O-Raly, Mac-Mahon and Mac-Guyer On the eighth of June, the Parliament met at Dublin, and seven hundred Marks were therein granted to the Lieutenant This Parliament continu'd sixteen days, and at last was prorogu'd || till the [|| *Ad ferium secundam.*] Monday after S Andrews, at Dublin The Debts of the Lord John Talbot late Lieutenant, were computed in this Parliament, which amounted to a great Sum

Also, on the morrow after S Michael's-day, Michael Bodly departed this life

Also, on S Francis's-eve, dy'd Frier Nicholas Talbot Abbot of the Monastery of S Thomas the Martyr, in Dublin, and was succeeded by Frier John Whiting

Also, the morrow after S Simon and Jude, the castle of Colmolin was taken by Thomas Fitz-Geffery

Also, on S Katherin the Virgins's-eve, was born Boteler, son and heir to the Earl of Ormond

Also, * on Monday after the feast of S Andrew, [* *Secunda fe-*] the foresaid Parliament met at Dublin, and sat thirteen days The Lieutenant had three hundred Marks granted him herein; and it was adjourn'd † till the Monday after S Ambrose [† *Ad feriam secundam*]

News came over at this time, that the Lord Thomas Fitz-John Earl of Desmond, dy'd on S Laurence's-day at Paris, and was buried in the Convent of the Friers-predicants there, the King being present at his Funeral James Fitz-Gerald, his Uncle by the Father's side, succeeded to the Seignory, who had thrice dispossess'd him of his Estate, and accus'd him of prodigality and waste both in Ireland and England, and that he had already given, or intended to give, Lands to the Abbey of S. James at Keynisham

MCCCCXXI [Dominica feria] The Parliament sat the third time at Dublin, || the Monday after the feast of S Ambrose, [|| *Feria secunda*] and therein it was resolv'd, That the Archbishop of Armagh and Sir Christopher Preston, Knight, should be sent to the King for redress of national Grievances

At the same time, Richard O-Hedian, Bishop of Cassel, was accus'd by John Gese Bishop of Lismore and Waterford, upon thirty distinct Articles; That he favour'd the Irish, and was averse to the English; That he presented none of the English to any Benefice, and had given order to other Bishops that they should not prefer them to any the least Living · That he counterfeited the King of England's Seal and the King's Letters-patents, and that he had attempted to make himself King of Mounster; That he took away a Ring from the Image of S Patrick (which the Earl of Desmond had offer'd) and gave it to his Whore, with several other enormous Crimes, all exhibited in Writing; which created a great deal of vexatious trouble to the Lords and Commons.

In this Parliament, there was also a Debate between Adam Pay Bishop of Clon [and another] for that the Bishop of Clon would have annex'd the Church of another to his See, and that other oppos'd it, so they were referr'd to the Court of Rome This session continu'd eighteen days

On the Nones of May, a great Slaughter was made among the Retinue of the Earl of Ormond, Lieutenant, near the Monastery of Leys, by O-Mordris; twenty seven of the English were cut off. The chief of them were Purcel and Grant. Ten Persons of Quality were taken Prisoners, and 200 fled to the foresaid Monastery, and were sav'd.

On the Ides of May, dy'd Sir John Bedley, Knight, and Geffery Galoo, formerly Mayor of Dublin, who was bury'd in the Convent of the Friers-predicants of that City

About this time, Mac-Mahon did great mischief in Urgal; plundering and burning.

On the seventh of June, the Lieutenant went into Leys against O-Mordris with a mighty Army, which kill'd all before them for four days, till the Irish promised peace and submission.

On S Michael's-day, Thomas Stanley, with all the Knights and 'Squires of Meth and Irel, took Moyl O-Downyl prisoner, and kill'd others, in the fourteenth year of King Henry the sixth

Thus far go the Annals of Ireland, *viz all that I could meet with These I have inserted here, to gratify such as delight in Antiquity As for the nice delicate Readers, who try all Writings by* Augustus's *Age, I am very sensible they will not relish them, because they are written in a rough, insipid, dry Stile, such as was common in that Age. But let these Persons remember,* That History bears and requires Authors of all Ages, and that they must look for *Things* in some Writers, as well as *Words* in others

THE

THE *O-NEALS, AND THEIR REBELLIONS In the † LAST AGE.

* See the Conclusion of the Description of Ireland

† This, C

[*By Mr.* CAMDEN.]

TO say nothing of *O-Neal* the Great, who before the arrival of St *Patrick* tyranniz'd in *Ulster* and a great part of Ireland, nor of those after him, who were too obscure for History. This family has been of no eminence since the English set foot in that Kingdom, save only during the space in which *Edward Brus* the Scot assum'd the title of *King of Ireland* In those troublesome times, *Dovenald O Neal* began to exert himself, and in his Letter to the Pope us'd this stile, *Dovenald O-Neal, King of Ulster and right heir by descent of all Ireland* Yet this new King soon vanish'd, upon the ceasing of those troubles, and his posterity continu'd in obscurity till the wars between the houses of *York* and *Lancaster* embroil'd the Kingdom of England, and the English then in *Ulster* were oblig'd to return home to support their respective parties, and commit the Province to the charge of the *O-Neals* At that time, *Henry O-Neal*, the son of *Oen* or *Eugenius O-Neal*, marry'd the daughter of *Thomas* Earl of *Kildare*; and his son *Con More*, or *Con* the Great, marry'd the daughter of *Girald* Earl of *Kildare*, his mother's Niece Being thus supported with the Power and Interest of the Earls of *Kildare*, who had administer'd the affairs of Ireland for many years, they began to lord it with great tyranny over the people, under no other title than the bare name of *O-Neal*; insolently slighting those of *Prince*, *Duke*, *Marquis*, *Earl*, &c as mean, and inferiour to it *Con*, the son of this *Con*, surnamed *Bacco*, i e *lame*, succeeded his father in this dignity of *O-Neal*; who denounced a curse upon such of his posterity, as should learn to speak English, or sow corn, or build houses; fearing that these would tempt the English to invade them King *Henry* VIII. had already humbled the Family of *Kildare*, and began to be jealous of the *O-Neals*, who had been aiding to the former in their rebellions; which terrify'd him so much, that he came into England voluntarily, and renounc'd the title of *O-Neal*, and surrender'd all he had into the King's hands who, by his Letters-Patents under the great Seal, restor'd them, with the title of Earl of *Tir Oen*, to have and to hold, to him and his *son* Matthew (falsly so call'd) and to the Heirs of their bodies lawfully begotten *Matthew* at the same time was created Baron of *Dunganon*; who, till the fifteenth year of his age, pass'd for the son of a Black-smith in *Dundalk*, whose wife had been a concubine of this *Con's*, and then presented the lad to him as his son Accordingly he receiv'd him as such, and set aside his own son *John*, or *Shan*, as they call him, with the rest of the children which he had had by his lawful wife *Shan*, seeing a Bastard preferr'd before him and advanc'd to this dignity, took fire immediately, and became an utter enemy to his father; with such violent hatred and enmity against *Matthew*, that he murther'd him; and so plagu'd the old man with affronts and indignities (attempting to dispossess him of his estate and honours) that he dy'd of grief

Scoto Chronicon l 11 c 26.

The first Earl of Tir Oen

Shan or John O Neal

Shan was presently chosen and proclaim'd *O Neal*, after which he enter'd upon the Estate; and, to secure himself in the enjoyment of it, made diligent search after the sons of *Matthew*; but they had made their escape. Yet *Brian*, the eldest, was slain not long after by *Mac-Donel Tetan*, of the family of *O-Neal*, and upon *Shan's* instigation, as was reported *Hugh* and *Cormack* made their escape by the assistance of the English, and are living † at this day *Shan* being possess'd of the Government, and being also of a bar-

† Ann 15[illegible]

a bar-a barbarous cruel temper, began to tyrannize among the Gentry of *Ulster* after an intolerable manner; boasting that he had the *Mac-Gennys*, *Mac-Guir*, *Mac-Mahon*, *O-Realy*, *O-Hanlon*, *O-Cahan*, *Mac-Brien*, *O-Hagan*, *O-Quin*, *Mac Canna*, *Mac-Cartan*, and the *Mac-Donells*, the *Galloglasses*, his Subjects.

Being called to account for these things by *H. Sidney*, who governed in the absence of the Earl of *Sussex* Lord Deputy, he answer'd, That as the undoubted and legitimate son and heir of *Con*, born by his lawful wife, he had enter'd upon his father's estate; that *Matthew* was the son of a Black-smith of *Dundalk*, born of his wife *Alison*, who had cunningly obtruded him upon his father *Con* as his son, to deprive him of the estate and dignity of the *O-Neals*; and that, supposing he had been so tame as to bear this injury, not another of the family of *O-Neal* would have endur'd it. That as for the Letters Patents of *Henry* VIII, they were null and void, forasmuch as *Con* had no right in any of those things which he surrender'd to the King, but for his own life; and that he had not the disposal of them, without the consent of the Nobility and People who elected him *O-Neal*: neither were Patents of this nature of any force, but where the true heir of the family was first certify'd upon the oath of twelve men, which was omitted in this case. Lastly, that he was right heir, both by the Laws of God and man, being the eldest son of his father, born in wedlock, and elected *O-Neal* by the unanimous consent of the Nobility and People, according to the Law of *Tanistry*, whereby a man at his full age is to be preferr'd before a boy, and an unkle before a nephew whose Grandfather surviv'd the Father, neither had he assum'd any greater authority over the Nobility of *Ulster*, than his Ancestors had ever done; as he could sufficiently prove from the Records.

Not long after, he fought *O-Rayly*, and defeated him, took *Callogh O-Donell*, put him in prison with all his children, ravish'd his wife and had issue by the adultery, seiz'd all his castles, lands and moveables, and made himself Monarch of *Ulster*.

But hearing, that *Thomas* Earl of *Sussex*, the Lord Deputy, was upon his march to chastise his insolence; he was so terrified, that upon the persuasion of his Kinsman *Gerald* Earl of *Kildare* (who had been restor'd to his estate by Queen Mary) he went into England, and threw himself on the mercy of Queen Elizabeth, who receiv'd him graciously, and so having promised allegiance for the future, he return'd home, where for some time he went on in a civiliz'd way both in diet and apparel, and drove the Scots out of *Ulster* (having slain *James Mac Conell* their Captain) kept himself and his people in good order, and protected the weak, but continued insolent and cruel to the Nobility; insomuch that they petition'd the Lord Deputy for protection and relief. Whereupon, he grew more outragious, dispossess'd *Mac-Guir*, Lord of *Fermanagh* (who had secretly inform'd against him) with fire and sword, burnt the Metropolitan Church of *Armagh*, and besieged *Dundalk*; but this last prov'd ineffectual, partly by the valour of the Garrison, and partly by the apprehension of being surpriz'd by *William Sarfield*, the Mayor of *Dublin*, who was on his march towards him with the flower of the City. However, he made cruel ravages in the adjacent Country. To put a stop to these bold and outragious proceedings, *Sidney* the Lord Deputy set out himself, and was advanc'd at the head of an Army against him, but wisely de-

Henry Sidney Lord Deputy 1565

tach'd seven companies of foot and a * troop of horse to go before-hand, under the conduct of *Edward Randolph* a famous old soldier, by sea, into the North parts of Ireland, where they encamp'd at *Derry* upon *Loghfoil*, to be upon the rear of the enemy. *Shan* fearing this, immediately march'd thither, and with all his force endeavour'd to remove them: upon this attack, *Randolph* gave him battel; and though he valiantly lost his own life in the engagement, yet he gave the enemy such a defeat, that from that time forward they were never able to keep the field. So that *Shan*, finding himself weaken'd by slight skirmishes, and deserted by his soldiers, was once resolv'd to go and throw himself, with a halter about his neck, at the mercy of the Lord Deputy. But his Secretary persuading him in the first place to solicit the friendship of the Scots, who under the conduct of *Alexander Oge*, i. e. *the younger*, were now encamp'd in *Claneboy*; he sent *Surley boy*, *Alexander*'s brother, whom he had detain'd prisoner a long time, to prepare the way, and soon after follow'd with the wife of *O-Donell*, whom he had ravish'd. The Scots received him kindly, and with a few of his adherents he was admitted into a tent, where, after some cups, they began to resent the fate of *James Mac-Conell*, the brother of *Alexander*, whom *Shan* had kill'd, and the dishonour done to *James*'s sister, whom *Shan* had marry'd and then put away, whereupon *Alexander Oge* and his brother *Mac-Gillaspic*, took fire, and giving the signal for revenge, all fell upon *Shan* with their drawn swords, and run him through and through: by whose death, peace was restored to that Province in the year 1567.

* Alias

Shan murder'd.

A little after this, a Parliament was held at *Dublin*, wherein an Act passed for the Attainder of *Shan*, and for annexing most of the Counties and Seignories of *Ulster* to the person of the Queen and her Successors; and it was also enacted, that none should hereafter assume the stile and title of *O-Neal*. Notwithstanding, it was soon after assum'd by *Turlogh Leinogh*, Brother's son to the *Con More O-Neal*, already spoken of, who was now towards the decline of his age, and therefore more calm and wary; and the rather, because he lay under apprehensions from *Shan*'s sons, and *Hugh* Baron of *Dungannon* his son, though he had marry'd his daughter to him; whom he put away soon after, and married another. This *Turlogh*, being very obsequious and dutiful to the Queen of England, gave no disturbance to the English, but prov'd a very troublesom neighbour to *O-Donell* and the Island-Scots, and in a skirmish cut off *Alexander Oge*, who had kill'd *Shan O-Neal*. *Hugh*, the son of *Matthew*, called Baron of *Dungannon*, who for a long while had liv'd, sometimes obscurely in his own country, and sometimes in England in the service of some of our Nobility; began to rise from this mean condition, to some degree of eminence. The Queen made him Captain of a troop of horse in the war against the Earl of *Desmond*, and allow'd him a yearly pension of a thousand marks: whereupon, he behaved himself gallantly against the rebels in all encounters, and at length exhibited a Petition in Parliament, That by virtue of a Grant made to his Grandfather, an Act might be pass'd for his restitution to the title and dignity of Earl of *Tir-Oen*, and the estate of his Ancestors.

The title of O Neal abolished.

As for the title and dignity of Earl of *Tir-Oen*, it was granted without difficulty; but the estate of his Ancestors being annex'd to the Crown by the Attainder of *Shan O-Neal*, it was wholly referr'd to the Queen, who graciously gave it

Hugh Son of Matthew made Earl of Tir Oen.

 him

him in consideration of his services already done her, and those she expected hereafter Yet, first, she provided that the Province should be survey'd and laid out into proper districts, and that one or two places should be reserv'd in her own hands for garrisons, particularly the Fort at *Black-water*; that provision should be made for the maintenance of the sons of *Shan* and *Turlogh*, and that he should pretend to no authority over any neighbouring Seignories beyond the County of *Tir-Oen.* Having willingly embrac'd these conditions, he return'd his most humble thanks to her Majesty, with great expressions of the reality of his Intentions and of his sincere resolution to be wanting in nothing which application could effect And indeed it must be said, that he performed his promise, and that the Queen could expect no more from the most faithful subject she had, than he did for her He had a body made to endure labour, watching, and want, his industry was great, his mind warlike and capable of the highest employments he had great knowledge in the affairs of war, and was so profound a dissembler, that some foretold at that time, *He would either prove the greatest good, or the greatest hurt, to Ireland* He gave such testimonies of his valour and loyalty, that the Queen herself interceded with *Turlogh Leinigh* for his Seignory, and got him to surrender it upon conditions After *Leinigh*'s death, he usurp'd the title of *O Neal,* notwithstanding it was made capital by Act of Parliament, excusing it, as done to anticipate others who were ready to assume it, and promis-
1588 ing to relinquish it, but beg'd earnestly that no oath might be press'd upon him for performance

Earl of *Tir-On* suspected of corresponding with the *Spaniards*

About this time, the Spanish Armada, which had in vain attempted to invade England, was dispersed and destroy'd, many of them in their return were shipwreck'd in the Irish Sea, and great numbers of the Spaniards thrown upon the coast of Ireland The Earl of *Tir-Oen* was said to have receiv'd some of them with great kindness, and to have treated with them about making a private league between him and the King of Spain Upon this account, he was accus'd before the Queen (and no slight evidence brought against him) by *Hugh Ne Gaveloc,* i e *in Fetters,* a natural son of *Shan,* and so call'd from his being kept in Fetters for a long time; which so enraged the Earl, that, afterwards, he had him apprehended, and commanded him to be strangled, but had much ado to find an Executioner, the people had so great a veneration for the blood of the *O-Neals* Queen Elizabeth had still such hopes of the Earl, that out of her Royal clemency, upon his Repentance and suit for mercy, she pardon'd this barbarous and inhuman Parricide; notwithstanding the dissuasions of some good men about her There was also another thing that gall'd him at this time the Lord Deputy had extinguish'd the name of *Mac-Mahon* in the next County, and, to suppress the power of that great family, had divided the County among several, whereupon the Earl was apprehensive he would go on, and serve him and the other Lords of *Ulster* after the same manner Dissensions between the Earl and Henry Bagnall, Marshal of Ireland, broke out likewise at this time, for the Earl had marry'd Bagnall's Sister by force The Earl complain'd that whatever he had reduc'd in Ulster to the subjection of the Queen, at the expence of his own blood and labour, was no way advantageous to him, but to the Marshal; that the Marshal, having suborn'd certain profligate fellows to witness against him, had impeach'd him of high treason, that by his arts and instigation he had made William Fitz-Williams, the Lord Deputy, his bitter enemy, and that he had lain in ambush for his life This is certain, that all that the Lord Deputy had writ upon that subject, was believ'd in the Court of England, till the Earl, to clear himself, writ into England, that he would stand his trial either there or in Ireland

New Rebellion in *Ulster*

And it is also plain, that he and the other Lords of Ulster enter'd into a secret combination about this time, That they would defend the Roman Catholick Religion (for rebellion is never set afoot now, but under pretence and colour of religion,) That they would suffer no Sheriffs nor Garrisons to be within the compass of their territories, and, That they would stand by one another in maintaining their rights, and jointly resist all Invasions of the English The first that gave the alarm, was *Mac-Gwire,* a man of a turbulent spirit, who ravag'd the country about him, and enter'd Conaght, accompanied with one *Gauran* a Priest, whom the Pope had made Primate of Ireland, and who exhorted him to depend upon God and try his fortune, and assur'd him that the Event would answer his expectation Yet it happen'd quite otherwise, for *Mac-Gwire* was routed by Richard Bingham, and the Primate himself was cut off, with many others Soon after, Mac Guire broke out into open Rebellion, and was pursu'd by the Marshal, and by the Earl himself under pretence of loyalty, who receiv'd a wound in the thigh, and great applause for his valour Yet at the same time he was so intent upon his own safety, that he intercepted the sons of Shan O-Neal, to prevent the mischief they might do him, and though the restitution of them was demanded, he answer'd nothing to the purpose, but made heavy complaints of the injuries done him by the Lord Deputy, the Marshal, and the Garrisons, which notwithstanding he dissembled so well, that he came afterwards to the Deputy as if he had forgot all, submitted himself, and, promising loyalty and entire obedience, return'd home

William Fitz Williams being recall'd out of Ireland, William Russel was made Lord Deputy in his place The Earl voluntarily went to him, promising a perfect obedience to his Lordship's commands in every thing, and sent letters to some of her Majesty's Council to the same effect, entreating earnestly that he might be receiv'd again into the Queen's favour, which he had lost by no demerit or disloyalty of his own, but purely by the false suggestions of Enemies Bagnal the Marshal at the same time exhibited articles of accusation against him; That the Earl himself had sent Mac-Gwire, with the Primate, into Conaght, that he was in the combination of *Mac-Gwire, O Donell,* and other Conspirators, that he had assisted them in wasting Monaghan, and in the siege of Inis Kellin, by his Brother Cormac Mac-Baron and his bastard son Con, and had by his threatnings drawn the Governors of Kilulto and Kilwarny from their allegiance to the Queen Upon this, it was warmly debated in Council, whether or no the Earl should be apprehended, to answer to this Information The Lord Deputy was for apprehending him, but most of the Council, out of fear or favour to the Earl, were for dismissing him at present, and deferring the tryal to another time Whereupon the Lord Deputy, *in respect to the majority, and their great experience* in the affairs of that Kingdom, desisted, though much against his own inclination, and the Earl was dismiss'd, but his accusers

1594 Russel Lord Deputy

Articles against the Earl of Tir-On

not

not so much as heard The Queen was extremely concern'd at this oversight (for his dangerous designs and actions began now to appear plain to every body,) and the more, because she had warn'd the Lord Deputy to detain the Earl in custody, till he should answer to the crimes charg'd upon him

The Earl takes *Black water*

As soon as the Earl got home, and heard of a reinforcement coming from England, and that 1300 veterans, who had serv'd under the command of *John Norris* in Bretagne, were now also transporting thither from Holland, as also that the English had a design upon *Ballishannon* and *Belyk*, two castles at the end of Lough *Ern*, and being conscious of what he had done, he surpriz'd the Fort upon *Black-water*, which open'd a passage into his County of *Ter-Oen*, and forc'd it to surrender His resolutions however were so various, and uncertain, that he wrote to the Earl of *Kildare*, to offer his assistance against the Injuries of the Lord Deputy, as also to the Earl of *Ormond*, and *Henry Wallop*, * Vice Treasurer of the Kingdom, assuring them of his intention to continue loyal, and to *John Norris* the General, desiring that he would not proceed roughly against him, and push him into rebellion against his will This letter to *Norris* was intercepted by *Bagnall* the Marshall, and (as the Earl afterwards complain'd) suppressed, to his great damage For he was, presently after, publickly declar'd an enemy and traitor to his Country

* *Proquaestori*

1595 *June* 17

By this time, the Rebels in *Ulster* amounted to 1000 horse or thereabouts, and 6280 foot, and in *Connaught*, to 2300, all at the entire dispotal of the Earl, and many of them tolerably disciplin'd, ever since *J Perrot*, the Lord Deputy, had commanded every Lord of *Ulster* to raise and exercise a certain number of men, to withstand the inroads of the Island Scots, or else being such as had serv'd in the wars of the Low-Countries, and were unadvisedly transported hither, by his means The number of the English army, under the command of *J Norris* (so eminent in the wars of Flanders) was not inferior Yet nothing memorable was done by him, by reason of a misunderstanding between the General and the Deputy, so that the Campaign was spent in ravages, cessations, and parleys Without doubt, both (being men of arms) were for prolonging the war, and as for the Earl, he daily expected a reinforcement out of Spain

Treaties with the Earl

Of these parleys, the most memorable was that between *Henry Wallop*, Vice Treasurer of the Kingdom, and *Robert Gardner*, Chief Justice, persons of great gravity and approv'd wisdom (who were appointed Commissioners,) and the Earl of *Tir-Oen*, and *O Donell*, wherein these, and others of the Rebels, summ'd up their grievances and demands

The Earl's Grievances

The Earl complain'd that *Bagnall*, the Marshal, had reap'd the fruits of his labours, that by his false suggestions and artifices he had wrought him out of the Queen's favour, and almost out of his honour, that, to his great prejudice, he had intercepted the letters he writ to the Lord-Deputy, *Norris*, and some others, and detain'd his wife's portion from him Protesting, that he had never enter'd into any Treaty with foreign Princes, till he was proclaim'd a Rebel, and humbly entreating, that his own Crimes and those of his adherents might be pardon'd, that they might be restor'd to their estates, and enjoy the free exercise of their Religion (which by the bye, was ever allow'd them,) that the Marshal might pay him 1000*l sterling*, in consideration of his wife's portion now deceas'd, that no Garrison, Sheriff, nor any Officer whatsoever, might be plac'd within his County; that his Troop of Horse which the Queen had formerly given him, might be restor'd, and that those who had pillaged his people, might be punished

O Donell's Grievances

O-Donell, after he had enlarg'd upon the loyalty of his Forefathers to the Kings of England, complain'd that one *Boin*, a Captain, was sent by *Perrot* the Lord Deputy into his Province with Soldiers, under pretence of civilizing his people, and that after his father had received him kindly, and assign'd him quarters, he treated him barbarously, and preferr'd a bastard to the dignity of *O-Donell* That the same Lord Deputy had intercepted this very Man at Sea, clap'd him in prison notwithstanding his innocence, and there unjustly detained him, till Providence set him at liberty That, moreover, the Lord Deputy *Fitz Williams* had kept *Owen O-Toole*, the greatest man in these parts next *O-Donell*, a close prisoner seven years together, notwithstanding he went to him upon Parol, and was indeed innocent That he was intolerably oppressive to his poor neighbours in *Fermanagh*, and, That himself had no better way to lay a foundation for his own Safety, but the assisting his neighbours in their necessity He likewise requir'd, what the Earl did, and demanded certain Castles and Possessions in the County of *Slego*, as of right belonging to him

Other Grievances

Shan Mac-Brian Mac-Phelim O-Neal complain'd, that the Earl of *Essex* had taken the Isle of *Magee* from him, and that *Henry Bagnall* had depriv'd him of the Barony of *Maughery Mourn*, both which had been enjoy'd by his Ancestors; that he was kept in chains till he surrender'd his right to *Bagnall*, besides injuries without number which he had receiv'd from the Garrison of *Knoc-Fergus* *Hugh Mac Guir* shew'd them likewise what he had suffer'd by the insolence of the neighbouring Garrison, who made booty of his Cattle, and that the Sheriff, who was sent into his territories, had cut off the head of his nearest Relation, and trod it under foot with scorn *Brian Mac-Hugh Oge*, *Mac-Mahon*, and *Ever Mac Couly*, exhibited, That besides other wrongs, the Lord Deputy *Fitz Williams*, whose goodness and honesty always gave place to money, was induc'd by corruption and bribery to establish *Hugh Roe* in the dignity of *Mac-Mahon*, and after that, hang'd him, for raising a fine by force of arms, according to the custom of the country, and divided his Estate among strangers, to extinguish the very name of *Mac-Mahon* In one word, every man was a Petitioner for every thing we have nam'd On the other side, the Commissioners having allow'd some of their demands, and referr'd others to the Queen, propos'd certain articles to the rebels But they were grown so insolent by this time, that they thought them unreasonable, and so broke off the short suspension of arms which they had agreed to Whereas, the Queen, both then and afterwards, would have condescended to any terms consistent with her honour, to prevent the effusion of Christian blood, and the consumption of her Treasures

[illegible] against the Earl

The time of the Truce being now expir'd, *Norris* (who by the Queen's order had the sole command of the Army conferr'd upon him by the Lord Deputy during his absence) advanc'd with his Army towards the Earl However, the Lord Deputy joyn'd him, and so, they marched as far as Armagh to the great terror of the Enemy; insomuch that the Earl was oblig'd to quit the fort of *Black-water*, and burn all the villages round about, and the town of *Dunganon*

non

ron; nay, to demolish a great part of his own house there, and, in this desperate condition, to consider where he might abscond But our Army could proceed no farther for want of Provision; and so return'd, after they had proclaim'd the Earl a Traitor, in his own territories, and put a Garrison into the Church of *Armagh* The Earl took care to watch them diligently in their return; notwithstanding which, they reinforc'd the Garrison at *Monaghan* When they had march'd almost as far at *Dundalk*, the Lord Deputy, according to the Queen's orders, left the war to the conduct of *Norris*, and after leave taken, with many kind expressions on both sides, return'd to *Dublin*, where he had a strict eye upon the Affairs of *Leinster*, *Conaght*, and *Munster*

Norris remain'd in *Ulster*; but whether out of envy to the Lord Deputy, or that fortune had now left him, as she often does great Generals, or whether out of favour to the Earl, to whom he was certainly as kind as the Lord Deputy was averse, he atchiev'd nothing answerable to his great Character For *Norris* had under-hand accused the Lord Deputy, that out of ill-will to the Earl he had resolv'd to make no peace with him. The Deputy would not be perswaded but that the Earl's design was to gain time, till his recruits from Spain might arrive, whereas *Norris* was more easy and credulous, and did not doubt but the Earl would be brought to reasonable terms: which opinion the Earl cherish'd so artificially, that he offer'd him a submission under his hand and seal, and fell upon his knees before him for mercy and pardon. Yet, at the same time, was he plying the King of Spain, by letters and agents, for assistance; so that one or two messengers were sent from Spain to the Rebels, who agreed and concluded with them, that if the King of Spain their master should send such an Army by a set day, as could face the English, they would join it; and in case he supply'd them with ammunition in the mean time, they would not treat with the English upon any terms whatsoever

A Treaty of the Rebels with *Spain*

This treaty was subscrib'd by *O-Rorck*, *Mac-William*, and others; but the Earl was too cautious to sign it, though it is not doubted but he gave his consent And, to disguise his designs, he sent to the Lord Deputy the King of Spain's answer to the Rebels (which was full of promises and assurances) as if he detested it; yet, relying upon the hopes of those Spanish recruits, he recanted the submission and promise he had made to *Norris* but a little before *Norris* finding himself thus deluded by his own credulity, attack'd him with angry and sharp expostulations for imposing upon him in this base manner But the Earl, knowing well how to temporize for his advantage, enter'd into another Parley with *Norris*, and *Fenton* his Secretary; and having given Hostages, concluded another Peace, or rather a bargain, which he soon after broke with the same levity; pretending, That he could not but think he was deceitfully dealt with, while the Lord Deputy and General vary'd with one another in their proceedings; That the Lord Deputy had treated those he had sent to him about Peace, very unworthily; That it appear'd he was wholly for the War, and had reinforc'd his horse from England, and detain'd the King of Spain's letter; and, That the Marshal, his bitter Enemy, was now return'd with a new Commission from England

Upon this, he began immediately to waste the adjacent country, burning the villages, and driving away the cattle, but being conscious of what he had done, and hearing that a peace was concluding between England and Spain, he sent again to desire a parley, and that reasonable terms might be allow'd him It would be tedious to unfold all the Arts and Intricacies of this man; but in short, whenever he found himself in danger from the English, he acted Submission and Repentance so well, in carriage, countenance, and address, that he still deluded them, till they lost their opportunity of pursuing the war, and were oblig'd to withdraw their forces Again, such was the supineness of the Commanders in Ireland, and the frugality of the Council in England, and the innate Clemency of the Queen, who was willing to hope that these *Robberies* in Ireland (for it could not be call'd a War) might be suppress'd without blood; that he was always believed, and hopes of pardon were given, to keep him from being desperate

Baron *Burough* Lord Deputy

In the year 1597 (by which time all *Ulster* beyond *Dundalk*, except the seven Garrison-Towns, *viz Newry*, *Knoc-Fergus*, *Carlingford*, *Green-Castle*, *Armagh*, *Dondrom*, and *Olde-fleet*, as also the greatest part of *Conaght*, had revolted from the Queen,) *Thomas* Lord *Burough*, a person of great courage and conduct, was sent Lord Deputy into Ireland The Earl, by letter, desir'd a cessation of arms, and his Lordship thought it his Interest at that time to allow it for one month The month being expir'd, the Lord Deputy drew his forces together (which he thought would be for his advantage and honour at his entrance upon the office,) and engag'd the Earl with some disadvantage in a narrow passage, but he made his way through by his valour, and took the Fort at *Black-water*, which had been repair'd by the Rebels, and which open'd a passage into the County of *Tir-Oen*, and was the only fence the Rebels had (besides their woods and marshes) to secure them This one action sufficiently shew'd, that if the war was well follow'd, it could not continue long The very day that the Fort was taken, as the Lord Deputy and his Army were giving God thanks for their success, an alarm was given on the sudden, that the enemy appear'd upon the hills hard by, so, *Henry* Earl of *Kildare*, with a troop of horse, and some volunteers of the Nobility, was detach'd against them, who fell upon the Enemy, and put them to flight Yet we lost of the English, *Francis Vaughan*, brother to the Lord Deputy's Lady, *R Turner* † Serjeant-Major, an experienc'd Soldier, and two foster-brothers of the Earl of *Kildare*; which so exceedingly troubled him, that he dy'd of grief some few days after: for there is no love so strong in any degree of relation, as between foster-brothers in Ireland. Many more of the English were wounded; and among the rest, *Thomas Waller*, who was particularly eminent for his great valour As soon as the Lord Deputy had strengthen'd the Fort with new works, and drawn off his Army; the Rebels, between hope, fear, and shame, thought it most adviseable to lay siege to it. The Earl was sensible how conveniently it was plac'd to annoy them, and that his fame and fortune would dwindle into nothing, unless he recover'd it Accordingly, he invested the Fort with a strong army The Lord Deputy, upon the news hereof, march'd against him with all speed but in his full career towards victory, sickness and death arrested

[illegible]

Black water retaken

† [illegible] *Major*

arrested him, to the grief of all good men, and the joy of the Rebels. For it was the opinion of very wise men, that if he had liv'd, he would certainly have reduc'd the enemy, and the State had not been plung'd into so great danger

Black-water attack'd upon the Lord Deputy's death

As soon as the Lord Deputy's death was known to the enemy, they attack'd the Fort with great clamour and violence, but were ever repelled with great loss those who scal'd the walls were push'd back headlong by the garrison, and many of them trod to pieces, so that, despairing of success by force, they resolv'd to starve them, believing that their provisions could not last many days, and that hunger would quickly shake their Loyalty and Courage But the Fort was gallantly defended by the valour of Thomas Williams the Governor and his garrison, who liv'd on herbs growing on the rocks, after they had eat their horses, and held it in spight of famine, and the Enemy, and extremities of all kinds

Earl of Ormond Lieutenant

By this time, the Government was committed by the Queen to the Earl of Ormond, under the title of Lieutenant General of the army, together with the Chancellor, and Robert Gardiner The Earl presently gave the Lieutenant General a long account by Letter of the grievances before-mention'd, not omitting the least miscarriage of any Soldier, or Sheriff, and coldly excusing his breach of covenant with Norris, but more especially urging that Feogh-Mac-Hugh, one of his relations, had been taken and executed, and lastly, that his letters to the Queen had been intercepted and concealed, and that the imposts and taxes were grown intolerable both to the Gentry and common People, adding, that he saw very well, that all the possessions of the nobility and gentry of Ireland, would be shortly parcell'd among Counsellors, Lawyers, Soldiers, and Secretaries At the same time he sent supplies to the sons of Feogh Mac-Hugh, that they might embroil the Province of Leinster So that now every body saw plainly, that the Earl's design from the very beginning was to extirpate the English in Ireland, notwithstanding all his pretences in order to disguise it

1598

The Earl's victory over the Marshal.

The Earl in the mean time carry'd on the siege at Black-water The Lieutenant General therefore (for a Lord Deputy was not yet appointed) had detach'd fourteen choice * Troops, under the conduct of Henry Bagnall the Marshal, a bitter enemy of the Earl's to relieve it The Earl, spurr'd on with an inveterate hatred of the man, fell upon him with great fury near Armach the Marshal himself, at whom he principally aim'd, was soon cut off in the midst of the Battle; whereby the Earl had the double satisfaction, to triumph over an enemy, and to gain a considerable victory over the English For this was the greatest defeat they had ever had in Ireland; no less than thirteen brave Captains, and fifteen hundred common soldiers cut off, either in the engagement, or after they were broken and dispers'd Those who escap'd, imputed the loss, not to cowardise in the soldiers, but to the ill conduct of the General; as is common in all such cases The Fort of Black-water presently surrender'd they had held out, with great loyalty and valour, against all the Extremities of famine, and saw there was now no relief to be expected This was indeed a famous victory, and of great importance to the Rebels, who got both arms and provisions by it The Earl being applauded throughout the Country, as the glorious restorer of their liberty, grew intolerably cruel and insolent, and sent Ouny Mac-Rory-Og-O More, and one Tirel (of English Extraction, but now an implacable enemy) with four thousand Rapparees into Munster Thomas Norris, President of the Province, march'd against them with a good body, as far as Kilmalock; but separated his forces without facing the enemy, and retur'd to Cork The Rebels, joyn'd by great numbers of the profligate sort, as soon as they understood this, began to waste the Country, and drive away the Cattle, and plunder and burn all castles, houses, and whatever else was in the possession of the English; putting the men themselves to the most cruel deaths. They made James Fitz-Thomas, one of the family of the Earls of Desmond, Earl of Desmond; yet so, that he should hold it of O-Neal, that is to say, of the Earl, and, having thus embroil'd Munster for a month, they march'd home with large booty The Earl forthwith sent a letter into Spain, with a long account of these victories; desiring no credit might be given to the English, in case they pretended he was desiring a Peace with them; that he had firmly resolv'd against accepting any terms, though never so advantageous, and that he would religiously observe his Engagements to the King of Spain And yet at the same time he pretended to intercede, both by letters and messages, with the Earl of Ormond, for leave to submit, upon such and such unreasonable terms

*[illegible]

This was the deplorable state of Ireland, when Queen Elizabeth made Robert Earl of Essex (eminent for his taking of Cadis from the Spaniards, and for his great prudence, as well as valor and loyalty) Lord Deputy there, to repair the losses which we had sustain'd, and with full commission to put an end to the war, and (which he gain'd with great importunity) a power to pardon even high treason; for this us'd to be excepted in all the Patents of former Lords Deputies in express words (*All treasons touching our own person, or the persons of our heirs and successors, excepted*) And without doubt, it was great wisdom in him to obtain authority for that, considering that the Lawyers hold, that all rebellions do *touch the person of the Prince* He was also allowed as great an army as he pleas'd, such a one as had never been seen before in Ireland; namely sixteen thousand foot, and thirteen hundred horse, which was augmented afterwards to twenty thousand compleat He had particular instructions to turn his chief strength against the Earl of Tir-Oen (as the heart and soul of this rebellion) without much regard to any other, and to straiten him with garrisons at Lough Foil and Bala-Shannon a thing, that he always reckon'd of great consequence, and charg'd as an oversight in the former Deputies

Robert Earl of Essex Lord Deputy 1599

Thus the Earl, accompany'd with the flower of the Nobility, and the acclamations of the common people, and with a clap of thunder in a clear sun-shine day; set out from London towards the end of March, and after a dangerous voyage, arriv'd in Ireland Having received the sword according to custom, he march'd (upon the persuasion of some of the Council, who had too much regard to their own private interests) against some petty Rebels in Munster, without regarding the Earl; which was directly contrary to his instructions and having taken Cahir (a Castle of Edward Butler, Baron of Cahir, which was encompass'd by the River Swire, and possess'd by the Rebels) and driven off vast numbers of Cattle, he made himself terrible to the whole Country, so that the Rebels dispers'd in to the woods and forests In the mean time, he

He marches not against the Earl

receiv'd

receiv'd no small loss by the cowardise of some soldiers under H Harrington, for which he punish'd them with great severity He return'd towards the end of July, with an army most sadly harass'd, and sick, and also incredibly diminish'd

The Queen displeas'd at it

Finding the Queen much displeas'd at this expensive and unfortunate expedition, and that she was above all things for their marching directly into Ulster against the Earl; he writ an excuse to her Majesty, laying the blame upon her Council in Ireland, who had advis'd him, and with whom he could not but comply, in respect of their experience in the affairs of that Kingdom, promising that he would now forthwith march into Ulster He had scarce deliver'd these letters out of his hands, when he was forc'd to send another dispatch, that now he was diverted, and oblig'd to march into Ophaly near Dublin against the O-Conors and the O-Moils, who had broken out into rebellion, but he soon suppress'd them by some few skirmishes Upon a review of his army after this expedition, he found himself so much weaken'd, that he wrote to the Queen, and got the hands of the Privy-Council to his letter, that it was necessary to reinforce his army with a thousand men before he went into Ulster

Clifford and the Deputy march against *Ulster*

Being now resolv'd to employ his whole power against that Province, he order'd Conyers Clifford, Governor of Conaught, to march towards *Belik* with a body of light horse, that the Earl's forces might be divided, while he should attack him on the other side Clifford set out accordingly with 1500 men, and notwithstanding the toil of a long march, and scarcity of powder, would not halt till he had pass'd the Curlew-mountains When most of his men had pass'd, the Rebels fell upon them by surprise, under the conduct of O-Rork Being easily repell'd, ours still continu'd their march, but the enemy perceiving the want of powder among them, renew'd the charge, and put them quickly to flight (being extremely fatigu'd with their journey,) killing Clifford himself, and Sir Henry Radcliff of Ordsall, Knight In the mean while, the supply which the Lord Deputy had desir'd, was rais'd in England, and transported But in a few days after, he acquainted the Queen by Letter, that he could do no more this year, than march to the frontiers of Ulster with 1300 foot and 300 horse, where he arriv'd the thirteenth of September The Earl shew'd himself from the hills at a great distance for two days together, and at length sent Hagan to the Lord Deputy for a parley His Lordship refus'd it, answering, That if the Earl had any thing to say to him, he might find him next morning at the head of his army The next morning, after some light skirmishes, a * trooper of the Earl's army told them with a loud voice, that the Earl did not intend to engage, but to parley with the Lord Lieutenant, but by no means now, between the armies in battalia As the Lord Deputy was advancing the next day, Hagan came up to him, declaring that the Earl desir'd the Queen's pardon and peace, and withal, that he might have audience of his Lordship; and if this favour was granted him, he would attend him at the ford of a river hard by, called *Balla Clinch* This ford is not far from Louth, the head town of the County, and near the Castle of Gerard Fleming The Lord Deputy sent Spies before hand to observe the place, who found the Earl there according to appointment; and he told them, that tho' the river was swell'd, a man might be very easily heard from one side of the ford to the other Whereupon, his Lordship having posted a troop of horse upon the next hill, went down to him alone The Earl riding his horse to the belly in the ford, saluted him with great respect, and, after about an hour's discourse between themselves, they withdrew to their respective armies Con, a bastard son of the Earl's, was sent to the Lord Deputy, to desire another conference before a select number on both sides The Lord Deputy granted this likewise, provided the number did not exceed six The Earl, taking with him his brother *Cormac*, Mac Gennys, Mac Guir, Ever Mac Cowley, Henry Ovington, and O-Quin, return'd to the Ford, and the Lord Deputy came down to him, accompany'd with the Earl of Southampton, and Sir George Bourgchier, Sir Warham S Leger, Sir Henry Danvers, Sir Edward Wingfield, and Sir William Constable, Knights The Earl saluted them singly with great respect, and, after some few words, it was concluded that Commissioners should be appointed the day following to treat of a Peace, who agreed upon a cessation from that day, for six weeks to six weeks, till the first of May, yet so that it should be lawful for both sides to renew the war after fourteen days warning, and that if any Confederate of the Earl's did not agree to it, the Earl should leave him to be treated as an Enemy, at the discretion of the Lord Deputy

Lord Deputy's Conferences with the Earl

8 Sept 1599

* Eques

The Queen much displeas'd with his Delays

In the mean while, the forementioned letter of the Lord Deputy was deliver'd to the Queen by Henry Cuff, an excellent Scholar, but an unfortunate man As soon as she found that the Deputy had done nothing in so long a time, with so great an army, and so much expence, nor was likely to do any thing that year, she was extremely offended, and wrote back to him and the Council, That she could not but wonder what the Lord Deputy meant, by prolonging the war, and letting slip those excellent opportunities he had, of marching against the Earl himself, considering, that this was his constant advice in England; and he had often promised by his Letters, that he would take that course She ask'd him, why he had made those chargeable expeditions into Munster and Ophaly, against his own judgment, and without giving her the least notice before hand, that so she might (as she certainly would) have countermanded them And if his army was now broken and weak, how it came to pass that he did not pursue the enemy, while it was entire, strong, and compleat? If the spring was not a fit season for the war in *Ulster*, why was the summer, why autumn, thus neglected? was there no part of the year fit for it? She told him, she saw that her Kingdom would be impoverished to a great degree by the charge of the war, and her honour blemish'd among foreign Princes by this ill success, and that whoever should give posterity an account of these times, would testify, that she had omitted nothing that could conduce to the preservation of Ireland, and that he had done every thing that was like to lose it; unless he resolv'd at last to take another course In conclusion, she admonish'd him and the Council, with some sharpness, to be more cautious in their resolutions, and from thence forward not to suffer themselves to be misled by ill advice, commanding them withal, to give her a true account of the condition into which they had brought the Kingdom, and to be very careful to prevent any future mischief

This

The Lord Deputy goes for England, 28 Sept 1599

This letter start'd, or rather gall'd, the Lord Deputy upon which, he took post, and arriv'd in England sooner than could possibly be expected, and early in the morning presented himself to the Queen upon his knees, as she was in her Bed-chamber and did not in the least expect him After she had talk'd a while to him (but not with the good countenance she us'd to do) she order'd him to withdraw to his own Lodgings, and not to stir thence For the Queen was angry, that he had left Ireland so suddenly, against her orders, and without leave, and also that he had agreed to a cessation which might end every fourteen days, when he had authority to make an end of the war, and pardon the Rebels What became of him afterwards, and how it appear'd by very good testimonies that he had higher matters in his mind than the war against the Rebels (while he could not sacrifice his own private resentments to the publick good, but rely'd too much upon popular Applause, which is ever a fickle and a very short support,) all this is foreign to my design and as I have no pleasure in the thoughts of it, so I leave it to those who are composing the History of that age.

The Earl breaks the Cessation of Arms

The Cessation had hardly expir'd above once or twice, when the Earl of Tir Oen drew his forces together, in order to renew the war Sir Wm Warren was sent by the Council, to know why he broke the Cessation He answer'd with an air of Insolence, that he did not, for he had given fourteen days warning of his design, and that he had good reason to break it, since he understood the Lord Deputy, upon whom alone he could rely for life and safety, was taken into custody in England, and said, he would have no more to do with any of the Council, who had already dealt perfidiously with him, and, as for the Cessation, he could not continue it now, if he would, because he had sent O Donell into Conaught, and others, his Confederates, into other parts, upon action

New Insurrections in Ireland

In the mean time, a rumor was spread among the Rebels by the Earl of Tir-Oen, not without some grounds, that the Kingdom of England would suddenly be imbroil'd, and so the Rebels increas'd daily, both in numbers and resolution They who were originally Irish, began to flatter themselves with the hopes of their ancient freedom and nobility; and the English who stood true in their inclinations grew dejected, when they saw all these preparations and expences vanish, without effect, complaining withal of their ill usage of late, in being excluded, as meer strangers, from all publick offices On the other side, the Earl was sanguine, boasted every where that he would restore religion and liberty to his Country, receiv'd all seditious persons into protection, sent recruits where they were needful, confirm'd the wavering, and took all imaginable care to subvert the English Government in Ireland To this he was encourag'd, by the supplies of stores and money which the King of Spain sent him from time to time; and by the promises and indulgences of the Pope, who had also sent him the plume of a Phœnix, in imitation perhaps of Pope Urban the third, who sent a little Coronet platted with Peacocks feathers, to John, Son of King Henry the second, when he was created Lord of Ireland

Thus flush'd with victory, the Earl went in pilgrimage, in the depth of winter, to a piece of Christ's Cross which was thought to be preserv'd in the Abbey of Holy Cross in Tipperary, for Religion, as he pretended; but really to show his greatness, and to blow up those flames by his own presence, which he had before kindled in Munster And he sent out some of his Rapparees, to ravage the Country belonging to the Queen's subjects, under the conduct of *Mac-Guir*, who happen'd to fall upon Sir * Warham Sentleger, who run him through with his spear, and was run through by *Mac-Guir*, at the same time As soon as the Earl had bury'd him, he march'd homewards, and return'd sooner than could be expected For he had heard, that the Earl of Ormond was appointed General of the Army, and was drawing his forces together from all parts, and that Charles Blunt, Baron Montjoy, the new Lord Deputy, was coming. The Queen, indeed, had design'd him this office before, but Robert Earl of Essex aiming at it himself (to the end he might be capable of establishing an interest in the military men, whom he always study'd to oblige,) had oppos'd him, alledging, that the Lord Montjoy had no more experience in war than what he had pick'd up in the Low Countrys, that he had no dependants, nor estate answerable, and that he was too bookish

* S Leodegarius

1600

Lord Montjoy, Lord Deputy

In February, the Lord Montjoy arriv'd in Ireland, without much noise or retinue, and enter'd upon the Government He found the state of affairs very ill, or rather desperate and beyond recovery All honest men dejected and in despair; the enemy flush'd with continual success, and the Earl himself marching from the furthest part of Ulster into the Province of Munster, which was the whole length of the Island, in a kind of triumph Nay, to daunt his Lordship, the Rebels welcom'd him with an alarm, in the very Suburbs of Dublin This gall'd him, yet he resolv'd to march directly against the Earl himself, who, he heard, was about to return from Munster, and so, with such forces as he could readily get together (for the best troops were in Munster already, under the command of the Earl of Ormond) he set forward, to stop the Earl in Fereal, and to give him battle But the Earl prevented him by his speedy march, having information of the design, for it is certain, that some of the Queen's Council were well wishers to the Earl and his proceedings As soon as the Lord Deputy return'd to Dublin, he employ'd himself wholly in reviewing his troops, and drawing out a detachment of Veterans to be transported by sea to Logh-Foil and Bala-Shannon, near the mouth of Lough-Erne, that a garrison being plac'd there, he might annoy the enemy both in the flank and the rear, and also to reinforce his garrisons in Lease and Ophaly, a matter of no small danger and difficulty, when the enemy was on all sides In the beginning of May, the Lord Deputy took his march towards Ulster, to divert the enemy on that side, while Henry Docwra planted a garrison at Logh Foil, and Morgan another at Bala Shannon The Earl was so well diverted by the Lord Deputy with successful skirmishes, that Docwra and the other easily compass'd their design, and the Earl himself grew sensible of a change of fortune, and that he was now beaten back to his old Corners The Lord Deputy having planted these garrisons, return'd about the middle of June, and sent into England for a supply of men and * provisions, that he might plant another garrison at Armach, on this side, to straiten the Rebels yet more In the mean time, he march'd into Leise, which was the refuge of all the Rebels in Leinster; and there cut off Ony Mac Rory Og, chief of the family of O More a bloody and desperate young fellow, who had lately raised those commotions in Munster with many others of the same profli-

* Commeatus

gate

gate spirit; and, having wasted the Country, drove them into the woods and boggs in such consternation, that they never made head again in those parts.

The Deputy marches against the Rebels

The supplies from England being now arrived, though his Lordship wanted both money and provision, and though the Equinox was now past, and winter already begun in this climate, yet he march'd to the Pass of Moyery, three miles beyond Dundalk. This Pass is, by nature, the most difficult in Ireland; and besides, the Rebels had with great art and industry obstructed it by fences, stakes, hurdles, stones, and clods of earth, as it lies between the hills, woods, and boggs on both sides, and had also lin'd it with soldiers. Moreover, the weather was very bad, and the great rains which had fallen for some days together, had made the rivers overflow, and to be impassable. As soon as the waters fell, the English open'd their way through this passage and the fences, with great courage; and, notwithstanding all the difficulties they had to encounter, they beat back the enemy, and marched towards Armagh; but Armagh itself was eaten up with Rebels; so that the Lord Deputy planted his garrison eight miles from the town, and in memory of John Norris (under whom his Lordship had learn'd the rudiments of war) call'd the place *Mount Norris*, committing it to the charge of *E. Blany*, a person of great diligence and valour, who sufficiently gall'd the enemy on this side, as Henry Docwra did on the other, and kept them in great awe. Not to mention the skirmishes in his return, in the Pass near Carlingford, which the Rebels had block'd up, he gave them a memorable defeat.

Lord Deputy marches into *Leinster*

Some few days after (though it was now the middle of winter) the Lord Deputy, to make the most of his time, march'd into the Glynnes, or the vallies of Leinster, which continu'd hitherto undistur'd, and having wasted the Country, he forc'd *Donel Spaniah*, Phelim Mac Feogh, and the seditious race of the O-Tools, to give hostages, and submit. After this, he enter'd Fereal, and drove Tirell, the best commander among the Rebels, out of his strong hold, such as they call a *Fastness* (being a boggy place, beset with thick bushes) into Ulster, whither he pursu'd the Enemy with a victorious army, by a winding-march. In the first place, he laid waste the Country of Ferney (having slain the two sons of Evar Mac Cowly;) and did the like to *Fues*, by a detachment under the command of Richard Monson. At the same time, he sent Oliver Lambard to plant a garrison in Breany, and then turn'd towards Drogheda, where he receiv'd such of the principal Rebels into his protection, as submitted themselves, namely *Turlogh Mac Henry*, Governour in Fues, *Ever Mac Cowly C-Hanlon*, who || claim'd the honour of hereditary Standard-bearer to the Kings of Ulster, and many of the *Mac Mahons* and *O-Realies*; who gave up their nearest friends and relations as hostages. As soon as the spring came on, the Lord Deputy, before all the forces were got together, march'd again to Moyery, and cut down the woods to make the way passable, and there erected a Fort. In this expedition, he drove the Mac Genniss out of Lecal, which they had seiz'd; and reduc'd all the castles of the enemy as far as Armagh, in which he also planted a garrison. Nay, he advanc'd so far, that the Earl, who was strongly encamp'd at Black-water, was oblig'd to retire; and the Deputy design'd to erect a Fort somewhat lower, but receiv'd certain advice that the Spaniards were landed in Munster;

|| Claim, C

as he had heard by flying reports before. Upon this, he was forc'd to stop; for he was not now to deliver Ireland from a civil war, but from a foreign invasion. However, to secure what he had gain'd, he reinforc'd his garrisons, and march'd with great speed at the head of two * troops of horse for Munster, commanding the foot to follow.

* A..

Spaniard invited by the Earl

For while the Lord Deputy was imploy'd in Ulster, the Earl and those of his party in Munster, had, by their agents, (viz. a certain Spaniard who was made Archbp of Dublin by the Pope, the Bp of Clonfort, the Bp of Killalo, and one Archer a Jesuit,) prevail'd with the K of Spain, after great Solicitation, to send a reinforcement to the Rebels in Munster, under the conduct of John de D'Aquila, in hopes that the whole Province would presently revolt, and that the titular Earl of Desmond, as also Florens Mac-Carty, would joyn them with a strong Body. But the President George Carew, had taken care to seize these two, and transport them into England. D'Aquila landed at Kingsale in Munster, with two thousand veteran Spaniards and some Irish Deserters, on the last of October, and forthwith publish'd a Manifesto, wherein he stil'd himself *Master-General, and Captain, of his Catholick Majesty, in the war of God, for preserving the Faith in Ireland*, and endeavour'd to persuade them, that Q. Elizabeth was depriv'd of her Kingdom by the sentences of several Popes, and her subjects absolv'd from their allegiance, and that he and his army had undertaken this expedition to deliver them from *the jaws of the Devil* and *the English Tyranny*, and, by these pretences he drew great numbers to him.

Lord Deputy besieges Kinsale

The Lord Deputy, with all the forces he could raise, prepar'd to besiege the town, and Richard Levison, Vice-Admiral, was sent out of England with two men of war to block up the harbour, which he did. The English invested the town, and began the siege briskly, battering it both by sea and land; but afterwards it was carry'd on more slowly, because Levison on the one side, with his Seamen, was sent against two thousand Spaniards, who had landed at Bere haven, Baltimore, and Castle-haven, and sunk five of their ships; and, at the same time, the President of Munster was sent with a detachment to intercept O-Donell, who was upon his march to joyn the supplies from Spain. And the frost being very hard, he got to the Spaniards safe and undiscover'd, by the shortest ways, in the night. Some few days after, the Earl of Tir-Oen, together with O-Rork, Reimund Burk, Mac-Mahon, Randall Mac-Surley, Tirell, and the Baron of Lixnaw, advanc'd with the choicest Troops of the Rebels, who, after Alphonsus O-Campo had joyn'd them with the fresh supply of Spaniards under his command, amounted to 6000 foot and 600 horse, all big with hopes of victory, which they thought was their own, as superior in numbers, and fresher and better provided in all kinds, than the English, who were harass'd with the fatigues of a winter-siege, themselves straiten'd in provisions, and their horses worn out with hard service and want of forage. The Lord Deputy call'd a Council of war, for their advice in these circumstances. Some thought it best to raise the siege, and retire to Cork, and not to venture the whole Kingdom upon a single Battle. On the other side, his Lordship advis'd them to persist in the design, and not to degenerate from the known resolution and bravery of their Ancestors, saying, that a better opportunity could not be had by men of valour, than was now put into

3 them

their hands, to dye with glory, or conquer with honour. So, he continu'd the ſiege with the utmoſt vigour, playing perpetually upon the walls, and fortifying his camp with new works.

On the twenty-firſt of December, the Earl of Tir-Oen appear'd with his army, from a hill, about a mile from our trenches, and there encamp'd; the next day he appear'd again in the ſame place, and the night following the Spaniards made a ſally, and the Iriſh attempted to throw themſelves into the town, but both were repulſed. On the twenty third the Engliſh began to play their heavy Cannon againſt the town, to ſhow how little they regarded the Earl, tho' at their backs, and the ſame day intercepted D'Aquila's letters to the Earl, deſiring him to throw the Spaniards, lately arriv'd, into the town, and to attack the enemy's camp on both ſides. That night, as the moon was ſetting, the Lord Deputy commanded Henry Poer, with eight companies of Veterans, to poſt himſelf on the weſt ſide of the Camp. Henry Gream, who that night commanded the Horſe-Guards, gave the Deputy notice betimes in the morning, that he foreſaw the Enemy would attack them, from the great number of matches which they had lighted. Whereupon, all were order'd to their arms, and the paſſes to the town were well guarded. The Lord Deputy himſelf, attended by the President of Munſter, and Richard Wingfield, Marſhall, † went out, and with the advice of Oliver Lambard, pitch'd upon a place to receive the Enemy, commanding the * Regiments of Henry Folliot and Oliver S John, and ſix hundred marines under the command of Richard Leviſon, to poſt themſelves there. But the Earl of Tir-Oen (who had reſolved, as it appear'd afterwards, to throw the new recruits of Spaniards and 800 Iriſh into the Town, by the benefit of the night,) as ſoon as day began to break, and he found the Marſhal and Henry Danvers with the horſe, and Poer with a body of Veterans, drawn up to receive him at the foot of the hill, deſpair'd of ſucceſs, and ſounded a retreat by his bag-pipers.

† *Verſus pro cultores tendit*

* *Vexillationes*

Tir-Oen and the *Spaniards* defeated

As ſoon as the Deputy had intelligence of this diſorderly retreat, he gave direction to purſue them, and march'd in the van himſelf to obſerve their retreat, that he might take his meaſures accordingly, but the fogg was ſo thick, and the rains ſo violent, that they could ſcarce ſee before them, for ſome time. As ſoon as it cleared up, and he found the enemy retir'd haſtily in three bodies with the horſe in the rear, he reſolv'd to attack them, but firſt commanded the Preſident of *Munſter* to return to the Camp with three troops of horſe, to make that good in caſe the Spaniards ſhould ſally out of the Town. The Lord Deputy himſelf purſu'd the rebels; and with ſuch ſpeed, that they were oblig'd to turn and face him on the brink of a deep bog, which was unacceſſible, but by one ford. As ſoon as the Marſhal and the Earl of *Clan Ricard* had routed the party of horſe that defended this paſs, they fell upon the whole body of the Enemy's cavalry; and were ſo well ſeconded by *William Godolphin* (who led up the Deputy's ‖ Horſe) and *Henry Danvers*, *Minshaw*, *Taff*, and *Fleming*, and by *J Barkly* * Serjeant major, who join'd them, that the rebels were put to flight. Yet it was not thought adviſeable to purſue them, but rather to unite again, and charge the Body of the enemy, which was in great conſternation. The charge was accordingly given, and the enemy broken. *Tyrell* with his men, and the Spaniards, kept their ground. Whereupon, the Lord Deputy commanded his rear to advance againſt them; and, to perform the duty of a ſoldier as well as the office of a General, he put himſelf at the head of three * companies of *Oliver S John's* (which were commanded by *Roe*,) and attack'd them with ſuch vigour, that they fled in diſorder to ſhelter themſelves among the Iriſh, who ſoon left them to the mercy of the enemy, and ſo they were defeated with great ſlaughter by the Lord Deputy's troop of Guards under the conduct of *William Godolphin*. *Tir Oen*, *O Donell*, and the reſt, upon this flung away their weapons, and betook themſelves to their heels. *Alphonſus O Campo* was taken Priſoner, with three Spaniſh Captains, and ſix Enſigns, 1200 of the enemy were ſlain, and nine Colours taken, whereof ſix were Spaniſh. The Engliſh had not above two or three kill'd, but many wounded, and among the reſt *Henry Danvers*, *William Godolphin*, and *Croft*: ſo little did this great victory coſt us. As ſoon as the Lord Deputy had ſounded a retreat, and given God thanks for his victory among the heaps of dead bodies, he knighted the Earl of *Clan Ricard* for his valour and bravery in this battle; and ſo return'd with acclamations into his camp, which he found ſafe as he had left it. For the Spaniards, ſeeing all ſtrongly guarded, and having found by experience that Sallies were always to their own loſs, kept cloſe within the town, expecting the iſſue of the battle.

‖ *Alæ ...*

* *... Ma... ...*

* *Vexillationibus*

This was a noble victory, and of mighty conſequence in many reſpects. Ireland wavering and ready to revolt, was hereby retained in Obedience, and the Spaniards ejected, and the Arch-Rebel *Tir-Oen* driven to his holes in *Ulſter*, *O-Donel* frighted into Spain, the reſt of the rebels diſperſed, the authority of the Queen (then at a very low ebb) recover'd, the dejected Loyaliſts confirm'd, and ſoon after, a firm and laſting peace eſtabliſhed throughout the Iſland.

Kingſale ſurrender'd

† *Vallorum Præfectus*

Next day, the Lord Deputy order'd *Bodley*, the † Camp-Maſter General, who both in the Siege and the Battle had behav'd himſelf valiantly, to finiſh the mount, and carry the banks and rampires nearer to the enemy. After ſix days ſpent in that work, *D'Aquila* ſent a Trumpeter with a letter to the Lord Deputy, that ſome perſon of honour and credit might be ſent into the town to treat with him. Sir *William Godolphin* was accordingly ſent. *D'Aquila* told him, that though the Lord Deputy was a terrible Enemy, he muſt own him to be alſo an honourable one, That the Iriſh were cowardly, and undiſciplin'd, and he fear'd treacherous too. That he was ſent thither by the King of Spain his Maſter to the aſſiſtance of two Earls, but now he queſtion'd whether there was one ſuch in being, this ſtorm having blown one of them into Spain, and the other into the north, and both were vaniſh'd. That he was willing, for this reaſon, to conclude ſuch a peace, as might be for the intereſt of England on one ſide, and no prejudice to Spain on the other, but yet that he wanted nothing for a defence, and daily expected more ſupplies from Spain to give the Engliſh further trouble. In ſhort, both ſides being fatigued and weary of the ſiege, they came to this concluſion on the ſecond of January. That the Spaniards ſhould yield up *Kingſale*, and the forts and caſtles of *Baltimore*, *Berehaven*, and *Caſtle Haven* to the Lord Deputy, and go out with baggage, and colours flying, That the Engliſh ſhould find ſhipping, but be paid for it, to tranſport them at two voyages into Spain, and if they happen'd to put in at any port in England, they ſhould be kindly entertained, and, That during their ſtay in Ireland for a fair wind, they ſhould be allow'd all neceſſary accommodations for their money

The *Spaniards* return home

After ſome few days, the wind ſtood fair, and the Spaniards embark'd, with great loſs and diſhonour, for their own Country The Earl of *Tir-Oen* in the mean while fled in great haſte and conſternation thro' by-ways, to recover his holes in *Ulſter*; miſſing abundance of his men, who were many of them drown'd in paſſing the rivers then ſwell'd with the winter floods From hence-forward the Earl was without reſt and without hopes, under continual apprehenſions of puniſhment for thoſe crimes of which he was conſcious, and ſo fearful of every body, that he was daily ſhifting from one hole to another The Lord Deputy plac'd his army in winter-quarters to refreſh them, and having ſettled the affairs of *Munſter*, return'd to *Dublin*

Lord Deputy quite ſubdues *Ulſter*

As ſoon as the rigour of the ſeaſon was a little abated, he return'd at the head of his victorious army into *Ulſter* (with ſhort marches, to ſtrike a terror in the Country,) intending to perfect his firſt deſign of penning up the rebels with forts and garriſons on all ſides When he came to *Blackwater*, he paſs'd over his army in floats, and having found a ford (till that time unknown) below the old fort, he built a new fort upon the bank, and call'd it from his own Chriſtian-name, *Charlemont*. The Earl of *Tir-Oen*, out of fear, burnt his own houſe at *Dungannon* about this time. The Lord Deputy march'd from hence beyond *Dungannon*, and encamp'd, till Henry Docwra could come from *Logh-Foil* to join him After that, he made incurſions on all ſides, ſpoil'd the corn, burnt all the houſes and villages that could be found, made booty of the cattle, and had the forts of *Logh Crew*, *Logh Reogh*, and *Mogherlecow*, ſurrender'd to him, but at this laſt place, we loſt Sir *John Barkley*, a valiant man, who was ſhot through with a bullet. After this he planted a garriſon at *Logh Eaugh*, or *Logh Sidney*, and call'd it *Mountjoy* from his own title, committing the charge of it to Sir *Arthur Chicheſter*, whoſe great deſerts * raiſed him afterwards to the honour of Lord Deputy of Ireland; and another at *Monaghan*, of which he made *Chriſtopher S Lawrence*, Governor, men of great experience and greater courage, who by their continual ſallies and excurſions did ſo gall the rebels, that theſe, finding themſelves pent-in with garriſons, and ſtreighten'd more and more every day, and that they muſt live hereafter like wild beaſts, ſculking up and down among woods and deſarts, did, moſt of them, begin to make their Allegiance bend to their fortune, and tender'd ſubmiſſions privately to the Lord Deputy; murmuring, that the Earl had brought the whole Kingdom to ruin, to ſerve his own ends; and ſaying, that the war was neceſſary for him only, and had prov'd the deſtruction of the reſt

* Have raiſed him at this time, C

The Earl offers ſubmiſſion

The Earl was ſenſible, that the fidelity, as well as the ſtrength of his party, was exceedingly ſhaken, and reſolv'd to be as much beforehand with danger as he could; being now tir'd out with his misfortunes, and alſo tender of his own life, which will generally be regarded in ſpite of all reſolutions Accordingly, he wrote ſeveral letters to the Queen with great ſubmiſſion, addreſſing himſelf with prayers and tears for mercy, which the Queen obſerv'd to be ſo ſincere in all appearance, that (being alſo in her own temper very merciful) ſhe gave the Lord Deputy Authority to pardon him, and receive him into favour, in caſe he deſir'd it at his hands. As ſoon as he had this news from ſome of his friends, he ſent a petition to that purpoſe; preſſing the Lord Deputy continually by his brother *Arth Mac Baron*, and others and, in *February* (after many refuſals, and a promiſe to ſurrender his life and fortune to the Queen's diſcretion,) the Lord Deputy, upon advice from the Court of England, that the Queen who was now of a great age, was dangerouſly ill, gave the Earl leave to repair to *Mellifont*, which he immediately did, attended with one or two Followers Being admitted into the preſence-chamber, where the Lord Deputy ſat in ‖ a chair of ſtate, with many Officers about him, he fell down upon his knees at the very entrance, with a dejected look, and a mean habit. And after he had continued a while in this poſture, the Lord Deputy ſignify'd that he might approach nearer, ſo he aroſe, and after ſome few ſteps fell upon his knees again, *Acknowledging his offences againſt God, and his moſt gracious Sovereign Queen Elizabeth upon whoſe royal mercy and goodneſs he now wholly relied, and to whoſe diſcretion he ſubmitted his life and fortune; beſeeching in the moſt humble manner, that as he felt her mercy heretofore, and her power at this time, ſo he might once more taſte her clemency, and be an example of it to future ages Adding, That neither his age was ſo great, nor his body ſo weak, nor his mind ſo much broken, but he might expiate this rebellion by his future loyalty and ſervice* He was beginning to plead, in extenuation of his crime, that through the malice and envy of ſome perſons, he had been hardly dealt with, but the Lord Deputy interrupted him, ſaying with an air of Authority (the moſt graceful eloquence in a ſoldier,) that he would ſuffer no excuſe for a crime ſo hainous; and ſo, in few words, order'd him to withdraw, and the day following took him to *Dublin*, deſigning to carry him from thence into England, that the Queen might take what courſe with him ſhe thought fit But this excellent Princeſs, a little after ſhe had receiv'd Advice that a rebellion, which had ſo long diſturb'd her reign, was now extinguiſh'd (the only thing wanting to compleat her glory) left her earthly kingdom, with great calmneſs and piety, for a heavenly one

‖ *Solio*

Thus the Iriſh war, or rather the Rebellion of the Earl of *Tir-Oen* (ſprung from private reſentment and ambition, ſuffered to grow up by the diſregard and frugality of the Engliſh Court, diffuſed over all Ireland under pretence of reſtoring religion and liberty, and continu'd by a baſe emulation among the Engliſh, the avarice of the veterans, the artifice and feign'd ſubmiſſions of the Earl, the * difficult ſituation of the Country, and the nature of the people, who depend more upon their heels than their arms; as alſo by the credulity of ſome miniſters, and the corruption of others, the encouragement of one or two ſucceſsful Engagements on the ſide of the Rebels, and the ſupplies of men and money ſent them from Spain,) this War (I ſay) in the eighth year from its firſt breaking out, was happily extinguiſh'd under the Adminiſtration of Queen Elizabeth of bleſſed memory, and the conduct of *Charles Blunt*, Baron of *Montjoy*, Lord Deputy (created upon that account Earl of *Devonſhire* by King James [the firſt],) which † we hope will be the foundation of a laſting Peace in that Kingdom

* *Impeditis locorum difficultatibus*

† So ſo ... ann ...

A CHRO

A CHRONICLE OF THE KINGS of MAN.

IN the year of our Lord 1065 dy'd Edward King of England of blessed memory, to whom Harold son of Godwin succeeded Harold Harfager King of Norway gave him battle at *Stamfordbridge*, but was beaten, and all his men fled After this flight, one Godred sirnamed Crovan the son of Harold the black, escaping out of Iseland, came to Godred the son of Syrric, King of *Man* at that time, and was honourably entertain'd by him

The same year William the Bastard conquered England, and Godred the son of Syrric King of Man dy'd, and was succeeded by his son Fingall

An 1066 Godred Crovan got a numerous fleet together, and arriv'd at *Man*, where he fought with the inhabitants, but was overcome and put to flight Having rally'd his forces, and his fleet, he landed again at *Man*, fought the inhabitants, and was routed by them Having rais'd a great army the third time, he came by night to the port called *Ramsa*, and laid an ambuscade of three hundred men in a wood upon the * bending brow of a hill call'd *Scacafel* As soon as the sun was up, the inhabitants put themselves in order of Battle, and fell upon Godred with great violence When both parties were close engag'd, the three hundred men that lay in ambush, came out to the assistance of their Country-men, and put the Inhabitants of the Island to flight When they saw themselves overcome, and no place to retreat to (for the tide was in, so that there was no passing the river *Ramsa*; and the enemy was at their heels, pursuing them) they petition'd Godred with cries and tears to spare their lives Godred, being mov'd with compassion at the calamitous condition of the people, among whom he had himself been brought up for some time; recall'd his army, and hinder'd them from making further pursuit The next day, Godred gave his army their choice, whether they would divide the lands of this Isle among them and live here, or seize the wealth and substance of the Country, and return home But his army was rather for spoiling the Island, and enriching themselves with the goods of it, and then for departing However, Godred himself, with some of the Islanders, who stay'd with him, settled in the south part of the Island, and granted the north part to the remains of the natives, upon condition that none of them should ever presume to claim any part of it by way of inheritance Hence, to this very day, the whole Island is the King's, and all the rents arising out of it, belong to him Godred then reduced *Dublin*, and a great part of *Laynestir* As for the Scots, he brought them to such subjection, that if any of them built a ship or a boat, they were not allowed to have * above three sterns in it He reign'd sixteen years, and dy'd in the Island call'd *Yle*; leaving three sons, *Lagman*, *Harald*, and *Olave*. *Lagman* being eldest, seiz'd the Kingdom, and reign'd seven years His brother *Harald* continued a long time in rebellion against him, but being at last taken by *Lagman*, he had his privy members cut off, and his eyes put out. Afterwards *Lagman* was so deeply concern'd for having put out his brother's eyes, that he renounc'd the Kingdom, and with the sign of the cross went in pilgrimage to *Jerusalem*; in which pilgrimage he dy'd

1089 As soon as the Nobility of the Island receiv'd the news of *Lagman's* death, they dispatch'd their Ambassadors to *Murecard O-Bren* King of Ireland, desiring that he would send them some diligent person of Royal extraction, to Rule here, during the minority of *Olave* the son of *Godred* The King readily consented, and sent one *Dopnald* the son of *Tade*, with orders and instructions to govern the Kingdom which belong'd not to him, with tenderness and modesty But as soon as he was advanc'd to the throne, without regarding the commands of his Lord, he grew grievous to the people by his tyrannies, and reigned three years with great cruelty and wickedness The Nobility, being no longer able to endure this oppression, unanimously

* *D vexo*

* *Plus quam tres clavos in ferere*

unanimously conspir'd, and took up arms, and banish'd him Upon that, he fled into Ireland, and never return'd

1097. One *Ingemund* was sent by the King of Norway, to obtain the soveraignty of these Islands When he came to the Isle *Leod*, he sent to all the great men of the Islands, commanding them to assemble and make him King In the mean while, he with his companions did nothing but plunder, and feast, and ravish the women, wives and virgins, giving himself wholly to such beastly lusts and pleasures As soon as the great men of the Islands were acquainted with these things, being now assembled to make him King, they were so enraged, that they immediately march'd thither, and coming to his house in the night, set it on fire; so that he and his whole retinue were destroy'd either by fire or sword

1098 Was founded the Abby of S *Mary* at *Cistercium* *Antioch* was taken by the Christians, and a Comet appeared

The same year was fought a battle between the Inhabitants of the Isle of *Man* at *Santwat*, those of the north part got the victory In this engagement were slain Earl *Other*, and *Macmarus*, the Leaders of the two Parties

The same year, *Magnus* King of *Norway*, the son of *Olave*, son of *Harald Harfager*, out of curiosity to know whether the Corps of St *Olave*, King and Martyr, did remain uncorrupted; commanded his tomb to be open'd This order being oppos'd by the Bishop and his Clergy, the King himself came in person, and had it open'd by force And when with his own eyes and hands, he found the body sound and unputrified, he fell into great fears, and went away in all haste The next night, *Olavus*, King and Martyr, appear'd to him, saying, *Take thy choice of these two offers, either to lose thy Life and Kingdom within thirty days, or to leave Norway, and be content never to see it more* As soon as the King awak'd, he call'd his Nobles and the Elders of his people together, and told them the vision Being frighten'd at it, they gave him this Counsel, That with all haste he should depart out of *Norway* Upon this, he prepar'd a fleet of a hundred and sixty ships, and set sail for the *Orcades*, which he soon conquer'd, from whence he went on with success and victory through all the Islands, till he came to that of *Man* Being landed there, he went to St *Patrick's* Isle, to see the place where the Islanders had engag'd a little before, for many of the dead bodies were yet unburied This sweet and pleasant Island pleased him so well, that he resolv'd to seat himself in it, and to that end built forts and strong holds, which retain his name to this day Those of *Gallway* were so much aw'd by him, that at his command they cut down wood, and brought it to the shore, to make his Bulwarks withal Next, he sailed to *Mona*, an Island of Wales, where he found two *Hughs*, both Earls, one of them he slew, the other he put to flight, and conquered the Island The Welch made him many Presents; and so, taking his leave of them, he return'd to *Man* To *Murecard*, King of Ireland, he sent his shoes, commanding him to carry them upon his shoulders through the middle of his house, on Christmas day in sight of his Messengers, to signify his subjection to King *Magnus* The Irish received this news with great wrath and indignation But the King consider'd better, and told them, he would not only carry, but also eat his shoes, rather than King *Magnus*

Mona for An[illegible] G[illegible] rald C[illegible] [illegible] [illegible]

should destroy one Province in *Ireland* So he comply'd with this order, and honourably entertained his Messengers, and sent them back with many Presents to him, and made a league with him Being return'd, they gave their Master an account of *Ireland*, describing its situation, and pleasantness, its fruitfulness, and the excellency of its air *Magnus* hearing this, turn'd his thoughts wholly upon the Conquest of that Country For this end, he gave orders to fit out a fleet, and went before with sixteen ships, to take a view of the Country but, having unwarily left his ships, he was beset by the Irish, and cut off, with most of those that were with him His body was bury'd near St *Patrick's* Church in *Down* He reigned six years After his death, the Noblemen of this Island sent for *Olave*, son of *Godred Crovan*, who liv'd in the Court of Henry King of England, the son of William

1102 *Olave*, son of *Godred Crovan*, began his reign, which continued forty years He was a peaceable Prince, and in league with all the Kings of Ireland and Scotland His wife was *Africa*, the daughter of *Farguse* of *Gallway*, by whom he had *Godred* By his Concubines he had also *Regnald*, *Lagman*, and *Herald*, besides many daughters, one of whom was marry'd to *Summerled* Prince of * *Hererga del*, which prov'd the ruin of the Kingdom of the Isles By her he had four sons, *Dugal*, *Raignald*, *Engus*, and *Olave*

* *Argyle*

1133 The Sun was so eclips'd on the fourth of the Nones of *August*, that the day was as dark as night

1134 *Olave* gave to *Yvo*, Abbot of *Furnes*, part of his lands in *Man*, towards building an Abby in a place called *Russin* He augmented the † Churches of the Islands both with new Revenues, and new Immunities

† *Rin. Ecclesiam*

1142 *Godred*, the son of *Olave*, sail'd over to the King of *Norway*, who was call'd *Hinge*, and did him homage he staid there some time, and was honourably received This same year, the three sons of *Harald* brother of *Olave*, who were bred at *Dublin*, came to *Man*, with a great multitude of people, and such as the King had banish'd, demanding one half of the Kingdom of the Isles for their share The King, being willing to please them, answer'd, That he would take the advice of his Council about it Having agreed upon the time and place for their meeting, these villains enter'd into a plot against the King's life At the day appointed, both Parties met at the haven call'd *Ramsa*, and sat in ranks, the King with his Council on the one side, and they and their gang on the other, and *Regnald* (who was to dispatch him) in the middle, talking, apart, with one of the Noblemen When the King call'd him, he turn'd himself as though he would salute him, but lifting up a shining ax, he cut off his head at one blow When they had executed this villany, and divided the Island among them, after some few days they got a fleet together, and set sail for *Gallway*, intending to make a Conquest of it But the people, being in arms ready to receive them, fell upon them with great violence Upon this, they fled back to *Man* in much disorder, where they either kill'd or banish'd all the *Gallway*-men they could meet with

1143 *Godred*, Son of *Olave*, returning from Norway, was made King of *Man* To revenge the death of his father, he put out the eyes of two of *Harald's* sons, and the third he put to death

1144 *Godred* began his reign, and reign'd thirty years. In the third year of his reign, the people of *Dublin* sent for him, and made him King of *Dublin* *Murecard* King of Ireland rais'd war against him, and as he lay encamp'd before the City call'd *Cendelis*, sent *Osibel*, his half brother, by the mother's side, with three thousand horse to *Dublin*, who was slain by *Godred* and the Dublinians, and his army routed After this, he return'd to *Man*, and began to tyrannize here, depriving his Nobles of their Estates one of them called *Thorfin*, the son of *Oter*, mightier than the rest, went to *Sumerled*, and made *Dubgall* his son, King of the Isles, many of which he reduced to subjection *Godred* hearing of these proceedings by one *Paul*, set out a fleet, and steer'd towards *Sumerled*, who came against him with a fleet of eighty sail

1156 They came to an engagement by sea, * the night before the feast of Epiphany, and after great slaughters on both sides, concluded a peace the next day, agreeing to divide the Kingdom of the Isles between them from which time it hath continued two several Kingdoms to this day So that from the moment that *Sumerled*'s sons had to do with the Kingdom of the Isles, we may date its downfall and overthrow

* *Nonæ Epiphaniæ*

1158 *Sumerled* came to *Man* with a fleet of fifty three sail, and put *Godred* to flight, and spoil'd the Island; upon which, *Godred* sail'd over to Norway for aid against *Sumerled*

1164 *Sumerled* set out a fleet of one hundred and sixty ships, and arriv'd with them at *Rhinfrin*, intending to conquer all Scotland But by the just judgment of God, he was vanquished there by a very few, and he, together with his son and a vast multitude, slain

The same year, a battle was fought at *Ramsa*, between *Reginald*, *Godred*'s brother, and the people of *Man*; wherein those of *Man* were put to flight, by the treachery of a certain Earl

Now also *Reginald* began his reign, which had not continued four days, till *Godred* his brother invaded him with a great army from Norway, and having taken him, put out his eyes, and cut off his privy members The same year dy'd *Malcolm* King of Scotland, and was succeeded by his brother William

1166 In August there appeared two Comets before sun-rise, one in the south, the other in the north

1171. Richard Earl of *Pembroke* sailed into Ireland, and subdu'd *Dublin*, and a great part of Ireland

1176 John *Curcy* conquer'd *Ulster*, and *Vivian* the Pope's Legat came into *Man*, and made King *Godred* to be lawfully marry'd to his wife *Phingola*, daughter to *Mac-Lotlen*, son of *Murkertac*, King of Ireland, the mother of *Olave*, then three years old They were marry'd by *Sylvan* the Abbot, to whom *Godred* the very same day gave a parcel of land at *Mirescoge*, where he built a Monastery; but this, together with the Monks, was at last made over to the Abbey of *Russin*

1172 *Reginald*, the son of *Eac-Marcat*, of the blood royal, coming into *Man* in the King's absence with a great body of men, presently put to flight those who guarded the Coast, and slew about thirty of them; but the inhabitants rising, fell upon him, and the same day slew him and most of his party

1183. *O-Fogolt* was * Sheriff of *Man*. † *Vice Comes*

1185. There happened an Eclipse of the sun on St. Philip and Jacob's day.

1187 On the fourth of the Ides of November, *Godred*, King of the Isles, departed this life; and the Summer following, his body was convey'd to the Isle of *Hy*. He left three sons, *Reginald*, *Olave*, and *Yvar*. In his life-time, he made *Olave* his heir; being the only legitimate son that he had But (*Olave* being scarce ten years old) the people sent for *Reginald* out of the Isles, and made him King.

1188. *Reginald*, the son of *Godred*, began his reign over the Islands; and *Murchard*, a man of great interest in the Isles, was slain

1192 A battle was fought between *Reginald* and *Engus*, the sons of *Sumerled*; wherein *Engus* got the victory

The same year the Abbey of *Russin* was translated to *Dufglass*; yet the Monks, about four years after, return'd to *Russin*.

1203 *Michael*, Bishop of the Isles, dy'd at *Fontans*, and was succeeded by *Nicholas*

1204. *Hugh de Lacy* brought an army into *Ulster*, and fought *John Curcy*, and took him prisoner, and conquer'd *Ulster* Afterwards, he set *John* at liberty; who thereupon came to King *Reginald*, and was honourably receiv'd, as being his son in-law for *Africa*, *Godred*'s daughter (she who founded the Abbey of St. *Mary de Jugo Domini*, and was bury'd there) was *John de Curcy*'s wife

1205 *John Curcy*, and *Reginald* King of the Isles, enter'd *Ulster* with an hundred ships, at the haven call'd *Stranfeord*, and laid siege to *Rath* Castle But *Walter de Lacy* came upon them with an army, and put them to flight. After that, *Curcy* could never recover his Territories

1210 *Engus*, the son of *Sumerled*, was slain, with his three sons

John, King of England, arriv'd in Ireland with a fleet of 500 ships, and conquer'd it, and sent a certain Earl, call'd *Fulco*, to *Man*; who wasted the whole Country in a fortnight, and taking hostages, return'd home King *Reginald* and his Nobles were not in *Man* at that time.

1217 Nicholas, Bishop of the Isles, dy'd, and was bury'd in *Ulster*, in the house of *Benchor*, and succeeded by *Reginald*.

I will, with the Reader's leave, add something further, concerning the two brothers, Olave *and* Reginald

REginald gave to his brother *Olave* the Isle of *Lodhus*; which is counted larger than any of the other Islands, but thinly peopled, because it is mountainous and stony, and almost every where unfit for tillage. The inhabitants live generally by hunting and fishing. *Olave*, thereupon, went to take possession of this Island, and dwelt there in a poor condition Finding it too little to maintain him and his army, he went boldly to his brother *Reginald*, who then liv'd in the Islands, and address'd him in this manner My brother, and my Sovereign; You know well, that the Kingdom of the Isles was mine by right of inheritance; but since God hath made you King over it, I envy not your happiness, nor do I grudge to see the crown upon your head I only beg of you so much land in these Islands, as may be an honourable main-

 tenance,

tenance, for I am not able to live upon the Island *Lodbus*, which you gave me *Reginald* hearing this, told his brother he would take the advice of his Council upon it, and the day after, when *Olave* was call'd in, he was apprehended by *Reginald*'s order, and carry'd to William King of Scotland, that he might be there kept in prison; where he continu'd in chains almost seven years For in the seventh year dy'd William King of Scotland, and was succeeded by his son *Alexander*; but before his death he commanded that all prisoners should be set at liberty *Olave* being thus freed, came to Man, and soon after, accompanied with no small train of Nobility, went to St *James* At his Return, his brother *Reginald* made him marry the daughter of a Nobleman of *Kentyre*, his own wife's sister, named *Lavon*, and gave him *Lodbus* again But a few days after, *Reginald* Bishop of the Isles, call'd a Synod, and divorced *Olave*, the son of *Godred*, and *Lavon* his wife, as being the Cousin-german of his former wife Afterwards *Olave* married *Scristina*, the daughter of *Ferkar* Earl of *Rosse*

Reginald's wife, the Queen of the Islands, was so troubled at this news, that she sent letters, in the name of her husband King *Reginald*, to her son *Godred* in the Island of *Sky*, commanding him to kill *Olave* As *Godred* was contriving to execute this order, and going to *Lodbus* for that end, *Olave* got off in a little cock-boat, and fled to his father-in-law the Earl of *Rosse*, while *Godred* in the mean time wasted the Island At the same time, *Pol*, the son of *Boke*, Sheriff of *Sky*, a man of great interest in all the Islands, fled likewise (having refus'd to side with *Godred*) and liv'd in the Earl of *Rosi*'s house with *Olave* Making a league with *Olave*, they went together in one vessel to *Sky* At last, they understood by their Spies, that Godred lay secure and negligent, with a very few men, in a certain Island call'd St. *Columbs* So, they got together their friends and companions, and with such volunteers as would go with them, they set sail in the middle of the night with five ships, which they got from the opposite shore, distant about two furlongs from the aforesaid Island, and beset St *Columbs* *Godred* and his company next morning, perceiving themselves encompass'd by an Enemy, were in great consternation However, they took arms, and, though to no purpose, manfully endeavour'd to withstand them For *Olave*, and *Pol* the aforesaid Sheriff, landed about nine a clock with their whole army, and cut off all they met with, those excepted, who had taken sanctuary in the Churches *Godred* was taken, and had his eyes put out, and his privy members cut off However, this was against *Olave*'s will; for he would have sav'd him but the son of *Boke*, the Sheriff aforesaid, would not suffer it This was done in the year 1223 Next summer, *Olave* having receiv'd pledges of the Noblemen of the Isles, set sail for Man with a fleet of thirty two ships, and arriv'd at *Rognolswabt* At this time, *Reginald* and *Olave* divided the Kingdom of the Isles between them; but *Reginald* was to have *Man* over and above, together with the title of King *Olave* having furnish'd himself with provisions in the Isle of Man, return'd with his company to his part of the Islands *Reginald*, the year following, taking *Alan* Lord of Galloway along with him, went with the people of the Isle of Man, to disseise his brother *Olave* of the land he had given him, and to reduce and add it to his own dominion But the people of Man being unwilling to fight against *Olave* and the Islanders, whom they lov'd very well, *Reginald* and Alan Lord of Gallway were forc'd to return home without effecting any thing. A little after, *Reginald* pretending a journey to the Court * of his Lord the King of England, rais'd an hundred marks upon the people of the Island, and then went to the Court of Alan Lord of Gallway. During his stay there, he marry'd his daughter to Alan's son The people of Man received this news with such indignation, that they sent for *Olave*, and made him King

* *Domini Regis Angliæ*

1226 *Olave* recover'd his inheritance, namely, the Kingdom of Man, and of the Isles, which his brother *Reginald* had govern'd for thirty years, and reign'd quietly two years

1228 *Olave*, accompany'd with all the Nobility, and the military part of the people of Man, sail'd over to the Isles A while after that, Alan Lord of Gallway, Thomas Earl of Athol, and King *Reginald*, came into Man with a great army, and wasted all the south part of the Island, and spoil'd the Churches, and put all the inhabitants they could meet with to the sword, so that the whole south part of the Island was in a manner desolate After Alan had thus ravaged the Country, he returned with his army, leaving his Bailiffs in *Man*, to collect the tribute of the Country, and send it to him King *Olave* coming upon them unawares, put them to flight, and recover'd his Kingdom Whereupon, the people who had been dispersed and scattered, got together again, and began to live securely in their old homes

The same year, King *Reginald* came by surprize in the dead of the night in winter, with five sail of ships, from Galway, and burnt all the ships that belong'd to his brother *Olave* and the Nobility of Man, at the Isle of S Patrick; and tarry'd forty days after in *Ragnollwath*-haven, desiring peace of his brother During his abode, he won-over to his interest all the inhabitants of the south part of Man; so that they swore they would lose their lives, rather than he should not be restor'd to half of the Kingdom *Olave*, on the other side, had secur'd those of the north to his interest; and so on the 14th of Feb at a place called *Tinguall*, the two brothers came to an engagement; wherein *Olave* had the victory, and King *Reginald* was slain, but without the knowledge of *Olave* Certain Pirates arrived in the south part of *Man*, and wasted it The Monks of Russin convey'd the Corps of King *Reginald* to the Abbey of S Mary *de Fournes*, and there it was bury'd in a certain place which he himself had appointed before *Olave*, after this, went to the King of Norway; but before his arrival, Haco King of Norway had made a certain Nobleman, call'd *Husbac*, the son of *Owmund*, King of the Sodorian Islands, and nam'd him *Haco* This Haco, accompany'd by Olave, and Godred Don the son of Reginald, and many Norwegians, came to the Isles; but in taking a certain castle in the Isle of *Both*, he was kill'd with a stone, and buried in Jona

1230 Olave came with Godred Don and the Norwegians to *Man*, and they divided the Kingdom Olave was to have *Man* Godred going to the Isles, was slain in Lodhus So, *Olave* came to be sole King of the Isles

1237 On the twelfth of the Calends of June, died *Olave* the son of *Godred*, King of Man, in St Patrick's Isle; and was bury'd in the Abbey of *Russin* He reign'd eleven years, two in the life-time of his brother, and nine after

His son *Harald*, then fourteen years old, succeeded, and reign'd twelve years In the first year of his reign, he went to the Isles, and made Loglen his Kinsman Keeper of *Man* In the autumn following, *Harald* sent three sons of *Nell*, *viz* Dufgald, Thorquel, and Molmore, and his friend *Joseph*, to Man, in order to a Conference Accordingly, on the twenty-fifth day, they met at *Tinguall*; where, upon a difference that happen'd between the sons of *Nell*, and Loglen, there ensu'd a fight, in which Dufgald, Mormor, and the said Joseph lost their lives. The spring following, King *Harald* came to the Isle of Man; and Loglen, who fled into Wales with Godred the son of *Olave* his pupil, was cast away with about forty others

1238 Gospatrick and Gillecrist the son of *Mac-Kerthac*, came from the King of Norway into Man, and drove out *Harald*, and converted the tribute of the Country to the service of the King of Norway; because he had refused to appear in person at the Court of that King

1239 *Harald* went to the King of Norway, who after two years confirm'd to him, his heirs and successors, under his Seal, all the Islands that his Predecessors had enjoy'd

1240 Gospatrick dy'd, and was buried in the Abbey of *Russin*

1242 *Harald* return'd out of Norway to Man, was honourably receiv'd by the Inhabitants, and was at peace with the Kings of England and Scotland

1247 *Harald*, as his father had been, was Knighted by the King of England, and return'd home with many presents The same year the King of Norway sent for him, and a match was made between *Harald* and his daughter In the year 1249, as he was on his voyage homeward with his wife, accompany'd with Laurence the elect King of Man, and many of the Nobility and Gentry, he was cast away by a sudden storm near the coasts of *Radland*

1249. *Reginald*, son of *Olave* and brother of *Harald*, began his reign the day before the Nones of May, and on the thirtieth day thereof was slain by one Yvar, a Knight, and his accomplices, in a meadow near Trinity-Church, on the south-side. He was bury'd in the Church of St Mary *Russin*.

Alexander, King of Scots, prepar'd a great fleet about this time, intending to conquer the Isles; but a fever seiz'd him in the Isle of Kerwaray, of which he dy'd

Harald, son of Godred Don, assum'd the title of King of the Islands, and banish'd all the Noblemen of *Harald*, King *Olave*'s son, and, instead of them, recall'd such as were fled

1250 Harald, the son of Godred Don, being summon'd by a letter from the King of Norway, went to him, and was there imprison'd for his unjust usurpation

The same year, *Magnus* son of *Olave*, and John son of Dugald, who stil'd himself King, arriv'd at *Roghalwaht*; but the people of Man, taking it ill that *Magnus* had not the title, beat them off their coast, and many of them were cast away

1252 *Magnus*, son of *Olave*, came to Man, and was made King. The next year, he took a voyage to the Court of Norway, and tarry'd there a year

1254 Haco, King of Norway, made *Magnus* son of *Olave*, King of the Isles, confirming them to him and his heirs, and by name to his brother *Harald*

1256 *Magnus*, King of Man, went into England, and there was Knighted by the King

1257 The Church of S Mary of *Russin* was consecrated by Richard Bishop of Sodor

1260 Haco, King of Norway, came to Scotland, and without effecting any thing, dy'd in his return to the Isles of Orkney, at Kirwas, and was buried at *Bergh*

1265 This year dy'd *Magnus* son of *Olave*, K of Man and of the Islands, at the castle of *Russin*, and was bury'd in S Mary's Church there

1266 The Kingdom of the Isles was translated, by means of Alexander King of Scots

What follows, is written in a different and later Character.

1270 *On the seventh of October, the Fleet of Alexander King of Scots arriv'd at* Roghalwath; *and, before sun-rise next morning, a battle was fought between the Inhabitants of Man, and the Scots, who slew five hundred and thirty five of the former, whence that of a certain Poet,*

L decies, X ter, & penta duo cecidere,
Mannica gens de te, damna futura cave.

1313 *Robert, King of Scots, besieg'd the castle of* Russin (*which was defended by* Dingawy Dowyll) *and at last took it*

1316 *Upon Ascension-day*, Richard de Mandevile *and his brothers, with others of the Irish Nobility, arriv'd at* Ramaldwath, *desiring a supply of provisions and money; for they had been stript of all by the continual depredations of the Enemy When the People deny'd their request, they took the field in two bodies against those of* Man, *advancing till they came to the side of* Warthfell-*hill, in a field where* John Mandevile *was posted Upon engaging, the Irish had the victory, and spoil'd the Isle and the Abbey of* Russin, *and, after a month's stay, return'd home, full-fraught with pillage* †

† Thus far out of that ancient Book

The end of the Chronicle of the Kings of Man.

A Con-

A Continuation of the foregoing HISTORY, *collected out of other Authors.*

ALexander the third, King of Scots, having made himself master of the Western Islands, partly by his sword, and partly by purchase from the King of Norway, at last invaded *Man* also, as one of that number, and by the valiant conduct of *Alexander Steward*, entirely subdu'd it, and set a King over the Isle, upon this condition, that he should be ready to assist him with ten ships in his wars by Sea, whenever he demanded them However, *Mary* the daughter of *Reginald*, King of *Man* (who was the *Liege-man* of John King of England,) address'd her self to the King of England for justice in this case Answer was made, That the King of Scots was then possess'd of the Island, and she ought to apply to him Her son's son, *John Waldebof* (for *Mary* married into this family) su'd again for his right in Parliament, the 33d of Edward the first, before the King of England, as Lord Para mount of Scotland Yet all the answer he could have, was (as it is in the Record,) *He may prosecute his title before the Justices of the King's Bench, let it be heard there, and let justice be done* But what he could not effect by law, his kinsman *William Montacute* (for he was of the royal family of *Man*) obtain'd by force of arms For having rais'd a body of English, with these raw soldiers he drove all the Scots out of the Isle But having plung'd himself into debt by the great expence of this war, and being insolvent, he was forced to mortgage the Island to *Anthony Bec* Bishop of *Durham*, and Patriarch of *Jerusalem*, and made over all the profits to him for seven years, and quickly after, the King gave the Island to the said *Anthony* for term of life Afterwards, King Edward II gave it to his great favourite *Peter de Gaveston*, at the same time that he made him Earl of Cornwall He being dead, the King gave it to *Henry Beaumont with all the demesns, and royal jurisdiction thereunto belonging* Soon after this, the Scots recover'd it again, under the conduct of *Robert Brus*, and from that time *Thomas Randolph* a warlike Scot (as Alexander Duke of Albany did a long time after) stil'd himself *Lord of Man*, and bore the same Arms that the later Kings of the Island did, namely *Three arm'd legs of a man linked together and bending in the hams*, like the three legs naked, which were formerly stamp'd on the coins of *Sicily*, to signify the three Promontories But before the Arms of the King of *Man* were a * *Ship* with the sail folded, and his title, *Rex Manniæ & Insularum, King of Man and of the Isles*, as I have seen both, in their Seals Afterwards, about the year 1340, *William Montacute* the younger, Earl of *Salisbury*, rescu'd it by force of arms out of the hands of the Scots; and in the year of our Lord 1393 sold *Man and the Crown thereof* to *William Scrope* for a great sum of money, as *Walsingham* tells us *Scrope* being afterwards beheaded, and his Estate confiscate for treason, it fell into Henry the IVth's hands, who bestow'd it upon *Henry Percy* Earl of *Northumberland* in a kind of triumph over *William Scrope* (whom he, while a private man, had taken and beheaded for aspiring to the Crown;) upon this condition, That he and his posterity, at the Coronation of the Kings of England, should carry the Sword before him, which the said King Henry wore by his side, at his return to England, commonly call'd *Lancaster-sword* But take the King's own words, as they stand in the Record *We of our special grace, have given and granted to Henry Earl of Northumberland, the Isle, Castle, Pile, and Lordship of* Man, *with all such Islands and seignories thereunto belonging, as were the possessions of Sir* William Le Scrope *Knight, deceased, whom in his life we conquer'd, and do declare conquer'd, and which, by reason of this our conquest, we seiz'd into our hands Which Conquest and Decree, as touching the person of the said William, and all the lands, tenements, goods, and chattels, as well within as without the Kingdom, belonging to him, are now, at the petition of the Commons of our Kingdom, and by the consent of the Lords Temporal assembled in Parliament, ratify'd and confirm'd*, &c *To have and to hold to the said Earl and his heirs*, &c *by service of carrying on every Coronation-day of us and our heirs, at the left shoulder of us and our heirs, by himself or by a sufficient and honourable deputy, that sword naked which we wore when we arriv'd in Holdrness, call'd Lancaster-sword*, &c However, this *Henry Percy* was attainted four years after, and though it was not long before he was restor'd in blood, yet he was depriv'd of *Man*, which was given first to *William Stanley*, and after that to *John Stanley*, together with the advowson of the Bishoprick, &c whose posterity were honour'd with the title of Earls of *Derby*, and commonly call'd *Kings of Man*

Lords of *Man*

The Arms of the Kings of *Man*

The old Coat of Arms of Sicily

* *Vide complicato*

An 1 H 4 Rot 2 bundle 2

Annals of Tho Otterborn an H 4

THE

THE

INSERTIONS

Made by

Dr. HOLLAND,

In his English Translation of

Mr. CAMDEN's

BRITANNIA,

WITH

The PAGES, and LINES, in this WORK, to which they relate.

THE

INSERTIONS

Made by

Dr. HOLLAND,

In his Engliſh Tranſlation of

Mr. *CAMDEN*'s Britannia.

[*Note*, That the word ſet here in the Roman letter at the beginning of each Addition, is the word, *after* which the Addition comes; and that the reaſons why they were not inſerted in the *body* of the Work, are given in the *General Preface* to this Edition.]

The PICTS.

Page Line.
cxxxix. 28 PLace — *Made againſt the Incurſion of the* Picts.

The SCOTS.

cxliv. 7. MAurus — *Doubtleſs out of him*

The Engliſh SAXONS

clxiv. 50. EAſter — *But rather, as I think, of the Riſing of Chriſt, which our Progenitors call Eaſt, as we do now that part whence the Sun riſeth*

The Degrees of ENGLAND

ccxxxvi. 40 DIgnity — *With the Coronet.*

ccxxxvii 20 Honour — Comes Domeſticorum, *Lord Great Maſter of the Houſhold*; Comes ſacrarum largitionum, *Lord High Treaſurer*; Comes ſacræ veſtis, *Maſter of the Wardrobe*; Comes Stabuli, *Maſter of the Horſe*, Comes Theſauri, *Treaſurer*; Comes Orientis, *Lieutenant of the Eaſt*, Comes Britanniæ, Comes Africæ, &c

ccxxxviii 62. Territories — *As for the Earl Marſhal of* England, *King* Richard *the ſecond gave that title firſt to* Thomas Mowbray, *Earl of* Nottingham, *whereas before they were ſimply ſtiled* Marſhals of England; *and after the baniſhment of* Mowbray, *he granted it to* T. Holland, *Duke of* Surrey, *ſubſtituted Earl Marſhal in his place, that he ſhould carry a Rod of gold enamell'd black at both ends, whenas before they us'd one of wood*

ibid 67 Time — *Who conferr'd that title upon* J. *Lord* Beaumont

ccxl 52. To Parliament — *And it is noted that the ſaid prudent King* Edward I *ſummoned always thoſe of ancient Families, that were moſt wiſe, to his Parliaments; but omitted their Sons after their death, if they were not anſwerable to their Parents in Underſtanding*

Chev-

Page. Line.

ccxl. 64 Chevalier—— For the Common Law doth not acknowledge Baron to be a Name of Dignity

The Law-Courts of ENGLAND.

cclvii 7 ARches——He is call'd Dean, for that he hath Jurisdiction in 13 Parishes of London, exempt from the Bishop of London; which Number maketh a Deanerie.

CORNWALL.

3 59. SEA-Coast—— Opposite to this County

4. 8 Make—— The Inhabitants do discover these Mines by certain Tin-stones lying on the face of the ground, which they call Shoad, being somewhat smooth and round

ibid 24 Breaking—Stamping, drying

ibid 26 Ingenious—— There are also two sorts of Tin; Black-tin, which is Tin ore, broken and washed, but not yet founded into Metal, and White-Tin, that is molten into Metal; and that is either soft Tin, which is best Merchantable, or hard Tin, less Merchantable

ibid 46 St Jerom—— Out of the Sclavonian Tongue.

ibid. 53 Saracens——If they did mean by that Name, the ancient Panims

ibid 69 Afterwards— This Richard began to make Ordinances for these Tin-works, and afterwards, &c

5 4 Rest——Called Lord Warden of the Stannaries of Stannum, that is, Tin

ibid 6 For, Every Month——Every three Weeks

ibid 8 Controversies——In Causes personal between tinner and tinner, and between tinner and foreigner, except in Causes of Land, Life or Member

ibid 12 Himself— From him to the Duke, from the Duke to the King In matters of moment, there are by the Warden, General Parliaments or several Assemblies summoned, whereunto Jurats are sent out of every Stannary, whose Constitutions do bind them As for those that deal with Tin, they are of four sorts, the Owners of the Soil, the Adventurers, the Merchants or Regraters, and the Labourers, called the Spadiards (of their Spade) who, poor men, are pitifully out-eaten by usurious Contracts But the Kings of England and Dukes of Cornwall in their times have reserved to themselves a Pre-emption of Tin (by the Opinion of the Learned in the Law) as well in regard of the Propriety, as being chief Lords and Proprietaries, as of their Royal Prerogative

ibid 20 Stamp'd—They call it Coynage

ibid 22 Without—Under forfeiture of their Tin

13 31 Main Amber— Which being a great Rock advanced upon some others of meaner size with so equal a Counterpoize, a man may stir, &c

14 16 Main-land—So they they say of it, It is Land and Island twice a day

17. 14 Harbour— And neighbour to it is Golden the Inheritance of Tregian, a House ancient and well ally'd But descending, to the haven's mouth you may see Fenten Gollan, in English Harteiwell, lately the seat of Carminow, a family anciently of high esteem for blood and wealth, between whom and the Lord Scroope two hundred years since, was a Plea commenced in the Court of Chivalry, for bearing in a Shield Azure, a Bend Or

ibid 62 Sand—— Whereunto fall many fresh Rivulets, amongst which that is principal which passe b by Lanladron, whose Lord S Serls Lanladron, wa

Temp. Ed I summoned a Baron to the Parliament, in that age when the fit t men for wisdom and worth among the Gentry were called to Parliaments, and their Posterity omitted, if they were defective therein

Page. Line

21 20. Aldermen——Somewhat westward from this lieth Cligarth, the Habitation of the Bevils, of especial good note for Antiquity and Gentry

ibid. 21. Memorable—But a small River passing by Minhevet, whereby is Pole, the seat of the Trelawnies, to whom with others, the Inheritance of the Courtneys Earls of Devonshire accrued

ibid. 52. Monte-Edgcombe—At the East-side of Tamar.

24. 62 Digression— Between Padstow and Tindagel inwardly there extendeth a fruitful vein, and therein flourish the Families of Roscarrock, Carnsew, Penkevel, Cavel, Penkavel, of ancient name and great respect in this Coast

25 6. Only Daughter—And sole Heir

ibid 35. Azores—— As I shall shew more fully in my Annals

ibid 54 Tamerton——By Tamar an ancient Manour of the Trevilions, to whom, by marriages, the Inheritance of Walesborough and Ralegh of Netlested descended

26 10 Tin—— So that the Countrey people had this Byword for it,

Hengston down well ywrought,
Is worth London deer ybought

ibid 19 Man—— Beneath it Tamar leaveth Halton [formerly] the habitation of the Rouses, anciently Lords of Little-Modbery in Devonshire

ibid 69 Besants—Five, Four, Three, Two and One

ibid 76 Honours—And at last turn'd Monk at Bermondsey

27 2 Henry the first— By the Daughter of Sir Robert Corbet.

ibid 33 Germany—— Among the Competitors of the Empire

28 8 Edward the second—Advanced thereunto by his Brother Edward the third

DEVONSHIRE

33 74 INhabitants——In Sea-services of all sorts

35 30 Call'd De Campo Arnulphi—— In old Deeds

37 17 Bruiers heretofore—— Who built here a Religious House

39 13 Religion----And, for that, was accounted the Apostle of Germany, and Canoniz'd a Saint

41 30. War——Against Henry the seventh

42 8. Soon after——For Conspiracy against the King

35 Henry the eighth---And designed Heir-Apparent

43 12 Ancestors—— Under Pouderham, Ken a pretty Brook enters into Ex, which riseth near Holcombe, where in a Park is a fair place built by Sir Thomas Denis, whose family fetcheth their first Off-spring and Surname from the Danes, and were anciently written Le Dan Denis, by which name the Cornish call'd the Danes

20 Parts——And was given by Isabel, heir to the Earls of Devonshire, to King Edward the first, when her Issue fail'd

74 Chanel—After it hath pass'd down by Ford, wh re Adelize, daughter to Baldewin of Okehampton, founded an Abbey for Cistercian Monks, 1140

45 31 Time---From whom it descended to the Courtneys Suddenly turning his Chanel, maketh ro b-ward, insu'ating in a manner Potheridge, the Mansion of the Famiy surnamed Monke Happily, for that some one of them being a profess'd Monk, by dispensation to continue his House, return'd to temporal estate as that noble House in France surnamed Archevelque, that is, Archbishop, t k that name to continue the memory that on of the Progenitors of an Archbishop, return'd b d [illegible]

Page. Line. *fallen to a temporal man. Certainly from whencesoever the name came, they have worshipfully match'd, and not long since with one of the Daughters of* Arthur Plantagenet, *Viscount* Lisley, *natural son to King* Edward *the fourth*

47 44 Day — *From the ancient* Gallick *Language, the same with old* British.

48 31 Vernon—*Because he was born there*

49 Devonshire — *And link'd as Cousin, and next heir to the said* Isabel

51 Title—*And by a Precept to the High-sheriff of the Shire, commanded he should be so acknowledg'd* Reginald Courtney *was the first of this Family that came into* England, *brought hither by King* Henry *the second, and by him advanced with the marriage of the heir of the Barony of* Okehampton, *for that he procured the marriage between the said King and* Elenor *heir of* Poictou *and* Aquitain *But whether he was branched from the House of* Courtney *before it was matched in the Royal Blood of* France, *or after, which our Monks affirm, but* du Tillet *Keeper of the Records of* France, *doubteth, I may say somewhat in another place*

60 Thomas—*Taken at* Towton field

63 Created—*Sir*

64 Devonshire—*Who within three months revolting from King* Edward, *his advancer, most ingratefully, was apprehended, and without Process executed at* Bridgewater

49 3 Ireland—*Which title he affected, as descended from a Cousin and Heir of* Humfrey Stafford *Earl of* Devonshire

13 Honour—*Which he enjoy'd a few years as his Predecessor* Humfrey Stafford *did Months.*

DORSETSHIRE

51 27. DEvonshire—*And some part of* Somersetshire

54. 65 Buildings—*By Sea-adventures*

77 Corffe—*Seated upon a great stately Hill*

78 Age—*Until of late it hath been repaired*

56 35 Ignorance—*Here was first bred among the religious men (as I have read)* John Morton *Cardinal and Archbishop of* Canterbury, *born at* St Andrews Milborne, *worthily advanced to so high places for his good service in working* England's *Happiness by the Union of the two Houses of* Lancaster *and* York, *and of this Family there hath issued both* Robert *Bishop of* Worcester, *and many Gentlemen of very good note in this Country and elsewhere*

46 Town—*Whereof one is called* Maumbury, *being an Acre inditched, another* Poundbury *somewhat greater, and the third a mile off, as a Camp, with five Trenches, containing some ten Acres, call'd* Maiden castle

59 Emperors—*Found there, and especially at* Fordington *hard by*

70 Romans— *It* [Dorchester] *had anciently a Castle in that place where the Grey-Friers built their Convent out of the ruins thereof, and hath now but three Parish-Churches, whereas the compass of the old Town seemeth to have been very large*

57 34 Brien—*A Baron*

36 For, Humphrey Stafford—Hugh Stafford

39 Lancashire—*And brought hither by the first Marquess of* Dorset

63 Viscount—*To the Lord* Thomas Howard

58. 36 Second — *Who, when he came to challenge the Crown of* England *in the year* 1142, *arrived here, besieged and took the Castle, which was defended by* Robert Lacy *against him in behalf of King* Stephen, *and afterward* Robert *of* Lincoln, *a man of mighty possessions in those parts defended the same against King* Stephen. *But*, &c

59 7 Seat — *Whereof, as some were famous, so* Hugh Turberville, *in the time of King* Edward *the first, was infamous for his infamous practices with the* French

74 *For*, Malbanch—Malbanc.

60 9 Hill—*Very defective of Water*

45. England—*And, I have been informed that it continued there till the time of King* Henry *the eighth, yet the Inhabitants have a Tradition, that an old City stood upon the place which is called the* Castle-green, *and by some* Bolt-bury, *now a fair plain so sited, that as of one side it joineth to the town; so of another it is a strange sight, to look down to the Vale under it; whereby in the west end of the Chapel of* St John *(as I hear now) standeth a Roman Inscription reversed*

52 Howard—*Brother of* Thomas *last Duke of* Norfolk *receiv'd of King* James *the Title*, &c.

61 36 *For*, Thomas Poynings—*Sir* Thomas Poynings, *son of Sir* Edward Poynings

38 Expir'd — *As bastardly Slips seldom take good root*

62 10 Well-inhabited—*But few fair Buildings*

50 Buried — Gertrude Blunt, *daughter to* William *Lord* Montjoy

54 Wife—Margaret, *daughter and heir to Sir* John Beauchamp *of* Bleteneshoe

63 74 Robert Cecil—*Now Earl of* Salisbury

79 Cranborne—*South from hence lieth* Woodland *emparked, sometime the seat of the worshipful Family of* Filioll, *the heirs whereof are married to* Edward Seymor, *after Duke of* Somerset, *and* Willoughby *of* Wallerton

64 59 Publick—*Who ended his life with sudden death,* An 1608, *and left* Robert *his son, his successor, who deceasing within the year, left the said honour again to* Richard *his hopeful son, whom he begat of the Lady* Margaret Howard, *daughter to the late Duke of* Norfolk

SOMERSETSHIRE

67 38 PAsturage—*And yet not without stony Hills.*

54 Somertun—*In the very first limit of the Shire westward, where* Ex *riseth in a solitary and hilly Moor, first appeareth* Dulverton, *a silly Market, according to the soil, and near unto it was a small religious House of black Canons at* Barelinch, *who in later times acknowledged the* Fettiplaces *their Founders*

69 62 People—*And between those* Clivers *was an old Abbey of white Monks, founded by* William de Romara, *Cousin to the Earl of* Lincoln

70 11 Evel—*Which rose by the decay of* Ilchester

16 Acres —*And there appear about the Hill five or six Ditches, so steep, that a man shall sooner slide down, than go down*

36 Camelion—*Hereby are two Towns,* West-Camelet *and* East Camelet, *or* Queens-Camelet, *happily for that it had been in Dowry to some Queen*

49 Courtney—*Here, to digress aside, from the River* Ivel, Winecaunton, *no mean Market, is neighbour to this* North-Cadbury, *and near thereunto is* Pen, &c

71 1 Ruins—*And two Towers upon the Bridge*

19 Inward—*By* Langport *a proper Market-town*

72 24 Family — *And here I must not forget* Preston, *sometimes the seat of* John Sturton, *younger son to the first Lord* Sturton, *one of whose heirs was married to* Sidenham *of* Brimston *thereby*

Page Lane

72 29 Who—*Who being taken up in the* New-forest *by* King Henry *the second, in a hunting journey, prov'd a great man*

32 Estate—*Married* Beatrix *of* Vannes, *Widow to* Reginald *Earl of* Cornwall

73. 1 Fields—*Near* Wivelscomb *assign'd anciently to the Bishop of* Bath

12 *For*, John Popham—*Sir* John Popham

74. 19 Beauchamp—*And Earl of* Hertford, *whom King* Edward *the sixth afterwards honour'd, first with the name of Lord and Baron* Seimor, *to be annex'd to his other Titles, lest (as the King saith in the Patent) the name of his mother's Family shou'd be overshadowed with any other Stile, and yet afterward created him Duke of* Somerset

75 20 Alone—Parret, *having received the same river, runneth alone swelling with certain sandy shelves sometime in his Chanel, by the Hundred of* N Pederton *anciently acknowledging the* Bluets *to have been Lords thereof, who are thought to have brought that Name from* Bluet *in* Little-Britain

21 East—*Which openeth itself near* Castle-Cary, *which* William Lovel *Ld thereof held against K* Stephen *in the behalf of* Maud *the Empress right inheritrix of the Crown of* England, *whose issue-male failing in the time of* K Edward *the third, by heir-female it came to* Nicholas de St Maure, *a Baron (of a distinct Family from that which was a few lines before mention'd,) and shortly after, about the time of* Henry *the fifth by an heir-female, again to the Lords* Zouch *of* Harringworth, *as a moiety of the Lands of Ld* Zouch *of* Ashby de la Zouch *came before by coheirs to the house of this* S Maures. *But when the Lord* Zouch *was attainted by K* Henry *the seventh for assisting K* Richard *the third, this Castle was given by the K to* Robert Willoughby *Lord* Brooke, *as his Lands at* Bridgewater *to the Lord* Daubeney, *and then he was restored in blood From* Castle-Cary *this water passeth by* Lites-Cary, *to be remember'd in respect to the late Owner* Thomas Lyte, *a Gentleman studious of all good knowledge, and so to* Somerton

76 21 Father—*Better'd this Haven*

25. *For*, Trivet—Strivet

ibid Cornwall—*Who founded also the Hospital of St* John *here, and* Durkeswell-*Abby*

28 *For*, De la Fert—De la Fort

31 Lancaster—*As some Lands hereabout, by another Sister, came to* Brees, *and so by* Cantalupe *to Lord* Zouch

77 13 Æstuarie—*Where we saw* Honispell *an ancient Manor of the* Cogans, *Men of great fame in the Conquest of* Ireland

37 There—*Of the* Fitz James

78. 10 Island—*Under a great Hill rising in great height with a Tower thereon, which they call the* Tor

79. 50 City—*Environ'd with a large Wall a mile about, and replenish'd with stately buildings*

54 Wallnut-tree—*In the holy Church-yard*

57 Abundance—*But that is now gone, and a young Tree in the place*

ibid Hawthorn-tree—*In* Wirral-*Park, hard by*

81. 3 Antiocheis—*Wherein he describ'd the Wars of the Christians for recovery of the Holy-land, and was there present with King* Richard *the first speaking of* Britain

83 37. Lead—*Which lay long at* Lambith *in the Duke of* Norfolk's-*house*

85 77. River—*Verily near the Church there is a Spring call'd St* Andrew's *Well, the fairest, deepest, and most plentiful that I have seen, by and by making a swift Brook*

86. 2 Antiquity—*And the Cloisters adjoyning very fair and spacious.*

Page. Line

86 58 Wall—*But this rich Church was despoiled of many fair possessions in the time of* Edward *the sixth, when* England *felt all Miseries which happen under a Child-King*

87 36. Since—*To the Lord* Hungerford.

57 Castle—*Consisting of four round Turrets*

61 Nunnery—*Which afterwards was the first House, and as it were Mother to the* Carthusians, *or* Charter-house-*Monks in* England, *as* Hinton, *not far off, near* Farnley-*Castle, was the second*

88 48 Drawers—*And have their guides.*

89 38 Deorham—*In* Glocestershire

90 9 Disturbances — *And the suppression of Religious Houses ensuing*

21 Strangers—*For Health twice a year*

90 34 Bath—*Who dy'd shortly after, leaving, by his wife the sister of* H Daubeney *Earl of* Bridgewater, John *second Earl of this family, who by the daughter of* George *Lord* Roos, *had* John *Lord* Fitz-warin, *who deceas'd before his father, having by* Frances *the daughter of Sir* Thomas Kitson *of* Hengrave, William, *now third Earl of* Bath

95 25 Shipward—*Alias* Barstaple

96 12 Robert — *Call'd by the Normans* Fitz-Harding

14 King Henry—*The second*

97 72 Invested—Sir Edward, *&c*

98 2 Foot-ball—*(Which never suffereth sudden Over greatness to last long)*

WILTSHIRE

99 71 PART — *Which they call* North Wiltshire

101 64 East-Angles—*In* Cambridgeshire *and* Suffolk

102 4 Crecklade—*By* Marianus

9 Oxford — *West from that is* Highworth *highly seated, a well-known Market,* &c

48. Wotton-Basset—*Having this primitive Name from* Wood

107 8 It—*Men of great Renown in their Time.*

10 Petronilla—*Or Parnel.*

32 Samond—*Or truly* De S Amando, St Amand. *Afterward of the* Baintons *from them.*

108. 36 Made—*Steward of his House and,* &c

110 23 Lancaster — *And sometime to the Earl of* Salisbury

52 House—*In a foul Soil, which,* &c

53 Fire—*Hath risen eftsoons more fair*

111 38 Sold—*But for remnants of* Roman *Antiquities, I could discover none here, only on the Eastside are seen some trenches upon the hills, and on the West a natural round and high cop'd Hill, called* Clay-hill

49 Hungerford—*But in the Church which hath been Collegiate, there is seen but one defaced Monument of them The last Lord* Hungerford, *created by* King Henry *the eighth, had his Denomination of this place, but enjoy'd that Honour a short while, being condemn'd of a Crime not to to be utter'd*

ibid 69 Yanesbury—*Opposite to this on the other side of the Water, is another less Camp-place singly ditch'd, call'd* Dunshat, *and about one mile and a half from* Yanesbury, *another likewise with a single Trench, call'd* Woldsbury *I have noted the names, as the Country-people term them, and others may collect some Matter thereby more than I can*

112 8 Owners — *And amongst them the Lord* Brook, *who repair'd it and dy'd at it*

40 Nobility—*And a few miles from thence, is* Hindon, *a quick Market, and known for nothing else that I could see*

Sarisbu

Page. Line

113 43 Sarisburia——*And Sarisburiaha.*

114 55 Soldiers——*Against the Churchmen*

ibid Water——*The Churchmen first, and then,* &c

118 31 Issue——*Having unhappily slain his own Son, while he trained him at Tilting.*

57 Edward—*Earl of* Warwick

60. Restor'd—*By* Henry *the eighth in a full Parliament about the fifth year of his Reign*

69. Third—*Duke of* Glocester, *and Brother to King* Edward *the fourth*

70 Edward—*Whom his Unkle King* Edward, *in the* 17th *year of his Reign, created Earl of* Salisbury, *and* Richard *his Father usurping the Kingdom, made,* &c.

119 39 Place—*Famous is this* Clarendon, *for that here in the year* 1164. *was made a certain Recognition and Record of the Customs and Liberties of the Kings of* England, *before the Prelates and Peers of this Kingdom, for avoiding dissensions between the Clergy, Judges and Barons of the Realm, which were call'd* The Constitutions of Clarendon *Of which so many as the Pope approved, have been set down in the Tomes of the Councils, the rest omitted albeit* Thomas Becket *then Archbishop of* Canterbury, *and the rest of the Bishops approved them also Hereby is* Ivy Church, *sometime a small Priory, where, as Tradition runneth, in our Grandfathers remembrance was found a Grave, and therein a Corps of twelve foot, and not far off a stock of wood hollowed, and the concave lin'd with Lead, with a Book therein of very thick Parchment, all written with Capital Roman Letters But, it had lain so long, that when the leaves were touched, they moulder'd to dust Sir* Thomas Eliot *who saw it, judged it to be an History No doubt he that so carefully laid it up, hoped it shou'd be found, and discover some things memorable to Posterity*

126. 25. Arles—*I have heard, that in the time of King* Henry *the eighth, there was found near this place a Table of Metal, as it had been Tin and Lead commix'd, inscrib'd with many Letters, but in so strange a Character, that neither Sir* Thomas Eliot *nor Mr* Lily *School-master of St* Paul's, *could read it, and therefore neglected it Had it been preserv'd, somewhat happily might have been discovered as concerning* Stone-henge, *which now lieth obscured*

127 45 Land-marks——*Within one mile of* Selbury *is* Albury, *an uplandish Village built in an old Camp, as it seemeth, but of no large Compass, for it is environed with a fair Trench, and hath four Gaps or Gates, in two of which stand huge Stones as jambs, but so rude, that they seem rather natural than artificial, of which sort there are some other in the said Village*

128 69 Runs—*Eastward*

130 28 Is—*Not long since the Seat of the* Darcls

32 Before—*And hereby runneth the limit between this Shire and* Berkshire

HAMSHIRE

135. 47 BAY——*As more inwardly, on the other side, are the two Castles of St* Andrew *and* Netley.

137 14 Second——*And afterward King* Henry *the sixth granted to the Mayor, Bailiffs and Burgesses, that it shou'd be a County by it self, with other Liberties.*

66 It——*From thence it runneth down, and receives from the East a Brook passing by* Bullingdon, *in whose Parish is a place call'd* Tilbury hill, *and contains a square Field, by estimation ten acres ditched about, in some places deeper than other,*

Page Line. *wherein hath been found tokens of Wells, and about which the Plough-men have found square Stones and Roman Coins, as they report; for the place I have not seen.*

138 16 River—*Out of the which,* Mary *daughter to King* Stephen *being their Abbess, and his only heir surviving, was convey'd secretly by* Matthew *of* Alsace *son to the Earl of* Flanders, *and to him married But after she had born to him two Daughters, was enforced by Sentence of the Church to return hither again according to her Vow*

142. 7 Devotion—*But among others St* Swithin *continues yet of greatest fame, not so much for his Sanctity, as for the Rain which usually falls about the Feast of his Translation in* July, *by reason the Sun then is Cosmically with* Præsepe *and* Aselli, *noted by ancient writers to be rainy Constellations, and not for his weeping, or other weeping Saints* Margaret *the Virgin, and* Mary Magdalen, *whose Feasts are shortly after, as some superstitiously credulous have believed.*

144 21 Quincy——*In these words,* Azur a dix Mascles D'or en orm d'un Canton de nostre propre Armes d'Engleterre, cest favour, de Goul un Leopard passant d'or, armée d'azur

24. *For,* William—*Sir* William

ibid England—*Earl of* Wiltshire, *and Lord St* John *of* Basing

26 Winchester—*A man prudently pliable to times; raised not suddenly, but by degrees in Court, excessive in vast informous buildings, temperate in all other things, full of years, for he lived* 97 *years, and fruitful in his generation, for he saw* 103 *issued from him by* Elizabeth *his wife, daughter to Sir* William Capel *Knight And now his Grandchild* William *enjoys the said Honours*

55 Bere—*Whereby is* Wickham, *a Mansion of that ancient Family of* Vuedal.

57 Winchester—*Where the marriage was solemniz'd between King* Henry *the sixth, and* Margaret *of* Anjou

147 9 *For,* Luke—*Sir* Luke

33 *For,* William—*Sir* William.

150 35 Market—*By it* Fremantle, *in a Park where King* John *much hunted*

BARKSHIRE.

162 10 PORtugal——*And widow to* Gilbert *Lord* Talbot

23 L'Isle—*By King* Henry *the sixth*

26 L'Isle—*By a Patent, without any such regard.*

47 Northumberland—*In the time of King* Edward *the sixth*

49 Attainted—*By Queen* Mary

52 L'Isle—*Who ended his Life issueless*

166 53 *For,* Thomas—*Sir* Thomas

58 Pembroke——*But Queen* Elizabeth *gave it to* John Baptista Castilion, *a Piemontese, of her Privy Chamber for faithful Service in her Dangers*

168 35 Henry——*With his Wife both veiled and crown'd, for that she had been a Queen and professed Nun*

170 40 Belongs—*Hereby falleth* Ladden, *a small water, into the* Thames

43 Dug-up—*And next to it* Billingshere, *the inhabitation of Sir* Henry Nevil, *issued from the Lords* Abergevenny

50. Montacutes—*And amongst them the first Earl of* Salisbury *of this Family founded a Priory, wherein, some say, he was buried Certes his Wife, the daughter of the Lord* Grandison, *was buried*

Page Line. buried there, and in the Inscription of his Tomb it was specified, that her Father was descended out of Burgundy, Cousin-german to the Emperor of Constantinople, the King of Hungary, and Duke of Bavaria, and brought into England by Edmund Earl of Lancaster.

170 59 Southealington——Afterwards, Maidenhuth

171 65 Fourth——And Sir Reginald Bray

173 11 For, William Paynell——Sir Walter Paveley

SUTH-REY

181 27 MONKS—— Commonly called White-Monks, which Abbey being a Grand-child, (as they term'd it) from Cisterce in Burgundy, was so fruitful here in England, that it was Mother to the Abbeys of Gerondon, Ford, Tame, Cumb, and Grandmother to Bordesley, Bidlesdon, Bruer, Bindon, and Dunkeswell For so Religious Orders were wont to keep in pedigree-manner the Propagation of their Order, as a Deduction of Colonies out of them

182 57 Knights—Better'd by an heir of T Camel.

ibid Seat——Where King Henry the seventh repair'd and enlarg'd the Manour-house, being the inheritance of the Lady Margaret Countess of Richmond, his Mother, who liv'd there in her later time Newark sometime a small Priory environed with divided streams

59 Clinton— And Admiral of England

67 Place— As of the next Village Ripley, G de Ripley a Ringleader of our Alchimists, and a mystical Impostor

185 36 For, Thomas—Sir Thomas

39 For, Anthony—Sir Anthony

186. ult Nottingham—Of whom more in my Annals.

187 21 Current— By Stoke-Dabernoun, so named of the ancient Possessors the Dabernouns, Gentlemen of great note Afterwards, by inheritance from them the possession of the Lord Bray And by Alsher, sometimes a Retiring-place belonging to the Bishops of Winchester

39 Inaugurated— Upon an open Stage in the Market-place

190 64. First——For Black-Canons

65 Surrey—In the year 1127, which was famous for the Statute of Merton, enacted in the 21st of Henry the eighth, and also for Walter de Merton, founder of Merton-College in Oxford, born and bred here

191 26 For, J —— Sir James.

28 Hoo—— And Hastings To digress a little from the river Eastward from Croydon standeth Addington, now the habitation of Sir Oliff Leigh, whereby is to be seen the ruble of a Castle of Sir Robert Agvilon, and from him of the Lords Bardolph, who held certain Lands here in fee by Seryeanty to find in the King's Kitchen at the Coronation one to make a dainty Dish which they called Mapigernoun & Dilgerunt What that was, I leave to the skilful in ancient Cookery

192. 32 Wandlesworth—— Between Putney, the native Soil of Thomas Cromwell, one of the flowting-Stocks of Fortune

193 51. Of—Humphrey Duke

194 11. Surrey—Who had married his Sister

21 Son——And married the Daughter of Hugh Earl of Vermandois; whereupon his Posterity (as some suppose) us'd the Arms of Vermandois His Son William dying in the Holy Land about 1142

32 John——Who slew Alan de la Zouch, in presence of the Judges of the Realm

45 Arundels—— For Richard their Son, who married in the House of Lancaster (after his Father was wickedly beheaded for siding with his Sovereign King Edward the second, by the malignant Envy of the Queen) was both Earl of Arundel and Surrey, and left both Earldoms to Richard his Son, who contrary-wise lost his head for siding against his Sovereign King Richard the second But Thomas his Son, to repair his Father's Dishonour, lost his life for his Prince and Country in France, leaving his Sisters his Heirs for the Lands not entailed, who were married to Thomas Mowbray Duke of Norfolk, &c to Sir Rowland Lenthall, and Sir William Beauchampe, Lord of Abergavenny

194. 49 Time——After the Execution of Richard Earl of Arundel

69 Surry—— And Richard second Son of King Edward the fourth, having married the Heir of Mowbray, receiv'd all the titles due to the Mowbrays by creation from his Father After ward, King Richard the third, having dispatch'd the said Richard, &c

SUTH-SEX

195 38 ROcks — And the South-west wind doth tyrannize thereon, casting up Beach infinitely

198 48 Domine — Neither he only adorned the Lord's House, but repaired also the Bishop's Houses

53 Castle— Near the Haven of Chichester is W Witering, where (as the Monuments of the Church testifie) Ælla the first founder of the Kingdom of Suth-sex arrived

199 20 Young— But now it is most famous for good Cockles and full Lobsters

201 43 Arundel— By virtue of an Entail

50 Fitz-Alans—— Edmund, second Earl, son to Richard, marry'd the heir of the Earl of Surrey, and was beheaded through the malicious fury of Queen Isabel, not lawfully convicted, for that he oppos'd himself in King Edward the second's behalf against her wicked practices His Son Richard petition'd in Parliament to be restor'd to blood, lands and goods, for that his father was put to death not try'd by his Peers, according to the Law and Great Charter of England Nevertheless, whereas the Attainder of him was confirm'd by Parliament, he was forc'd to amend his Petition, and upon the amendment thereof, he

4 Edw III was restor'd by the King's meer grace Richard his Son, as his grandfather died for his Sovereign, lost his life for banding against his Sovereign King Richard the second But Thomas his Son more honourably ended his life, serving King Henry the fifth valorously in France, and leaving his Sisters his heirs general Sir John of Arundel Lord Maltravers, his next Cousin and Heir Male, obtain'd of King Henry the sixth, the Earldom of Arundel, as we even now declared (See before the Earls of Surrey) and also was by the said King for his good Service created Duke of Touraine Of the succeeding Earls I find nothing memorable

204 4 Montacute——Which for building oweth much to the late Viscount, and formerly to Sir William Fitz-Williams, Earl of Southampton

ibid Midherst——That is Middle wood

56 Arun—— Inwardly is Michelgrove, that is, Great Grove, the Heir general, whereof so surnamed, was married to John Shelley, whereby with the Profession of the Law, and a marriage with one of the Coheirs of Beknap, the family of Shelley was greatly enriched

205 29 Thence—— Upon a Statute made against Women absenting themselves from their Husbands, &c

Page. Line

205. 57 Steningham— *In latter times it had a Cell of Black Monks, wherein was enshrined St* Cudman *an obscure Saint, and visited by Pilgrims with Oblations*

206 17. Knighthood — *Thence by* Cuckfield *to* Linfeld, *where, in former Ages, was a small Nunnery, and so by* Malling *sometime a Manour appertaining to the Archbishops of* Canterbury

23 County—*Seated it is upon a rising almost on every side That it hath been walled, there are no apparent tokens Southward it hath under it, as it were, a great* Suburb, *called* South-over, *another westward, and beyond the River a third eastward called* Cliffe, *because it is under a Chalky Cliff In the time of the English-Saxon Government, when King* Athelstan *made a Law, that Money shou'd not be coined but in good Town*, *he appointed two Minters or Coiners for this Place*

207. 26 Hands — *From* Lewis, *the river as it descendeth, so swelleth, that the bottom cannot contain it, and therefore maketh a large Mere, and is fed more full with a Brooket falling from* Laughton, *a Seat of the* Pelhams (*a Family of especial respect*) *by* Gline, *that is, in the British tongue, the* Vale, *the habitation of the* Morleys, *whose Antiquity the name doth testify And afterward, albeit it gathereth it self into a chanel, yet oftentimes it overfloweth the low Lands about it, to no small detriment*

36 Cuckmer — *Which yet affordeth no commodious haven, though it be fed with a* Fresh *which insulateth* Michelham, *where* Gilbert de Aquila *founded a Priory for Black Canons And then at* East-bourn *the Shore ariseth into so high a Promontory, called of the* Beach, Beachy-Points *and* Beau-Cliff (*for the fair shew being utter changeably compounded with rows of Chalk and Flint*) *that it is esteem'd the highest Cliff of all the South-coast of* England *As hitherto from* Arundel *and beyond, the Countrey along the Coast, for a great breadth, mounteth up into high hills, called the* Downes, *which for rich fertility giveth place to few Valleys and Plains, so now it falleth into such a low Level and Marsh, that the People think it hath been overflowed by the Sea They call it* Pevensey-Marsh, *of* Pevensey.

44 Conqueror——*And then had fifty six Burgesses After the Attainder of his Son* William *Earl of* Moriton, *it came to King* Henry *the first by Escheat In the composition between* Stephen *and King* Henry *the second, both Town and Castle, with whatsoever* Richard de Aquila *had of the honour of* Pevensey, *which after his name was called* Honor de Aquila *and* Baronia de Aquila, *or of the Eagle, was assigned to* William *Son to King* Stephen *But he surrender'd it, with* Norwich, *into King* Henry *the second's hands, in the year* 1158 *when he restor'd to him all such Lands as* Stephen *was seised of before he usurped the Crown of* England

208 2 It—*Which had fallen to the Crown by Escheat; for that* Gilbert de Aquila *had passed into* Normandy, *against the King's good will, to* Peter *Earl of* Savoy *the Queen's Uncle But he, fearing the envy of the* English *against Foreigners, relinquish'd it to the King, and so at length it came to the Dutchy of* Lancaster

36 Bologne——*About the time of King* Edward *the second, Sir* John Fienes *married the heir of* Monceaux, *his Son* William *married one of the heirs of the Lord* Say, *his Son likewise the heir of* Balisford, *whose Son Sir* Roger Fienes *married the daughter of* Holland, *and in the first year of King* Henry *the sixth, built of Brick the large, fair, uniform and convenient house here, Castle-like within a deep Moat*

208. 43 Dacre —— *And to have precedence before the Lord* Dacre *of* Gilesland *heir-male of the Family*

44 Time —— *The heirs lineally descending from him being enrich'd by one of the heirs of the Lord* Fitz-Hugh.

46. Dacre —— *Son to the unfortunate* Thomas *Lord* Dacre

49 Civility—— *And by her hath fair issue In whose behalf it was published, declared and adjudged by the Lords Commissioners for Martial Causes, in the second year of the Reign of King* James, *with his privity and assent Royal, That the said* Margaret *ought to bear, have, and enjoy, the name, state, degree, title, stile, honour, place, and precedency of the Barony of* Dacre; *to have and to hold, to her, and the issue of her body in as full and ample manner, as any of her Ancestors enjoy'd the same And that her Children may and shall have, take, and enjoy the place and precedence respectively, as the Children of her Ancestors Barons* Dacre *have formerly had and enjoy'd*

53 Return —— *About three miles from* Pevensey, *is* Beckes-hill, *a place much frequented by St* Richard *Bishop of* Chichester, *and where he died Under this is* Bulverhith *in an open shore, with a roofless Church, not so named of a* Bull's Hide, *which, cut into Thongs by* William *the Conqueror, reach'd to* Battaile (*as the fable*) *for it had that name before his coming But here he arriv'd, &c*

61. Victory—— *After two days march'd to* Hastings

62 Hastings——*Then to an hill near* Ninfield, *now call'd* Standard-Hill, *because* (*as they say*) *he there pitched his Standard, and from thence two miles further, where in a Plain, &c*

209 18 Victory —— *And therein he offer'd his Sword and Royal Robe which he ware the day of his Coronation These the Monks kept until their suppression, as also a Table of the Normans Centry which entred with the Conqueror, but so corruptly in later times, that they inserted therein the names of such as were their Benefactors, and whosoever the favour of Fortune or Virtue had advanc'd to any eminence in the subsequent ages*

210 13 Kent —— *The tradition is, that the old Town of* Hastings *is swallowed up of the Sea That which standeth now, as I observ'd, is couched between a high Cliff Sea-ward, and as high an Hill landward, having two Streets extended in length from North to South, and in each of them a* Parish-Church *The Haven, such as it is, being fed but with a poor small Rill, is at the south end of the Town, and hath had a great Castle upon the hill, which over-commanded it now there are only ruins thereof, and on the said hill Lighthouses to direct Sailors in the night-time*

40 Day ——*Thus* Hastings *flourish'd long, inhabited with a warlike People and skilful Sailors, well stor'd with Barks and Craies, and gained much by fishing, which is plentiful along the shore But after that the Peer made of Timber was at length violently carry'd away by extream rage of the Sea, it hath decay'd, and the fishing less used by the reason of the dangerous landing; for they are enforced to work their Vessels to land by a Capstall or Crain In which respect, for the bettering of the Town, Queen* Elizabeth *granted a Contribution toward the making of a new Harbour, which was begun, but the Contribution was quickly converted into private purses, and the publick good neglected Nevertheless, both Court, the Country, and City of* London *is served with much Fish from thence.*

 6 E Allega-

Page Line.

210. 49 Allegiance —— When King Henry the third had seiz'd their Lands into his hands, he granted the Rape of Hastings first to Peter Earl of Savoy, then to Prince Edward his Son, and after, upon his surrender, to John, Son to the Duke of Little Britain, upon certain exchanges of Lands pertaining to the Honour of Richmond, which Peter Earl of Savoy had made over for the use of the Prince. Long time after, when the Dukes of Britain had lost their Lands in England for adhering to the French King, King Henry the fourth gave the Rape of Hastings, with the Manour of Crowherst, Burgwash, &c to Sir John Pelham the elder, upon whose loyalty, wisdom and valour he much relied

211 32 Sudden — And now only beareth the countenance of a fair Town, and hath under it in the level, which the Sea relinquished, a Castle fortify'd by Henry the eighth, and large Marshes defended from Sea-rages with Works very chargeable

212. 16 Normandy — Yet now it beginneth to complain that the Sea abandoneth it (such is the variable and interchangeable course of that Element) and in part imputeth it, that the River Rother is not contain'd in his Chanel, and so loseth it's force to carry away the Sands and Beach which the Sea doth inbear into the haven Notwithstanding, it hath many Fishing-Vessels, and serveth London and the Court with variety of Sea-fish

24. Ripa — These two Towns (neither may it seem impertinent to note it) belong'd to the Abbey of Fescampe in Normandy But when King Henry the third perceiv'd that Religious Men intermingled secretly in matters of State, he gave them in exchange for these two, Chultenham and Sclover, two Manours in Gloucestershire, and other Lands; adding for the reason, that the Abbots and Monks might not lawfully fight with temporal Arms against the enemies of the Crown

76. Forest — And not far off East-Grensted, anciently a Parcel of the Barony of Eagle, and made a Market by King Henry the seventh

213. 1. Sackvil — Her Allie by the Bullens

6. Forest — Where I saw Endge, a Lodge of the Lord Abergavenny, and by it craggy Rocks rising up so thick, as though sporting Nature had there purposed a Sea Hereby, in the very confines of Kent is Groomebridge, an habitation of the Wallers, whose House there was built by Charles Duke of Orleans, father to King Lewis the 12th of France, when he, being taken Prisoner in the Battle of Agincourt by Richard Waller of this place, was here a long time detained Prisoner.

KENT

215 27. KENT — Extendeth it self in length from West to East fifty miles, and from South to North twenty-six

52. Towns — And well-peopled

55 Waters — At a word, the Revenues of the Inhabitants are greater both by the Fertility of the Soil, and also by the neighbourhood of a great City, of a great River, and the Main Sea

218 18. Them —— And representing afar off a moving Wood.

24 Which — By which they are not so bound by Copyhold, Customary Tenures, or tenant-right, as in other parts of England; but in a manner every Man is a Free-holder, and hath some part of his own to live upon

77. Admiral — A Chancellor and, &c.

219. 5 Above — Doth there admit into his Chanel into the first limit of this Shire Ravensburne, a small water, and of short course, which riseth in Keston-heath hard under the pitching of an ancient Camp, strange for the height as double rampires, and depth as double Ditches, of all that I have seen doubtless the work of many labouring hands Of what capacity it was, I could not discover, for that the greatest part thereof is now several, and overgrown with a thicket, but verily great it was, as may be gather'd by that which is apparent We may probably conjecture that it was a Roman Camp; but I might seem to rove, if I should think it that Camp which Julius Cæsar pitch'd, when the Britains gave him the last battel with their whole Forces, and then having bad success, retired themselves, and gave him leave to march to the Thames-side And yet certes Keston the name of the place seemeth to retain a parcel of Kæsar's name, for so the Britains call'd him, and not Cæsar, as we do As for the other small Intrenchment not far off by W Wickham, it was cast in fresh memory, when old Sir Christopher Heydon, a man then of great command in these parts, trained the Country People This water having passed by Bromeley, a Mansion-house of the Bishops of Rochester, after it hath gathered strength, the depth of his Ford giveth name to Depeford

220 74 Sticks — And to the memory of this St Ealpheg, the Parish-Church here consecrated

221 1 Tower — Famous in Spanish Fable.

4 Meadows — To the City of London, and the Country round about

8 Northampton — Lord Privy Seal, &c

222 28. Poor — And, as the prying Adversaries of our Religion then observ'd, was the first Protestant that built an Hospital

40 Kings — But unwholsomly, by reason of the Moat

50 Done — But despoil'd him of Alnwick-Castle, this, and other fair Lands

57 Stream — Which the Canons of Liesness adjoyning kept sweet and sound Land in their times This Abbey was founded 1179, by Lord Richard Lucy Chief Justice of England, and by him dedicated to God, and the memory of Thomas of Canterbury, whom he so admired for his Piety, while others condemn'd him for Pervicacy against his Prince; as he became here a devoted Canon to him

223 45 Height —— Now cut down, which commendeth Sir William Sevenok, an Alderman of London, who being a Foundling, and brought up here, and therefore so named, built here, in grateful remembrance, an Hospital and a School On the east-side of it standeth Knoll, so called for that it is seated upon a Hill, which Thomas Bourchier, Archbishop of Canterbury, purchasing of Sir William Fienes, Lord Say and Seale, adorn'd with a fair House; and now lately Thomas Earl of Dorset, Lord Treasurer, hath furnish'd, and beautified the old Work with new chargeable Additaments

224 19 Name —— But now of Sir Percival Hart, descended from one of the Coheirs of the Lord Bray

23. Market — Where King Edward the third built a Nunnery, which King Henry the eighth converted into a House for himself and his Successors

29 Crecce — Anciently call'd Creccan; when in his short course he hath imparted his name to five Townlets, which he watereth, as St Mary-Crey, Paul's-Crey, Vote's-Crey, North-Crey, and Crey-Ford

40. Else — Yet amongst them is * Swanscomb (of which I have heretofore spoken) of honourable Memory amongst the Kentish-men, for obtaining there the continuance of their ancient Franchises After-wards

Page Line.

wards it was well known by the Montceusies, Men of great Nobility, the Owners thereof, who had their Barony hereabout. [* In the Margin Swanscomb, i e K, Swane's Camp.]

224 50. Graves-end—So called (as Mr Lambard is my Author) as the Gereves-end, i e. the limit of the Gereve or Reve

51. England—For the usual passage by water between it and London, since the Abbot of Grace by the Tower of London, to which it appertained, obtained of King Richard the second, that the Inhabitants of it and Milton only shou'd transport Passengers from thence to London

53 Eighth—When he fortified the Sea-Coasts

ibid River—Beyond Gravesend is Shorn, held anciently by Sir Roger Northwood, by Service to carry with others the King's Tenants a white Ensign forty days at his own Charges, when the King warred in Scotland. (Inq 39 Edw III)

62 For, John—Sir John Oldcastle

225 1 Wholsom—At the entry hereof is Cowling-castle, built by John Lord Cobham in a Moorish ground

51 Small—It receiveth the Eden

ibid Pens-hurst—The Seat anciently (as it seemeth by the name) of Sir Stephen de Penherst, who was also called de Penshester, a famous Warden of the Cinque-Ports

54 Was—Sir Henry Sidney

63 For, Philip—Sir Philip

226. 10. Medway—Branching it self into five Streamlets, is joyned with as many Stone-bridges, and thereof groweth the name of Tunbridge to the Town there situate, as the Town of Bridges This, about King William Rufus's time, Richard son of Count Gilbert, grandchild to Godfrey Earl of Ewe and Lord of Briony, &c

22 England—Shortly after, he built here a fair large Castle, fenced with the river, a deep ditch, and strong Walls And albeit it is now ruinous, and the Keep attir'd with Ivy, yet it manifestly sheweth what it was

23. Glocester—And sirnam'd de Clare (for that they were Lords of Clare in Suffolk) built he e a Priory for Canons of St Austin's Orde, founded the Parish-Church, which was impropriated to the Knights of St John of Jerusalem, and compounded about the Tenure of the Manor, for which there had been long suit

28. Children—From those Clares Earls of Glocester, it came by an heir general to Sir Hugh Audley Earl of Glocester, and by his only daughter to the Earls of Stafford, who were afterward Dukes of Buckingham; and from them, by attainder, to the Crown. It hath in latter ages been beholden to Sir Andrew Jude of London, for a fair Free-school, and to John Wilford for a Causey toward London Three miles directly south from hence, in the very limit of Sussex, and near Frant, I saw in a white sandy ground divers vasty, craggy stones of strange forms, where of two of the greatest stand so close together, and yet severed with so streight a line, as you would think they had been sawed asunder· and Nature, when she reared these, might seem sportingly to have thought of a Sea

52 Forward—From Tunbridge, Medway passeth by Haudelo, from whence came that John Haudelo, who happily marrying the heir of the Lord Burnell, had issue by her a son, who was called Nicholas, summon'd to Parliament among the Barons, by the name of Burnell Then Medway, encreased with another Water, call'd Twist, which twisteth about and insulateth a large Plot of good ground, runneth on not far from Mereworth, &c

226 72 Medway—Having receiv'd a Rivulet, that loseth it self under-ground, and riseth again at Loose, serving thirteen Fulling-mills

227 16. Town—For the fair Stone-bridge, it hath been beholding to the Archbishops of Canterbury Among whom, to grace this place of the confluence of waters, Boniface of Savoy built a small College

23 Islip—And between them, which standeth in plight, William Courtney erected a fair Collegiate Church, in which he so great a Prelate, and so high born, lieth lowly entomb'd

48 County—And it hath been endow'd with sundry Privileges by King Edward the sixth, incorporated by the name of Mayor and Jurates, all which, in short time, they lost by favouring Rebels But Queen Elizabeth amply restor'd them, &c

229 57 For Edward—Sir Edward

61 Merlay—Here under is Ulcomb, anciently a Mansion of the Family De Sancto Leodegario, commonly called Sentleger and Sellinger, and Motinden, where Sir R Rockesley descended from Kriol and Crevecer built a house, who held Lands at Seaton by Serjeanty to be Vantrarius Regis, when the King goeth into Gascoin, donec perusus fuerit pari solutarum pretii 4 d which, as they that understand Law-Latin (for I do not) translate, that he should be the King's fore-footman, until he had worn out a pair of Shooes prized 4 d (Fin Mich 11 Edw II)

230 27 House—Now decay'd, whose son Sir Thomas enrich'd by an heir of Sir T Haut, proposing to himself great hopes upon fair pretences, pitifully overthrew himself and his State

48 Where—Under the side of a Hill——but not so artificially with mortis and tenents

53 House—In Ailsford it self, for the Religious House of the Carmelites founded by Richard Lord Grey of Codnor in the time of King Henry the third, is now seen a fair habitation of Sir William Siddey a learned Knight, painfully and expencefully studious of the common good of his Country, as both his endow'd House for the poor, and the Bridge here, with the common voice do plentifully testify

231 2 Burgundy—Medway having wound himself higher, from the east receiveth a Brook springing near Wrotham or Wirtham, so named for plenty of Wort, where the Archbishops had a Palace until Simon Islip pull'd it down, watereth Malling, which grew to be a Town after Gundulph Bishop of Rochester had there founded an Abby of Nuns, and watereth Leibourn, which hath a Castle sometime the Seat of a Family thereof sirnamed, out of which Sir Roger Leibourn was a great Agent in the Barons Wars, and William was a Parliamentary Baron in the time of King Edward the first,

4 Birling—Now the habitation of the Lord Abergeveny

35 Encompass'd—With a marsh, river, &c

56 Gundulphus—A Norman

70 Rufus—At which time there passed a Proclamation thro' England, That whosoever would not be reputed a Niding, should repair to recover Rochester-Castle whereupon the youth fearing that name, most reproachful and opprobrious in that Age, swarm'd thither in such number, that Odo was enforced to yield the place

232 2 For, Robert—Sir Robert

20 Montefort—Earl of Leicester

26, Cobham—Which was after repair'd But, in the time of K Richard the second, Sir Robert, &

28 Honour—At the end of the said Bridge, Sir John Cobham, who much further'd the Work, erected a Chapel (for our Elders built not one bridge

Page. Line. *without a Chapel,) upon which, besides the Arms of Saints, are seen the Arms of the King and his three Uncles then living And long after, Archbishop* Warham, *copied a great part of the said Bridge with iron-bars*

232. 45 Dock—*At* Gillingham *and* Chetham.

51 Bank—*At* Upnore

233 54. *For*, Edward—*Sir* Edward

59 *For*, Philip—*Sir* Philip

234. 62. Neighbourhood—*With his new Mayor and Corporation——which, as some write, was so called for that* Hengist *built it by a measure of thongs cut out of a Beast's hide, when* Vortigern *gave so much Land to fortify upon, as he could encompass with a Beast's hide cut into thongs Since the Conquest*, &c

235 2 Seditious—*Sir* Bartholomew *Lord* Badilsmere

3 Had—*Sir* Giles *Lord* Badilsmere.

8 Of—*Sir* John

10 Noblemen—*Then saw I* Tenham, *not commended for Health, but the Parent as it were of all the choice Fruit-gardens and Orchards of* Kent, *and the most large and delightsome of them all, planted in the time of King* Henry *the eighth by* Richard Harris *his Fruiterer, to the publick good, for thirty Parishes thereabout are replenished with Cherry-gardens, and Orchards beautifully disposed to direct lines*

236 41 Show—*Who had the Command then of nine ports, as the Lord Warden hath now of five ports*

237 11 Deriv'd — *From the Salt savoury Oysters there dredged*

52 Of— Eustace

55 Miracles—*As how the blind by drinking thereof recovered sight, the dumb their Speech, the deaf their Hearing, the lame their Limbs And how a Woman possess'd of the Devil, sipping thereof vomited two Toads, which immediately were first transformed into huge black Dogs and again into Asses And much more no less strange than ridiculous, which some in that age are as easily believ'd, as others falsely forg'd Thence, the* Stour *leaving* Eastwell, *the inhabitation of the family of the* Finches, *worshipful of itself, and by descent from* Philip Belknap *and* Peplesham, *goeth on to* Chilham, *&c*

67 Scotland— *Afterward, of Sir* Alexander Baliol, *who was called to Parliament by the name of Lord of* Chilham

238 6 To— *Sir* Bartholomew

239 4 Says—*Four hundred years since*

13 Austin—*The Apostle, as they called him*

242. 65 Sturemouth—*Which it hath now forsaken a mile and more, yet left and bequeathed his name to it*

Inq 2 *Edw* III *But now by* Stoure-mouth *runneth a Brook, which issuing out of St* Eadburgh's *Well at* Liming, *(where the daughter to King* Ethelbert, *first of our Nation took the Veil) while it seeketh the Sea, seeth* Elham *a Market-town, of which I have read nothing, but that the Manour was the inheritance of* Julian Leibourn, *a Lady of great honour in her time, who was mother of* Laurence Hastings *first Earl of* Pembroke *of that sirname, and after wife to* William Clinton *Earl of* Huntington *Then it holdeth his course by divers Villages, which thereof receive the addition of* Bourn, *as* Bishops bourn, Hawles-bourn, Patricks bourn, *and* Beaks-bourn *This* Bourn *is that river* Stoure, *as* Cæsar *calleth it (as I have observ'd travelling lately in these parts) which* Cæsar *came unto, when he had marched by night almost twelve Italian miles from the Sea-coast, and where he had the first encounter, in his second expedition into* Britain, *with the* Britains, *whom he drave into the woods, where they had a place fortified both by nature and men's labour, with a number of Trees hewen down, and plashed to fore-close the Entries But yet the Romans forc'd an entry, drave them out, and thereabout encamped. The place of Camp, as I hear, is near* Hardes, *a place of ancient Gentlemen of that sirname, descended from* Estengrave, Herenged, *and the* Fitz-Bernards

Page Line.

244. 10 Government—*Here also landed* Lewis *of* France, *who, called in by the tumultuous Barons of* England *against King* John, *published, by their instigation, a pretended right to the Crown of* England *For that whereas King* John *for his notorious Treason against King* Richard *his brother, absent in the Holy Land, was by his Peers lawfully condemned, and therefore after the death of King* Richard, *the Right of the Crown was devolved to the Queen of* Castile, *sister to the said King* Richard; *and that she and her heirs had convey'd over their right to the said* Lewis *and his wife her daughter Also that King* John *had forfeited his Kingdom both by the murther of his Nephew* Arthur, *whereof he was found guilty by his Peers in* France, *and also by subjecting his Kingdoms, which were always free, to the Pope, as much as in him lay, contrary to his Oath at his Coronation, and that without the consent of the Peers of the Realm*, &c *Which I leave to the Historians, with the success of his Expedition, lest I might seem to digress extraordinarily*

246 19 Tower—*Of rough Flint, and long Britain Bricks ——mightily strengthe ed by tracts of time, so that the cement is as hard as the stone Over the entry whereof is fixed a head of a personage engraven in stone; some say it was Queen* Bertha's *head, but I take it to be a Roman work*

54. Sort—*In ancient times it sundry times felt the furious Forces of the* Danes *Afterward, King* Kanutus *the Dane, when he had gained the Crown of* England, *bestow'd it upon* Christ's *Church in* Canterbury, *with the Royalty of the water on each side, so far forth as a Ship being afloat a Man might cast a* Danish *Hatchet out of the Vessel to the bank In the Norman Reign it was reckon'd one of the Cinque Ports, and to find five Ships In the year* 1217 Lewis *of* France, *of whom we spake lately, burned it. King* Edward *the first for a time placed here the Staple; and King* Edward *the third by exchange re-united it to the Crown About which time there flourished here a Family sirnamed* de Sandwico, *which had match'd with one of the Heirs of* Creveceur *and* D'Auranches *Lord of* Folkeston, *and deserved well of this place In the time of King* Henry *the sixth it was burned by the* French. *In our days, Sir* Roger Manwood, *Chief Baron of the Exchequer, a Native of this place, built and endowed here a Free-School; and the* Netherlanders *have better'd the Town by making and trading of* Baies *and other Commodities*

247 27 And — Deale *and* Walmar *three Neighbour Castles*

248 33 History—*But a Topography.*

249 44. Been—*Then and many years after, before the Invention of great Ordnance, out of Engines called* Balliste, *like huge Cross-bows, bent by force of two or four men*

75 When—*Sir* Hubert

250. 8. Cities — *And Forts; and could not get this, being manfully defended by the said Sir* Hubert de Burgh.

33. Labour—*And sixty-three thousand Pounds Charges*

251 15 Field—*If it be not raised with winds and counter-Seas*

253 21 Deep—*But within half a League to the Southward is* 27 *Fathom deep, and to the Northward twenty five.*

Page Line.

154. 29 Histories — *Insomuch that certain Lands were held in* Coperland *near* Dover, *by service to hold the King's head between* Dover *and* Whitsand, *whensoever he cross'd the Sea there, and,* &c

155 8 Memory—*And that Victory so glorious*

19 Dover—*Leaving the little Abbey of* Bradsole *dedicated to St* Radegund, *whereof* Hugh *the first Abbot was Founder*

23 Coins—*And* British *Bricks*

36 To—*Sir* Hamon Crevequer

37 To—*Sir* John

43 Shore—*Turning South-westward,* Sandgate-*castle, built by King* Henry *the eighth, defendeth the Coast, and upon a Castle-hill thereby are seen reliques of an ancient Castle*

46 Where — *Sir* Edward Poinings — *and among them of* Thomas *Lord* Poining *Lieutenant of* Bolen

48 House — *But left it imperfect, when death had bereft him of his only lawful Child, which he had by his lawful Wife the daughter of Sir* J Scot *his neighbour at* Scots-hall, *where the Family of* Scots *hath lived in worshipful Estimation a long time, as descended from* Pasheley *and* Serjeaux, *by* Pimpe

59 It—*So are Sea-towns subject to the uncertain Vicissitude of the Sea*

73 Way—*Called* Stony-street

157. 9 It—*Certain Laws of* Sewers *were made in the time of King* Henry *the third, and,* &c

58. Nose—*Before which lieth a dangerous Flat in the Sea*

158. 9 Antiquity—*Whereof they shew the Plot*

22 Supplies—*Of his own Nation*

39 Of—*Sir*

43. Valley — *I saw nothing there now, but a mean Village with a poor Church, and a wooden Bridge to no great purpose, for a Ferry is in most use, since that the river* Rother *not containing himself in his Chanel, hath overlaid and is like to endanger and surround the level of rich lands thereby Whereupon, the Inhabitants of* Rhie *complain that their haven is not scour'd by the stream of* Rother, *as heretofore, and the owners here suffer great loss, which their neighbours in* Oxency *do fear, if it were remedy'd, would fall upon them This is a river-Isle ten miles about, encompass'd with the river* Rother, *dividing his streams, and now brackish, having his name either of mire, which our Ancestors called* Hox, *or of* Oxen, *which it feedeth plentifully with rank grass Opposite to this is,* &c

159 2 Towns—Sisinghurst, *a fair House of the Family of* Bakers, *advanced by Sir* John Baker, *not long since Chancellour of the Exchequer, and his marriage with a daughter and heir of* Dingley Bengebury, *an habitation of the ancient Family of* Colepepper, *and near adjoyning,* Hemsted *a Mansion of the* Guildfords, *an old Family, but most eminent since Sir* John Guildford *was Controuler of the House to King* Edward *the fourth For his son and heir Sir* Richard Guildford *was by King* Henry *the seventh made Knight of the Garter Of his sons again, Sir* Edward Guildford *was Marshal of* Calais, *Lord Warden of the Cinque Ports, and Master of the Ordnance, Father to* Jane *Dutchess of* Northumberland, *Wife to Sir* J Dudley *Duke of* Northumberland, *Mother to the late Earls of* Warwick *and* Leicester, *and Sir* Henry *was chosen Knight of the Garter by King* Henry *the 8th, and had his Arms ennobled with a* Canton of Granado, *by* Ferdinand *King of* Spain, *for his worthy service in that Kingdom when it was recover'd from the* Moors, *and* Edward *liv'd in great esteem at*

Page Line

home To be brief, from the said Sir John *are issued by Females immediately the* Darels *of* Calehill, Gages, Brownes *of* Beechworth, Walsinghams, Cromers, Isaacs, *and* Iseleies, *Families of prime and principal note in these parts But now I digress, and therefore crave pardon*

259 10 Kingdom — *Thus much of* Kent, *which (to conclude summarily) hath this part last spoken of for* Drapery, *the Isle of* Tenet *and the east parts for the* Granary; *the Weald for the* Wood; Rumney *marsh for the Meadow-plot, the north* Downs *towards the* Thames *for the* Conygarthe; Tenham *and thereabout for an Orchard, and* Head-corne *for the brood and poultry of fat, big, and commended Capons*

13 Godwin—*And* Leofwin *his Brother*

21 Whereupon — *Whereupon he was committed to prison by a subtil distinction, as Earl of* Kent, *and not Bishop of* Bayeux, *in regard of his Holy Orders*

31 Eyes—*And so became a Monk*

47 Third — *Who also made him Chief Justice of* England

61 Prison—*Persuaded thereto by such as covertly practised his Destruction*

62. John—*Who were restored by Parliament to Blood and Land shortly after And withal it was enacted, That no Peer of the Land, or other that procur'd the death of the said Earl should be impeached therefore, than* Mortimer *Earl of* Marsh, *Sir* Simon Beresford, John Matravers, Barons *and* John Devoroil

66 For—*Sir* Thomas

67 Kent — *And she after married by dispensation to the Black-Prince, bare to him, King* Richard *the second*

68 By— *Sir* Thomas

73 Beheaded—*Leaving no Child*

76 1408—*Leaving likewise no Issue.*

260. 3 First — *Sir* William

9 Issue — 1523

12 Knight—*Of Wrest*

GLOCESTERSHIRE.

267 36 WArwickshire — *And* Barkshire

270 15 Knight—*For Sea Services, as his brother* Arthur, *slain in* Orkney-*Isles*

69 By—*Sir* Walter Clifford

271. 17 Tract — *Beside* Newnham *a pretty Market, and* Westbury *thereby, a Seat of the* Bainhams *of ancient descent*

64 Norman — *Lord of* Corboile *and* Thorigny *in* Normandy, *translating Monks from* Cranborn *in* Dorsetshire *hither*

273 15 Severn — *Runneth down by* Haresfield, *which King* Henry *the third gave to* Richard Pauncefote, *whose Successors built a fair House here, and whose Predecessors were possess'd of fair Lands in this Country, before, and in the Conqueror's time, in* Wiltshire

52 Brightstow — *And* Shirley.

53 Fairford—Fairley, *&c*

275. 5 Monument—*Who was bereft of the Kingdom of* England, *for that he was born before his Father was King, depriv'd of his two Sons, the one by strange death in the New Forest, the other despoiled of the Earldom of* Flanders, *his inheritance, and slain; he himself dispossess'd of the Dukedom of* Normandy *by his Brother King* Henry *the first, his eyes pluck'd out, and kept close prisoner twenty six years with all contumelious indignities, until through extream anguish he ended his life*

Page Line

276 69 Streams — *Windeth itself by* Elmore, *a Mansion House of the* Gises, *ancient by their own lineal descent being in elder times owners of* Apseley-Gise *near* Brickhill, *and from the* Beauchamps *of* Holt, *who acknowledge* Hubert de Burgo *Earl of* Kent (*whom I lately mention'd*) *beneficious to them, and testify the same by their Armories Lower upon the same side*, Stroud *a pretty river slideth into* Severn *out of* Cotefwold, *by* Stroud *a Market-town sometimes better peopled with Clothiers, and not far from* Minching-Hampton, *which anciently had a Nunnery, or belong'd to Nuns, whom our Ancestors named* Minchings

277 15 Family—*Descended from* Robert Fitz-Harding, *to whom King* Henry *the second gave this place and* Barkley Hearnes *Out of this House descended many Knights and Gentlemen of signal note*

16 Barkley—*Who was honoured by King* Edward *the fourth with the stile of Viscount* Barkley, *by King* Richard *the third, with the Honour of Earl of* Nottingham (*in regard of his mother, daughter of* Thomas Mowbray *Duke of* Norfolk, *and Earl of* Nottingham) *and by King* Henry *the seventh with the Office of* Marshal of England *and dignity of Marquess* Barkley

279 28 Testifies — *When he had taken down an ancient House which* Hugh Audeley *Earl of* Glocester *had formerly built*

280 24 Lords — *Among whom* Sir Thomas *was summon'd among the Barons in the time of King* Edward *the third*

56 Name — *But from* Ralph Russel *the heir, this* Deorham *descended to the Family of* Venis *Above these is* Sodbury, *known by the family of* Walsh, *and neighbours thereunto are* Wike ware *the ancient seat of the family* De-la-Ware; Woton *under* Edge, *which yet remembereth the slaughter of* Sir Thomas Talbot *Viscount* Lisle, *here slain in the time of King* Edward *the fourth, in an encounter with the Lord* Barkley, *about possessions, since which time have continued Suits between their Posterity, until now lately they were finally compounded*

281 25 Duresley—*Who built here a Castle now more than ruinous*

26 Order—*Derived from* Tintern, *whom* Maud *the Empress greatly enrich'd The males of this House failed in the time of K* Richard *the second, and the Heir-General was married to* Cantelow *Within one mile of this, where the river* Cam *lately spoken of, springeth, is* Uleigh, *a seat also of the* Barkleys *descended from the Barons* Barkley, *stiled of* Uleigh, *and* Stoke-Giffard, *who were found Coheirs to* J *Baron* Boutetort, *descended from the Baron* Zouch *of* Richard Castles *alias* Mortimer, *and the* Somerys *Lords of* Dueley

65 Hills—*Without Woods*

74 Antiquity — *Beginning at the north-east end of them*

282 1 Town - Weston *and* Biselay *were in the possession of* Hugh *Earl of* Chester

4 Descended—*By* Nicolao de Albeniaco, *an Inheritrice to the ancient Earls of* Arundel, *unto* Roger de Somery

30 Romans - *Who was there buried with his wife* Sanchia *daughter to the Earl of* Provence

33. Divinity — *As he carried away the firname of* Doctor Irrefragabilis, *that is, the* Doctor Ungainsaid, *as he could not be gainsaid*

46 Seat — *Of* Sir Thomas Seimor, *Baron* Seimor *of* Sudley, *and Admiral of* England, *attainted in the time of King* Edward *the sixth, and afterward of* Sir John Bruges, *whom Queen* Mary, *&c.*

Page Line

282 54 John Chandos — *Sir* John, *a famous Banneret Lord of* Caumont *and* Kerkitou *in* France

64 For, William — *Sir* William

68 Sudley — *With a fee of two hundred Marks yearly*

283 38 Glocester — *Thence I found nothing memorable, but near the Fountain of* Churn *river*, Coberley, *a seat of a Stem of* Barklies, *so often named even from the Conquest, which matched with an heir of* Chandos, *and so came hereditarily to the* Bruges *Progenitors to the Lords* Chandos *Then, by* Bird-lip-hill, *whereby we ascended to this high* Cotefwold

284 21 Hills—*Near* Corbeiley

285 11 Gurmundus—*So that it may seem he was that* Gurmund *which they so much speak of, for certes when he raged, about the year* 879 *a rabblement of* Danes *rousted here one whole year*

15. Second—*For black Canons*

39 Kent — *Late Duke of* Surrey

ibid Huntingdon—*Late Duke of* Exeter

286. 36 Miles—*Near to* Dounamveny *an ancient seat of the* Hungerfords

288 14 Honour — *Who dejected with comfortless grief, when death had deprived him of his only son and heir, assured his estate, with his eldest daughter, to* John *son to King* Henry *the second, with certain Proviso's for his other daughters*

15 Families—John, *when he had obtain'd the Kingdom, repudiated her upon pretences as well that she was barren, as that they were within prohibited degrees of consanguinity and reserving the Castle of* Bristow *to himself, after some time passed over his repudiated wife, with the honour of* Glocester, *to* Geoffry Mandeville, *son of* Geoffry Fitz-Peter *Earl of* Essex, *for twenty thousand marks, who thus over-marrying himself, was greatly impoverished, and wounded in Tournament, died soon after without issue she being remarried to* Hubert *of* Burgh, *died immediately*

24 Mabel—*The eldest*

30 Glocester — *Who was stiled Earl of* Glocester *and* Hereford, *and mightily enrich'd his House by marrying one of the heirs of* William Marshall *Earl of* Pembroke *His son and successor* Richard, *in the beginning of the Barons Wars against King* Henry *the third, ended his life, leaving* Gilbert *his son to succeed him, who powerfully and prudently sway'd much in the said Wars, as he enclined to them or the King H., obnoxious to King* Edward *the first, surrender'd his Lands unto him, and receiv'd them again by marrying* Joan *the King's daughter (sirnamed of* Acres *in the Holy Land, because she was there born) to his second wife, who bore unto him* Gilbert Clare, *last Earl of* Glocester *of this sirname, slain in the flower of his youth in* Scotland, *at the battle of* Sterling, *in the sixth year of King* Edward *the second*

34 For, Ralph—*Sir* Ralph

37 First—*For which he incurr'd the King's high displeasure, and a short imprisonment, but after reconciled, was summoned to Parliaments by the name of* Earl of Glocester and Hereford *But when* Gilbert *was out of minority, he was summoned among the Barons by the name of Sir* Ralph de Mont-hermer *as long as he lived Which I note more willingly for the rareness of the example*

42 Issue—*Sir* Hugh Le de Spencer

47. Was—*Sir* Hugh Audley

75 De-Spencer — *In the right of his Great Grand-mother*

76 Grandfather—*Sir* Hugh

Bristol

Page. Line.

288. ult. Bristol—*By the people's fury*

289. 3 Himself—*In the first year of King* Henry *the sixth, as I have seen in an Instrument of his,* Humphrey, *by the Grace of God, Son, Brother and Uncle to Kings, Duke of* Glocester, *Earl of* Hainault, Holland, Zeeland, *and* Pembroke, *Lord of* Friseland, *Great Chamberlain of the Kingdom of* England, *Protector and Defender of the same Kingdom and Church of* England

7 Contrivance—*Of a Woman*

OXFORDSHIRE

294 43 Confirmed—*To the Benedictine Monks*

295 ibid. Intimates — *Certainly in an Exchequer-book the Town adjacent is called* Rollendrich, *whereas it is there specified* Turstan le Dispenser *held Land by Serjeanty of the King's Dispensary, i e to be the King's Steward*

297 58. Remarkable — *But* la Bruer, *now* Bruern, *sometime an Abbey of White Monks.*

299 40 Well — *We read, that* Hugh *Bishop of* Lincoln, *Diocesan of this place coming hither, caused her Bones to be removed out of the Church, as unworthy of Christian burial for her unchaste life Nevertheless, the holy Sisters there translated them again into the Church, and laid them up in a perfumed leather Bag enclos'd in Lead, as was found in her Tomb at the dissolution of the House and they erected a Cross there, whereby the Passengers were put in mind with two rhiming Verses to serve God, and pray for her but I remember them not*

301. 5 Place — *Near to* Banbury *is* Hanwell, *where the Family of* Cope *hath flourished many years in great and good esteem*

17 Sixth—— *Who was cruelly beheaded by a rabble of Rebels in the time of King* Henry *the sixth*

20 Stands—— Haford-warine, *so denominated from* Warine Fitz-Gerold *Lord thereof* Heyford Purcell *likewise, so named of the* Purcells *or* de Porcellis, *ancient Gentlemen, the old owners* Blechingdon, *an ancient possession of the Family of* Povre

308. 52 College—*And these two were the first endow'd Colleges for Students in Christendom*

310 6 Hither — *Recall'd by Proclamation directed to the High-Sheriff of* Lincolnshire, *upon penalty to forfeit their Books and the King's displeasure*

14 Winchester— *And be about the same, by the tract of the City wall, built a fair high wall, embattled and turretted*

57 Monks— *By a Chapter held among them laid their Monies together and encreased* Glocester-Hall, *built before by* John *Lord* Giffard *of* Brimsfield *for Monks of* Glocester

62 Convents — Nicholas Wadham *of* Merefield *in the County of* Somerset *hath assign'd a fair portion of Lands and Money for the propagation of Religion and Learning, which I note incidently by way of congratulation to our age, that there are yet some who graciously respect the advancement of good learning*

311 54 Uses—*In the giddy time of King* Edward *the sixth*

312 69 Others — *For Professors and two hundred Students*

71 Christ-Church—*Assign'd to a Dean, Prebends, and Students*

313 61 Foundation — *With good speed and happy success, as I wish*

314 75 Minutes—*And thus much briefly of my dear Nurse-Mother* Oxford

315 47 Alms-house—*But this Title soon determin'd, when he left but Daughters, married into the Families of* Norris *and* Wenman

315 74. Is — Husely, *where sometimes the names of* Buttentines *flourished as at* Chalgrave.

320 35 Lincoln—*Who by King* Richard *the third had been declared heir apparent to the Crown*

41 Battle—*At* Stoke, *and* Edmund *his brother*

59 Cæsar — *Here is* Bixbrond *and* Stonor, *ancient possessions of the Families of* Stonors, *who since the time of King* Edward *the third, when Sir* John Stonor *was Chief Justice in the Common Pleas, flourished with great Alliance and fair Revenues, until they were transferred by an heir general to Sir* Adrian Fortescue *unhappily attainted, whose daughter, heir to her mother, was married to the first Baron* Wentworth *Next neighbour hereunto is* Pus-hall, *which the Family of* D'oily *held by yielding yearly to the King a Table-cloth of three Shillings price, or Three Shillings for all Services*

321 69 Enjoy'd—*To omit* Edgar, Algar, *and other English* Saxons, *Official Earls of* Oxford

322 35 Banishment—John *the first of that name, so trusty and true to the House of* Lancaster, *that both he and his Son and heir* Aubrey *lost their heads therefore together, in the first year of King* Edward *the fourth*

BUCKINGHAMSHIRE

327 32 WICK—*And* Comb *a low Valley*

74 Family—*Whose Father Sir* Andrew, *descended from the old Stem of ancient Barons, King* Henry *the eighth dignified with the honour of Baron* Windsor.

328 39 Called—*And our* Tunbridge, *and others*

65 By — Burnham, *better known by the* Hodengs, *Lord* Huntercombs *and* Scudamores *(who were Lords thereof and of* Beconsfield *successively by inheritance) than by it self*

329 21 Missenden —— *Upon a Vow for escaping Shipwrack*

39 Adjoyneth—*On the one side*

44 Seat—*On the other side* Chesham Bois, *where, and at* Draiton Beauchamp *the Family of* Cheneis *hath anciently flourish'd*

330 13 Bon-hommes—*Who profess'd the Rule of St.* Austin

35 Bernwood — *Whose Foresters surnam'd* de Borstal *were famous in former times* Nigell de Borstall *was so surnam'd from having kill'd a wild Boar in that Forest, for which he had from the King one Hide of arable Land, call'd* Derehide ; *and on that he built a Mansion, and call'd it* Borestale *in memory of the slain Boar.*

331 45 Staffords—*Of* Grafton, &c

332 10 Conquest —*Whose Son, the second Earl of* Buckingham, *and* Ermingard *his wife, built the Abbey of* Notelcy *thereby in the year* 1112

16 Whitchurch—*Near unto which is* Ascot, *the principal Mansion-house of the* Dormers, *from whence descended the Dutchess of* Feria *in* Spain, *and others of noble note*

61 Rumbald—*A child*

63. Saint—*Child Saint, and much fam'd with many Miracles*

333 51 Exchequer —— *And of the Dutchy of* Lancaster

54 Are—Stow *of the Family of the* Temples

55 Seat—*Of the* Greenwaies

334 33 Wolverton—*Anciently* Wolverington, *the Seat of an ancient Family so surnam'd, whose Lands are nam'd in Records,* The Barony of Wolverington, *from whom it came to the House of* Longviles *of ancient descent in these parts*

Dr. HOLLANDS's Insertions

Page Line
334. 75. Dy'd——*Issueless.*
ult Pembroke—*Called Conqueror of* Ireland.
335. 10. Sixth—— *With an invidious precedence before all Dukes in* England.
336 4 Said——*As it is written in his Life*
5 England—*To the name* Buckingham, *and*, &c.
9 Stafford—*Whereas they were stiled before Dukes of* Buckingham, *Earls of* Stafford, Hereford, Northampton *and* Perch; *Lords of* Brecknock, Kimbolton *and* Tunbridge

BEDFORDSHIRE.

41. BEholders—*They who saw it, took it as a plain Presage of the Division ensuing*
51. Nobility—*Whose Barony consisted of three hundred Knight-fees in divers Countreys*
ibid Castle—— *Which is now hereditarily descended to Sir* R Chetwood *Knight, as the Inheritance of the* Chetwoods *came formerly to the* Wahuls
62 Wales—*In* Glamorganshire.
64 Memory—*When she created Sir* Oliver, *the second Baron of her Creation, Lord* St John *of* Bletnesho, *unto whom it came by*, &c
337 25 Hastens—*By* Brumham, *a Seat of the* Dives, *of very ancient parentage in these parts*
339 64 Town — Wardon *more inward, where was a House of* Cistercian *Monks, and was Mother to the Abbeys of* Saultry, Sibton, *and* Tilthey
72 Hill——*A parcel of the Barony of* Kainho
75 By——*Sir* John
340. 4 Kent—*Whose grandchild* Ruthin *passed both it and* Ruthin *over to* Henry *the seventh.*
55 For, H — Henry
67 Cheney——*Made by Queen* Elizabeth *Baron* Cheney *of* Tuddington, *built, and shortly after dy'd* sans-issue.
77. Winter-time—*For the old* Englishmen, *our Progenitors, call'd deep Mire*, Hock *and* Hocks.
341. 18 Carry'd—*Out of* Lincolnshire.
57. Immunities—*As for* Leighton-Buzard *on the one side of* Dunstable, *and* Luton *on the other, neither have I read nor seen any thing memorable in them, unless I should say, that at* Luton *I saw a fair Church, but the Quire then roofless and overgone with Weeds, and adjoyning to it an elegant Chapel founded by* J *Lord* Wenlock, *and well main tain'd by the Family of* Rotheram, *planted here by* Thomas Rotheram *Archbishop of* York, *and Chancellor of* England *in the time of King* Edward *the fourth*
342 35 France——*Son to* Engelrame *Lord of* Coucy, *and his wife daughter to the Duke of* Austria.
41. France——*Slain*
65. But——*Some ten years after his Creation*
70 Son——*Sir* Francis

HERTFORDSHIRE.

345 8 PLACE—— *Which was thought in that age a pious Work, to put Passengers in mind of Christ's Passion*
11 Honour—*Of* Thomas *of* Canterbury
34 That——*Sir* John
45 To——*Sir* Robert
5 . To——*Sir* Anthony
65 Telbridge—*The Manour of* Barkway *hereby appertain'd also to those Lords* Scales, *a well known Thorough-fare Beyond which, is* Barley, *that imparted surname to the ancient and well allied Family of the* Barleys; *and on this side* Anestie, *which was not long since the Inheritance of the House of* York. *and in elder times, the Castle there was a Nest of Rebels; wherefore* Nicholas *of* Anestie *Lord thereof, was expresly commanded by* Henry *the third, to demolish so much of it as they raised since the Barons wars against his Father King* John. *But now time hath wholly rased it all.*
346. 53. Is—*Sir* Giles.
75. Littons —— *Descended from* Litton *in* Derbyshire.
348. 13 Burgesses—*And at that time* Ralph Limsey *a Nobleman, built here a Cell for St* Alban's *Monks.*
74 Hither—*And at that time* Ralph Limsey *a Nobleman, built here a Cell for St* Alban's *Monks.*
349. 64. Castle—*And also* Woodhall, *an habitation of the* Butlers, *who being branch'd from Sir* Ralph Butler *Baron of* Wem *in* Shropshire, *and his wife heir to* William Pantulfe *Lord of* Wem, *were Lords of* Pulre-bach, *and enrich'd much by an heir of Sir* Richard Gobion, *and another of* Peletot *Lord of this place in the time of King* Edward *the third*
69 Bland—*Whereupon also neighboureth* Standon, *with a seemly House built by Sir* Ralph Sadleir, *Chancellor of the Dutchy of* Lancaster, *Privy Counsellor to three Princes, and the last Knight Banneret of* England; *a man so advanc'd for his great Services and stay'd wisdom*
71 Account—*That* Gefferey *Earl of* Britain *gave it to* Gerard, *&c.*
350. 27 It—*From thence it maketh his way by* Sabridgworth, *a parcel of the honour of Earl* William Mandevile, *and sometime the possession of* Geffry Say, *near* Shingle-hall, *honested by the owners the* Leventhorpes *of ancient Gentry. So on, not far from* Honsdon, *&c*
49 Thames — *Under* Hodsdon, *a fair through-far, to which* H Bourchier *Earl of* Essex, *having a fair House at* Baise *thereby (while it stood) procured a Market*
356. 72. Where—*Sir* Nicholas
357 8 Place—*from* Mergrate, *sometime a Religious House, now a Seat of the* Ferrers, *out of the House of* Groby
358 34. Cornwal—*His half-brother*
50 Devonshire — *And the* Beauforts *Dukes of* Somerset.
359. 11 Son—*Sir* Charles
360 16 Under — Barnet *hath for his neighbours* Mimmes, *a Seat of the worshipful Family of the* Coningsbies, *descended to them by* Frowick *from the* Knolles, *ancient possessors thereof, and* Northhall, *where* Ambrose Dudley, *last Earl of* Warwick, *raised a stately House from the Foundations.*
46 Honoured—*Sir* Edward
49 Somerset—*By King* Edward *the sixth*

MIDDLESEX

365 14 COLE——*Which the* Britains *called* Co.
32. Of——*Count.*
34. Uxbridge——*Anciently* Woxbridge.
33 Was—*Made an Honour.*
368 31. For—*To the Honour of our* Saviour, *the Virgin* Mary, *and*, &c
83. Call'd—*Jesu of*
49. House—*Under this the small river* Brent *issueth into the* Thames, *and springeth out of a Pond vulgarly call'd* Browns well *for* Brent-well, *that is in old English* Frogwell, *passeth down between* Hendon, *which Archbishop* Dunstan, *born for the advancement of Monks, purchased for some* fe-

Page Line

few gold Bizantines, which were Imperial pieces of Gold coined at Byzantium or Constantinople, and gave to the Monks of St Peter of Westminster And Hamsted-hill, from whence you have a most pleasant prospect to the most beautiful City of London, and the lovely Country about it Over which the ancient Roman Military way led to Verulam or St Albans by Edgworth, and not by High gate, as now, which new way was open'd by the Bishops of London about some three hundred years since But to return Brent, into whom all the small rivers of these parts resort, runneth on by Brent-street, an Hamlet to which it imparted its name, watereth Hangerwood, Hanwell, Oisterley-Park, where Sir Thomas Gresham built a fair large House, and so near her fall into the Thames, giveth name to Brentford, a fair thorough fare and frequent Market

369 30 And—To the Thames-side

34 Seat—Standing there conveniently, not far from the City, albeit not so healthfully

45 Thames—— (as some suppose) but in Records 'tis nam'd Chelche-hith

370 40 Inconstancy—While I disport in Conjecture

371 53 Omen—— Mark'd for life and long continuance

58 Nero——1540 years since

373 27 One——Francerius Falconer Lord Mayor, A D 1414

34 Elbegate—— Which at this present is by the Cities Charge re-edify'd

374 4 London— And amongst them, Robert Fitz-Walter had Licence of King Edward the first to sell the site of Bainard-Castle to the said Archbishop Robert

379 26 Knight—— A right noble Knight of the Garter executed by encroached Authority without the King's Consent

27 For, J de— Sir John de Bellocampo or Beauchamp

32 And—Sir Christopher Hatton

379 35 Nephew—Sir William Hatton

380 40 Delign'd——The good of England against those spoilers

382 7 Chancery—Besides two Inns moreover for the Serjeants at Law

11 As—Sir John Fortescue

20 For—— At their first institution about A D 1113

24 Religion- The Holy Land

26 Mahometans— Professing to live in Charity and Obedience

28 Princes—Devout People

30 Piety—Yea and in the opinion, both of the holiness of the men and of the place, King Henry the third, &c

37 William— Marshal the elder a most powerful man in his time

39 Pembroke — Upon William the elder his Tomb I some years since read in the upper part Comes Pembrochiæ, and upon the side this Verse

Miles eram Martis, Mars multos vicerat armis

ibid But — But in process of time, when with insatiable greediness they had hoarded great wealth by withdrawing Tithes from Churches, appropriating spiritual Livings to themselves, and other hard means, their riches turn'd to their ruin For thereby their former piety was after a manner stifled, they fell at jarr with other Religious Orders, their professed Obedience to the Patriarch of Jerusalem was rejected, envy among the common

Page Line

Sort was procured, which hope of gain among the better sort so enkindled, that, &c

382 50 That—Sir Hugh Spencer

52 Of—Sir Aimer de Valentia or Valence

58 Grey—Of Wilton.

383 38 House—Or Salisbury Court.

39 Salisbury— The White-Friers, or, &c

40 Mentioned—Then without the Barrs

41 House—Before called Hampton-place

49 Hospital— Worcester-house, late Bedford-house, Salisbury-house

51 Jerusalem —And thereby the only Ornament of this part, the Britain-Burse built by the Earl of Salisbury, and so named of King James the first

52 Formerly—And Northampton-house, now begun by Henry Earl of Northampton

385 9 It —Surrender'd it to the Spoil of Courtiers

20 Dean —Over these she placed Dr Bill Dean, whose Successor was, &c

55 First—And first Christian

70 Elizabeth —— Daughter to King Edward the fourth

387 45 Fourth - Sir Giles Daubeney

58 Sussex James Butler.

62 Another—Sir Humfrey Bourchier

63 Barnet— Sir Nicholas Carew, Baron Carew

67 Douglasia --H Howard

69 Of---Sir Arthur Gorges

71 Cecil---Sir John Puckering.

388 4 Pyramid---Sir Charles Blunt, Earl, &c

57 College---Of a Dean and, &c

389 5 Edward---Because the Tradition holds, that the said King Edward therein dy'd

10 Arch traitor---Robert Catesby

390 23 St James's---Where anciently was a Spittle for Maiden Lepers

391 48 Oldburn- - Wherein stood anciently the first House of Templers only in the place now called Southampton-House

61 Institution ---- About the year 1124 and long after

66 Temple ---- This religious Order was instituted shortly after Geoffrey of Bollen had recover'd Jerusalem The Brethren whereof wore a white Cross upon their upper black garment, and by solemn Profession were bound to serve Pilgrims and poor People in the Hospital of St John of Jerusalem, and to secure the passages thither they charitably buried the dead, they were continual in prayer, mortified themselves with watchings and fastings they were courteous and kind to the poor, whom they called their Masters, and fed with white Bread, while themselves liv'd with brown, and carried themselves with great austerity Whereby they purchased to themselves the love and liking of all Sorts

392 11 By---Sir Walter Many

75 To --Sir Peregrine Berty

393 20 Ways -To put Passengers in mind that they are, as those were, subject to mortality

394 21 For---Black Canons

395 6 By---Sir Thomas Knowles

41 Company--- Commonly called the Stil-yard, as the Easterlings yard

56 Rome--- As great and holy as it is

397 8 Stephen--- About four hundred years since

398 44 County -- When it hath collected his divided Stream, and cherished fruitful Marish-Meadows

58 Seventh ----- And Durance neighbour thereto a House of the Wrothes of ancient name in this County

ult Essex - As for the title of Middlesex, the Kings of England have vouchsafed to none, neither Duke, Marquess, Earl, or Baron

Page Line.

ESSEX.

405 60 CROSS--- *Found far westward, and brought hither, as they write, by Miracles*

66 In---*Sir* Edward

407 15 By---*So it passeth by* Lambourn *Manour, which is held by service of the* Wardstaffe, *viz to carry a load of Straw in a Cart with six horses, two ropes, two men in harness to watch the said Wardstaffe, when it is brought to the Town of* Aibridge, *&c and then by* Wansted Park, *where the late Earl of* Leicester *built much for his pleasure*

408 34 To---*Sir* Thomas

38 Descended -- *Here I have heard much speech of a* Lawless-Court *(as they called it) holden in a strange manner about* Michaelmas *in the first peep of the day, upon the first cock-crowing in a silent sort, yet with shrewd fines eftsoons redoubled if not answered, which servile attendance, they say was impos'd upon certain Tenants thereabout, for conspiring there, at such unseasonable time, to raise a commotion But I leave this, knowing neither the original nor the certain form thereof Only I heard certain obscure barbarous Rhimes of it;* Curia de Domino Rege tenetur sine Lege Ante ortum solis, luceat nisi polus, *&c not worth remembering*

409 15 To--- *Sir* Thomas

23 Brentwood---*Called by the* Normans Bois arse *in the same sense, and by that name King* Stephen *granted a Market and a Fair there, to the Abbot of St* Osith *and many years after,* Isabel *Countess of* Bedford, *Daughter to King* Edward *the third, built a Chapel to the memory of St* Thomas *of* Canterbury, *for the ease of the Inhabitants*

410 61 Knight ---*Created by our Sovereign King* James, *&c*

411 19 Born---*Sir* Robert de Essex

28 Till---*Sir* Hubert de Burgh

412 7 Design---*Yet there remaineth a huge ruin of a thick Wall, where-by many Roman Coins have been found*

413 53 Us--- *At this Town, the first* William de Mandevill *Earl of* Essex *began a Castle, and two,* &c

58 Essex---*Who founded here a College*

414 7 And --*Sir* Payne

66 John-- *Surnamed* Scot

• 76 Father --*Sir* William

415 7 Engerston---*Where he lieth buried*

28 Monks---*And the habitation of ancient Knights thence surnamed* de Cogeshall, *from whose Heir General, married into the old Family of* Tirrel, *there branched forth a fair propagation of the* Tirrels *in this Shire and elsewhere Then goeth on this water by* Eastertord; *some call it* East-Sturford

44 To---*Sir* Thomas

•418 60 Length---*Upon the ridge of an Hill answerable to the termination of* Dunum, *which signified an hilly and high situation, wherein I saw nothing memorable, unless I should mention two silly Churches, a desolate place of White-Friers, and a small pile of Bricks built not long since by* R Darcy, *which name hath been respective here about Hence passing down over the brackish water divided into two streamlets, by* Highbridge, *&c*

419 28. Purpose-- *Yet I will here impart what I incidentally happen'd upon in a private Note which I was inquisitive here about for* Ad Ansam *In a place call'd* Westfield, *three quarters of a mile distant from* Cogeshall, *and belonging to the Abbey there, was found by touching of a Plough a great brazen Pot The Ploughmen, supposing it to have been hid treasure, sent for the Abbot of* Cogeshall *to see the taking up of it, and he going thither met with Sir* Clement Harleston, *and desired him also to accompany him thither The mouth of the Pot was closed with a white substance like paste or clay, as hard as burn'd Brick, when that by force was remov'd, there was found within it another Pot, but that was of earth, that being opened, there was found in it a lesser Pot of earth of the quantity of a gallon, cover'd with a matter like velvet, and fasten'd at the mouth with a silk Lace In it they found some whole bones, and many pieces of small bones wrapp'd up in fine Silk of fresh colour, which the Abbot took for the Reliques of some Saints, and laid up in his vestuary*

420 47 Oxford---*Who procured a Market thereunto*

50 Famous---*Sir* [John Hawkwood]

ult Save---*This renown'd Knight thus celebrated abroad, was forgotten at home, save that some of his kind soldierly followers founded a Chantery at* Castle Hemingham *for him, and for two of his military Companions,* John Oliver, *and* Thomas Newenton, *Esquires*

421 24 Vere——*In the time of King* Henry *the first*

66 Wars——*And long after* Maud *the Empress gave it to* Alberic Vere *to assure him to her Party*

422 62 Sixth—— *When he created Sir* Thomas Darcy *his Counsellor, Vice-Chamberlain, and Captain of the Guard, Lord* Darcy *of* Chich

423 58 Lies---*The Town is not great, but well peopled, fortified by Art and Nature, and made more fencible by Queen* Elizabeth *The Salt Water so creeketh about it, that it almost insulateth it, but thereby maketh the Springs so brackish that there is a defect of fresh water, which they fetch some good way off*

424. 73 Barony---*From whom the* Wentworths *of* Gosfield *are descended*

425 16 Saffron-Walden---*Incorporated by King* Edward *the sixth with a Treasurer, two Chamberlains and the Commonalty*

20 Monastery- - *Founded in a place very commodious in the year* 1136

47 From——*Sir* Thomas

59 Chamberlain- - *Who in this place hath begun a magnificent Building*

426 3 Saffron---*A Commodity brought into* England *in the time of* Edward *the third*

50 To --*Sir* Robert Fitz Roger

73 By-- *Sir* George Vere

427 6 Of --*Sir* Henry Pole.

9 Blood- -*Neither is* Hatfield Regis, *commonly called of a broad spread Oak* Hatfield Brad Oak *to be omitted where* Robert Vere *Earl of* Oxford *built a Priory, and there lieth entomb'd cross-legg'd with a French Inscription, wherein he is noted to be the first of that name* Robert, *the third Earl of* Oxford

17 Stephen---*Despoiled of his estate*

28. Tree - *For in a reverent awe of the Church they durst not bury him, because he was excommunicated*

29 Sons Geoffrey *his Son, who was restored by* Henry *the second to his Father's Honours and [illegible] to him and his heirs,* William, *who by his wife was also Earl of* Albemarle

49 Service- *And so was girt with the Sword of the Earldom of* Essex *by King* John *at the Solemnity of his Coronation This* Geoffrey Fitz [illegible] *was advanced to the high estate of Justice of* England *by King* Richard *the first,* [illegible]

[illegible]

Page Line

removed Hubert *Archbishop of* Canterbury *from that Office by the Pope's peremptory command, for that Bishops ought not to intermeddle in secular Affairs This place the said* Geoffry Fitz-Petre *executed with great commendation, preserving by his wisdom the Realm from that confusion, which it after fell into by King* John's *unadvised carriage*

427. 53 These—*By his wife, was Earl of* Glocester *also, and*, &c

56 To — *Their sister's son.*

428 3 To — *Sir* William

8 Fourth—*In regard he had married his Aunt, and was descended from* Thomas *of* Woodstock

27 Essex — *Sir* William

SUFFOLK.

435. 13 VEterans — *Planted at* Maldon *abovesaid*

439 14. Sueno — *Being terrified with a Vision of* St Edmund

27 Seen—*And Abbot* Newport, *in like manner walled in the Abbey*

440 13. Getting—*Through the means of* St Edmund's *Shrine, and the Monument of* Alan Rufus *Earl of* Britain *and* Richmond, Sir Thomas *of* Brotherton, *son to King* Edward *the first, Earl of* Norfolk, *and Marshal of* England, Thomas *of* Beaufort, *Duke of* Exeter, William *Earl of* Stafford, Mary *Queen* Dowager *of* France, *daughter to King* Henry *the seventh, and many other illustrious Personages there interred*

74 Heirs—*Afterward, both here at* Haulsted *near* Rougham, *and elsewhere, the Family of* Drury *(which signifies in old English a* precious Jewel*) hath been of great reputation, more especially since they were marry'd with the Heiress of* Fresil *of* Saxham

441. 54. Clarence — *With a fuller sound than that of* Clare

442. 22 Normandy—*As also Lord High Steward of* England, *and Earl of* Albemarle

443 2 Marks — *No small Wealth, as the Standard was then From a younger brother or cadet of this House of* Montchensie, *issu'd by an heir-general the Family of the* Waldgraves, *who having long flourish'd in Knightly degree at* Smaltbridge *nearer to* Stour, *as another Family of great account in elder ages at* Buers, *which was thereof sirnamed*

36 Nettlested — *Whence was* Sir Thomas Wentworth, *whom King* Henry *the eighth honour'd with the title of Baron* Wentworth

44 Kingdom—*But to return to the river* Breton, *on the banks of another Brook that is joyn'd thereto, stands* Lancham, *a fair Market-town, and near it the Manour of* Burnt-Elleie, *to which King* Henry *the third granted a Market at the request of* Sir Henry Shelton *Lord thereof, whose posterity flourish'd here for a long time*

57 Runs — *Runs swiftly by* Higham, *whence the Family of* Higham *takes its name, to* Stour, *&c*

62 Bacons—*Who held this Manour of* Brome, *by conducting all the Footmen of* Suffolk *and* Norfolk *from* St Edmund's *dike, in the Wars of* Wales

444 26 Leicester—*During the intestine War between King* Henry *the second and his disloyal son.*

445 60 Frevil—Barkley *of* Stoke

446 36 Bigods—*Through the Bounty of King* Henry *the first*

447 7 Family—*Descended from the* Bacons *and* Brandons

Page Line.

449 27 Place—*On the farthest part of the same Promontory, stands* Easton, *a Village of Fishermen almost entirely swallowed up of the sea, and on the southern side thereof,* Southwold, *&c*

450 60 He—*Having surrender'd his Estate to King* Henry *the second*

452 59 Merchant—Michael *his son being restor'd, dy'd at the siege of* Harflew, *and within the space of one month, his son* Michael *was in like manner slain in the battle of* Agincourt, *leaving daughters only*

63 Suffolk—*As also Earl of* Pembroke

453 16 People—*Insomuch that being vehemently accus'd of Treason and Misprisions, and on that account summon'd to appear before the King and Lords in Parliament assembled, after having answer'd the Articles objected, he referr'd himself to the King's Order Whereupon the Chancellor by his Majesty's special Command, pronounc'd, That whereas the Duke did not put himself on his Peers, the K (as for what related to the Articles of Treason) would remain doubtful, and with respect to those of Misprision, not as a Judge by advice of the Lords, but as a person to whose order the Duke had voluntarily submitted himself, did banish him from the Realms, and all other his Dominions, for five years But he was surpriz'd*, &c

27 Cut-off—*In the battle at* Stoke

55 Upon—*Sir* Charles

58 Marriage — *And granted to him all the Honours and Manours which* Edmund *Earl of* Suffolk *had forfeited*

61 Sickness—*On one day*

NORFOLK

457 35 COnsul—*Which name may intimate that it was a Roman town*

458 51 Of—*Sir* John

56 And—*Sir* Thomas Knevet, *Lord* Knevet.

459 18 Upon—*Sir* Richard Lucy

25 Be—Harleston—*a good Market, and*, &c

41 Mareschals—*To the Lord* Morleys

47 Burdos—*Or* Burdelos

50 Him——*Joint-neighbour to* Skulton, *is* Woodrising, *the fair seat of the family of* Southwells, *which received the greatest Reputation and Increase from* Sir Richard Southwell, *Privy-Counsellor to K* Edward *the sixth, and his brother* Sir Robert *Master of the* Rowles

67 Here--*Which afterwards was advanced to an Abby*

460 4 To——*Sir* Ralph

62 Course — *By* Fakenham, *which King* Henry *the first gave to* Hugh Capel, *and King* John, *afterward, to the Earl of* Arundel

77 As — *Archbishop*

463 29 Thereof — *They obtain'd of King* Richard *the second, that the* Worsted *made there might be transported*

42 Of — *Of* Sales, Baies, *and other Stuffs now much in use*

464 48 Pleas—*It receiveth a Brook which passeth by nothing memorable but* Halles-hall, *and that only memorable for its ancient owner* Sir James Hobart *Attorney-General, and of the Privy Council to King* Henry *the seventh (by him dubb'd Knight at such time as he created* Henry *his son Prince of* Wales*) who, by building from the ground the fair Church at* Loddon *being his Parish-Church,* St Olave's *Bridge over* Wavency *that divideth* Norfolk *and* Suffolk, *the Cawsey thereby, and other Works of Piety, deserv'd well of the Church, his Country, and the Common weal, and planted*

three

Page Line three Houses out of his own issue, out of the second whereof Sir Henry Hobart his great grandchild, now likewise Attorney-General to King James, is lineally descended

465 30 Knight—And now appertaining to the Pastans

466. 74 Possessions — Nor far from Worsted, where (as I read) the Stuff-worsted, in so great request among our Ancestors, was first made, and hence so nam'd, as Dornicks, Cameric, Calecut, &c had in like manner their denomination from the places where they were first invented and made

467 61 Veneration — Next is Paston, a small Townlet, which yet hath given firname to a family grown great both in estate and alliance, since they match'd with the heiress of Beary and Maultbye

468. 16 By—Sir Robert.

ibid Roos—Sir Robert

475. 3 To—Sir William

42 To—Sir Hugh

45 To—Sir Hamon

46 Of—Sir Anthony

476 56 England — This is he, that before the King was challeng'd and accus'd by Henry of Lancaster Duke of Hereford

477 15 Upon—John Lord Howard

25 Surrey — And by King Henry the seventh made Lord Treasurer

26 Norfolk —And his son the same day created Earl of Surrey

27 Army—At Branxton

37 Thomas — As well in his honours, as in the Office of Lord Treasurer of England, and liv'd in the time of Queen Mary

CAMBRIDGESHIRE

479 58 JErmins—Above Caxton before-mention'd, is Eltesley, where was in elder ages a Religious House of holy Virgins, among whom was celebrated the incertain memory of Saint Pandionia, the daughter of a Scottish King, as the Tradition is But long since they were translated to Hinchinbroke And again, above Eltesley was the Priory of Swasey, founded for black Monks by Alan la Zouch, brother to the Viscount of Rohan in the lesser Britain, and was the common sepulture a long time for the family of Zouch

486 35 11 Min —Cam, from Cambridge continuing his course by Waterbeach, an ancient seat of Nuns, which Lady Mary St Paul translated from thence to Denny somewhat higher, but nothing healthfuller, when in a low ground he hath spread a Mere, associateth himself with the river Ouse

487 42 Office—The Earls of Oxford also (that I may note it incidently) by the heir of R Sandford, held the Manours of Fingrey and Walfelmeston by Serjeanty of Chamberlainship to the Queens at the Coronation of their Kings

488. 73 Cottons—From which Wicken is not far distant; which came to the family of the Peytons by a daughter and coheir of the Gernons, about Edward the third's time.

492 33 Fens—He began the fair Palace at Ely for his successors

493 7 Air—Although it be seated somewhat higher Near to it is Downham, where the Bishop hath his residing house with a Park Near to Downham is Cowney, the ancientest seat of the family, firnam'd for their habitation here, Lisle and De Insula, and first planted here by Nigellus the second Bishop of Ely, their allie in the time of King Henry the first, as is set down in a Leiger-book of Ely Chateries or Cheaterich is not far hence westward, where Alwena a devout woman, founded a Nunnery upon a copp'd ground encompass'd with Fens, while her Husband founded Ramsey

HUNTINGDONSHIRE

504 16 PLace—And by the name of Gumicester King Henry the third granted it to his son Edmund Earl of Lancaster

506 35 Broad—Which (as other Meres in this tract) doth sometimes in calms and fair weather rise tempestuously as it were into violent water-quakes, to the danger of the poor Fisher-men, by reason, as some think, of Evaporations breaking violently out of the earth.

40 Place—Whereunto strangers, and not the natives there, are subject, who live long and healthfully

509 21 John—(Who was stiled Duke of Excester, Earl of Huntingdon and Ivory, Lord of Sparre, Admiral of England and Ireland, Lieutenant of Aquitain, and Constable of the Tower of London)

NORTHAMPTONSHIRE

513 3 EXpir'd — And, being canoniz'd by the People amongst the Saints, had his commemoration kept both here and at Buckingham

514 37 Appeal—Moreover, about that time he was made Lord Treasurer of England

519 74 Belong'd—And, to turn a little aside, I may not omit Horton, whenas King Henry the eighth created Sir W Par Lord thereof, Uncle and Chamberlain to Queen Catharine Par, Baron Par of Horton; which Honour shortly vanish'd with him, when he left only daughters, who were married into the families of Tresham and Lane But to return, &c

520 1 Wedlingborough— And Wodlingborough, made a Market by King John at the suit of the Monks of Crowland

52 Whereof—Sir Nicholas

56 Town—In times past of the Peverells, and after by them of the Ferrers

66 Thrapston — Belonging likewise to them

521 10 Synod — Of one hundred and thirteen Bishops

19 Huntingdon — Who were of the Royal race of Scotland

25 Fetter — Which, both of it self, and with a Falcon in it, was his Device or Emprese, as implying that he was lock'd up from all great hope, as a younger Brother

36 Church—In King Edward the sixth's time

44 Descended — The form of the Keep belonging [illegible], built like a Fetterlock, occasioneth me to [illegible] little, and I hope with your pardon, [illegible] the gravest Authors in as small matters [illegible] the like Edmund of Langly Duke of York, who built that Keep, and garnish'd the [illegible] windows there with Fetter locks, [illegible] his Sons, being young Scholars, gazing upon the painted Windows, ask'd them, [illegible] for a Fetter lock? They [illegible] and looking silently one upon another, not able to answer, If you cannot tell me, says he, I will tell you, Hic, haec, hoc Taceatis, that is, [illegible] but be silent, and quiet, and therewithal added, God knoweth what may happen hereafter This King Edward the fourth, his great grandchild, reported publickly, when he, having attained the Crown, created Richard his younger son Duke of York, and then commanding that he should use for his Badge the Fetter-lock open, to verify the presage of his great grandfather But this by the way

Page Line

521. 53 The — *Deprived of the same, recovering it again*

55 Away—*Her second son, and,* &c

523 15 Lord—*546*

18 Girvians—*Or Finn-Country*

527 36 By—Suleby, *sometimes an Abbey of black Monks, and by,* &c

528 5 Seen—*And called* Burrows.

LEICESTERSHIRE.

530 17. GUIDE.—*For the finding out of those said Towns which* Antonine *the Emperor specifieth in his Itinerary*

50 Poultneys — *Who took that name of* Poulteney, *a place now decay'd within the said Lordship*

53 Verdons—*Which only sheweth a fair Church, which hath been encreas'd by the* Feldings *of Knights Degree and ancient Gentry in this Shire*

60. Rome—*And Religious Men*

531 46 Grantmaisnill—*A* Norman

533 63 Zouch — *Who descended from* Alan *Viscount of* Rohan *in* Little Britain, *and* Constantia *his wife, daughter to* Conan le Grosse *Earl of* Britain, *and* Maud *his wife, the natural daughter of* Henry *the first*

534 10 Seymour—*Of* Castle-Cary

ibid. Holland—*Yet their Father first bestow'd this* Ash by *upon* Sir Richard Mortimer *of* Richards-Castle *his Cousin, whose younger issue thereupon took the sirname of* Zouch, *and were Lords of* Ashby *But from* Eudo *a younger Son of* Alane, *who was slain in* Westminster-hall, *the Lords* Zouch *of* Haringworth *branch'd out, and have been for many descents Barons of the Realm*

50 Beaumont — *Descended from Sir* Thomas Beaumont, *Lord of* Bachevill *in* Normandy, *brother to the first Viscount Which Sir* Thomas *(as some write) was he who was slain manfully fighting at such time as the* French *recover'd* Paris *from the* English, *in the time of King* Henry *the sixth*

535 58 Ore—*That is, by weight*

536. 46. Hospital — *As for this Hospital, it continueth in some good state, as another Beadhouse in the town, built by* W Wigeston *But the Collegiate Church, which was a magnificent Work, and the greatest ornament of* Leicester, *was demolished when Religious Houses were granted to the King*

59 Leicester—*When he began* Gerondon-Abbey *for* Cistercians

537 8 Raw-dikes—*Or Road-dikes*

538 24 Not—*North-west from* Leicester

539 26 Trent—*A little above* Cotes, *now the habitation of the Family of* Skipwith, *originally descended out of* Yorkshire, *and enrich'd many years since with fair possessions in* Lincolnshire, *by an heir of* Ormesby

540 34 Wall—*These* Beaumonts *descended from a younger son of* John *Count of* Brene *in* France, *who for his high honour and true valour was preferr'd to marry the heir of the Kingdom of* Jerusalem, *and with great pomp crown'd King of* Jerusalem *in the year of our Lord* 1248 *Hence it is, that we see the Arms of* Jerusalem *so often quarter'd with those of* Beaumont, *in sundry places of* England *Sir* Henry Beaumont *was the first that planted himself in* England, *about the year* 1308

54 Treason—*By attainder of* Lovel, *it fell into the hands of King* Henry *the seventh*

540 57 Dieu—*Now belonging to a younger House of the* Beaumonts

67 Younger—*The hereditaments of* Thomas *Earl of* Lancaster; *and* Alice Lacy *his wife, were seiz'd into the King's hands, and alienated in divers sorts; the King enforc'd her to release this Manour to* Hugh le Dispenser *the younger.*

541. 19 Burgh—*And under it a town call'd* Burrough, *belonging to an old family of Gentlemen so sirnam'd*

542 2 Elephantiasis—*Because the skins of Lepers are like those of Elephants*

8 History—*Whether by celestial influence, or other hidden causes, I leave to the learned*

31. Same—*The river that watereth this part of the Shire, is by the Inhabitants about it call'd the* Wreken, *along which, upon resemblance of the name, I have sought* Vernometum, *but in vain This* Wreken *gathereth a strong stream by many lively Brooks resorting unto it, whereof one passeth by* Wimondham, *an ancient habitation of a younger branch of the House of the Lords* Barkleis, *well encreased by an heir of* Dela-Laund, *and so on by* Melton Mowbray *before mention'd, by* Kirkby-Bellers *(where there was a Priory,) having that addition of the* Bellers, *a respective, rich, and noble Family in their time, by* Brokesby *a seat now of the* Villiers *of an old* Norman *race, and descended from an heir of* Bellers *which* Brokesby *imparted formerly the sirname to the* Brokesbies *of especial Antiquity in these parts Then the* Wreken *speedeth by* Ratcliffe, *high mounted upon a Cliff, and within few miles conjoyneth it self to* Soar, *near unto* Mont-Soar-hill *before-mention'd Whatsoever of this Shire lieth beyond the* Wreken *northward, is not so frequently inhabited, and part of it is call'd the* Wold, *as being hilly without wood, wherein* Dalby, *a seat of the old family of the* Noels, *of whom I shall speak elsewhere, and* Waltham on the Wold, *a mean Market, are most notable Through this part, as I have been informed, passeth the* Fosse-way, *made by the* Romans *from* Lewing Bridge, *by* Segrave, *which gave sirname to the honourable family often mention'd, and the* Lodge on the Wold *toward the* Vale of Bever, *but the Track thereof as yet I know not*

62 Bossu—*Because he was crook back'd, who, after he had rebell'd against King* Henry *the first, weary of his loose irregular life, became a Canon-Regular*

63 Blanchmaines — *Of his Lily-white hands; who sided with the young King against King* Henry *the second, and died in the expedition of King* Richard *the first to the Holy Land*

67 Grant maisnil — *In whose right he was Seneschal or Steward of* England, *and died issueless in the time of King* John

73 1200—*As wholly devoted to the* French

543 5 Leicester — *Granted to him the Stewardship of* England

544 9 Sword — *And extraordinarily favoured*

13 1588 — *Leaving the Fame only of his Greatness behind him*

RUTLANDSHIRE

545 4 WHich — *(I grieve to utter it, but all Men know it)*

8 Country *More eastward, upon the river* Welland, *I saw nothing remarkable, unless it be* Berohdon, *now* Barodon, *which* Thomas Beauchamp *Earl of* Warwick *held with* South Luttenham

Esc. 14 *Edw.* III

Page Line

fenham and other Hamlets, by service to the King's Chamberlain in the Exchequer

545 27. Church—Which is large and fair

546. 24. Harrington—Branch'd from the stem of the ancient Lords Harrington.

26 Exton—A Town adjacent, where he hath also another fair House

LINCOLNSHIRE

549. 29 HAY—Which our Progenitors broadly called Hoy

552. 56 Things—But hereby you may see how by small Contributions great Works arose

555 61. Oxford—Upon the King's Proclamation

556 31 Britain—Sir William

557 71. Of—Sir Andrew

558. 53 To—Sir Henry.

70 Also—Sir John

ult Name—Created by King Henry the eighth

559 51 To—Sir William

561 75. To—Sir William

563 56 Hill—At the foot whereof they built (as it seemeth) the gate yet standing, compiled of vast Stones

564. ult First—Who dy'd at Hardby in this Shire

565. 1 Of—Sir Nicholas.

567 35 By—Sir John

59 To—Sir Ralph

ult Was—Sir Robert

569 20 Hos—More inward are Driby and Ormesby, neighbour Towns, which gave sirnames to two great Families in their times From the Dribyes descended the elder Lords Cromwell, now determined, and from Ormesbies, the House of Skipwith, still continuing.

39 Night—But the honour and ornament of this place, was the right reverend Doctor Whitgift, late Archbishop of Canterbury, a peerless Prelate for piety and learning in our days.

570 23 Family—Of Semarc.

34. Knights—Descended from Grovil, Oxenbridge, and Echingham.

571. 51 Of—Sir William.

573 13 Gall—It yieldeth also Pets in the Mores, and dead roots of Fir-wood, which in burning give a rank sweet savour There also have been found great and long fir-trees while they digg'd for Pet, both within the Isle, and also without, at Laughton upon Trent bank, the old habitation of the Family of Delanson, now contractly call'd Dalison

42 Whereof—Sir Edmund Sheffeld

49 Garter—President of the Council establish'd in the North.

574 25 Marry'd—Sir Eubul

28 Estate—Yet both Sir Eubul Strange and Sir Hugh Frene her third husband, are in some Records nam'd Earls of Lincoln

56 On—Sir John.

NOTTINGHAMSHIRE

576 39 WAY—And received into its Chanel the River Soure, running hither from the County of Leicester

47 Clistons—Much enrich'd by one of the heirs of Cressy

579 53 Shelford—Where Ralph Hanselin founded a Priory, and the Lords Randolphs had a Mansion, but now the seat of, &c

580 2 Parts—Since they match'd with an heir of Mallovel

Page Line

580. 32 Hence—Is Thurgarton, where Sir Ralph D'eincourt founded a Priory, and somewhat higher Southwell, &c.

581 38 Self—Near Averham or Aram, an ancient habitation of the Suttons, Gentlemen of respective worth

582 11 Castle—And King Edward the sixth incorporated it of one Alderman, and twelve Assistants

583 49 Some—Who delineate the pedigree of the Graves of the great Family of Mansfield in Germany.

58 Mansfeld—And the hereditary Foresters or Keepers of this Forest of Shirewood, were men in their times of high estimation, viz Sir Gerard de Normanvile, in the time of the Conquest, the Cauzes and Birkins, by whose heir it came to the Everinghams Of which Family Sir Adam Everingham was summon'd to Parliaments in the reigns of King Edward the second, and King Edward the third At which time they were seated at Laxton anciently call'd Lexinton, where also flourish'd a great Family so sirnam'd, whose heirs were marry'd into the Houses of Sutton of Averham and Markham

584. 5 Valour—Being descended from one of the heirs of Cressy, and formerly from an heir of Lexinton, as I lately shewed

585 10 Others—By his wife, the heir of the Mowbrays

13 Son—When he created him Duke of Richmond

DERBYSHIRE

586. 53 CRoxton—But whether Sir Robert Curson, Knighted by King Henry the seventh, and created a Baron of the Empire by the Emperor Maximilian, A D 1500 on the account of his singular Valour, on whom King Henry the eighth in like manner conferr'd the title of a Baron of England, assigning to him a liberal Pension, were descended from these Cursons, I dare not affirm.

589. 41 Montjoy—With a Pension

590. 22 Musards—That is to say, Doubters and Delayers

57 Lost—King John erected it into a Free-borough, and gave it to William Briewer, his particular Favourite

591 25 Also—(By reason that under the upper crust of the Earth there is Lime-stone, which yields a fruitful Slugh or Humour)

76 Mannours—Son of Thomas Earl of Rutland, and to Sir Thomas Stanley, Son of Edward Earl of Derby

594 11 Sight—To these wonders may be added a wonderful Well in the Peake-forest not far from Buxtons, which ordinarily ebbeth and floweth four times in the space of one hour, or thereabouts, keeping his just tides and I know not whether Tideswel, a Market-town hereby, hath his name thereof

29. Son—Who, being bruis'd with a fall out of his Coach, dy'd in the year 1254

46 Mother—To him and his heirs males He had for his Successor his grandson Thomas, begotten by George his Son on the body of Joan the heiress of the Lord Strange of Knocking This same Thomas had by the sister of George Earl of Huntingdon, Edward the third Earl of this Family, highly commended for his courteousness and hospitality, who, of the Lady Dorothy, daughter to the first Thomas Howard, Duke of Norfolk, begat Henry the fourth Earl, who soon obtain'd very honourable employments, and

Page Line

left, by the Lady Margaret, daughter of Henry Earl of Cumberland, Ferdinand and William successively Earls of Derby Ferdinand dy'd after a strange manner in the flower of his youth, having by Margaret his wife, daughter of Sir John Spenser of Althorp, three daughters, viz Anne, marry'd to Grey Bruges Lord Chandos, Frances, espous'd to Sir John Egerton, and Elizabeth the wife of Henry Earl of Huntingdon William the sixth Earl now enjoyeth the honour, and hath issue by Elizabeth, daughter to Edward late Earl of Oxford

WARWICKSHIRE

603 8 Notitia)— Or Abstract of Provinces.

32. Præsidium —— That is, the Garrison-town

604 14. Pomp — And after a sumptuous Funeral solemniz'd, in this Church lies entomb'd in a magnificent Tomb with this Inscription Pray devoutly for the Soul, whom God assoil, of one of the most worshipful Knights in his days of manhood and cunning, Richard Beauchamp, late Earl of Warwick, Lord Dispenser of Bergavenny, and of many other great Lordships, whose body resteth here under this Tomb, in a full fair Vault of Stone, set in the bare Roche The which visited with long sickness in the Castle of Roan, therein deceased full Christianly the last day of April, in the year of our Lord God 1439 He being at that time Lieutenant General of France, and of the Dutchy of Normandy, by sufficient authority of our Sovereign Lord King Henry the sixth The which body, by great deliberation and worshipful conduct by Sea and Land, was brought to Warwick the fourth of October, the year abovesaid, and was laid with full solemn exequies in a fair Chest made of Stone in the west door of this Chapel, according to his last Will and Testament, therein to rest till this Chapel, by him devised in his life, were made the which Chapel founded on the Roche, and all the members thereof, his Executors did fully make and apparel, by the authority of his said last Will and Testament And thereafter by the said authority they did translate worshipfully the said body into the Vault aforesaid Honoured be God therefore

606 71 Others—Who have better observed the nature of this River

607 70 To—Sir William

76 Chaundois — But now it is decay'd, and of a very great Town become a small Market of wares and trade Howbeit exceeding much frequented for the Corn-fair there holden. This hath for a near neighbour Arrow, according to the name of the river, whose Lord Thomas Burdet, for his dependance upon George Duke of Clarence, words unadvisedly uttered, and hardly construed through the iniquity of the time, lost his life But by his grand-daughter, married to Edward Conway brother to Sir Hugh Conway of Wales, a gracious favourite of King Henry the seventh, the Knightly Family of the Conways have ever since flourished, and laudably followed the Profession of Arms

608 ult. Wars—Which he had raised upon fair pretext against his Sovereign

609 2 Third—Who annex'd this Castle as an Inheritance to Edmund his Son, Earl of Lancaster

Page Line

62. Bremichams—Earls of Louth, &c

611 49. Bayliffs—And to build and embattle a Wall about it

613. 14. Asteleys — Out of which flourish'd Barons in the time of King Edward the first, second, and third

17 Inter'd— In a most fine and fair Collegiate Church, which Thomas Lord Astley founded with a Dean and Secular Canons

57. The—Augustine Friers

615 23 That— After his death, Anne his wife by Act of Parliament was excluded and debarred from all her Lands for ever, and his two daughters, heirs to him, and heirs apparent to their mother, being married to George Duke of Clarence, and Richard Duke of Glocester, were enabled to enjoy all the said Lands, in such wise as if the said Anne their mother were naturally dead Whereupon the name, stile and title of Earl of Warwick and Salisbury was granted to George Duke of Clarence, who soon after was unnaturally dispatch'd by a sweet death in a Butt of Malvesey by his suspicious brother King Edward the fourth His young Son Edward was stiled Earl of Warwick, and being but a very child, was beheaded by King Henry the seventh, to secure himself and his posterity The death of this Edward, our Ancestors accounted to be the full period and final end of the long lasting War between the two Royal Houses of Lancaster and York Wherein, as they reckon'd, from the 28th year of Henry the sixth, unto this, being the 15th of Henry the seventh, there were thirteen Fields fought, three Kings of England, one Prince of Wales, twelve Dukes, one Marquis, eighteen Earls, with one Viscount, and twenty three Barons, besides Knights and Gentlemen, lost their lives

45 Him—And his heirs males, and for defect of them, to Robert his brother, and the heirs males of his body lawfully begotten

46 Issue— This Honour Ambrose bare with great commendation, and died without Children in the year 1589, shortly after his brother Robert Earl of Leicester

WORCESTERSHIRE

618 11 Plenty—And in one part for dainty Cheese surpasseth them

62 Arthur — At which time he granted some privileges to Beawdley

620 10 Salwarp — This hath its first veins out of the Lickey-hill, most eminent in the North-part of this Shire; near unto which, at Frankley, the Family of the Littletons were planted by John Littleton alias Westcote, the famous Lawyer, Justice in the King's Bench in the time of King Edward the fourth, to whose Treatise of Tenures, the Students of our Common Law are no less beholden, than the Civilians to Justinian's Institutes

621 13 Bullions—Salwarp having now entertain'd a small Brook descending from Chedesley, where anciently the Family of Foliot flourish'd, as after at Longdon, makes haste to Severne

629 23 Westminster—Then receiveth Avon, a riveret, from the north, upon which stands Hodington a Seat of the Winters, of which were Robert Winter and his brother Thomas, who whereas they were in the Gun-powder Treason, &c

631 36. Mellent--Twin brother

STAFFORD

Page Line

STAFFORDSHIRE

633. 34. WOrcestershire—On the river Stoure stands Stourton-Castle, sometime appertaining to the Earls of Warwick, the place of the nativity of Cardinal Pole, and then Dudley-Castle, &c

42. Knight—Descended from the Suttons of Nottinghamshire

46 Dudley——But first summoned to Parliament by King Henry the sixth

47 Family——Here is situated Penkneth-chace, in former times better stored with Game than at present, where are found many Coal-Pits, in which (as it hath been related to me) here as yet continueth a Fire begun by a Candle long since by the negligence of a certain grover or digger The Smoak of this fire, and sometimes the flame, is seen, but the scent oftener smelt And other places of the like nature were shew'd to me not far off On the confines of Shropshire, to the northwest, I saw Pateshall, a Seat of the Astleys, descended from honourable Progenitors; and Wrotesley, an habitation of a race of Gentlemen so surnamed, out of which, Sir Hugh Wrotesley, on the account of his singular Valour, was chosen by King Edward the third Knight of the Garter at the first Institution, and therefore esteemed as one of the Founders of the said honourable Order

636 8. Honour — When Baldwin Frevil inhibited his Petition for the same, it was adjudg'd from this Family to Sir John Dimock his Competitor, descended also from Marmion, and producing more authentick Records and Evidences

637. 15 Way——But, at a small distance from thence is Breewood, a Market-town, where the Bishops of the Diocese had a Seat before the Conquest, and then near Weston is that clear, &c

24. Fountains——In the north part of this Shire, and amidst the Moors or Marshes

638 17 Derby——Strange it is to read, what Lands King Henry the third confirm'd to Henry Audeley, which were bestow'd on him through the bounty of the Peers, and even of private Gentlemen, not only in England, but also in Ireland, where Hugh Lacy Earl of Ulster gave him Lands, together with the Constableship of Ulster; so that without doubt he was either a person of singular virtue, or a very great Favourite, or an able Lawyer, or perhaps was endu'd with all these qualifications His posterity were ally'd in marriage with the heirs of the Lord Giffard of Brimsfield, of Baron Martin Lord of Keimeis and Barstaple, as also a younger brother of this House, with one of the heirs of the Earl of Glocester, who was by King Edward the third created Earl of Glocester About which time James Lord Audley acquir'd a very great reputation, on the account of his valour and skill in war like Affairs, (who as it is related by French Historians) being dangerously wounded in the battle of Poitiers, when the Black Prince with many high commendations had given to him a pension of four hundred marks per annum, bestow'd it immediately on his four Esquires, that always valiantly attended him, and satisfy'd the Prince, doubting that his gift might be too little for so great service, with this answer, gratefully acknowledging his bounty These my Esquires sav'd my life amidst my enemies; and God be thank'd, my Ancestors have left me sufficient Revenues to maintain me in your Service Whereupon the Prince, approving the prudent Liberality, both confirm'd his Donation to his Esquires, and besides assign'd to him Lands to the value of six hundred marks yearly. But by his daughter, one of the co-heirs to her brother, the title of Lord Audley came afterwards to the Touchets, and in them continueth

638 36 Chebsey — Reckon'd among the principal Noblemen in the time of King Edward the first

68 Deniers — And had thirteen Canons Prebendaries, who held in Frank-Almoin.

76 It——Which the Barons of Stafford, of whose Progeny were the Dukes of Buckingham, built for their own Seat who prevail'd with King John to erect it into a Burrough with ample liberties and privileges, caus'd to be partly enclos'd with a Wall, and founded a Priory of Black-Canons in honour of St Thomas of Canterbury

639 68 Sixth —— He was (as it may be collected from his Epitaph) Secretary and Privy Counsellor to King Henry the eighth, and constituted by his Testament Counsellor and Adjutant to King Edward the sixth during his minority, to whom he was Chancellor of the Dutchy of Lancaster, Comptroller of the Houshold, and by him created (as I have already intimated) Baron, and Knight of the Garter, as also by Queen Mary, Lord Privy Seal Whose grandson William is now the fourth Baron Pagett

641 48 Ferrars——Built in the Conqueror's time

642 42 Never —— Neverthelefs in so hard a Soil it brings forth and feeds Beasts of a large size

643 16 Verdons —— Who founded here the Abbey of Croxden

33 Say—— As for Blith, it hath in this Moorland a little Castle named Careswell, which Sir William Careswell built, with great Ponds, having their heads made of square Stones, and Draicot, which gave a surname to a Family of great Antiquity in this County

39 Dove——After it hath receiv'd Tine

644. 31. Stafford—Then sew of them Earls, viz Ralph created by King Edward the third Earl of Stafford, who married the heiress of Hugh Audley Earl of Glocester Hugh his Son, who dy'd in Pilgrimage at Rhodes, and his three Sons successively Thomas and William both without issue, and Edmund, who took to wife the daughter and heiress of Thomas of Woodstock Duke of Buckingham Afterward, three of them were Dukes of Buckingham, and Earls of Stafford, &c as it hath been before declared By the Attainder of the last of them, those ample Inheritances, &c

SHROPSHIRF

645 66 LORDS — Which they enjoy'd, and insolently exercis'd over the poor Inhabitants in the Marches

648 18 To—Sir Foulk of Dinan

19 To—Sir Jeffrey

63 To—Sir Jeffrey

649 61 Prince—Sir Robert Syncler

63 Also—Sir Ralph

67 Of—Burgh

75 Of—Sir Warner

650 9 To—Robert Blunt.

17 Montgomery — In later times, Sir John Winell, call'd also Wenlock, because he here inhabited, for his faithful Service to King Henry the sixth, was by him advanc'd to the state and honour of Baron Wenlock, and elected Knight of the Garter; in whose cause he manfully lost his life in the battle of Tewksbury, leaving no issue but from his Cousin and heir-general, the Lawleys of this County are lineally descended A little more west, is Acton-Burnell, &c

Of

Page Line.

651 14 Of—*Sir* Ralph Butler, *the younger Son of* Ralph Butler *of* Wem

21 Tewion — *But whereas these seem natural, I dare not*, &c

36 Of—*Sir* Peter.

46 Of—*Sir* Foulque

653 8. Without—*In equal distance*

654 4. Of—*Sir* Ralph

5 Shrewsbury — *But above* Tong *was* Lilleshul-*Abbey, in a wood-land Country, founded by the Family of* Beaumeis, *whose heir was marry'd into the House of* De la Zouch *But seeing there is little left but ruins, I will leave it, and proceed*

48 Walls—*Which yet make a fair shew*

57 Days—*as the common sort ascribe whatsoever is ancient and strange to King* Arthur's *glory*

59 Corbet —— *Anciently an House of the Family of* Turet

62. Building — *In a barren place—after the Italian model*

65 Unfinish'd—*And the old Castle defac'd*

74 Udecot——*And in later age, this Family far and fairly propagated, receiv'd encrease both of revenue and great alliance by the marriage of an heir of* Hopton

75 Newports — *Knights of great worship, descended from the Barons* Grey *of* Codnor *and the Lords of* Mothwy

655 59 Book — *In King* Edward *the Confessor's time, it paid Gelt according to an hundred Hides In the Conqueror's time, it paid yearly seven pounds*, &c

656 52 Erected — *A school wherein were more Scholars in number, when I first saw it, than any School in* England

56. Salary—*It shall not now, I hope, be impertinent to note, that when divers of the Nobility conspir'd against King* Henry *the fourth, with a purpose to advance* Edmund Mortimer *Earl of* March *to the Crown, as the undoubtful and right Heir, whose Father King* Richard *the second had also declar'd Heir apparent, and Sir* Henry Percy *call'd* Hotspur, *then addressed himself to give the assault to* Shrewsbury, *&c*

ult. Dispute —— *Wherein the Scottish-men which follow'd him, shew'd much manly Valour (when the Earl of* Worcester *his Uncle, and the Earl of* Dunbar *were taken) he despairing*, &c

657 51 To—*Such as attribute nothing at all to celestial Influence and learned Experience*

658 3 Honourable—*Sir* Thomas

659 23 From—*Sir* Guarin

27 Renown'd—*Sir* Fulk Fitz-Warren

29 Ancestors—*And had Poems compos'd upon it*

45 Needhams—Blackmere, *an ancient Family of the Lords* L'estrange

57 Achilles—*Sir* John

660 7 Blackmere—*Who were Surnam'd* Le Strange *commonly, and* Extranei *in Latin Records, for that they were strangers brought hither by King* Henry *the second, and in a short time their House was far propagated Those of* Blackmere *were much enrich'd by an heir of* W de Albo Monasterio *or this* Whit-church, *and also by one of the heirs of* John *Lord* Giffard *of* Brimsfield, *of ancient Nobility in* Glocestershire, *by the only daughter of* Walter *Lord* Clifford

18 More—*Westward*

23 And—Joan *his base-daughter*

ibid Then—*In the time of King* Henry *the third*

25 Baron—— *Sir* Thomas

63 Chatillon—*Upon* Dordan *near* Bourdeaux

ibid Son—— *Sir* John Talbot

68 Of——*Sir* Thomas

660. 71 Him —— *By a daughter of the Earl of* Ormond

72. And —— *Sir* Gilbert Talbot, *Captain of* Calais

73 Descended — *This third* John *had by his wife* Katharine, *daughter to* Henry *Duke of* Buckingham, George *the fourth Earl, who serv'd King* Henry *the seventh valiantly and constantly at the battle of* Stoke *And he, by* Anne *his wife, daughter of* William *Lord* Hastings, *had* Francis *the fifth Earl, who begat, of* Mary *daughter to* Thomas *Lord* Dacre *of* Gillesland, George *the sixth Earl, a man of approv'd fidelity in weighty Affairs of State; whose Son* Gilbert *by his wife* Gertrude, *daughter to* Thomas *Earl of* Rutland, *the seventh Earl, maintaineth at this day*, &c

CHESHIRE

667 58 REIGN—*Sir* Ralph

671 31. Churches——*But that of St* John's, *without the North-gate, was the fairest, being a stately and solemn building, as appears by the remains, wherein were anciently Prebendaries, and (as some write) the Bishop's See*

36 Street——*They call them* Rowes, *having Shops on both sides, through which a Man may walk dry from one end unto the other*

674 10 Bunbury—*Contractly so called for* Boniface Bury, *for St* Boniface *was the Patron Saint there.*

11 Beeston castle—— *Which gave Surname to an ancient Family*

675 68 Where—— *Very near the brink of the river* Dan

677 44 To—*Sir* John

678 42 Baron —— *Of the Earls of* Chester, *and* Warburgton, *so named of St* Werburgh, *the habitation of a Family thereof surnamed, but branched from the* Duttons

44 Maclesfeld — *One of the fairest Towns in this County*

679 12 From——*Sir* Hamon

39 Ethelfleda—*Commonly call'd* Elfled

682 57 Chamberlain——*Who hath all jurisdiction of a Chancellor, within the said County* Palatine

58 Special—*For matters in Common-Plees, and Plees of the Crown, to be heard and determin'd in the said County*

59 Escheator—*And the inhabitants of the said County, for the enjoying of their Liberties, were to pay at the change of every owner of the said Earldom, a Sum of Money (about three thousand marks) by the name of a* Mize, *as the County of* Flint *being a parcel thereof about two thousand Marks, if I have not been misinformed*

HEREFORDSHIRE.

685 21 FErtility — *And therefore says, that for three* W W W *Wheat, Wool and Water, it yieldeth to no Shire of* England

691 20 Year—— 1,71

68 Rosse—— *Made a free Borough by King* Henry *the third*

692 29 The—*Assisting the Earl of* Flanders

31 Dy'd—*Condemn'd to perpetual Prison for a Conspiracy against the Conqueror*

33 Leicester—*Who had married* Emme *or* Itta *heir of* Breteuill

41 And —— *Also granted to him* Constabulariam Curiæ suæ, *the Constableship of her Court, whereupon his Posterity were Constables of* England,

Page Line

as the Marshalship was granted at the first by the name of Magistratus Mariscalliæ Curiæ nostræ

692 *ult.* Elizabeth——*Daughter.*

MONMOUTHSHIRE.

714. 60. KAradok —— *And adjoining to it, is* Sudbroke, *the Church whereof, call'd* Trinity-Chapel, *standeth so near the Sea, that the vicinity of so tyrannous a neighbour, hath spoil'd it of half the Church-yard, as it hath done also of an old Fortification lying thereby, which was compassed with a triple Ditch and three Rampires, as high as an ordinary house, cast in form of a Bow, the string whereof is the Sea-cliff That this was a* Roman *work, the* Britain *Bricks and* Roman *Coins there found, are most certain arguments, among which, the Reverend Father in God,* Francis *Bishop of* Landaffe *(by whose information I write this) imparted unto me of his kindness o e of the greatest pieces that ever I saw coin'd, of* Corinthian *Copper, by the City of* Elaia *in the lesser* Asia, *to the honour of the Emperor* Severus, *with this Greek Inscription,* ΑΥΤ ΚΑΙ Λ ΣΕΠΤΙ ΣΕΒΗΡΟΣ ΠΕΡ *that is, the Emperor* Cæsar Lucius Septimius Severus Pertinax *And on the reverse, an Horse-man with a Trophee erected before him, but the Letters not legible, save under him* ΕΛΑΙΤΩΝ *that is, of the* Elaians, *which kind of great pieces the* Italians *call* Medaglioni, *and were extraordinary Coins, not for common use, but coin'd by the Emperors, either to be distributed by the way of largess in Triumphs, or to be sent for Tokens to men well deserving, or else by free Cities to the glory and memory of good Princes What name this place anciently had, is hard to be found, but seemeth to have been the Port and Landing-place for* Venta Silurum, *when as it is but two miles from it*

728. 49 Clare — Miles *of* Glocester, Robert Chandos, Pain Fitz-John, Richard Fitz-Punt, *and,* &c

CAER-MARDHIN-SHIRE

744 20 OF—*Sir* Thomas *of* London

747 57 Howel—*Surnamed* Dha, *that is Good*

749 47 By—*Sir* Rhise ap Thomas

PENBROKSHIRE

753 33 TOWN—*Well govern'd by a Mayor, and strongly wall'd toward the Land*

754 17 Haven—*In the most pleasant Country of all* Wales, *standeth* Penbroke *the Shire-town, one direct Street upon a long narrow point all rock, and a forked arm of* Milford-*haven, ebbing and flowing close to the Town-walls on both sides It hath a Castle, but now ruinate, and two Parish-Churches within the walls, and is incorporate of a Mayor, Bailiffs, and Burgesses. But hear* Giraldus, &c

756 29 Inhabitants—— *Situate upon an hill-side, having scarce one even Street, but is steep one way or other*

757. 2 Are—*Twenty-two*

3 Wall—*Whereupon they call it,* The Close

758. 35 Newport—*At the foot of a high Mountain*

37 Sand——*And, in Latin Records,* Novus Burgus

43 Dogmael—*According to the Order of* Tours

Page Line

765 64 Anselm — *Who enjoy'd this Honour but a few days*

766 3 His—*Eldest.*

6 Son—*Lord of* Weishford, *and,* &c.

47 1391—*By Sir* John St John, *casually*

55 Penbroke——*Not long after,* Humfrey, *Son to King* Henry *the fourth, before he was Duke of* Glocester, *receiv'd this title of his brother King* Henry *the fifth, and before his death King* Henry *the sixth granted the same in reversion (a thing not before heard of) to* William de la Pole, *Earl of* Suffolk, *after whose downfall, the said King, when he had enabled* Edmund *of* Hadham, *and* Jasper *of* Hatfield, *the sons of Queen* Catharine *his mother, to be his lawful half-brethren, created* Jasper *Earl of* Penbroke, *and* Edmund *Earl of* Richmond, *with pre-eminence to take place above all Earls For Kings have absolute authority in dispensing honours*

64 By—— *Sir* William Herbert, *for his good service against* Jasper *in* Wales

73 Penbroke—*With a Mantle and Coronet, in regard both of her Nobility and also her Vertues (for so run the words of her Patent)*

74 Invested—*Sir* William.

MONTGOMERYSHIRE

778 34 WHERE—*In the time of the Emperor* Theodosius *the younger*

780 34 Shrewsbury—*Who winning much Land here from the* Welsh, *as we find in* Domesday, &c

45 Liberties——*Now the* Herberts *are here seated, branched out from a Brother of Sir* William Herbert, *the first Earl of* Penbroke *of that name*

783 4 Rivers—*But this may seem overmuch of* Mediolanum, *which I have sought here and about* Alcester, *not far off*

784 5 To—*Sir* John

10. Gules——*Which he received from his Wife's Progenitors*

MEIRIONYDHSHIRE

785. 7 COuntries—*And* Wales

28 To—*Sir* Hugh Burgh

66 Until—*Sir* William

ANGLESEY

806 59 CATTEL—*And sendeth out great multitudes*

808 65 Time——*Shot the said* Hugh *Earl of* Shrewsbury, &c

DENBIGHSHIRE

818 44 MOrtimer—*Earl of* Winchester

47 It—*With the* Cantreds *of* Ross *and* Riewinock, &c

48 Montacute—*After Earl of* Salisbury

ibid Salisbury—*For surprising of* Mortimer

819 17 1566—*To him and the heirs of his body lawfully begotten*

61 Built—*By* Reginald Grey, *to whom King* Edward *the first granted it, and* Roger, &c

820 18 Monastery—*Now wholly decayed*

42 To—*Sir* William

44 To—*Sir* William Stanley, *Chamberlain to King* Henry *the* [illegible]

Page Line. *vereign about his good services (when he was honourably recompens'd) lost his head, forgetting that Sovereigns must not be beholden to subjects, howsoever subjects fansy their own good services*

FLINTSHIRE

824 18 Winifrid — *How her head was cut off, and set on again by* St Benno

19. Giraldus — *Who yet knew not this Well*

825 76. First — *Where King* Richard *the second, circumvented by them who should have been most trusty, was cunningly induced to renounce the Crown, as unable, for certain defects, to rule, and was delivered into the hands of* Henry *of* Lancaster *Duke of* Hereford, *who soon after claimed the Kingdom and Crown, being then void by his cession, as his inheritance descended from King* Henry *the third, and to this his devis'd Claim the Parliament assented, and he was establish'd in the Kingdom*

831 21 Kingdom — *And by that title summon'd him to Parliament, being then nine years old*

22 Title — *With a Cap of Estate, and a Coronet set on his head, a gold Ring put on his finger, and a * silver Verge deliver'd into his hand, with the assent of Parliament,*

* Afterward, a golden Verge was used

28. Fourth — *At the formal request of the Lords and Commons*

832 24 Privileges — *Or that you may read it abridg'd out of the Act of Parliament* The King's Country or Dominion of *Wales*, shall stand and continue for ever incorporated, united, and annex'd to and with the Realm of *England*, and all and singular person and persons, born and to be born in the said Principality, Country, or Dominion of *Wales*, shall have, enjoy, and inherit, all and singular Freedoms, Liberties, Rights, Privileges, and Laws within this Realm and other the King's Dominions, as other the King's Subjects naturally born within the same, have, enjoy, and inherit and the Laws, Ordinances, and Statutes of the Realm of *England* for ever, and none other, shall be had, used, practised, and executed, in the said Country, or Dominion of *Wales*, and every part thereof, in like manner, form, and order, as they be and shall be in this Realm, and in such like manner and form, as hereafter shall be farther establish'd and ordain'd *This Act, and the calm command of King* Henry *the seventh preparing way for it, effected that in a short time, which the violent power of other King's arms, and especially of* Henry *the 4th, with extream rigour also of Laws, could not draw on in many years For ever since, the British Nation hath continued as faithful and dutiful in their loyal Allegiance to the Crown of* England, *as any other part of the Realm*

YORKSHIRE West-Riding

846 23 FUrnival — *And* Thomas *Lord* Nevil *of* Furnival

847 62 Business — *But this* Coningsborough *in later ages was the possession of the Earls of* Warren

848 25 Of — *Sir* William

851 34 Exchequer — *But now among Sir* Robert Cotton' *Antiquities*

857. 36 Of — *Sir* Robert

865 10 Lancaster — *The first of the* Lancastrian *House, that in right of his wife possess'd it, stained and embrued the same with his own blood*

Page Line

865 29 Of — *Sir* Robert

72 That — *Sir* William

866 49 Harden — *But (to return)* Cor, *making no long course, sheadeth himself into* Wherf

871 8 Cold — *Whereupon, in his return, he finding here Dirt for Dust, and full current water under the Bridge, recanted with these Verses*

> Quæ Tadcaster erat fine flumine, pulvere plena,
> Nunc habet immensum fluvium, & pro pulvere lutum

873 59 York — *And addicted themselves to the Ordinances of Saint* Bernard

60 Purpose — *Which Abbey was acknowledged an immediate daughter of* Clarevalle, *and in a few years became a daughter to many others, as* Kirkstall, Salley, Meaux, *&c*

879 27 Ptolemy — *And* Antonine *himself*

886 20 Humber — *Leaving first* Escricke *a seat of the* Lascelles, *sometimes to be remember'd for that King* James *advanced Sir* Thomas Knivet, *the Owner thereof, Lord* Knivet, *in the honour of Baron* Knivet *of* Escricke *in the year* 1607

36 Monastery — *Founded there by Sir* William Painell.

EAST-RIDING

888 12 BY — *Sir* Thomas

889 23 Humber — *Whereof also the Country beyond it, by a general name, was call'd* Northumberland

891 18 Immunities — *And* Athelstan *granted them Liberties in these general words,*

> Alls free, make I thee,
> As heart may think, or eye may see.

894 55 Son — *Sir* Michael

NORTH-RIDING

907 63 ISSUE — *The Inheritance of* Dancaster, Bainton, Bidesalle, *&c were parted,* &c

909 44 To — *Sir* William.

911 22 Follows — *Whereupon they have a proverbial Rhime,*

> When *Rosebery Topping* wears a Cap,
> Let *Cliveland* then beware of a Clap

54 Strangwaies — *And* Darcies, *descended,* &c

68 Durham — *Between* Tine *and* Tees

913 5 And — *Sir* Guarin

24 Of — *Sir* Guarin

914 8 By — *Sir* Bertrand Bulmer

916 41 Kingdom — *He and his heirs to succeed after him*

75 Ardmanoch — *A little child, not full four years of age*

RICHMONDSHIRE

920 45 ABBEY — *Of* Cistercians, *founded first at* Fors, *and after translated hither by* Stephen *Earl of* Britain *and* Richmond

Mother

Dr. HOLLAND's Insertions

Page Line

920 71 Mother — John, that assumed the surname of Marmion, and dy'd issueless; and Robert, who left behind him one only daughter and sole heir Elizabeth, wife to Sir Henry Fitz-Hugh, a noble Baron

924 3 Baron—Sir Brian

4 Descended — From the Earls of Britain and Richmond

926 12. Travellers——Called the Spittle on Stanemore

31. Can—The first Earls were out of the House of Little Britain in France, whose descent is confusedly intricate amongst their own Writers, for that there were two principal Earls at once, one of Haulte Britain, and another of Base Britain, for many years, and every one of their Children had their part in Gavelkind, and were stiled Earls of Britain without distinction But of these the first Earl of Richmond, according to our Writings and Records, was Alane surnam'd Feregaunt, that is, The Red, son of Hoel Earl of Britain, descended from Hawise great Aunt to William the Conqueror, who gave this Country unto him by name of the Lands of Earl Edwin in Yorkshire, and withal bestowed his daughter upon him, by whom he had no issue He built Richmond castle, as is before specified, to defend himself from disinherited and out-law'd Englishmen in those parts and dying, left Britain to his son Conan le Grosse by a second wife But Alane the Black son of Eudo, son of Geffrey Earl of Britain and Hawise aforesaid, succeeded in Richmond, and he having no child, left it to Stephen his brother This Stephen begat Alane, surnam'd Le Savage, his son and successor, who assisted King Stephen against Maude the Empress in the battle at Lincoln, and married Bertha one of the heirs of Conan le Gross Earl of Hault Britain, by whom he had Conan le Petit Earl of both Britains by hereditary right, as well as of Richmond II, by the assistance of King Henry the second of England, dispossessed Eudo Viscount of Porhoet his father-in-law, who usurp'd the title of Britain in right of the said Bertha his wife and ending his life, having only one daughter Constance, by Margaret sister to Malcolme King of the Scots Geffrey, third son to King Henry the second of England, was advanced by his Father to the marriage of the said Constance, whereby he was Earl of Britain and Richmond, and begat of her Arthur, who succeeded him, and, as the French write, was made away by King John his Uncle

927 7 Thouars—Then upon dislike of the House of Britain, Peter of Savoy, &c

29 For — Between John Earl of Montfort of the half-blood, and Joan his brother's daughter, and heir of the whole blood, married to Charles of Bloys

35 Deceased — To whom the Parliament of France had adjudg'd it

73 Issue— As for Sir Thomas Grey who was made Baron of Richmond, by King Henry the sixth, he was not Lord of this Richmond, but of a place in Bedfordshire, called Rugemound and Richmount-Greies.

The BISHOPRICK of DURHAM

949 16 BODY — And unwilling I am to remember, how this Bishoprick was dissolv'd by a private Statute, and all the possessions thereof given to Edward the sixth, when private Greediness edg'd by Churchmen did grind the Church, and withdraw much from God, wherewith Christian Piety had formerly honoured God. But Queen Mary repeal'd that Statute, and restored the said Bishoprick, with all the Possessions and Franchises thereof, that God might enjoy his own

Page Line.

950 38 Money — Buried, as it is thought, by the Romans

44 Durham — And Patriarch of Jerusalem

960. 56. Piety — And great wisdom approved in domestical and foreign Employments

LANCASHIRE

962 62 LA-Ware—Being summon'd to Parliament among the Lords Temporal, by the name of Magister Thomas de la Ware

65 Town — And by Joanna, sister of the said Sir Thomas, it came to the Wests, now Lord de la Ware

967 7 Virtuosi—To whom I recommend them, and to their farther disquisition, whether there are not subterranean Trees, growing under the earth, as well as Plants, and other Creatures

970 11 Brother—But I forget my self now, when as I have formerly remember'd as much

973 16. Inscription—And dedicated to the Mother Goddesses by a Captain of the Asturians

976 49 Derby—And advanced to that title by King Henry the eighth

977 18 Aliens—Founded by Roger of Poictiers

978 59 Abbey—Of Cistercian Monks

73 Bonvill—Of Somersetshire.

980 60 Albemarle —— Of William de Fortibus Earl, &c

981 48 Aquitain—To have and to hold the same title for term of life, of the King of England and Monarch of France, but to the general disgust of the Inhabitants of the Province of Aquitain, who gave it out that their Seigniory was inseparably annex'd to the Crown of England

54 Lancaster—Who when he had dispossess'd Richard the second, and obtain'd the Kingdom of England, he considering that being now King, he could not bear the title of Duke of Lancaster, and unwilling that the said title should be discontinued, ordain'd by assent of Parliament, that Henry his present son should enjoy the same, and be stil'd Prince of Wales, Duke of Aquitain, Lancaster, and Cornwall, and Earl of Chester and also, that the Liberties and Franchises of the Dutchy of Lancaster should remain to his said son, sever'd from the Crown of England

982 12 Mother — Dame Mary.

WESTMORELAND

984 37 CAndale—Or Kendale

985 2 Parts—Of whom Sir William Parr was made Lord Par, by King Henry the eighth

988 38 Was — Sir Thomas Wharton

989 46 Government —The northern English

995 12 Age — Or thrust out by the root of a Tree .. growing

999 27 Daughters — Isabel

29. Of — Sir Roger

34 Posterity—By his former wife Margaret

38 Country — And covert g Treason under the ma.. 't of Religion

40 Honour — By actual Rebellion, in the year 1[illegible]

46 Family—Beside the Earl of Westmorland

48 Montacute — A Duke of Bedford.

Page Line

CUMBERLAND

1001 67 PRospect—*And giveth Contentment to as many as travel it*

1004 34 Notwithstanding—Sir Thomas.

1006 24 Miners—*Who have here their Smelting-house by* Derwent *side, which with his forcible Stream and their ingenious Inventions, serveth them in notable stead for easy bellows-works, hammer-works, forge-works, and sawing of Boards, not without admiration of those that behold it*

1008 7 Baptiz'd — *As saith* Pontius Paulinus *For in the first plantation of Christianity among the Gentiles, such only as were of full age, after they were instructed in the Principles of Christian Religion, were admitted to Baptism, at that but twice in the year, at* Easter *and* Whitsontide, *except upon urgent necessity At which time, they which were to be baptiz'd, were attir'd in white garments exorcis'd and exsuffled, with sundry Ceremonies, which I leave to the learned in Christian Antiquities*

1010 48 Stilico——*The potent Commander in the* Roman *State*

68 Garrison'd — *The near resemblance of the name* Elenborough *with* Olenacum, *where the first* Herculean *Wing lay in garrison in the time of* Theodosius *the younger, is some motive to think that this was that* Olenacum, *but yet I dare not affirm it*

1013 42 Engraven—*And erected for some Victory of the Emperor's.*

1015 42 COSS—*This votive Altar also of a rude Stone was erected for the happy health of the Emperor* Gordian *the third, and his wife* Furio Sabina Tranquilla, *and their whole Family, by the troop of Horsemen, surnam'd* Augusta Gordiana, *when* Æmilius Crispinus, *a native of* Africa, *govern'd the same under* Nonnius Philippus, *Lieutenant General of* Britain *in the year of Christ* 243, *as appeareth by the Consuls therein specified*

1016 ult Inscription — *To the honour of* Philip *the Emperor and his son, who flourish'd about the year of our Lord* 248

1018 15 Dew——*In Summer*

1021 52 That——*Sir* Hugh

1022 20 Place——*In this dangerous Country*

Honour—*With the title of Lord* Greystock

53 To—Philip *Earl of* Arundel, *and Lord* William Howard

1025 60 Viz —— *Sir* Andrew

1027 63 Kent—— *Of the Blood-royal*

1028 7 By——*Sir* Thomas

48 To — *Sir* John *of* Strivelin, *a Baron*

1037 17 Flight—*But of him more in my Annals Nearer the Wall, beyond the river* Irthing, *was lately found this fair votive Altar, erected to the Goddess* Nymphe *of the* Brigantes, *for the health of the Empress* Plautilla, *Wife to* M Aurelius Antoninus Severus, *and the whole Imperial Family, by* M Cocceius Nigrinus *a Treasurer to the Emperor, when* Lætus *was second time Consul, with intricate connexion of Letters, which I read thus*

Page Line

DEÆ NYMPHÆ BRIGantum
QUOD VOVERAT PRO
SALUTE PLAUTILIÆ COnjugis INVITÆ
DOMini NOSTRI INVICTI
IMP M AVRELii SEVERI
ANTONINI PII FELicis CÆSaris
AUGusti TOTIUSQUE DO
MUS DIVINÆ EJUS
M COCCEIUS NIGRINUS
Questor AUGusti Numini DEVOTUS
LIBENS SUSCEPTUM Solvit
LÆTO II ——

1042 13 Anne—*Now Countess of* Dorset *But his Brother Sir* Francis, *&c*

16 Ancestors — *As for the Wardens of the West-Marches against* Scotland *in this County, which were Noblemen of especial trust, I need to say nothing, when as by the Union of both Kingdoms under one head, that Office is now determin'd*

NORTH-HUMBERLAND

1070 ult MElkrigg — *Where now Women beat their Bucks on it*

1071 27 Call'd — *But what the old name was, will not easily be found*

1079 14 The—Hairuns, *now commonly call'd* Heron

1089 18 Account — *King* Richard *the second granted, That a Sword should be carry'd before the Mayor; and King* Henry *the sixth, &c*

1090 46 Gual—Bal, Val, *and* Gual

1096 38 Necham—*Insinuating that the hither part of* Scotland *was called* Pict-land.

1097 75 And—*In barbarous Latin*

1098 25 Floddon—*Near* Bramton

41 Howards—*As I have formerly specified*

1104 17 Treason - *When he devised to deprive King* William Rufus *of his Royal Estate, and to advance* Stephen *Earl of* Albemarle, *a son to the Conqueror's sister, thereunto*

69 King — *Who also made him Constable of* England

1105 2 Kinsman — *Grievously complaining, and charging him* [*King* Henry] *with Perjury, That whereas he had solemnly sworn to him and others, that he would not challenge the Crown, but only his own Inheritance, and that King* Richard *should be govern'd during his life by the good Advice of the Peers of the Realm, he, to the contrary, had (by imprisonment and terror of death) enforc'd him to resign his Crown, and usurp'd the same by the concurrence of his Faction, horribly murdering the said King, and defrauding* Edward Mortimer *Earl of* March *of his lawful right to the Crown, whom he had suffer'd to languish long in prison under* Owen Glendowr, *reputing those Traytors who with their own Money had procur'd his enlargement*

ult Northumberland — *By the name of* John *Earl of* Warwick, *Marshal of* England, *Viscount* Lisle, *Baron* Somery, Basset, *and* Lies, *Lord of* Dudley, *Great Master and Steward of the King's House*

SCOTLAND.

LENNOX

Page Line
1220 5 SON—Lodowick Esme
26 Born — *Quarterly with the Arms of* Steward

STERLING

1222. 55. PACIS — *That is,* Knolls *of Peace*

CALEDONIA

1229. 31. CAlled — *In the Book of Triplicites*

FIFE

1235 41 ELphinston — *Advanced to that honour by* James *King of* Great Britain
1236. 64 First—*For their violent Oppressions*

STRATHERN

1238 39 LOrn — Inch-chafra, i e *in the old* Scottish *tongue, the* Isle of Masses, *hereby may be remember'd whenas it was a most famous Abbey of the Order of St* Augustin, *founded by the Earl of* Strathern, *about the year* 1200
54. Was—Malisse, *who, in the time of King* Henry *the third of* England, *marry'd one of the heirs of* Robert Muschamp *a potent Baron of* England. *Long afterward,* &c.

Page Line.

CANTIRE.

1244 17 MILES — *From* Æmonia *to the Shores of* Thessalia

BRAIDALBIN

1246 8 MARY — *In our memory*
40 Death — *Whereas the whole* Clan *commonly beareth feud, for any hurt receiv'd by any one Member thereof, by Execution of Laws, Order of Justice, or otherwise*

PERTHSHIRE

1250 58 ARMS —— *Three Escutcheons Gules in Argent*

BUQUHAN

1265 42 KNight — *Whom he had by Queen* Joan *Sister to the Duke of* Somerset, *and Widow to King* James *the first,* &c

LOQHUABRE

1271 *ult* BRITAIN — *And the Isles adjacent*

CATHNES

1278 13 REquire —— *For the Administration of Justice*

IRELAND.

IRELAND in General.

Page Line
1317 27 TO——*Sir* Martin
1320 12 Eminent—*Sir* Thomas.

The Courts of IRELAND

1325 8 YEAR — *Which seemeth yet not to have been effected*
1326 4. Same — *Nevertheless, the meer* Irish *did not admit them, but retain'd their own* Brehon-*Laws and leud Customs And the Kings of* England *used a connivance therein upon some deep consideration, not vouchsafing to communicate the benefit of the* English *Laws, but upon special grace to especial Families or Sects, namely, the* O Neiles, O Conors, O Brien, O Maloghlins, *and* Mac Murough, *which were reputed of the blood Royal among them*
8 Ireland—*In the time of Sir* Edward Poinings's *government*

Page Line.

The Division of IRELAND.

1330 29 DEarrih—Cloemacniso
55 Achad —Achonry

DESMOND

1338 1 YEAR —*Nevertheless, in the last Rebellion, the Rebels erected a titulary Earl, and against him Queen* Elizabeth *granted the Title of Earl of* Desmond *unto* James Fitz-Girald, *son to the aforesaid Rebel, who shortly after dy'd issueless in the year* 1601

CORK

18 THESE—*Sir* Charles
1340 30 To—*Sir* Robert
ibid And—*Sir* Miles
36 Stephen—*Sir* George

Page. Line

TIPPERARY

1348 69 TO——*Sir* James.

ult. Issue—*Sir* Thomas

1349 7 Bullein—*Without issue-male Sir* Pierce, &c

CATERLOGH

1355 35. DEvonshire — *For Sir* John Carew, *an English Knight, died seised thereof in the time of King* Edward *the third*

KILDARE

1358 37 DArensis —— *And after the entrance of the* English *into* Ireland, *was*, &c

49 Son——William *Lord* Vesey

1359 39 Ofaly——*He ended this life about the year* 1558 *His eldest Son* Girald *died before his Father, leaving only one Daughter married to Sir* Robert Digby Henry *his second Son succeeded, who, when he had by his wife Lady* Frances, *daughter to* Charles *Earl of* Nottingham, *only two daughters*, William *the third Son succeeded to the Earldom, who was drowned in passing into* Ireland *in the year* 1599, *having no issue And then the title of Earl of* Kildare *came to* Girald Fitz-Girald, *Son to* Edward *their Uncle, who was restored to his blood in lineage, to make title by descent lineal and collateral, from his Father and Brother and all his Ancestors, any attainder or corruption of blood to the contrary notwithstanding*

1360 14 Lost—*With a fair Patrimony, seduced by the Religious pretext into Rebellion*

WEISFORD

1362 9 MEntioned —*In the Records*

34 Was —*Richard*

WICKLOW

1364 9 SEA— *Making a Creek*

DUBLIN

1366 4 TEstifies—*Wherein he calleth it the noble City of* Ireland

72 Palace —*Or rather Banqueting house*

1368 11 By—*Sir* Henry

40 Here—*Yet I will note thus much, which I have since happened upon in the Records Whenas* King Richard *aforesaid had advanced that* Robert Vere, *Earl of* Oxford, *to be Marquiss of* Dublin, *and had given to him the Seignory of* Ireland *during his life, he, desirous to augment his honour by more ennobling him with honourable Arms, granted also, that as long as he should live, and hold the said Seignory, he should bear these Arms*, Azure three Crowns, Or in a Border, *in his Standards, Pennons, Coat armors, and other things wherein Arms are to be shew'd in all Marshall matters, and elsewhere at his pleasure But this grant was soon after recalled, and those Arms abolished*

Pr pat an 9 *Rich.* II m 1

Page Line

The County of METH

1371. 2 SINCE—*Sir* Christopher

12. For—*Sir* Robert Barnwell

West METH.

1373 17 FROM— *Sir* Gilbert

1374 33 England —*As* Furnivall, Burghersh, Crophull, &c

LONGFORD.

1373 39 BY— *Sir* Henry Sidney

TWOMOND.

1379 9 TILL—*Sir* Henry

20 By—*Sir* Robert

1380 4 Which—*Sir* Robert

33 Brother—*Sir* Donell

MAIO.

1383 46 THEM —*Sir* Richard

1384 50 Related—*Out of my Annals*

ROSCOMAN.

1387 16 OF —*Sir* Coniers Clifford

The Lords of CONAGHT

1390 10 MEntioned — *Under countenance of which name, they for a long time tyranniz'd over the poor Inhabitants with most grievous Exactions*

ULSTER.

1391 14 OF—*Sir* John

LOUTH.

1394 1 TO— *Sir* John

CAVON

1393 34 OF—*Sir* Henry

FERMANAGH

1396 17 HERE— *Was* Mac-Gwir, *until he overthrew himself and his State in the late Rebellion*

MONAGHAN

37 DEputy—*Sir* William.

ARMAGH

1397 44 MAgonius— *As a* Nurse Father, *out of a* British *word*

1398 *ult* By—*Sir* John Curcy.

Page Line

DOWN

1399. 33. BY—*Sir* Nicholas
42. Ulster—*Whether they were Vassals to* O-Neal, *and whether*, &c
1400. 51 Too—*At* Kirk-Patrick
1401. 44 Peninsula—*Called the* Andes
1403 12 Saying—*When he was moved to build a Castle for his own defence*

ANTRIM

56. BY—*Sir* Henry.
1405 1 Till—*Sir* John
4 By—*Sir* Richard
21 Till—*Sir* John

LONDONDERRY

1408 4 IT—*But this County, without confining, is escheated to the King, who graciously purposing a civil Plantation of those unreformed and waste parts, is pleased to distribute the said Lands to his civil Subjects and the City of* London *hath undertaken to plant Colonies there*

TIR-OEN

1407 12. EUgenius—*Which name the Irish have contracted into* Eogain *and* Oen

TIR-CONEL.

1411 5 O-Neal—*Who had then assembled and armed all the power he cou'd possibly against the* English
53 Donegall—*That is, the town of the* Gallicians *in* Spain
68 Died—*And this* Rory *his Successor, practising new Treason against King* James *his Advancer, upon the Terror of a guilty Conscience, fled the Realm in the year* 1607, *and died at* Rome
1412 58 Day—*Sir* John
1414 *ult* Care—*If they were wrought and confirm'd to orderly Civility*

The ancient and modern Customs of the IRISH

1417 44 SAY—*But whereas I have incidently happened of better Observations concerning this* Brehon *Law and* Tanistry, *diligently collected by Sir* John Davis, *his Majesty's Attorney General in* Ireland, *I hope I may with his good leave impart some of them to publick knowledge in his own words The several Countries or Territories possess'd by the* Irishry *were in number sixty and upwards, and some being greater, and some less, did in extent and scope of Land contain two parts of the Kingdom at least In every one of these Countries there was a chief Lord or Captain, and under him a* Tanist, *which was his successor apparent, both these were elected of the Country, who commonly made choice of such as were most active, and had most sword-men, and followers depending upon him The chief Lord had certain Lands in Demesne, which were called his* Loghtin, *or Mensall Lands in Demesne, where he placed his principal Officers, namely, his* Brehon, *his Marshal, his Cup-bearer, his Physician, his Surgeon, his Chronicler, his Rhimer, and others which Offices and Professions were hereditary and peculiar to certain Septs and Families He had also small rents of Money, and Cows, and customary Duties of Oatmeal, Butter, and the like, out of the Lands in the Country, except the Lands of the Church, and such of his kinsmen and followers, to whom he granted a special privilege or freedom Besides, he had a general Tallage, or cutting high or low at his pleasure, upon all the Inheritance, which he took commonly when he made war, either with his neighbours, or against the Crown of* England, *or made a journey to the State, or gave any entertainment, so as the whole Profits of the Country were at his disposition when he listed and so made the Inhabitants like the Villains of* England, *upon whom their Lords had power* Tallier Haut *and* Bas, *as the Phrase of our Law is, whereupon the* English *call this kind of exaction by the name of cutting The chief Lord had his Cosharies upon his tenants, that is, he and his would lie upon them until they had eat up all their Provisions He would likewise employ upon them his horsemen, his kernes, his horse-boys, his dog-boys, and the like, to be fed and maintained by them, which kept the poor people in continual slavery and beggary The* [illegible] *had also a special portion of Land, and certain Chiefry proper to the* Tanist, *and within the* [illegible] *mits of his portion he had also his cuttings and his Cosharies The rest of the Land being distributed among several Septs, every Sept had a Chief or* Canfinic, *as they called them, with a* Tanist *of that Sept, both which were chosen by the chief Lord or Captain of the Country, and had likewise their several Portions and Chiefries These Captainships or Chiefries were not partable, but were entirely enjoyed by such as were elected thereunto All the rest of the Lands, except the portions of the chiefs and* Tanists, *descended in course of Gavelkind, and were partable among the Males only, in which division, the Bastards had their Portions as well as the legitimate For offences and matters criminal, none was so hainous or of so high a nature, as that it was capital, for Treason against the chief Lord, and Murder, were finable, the Fine they called an* Ericke, *which was assessed by the Lord and his* Brehons *In case of Treason, the Lord had all the Fine, in case of Murder, the Lord had one Moiety, and the kindred of the Party slain the other Moiety, so as they never forfeited their possessions or their lands for any offence Howbeit, their Lands were seized by the Lord for their Fines, until the same were levied thereupon, and then restored Rote was finable in like sort, but theft deserved praise and reward, if the stealth were brought into the Country, because the Lord had a share, and the Country thereby became the richer But the theft committed in the Country, and carried out, if the Thief were apprehended before his Friend made offer of his Fine, he was commonly punished with death But the Lord in that case might take an* Ericke *if he wou'd Upon the stealth of any Cattle, if the owner followed the track (wherein the* Irish *are incredible cunning, insomuch as they will find the same by the bruising of a grass in the summer-time) if the party unto whose land the Track is brought, cannot make it off to some other Land, he is to answer the stealth to the owner And this being an* Irish *Law or Custom, is at this day observ'd both by the* English *and* Irish, *the same being ratified by an Act of Council in the Earl of* Sussex *his government, as fit and necessary for that Kingdom The* Brehons [illegible]

f[illegible]d

Page Line.

fifted by certain Scholars, who had learned many rules of the Civil and Canon Law, rather by tradition than by reading, gave judgment in all Causes, and had the eleventh part of the thing adjudged for their Fee, and the chief Lord's Marshal did execution These are the principal rules and grounds of the Brehon *Law, which the makers of the Statutes of* Kilkenny *did not without cause call a lewd custom; for it was the cause of much lewdness and barbarism It*

Page Line

gave countenance and encouragement to theft, rape, and murder, it made all possessions uncertain, whereby it came to pass that there was no building of Houses and Towns, nor education of Children in learning or civility, no exercise of trades or handicrafts, no improvement or manuring of lands, no industry or virtue in use among them, but the people were bred in looseness and idleness, which hath been the true cause of all the mischiefs and miseries in that Kingdom

The Smaller

ISLANDS

IN THE

BRITISH OCEAN.

Page. Line

1435. 3. DEmetrius—*Who seemeth to have liv'd in* Hadrian's *time*

The HEBRIDES, *or* Western Isles

1461. 28. Ἐβέδαι —— *Which names have some consonant affinity with* Epidium, *the Promontory of* Britain *opposite to them, and an Isle among these so named*

1462. 12. English —— *Under the Conduct of Sir* William Norris, *in the year* 1575

The ORCADES, or Isles of Orkney

1469. 57. THEM — *If we may believe* Tacitus, *but questionless they were known in the time of* Claudius *the Emperor; for* Pomponius Mela, *who then lived, mentioneth them Yet doubtless,* Orosius *is untrue, in that he writeth, that* Claudius *conquered them*

1470 1 *For,* Picts——*The* Saxons

9. vi — 40.

26. 1468 —— 1498

The Thule of the Ancients.

1484. 19. FISH — *Which we call Stockfish.*

Islands in the German Ocean.

1502. 55 AFterwards — *When the* Danes *rifled and robbed all the Sea-coasts*

1504 44. Franks — *Call'd* SALII.

British Islands on the Coast of FRANCE

1507 25. WEather —— *This* Alderney *lieth in the chief trade of all shipping passing from the Eastern parts to the West three leagues distant from the coast of* Normandy, *thirty from the nearest part of* England, *extended from South east to the North west, and containeth about eight*

Page Line

miles in circuit, the South shore consisting of high Cliffs The Air is healthful, the soil sufficiently rich, full of fresh Pastures and Corn-fields yet the Inhabitants poor, through a custom of parting their Lands into small parcels by Gavelkind The Town is situate well-near in the midst of the Isle, having a Parish-Church, and about eighty Families, with an Harbour call'd Crabbic *some miles off On the East-side there is an ancient Fort, and a dwelling-house built at the charge of the* Chamberlans *for the fee-farm of the Isle was granted by Queen* Elizabeth *to* G Chamberlane, *son to Sir* Leonard Chamberlane *of* Shirburne *in* Oxfordshire, *when he recovered it from the* French *And under this Fort, the Sand with violent drifts from the North-west overlaid the Land, so that now it serveth thereabout most for Conies*

1507 65 Rocks — *Which have their several Eddies, and therefore are dreaded, &c*

65 Casquets--*Out of one of the which properly named* Casquet, *there gusheth a most sweet Spring of fresh water, to the great comfort of the Island-fishermen beating up and down hereabout At these, to remember incidently (that the memory of a well-deserving Patriot may not perish) the Fleet, which* John Philpot *Citizen of* London *set forth and manned at his own private charges, had a glorious Victory over a rabble of Pirates, who impeached all traffick, taking their Captain, and fifteen* Spanish *Ships that consorted with them. Which worthy man also maintained one thousand Soldiers at his own pay for the defence of the Realm against the* French, *who sore infested the southern coast in the beginning of the reign of King* Richard II *to omit his great loans to the King, and other good and laudable offices to the Country*

1514. 22 Him — *Under Queen* Elizabeth

1515 57 Possession — *And verily* Evan *a Welsh Gentleman, descended from the Princes of* Wales, *and serving the* French *King, surprized* Garnsey *in the time of King* Edward *the third, but soon lost it*

Page. Line.

The Cassiterides, or Silly Islands.

1523 10. ST Mary—*Having a Town so named, and is about eight miles in compass, offereth a good Harbour to Sailors in a sandy Bay, wherein they may anchor at six, seven and eight fathom; but in the entry lie some Rocks on either side It hath had anciently a Castle, which hath yielded to the force of time But for the same Queen* Elizabeth *in the year* 1593 *when the* Spaniards, *called-in by the Leaguers of* France, *began to nestle in* Little Britain, *built a new Castle with fair and strong Ravelins, and named the same* Stella Maria, *in respect both of the Ravelins, which resemble the rays of a Star, and the name of the Isle; for defence whereof she there placed a garrison under the command of Sir* Francis Godolphin

1525 25 Samothracia — *Hitherto have I extended the* British *Sea, both upon the credit of* Pomponius Mela, *who stretcheth it to the coast of* Spain; *and upon the authority of the Lord Great Admiral of* England, *which extendeth so far For the Kings of* England *were, and are rightful Lords of all the North and West Sea coasts of* France *(to say nothing of the whole Kingdom and Crown of* France*) as who, to follow the track of the Sea-coast, wan the Counties of* Guines, Mark, *and* Oye, *by the Sword, were true heirs to the county of* Ponthieu *and* Monstreville *by* Eleanor *the wife of King* Edward *the first, the only heir thereof In like manner most certain heirs to the Dutchy of* Normandy *by King* William *the Conqueror, and thereby superior Lords of* Little Britain *dependant thereof, undoubted heirs of the counties of* Anjou, Touraın, *and* Maine, *from King* Henry *the second, whose Patrimony they were likewise of the County of* Poictou, *and Dutchy of* Aquitaine *or* Guyenne, *by* Eleanor *the true heir of them, wife to the said* Henry *the second, to omit the counties of* Tholouse, March, *the homage of* Avergne, *&c Of all which the* French *by their arrests of pretended forfeitures and confiscations have disseized the Crown of* England, *and annex'd them to the Crown of* France, *taking advantage of our most unhappy civil dissentions whereas in former ages the* French *Kings were so fore-closed by these territories, as they had no access at all to the Ocean*

THE

History of the O-Neals,

AND

Their REBELLIONS in *IRELAND*.

Page. Line

1 10 BRUS — *Brother to* Robert *King of* Scotland

2. 1 Them—*Often saying, that Language bred Conversation, and consequently their confusion, that Wheat gave sustenance with like effect. and by building they should do as the Crow doth; Make her Nest, to be beaten out by the Hawk*

31 O-Neal—*By an old shoe cast over his head*

3 10. *For*, H — *Sir* Henry

77 Proceedings — *Sir* Henry

5. 70 *For*, Henry—*Sir* Henry

6. 2 William — *Sir* William

28 Richard — *Sir* Richard

47 William — *Sir* William

48 William — *Sir* William.

50. Him — *Exhibited an humble submission upon his knees to the Lord Deputy, wherein he dolefully expressed his great grief that the Queen had conceived indignation against him, as of one undutiful and disloyal He acknowledged that the late absenting himself from the state was disagreeable to his obedience; albeit it was occasioned by some hard measures of the late Lord Deputy, as though he and the Marshal had combined for his destruction He acknowledged that the Queen advanced him to high title and great livings, that she ever upheld him and enabled him; that she, who by grace had advanced him, was able by her force to subvert him; and therefore if he were void of gratitude, yet he could not be so void of reason, as to word his own ruin*

6 71 Him—*But when it was put to question generally*

74 Time—*Pretending certain weighty considerations, and that the Articles exhibited were without proof or time*

7 11 *For*, John—*Sir* John

23 Henry—*Sir* Henry

25 John—*Sir* John

33 Country— *Both in* Irish *and* English, *and pardon offered to all that would submit*

37 *For*, J. — *Sir* John

45. J — *Sir* John

46. Flanders — *For the Queen had selected him as a man of especial trust and reputation, to be used martially in such Journeys, as the Deputy himself in person could not undertake, in consideration that he had performed divers honourable service, was now President of* Mounster, *and had formerly commanded the* Britain *Companies, which were to serve principally in this action*

55 *For*, Henry — *Sir* Henry

56 Robert — *Sir* Robert.

62 That — *Sir* Henry

8 21. *For*, Owen — *Sir* Owen

34 Henry — *Sir* Henry

48 Deputy — *Sir* William

61. Rebells — *That they should lay down their Arms, disperse their Forces, acknowledge submissively their Disloyalties, admit Sheriffs in their Government, re-edify the Forts they had defaced, suffer the Garrisons to live without disturbance, make restitution*

Page	Line.	
		tution of Spoils taken, confess upon their Oath how far they have dealt with foreign Princes, and renounce all foreign Aid, &c.
10.	39.	Passage—*Within the space of the* Moiry
	65.	*For*, Thomas—*Sir* Thomas
11.	26	Robert—*Sir* Robert.
	31	With—*Sir* John
	53	*For*, Henry—*Sir* Henry
	57.	Armach—*As he marched with divers Troops*
12	4.	*For*, Thomas—*Sir* Thomas
13	2	H—*Sir* Henry
	31	Coigniers—*Sir* Coniers
14.	42	Council—*That his Proceeding answer'd neither her direction, nor the World's expectation*
	64	Princes —— *And the Rebels encouraged by this unfortunate Success.*
15	3	England—*Accompanied with some Men of Quality*
	12	Leave — *And also had treated with the Rebels to her dishonour privately, and upon equal terms, with condition of Toleration of Religion, and to her disservice, when as the Rebels made profit of all Cessations*
16	13	*For*, Charles—*Sir* Charles
	60.	Henry—*Sir* Henry.
	61	And—*Sir* Matthew

Page.	Line.	
16	64.	That—*Sir* Henry.
17.	27	*For*, John—*Sir* John.
	32	Henry—*Sir* Henry
	41	Leinster—*A secure Receptacle of Rebels.*
	55	*For*, Richard—*Sir* Richard.
	56.	Oliver—*Sir* Oliver.
18.	21	George—*Sir* George
	40	Richard—*Sir* Richard.
19	21	Henry—*Sir* Henry.
	23	Henry—*Sir* Henry.
	32	Richard—*Sir* Richard.
	33.	Oliver—*Sir* Oliver
	35.	Henry—*Sir* Henry.
	ibid	Oliver—*Sir* Oliver
	37	Richard—*Sir* Richard
	43	Henry—*Sir* Henry
	69	William—*Sir* William
	70	Henry—*Sir* Henry.
	71	J —*Sir* John
20	20	Henry---*Sir* Henry
	ibid	William---*Sir* William.
21	37	Henry---*Sir* Henry
	51	Christopher---*Sir* Christopher
22	72	Charles---*Sir* Charles.

A Continuation of the

History of the Kings of Man.

Page	Line.	
33	27.	*For*, WILLIAM---*Sir* William.

INDEX.

INDEX.

INDEX.

Almondbury

man

Auguſtin

Bindon,

Brounsover,

C

Cæsar

Castle-

Chal

Chri

Crom-

D.

Douſa

Exan-

3 gre

INDEX.

Groffe

INDEX.

Hen-

K

Katwal

Kilmore,

Leonard

M.

N.

O

Oswald

 boy

Pryfetes

Singuelie,

Tyln,

INDEX.

UXAN-

CPSIA information can be obtained at www.ICGtesting.com
Printed in the USA
LVOW052042261012

304632LV00013B/5/P